See the Difference with LearningCurve.

LearningCurve
macmillan learning

learningcurveworks.com

LearningCurve is a winning solution for everyone: students come to class better prepared and instructors have more flexibility to go beyond the basic facts and concepts in class. LearningCurve's game-like quizzes are book-specific and link back to the textbook in LaunchPad so that students can brush up on the reading when they get stumped by a question. The reporting features help instructors track overall class trends and spot topics that are giving students trouble so that they can adjust lectures and class activities.

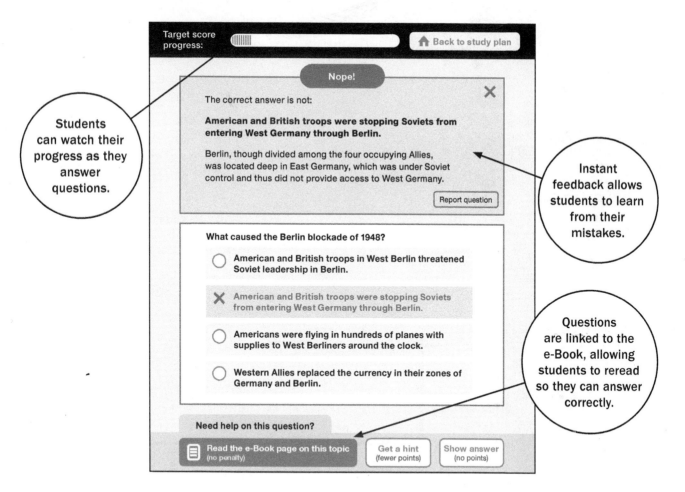

Students can watch their progress as they answer questions.

Instant feedback allows students to learn from their mistakes.

Questions are linked to the e-Book, allowing students to reread so they can answer correctly.

Target score progress:

Back to study plan

Nope!

The correct answer is not:

American and British troops were stopping Soviets from entering West Germany through Berlin.

Berlin, though divided among the four occupying Allies, was located deep in East Germany, which was under Soviet control and thus did not provide access to West Germany.

Report question

What caused the Berlin blockade of 1948?

○ American and British troops in West Berlin threatened Soviet leadership in Berlin.

✗ American and British troops were stopping Soviets from entering West Germany through Berlin.

○ Americans were flying in hundreds of planes with supplies to West Berliners around the clock.

○ Western Allies replaced the currency in their zones of Germany and Berlin.

Need help on this question?

Read the e-Book page on this topic (no penalty) | Get a hint (fewer points) | Show answer (no points)

LearningCurve is easy to assign, easy to customize, and easy to complete. See the difference LearningCurve makes in teaching and learning history.

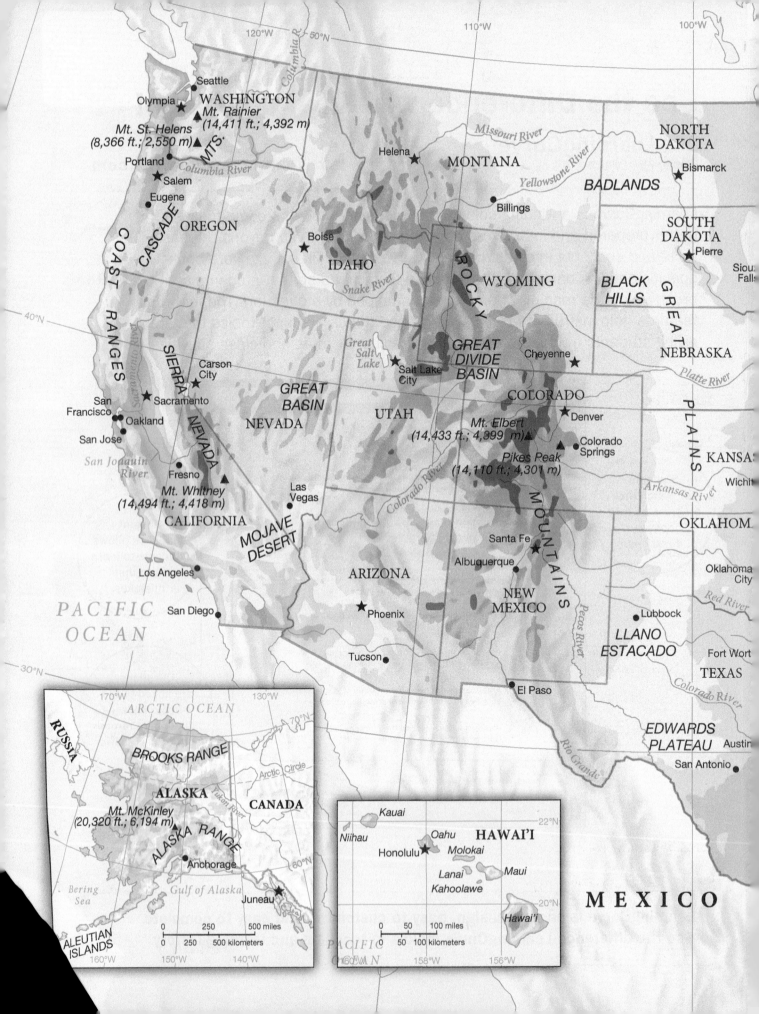

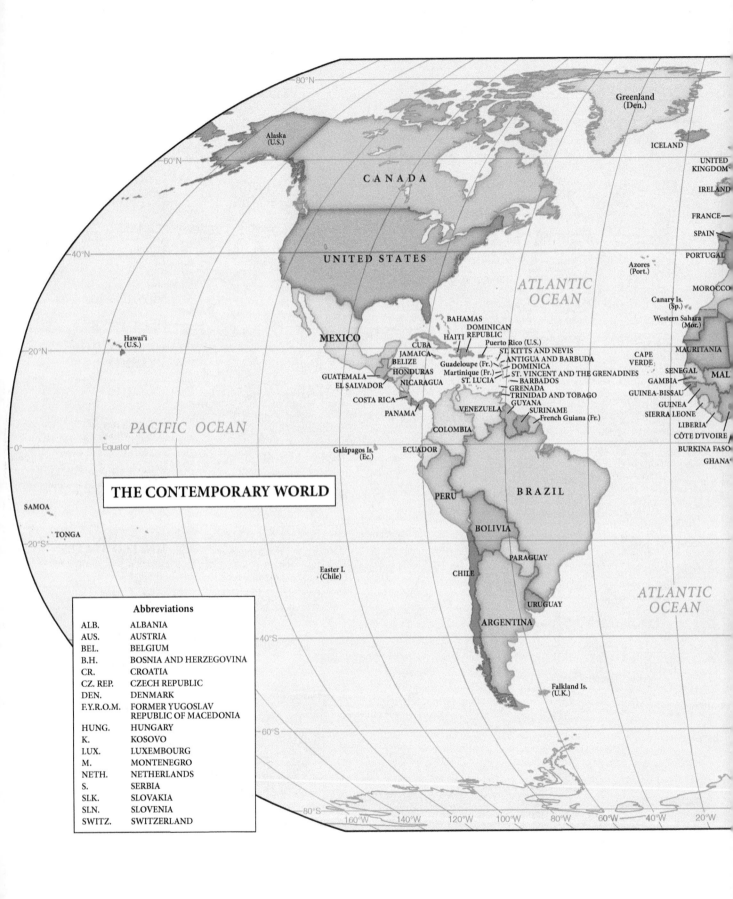

THE CONTEMPORARY WORLD

CANADA

UNITED STATES

MEXICO

Alaska (U.S.)

Greenland (Den.)

ICELAND

UNITED KINGDOM

IRELAND

FRANCE

SPAIN

PORTUGAL

Azores (Port.)

MOROCCO

Canary Is. (Sp.)

Western Sahara (Mor.)

MAURITANIA

CAPE VERDE

SENEGAL

MAL

GAMBIA

GUINEA-BISSAU

GUINEA

SIERRA LEONE

LIBERIA

CÔTE D'IVOIRE

BURKINA FASO

GHANA

ATLANTIC OCEAN

Hawai'i (U.S.)

BAHAMAS

DOMINICAN REPUBLIC

HAITI

Puerto Rico (U.S.)

CUBA

ST. KITTS AND NEVIS

JAMAICA

ANTIGUA AND BARBUDA

BELIZE

Guadeloupe (Fr.)

DOMINICA

GUATEMALA

Martinique (Fr.)

ST. VINCENT AND THE GRENADINES

HONDURAS

ST. LUCIA

BARBADOS

EL SALVADOR

NICARAGUA

GRENADA

TRINIDAD AND TOBAGO

COSTA RICA

GUYANA

PANAMA

VENEZUELA

SURINAME

French Guiana (Fr.)

COLOMBIA

PACIFIC OCEAN

Galápagos Is. (Ec.)

ECUADOR

PERU

BRAZIL

SAMOA

BOLIVIA

TONGA

PARAGUAY

Easter I. (Chile)

CHILE

URUGUAY

ARGENTINA

ATLANTIC OCEAN

Falkland Is. (U.K.)

Equator

Abbreviations	
ALB.	ALBANIA
AUS.	AUSTRIA
BEL.	BELGIUM
B.H.	BOSNIA AND HERZEGOVINA
CR.	CROATIA
CZ. REP.	CZECH REPUBLIC
DEN.	DENMARK
F.Y.R.O.M.	FORMER YUGOSLAV REPUBLIC OF MACEDONIA
HUNG.	HUNGARY
K.	KOSOVO
LUX.	LUXEMBOURG
M.	MONTENEGRO
NETH.	NETHERLANDS
S.	SERBIA
SLK.	SLOVAKIA
SLN.	SLOVENIA
SWITZ.	SWITZERLAND

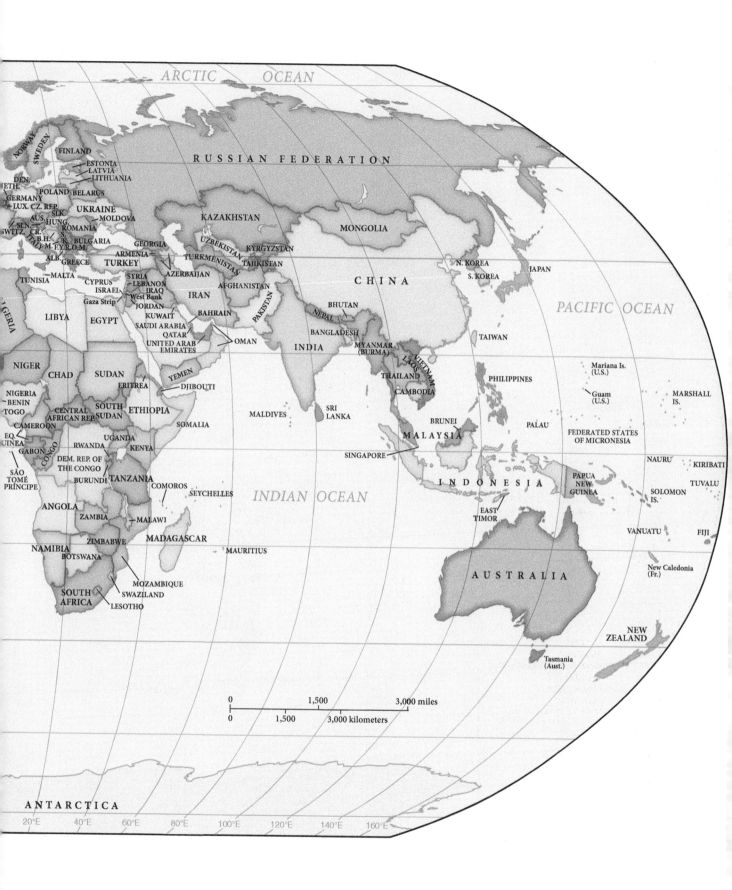

ARCTIC OCEAN

RUSSIAN FEDERATION

NORWAY
SWEDEN
FINLAND
ESTONIA
LATVIA
LITHUANIA
DEN.
ETH.
GERMANY
LUX. CZ. REP.
AUS.
SWITZ. CR.
ITALY M. F.Y.R.O.M.
ALB.
TUNISIA
MALTA
POLAND BELARUS
UKRAINE
MOLDOVA
SLK.
HUNG.
ROMANIA
S.
BULGARIA
GREECE
TURKEY
CYPRUS
ISRAEL

KAZAKHSTAN

MONGOLIA

GEORGIA
ARMENIA
AZERBAIJAN
SYRIA
LEBANON
IRAQ
West Bank
JORDAN
Gaza Strip

UZBEKISTAN
TURKMENISTAN
KYRGYZSTAN
TAJIKISTAN

CHINA

N. KOREA
S. KOREA
JAPAN

PACIFIC OCEAN

LIBYA
EGYPT

IRAN
AFGHANISTAN

KUWAIT
SAUDI ARABIA
QATAR
UNITED ARAB
EMIRATES
BAHRAIN
OMAN

PAKISTAN

NEPAL
BHUTAN
INDIA
BANGLADESH
MYANMAR
(BURMA)

TAIWAN

NIGER
CHAD
SUDAN
YEMEN
ERITREA
DJIBOUTI

NIGERIA
BENIN
TOGO
CENTRAL
AFRICAN REP.
CAMEROON
EQ.
GUINEA
GABON
CONGO
SÃO
TOMÉ
PRÍNCIPE

SOUTH
SUDAN
ETHIOPIA
SOMALIA

RWANDA
UGANDA
KENYA
DEM. REP. OF
THE CONGO
BURUNDI
TANZANIA

MALDIVES

SRI
LANKA

LAOS
THAILAND
VIETNAM
CAMBODIA

PHILIPPINES

Mariana Is.
(U.S.)
Guam
(U.S.)

MARSHALL
IS.

BRUNEI

MALAYSIA

PALAU

FEDERATED STATES
OF MICRONESIA

SINGAPORE

NAURU
KIRIBATI

TUVALU

COMOROS
SEYCHELLES

INDIAN OCEAN

INDONESIA

PAPUA
NEW
GUINEA

SOLOMON
IS.

ANGOLA
ZAMBIA
MALAWI
ZIMBABWE
MADAGASCAR

EAST
TIMOR

VANUATU
FIJI

NAMIBIA
BOTSWANA
MAURITIUS

New Caledonia
(Fr.)

SOUTH
AFRICA
MOZAMBIQUE
SWAZILAND
LESOTHO

AUSTRALIA

NEW
ZEALAND

Tasmania
(Aust.)

0   1,500   3,000 miles
0   1,500   3,000 kilometers

ANTARCTICA

20°E   40°E   60°E   80°E   100°E   120°E   140°E   160°E

The
American
Promise

A History of
the United States

The American Promise

A History of the United States

SEVENTH EDITION

James L. Roark
Emory University

Michael P. Johnson
Johns Hopkins University

Patricia Cline Cohen
University of California, Santa Barbara

Sarah Stage
Arizona State University

Susan M. Hartmann
The Ohio State University

bedford/st.martin's
Macmillan Learning
Boston | New York

FOR BEDFORD/ST. MARTIN'S

Vice President, Editorial, Macmillan Learning Humanities: Edwin Hill
Publisher for History: Michael Rosenberg
Senior Executive Editor for History: William J. Lombardo
Director of Development for History: Jane Knetzger
Developmental Editor: Robin Soule
Associate Editor: Tess Fletcher
Assistant Editor: Mary Posman
Editorial Assistant: Lexi DeConti
Senior Production Editor: Rosemary Jaffe
Media Producer: Michelle Camisa
Media Editor: Jennifer Jovin
Production Manager: Joe Ford
History Marketing Manager: Melissa Famiglietti
Copy Editor: Lisa Wehrle
Indexer: Mary White
Cartography: Mapping Specialists, Ltd.
Photo Editor: Cecilia Varas
Photo Researcher: Naomi Kornhauser
Permissions Editor: Eve Lehmann
Senior Art Director: Anna Palchik
Text Design: Cenveo Publisher Services
Cover Design: William Boardman
Cover Photo: Workers during the Construction of the Grand Coulee Dam, Washington (between 1936 and 1946). Library of Congress, Prints & Photographs Division, Reproduction number LC-DIG-ppmsca-17400.
Composition: Cenveo Publisher Services
Printing and Binding: King Printing Co., Inc.

For information, write: Bedford/St. Martin's, 75 Arlington Street, Boston, MA 02116   (617-399-4000)

ISBN 978-1-319-29275-1 (Combined Edition)
ISBN 978-1-319-29278-2 (Volume 1)
ISBN 978-1-319-29281-2 (Volume 2)

Acknowledgments

Acknowledgments and copyrights appear on the same page as the text and art selections they cover; these acknowledgments and copyrights constitute an extension of the copyright page.

Preface: Why This Book This Way

What is the best way to engage and teach students in their history survey course? From the beginning, *The American Promise* has been shaped by our firsthand knowledge that the survey course is one of the most difficult to teach and, for many, also the most difficult to take. From the outset we have met this challenge by providing a story students enjoy for its readability, clear chronology, and lively voices of ordinary Americans, and by providing a full-featured text that instructors prize for its full narrative with political backbone, abundant documents and features for analysis and discussion, and the overall support for teaching. We remain committed to making the book the most teachable and readable introductory American history text available.

With **LaunchPad** we have made meeting the challenges of the survey course a great deal easier by providing an intuitive, interactive e-Book and course space with a wealth of primary sources. Ready to assign as is with key assessment resources built into each chapter, LaunchPad can also be edited and customized as instructors' imaginations and innovations dictate. Free when packaged with the print text, LaunchPad grants students and teachers access to a wealth of online tools and resources built specifically for our text to enhance reading comprehension and promote in-depth study. LaunchPad is loaded with the full-color e-Book plus **LearningCurve**, an adaptive learning tool; the popular ***Reading the American Past*** primary documents collection; **additional primary sources**; special **skills-based assessment activities**; **videos**; **chapter summative quizzes**; and more.

What Makes *The American Promise* Special

Our experience as teachers and our frustrations with available textbooks inspired us to create a book that we could use effectively with our own students. Our knowledge of classroom realities has informed every aspect of each edition and version of *The American Promise*. We began with **a clear chronological**, **political framework**, as we have found that students need both the structure a political narrative provides *and* the insights gained from examining social and cultural experience. To write a comprehensive, balanced account of American history, we focus on the public arena—the place where politics intersects social and cultural developments—to show how Americans confronted the major issues of their day and created far-reaching historical change.

The unique approach of our narrative is reflected in our title, *The American Promise*. We **emphasize human agency** and demonstrate our conviction that the essence of America has been its promise. For millions, the nation has held out the promise of a better life, unfettered worship, equality before the law, representative government, democratic politics, and other freedoms seldom found elsewhere. But none of these promises has come with guarantees. Throughout the narrative we demonstrate how much of American history is a **continuing struggle over the definition and realization of the nation's promise**.

To engage students in this American story and to portray fully the diversity of the American experience, we stitch into our narrative **the voices of hundreds of contemporaries**. We further animate this story with a vivid art and map program. **Four visual activities and two map activities per chapter** prompt students to think critically about what they see. To help students of all levels understand American history, we provide the best in **primary sources** and **pedagogical aids**. To help instructors teach important skills and evaluate student learning, we provide a **rich assortment of assignments and assessments** in both the print and LaunchPad formats. While this edition rests solidly on our original goals and premises, it breaks new ground in addressing the specific needs of today's courses.

A New Skills Focus for the Special Features

For this revision we focused our attention on *The American Promise*'s acclaimed feature program by looking for ways to make the features more useful, skills-oriented assignments. In print, the features offer primary sources, visuals, essays, and discussion questions; in Launchpad, the feature program comes fully to life with both short-answer and multiple-choice questions that test students' critical reading skills. **Making Historical Arguments** (formerly **Historical Question**) now offers active, skills-based activities that demonstrate to students how historians make and support historical arguments. **Analyzing Historical Evidence** (formerly **Documenting the American Promise**) then gives students the opportunity to practice the skills introduced in **Making Historical Arguments** through analysis of text and visual sources. **Experiencing the American Promise** (formerly **Seeking the American Promise**) offers essays that illuminate the stories of individuals who sought their dream in America, helping students evaluate to what extent individuals make history. Finally, an enhanced **Beyond America's Borders** continues to offer students a global perspective on the narrative's themes with essays that connect U.S. history to developments around the globe.

Collectively these features provide a range of new topics and content that includes increased attention to white servant women and slave men in the seventeenth-century Chesapeake; a new focus on the weak opposition to the African slave trade in the eighteenth century; a nuanced look at urban workers' standard of living in the Gilded Age; a spotlight on Franklin D. Roosevelt's use of New Deal programs to rebuild the navy during the 1930s; an exploration of the federal government's influence on the economy in the post–World War II years; a study of the impact of the Voting Rights Act; an in-depth look at the use of air power in Vietnam; an investigation of the loss of American manufacturing jobs in the twenty-first century; and much more.

Evaluation of Primary Sources

Primary sources form the heart of historical study, and we are pleased to offer **the new Analyzing Historical Evidence** feature, which asks students to use historical thinking skills to consider a range of documents. Each feature juxtaposes two to four primary documents to reveal varying perspectives on a topic or issue and to provide students with opportunities to build and practice their skills of historical interpretation. Because students are so attuned to visuals and instructors deeply value their usefulness as primary sources, we have included both text and visual sources in this new feature. Images, including artifacts of daily life in Chaco Canyon, paintings of the Battle of the Little Big Horn, a 1920s mouthwash advertisement, political cartoons, and more, show students how to mine visual documents for evidence about the past.

In **Analyzing Historical Evidence**, feature introductions and document headnotes contextualize the sources, and short-answer questions at the end of the feature promote critical thinking about primary sources. New topics have been added that are rich with human drama and include "Enslavement by Marriage" and "The Nation's First Formal Declaration of War." These features are available both in print and online, and they are easily assigned in LaunchPad, along with multiple-choice quizzes that measure student comprehension.

In addition, more than 150 documents in the accompanying collection *Reading the American Past* are available free to users who package the reader with the main print text, and they are automatically included in the LaunchPad e-Book. Multiple-choice questions are also available for assignment to measure comprehension and hold students accountable for their reading.

LaunchPad for *The American Promise* also comes with a collection of **more than 135 additional primary sources** that instructors can choose to assign. These sources include letters, memoirs, court records, government documents, and more, and they include items by or about such people as John Smith, William Penn, Anne Hutchinson, Jonathan Edwards, Mary Jemison, Black Hawk, Rebecca Neugin, John C. Calhoun, Frederick Douglass, Abraham Lincoln, Mary Elizabeth Lease, William Jennings Bryan, Rose Pastor Stokes, Theodore Roosevelt, Nicola Sacco and Bartolomeo Vanzetti, Franklin D. Roosevelt, Harry S. Truman, Paul Robeson, Ronald Reagan, and more.

To give students ample opportunity to practice thinking critically about primary source images, four pictures in each chapter include a special **visual activity caption** that reinforces this essential skill. One set of questions in these activities prompts analysis of the image, while a second set of questions helps students connect the images to main points in the narrative.

Distinctive Essay Features Practice Historical Thinking Skills

To demonstrate and engage students in various methods of historical thinking, our **Making Historical Arguments** feature essays, which occur in every chapter, pose and interpret specific questions of continuing interest. We pair perennial favorites such as "Was the New United States a Christian Country?," "How Often Were Slaves Whipped?," "Was There a Sexual Revolution in the 1920s?," and "Why Did the Allies Win World War II?," with brand-new entries including "How Did Seventeenth-Century Colonists View Nature?" and "What Did African Americans Want from World War I, and What Did They Get?"

Short-answer questions at the end of the features prompt students to consider things such as evidence, beliefs and values, and cause and effect as they relate to the historical question at hand. Available both in print and online, these features can be easily assigned in LaunchPad, along with multiple-choice quizzes that measure student comprehension.

Helping Students Understand the Narrative

Every instructor knows it can be a challenge to get students to complete assigned readings, and then to fully understand what is important once they do the reading. *The American Promise* addresses these problems head-on with a suite of tools in LaunchPad that instructors can choose from.

To help students come to class prepared, instructors who adopt LaunchPad for *The American Promise* can assign the **LearningCurve** formative assessment activities. This online learning tool is popular with students because it helps them comprehend content at their own pace in a nonthreatening, game-like environment. LearningCurve is also popular with instructors because the reporting features allow them to track overall class trends and spot topics that are giving their students trouble so they can adjust their lectures and class activities.

Encouraging active reading is another means for making content memorable and highlighting what is truly important. To help students read actively and understand the central idea of the chapter, instructors who use LaunchPad can also assign **Guided Reading Exercises**. These exercises appear at the start of each chapter, prompting students to collect information to be used to answer a broad analytic question central to the chapter as a whole.

To further encourage students to read and fully assimilate the text as well as measure how well they do this, instructors can assign the **multiple-choice summative quizzes** in LaunchPad, where they are automatically graded. These secure tests not only encourage students to study the book, they can be assigned at specific intervals as higher-stakes testing and thus provide another means for analyzing class performance.

Another big challenge for survey instructors is meeting the needs of a range of students, particularly the students who need the most support. In addition to the formative assessment of LearningCurve, which adapts to the needs of students at any level, *The American Promise* offers a number of print and digital tools for the underprepared. Each chapter opener includes **Content Learning Objectives** to prepare students to read the chapter with purpose. Once into the heart of the chapter, students are reminded to think about main ideas through **Review Questions** placed at the end of every major section. Some students have trouble connecting events and ideas, particularly with special boxed features. To address this, we have added a set of **Questions for Analysis** to the end of each feature to help students understand the significance of the featured topic, its context, and how it might be viewed from different angles. These questions are also available in the print and LaunchPad versions of the book.

With this edition we also bring back two popular sets of end-of-chapter questions that help widen students' focus as they consider what they have read. **Making Connections** questions ask students to think about broad developments within the chapter, while **Linking to the Past** questions cross-reference developments in earlier chapters, encouraging students to draw connections to the modern world and consider how the issues addressed in the chapter are still relevant today.

Helping Instructors Teach with Digital Resources

With requests for clear and transparent learning outcomes coming from all quarters and with students who bring increasingly diverse levels of skills to class, even veteran teachers can find preparing for today's courses a trying matter. With **LaunchPad** we have reconceived the textbook as a suite of tools in multiple formats that allows each format to do what it does best to capture students' interest and help instructors create meaningful lessons.

But one of the best benefits is that instructors using LaunchPad have a number of assessment tools that allow them to see what it is their students do and don't know and measure student achievement all in one convenient space. For example, **LearningCurve**, an adaptive learning tool that comes with LaunchPad, garners more than a 90 percent student satisfaction rate and helps students master book content. When LearningCurve is assigned, the grade book results show instructors where the entire class or individual students may be struggling, and this information in turn allows instructors to adjust lectures and course activities accordingly—a benefit not only for traditional classes but invaluable for hybrid, online, and newer "flipped" classes as well. In addition, not only can instructors assign all of the questions that appear in the print book and view the responses in the grade book, they have the option to assign automatically graded multiple-choice questions for all of the book features.

With LaunchPad for *The American Promise* we make the tough job of teaching simpler by providing everything instructors need in one convenient space so they can set and achieve the learning outcomes they desire. To learn more about the benefits of LearningCurve and LaunchPad, see the "Versions and Supplements" section on page xvii.

Acknowledgments

We gratefully acknowledge all of the helpful suggestions from those who have read and taught from previous editions of *The American Promise,* and we hope that our many classroom collaborators will be pleased to see their influence in the seventh edition. In particular, we wish to thank the talented scholars and teachers who gave generously of their time and knowledge to review the previous edition in preparation for its revision: LeNie Adolphson, *Sauk Valley Community College*; Daniel Anderson, *Cincinnati State Technical and Community College*; Ian Baldwin, *University of Nevada, Las Vegas*; Veronica Bale, *MiraCosta College*; Karen Cook Bell, *Bowie State University*; Dustin Black, *El Camino College*; Nawana Britenriker, *Pikes Peak Community College*; Elizabeth Broen, *South Florida State College*; Robert Browning, *University of Texas, San Antonio*; Robert Bush, *Front Range Community College*; Brian David Collins, *El Centro College*; Alexandra Cornelius, *Florida International University*; Sondra Cosgrove, *College of Southern Nevada*; Rodney E. Dillon, Jr., *Palm Beach State College*; Wayne Drews, *Georgia Institute of Technology*; Edward J. Dudlo, *Brookhaven College*; E. J. Fabyan, *Vincennes University*; Randy Finley, *Georgia Perimeter College*; Cecilia Gowdy-Wygant, *Front Range Community College*; Elizabeth Green, *University of South Alabama*; William Grose, *Wytheville Community College*; Steven Heise, *Holyoke Community College*; Jeff Janowick, *Lansing Community College*; Juneann Klees, *Bay College*; Leonard V. Larsen, *Des Moines Area Community College*; Charles Levine, *Mesa Community College*; Kerima Lewis, *Bridgewater State University*; Mary Linehan, *University of Texas at Tyler*; Annie Liss, *South Texas College*; Patricia Loughlin, *University of Central Oklahoma*; Veronica McComb, *Lenoir-Rhyne University*; Walter Miszczenko, *College of Western Idaho*; Rick Murray, *Los Angeles Valley College*; Richard Owens, *West Liberty University*; Stacey Pendleton, *University of Colorado Denver*; Michael J. Pfeifer, *John Jay College of Criminal Justice*; Robert Lynn Rainard, *Tidewater Community College*; Chris Rasmussen, *Fairleigh Dickinson University*; George D. Salaita, *Eastern Tennessee University*; Robert Sawvel, *University of Northern Colorado*; Benjamin G. Scharff, *West Virginia University*; Mark Simon, *Queens College of the City of New York*; Christopher Sleeper, *MiraCosta College*; Janet P. Smith, *East Tennessee State University*; John Howard Smith, *Texas A&M University–Commerce*; William Z. Tannenbaum, *Missouri Southern State University*; Ramon C. Veloso, *Palomar College*; Kenneth A. Watras, *Paradise Valley Community College*; and Eric Weinberg, *Viterbo University*.

A project as complex as this requires the talents of many individuals. First, we would like to acknowledge our families for their support, forbearance, and toleration of our textbook responsibilities. Naomi Kornhauser contributed her vast knowledge, tireless energy, and diligent research to make possible the useful and attractive illustration program. We would also like to thank the many people at Bedford/St. Martin's and Macmillan Learning who have been crucial to this project. Thanks are due to Robin Soule, developmental editor; Edwin Hill, vice president; Michael Rosenberg, publisher; William J. Lombardo, senior executive editor for history; and Jane Knetzger, director of development for history, for their support and guidance. Thanks are also due to Heidi Hood, senior editor; Jennifer Jovin, media editor; Tess Fletcher, associate editor; Mary Posman, assistant editor; and Lexi DeConti, editorial assistant. For their imaginative and tireless efforts to promote the book, we want to thank history marketing manager Melissa Famiglietti, and marketing assistant Morgan Ratner. With great skill and professionalism, senior production editor Rosemary Jaffe pulled together the many pieces related to copyediting, design, and composition. Production manager Joe Ford oversaw the manufacturing of the book. Designer Jerilyn Bockorick, copy editor Lisa Wehrle, and proofreaders Roberta Sobotka and Linda McLatchie attended to the myriad details that help make the book shine. Mary White provided an outstanding index. The covers for the book's many versions were researched and designed by William Boardman. Media producer Michelle Camisa oversaw the timely and complex production of digital components of *The American Promise*.

Versions and Supplements

Adopters of *The American Promise* and their students have access to abundant print and digital resources and tools, the acclaimed Bedford Series in History and Culture volumes, and much more. The LaunchPad course space provides access to the narrative as well as a wealth of primary sources and other features, along with assignment and assessment opportunities. See below for more information, visit the book's catalog site at **macmillanlearning.com**, or contact your local Bedford/St. Martin's sales representative.

Get the Right Version for Your Class

The American Promise franchise offers a variety of versions to best suit your course needs. The comprehensive *The American Promise* includes a full-color art program and a robust set of features. *Understanding the American Promise*, with a more modest feature program, enhances the full narrative with a question-driven approach and innovative active learning pedagogy. *The American Promise: A Concise History* also provides the full narrative, with a streamlined art and feature program, at a lower price. *The American Promise, Value Edition* offers a trade-sized two-color option with the full narrative and selected art and maps at a steeper discount. The *Value Edition* is also offered at the lowest price point in loose-leaf, and all versions are available as low-priced PDF e-Books. For the best value of all, package a new print book with LaunchPad at no additional charge to get the best each format offers—a print version for easy portability with a LaunchPad interactive e-Book and course space with LearningCurve and loads of additional assignment and assessment options.

- **Combined Volume** (Chapters 1–31): available in the comprehensive, *Understanding*, Concise, Value, loose-leaf, and e-Book formats and in LaunchPad

- **Volume 1, To 1877** (Chapters 1–16): available in the comprehensive, *Understanding*, Concise, Value, loose-leaf, and e-Book formats and in LaunchPad

- **Volume 2, From 1865** (Chapters 16–31): available in the comprehensive, *Understanding*, Concise, Value, loose-leaf, and e-Book formats and in LaunchPad

As noted below, any of these volumes can be packaged with additional titles for a discount. To get ISBNs for discount packages, visit **macmillanlearning.com** or contact your Bedford/St. Martin's representative.

Assign LaunchPad—an Assessment-Ready Interactive e-Book and Course Space

Available for discount purchase on its own or for packaging with new books at no additional charge, LaunchPad is a breakthrough solution for history courses. Intuitive and easy-to-use for students and instructors alike, LaunchPad is ready to use as is; it can be edited, customized with your own material, and assigned quickly. LaunchPad for *The American Promise* includes Bedford/St. Martin's high-quality content all in one place, including the full interactive e-Book and the companion reader *Reading the American Past*, plus LearningCurve formative quizzing, guided reading activities designed to help students read actively for key concepts, auto-graded quizzes for each primary source, and chapter summative quizzes.

Through a wealth of formative and summative assessments, including the adaptive learning program of LearningCurve (see the full description ahead), students gain confidence and get into their reading *before* class. These features, plus additional primary-source documents, video sources and tools for making video assignments, map activities, flashcards, and customizable test banks, make LaunchPad an invaluable asset for any instructor. For more information, visit **launchpadworks.com** or to arrange a demo, contact us at **history @macmillan.com**.

Assign LearningCurve So Your Students Come to Class Prepared

Students using LaunchPad receive access to LearningCurve for *The American Promise*. Assigning LearningCurve in place of reading quizzes is easy for instructors, and the reporting features help instructors track overall class trends and spot topics that are giving students trouble so they can adjust their lectures and class activities. This online learning tool is popular with students because it was designed to help them comprehend content at their own pace in a non-threatening, game-like environment. The feedback for wrong answers provides instructional coaching and sends students back to the book for review. Students answer as many questions as necessary to reach a target score with repeated chances to revisit material they haven't mastered. When LearningCurve is assigned, students come to class better prepared.

Take Advantage of Instructor Resources

Bedford/St. Martin's has developed a rich array of teaching resources for this book and for this course. They range from lecture and presentation materials and assessment tools to course management options. Most can be found in LaunchPad or can be downloaded or ordered from the Instructor Resources tab of the book's catalog site at **macmillanlearning.com**.

Bedford Coursepack for Blackboard, Canvas, Brightspace by D2L, or Moodle. We can help you integrate our rich content into your course management system. Registered instructors can download coursepacks that include our popular free resources and book-specific content for *The American Promise*.

Instructor's Resource Manual. The instructor's manual offers both experienced and first-time instructors tools for presenting textbook materials in engaging ways. It includes chapter content learning objectives, annotated chapter outlines, and strategies for teaching with the textbook, plus suggestions on how to get the most out of LearningCurve and a survival guide for first-time teaching assistants.

Guide to Changing Editions. Designed to facilitate an instructor's transition from the previous edition of *The American Promise* to this new edition, this guide presents an overview of major changes as well as of changes in each chapter.

Online Test Bank. The test bank includes a mix of fresh, carefully crafted multiple-choice, matching, short-answer, and essay questions for each chapter. Many of the multiple-choice questions feature a map, an image, or a primary-source excerpt as the prompt. All questions appear in easy-to-use test bank software that allows instructors to add, edit, resequence, filter by question type or learning objective, and print questions and answers. Instructors can also export questions into a variety of course management systems.

The Bedford Lecture Kit: Lecture Outlines, Maps, and Images. Look good and save time with *The Bedford Lecture Kit*. These presentation materials are downloadable individually from the Instructor Resources tab at **macmillanlearning.com/roark/catalog**. They include fully customizable multimedia presentations built around chapter outlines that are embedded with maps, figures, and images from the textbook and are supplemented by more detailed instructor notes on key points and concepts.

America in Motion: Video Clips for U.S. History. Set history in motion with *America in Motion*, an instructor DVD containing dozens of short digital movie files of events in twentieth-century American history. From the wreckage of the battleship *Maine* to FDR's fireside chats to Ronald Reagan speaking before the Brandenburg Gate, *America in Motion* engages students with dynamic scenes from key events and challenges them to think critically. All files are classroom-ready, edited for brevity, and easily integrated with presentation slides or other software for electronic lectures or assignments. An accompanying guide provides each clip's historical context, ideas for use, and suggested questions.

Print, Digital, and Custom Options for More Choice and Value

For information on free packages and discounts up to 50 percent, visit **macmillanlearning.com** or contact your local Bedford/St. Martin's sales representative.

Reading the American Past, Fifth Edition.
Edited by Michael P. Johnson, one of the authors of *The American Promise*, and designed to complement the textbook, *Reading the American Past* provides a broad selection of more than 150 primary-source documents, as well as editorial apparatus to help students understand the sources. Available free when packaged with the print text and included in the LaunchPad e-Book. Also available on its own as a downloadable PDF e-Book.

NEW Bedford Custom Tutorials for History.
Designed to customize textbooks with resources relevant to individual courses, this collection of brief units, each sixteen pages long and loaded with examples, guides students through basic skills such as using historical evidence effectively, working with primary sources, taking effective notes, avoiding plagiarism and citing sources, and more. Up to two tutorials can be added to a Bedford/St. Martin's history survey title at no additional charge, freeing you to spend your class time focusing on content and interpretation. For more information, visit **macmillanlearning.com /historytutorials**.

NEW Bedford Digital Collections for U.S. History. This source collection provides a flexible and affordable online repository of discovery-oriented primary-source projects ready to assign. Each curated project—written by a historian about a favorite topic—poses a historical question and guides students step by step through analysis of primary sources. Examples include What Caused the Civil War?; The California Gold Rush: A Trans-Pacific Phenomenon; and War Stories: Black Soldiers and the Long Civil Rights Movement. For more information, visit **macmillanlearning.com/bdc/ushistory/catalog**. Available free when packaged.

NEW Bedford Digital Collections Custom Print Modules. Choose one or two document projects from the collection (see above) and add them in print to a Bedford/St. Martin's title, or select several to be bound together in a custom reader created specifically for your course. Either way, the modules are affordably priced. For more information visit **macmillanlearning .com/custombdc/ushistory** or contact your Bedford/St. Martin's representative.

The Bedford Series in History and Culture.
More than 100 titles in this highly praised series combine first-rate scholarship, historical narrative, and important primary documents for undergraduate courses. Each book is brief, inexpensive, and focused on a specific topic or period. Revisions of several best-selling titles, such as *The Cherokee Removal: A Brief History with Documents* by Theda Perdue; *Narrative of the Life of Frederick Douglass*, edited by David Blight; and *The Triangle Fire: A Brief History with Documents* by Jo Ann Argersinger, are now available. For a complete list of titles, visit **macmillanlearning.com**. Package discounts are available.

Rand McNally Atlas of American History.
This collection of more than eighty full-color maps illustrates key events and eras from early exploration, settlement, expansion, and immigration to U.S. involvement in wars abroad and on U.S. soil. Introductory pages for each section include a brief overview, timelines, graphs, and photos to quickly establish a historical context. Free when packaged.

The Bedford Glossary for U.S. History. This handy supplement for the survey course gives students historically contextualized definitions for hundreds of terms—from *abolitionism* to *zoot suit*—that they will encounter in lectures, reading, and exams. Free when packaged.

Trade Books. Titles published by sister companies Hill and Wang; Farrar, Straus and Giroux; Henry Holt and Company; St. Martin's Press; Picador; and Palgrave Macmillan are available at a 50 percent discount when packaged with Bedford/St. Martin's textbooks. For more information, visit **macmillanlearning.com/tradeup**.

A Pocket Guide to Writing in History. This portable and affordable reference tool by Mary Lynn Rampolla provides reading, writing, and research advice useful to students in all history courses. Concise yet comprehensive advice on approaching typical history assignments, developing critical reading skills, writing effective history papers, conducting research, using and documenting sources, and avoiding plagiarism—enhanced with practical tips and examples throughout—have made this slim reference a best seller. Package discounts are available.

A Student's Guide to History. This complete guide to success in any history course provides the practical help students need to be successful.

In addition to introducing students to the nature of the discipline, author Jules Benjamin teaches a wide range of skills from preparing for exams to approaching common writing assignments, and explains the research and documentation process with plentiful examples. Package discounts are available.

Going to the Source: The Bedford Reader in American History. Developed by Victoria Bissell Brown and Timothy J. Shannon, this reader combines a rich diversity of primary and secondary sources with in-depth instructions for how to use each type of source. Mirroring the chronology of the U.S. history survey, each of the main chapters familiarizes students with a single type of source—from personal letters to political cartoons—while focusing on an intriguing historical episode such as the Cherokee Removal or the 1894 Pullman strike. The reader's wide variety of chapter topics and sources provoke students' interest as it teaches them the skills they need to successfully interrogate historical sources. Package discounts are available.

America Firsthand. With its distinctive focus on first-person accounts from ordinary people, this primary documents reader by Anthony Marcus, John M. Giggie, and David Burner offers a remarkable range of perspectives on America's history from those who lived it. Popular Points of View sections expose students to different perspectives on a specific event or topic. Package discounts are available.

Brief Contents

Contents

CHAPTER 1
Ancient America,
Before 1492   1

Photo by John Bigelow Taylor.

CHAPTER 2
Europeans Encounter the New World, 1492–1600   25

Photo: © Chico Sanchez/Alamy Stock Photo.

CHAPTER 3
The Southern Colonies in the Seventeenth Century, 1601–1700 51

Photo: Courtesy Jamestown Rediscovery (Preservation Virginia).

CHAPTER 4
The Northern Colonies in the Seventeenth Century, 1601–1700 77

Photo: Polaris/Newscom.

CHAPTER 7
The War for America,
1775–1783 165

Photo: National Museum of American History, Smithsonian Institution, USA/Bridgeman Images.

CHAPTER 8
Building a Republic,
1775–1789 195

Photo: Courtesy of Independence National Historic Park.

CHAPTER 11
The Expanding Republic, 1815–1840   283

Photo: Willard House and Clock Museum.

CHAPTER 12
The New West and the Free North, 1840–1860   315

Photo: CSP_Fireflyphoto/age fotostock.

Photo: National Museum of American History, Smithsonian Institution, USA/ Bridgeman Images.

Photo: © Chicago History Museum, USA/Bridgeman Images.

Photo: Private Collection, photograph American Hurrah Archive, NYC.

Photo: David J. & Janice L. Frent Collection/Corbis.

CHAPTER 21
Progressivism from the Grass Roots to the White House, 1890–1916   587

Photo: David J. & Janice L. Frent Collection/Corbis.

CHAPTER 22
World War I: The Progressive Crusade at Home and Abroad, 1914–1920   617

Photo: Collection of Colonel Stuart S. Corning Jr./Picture Research Consultants & Archives.

Photo: Division of Work & Industry, National Museum of American History, Smithsonian Institution.

Photo: David J. & Janice L. Frent Collection/Corbis.

Photo: National Museum of American History, Smithsonian Institution, USA/Bridgeman Images.

Image Courtesy of The Advertising Archives.

Photo: Bill Philpot/Alamy Stock Photo.

Photo: Collection of Mark Hooper.

Photo: Doug Steley B/Alamy.

Photo: Division of Political History, National Museum of American History, Smithsonian Institution.

CHAPTER 31
The Promises and Challenges of Globalization, Since 1989   891

APPENDICES

Maps, Figures, and Tables

Maps

Figures and Tables

Special Features

MAKING HISTORICAL ARGUMENTS

The
American
Promise

A History of
the United States

1

Ancient America

Before 1492

CONTENT LEARNING OBJECTIVES

After reading and studying this chapter, you should be able to:

- Distinguish archaeology and history as disciplines, and understand the possibilities and limitations of both.

- Identify the earth's first human inhabitants and what developments allowed them to migrate to the Western Hemisphere.

- Differentiate between Archaic hunter-gatherers and the Paleo-Indians, and identify the main characteristics of their cultures.

- Explain how the Archaic peoples transitioned from being nomadic hunter-gatherers to relying on agriculture and permanent settlements.

- Identify the major Native American cultures that flourished in North America on the eve of Columbus's arrival and the similarities among them.

- Describe the structure, influence, and expanse of the Mexica (Aztec) empire on the eve of Columbus's arrival.

MISSISSIPPIAN WOODEN MASK
Between AD 1200 and 1350, a Mississippian in what is now central Illinois fashioned this mask. Influenced by the culture of Cahokia, it was probably used in rituals. Photo by John Bigelow Taylor.

NOBODY TODAY KNOWS HIS NAME. BUT ALMOST A THOUSAND years ago, more than four hundred years before Europeans arrived in the Western Hemisphere, many ancient Americans celebrated this man—let's call him Sun Falcon. They buried Sun Falcon during elaborate rituals at Cahokia, the largest residential and ceremonial site in ancient North America, the giant landmass north of present-day Mexico. Located near the eastern shore of the Mississippi River in what is now southwestern Illinois, Cahokia stood at the spiritual and political center of the world of more than 20,000 ancient Americans who lived there and nearby. The way Cahokians buried Sun Falcon suggests that he was a very important person who represented spiritual and political authority.

What we know about Sun Falcon and the Cahokians who buried him has been discovered by archaeologists—scientists who study artifacts, material objects left behind by ancient peoples. Cahokia attracted the attention of archaeologists because of the hundreds of earthen mounds that ancient Americans built in the region. The largest surviving mound, Monks Mound, is a huge pyramid that covers sixteen acres, making it the biggest single structure ever built by ancient North Americans.

Atop Monks Mound, political and religious leaders performed ceremonies watched by thousands of Cahokians who stood on a fifty-acre plaza at the base of the mound. Their ceremonies were probably designed to demonstrate to onlookers the leaders' access to supernatural forces. At the far edge of the plaza, Cahokians buried Sun Falcon in an oblong mound about 6 feet high and 250 feet long.

Before Cahokians lowered Sun Falcon into his grave sometime around AD 1050, they first placed the body of another man facedown in the dirt. On top of that man, Cahokians draped a large cape made of 20,000 shell beads crafted into the likeness of a bird. They then put Sun Falcon faceup on the beaded cape with his head pointing southeast, aligned with the passage of the sun across the sky during the summer solstice. Experts speculate that Cahokians who buried Sun Falcon sought to pay homage not only to him but also to the awe-inspiring forces of darkness and light, of earth and sun, that governed their lives.

To accompany Sun Falcon, Cahokians also buried hundreds of exquisitely crafted artifacts and the bodies of seven other adults who probably were relatives or servants of Sun Falcon. Not far away, archaeologists discovered several astonishing mass graves. One contained 53 women, all but one between the ages of fifteen and twenty-five, who had been sacrificed by poison, strangulation, or having their throats slit. Other graves contained 43 more sacrificed women, and 43 other men and women who had been executed at the burial site. In all, more than 270 people were buried in the mound with Sun Falcon.

Nobody knows exactly who Sun Falcon was or why Cahokians buried him as they did. To date, archaeologists have found no similar burial site in ancient North America. Most likely, Sun Falcon's burial and the human sacrifices that accompanied it were major public rituals that communicated to the many onlookers the fearsome power he wielded, the respect he commanded, and the authority his survivors intended to honor and maintain. Much remains unknown and unknowable about him and his fellow Cahokians, just as it does with other ancient Americans. The

VISUAL ACTIVITY

Cahokia Burial

The excavation of a burial site at Cahokia revealed the remains of a man—presumably a revered leader—whom Cahokians buried atop a large bird-shaped cape covered with shell beads. Nearby in the same mound, excavators found mass graves of scores of other Cahokians, many of them executed just before burial, evidently during ceremonies to honor their leader. Photo courtesy of University of Wisconsin–Milwaukee Archaeological Research Laboratory (ARL image 1967.2.31).

READING THE IMAGE: What does the cape or blanket suggest about patterns of trade and craftsmanship at Cahokia?

CONNECTIONS: Where was Cahokia located and for approximately how many ancient Americans was this an important spiritual and political center?

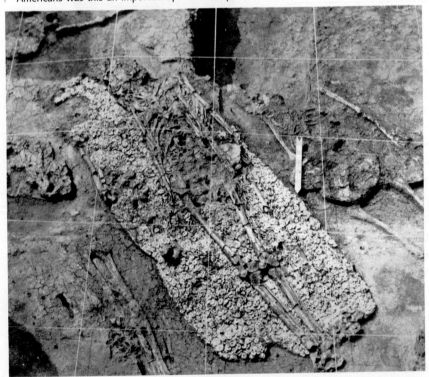

history of ancient Americans is therefore necessarily incomplete and controversial. Still, archaeologists have learned enough to understand where ancient Americans came from and many basic features of the complex cultures they created and passed along to their descendants, who dominated the history of America until 1492.

▶ Archaeology and History

Archaeologists and historians share the desire to learn about people who lived in the past, but they usually employ different methods to obtain information. Both archaeologists and historians study artifacts as clues to the activities and ideas of the humans who created them. They concentrate, however, on different kinds of artifacts. Archaeologists tend to focus on physical objects such as bones, spear points, pots, baskets, jewelry, clothing, and buildings. Historians direct their attention mostly to writings, such as letters, diaries, laws, speeches, newspapers, and court cases. The concentration of historians on writings and of archaeologists on other physical objects denotes a rough cultural and chronological boundary between the human beings studied by the two groups of scholars, a boundary marked by the use of writing.

Writing is defined as a system of symbols that record spoken language. Writing originated among ancient peoples in China, Egypt, and Central America about eight thousand years ago, within the most recent 2 percent of the four hundred millennia (a *millennium* is a thousand years) that modern human beings have existed. While the ancient Americans who buried Sun Falcon at Cahokia about AD 1050 and all those who inhabited North America in 1492 possessed many forms of symbolic representation, they did not use writing. Ancient Americans invented hundreds of spoken languages; they learned to survive in almost every natural environment; they chose and honored leaders; they traded, warred, and worshipped; and above all, they learned from and taught one another. However, much of what we would like to know about their experiences and those of other ancient Americans remains unknown because they did not write about it.

Archaeologists specialize in learning about people who did not document their history in

CHRONOLOGY

ca. 400,000 BP	• *Homo sapiens* evolve in Africa.
ca. 25,000–14,000 BP	• Glaciation exposes Beringia land bridge.
ca. 15,000 BP	• Humans arrive in North America.
ca. 13,500–13,000 BP	• Paleo-Indians use Clovis points.
ca. 11,000 BP	• Mammoths become extinct.
ca. 10,000–3000 BP	• Archaic hunter-gatherer cultures dominate ancient America.
ca. 5000 BP	• Chumash culture emerges in southern California.
ca. 4000 BP	• Eastern Woodland peoples grow gourds, make pottery.
ca. 3500 BP	• Southwestern cultures cultivate corn.
ca. 2500 BP	• Eastern Woodland cultures build burial mounds, cultivate corn.
ca. 2500–2100 BP	• Adena culture develops in Ohio.
ca. 2100 BP–AD **400**	• Hopewell culture emerges in Ohio and Mississippi valleys.
ca. AD 200–900	• Mogollon culture develops in New Mexico.
ca. AD 500	• Bows and arrows appear south of Arctic.
ca. AD 500–1400	• Hohokam culture develops in Arizona.
ca. AD 800–1500	• Mississippian culture flourishes in Southeast.
ca. AD 1000–1200	• Anasazi peoples build cliff dwellings and pueblos.
ca. AD 1325–1500	• Mexica establish Mexican empire.
AD 1492	• Christopher Columbus arrives in New World.

writing. They study the millions of artifacts these people created. They also scrutinize geological strata, pollen, and other environmental features to reconstruct as much as possible about the world inhabited by ancient peoples. This chapter relies on studies by archaeologists to sketch a brief overview of ancient America, the long first phase of the history of the United States.

Ancient Americans and their descendants resided in North America for thousands of years before Europeans arrived. While they created societies and cultures of remarkable diversity and complexity, their history cannot be reconstructed with the detail and certainty made possible by writing.

REVIEW   Why must historians rely on the work of archaeologists to write the history of ancient America?

▶ The First Americans

The first human beings to arrive in the Western Hemisphere emigrated from Asia. They brought with them hunting skills, weapon- and tool-making techniques, and other forms of human knowledge developed millennia earlier in Africa, Europe, and Asia. These first Americans hunted large mammals, such as the mammoths they had learned in Europe and Asia to kill, butcher, and process for food, clothing, and building materials. Most likely, these first Americans wandered into the Western Hemisphere more or less accidentally in pursuit of prey.

African and Asian Origins

Human beings lived elsewhere in the world for hundreds of thousands of years before they reached the Western Hemisphere. They lacked a way to travel to the Western Hemisphere because millions of years before humans existed anywhere on the globe, North and South America became detached from the gigantic common landmass scientists now call Pangaea. About 240 million years ago, powerful forces deep within the earth fractured Pangaea and slowly pushed continents apart to their present positions (Map 1.1). This

process of continental drift encircled the land of the Western Hemisphere with large oceans that isolated it from the other continents long before early human beings (*Homo erectus*) first appeared in Africa about two million years ago.

More than 1.5 million years after *Homo erectus* appeared, or about 400,000 BP, modern humans (*Homo sapiens*) evolved in Africa. (The abbreviation *BP*—for "years before the present"—indicates dates earlier than two thousand years ago; for more recent dates, the common and familiar notation *AD* is used, as in AD 1492.) All human beings throughout the world today are descendants of these ancient Africans. Their DNA was the template for ours. Slowly, over many millennia, *Homo sapiens* migrated out of Africa and into Europe and Asia, which retained land connections to Africa that allowed ancient humans to migrate on foot. For roughly 97 percent of the time *Homo sapiens* have been on earth, none migrated across the enormous oceans isolating the Eurasian landmass from North and South America.

Two major developments made it possible for ancient humans to migrate to the Western Hemisphere. First, people successfully adapted to the frigid environment near the Arctic Circle. Second, changes in the earth's climate reconnected North America to Asia.

By about 25,000 BP, *Homo sapiens* had spread from Africa throughout Europe and Asia. People, probably women, had learned to use bone needles to sew animal skins into warm clothing that permitted them to become permanent residents of extremely cold regions such as northeastern Siberia. A few of these ancient Siberians clothed in animal hides walked to North America on land that now lies submerged beneath the sixty miles of water that currently separates easternmost Siberia from westernmost Alaska. A pathway across this watery chasm opened during the last global cold spell—which endured from about 25,000 BP to 14,000 BP—when snow piled up in glaciers, causing the sea level to drop, thereby exposing a land bridge hundreds of miles wide called **Beringia** that connected Asian Siberia to American Alaska.

Siberian hunters roamed Beringia for centuries in search of mammoths, bison, and numerous smaller animals. As the hunters ventured farther east, they eventually became pioneers of human life in the Western Hemisphere. Although they did

Beringia

MAP ACTIVITY

Map 1.1 Continental Drift

Massive geological forces separated North and South America from other continents eons before human beings evolved in Africa two million years ago.

READING THE MAP: Which continents separated from Pangaea earliest? Which ones separated from each other last? Which are still closely connected to each other?

CONNECTIONS: How does continental drift explain why human life developed elsewhere on the planet for hundreds of thousands of years before the first person entered the Western Hemisphere 15,000 years ago?

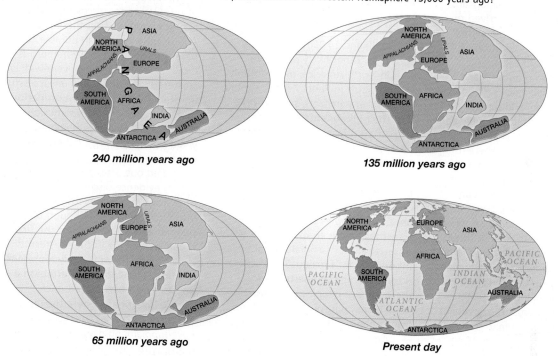

240 million years ago

135 million years ago

65 million years ago

Present day

not know it, their migrations revolutionized the history of the world.

Archaeologists refer to these first migrants and their descendants for the next few millennia as **Paleo-Indians**. They speculate that these Siberian hunters traveled in small bands of no more than twenty-five people. How many such bands arrived in North America before Beringia disappeared beneath the sea will never be known.

When the first migrants came is hotly debated by experts. They probably arrived sometime after 15,000 BP. Scattered and inconclusive evidence suggests that they may have arrived several thousand years earlier. (See "Making Historical Arguments," page 6.) Certainly, humans who came from Asia—whose ancestors left Africa hundreds of thousands of years earlier—inhabited the Western Hemisphere by 14,000 BP.

Paleo-Indian Hunters

When humans first arrived in the Western Hemisphere, massive glaciers covered most of present-day Canada. Many archaeologists believe that Paleo-Indians probably migrated in pursuit of game along an ice-free passageway on the eastern side of Canada's Rocky Mountains. Other Paleo-Indians may have traveled along the Pacific coast in small boats, hunting marine life and hopscotching from one desirable landing spot to another. At the southern edge of the glaciers, Paleo-Indians entered a hunters' paradise teeming with wildlife that had never before confronted human predators armed with razor-sharp spears. The abundance of game presumably made hunting relatively easy. Ample food permitted the Paleo-Indian population to grow. Within a thousand years or so of their arrival, Paleo-Indians had migrated throughout the Western Hemisphere.

Early Paleo-Indians used a distinctively shaped spearhead known as a **Clovis point**, named for the place in New Mexico where it was first excavated. Archaeologists' discovery of abundant Clovis points throughout North and Central America in sites occupied between 13,500 BP and 13,000 BP provides evidence that these

Who Were the First Americans?

To learn who the first Americans were and when they arrived requires following a trail of evidence that has grown very cold during the past 15,000 or 20,000 years.

After millennia of erosion and environmental change, much of the land they walked, hunted, and camped on is now submerged and inaccessible beneath the Bering Sea and along the Atlantic and Pacific coasts, where rising sea levels have flooded wide, previously exposed coastal plains. Most of the numerous Paleo-Indian sites archaeologists have excavated were occupied more than a hundred centuries after the first migrants arrived. These sites often yield spear points and large animal bones, but Paleo-Indian human skeletal remains are very rare. And yet evidence that Paleo-Indians inhabited the Western Hemisphere is overwhelming and indisputable. Human craftsmanship is the only credible explanation for Clovis points, and carbon dating establishes that the oldest Clovis sites are about 13,500 years old.

Scattered and controversial evidence suggests, however, that Clovis peoples were not the first arrivals. The Monte Verde excavation in Chile has persuaded many archaeologists that the first Americans resided in South America sometime between 14,750 BP and 14,000 BP. This site and a few other likely pre-Clovis sites in North America, most notably Meadowcroft in Pennsylvania, contain no Clovis-era artifacts, suggesting that their inhabitants arrived earlier and differed from the later Clovis peoples. But if the first Americans already lived in Chile and Pennsylvania 14,000 or more years ago, when did they first arrive and from where?

Some experts hypothesize that pre-Clovis peoples sailed or floated across the Pacific from Australia or Antarctica. Most scholars consider those ideas far-fetched. The Pacific is too wide and tempestuous for these ancient peoples and their small boats to have survived a long transoceanic trip.

Ancient Siberians had the means (hunting skills and adaptation to the frigid climate), motive (pursuit of game animals), and opportunity (the Beringian land bridge) to become the first humans to arrive in America, and most archaeologists believe they did just that. But when they came is difficult to determine since the Beringian land bridge existed for thousands of years. The extreme rarity of the earliest archaeological sites in North America also makes it difficult to estimate with confidence when pre-Clovis hunters arrived. A rough guess is 15,000 BP, although it might have been earlier. The scarcity of pre-Clovis sites discovered so far strongly suggests that these ancient Americans were few in number (compared to the much more numerous Clovis-era Paleo-Indians), very widely scattered, and ultimately unsuccessful in establishing permanent residence in the hemisphere. Although they and their descendants may have survived in America for a millennium or more, pre-Clovis peoples appear to have died out. The sparse archaeological evidence discovered to date does not suggest that they evolved into Clovis peoples. Although Clovis peoples evidently were not the first humans to arrive in the Western Hemisphere, they probably represent the first Paleo-Indians to establish a permanent American presence.

To investigate where the mysterious first Americans came from, experts have supplemented archaeological evidence with careful study of modern-day Native Americans. Although many millennia separate today's Native Americans from those ancient hunters, most scholars agree that telltale clues to the identity of the first Americans can be gleaned from den-

nomadic hunters shared a common ancestry and way of life. At a few isolated sites, archaeologists have found still-controversial evidence of pre-Clovis artifacts that suggests the people who used Clovis spear points may have followed a few pre-Clovis pioneers who arrived several hundred years earlier. Paleo-Indians hunted large game such as mammoths and bison, but they probably also killed smaller animals. Concentration on large animals, when possible, made sense because just one mammoth could supply meat for months. Some Paleo-Indians even refrigerated killed mammoths by filling their body cavities with stones and submerging the carcasses in icy lakes for later use. In addition to food, mammoths provided Paleo-Indians with hides and bones for clothing, shelter, tools, and much more.

About 11,000 BP, Paleo-Indians confronted a major crisis. The mammoths and other large mammals they hunted became extinct. The extinction was gradual, stretching over several hundred years. Scientists are not completely certain why it occurred, although environmental change probably contributed to it. About this time, the earth's climate warmed, glaciers melted,

Clovis Point

This spear point excavated along the Columbia River in what is now Washington State was crafted by Clovis people around 11,000 BP. It illustrates how small fragments of stone were chipped away to create the point used for killing animals—a feature common to Clovis points throughout the hemisphere. Archaeologists believe that such commonalities document a widely shared Clovis culture practiced for many generations. Washington State Historical Society.

netic characteristics commonly found among Asians. Estimates of the evolutionary time required to produce the subtle differences between Asian and Native American DNA suggest a migration from Asia as early as 25,000 BP or before. But like the other high-tech evidence, this genetic evidence is sharply disputed by experts.

Fascinating as the genetic, linguistic, and dental studies are, they are unlikely to win widespread support among experts until they can be corroborated by archaeological evidence that, so far, has not been found. Until then, specialists will continue to debate when the first Americans arrived and how they were related to subsequent generations of ancient Americans.

tal, linguistic, and genetic evidence collected from their descendants who still live throughout the hemisphere.

Detailed scientific analyses of the teeth of thousands of ancient and modern Native Americans have identified distinctive dental shapes—such as incisors with a scooped-out inner surface—commonly found among ancient Siberians, ancient Americans, and modern Native Americans, but rare elsewhere. This dental evidence strongly supports the theory that the first Americans originated in Asia and migrated across the Beringian land bridge.

Linguistic analysis of more than a thousand modern Native American languages demonstrates that Native Americans throughout the hemisphere speak some form of Amerind—an ancient root-language—which (presumably) arrived with the earliest wave of ancient migrants around 13,000 BP. This migration chronology and linguistic analysis remain controversial among experts, but they suggest that Clovis peoples spoke some ancient form of Amerind.

Genetic research into the mutation rate of DNA reveals that many modern Native Americans share ge-

---

Questions for Analysis

Summarize the Argument: Were Clovis people the first Americans?

Analyze the Evidence: What evidence suggests ancient migrants arrived before Clovis people? What evidence suggests the origins and ancestry of ancient Americans?

Consider the Context: How were the first Americans related to their ancestors elsewhere in the world? How did they differ from their descendants among later ancient Americans? What might account for the changes?

---

and sea levels rose. Mammoths and other large mammals probably had difficulty adapting to the warmer climate. Many archaeologists also believe, however, that Paleo-Indians probably contributed to the extinctions in the Western Hemisphere by killing large animals more rapidly than the animals could reproduce. Some experts dispute this overkill interpretation, but similar environmental changes had occurred for millions of years before the arrival of Paleo-Indians without triggering the extinction of large animals—the presence of skilled hunters seems to have made a decisive difference.

Whatever the causes, after the extinction of large mammals, Paleo-Indians literally inhabited a new world.

Paleo-Indians adapted to this drastic environmental change by making at least two important changes in their way of life. First, hunters began to prey more intensively on smaller animals. Second, Paleo-Indians devoted more energy to foraging—that is, to collecting wild plant foods such as roots, seeds, nuts, berries, and fruits. When Paleo-Indians made these changes, they replaced the apparent uniformity of the big-game-oriented Clovis culture with great

Folsom Discovery
The discovery of this spear point stuck between the ribs of an ancient bison near Folsom, New Mexico, revolutionized our understanding of ancient Americans. Since the bison was known to have been extinct for about 10,000 years, ancient Americans must have been hunting them at least 10,000 years ago. This discovery prompted the search for more human artifacts, such as spear points, that proved humans resided in America for thousands of years before the extinction of the ancient bison. Courtesy of the Center for the Study of the First Americans, Texas A&M University.

cultural diversity adapted to the many natural environments throughout the hemisphere.

These post-Clovis adaptations to local environments resulted in the astounding variety of Native American cultures that existed when Europeans arrived in AD 1492. By then, hundreds of tribes inhabited North America alone. Hundreds more lived in Central and South America. Still more hundreds of ancient American cultures had disappeared or transformed as their people constantly adapted to environmental and other challenges.

REVIEW   Why and how did Paleo-Indians adapt to environmental change?

▶ Archaic Hunters and Gatherers

Archaeologists use the term *Archaic* to describe the many different hunting and gathering cultures that descended from Paleo-Indians and

the long period of time when those cultures dominated the history of ancient America— roughly from 10,000 BP to somewhere between 4000 BP and 3000 BP. The term describes the era in the history of ancient America that followed the Paleo-Indian big-game hunters and preceded the development of agriculture. It denotes a **hunter-gatherer** way of life that persisted in North America long after European colonization.

Like their Paleo-Indian ancestors, **Archaic Indians** hunted with spears, but they also took smaller game with traps, nets, and hooks. Unlike their Paleo-Indian predecessors, many Archaic peoples became excellent basket makers in order to collect and store seeds, roots, nuts, and berries they gathered from wild plants. They prepared food from these plants by using a variety of stone tools. A characteristic Archaic artifact is a grinding stone used to pulverize seeds into edible form. Most Archaic Indians migrated from place to place to harvest plants and hunt animals. They usually did not establish permanent villages, although they often returned to the same river valley or fertile

MAP ACTIVITY

Map 1.2 Native North American Cultures
Environmental conditions defined the boundaries of the broad zones of cultural similarity among ancient North Americans.

READING THE MAP: What crucial environmental features set the boundaries of each cultural region? (The topography indicated on Map 1.3, "Native North Americans about 1500," may be helpful.)

CONNECTIONS: How did environmental factors and variations affect the development of different groups of Native American cultures? Why do you think historians and archaeologists group cultures together by their regional positions?

meadow year after year. In regions with especially rich resources—such as present-day California and the Pacific Northwest—they developed permanent settlements. Archaic peoples followed these practices in distinctive ways in the different environmental regions of North America (Map 1.2).

Great Plains Bison Hunters

After the extinction of large game animals, some hunters began to concentrate on bison in the huge herds that grazed the plains stretching hundreds of miles east of the Rocky Mountains. For almost a thousand years after the big-game extinctions, Archaic Indians hunted bison with Folsom points, named after a site near Folsom, New Mexico. In 1908, George McJunkin, an African American cowboy, discovered this site, which contained a deposit of large fossilized bones. In 1926, archaeologists excavated this site and found evidence that proved conclusively for the first time that ancient Americans were contemporaries of giant bison—which were known to have been extinct for at least ten thousand years. One Folsom point remained stuck between two ribs of a giant bison, where a Stone Age hunter had plunged it more than ten thousand years earlier. Until this discovery, leading experts had believed that ancient Americans had arrived in the New World fairly recently, some three thousand years ago. Since the 1920s, thanks to McJunkin's discovery, archaeologists and historians have come to understand that the history of ancient Americans was far more ancient than experts previously imagined.

Like their nomadic predecessors, Folsom hunters moved constantly to maintain contact with their prey. Great Plains hunters often stampeded bison herds over cliffs and then slaughtered the animals that plunged to their deaths. At the Folsom site McJunkin discovered, hunters drove bison into a narrow gulch and then speared twenty-three of the trapped animals.

Bows and arrows reached Great Plains hunters from the north about AD 500. They largely replaced spears, which had been the hunters' weapons of choice for millennia. Bows permitted hunters to wound animals from farther away, arrows made it possible to shoot repeatedly, and arrowheads were easier to make and therefore less costly to lose than the larger, heavier spear points. These new weapons did not otherwise alter age-old ways of hunting. Although we often imagine bison hunters on horseback, in reality ancient Great Plains people hunted on foot. Horses did not arrive on the Great Plains until decades after 1492, when Europeans imported them. Only then did Great Plains bison hunters obtain horses and become expert riders.

Ancient California Peoples

Great Basin Cultures

Archaic peoples in the Great Basin between the Rocky Mountains and the Sierra Nevada inhabited a region of great environmental diversity defined largely by the amount of rain. While some lived on the shores of lakes and marshes fed by the rain and ate fish, others hunted deer, antelope, bison, and smaller game. To protect against shortages in fish and game caused by the fickle rainfall, Great Basin Indians relied on plants as their most important food. Unlike meat and fish, plant food could be collected and stored for long periods. Many Great Basin peoples gathered piñon nuts as a dietary staple. Great Basin peoples adapted to the severe environmental challenges of the region and maintained their Archaic hunter-gatherer way of life for centuries after Europeans arrived in AD 1492.

Pacific Coast Cultures

The richness of the natural environment made present-day California the most densely settled area in all of ancient North America. The land and ocean offered such ample food that California peoples remained hunters and gatherers for hundreds of years after AD 1492. The diversity of California's environment also encouraged corresponding variety among native peoples. The mosaic of Archaic settlements in California included about five hundred separate tribes speaking some ninety languages, each with local dialects. No other region of comparable size in ancient North America exhibited such cultural variety.

The Chumash, one of the many California cultures, emerged in the region surrounding what is now Santa Barbara about 5000 BP. Comparatively plentiful food resources—especially acorns—permitted Chumash people to establish relatively permanent villages. Conflict, probably caused by competition for valuable acorn-gathering territory, often broke out among the villages, as documented by Chumash skeletons that display unmistakable signs of violence. Although few other California cultures achieved the population density and village settlements of the Chumash, all shared the hunter-gatherer way of life and reliance on acorns as a major food source.

Another rich natural environment lay along the Pacific Northwest coast. Like the Chumash, Northwest peoples built more or less permanent villages. After about 5500 BP, they concentrated on catching whales and large quantities of salmon, halibut, and other fish, which they dried to last throughout the year. They also traded with people who lived hundreds of miles from the coast. Fishing freed Northwest peoples to develop sophisticated woodworking skills. They fashioned elaborate wood carvings that denoted wealth and status, as well as huge canoes for fishing, hunting, and conducting warfare against neighboring tribes. Archaic northwesterners often fought with one another over access to prime fishing sites.

Eastern Woodland Cultures

East of the Mississippi River, Archaic peoples adapted to a forest environment that included

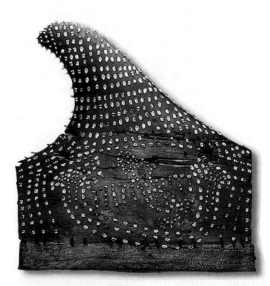

Ozette Whale Effigy
This carving of a whale fin decorated with hundreds of sea otter teeth was discovered along with thousands of other artifacts of daily life at Ozette, an ancient village on the tip of the Olympic Peninsula in present-day Washington that was inundated by a catastrophic mud slide about five hundred years ago. The fin illustrates the importance of whale hunting to the residents of Ozette. Richard Alexander Cooke III.

the major river valleys of the Mississippi, Ohio, Tennessee, and Cumberland; the Great Lakes region; and the Atlantic coast (see Map 1.2). Throughout these diverse locales, Archaic peoples pursued similar survival strategies.

Woodland hunters stalked deer as their most important prey. Deer supplied Woodland peoples with food as well as hides and bones that they crafted into clothing, weapons, and many other tools. Like Archaic peoples elsewhere, Woodland Indians gathered edible plants, seeds, and nuts. About 6000 BP, some Woodland groups established more or less permanent settlements of 25 to 150 people, usually near a river or lake that offered a wide variety of plant and animal resources. Woodland burial sites suggest that life expectancy was about eighteen years, a relatively short time to learn all the skills necessary to survive, reproduce, and adapt to change.

Around 4000 BP, Woodland cultures added two important features to their basic hunter-gatherer lifestyle: agriculture and pottery. Trade and migration from Mexico brought gourds and pumpkins to Woodland peoples, who also began to cultivate sunflowers and small quantities of tobacco. Corn, which had been grown in Mexico and South America since about 7000 BP, also traveled north and became a significant food crop among Eastern Woodland peoples around 2500 BP. Most likely, women learned how to plant, grow, and harvest these crops as an outgrowth of their work gathering edible wild plants. Cultivated crops did not alter Woodland peoples' dependence on gathering wild plants, seeds, and nuts.

Like agriculture, pottery probably originated in Mexico. Pots were more durable than baskets for cooking and storing food and water, but they were also much heavier, and therefore nomadic peoples shunned them. The permanent settlements of Woodland peoples made the heavy weight of pots much less important than their advantages compared to leaky and fragile baskets. While pottery and agriculture introduced changes in Woodland cultures, ancient Woodland Americans retained the other basic features of their Archaic hunter-gatherer lifestyle until 1492 and beyond.

REVIEW   Why did Archaic Native Americans shift from big-game hunting to foraging and hunting smaller animals?

Corn: An Ancient American Legacy

Corn on the cob slathered with butter, salted popcorn, corn chips—Americans consume and produce more corn than any other nation on earth. Today, each American eats an average of 52 quarts of popped corn a year. Popcorn grown in the United States is also munched in Mexico City, Tokyo, Seoul, Beijing, and London, and corn on the cob is even sold at Moscow's famed Gorky Park. Yet popcorn and corn on the cob account for a minuscule fraction of the gigantic mountain of 34 billion bushels of corn produced across the globe each year, one-third of it in the United States. All of that corn is descended from a plant domesticated and cultivated by ancient Americans beginning about ten thousand years ago.

The ancient ancestor of what we know today as corn is a grass called *teosinte*. Ancient people in central Mexico, probably women, selected desirable seeds from *teosinte* and over many generations managed to transform the small grass seeds into rows of corn kernels arrayed around a central cob. Slowly, during thousands of years, ancient agriculturalists developed many varieties of corn adapted to different growing conditions, with different nutritional qualities and varying productivity (the number of kernels grown from one corn seed). The remarkable adaptability of the corn plant and the high food value of the corn kernels caused the crop to spread among ancient Americans throughout the Western Hemisphere.

Entirely unknown to Europeans when they arrived in the New World in 1492, corn acquired the name by which it is known in most of the world today: *maize*, which is derived from *mahiz* ("life-giver"), the word for corn Christopher Columbus learned from the Taino Indians he first encountered. It is no wonder ancient Americans worshipped maize gods, given how important corn was to their survival. Columbus and other Spaniards carried corn back to Europe in 1493, and within a generation corn seeds had sprouted for the first time not only in Europe but also in the Middle East, Africa, India, and China.

At first, people outside the Americas did not find corn an appetizing food. An English botanist in the seventeenth century spoke for many others when he declared corn a food of the "barbarous Indians which know no better." He pronounced corn "a more convenient food for swine than for man." But Europeans in the New World, following Native American foodways, soon learned to eat corn ground into meal, often mixed with vegetables or meat, moistened, and served as a kind of mush they called samp or hominy or grits. Or they made a cornmeal dough that they baked in the coals of a fire or on an iron griddle to produce corn bread, which they also called hoecake, johnnycake, or corn pone—all of them adaptations of ancient American tortillas. Corn helped sustain Euro-Americans in the New World for centuries after 1492, just as it had ancient Americans for thousands of years before Europeans arrived.

Today corn is grown throughout the world and is a major commodity in global trade. The United States produces more than half of global corn exports, while Argentina, Brazil, and Ukraine account for another third. This exported corn goes to countries all around the world. Japan takes about a fifth of the global corn imports, and another third of corn imports goes to South Korea, Mexico, Egypt, and Taiwan.

Corn connects the United States to the rest of the world in many more ways than the export of mil-

▶ Agricultural Settlements and Chiefdoms

Among Eastern Woodland peoples and most other Archaic cultures, agriculture supplemented but did not replace hunter-gatherer subsistence strategies. Reliance on wild animals and plants required most Archaic groups to remain small and mobile. But beginning about 4000 BP, distinctive southwestern cultures began to *depend* on agriculture and to build permanent settlements. Later, around 2500 BP, Woodland peoples in the vast Mississippi valley began to construct burial mounds and other earthworks that suggest the existence of social and political hierarchies that archaeologists term *chiefdoms*. Although the hunter-gatherer lifestyle never entirely disappeared, the development of agricultural settlements and chiefdoms represented important innovations to the Archaic way of life.

Southwestern Cultures

Ancient Americans in present-day Arizona, New Mexico, and southern portions of Utah and

Florida Woman

This sixteenth-century drawing with watercolor of a Native American woman in Florida shows her extending a gift of hospitality with ears of corn in one hand and a basket of corn mush in the other. The watercolor captures the gift of corn ancient Americans bestowed on people throughout the world today. The Trustees of the British Museum/Art Resource, NY.

Of Florida.

livestock. Chances are that the beef, chicken, pork, and dairy products in American supermarkets came from animals that ate corn. And the United States exports billions of dollars' worth of corn-fed meat and dairy products to the rest of the world every year. A similar pattern prevails in many of the other products corn is used to create, such as corn sugar used to sweeten hundreds of processed foods and corn by-products used, for example, in products as varied as skateboards, toothpaste, tires, batteries, and lipstick. Even pulling into a gas station for a fill-up often means pumping gasoline mixed with ethanol made from corn—about a fourth of the American corn crop is used to make ethanol fuel, a product that reduces American dependence on foreign sources of oil.

Questions for Analysis

Ask Historical Questions: How did ancient Americans contribute to the evolution of corn? Why does the United States produce so much corn today?

Consider the Context: How did corn contribute to changes in ancient American cultures and societies? Why did corn spread so rapidly throughout the world?

Analyze the Evidence: In what ways is corn used today? How do these compare to how ancient Americans used corn?

lions of bushels of corn kernels. Only about a fifth of the U.S. corn crop is exported annually. The rest is used in dozens of products that Americans consume themselves as well as export

to countries around the globe. The seventeenth-century English botanist was correct that corn is an excellent food for animals. Today, about half of the American corn crop is fed to

Colorado developed cultures characterized by agricultural settlements and multiunit dwellings called **pueblos**. All southwestern peoples confronted the challenge of a dry climate and unpredictable fluctuations in rainfall that made the supply of wild plant food very unreliable. These ancient Americans probably adopted agriculture in response to this basic environmental uncertainty.

About 3500 BP, southwestern hunters and gatherers began to cultivate corn, their signature food crop. (See "Beyond America's Borders," above.) The demands of corn cultivation encouraged hunter-gatherers to restrict their migratory

habits in order to tend the crop. A vital consideration was access to water. Southwestern Indians became irrigation experts, conserving water from streams, springs, and rainfall and distributing it to thirsty crops.

About AD 200, small farming settlements began to appear throughout southern New Mexico, marking the emergence of the Mogollon culture. Typically, a Mogollon settlement included a dozen pit houses, each made by digging out a pit about fifteen feet in diameter and a foot or two deep and then erecting poles to support a roof of branches or dirt. Larger villages usually had one or two bigger pit houses that may have been the

VISUAL ACTIVITY

Ancient Agriculture

Dropping seeds into holes punched in cleared ground by a pointed stick known as a "dibble," this ancient American farmer sows a new crop while previously planted seeds—including the corn and beans immediately opposite him—bear fruit for harvest. Created by a sixteenth-century European artist, the drawing misrepresents who did the agricultural work in many ancient American cultures—namely, women rather than men. The Pierpont Morgan Library/Art Resource, NY.

READING THE IMAGE: In what ways has this ancient farmer modified and taken advantage of the natural environment?

CONNECTIONS: What were the advantages and disadvantages of agriculture compared to hunting and gathering?

predecessors of the circular kivas, the ceremonial rooms that became a characteristic of nearly all southwestern settlements. About AD 900, Mogollon culture began to decline, for reasons that remain obscure.

Around AD 500, while the Mogollon culture prevailed in New Mexico, other ancient people migrated from Mexico to southern Arizona and established the distinctive Hohokam culture. Hohokam settlements used sophisticated grids of irrigation canals to plant and harvest crops twice a year. Hohokam settlements reflected Mexican cultural practices that northbound migrants brought with them, including the building of sizable platform mounds and ball courts. About AD 1400, Hohokam culture declined for reasons that remain a mystery, although the rising salinity of the soil brought about by centuries of irrigation probably caused declining crop yields and growing food shortages.

North of the Hohokam and Mogollon cultures, in a region that encompassed southern Utah and Colorado and northern Arizona and New Mexico, the Anasazi culture began to flourish about AD 100. The early Anasazi built pit houses on mesa tops and used irrigation much as did their neighbors to the south. Beginning around AD 1000, some Anasazi began to move to large, multistory

cliff dwellings whose spectacular ruins still exist at Mesa Verde, Colorado, and elsewhere. Other Anasazi communities—like the one known as **Pueblo Bonito** whose impressive ruins can be visited at Chaco Canyon, New Mexico—erected huge stone-walled pueblos with enough rooms to house everyone in the settlement. (See "Analyzing Historical Evidence," page 16.) Anasazi pueblos and cliff dwellings typically included one or more kivas used for secret ceremonies, restricted to men, that sought to communicate with the supernatural world. The alignment of Chaco buildings with solar and lunar events (such as the summer and winter solstices) also suggests that the Anasazi studied the sky carefully, probably because they believed supernatural celestial powers influenced their lives in every way. Pueblo Bonito stood at the center of thousands of smaller pueblos that sent food and other goods to support Bonito's spiritual and political elites. Exactly how the Pueblo Bonito elites exercised power over the satellite pueblos is not known, but it probably involved a combination of violence and spiritual ceremonies performed in the kivas. Drought began to plague the region about AD 1130, and it lasted for more than half a century, triggering the disappearance of the Anasazi culture. By AD 1200, the large Anasazi pueblos had been abandoned.

complex and labor-intensive burial mounds is to assume that one person—whom scholars term a *chief*—commanded the labor and obedience of very large numbers of other people, who made up the chief's chiefdom.

Between 2500 BP and 2100 BP, Adena people built hundreds of burial mounds radiating from central Ohio. In the mounds, the Adena usually included grave goods such as spear points and stone pipes as well as thin sheets of mica (a glasslike mineral) crafted into animal or human shapes. Sometimes burial mounds were constructed all at once, but often they were built up slowly over many years.

About 2100 BP, Adena culture evolved into the more elaborate Hopewell culture, which lasted about five hundred years. Centered in Ohio, Hopewell culture extended throughout the enormous drainage of the Ohio and Mississippi rivers. Hopewell people built larger mounds than did their Adena predecessors and filled them with more magnificent grave goods. Burial was probably reserved for the most important members of Hopewell groups. Most people were cremated, not buried. Burial rituals appear to have brought many people together to honor the dead person and to help build the mound. Hopewell mounds were often one hundred feet high and thirty feet in diameter. Grave goods at Hopewell sites testify to the high quality of Hopewell crafts and to a thriving trade network that ranged from present-day Wyoming to Florida.

Hopewell culture declined about AD 400 for reasons that are obscure. Archaeologists speculate that bows and arrows, along with increasing reliance on agriculture, made small settlements more self-sufficient and therefore less dependent on the central authority of the Hopewell chiefs who were responsible for the burial mounds.

Four hundred years later, another mound-building culture flourished. The Mississippian

The prolonged drought probably intensified conflict among the pueblos and made it impossible to depend on the techniques of irrigated agriculture that had worked for centuries. Some Anasazi migrated toward regions with more reliable rainfall and settled in Hopi, Zuñi, and Acoma pueblos that their descendants in Arizona and New Mexico have occupied ever since.

Woodland Burial Mounds and Chiefdoms

No other ancient Americans created dwellings similar to pueblos, but around 2500 BP, Woodland cultures throughout the Mississippi River watershed began to build **burial mounds**. The size of the mounds, the labor and organization required to erect them, and differences in the artifacts buried with certain individuals suggest the existence of a social and political hierarchy that archaeologists term a **chiefdom**. Experts do not know the name of a single chief, nor do they understand the organizations chiefs headed. But the only way archaeologists can account for the

Artifacts of Daily Life in Chaco Canyon

Pueblo Bonito, Chaco Canyon, New Mexico Richard A. Cooke/Corbis.

Like archaeologists, historians study artifacts—physical objects—to investigate the past. Since ancient Americans did not use writing, their artifacts serve as documents of a sort that historians examine for evidence of ancient societies and cultures. Pictured here are artifacts made and used more than a thousand years ago by residents of Pueblo Bonito in Chaco Canyon, located in the arid region at the intersection of present-day Utah, Colorado, Arizona, and New Mexico.

The largest of many buildings in Chaco Canyon, Pueblo Bonito originally stood four or five stories tall and housed more than 600 rooms, including 35 kivas, the circular structures visible around the perimeter of the large plazas. Chaco residents covered each kiva with a roof, creating a

Sandal Courtesy National Park Service, Chaco Culture National Historical Park.

darkened underground space for ceremonial rituals. The ceremonies remain a mystery, but less mysterious are the routines of daily life that for centuries sustained Chacoan people at Pueblo Bonito.

Among the many thousands of artifacts excavated by archaeologists at Pueblo Bonito are these

VISUAL ACTIVITY

Ancient Petroglyph

More than a thousand years ago one or more members of the Fremont people crafted this hunting scene on a sandstone surface in Cottonwood Canyon in northeastern Utah. Four hunters aim their arrows into a flock of bighorn sheep. Other human-like forms appear in the image—perhaps shamans or decoys to move the flock toward the hunters. Lisa Werner/Getty Images.

READING THE IMAGE: What techniques might have allowed the hunters to concentrate the flock in the way depicted?

CONNECTIONS: What weapons did earlier Paleo-Indians and Archaic Indians use for killing and capturing game?

objects Chaco residents used routinely in their daily lives. Imagine a woman at Pueblo Bonito setting out on a spring day to plant corn, her family's most important food. She might strap on sandals, like the one shown on page 16 woven from fibers of the yucca plant. To dig a hole for planting corn seeds, the woman

Digging Stick

might use a digging stick like the one shown here, tipped by the horn of a mountain sheep and tightly bound with sinew to a cottonwood branch and covered with animal hide to protect the binding.

Once harvested and dried, corn needed to be ground in order to be cooked and eaten. Our imagined woman used the small flat stone (the

Mano and Metate

Ladle

mano) and the larger stone slab (the metate) to grind the corn. Some rooms at Pueblo Bonito contained numerous grinding stones.

To cook the cornmeal the woman mixed it with water, perhaps using a ceramic ladle—like the one shown here crafted by a Chaco pottery maker—to dip water from a storage pot. To kindle a fire, she might use the Chacoan fire starter kit shown here. After heating the cornmeal gruel in a ceramic pot, she might use the ladle again to transfer servings into small bowls for eating.

Examine these objects and think carefully about them. Each object required a great deal of learning and experience to create it and use it effectively. Consider in detail, step by step, what activities went into the making and use of each artifact.

Source: All images courtesy National Park Service, Chaco Culture National Historical Park.

Questions for Analysis

Analyze the Evidence: What kinds of material, knowledge, skill, and activity were required to make and use each of these artifacts? What do the decorations on the ladle suggest about Chacoan artistry?

Consider the Context: What do these artifacts suggest about food production and consumption in Chaco Canyon? What do these artifacts reveal about the society and culture of Chacoan people?

Ask Historical Questions: How did Chacoan culture, as revealed by these artifacts, compare to the lifestyles of ancient Americans in other regions at about the same time? How do these artifacts differ from artifacts of Paleo-Indians and Archaic hunters and gatherers described in the chapter? What changes might account for the differences?

Fire Starter Kit

culture emerged in the floodplains of the major southeastern river systems about AD 800 and lasted until about AD 1500. Major Mississippian sites, such as the one at **Cahokia**, included huge mounds with platforms on top for ceremonies and for the residences of great chiefs. Most likely, the ceremonial mounds and ritual practices were influenced by Mexican cultural expressions brought north by traders and migrants. At Cahokia, skilled farmers supported the large population with ample crops of corn. In addition to mounds, Cahokians erected what archaeologists call woodhenges (after the famous Stonehenge in England)—long wooden poles set upright in the ground and carefully arranged in huge circles. Experts believe that Cahokians probably built

woodhenges partly for ceremonies linked to celestial observations. The large plazas at Cahokia were used for religious and political ceremonies as well as for playing the Cahokians' signature game of chunkey, which involved rolling a concave stone disk and trying to throw a spear that landed as close as possible to where the stone stopped. The game of chunkey spread throughout the region of Cahokians' cultural influence, and chunkey stones are commonly found in Mississippian graves, signifying the importance Cahokians attached to chunkey in the hereafter as well as the here and now.

Cahokia and other Mississippian cultures dwindled by AD 1500. When Europeans arrived, most of the descendants of Mississippian cultures,

Cahokia Pipe
This pipe bowl excavated at Cahokia depicts a chunkey player preparing to roll the concave chunkey stone with his right hand. Chunkey stones are frequently found in Cahokian and other Mississippian burials, suggesting the importance of the chunkey game in their culture. The man shown here also wears the characteristic skullcap of chunkey players. Ira Block/Corbis.

like those of the Hopewell culture, lived in small dispersed villages supported by hunting and gathering, supplemented by agriculture. Clearly, the conditions that caused large chiefdoms to emerge—whatever they were—had changed, and chiefs no longer commanded the sweeping powers they had once enjoyed.

> **REVIEW**   How and why did the societies of the Southwest differ from eastern societies?

▶ Native Americans in the 1490s

On the eve of European colonization in the 1490s, Native Americans lived throughout North and South America, but their total population is uncertain. Some experts claim that Native Americans inhabiting what are now the United States and Canada numbered 18 million to 20 million, while others place the population at no more than 1 million. A prudent estimate is about 4 million, or about the same as the number of people living on the small island nation of England at that time. The vastness of the territory meant that the overall population density of North America was low, just 60 people per 100 square miles, compared to more than 8,000 in England. Native Americans were spread thin across the land because of their survival strategies of hunting, gathering, and agriculture, but regional populations varied (Figure 1.1).

Eastern and Great Plains Peoples

About one-third of native North Americans inhabited the enormous Woodland region east of the Mississippi River; their population density

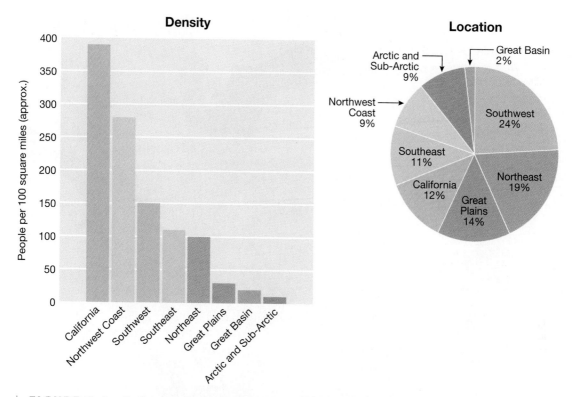

FIGURE 1.1   **Native American Population in North America about 1492 (Estimated)**
Just before Europeans arrived, Native American population density varied widely, depending in large part on the availability of natural resources. The Pacific coast, with its rich marine resources, had the highest concentration of people. Overall, the population density of North America was less than 1 percent that of England, which helps explain why Europeans viewed North America as a relatively empty wilderness.

approximated the average for North America as a whole. Eastern Woodland peoples clustered into three broad linguistic and cultural groups: Algonquian, Iroquoian, and Muskogean.

Algonquian tribes inhabited the Atlantic seaboard, the Great Lakes region, and much of the upper Midwest (Map 1.3). The relatively mild climate along the Atlantic permitted the coastal Algonquians to grow corn and other crops as well as to hunt and fish. Around the Great Lakes and in northern New England, however, cool summers and severe winters made agriculture impractical. Instead, the Abenaki, Penobscot, Chippewa, and other tribes concentrated on hunting and fishing, using canoes both for transportation and for gathering wild rice.

Inland from the Algonquian region, Iroquoian tribes occupied territories centered in Pennsylvania and upstate New York, as well as the hilly upland regions of the Carolinas and Georgia. Three features distinguished Iroquoian tribes from their neighbors. First, their success in cultivating corn and other crops allowed them to build permanent settlements, usually consisting of several long-houses housing five to ten families. Second, Iroquoian societies adhered to matrilineal rules of descent. Property of all sorts belonged to women. Women headed family clans and even selected the chiefs (normally men) who governed the tribes. Third, for purposes of war and diplomacy, an Iroquoian confederation—including the Seneca, Onondaga, Mohawk, Oneida, and Cayuga tribes—formed the League of Five Nations, which remained powerful well into the eighteenth century.

Muskogean peoples spread throughout the woodlands of the Southeast, south of the Ohio River and east of the Mississippi. Including the Creek, Choctaw, Chickasaw, and Natchez tribes, Muskogeans inhabited a bountiful natural environment that provided abundant food from hunting, gathering, and agriculture. Remnants of the earlier Mississippian culture still existed in Muskogean religion. The Natchez, for example, worshipped the sun and built temple mounds modeled after those of their Mississippian ancestors, including Cahokia.

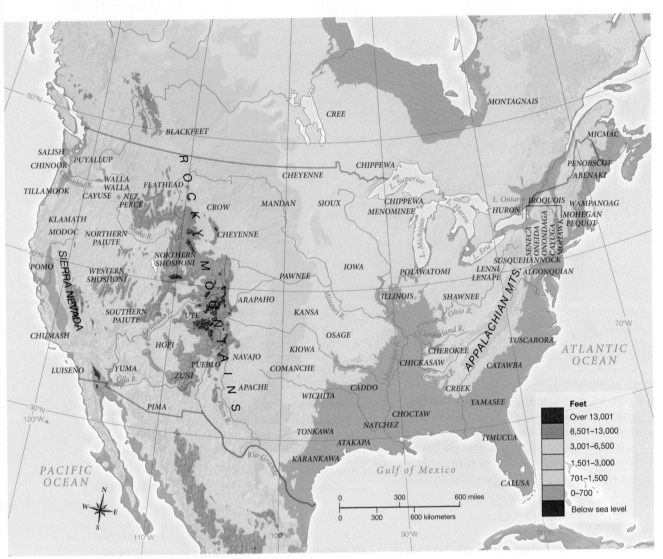

Map 1.3   Native North Americans about 1500
Distinctive Native American peoples resided throughout the area that, centuries later, became the United States. This map indicates the approximate location of some of the larger tribes about 1500. In the interest of legibility, many other peoples who inhabited North America at the time are omitted from the map.

Great Plains peoples accounted for about one out of seven native North Americans. Inhabiting the huge region west of the Eastern Woodland people and east of the Rocky Mountains, many tribes had migrated to the Great Plains within the century or two before the 1490s, forced westward by Iroquoian and Algonquian tribes. Some Great Plains tribes—especially the Mandan and Pawnee—farmed successfully, growing both corn and sunflowers. But the Teton Sioux, Blackfeet, Comanche, Cheyenne, and Crow on the northern plains and the Apache and other nomadic tribes on the southern plains depended on buffalo (American bison) for their subsistence.

Southwestern and Western Peoples

Southwestern cultures included about a quarter of all native North Americans. These descendants of the Mogollon, Hohokam, and Anasazi cultures lived in settled agricultural communities, many of them pueblos. They continued to grow corn, beans, and squash using methods they had refined for centuries.

However, their communities came under attack by a large number of warlike Athapascans who invaded the Southwest beginning around AD 1300. The Athapascans—principally Apache and Navajo—were skillful warriors who preyed on the sedentary pueblo Indians, reaping the fruits of agriculture without the work of farming.

About a fifth of all native North Americans resided along the Pacific coast. In California, abundant acorns and nutritious marine life continued to support high population densities, but this abundance retarded the development of agriculture. Similar dependence on hunting and gathering persisted along the Northwest coast, where fishing reigned supreme. Salmon were so plentiful at The Dalles, a prime fishing site on the Columbia River on the border of present-day Oregon and Washington, that Northwest peoples caught enough to use themselves as well as to trade dried fish as far away as California and the Great Plains. It is likely that The Dalles was the largest Native American trading center in ancient North America, although other ancient trading centers, such as Pueblo Bonito and Cahokia, also existed.

Cultural Similarities

While trading was common, all native North Americans in the 1490s still depended on hunting and gathering for a major portion of their food. Most of them also practiced agriculture. Some used agriculture to supplement hunting and gathering; for others, the balance was reversed. People throughout North America used bows, arrows, and other weapons for hunting and warfare. To express themselves, they drew on stones, wood, and animal skins; wove baskets and textiles; crafted pottery, beads, and carvings; and created songs, dances, and rituals.

North American life did not include features common in Europe during the 1490s. Native North Americans did not use writing, wheels, or sailing ships; they had no large domesticated animals such as horses or cows; their only metal was copper. However, the absence of these European conveniences mattered less than Native Americans' adaptations to local natural environments and to the social environment among neighboring peoples, adaptations that all native North Americans held in common.

It would be a mistake, however, to conclude that native North Americans lived in blissful harmony. Archaeological sites provide ample evidence of violent conflict. Warfare was common, making violence and fear typical features of ancient American life. Warfare not only killed people and destroyed their settlements, but victors often took captives, especially women and children, and often treated them as slaves. Skeletons, like those at Cahokia, not only bear marks of wounds but also exhibit clear signs of ritualistic human sacrifice. Religious, ethnic, economic, and familial conflicts must have occurred, but they remain in obscurity because they left few archaeological traces. In general, anxiety and instability must have been at least as common among ancient North Americans as feelings of peace and security.

Native North Americans not only adapted to the natural environment but also changed it in many ways. They built thousands of structures, from small dwellings to massive pueblos and enormous mounds, permanently altering the landscape. Their gathering techniques selected productive and nutritious varieties of plants, thereby shifting the balance of local plants toward useful varieties. The first stages of North American agriculture, for example, probably involved Native Americans gathering wild seeds and then sowing them in a meadow for later harvest. To clear land

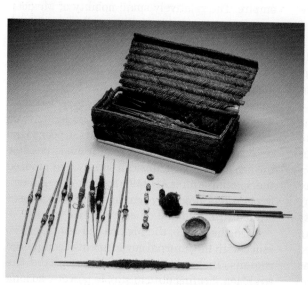

VISUAL ACTIVITY

Ancient American Weaving

This workbasket of a master weaver illustrates the technology of ancient American textile production. Found in a woman's grave in the Andes dating from one thousand years ago, the workbasket contains tools and thread for every stage of textile production. Weaving—like cooking, hunting, and worship—depended on human knowledge that survived only when passed from an experienced person to a novice. Museum of Fine Arts, Boston, Massachusetts, USA/Gift of Charles H. White/Bridgeman Images.

READING THE IMAGE: What human activities were required to produce the tools in the workbasket?

CONNECTIONS: The production of woven materials such as baskets and textiles was common in the North American cultures of the 1490s. What other similarities did these cultures hold?

for planting seeds, native North Americans set fires that burned off thousands of acres of forest.

Ancient North Americans also used fires for hunting. Hunters often started fires to frighten and force together deer, buffalo, and other animals and make them easy to slaughter. Indians also started fires along the edges of woods to burn off shrubby undergrowth, encouraging the growth of tender young plants that attracted deer and other game, bringing them within convenient range of hunters' weapons. The burns also encouraged the growth of sun-loving food plants that Indians relished, such as blackberries, strawberries, and raspberries.

Because the fires set by native North Americans usually burned until they ran out of fuel or were extinguished by rain or wind, enormous regions of North America were burned over. In the long run, fires created and maintained a diverse and productive natural environment. Fires, like other activities of native North Americans, shaped the landscape of North America long before Europeans arrived in 1492.

REVIEW   What cultural similarities did native peoples of the Western Hemisphere share in the 1490s, and why?

► The Mexica: A Mesoamerican Culture

The vast majority of the millions of people who lived in the Western Hemisphere in the 1490s inhabited Mesoamerica and South America, where the population approximately equaled that of Europe. Like their much less numerous counterparts north of the Rio Grande, these people lived in a natural environment of tremendous diversity. Among all these cultures, the **Mexica** stood out. Their empire stretched from coast to coast across central Mexico, encompassing approximately six million people. Their significance in the history of the New World after 1492 dictates a brief survey of their culture and society.

The Mexica began their rise to prominence about 1325, when small bands settled on a marshy island in Lake Texcoco, the site of the future city of Tenochtitlán, the capital of the Mexican empire. Resourceful, courageous, and cold-blooded warriors, the Mexica were often hired out as mercenaries for richer, more settled tribes.

By 1430, the Mexica succeeded in asserting their dominance over their former allies and leading their own military campaigns in an ever-widening arc of empire building. Despite pockets of resistance, by the 1490s the Mexica ruled an empire that contained about as many people as lived in Spain. The empire exemplified the central values of Mexican society. The Mexica worshipped the war god Huitzilopochtli. Warriors held the most exalted positions in the social hierarchy, even above the priests who performed the sacred ceremonies that won Huitzilopochtli's favor. In the almost constant battles necessary to defend and extend the empire, young Mexican men exhibited the courage and daring that would allow them to rise in the carefully graduated ranks of warriors. The Mexica considered capturing prisoners the ultimate act of bravery. Warriors usually turned over the captives to Mexican priests, who sacrificed them to Huitzilopochtli by cutting out their hearts. The Mexica believed that human sacrifice fed the sun's craving for blood, which kept the sun aflame and prevented the fatal descent of everlasting darkness and chaos.

The empire contributed far more to Mexican society than victims for sacrifice. At the most basic level, the empire functioned as a military and political system that collected **tribute** from subject peoples. The Mexica forced conquered tribes to pay tribute in goods, not money. Tribute redistributed to the Mexica was as much as one-third of the goods produced by conquered tribes. It included everything from candidates for human sacrifice to textiles and basic food products as well as exotic luxury items such as gold, turquoise, and rare bird feathers.

Tribute reflected the fundamental relations of power and wealth that pervaded the Mexican empire. The relatively small nobility of Mexican warriors, supported by a still smaller priesthood, possessed the military and religious power to command the obedience of thousands of non-noble Mexicans and of millions of non-Mexicans in subjugated colonies. The Mexican elite exercised their power to obtain tribute and thereby to redistribute wealth from the conquered to the conquerors, from the commoners to the nobility, from the poor to the rich. This redistribution of wealth made possible the achievements of Mexican society that amazed the Spaniards after AD 1492: the huge cities, teeming markets, productive gardens, and storehouses stuffed with gold and other treasures.

On the whole, the Mexica did not interfere much with the internal government of conquered regions. Instead, they usually permitted the traditional ruling elite to stay in power—so long

Mexican Human Sacrifice
This late-sixteenth-century painting depicts human sacrifice, a common Mexican ritual, at the temple of Tenochtitlán, before Spanish conquest. Mexicans believed that cutting the heart from a sacrifice victim fed the sun with human blood and assured that the sun would continue to warm and nourish the world. Spaniards considered these rituals barbaric and banned them. DEA/G. Dagli Orti/De Agostini/Getty Images.

as they paid tribute. Subjugated communities felt exploited by the constant payment of tribute to the Mexica. The high level of discontent among subject peoples constituted the soft, vulnerable underbelly of the Mexican empire, a fact that Spanish intruders exploited after 1492 to conquer the Mexica.

REVIEW How did the conquest and creation of an empire exemplify the central values of Mexican society?

► Conclusion: The World of Ancient Americans

Ancient Americans shaped the history of human beings in the New World for more than thirteen thousand years. They established continuous human habitation in the Western Hemisphere from the time the first big-game hunters crossed Beringia until 1492 and beyond. Much of their history remains lost because they relied on oral rather than written communication. But much can be pieced together from artifacts they left behind at camps, kill sites, and ceremonial and residential centers such as Cahokia and Pueblo Bonito. Ancient Americans achieved their success through resourceful adaptation to the hemisphere's many and changing natural environments. They also adapted to social and cultural changes caused by human beings—such as marriages and deaths, as well as political struggles and warfare among chiefdoms. Their creativity and artistry are unmistakably documented in their numerous artifacts. Those material objects sketch the only likenesses of ancient Americans we will ever have—blurred, shadowy images that are indisputably human but forever silent.

When European intruders began arriving in the Western Hemisphere in 1492, their attitudes about the promise of the New World were heavily influenced by the diverse peoples they encountered. Europeans coveted Native Americans' wealth, labor, and land, and Christian missionaries sought to save their souls. Likewise, Native Americans marveled at such European technological novelties as sailing ships, steel weapons, gunpowder, and horses, while often reserving judgment about Europeans' Christian religion.

In the centuries following 1492, as the trickle of European strangers became a flood of newcomers from both Europe and Africa, Native Americans and settlers continued to encounter one another. Peaceful negotiations as well as violent conflicts over both land and trading rights resulted in chronic fear and mistrust. While the era of European colonization marked the beginning of the end of ancient America, the ideas, subsistence strategies, and cultural beliefs of native North Americans remained powerful among their descendants for generations and continue to persist to the present.

See the Selected Bibliography for this chapter in the Appendix.

1 Chapter Review

KEY TERMS

Beringia (p. 4)
Paleo-Indians (p. 5)
Clovis point (p. 5)
hunter-gatherer (p. 8)
Archaic Indians (p. 8)
pueblos (p. 13)
Pueblo Bonito (p. 14)
burial mounds (p. 15)
chiefdom (p. 15)
Cahokia (p. 17)
Mexica (p. 22)
tribute (p. 22)

REVIEW QUESTIONS

1. Why must historians rely on the work of archaeologists to write the history of ancient America? (pp. 3–4)

2. Why and how did Paleo-Indians adapt to environmental change? (pp. 4–8)

3. Why did Archaic Native Americans shift from big-game hunting to foraging and hunting smaller animals? (pp. 8–11)

4. How and why did the societies of the Southwest differ from eastern societies? (pp. 12–18)

5. What cultural similarities did native peoples of the Western Hemisphere share in the 1490s, and why? (pp. 18–22)

6. How did the conquest and creation of an empire exemplify the central values of Mexican society? (pp. 22–23)

MAKING CONNECTIONS

1. How did ancient peoples' different approaches to survival contribute to the diversity of Native American cultures?

2. Native Americans both adapted to environmental changes in North America and produced changes in the environments around them. Discuss specific examples of such changes.

3. How did the Mexica establish and maintain their expansive empire?

LINKING TO THE PAST

1. Did the history of ancient Americans make them unusually vulnerable to eventual conquest by European colonizers? Why or why not?

2. Do you think that ancient American history would have been significantly different if North and South America had never separated from the Eurasian landmass? If so, how and why? If not, why not?

2 Europeans Encounter the New World

1492–1600

After reading and studying this chapter, you should be able to:

- Recognize the demographic shifts and technological innovations of the fifteenth century that allowed Europeans to explore regions outside their own continent.

- Follow the Columbian exchange, including its costs and benefits to Europeans and Indians.

- Understand how Spain created its empire in the Caribbean and in Central and South America, including the costs of Spanish conquest and colonization.

- Explain how Spain's New World colonies affected its political ambitions in Europe.

QUEEN ISABELLA'S CROWN
Queen Isabella probably wore this crown when she commissioned the voyage of Columbus and when he returned to report the good news of discoveries across the Atlantic. Made of silver covered with gold, the crown is relatively plain compared to crowns of other monarchs of the era. Only about five and a half inches in diameter, the crown would have perched on Isabella's hair rather than encircling her head. Pomegranates decorate the crown, a symbol of Isabella's court in Granada in what is now Spain. © Chico Sanchez/Alamy Stock Photo.

TWO BABIES WERE BORN IN SOUTHERN EUROPE IN 1451, separated by about seven hundred miles and a chasm of social, economic, and political power. The baby girl, Isabella, was born in a king's castle in what is now Spain. The baby boy, Christopher, was born in the humble dwelling of a weaver near Genoa in what is now Italy. Forty-one years later, the lives and aspirations of these two people intersected in southern Spain and permanently changed the history of the world.

Isabella was named for her mother, the wife of the king of Castile, whose monarchy encompassed the large central region of present-day Spain. As a young girl, Isabella was well educated, and she became a strong, resolute woman. When her half-brother Henry became king and tried to arrange her marriage, Isabella refused to accept Henry's choices and maneuvered to marry Ferdinand, the king of Aragon, a region of northeastern Spain. The couple married in 1469, and Isabella became queen when Henry died in 1474.

Queen Isabella and King Ferdinand battled to unite the monarchies of Spain under their rule, to complete the long campaign known as the Reconquest to eliminate Muslim strongholds on the Iberian Peninsula, and to purify Christianity. In their intense efforts to defend Christianity, persecute Jews, and defeat Muslims, Isabella and Ferdinand traveled throughout their realm, meeting local notables, hearing appeals and complaints, and impressing all with their regal splendor.

Tagging along in the royal cavalcade of advisers, servants, and hangers-on that moved around Spain in 1485 was Christopher Columbus, a deeply religious man obsessed with obtaining support for his scheme to sail west across the Atlantic Ocean to reach China and Japan. An experienced sailor, Columbus had become convinced that it was possible to reach the riches of the East by sailing west. Columbus finally won an audience with the monarchs in January 1486. They rejected his plan. The earth was too big, the ocean between Europe and China was too wide, and no sailors or ships could possibly withstand such a long voyage. Doggedly, year after year, Columbus kept trying to interest Isabella until mid-April 1492, when she summoned him and agreed to support his risky scheme, hoping to expand the wealth and influence of her monarchy.

Columbus hurriedly organized his expedition, and just before sunrise on August 3, 1492, three ships under his command caught the tide out of a harbor in southern Spain and sailed west. Barely two months later, in the predawn moonlight of October 12, 1492, he glimpsed an island on the western horizon. At daybreak, Columbus rowed ashore, and as the curious islanders crowded around, he claimed possession of the land for Isabella and Ferdinand.

Columbus's encounters with Isabella and those islanders in 1492 transformed the history of the world and unexpectedly made Spain the most important European power in the Western Hemisphere for more than a century. Long before 1492, other Europeans had restlessly expanded the limits of the world known to them, and their efforts helped make possible Columbus's voyage. But without Isabella's sponsorship, it is doubtful that Columbus could have made his voyage. With her support and his own unflagging determination, Columbus blazed a watery trail to a world that neither he nor anyone else in Europe knew existed. As Isabella, Ferdinand, and subsequent Spanish monarchs sought to reap the rewards of what they considered their emerging empire in the West, they created a distinctively Spanish colonial society that conquered and killed Native Americans, built new institutions, and extracted great wealth that enriched the Spanish monarchy and made Spain the envy of other Europeans.

Spanish Tapestry
This detail from a lavish sixteenth-century tapestry depicts Columbus (kneeling) receiving a box of jewels from Queen Isabella (whose husband, King Ferdinand, stands slightly behind her) in appreciation for his voyages to the New World.
© Julio Donoso/Corbis.

► Europe in the Age of Exploration

Historically, the East—not the West—attracted Europeans. Europeans did not venture across the North Atlantic until around AD 1000, when Norsemen founded a small fishing village at L'Anse aux Meadows on the tip of Newfoundland that lasted only a decade or so. When the world's climate cooled, choking the North Atlantic with ice, the Norse left and other Europeans remained unaware of North America. Instead of looking to the West, wealthy Europeans developed tastes for luxury goods from Asia and Africa, and merchants competed to satisfy those desires. As Europeans traded with the East and with one another, they acquired new information about the world they inhabited. A few people—sailors, merchants, and aristocrats—took the risks of exploring beyond the limits of the world known to Europeans. Those risks could be deadly, but sometimes they paid off in new information, new opportunities, and eventually the discovery of a world entirely new to Europeans.

Mediterranean Trade and European Expansion

From the twelfth through the fifteenth centuries, spices, silk, carpets, ivory, and gold traveled overland from Persia, Asia Minor, India, and Africa and then funneled into continental Europe through Mediterranean trade routes (Map 2.1). Dominated primarily by the Italian cities of Venice, Genoa, and Pisa, this lucrative trade enriched Italian merchants and bankers, who fiercely defended their near monopoly of access to Eastern luxuries. The vitality of the Mediterranean trade offered merchants few incentives to look for alternatives. New routes to the East and the discovery of new lands were the stuff of fantasy.

Preconditions for turning fantasy into reality developed in fifteenth-century Europe. In the mid-fourteenth century, a catastrophic epidemic of bubonic plague (or the **Black Death**, as it was called) killed at least a third of the European population. This devastating pestilence had major long-term consequences. By drastically reducing the population, it made Europe's limited supply of food more plentiful for survivors. Many survivors inherited property from plague victims, giving them new chances for advancement.

Understandably, most Europeans perceived the world as a place of alarming risks where the

CHRONOLOGY

1480	• Portuguese ships reach Congo.
1488	• Bartolomeu Dias rounds Cape of Good Hope.
1492	• Christopher Columbus lands in Caribbean.
1493	• Columbus makes second voyage to New World.
1494	• Portugal and Spain sign Treaty of Tordesillas.
1497	• John Cabot searches for Northwest Passage.
1498	• Vasco da Gama sails to India.
1513	• Vasco Núñez de Balboa crosses Isthmus of Panama.
1517	• Protestant Reformation begins in Germany.
1519	• Hernán Cortés searches for wealth in Mexico. • Ferdinand Magellan sets out to sail around world.
1520	• Mexica in Tenochtitlán revolt against Spaniards.
1521	• Cortés conquers Mexica.
1532	• Francisco Pizarro begins conquest of Peru.
1535	• Jacques Cartier explores St. Lawrence River.
1539	• Hernando de Soto explores southeastern North America.
1540	• Francisco Vásquez de Coronado starts to explore Southwest and Great Plains.
1542	• Juan Rodríguez Cabrillo explores California coast.
1549	• Repartimiento reforms replace encomienda.
1565	• St. Augustine, Florida, is settled.
1576	• Martin Frobisher explores northern Canadian waters.
1587	• English settle Roanoke Island.
1598	• Juan de Oñate explores New Mexico.
1599	• Acoma pueblo revolts against Oñate.

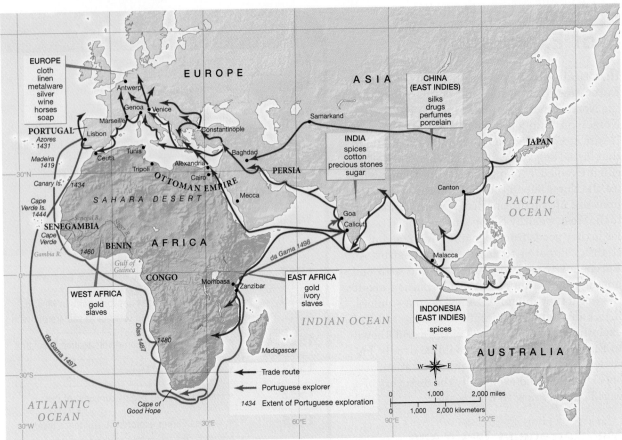

Map 2.1 European Trade Routes and Portuguese Exploration in the Fifteenth Century
The trade of Italian cities from Asia was slowly undermined during the fifteenth century by Portuguese explorers who hopscotched along the coast of Africa and eventually found a sea route that opened the rich trade of the East to Portuguese merchants.

delicate balance of health, harvests, and peace could quickly be tipped toward disaster by epidemics, famine, and violence. Most people protected themselves from the constant threat of calamity by worshipping the supernatural, by living amid kinfolk and friends, and by maintaining good relations with the rich and powerful. But the insecurity and uncertainty of fifteenth-century European life also encouraged a few people to take greater risks, such as embarking on dangerous sea voyages through uncharted waters to points unknown.

In European societies, exploration promised fame and fortune to those who succeeded, whether they were kings or commoners. Monarchs such as Isabella hoped to enlarge their realms and enrich their dynasties by sponsoring journeys of exploration. More territory meant more subjects who could pay more taxes, provide more soldiers, and participate in more commerce, magnifying

the monarch's power and prestige. Voyages of exploration also could stabilize the monarch's regime by diverting unruly noblemen toward distant lands. Some explorers, such as Columbus, were commoners who hoped to be elevated to the aristocracy as a reward for their daring achievements.

Scientific and technological advances also helped set the stage for exploration. The invention of movable type by Johannes Gutenberg around 1450 in Germany made printing easier and cheaper, stimulating the diffusion of information, including news of discoveries, among literate Europeans such as Isabella and Columbus. By 1400, crucial navigational aids employed by maritime explorers like Columbus were already available: compasses; hourglasses; and the astrolabe and quadrant, which were devices for determining latitude. Although many people throughout fifteenth-century Europe knew about such technological advances, the Portuguese were the first to use them in a campaign to sail beyond the limits of the world known to Europeans.

A Century of Portuguese Exploration

With only 2 percent of the population of Christian Europe, Portugal devoted far more energy and wealth to the geographic exploration of the world between 1415 and 1460 than all other European countries combined. As a Christian kingdom, Portugal cooperated with Spain in the **Reconquest**, the centuries-long drive to expel the Muslims from the Iberian Peninsula. The religious zeal that propelled the Reconquest also justified expansion into what the Portuguese considered heathen lands. A key victory came in 1415 when Portuguese forces conquered Ceuta, the Muslim bastion at the mouth of the Strait of Gibraltar that had previously blocked Portugal's access to the Atlantic coast of Africa.

The most influential advocate of Portuguese exploration was Prince Henry the Navigator, son of the Portuguese king. From 1415 until his death in 1460, Henry collected the latest information about sailing techniques and geography, supported new crusades against the Muslims, sought fresh sources of trade to fatten Portuguese pocketbooks, and pushed explorers to go farther still. Expeditions to Africa promised to capture wheat fields from their Moroccan owners and to obtain gold for currency, which had become scarce due to the quickening pace of European commerce and the luxury trade in Eastern goods.

Neither the Portuguese nor anybody else in Europe knew the immensity of Africa or the length of its coastline, which fronted the Atlantic for more than seven thousand miles. At first, Portuguese mariners cautiously hugged the west coast of Africa, seldom venturing beyond sight of land. By 1434, they had reached the northern edge of the Sahara Desert, where they learned to ride strong westerly currents before catching favorable easterly winds that turned them back toward land, which allowed them to reach Cape Verde by 1444.

To stow the supplies necessary for long sea voyages and to withstand the battering of waves in the open ocean, the Portuguese developed the caravel, a fast, sturdy ship that became explorers' vessel of choice. In caravels, Portuguese mariners sailed into and around the Gulf of Guinea and as far south as the Congo by 1480.

Ivory Saltcellar
This exquisitely carved sixteenth-century ivory saltcellar combines African materials, craftsmanship, and imagery in an artifact for Portuguese tables. Designed to hold table salt in the central globe, the saltcellar dramatized African trade and quietly suggested the beneficial influence of Portuguese in Africa. akg-images.

Fierce African resistance confined Portuguese expeditions to coastal trading posts, where they bartered successfully for gold, slaves, and ivory. Powerful African kingdoms welcomed Portuguese trading ships loaded with iron goods, weapons, textiles, and ornamental shells. Portuguese merchants learned that establishing relatively peaceful trading posts on the

Portuguese Merchant Fleet
This 1533 drawing of the Portuguese merchant fleet on the way to trade in the East Indies illustrates the kinds of ships able to withstand the long ocean voyage as well as the large scale of Portugal's investment in the trade. The drawing suggests the pride in the trade felt by the Portuguese monarchy as well as by the merchants and sailors aboard the vessels, each of which is carefully named. akg-images.

coast offered more profit than attempting violent conquest and colonization of inland regions. In the 1460s, the Portuguese used African slaves to develop sugar plantations on the Cape Verde Islands, inaugurating an association between enslaved Africans and plantation labor that would be transplanted to the New World in the centuries to come.

About 1480, Portuguese explorers, eager to bypass the Mediterranean merchants, began a conscious search for a sea route to Asia. In 1488, Bartolomeu Dias sailed around the Cape of Good Hope at the southern tip of Africa and hurried back to Lisbon with the exciting news that it appeared to be possible to sail on to India and China. In 1498, after ten years of careful preparation, Vasco da Gama commanded the first Portuguese fleet to sail to India. Portugal quickly capitalized on the commercial potential of da Gama's new sea route. By the early sixteenth century, the Portuguese controlled a far-flung commercial empire in India, Indonesia, and China (collectively referred to as the East Indies). Their new sea route to the East eliminated overland travel and allowed Portuguese merchants to charge much lower prices for the Eastern goods they imported.

Portugal's African explorations during the fifteenth century broke the monopoly of the old Mediterranean trade with the East, dramatically expanded the world known to Europeans, established a network of Portuguese outposts in Africa and Asia, and developed methods of sailing the high seas that Columbus employed on his revolutionary voyage west.

REVIEW   Why did European exploration expand dramatically in the fifteenth century?

▶ A Surprising New World in the Western Atlantic

The Portuguese and other experts believed that sailing west across the Atlantic to Asia was literally impossible. The European discovery of America required someone bold enough to believe that the experts were wrong. That person was Christopher Columbus. His explorations inaugurated a geographic revolution that forever altered Europeans' understanding of the world and its peoples, including themselves. Columbus's landfall in the Caribbean initiated a thriving exchange between the people, ideas, cultures, and institutions of the Old and New Worlds that continues to this day.

The Explorations of Columbus

Columbus went to sea when he was about fourteen and eventually made his way to Lisbon, where he married Felipa Moniz, whose father had been raised in the household of Prince Henry the Navigator. Through Felipa, Columbus gained access to explorers' maps and information about sailing in the tricky currents and winds of the Atlantic. Like other educated Europeans, Columbus believed that the earth was a sphere and that theoretically it was possible to reach the East Indies by sailing west. With flawed calculations, he estimated that Asia was only about 2,500 miles away, a shorter distance than Portuguese ships routinely sailed between Lisbon and the Congo. In fact, the shortest distance to Japan from Europe's jumping-off point was nearly 11,000 miles. Convinced by his erroneous calculations, Columbus became obsessed with a scheme to prove he was right.

In 1492, after years of unsuccessful lobbying in Portugal, Spain, England, and France, Columbus finally won financing for his journey from the Spanish monarchs, Queen Isabella and King Ferdinand. They saw Columbus's venture as an inexpensive gamble: The potential loss was small, but the potential gain was huge. They gave Columbus a letter of introduction to China's Grand Khan, the ruler they hoped he would meet on the other side of the Atlantic.

After frantic preparation, Columbus and his small fleet—the *Niña* and *Pinta*, both caravels, and the *Santa María*, a larger merchant vessel—headed west. Six weeks after leaving the Canary Islands, Columbus landed on a tiny Caribbean island about three hundred miles north of the eastern tip of Cuba.

Columbus claimed possession of the island for Spain and named it San Salvador, in honor of the Savior, Jesus Christ. He called the islanders "Indians," assuming that they inhabited the East Indies somewhere near Japan or China. The islanders called themselves **Tainos**, which in their language meant "good" or "noble." An agricultural people, Tainos grew cassava, corn, cotton, tobacco, and other crops. Instead of dressing in the finery Columbus had expected to find in the East Indies, Tainos "all . . . go around as naked as their mothers bore them," Columbus wrote. Although Columbus

Columbus's First Voyage to the New World, 1492–1493

concluded that Tainos "had no religion," in reality they worshipped gods they called *zemis*, ancestral spirits who inhabited natural objects such as trees and stones. Tainos had no riches. "It seemed to me that they were a people very poor in everything," Columbus wrote.

What Tainos thought about Columbus and his sailors we can only surmise since they left no written documents. At first, Columbus got the impression that Tainos believed Spaniards came from heaven. But after six weeks of encounters, Columbus decided that "the people of these lands do not understand me nor do I, nor anyone else that I have with me, [understand] them." The confused communication between Spaniards and Tainos suggests how strange each group seemed to the other. Columbus's perceptions of Tainos were shaped by European attitudes, ideas, and expectations, just as Tainos' perceptions of the Europeans were no doubt colored by their own culture.

Columbus and his men understood that they had made a momentous discovery. In 1493, when Queen Isabella and King Ferdinand learned Columbus's news, they were overjoyed. With a voyage that had lasted barely eight months, Columbus appeared to have catapulted Spain into a serious challenger to Portugal, whose explorers had not yet sailed to India or China. Columbus was elevated to the nobility and given the title "Admiral of the Ocean Sea," and the seven Tainos he brought to Spain were baptized as Christians with King Ferdinand as their godfather. Soon after Columbus returned to Spain, the Spanish monarchs rushed to obtain the pope's support for their claim to the new lands in the West. When the pope, a Spaniard, complied, the Portuguese feared that their own claims to recently discovered territories were in jeopardy. To protect their claims, the Portuguese and Spanish monarchs negotiated the **Treaty of Tordesillas** in 1494. The treaty drew an imaginary line eleven hundred miles west of the Canary Islands (see Map 2.2). Land discovered west of the line (namely, the islands that Columbus discovered and any additional land that might be found) belonged to Spain; Portugal claimed land to the east (namely, its African and East Indian trading empire).

Taino Zemi Effigy

This sixteenth-century carving of a manatee bone depicts a Taino zemi in the form of a pipe-like container for inhaling cohoba, a psychedelic substance the Taino smoked to induce trances that revealed the supernatural world. Holes barely visible here in the feet placed behind the head of the zemi allowed the user to inhale with both nostrils simultaneously. Fundación Garcia Arevalo, Dominican Republic/ Photo © Dirk Bakker/ Bridgeman Images.

Isabella and Ferdinand moved quickly to realize the promise of their new claims. In the fall of 1493, they dispatched Columbus once again, this time with a fleet of seventeen ships and more than a thousand men who planned to locate the Asian mainland, find gold, and get rich. Before Columbus died in 1506, he returned to the New World two more times (in 1498 and 1502) without relinquishing his belief that the East Indies were there, someplace. Other explorers continued to search for a passage to the East or some other source of profit. Before long, however, prospects of beating the Portuguese to Asia began to dim along with the hope of finding vast hoards of gold.

Nonetheless, Columbus's discoveries forced sixteenth-century Europeans to think about the world in new ways. He proved it was possible to sail from Europe to the western rim of the Atlantic and return to Europe. Most important, Columbus's voyages demonstrated that lands and peoples entirely unknown to Europeans lay across the Atlantic.

The Geographic Revolution and the Columbian Exchange

Within thirty years of Columbus's initial discovery, Europeans' understanding of world geography underwent a revolution. An elite of perhaps twenty thousand people with access to Europe's royal courts and trading centers learned the exciting news about global geography. But it took a generation of additional exploration before they could comprehend the larger contours of Columbus's discoveries.

European monarchs hurried to stake their claims to the newly discovered lands. In 1497, King Henry VII of England sent John Cabot to look for a Northwest Passage to the Indies across the North Atlantic (Map 2.2). Cabot reached the tip of Newfoundland, which he believed was part of Asia, and hurried back to England, where he assembled a small fleet and sailed west in 1498. But he was never heard from again.

Three thousand miles to the south, a Spanish expedition landed on the northern coast of South America in 1499 accompanied by Amerigo Vespucci, an Italian businessman. In 1500, Pedro Álvars Cabral commanded a Portuguese fleet that looped westward into the Atlantic bound for the Indian Ocean, but accidentally made landfall on the east coast of Brazil.

By 1500, European experts knew that several large chunks of land cluttered the western Atlantic. A few cartographers speculated that these chunks were connected to one another in a landmass that was not Asia. In 1507, Martin Waldseemüller, a German cartographer, published the first map that showed the New World separate from Asia; he named the land America, in honor of Amerigo Vespucci.

Two additional discoveries confirmed Waldseemüller's speculation. In 1513, Vasco Núñez de Balboa crossed the Isthmus of Panama and reached the Pacific Ocean. Clearly, more water lay between the New World and Asia. Ferdinand Magellan discovered just how much water when he led an expedition to circumnavigate the globe in 1519. Sponsored by Spain, Magellan's voyage took him first to the New World, around the southern tip of South America, and into the Pacific. Crossing the Pacific took almost four months, decimating his crew with hunger and thirst. Magellan himself was killed by Philippine tribesmen. A remnant of his expedition continued on to the Indian Ocean and managed to transport a cargo of spices back to Spain in 1522.

In most ways, Magellan's voyage was a disaster. One ship and 18 men crawled back from an expedition that had begun with five ships and more than 250 men. But the geographic information it provided left no doubt that America was a continent separated from Asia by the enormous Pacific Ocean. Magellan's voyage made clear that

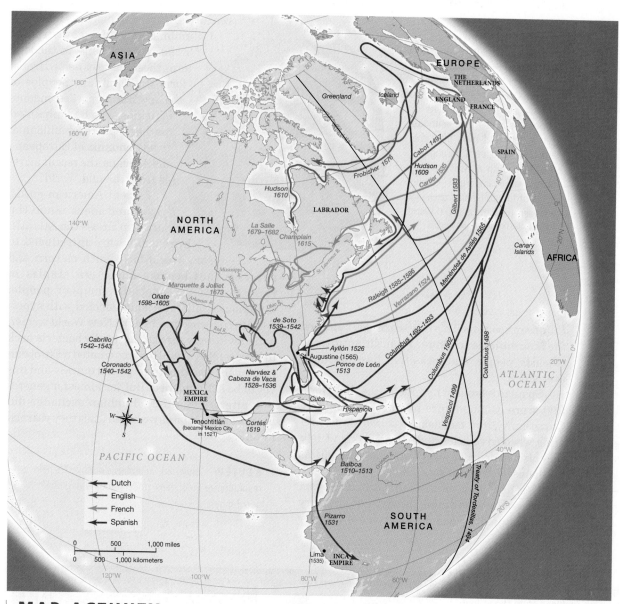

MAP ACTIVITY

Map 2.2   European Exploration in Sixteenth-Century America
This map illustrates the approximate routes of early European explorations of the New World.

READING THE MAP: Which countries were most actively exploring the New World? Which countries were exploring later than others?

CONNECTIONS: What were the motivations behind the explorations? What were the motivations for colonization?

it was possible to sail west to reach the East Indies, but that was a terrible way to go. After Magellan, most Europeans who sailed west set their sights on the New World, not on Asia.

Columbus's arrival in the Caribbean anchored the western end of what might be imagined as a sea bridge that spanned the Atlantic, connecting the Western Hemisphere to Europe. Somewhat

like the Beringian land bridge traversed by the first Americans millennia earlier (see "African and Asian Origins" in chapter 1), the new sea bridge reestablished a connection between the Eastern and Western Hemispheres. The Atlantic Ocean, which had previously isolated America from Europe, became an aquatic highway, thanks to sailing technology, intrepid seamen, and their

Inca Goddess
This sixteenth-century Inca effigy depicts a goddess of agriculture clothed in ears of corn and varieties of squash. Over millennia, these foods became staples of the diets of ancient peoples throughout the hemisphere and then, after the arrival of Europeans, throughout the globe. Such ancient American plants were important components of the Columbian exchange between the New and Old Worlds. Private Collection/Bridgeman Images.

centuries. European diseases made the Columbian exchange catastrophic for Native Americans. In the long term, these diseases helped transform the dominant peoples of the New World from descendants of Asians, who had inhabited the hemisphere for millennia, to descendants of Europeans and Africans, the recent arrivals from the Old World.

Ancient American goods, people, and ideas made the return trip across the Atlantic. Europeans were introduced to New World foods such as corn and potatoes that became important staples in European diets, especially for poor people. Columbus's sailors became infected with syphilis in sexual encounters with New World women and unwittingly carried the deadly bacteria back to Europe. New World tobacco created a European fashion for smoking that ignited quickly and has yet to be extinguished. But for almost a generation after 1492, this Columbian exchange did not reward Spaniards with the riches they yearned to find.

European sponsors. This new sea bridge launched the **Columbian exchange**, a transatlantic trade of goods, people, and ideas that has continued ever since.

Spaniards brought novelties to the New World that were commonplace in Europe, including Christianity, iron technology, sailing ships, firearms, wheeled vehicles, and horses. Unknowingly, they also carried many Old World microorganisms that caused devastating epidemics of smallpox, measles, and other diseases that killed the vast majority of Indians during the sixteenth century and continued to decimate survivors in later

REVIEW How did Columbus's discoveries help revolutionize Europeans' understanding of global geography?

Smallpox Victims
This sixteenth-century picture shows four Mexican smallpox victims lying on woven mats while a fifth victim is treated by a Mexican healer. In reality, there were no known remedies for smallpox, which Spaniards brought to Mexico. Millions died from smallpox, and those who survived were often horribly disfigured and demoralized. The Granger Collection, New York.

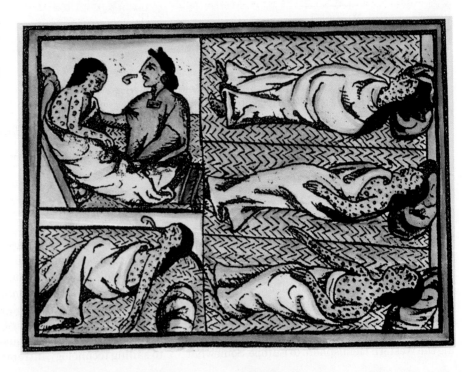

► Spanish Exploration and Conquest

During the sixteenth century, the New World helped Spain become the most powerful monarchy in both Europe and the Americas. Initially, Spaniards enslaved Caribbean tribes and put them to work growing crops and mining gold. But the profits from these early ventures barely covered the costs of maintaining the settlers. After almost thirty years of exploration, the promise of Columbus's discovery seemed illusory.

In 1519, however, that promise was spectacularly fulfilled by Hernán Cortés's march into Mexico. By about 1545, Spanish conquests extended from northern Mexico to southern Chile, and New World riches filled Spanish treasure chests. Cortés's expedition served as the model for Spaniards' and other Europeans' expectations that the New World could yield bonanza profits for its conquerors, while forced labor and deadly epidemics decimated native populations.

The Conquest of Mexico

Hernán Cortés, an obscure nineteen-year-old Spaniard, arrived in the New World in 1504. Throughout his twenties, he fought in the conquest of Cuba and elsewhere in the Caribbean. In 1519, the governor of Cuba authorized Cortés to organize an expedition of about six hundred men and eleven ships to investigate rumors of a fabulously wealthy kingdom somewhere in the interior of the mainland.

A charismatic and confident man, Cortés could not speak any Native American languages. Landing first on the Yucatán peninsula with his ragtag army, he had the good fortune to receive from a local Tobascan chief the gift of a young girl named Malinali. She spoke several native languages, including Nahuatl, the language of the Mexica, the most powerful people in what is now Mexico and Central America (see "The Mexica: A Mesoamerican Culture" in chapter 1). Malinali, whom Spaniards called Marina, had acquired her linguistic skills painfully. Born into a family of Mexican nobility, she learned Nahuatl as a child. After her father died and her mother

remarried, her stepfather sold her as a slave to Mayan-speaking Indians, who subsequently gave her to the Tobascans, who in turn presented her to Cortés. She soon learned Spanish and became Cortés's interpreter, one of his several mistresses, and the mother of his son. Malinali was the Spaniards' lifeline of communication with the Indians. "Without her help," wrote one Spaniard who accompanied Cortés, "we would not have understood the language of New Spain and Mexico." By the time Marina died at age twenty-four, the people she had grown up among—the people who had taught her languages, enslaved her, and given her to Cortés—had been conquered by the Spaniards with her help.

In Tenochtitlán, the capital of the Mexican empire, the emperor Montezuma heard about some strange creatures sighted along the coast. (Montezuma and his people called themselves Mexica.) The emperor sent representatives to bring the strangers large quantities of food. Before the Mexican messengers served food to the Spaniards, they sacrificed several hostages and soaked the food in their blood. This fare disgusted the Spaniards and might have been enough to turn them back to Cuba. But along with the food, the Mexica also brought the Spaniards another gift, a "disk in the shape of a sun, as big as a cartwheel and made of very fine gold," as a Mexican recalled. Here was conclusive evidence that the rumors of fabulous riches heard by Cortés had some basis in fact.

In August 1519, Cortés marched inland to find Montezuma. Leading about 350 men, Cortés had to live off the land, establishing peaceful relations with indigenous tribes when he could and killing them when he thought it necessary. On November 8, 1519, Cortés reached Tenochtitlán, where Montezuma welcomed him and showered the Spaniards with lavish hospitality. Quickly, Cortés took Montezuma hostage and held him under house arrest, hoping to make him a puppet through whom the Spaniards could rule the Mexican empire. This uneasy peace existed for several months until one of Cortés's men led a brutal massacre of many Mexican nobles, causing the people of Tenochtitlán to revolt. Montezuma was killed, and the Mexica mounted a ferocious assault on the Spaniards. On June 30, 1520, Cortés and about a hundred other Spaniards

Cortés's Invasion of Tenochtitlán, 1519–1521

0 25 50 mi.
0 25 50 km.

Gulf of Mexico

Texcoco
Otumba   Zautla
                    Jalapa
                    Veracruz
Tlaxcala
Tenochtitlán Cholula

➤ Cortés's original route, 1519
➤ Cortés's retreat, 1520
➤ Cortés's return route, 1520–1521

Why Did Cortés Win?

By conquering Mexico, Hernán Cortés demonstrated that the New World could enrich the Old. But how did a few hundred Spaniards so far away from home defeat millions of Indians fighting on their home turf?

First, several military factors favored the Spaniards. They possessed superior military technology, which partially offset the Mexicans' superior numbers. They fought with weapons of iron and steel against the Mexicans' stone, wood, and copper. They charged on horseback against Mexican warriors on foot. They ignited gunpowder to fire cannon and muskets toward attacking Mexicans, whose only source of power was human muscle. However, the Spaniards' weaponry alone was not enough to overpower the Mexicans' immense numerical superiority.

The Spanish forces also had superior military organization, although they were far from a highly disciplined, professional fighting force. Cortés's army was composed of soldiers of fortune, young men who hoped to fight for God and king and get rich. The unsteady discipline among the Spaniards is suggested by Cortés's decision to beach and dismantle the ships that had brought his small army to the Mexican mainland, thereby leaving his men with no choice but to go forward. Still, the Spaniards formed a well-oiled military machine compared to the Mexicans. Spanish tactics concentrated soldiers to magnify the effect of their firepower and to maintain communication during the thick of battle. In contrast, Mexicans tended to attack from ambush or in waves of frontal assaults, showing great courage but little organization or discipline. In the siege of Tenochtitlán, for example, when Mexicans had Spaniards on the run, they often paused to sacrifice Spanish soldiers they had captured, taking time to skin "their faces," one Spaniard recalled, "which they afterward prepared like leather gloves, with their beards on."

But perhaps the Spaniards' most fundamental military advantage was their concept of war. The Mexican concept was shaped by the nature of the empire. The Mexicans fought to impose their tribute system on others and to take captives for sacrifices. They believed that war would make their adversaries realize the high cost of continuing to fight and would give them incentive to surrender and pay tribute. To the Spaniards, war meant destroying the enemy's ability to fight. In short, the Spaniards sought total victory; the Mexicans sought surrender. All these military factors weakened the Mexicans' resistance but were still insufficient to explain Cortés's victory.

European viruses proved to be at least as significant as military technology. When the Mexicans confronted Cortés and his men, they were weakened by the smallpox and measles viruses that the Spaniards had brought with them to Mexico. A smallpox epidemic struck the Caribbean in 1519 and lasted

---

fought their way out of Tenochtitlán (losing much of the gold they had confiscated since it proved too heavy to carry away in haste) and retreated about one hundred miles to Tlaxcala, a stronghold of bitter enemies of the Mexica. Tlaxcalans—who had long resented Mexican power—allowed Cortés to regroup, obtain reinforcements, and plan a strategy to conquer Tenochtitlán.

In the spring of 1521, Cortés and thousands of Indian allies laid siege to the Mexican capital. With a relentless, scorched-earth strategy, Cortés finally defeated the last Mexican defenders on August 13, 1521. The great capital of the Mexican empire "looked as if it had been ploughed up," one of Cortés's soldiers remembered. (See "Making Historical Arguments," above.)

The Search for Other Mexicos

Lured by their insatiable appetite for gold, Spanish conquistadors (soldiers who fought in conquests) quickly fanned out from Tenochtitlán in search of other sources of treasure. The most spectacular prize fell to Francisco Pizarro, who conquered the Incan empire in Peru. The Incas controlled a vast, complex region that contained more than nine million people and stretched along the western coast of South America for more than two thousand miles. In 1532, Pizarro and his army of fewer than two hundred men captured the Incan emperor Atahualpa and held him hostage. As ransom, the Incas gave Pizarro the largest treasure yet produced by the conquests: gold and silver equivalent to half a century's worth of precious-metal production in Europe. With the ransom safely in their hands, the Spaniards murdered Atahualpa. The Incan treasure proved that at least one other Mexico did indeed exist, and it spurred Spaniards' search for others.

Juan Ponce de León sailed to Florida in 1521 to find riches, only to be killed in battle with Calusa Indians. A few years later, Lucas Vázquez de Ayllón explored the Atlantic coast north of Florida to present-day South Carolina. In 1526, he established a small settlement on the Georgia

through 1522, killing thousands of Indians and leaving many others too sick to fight. As one Mexican explained to a Spaniard shortly after the conquest, the plague lasted for months, "striking everywhere in the city and killing a vast number of our people." While Mexicans were decimated by their first exposure to smallpox and measles, Spaniards were for all practical purposes immune, having previously been exposed to the diseases.

Christianity was as much a part of the conquistadors' armory as swords and gunpowder. Spaniards' Christianity was a confident and militant faith that commanded its followers to destroy idolatry, root out heresy, slay infidels, and subjugate nonbelievers. Mexicans' religious doctrine caused them to be hesitant and uncertain in confronting Spaniards when they were most vulnerable. At first, Mexicans worried that Spaniards were immortal, an illusion Cortés tried to maintain by hiding the bodies of Spaniards who died.

Mexican military commanders often turned to their priests for military guidance. Spaniards routinely celebrated mass and prayed before battles, but Cortés and his subordinates—tough, wily, practical men—made the military and diplomatic decisions. When Spaniards suffered defeats, they did not worry that God had abandoned them. In contrast, when Mexicans lost battles advised by their priests, they confronted the distressing fear that their gods no longer seemed to listen to them. The deadly sickness sweeping through the countryside also seemed to show that their gods had abandoned them. "Cut us loose," one Mexican pleaded, "because the gods have died."

Finally, politics proved decisive in the Mexicans' defeat. Cortés shrewdly exploited the tensions between Mexicans and the people in their empire. Cortés reinforced his small army with thousands of Indian allies who were eager to seek revenge against their Mexican conquerors. With skillful diplomacy, Cortés obtained cooperation from thousands of Indian porters and food suppliers. Besides fighting alongside Cortés, Spaniards' Indian allies provided the invaders with a fairly secure base from which to maneuver against Mexicans' stronghold. Hundreds of thousands of other Indians helped Cortés by failing to come to Mexicans' defense. These passive allies of the Spaniards prevented Mexicans from fully capitalizing on their overwhelming numerical superiority. In the end, the political tensions created by the Mexican empire proved to be its crippling weakness.

coast that he named San Miguel de Gualdape, the first Spanish attempt to establish a foothold in what is now the United States. This settlement was soon swept away by sickness and hostile Indians. In 1528, Pánfilo de Narváez surveyed the Gulf coast from Florida to Texas, but his expedition ended disastrously with a shipwreck near present-day Galveston, Texas.

In 1539, Hernando de Soto, a seasoned conquistador, set out with more than six hundred

men to find another Peru in North America. Landing in Florida, de Soto slashed his way through much of southeastern North America for three years. De Soto typified the viewpoint of other conquistadors when he told an Indian leader in Georgia that he "was the child of the Sun, coming from its abode, and that he was going about the country seeking the greatest prince there and the richest region." After the brutal slaughter of many Native Americans and much hardship, de Soto died in 1542. His men buried him in the Mississippi River and turned back to Mexico, disappointed.

VISUAL ACTIVITY

Zuñi Defend Their Pueblo against Coronado

This sixteenth-century drawing by a Mexican artist shows Zuñi bowmen fighting back against Coronado's men and the entreaties of Christian missionaries. The drawing depicts a Zuñi defender aiming his arrow at a Mexican missionary armed with a crucifix, a rosary, and the Bible. Ms Hunter 242 f.317r *The Spanish Conquest*, from "Historia de Tlaxcala" by Diego Munoz Camargo (pen & ink on paper)/Mexican School, (16th century)/UNIVERSITY OF GLASGOW LIBRARY/© Glasgow University Library, Scotland/Bridgeman Images.

READING THE IMAGE: How did this picture convey Spaniards' point of view about Zuñi opposition to Coronado and his men?

CONNECTIONS: Why did missionaries seek to convert Native Americans to Christianity, and why did many Native Americans resist the missionaries' efforts?

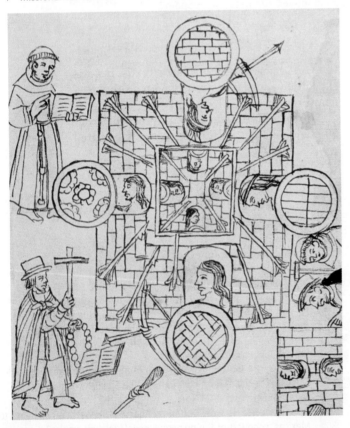

Tales of the fabulous wealth of the mythical Seven Cities of Cíbola also lured Francisco Vásquez de Coronado to search the Southwest and Great Plains of North America. In 1540, Coronado left northern Mexico with more than three hundred Spaniards, a thousand Indians, and a priest who claimed to know the way to what he called "the greatest and best of the discoveries." Cíbola turned out to be a small Zuñi pueblo of about a hundred families. When the Zuñi shot arrows at the Spaniards, Coronado attacked the pueblo and routed the defenders after a hard battle. Convinced that the rich cities must lie somewhere over the horizon, Coronado kept moving all the way to central Kansas before deciding in 1542 that the rumors he had pursued were just that.

The same year Coronado abandoned his search for Cíbola, Juan Rodríguez Cabrillo's maritime expedition sought to find wealth along the coast of California. Cabrillo died on Santa Catalina Island, offshore from present-day Los Angeles, but his men sailed on to Oregon, where a ferocious storm forced them to turn back toward Mexico.

These probes into North America by de Soto, Coronado, and Cabrillo persuaded other Spaniards that although enormous territories stretched northward from Mexico, their inhabitants had little to loot or exploit. After a generation of vigorous exploration, the Spaniards concluded that there was only one Mexico and one Peru.

Spanish Outposts in Florida and New Mexico

Disappointed by the explorers' failure to discover riches in North America, the Spanish monarchy insisted that a few settlements be established in Florida and New Mexico to give a token of reality to Spain's territorial claims. Settlements in Florida would have the additional benefit of protecting Spanish ships from pirates and privateers who lurked along the southeastern coast, waiting for the Spanish treasure fleet sailing toward Spain.

In 1565, the Spanish king sent Pedro Menéndez de Avilés to found St. Augustine in Florida, the first permanent European settlement within what became the United States. By 1600, St. Augustine had a population of about five hundred, the only remaining Spanish beachhead on North America's vast Atlantic shoreline.

More than sixteen hundred miles west of St. Augustine, Spaniards founded another outpost in 1598. Juan de Oñate led an expedition of about five hundred people to settle northern Mexico, now called New Mexico, and claim the booty rumored to exist there. Oñate had impeccable credentials for both conquest and mining. His father helped to discover the bonanza silver mines of Zacatecas in central Mexico, and his wife Isabel Tolsa Cortés Montezuma was the granddaughter of Cortés and the great-granddaughter of Montezuma. When Oñate and his companions reached pueblos near present-day Albuquerque and Santa Fe, he sent out scouting parties to find the legendary treasures of the region and to locate the ocean, which he believed must be nearby. Meanwhile, many of his soldiers planned to mutiny, and relations with the Indians deteriorated. When Indians in the Acoma pueblo revolted against the Spaniards, Oñate ruthlessly suppressed the uprising, killing eight hundred men, women, and children. Oñate's response to the **Acoma pueblo revolt** reconfirmed Spaniards' military superiority, but he did not bring peace or stability to the region. After another pueblo revolt occurred in 1599, many of Oñate's settlers returned to Mexico, leaving New Mexico a small, dusty assertion of Spanish claims to the North American Southwest.

New Spain in the Sixteenth Century

For all practical purposes, Spain was the dominant European power in the Western Hemisphere during the sixteenth century (Map 2.3). Portugal claimed the giant territory of Brazil under the Tordesillas Treaty but was far more concerned with exploiting its hard-won trade with the East Indies than with colonizing the New World. England and France were absorbed by domestic and diplomatic concerns in Europe and largely lost interest in America until late in the century. In the decades after 1519, Spaniards created the distinctive colonial society of **New Spain**, which showed other Europeans how the New World could be made to serve the purposes of the Old.

The Spanish monarchy gave the conquistadors permission to explore and plunder what they found. (See "Analyzing Historical Evidence," page 42.) The crown took one-fifth, called the "royal fifth," of any loot confiscated and allowed the conquerors to divide the rest. In the end, most conquistadors received very little after the plunder was divided among leaders such as Cortés and his favorite officers. To compensate his disappointed, battle-hardened soldiers, Cortés gave them towns Spaniards had subdued.

The distribution of conquered towns institutionalized the system of **encomienda**, which empowered the conquistadors to rule the Indians and the lands in and around their towns. The concept of encomienda was familiar to Spaniards who had used it to govern regions captured from Muslims during the Reconquest. In New Spain, encomienda transferred to the Spanish *encomendero* (the man who "owned" the town) the tribute that the town had previously paid to the Mexican empire. In theory, the encomendero was supposed to guarantee order and justice, be responsible for the Indians' material welfare, and encourage them to become Christians.

Catholic missionaries worked hard to convert Indians. They fervently believed that God expected them to save Indians' souls by convincing them to abandon their old sinful beliefs and to embrace the one true Christian faith. (See "Experiencing the American Promise," page 44.) But after baptizing tens of thousands of Indians, the missionaries learned that many Indians continued to worship their own gods. Most priests came to believe that Indians were lesser beings inherently incapable of fully understanding Christianity.

In practice, encomenderos were far more interested in what Indians could do for them than in what they or the missionaries could do for Indians. Encomenderos subjected Indians to chronic overwork, mistreatment, and abuse. According to one Spaniard, "Everything [Indians] do is slowly done and by compulsion. They are malicious, lying, [and] thievish." Economically, however, encomienda recognized a fundamental reality of New Spain: The most important treasure Spaniards could plunder from the New World was not gold but uncompensated Indian labor.

The practice of coerced labor in New Spain grew directly out of Spaniards' assumption that they were superior to Indians. As one missionary put it, Indians "are more stupid than asses and refuse to improve in anything." Therefore, most Spaniards assumed, Indians' labor should be organized by and for their conquerors. Spaniards seldom hesitated to use violence to punish and intimidate recalcitrant Indians.

Encomienda engendered two groups of influential critics. A few missionaries were horrified at the brutal mistreatment of Indians. "What will [Indians] think about the God of the Christians," Friar Bartolomé de Las Casas asked,

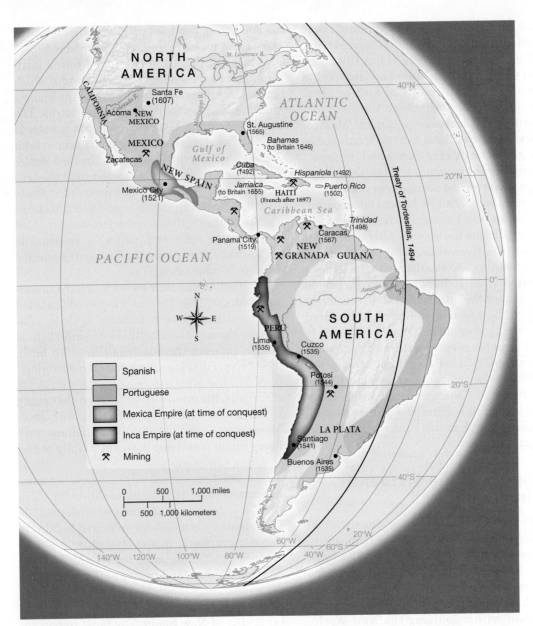

MAP ACTIVITY

Map 2.3 Sixteenth-Century European Colonies in the New World

Spanish control spread throughout Central and South America during the sixteenth century, with the important exception of Portuguese Brazil. North America, though claimed by Spain under the Treaty of Tordesillas, remained peripheral to Spain's New World empire.

READING THE MAP: Track Spain's efforts at colonization by date. How did political holdings, the physical layout of the land, and natural resources influence where Spaniards directed their energies?

CONNECTIONS: What was the purpose of the Treaty of Tordesillas? How might the location of silver and gold mines have affected Spain's desire to assert its claims over regions still held by Portugal after 1494, and Spain's interest in California, New Mexico, and Florida?

when they see their friends "with their heads split, their hands amputated, their intestines torn open? . . . Would they want to come to Christ's sheepfold after their homes had been destroyed, their children imprisoned, their wives raped, their cities devastated, their maidens deflowered, and their provinces laid waste?" Unlike most Spaniards, Las Casas believed that Indians "are by nature of very subtle, lively, clear, and most capable understanding." While he and other

Connections between Spanish Christianity and Mexican Traditional Religions
Spanish missionaries struggled to eradicate all forms of Mexicans' traditional religion. The painting portrays a Catholic priest instructing two Mexican children while another priest shelters a group of children and wields a cross to protect them from the diabolical creatures seeking to tempt them to embrace evil. Even Mexicans who converted to Christianity continued to express their spirituality in traditional ways. The Granger Collection, New York.

outspoken missionaries softened few hearts among the encomenderos, they won some sympathy for Indians from the Spanish monarchy and royal bureaucracy. The Spanish monarchy moved to abolish encomienda in an effort to replace swashbuckling old conquistadors with royal bureaucrats as the rulers of New Spain.

In 1549, a reform called the *repartimiento* began to replace encomienda. It limited the labor an encomendero could command from his Indians to forty-five days per year from each adult male. The repartimiento, however, did not challenge the principle of forced labor, nor did it prevent encomenderos from continuing to cheat, mistreat, and overwork their Indians, many of whom were put to work in silver mines.

Mining was grueling and dangerous work. One Spaniard claimed that ten Indians died for every peso earned in the mines, an exaggeration. But the mines were fabulously profitable for the Spaniards. During the entire sixteenth century, precious-metal exports from New Spain to Spain were worth twenty-five times more than the next most important export, leather hides (Figure 2.1).

For Spaniards, life in New Spain after the conquests was relatively easy. As one colonist wrote to his brother in Spain, "Don't hesitate [to come]. . . . This land [New Spain] is as good as ours [in Spain], for God has given us more here than there, and we shall be better off." During the century after 1492, about 225,000 Spaniards

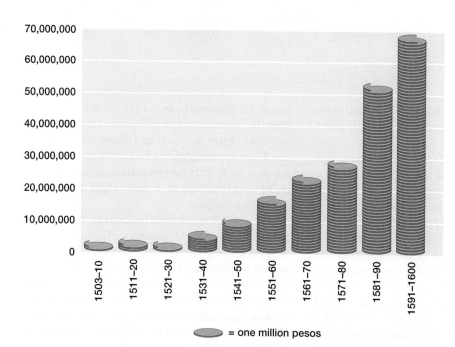

= one million pesos

FIGURE 2.1 New World Gold and Silver Imported into Spain during the Sixteenth Century, in Pesos
Spain imported more gold than silver during the first three decades of the sixteenth century, but the total value of this treasure was quickly eclipsed during the 1530s and 1540s, when rich silver mines were developed. Silver accounted for most of the enormous growth in Spain's precious-metal imports from the New World.

Justifying Conquest

The immense riches Spain reaped from its New World empire came largely at the expense of Native Americans. A few individual Spaniards raised their voices against the brutal exploitation of Indians. Their criticisms prompted the Spanish monarchy to formulate an official justification of conquest that, in effect, blamed Indians for resisting Spanish dominion.

DOCUMENT 1
Montecino's 1511 Sermon

In 1511, a Dominican friar named Antón Montecino delivered a blistering sermon that astonished the Spaniards gathered in the church in Santo Domingo, headquarters of the Spanish Caribbean.

Your greed for gold is blind. Your pride, your lust, your anger, your envy, your sloth, all blind. . . . You are in mortal sin. And you are heading for damnation. . . . For you are destroying an innocent people. For they are God's people, these innocents, whom you destroyed. By what right do you make them die? Mining gold for you in your mines or working for you in your fields, by what right do you unleash enslaving wars upon them? They have lived in peace in this land before you came, in peace in their own homes. They did nothing to harm you to cause you to slaughter them wholesale. . . .

Are you not under God's command to love them as you love yourselves?

Are you out of your souls, out of your minds? Yes. And that will bring you to damnation.

Source: Zvi Dor-Ner, *Columbus and the Age of Discovery* (New York: William Morrow, 1991), 220–21.

DOCUMENT 2
The Requerimiento

In 1512 and 1513, King Ferdinand met with philosophers and theologians, and concluded that their holy duty to spread Christianity justified conquest. To buttress this claim, the king had his advisers prepare the requerimiento.

According to the requerimiento, Indians who failed to welcome Spanish conquest and all its blessings deserved to die. Conquistadors were commanded to read the requerimiento to the Indians before any act of conquest.

On the part of the King . . . [and] queen of [Spain], subduers of the barbarous nations, we their servants notify and make known to you, as best we can, that the Lord our God, living and eternal, created the heaven and the earth, and one man and one woman, of whom you and we, and all the men of the world, were and are descendants. . . .

God our lord gave charge to one man called St. Peter, that he should be lord and superior to all the men in the world, that all should obey him, and that he should be the head of the whole human race, wherever men should live . . . and he gave him the world for his kingdom and jurisdiction. . . .

[The Pope] who succeeded that St. Peter as lord of the world . . . made donation of these islands and mainland to the . . . king and queen [of Spain]. . . .

So their highnesses are kings and lords of these islands and mainland by virtue of this donation; and . . . almost all those to whom this has been notified, have received and served their highnesses, as lords and kings, in the way that subjects ought to do, with good will, without any resistance, immediately, without delay, when they were in-

settled in the colonies. Virtually all of them were poor young men of common (non-noble) lineage who came directly from Spain. Laborers and artisans made up the largest proportion, but soldiers and sailors were also numerous. Men vastly outnumbered women.

The gender and number of Spanish settlers shaped two fundamental features of the society of New Spain. First, Europeans never made up more than 1 or 2 percent of the total population. Although Spaniards ruled New Spain, the population was almost wholly Indian. Second, the shortage of Spanish women meant that Spanish men frequently married Indian women or used them as concubines. As a Spanish merchant in Mexico City wrote to a relative in Castile, "though there in Spain it might shock you that I have married an Indian woman, here one loses nothing of his honor." The relatively few women from Spain usually married Spanish men, contributing to a tiny elite defined by European origins.

The small number of Spaniards, the masses of Indians, and the frequency of intermarriage created a steep social hierarchy defined by perceptions of national origin and race. Natives of Spain—*peninsulares* (people born on the Iberian Peninsula)—enjoyed the highest social status in New Spain. Below them but still within the white elite were *creoles*, the children born in

formed of the aforesaid facts. And also they received and obeyed the priests whom their highnesses sent to preach to them and to teach them our holy faith; and all these, of their own free will, without any reward or condition have become Christians, and are so, and their highnesses have joyfully and graciously received them, and they have also commanded them to be treated as their subjects and vassals; and you too are held and obliged to do the same. Wherefore, as best we can, we ask and require that you consider what we have said to you, and that you take the time that shall be necessary to understand and deliberate upon it, and that you acknowledge the Church as the ruler and superior of the whole world, and the high priest called Pope, and in his name the king and queen [of Spain] our lords, in his place, as superiors and lords and kings of these islands and this mainland . . . and that you consent and permit that these religious fathers declare and preach to you. . . .

If you do so . . . we . . . shall receive you in all love and charity, and shall leave you your wives and your children and your lands free without servitude, that you may do with them and with yourselves freely what you like and think best, and they shall not compel you to turn to Christians unless you yourselves, when informed of the truth, should wish to be converted to our holy

Catholic faith. . . . And besides this, their highnesses award you many privileges and exemptions and will grant you many benefits.

But if you do not do this or if you maliciously delay in doing it, I certify to you that with the help of God we shall forcefully enter into your country and shall make war against you in all ways and manners that we can, and shall subject you to the yoke and obedience of the Church and of their highnesses; we shall take you and your wives and your children and shall make slaves of them, and as such shall sell and dispose of them as their highnesses may command; and we shall take away your goods and shall do to you all the harm and damage that we can, as to vassals who do not obey and refuse to receive their lord and resist and contradict him; and we protest that the deaths and losses which shall accrue from this are your fault, and not that of their highnesses, or ours, or of these soldiers who come with us.

Indians who heard the requerimiento could not understand Spanish, of course. No native documents survive to record the Indians' thoughts upon hearing the Spaniards' official justification for conquest, even when it was translated into a language they recognized. But one conquistador reported that when the requerimiento was

translated for two chiefs in Colombia, they responded that if the pope gave the king so much territory that belonged to other people, "the Pope must have been drunk."

Source: Adapted from A. Helps and M. Oppenheim, eds., *The Spanish Conquest in America and Its Relation to the History of Slavery and to the Government of the Colonies,* 4 vols. (London, 1900–1904), 1:264–67.

Questions for Analysis

Ask Historical Questions: To what degree did Spaniards believe their New World conquests were moral and just? How did Christianity influence Spaniards' ideas about conquest?

Analyze the Evidence: How did the requerimiento address the criticisms of Montecino? According to the requerimiento, what choices did Native Americans and Spaniards have?

Consider the Context: Since few Native Americans could understand the requerimiento when it was read to them, what purpose did the requerimiento serve? Who were its intended audiences?

Recognize Viewpoints: According to the requerimiento, why were Native Americans responsible for Spanish cruelty? What arguments might Native American leaders have made against the requerimiento?

the New World to Spanish men and women. Together, peninsulares and creoles made up barely 1 or 2 percent of the population. Below them on the social pyramid was a larger group of *mestizos*, the offspring of Spanish men and Indian women, who accounted for 4 or 5 percent of the population. Some mestizos worked as artisans and labor overseers and lived well, and a few rose into the ranks of the elite, especially if their Indian ancestry was not obvious from their skin color. Most mestizos, however, were lumped with Indians, the enormous bottom slab of the social pyramid.

The society of New Spain established the precedent for what would become a pronounced pattern in the European colonies of the New World: a society stratified sharply by social origin and race. All Europeans of whatever social origin considered themselves superior to Native Americans; in New Spain, they were a dominant minority in both power and status.

The Toll of Spanish Conquest and Colonization

By 1560, the major centers of Indian civilization had been conquered, their leaders overthrown, their religion held in contempt, and their people forced to work for the Spaniards. Profound demoralization pervaded Indian society. A Mexican poet wrote:

Spreading Christianity in New Spain

Spanish officials aspired to accompany the military and political conquest of the New World with spiritual conquest. With royal support, priests flocked to New Spain to save the millions of souls unexpectedly disclosed by the voyages of Columbus. In 1529, a young priest named Bernardino de Sahagún sailed to New Spain, where he spent the remaining sixty-one years of his life seeking to realize the promise of spreading Christianity to people who had never heard of it.

Sahagún believed that preaching the gospel in the New World was a heaven-sent opportunity to revitalize global Christianity. In Asia, he wrote, "there are nothing but Turks and Moors"; in Africa, "there are no longer any Christians"; in Germany, "there are nothing but heretics"; and in Europe, "in most places there is no obedience to the Church." Now, Sahagún wrote, "Our Lord [ordained] the Spanish people to traverse the Ocean Sea to make discoveries in the West" and to "bring into the embrace of the Church that multitude of peoples, kingdoms, and nations." In pursuit of his goal to rescue Christianity by converting the New World Indians, Sahagún compiled the most important collection of information in existence about the lives and beliefs of sixteenth-century Mexicans.

Sahagún and other Spaniards considered Christianity the one true faith. When Cortés and his men marched into Mexico a decade before Sahagún arrived, they went out of their way to destroy effigies of Mexican gods and to replace them with crosses, the icons of Christianity. "It was necessary," Sahagún wrote, "to destroy the idolatrous things, and all the idolatrous buildings, and even the customs of the [Mexicans] . . . that were intertwined with idolatrous rites and accompanied by idolatrous ceremonies."

What Sahagún considered idolatry was rooted in individual Mexicans' belief in what he called their own "innumerable insanities and gods without number." Sahagún and other priests set out to persuade Indians to reject belief in traditional deities and to have faith instead in the divinity of Jesus Christ and in the Catholic Church as Christ's representative on earth.

At first, the conversion campaign seemed amazingly successful. One priest claimed that more than nine million Mexicans had been baptized by 1539. But after a few years, Sahagún and other priests realized that many Indians simply "took [Jesus Christ] as yet another god . . . without . . . relinquishing their ancient gods." Adopting some of the outward rituals of Christianity while maintaining belief in what Spaniards considered pagan idols was a "twisted perversity," Sahagún wrote, one that caused the New World church "to be founded on falsehood."

Unlike many other Spaniards, Sahagún believed that to purge Mexicans' idolatries, church leaders needed to become familiar with Mexicans' traditional religious ideas. To diagnose what he called Mexicans' "spiritual illnesses," Sahagún set out to record everything he could learn about Indians' beliefs.

As a first step, Sahagún learned Nahuatl, the Mexicans' unwritten language. Next, he and other priests started schools to teach Latin and eventually Spanish to young Indian students, usually drawn from elite families. These "trilinguals," as Sahagún called them, could translate religious texts into Nahuatl, which the priests could use in their missionary efforts.

Beginning in 1558, Sahagún used his trilinguals to undertake a systematic investigation of every facet of Mexican life. Sahagún and his assistants interviewed Mexican elders, asking them not only about gods and religious ceremonies but also about farming, family life, education, poetry, songs, and even their conquest by the Spaniards. Sahagún developed great admiration for both the Mexicans and their language. "They are quick to learn," he wrote. "There is no art for which they do not have the talent to learn and use it." In fact, Sahagún declared, the Mexicans "are held to be barbarians and a people of little

Nothing but flowers and songs of sorrow are left in Mexico . . .

Where once we saw warriors and wise men . . .

We are crushed to the ground; we lie in ruins.

There is nothing but grief and suffering in Mexico.

Adding to the culture shock of conquest and colonization was the deadly toll of European diseases. As conquest spread, Indians succumbed to epidemics of measles, smallpox, and respiratory illnesses. They had no immunity to these diseases because they had not been exposed to them before the arrival of Europeans. By 1570

lloro nono

inizquicacan catca icalpiscah
oan inquitlapicliaia. Auh in
cequintin moteneheaia calla a
manteca: inichoantin, y, canquis
caluaia intlauiztli quichioaia
quimotiamictiaia, aço chimalli
anoço tozehoatl: inçaço quena
mi quichioaia. Auh inascan, ma
ciui inaocmo cenca monequi tla
uiztli: çacan icuih otlatoca, can
icuih motocatiuh intlachioalli, in
tlachichioaliztli: iniuh otlacauh
tiaque, otlanelhoaiotitiaque in
amanteca ueuetque inicquiziui
intultecaio: caçan iee inimiis, inin
iollo motitlani, inictlachichioa
lo ascan, camochioa inchimalli:
ihuitica motzacoa mopepechoa
inicoac monequi: auh mochioa
intlamamalli inipan macehoalo,
ioan inisquich macehoallatquitl
innetotiloni, innechichioaloni in
quezalli, inicpax xochitl, inmachō
cōtl, inmatemecatl inêcacehoaz
tli, aztaecacehoaztli, quauhque
cholecacehoaztli, caquaneca ca
hoaztli, coxoleca cehoaztli, que

officials wanted to stamp out the Mexicans' beliefs, not preserve them. Sahagún dutifully sent his volumes to Spain, but he was still working on a final copy, which he later gave to a priest friend, who saved it, and it survives to this day. Unbeknownst to him, Sahagún's masterwork preserved for posterity an unrivaled account of the hearts and souls of sixteenth-century Mexicans in their own words.

Questions for Analysis

Ask Historical Questions: How did Sahagún contribute to Spaniards' conquest of the New World?

Analyze the Evidence: According to Sahagún, what steps had to be taken to convert Indians to Christianity?

Consider the Context: How did Sahagún's efforts differ from those of most other Catholic missionaries? Why did the church want to destroy Sahagún's information?

Recognize Viewpoints: Why did Sahagún collect information about the social and cultural lives of Indians? How did Indians' religious views differ from Sahagún's?

worth, yet in truth, in matters of culture, they are a step ahead of many nations that presume to be civilized."

For years, Sahagún edited and organized this massive treasure trove of information about Mexican life and beliefs, all in the hope that it would ultimately help priests make converts to Christianity. When church officials heard about Sahagún's great work, they obtained a royal order in 1577 to collect all copies and send them immediately to Spain for destruction. The Spanish monarchy and most church

the Indian population of New Spain had fallen about 90 percent from what it was when Columbus arrived, a catastrophe unequaled in human history. A Mayan Indian recalled that when sickness struck his village, "The dogs and vultures devoured the bodies. The mortality was terrible. . . . So it was that we became orphans. . . . We were born to die." For most Indians, New Spain was a graveyard.

For Spaniards, Indian deaths meant that the most valuable resource of New Spain—Indian labor—dwindled rapidly. By the last quarter of the sixteenth century, Spanish colonists began to import African slaves. Some Africans had

Español con India, Mestizo.

Mestizo con Española Castizo.

Castizo con Española Español.

Español con Mora Mulato.

5

Mulato con Española Morisco.

6

Morisco con Española Chino.

7

Chino con India Salta atas.

Salta atas con Mulata Lobo.

VISUAL ACTIVITY

Mixed Races

These eighteenth-century paintings illustrate forms of racial mixture common in the sixteenth century. In the first painting, a Spanish man and an Indian woman have a mestizo son; in the fourth, a Spanish man and a woman of African descent have a mulatto son. Can you detect any meanings of racial categories in the clothing? Schalkwijk/Art Resource, NY.

READING THE IMAGE: What do these paintings reveal about social status in New Spain?

CONNECTIONS: How do the paintings illustrate the power Spaniards exercised in their New World colonies? What were some other aspects of colonial society that demonstrated Spanish domination?

come to Mexico with the conquistadors. One Mexican recalled that among Cortés's men were "some black-skinned one[s] with kink[y] hair." In the years before 1550, while Indian labor was still adequate, only 15,000 slaves were imported from Africa. The relatively high cost of African slaves kept imports low, totaling approximately 36,000 from 1550 to the end of the century. During the sixteenth century, New Spain continued to rely primarily on a shrinking number of Indians.

REVIEW   How did New Spain's distinctive colonial population shape its economy and society?

▶ The New World and Sixteenth-Century Europe

The riches of New Spain helped make the sixteenth century the Golden Age of Spain. After Queen Isabella and King Ferdinand died, their sixteen-year-old grandson became King Charles I of Spain in 1516. Three years later, just as Cortés ventured into Mexico, King Charles became Holy Roman Emperor Charles V. His empire encompassed more territory than that of any other European monarch. He used the wealth of New Spain to promote his interests in sixteenth-century Europe. He also sought to defend orthodox Christianity from the insurgent heresy of the Protestant Reformation. The power of the Spanish monarchy spread the message throughout sixteenth-century Europe that a New World empire could bankroll Old World ambitions.

The Protestant Reformation and the Spanish Response

In 1517, Martin Luther, an obscure Catholic priest in central Germany, initiated the **Protestant Reformation** by publicizing his criticisms of the Catholic Church. Luther's ideas won the sympathy of many Catholics, but they were considered extremely dangerous by church officials and by monarchs such as Charles V, who believed that just as the church spoke for God, they ruled for God.

Luther preached a doctrine known as "justification by faith": Individual Christians could obtain salvation and life everlasting only by having faith that God would save them. Giving monetary offerings to the church, following the orders of priests, or participating in church rituals would not bring believers closer to heaven. The only true source of information about God's will was the Bible, not the church. By reading the Bible, any Christian could learn as much about God's commandments as any priest. Indeed, Luther called for a "priesthood of all believers."

In effect, Luther charged that the Catholic Church was in many respects fraudulent. Luther declared that the church had neglected its true purpose of helping individual Christians understand the spiritual realm revealed in the Bible and had wasted its resources in worldly conflicts of politics and wars. Luther hoped his ideas would reform the Catholic Church, but instead they ruptured forever the unity of Christianity in western Europe.

Charles V pledged to exterminate Luther's Protestant heresies. The wealth pouring into Spain from the New World fueled his efforts to defend orthodox Catholic faith against Protestants, as well as against any other challenge to Spain's supremacy. As the most powerful monarch in Europe, Charles V, followed by his son and successor Philip II, assumed responsibility for upholding the existing order of sixteenth-century Europe.

American wealth, particularly Mexican silver, fueled Spanish ambitions, but Charles V's and Philip II's expenses for constant warfare far outstripped the revenues arriving from New Spain. To help meet military expenditures, both kings raised taxes in Spain more than fivefold during the sixteenth century. Since the wealthy nobility were exempted from taxation, the tax burden fell mostly on poor peasants. The monarchy's ambitions impoverished the vast majority of Spain's population and brought the nation to the brink of bankruptcy. When taxes failed to produce enough revenue to fight its wars, the monarchy borrowed heavily from European bankers. By the end of the sixteenth century, interest payments on royal debts swallowed two-thirds of the crown's annual revenues. In retrospect, the riches from New Spain proved a short-term blessing but a long-term curse.

Most Spaniards, however, looked upon New Spain as a glorious national achievement that displayed Spain's superiority over Native Americans and other Europeans. They had added enormously to their own knowledge and wealth. They had built mines, cities, Catholic churches, and even universities on the other side of the Atlantic. These military, religious, and economic achievements gave them great pride and confidence.

Europe and the Spanish Example

The lessons of sixteenth-century Spain were not lost on Spain's European rivals. Spain proudly displayed the fruits of its New World conquests. In 1520, for example, the German artist Albrecht Dürer wrote in his diary that he "marveled over the subtle ingenuity of the men in these distant lands [of New Spain]" who created such things as "a sun entirely of gold, a whole fathom [six feet] broad." But the most exciting news about "the men in these distant lands" was that they could serve the interests of Europeans, as Spain had shown. With a few notable exceptions, Europeans saw the New World as a place for the expansion of European influence, a place where, as one Spaniard wrote, Europeans could "give to those strange lands the form of our own."

France and England tried to follow Spain's example. Both nations warred with Spain in Europe, preyed on Spanish treasure fleets, and ventured to the New World, where they too hoped to find an undiscovered passageway to the East Indies or another Mexico or Peru.

In 1524, France sent Giovanni da Verrazano to scout the Atlantic coast of North America from North Carolina to Canada, looking for a Northwest Passage (see Map 2.2). Eleven years later, France probed farther north with Jacques Cartier's voyage up the St. Lawrence River. Encouraged, Cartier returned to the region with a group of settlers in 1541, but the colony they established—like the search for a Northwest Passage—came to nothing.

English attempts to follow Spain's lead were slower but equally ill fated. Not until 1576, almost eighty years after John Cabot's voyages, did the English try again to find a Northwest Passage. This time Martin Frobisher sailed into the frigid waters of northern Canada (Map 2.2). Like many other explorers mesmerized by the Spanish

Roanoke Settlement, 1585–1590

example, Frobisher believed he had found gold. But the tons of "ore" he hauled back to England proved worthless, and English interests shifted southward to the giant region on the northern margins of New Spain.

English explorers' attempts to establish North American settlements were no more fruitful than their search for a northern route to China. Sir Humphrey Gilbert led expeditions in 1578

VISUAL ACTIVITY

Algonquian Ceremonial Dance

When English artist John White visited the coast of present-day North Carolina in 1585 as part of Raleigh's expedition, he painted this Algonquian ceremonial dance. This is one of the only likenesses of sixteenth-century North American Indians that were drawn from direct observation. British Museum, London, UK/Bridgeman Images.

READING THE IMAGE: What features of Algonquian life does the image show?

CONNECTIONS: How did this Algonquian dance compare with common Mexican rituals?

and 1583 that made feeble efforts to found colonies in Newfoundland until Gilbert vanished at sea. Sir Walter Raleigh organized an expedition in 1585 to settle Roanoke Island off the coast of present-day North Carolina. The first group of explorers left no colonists on the island, but in 1587 Raleigh sent a contingent of more than one hundred settlers to Roanoke under John White's leadership. White went back to England for supplies, and when he returned to Roanoke in 1590, the colonists had disappeared. Roanoke colonists most likely died from a combination of natural causes and unfriendly Indians. Neither mines nor a route to Asia was found, and the colony was abandoned. By the end of the century, England had failed to secure a New World beachhead.

REVIEW   How did Spain's conquests in the New World shape Spanish influence in Europe?

▶ Conclusion: The Promise of the New World for Europeans

The sixteenth century in the New World belonged to the Spaniards who employed Columbus and to the Indians who greeted him as he stepped ashore. The Portuguese, whose voyages to Africa and Asia set the stage for Columbus's voyages, won the important consolation prize of Brazil, but Spain hit the jackpot. Isabella of Spain helped initiate the Columbian exchange between the New World and the Old, which massively benefited first Spain and later other European countries and which continues to this day. The exchange also subjected Native Americans to the ravages of European diseases and Spanish conquest. Spanish explorers, conquistadors, and colonists forced Indians to serve the interests of Spanish settlers and the Spanish monarchy. The exchange illustrated one of the most important lessons of the sixteenth century: After millions of years, the Atlantic no longer was an impermeable barrier separating the Eastern and Western Hemispheres. After the voyages of Columbus, European sailing ships regularly bridged the Atlantic and carried people, products, diseases, and ideas from one shore to the other.

No European monarch could forget the seductive lesson taught by Spain's example: The New World could vastly enrich the Old. Spain remained a New World power for almost four centuries, and its language, religion, culture, and institutions left a permanent imprint. By the end of the sixteenth century, however, other European monarchies had begun to contest Spain's dominion in Europe and to make forays into the northern fringes of Spain's New World preserve. To reap the benefits Spaniards enjoyed from their New World domain, the others had to learn a difficult lesson: how to deviate from Spain's example. That discovery lay ahead.

While England's rulers eyed the huge North American hinterland of New Spain, they realized that it lacked the two main attractions of Mexico and Peru: incredible material wealth and large populations of Indians to use as workers. In the absence of gold and silver booty and plentiful native labor in North America, England would need to find some way to attract colonizers to a region that—compared to New Spain—did not appear very promising. During the next century, England's leaders overcame these dilemmas by developing a distinctive colonial model, one that encouraged land-hungry settlers from England and Europe to engage in agriculture and that depended on other sources of unfree labor: indentured servants from Europe and slaves from Africa.

See the Selected Bibliography for this chapter in the Appendix.

2 Chapter Review

REVIEW QUESTIONS

1. Why did European exploration expand dramatically in the fifteenth century? (pp. 27–30)

2. How did Columbus's discoveries help revolutionize Europeans' understanding of global geography? (pp. 30–34)

3. How did New Spain's distinctive colonial population shape its economy and society? (pp. 35–46)

4. How did Spain's conquests in the New World shape Spanish influence in Europe? (pp. 46–49)

MAKING CONNECTIONS

1. How did the Columbian exchange lead to redistributions of power and population? Discuss these changes, being sure to cite examples from both contexts.

2. Why did the Spanish conquest of Mexicans succeed, and how did Spaniards govern the conquered territory to maintain their dominance?

3. How did Spaniards' and Indians' perceptions of each other shape their interactions? How did perceptions change over time?

4. How did the wealth generated by the Spanish conquest of the New World influence interest in European colonial exploration throughout the sixteenth century?

LINKING TO THE PAST

1. How did the legacy of ancient Americans influence their descendants' initial encounters and subsequent economic, social, and military relations with Europeans in the sixteenth century? (See chapter 1.)

2. Before the arrival of Europeans, Native Americans in the New World had no knowledge of Christianity, just as Europeans had no knowledge of Native American religions. To what extent did contrasting religious beliefs and assumptions influence relations among Europeans and Native Americans in the New World in the sixteenth century? (See chapter 1.)

3 The Southern Colonies in the Seventeenth Century

1601–1700

CONTENT LEARNING OBJECTIVES

After reading and studying this chapter, you should be able to:

- Explain why England decided to establish colonies in the New World and what challenges the early colonists faced.

- Recognize how the introduction of tobacco into the Chesapeake region shaped the Virginia colony.

- Define the social, political, and economic inequalities that led to Bacon's Rebellion.

- Differentiate the Spanish colonies in New Mexico and Florida from the Chesapeake, and explain why the Pueblo Indians in New Mexico revolted against Spanish rule in the late seventeenth century.

- Describe how the British developed slave labor systems in the West Indies, Carolina, and the Chesapeake, and identify the similarities and differences between the systems.

IN DECEMBER 1607, AFTER ARRIVING AT JAMESTOWN with the first English colonists, Captain John Smith was captured by warriors of Powhatan, the supreme chief of about fourteen thousand Algonquian Indians who inhabited the coastal plain of present-day Virginia. According to Smith, Powhatan "feasted him after their best barbarous manner." Then, Smith recalled, "two great stones were brought before Powhatan: then as many [Indians] as could layd hands on [Smith], dragged him to [the stones], and thereon laid his head, and being ready with their clubs, to beate out his braines." At that moment, Pocahontas, Powhatan's eleven-year-old daughter, rushed forward and "got [Smith's] head in her armes, and laid her owne [head] upon his to save him from death." Pocahontas, Smith wrote, "hazarded the beating out of her owne braines to save mine, and . . . so prevailed with her father, that I was safely conducted [back] to James towne."

Historians believe that this episode happened more or less as Smith described it. But Smith did not understand why Pocahontas acted as she did. Most likely, what Smith interpreted as Pocahontas's saving him from certain death was instead a ritual enacting Powhatan's willingness to incorporate Smith and the white strangers at Jamestown into Powhatan's

COPPER PENDANT
About four hundred years ago, an early Jamestown resident crafted this small copper pendant in the likeness of a Native American, possibly the Algonquian leader Powhatan, the ruler of most of the nearby Indians. Recently excavated from the site of the Jamestown fort, the pendant probably was an identification badge intended to be given to a Native American the colonists considered friendly. The pendant illustrates the colonists' desire to identify Indians they considered nonthreatening and possibly helpful and to distinguish them from other Native Americans the colonists considered dangerous. Courtesy Jamestown Rediscovery (Preservation Virginia).

Pocahontas in England
Shortly after Pocahontas and her husband, John Rolfe, arrived in England in 1616, she posed for this portrait dressed in English clothing. The portrait captures the dual novelty of England for Pocahontas and of Pocahontas for the English. The ambiguity about Pocahontas's identity is displayed in the identification of her as "Matoaks" or "Rebecka." National Portrait Gallery, Smithsonian Institution/Art Resource, NY.

empire. By appearing to save Smith, Pocahontas was probably acting out Smith's new status as an adopted member of Powhatan's extended family.

After Smith returned to England about two years later, relations between Powhatan and the English colonists deteriorated into bloody raids. In 1613, the colonists captured Pocahontas and held her hostage at Jamestown. Within a year, she converted to Christianity and married a colonist named John Rolfe. After giving birth to a son named Thomas, Pocahontas, her husband, and the new baby sailed for England in the spring of 1616. There, promoters of the Virginia colony dressed her as a proper Englishwoman and arranged for her to go to a ball attended by the king and queen.

Pocahontas died in England in 1617. Her son, Thomas, ultimately returned to Virginia, but the world he and his descendants inhabited was shaped by a reversal of the power ritualized when his mother "saved" John Smith. By the end of the seventeenth century, Native Americans no longer dominated the newcomers who had arrived in the Chesapeake with John Smith.

During the seventeenth century, English colonists learned how to deviate from the example of New Spain (see "Europe and the Spanish Example" in chapter 2) by growing tobacco, a crop Native Americans had cultivated in small quantities for centuries. The new settlers grew enormous quantities of tobacco and exported most of it to England. Instead of incorporating Powhatan's people into their emerging society, the settlers encroached on Indian land and built new societies on the foundation of tobacco and transatlantic trade.

Producing large crop surpluses for export required hard labor and people who were willing—or could be forced—to do it. While New Spain took advantage of Native American labor, for the most part the Native Americans in British North America refused to be conscripted into the English colonists' fields. Instead, the settlers depended on the labor of family members, indentured servants, and, by the last third of the seventeenth century, African slaves.

By the end of the century, the southern colonies had become sharply different both from the world dominated by Powhatan when the Jamestown settlers first arrived and from seventeenth-century English society. In ways unimaginable to Powhatan, Pocahontas, and John Smith, the colonists paid homage to the international market and the English monarch by working hard to make a good living growing crops for sale to the Old World.

▶ An English Colony on Chesapeake Bay

In 1606, England's King James I granted the Virginia Company more than six million acres in North America in hopes of establishing the English equivalent of Spain's New World empire. Enthusiastic reports from the Roanoke voyages twenty years earlier (see "Europe and the Spanish Example" in chapter 2) claimed that in Virginia "the earth bringeth foorth all things in aboundance . . . without toile or labour." Investors hoped to profit by growing some valuable exotic crop, finding gold or silver, or raiding Spanish treasure ships. Their hopes failed to confront the difficulties of adapting English desires and expectations to the New World already inhabited by Native Americans. The Jamestown settlement struggled to survive for nearly two decades, until the royal government replaced the private Virginia Company, which never earned a profit for its investors.

The Fragile Jamestown Settlement

Although Spain claimed all of North America under the 1494 Treaty of Tordesillas (see "The Explorations of Columbus" in chapter 2), King James believed that England could encroach on the outskirts of Spain's New World empire. An influential proponent of colonization claimed that "God hath reserved" the lands "lying north of Florida" to be brought "unto Christian civility by the English nation." In effect, the king acted upon this claim by granting to the **Virginia Company**, a joint-stock company, a royal license to poach on both Spanish claims and Powhatan's chiefdom.

English merchants had pooled their capital and shared risks for many years by using joint-stock companies for trading voyages to Europe, Asia, and Africa. The London investors of the Virginia Company, however, had larger ambitions: They hoped to found an empire that would strengthen England both overseas and at home. Richard Hakluyt, a strong proponent of colonization, claimed that a colony would provide work for swarms of poor "valiant youths rusting and hurtfull by lack of employment" in England. Colonists could buy English goods and supply products that England now had to import from other nations.

In December 1606, the ships *Susan Constant*, *Discovery*, and *Godspeed* carried 144 Englishmen toward Virginia. A few weeks after they

CHRONOLOGY

1606	• Virginia Company receives royal charter.
1607	• English colonists found Jamestown; Pocahontas "rescues" John Smith.
1607–1610	• Starvation plagues Jamestown.
1612	• John Rolfe begins to plant tobacco in Virginia.
1617	• First commercial tobacco shipped to England. • Pocahontas dies in England.
1618	• Powhatan dies; Opechancanough becomes Algonquian chief.
1619	• First Africans arrive in Virginia. • House of Burgesses begins to meet.
1622	• Opechancanough leads first uprising in Virginia.
1624	• Virginia becomes royal colony.
1630s	• Barbados colonized by English.
1632	• Colony of Maryland founded.
1634	• Colonists begin to arrive in Maryland.
1640s	• Barbados colonists grow sugarcane with slave labor.
1644	• Opechancanough leads second uprising.
1660	• Navigation Act requires colonial products be shipped only to English ports. • Virginia law defines slavery as inherited, lifelong servitude.
1663	• Royal charter granted for Carolina colony.
1670	• Charles Towne, South Carolina, founded.
1670–1700	• Slave labor system emerges in Carolina and Chesapeake colonies.
1676	• Bacon's Rebellion erupts.
1680	• Pueblo Revolt takes place.

VISUAL ACTIVITY

Secotan Village

This engraving was copied from an original drawing John White made in 1585 when he visited the village of Secotan on the coast of North Carolina. The drawing shows daily life in the village, which may have resembled one of Powhatan's settlements. This drawing conveys the message that Secotan was orderly, settled, religious, harmonious, and peaceful, and very different from English villages. Service Historique de la Marine, Vincennes, France/Bridgeman Images.

READING THE IMAGE: What does this image say about Indian life in Secotan?

CONNECTIONS: How did Indian society differ from the English tobacco society that emerged later?

arrived at the mouth of Chesapeake Bay on April 26, 1607, they went ashore on a small peninsula in the midst of the territory ruled by Powhatan and quickly built a fort, the first building in **Jamestown**. The fort showed the colonists' awareness that they needed to protect themselves from Indians and Spaniards. Spanish plans to wipe out Jamestown were never carried out. Powhatan's people, however, defended Virginia as their own. For weeks, the settlers and Powhatan's **Algonquian** warriors skirmished repeatedly. English firearms repelled Indian attacks, but the Indians' superior numbers and knowledge of the wilderness made it risky for settlers to venture far beyond the fort.

The settlers soon confronted invisible dangers: disease and starvation. Saltwater and freshwater mixed in the swampy marshland surrounding Jamestown, creating an ecological zone where

diseases thrived, especially since the colonists neglected careful sanitary habits. During the summer, many of the Englishmen lay "night and day groaning in every corner of the Fort most pittiful to heare," wrote George Percy, one of the settlers. The colonists increased their misery by bickering among themselves, leaving crops unplanted and food supplies shrinking. "For the most part [the settlers] died of meere famine," Percy wrote; "there were never Englishmen left in a forreigne Countrey in such miserie as wee were in this new discovered Virginia."

Powhatan's people came to the rescue of the weakened and demoralized Englishmen. Early in September 1607, they began to bring corn to the colony for barter. Accustomed to eating food derived from wheat, English people considered corn the food "of the barbarous Indians which know no better . . . a more convenient food for

Chief Powhatan

In 1612, John Smith published a map of early Virginia that included this drawing of Powhatan, surrounded by some of his many wives, smoking a pipe, and adorned with a feathered headdress. The illustration was almost certainly made by an English artist who had never been to Virginia or seen Powhatan but who tried to imagine the scene as described by John Smith. Newberry Library/SuperStock.

Cooperation and Conflict between Natives and Newcomers

Powhatan's people stayed in contact with the English settlers but maintained their distance. The Virginia Company boasted that the settlers bought from the Indians "the pearles of earth [corn] and [sold] to them the pearles of heaven [Christianity]." In fact, few Indians converted to Christianity, and the English devoted scant effort to proselytizing. Marriage between Indian women and English men also was rare, despite the acute shortage of English women in Virginia in the early years. Few settlers other than John Smith bothered to learn the Indians' language.

Powhatan's people regarded the English with suspicion, for good reason. Although the settlers often made friendly overtures to the Indians, they did not hesitate to use their guns and swords to enforce English notions of proper Indian behavior. When Indians refused to trade their corn to the settlers, the English pillaged their villages and confiscated their corn.

The Indians retaliated against English violence, but for fifteen years they did not organize an all-out assault on the European intruders, probably for several reasons. Although Christianity held few attractions for the Indians, the power of the settlers' God impressed them. One chief told John Smith that "he did believe that our [English] God as much exceeded theirs as our guns did their bows and arrows." Powhatan probably concluded that these powerful strangers would make better allies than enemies. As allies, the English strengthened Powhatan's dominion over the tribes in the region.

The colonists also traded with Powhatan's people, usually exchanging European goods for corn. Native Virginians quickly recognized the superiority of the intruders' iron and steel knives, axes, and pots, and they eagerly traded corn to get them.

But why were the settlers unable to feed themselves for more than a decade? First, as the staggering death rate suggests, many settlers were too sick to be productive. Second, very few farmers came to Virginia in the early years. Instead, most of the newcomers were gentlemen and their servants who, in John Smith's words, "never did know what a day's work was." The proportion of gentlemen in Virginia in the early years was six times greater than in England, a reflection of the Virginia Company's urgent need for investors and settlers. Smith declared repeatedly that in Virginia "there is no country to pillage

swine than for man." The famished colonists soon overcame their prejudice against corn. Jamestown leader Captain John Smith recalled that the settlers were so hungry that "they would have sould their soules" for half a basket of Powhatan's corn. Indians' corn acquired by both trade and plunder managed to keep 38 of the original settlers alive until a fresh supply of food and 120 more colonists arrived from England in January 1608.

It is difficult to exaggerate the fragility of the early Jamestown settlement. One colonist lamented that "this place [is] a meere plantacion of sorrowes and Cropp of trobles, having been plentifull in nothing but want and wanting nothing but plenty." When a new group of colonists arrived in 1610, they found only 60 of the 500 previous settlers still alive. The Virginia Company sent hundreds of new settlers to Jamestown each year, each of them eager to find the paradise promised by the company. But most settlers went instead to early graves.

[as in New Spain]. . . . All you can expect from [Virginia] must be by labor." For years, however, colonists clung to English notions that gentlemen should not work with their hands and that tradesmen should work only in trades for which they had been trained, ideas that made more sense in labor-rich England than in labor-poor Virginia.

The persistence of the Virginia colony created difficulties for Powhatan's chiefdom. Steady contact between natives and newcomers spread European diseases among the Indians, who suffered deadly epidemics. To produce enough corn for trade with the English required the Indian women to spend more time and effort growing crops. But from the Indians' viewpoint, the most important fact about the always-hungry English colonists was that they were not going away.

Powhatan died in 1618, and his brother Opechancanough replaced him as supreme chief. In 1622, Opechancanough organized an all-out assault on the English settlers. As an English colonist observed, "When the day appointed for the massacre arrived [March 22], a number of savages visited many of our people in their dwellings, and while partaking with them of their meal[,] the savages, at a given signal, drew their weapons and fell upon us murdering and killing everybody they could reach[,] sparing neither women nor children." In all, the Indians killed 347 colonists, nearly a third of the English population. But the attack failed to dislodge the colonists. Instead, in the years to come the settlers unleashed a murderous campaign of Indian extermination that pushed the Indians beyond the small circumference of white settlement. After 1622, most colonists considered Indians their perpetual enemies. As

an Englishman declared, the "murdered carcasses" of the colonists "speak, proclaim, and cry, *This our earth is truly English, and therefore this Land [of Virginia] is justly yours O English.*"

From Private Company to Royal Government

In the immediate aftermath of the 1622 uprising, the survivors became demoralized because, as one explained, the "massacre killed all our Countrie . . . [and] burst the heart of all the rest." The disaster prompted a royal investigation of affairs in Virginia. The investigators discovered that the appalling mortality among the colonists was caused more by disease and mismanagement than by Indian raids. In 1624, King James revoked the charter of the Virginia Company and made Virginia a **royal colony**, subject to the direction of the royal government rather than to the company's private investors, an arrangement that lasted until 1776.

The king now appointed the governor of Virginia and his council, but most other features of local government established under the Virginia Company remained intact. In 1619, for example, the company inaugurated the **House of Burgesses**, an assembly of representatives (called burgesses) elected by the colony's inhabitants. Under the new royal government, laws passed by the burgesses had to be approved by the king's bureaucrats in England rather than by the company. Otherwise, the House of Burgesses continued as before, acquiring distinction as the oldest representative legislative assembly in the English colonies. Under the new royal government, all free adult men in

VISUAL ACTIVITY

Jamestown Trade Goods
Jamestown colonists used these objects to trade with Powhatan's people. The bead (upper right) was made in Venice, Italy, while Jamestown settlers crafted the triangular copper pendant and the incised bone pendant. All images courtesy Jamestown Rediscovery (Preservation Virginia).
READING THE IMAGE: What do these trade goods suggest about the needs and desires of the settlers and the Native Americans?
CONNECTIONS: Why was trade between settlers and Indians important to each group?

Virginia could vote for the House of Burgesses, giving it a far broader and more representative constituency than the English House of Commons.

The demise of the Virginia Company marked the end of the first phase of colonization of the Chesapeake region. From the first 105 adventurers in 1607, the population had grown to about 1,200 by 1624. Despite mortality rates higher than the worst epidemics in London, new settlers still came. Their arrival and King James's willingness to take over the struggling colony reflected a fundamental change in Virginia. After years of fruitless experimentation, it was becoming clear that English settlers could make a fortune in Virginia by growing tobacco.

REVIEW Why did Powhatan behave as he did toward the English colonists?

▶ A Tobacco Society

Tobacco grew wild in the New World, and Native Americans used it for thousands of years before Europeans arrived. Many sixteenth-century European explorers noticed the Indians' habit of "drinking smoke." During the sixteenth century, tobacco was an expensive luxury used sparingly by a few in Europe. During the next century, English colonists in North America sent so much tobacco to European markets that it became an affordable indulgence used often by many people. (See "Beyond America's Borders," page 58.)

By 1700, nearly 100,000 colonists lived in the Chesapeake region, encompassing Virginia, Maryland, and northern North Carolina (Map 3.1). Although they differed in wealth, landholding, access to labor, and religion, they shared a dedication to growing tobacco. They exported

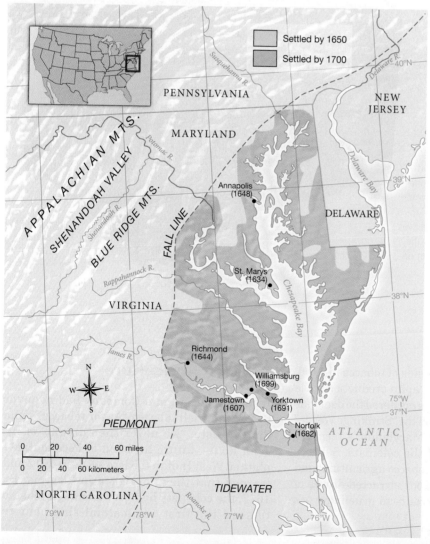

MAP ACTIVITY

Map 3.1 Chesapeake Colonies in the Seventeenth Century
This map illustrates the intimate association between land and water in the settlement of the Chesapeake in the seventeenth century. The fall line indicates the limit of navigable water, where rapids and falls prevented travel farther upstream.

READING THE MAP: Using the notations on the map, create a chronology of the establishment of towns and settlements. What physical features correspond to the earliest habitation by English settlers?
CONNECTIONS: Why was access to navigable water so important? Given the settlers' need for defense against native tribes, what explains the distance between settlements?

American Tobacco and European Consumers

English colonies in the Chesapeake were "wholly built upon smoke," King Charles I observed during the second quarter of the seventeenth century. The king's shrewd observation highlighted the fundamental reason the seventeenth-century Chesapeake colonies prospered by growing ever-larger crops of tobacco: namely, because people on the eastern side of the Atlantic were willing to buy ever-greater quantities of tobacco to smoke—and to sniff and chew. Europeans' desire for tobacco was the only reason it had commercial value.

Some Europeans hated tobacco, most notably England's King James I (who preceded Charles I). In *A Counterblaste to Tobacco,* a pamphlet published in 1611, James declared that smoking was "A custome lothsome to the eye, hatefull to the

Nose, harmefull to the braine, [and] dangerous to the Lungs." He reviled the "filthy smoke," the "stinking Suffumigation," the "spitting," the

"lust," the "shameful imbecilitie," and the "sin" of tobacco. James's fulminations acknowledged that "the generall use of Tobacco" was

Tobacco Cutter
Planters in the southern colonies of British North America shipped tobacco to England, where tobacconists used machines like the one shown here to chop the leaves into small pieces for smoking. Tobacco merchants often flavored the chopped leaves with oils, herbs, and spices. The illustration on the side of the cutter refers to the Native American origins of tobacco. Historisch Museum Haarlem.

more than 35 million pounds of tobacco in 1700, a fivefold increase in per capita production since 1620. Chesapeake colonists mastered the demands of tobacco agriculture, and the "Stinkinge Weede" (a seventeenth-century Marylander's term for tobacco) also mastered the colonists. Settlers lived by the rhythms of tobacco agriculture, and their endless need for labor attracted droves of English indentured servants to grueling work in tobacco fields.

Tobacco Agriculture

Initially, the Virginia Company had no plans to grow and sell tobacco. "As for tobacco," John Smith wrote, "we never then dreamt of it." John Rolfe—future husband of Pocahontas—planted West Indian tobacco seeds in 1612 and learned that they flourished in Virginia. By 1617, the colonists had grown enough tobacco to send the first commercial shipment to

"daily practiced . . . by all sorts and complexions of people." He noted, "The publike use [of tobacco], at all times, and in all places, hath now so farre prevailed that a man cannot heartily welcome his friend now, but straight they must bee in hand with Tobacco." Clearly, James championed a lost cause.

When the Spaniards first brought tobacco to Europe during the sixteenth century, physicians praised it as a wonder drug. One proclaimed that "this precious herb is so general a human need [that it is] not only for the sick but for the healthy." Such strong recommendations from learned men were reinforced by everyday experiences of commoners. Sailors returning from the New World "suck in as much smoke as they can," one Spaniard observed, "[and] in this way they say that their hunger and thirst are allayed, their strength is restored and their spirits are refreshed; [and] . . . their brains are lulled by a joyous intoxication." That joyous intoxication—"a bewitching quality," King James called it— made tobacco irresistible to most Europeans.

At the beginning of the seventeenth century, tobacco was scarce and therefore expensive. In 1603, for example, England imported only about 25,000 pounds of tobacco, all from New Spain. By 1700, England imported nearly 40 million pounds of tobacco, almost all from the Chesapeake colonies. The huge increase in the tobacco supply caused prices to plummet. A quantity of

tobacco that sold for a dollar in 1600 cost less than two and a half cents by 1700.

The low prices made possible by bumper crops harvested by planters in the Chesapeake transformed tobacco consumption in England and elsewhere in Europe. Annual per capita tobacco use in England grew more than 200-fold during the seventeenth century. American tobacco became the first colonial product of mass consumption by Europeans, blazing a trail followed by New World sugar, coffee, and chocolate.

Tobacco altered European culture. It spawned new industries, new habits, and new forms of social life. Smoking was the most common form of tobacco consumption in the seventeenth century. Smokers needed pipes, boxes, or tins to hold their tobacco; a flint and steel to strike sparks; pipe cleaners; and spittoons, if they were smoking in a respectable place that disapproved of spitting on the floor. European merchants and manufacturers supplied all these needs, along with the tobacco itself, which had to be graded, chopped, flavored, packaged, stored, advertised, and sold. Men and women smoked in taverns, in smoking clubs, around dinner tables, and in bed.

The somewhat cumbersome paraphernalia of smoking caused many tobacco users to shift to snuff, which became common in the eighteenth century. Snuff use eliminated smoke, fire, and spitting, replacing them with the more refined gesture

of taking a pinch of powdered, flavored tobacco from a snuffbox and sniffing it into one or both nostrils, which produced a fashionable sneeze followed by a genteel wipe with a dainty handkerchief. One snuff taker explained the health benefits of such a sneeze: "by its gently pricking and stimulating the membranes, [snuff] causes Sneezing or Contractions, whereby the Glands like so many squeezed Sponges, dismiss their Seriosities and Filth."

Whether consumed by sniffing, by smoking, or in other ways, tobacco profoundly changed European habits, economies, and societies. And its popularity turned the Chesapeake colonies into invaluable assets for England.

Questions for Analysis

Consider the Context: What were the consequences of the transatlantic tobacco market both in the southern colonies and in Europe? Why did European demand for tobacco grow so dramatically during the seventeenth century?

Analyze the Evidence: How did Europeans use tobacco, and why? Why did some people object to tobacco use?

Summarize the Argument: How did tobacco produced in the seventeenth-century southern colonies change European social and economic life? How did tobacco shape the southern colonies?

England, where it sold for a high price. After that, Virginia pivoted from a colony of rather aimless adventurers to a society of dedicated tobacco planters.

A demanding crop, tobacco required close attention and a great deal of hand labor year-round. Like the Indians, the colonists "cleared" fields by cutting a ring of bark from each tree (a procedure known as "girdling"), thereby killing the tree. Girdling brought sunlight to

clearings but left fields studded with tree stumps, requiring colonists to use heavy hoes to till their tobacco fields. To plant, a visitor observed, they "just make holes [with a stick] into which they drop the seeds," much as the Indians did. Colonists young and old enjoyed the fruits of their labor. "Everyone smokes while working or idling," a traveler observed, including "men, women, girls, and boys, from the age of seven years."

Tobacco Plantation
This engraving of a West Indian tobacco plantation illustrates both similarities with and differences from Chesapeake tobacco production in the seventeenth century. As in the Chesapeake, tobacco plants were planted in individual mounds that required careful tending by hand. In the Chesapeake, however, most of the laborers were white servants until the last third of the seventeenth century, not slaves as shown here. Chesapeake producers commonly packed tobacco in barrels rather than winding it into rope-like twists as shown in the open-sided huts here. Courtesy of the John Carter Brown Library at Brown University.

English settlers worked hard because their labor promised greater rewards in the Chesapeake region than in England. One colonist proclaimed that "the dirt of this Province affords as great a profit to the general Inhabitant, as the Gold of Peru doth to . . . the Spaniard." Although he exaggerated, it was true that a hired man could expect to earn two or three times more in Virginia's tobacco fields than in England. Better still, in Virginia land was so abundant that it was extremely cheap compared with land in England.

By the mid-seventeenth century, common laborers could buy a hundred acres for less than their annual wages—an impossibility in England. New settlers who paid their own transportation to the Chesapeake received a grant of fifty acres of free land (termed a headright). The Virginia Company granted headrights to encourage settlement, and the royal government continued them for the same reason.

A Servant Labor System

Headrights, cheap land, and high wages gave poor English folk powerful incentives to immigrate to the New World. Yet many potential immigrants could not scrape together the money to pay for a trip across the Atlantic. Their poverty and the colonists' crying need for labor formed the basic context for the creation of a servant labor system.

About 80 percent of the immigrants to the Chesapeake during the seventeenth century came as **indentured servants**. Instead of a slave society, the seventeenth-century Chesapeake region was fundamentally a society of white servants and ex-servants.

Relatively few African slaves were brought to the Chesapeake in the first half century after settlement. The first known Africans arrived in Virginia in 1619 aboard the *White Lion*, an English privateer that had seized them from a

Portuguese slave ship bound for South America. The "20. And odd Negroes," as John Rolfe called them, were slaves captured in Angola in west-central Africa. A few more slaves trickled into the Chesapeake region during the next several decades. Until the 1670s, however, only a small number of slaves labored in Chesapeake tobacco fields. Men and women of African descent occasionally became indentured servants, served out their terms of servitude, and became free. A few slaves purchased their way out of bondage and lived as free people. These people were exceptions, however. Almost all people of African descent were slaves and remained enslaved for life.

The overwhelming majority of indentured servants were white immigrants from England. To buy passage aboard a ship bound for the Chesapeake, an English servant or laborer had to come up with about a year's wages. Earning wages at all was difficult in England since job opportunities were shrinking. Many country landowners needed fewer farmhands because they shifted from growing crops to raising sheep in newly enclosed fields. Unemployed people drifted into seaports such as Bristol, Liverpool, and London, where they learned about the plentiful jobs in North America. Unable to pay for their trip across the Atlantic, poor immigrants agreed to a contract called an indenture, which functioned as a form of credit. By signing an indenture, an immigrant borrowed the cost of transportation to the Chesapeake from a merchant or ship captain in England. To repay this loan, the indentured person agreed to work as a servant for four to seven years in North America.

Once the indentured person arrived in the colonies, the merchant or ship captain sold his right to the immigrant's labor to a local tobacco planter. To obtain the servant's labor, the planter paid about twice the cost of transportation and agreed to provide the servant with food and shelter during the term of the indenture. When the indenture expired, the planter owed the former servant "freedom dues," usually a few barrels of corn and a suit of clothes.

Ideally, indentures allowed poor immigrants to trade their most valuable assets—their freedom and their ability to work—for a trip to the New World and a period of servitude followed by freedom in a land of opportunity. "What's a four years Servitude," a Maryland servant asked, "to advantage a man all the remainder of his dayes?" Planters reaped more immediate benefits.

Servants meant more hands to grow more tobacco. A planter expected a servant to grow enough tobacco in one year to cover the price the planter paid for the indenture. Servants' labor during the remaining three to six years of the indenture promised a handsome profit for the planter. No wonder one Virginian declared, "Our principall wealth . . . consisteth in servants." Although many servants died before their indentures expired, planters still profited because they received a **headright** of fifty acres of land from the colonial government for every newly purchased servant.

About three out of four servants were young men between the ages of fifteen and twenty-five when they arrived in the Chesapeake. Typically, they shared the desperation of sixteen-year-old Francis Haires, who indentured himself for seven years because, according to his contract, "his father and mother and All friends [are] dead and he [is] a miserable wandering boy." Like Francis, most servants had no special training or skills, although the majority had some experience with agricultural work. "Hunger and fear of prisons bring to us onely such servants as have been brought up to no Art of Trade," one Virginia planter complained. A skilled craftsman could obtain a shorter indenture, but few risked coming to the colonies since their prospects were better in England.

Women were almost as rare as skilled craftsmen in the Chesapeake and more ardently desired. In the early days of the tobacco boom, the Virginia Company shipped young single women servants to the colony as prospective wives for male settlers willing to pay "120 weight [pounds] of the best leaf tobacco for each of them," in effect getting both a wife and a servant. The company reasoned that, as one official wrote in 1622, "the plantation can never flourish till families be planted, and the respect of wives and children fix the people on the soil." Nonetheless, women remained a small minority of the Chesapeake population until late in the seventeenth century.

The servant labor system perpetuated the gender imbalance. Although female servants cost about the same as males and generally served for the same length of time, planters preferred male servants, as one explained, because they were "the mor[e] excellent and yousefull Cretuers," especially for field work. Although many servant women hoed and harvested tobacco fields, most also did household chores such as cooking, washing, cleaning, gardening, and milking.

VISUAL ACTIVITY

Bristol Docks
This painting of the docks in Bristol, England, portrays a scene common at ports throughout the seventeenth-century Atlantic world. Tobacco flooded into Bristol in the seventeenth century while Bristol merchants also became active in the African slave trade, trading British goods on the West African coast for slaves, who were then taken to the New World to be sold to eager sugar and tobacco planters.
© Bristol Museum and Art Gallery, UK/Bridgeman Images.
READING THE IMAGE: What kinds of work are being done by the people shown on the dock?
CONNECTIONS: Why was transatlantic commerce important to settlers in the seventeenth-century Chesapeake region?

The Rigors of Servitude

Servants—whether men or women, whites or blacks, English or African—tended to work together and socialize together. During the first half century of settlement, racial intermingling occurred, although the small number of blacks made it infrequent. In general, the commonalities of servitude caused servants—regardless of their race and gender—to consider themselves apart from free people, whose ranks they longed to join eventually.

Servant life was harsh by the standards of seventeenth-century England and even by the frontier standards of the Chesapeake. Unlike servants in England, Chesapeake servants had no control over who purchased their labor—and thus them—for the period of their indenture. They were "sold here upp and downe like horses," one observer reported. A Virginia servant complained in 1623 that his master "hath sold me for £150 sterling like a damnd slave." But tobacco planters' need for labor muffled complaints about treating servants as property.

"The Servants of this Province," one boasted, "live more like Freemen than the most Mechanick Apprentices in London, wanting for nothing that is convenient and necessary, and . . . are extraordinary well used and respected." For many other servants, such promises withered when confronted by the rigors of labor in tobacco fields. Severe laws aimed to keep servants in their proper places. James Revel, an eighteen-year-old thief punished by being indentured to a Virginia tobacco planter, declared he was a "slave" sent to hoe "tobacco plants all day" from dawn to dusk. Punishments for petty crimes stretched servitude far beyond the original terms of indenture. Richard Higby, for example, received six extra years of servitude for killing three hogs. After midcentury, the Virginia legislature added three or more years to the indentures of most servants by requiring them to serve until they were twenty-four years old.

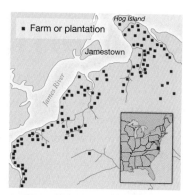

Settlement Patterns along the James River

Women servants were subject to special restrictions and risks. They were prohibited from marrying until their servitude had expired. A servant woman, the law assumed, could not serve two masters at the same time: one who owned her indentured labor and another who was her husband. As a rule, if a woman servant gave birth to a child, she had to serve two extra years and pay a fine. Inevitably, the predominance of men in the colonial population pressured servant women to engage in sexual relations, and about a third of immigrant women were pregnant when they married.

Harsh punishments reflected four fundamental realities of the servant labor system. First, planters' hunger for labor caused them to demand as much labor as they could get from their servants. Second, servants hoped to survive their servitude and use their freedom to obtain land and start a family. Third, since servants saw themselves as free people in a temporary status of servitude, they often made grudging, halfhearted workers. Finally, planters put up with this contentious arrangement because the alternatives were less desirable.

Planters could not easily hire free men and women because land was readily available and free people preferred to work for themselves on their own land. Nor could planters depend on much labor from family members because families were few, were started late, and thus had few children. And, until the 1680s and 1690s, slaves were expensive and hard to come by. Before then, masters who wanted to grow more tobacco had few alternatives to buying indentured servants. (See "Analyzing Historical Evidence," page 64.)

Cultivating Land and Faith

Villages and small towns dotted the rural landscape of seventeenth-century England, but in the Chesapeake towns were few and far between. Instead, tobacco farms occupied small clearings surrounded by hundreds of acres of wilderness. Since tobacco was a labor-intensive crop that quickly exhausted the fertility of the soil, each farmer cultivated only 5 or 10 percent of his land at any one time. Tobacco planters sought land that fronted a navigable river in order to minimize the work of transporting the heavy barrels of tobacco onto ships. A settled region thus resembled a lacework of farms stitched around waterways.

Portrait of Cecilius Calvert
Cecil Calvert, Lord Baltimore, served as the proprietor of Maryland from 1633 to 1675. Pictured here with his grandson and an enslaved boy, Calvert lived in sumptuous luxury in England and never set foot in the colony populated mostly by tobacco-growing farmers. Calvert's descendants eventually moved to Maryland, continued to govern the colony for more than a century, and remain a prominent family today. Private Collection/Peter Newark American Pictures/Bridgeman Images.

Enslavement by Marriage

A white indentured servant woman named Eleanor Butler—Irish Nell—immigrated to Maryland and married a slave named Charles in 1681. More than eighty years later, Mary and William Butler, descendants of Irish Nell and Charles, petitioned a Maryland court to free them from "a state of perpetual Slavery" in which they were held by a planter named Richard Boarman. Since seventeenth-century documents that could prove the race and status of Irish Nell and Charles did not exist, the court collected testimony in 1767 from white witnesses who knew the couple or had heard about them. The court eventually refused to grant freedom to Mary and William, but the testimony the court gathered about Irish Nell and Charles, excerpted here, reveals assumptions about race, status, and gender that were common in the seventeenth-century Chesapeake region.

Samuel Abell, Junior, 49: said "that . . . Mr Richard Boarman the Defendant . . . told him . . . that Lord Baltimore a good many years ago, came into this Country to live and brought with him a woman named Butler . . . to wash and Iron and boarded with his Grand Father, and that sometime after they had been there, the said woman called Butler fell in Love with one of his Grand Father's Negroes and wanted to marry him, and upon my Lord, being informed that she wanted to marry the negro, my Lord sent for her in, and chid [chided] her, and told her that if she married the negro she would by that means enslave herself, and her posterity, upon which the woman told him that she had rather marry the negro under them circumstances, than to marry his Lordship with all his Country, upon which he told her she might go and marry him, and be dammed, accordingly she went and was married to the negro. . . . [Abell] asked . . . [Boarman] if there were not a good many of that Family; he said there was about one hundred and twenty of them, but the negroes by their Count made near three hundred of them, for that they had taken even some Salt water [African-born] negroes, into their count, and upon asking . . . [Boarman] how they came to be slaves as they came of a white woman; he said he claimed them by a Law of this province whereby white women marrying of slaves should become slaves to the house of her Husband's master, and he took out of his pocket a paper which he said was a copy of the act, and it appeared to be a copy of an act."

Thomas Bowling, 63: said "that . . . Irish Nell told [his mother] the day she expected to be married, she was early up intending to clear the house out, and a Gentleman . . . asked her if she was the Girl that was to be married that day to the negro? She said Yes, he then chid her, and told her, she would put a mark by that upon her Children and bring them into Slavery, that if she would marry a white man her Children might be of Credit in the world, otherwise they wou'd be in Slavery, upon which she fell a crying, and said it was to her Choice, she wou'd rather have Charles than have your Lordship."

Edward Edelen, 50: said "that . . . his Father . . . heard Lord Baltimore ask for Eleanor Butler a servant woman of Major Boarmans, when she came to him he said, I understand you are going to be married today to Negro

---

Most Chesapeake colonists were nominally Protestants. Attendance at Sunday services and conformity to the doctrines of the Church of England were required of all English men and women. Few clergymen migrated to the Chesapeake, however, and too few of those who did were models of piety. Certainly, some colonists took their religion seriously. Church courts punished fornicators, censured blasphemers, and served notice on parishioners who spent Sundays "goeing a fishing." But on the whole, religion did not awaken the zeal of Chesapeake settlers, certainly not as it did the zeal of New England settlers in these same years (as discussed in "Church, Covenant, and Conformity" in chapter 4). The religion of the Chesapeake colonists was Anglican, but their faith lay in the turbulent, competitive, high-stakes gamble of survival as tobacco planters.

The situation was similar in the Catholic colony of Maryland. In 1632, England's King Charles I granted his Catholic friend Lord Baltimore about six and a half million acres in the northern Chesapeake region. Lord Baltimore intended to create a refuge for Catholics, who suffered severe discrimination in England. He fitted out two ships, the *Ark* and the *Dove*; gathered about 150 settlers; and sent them to the new colony, where they arrived on March 25,

Charles, he said to her what a pitty so likely a young Girl as you are should fling herself away so as to marry a negro, and he said not only that, but you'l make slaves of your Children and their posterity."

Benjamin Jameson, 48: said "that . . . [he] heard old Mrs Ruthom . . . say, that she was at Major Boarmans when the same Nell and Charles . . . was married . . . that she heard several people wish them much Joy, and that she behaved as a Bride, and that he has heard his mother say that . . . my Lord asked . . . [Nell] how she would like to go to bed to a Negro? She answered him that she rather go to bed to Charles than his Lordship."

Mary Crossen, 74: said "that she knew Eleanor Butler a white woman commonly called Irish Nell . . . that she does not know that Nell was a free woman but appeared to her, to do as she pleased, that she was a hard labouring body, and made Good Crops."

William Simpson, 49: said . . . "that he remembers Nell Butler and Negro Charles, and they passed as man and wife and called themselves so, and that Charles he believes was a salt water negro, and always understood was a slave of Major William Boarmans."

Joseph Jameson, 52: said "that he knew Irish Nell very well, that she lived . . . within a [mile?] of his Fathers, that she had a Daughter living with her, who died as a slave of Mr Boarman, and being asked how he knew she was a slave? Says she worked among the other slaves and lived as they did, she there died . . . that all the Descendants of the said Nell that he knew lived and died slaves they working and living as such except the said Kate who he had heard from the neighbourhood . . . has purchased her freedom."

William McPherson, 60: said "that he knew Eleanor Butler, commonly called Irish Nell about fifty years ago . . . that he has seen Nell and Charles together and the Negro Charles called the said Nell his old woman, and she called him her old man, that he never knew of the said Nell being held as a slave, that when Charles went to [John] Saunders's quarter Nell went there also and acted as a Cook . . . that [when] John Saunders hired Negro Charles . . . that Eleanor Butler either came with him or followed him there and acted as a free woman and took in spinning and acted as a midwife . . . that . . . he has heard, that the Children of Nell . . . were held as slaves."

Source: Depositions from *Butler v. Boarman*, 1H. & McH. 371 (1770), Provincial Court, Judgment Record, Liber DD 17, Folio 236–243, Maryland State Archives.

Questions for Analysis

Ask Historical Questions: Why were Irish Nell and her descendants enslaved? What assumptions about race, gender, and social order contributed to their enslavement?

Analyze the Evidence: According to the witnesses, why did Irish Nell marry Charles? Why did Charles marry Irish Nell? What did it mean to the witnesses that Irish Nell was a white woman? To what extent are the testimonies reliable evidence?

Consider the Context: How did the witnesses learn about Irish Nell and Charles? What do the testimonies suggest about the neighborhood where Irish Nell and Charles resided? What do they suggest about the relationship between servants and slaves?

Recognize Viewpoints: Why did Lord Baltimore warn Irish Nell about marrying Charles? How did Nell's viewpoint differ from that of Lord Baltimore and other white Marylanders?

1634. However, Maryland failed to live up to Baltimore's hopes. The colony's population grew very slowly for twenty years, and most settlers were Protestants rather than Catholics. The religious turmoil of the Puritan Revolution in England (see "Religious Controversies and Economic Changes" in chapter 4) spilled across the Atlantic, creating conflict between Maryland's few Catholics—most of them wealthy and prominent—and the Protestant majority, most of them neither wealthy nor prominent. Maryland's leaders hoped to attract decent people as servants, unlike those in Virginia who were described by one Marylander as "the scumme of the people, . . . vagrants and runnewayes from their m[aste]rs, deabauched, idle, lazie squanderers, [and] jaylbirds." During the 1660s, however, Maryland began to attract settlers very much like Virginia's, and most of them were Protestants. Although Catholics and the Catholic faith continued to exert influence in Maryland, the colony's society, economy, politics, and culture became nearly indistinguishable from Virginia's. Both colonies shared a devotion to tobacco, the true faith of the Chesapeake.

REVIEW Why did the vast majority of European immigrants to the Chesapeake come as indentured servants?

► Hierarchy and Inequality in the Chesapeake

The system of indentured servitude sharpened inequality in Chesapeake society by the mid-seventeenth century, propelling social and political polarization that culminated in 1676 with Bacon's Rebellion. The rebellion prompted reforms that stabilized relations between elite planters and their lesser neighbors and paved the way for a social hierarchy that muted differences of landholding and wealth and amplified racial differences. Amid this social and political evolution, Chesapeake colonists' dedication to growing tobacco did not change.

Social and Economic Polarization

The first half of the seventeenth century in the Chesapeake was the era of the yeoman—a farmer who owned a small plot of land sufficient to support a family and tilled largely by servants and a few family members. A small number of elite planters had larger estates and commanded ten or more servants. But for the first several decades, few men lived long enough to accumulate fortunes sufficient to set them much apart from their neighbors.

Until midcentury, the principal division in Chesapeake society was less between rich and poor planters than between free farmers and unfree servants. Although these two groups contrasted sharply in their legal and economic status, their daily lives had many similarities. Servants looked forward to the time when their indentures would expire and they, too, would become free and eventually own land.

Three major developments splintered this rough frontier equality during the third quarter of the century. First, as planters grew more and more tobacco, the ample supply depressed tobacco prices in European markets. Cheap tobacco reduced planters' profits and made saving enough to become landowners more difficult for freed servants. Second, because the mortality rate in the Chesapeake colonies declined, more and more servants survived their indentures, causing landless freemen to become more numerous and discontent. Third, declining mortality also encouraged the formation of a planter elite. By living longer, the most successful planters compounded their success. The wealthiest planters also began to buy slaves as well as to serve as merchants.

By the 1670s, the society of the Chesapeake had become polarized. Landowners—the planter elite and the more numerous yeoman planters—clustered around one pole. Landless colonists, mainly freed servants, gathered at the other. Each group eyed the other with suspicion and mistrust. For the most part, planters saw landless freemen as a dangerous rabble rather than as fellow colonists with legitimate grievances. Governor William Berkeley feared the political threat to the governing elite posed by "six parts in seven [of Virginia colonists who] . . . are poor, indebted, discontented, and armed."

Government Policies and Political Conflict

In general, government enforced the distinction separating servants and masters with an iron fist. Poor men complained that "nether the Governor nor Counsell could or would doe any poore men right, but that they would shew favor to great men and wronge the poore." Most Chesapeake colonists, like most Europeans, assumed that "great men" should bear the responsibilities of government. Until 1670, all freemen could vote, and they routinely elected prosperous planters to the legislature. No former servant served in either the governor's council or the House of Burgesses after 1640. Yet poor Virginians believed that the "great men" used their government offices to promote their selfish personal interests rather than governing impartially.

As discontent mounted among the poor during the 1660s and 1670s, colonial officials tried to keep political power in safe hands. Beginning in 1661, for example, Governor William Berkeley did not call an election for the House of Burgesses for fifteen years. In 1670, the House of Burgesses outlawed voting by poor men, permitting only men who were landowners and headed households to vote.

The king also began to tighten the royal government's control of trade and to collect substantial revenue from the Chesapeake colonies. A series of English laws funneled colonial trade exclusively into the hands of English merchants and shippers. The **Navigation Acts** of 1650 and 1651 specified that colonial goods had to be transported in English ships with predominantly English crews. A 1660 act required colonial products to be sent only to English ports. A 1663 law stipulated further that all goods sent to the

Governor William Berkeley
This portrait illustrates the distance that separated Governor Berkeley and the other Chesapeake grandees from poor planters, landless freemen, servants, and slaves. Berkeley's clothing suited the genteel homes of Jamestown, not the rustic dwellings of lesser Virginians. His haughty, satisfied demeanor suggests his lack of sympathy for poor Virginians, who, he was certain, deserved their lot. National Gallery of Art, Washington, D.C./SuperStock.

colonies must pass through English ports and be carried on English ships manned by English sailors. Taken together, these navigation acts reflected the English government's mercantilist assumption that what was good for England (channeling all trade through English hands) should determine colonial policy.

Assumptions about mercantilism also underlay the import duty on tobacco inaugurated by the Navigation Act of 1660. The law assessed an import tax of two pence on every pound of colonial tobacco brought into England, about the price a Chesapeake tobacco farmer received. The tax gave the king a major financial interest in the size of the tobacco crop, which yielded about a quarter of all English customs revenues during the 1660s.

Bacon's Rebellion

Colonists, like residents of European monarchies, accepted class divisions and inequality as long as they believed that government officials ruled for the general good. When rulers violated that precept, ordinary people felt justified in rebelling. In 1676, **Bacon's Rebellion** erupted as a dispute over Virginia's Indian policy. Before it was over, the rebellion convulsed Chesapeake politics and society, leaving in its wake death, destruction, and a legacy of hostility between the great planters and their poorer neighbors.

Opechancanough, the Algonquian chief who had led the Indian uprising of 1622 in Virginia, mounted another surprise attack in 1644 and killed about five hundred Virginia colonists in two days. During the next two years of bitter fighting, the colonists eventually gained the upper hand, capturing and murdering the old chief. After the war, the Indians relinquished all claims to land already settled by the English. Wilderness land beyond the fringe of English settlement was supposed to be reserved exclusively for Indian use. The colonial government hoped this arrangement would minimize contact between settlers and Indians and thereby maintain the peace.

If the Chesapeake population had not grown, the policy might have worked. But the number of land-hungry colonists multiplied. In their quest for land, they encroached steadily on Indian land. During the 1660s and 1670s, violence between colonists and Indians repeatedly flared along the frontier. The government, headquartered in the tidewater region near the coast, far from the danger of Indian raids, tried to calm the disputes and reestablish the peace.

Frontier settlers thirsted for revenge against what their leader, Nathaniel Bacon, termed "the protected and Darling Indians." Bacon proclaimed his "Design not only to ruine and extirpate all Indians in Generall but all Manner of Trade and Commerce with them." Bacon also urged the colonists to "see what spounges have suckt up the Publique Treasure." (See "Making Historical Arguments," page 68.) He charged that grandees, or elite planters, operated the government for their private gain, a charge that made sense to many colonists. In fact, officeholders had profited enough to buy slaves to replace their servants; by the 1660s, they owned about 70 percent of all the colony's slaves. Bacon crystallized the grievances of the small planters and poor farmers against both the Indians and the colonial rulers in Jamestown.

Hoping to maintain the fragile peace on the frontier in 1676, Governor Berkeley pronounced Bacon a rebel, threatened to punish him for treason, and called for new elections of

Why Did English Colonists Consider Themselves Superior to Indians and Africans?

Were seeds of the racial prejudice that has been such a powerful force in American history planted in the seventeenth-century Chesapeake? To answer that question, historians have paid close attention to the language colonists used to describe Indians, Africans, and themselves.

In the mid-1500s, the English adopted the words *Indian* and *Negro* from Spanish, where they had come to mean, respectively, an aboriginal inhabitant of the New World and a black person of African ancestry. Both terms were generic, homogenizing an enormous diversity of tribal affiliations, languages, and cultures. Neither term originated with the people to whom it referred. The New England minister Roger Williams, who published a book on Indian languages in 1643, reported, "They have often asked mee, why we call them Indians," a poignant question that reveals the European origins of the term, dating back to Columbus.

After *Indians,* the word the settlers used most frequently to describe Native Americans was *savages.* The Indians were savages in the colonists' eyes because they lacked the traits of English civilization. As one Englishman put it in 1625, the natives of Virginia were "so bad a people, having little of

humanitie but shape, ignorant of Civilitie, of Arts, of Religion; more brutish than the beasts they hunt, more wild and unmanly than that unmanned wild countrey, which they range rather than inhabite; captivated also to Satans tyranny in foolish pieties, mad impieties, wicked idlenesse, busie and bloudy wickednesse." Some English colonists counterbalanced this harsh indictment with admiration for certain features of Indian behavior. They praised Indians' calm dignity and poise, their tender love and care for family members, and their simple, independent way of life in apparent harmony with nature.

Color was not a feature of the Indians' savagery. During the seventeenth century, colonists never referred to Indians as "red." Instead, they saw Indians' skin color as tawny or tanned, the "Sun's livery," as one settler wrote. To the English, tanned skin denoted a member of the working class who spent his or her days toiling under the sun; pale skin was the fashion. Many settlers held the view that Indians were innately white like the English but in other ways woefully un-English.

Despite their savagery in English eyes, Indians controlled two things colonists desperately wanted: land

and peace. Early in the seventeenth century, when English settlements were small and weak, peace with the Indians was a higher priority than land. In this period, English comments on Indian savagery noted the obvious differences between settlers and Indians, but the colonists' need for peace kept them attuned to ways to coexist with the Indians. By the middle of the seventeenth century, as colonial settlements grew and the desire for land increased, violent conflict with Indians erupted repeatedly. The violence convinced settlers that the only way to achieve both land and peace was to eliminate the Indians, by either killing them or pushing them far away from colonial settlements. English assumptions of their superiority to savage Indians provided justification and a gloss of respectability to the colonists' violent and relentless grab of Indian land.

The colonists identified Africans quite differently. Their most common term for Africans was *Negroes,* but the other was not *savage* or *heathen* but *black.* What struck English colonists most forcefully about Africans was not their un-English ways but their un-English skin color.

Black was not a neutral color to the colonists. According to the *Oxford English Dictionary* (which

burgesses who, Berkeley believed, would endorse his get-tough policy. To Berkeley's surprise, the elections backfired. Almost all the old burgesses were voted out of office and replaced by local leaders, including Bacon, who chafed at the rule of the elite planters.

In June 1676, the new legislature passed a series of reform measures known as Bacon's

Laws. Among other changes, the laws gave local settlers a voice in setting tax levies, forbade officeholders from demanding bribes or other extra fees for carrying out their duties, placed limits on holding multiple offices, and restored the vote to all freemen. But elite planters soon convinced Berkeley that Bacon and his men were a greater threat than Indians.

hardened English notions about social hierarchy, about superiority and inferiority. Colonists' convictions of their own superiority to Indians and Africans justified, they believed, their exploitation of Indians' land and Africans' labor. Those justifications planted the seeds of pernicious racial prejudices that flourished in America for centuries.

catalogs the changing meaning of words), *black* meant to the English people who settled the Chesapeake "deeply stained with dirt; soiled, dirty, foul . . . having dark or deadly purposes, malignant; pertaining to or involving death, deadly; baneful, disastrous, sinister . . . foul, iniquitous, atrocious, horrible, wicked." Black was the opposite of white, which connoted purity, beauty, and goodness—attributes the colonists identified with themselves. By the middle of the seventeenth century, the colonists referred to themselves not only as English but also as free, hinting that they believed that people who were not English were not

free. After about 1680, colonists often referred to themselves as white, acknowledging the color of free people. By the end of the seventeenth century, blacks were triply cursed in English eyes: un-English, un-white, and un-free.

Virginians did not legally define slavery as permanent, lifelong, inherited bondage until 1660. The sparse surviving evidence demonstrates, however, that colonists practiced slavery from the start. The debasements of slavery strengthened the colonists' prejudice toward blacks, while racial prejudices buttressed slavery.

Colonists' attitudes toward Indians and Africans exaggerated and

Questions for Analysis

Summarize the Argument: How did colonists' views of Indians and Africans indicate their views about themselves? What were the consequences of English colonists' belief in their own superiority?

Analyze the Evidence: How did the words colonists used to describe Indians and Africans indicate their beliefs? How did colonists' views of Indians differ from their views of Africans?

Consider the Context: What basic contexts of ideas, identities, and desires shaped the colonists' views of Indians and Africans?

When Bacon learned that Berkeley had once again branded him a traitor, he declared war against Berkeley and the other grandees. For three months, Bacon's forces fought the Indians, sacked the grandees' plantations, and attacked Jamestown. Berkeley's loyalists retaliated by plundering the homes of Bacon's supporters. The fighting continued until Bacon unexpectedly

died, most likely from dysentery, and several English ships arrived to bolster Berkeley's strength. With the rebellion crushed, Berkeley hanged several of Bacon's allies and destroyed farms that belonged to Bacon's supporters.

The rebellion did nothing to dislodge the grandees from their positions of power. If anything, it strengthened them. When the king learned of the turmoil in the Chesapeake and its devastating effect on tobacco exports and customs duties, he ordered an investigation. Royal officials replaced Berkeley with a governor more attentive to the king's interests, nullified Bacon's Laws, and instituted an export tax on tobacco as a way to pay the expenses of the colony's government without having to obtain the consent of the tightfisted House of Burgesses.

In the aftermath of Bacon's Rebellion, tensions between great planters and small farmers moderated. Bacon's Rebellion showed, a governor of Virginia said, that it was necessary "to steer between . . . either an Indian or a civil war." The ruling elite concluded that it was safer for the colonists to fight the Indians than to fight each other, and the government made little effort to restrict settlers' encroachment on Indian land. Tax cuts also were welcomed by all freemen. The export duty on tobacco imposed by the king allowed the colonial government to reduce taxes by 75 percent between 1660 and 1700. In the long run, however, the most important contribution to political stability was the declining importance of the servant labor system. During the 1680s and 1690s, fewer servants arrived in the Chesapeake, partly because of improving economic conditions in England. Accordingly, the number of poor, newly freed servants also declined, reducing the size of the lowest stratum of free society. In 1700, when about one-third of the free colonists still worked as tenants on land owned by others, the Chesapeake was in the midst of transitioning to a slave labor system that minimized the differences between poor farmers and rich planters and magnified the differences between whites and blacks.

REVIEW   Why did Chesapeake colonial society become increasingly polarized between 1650 and 1670?

▶ Toward a Slave Labor System

Unlike the Spaniards in New Spain, English colonists were unsuccessful in conscripting Indian labor. They looked instead to another source of workers used by the Spaniards and Portuguese: enslaved Africans. On this foundation, European colonizers built African **slavery** into the most important form of coerced labor in the New World.

During the seventeenth century, English colonies in the West Indies followed the Spanish and Portuguese examples and developed sugar plantations with slave labor. In the English North American colonies, however, a slave labor system did not emerge until the last quarter of the seventeenth century. During the 1670s, settlers from Barbados brought slavery to the new English mainland colony of Carolina, where the imprint of the West Indies remained strong for decades. In Chesapeake tobacco fields at about the same time, slave labor began to replace servant labor, marking the transition toward a society of freedom for whites and slavery for Africans.

Religion and Revolt in the Spanish Borderland

While English colonies in the Chesapeake grew and prospered with the tobacco trade, the northern outposts of the Spanish empire in New Mexico and Florida stagnated. Only about fifteen hundred Spaniards lived in Florida, and roughly twice as many inhabited New Mexico, yet both colonies required regular deliveries of goods and large subsidies. One royal governor complained that "no [Spaniard] comes . . . to plow and sow [crops], but only to eat and loaf."

Instead of attracting settlers and growing crops for export, New Mexico and Florida appealed to Spanish missionaries seeking to convert Indians to Christianity. In both colonies, Indians outnumbered Spaniards ten or twenty to one. Royal officials hoped that the missionaries' efforts would pacify the Indians and be a relatively cheap way to preserve Spanish footholds in North America. The missionaries baptized thousands of Indians in Spanish North America during the seventeenth century, but they also planted the seeds of Indian uprisings against Spanish rule.

Dozens of missionaries came to Florida and New Mexico, as one announced, to free the Indians "from the miserable slavery of the demon and from the obscure darkness of their idolatry." The missionaries followed royal instructions that Indians should be taught "to live in a civilized manner, clothed and wearing shoes . . . [and] given the use of . . . bread, linen, horses, cattle, tools, and weapons, and all the rest that Spain has had." In effect, the missionaries sought to convert the Indians not just into Christians but also into substitute Spaniards.

The missionaries supervised the building of scores of Catholic churches across Florida

VISUAL ACTIVITY

Spanish Missionary in Florida
This sixteenth-century picture illustrates the methods Spanish missionaries used to teach Christianity to Native Americans. The picture shows the importance of reading and the punishment for students who did not measure up to the missionaries' expectations. The Granger Collection, New York.

READING THE IMAGE: Aside from the doctrines of Christianity, what are the Native American students being taught by these methods of instruction?

CONNECTIONS: How did missionary activity among the English colonists in the seventeenth-century southern colonies differ from that among the Spanish colonies?

and New Mexico. Adopting practices common elsewhere in New Spain, they forced the Indians both to construct these churches and to pay tribute in the form of food, blankets, and other goods. Although the missionaries congratulated themselves on the many Indians they converted, their coercive methods undermined their goals. A missionary reported that an Indian in New Mexico asked him, "If we [missionaries] who are Christians caused so much harm and violence [to Indians], why should they become Christians?"

The Indians retaliated repeatedly against Spanish exploitation, but the Spaniards suppressed the violent uprisings by taking advantage of the disunity among the Indians, much as Cortés did in the conquest of Mexico (see chapter 2). In 1680, however, the native leader Popé organized the **Pueblo Revolt**, ordering his followers, as one recounted, to "break up and burn the images of the holy Christ, the Virgin Mary, and the other saints, the crosses, and everything pertaining to Christianity." During the revolt, Indians desecrated churches, killed two-thirds of the Spanish missionaries, and drove the Spaniards out of New Mexico to present-day El Paso, Texas. The Spaniards managed to return to New Mexico by the end of the seventeenth century, but only by

curtailing the missionaries and reducing labor exploitation. Florida Indians never mounted a unified attack on Spanish rule, but they too organized sporadic uprisings and resisted conversion, causing a Spanish official to report by the end of the seventeenth century that "the law of God and the preaching of the Holy Gospel have now ceased."

The West Indies: Sugar and Slavery

The most profitable part of England's New World empire in the seventeenth century lay in the Caribbean (Map 3.2). The tiny island of **Barbados**, colonized in the 1630s, was the jewel of the English West Indies. During the 1640s, a colonial official proclaimed Barbados "the most flourishing Island in all those American parts, and I verily believe in all the world for the production of sugar." Sugar commanded high prices in England, and planters rushed to grow as much as they could. By midcentury, annual sugar exports from the English Caribbean totaled about 150,000 pounds; by 1700, exports reached nearly 50 million pounds.

Sugar transformed Barbados and other West Indian islands. Poor farmers could not afford the

MAP ACTIVITY

Map 3.2 The West Indies and Carolina in the Seventeenth Century

Although Carolina was geo-graphically close to the Chesapeake colonies, it was cul-turally closer to the West Indies in the seventeenth century be-cause its early settlers—both blacks and whites—came from Barbados. South Carolina main-tained strong ties to the West Indies for more than a century.

READING THE MAP: Locate English colonies in America and English holdings in the Caribbean. Which European country controlled most of the mainland bordering the Caribbean? Where was the closest mainland English territory?

CONNECTIONS: Why were colonists in Carolina so interested in Barbados? What goods did they export? Describe the relationship between Carolina and Barbados in 1700.

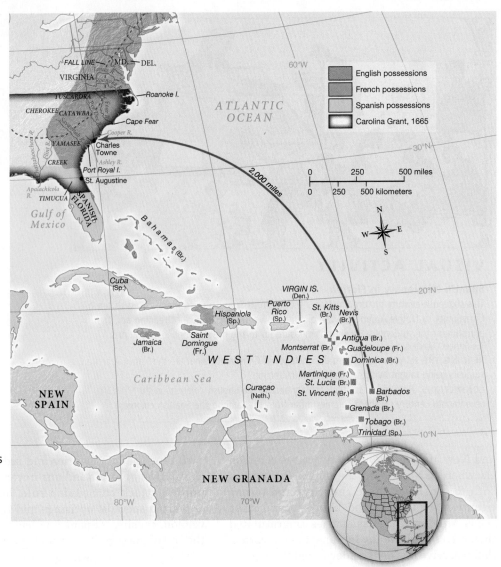

expensive machinery that extracted and refined sugarcane juice, but planters with enough capi-tal to grow sugar got rich. By 1680, the wealthiest Barbadian sugar planters were, on average, four times richer than tobacco grandees in the Chesapeake. The sugar grandees differed from their Chesapeake counterparts in another crucial way: The average sugar baron in Barbados owned 115 slaves in 1680.

African slaves planted, cultivated, and har-vested the sugarcane that made West Indian planters wealthy. Beginning in the 1640s, Barbadian planters purchased thousands of slaves to work their plantations, and the African popu-lation on the island mushroomed. During the 1650s, when blacks made up only 3 percent of the Chesapeake population, they had already become the majority in Barbados. By 1700, slaves constituted more than three-fourths of the island's population (Figure 3.1).

For slaves, work on a sugar plantation was a life sentence to brutal, unremitting labor. Slaves suffered high death rates. Since slave men outnumbered slave women two to one, few slaves could form families and have children. These grim realities meant that in Barbados and else-where in the West Indies, the slave population did not grow by natural reproduction. Instead, planters continually purchased enslaved Africans. Although sugar plantations did not gain a foot-hold in North America in the seventeenth century, the West Indies nonetheless exerted a powerful influence on the development of slavery in the mainland colonies.

Carolina: A West Indian Frontier

The early settlers of what became South Carolina were immigrants from Barbados. In 1663, a

Barbadian planter named John Colleton and a group of seven other men obtained a charter from England's King Charles II to establish a colony north of the Spanish territories in Florida. The men, known as "proprietors," hoped to siphon settlers from Barbados and other colonies and encourage them to develop a profitable export crop comparable to West Indian sugar and Chesapeake tobacco. The proprietors enlisted the English philosopher John Locke to help draft the *Fundamental Constitutions of Carolina*, which provided for religious liberty and political rights for small property holders while envisioning a landed aristocracy supported by bound laborers and slaves. Following the Chesapeake example, the proprietors also offered headrights of up to 150 acres of land for each settler, a provision that eventually undermined the *Constitutions*'s goal of a titled aristocracy. In 1670, the proprietors established the colony's first permanent English settlement, Charles Towne, later spelled Charleston (see Map 3.2).

As the proprietors had planned, most of the early settlers were from Barbados, and they brought their slaves with them. More than a fourth of the early settlers were slaves, and by 1700 slaves made up about half the Carolina population. The new colony's close association with Barbados caused English officials to refer routinely to "Carolina in ye West Indies."

The Carolinians experimented unsuccessfully to match their semitropical climate with profitable export crops of tobacco, cotton, indigo, and olives. In the mid-1690s, colonists identified a hardy strain of rice and took advantage of the knowledge of rice cultivation among their many African slaves to build rice plantations. Settlers also sold livestock and timber to the West Indies, as well as another "natural resource": They captured and enslaved several thousand local Indians and sold them to Caribbean planters. Both economically and socially, seventeenth-century Carolina was a frontier outpost of the West Indian sugar economy.

Slave Labor Emerges in the Chesapeake

By 1700, more than eight out of ten people in the southern colonies of English North America lived in the Chesapeake. Until the 1670s, almost all Chesapeake colonists were white people from England. By 1700, however, one out of eight people in the region was a black person from Africa. A few black people had lived in the Chesapeake since the 1620s, but the black

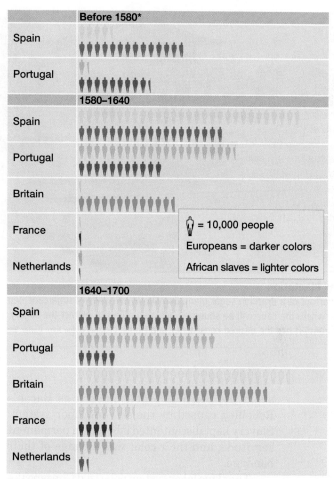

*Note: Before 1580, migration from Britain, France, and the Netherlands was negligible.

FIGURE 3.1   Global Comparison: Migration to the New World from Europe and Africa, 1492–1700
Before 1640, Spain and Portugal sent four out of five European migrants to the New World, virtually all of them bound for New Spain or Brazil. But from 1640 to 1700, nearly as many migrants came from England as from all other European nations combined, a measure of the growing significance of England's colonies. From 1492 to 1700, more enslaved Africans than Europeans arrived in the New World. What might explain the shifts in the destinations of enslaved Africans? Were those shifts comparable to shifts among European immigrants?

population grew fivefold between 1670 and 1700 as hundreds of tobacco planters made the transition from servant to slave labor.

Planters saw several advantages to purchasing slaves rather than servants. Although slaves cost three to five times more than servants, slaves never became free. Because the mortality rate had declined by the 1680s, planters could reasonably expect a slave to live longer than a servant's period of indenture. Slaves also promised to be a perpetual labor force since children of slave mothers inherited the status of slavery. And unlike servants, they could be controlled politically. A slave labor system promised to

Sugar Plantation
This portrait of a Brazilian sugar plantation shows cartloads of sugarcane being hauled to the mill, which is powered by a waterwheel (far right), where the cane will be squeezed between rollers to extract the sugary juice. The juice will then be distilled over a fire tended by the slaves until it has the desired consistency and purity. Courtesy of the John Carter Brown Library at Brown University.

avoid the political problems such as Bacon's Rebellion caused by the servant labor system. Slavery kept discontented laborers in permanent servitude, and their color was a badge of their bondage.

The slave labor system polarized Chesapeake society along lines of race and status: All slaves were black, and nearly all blacks were slaves; almost all free people were white, and all whites were free or only temporarily bound in indentured servitude. Unlike Barbados, however, the Chesapeake retained a vast white majority. Among whites, huge differences of wealth and status still existed. By 1700, more than three-quarters of white families had neither servants nor slaves. Nonetheless, poor white farmers enjoyed the privileges of free status. They could own property, get married, have families, and bequeath their property and their freedom to their descendants; they could move when and where they wanted; they could associate freely with other people; they could serve on juries, vote, and hold political office; and they could work, loaf, and sleep as they chose. These privileges of freedom—none of them possessed by slaves—made lesser white folk feel they had a genuine stake in the existence of slavery, even if they did not own a single slave. By emphasizing the privileges of freedom shared by all white people, the slave labor system reduced the tensions between poor folk and grandees that had plagued the Chesapeake region in the 1670s.

In contrast to slaves in Barbados, most slaves in the seventeenth-century Chesapeake colonies had frequent and close contact with white people. Slaves and white servants performed the same tasks on tobacco plantations, often working side by side in the fields. Slaves took advantage of every opportunity to slip away from white supervision and seek out the company of other slaves. Planters often feared that slaves would turn such seemingly innocent social pleasures to political ends, either to run away or to conspire to strike against their masters. Slaves often did run away, but they were usually captured or returned after a brief absence. Despite planters' nightmares, slave insurrections did not occur.

Although slavery resolved the political unrest caused by the servant labor system, it created new political problems. By 1700, the bedrock political issue in the southern colonies was keeping slaves in their place, at the end of a hoe. The slave labor system in the southern colonies stood roughly midway between the sugar plantations and black majority of Barbados to the south and the small farms and homogeneous villages that developed in seventeenth-century New England to the north (see "Religious Controversies and Economic Changes" in chapter 4).

REVIEW   Why had slave labor largely displaced indentured servant labor by 1700 in Chesapeake tobacco production?

Tobacco Wrapper
This wrapper labeled a container of tobacco from the English colonies sold at Reighly's shop in Essex. The wrapper was much like a brand, promising consumers consistency in quality and taste. The wrapper illustrates tobacco growing in a field and harvested leaves ready to be packed into a barrel, ferried to the ships waiting offshore, and transported to Reighly's and other tobacconists in England. The Granger Collection, New York.

▶ ## Conclusion: The Growth of English Colonies Based on Export Crops and Slave Labor

By 1700, the colonies of Virginia, Maryland, and Carolina were firmly established. The staple crops they grew for export provided a livelihood for many, a fortune for a few, and valuable revenues for shippers, merchants, and the English monarchy. Their societies differed markedly from English society in most respects, yet the colonists considered themselves English people who happened to live in North America. They claimed the same rights and privileges as English men and women, while they denied those rights and privileges to Native Americans and African slaves.

The English colonies also differed from the example of New Spain. Settlers and servants flocked to English colonies, in contrast to Spaniards who trickled into New Spain. Few English missionaries sought to convert Indians to Protestant Christianity, unlike the numerous Catholic missionaries in the Spanish settlements in New Mexico and Florida. Large quantities of gold and silver never materialized in English North America. English colonists never adopted the system of encomienda (see "New Spain in the Sixteenth Century" in chapter 2). Yet important forms of coerced labor and racial distinction that developed in New Spain had North American counterparts, as English colonists employed servants and slaves and defined themselves as superior to Indians and Africans.

By 1700, the remnants of Powhatan's people still survived. As English settlement pushed north, west, and south of Chesapeake Bay, the Indians faced the new colonial world that Powhatan and Pocahontas had encountered when John Smith and the first colonists had arrived at Jamestown. By 1700, the many descendants of Pocahontas's son, Thomas, as well as other colonists and Native Americans, understood that the English had come to stay.

Economically, the southern colonies developed during the seventeenth century from the struggling Jamestown settlement that could not feed itself into a major source of profits for England. The European fashion for tobacco provided livelihoods for numerous white families and riches for elite planters. But after 1700, enslaved Africans were conscripted in growing numbers to grow tobacco in the Chesapeake and rice in Carolina. The slave society that dominated the eighteenth-century southern colonies was firmly rooted in the developments of the seventeenth century.

A desire for land, a hope for profit, and a dream for security motivated southern white colonists. Realizing these aspirations involved great risks, considerable suffering, and frequent disappointment, as well as seizing Indian lands and coercing labor from servants and slaves. By 1700, despite huge disparities in individual colonists' success in achieving their goals, tens of thousands of white colonists who were immigrants or descendants of immigrants now considered the southern colonies their home, shaping the history of the region and of the nation as a whole for centuries to come.

See the Selected Bibliography for this chapter in the Appendix.

3 Chapter Review

REVIEW QUESTIONS

1. Why did Powhatan behave as he did toward the English colonists? (pp. 53–57)

2. Why did the vast majority of European immigrants to the Chesapeake come as indentured servants? (pp. 57–65)

3. Why did Chesapeake colonial society become increasingly polarized between 1650 and 1670? (pp. 66–70)

4. Why had slave labor largely displaced indentured servant labor by 1700 in Chesapeake tobacco production? (pp. 70–74)

MAKING CONNECTIONS

1. Given the vulnerability of the Jamestown settlement in its first two decades, why did its sponsors and settlers not abandon it?

2. How did tobacco agriculture shape the Chesapeake region's development? In your answer, be sure to address the demographic and geographic features of the colony.

3. Bacon's Rebellion highlighted significant tensions within Chesapeake society. What provoked the rebellion, and what did it accomplish?

4. How did European colonists' relations with Native Americans and enslaved Africans contribute to political friction and harmony within the colony?

LINKING TO THE PAST

1. How did England's colonization efforts in the Chesapeake and Carolina during the seventeenth century compare with Spain's conquest and colonization of Mexico? (See chapter 2.)

2. How did the development of the transatlantic tobacco trade exemplify the Columbian exchange? (See chapter 2.)

4

The Northern Colonies in the Seventeenth Century

1601–1700

After reading and studying this chapter, you should be able to:

• Explain why England became a Protestant nation and who the Puritans were.

• Understand how the Puritans came to dominate New England society.

• Recognize how Puritanism influenced the development of New England.

• Describe how the middle colonies were founded and how the founding and settlement of New York, New Jersey, and Pennsylvania differed from the founding and settlement of the New England colonies.

• Explain how the English monarchy consolidated its authority over the American colonies.

ROGER WILLIAMS AND HIS WIFE, MARY,
arrived in Massachusetts in February 1631. Fresh from a superb education at Cambridge University, the twenty-eight-year-old Williams was "a godly [Puritan] minister," noted Governor John Winthrop, whose Boston church asked Williams to become its minister. But Williams refused the invitation because the church had not openly rejected the corrupt Church of England. New England's premier Puritan church was not pure enough for Roger Williams.

Williams and his wife moved to Plymouth colony, where he spent time among the Narragansett Indians. Williams believed that "Nature knows no difference between Europeans and [Native] Americans in blood, birth, [or] bodies . . . God having made of one blood all mankind." He insisted that the colonists respect the Indians' religion and culture since all human beings—Christians and non-Christians alike—should live according to their consciences as revealed to them by God.

BAY PSALM BOOK
This first book printed in America contains psalms that Puritans sang as routine parts of their religious services. Although 1,700 copies of the Bay Psalm book were printed in 1640—enough for wide distribution among the early settlers—heavy use (indicated by the handwriting on the left-hand page) and the ravages of time have left only eleven surviving copies. This rare book recently sold for more than $14 million.
Polaris/Newscom.

Williams condemned English colonists for their "sin of unjust usurpa- tion" of Indian land. He believed that English claims were legally, morally, and spiritually invalid. In contrast, Massachusetts officials defended colo- nists' settlement on Indian land. Governor Winthrop declared, "if we leave [the Indians] sufficient [land] for their use, we may lawfully take the rest, there being more than enough for them and us." Winthrop's argu- ments prevailed, but Williams refused to knuckle under. "God Land," he said, "[is] as great a God with us English as God Gold was with the Spaniards."

In 1633, Williams believed that the Bible shrouded the Word of God in "mist and fog." That observation led him to denounce the emerging New England order as impure, ungodly, and tyrannical. He disagreed with the New England government's requirement that everyone attend church ser- vices. He argued that forcing people who were not Christians to attend church was "False Worshipping" that only promoted "spiritual drunken- ness and whoredom." He believed that to regulate religious behavior would be "spiritual rape"; that governments should tolerate all religious beliefs because only God knows the Truth. "I commend that man," Williams wrote, "whether Jew, or Turk, or Papist, or whoever, that steers no otherwise than his conscience dares."

New England's leaders denounced Williams's arguments and banished him for his "extreme and dangerous" opinions. In January 1636, he fled south to Narragansett Bay, where he and his followers established the colony of Rhode Island, which enshrined "Liberty of Conscience" as a fun- damental ideal and became a refuge for other dissenters. Although New England's leaders expelled Williams from their holy commonwealth, his dissenting ideas arose from orthodox Puritan doctrines. Puritanism in- spired believers such as Roger Williams to draw their own conclusions and stick to them.

During the seventeenth century, New England's Puritan zeal cooled, and the promise of a holy New England faded. Late in the century, the new "middle" colonies of New York, New Jersey, and Pennsylvania were founded, featuring greater religious and ethnic diversity than did New England. Religion remained important throughout all the colonies, but it competed with the growing faith that a better life required less focus on salvation and more attention to worldly concerns of family, work, and trade.

Throughout the English mainland colonies, settlements encroached on Indian land, causing violent conflict to flare up repeatedly. Political conflict also arose among colonists, particularly in response to major political up- heavals in England. By the end of the seventeenth century, the English monarchy exerted greater control over North America and the rest of its Atlantic empire, but the products, people, and ideas that pulsed between England and the colonies energized both.

▶ Puritans and the Settlement of New England

Puritans who emigrated to North America aspired to escape the turmoil and persecution they suffered in England, a long-term consequence of the English Reformation. They also sought to build a new, orderly, Puritan version of England. Puritans established the first small settlement in New England in 1620, followed a few years later by additional, larger settlements of the Massachusetts Bay Company. Allowed self-government through royal charter, these Puritans were in a unique position to direct the new colonies according to their faith. Although many New England colonists were not Puritans, Puritanism remained a paramount influence in New England's religion, politics, and community life during the seventeenth century.

Puritan Origins: The English Reformation

The religious roots of the Puritans who founded New England reached back to the Protestant Reformation, which arose in Germany in 1517 (see "The Protestant Reformation and the Spanish Response" in chapter 2). The English church initially remained within the Catholic fold. Henry VIII, who reigned from 1509 to 1547, saw that the Reformation offered him an opportunity to break with Rome and take control of the church in England. In 1534, Henry formally initiated the **English Reformation**. At his insistence, Parliament outlawed the Catholic Church and proclaimed the king "the only supreme head on earth of the Church of England." Henry seized the vast properties of the Catholic Church in England as well as the privilege of appointing bishops and others in the church hierarchy.

In the short run, the English Reformation allowed Henry VIII to achieve his political goal of controlling the church. In the long run, however, the Reformation brought to England the political and religious turmoil that Henry had hoped to avoid. Henry himself sought no more than a halfway Reformation. Protestant doctrines held no attraction for him; in almost all matters of religious belief and practice he remained an orthodox Catholic. Many English Catholics wanted to revoke the English Reformation; they hoped to return the Church of England to the pope and to restore Catholic doctrines and ceremonies.

CHRONOLOGY

1534	• English Reformation begins.
1609	• Henry Hudson searches for Northwest Passage.
1620	• Plymouth colony founded.
1626	• Manhattan Island purchased; New Amsterdam founded.
1629	• Massachusetts Bay Company receives royal charter.
1630	• John Winthrop leads Puritan settlers to Massachusetts Bay.
1636	• Rhode Island colony established. • Connecticut colony founded.
1636–1637	• Pequot War fought between colonists and Pequot Indians.
1638	• Anne Hutchinson excommunicated.
1642	• Puritan Revolution inflames England.
1649	• English Puritans win civil war.
1656	• Quakers arrive in Massachusetts and are persecuted.
1660	• Monarchy restored in England.
1662	• Many Puritan congregations adopt Halfway Covenant.
1664	• English seize Dutch colony, rename it New York. • Colony of New Jersey created.
1675–1676	• King Philip's War fought between colonists and Indians.
1681	• Colony of Pennsylvania founded.
1686	• Dominion of New England created.
1688	• England's Glorious Revolution restores Protestant monarchy.
1689–1697	• King William's War pits Britain against France in North America.
1692	• Salem witch trials held.

But many other English people insisted on a genuine, thoroughgoing Reformation; these people came to be called **Puritans**.

During the sixteenth century, Puritanism was less an organized movement than a set of ideas and religious principles that appealed strongly to many dissenting members of the Church of England. They sought to eliminate what they considered the offensive features of Catholicism that remained in the religious doctrines and practices of the Church of England. For example, they wanted to do away with the rituals of Catholic worship and instead emphasize that an individual Christian's relationship with God developed through Bible study, prayer, and introspection. All Puritans shared a desire to make the English church thoroughly Protestant.

The fate of Protestantism waxed and waned under the monarchs who succeeded Henry VIII. In 1558 Elizabeth I, the daughter of Henry and his second wife, Anne Boleyn, became queen. During her long reign, Elizabeth reaffirmed the English Reformation and tried to position the English church between the extremes of Catholicism and Puritanism. Like her father, she desired a church that would strengthen the monarchy and the nation. By the time Elizabeth died in 1603, many people in England looked on Protestantism as a defining feature of national identity.

When Elizabeth's successor, James I, became king, English Puritans petitioned for further reform of the Church of England. James authorized a new translation of the Bible, known ever since as the King James Version. However, neither James I nor his son Charles I, who became king in 1625, was receptive to the ideas of Puritan reformers. James and Charles moved the Church of England away from Puritanism. They enforced conformity to the Church of England and punished dissenters. In 1629, Charles I dissolved Parliament—where Puritans were well represented—and initiated aggressive anti-Puritan policies. Many Puritans despaired about continuing to defend their faith in England and made plans to emigrate to Europe, the West Indies, or America.

The Pilgrims and Plymouth Colony

One of the first Protestant groups to emigrate, later known as Pilgrims, professed an unorthodox view known as separatism. These **Separatists** sought to withdraw—or separate—from the Church of England, which they considered hopelessly corrupt. In 1608 they moved to Holland; by 1620 they realized that they could not live and worship there as they had hoped. William Bradford, a leader of the Separatists, recalled

English Monarchy and the Protestant Reformation

1509–1547	Henry VIII	Leads the English Reformation, outlawing the Catholic Church in England and establishing the English monarch as supreme head of the Church of England.
1547–1553	Edward VI	Moves religious reform in a Protestant direction.
1553–1558	Mary I	Outlaws Protestantism and strives to reestablish the Catholic Church in England.
1558–1603	Elizabeth I	Tries to position the Church of England between extremes of Catholicism and Protestantism.
1603–1625	James I	Authorizes a new, Protestant translation of the Bible but is unsympathetic to Puritan reformers.
1625–1649	Charles I	Continues move away from Puritan reformers. Beheaded during the Puritan Revolution.
1642		Puritan Revolution (English Civil War) begins.
1644–1660	Oliver Cromwell	Leads Puritan side to victory in the English Civil War. Parliament proclaims England a Puritan republic (1649) and declares Cromwell the nation's "Lord Protector" (1653).
1660–1685	Charles II	Restored to the monarchy by Parliament and attempts to enforce religious toleration of Catholics and Protestant dissenters from the Church of England.
1685–1688	James II	Ousted by Parliament for pro-Catholic policies and replaced by his Protestant son-in-law, William, and his daughter (William's wife) in the "Glorious Revolution" (1688).
1689–1694	William III and Mary II	Reassert Protestant influence in England and its empire.

Queen Elizabeth
This sixteenth-century portrait of Queen Elizabeth celebrates English victory over the Spanish Armada in 1588 (shown in the panels on either side of Elizabeth's head) that resulted in England's empire reaching North America (notice her right hand covering North America on the globe). Corbis.

that "many of their children, by . . . the great licentiousness of youth [in Holland], and the manifold temptations of the place, were drawn away by evil examples." Bradford and other Separatists believed that America promised to better protect and preserve their children and their community. Separatists obtained permission to settle in the extensive territory granted to the Virginia Company (see "The Fragile Jamestown Settlement" in chapter 3). In August 1620, Pilgrim families boarded the *Mayflower*, and after eleven weeks at sea all but one of the 102 immigrants arrived at the outermost tip of Cape Cod in present-day Massachusetts.

The Pilgrims realized immediately that they had landed far north of the Virginia grants and had no legal authority to settle in the area. To provide order, security, and a claim to legitimacy, they drew up the Mayflower Compact on the day they arrived. They pledged to "covenant and combine ourselves together into a civil Body Politick, for our better Ordering and Preservation." The signers (all men) agreed to enact and obey necessary and just laws.

VISUAL ACTIVITY

Plymouth Village
This historically accurate modern-day reconstruction of the Plymouth settlement depicts the simple dwellings the Pilgrims built with materials readily at hand. Even the chimneys were built with wood. Notice that the buildings are huddled together rather than scattered across the landscape, all the better to promote community cohesion and protection against Indians. © Plus One Pix/Alamy Stock Photo.
READING THE IMAGE: What kinds of work were required to erect these buildings?
CONNECTIONS: How did New England settlements reflect Puritan religious ideas?

Seal of Massachusetts Bay Colony
In 1629, the Massachusetts Bay Company designed this seal depicting an Indian man inviting English settlers to "come over and help us." Of course, such an invitation was never issued. The seal was an attempt to lend an aura of altruism to the Massachusetts Bay Company's colonization efforts. What does the seal suggest about English views of Indians? Private Collection/Peter Newark American Pictures/Bridgeman Images.

The Pilgrims settled at Plymouth and elected William Bradford their governor. That first winter, which they spent aboard their ship, "was most sad and lamentable," Bradford wrote later. "In two or three months' time half of [our] company died . . . being the depth of winter, and wanting houses . . . [and] being infected with scurvy and other diseases."

In the spring, Indians rescued the floundering Plymouth settlement. First Samoset and then Squanto befriended the settlers. Samoset had learned English from previous contacts with sailors and fishermen who had visited the coast to dry fish before the Plymouth settlers arrived. Squanto had been kidnapped by an English trader in 1614 and taken as a slave to Spain, where he escaped to London and learned English before finally making his way back home. Samoset arranged for the Pilgrims to meet and establish good relations with Massasoit, the chief of the Wampanoag Indians, whose territory included Plymouth. Squanto, Bradford wrote, "was a special instrument sent of God for their [the Pilgrims'] good. . . . He directed them how to set their corn, where to take fish, and to procure other commodities." With the Indians' guidance, the Pilgrims managed to harvest enough food to guarantee their survival through the coming winter, an occasion they celebrated in the fall of 1621 with a feast of thanksgiving attended by Massasoit and other Wampanoags.

Plymouth colony remained precarious for years, but the Pilgrims persisted, living simply and coexisting in relative peace with the Indians. One settler contrasted the group's improved circumstances with their former homes in England by noting, "We are all free-holders [here], the [landlords'] rent-day doth not trouble us." By 1630, Plymouth had become a small permanent settlement, but it failed to attract many other English Puritans.

The Founding of Massachusetts Bay Colony

In 1629, shortly before Charles I dissolved Parliament, a group of Puritans obtained a royal charter for the Massachusetts Bay Company. The charter provided the usual privileges granted to joint-stock companies, including land for colonization that spanned present-day Massachusetts, New Hampshire, Vermont, Maine, and upstate New York. A unique provision of the charter permitted the government of the Massachusetts Bay Company to be located in the colony rather than in England. This provision allowed Puritans to exchange their status as a harassed minority in England for self-government in Massachusetts.

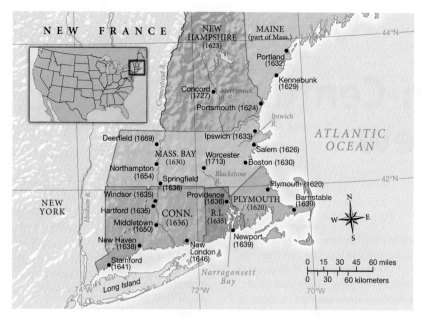

MAP ACTIVITY

Map 4.1 New England Colonies in the Seventeenth Century

New Englanders spread across the landscape town by town during the seventeenth century. (For the sake of legibility, only a few of the more important towns are shown on the map.)

READING THE MAP: Using the dates on the map, create a chronology of the establishment of New England towns. What physical features correspond to the earliest habitation by English settlers?

CONNECTIONS: Why were towns so much more a feature of seventeenth-century New England than of the Chesapeake (see "Cultivating Land and Faith" in chapter 3)? How did Puritan dissent influence the settlement of New England colonies?

To lead the emigrants, the Massachusetts Bay Company selected John Winthrop, a prosperous lawyer and landowner, to serve as governor. In March 1630, eleven ships crammed with seven hundred passengers sailed for Massachusetts; six more ships and another five hundred emigrants followed a few months later. Unlike the Separatists, Winthrop's Puritans aspired to reform the corrupt Church of England (rather than separate from it) by setting an example of godliness in the New World. "For England's sake they are going from England to pray without ceasing for England," wrote one Puritan emigrant. Winthrop and a small group chose to settle on the peninsula that became Boston, and other settlers clustered at promising locations nearby (Map 4.1).

In a sermon to his companions aboard the *Arbella* while they were still at sea—probably the most famous sermon in American history—Winthrop proclaimed the cosmic significance of their journey. The Puritans had "entered into a covenant" with God to "work out our salvation under the power and purity of his holy ordinances," Winthrop declared. This sanctified agreement with God meant that the Puritans had to make "extraordinary" efforts to "bring into familiar and constant practice" religious principles that most people in England merely preached. To achieve their pious goals, the Puritans had to subordinate their individual interests to the common good. "We must be knit together in this work as one man," Winthrop

preached. "We must delight in each other, make others' conditions our own, rejoice together, mourn together, labor and suffer together." The stakes could not be higher, Winthrop told his listeners: "We must consider that we shall be as a city upon a hill. The eyes of all people are upon us."

That belief shaped seventeenth-century New England as profoundly as tobacco shaped the Chesapeake. Winthrop's vision of a city on a hill fired the Puritans' fierce determination to keep their covenant and live according to God's laws, unlike the backsliders and compromisers who accommodated to the Church of England. Their resolve to adhere strictly to God's plan charged nearly every feature of life in seventeenth-century New England with a distinctive, high-voltage piety. (See "Making Historical Arguments," page 84.)

The new colonists had "all things to do, as in the beginning of the world," as Winthrop's son wrote later. Unlike the early Chesapeake settlers, the first Massachusetts Bay colonists encountered few Indians because the local population had been almost entirely exterminated by an epidemic. Still, many of the colonists succumbed to diseases. During the first year, more than two hundred settlers died, including one of Winthrop's sons and eleven of his servants. Winthrop himself remained confident and optimistic. He wrote to his wife that "I like so well to be heer as I do not repent my comminge.... I would not have altered my course, though I had forseene all these

How Did Seventeenth-Century Colonists View Nature?

A cascade of novelty swept across Europe during the sixteenth and seventeenth centuries. New continents, new peoples, new plants and animals, new religions, and new ideas caused some thinkers to reconsider the basic nature of the world and the place of human beings within it. Building on discoveries made in the sixteenth century by Copernicus and other astronomers, Galileo insisted, for example, that the earth did not rest at the center of the universe, but instead moved around the sun, demoting the globe and its inhabitants from the hub to an outer orbit. Isaac Newton, to take another example, invented the mathematics of bodies in motion—calculus, familiar to students for hundreds of years afterward—and worked out the theory of the invisible force that governs all matter—gravity. These and other scientific advances seemed to some to contradict Christian ideas about God's sovereignty and much else. Was gravity just another name for God? Or was gravity the way God chose to order creation? Newton and most other seventeenth-century scientists believed that God created gravity and the rest of the natural order much like a watchmaker built a complex mechanical clock. Setting the clock in motion, God then stepped back and allowed the universe to operate by natural laws like gravity that did not need his constant supervision or intervention.

Settlers in seventeenth-century New England and the middle colonies lived thousands of miles and a mental world away from centers of advanced scientific thinking in London, Paris, Berlin, and elsewhere in Europe. Seventeenth-century colonists believed they and the earth stood at the center of God's vision, and that God constantly intervened in the world to express his pleasure or displeasure with humans' behavior. Violent thunderstorms, destructive winds, hail, floods, droughts, disease epidemics, and much else that we might consider acts of nature, seventeenth-century colonists interpreted instead as signs of God's anger that people were not living up to his expectations. New Englanders in particular searched for evidence that God was punishing them for falling short of his biblical commandments.

God also sometimes rewarded colonists for obeying his divine laws. A Connecticut man, for example, reported that "we have had of late, great stormes of rain & wind, & sometimes of thunder and lightning, whereby some execution hath been done by the Lord's holy Hand, though with sparing mercy to mankind." The

Afflictions." And each year from 1630 to 1640, ship after ship followed in the wake of Winthrop's fleet, bringing more than twenty thousand new settlers.

Often, when the Church of England cracked down on a Puritan minister in England, he and many of his followers moved together to New England. Smaller groups of English Puritans moved to the Chesapeake and elsewhere in the colonies, including New Amsterdam (present-day New York). By 1640, New England had one of the highest ratios of preachers to population in all of Christendom. Several ministers sought to carry the message of Christianity to the Indians in order to replace what missionary John Eliot termed the Indians' "unfixed, confused, and ungoverned . . . life, uncivilized and unsubdued to labor and order," and they established "praying towns" to encourage Indians to adopt English ways. But the colonists focused far less on saving Indians' souls than on saving their own.

The occupations of New England immigrants reflected the social origins of English Puritans. On the whole, the immigrants came from the middle ranks of English society. The vast majority were either farmers or tradesmen. Indentured servants, whose numbers dominated the Chesapeake settlers, accounted for only about a fifth of those headed for New England. Most New England immigrants paid their way to Massachusetts. They were encouraged by the promise of bounty in New England reported in Winthrop's letter to his son: "Here can be no want of anything to those who bring means to raise [it] out of the earth and sea."

In contrast to Chesapeake newcomers, New England immigrants usually arrived as families.

storms killed nine oxen, seven hogs, and a dog, but a nearby family of children left alone by their parents suffered "no hurt to any of them, more than amazing fear." We might believe these children were lucky, having avoided harm by accident or coincidence. But colonists saw the children's safety as a "remarkable providence," an instance of God's gracious protection of his precious loved ones. Puritans welcomed remarkable providences as reassuring evidence of God's satisfaction that they were fulfilling the obligations of their holy covenant, at least temporarily. When a bolt of lightning stunned another colonist, God's divine intervention shielded him and he survived unhurt, as did the Bible he was carrying under his arm, which was "left untouched" by the lightning except for the "whole book of Revelation [which] was carried away."

Colonists stayed alert to any unusual happening: a strange cloud formation; an unusual noise in the night; an ominous comet streaking across the sky; the "monstrous" birth of a calf with two heads or, worse, of a deformed human fetus. Colonists referred to such events as "wonders" that signaled God's awareness of every detail of their lives. Wonders seemed to be omens of God's judgment, but it was often difficult to decipher whether an omen meant God was angry or pleased. Overall, signs of an angry, vengeful God seemed to predominate, worrisome evidence to many colonists that they were failing—individually and collectively—to win God's favor. But another interpretation of wonders worried colonists even more. Maybe that two-headed calf or fiery comet was the work of Satan, whose powers for evil always warred against colonists' desires to live in godly ways.

Wonders and remarkable providences revealed seventeenth-century colonists' view of nature as suffused with mysterious, supernatural power. To them, nature was not a Newtonian clock set in motion by a distant God, but an enchanted environment that God and Satan battled over constantly, storm by storm, comet by comet. Colonists could try to align themselves with God and reject Satan, but they could scarcely comprehend, much less alter, the mysterious forces that governed nature and themselves. The orderly, harmonious, and law-abiding nature posited by a Newtonian "watchmaker God" made no sense to seventeenth-century colonists. Instead, God watched and cared about every second of the lives of every creature on earth. They mattered to him, and, if they knew what was good for them, he better matter to them lest their chance for salvation slip away for all eternity.

Questions for Analysis

Summarize the Argument: According to this essay, how did seventeenth-century colonists' views of nature differ from those of leading European scientists?

Analyze the Evidence: What does the colonial reaction to "wonders and remarkable providences" discussed in this essay reveal about colonists' view of nature? How might leading European scientists of the era have interpreted these events differently?

Consider the Context: How might life in the seventeenth-century colonies have influenced colonists' views about nature and themselves? Why might colonists and European scientists have had such contrasting views of God and nature?

In fact, more Puritans came with family members than did any other group of immigrants in all of American history. Unlike immigrants to the Chesapeake, women and children made up a solid majority in New England.

As Winthrop reminded the first settlers in his *Arbella* sermon, each family was a "little commonwealth" that mirrored the hierarchy among all God's creatures. Just as humankind was subordinate to God, so young people were subordinate to their elders, children to their parents, and wives to their husbands. The immigrants' family ties reinforced their religious beliefs with the interlocking institutions of family, church, and community.

> **REVIEW** What was a "little commonwealth," and why was it so important to New England settlement?

▶ The Evolution of New England Society

The New England colonists, unlike their counterparts in the Chesapeake, settled in small towns, usually located on the coast or by a river (see Map 4.1). Massachusetts Bay colonists founded 133 towns during the seventeenth century, each with one or more churches. Church members' fervent piety, buttressed by the institutions of local government, enforced remarkable religious and social conformity in the small New England settlements. During the century, tensions within the Puritan faith and changes in New England communities splintered religious orthodoxy and weakened Puritan zeal. By 1700, however, Puritanism retained a distinctive influence in New England.

Church, Covenant, and Conformity

Puritans believed that a church consisted of men and women who had entered a solemn covenant with one another and with God. Winthrop and others who signed the covenant of the first Boston church in 1630 agreed to "Promisse, and bind our selves, to walke in all our wayes according to the Rule of the Gospell, and in all sincere Conformity to His holy Ordinaunces." Each new member of the covenant had to persuade existing members that she or he had fully experienced conversion.

Puritans embraced a distinctive version of Protestantism derived from **Calvinism**, the doctrines of John Calvin, who insisted that Christians strictly discipline their behavior to conform to God's commandments announced in the Bible. Like Calvin, Puritans believed in **predestination**— the idea that the all-powerful God, before the creation of the world, decided which few human souls would receive eternal life. Only God knows the identity of these fortunate predestined individuals—the "elect" or "saints." Nothing a person did in his or her lifetime could alter God's choice or provide assurance that the person was predestined for salvation with the elect or damned to hell with the doomed multitude.

Despite the looming uncertainty about God's choice of the elect, Puritans believed that if a person lived a rigorously godly life—constantly winning the daily battle against sin—his or her behavior was likely to be a hint, a visible sign, that he or she was one of God's chosen few. Puritans thought that "sainthood" would become visible in individuals' behavior, especially if they were privileged to know God's Word as revealed in the Bible.

The connection between sainthood and saintly behavior, however, was far from certain. Some members of the elect, Puritans believed, had not heard God's Word. One reason Puritans required all town residents to attend church services was to enlighten anyone who was ignorant of God's Truth. The slippery relationship between saintly behavior and God's predestined election caused Puritans to worry constantly that individuals who acted like saints were fooling themselves and others. Nevertheless, Puritans thought that **visible saints**—persons who passed their demanding tests of conversion and church membership— probably were among God's elect.

Members of Puritan churches ardently hoped that God had chosen them to receive eternal life and tried to demonstrate saintly behavior. Their covenant bound them to help one another attain salvation and to discipline the entire community by saintly standards. Church members kept an eye on the behavior of everybody in town. By overseeing every aspect of life, the visible saints enforced a remarkable degree of righteous conformity in Puritan communities. Total conformity, however, was never achieved. Ardent Puritans differed among themselves, and non-Puritans shirked orthodox rules, such as the Roxbury servant who declared that "if hell were ten times hotter, [I] would rather be there than [I] would serve [my] master."

Despite the central importance of religion, churches played no direct role in the civil government of New England communities. Puritans did not want to mimic the Church of England, which they considered a puppet of the king rather than an independent body that served the Lord. They were determined to insulate New England churches from the contaminating influence of the civil state and its merely human laws. Ministers were prohibited from holding government office.

Puritans had no qualms, however, about their religious beliefs influencing New England governments. As much as possible, the Puritans tried to bring public life into conformity with their view of God's law. For example, fines were issued for Sabbath-breaking activities such as working, traveling, playing a flute, smoking a pipe, and visiting neighbors.

Puritans mandated other purifications of what they considered corrupt English practices. They refused to celebrate Christmas or Easter because the Bible did not mention either one. They outlawed religious wedding ceremonies; couples were married by a magistrate in a civil ceremony. They banned cards, dice, shuffleboard, and other games of chance, as well as music and dancing. "Mixt or Promiscuous Dancing . . . of Men and Women" could not be tolerated since "the unchaste Touches and Gesticulations used by Dancers have a palpable tendency to that which is evil."

Government by Puritans for Puritanism

It is only a slight exaggeration to say that seventeenth-century New England was governed by Puritans for Puritanism. The charter of the Massachusetts Bay Company empowered the company's stockholders, known as freemen, to meet as a body known as the General Court and make the laws needed to govern the company's

THE
World turn'd upfide down:
OR
A briefe defcription of the ridiculous Fafhions
of thefe dultracted Times.

By T.J. a well-wilker to King, Parliament and Kingdom.

affairs. The colonists transformed this arrangement for running a joint-stock company into a structure for governing the colony. Hoping to ensure that godly men would decide government policies, the General Court expanded the number of freemen in 1631 to include all male church members. Only freemen had the right to vote for governor and other officials. When the size of the General Court grew too large to meet conveniently, the freemen agreed in 1634 that each town would send two deputies to the General Court to act as the colony's legislative assembly. All other men were classified as "inhabitants," who had the right to vote, hold office, and participate fully in town government.

A "town meeting," composed of a town's inhabitants and freemen, chose the selectmen who administered local affairs. New England town meetings routinely practiced a level of popular participation in political life that was unprecedented elsewhere in the world during the seventeenth century. Almost every adult man could speak out and vote in town meetings, but all women—even church members—were prohibited from voting. This widespread political participation tended to reinforce conformity to Puritan ideals.

The General Court granted land for town sites to pious petitioners, once the Indians agreed to relinquish their claim to the land, usually in exchange for manufactured goods. William Pynchon, for example, purchased the site of Springfield, Massachusetts, from the Agawam Indians for "eighteen fathams [arm's lengths] of Wampum [strings of shell-beads used in trade], eighteen coates, 18 hatchets, 18 hoes, [and] 18 knives." Town founders then apportioned land among themselves and any newcomers they approved. Most family plots clustered between about fifty to one hundred acres, resulting in a more nearly equal distribution of land in New England than in the Chesapeake.

The physical layout of New England towns encouraged settlers to look inward toward their neighbors, multiplying the opportunities for godly vigilance. Most people considered the forest that lay just beyond every settler's house an alien environment. Footpaths connecting one town to another were so rudimentary that even John Winthrop once got lost and spent a sleepless night in the forest only a half mile from his house.

Connecticut Church
Puritans erected this church in Hartford, Connecticut, in 1636. The church displays the plain, unadorned style Puritans championed, a flagrant repudiation of the elaborate buildings and lavish ornamentation common in Anglican churches in England. Note that the church lacks even the Christian symbol of the cross. The Granger Collection, New York.

The Splintering of Puritanism

Almost from the beginning, John Winthrop and other leaders had difficulty enforcing their views of Puritan orthodoxy. In England, persecution as a dissenting minority had unified Puritan voices in opposition to the Church of England. In New England, the promise of a godly society and the Puritans' emphasis on individual Bible study led toward different visions of godliness. Puritan leaders, however, interpreted dissent as an error caused either by a misguided believer or by the malevolent power of Satan. As one Puritan minister proclaimed, "The Scripture saith . . . there is no Truth but one."

Shortly after banishing Roger Williams, Winthrop confronted another dissenter, this time a devout Puritan woman steeped in Scripture and absorbed by religious questions: Anne Hutchinson. The mother of fourteen children, Hutchinson assisted neighboring women during childbirth and in 1634 began to give weekly lectures on recent sermons attended by women who gathered at her home. Hutchinson lectured on the "covenant of grace"—the idea that individuals could be saved only by God's grace in choosing them to be members of the elect. This familiar Puritan doctrine contrasted with the covenant of works, the erroneous belief that a person's behavior—one's works—could win God's favor and ultimately earn a person salvation.

The meetings at Hutchinson's house alarmed her nearest neighbor, Governor John Winthrop, who believed that she was subverting the good order of the colony. In 1637, Winthrop had formal charges brought against Hutchinson and denounced her lectures as "not tolerable nor comely in the sight of God nor fitting for your sex." A leading minister told her, "You have stept out of your place, you have rather bine a Husband than a Wife and a preacher than a Hearer; and a Magistrate than a Subject."

Winthrop and other Puritan elders referred to Hutchinson and her followers as **antinomians**, people who believed that Christians could be saved by faith alone and did not need to act in accordance with God's law as set forth in the Bible and as interpreted by the colony's leaders. Hutchinson nimbly defended herself against the accusation of antinomianism. Yes, she acknowledged, she believed that men and women were saved by faith alone; but no, she did not deny the need to obey God's law. "The Lord hath let me see which was the clear ministry and which the wrong," she said. How could she tell, Winthrop asked, which ministry was which? "By an immediate revelation," she replied, "by the voice of [God's] own spirit to my soul." Winthrop seized this statement as the heresy of prophecy, the view that God revealed his will directly to a believer instead of exclusively through the Bible, as every right-minded Puritan knew.

In 1638, the Boston church formally excommunicated Hutchinson. The minister decreed, "I doe cast you out and . . . deliver you up to Satan." Banished, Hutchinson and her family moved first to Roger Williams's Rhode Island and then to present-day New York, where she and most of her family were killed by Indians.

The strains within Puritanism exemplified by Anne Hutchinson and Roger Williams caused communities to splinter repeatedly during the seventeenth century. Thomas Hooker, a prominent minister, clashed with Winthrop and other leaders over the composition of the church. Hooker argued that men and women who lived godly lives should be admitted to church membership even if they had not experienced conversion. In 1636, Hooker led an exodus of more than eight hundred colonists from Massachusetts to the Connecticut River valley, where they founded Hartford and neighboring towns. In 1639, the towns adopted the Fundamental Orders of Connecticut, a quasi-constitution that could be altered by the vote of freemen, who did not have to be church members, though nearly all of them were.

Other Puritan churches divided and subdivided throughout the seventeenth century as acrimony developed over doctrine and church government. Sometimes churches split over the appointment of a controversial minister. These schisms arose from ambiguities and tensions within Puritan belief. As the colonies matured, other tensions developed as well.

Religious Controversies and Economic Changes

A revolutionary transformation in the fortunes of Puritans in England had profound consequences in New England. Disputes between King Charles I and Parliament, which was dominated by Puritans, escalated in 1642 to civil war in England, a conflict known as the **Puritan Revolution**. Parliamentary forces led by the staunch Puritan Oliver Cromwell were victorious, executing Charles I in 1649 and proclaiming England a Puritan republic. From 1649 to 1660, England's rulers were not monarchs who suppressed Puritanism but believers who championed it.

When the Puritan Revolution began, the stream of immigrants to New England dwindled to a trickle, creating hard times for the colonists. They could no longer consider themselves a city on a hill setting a godly example for humankind. Puritans in England, not New England, were reforming English society. Furthermore, when immigrant ships became rare, the colonists faced sky-high prices for scarce English goods and few customers for their own colonial products. As they searched to find new products and markets, they established the enduring patterns of New England's economy.

New England's rocky soil and short growing season ruled out cultivating the southern colonies' crops of tobacco and rice that found ready markets in Atlantic ports. Exports that New Englanders could not get from the soil they took instead from the forest and the sea. By the 1640s, furbearing animals had become scarce unless traders ventured far beyond the frontiers of English settlement. Trees from the seemingly limitless forests of New England proved a longer-lasting resource. Masts for ships and staves for barrels of Spanish wine and West Indian sugar were crafted from New England timber.

The most important New England export was fish. Dried, salted codfish from the rich North Atlantic fishing grounds found markets in southern Europe and the West Indies. The fish trade also stimulated colonial shipbuilding and trained generations of fishermen, sailors, and merchants. But the lives of most New England colonists revolved around their farms, churches, and families.

Although immigration came to a standstill in the 1640s, the colonial population continued to boom, doubling every twenty years. In New England, almost everyone married, and women often had eight or nine children. Long, cold winters minimized the presence of warm-weather ailments such as malaria and yellow fever, so the mortality rate was lower than in the South. By the end of the seventeenth century, the New England population roughly equaled that of the southern colonies (over 100,000 colonists).

During the second half of the seventeenth century, under the pressures of steady population growth (Figure 4.1) and integration into the Atlantic economy, the red-hot piety of the founders cooled. After 1640, the population grew faster than church membership. Boston's churches in 1650 could house only about a third of the city's residents. By the 1680s, women were the majority of church members throughout New England. In some towns, only 15 percent of the adult men were members. A growing fraction of New Englanders, especially men, practiced what one historian has called "horse-shed Christianity." They attended sermons but afterward loitered outside near the horse shed, gossiping about the weather, fishing, their crops, or the scandalous behavior of neighbors. This slackening of piety led the Puritan minister Michael Wigglesworth to ask, in verse:

How is it that
I find In stead of holiness Carnality;
In stead of heavenly frames an Earthly mind,
For burning zeal luke-warm Indifferency,
For flaming love, key-cold Dead-heartedness....
Whence cometh it, that Pride, and Luxurie
Debate, Deceit, Contention and Strife,
False-dealing, Covetousness, Hypocrisie
. . . amongst them are so rife,
. . . that an honest man can hardly
Trust his Brother?

Most alarming to Puritan leaders, many of the children of the visible saints of Winthrop's generation failed to experience conversion and attain full church membership. Puritans tended to assume that sainthood was inherited—that the children of visible saints were probably also among the elect. As these children grew up during the 1640s and 1650s, however, they seldom experienced the inward transformation that

FIGURE 4.1   Population of the English North American Colonies in the Seventeenth Century
The colonial population grew at a steadily accelerating rate during the seventeenth century. New England and the southern colonies each accounted for about half the total colonial population until after 1680, when growth in Pennsylvania and New York contributed to a surge in the population of the middle colonies.

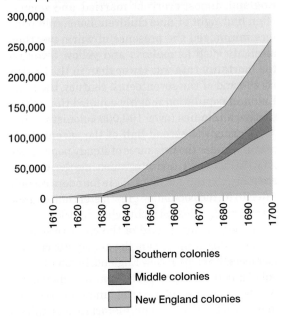

Southern colonies

Middle colonies

New England colonies

signaled conversion and qualification for church membership. The problem of declining church membership and the watering-down of Puritan orthodoxy became urgent during the 1650s when the children of saints, who had grown to adulthood in New England but had not experienced conversion, began to have children themselves. Their sons and daughters—the grandchildren of the founders of the colony—could not receive the protection that baptism afforded against the terrors of death because their parents had not experienced conversion.

Puritan churches debated what to do. To allow anyone, even the child of a saint, to become a church member without conversion was an unthinkable retreat from fundamental Puritan doctrine. In 1662, a synod of Massachusetts ministers reached a compromise known as the **Halfway Covenant**. Unconverted children of saints would be permitted to become "halfway" church members. Like regular church members, they could baptize their infants. But unlike full church members, they could not participate in communion or have the voting privileges of church membership. The Halfway Covenant generated a controversy that sputtered through Puritan churches for the remainder of the century. With the Halfway Covenant, Puritan churches came

VISUAL ACTIVITY

New England Mother and Child
This seventeenth-century painting of Elizabeth Freake and her baby Mary illustrates the evolution of New England society away from the Puritan austerity of the founders and toward worldly elegance and display. Both mother and daughter appear prosperous, healthy, and somewhat proud. Worcester Art Museum, Massachusetts, USA/Bridgeman Images.
READING THE IMAGE: What does the clothing of Elizabeth and Mary suggest about their religion?
CONNECTIONS: Why did New England's Puritan zeal diminish in the latter third of the seventeenth century?

to terms with the lukewarm piety that had replaced the founders' burning zeal.

Nonetheless, New England communities continued to enforce piety with holy rigor. Beginning in 1656, small bands of **Quakers**—members of the Society of Friends, as they called themselves—began to arrive in Massachusetts. Quakers believed that God spoke directly to each individual through an "inner light" and that individuals needed neither a preacher nor the Bible to discover God's Word. Maintaining that all human beings were equal in God's eyes, Quakers refused to conform to mere temporal powers such as laws and governments unless God requested otherwise. Women often took a leading role in Quaker meetings, in contrast to Puritan congregations, where women usually outnumbered men but remained subordinate.

New England communities treated Quakers with ruthless severity. Some Quakers were branded on the face "with a red-hot iron with [an] H. for heresie." When Quakers refused to leave Massachusetts, Boston officials hanged four of them between 1659 and 1661. New Englanders' partial success in realizing the promise of a godly society ultimately undermined the intense appeal of Puritanism. In the pious Puritan communities of New England, leaders tried to eliminate sin. In the process, they diminished the sense of utter human depravity that was the wellspring of Puritanism. Minister Cotton Mather bemoaned, "*Religion* brought forth *Prosperity*, and the *Daughter* destroy'd the *Mother*."

Witch trials held in Salem, Massachusetts, signaled the erosion of religious confidence and assurance. From the beginning of English settlement in the New World, more than 95 percent of all legal accusations of witchcraft occurred in New England, a hint of the Puritans' preoccupation with sin and evil. In Salem in 1692, witnesses accused more than one hundred people of witchcraft, a capital crime. (See "Analyzing Historical Evidence," page 92.) Bewitched young girls shrieked in pain, their limbs twisted into strange contortions, as they pointed out the witches who tortured them. According to the trial court record, the bewitched girls declared that "the shape of [one accused witch] did oftentimes very grievously pinch them, choke them, bite them, and afflict them; urging them to write their names in a book"—the devil's book. Most of the accused witches were older women, and virtually all of them were well known to their accusers. The Salem court hanged nineteen accused witches and pressed one to death, signaling enduring belief in the supernatural origins of evil and gnawing doubt about the strength of Puritan New Englanders' faith. Why else, after all, had so many New Englanders succumbed to what their accusers and the judges believed were the temptations of Satan?

REVIEW   Why did Massachusetts Puritans adopt the Halfway Covenant?

Witches Show Their Love for Satan
Witches debased themselves by standing in line to kiss Satan's buttocks—or so it was popularly believed. This seventeenth-century print portrays Satan with clawlike hands and feet, the tail of a rodent, the wings of a bat, and the head of a lustful ram attached to the torso of a man. Notice that women predominate among the witches eager to express their devotion to Satan. The Granger Collection, New York.

Hunting Witches in Salem, Massachusetts

In the summer of 1692, many people in and around Salem, Massachusetts, accused dozens of their neighbors and kinfolk of being witches. Officials convened a special court to hear the testimony of the accusers and to examine the accused. In the end, nineteen convicted witches were hanged, and more than 150 accused witches crammed the jails before the trials were finally called off.

DOCUMENT 1
Witnesses against Accused Witch Susanna Martin, 1692

Neighbors lined up to give testimony that, in their minds, proved that the accused were witches. Like many other accused people, Susanna Martin pleaded not guilty to witch-craft. The court, persuaded by the testimony of witnesses, sentenced her to death, and she was executed on July 19, 1692.

Bernard Peache testify'd, That being in Bed on a Lords-day Night, he heard a scrabbling at the Window, whereat he then saw, *Susanna Martin* come in, and jump down upon the Floor. She took hold of this Deponents Feet, and drawing his Body up into an Heap, she lay upon him, near Two Hours; in all which time he could neither speak nor stirr. At length, when he could begin to move, he laid hold on her Hand, and pulling it up to his mouth, he bit three of her Fingers, as he judged, unto the Bone. Whereupon she went from the Chamber, down the Stairs, out at the Door. . . .

John Kembal . . . Being desirous to furnish himself with a Dog, he applied himself to buy one of this Martin. . . . But she not letting him have his Choice [Kembal went to another neighbor to get a puppy]. Within a few days after, [when] this *Kembal* . . . came below the Meeting-House, there appeared unto him, a little thing like a *Puppy*, of a Darkish Colour; and it shot Backwards and forwards between his Leggs. He had the Courage to use all possible Endeavors of Cutting it, with his Axe; but he could not Hit it. . . . Going a little further, there appeared unto him a Black Puppy, somewhat bigger than the first; but Black as Cole. Its motions were quicker than those of his Ax; it Flew at his Belly and away; then at his Throat, also over his Shoulder. . . . His heart now began to fail him, and he thought the Dog would have Tore his Throat out. But he recovered himself, and called upon God in his Distress; and Naming the Name of JESUS CHRIST, it Vanished away at once. . . . [The next day, Susanna Martin told other people that he had been frightened by puppies, although] Kembal [said he] had mentioned the Matter to no Creature Living.

Joseph Ring . . . has been strangely carried about by *Demons*, from one *Witch-Meeting* to another, for near two years together. . . . Afterwards . . . this poor man would be visited with unknown shapes . . . which would force him away with them, unto unknown Places, where he saw meetings, Feastings, Dancings. . . . When he was brought into these Hellish meetings, one of the First things they still did unto him, was to give him a knock on the

▶ The Founding of the Middle Colonies

South of New England and north of the Chesapeake, a group of middle colonies were founded in the last third of the seventeenth century. Before the 1670s, few Europeans settled in the region. For the first two-thirds of the seventeenth century, the most important European outpost in the area was the relatively small Dutch colony of New Netherland. By 1700, however, the English monarchy had seized New Netherland, renamed it New York, and encouraged the creation of a Quaker colony in Pennsylvania led by William Penn. Unlike the New England colonies, the middle colonies of New York, New Jersey, and Pennsylvania originated as land grants by the English monarch to one or more proprietors, who then possessed both the land and the extensive, almost monarchical, powers of government (Map 4.2). These middle colonies attracted settlers of more diverse European origins and religious faiths than were found in New England.

Back, whereupon he was . . . as if Bound with chains, uncapable of Stirring out of the place, till they should Release him. . . . There often came to him a man, who presented him a Book, whereto he would have him set his Hand; promising to him, that he should then have even what he would; and presenting him with all the delectable Things, persons, and places that he could imagine. But he refusing to subscribe, the business would end with dreadful Shapes, Noises and Screechings, which almost scared him out of his witts. . . . He saw the Prisoner [Susanna Martin], at several of those Hellish Randezvouzes. Note, This Woman was one of the most Impudent, Scurrilous, wicked creatures in the world & she did now throughout her whole Trial, discover herself to be such an one. Yet when she was asked what she had to say for her self, her Cheef Plea was, *That she had Led a most virtuous and Holy Life.*

Source: Cotton Mather, *The Wonders of the Invisible World* (Boston, 1692), 115–26.

**DOCUMENT 2
Robert Calef, *More Wonders of the Invisible World*, 1700**

A few New Englanders spoke out against the witch-hunt as the

persecution of innocent people. Robert Calef, a Boston merchant, wrote a scathing criticism of the witch trials and their supporters.

And now to sum up all in a few words, we have seen a biggotted zeal, stirring up a blind, and most bloody rage, not against enemies, or irreligious, profligate persons— but . . . against as virtuous and religious as any they have left behind them in this country . . . and this by the testimony of vile varlets, as not only were known before, but have been further apparent since, by their manifest lives, whoredoms, incest &c. The accusations of these, from their spectral sight, being the chief evidence against those that suffered; in which accusations they were upheld by both magistrates and ministers, so long as they apprehended themselves in no danger. And then, tho' they could defend neither the doctrine nor the practice, yet none of them have in such a publick manner as the case requires, testified against either; tho', at the same time they could not but be sensible what a stain and lasting infamy they have brought upon the whole country, to the indangering of the future welfare not only of this but of other places, induced by their example . . . occasioning the great dishonour and blasphemy of the name of God . . . and as a

natural effect thereof, to the great increase of Atheism.

Source: Robert Calef, *More Wonders of the Invisible World* (London, 1700), unpaginated "Epistle to the Reader."

Questions for Analysis

Ask Historical Questions: Why were witnesses, the Salem court, and many people in the region so obsessed with witches that they seemed to suspect their malevolent influence in the ordinary events of daily life?

Analyze the Evidence: What evidence did accusers offer as proof that Susanna Martin was a witch? What did Calef think about such evidence? If the evidence was not the work of the devil or witches, what did it indicate?

Consider the Context: How did the 1692 witchcraft trials reflect changes in New England society since the time of John Winthrop and the founding generation? What do the testimonies of the accusers and the criticisms of Calef suggest about the strength and confidence of Puritans' belief in their covenant with God?

Recognize Viewpoints: Why did Calef denounce the witchcraft trials? How would the witnesses respond to Martin's claim that she had led a most virtuous and holy life?

From New Netherland to New York

In 1609, the Dutch East India Company dispatched Henry Hudson to search for a Northwest Passage to the Orient. Hudson ventured up the large river that now bears his name until it dwindled to a stream that obviously did not lead to China. A decade later, the Dutch government granted the West India Company—a group of Dutch merchants and shippers—exclusive rights to trade with the Western Hemisphere. In 1626,

Peter Minuit, the resident director of the company, purchased Manhattan Island from the Manhate Indians for trade goods worth the equivalent of a dozen beaver pelts. New Amsterdam, the small settlement established at the southern tip of Manhattan Island, became the principal trading center in **New Netherland** and the colony's headquarters.

Unlike the English colonies, New Netherland did not attract many European immigrants. Like New England and the Chesapeake colonies, New Netherland never realized its sponsors' dreams

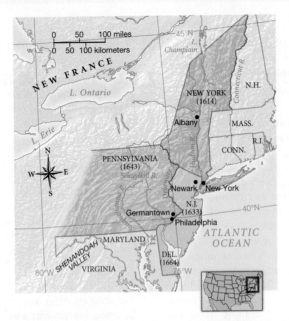

Map 4.2 Middle Colonies in the Seventeenth Century
For the most part, settlers in the middle colonies in the seventeenth century clustered along the Hudson and Delaware rivers. The geographic extent of the colonies shown in this map reflects land grants authorized in England. Most of this area was inhabited by Native Americans rather than colonists.

of great profits. The company tried to stimulate immigration by granting patroonships—allotments of eighteen miles of land along the Hudson River—to wealthy stockholders who would bring fifty families to the colony and settle them as serflike tenants on their huge domains. Only one patroonship succeeded; the others failed to attract settlers, and the company eventually recovered much of the land.

Though few in number, New Netherlanders were remarkably diverse, especially compared with the homogeneous English settlers to the north and south. Religious dissenters and immigrants from Holland, Sweden, France, Germany, and elsewhere made their way to the colony. A minister of the Dutch Reformed Church complained to his superiors in Holland that several groups of Jews had recently arrived, adding to the religious mixture of "Papists, Mennonites and Lutherans among the Dutch [and] many Puritans . . . and many other atheists . . . who conceal themselves under the name of Christians."

The West India Company struggled to govern the motley colonists. Peter Stuyvesant, governor from 1647 to 1664, pointed out to company officials

in Holland that "the *English* and *French* colonies are continued and populated by their own nation and countrymen and consequently [are] bound together more firmly and united," while the "colonies in *New-Netherland* are only gradually and slowly peopled by the scrapings of all sorts of nationalities (few excepted), who consequently have the least interest in the welfare and maintenance of the commonwealth." Stuyvesant tried to enforce conformity to the Dutch Reformed Church, but the company—eager for more immigrants—declared that "the consciences of men should be free and unshackled," making a virtue of New Netherland necessity. The company never permitted the colony's settlers to form a representative government. Instead, the company appointed government officials who established policies, including taxes, that many colonists deeply resented.

In 1664, New Netherland became New York. Charles II, who became king of England in 1660 when Parliament restored the monarchy, gave his brother James, the Duke of York, an enormous grant of land that included New Netherland. The duke quickly organized a small fleet of warships, which appeared off Manhattan Island in late summer 1664, and demanded that Stuyvesant surrender. With little choice, he did.

As the new proprietor of the colony, the Duke of York exercised almost the same unlimited authority over the colony as had the West India Company, although the duke never set foot in the colony. Like the Dutch, the duke permitted "all persons of what Religion soever, quietly to inhabit . . . provided they give no disturbance to the publique peace, nor doe molest or disquiet others in the free exercise of their religion." This policy of religious toleration was less an affirmation of liberty of conscience than a recognition of the reality of the most heterogeneous colony in seventeenth-century North America.

New Jersey and Pennsylvania

The creation of New York led indirectly to the founding of two other middle colonies, New Jersey and Pennsylvania. In 1664, the Duke of York subdivided his grant and gave the portion between the Hudson and Delaware rivers to two of his friends. The proprietors of this new colony, New Jersey, quarreled and called in a prominent English Quaker, William Penn, to arbitrate their dispute. Penn eventually worked out a settlement that continued New Jersey's proprietary government. In the process, Penn became intensely

N. AMSTERDAM, ou N. IORK in Amerig:

VISUAL ACTIVITY

New Amsterdam

The settlement on Manhattan Island appears in the background of this 1673 Dutch portrait of New Amsterdam. In the foreground, the Dutch artist placed native inhabitants of the mainland, drawing them to resemble Africans rather than Lenni Lenape (Delaware) Indians. The portrait contrasts orderly, efficient, businesslike New Amsterdam with the exotic natural environment of America. © Collection of the New-York Historical Society, USA/Bridgeman Images.

READING THE IMAGE: What features of New Amsterdam contrast with the natural environment of Native Americans?

CONNECTIONS: How did New Amsterdam differ from New England?

interested in what he termed a "holy experiment" of establishing a genuinely Quaker colony in America.

Unlike most Quakers, William Penn came from an eminent family. His father had served both Cromwell and Charles II and had been knighted. Born in 1644, the younger Penn trained for a military career, but the ideas of dissenters from the reestablished Church of England appealed to him, and he became a devout Quaker. By 1680 Penn had published fifty books and spoken at countless public meetings, but he had failed to win public toleration for Quakers in England.

The Quakers' concept of an open, generous God who made his love equally available to all people continually brought them into conflict with the English government. Quaker leaders were ordinary men and women, not specially trained preachers. Quakers allowed women to assume positions of religious leadership. "In souls there is no sex," they said. Since all people were equal in the spiritual realm, Quakers considered social hierarchy false and evil. They called everyone "friend" and shook hands instead of curtsying or removing their hats—even when meeting the king. These customs enraged many non-Quakers and provoked innumerable beatings

Quaker Couple
This seventeenth-century picture of a Quaker couple illustrates their plain clothing and modest habits. The woman and man do not appear poor; their clothing fits them and is well made, but the colors in their clothing are somber and muted, unlike the richly ornamented and brightly colored clothes worn by prosperous non-Quakers. Private Collection/The Stapleton Collection/Bridgeman Images.

and worse. Penn was jailed four times for such offenses, once for nine months.

Despite his many run-ins with the government, Penn remained on good terms with Charles II. Partly to rid England of the troublesome Quakers, in 1681 Charles made Penn the proprietor of a new colony of some 45,000 square miles called Pennsylvania.

Toleration and Diversity in Pennsylvania

Quakers flocked to Pennsylvania in numbers exceeded only by the great Puritan migration to New England fifty years earlier. Between 1682 and 1685, nearly eight thousand immigrants arrived. Penn wrote in 1685 that the settlers were "a collection of divers nations in Europe: as, French, Dutch, Germans, Swedes, Danes, Finns, Scotch-Irish, and English; and of the last equal to all the rest." The settlers represented a cross section of the artisans, farmers, and laborers who predominated among English Quakers. Quaker missionaries also encouraged immigrants from the European continent, and many came, giving Pennsylvania greater ethnic diversity

than any other English colony except New York. The Quaker colony prospered, and the capital city, Philadelphia, soon rivaled New York as a center of commerce. By 1700, the city's five thousand inhabitants participated in a thriving trade exporting flour and other food products to the West Indies and importing English textiles and manufactured goods.

Penn was determined to live in peace with the Indians who inhabited the region. His Indian policy expressed his Quaker ideals and contrasted sharply with the hostile policies of the other English colonies. As he explained to the chief of the Lenni Lenape (Delaware) Indians, "God has written his law in our hearts, by which we are taught and commanded to love and help and do good to one another . . . [and] I desire to enjoy [Pennsylvania lands] with your love and consent." Penn instructed his agents to obtain the Indians' consent by purchasing their land, respecting their claims, and dealing with them fairly.

Penn declared that the first principle of government was that every settler would "enjoy the free possession of his or her faith and exercise of worship towards God." Accordingly,

Pennsylvania tolerated Protestant sects of all kinds as well as Roman Catholicism. All voters and officeholders had to be Christians, but the government did not compel settlers to attend religious services, as in Massachusetts, or to pay taxes to maintain a state-supported church, as in Virginia.

Despite its toleration and diversity, Pennsylvania was as much a Quaker colony as New England was a stronghold of Puritanism. "Government seems to me a part of religion itself," Penn wrote, "for there is no power but of God. The powers that be, are ordained of God: whosoever therefore resists the power [of government] resists the ordinance of God." Penn believed that government had two basic purposes: "to terrify evildoers . . . [and] to cherish those that do well." Penn had no hesitation about using civil government to enforce religious morality. One of the colony's first laws provided severe punishment for "all such offenses against God, as swearing, cursing, lying, profane talking, [and] drunkenness . . . which excite the people to rudeness, cruelty, looseness, and irreligion."

As proprietor, Penn had extensive powers subject only to review by the king. He appointed a governor, who maintained the proprietor's power to veto any laws passed by the colonial council, which was elected by property owners who possessed at least one hundred acres of land or who paid taxes. The council had the power to originate laws and administer all the affairs of government. A popularly elected assembly served as a check on the council; its members had the authority to reject or approve laws framed by the council.

Penn stressed that the exact form of government mattered less than the men who served in it. In Penn's eyes, "good men" staffed Pennsylvania's government because Quakers dominated elective and appointive offices. Quakers, of course, differed among themselves. Members of the assembly struggled to win the right to debate and amend laws, especially tax laws. They finally won the battle in 1701 when a new Charter of Privileges gave the proprietor the power to appoint the council and in turn stripped the council of all its former powers and gave them to the assembly, which became the only single-house legislature in all the English colonies.

REVIEW   How did Quaker ideals shape the colony of Pennsylvania?

▶ The Colonies and the English Empire

Proprietary grants to faraway lands were a cheap way for the king to reward friends. As the colonies grew, however, the grants became more valuable. After 1660, the king took initiatives to channel colonial trade through English hands and to consolidate royal authority over colonial governments. Occasioned by such economic and political considerations and triggered by King Philip's War between colonists and Native Americans, these initiatives defined the basic relationship between the colonies and England that endured until the American Revolution (Map 4.3).

Royal Regulation of Colonial Trade

English economic policies toward the colonies were designed to yield customs revenues for the monarchy and profitable business for English merchants and shippers. Also, the policies were intended to divert the colonies' trade from England's enemies, especially the Dutch and the French.

The Navigation Acts of 1650, 1651, 1660, and 1663 (see "Government Policies and Political Conflict" in chapter 3) set forth two fundamental rules governing colonial trade. First, goods shipped to and from the colonies had to be transported in English ships using primarily English crews. Second, the Navigation Acts listed colonial products that could be shipped only to England or to other English colonies. While these regulations prevented Chesapeake planters from shipping their tobacco directly to the European continent, they interfered less with the commerce of New England and the middle colonies, whose principal exports—fish, lumber, and flour—could legally be sent directly to their most important markets in the West Indies.

By the end of the seventeenth century, colonial commerce was defined by regulations that subjected merchants and shippers to royal supervision and gave them access to markets throughout the English empire. In addition, colonial commerce received protection by the English navy. By 1700, colonial goods (including those from the West Indies) accounted for one-fifth of all English imports and for two-thirds of all goods reexported from England to the European continent. In turn, the colonies absorbed more than

MAP ACTIVITY

Map 4.3 American Colonies at the End of the Seventeenth Century

By the end of the seventeenth century, settlers inhabited a narrow band of land that stretched from Boston to Norfolk, with pockets of settlement farther south. The colonies' claims to enormous tracts of land to the west were contested by Native Americans as well as by France and Spain.

READING THE MAP: What geographic feature acted as the western boundary for colonial territorial claims? Which colonies were the most settled and which the least?

CONNECTIONS: The map divides the colonies into four regions. Can you think of an alternative organization? On what criteria would it be based?

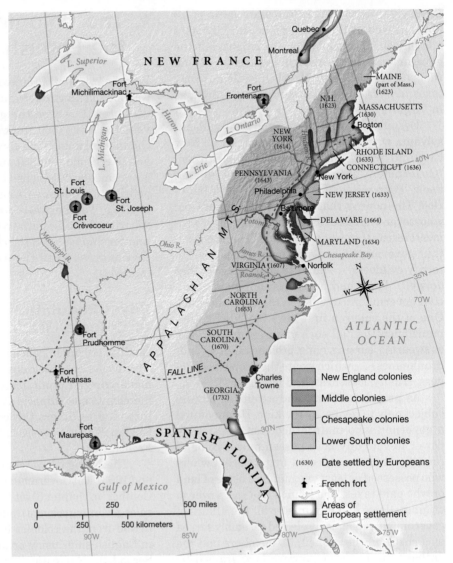

one-tenth of English exports. The commercial regulations gave economic value to England's proprietorship of the American colonies.

King Philip's War and the Consolidation of Royal Authority

The monarchy also took steps to exercise greater control over colonial governments. Virginia had been a royal colony since 1624; Maryland, South Carolina, and the middle colonies were proprietary colonies with close ties to the crown. The New England colonies possessed royal charters, but they had developed their own distinctively Puritan governments. Charles II, whose father, Charles I, had been executed by Puritans in England, took a particular interest in harnessing the New England colonies more firmly to the

English empire. The occasion was a royal investigation following **King Philip's War**.

A series of skirmishes in the Connecticut River valley between 1636 and 1637 culminated in the Pequot War when colonists massacred hundreds of Pequot Indians. In the decades that followed, New Englanders established relatively peaceful relations with the more potent Wampanoags, but they steadily encroached on Indian land. In 1642, a native leader urged warring tribes to band together against the English. "We [must] be one as they [the English] are," he said; "otherwise we shall be gone shortly, for . . . these English having gotten our land, they with scythes cut down the grass, and with axes fell the trees, and their cows and horses eat the grass, and their hogs spoil our clam banks, and we shall all be starved."

Such grievances accumulated until 1675, when the Wampanoags led by their chief

Metacomet—whom the colonists called King Philip—attacked English settlements in western Massachusetts. Militias from Massachusetts and other New England colonies counterattacked the Wampanoags, Nipmucks, and Narragansetts in a deadly sequence of battles that killed more than a thousand colonists and thousands more Indians. The Indians destroyed thirteen English settlements and partially burned another half dozen. Mary Rowlandson, a minister's wife in Lancaster, Massachusetts, who was captured by Indians, recalled later that it was a "solemn sight to see so many Christians lying in their blood . . . like a company of sheep torn by wolves. All of them stripped naked by a company of hell-hounds, roaring, singing, ranting and insulting, as if they would have torn our very hearts out."

By the spring of 1676, Indian warriors ranged freely within seventeen miles of Boston. The

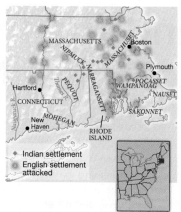

King Philip's War, 1675

colonists finally defeated the Indians, principally with a scorched-earth policy of burning their food supplies. But King Philip's War left the New England colonists with a large war debt, a devastated frontier, and an enduring hatred of Indians. "A Swarm of Flies, they may arise, a Nation to Annoy," a colonial officer wrote in justification of destroying the Indians; "Yea Rats and Mice, or Swarms of Lice a Nation may destroy."

In 1676, an agent of the king arrived to investigate whether New England was abiding by English laws. Not surprisingly, the king's agent found all sorts of deviations from English rules, and the monarchy decided to govern New England more directly. In 1684, an English court revoked the Massachusetts charter, the foundation of the distinctive Puritan government. Two years later, royal officials incorporated Massachusetts and the other colonies north of

Metacomet

This eighteenth-century engraving illustrates the artist's image of Metacomet, the native leader of what colonists recalled as King Philip's War. The engraving depicts Metacomet's Indian style of dress, a sharp contrast to colonists' clothing. Yet the clothing is made of textiles obtained in trade with colonists, indicating the partial adoption of colonial goods. Metacomet's musket and powder horns emphasize the danger Metacomet and other Indians posed to the colonists by making effective use of the colonists' own weaponry. Library of Congress, 3b42346.

New France and the Indians: The English Colonies' Northern Borderlands

North of New England, French explorers, traders, and missionaries carved out a distinctive North American colony that contrasted, competed, and periodically fought with the English colonies to the south.

The explorer Jacques Cartier sailed into the St. Lawrence River in 1535 and claimed the region for France. Cartier's attempts to found a permanent colony failed, but French ships followed in his wake and began to trade with Native Americans for wild animal pelts. By the time King Louis XIV made New France a royal colony in 1663, the fur trade had become the colony's economic foundation.

The French monarchy hoped to channel the fur trade through French hands into the broader European market and to compete against rival Dutch traders, whose headquarters at Albany (in what is now New York) funneled North American furs down the Hudson River to markets in the Netherlands. The crown also hoped the fur trade would allow the creation of a North American colony on the cheap.

The fur trade required little investment other than the construction and staffing of trading outposts at Quebec, Montreal, and elsewhere.

In exchange for textiles and various metal trade goods, the Iroquois, Huron, Ottawa, Ojibwa, and other Native Americans did the arduous, time-consuming, and labor-intensive work of tracking, trapping, and skinning the animals and transporting the pelts—usually by canoe—to French traders. Unlike the English colonies, which attracted numerous settlers to engage in agriculture and produce food as well as valuable export crops, New France needed only a few colonists to keep the trading posts open and to maintain friendly relations with their Indian suppliers. By 1660, English colonists in North America outnumbered their French counterparts by more than twenty to one.

After England seized control of New York in 1664, English fur traders replaced the Dutch at Albany and eagerly competed to divert the northern fur trade away from New France. By then, the Iroquois—strategically located between the supply of furs to the north and west, New France to the east, and New York to the south—had become middlemen, collecting pelts from Huron, Ottawa, and other Indians and swapping them with French or English traders, depending on who offered the better deal.

Able to mobilize scores of fierce warriors to threaten European traders as well as their Indian suppliers, the Iroquois managed to play the French and English off against each other and to maintain a near choke hold on the supply of furs.

Native Americans preferred English trade goods, which tended to be of higher quality and less expensive than those available at French outposts, but New France cultivated better relationships with the Indians. When English colonists had the required military strength, they seldom hesitated to kill Indians, especially those who occupied land the colonists craved. Since the small number of colonists in New France never had as much military power as the English colonists, they sought to stay on relatively peaceful and friendly terms with the Indians. French men commonly married or cohabited with Indian women, an outgrowth of both the shortage of French women among the colonists and the acceptance of such couplings, compared with the strong taboo prevalent in the English colonies.

Jesuit missionaries led the spiritual colonization of New France. Zealous enemies of what they considered Protestant heresies and stout

Maryland into the Dominion of New England. To govern the dominion, the English sent Sir Edmund Andros to Boston. Some New England merchants cooperated with Andros, but most colonists were offended by his flagrant disregard of such Puritan traditions as keeping the Sabbath. A visiting Englishman claimed that Bostonians were "great Censors of other Men's Manners, but extremely careless of their own." Worst of all, the Dominion of New England invalidated all land titles, confronting landowners in New England with the horrifying prospect of losing their land.

Events in England, however, permitted Massachusetts colonists to overthrow Andros and retain title to their property. When

American continent by canoeing down the Mississippi River to what is now Arkansas. Jolliet and Marquette made grandiose claims to the Mississippi valley, but in reality these claims amounted to little more than a colored patch on European maps. The dominant military power in New France remained the Iroquois, not the French.

England and France clashed repeatedly in North America over the fur trade and in a colonial extension of their rivalry at home. European conflict between France and England spread to North America during King William's War (1689–1697), when the colonists and their Indian allies carried out numerous deadly raids, marking the contested boundary between New France and the English colonies as a bloody zone controlled by none of its claimants or inhabitants.

Questions for Analysis

Analyze the Evidence: How did New France differ from the English colonies in seventeenth-century North America?

Consider the Context: How did European rivalries influence the encounters of Indians with French and English colonists? In what ways did New France reflect the colonial objectives of the French monarchy? Why was New France important to the seventeenth-century English colonists?

Recognize Viewpoints: How did the viewpoint of the Iroquois toward the fur trade compare to that of other Indians, the French, and the English?

defenders of Catholicism, the Jesuits fanned out to Indian villages throughout New France, determined to convert the Native Americans and to preserve the colony as a Catholic stronghold. Unwittingly, the missionaries also spread European diseases among the Native Americans, repeatedly causing deadly epidemics. Above all, the missionaries worked hand in hand with the fur traders and royal officials to make New

France a low-cost Catholic colony on the thinly defended borders of the predominantly Protestant English colonies.

To extend the boundaries of New France far to the west and south, almost encircling the English colonies along the Atlantic coast, royal officials in 1673 sponsored a voyage by the explorer Louis Jolliet and the priest Jacques Marquette to explore the vast interior of the North

Charles II died in 1685, he was succeeded by his brother James II, a zealous Catholic. James's aggressive campaign to appoint Catholics to government posts engendered such unrest that in 1688 a group of Protestant noblemen in Parliament invited the Dutch ruler William III of Orange, James's son-in-law, to claim the English throne.

When William III landed in England at the head of a large army, James fled to France, and William III and his wife, Mary II (James's daughter), became corulers in the relatively bloodless "Glorious Revolution," reasserting Protestant influence in England and its empire. Rumors of the revolution raced across the Atlantic and emboldened colonial uprisings against royal authority in Massachusetts, New York, and Maryland.

In Boston in 1689, rebels tossed Andros and other English officials in jail, destroyed the Dominion of New England, and reestablished the former charter government. New Yorkers followed the Massachusetts example. Under the leadership of Jacob Leisler, rebels seized the royal governor in 1689 and ruled the colony for more than a year. That same year in Maryland, the Protestant Association, led by John Coode, overthrew the colony's pro-Catholic government, fearing it would not recognize the new Protestant king.

But these rebel governments did not last. When King William III's governor of New York arrived in 1691, he executed Leisler for treason. Coode's men ruled Maryland until the new royal governor arrived in 1692 and ended both Coode's rebellion and Lord Baltimore's proprietary government. In Massachusetts, John Winthrop's city on a hill became another royal colony in 1691. The new charter said that the governor of the colony would be appointed by the king rather than elected by the colonists' representatives. But perhaps the most unsettling change was the new qualification for voting. Possession of property replaced church membership as a prerequisite for voting in colony-wide elections. Wealth replaced God's grace as the defining characteristic of Massachusetts citizenship.

Colonists chafed under increasing royal control, but they still valued English protection from hostile neighbors. Colonists worried that the Catholic colony of New France menaced frontier regions by encouraging Indian raids and by competing for the lucrative fur trade. (See "Beyond America's Borders," page 100.) Although French leaders tried to buttress the military strength of New France during the last third of the seventeenth century to block the expansion of the English colonies, most of the military efforts mustered by New France focused on defending against attacks by the powerful Iroquois. However, when the English colonies were distracted by the Glorious Revolution, French forces from the fur-trading regions along the Great Lakes and in Canada attacked villages in New England and New York. Known as King William's War, the conflict with the French was a colonial outgrowth of William's war against France in Europe. The war dragged on until 1697 and ended inconclusively in both Europe and the colonies. But it made clear to many colonists that along with English royal government came a welcome measure of military security.

> **REVIEW** Why did the Glorious Revolution in England lead to uprisings in the American colonies?

▶ Conclusion: An English Model of Colonization in North America

By 1700, the northern English colonies of North America had developed along lines quite different from the example set by their southern counterparts. Emigrants came with their families and created settlements unlike the scattered plantations and largely male environment of early Virginia. Puritans in New England built towns and governments around their churches and placed worship of God, not tobacco, at the center of their society. They depended chiefly on the labor of family members rather than on that of servants and slaves.

The convictions of Puritanism that motivated John Winthrop and others to reinvent England in the colonies became muted, however, as New England matured and dissenters such as Roger Williams multiplied. Catholics, Quakers, Anglicans (members of the Church of England), Jews, and others settled in the middle and southern colonies, creating considerable religious toleration, especially in Pennsylvania and New York. At the same time, northern colonists, like their southern counterparts, developed an ever-increasing need for land that inevitably led to bloody conflict with the Indians who were displaced. By the closing years of the seventeenth century, the royal government in England intervened to try to moderate those conflicts and to govern the colonies more directly for the benefit of the monarchy. Assertions of royal control triggered colonial resistance that was ultimately suppressed, resulting in Massachusetts losing its special charter status and becoming a royal colony much like the other British North American colonies.

During the next century, the English colonial world would undergo surprising new developments built on the achievements of the seventeenth century. Immigrants from Scotland, Ireland, and Germany streamed into North America, and unprecedented numbers of African slaves poured into the southern colonies. On average, white colonists attained a relatively comfortable standard of living, especially compared with most people in England and continental Europe. While religion remained important, the intensity of religious concern that characterized the seventeenth century waned during the eighteenth century. Colonists worried more about prosperity than about providence, and their societies grew increasingly secular, worldly, and diverse.

See the Selected Bibliography for this chapter in the Appendix.

4 Chapter Review

KEY TERMS

English Reformation (p. 79)
Puritans (p. 80)
Separatists (p. 80)
Calvinism (p. 86)
predestination (p. 86)
visible saints (p. 86)
antinomians (p. 88)
Puritan Revolution (p. 89)
Halfway Covenant (p. 90)
Quakers (p. 91)
New Netherland (p. 93)
King Philip's War (p. 98)

REVIEW QUESTIONS

1. What was a "little commonwealth," and why was it so important to New England settlement? (pp. 79–85)

2. Why did Massachusetts Puritans adopt the Halfway Covenant? (pp. 85–91)

3. How did Quaker ideals shape the colony of Pennsylvania? (pp. 92–97)

4. Why did the Glorious Revolution in England lead to uprisings in the American colonies? (pp. 97–102)

MAKING CONNECTIONS

1. How did the religious dissenters who flooded into the northern colonies address the question of religious dissent in their new homes? Comparing two colonies, discuss their different approaches.

2. John Winthrop spoke of the Massachusetts Bay colony as "a city upon a hill." What did he mean? How did this expectation influence life in New England during the seventeenth century?

3. How did religious and political turmoil in seventeenth-century England affect life in the colonies? In your answer, consider the establishment of the colonies and the crown's attempts to exercise authority over them.

4. To what extent did the New England and middle colonies become more alike during the seventeenth century? To what extent did they remain distinctive?

LINKING TO THE PAST

1. How did the communal goals of New England settlers compare with the aspirations of the tobacco and rice planters of the southern colonies? (See chapter 3.)

2. To what degree did religious intolerance shape events in the New World colonies of Spain, France, and England? (See chapters 2 and 3.)

5 Colonial America in the Eighteenth Century

1701–1770

CONTENT LEARNING OBJECTIVES

After reading and studying this chapter, you should be able to:

• Understand the link between eighteenth-century colonial population growth and economic growth.

• Explain how the market economy developed in New England and in what ways Puritanism was weakened.

• Discern how the population growth of the middle colonies differed from that of New England and the South.

• Recognize how the large influx of slaves into the southern colonies shaped the region's economy, society, and politics.

• Identify the shared experiences that unified the culture of the colonies of British North America.

• Understand how the policies of the British empire provided a common framework of political expectations and experiences for American colonists, including their relations with Native Americans throughout North America.

TEXTILE SAMPLE BOOK
These cloth samples assembled by an English textile manufacturer allowed North American colonial merchants to choose from a wide range of designs, textures, and fibers that they believed customers would purchase. Norfolk Museums Service.

THE BROTHERS AMBOE ROBIN JOHN AND LITTLE EPHRAIM ROBIN JOHN lived in Old Calabar on the Bight of Biafra in West Africa. The Robin Johns were part of a slave-trading dynasty headed by their kinsman Grandy King George, one of the most powerful leaders of the Efik people. Grandy King George owned hundreds of slaves whom he employed to capture still more slaves in the African interior. He sold these captives to captains of European slave ships for transport to the sugar, tobacco, and rice fields in the New World.

British slave ship captains and Grandy King George's African rivals conspired in 1767 to destroy the king's monopoly. In a bloody battle, Little Ephraim and Ancona Robin John were enslaved and transported across the Atlantic to the West Indies.

Unlike most slaves, the Robin Johns spoke and wrote English, a skill they had learned as slave traders in Old Calabar. The Robin Johns escaped from the man who bought them in the West Indies and boarded a ship "determined to get home," Little Ephraim wrote. But the ship captain took them to Virginia instead and sold them as slaves. Their new master "would tie me up & whip me many times for nothing at all," Ancona testified, adding that he "was exceedingly badly man ever I saw." After their master died in 1772, the Robin Johns heard that a slave ship from Old Calabar had recently arrived in Virginia, and the captain promised to take them back to Africa if they would run away. They did, but the captain took the Robin Johns to Bristol, England, and sought to sell them as slaves yet again.

While imprisoned in Bristol harbor, the Robin Johns smuggled letters to a Bristol slave trader they had known in Old Calabar. With his help, the Robin Johns appealed to the chief justice of England for their freedom on the grounds that they were unjustly enslaved because they "were free people . . . [who] had not done anything to forfeit our liberty." After complex negotiations, they won their freedom.

As free Africans in Bristol, the Robin Johns converted to Christianity, but they longed to return to Africa. In 1774, they left Bristol as free men on a slave ship bound for Old Calabar, where they resumed their careers as slave traders.

The Middle Passage
This nineteenth-century print illustrates conditions common during the eighteenth century aboard African slave trade ships on the Middle Passage between West Africa and the New World. Here enslaved Africans have been brought onto the upper deck to be fed. A barricade separated enslaved men and women, preventing the men from protecting the women. On the right, a crewman beats a shackled enslaved man while another African appears to dance, perhaps to avoid a beating. On the left, crewmen abuse enslaved women. Prudery kept the artist from realistically portraying the rapes crewmen routinely inflicted on the African women. Musée des Beaux-Arts, Chartres, France/Bridgeman Images.

The Robin Johns' quest to escape enslavement and redeem their freedom was shared but not realized by millions of Africans who were victims of slave traders such as Grandy King George and numberless merchants, ship captains, and colonists. In contrast, tens of thousands of Europeans voluntarily crossed the Atlantic to seek opportunities in North America—often by agreeing to several years of contractual servitude. Both groups illustrate the undertow of violence and deceit beneath the surface of the eighteenth-century Atlantic commerce linking Britain, Africa, the West Indies, and British North America. Many people, like the Robin Johns, turned to the consolations of religious faith as a source of meaning and hope in an often cruel and unforgiving society.

The flood of free and unfree migrants crossing the Atlantic contributed to unprecedented population growth in eighteenth-century British North America. In contrast, Spanish and French colonies in North America remained thinly populated outposts of European empires interested principally in maintaining a toehold in the vast continent. While the New England, middle, and southern colonies retained regional distinctions, commercial, cultural, and political trends built unifying experiences and assumptions among British North American colonists.

► A Growing Population and Expanding Economy in British North America

The most important fact about eighteenth-century British America is its phenomenal population growth: from about 250,000 in 1700 to more than two million by 1770. The eightfold growth of the colonial population signaled the maturation of a distinctive colonial society. A sign of the emerging significance of colonial North America is that in 1700 there were nineteen people in England for every American colonist, while by 1770 there were only three. Colonists of different ethnic

CHRONOLOGY

1711	• North Carolina founded.
1730s	• Jonathan Edwards promotes Great Awakening.
1732	• Georgia founded.
1733	• Benjamin Franklin publishes *Poor Richard's Almanack*.
1739	• Stono Rebellion takes place in South Carolina.
1740s	• George Whitefield preaches religious revival.
1745	• Olaudah Equiano born.
1750s	• Colonists move down Shenandoah Valley.
1754	• Seven Years' War begins.
1769	• First California mission established.
1770	• Mission and presidio established at Monterey, California. • British North American colonists number more than two million.

groups, races, and religions lived in varied environments under thirteen different colonial governments, all of them part of the British empire.

In general, the growth and diversity of the eighteenth-century colonial population derived from two sources: immigration and **natural increase** (growth through reproduction). Natural increase contributed about three-fourths of the population growth, immigration about one-fourth. Immigration shifted the ethnic and racial balance among the colonists, making them by 1770 less English and less white than ever before. Fewer than 10 percent of eighteenth-century immigrants came from England; about 36 percent were Scots-Irish, mostly from northern Ireland; 33 percent arrived from Africa, almost all of them slaves; nearly 15 percent had left the many German-language principalities (the nation of Germany did not exist until 1871); and almost 10 percent came from Scotland. In 1670, more than 9 out of 10 colonists were of English ancestry, and only 1 out of 25 was of African ancestry. By 1770, only about half of the colonists were of English descent, while more than 20 percent descended from Africans. Thus, by 1770, the people of the colonies had a distinctive colonial—rather than English—profile (Map 5.1).

The booming population of the colonies hints at a second major feature of eighteenth-century colonial society: an expanding economy. The nearly limitless wilderness stretching westward made land relatively cheap compared with its price in the Old World. The abundance of land made labor precious, and the colonists always needed more. The insatiable demand for labor was the fundamental economic environment that sustained the mushrooming population. Economic historians estimate that free colonists (those who were not indentured servants or slaves) had a higher standard of living than the majority of people elsewhere in the Atlantic world.

> **REVIEW**   How did the North American colonies achieve the remarkable population growth of the eighteenth century?

Map 5.1   Europeans and Africans in the Eighteenth Century
This map illustrates regions where Africans and certain immigrant groups clustered. It is important to avoid misreading the map. Predominantly English and German regions, for example, also contained colonists from other places. Likewise, regions where African slaves resided in large numbers also included many whites, slave masters among them. The map suggests the diversity of eighteenth-century colonial society.

▶ New England: From Puritan Settlers to Yankee Traders

The New England population grew sixfold during the eighteenth century but lagged behind the growth in the other colonies. Most immigrants chose other destinations because of New England's relatively densely settled land and because Puritan orthodoxy made these colonies comparatively inhospitable to those of other faiths. As the population grew, many settlers in search of farmland dispersed from towns, and Puritan communities lost much of their cohesion. Nonetheless, networks of economic exchange laced New Englanders to their neighbors, to Boston merchants, and to the broad currents of Atlantic commerce. In many ways, trade became a faith that competed strongly with the traditions of Puritanism.

Natural Increase and Land Distribution

The New England population grew mostly by natural increase, much as it had during the seventeenth century. The perils of childbirth gave wives a shorter life expectancy than husbands, but wives often lived to have six, seven, or eight babies. Anne Franklin and her husband Josiah, a soap and candle maker in Boston, had seven children before Anne died. Josiah quickly married his second wife, Abiah, and the couple had ten more children, including their son Benjamin, who became one of the most prominent colonial leaders of the eighteenth century. Like many other New Englanders, Benjamin Franklin felt hemmed in by family pressures and lack of opportunity and moved away from Boston when he was seventeen to "assert my freedom," as he put it, first in New York and then in Philadelphia.

The growing New England population pressed against a limited amount of land (see Map 5.1). Moreover, as the northernmost group of British colonies, New England had contested frontiers where powerful Native Americans, especially the Iroquois and Mahicans, jealously guarded their territory. The French (and Catholic) colony of New France also menaced the British (and mostly Protestant) New England colonies when provoked by colonial or European disputes.

During the seventeenth century, New England towns parceled out land to individual families. In most cases, the original settlers practiced **partible inheritance**—that is, they subdivided land more or less equally among sons. By the eighteenth century, the original land allotments had to be further subdivided, and many plots of land became too small to support a family. Sons who could not hope to inherit sufficient land had to move away from the town where they were born.

During the eighteenth century, colonial governments in New England abandoned the seventeenth-century policy of granting land to towns. Needing revenue, the governments of both Connecticut and Massachusetts sold

VISUAL ACTIVITY

New York Harbor

This portrait of New York harbor in about 1756 illustrates the importance of Atlantic commerce to the prosperous city in the background. The painting emphasizes a variety of oceangoing ships in the foreground. During its busiest seasons, the harbor commonly had ten times as many ships at anchor, which was nearly impossible for the artist to depict. © Collection of the New-York Historical Society, USA/Bridgeman Images.
READING THE IMAGE: How does the painting reflect New York's participation in Atlantic commerce?
CONNECTIONS: Why were port cities the largest and most prosperous cities in eighteenth-century America?

A Sailor's Life in the Eighteenth-Century Atlantic World

Although most eighteenth-century North American colonists made their living on farms, tens of thousands manned the vessels that ferried people, animals, commodities, consumer goods, ideas, and microorganisms from port to port throughout the Atlantic world. Built almost entirely from wood and fiber, ships were the most complex machines in the eighteenth century. Seamen needed to learn how to handle the intricacies of a sailing vessel quickly, smoothly, and reliably. The ship, cargo, and their own lives depended on their knowledge and dexterity. They had to endure hard physical labor for weeks or months on end in a cramped, crowded space. Sailors followed "one of the hardest and dangerousest callings," one old salt declared.

Despite the certainty of strenuous work and spartan accommodations, young men like Ashley Bowen made their way to wharves in small ports such as Marblehead, Massachusetts—Bowen's hometown—or large commercial centers such as Boston, Philadelphia, New York, and Charleston. There they boarded vessels and launched a life of seafaring, seeking the promise of a future sailing on the surface of the deep rather than rooted below the surface of the soil.

Born in 1728, Bowen grew up in Marblehead, one of the most important fishing ports in North America. Like other boys who lived in or near ports, Bowen probably watched ships come and go; heard tales of adventure, disaster, and intrigue; and learned from neighbors and pals how to maneuver small, shallow-draft boats within sight of land. Young girls sometimes learned to handle a small boat, but they almost never worked as sailors aboard Atlantic vessels. When Bowen was only eleven years old, he sailed as a ship's boy aboard a vessel captained by the father of a friend to pick up a load of tar bound for Bristol, England. The ship then loaded a cargo of coal in Wales and carried it to Boston, where Bowen, now twelve, arrived with a yearlong seafaring education under his belt.

Most commonly, young men first went to sea when they were fifteen to eighteen years old. Like Bowen, they were single, living with their parents, and looking for work. They usually sailed with friends, neighbors, or kinfolk, and they sought an education in the ways of the sea. Also like Bowen, they aspired to earn some wages, to rise in the ranks eventually from seaman to mate and possibly to master (the common term for captain), to save enough to marry and support a family, and after twenty years or so to retire from the rigors of the seafaring life with a

"competency"—that is, enough money to live modestly.

It usually took about four years at sea to become a fully competent seaman. Shortly after Bowen returned from his first voyage, his father apprenticed him to a sea captain for seven years. In return for a hefty payment, the captain agreed to tutor young Bowen in the art of seafaring, which ideally promised to ease his path to become a captain himself. In reality, the captain employed him as a cabin boy, taught him little except to obey, and beat him for trivial mistakes, causing Bowen to run away after four years of servitude.

Now seventeen years old, Bowen had already sailed to dozens of ports in North America, the West Indies, the British Isles, and Europe. For the next eighteen years, he shipped out as a common seaman on scores of vessels carrying nearly every kind of cargo afloat on the Atlantic. He sailed mostly aboard merchant freighters, but he also worked on whalers, fishing boats, privateers, and warships. He survived sickness, imprisonment, foul weather, accidents, and innumerable close calls. But when he retired from seafaring at age thirty-five, he still had not managed to attain command. In twenty-four years at sea, he had worked as either a common seaman or a mate. For whatever

land directly to individuals, including speculators. Now money, rather than membership in a community bound by a church covenant, determined whether a person could obtain land. The new land policy eroded the seventeenth-century pattern of settlement. As colonists spread north and west, they tended to settle on individual farms rather than in the towns and villages that characterized the seventeenth century. Far more than in the seventeenth century, eighteenth-century New Englanders regulated their behavior by their own individual choices.

Farms, Fish, and Atlantic Trade

A New England farm was a place to get by, not to get rich. New England farmers grew food for their families, but their fields did not produce huge marketable surpluses. Instead of one big crop, a farmer grew many small ones. If farmers had extra, they sold to or

reason, when most shipowners eyed Bowen, they did not see a man they would trust to command their vessels.

Like Bowen, about three out of ten seamen spent their entire seafaring lives as seamen or mates, earning five dollars or so a month in wages, roughly comparable to the wages of farm laborers. Another three out of ten seamen died at sea, many by drowning or as a result of injuries or, most commonly, from tropical diseases usually picked up in the West Indies. Bowen lived to the age of eighty-five, working as a rigger, crafting nautical fittings for sailing vessels. When Bowen, like thousands of other seafarers, looked at the world, his gaze did not turn west toward the farms and forests of the interior but rather turned east, toward the promise of the Atlantic deep beyond.

Ashley Bowen's Journal
Ashley Bowen painted these watercolors of ships he sailed aboard in 1754, 1755, and 1756. He paid attention to the distinctive rigging and flags of each vessel, and he kept notes about the vessels' owners, masters, mates, passengers, and destinations. The vessels dwarf the buildings of Marblehead, Massachusetts, in the background. Why might the differences among ships be important to Bowen? Photo courtesy of the Marblehead Museum, Marblehead, MA.

Questions for Analysis

Summarize the Argument: What promise did Bowen see in a seafaring life? To what degree did he realize that promise?

Analyze the Evidence: How did Bowen's experiences at sea compare to those of other seamen? What specific challenges and opportunities did he encounter?

Consider the Context: How did Bowen's experiences as a seaman compare to those of farmers in the colonies?

Recognize Viewpoints: How might Bowen's outlook on the world compare to that of the vast majority of colonists who seldom or never went to sea?

traded with neighbors. Poor roads made travel difficult, time-consuming, and expensive, especially with bulky and heavy agricultural goods. The one major agricultural product the New England colonies exported—livestock—walked to market on its own legs. By 1770, New Englanders had only one-fourth as much wealth per capita as free colonists in the southern colonies.

As consumers, New England farmers participated in a diversified commercial economy that linked remote farms to markets throughout the Atlantic world. Merchants large and small stocked imported goods—British textiles, ceramics, and metal goods; Chinese tea; West Indian sugar; and Chesapeake tobacco. Farmers' needs supported local shoemakers, tailors, wheelwrights, and carpenters. Larger towns, especially Boston, housed skilled tradesmen such as cabinetmakers, silversmiths, and printers. Shipbuilders were among the many New Englanders who made their fortunes at sea.

Fish accounted for more than a third of New England's eighteenth-century exports; livestock and timber made up another third. The West Indies absorbed two-thirds of all New England's exports. Slaves on Caribbean sugar plantations ate dried, salted codfish caught by New England fishermen, filled barrels crafted from New England timber with molasses and refined sugar, and loaded those barrels aboard ships bound ultimately for Europeans with a taste for rum (made from molasses) and sweets. Almost all of the rest of New England's exports went to Britain and continental Europe (Map 5.2).

This Atlantic commerce benefited the entire New England economy, providing jobs for laborers and tradesmen as well as for ship captains, clerks, merchants, and sailors. (See "Experiencing the American Promise," page 110.)

Merchants dominated Atlantic commerce. The largest and most successful New England merchants lived in Boston at the hub of trade between local folk and the international market. The magnificence of a wealthy Boston merchant's home stunned John Adams, who termed it a house that seemed fit "for a noble Man, a Prince." Such luxurious Boston homes contrasted with

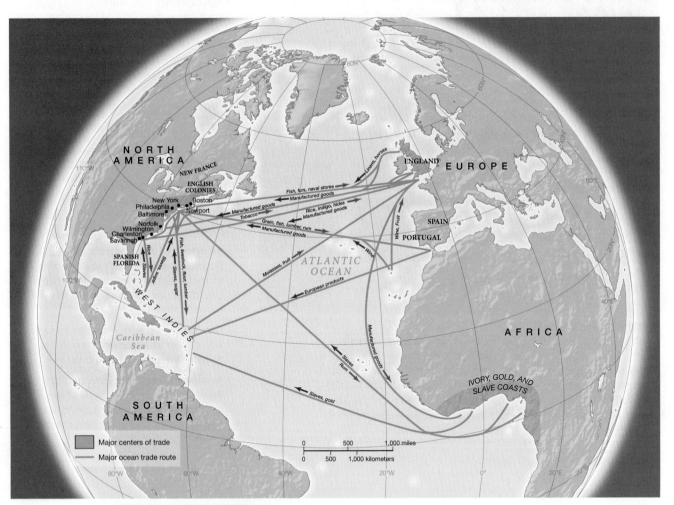

MAP ACTIVITY

Map 5.2   Atlantic Trade in the Eighteenth Century

This map illustrates the economic outlook of the colonies in the eighteenth century—east toward the Atlantic world rather than west toward the interior of North America. The long distances involved in the Atlantic trade and the uncertainties of ocean travel suggest the difficulties Britain experienced governing the colonies and regulating colonial commerce.

READING THE MAP: What were the major markets for trade coming out of Europe? What goods did the British colonies import and export?

CONNECTIONS: In what ways did the flow of raw materials from the colonies affect British industry? How did British colonial trade policies influence the Atlantic trade?

the modest dwellings of Adams and other New Englanders, a measure of the polarization of wealth that developed in Boston and other seaports during the eighteenth century.

By 1770, the richest 5 percent of Bostonians owned about half the city's wealth; the poorest two-thirds of the population owned less than one-tenth. Still, the incidence of genuine poverty did not change much. About 5 percent of New Englanders qualified for poor relief throughout the eighteenth century. Overall, colonists were better off than most people in England.

New England was more homogeneously English than any other colonial region. People of African ancestry (almost all of them slaves) numbered more than fifteen thousand by 1770, but they barely diversified the region's 97 percent white majority. Most New Englanders had little use for slaves on their family farms. Instead, the few slaves concentrated in towns, especially Boston, where most of them worked as domestic servants and laborers.

By 1770, the population, wealth, and commercial activity of New England differed from what they had been in 1700. Ministers still enjoyed high status, but Yankee traders had replaced Puritan saints as the symbolic New Englanders. Atlantic commerce competed with religious convictions in ordering New Englanders' daily lives.

REVIEW   Why did settlement patterns in New England change from the seventeenth to the eighteenth century?

VISUAL ACTIVITY

Boston Common in Needlework

Hannah Otis embroidered this portrait of Boston Common in 1750 when she was eighteen years old. The house belonged to the Hancock family. John Hancock, who later signed the Declaration of Independence, is shown on horseback. The needlework reveals that eighteenth-century Bostonians owned slaves. Museum of Fine Arts, Boston, Massachusetts, USA/Gift of a Friend of the Department of American Decorative Arts and Sculpture and 15 other funds/Bridgeman Images.

READING THE IMAGE: What features of the portrait would communicate to an eighteenth-century viewer that it portrays a city?

CONNECTIONS: How did life in Boston differ from that on rural farms in New England?

▶ The Middle Colonies: Immigrants, Wheat, and Work

In 1700, the middle colonies of Pennsylvania, New York, New Jersey, and Delaware had only half the population of New England. But by 1770, the population of the middle colonies had multiplied tenfold and nearly equaled the population of New England. Immigrants—mainly German, Irish, Scottish—made the middle colonies a uniquely diverse society. By 1800, barely one-third of Pennsylvanians and less than half the total population of the middle colonies traced their ancestry to England. New white settlers, both free and in servitude, poured into the middle colonies because they perceived unparalleled opportunities.

German and Scots-Irish Immigrants

Germans made up the largest contingent of migrants from the European continent to the middle colonies. By 1770, about 85,000 Germans had arrived in the colonies. Their fellow colonists often referred to them as **Pennsylvania Dutch**, an English corruption of *Deutsch*, the word the immigrants used to describe themselves.

Most German immigrants came from what is now southwestern Germany, where, one observer noted, peasants were "not as well off as cattle elsewhere." German immigrants included numerous artisans and a few merchants, but the great majority were farmers and laborers. Economically, they represented "middling folk," neither the poorest (who could not afford the trip) nor the better-off (who did not want to leave).

By the 1720s, Germans who had established themselves in the colonies wrote back to their friends and relatives, as one reported, "of the civil and religious liberties [and] privileges, and of all the goodness I have heard and seen." Such letters prompted still more Germans to pull up stakes and embark for the middle colonies.

Similar motives propelled the **Scots-Irish**, who considerably outnumbered German immigrants. The "Scots-Irish" actually hailed from northern Ireland, Scotland, and northern England. Like the Germans, the Scots-Irish were Protestants, but with a difference. Most German immigrants worshipped in Lutheran or German Reformed churches; many others belonged to dissenting sects such as the Mennonites, Moravians, and Amish, whose adherents sought relief from persecution they had suffered in Europe for their refusal to bear arms and to swear oaths, practices they shared with the Quakers. In contrast, the Scots-Irish tended to be militant Presbyterians who seldom hesitated to bear arms or swear oaths. Like German settlers, however, Scots-Irish immigrants were clannish, residing when they could among relatives or neighbors from the old country.

In the eighteenth century, wave after wave of Scots-Irish immigrants arrived, culminating in a flood of immigration in the years just before the American Revolution. Deteriorating economic conditions in northern Ireland, Scotland, and England pushed many toward America. One Ulster Scot remarked that "oppression has brought us" to the "deplorable state . . . [that] the very marrow is screwed out of our bones." Most of the immigrants were farm laborers or tenant farmers fleeing droughts, crop failures, high food prices, or rising rents. They came, they told British officials, because of "poverty," the "tyranny of landlords," and their desire to "do better in America."

Both Scots-Irish and Germans probably heard the common saying "Pennsylvania is heaven for farmers [and] paradise for artisans," but they almost certainly did not fully understand the risks of their decision to leave their native lands. Ship captains, aware of the hunger for labor in the colonies, eagerly signed up the penniless German emigrants as **redemptioners**, a variant of indentured servants. A captain would agree to provide transportation to Philadelphia, where redemptioners would obtain the money to pay for their passage by borrowing it from a friend or relative who was already in the colonies or, as most did, by selling themselves as servants. Many redemptioners traveled in family groups, unlike impoverished Scots-Irish emigrants, who usually traveled alone and paid for their passage by contracting as indentured servants before they sailed to the colonies.

Redemptioners and indentured servants were packed aboard ships "as closely as herring," one migrant observed. Seasickness compounded by exhaustion, poverty, poor food, bad water, inadequate sanitation, and tight quarters encouraged the spread of disease. When one ship finally approached land, a passenger wrote, "everyone crawls from below to the deck . . . and people cry for joy, pray, and sing praises and thanks to God." Unfortunately, their troubles were far from over. Unlike indentured servants, redemptioners negotiated independently with their purchasers about their period of servitude. Typically, a healthy adult redemptioner agreed to four years of labor. Indentured servants commonly served five, six, or seven years.

"God Gives All Things to Industry": Urban and Rural Labor

An indentured servant in 1743 wrote that Pennsylvania was "the best poor Man's Country in the World." Although the servant reported that "the Condition of bought Servants is very hard" and masters often failed to live up to their promise to provide decent food and clothing, opportunity abounded in the middle colonies because there was more work to be done than workers to do it.

Most servants toiled in Philadelphia, New York City, or one of the smaller towns or villages. Artisans, small manufacturers, and shopkeepers prized the labor of male servants. Female servants made valuable additions to households, where nearly all of them cleaned, washed, cooked, or minded children. From the masters' viewpoint, servants were a bargain. A master could purchase five or six years of a servant's labor for approximately the wages a common laborer would earn in four months.

Since a slave cost about three times more than a servant, only affluent colonists could afford the long-term investment in slave labor. Most farmers in the middle colonies used family labor, not slaves. Wheat, the most widely grown crop, did not require more labor than farmers could typically muster from relatives, neighbors, and a hired hand or two. Consequently, although people of African ancestry (almost all slaves) increased to more than thirty thousand in the middle colonies by 1770, they accounted for only about 7 percent of the total population and much less outside the cities.

Most slaves came to the middle colonies and New England after a stopover in the West Indies, as the Robin Johns did. Very few came directly from Africa. Slaves—unlike servants—could not charge masters with violating the terms of their contracts. Colonial laws punished slaves much more severely than servants for the same offense. Officials worried, for example, about "tippling" houses where "Negro Slaves and divers other person of Idle and suspected character . . . [were] drinking and behaving disorderly to the Great Disturbance of the Inhabitants . . . [by] offending against the peace of our . . . Lord the King his Crown and Dignity." Small numbers of slaves managed to obtain their freedom, but no African Americans escaped whites' firm convictions about black inferiority.

Whites' racism and blacks' lowly social status made African Americans scapegoats for European Americans' suspicions and anxieties. In 1741, when arson and several unexplained thefts plagued New York City, officials suspected a murderous slave conspiracy and executed thirty-one slaves. On the basis of little evidence other than the slaves' "insolence" (refusal to conform fully to whites' expectations of servile behavior), city authorities burned thirteen slaves at the stake and hanged eighteen others. Although slaves were certifiably impoverished, they were not among the poor for whom the middle colonies were reputed to be the best country in the world. (See "Making Historical Arguments," page 116.)

Immigrants swarmed to the middle colonies because of the availability of land. The Penn family (see "New Jersey and Pennsylvania" in chapter 4) encouraged immigration to bring in potential buyers for their enormous tracts of land in Pennsylvania. From the beginning, Pennsylvania followed a policy of negotiating with Indian tribes to purchase additional land. This policy reduced the violent frontier clashes more common elsewhere in the colonies. Few colonists drifted beyond the northern boundaries of Pennsylvania. Owners of the huge estates in New York's Hudson valley preferred to rent rather than sell their land, and therefore they attracted fewer immigrants. The Iroquois Indians dominated the lucrative fur trade of the St. Lawrence valley and eastern Great Lakes, and they vigorously defended their territory from colonial encroachment, causing most settlers to prefer the comparatively safe environs of Pennsylvania.

Since the cheapest land always lay at the margin of settlement, would-be farmers tended to migrate to promising areas just beyond already improved farms. By midcentury, settlement had reached the eastern slopes of the Appalachian Mountains, and newcomers spilled south down the fertile valley of the Shenandoah River into western Virginia and the Carolinas. Thousands of settlers migrated from the middle colonies through this back door to the South. Abraham Lincoln's great-grandfather, John Lincoln—whose own grandfather, Mordecai, had migrated from England to Puritan Massachusetts in the 1630s—moved his family in the 1760s from Pennsylvania down the Shenandoah Valley into Virginia, where the future president's grandfather, also named

Patterns of Settlement, 1700–1770

Why Did Few Colonists Oppose the African Slave Trade?

During the eighteenth century, the African slave trade carried more enslaved Africans across the Atlantic than ever before or since. From today's perspective, we might expect the booming trade to have engendered numerous outspoken opponents. But before the American Revolution, critics of the African slave trade were few, far between, and not influential. Why?

Enslaved Africans universally opposed becoming commodities in the trans-Atlantic slave trade, but they had little power to resist. For centuries, in Europe, Africa, Asia, and the Middle East, enslavement had been considered a legitimate fate for people captured during a war. Kidnapping for the purpose of enslavement was widely thought to be illegitimate, but in practice the boundary between legitimate and illegitimate enslavement was murky and almost impossible to enforce. Africans captured other Africans, whether legitimately or illegitimately, and ultimately sold the captives to European slave traders. Slaves aboard as many as one-tenth of all ships in the African trade tried to escape their bondage by revolting. But nearly all revolts occurred while slaves and ships were in sight of the African coast, strong evidence that hopes of escape evaporated as Africa slipped beneath the eastern horizon.

The horrors of the slave trade were no secret, but most people in the colonies as well as in Britain and on the European continent considered pain and suffering a regrettable but inescapable part of life. The brutality inflicted on enslaved Africans seemed to many colonists an extreme form of the harsh conditions of life everyone confronted and took for granted. Occasionally colonists acknowledged the miseries of enslavement by referring to slaves as "poor Negroes" or "poor Africans," terminology that reflected a measure of sympathy and a sense that slaves were unlucky victims of circumstance. But this sympathy was tempered by deeply held racial prejudices that justified vicious mistreatment of blacks, who were considered inferior to Euro-Americans.

Leading merchants who bought and sold enslaved Africans in ports such as Charleston, Philadelphia, Providence, New York, and Boston profited from the trade and did all they could to keep it going. They wanted enslaved Africans to be healthy and robust because then they could be sold for higher prices. Slave traders believed, however, that brutality was necessary to prevent revolts by enslaved Africans, who greatly outnumbered the crewmen

---

Abraham, raised his family, including the future president's father, Thomas Lincoln.

Farmers like the Lincolns made the middle colonies the breadbasket of North America. They planted a wide variety of crops to feed their families, but they grew wheat in abundance. Flour milling was the number one industry and flour the number one export, constituting nearly three-fourths of all exports from the middle colonies. Farmers profited from the grain market in the Atlantic world. By 1770 a bushel of wheat was worth twice as much (adjusted for inflation) as it had been in 1720. The steady rise of grain prices after 1720 helped make the standard of living in rural Pennsylvania higher than in any other agricultural region of the eighteenth-century world. The comparatively widespread prosperity of all the middle colonies permitted residents to indulge in a half-century shopping spree for British imports. Commerce was so popular that a prominent New Yorker asked a friend in London to send him a few goods to "please a little boy & Girl who want to be merchants as soon as they can speak like their play fellows the Dutch Children here." The middle colonies' per capita consumption of imported goods from Britain more than doubled between 1720 and 1770, far outstripping the per capita consumption of British goods in New England and the southern colonies.

Philadelphia stood at the crossroads of trade in wheat exports and British imports. Merchants occupied the top stratum of Philadelphia society. In a city where only 2 percent of the residents owned enough property to qualify to vote, merchants built grand homes and dominated local government. Many of Philadelphia's wealthiest merchants were Quakers. Quaker traits of industry, thrift, honesty, and sobriety encouraged the accumulation of wealth. A colonist complained that a Quaker "prays for his neighbors on First Days [Sabbaths] and then preys on him the other six."

aboard slave ships. Far from condemning or stigmatizing slave traders, other colonists respected them, bought slaves from them, borrowed money from them, and did not object to their daughters marrying them. Indeed, the slave trade was often seen as a sterling example of the great freedom colonists enjoyed as members of the British empire. Even most Christians who sought to live up to the biblical commandment to "do unto others as you would have them do unto you" felt few pangs of conscience about the African slave trade.

A few renegade Quakers became outspoken antislavery activists during the first half of the eighteenth century. Although Quakers were a tiny minority of colonists, they often prospered and bought slaves. A small number of Quakers denounced slavery and the trade in slaves for promoting worldliness and luxury rather than the simple life of faith and suffering professed by Quakers. In 1738, Pennsylvania Quaker Benjamin Lay went so far as to kidnap a white child belonging to a Quaker slaveholder to demonstrate the violence of the slave trade. Lay believed owning slaves corrupted all Quakers' faith, a point

he dramatized at the 1738 Philadelphia Yearly Meeting of Quakers meeting by plunging a sword into a Bible hollowed out to hold a container of pokeberry juice and splattering the blood-like fluid on his coreligionists. Beginning in the 1740s, New Jersey Quaker John Woolman visited individual Quaker slaveholders and quietly talked to them about his belief that God expected people "to exercise goodness toward every living creature," especially those like slaves who were suffering. Like Lay, Woolman worked to persuade slaveholders to liberate their slaves and thereby purge slaveholding from the Quaker faith in order to purify their church and fulfill their divine obligation to be kind to all creatures. Anthony Benezet, another Philadelphia Quaker, proclaimed that "nothing can be more inconsistent with the Doctrines and Practice of our meek Lord and Master, nor stained with a deeper Dye or Injustice, Cruelty and Oppression . . . [than] the SLAVE TRADE." The efforts of Lay, Woolman, Benezet, and others led the Philadelphia Quaker meeting in 1758 to encourage Quakers to free their slaves and to exclude slaveholders

from participating in the affairs of the church. But for the most part, these pioneering antislavery initiatives were confined to a small number of Quakers and ignored by the vast majority of colonists, for whom the African slave trade was business as usual.

Questions for Analysis

Summarize the Argument: Why did the African slave trade engender so little opposition among colonists? What motivated a few Quakers to oppose the trade?

Analyze the Evidence: How did supporters of the African slave trade justify its cruelty and violence? What arguments did Quakers use to denounce slavery and the slave trade?

Consider the Context: What did slave traders consider the fundamental context of the African slave trade? How did their view contrast with that of antislavery Quakers? How did colonists' attitudes toward the slave trade reflect their thinking about markets, freedom, inequality, and race?

The lower ranks of merchants included aspiring tradesmen such as Benjamin Franklin. In 1728, Franklin opened a small shop, run mostly by his wife, Deborah, that sold a little of everything: cheese, codfish, coffee, goose feathers, soap, and occasionally a slave. In 1733, Franklin began to publish *Poor Richard's Almanack*, which preached the likelihood of long-term rewards for tireless labor and quickly became Franklin's most profitable product. The popularity of *Poor Richard's Almanack* suggests that many Pennsylvanians thought less about the pearly gates of heaven than about their pocketbooks. Poor Richard's advice that "God gives all Things to Industry" might be considered the motto for the middle colonies. The promise of a worldly payoff made work a secular faith. Poor Richard advised, "Work as if you were to live 100 years, Pray as if you were to die Tomorrow."

Although Quakers remained influential in Pennsylvania, Franklin spoke for most colonists

with his aphorisms of work, discipline, and thrift that celebrated the spark of ambition and the promise of worldly gain.

> **REVIEW** Why did immigrants flood into Pennsylvania during the eighteenth century?

▶ The Southern Colonies: Land of Slavery

Between 1700 and 1770, the population of the southern colonies of Virginia, Maryland, North Carolina, South Carolina, and Georgia grew almost ninefold. By 1770, about twice as many people lived in the South as in either the middle colonies or New England. As elsewhere, natural increase and immigration accounted for the rapid population growth. Many Scots-Irish and German immigrants funneled from the middle colonies into the southern backcountry. Other immigrants were indentured servants (mostly English and Scots-Irish). But slaves made the most striking contribution to the booming southern colonies, transforming the racial composition of the population. Slavery became the defining characteristic of the southern colonies during the eighteenth century, shaping the region's economy, society, and politics.

The Atlantic Slave Trade and the Growth of Slavery

The number of southerners of African ancestry (nearly all of them slaves) rocketed from just over 20,000 in 1700 to well over 400,000 in 1770. The black population increased nearly three times faster than the South's briskly growing white population. Consequently, the proportion of southerners of African ancestry grew from 20 percent in 1700 to 40 percent in 1770.

Southern colonists clustered into two distinct geographic and agricultural zones. The colonies in the upper South, surrounding the Chesapeake Bay, specialized in growing tobacco, as they had since the early seventeenth century. Throughout the eighteenth century, nine out of ten southern whites and eight out of ten southern blacks lived in the Chesapeake region. The upper South retained a white majority during the eighteenth century.

In the lower South, a much smaller cluster of colonists inhabited the coastal region and specialized in the production of rice and indigo (a plant used to make blue dye). Lower South colonists made up only 5 percent of the total population of the southern colonies in 1700 but inched upward to 15 percent by 1770. South Carolina was the sole British colony along the southern Atlantic coast until 1732. (North Carolina, founded in 1711, was largely an extension of the Chesapeake region.) Georgia was founded in 1732 as a refuge for poor people from England. Georgia's leaders banned slaves from 1735 to 1750, but few settlers arrived until after 1750, when the prohibition on slavery was lifted and slaves flooded in. In South Carolina, in contrast to Georgia and every other British mainland colony, slaves outnumbered whites almost two to one; in some low-country districts, the ratio of blacks to whites exceeded ten to one.

The enormous growth in the South's slave population occurred through natural increase

TABLE 5.1	SLAVE IMPORTS, 1451–1870
Estimated Slave Imports to the Western Hemisphere	
1451–1600	275,000
1601–1700	1,341,000
1701–1810	6,100,000
1811–1870	1,900,000

and the flourishing Atlantic slave trade (Table 5.1 and Map 5.3). Slave ships brought almost 300,000 Africans to British North America between 1619 and 1780. Of these Africans, 95 percent arrived in the South and 96 percent arrived during the eighteenth century. Unlike indentured servants and redemptioners, these Africans did not choose to come to the colonies. Like the Robin Johns, most of them had been born into free families in villages located within a few hundred miles of the West African coast. Although they shared African origins, they came from many different African cultures, such as Akan, Angolan, Asante, Bambara, Gambian, Igbo, and Mandinga, among others. They spoke different languages, worshipped different deities, observed different rules of kinship, grew different crops, and recognized different rulers. The most important experience they had in common was enslavement.

Captured in war, kidnapped, or sold into slavery by other Africans, they were brought to the coast, sold to African traders like the Robin Johns who assembled slaves for resale, and sold again to European or colonial slave traders or ship captains, who packed two hundred to three hundred or more aboard ships that carried them on the **Middle Passage** across the Atlantic and then sold them yet again to colonial slave merchants or southern planters.

Olaudah Equiano published an account of his enslavement that hints at the common experiences of millions of other Africans swept up in the slave trade. In 1756 when he was eleven years old, Equiano was kidnapped by Africans in what is now Nigeria, who sold him to other Africans, who in turn eventually sold him to a slave ship on the coast. Equiano wrote that he "had never heard of white men or Europeans, nor of the sea," and he feared that he was "going to be killed" and "eaten by those white men with horrible looks, red faces, and loose hair." Once the ship set sail, many of the slaves, crowded together in suffocating heat fouled by filth of all descriptions, died from sickness. "The shrieks of the women

VISUAL ACTIVITY

Bethlehem, Pennsylvania
This view of Bethlehem, Pennsylvania, in 1757 dramatizes the profound transformation of the natural land-scape humans wrought in the eighteenth century. In less than twenty years, precisely laid-out orchards and fields replaced forests and glades. By carefully penning their livestock (lower center right) and fencing their fields (lower left), farmers safeguarded their livelihoods from the risks and disorders of untamed nature. In-dividual farmsteads (lower center) and brick town buildings (upper center) integrated the bounty of the land with community life. Few eighteenth-century communities were as orderly as Bethlehem, but many effected a comparable transformation of the environment. The New York Public Library/Art Resource, NY.
READING THE IMAGE: What does this painting indicate about the colonists' priorities?
CONNECTIONS: Why might Pennsylvanians have been so concerned about maintaining order?

and the groans of the dying rendered the whole a scene of horror almost inconceivable," Equiano recalled. Most of the slaves on the ship were sold in Barbados, but Equiano and other leftovers were shipped off to Virginia, where he "saw few or none of our native Africans and not one soul who could talk to me." Equiano felt isolated and

"exceedingly miserable" because he "had no per-son to speak to that I could understand." Finally, the captain of a tobacco ship bound for England purchased Equiano, and he traveled as an enslaved sailor between North America, England, and the West Indies for ten years until he succeeded in buying his freedom in 1766.

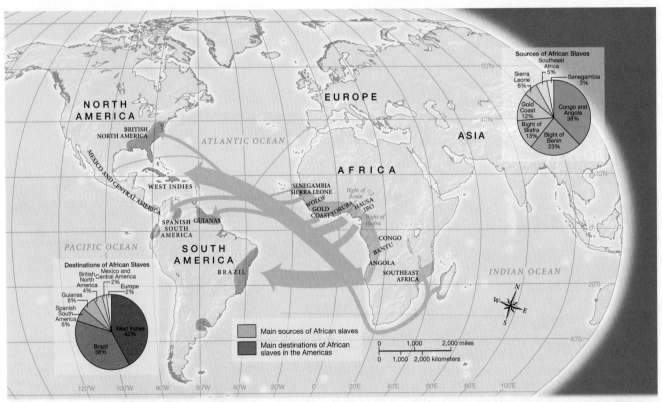

MAP ACTIVITY

Map 5.3   The Atlantic Slave Trade

Although the Atlantic slave trade lasted from about 1450 to 1870, it peaked during the eighteenth century, when more than six million African slaves were imported to the New World. Only a small fraction of these slaves were taken to British North America. Most went to sugar plantations in Brazil and the Caribbean.

READING THE MAP: Where in Africa did most slaves originate? Approximately how far was the trip from the busiest ports of origin to the two most common New World destinations?

CONNECTIONS: Why were so many more African slaves sent to the West Indies and Brazil than to British North America?

Only about 15 percent of the slaves brought into the southern colonies came aboard ships from the West Indies, as Equiano and the Robin Johns did. All the other slaves brought into the southern colonies came directly from Africa, and almost all the ships that brought them (roughly 90 percent) belonged to British merchants. Most of the slaves on board were young adults, with men usually outnumbering women two to one. Children under the age of fourteen, like Equiano, typically accounted for no more than 10 to 15 percent of a cargo.

Mortality during the Middle Passage varied considerably from ship to ship. On average, about 15 percent of the slaves died, but sometimes half or more perished. The average mortality among the white crew of slave ships was often nearly as bad. In general, the longer the voyage lasted, the more people died. Slaves and crew succumbed not only to epidemic diseases such as smallpox and

dysentery but also to acute dehydration caused by fluid loss from perspiration, vomiting, and diarrhea combined with a severe shortage of drinking water.

Normally, an individual planter purchased at any one time a relatively small number of newly arrived Africans, or **new Negroes**, as they were called. New Negroes were often profoundly depressed, demoralized, and disoriented. Planters expected their other slaves—either those born into slavery in the colonies (often called country-born or creole slaves) or Africans who had arrived earlier—to help new Negroes become accustomed to their strange new surroundings. Planters' preferences for slaves from specific regions of Africa aided slaves' acculturation (or seasoning, as it was called) to the routine of bondage in the southern colonies. Chesapeake planters preferred slaves from Senegambia, the Gold Coast, or—like Equiano and the Robin Johns—the Bight of

Biafra, which combined accounted for about 40 percent of Africans imported to the Chesapeake. South Carolina planters favored slaves from the central African Congo and Angola regions, the origin of about 40 percent of the slaves they imported. Although slaves spoke many different languages, enough linguistic and cultural similarities existed that they could usually communicate with other Africans from the same region.

New Africans had to adjust to the physical as well as the cultural environment of the southern colonies. Slaves who had just endured the Middle Passage were poorly nourished, weak, and sick. In this vulnerable state, they encountered the alien diseases of North America without having developed a biological arsenal of acquired immunities. As many as 10 to 15 percent of newly arrived Africans died during their first year in the southern colonies. Nonetheless, the large number of newly enslaved Africans made the influence of African culture in the South stronger in the eighteenth century than ever before—or since.

While newly enslaved Africans poured into the southern colonies, slave mothers bore children, which caused the slave population in the South to grow rapidly. Slave owners encouraged these births. Thomas Jefferson explained, "I consider the labor of a breeding [slave] woman as no object, that a [slave] child raised every 2 years is of more profit than the crop of the best laboring [slave] man." Although slave mothers loved and nurtured their children, the mortality rate among slave children was high, and the ever-present risk of being separated by sale brought grief to many slave families. Nonetheless, the growing number of slave babies set the southern colonies apart from other New World slave societies, where mortality rates were so high that deaths exceeded births. The high rate of natural increase in the southern colonies meant that by the 1740s the majority of southern slaves were country-born.

Slave Labor and African American Culture

Southern planters expected slaves to work from sunup to sundown and beyond. George Washington wrote that his slaves should "be at their work as soon as it is light, work til it is dark, and be diligent while they are at it." The conflict between the masters' desire for maximum labor and the slaves' reluctance to do more than necessary made the threat of physical punishment a constant for eighteenth-century slaves. Masters preferred black slaves to white indentured servants, not just because slaves served for life but also because colonial laws did not limit the force masters could use against slaves. Slaves often resisted their masters' demands, one traveler noted, because of their "greatness of soul"—their stubborn unwillingness to conform to their masters' definition of them as merely slaves.

Some slaves escalated their acts of resistance to direct physical confrontation with the master, the mistress, or an overseer. But a hoe raised in anger, a punch in the face, or a desperate swipe with a knife led to swift and predictable retaliation by whites. Throughout the southern colonies, the balance of physical power rested securely in the hands of whites.

Rebellion occurred, however, at Stono, South Carolina, in 1739. A group of about twenty slaves attacked a country store, killed the two storekeepers, and confiscated the store's guns, ammunition, and powder. Enticing other slaves to join, the group plundered and burned more than half a dozen plantations and killed more than twenty white men, women, and children. A mounted force of whites quickly suppressed the rebellion. They placed the rebels' heads atop mileposts along the

Olaudah Equiano
Painted after he had bought his freedom, this portrait evokes Equiano's successful acculturation to eighteenth-century English customs. In his *Interesting Narrative*, Equiano wrote that he "looked upon [the English] . . . as men superior to us [Africans], and therefore I had the stronger desire to resemble them, to imbibe their spirit and imitate their manners." Library of Congress, 3b01988.

main road, grim reminders of the consequences of rebellion. The South Carolina legislature enacted a draconian slave code in 1740 to punish with the utmost severity enslaved "negroes from the coast of Africa who are generally of a barbarous and savage disposition." The **Stono Rebellion** illustrated that eighteenth-century slaves had no chance of overturning slavery and very little chance of defending themselves in any bold strike for freedom. No other similar uprisings occurred during the colonial period.

Slaves maneuvered constantly to protect themselves and to gain a measure of autonomy within the boundaries of slavery. In Chesapeake tobacco fields, most slaves were subject to close supervision by whites. In the lower South, the **task system** gave slaves some control over the pace of their work and some discretion in the use of the rest of their time. A "task" was typically defined as a certain area of ground to be cultivated or a specific job to be completed. A slave who completed the assigned task might use the remainder of the day, if any, to work in a garden, fish, hunt, spin, weave, sew, or cook. When masters sought to boost productivity by increasing tasks, slaves did what they could to defend their customary work assignments.

Eighteenth-century slaves also planted the roots of African American lineages that branch out to the present. Slaves valued family ties, and, as in West African societies, kinship structured slaves' relations with one another. Slave parents often gave a child the name of a grandparent, aunt, or uncle. In West Africa, kinship identified a person's place among living relatives and linked the person to ancestors in the past and to descendants in the future. Newly imported African slaves usually arrived alone, like Equiano, without kin. Often slaves who had traversed the Middle Passage on the same ship adopted one another as "brothers" and "sisters." Likewise, as new Negroes were seasoned and incorporated into existing slave communities, established families often adopted them as fictive kin.

When possible, slaves expressed many other features of their West African origins in their lives on New World plantations. They gave their children African names such as Cudjo or Quash, Minda or Fuladi. They grew food crops they had known in Africa, such as yams and okra. They constructed huts with mud walls and thatched roofs similar to African residences. They fashioned banjos, drums, and other musical instruments, held dances, and observed funeral rites that echoed African practices. In these and many other ways, slaves drew upon their African her-

itages as much as the oppressive circumstances of slavery permitted.

Tobacco, Rice, and Prosperity

Slaves' labor bestowed prosperity on their masters, British merchants, and the monarchy. Slavery was so important and valuable that one minister claimed in 1757 that "to live in Virginia without slaves is morally impossible." The southern colonies supplied 90 percent of all North American exports to Britain. Rice exports from the lower South exploded from less than half a million pounds in 1700 to eighty million pounds in 1770, nearly all of it grown by slaves. Exports of indigo also boomed. Together, rice and indigo made up three-fourths of lower South exports, nearly two-thirds of them going to Britain and most of the rest to the West Indies, where sugar-growing slaves ate slave-grown rice.

Tobacco was by far the most important export from British North America; by 1770, it represented almost one-third of all colonial exports and three-fourths of all Chesapeake exports.

Colonial Slave Drum
An African in Virginia made this drum sometime around the beginning of the eighteenth century. The drum combines deerskin and cedarwood from North America with African workmanship and designs. During rare moments of respite from their work, slaves played drums to accompany dances learned in Africa. They also drummed out messages from plantation to plantation. © The Trustees of the British Museum/Art Resource, NY.

Under the provisions of the Navigation Acts (see "Royal Regulation of Colonial Trade" in chapter 4), nearly all of it went to Britain, where the monarchy collected a lucrative tax on each pound. British merchants then reexported more than 80 percent of the tobacco to the European continent, pocketing a nice markup for their troubles.

These products of slave labor made the southern colonies by far the richest in North America. The per capita wealth of free whites in the South was four times greater than that in New England and three times that in the middle colonies. At the top of the wealth pyramid stood the rice grandees of the lower South and the tobacco gentry of the Chesapeake. These elite families commonly resided on large estates in handsome mansions adorned by luxurious gardens, all maintained and supported by slaves.

The vast differences in wealth among white southerners engendered envy and occasional tension between rich and poor, but remarkably little open hostility. In private, the planter elite spoke disparagingly of humble whites, but in public the planters acknowledged their lesser neighbors as equals, at least in belonging to the superior—in their minds—white race. Looking upward, white yeomen and tenants (who owned neither land nor slaves) sensed the gentry's condescension and veiled contempt. But they also appreciated the gentry for granting favors, upholding white supremacy, and keeping slaves in their place. Although racial slavery made a few whites much richer than others, it also gave those who did not get rich a powerful reason to feel similar in race to those who were so different in wealth.

The slaveholding gentry dominated the politics and economy of the southern colonies. In Virginia, only adult white men who owned at least one hundred acres of unimproved land or twenty-five acres of land with a house could vote. This property-holding requirement prevented about 40 percent of white men in Virginia from voting for representatives to the House of Burgesses. In South Carolina, the property requirement was only fifty acres of land, and therefore most adult white men qualified to vote. In both colonies, voters elected members of the gentry to serve in the colonial legislature. The gentry passed elected political offices from generation to generation, almost as if they were hereditary. Politically, the gentry built a self-perpetuating oligarchy—rule by the elite few—with the votes of their many humble neighbors.

The gentry also set the cultural standard in the southern colonies. They entertained lavishly, gambled regularly, and attended Anglican (Church of England) services more for social than for religious reasons. Above all, they cultivated the leisurely pursuit of happiness. They did not condone idleness, however. Their many pleasures and responsibilities as plantation owners kept them busy. Thomas Jefferson, a phenomenally productive member of the gentry, recalled that his earliest childhood memory was of being carried on a pillow by a family slave—a powerful image of the slave hands supporting the gentry's leisure and achievement.

> **REVIEW**   How did slavery influence the society and economy of the southern colonies?

▶ Unifying Experiences

The societies of New England, the middle colonies, and the southern colonies became more sharply differentiated during the eighteenth century, but colonists throughout British North America also shared unifying experiences that eluded settlers in the Spanish and French colonies. The first was economic. All three British colonial regions had their economic roots in agriculture. Colonists sold their distinctive products in markets that, in turn, offered a more or less uniform array of goods to consumers throughout British North America. Another unifying experience was a decline in the importance of religion. Some settlers called for a revival of religious intensity, but most people focused less on religion and more on the affairs of the world than they had in the seventeenth century. Also, white inhabitants throughout British North America became aware that they shared a distinctive identity as *British* colonists. Thirteen different governments presided over these North American colonies, but all of them answered to the British monarchy. British policies governed not only trade but also military and diplomatic relations with the Indians, French, and Spanish arrayed along colonial borderlands. Royal officials who expected loyalty from the colonists often had difficulty obtaining obedience. The British colonists asserted their prerogatives as British subjects to defend their special colonial interests.

Commerce and Consumption

Eighteenth-century commerce whetted colonists' appetites to consume. Colonial products spurred the development of mass markets throughout the Atlantic world (Figure 5.1). Huge increases in the supply of colonial tobacco and sugar

FIGURE 5.1   Colonial Exports, 1768–1772

These pie charts provide an overview of the colonial export economy in the 1760s. The first two show that almost two-thirds of colonial exports came from the South and that the majority of the colonies' exports went to Great Britain. The remaining charts illustrate the distinctive patterns of exports in each colonial region. What do these patterns reveal about regional variations in Britain's North American colonies? What do they suggest about Britain's economic interest in the colonies?

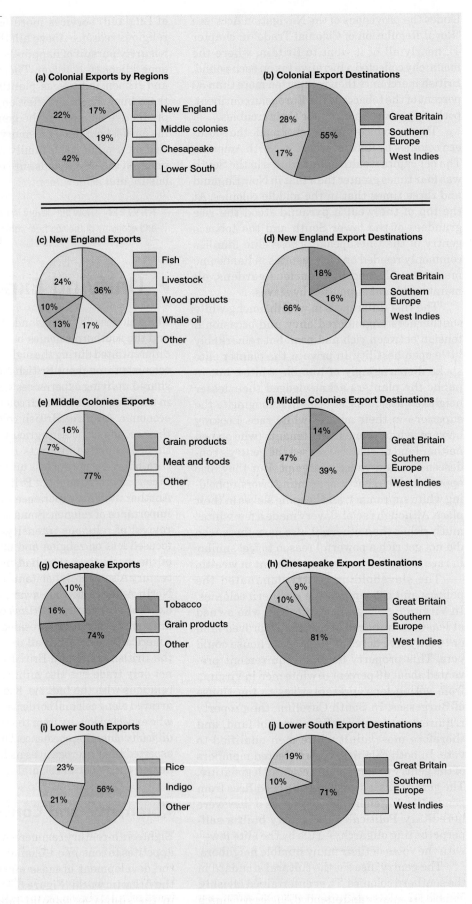

(a) Colonial Exports by Regions

- 17% New England
- 19% Middle colonies
- 42% Chesapeake
- 22% Lower South

(b) Colonial Export Destinations

- 55% Great Britain
- 17% Southern Europe
- 28% West Indies

(c) New England Exports

- 36% Fish
- 17% Livestock
- 13% Wood products
- 10% Whale oil
- 24% Other

(d) New England Export Destinations

- 18% Great Britain
- 16% Southern Europe
- 66% West Indies

(e) Middle Colonies Exports

- 77% Grain products
- 7% Meat and foods
- 16% Other

(f) Middle Colonies Export Destinations

- 14% Great Britain
- 39% Southern Europe
- 47% West Indies

(g) Chesapeake Exports

- 74% Tobacco
- 16% Grain products
- 10% Other

(h) Chesapeake Export Destinations

- 81% Great Britain
- 10% Southern Europe
- 9% West Indies

(i) Lower South Exports

- 56% Rice
- 21% Indigo
- 23% Other

(j) Lower South Export Destinations

- 71% Great Britain
- 10% Southern Europe
- 19% West Indies

Robert "King" Carter
Virginia grandee Robert "King" Carter amassed one of the largest estates in the Chesapeake during the early eighteenth century. Carter owned 45 plantations worked by more than 700 slaves who grew tobacco on some of his 30,000 acres of land. Carter matched his economic prowess with political influence, serving in the Virginia House of Burgesses and as governor. His wig hints at his embrace of English fashions while his somewhat plain clothing suggests an understated colonial restraint compared to the lavish outfits worn by wealthy Englishmen.
National Portrait Gallery, Smithsonian Institution/Art Resource, NY.

brought the price of these small luxuries within the reach of most free whites. Colonial goods brought into focus an important lesson of eighteenth-century commerce: Ordinary people, not just the wealthy elite, would buy the things that they desired in addition to what they absolutely needed. Even news, formerly restricted mostly to a few people through face-to-face conversations or private letters, became an object of public consumption through the innovation of newspapers and the rise in literacy among whites. With the appropriate stimulus, market demand seemed unlimited.

The Atlantic commerce that took colonial goods to markets in Britain brought objects of consumer desire back to the colonies. British merchants and manufacturers recognized that colonists made excellent customers, and the Navigation Acts gave British exporters privileged access to the colonial market. By midcentury, export-oriented industries in Britain were growing ten times faster than firms attuned to the home market.

When the colonists' eagerness to consume exceeded their ability to pay, British exporters willingly extended credit, and colonial debts soared. Imported mirrors, silver plates, spices, bed and table linens, clocks, tea services, wigs, books, and more infiltrated parlors, kitchens, and bedrooms throughout the colonies. Despite the many differences among the colonists, the consumption of British exports built a certain material uniformity across region, religion, class, and status.

The dazzling variety of imported consumer goods also presented women and men with a novel array of choices. In many respects, the choices might appear trivial: whether to buy knives and forks, teacups, a mirror, or a clock. But such small choices confronted eighteenth-century consumers with a big question: What do you want? As colonial consumers defined and expressed their desires with greater frequency during the eighteenth century, they became accustomed to thinking of themselves as individuals who had the power to make decisions that influenced the quality of their lives.

Religion, Enlightenment, and Revival

Eighteenth-century colonists could choose from almost as many religions as consumer goods. Virtually all of the many religious denominations represented some form of Christianity, almost all of them Protestant. Slaves made up the largest group of non-Christians. A few slaves converted to Christianity in Africa or after they arrived in North America, but most continued to embrace elements of indigenous African religions. Roman Catholics concentrated in Maryland as they had since the seventeenth century, but even there they were far outnumbered by Protestants.

The varieties of Protestant faith and practice ranged across a broad spectrum. The middle colonies and the southern backcountry included militant Baptists and Presbyterians. Huguenots who had fled persecution in Catholic France peopled congregations in several cities. In New England, old-style Puritanism splintered into strands of Congregationalism that differed over fine points of theological doctrine. The Congregational Church was the official established church in New England, and all residents paid taxes for its support. Throughout the plantation South and in urban centers such as Charleston, New York, and Philadelphia, prominent colonists belonged to the Anglican Church, which received tax support in the South. But dissenting faiths grew everywhere, and in most colonies their adherents won the right to worship publicly, although the established churches retained official support.

Many educated colonists became deists, looking for God's plan in nature more than in the Bible. Deism shared the ideas of eighteenth-century European Enlightenment thinkers, who tended to agree that science and reason could disclose God's laws in the natural order. In the colonies as well as in Europe, **Enlightenment** ideas encouraged people to study the world around them, to think for themselves, and to ask whether the disorderly appearance of things masked the principles of a deeper, more profound natural order. Leading colonial thinkers such as Benjamin Franklin and Thomas Jefferson communicated with each other seeking both to understand nature and to find ways to improve society. Franklin's interest in electricity, stoves, and eyeglasses exemplified the shift of focus among many eighteenth-century colonists from heaven to the here and now.

Most eighteenth-century colonists went to church seldom or not at all, although they probably considered themselves Christians. A minister in Charleston observed that on the Sabbath "the Taverns have more Visitants than the Churches." In the leading colonial cities, church members were a small minority. Anglican parishes in the South rarely claimed more than one-fifth of adults as members. In some regions of rural New England and the middle colonies, church membership embraced two-thirds of adults, while in other areas only one-quarter of the residents belonged to a church. The dominant faith overall was religious indifference. As a late-eighteenth-century traveler observed, "Religious indifference is imperceptibly disseminated from one end of the continent to the other."

George Whitefield

An anonymous artist portrayed George Whitefield preaching, emphasizing the power of his sermons to transport his audience to a revived awareness of divine spirituality. The woman below his hands appears transfixed. Her eyes and Whitefield's do not meet, yet the artist's use of light suggests that she and Whitefield see the same core of holy Truth.

National Portrait Gallery/SuperStock.

The spread of religious indifference, of deism, of denominational rivalry, and of comfortable backsliding profoundly concerned many Christians. A few despaired that, as one wrote, "religion . . . lay a-dying and ready to expire its last breath of life." To combat what one preacher called the "dead formality" of church services, some ministers set out to convert nonbelievers and to revive the piety of the faithful with a new style of preaching that appealed more to the heart than to the head. Historians have termed this wave of revivals the **Great Awakening**. In Massachusetts during the mid-1730s, the fiery Puritan minister Jonathan Edwards reaped a harvest of souls by reemphasizing traditional Puritan doctrines of humanity's utter depravity and God's vengeful omnipotence. A member of Edwards's church noted that his sermons caused "great moaning and crying through the whole [church]—What shall I do to be saved—oh I am going to Hell . . . the shrieks and cries were piercing and amazing." In Pennsylvania and New Jersey, William Tennent led revivals that dramatized spiritual rebirth with accounts of God's miraculous powers. The most famous revivalist in the eighteenth-century Atlantic world was George Whitefield. An Anglican, Whitefield preached well-worn messages of sin and salvation to large audiences in England using his spellbinding, unforgettable voice. Whitefield visited the North American colonies seven times, staying for more than three years during the mid-1740s and attracting tens of thousands to his sermons, including Benjamin Franklin and Olaudah Equiano. Whitefield's preaching transported many in his audience to emotion-choked states of religious ecstasy, as he wrote, with "most lifting their eyes to heaven, and crying to God for mercy."

Whitefield's successful revivals spawned many lesser imitations. Itinerant preachers, many of them poorly educated, roamed the colonial backcountry after midcentury. Bathsheba Kingsley, a member of Jonathan Edwards's flock, preached the revival message informally—as did an unprecedented number of other women throughout the colonies—causing Edwards's congregation to brand her a "brawling woman" who had "gone quite out of her place."

The revivals awakened and refreshed the spiritual energies of thousands of colonists struggling with the uncertainties and anxieties of eighteenth-century America. The conversions at revivals did not substantially boost the total number of church members, however. After the revivalists moved on, the routines and pressures of everyday existence reasserted their primacy in the lives of many converts. But the revivals communicated the important message that every soul mattered, that men and women could choose to be saved, that individuals had the power to make a decision for everlasting life or death. Colonial revivals expressed in religious terms many of the same democratic and egalitarian values expressed in economic terms by colonists' patterns of consumption. One colonist noted the analogy by referring to itinerant revivalists as "Pedlars in divinity." Like consumption, revivals contributed to a set of common experiences that bridged colonial divides of faith, region, class, and status.

Trade and Conflict in the North American Borderlands

British power defended the diverse inhabitants of its colonies from Indian, French, and Spanish enemies on their borders—as well as from foreign powers abroad. Royal officials warily eyed the small North American settlements of New France and New Spain for signs of threats to the colonies.

Alone, neither New France nor New Spain jeopardized British North America, but with Indian allies they could become a potent force that kept colonists on their guard (Map 5.4). Native Americans' impulse to defend their territory from colonial incursions competed with their desire for trade, which tugged them toward the settlers. As a colonial official observed in 1761, "A modern Indian cannot subsist without Europeans. . . . [The European goods that were] only conveniency at first [have] now become necessity." To obtain such necessities as guns, ammunition, clothing, and sewing utensils manufactured largely by the British, Indians trapped beavers, deer, and other furbearing animals.

British, French, Spanish, and Dutch officials competed for the fur trade. Indians took advantage of this competition to improve their own prospects, playing one trader and empire off another. Indian tribes and confederacies also competed among themselves for favored trading rights with one colony or another, a competition colonists encouraged.

The shifting alliances and complex dynamics of the fur trade struck a fragile balance along the frontier. The threat of violence from all sides was ever present, and the threat became reality often enough for all parties to be prepared for

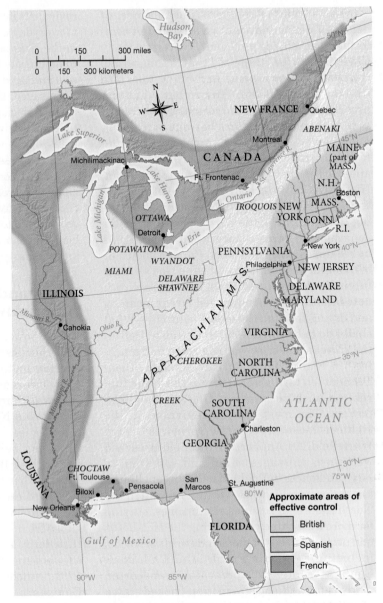

Map 5.4   Zones of Empire in Eastern North America

The British zone, extending west from the Atlantic coast, was much more densely settled than the zones under French, Spanish, and Indian control. The comparatively large number of British colonists made them more secure than the relatively few colonists in the vast regions claimed by France and Spain or the settlers living among the many Indian peoples in the huge area between the Mississippi River and the Appalachian Mountains. Yet the British colonists were not powerful enough to dominate the French, Spanish, or Indians. Instead, they had to guard against attacks by powerful Indian groups allied with the French or Spanish.

the worst. In the Yamasee War of 1715, for example, the Yamasee and Creek Indians—with French encouragement—mounted a coordinated attack against colonial settlements in South Carolina. The Cherokee Indians, traditional enemies of the Creeks, refused to join the attack. Instead, they protected their access to British trade goods by allying with the colonists and turning the tide of battle, triggering a murderous rampage of revenge by the colonists against the Creeks and Yamasee.

Relations between Indians and colonists differed from colony to colony and from year to year. But the British colonists' nagging perceptions of menace on the frontier kept them continually hoping for help from the British to keep the Indians at bay and to maintain the essential flow of trade.

In 1754, the British colonists' endemic competition with the French flared into the Seven Years' War (also known as the French and Indian War), which would inflame the frontier for years (see "French-British Rivalry in the Ohio Country" in chapter 6). Colonists agreed that Indians made deadly enemies, profitable trading partners, and powerful allies.

The Spanish kept an eye on the Pacific coast, where Russian hunters in search of seals and sea otters threatened to become a permanent presence on New Spain's northern frontier. To block Russian access to present-day California, officials in New Spain mounted a campaign to build forts (called **presidios**) and missions there. In 1769, an expedition headed by a military man, Gaspar de Portolá, and a Catholic priest, Junípero Serra, traveled north from Mexico to present-day San Diego, where they founded the first California mission, San Diego de Alcalá. They soon journeyed all the way to Monterey, which became the capital of Spanish California. There Portolá established a presidio in 1770 "to defend us from attacks by the Russians," he wrote. The same year, Serra founded Mission San Carlos Borroméo de Carmelo in Monterey to convert the Indians and recruit them to work to support the soldiers and other Spaniards in the presidio. By 1772, Serra had founded other missions along the path from San Diego to Monterey.

One Spanish soldier praised the work of the missionaries, writing that "with flattery and presents [the missionaries] attract the savage Indians and persuade them to adhere to life in society and to receive instruction for a knowledge of the Catholic faith, the cultivation of the land, and the arts necessary for making the instruments most needed for farming." Yet for the Indians, the Spaniards' California missions had horrendous consequences, as they had elsewhere in the Spanish borderlands. European diseases decimated Indian populations, Spanish soldiers raped Indian women, and missionaries beat Indians and subjected them to near slavery. Indian uprisings against the Spaniards occurred repeatedly, but the presidios and missions endured as feeble projections of the Spanish empire along the Pacific coast. (See "Analyzing Historical Evidence," page 130.)

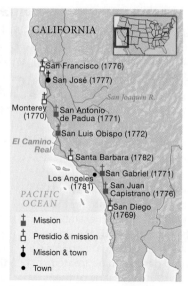

Spanish Missions in California

CALIFORNIA

San Francisco (1776)
San José (1777)
San Joaquin R.
Monterey (1770)
San Antonio de Padua (1771)
El Camino Real
San Luis Obispo (1772)
Santa Barbara (1782)
San Gabriel (1771)
Los Angeles (1781)
San Juan Capistrano (1776)
PACIFIC OCEAN
San Diego (1769)

✝ Mission
✝ Presidio & mission
● Mission & town
● Town

Colonial Politics in the British Empire

The plurality of peoples, faiths, and communities that characterized the North American colonies arose from the somewhat haphazard policies of the eighteenth-century British empire. Unlike Spain and France—whose policies of excluding Protestants and foreigners kept the population of their North American colonial territories tiny—Britain kept the door to its colonies open to anyone, and tens of thousands of non-British immigrants settled in the North American colonies and raised families. The open door did not extend to trade, however, as the seventeenth-century Navigation Acts restricted colonial trade to British ships and traders. These policies evolved because they served the interests of the monarchy and of influential groups in Britain and the colonies. The policies also gave the colonists a common framework of political expectations and experiences.

British attempts to exercise political power in their colonial governments met with success so long as British officials were on or very near the sea. Colonists acknowledged—although they did not always readily comply with—British authority to collect customs duties, inspect cargoes, and enforce trade regulations. But when royal officials tried to wield their authority in the internal affairs of the colonies on land, they invariably encountered colonial

Spanish Priests Report on California Missions

Catholic missionaries sent regular reports to their superiors in Mexico City, New Spain's capital city. The reports described what the missionaries considered their successes in converting pagan Indians—whom they called gentiles—as well as the difficulties caused by the behavior of both Spaniards and Indians.

DOCUMENT 1
Father Luís Jayme Describes Conditions at Mission San Diego de Alcalá, 1772

Father Luís Jayme, a Franciscan missionary, reported on the deplorable behavior of some of the Spanish soldiers at Mission San Diego de Alcalá; they frequently raped Indian women, causing many Indians to resist the efforts of the missionaries.

With reference to the Indians, I wish to say that great progress [in converting Indians] would be made if there was anything to eat and the soldiers would set a good example. . . . As for the example set by the soldiers, no doubt some of them are good exemplars and deserve to be treated accordingly, but very many of them deserve to be hanged on account of the continuous outrages which they are committing in seizing and raping the women. There is not a single mission where all the gentiles have not been scandalized, and even on the roads. . . . Surely, as the gentiles themselves state, they [the soldiers] are committing a thousand evils, particularly of a sexual nature. . . .

At one of these Indian villages near this mission of San Diego . . . the gentiles therein many times have been on the point of coming here to kill us all, and the reason for this is that some soldiers went there and raped their women, and other soldiers who were carrying the mail to Monterey turned their animals into their fields and they ate up their crops. Three other Indian villages . . . [near] here have

reported the same thing to me several times. For this reason on several occasions when . . . I have gone to see these Indian villages, as soon as they saw us they fled from their villages and fled to the woods or other remote places. . . . They do this so that the soldiers will not rape their women as they have already done so many times in the past. . . .

Now [the Indians] all want to be Christians because they know that there is a God who created the heavens and earth and all things, that there is a Hell and Glory, that they have souls, etc. . . . [Now] they . . . do not have idols; they do not go on drinking sprees; they do not marry relatives; and they have but one wife. The married men sleep with their wives only. . . . Some of the first adults whom we baptized, when we pointed out to them that it was wrong to have sexual intercourse with a woman to whom they were not married, told me that they already knew that, and that among them it was considered to be very

resistance. A governor appointed by the king in each of the nine royal colonies (Rhode Island and Connecticut selected their own governors) or by the proprietors in Maryland and Pennsylvania headed the government of each colony. The British envisioned colonial governors as mini-monarchs able to exert influence in the colonies much as the king did in Britain. But colonial governors were not kings, and the colonies were not Britain.

Even the best-intentioned colonial governors had difficulty developing relations of trust and respect with influential colonists because their terms of office averaged just five years and could be terminated at any time. Colonial governors controlled few patronage positions to secure political friendships in the colonies. Obedient and loyal to their superiors in Britain, colonial governors fought incessantly with the colonists' assemblies. They battled over issues such as governors' vetoes of colonial legislation, removal of colonial judges, and dismissal of the representative assemblies. But during the eighteenth century, the assemblies gained the upper hand.

Since British policies did not clearly define the colonists' legal powers, colonial assemblies

bad, and so they do not do so at all. "The soldiers," they told me, "are Christians and, although they know that God will punish them in Hell, do so, having sexual intercourse with our wives." . . . When I heard this, I burst into tears to see how these gentiles were setting an example for us Christians.

Source: Maynard Geiger, trans. and ed., *The Letter of Luís Jayme, O.F.M.: San Diego, October 17, 1772* (Los Angeles, 1979), 38–42. Courtesy of the Academy of American Franciscan History.

DOCUMENT 2
Father Junípero Serra Describes the Indian Revolt at Mission San Diego de Alcalá, 1775

Father Junípero Serra, the founder of many of the California missions, reported to his superiors in Mexico City that an Indian uprising had destroyed Mission San Diego de Alcalá. He recommended rebuilding and urged officials to provide additional soldiers to defend the missions, but not to punish the rebellious Indians.

I have just received [news] of the total destruction of the San Diego Mission, and of the death of the senior of its two religious ministers, called Father Luís Jayme, at the hand of the rebellious gentiles and of the Christian neophytes [Indians who lived in the mission]. All this happened . . . about one or two o'clock at night. The gentiles came together from forty rancherías [settlements] . . . and set fire to the church, after sacking it. They then went to the storehouse, the house where the Fathers lived, the soldiers' barracks, and all the rest of the buildings. They killed a carpenter . . . and a blacksmith. . . . They wounded with their arrows the four soldiers, who alone were on guard at the . . . mission. . . .

And now, after the Father has been killed, the Mission burned, its many and valuable furnishings destroyed, together with the sacred vessels, its paintings, its baptismal, marriage, and funeral records, and all the furnishings for the sacristy, the house, and the farm implements—now the forces [of soldiers] of both presidios [nearby] come together to set things right. . . . What happened was that before they set about reestablishing the Mission, they wanted to . . . lay hands on the guilty ones who were responsible for the burning of the Mission, and the death of the Fathers, and chastise them. The harassed Indians rebelled anew and became more enraged. . . . And so the soldiers there are gathered together in their presidios, and the Indians in their state of heathenism. . . .

But . . . what can be gained by campaigns [against the rebellious Indians]? Some will say to frighten them and prevent them from killing others. What I say is that, in order to prevent them from killing others, keep better guard over them than they did over the one who has been killed; and, as to the murderer, let him live, in order that he should be saved—which is the very purpose of our coming here, and the reason which justifies it.

Source: Antonine Tibesar, O.F.M., ed., *The Writings of Junípero Serra* (Washington, DC, 1956), 2:401–7. Courtesy of the Academy of American Franciscan History.

Questions for Analysis

Analyze the Evidence: How did the goals and activities of the Spanish soldiers compare with those of the Catholic missionaries?

Recognize Viewpoints: In what ways did Jayme and Serra agree or disagree about the motivations of Indians in and around Mission San Diego de Alcalá? What might Spanish soldiers or Indians have said about these events? What might they have said about missionaries like Jayme and Serra?

Consider the Context: How did Indian resistance to the Spanish in missions compare to Native Americans' resistance to the British and French in the fur trade?

seized the opportunity to make their own rules. Gradually, the assemblies established a strong tradition of representative government analogous, in their eyes, to the British Parliament. Voters often returned the same representatives to the assemblies year after year, building continuity in power and leadership that far exceeded that of the governor.

By 1720, colonial assemblies had won the power to initiate legislation, including tax laws and authorizations to spend public funds. Although all laws passed by the assemblies (except in Maryland, Rhode Island, and Connecticut) had to be approved by the governor and then by the Board of Trade in Britain, the difficulties in communication about complex subjects over long distances effectively ratified the assemblies' decisions. Years often passed before colonial laws were repealed by British authorities, and in the meantime the assemblies' laws prevailed.

The heated political struggles between royal governors and colonial assemblies that occurred throughout the eighteenth century taught colonists a common set of political lessons. They learned to employ traditionally British ideas of representative government to defend their own

Ambush of Spanish Expedition In 1720, the New Mexico governor sent forty-three Spanish soldiers and sixty Pueblo Indians to expel French intruders from New Spain's northern borderlands. The French and their Indian allies ambushed the expedition, killing thirty-three Spaniards and twelve Pueblos. Shortly afterward, an unknown artist recorded the event in this hide painting. Shown in the center of the painting is Father Juan Minguez of Albuquerque, and the Indian directly in front of him is Joseph Naranjo, leader of the Spaniards' Pueblo allies; both were killed in the ambush. MPI/Getty Images.

colonial interests. More important, they learned that power in the British colonies rarely belonged to the British government.

> **REVIEW** How did culture, commerce, and consumption shape the collective identity of Britain's North American colonists in the eighteenth century?

► Conclusion: The Dual Identity of British North American Colonists

During the eighteenth century, a society that was both distinctively colonial and distinctively British emerged in British North America. Tens of thousands of immigrants and slaves gave the colonies an unmistakably colonial complexion and contributed to the colonies' growing population and expanding economy. People of different ethnicities and faiths sought their fortunes in the colonies, where land was cheap, labor was

dear, and work promised to be rewarding. Indentured servants and redemptioners risked temporary periods of bondage for the potential reward of better opportunities in the colonies than on the Atlantic's eastern shore. Slaves arrived in unprecedented numbers and endured lifelong servitude, which they neither chose nor desired but from which their masters greatly benefited.

None of the European colonies could claim complete dominance of North America. The desire to expand and defend their current claims meant that the English, French, and Spanish colonies were drawn into regular conflict with one another, as well as with the Indians upon whose land they encroached. In varying degrees, all sought control of the Native Americans and their land, their military power, their trade, and even their souls. Spanish missionaries and soldiers sought to convert Indians on the West Coast and exploit their labor; French alliances with Indian tribes posed a formidable barrier to westward expansion of the British empire.

Yet despite their attempts to tame their New World holdings, Spanish and French colonists did not develop societies that began to rival the European empires that sponsored and supported them. They did not participate in the cultural, economic, social, and religious changes experienced by their counterparts in British North America, nor did they share in the emerging political identity of the British colonists.

Identifiably colonial products from New England, the middle colonies, and the southern colonies flowed to the West Indies and across the Atlantic. Back came unquestionably British consumer goods along with fashions in ideas, faith, and politics. The bonds of the British empire required colonists to think of themselves as British subjects and, at the same time, encouraged them to consider their status as colonists. By 1750, British colonists in North America could not imagine that their distinctively dual identity—as British and as colonists—would soon become a source of intense conflict.

See the Selected Bibliography for this chapter in the Appendix.

5 Chapter Review

REVIEW QUESTIONS

1. How did the North American colonies achieve the remarkable population growth of the eighteenth century? (pp. 107–108)

2. Why did settlement patterns in New England change from the seventeenth to the eighteenth century? (pp. 108–113)

3. Why did immigrants flood into Pennsylvania during the eighteenth century? (pp. 114–117)

4. How did slavery influence the society and economy of the southern colonies? (pp. 117–123)

5. How did culture, commerce, and consumption shape the collective identity of Britain's North American colonists in the eighteenth century? (pp. 123–132)

MAKING CONNECTIONS

1. How did consumption influence the relationship between the American colonies and Britain in the eighteenth century?

2. Why did the importance of religion decline throughout the colonies from the seventeenth to the eighteenth century?

3. How did colonists and Indians manage relationships with each other?

4. Compare patterns of immigration to the middle and southern colonies. Who came, and how did they get there? How did they shape the economic, cultural, and political character of each colony?

LINKING TO THE PAST

1. How did the British North American colonies in 1750 differ politically and economically from those in 1650? Were there important continuities? (See chapters 3 and 4.)

2. Is there persuasive evidence that colonists' outlook on the world shifted from the seventeenth to the eighteenth century? Why or why not? (See chapters 3 and 4.)

6

The British Empire and the Colonial Crisis

1754–1775

CONTENT LEARNING OBJECTIVES

After reading and studying this chapter, you should be able to:

- Recognize how the American colonies fit into the British empire's campaigns against other European powers and how the Seven Years' War laid the groundwork for the imperial crisis of the 1760s in British North America.

- Define the Sugar and Stamp Acts, and explain why and how American colonists opposed them.

- Explain how the British government responded to colonists' growing opposition to royal authority.

- Identify the events that escalated tensions between British leaders and the colonists.

- Explain the Intolerable Acts and the purposes and goals of the First Continental Congress.

- Identify the origins of the battles of Lexington and Concord.

IN 1771, THOMAS HUTCHINSON BECAME THE ROYAL GOVERNOR OF THE colony of Massachusetts. Most royal governors were British aristocrats sent over by the king for short tours of duty, but Hutchinson was a fifth-generation American with a long record of public service in local institutions. He lived in the finest mansion in Boston; wealth, power, and influence were his in abundance. He was proud of his connection to the British empire and loyal to his king.

Hutchinson had the misfortune to be a loyal colonial leader during the two tumultuous decades leading up to the American Revolution. He worked hard to keep the British and colonists aligned in interests, even promoting a plan to unify the colonies with a limited government (the Albany Plan of Union) to deal with Indian policy. His plan of union ultimately failed, however, and a major war—the Seven Years' War—ensued, pitting the British and colonists against the French and their Indian allies in the backcountry of the American colonies. When the war ended and the British government proposed to tax colonists to help pay for it, Hutchinson was certain that the new British taxation policies were legitimate—unwise, perhaps, but legitimate.

Not everyone in Boston shared his opinion. Enthusiastic crowds protested a succession of taxation policies enacted after 1763, from the Sugar

POWDER HORN FROM THE SEVEN YEARS' WAR
To reload muskets, soldiers carried this handy moisture-tight powder horn. Made from the durable horn of an ox or a bull, many powder horns survived the harsh rigors of wartime to become treasured souvenirs. Elaborate carvings, often with names and dates, individualized each horn. This horn from 1758 charts the forts and river systems extending from New York City to Canada, providing a convenient map of unfamiliar territory. Mickael Almonds/ The New-York Historical Society/Getty Images.

Act to the Tea Act. But Hutchinson maintained his steadfast loyalty to Britain. His love of order and tradition inclined him to unconditional support of the British empire, and by nature he was a measured and cautious man. "My temper does not incline to enthusiasm," he once wrote.

Privately, he lamented the stupidity of the British acts that provoked trouble, but his rigid sense of duty always prevailed, making him an inspiring villain to the emerging revolutionary movement. The man not inclined to enthusiasm unleashed popular enthusiasm all around him. He never appreciated that irony.

In another irony, Thomas Hutchinson early recognized the difficulties of maintaining full rights and privileges for colonists so far from their supreme government, the king and Parliament in Britain. At a crisis point in 1769, when British troops occupied Boston, he wrote privately to a friend in England, "There must be an abridgement of what are called English liberties. . . . I doubt whether it is possible to project a system of government in which a colony three thousand miles distant from the parent state shall enjoy all the liberty of the parent state." He could not imagine the colonies without a parent state, existing independently.

Thomas Hutchinson was a loyalist, as were most English-speaking colonists in the 1750s. But the Seven Years' War, in which Britain and its colonies were allies, shook that affection, and imperial policies in the decade following the war shattered it completely. Over the course of 1763 to 1773, Americans insistently raised serious questions about Britain's governance of its colonies. Many came to believe what Thomas Hutchinson could never accept—that a tyrannical Britain had embarked on a course to enslave the colonists by depriving them of their traditional English liberties.

The opposite of liberty was slavery, a coerced condition of nonfreedom. Political rhetoric about liberty, tyranny, and slavery heated up the emotions of white colonists during the many crises of the 1760s and 1770s. But this rhetoric turned out to be a two-edged sword. The call for an end to tyrannical slavery meant one thing when sounded by Boston merchants whose commercial shipping rights had been curtailed, but the same call meant something quite different in 1775 when sounded by black Americans locked in the bondage of slavery.

Thomas Hutchinson

The only formal portrait of Thomas Hutchinson still in existence shows an assured young man in ruffles. Doubtless he sat for other portraits, but none survive. One portrait in his summer house outside Boston was mutilated by a revolutionary crowd. In 1775, Hutchinson fled to Britain, the country he regarded as his cultural home, only to realize how very American he was.
© Massachusetts Historical Society, Boston, MA/Bridgeman Art Library.

► The Seven Years' War, 1754–1763

For the first half of the eighteenth century, Britain was at war intermittently with France or Spain. Often the colonists in America experienced reverberations from these conflicts, most acutely along the frontier of New France in northern New England. In 1754, international tensions returned, this time sparked by events in America's Ohio Valley. The land—variously claimed by Virginians, Pennsylvanians, and the French—was actually inhabited by more than a dozen Indian tribes. The result was the costly **Seven Years' War** (its British name—Americans called it the French and Indian War), which spread in 1756 to encompass much of Europe, the Caribbean, and even India. The British and their colonial allies won the war, but the immense costs of the conflict—in money, death, and desire for revenge by losers and even winners—laid the groundwork for the imperial crisis of the 1760s between the British and Americans.

French-British Rivalry in the Ohio Country

For several decades, French traders had cultivated alliances with the Indian tribes in the Ohio Country, a frontier region they regarded as part of New France, establishing a profitable exchange of manufactured goods for beaver furs (Map 6.1). But in the 1740s, aggressive Pennsylvania traders began to infringe on the territory. Adding to the tensions, a group of enterprising Virginians, including the brothers Lawrence and Augustine Washington, formed the Ohio Company in 1747 and advanced on the same land. Their hope for profit lay not in the fur trade but in land speculation, fueled by American population expansion.

In response to these incursions, the French sent soldiers to build a series of military forts to secure their trade routes and to create a western barrier to American expansion. In 1753, the royal governor of Virginia, Robert Dinwiddie, himself a shareholder in the Ohio Company, dispatched a messenger to warn the French that they were trespassing on Virginia land. For this dangerous mission, he chose the twenty-one-year-old George Washington, half-brother of the Ohio Company leaders, who did not disappoint. Washington returned with crucial intelligence confirming French military intentions. Impressed,

CHRONOLOGY

1754	• Seven Years' War begins. • Albany Congress convenes.
1755	• Braddock defeated in western Pennsylvania.
1757	• William Pitt fully commits to war.
1760	• Montreal falls to British. • George III becomes British king.
1763	• Treaty of Paris ends Seven Years' War. • Pontiac's Rebellion begins. • Proclamation of 1763 forbids colonial settlers west of Appalachian Mountains. • Paxton Boys massacre friendly Indians.
1764	• Parliament enacts Sugar Act.
1765	• Parliament enacts Stamp Act. • Virginia Resolves challenge Stamp Act. • Sons of Liberty stage crowd actions. • Stamp Act Congress meets.
1766	• Parliament repeals Stamp Act, passes Declaratory Act.
1767	• Parliament enacts Townshend duties.
1768	• British station troops in Boston.
1768–1769	• Merchants sign nonimportation agreements.
1770	• Boston Massacre occurs. • Parliament repeals Townshend duties.
1772	• British navy ship *Gaspée* burned. • Committees of correspondence begin forming.
1773	• Parliament passes Tea Act. • Tea dumped in Boston harbor.
1774	• Parliament passes Coercive Acts. • Powder Alarm shows colonists' readiness to fight. • First Continental Congress meets.
1775	• Battles of Lexington and Concord fought. • Lord Dunmore promises freedom to defecting slaves.

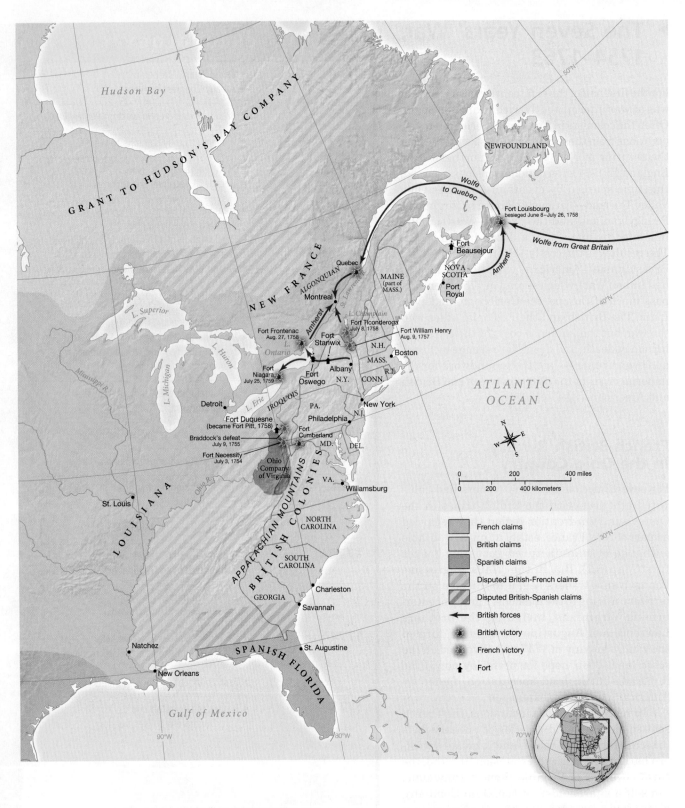

Map 6.1 European Areas of Influence and the Seven Years' War, 1754–1763

In 1750, the French and Spanish empires had relatively few people on the ground, compared to the exploding population of the Anglo-American colonies. The disputed lands shown here, contested by the imperial powers, were inhabited by a variety of Native American tribes.

Washington Crossing the Allegheny, 1753
Experienced backwoodsman Christopher Gist proved essential to George Washington's mission. When snowstorms halted Washington's band of men in December, Gist and Washington set out alone on foot. Their trek as narrated by Washington reads like a modern action movie, with attacks by Indians and passage over a swift river filled with tossing chunks of ice. Washington fell off the crude raft they constructed; Gist saved him from drowning. PhotoQuest/Getty Images.

Dinwiddie appointed the youth to lead a small military expedition west to assert Virginia's claim and chase the French away—but without attacking them.

In the spring of 1754, Washington set out with 160 Virginians and a small contingent of Mingo Indians equally concerned about the French military presence in the Ohio Country. Early one morning the Mingo chief Tanaghrisson led a detachment of Washington's soldiers to a small French encampment in the woods. Who fired first was in dispute, but fourteen Frenchmen (and no Virginians) were wounded. While Washington, lacking a translator, struggled to communicate with the injured French commander, Tanaghrisson and his men intervened to kill and then scalp the wounded soldiers, including the commander, probably with the aim of inflaming hostilities between the French and the colonists.

This sudden massacre violated Dinwiddie's instructions to Washington and raised the stakes considerably. Fearing retaliation, Washington ordered his men to throw together a makeshift "Fort Necessity." Several hundred Virginia reinforcements arrived, but the Mingos, sensing disaster and displeased by Washington's style of command, fled. (Tanaghrisson later said, "The Colonel was a good-natured man, but had no experience; he took upon him to command the Indians as his slaves, [and] would by no means take advice from the Indians.") Retaliation arrived in the form of six hundred French soldiers aided by one hundred Shawnee and Delaware warriors, who attacked Fort Necessity, killing or wounding a third of Washington's men. The message was clear: The French would not depart from the disputed territory.

Ohio River Valley, 1753

Fort Presqu'isle
Lake Erie
Fort Le Boeuf
Fort Machault (Venango)
Allegheny R.
PA.
Fort Duquesne
Redstone Old Fort
Fort Necessity
Fort Cumberland
Ohio Company
VIRGINIA
Muskingum R.
Scioto R.
Ohio R.
Kanawha R.

British fort
French fort

The Albany Congress

British imperial leaders hoped to prevent the conflict in the Ohio Country from leading to a larger war. One obvious strategy was to strengthen an old partnership with the Mohawks of New York's Iroquois Confederacy, who since 1692 had joined

Why Did the Mohawk Chief Hendrick Fight with the British against the French in 1755?

When a thousand provincial troops marched north through New York to engage the French enemy in fall of 1755, they were joined by just one Indian tribe, the Mohawks. Despite his advanced age, the white-haired Chief Hendrick Peters Thayanoguin rode at the head of a company of two hundred warriors, putting his life on the line for the British.

Most Native Americans of the 1750s favored the French in the Seven Years' War, seeing the British as more intrusive and land hungry. But Chief Hendrick's particular experiences gave him a more nuanced perspective on the British. Mohawk lands were not isolated; they lay close to the British seat of government in New York City and even closer to Dutch-descended merchants centered in Albany, who were vital participants in the fur trade. Hendrick engineered alliances with other tribes of the Iroquois Confederacy, and he maintained relationships, sometimes uneasy ones, with rising numbers of settlers— German, British, and Dutch—who were taking up farming near Mohawk villages. An astute politician, Hendrick orchestrated a complex balance of power within a diverse set of rival players.

Hendrick's most notable success was a decades-long trade alliance with the British called the Covenant Chain, a pact renewed at frequent intervals in ceremonial meetings where a valuable belt made of beads exchanged hands. On a personal level, Hendrick's closest alliance was his warm friendship with Sir William Johnson, an Irish-born gentleman with a large estate nearby. Johnson's family lineage gained him respect from British leaders, while his ready acceptance of—indeed, immersion in—Mohawk culture raised respect from Native Americans. Like Hendrick, Johnson was an astute broker between cultures.

In 1753, Hendrick's diplomatic efforts were in danger, with French-British tensions mounting. The fur trade with Albany merchants was threatened by a breakaway group of Mohawks based in Montreal; and more settlers, backed by the provincial assembly, were encroaching on nearby lands.

Hendrick staged a forceful complaint in New York City, accusing the assembly of breaking the Covenant Chain and ending with stern words for the royal governor: "So brother you are not to expect to hear of me any more, and Brother we desire to hear no more of you." When news of this speech reached London, alarmed British officials called for the Albany Congress to repair the Mohawk alliance. From the imperial perspective, this was no time for Britain to lose its best Indian ally—precisely the outcome Hendrick hoped to provoke.

At the Albany Congress, held in summer of 1754, delegates from New York extended a peaceful but not fully welcoming hand to reestablish the Covenant Chain. The Indians in attendance judged the effort to be insufficiently apologetic for past neglect. While accepting the belt symbolizing the alliance, Hendrick again gave a powerful speech designed to shame the colonial delegates. He grasped a stick and threw it behind him, saying, "You have thus thrown us behind your back, and disregarded us, whereas the French are a subtle and vigilant people, ever using their utmost endeavours to seduce and bring our

with New York fur merchants in an alliance called the Covenant Chain to foster trade and mutual protection. Yet unsavory land specula-tors had caused the Mohawks to doubt British friendship, leading Chief Hendrick to proclaim the alliance broken. (See "Making Historical Arguments," above.) Authorities in London directed New York's royal governor to convene a colonial conference to repair trade relations and secure the Indians' help—or at least their

neutrality—against the looming French threat. The conference convened at Albany, in June and July 1754. All six tribes of the Iroquois Confederacy attended, along with twenty-four delegates from seven colonies, making this an unprecedented pan-colony gathering.

Two colonial delegates at the congress seized the occasion to present an additional plan. Benjamin Franklin of Pennsylvania and Thomas Hutchinson of Massachusetts, both rising political

Chief Hendrick
A Philadelphia artist painted Chief Hendrick wearing a gold-braided coat, ruffled shirt, and cocked hat of a stylish English gentleman. After Hendrick's death, lithographed copies were sold in London, New York, Boston, and Philadelphia. What statement do the clothes make about Hendrick's political allegiance? Courtesy of the John Carter Brown Library at Brown University.

British rivalry in starkly gendered terms: "Brethren. You were desirous that we should open our minds, and our hearts to you; look at the French, they are Men, they are fortifying everywhere—but, we are ashamed to say it, you are like women, bare and open, without any fortifications."

Hendrick's fame spread far with this astute speech, and his reproach of the colonists gained him favor with war hawks in Britain. In 1755, the governor of Pennsylvania invited him to Philadelphia, hopeful the chief could have influence on disputed land deals with Indians in western Pennsylvania. The Pennsylvania assembly treated him as an honored guest, as did an elite men's club whose members raised private donations to win his favor.

By fall of 1755, the Seven Years' War had spread to the northern front. Sir William Johnson commanded the thousand provincial troops who marched north into French territory, and with him was his close friend Chief Hendrick with two hundred warriors. French troops and their Montreal Indian allies staged an ambush, but before the trap could be sprung, one of the French Mohawks in hiding recognized Hendrick, a white-haired standout on a lead horse. The man called to Hendrick, rebuking him for joining a white man's war. In short order, shots were fired and a general fight ensued. In the end, Hendrick was killed, but with the ambush spoiled, the provincial troops prevailed and claimed victory.

Chief Hendrick was mourned as a hero by the British Americans. Ships were named for him, as were two taverns in Philadelphia. Periodicals in Britain and America published a detailed account of his death in battle. Celebrated for his stirring speeches and courageous death, Hendrick above all was valued for his singular loyalty to the British.

Questions for Analysis

Summarize the Argument: In light of his scolding speeches criticizing the British, how was it that Chief Hendrick came to be so celebrated by the British Americans in 1755?

Analyze the Evidence: What evidence does the author cite to build the case that Hendrick was an unusually talented intercultural broker?

Consider the Context: The British had slender support of Native Americans in the Seven Years' War, yet they won on the American continent. Why?

people over to them." Hendrick reminded them of French fort building in the Ohio Country, met with inaction by the British. He concluded by casting the French-

stars, coauthored the Albany Plan of Union, a proposal for a unified but limited government with a president and a council to exercise sole authority over questions of war, peace, and trade with the Indians. No challenge to Parliament's authority was intended.

Delegates at the Albany Congress, alarmed by news of the Virginians' defeat at Fort Necessity, agreed to present the plan to their respective assemblies. To Franklin's surprise, not a single colony approved the Albany Plan. The Massachusetts assembly feared it was "a Design of gaining power over the Colonies," especially the power of taxation. Others objected that it would be impossible to agree on unified policies toward scores of quite different Indian tribes. The British government never backed the Albany Plan; instead, it appointed two superintendents of Indian affairs, one for the northern and another for the southern colonies, each with exclusive powers to negotiate treaties, trade, and land sales with all tribes. This move centralized control of Indian policy on officials supposedly reporting to London and decentered the policy role of the colonial assemblies.

The Indians at the Albany Congress were also not impressed with the Albany Plan. The Covenant Chain alliance with the Mohawk tribe was reaffirmed, but the other nations left without pledging to help the British battle the French. Some of the Iroquois figured that the French military presence around the Great Lakes would discourage the westward push of American colonists and therefore better serve the Indians' interests.

The War and Its Consequences

By 1755, George Washington's frontier skirmish had turned into a major war. The British expected quick victories on three fronts. General Edward Braddock, recently arrived from England, marched his army toward Fort Duquesne in western Pennsylvania. Farther north, British troops moved toward Fort Niagara, critically located between Lakes Erie and Ontario. And William Johnson, a New Yorker recently appointed superintendent of northern Indian affairs, led forces north toward Lake Champlain, intending to defend the border against the French in Canada (see Map 6.1).

Unfortunately for the British, the French were prepared to fight and had enlisted many Indian tribes in their cause. When Braddock's army of 2,000 British soldiers marched west toward Fort Duquesne, a mere 8 Oneida warriors came as guides. They were ambushed by 250 French soldiers joined by 640 Indian warriors. Surviving soldiers reported that they never saw more than a half dozen Indians at a time, so hidden were they in the woods. But the soldiers could hear them. One soldier wrote weeks later that "the yell of the Indians is fresh on my ear, and the terrific sound will haunt me until the hour of my dissolution." The disciplined British troops stood their ground, making them easy targets. In the bloody battle, nearly a thousand on the British side were killed or wounded, including General Braddock.

For the next two years, British leaders stumbled badly, deploying inadequate numbers of undersupplied troops. What finally turned the war around was the rise to power in 1757 of William Pitt, Britain's prime minister, a man ready to com-

MAP ACTIVITY

Map 6.2   Europe Redraws the Map of North America, 1763
In 1763, France ceded to Britain its interior territory from Quebec to New Orleans, retaining fishing rights in the north and sugar islands in the Caribbean. France transferred to Spain its claim to extensive territory west of the Mississippi River.

READING THE MAP: Who actually lived on and controlled the lands ceded by France? In what sense, if any, did Britain or Spain own these large territories?
CONNECTIONS: What was the goal of the Proclamation of 1763? Could it ever have worked?

mit massive resources to fight France and Spain worldwide. In America, British troops aided by American provincial soldiers at last captured Forts Duquesne, Niagara, and Ticonderoga, followed by the French cities of Quebec and finally Montreal, all from 1758 to 1760. By 1761, the war subsided in America but expanded globally, with battles in the Caribbean, Austria, Prussia, and India. The British captured the French sugar islands Martinique and Guadeloupe and then invaded Spanish Cuba with an army of some four thousand provincial soldiers from New York and New England. By the end of 1762, France and Spain capitulated, and the Treaty of Paris was signed in 1763.

In the complex peace negotiations that produced the treaty, Britain gained control of Canada, eliminating the French threat from the north. British and American title to the eastern half of North America was confirmed. But French territory west of the Mississippi River, including New Orleans, was transferred to Spain as compensation for Spain's assistance during the war. Strangely, Cuba was returned to Spain, and Martinique and Guadeloupe were returned to France (Map 6.2).

The British credited their army for their victory and criticized the colonists for inadequate support. William Pitt was convinced that colonial smuggling—beaver pelts from French fur traders and illegal molasses in the French Caribbean—"principally, if not alone, enabled France to sustain and protract this long and expensive war."

Colonists read the lessons of the war differently. American soldiers had turned out in force, they claimed, but had been relegated to grunt work by British commanders and subjected to harsh military discipline, including floggings and executions. They bristled at British arrogance, as when Benjamin Franklin heard General Braddock brag that "these savages may, indeed, be a formidable enemy to your raw American militia, but upon the king's regular and disciplined troops, sir, it is impossible they should make any impression." Braddock's crushing defeat "gave us Americans," Franklin wrote, "the first suspicion that our exalted ideas of the prowess of British regulars had not been well founded."

Perhaps most important, the enormous expense of the war cast a huge shadow over the victory. By 1763, Britain's national debt, double what it had been when Pitt took office, posed a formidable challenge to the next decade of leadership in Britain.

Pontiac's Rebellion and the Proclamation of 1763

One glaring omission marred the Treaty of Paris: The major powers at the treaty table failed to include or consult the Indians. Minavavana, an Ojibwa chief of the Great Lakes region, put it succinctly to an English trader: "Englishman, although you have conquered the French, you have not yet conquered us! We are not your slaves. These lakes, these woods and mountains were left to us by our ancestors . . . ; and we will part with them to none." Furthermore, Minavavana pointedly noted, "your king has never sent us any presents, nor entered into any treaty with us, wherefore he and we are still at war."

Minavavana's complaint about the absence of British presents was significant. To Indians, gifts

The Seven Years' War	
1692–1750s	English and Iroquois create and affirm the Covenant Chain alliance in western New York.
1700–1740s	French settlers enjoy exclusive trade with Indians in Ohio Valley.
1747	Ohio Company receives land grant from British king.
1753	Mohawk chief Hendrick accuses English of breaking Covenant Chain.
	French soldiers advance from Canada into Ohio Country.
	George Washington delivers message telling French they are trespassing.
1754	French build Fort Duquesne.
	Washington returns to Ohio Country with troops and Mingo allies.
	May. Washington, guided by Mingo chief Tanaghrisson, attacks French.
	June–July. Albany Congress convenes.
	July. French and Indian soldiers defeat Washington at Fort Necessity.
1755	British authorities appoint two superintendents of Indian affairs.
	July. Braddock defeated at Monongahela.
1756	William Pitt becomes British prime minister.
1758	British capture Fort Duquesne.
1759	British capture Forts Niagara and Ticonderoga.
1760	British capture Montreal.
1762	British capture Cuba.
1763	Treaty of Paris signed.

cemented social relationships, symbolizing honor and establishing obligation. Over many decades, the French had mastered the subtleties of gift exchange, distributing textiles and hats and receiving calumets (ceremonial pipes) in return. British military leaders, new to the practice, often discarded the calumets as trivial trinkets, thereby insulting the givers. From the British view, a generous gift might signify tribute (thus demeaning the giver), or it might be positioned as a bribe. "It is not my intention ever to attempt to gain the friendship of Indians by presents," Major General Jeffery Amherst declared. The Indian view was the opposite: Generous givers expressed dominance and protection, not subordination, in the ceremonial practices of giving.

Despite Minavavana's confident words, Indians north of the Ohio River had cause for concern. Old French trading posts all over the Northwest were beefed up by the British into military bases. Fort Duquesne, renamed Fort Pitt to honor the victorious leader, gained new walls sixty feet thick at their base, announcing that this was no fur trading post. Tensions between the British and the Indians in this area ran high.

A religious revival among the Indians magnified feelings of antagonism toward the British. In 1763, the renewal of commitment to Indian ways and the formation of tribal alliances led to open warfare, which the British called **Pontiac's Rebellion**, named for the chief of the Ottawas. In mid-May, Ottawa, Potawatomi, and Huron warriors attacked Fort Detroit. Six more attacks on forts followed within weeks, and frontier settlements were raided by tribes from western New York, the Ohio Valley, and the Great Lakes region. By fall, Indians had captured every fort

west of Detroit. More than four hundred British soldiers were dead and another two thousand colonists killed or taken captive.

Some Americans exacted revenge. The worst violent aggression occurred in late 1763, when some fifty Pennsylvania vigilantes known as the Paxton Boys descended on a peaceful village of friendly Conestoga Indians, murdering twenty. The vigilantes, now numbering five hundred, marched on Philadelphia to try to capture and murder some Christian Indians held in protective custody there. British troops prevented that, but the Paxton Boys escaped punishment for their murderous attack on the Conestoga village.

In early 1764, the uprising faded. The Indians were short on ammunition, and the British were tired and broke. The British government recalled the imperious general Amherst, blaming him for mishandling the conflict, and his own soldiers toasted his departure. A new military leader, Thomas Gage, took command and began distributing gifts profusely among the Indians.

To minimize violence, the British government issued the Proclamation of 1763, forbidding colonists to settle west of the Appalachian Mountains in order to protect Indian territory. But the Proclamation's language also took care not to identify western lands as belonging to the Indians. Instead, it spoke of lands that "are reserved to [Indians], as their Hunting Grounds."

Other parts of the Proclamation of 1763 referred to American and even French colonists in Canada as "our loving subjects," entitled to

Silver Medal to Present to Indians
After Pontiac's uprising, the British distributed gifts to foster peace. This 1766 silver medal shows King George III on the front and an Indian and a Briton smoking a peace pipe on the back. How would an English translator explain what HAPPY WHILE UNITED might mean? Both images courtesy of the American Numismatic Society.

Pontiac's Uprising, 1763

English rights and privileges. In contrast, the Indians were rejected as British subjects and described more vaguely as "Tribes of Indians with whom We are connected." Of course, the British were not really well connected with any Indians, nor did they wish connections to form among the tribes. As William Johnson, the superintendent of northern Indian affairs, advised in 1764, "It will be expedient to treat with each nation separately . . . for could they arrive at a perfect union, they must prove very dangerous Neighbours."

The 1763 boundary was a further provocation to American settlers and also to land speculators who (like the men of the Ohio Company) had already staked claims to huge tracts of western lands in hopes of profitable resale. Yet the boundary proved impossible to enforce. Surging population growth had already sent many hundreds of settlers, many of them squatters, west of the Appalachians. Periodic bloodshed continued and left the settlers fearful, uncertain about their futures, and increasingly wary of British claims to be a protective mother country.

REVIEW How did the Seven Years' War erode relations between colonists and British authorities?

▶ The Sugar and Stamp Acts, 1763–1765

In 1760, George III, twenty-two years old, became king of England. Timid and insecure, George struggled to gain his footing in his new job. He rotated through a succession of leaders, searching for a prime minister he could trust. A half dozen ministers in seven years took turns dealing with one basic underlying British reality: A huge war debt needed to be serviced, and the colonists, as British subjects, should help pay it off. To many American colonists, however, that proposition seemed in deep violation of what they perceived to be their rights and liberties as British subjects, and it created resentment that eventually erupted in large-scale street protests. The first provocative revenue acts were the work of Sir George Grenville, prime minister from 1763 to 1765.

Grenville's Sugar Act

To find revenue, George Grenville scrutinized the customs service, which monitored the shipping trade and collected all import and export duties. Grenville found that the salaries of customs officers cost the government four times what was collected in revenue. The shortfall was due in part to bribery and smuggling, so Grenville began to insist on rigorous attention to paperwork and a strict accounting of collected duties. The hardest duty to enforce was the one imposed by the Molasses Act of 1733—a stiff tax of six pence per gallon on any molasses imported to British colonies from non-British sources. Rum-loving Americans, however, were eager to buy molasses from French Caribbean islands—cheap because the French scorned rum, preferring wines and brandy. Americans had ignored the Molasses Act for decades.

Grenville's inspired solution was the **Revenue Act** of 1764, popularly dubbed the **Sugar Act**. It lowered the duty on French molasses to three pence, making it more attractive for shippers to obey the law, and at the same time raised penalties for smuggling. The act appeared to be in the tradition of navigation acts meant to regulate trade (see "Royal Regulation of Colonial Trade" in chapter 4), but Grenville's actual intent was to raise revenue. The Sugar Act toughened enforcement policies. From now on, all British naval crews could act as impromptu customs officers, boarding suspicious ships and seizing cargoes found to be in violation. Smugglers caught without proper paperwork would be prosecuted, not in a local court with a friendly jury but in a vice-admiralty court located in Nova Scotia, where a crown judge presided. The implication was that justice would be sure and severe. Grenville's hopes for the Sugar Act did not materialize. The small decrease in duty did not offset the attractions of smuggling, while the increased vigilance in enforcement led to several ugly confrontations in port cities. Reaction to the Sugar Act foreshadowed questions about Britain's right to tax Americans, but in 1764 objections to the act came principally from the small numbers of Americans engaged in the shipping trades. From the British point of view, the Sugar Act seemed to be a reasonable effort to administer the colonies. To Americans, however, the British supervision appeared to be a disturbing intrusion on colonial practices of self-taxation by elected colonial assemblies. Benjamin Franklin, Pennsylvania's lobbyist in London, warned that "two distinct Jurisdictions or Powers of Taxing cannot well subsist together in the same country."

The Stamp Act

In February 1765, Grenville escalated his revenue program with the **Stamp Act**, precipitating

VISUAL ACTIVITY

Tea and Sugar in the 1760s

In the mid-eighteenth century, rising sugarcane production in the West Indies transformed sugar into a commonplace commodity in the English-speaking world. It became a desired taste indulged in by the elite classes (as pictured here) and by non-elites. At the center of this 1764 painting, titled *The Honeymoon*, an alluring young bride delicately drops a sugar cube into her husband's cup of tea. The Colonial Williamsburg Foundation. Museum Purchase.

READING THE IMAGE: How does the artist convey the relationship between the two people? How does the sugar contribute to the theme of youthful romance?

CONNECTIONS: Why did sugar and molasses—newly popular and exotic stimulants—become politicized in the 1760s?

a major conflict between Britain and the colonies over Parliament's right to tax. The Stamp Act imposed a tax on all paper used for official documents—newspapers, pamphlets, court documents, licenses, wills, ships' cargo lists—and required an affixed stamp as proof that the tax had been paid. Unlike the Sugar Act, which regulated trade, the Stamp Act was designed plainly and simply to raise money. It affected nearly everyone who used any taxed paper but, most of all, users of official documents in the business and legal communities. Anticipating that the stamp tax would be unpopular—Thomas Hutchinson had forewarned him—Grenville delegated the administration of the act to Americans to avoid taxpayer hostility toward British enforcers. In each colony, local stamp distributors would be hired at a handsome salary of 8 percent of the revenue collected.

English tradition held that taxes were a gift of the people to their monarch, granted by the people's representatives. This view of taxes as a freely given gift preserved an essential concept of English political theory: the idea that citizens have the liberty to enjoy and use their property without fear of confiscation. The king could not demand taxes; only the House of Commons could grant it. Grenville agreed with the notion of taxation by consent, but he argued that the colonists were already "virtually" represented in Parliament. The House of Commons, he insisted, represented all British subjects, wherever they were.

Colonial leaders emphatically rejected this view, arguing that **virtual representation** could not withstand the stretch across the Atlantic. Colonists willingly paid local and provincial taxes, levied by their town, county, or colonial

Symbolic Death to Stamp Agents
Protesters in many towns staged threatening demonstrations designed to make any stamp distributor reconsider selling the hated stamps. In this contemporary cartoon, a dummy wearing a hat and waistcoat is being led to destruction. One protester carries a hangman's gallows, another a large bundle of sticks to burn the dummy. Do you think the cartoonist was in sympathy with the demonstrators? The Granger Collection, New York.

assemblies, to fund government administrative expenses and shared necessities like local roads, schools, and poor relief. In contrast, the stamp tax was a clear departure as a fee-per-document tax, levied by a distant Parliament on unwilling colonies.

Resistance Strategies and Crowd Politics

News of the Stamp Act arrived in the colonies in April 1765, seven months before it was to take effect. There was time, therefore, to object. Governors were unlikely to challenge the law, for most of them owed their offices to the king. Instead, the colonial assemblies took the lead; eight of them held discussions on the Stamp Act.

Virginia's assembly, the House of Burgesses, was the first. At the end of its May session, after two-thirds of the members had left, Patrick Henry, a young political newcomer, presented a series of resolutions on the Stamp Act that were debated and passed, one by one. They became known as the Virginia Resolves. Henry's resolutions inched the assembly toward radical opposition to the Stamp Act. The first three stated the obvious:

that Virginians were British citizens, that they enjoyed the same rights and privileges as Britons, and that self-taxation was one of those rights. The fourth resolution noted that Virginians had always taxed themselves, through their representatives in the House of Burgesses. The fifth took a radical leap by pushing the other four unexceptional statements to one logical conclusion—that the Virginia assembly alone had the right to tax Virginians.

Two more fiery resolutions were debated as Henry pressed the logic of his case to the extreme. The sixth resolution denied legitimacy to any tax law originating outside Virginia, and the seventh boldly called anyone who disagreed with these propositions an enemy of Virginia. This was too much for the other representatives. They voted down resolutions six and seven and later rescinded their vote on number five as well.

Their caution hardly mattered, however, because newspapers in other colonies printed all seven Virginia Resolves, creating the impression that a daring first challenge to the Stamp Act had occurred. Consequently, other assemblies were willing to consider even more radical questions, such as this: By what authority could Parliament

Pursuing Liberty, Protesting Tyranny

In August 1765, a little-known Boston shoemaker gained sudden prominence as the leader of crowd actions opposing the Stamp Act. Ebenezer Mackintosh boldly encouraged thousands of ordinary men in Massachusetts to assert a claim to liberty against what they identified as British tyranny. Mackintosh's story offers a glimpse into the political thinking of the man in the street during the decade of pre-Revolutionary turmoil. By 1776, this quest for liberty would be a defining feature of the fledgling United States.

Born in poverty in 1737, Ebenezer Mackintosh lacked family resources to ease his way in the world. His ancestors arrived in the Puritan migration of the 1630s; a century later, his family was quite poor. Ebenezer's father, an orphan, struggled against bad fortune. He owned no land and lacked a trade; he married and buried wives at least three times. The best he could do for young Ebenezer was to apprentice him to a shoemaker. During the Seven Years' War, Ebenezer joined the army to secure a signing bonus. He saw brief action and returned to Boston in 1758 to resume shoemaking. He was twenty-one.

A major fire in Boston in 1760 marked a dramatic change in direction for Mackintosh. In the aftermath of the fire, the city looked to young, able-bodied men to reinvigorate its volunteer fire companies and picked Ebenezer to join a select firemen's association in the city's South End. Fighting fires demonstrated one's sense of civic duty and manly responsibility. Fire clubs also generated fraternal sociability, with firemen regularly meeting in taverns over pitchers of beer, cementing the team spirit so critical to successful firefighting. Mackintosh proved to be a leader of men in times of emergency; he soon became head of the South End gang, which staged a mock battle once a year against the rival North End gang. In this traditional street festival, Mackintosh gained direct experience managing rowdy crowds.

Expertise in fire and crowd control paved the way for Mackintosh's transition from community leader to community activist in 1765. Stamp Act protests erupted twice in August of that year. In the first event, Mackintosh presided over the mock hanging of a dummy representing Andrew Oliver, the stamp distributor, at a century-old elm tree known as the Liberty Tree. The shoemaker led several thousand protesters in a march on the new stamp office, which was pulled down and burned.

Twelve days later, a smaller but far more destructive demonstration almost certainly led by Mackintosh demolished the mansion of Governor Thomas Hutchinson. Hutchinson ordered Mackintosh arrested, but no witnesses cared to identify him. Hours later, the sheriff—a member of Mackintosh's fire company—released him, predicting worse trouble if he was kept in jail.

The shoemaker continued to lead large demonstrations in November and December, forcing Andrew Oliver to repudiate his stamp distributor duties. Ordinary people like Mackintosh exerted a new authority and confidence, commanding their social betters to do their bidding.

In 1766, the Stamp Act was repealed, and Mackintosh went back to shoemaking. He married Elizabeth Maverick and had two children by 1769. Perhaps he took a break from activism; no record links him to protest activities when British troops came to town in 1769–1770, nor was his presence recorded at the Boston Massacre in March 1770. In 1773, he was apparently back at it, bragging later in life that he helped throw tea into Boston harbor.

A well-publicized rumor spread in 1774 that a ship en route from London carried official orders to

legislate for the colonies without also taxing them? No one disagreed, in 1765, that Parliament had legislative power over the colonists, who were, after all, British subjects. Several assemblies advanced the argument that there was a distinction between *external taxes*, imposed to regulate trade, and *internal taxes*, such as a stamp tax or a property tax, which could only be self-imposed.

Reaction to the Stamp Act ran far deeper than political debate in assemblies. Every person whose livelihood required official paper had to decide whether to comply with the act. The first organized resistance to the Stamp Act began in Boston in August 1765 under the direction of town leaders, chief among them Samuel Adams, John Hancock, and Ebenezer Mackintosh. Adams and Hancock, both Harvard graduates, were town officers. Adams, in his forties, had shrewd political instincts and a gift for organizing. Hancock, not yet thirty, had inherited an uncle's shipping business and was one of the wealthiest men in Massachusetts. Mackintosh, also a young man, was a shoemaker and highly experienced street activist. (See "Experiencing the American Promise,"

Mackintosh the Fireman
Skilled Boston firemen tapped water from underground water mains made from hollowed logs and pumped it vigorously by hand to douse fires. Demolition to halt the spread of fires was also essential work. Mackintosh's fire-control skills transferred easily to anti–Stamp Act actions, whether burning effigies and small buildings or pulling down Hutchinson's house. The Granger Collection, New York.

arrest four rebellious subjects, most notably Samuel Adams and Mackintosh. Adams stayed put, but Mackintosh, still lacking resources and at a low moment in life—his young wife had recently died—decided that flight was his best option. Carrying his two young children and his meager belongings, he walked 150 miles to a village in northern New Hampshire, where he set up shop as a shoemaker. He served locally and briefly as a soldier in the Revolution and then remarried and fathered four more children.

An especially telling clue to Mackintosh's idealization of liberty appears in the unusual name he gave his son born in 1769: Paschal Paoli

Mackintosh, named in honor of Pasquale Paoli of Corsica, an anti-monarchical freedom fighter who battled Italian foes and who won approving coverage in American newspapers in 1767–1769. (In those years, some scores of babies throughout the colonies were named Paschal.) Mackintosh enjoyed his brief moment of fame, and he lived to see liberty defined and enshrined in the foundational documents of the United States. Although his life ended in 1816 in obscurity, as it had begun, Mackintosh's activism in 1765 helped ensure that the thousands of people he mobilized learned a new political language of rights and liberties—a language that still resonates loudly today.

Questions for Analysis

Recognize Viewpoints: Why would a twenty-eight-year-old shoemaker of low social status get upset about Britain's passage of the Stamp Act?

Ask Historical Questions: What was at stake for Mackintosh in the American Revolution? What did he gain? What stayed the same?

Consider the Context: How did many ordinary Americans of limited means, limited tax liabilities, limited political experience, and limited literacy get drawn into the developing political crisis with Britain?

above.) Many other artisans, tradesmen, printers, tavern keepers, dockworkers, and sailors—the middling and lower orders—mobilized to oppose the Stamp Act, taking the name "Sons of Liberty."

The plan hatched in Boston called for a large street demonstration highlighting a mock execution designed to convince Andrew Oliver, the designated stamp distributor, to resign. On August 14, 1765, a crowd of two thousand to three thousand demonstrators, led by Mackintosh, hung an effigy of Oliver in a tree and then paraded it around town before finally beheading and burn-

ing it. In hopes of calming tensions, the royal governor Francis Bernard took no action. The next day Oliver resigned his office in a well-publicized announcement.

The demonstration provided lessons for everyone. Oliver learned that stamp distributors would be very unpopular people. Governor Bernard, with no police force to call on, learned the limitations of his power to govern. The demonstration's leaders learned that street action was effective. And hundreds of ordinary men not only learned what the Stamp Act was all about but also gained pride in their ability to have a decisive impact on politics.

Twelve days later, a second crowd action showed how well these lessons had been learned. On August 26, a crowd visited the houses of three detested customs and court officials, breaking windows and raiding wine cellars. A fourth target was the finest dwelling in Massachusetts, owned by Thomas Hutchinson, lieutenant governor of Massachusetts and the chief justice of the colony's highest court. Rumors abounded that Hutchinson had urged Grenville to adopt the Stamp Act. Although he had actually done the opposite, Hutchinson refused to set the record straight, saying curtly, "I am not obliged to give an answer to all the questions that may be put me by every lawless person." The crowd attacked his house, and by daybreak only the exterior walls were standing. Governor Bernard gave orders to call out the militia, but he was told that many militiamen were among the crowd.

The destruction of Hutchinson's house brought a temporary halt to protest activities in Boston. The town meeting issued a statement of sympathy for Hutchinson, but a large reward for the arrest and conviction of rioters failed to produce a single lead. Hutchinson believed that Adams commanded Mackintosh, but Adams denied involvement and professed shock at the "truly mobbish Nature" of the violence. Essentially, the opponents of the Stamp Act in Boston had triumphed; no one replaced Oliver as distributor. When the act took effect on November 1, ships without stamped permits continued to clear the harbor. Since he could not bring the lawbreakers to court, Hutchinson, ever principled, felt obliged to resign his office as chief justice. He remained lieutenant governor, however, and within five years he became the royal governor.

Liberty and Property

Boston's crowd actions of August sparked similar eruptions by groups calling themselves Sons of Liberty in nearly fifty towns throughout the colonies, and stamp distributors everywhere hastened to resign. A crowd forced one Connecticut distributor to throw his hat and powdered wig in the air while shouting a cheer for "Liberty and property!" This man fared better than another Connecticut stamp agent who was nearly buried alive by Sons of Liberty. Only when the thuds of dirt sounded on his coffin did he have a sudden change of heart, shouting out his resignation to the crowd above. Luckily, he was heard. In Charleston, South Carolina, the stamp distributor

resigned after crowds burned effigies and chanted "Liberty! Liberty!"

Some colonial leaders, disturbed by the riots, sought a more moderate challenge to parliamentary authority. In October 1765, twenty-seven delegates representing nine colonial assemblies met in New York City as the Stamp Act Congress. For two weeks, the men hammered out a petition about taxation addressed to the king and Parliament. Their statement closely resembled the first five Virginia Resolves, claiming that taxes were "free gifts of the people," which only the people's representatives could give. They dismissed virtual representation: "The people of these colonies are not, and from their local circumstances, cannot be represented in the House of Commons." At the same time, the delegates carefully affirmed their subordination to Parliament and monarch in deferential language. Nevertheless, the Stamp Act Congress, by the mere fact of its meeting, advanced a radical potential—the notion of intercolonial political action.

The rallying cry of "Liberty and property" made perfect sense to many white Americans of all social ranks, who feared that the Stamp Act threatened their traditional rights to liberty as British subjects. The liberty in question was the right to be taxed only by representative government. "Liberty and property" came from a trinity of concepts—"life, liberty, property"—that had come to be regarded as the birthright of freeborn British subjects since at least the seventeenth century. A powerful tradition of British political thought invested representative government with the duty to protect individual lives, liberties, and property against potential abuse by royal authority. Up to 1765, Americans had consented to accept Parliament as a body that represented them. But now, in this matter of taxation via stamps, Parliament seemed a distant body that had failed to protect Americans' liberty and property against royal authority.

Alarmed, some Americans began to speak and write about a plot by British leaders to enslave them. A Maryland writer warned that if the colonies lost "the right of exemption from all taxes without their consent," that loss would "deprive them of every privilege distinguishing freemen from slaves." In Virginia, a group of planters headed by Richard Henry Lee issued a document called the Westmoreland Resolves, claiming that the Stamp Act was an attempt "to reduce the people of this country to a state of abject and detestable slavery." The opposite meanings of *liberty* and *slavery* were utterly clear to white Americans, but they stopped short of applying similar logic to the half million black Americans they held in bondage. Many blacks, however, could see the contradiction. When a crowd of Charleston blacks paraded with shouts of "Liberty!" just a few months after white Sons of Liberty had done the same, the town militia turned out to break up the demonstration.

Politicians and merchants in Britain reacted with distress to the American demonstrations and petitions. Merchants particularly feared trade disruptions and pressured Parliament to repeal the Stamp Act. By late 1765, yet another new minister, the Marquess of Rockingham, headed the king's cabinet and sought a way to repeal the act without losing face. The solution came in March 1766: The Stamp Act was repealed, but with the repeal came the **Declaratory Act**, which asserted Parliament's right to legislate for the colonies "in all cases whatsoever." Perhaps the stamp tax had been inexpedient, and indeed a failure, but the power to tax—one prime case of a legislative power—was stoutly upheld.

REVIEW Why did the Sugar Act and the Stamp Act draw fierce opposition from colonists?

▶ The Townshend Acts and Economic Retaliation, 1767–1770

Rockingham did not last long as prime minister. By the summer of 1766, George III had persuaded William Pitt to resume that position. Pitt appointed Charles Townshend to be chancellor of the exchequer, the chief financial minister. Facing both the old war debt and the cost of the British troops in America, Townshend turned again to taxation, but his plan to raise revenue touched off coordinated boycotts of British goods in 1768 and 1769. Even women were politicized as self-styled "Daughters of Liberty." Boston led the uproar, causing the British to send peacekeeping soldiers to assist the royal governor. The stage was thus set for the first fatalities in the brewing revolution.

The Townshend Duties

Townshend proposed new taxes in the old form of a navigation act. Officially called the Revenue Act of 1767, it established new duties on tea, glass, lead, paper, and painters' colors imported into the colonies, to be paid by the importer but passed on to consumers in the retail price. A recent further reduction in the duty on French molasses had persuaded some American shippers to quit smuggling, and finally Britain was deriving a moderate revenue stream from its colonies. Townshend naively concluded that Americans accepted external taxes.

The **Townshend duties** were not especially burdensome, but the principle they embodied—taxation through trade duties—looked different to the colonists in the wake of the Stamp Act crisis. Although Americans once distinguished between external and internal taxes, accepting external duties as a means to direct the flow of trade, that distinction was wiped out by an external tax meant only to raise money. John Dickinson, a Philadelphia lawyer, articulated this view in an essay titled *Letters from a Farmer in Pennsylvania*, widely circulated in late 1767. "We are taxed without our consent. . . . We are therefore—SLAVES," Dickinson wrote, calling for "a total denial of the power of Parliament to lay upon these colonies any 'tax' whatever."

A controversial provision of the Townshend duties directed that some of the revenue generated would pay the salaries of royal governors. Before 1767, local assemblies set the salaries of their own officials, giving them significant influence over crown-appointed officeholders. Through his new provision, Townshend aimed to strengthen the governors' position as well as to curb what he perceived to be the growing independence of the assemblies.

Massachusetts again took the lead in protesting the Townshend duties. Samuel Adams, now an elected member of the provincial assembly, argued that any form of parliamentary taxation was unjust because Americans were not represented in Parliament. Further, he argued that the new way to pay governors' salaries subverted the proper relationship between the people and their rulers. The assembly circulated a letter with Adams's arguments to other colonial assemblies for their endorsement. As with the Stamp Act Congress of 1765, colonial assemblies were starting to coordinate their protests.

In response to Adams's letter, Lord Hillsborough, the new man in charge of colonial affairs in Britain, instructed Massachusetts governor Bernard to dissolve the assembly if it refused to repudiate the letter. The assembly refused, by a vote of 92 to 17, and Bernard carried out his instruction. In the summer of 1768, Boston was in an uproar.

Nonconsumption and the Daughters of Liberty

The Boston town meeting led the way with nonconsumption agreements calling for a boycott of all British-made goods. Dozens of other towns passed similar resolutions in 1767 and 1768. For example, prohibited purchases in the town of New Haven, Connecticut, included carriages, furniture, hats, clothing, lace, clocks, and textiles. The idea was to encourage home manufacture and to hurt trade, causing London merchants to pressure Parliament for repeal of the duties.

Nonconsumption agreements were very hard to enforce. With the Stamp Act, there was one hated item, a stamp, and a limited number of official distributors. In contrast, an agreement to boycott all British goods required serious personal sacrifice, which not everyone was prepared to make. A more direct blow to trade came from nonimportation agreements, but getting merchants to agree to these proved more difficult because of fears that merchants in other colonies might continue to import goods and make handsome profits. Not until late 1768 could Boston merchants agree to suspend trade through a nonimportation agreement lasting one year starting January 1, 1769. Sixty signed the agreement. New York merchants soon followed suit, as did Philadelphia and Charleston merchants in 1769.

Many of the British products specified in nonconsumption agreements were household goods traditionally under the control of the "ladies." By 1769, male leaders in the patriot cause clearly understood that women's cooperation in nonconsumption and home manufacture was beneficial to their cause. The Townshend duties thus provided an unparalleled opportunity for encouraging female patriotism. During the Stamp Act crisis, Sons of Liberty took to the streets in protest. During the difficulties of 1768 and 1769, the concept of Daughters of Liberty emerged to give shape to a new idea—that women might play a role in public affairs. Any woman could express affiliation with the colonial protest through conspicuous boycotts of British-made goods. In Boston, more than three hundred women signed a petition to abstain from tea, "sickness excepted," in order to "save this abused Country from Ruin and Slavery."

Homespun cloth became a prominent symbol of patriotism. A young Boston girl learning to spin called herself "a daughter of liberty," noting that "I chuse to wear as much of our own manufactory as pocible." In the boycott period of 1768 to 1770, newspapers reported on spinning matches, or bees, in some sixty New England towns, in which women came together in public to make yarn. Newspaper accounts variously called the spinners "Daughters of Liberty" or "Daughters of Industry."

This surge of public spinning was related to the politics of the boycott, which infused traditional women's work with new political purpose. But the women spinners were not equivalents of the Sons of Liberty. The Sons marched in streets, burned effigies, threatened hated officials, and celebrated anniversaries of their successes with raucous drinking in taverns. The Daughters manifested their patriotism quietly, in ways marked by piety, industry, and charity. The difference was due in part to cultural ideals of gender, which prized masculine self-assertion and feminine selflessness. It also was due to class. The Sons were a cross-class alliance, with leaders from the middling orders reliant on men and boys of the lower ranks to fuel their crowds. The Daughters dusting off spinning wheels and shelving their teapots were genteel ladies accustomed to buying British goods. The difference between the Sons and the Daughters also speaks to two views of how best to challenge authority: violent threats and street actions, or the self-disciplined, self-sacrificing boycott of goods?

On the whole, the anti-British boycotts were a success. Imports fell by more than 40 percent; British merchants felt the pinch and let Parliament know it. In Boston, the extended Hutchinson family—whose fortune rested on British trade—also endured losses, but even more alarming to the lieutenant governor, Boston seemed overrun with anti-British sentiment. The Sons of Liberty staged rollicking annual celebrations of the Stamp Act riot, and both Hutchinson and Governor Bernard concluded that British troops were necessary to restore order.

Military Occupation and "Massacre" in Boston

In the fall of 1768, three thousand uniformed troops arrived to occupy Boston. The soldiers drilled conspicuously on the town Common, played loud music on the Sabbath, and in general grated on the nerves of Bostonians. Although the situation was frequently tense, no major troubles occurred that winter and through most of 1769. But as January 1, 1770, approached, marking the end of the nonimportation agreement, it was

Edenton Tea Ladies
Patriotic women in Edenton, North Carolina, pledged to renounce British tea and were satirized in this British cartoon, which shows brazen women shedding their femininity. Neglected babies, urinating dogs, wanton sexuality, and mean-looking women were the consequences, according to the artist. The cartoon was humorous to the British because of the gender reversals it predicts and because of the insult it directs at American men. Library of Congress, 3g04617.

clear that some merchants—such as Thomas Hutchinson's two sons, both importers—were ready to break the boycott.

Trouble began in January, when a crowd smeared the door of the Hutchinson brothers' shop with excrement. In February, a crowd surrounded the house of a confrontational customs official who panicked and fired a musket, accidentally killing a young boy passing on the street. The Sons of Liberty mounted a massive funeral procession to mark this first instance of violent death in the struggle with Britain.

For the next week, tension gripped Boston. The climax came on Monday evening, March 5, 1770, when a crowd taunted eight British soldiers guarding the customs house. Onlookers threw snowballs and rocks and dared the soldiers to fire; finally one did. After a short pause, someone yelled "Fire!" and the other soldiers shot into the crowd, hitting eleven men, killing five of them.

The **Boston Massacre**, as the event was quickly labeled, was over in minutes. Hutchinson,

now acting governor of the colony, showed courage in addressing the crowd from the balcony of the statehouse. He immediately removed the regiments to an island in the harbor to prevent further bloodshed, and he jailed Captain Thomas Preston and his eight soldiers for their own protection, promising they would be held for trial.

The Sons of Liberty staged elaborate martyrs' funerals for the five victims. Significantly, the one nonwhite victim shared equally in the public's veneration. Crispus Attucks, a sailor and rope maker in his forties, was the son of an African man and a Natick Indian woman. A slave in his youth, he was at the time of his death a free laborer at the Boston docks. Attucks was one of the first American partisans to die in the revolutionary struggle with Britain, and certainly the first African American.

At trial in the fall of 1770, the eight soldiers were ably defended by two Boston attorneys, John Adams and Josiah Quincy. While both had direct ties to the leadership of the Sons of Liberty, Adams was deeply committed to the principle

VISUAL ACTIVITY

The Bloody Massacre Perpetrated in King Street, Boston, on March 5, 1770
Paul Revere's mass-produced engraving shows the patriot version of events. Soldiers appear as a firing squad, shooting simultaneously at an unarmed and bewigged crowd; more likely the shooting was chaotic and the fatalities were from lower classes who were not the sort to wear wigs. Crispus Attucks, an African-Indian dockworker, was killed, but Revere depicts only whites among the injured. Anne S. K. Brown Military Collection, Brown University Library.
READING THE IMAGE: How does this picture attempt to enlist its viewers' sympathies?
CONNECTIONS: Does this picture accurately represent the events of the Boston Massacre? What might account for its biases?

that even unpopular defendants deserved a fair trial. Samuel Adams respected his cousin's decision to take the case, for there was a tactical benefit as well. It showed that the Boston leadership was not lawless but could be seen as defenders of British liberty and law. The five-day trial resulted in acquittal for Preston and for all but two of the soldiers, who were convicted of manslaughter, branded on the thumbs, and released.

REVIEW Why did British authorities send troops to occupy Boston in the fall of 1768?

▶ The Destruction of the Tea and the Coercive Acts, 1770–1774

In the same week as the Boston Massacre, yet another new British prime minister, Frederick North, acknowledged the harmful impact of the boycott on trade and recommended repeal of the Townshend duties. A skillful politician, Lord North took office in 1770 and kept it for twelve years; at last King George had stability at the helm. Seeking peace with the colonies and prosperity for British merchants, Lord North persuaded Parliament to remove all the duties except the tax on tea, kept as a symbol of Parliament's power. For nearly two years following repeal of the Townshend duties, peace seemed possible, but tense incidents in 1772, followed by a renewed struggle over the tea tax in 1773, precipitated a full-scale crisis in the summer and fall of 1774. In response, men from nearly all the colonies came together in a special "Continental Congress" to debate the crisis.

The Calm before the Storm

Repeal of the Townshend duties brought an end to nonimportation. Trade boomed in 1770 and 1771, driven by pent-up demand. Moreover, the leaders of the popular movement seemed to be losing their power. Samuel Adams, for example, ran for a minor local office and lost to a conservative merchant. Then in 1772, several incidents again brought the conflict with Britain into sharp focus. One was the burning of the *Gaspée*, a Royal Navy ship pursuing suspected smugglers near

Rhode Island. A British investigating commission failed to arrest anyone but announced that it would send suspects, if any were found, to Britain for trial on charges of high treason. This ruling seemed to fly in the face of the traditional English right to trial by a jury of one's peers.

When news of the *Gaspée* investigation spread, it was greeted with disbelief in other colonies. Patrick Henry, Thomas Jefferson, and Richard Henry Lee in the Virginia House of Burgesses proposed that a network of standing committees be established to link the colonies and pass along alarming news. By mid-1773, all but one colonial assembly had set up a "committee of correspondence."

Massachusetts, the continuing hotspot of the conflict, developed its own rapid communications network, with urgency provided by a new proposal by Lord North to pay the salaries of county court justices out of the tea revenue, reminiscent of Townshend's plan for paying royal governors. By spring 1773, more than half the towns in Massachusetts had set up **committees of correspondence** to receive, discuss, distribute, and act on political news. The first message to circulate came from Boston; it framed North's salary plan for judges as the latest proof of a British conspiracy to undermine traditional liberties: first taxation without consent, then military occupation and a massacre, and now a plot to subvert the justice system. Express riders swiftly distributed the message, which sparked ordinary townspeople to embrace a revolutionary language of rights and constitutional duties. Eventually the committees of correspondence would foster rapid mobilization to defend a countryside feeling under literal attack.

The paramount incident shattering the relative calm of the early 1770s was the **Tea Act of 1773**. After nonimportation ended, Americans had resumed buying the taxed British tea, but they were also smuggling much larger quantities of tea obtained from Dutch sources, greatly undercutting the sales of Britain's East India Company. To reverse this trend, Parliament lowered the colonists' tax on East India Company tea and, at the same time, allowed the Company to sell its product directly to a few selected merchants in four colonial cities, cutting out British middlemen. The combined effect was to lower the retail price of the East India tea well below that of smuggled Dutch tea, thus motivating Americans to obey the law.

Tea in Boston Harbor

In the fall of 1773, news of the Tea Act reached the colonies. Parliamentary legislation to make tea inexpensive struck many colonists as an insidious plot to trick Americans into buying the duties tea. The real goal, some argued, was the increased revenue that would pay the salaries of royal governors and judges and the reassertion of Britain's right to tax the colonists.

But how to resist the Tea Act? Nonimportation was not viable because the tea trade was too lucrative to expect merchants to give it up willingly. Consumer boycotts seemed ineffective because it was impossible to distinguish between duties tea and smuggled tea once it was in the teapot. The appointment of official tea agents, parallel to the Stamp Act distributors, suggested one solution. In every port city, revived Sons of Liberty pressured tea agents to resign. Without agents, governors yielded, and tea cargoes either landed duty-free or were sent home.

Governor Hutchinson, however, would not bend any rules. Three ships bearing tea arrived in Boston in November 1773. The ships cleared customs, and the crews, sensing the town's extreme tension, unloaded all cargo except the tea. Picking up on the tension on the town, the captains wished to return to England, but Hutchinson would not grant them clearance to leave without paying the tea duty. To add to the difficulties, another long-standing law imposed a twenty-day limit for the payment of duties, after which time cargo would be confiscated. Hutchinson made it clear he planned to enforce that law.

For the full twenty days, crowds swelled by concerned people from surrounding towns kept the pressure high. On the final day, December 16, a large crowd gathered at Old South Church to debate a course of action. No solution emerged at that meeting, but immediately after, 100 to 150 men disguised as Mohawk Indians, with soot-darkened faces and blankets wrapped around them, boarded the ships and dumped over 90,000 pounds of tea into the harbor. Their disguises served to distinguish them from the Boston townsmen at Old South Church, whose leaders did not join the crowd of 2,000 bystanders watching the near-silent and efficient destruction of the tea. In admiration, John Adams wrote in his diary, "This Destruction of the Tea is so bold, so daring, so firm, intrepid and inflexible, and it must have so important Consequences."

The Coercive Acts

Lord North's response was swift and stern: He persuaded Parliament to issue the **Coercive Acts**, four laws meant to punish Massachusetts for destroying the tea. In America, those laws,

The Bostonians Paying the Excise-Man, or Tarring and Feathering, 1774

In January 1774, Boston customs collector John Malcolm beat a patriot shoemaker with his cane. An incensed crowd nabbed him and subjected him to a painful tarring and feathering. This ritualized humiliation involved stripping a victim and dipping him in warm tar followed by chicken feathers. Note the pictorial references to other events in Boston. Does this artist support the American cause? What's your evidence? Gilder Lehrman Collection, New York, USA/ Bridgeman Images.

could now appoint all judges, sheriffs, and officers of the court. No town meeting beyond the annual spring election of town selectmen could be held without the governor's approval, and every agenda item required prior approval. Every Massachusetts town was affected.

The third Coercive Act, the Impartial Administration of Justice Act, stipulated that any royal official accused of a capital crime—for example, Captain Preston and his soldiers at the Boston Massacre—would be tried in a court in Britain. It did not matter that Preston had received a fair trial in Boston. What this act ominously suggested was that down the road, more Captain Prestons and soldiers might be firing into unruly crowds. The fourth act amended the 1765 Quartering Act and permitted military commanders to lodge soldiers wherever necessary, even in private households. In a related move, Lord North appointed General Thomas Gage, the commander of the Royal Army in New York, to be governor of Massachusetts. Thomas Hutchinson was out, relieved at long last of his duties. Military rule, including soldiers, returned once more to Boston.

The fifth act, concerning Quebec, now part of the British empire, was unrelated to the four Coercive Acts, but it magnified American fears. It confirmed the continuation of French civil law as well as Catholicism for Quebec—an affront to Protestant New Englanders who had recently been denied their own representative government. It also awarded Quebec land (and the lucrative fur trade) in the Ohio Valley, an area also claimed by Virginia, Pennsylvania, and a number of Indian tribes.

The five Intolerable Acts spread alarm in all the colonies. (See "Analyzing Historical Evidence," page 158.) If Britain could squelch Massachusetts—change its charter, suspend local government, inaugurate military rule, and on top of that give Ohio to Catholic Quebec—what liberties were secure? Fearful royal governors in a half dozen colonies dismissed the sitting assemblies, adding to the sense of urgency. A few of the assemblies defiantly continued to meet in new locations. Via the committees of correspondence, colonial leaders arranged to convene in Philadelphia in September 1774 to respond to the crisis.

Beyond Boston: Rural New England

The Coercive Acts fired up all of New England to open insubordination. With a British general occupying the Massachusetts governorship and

along with a fifth one, the Quebec Act, were soon known as the **Intolerable Acts**. The first act, the Boston Port Act, closed Boston harbor to all shipping as of June 1, 1774, until the destroyed tea was paid for. Britain's objective was to halt the commercial life of the city. The second act, called the Massachusetts Government Act, greatly altered the colony's charter, underscoring Parliament's claim to supremacy over Massachusetts. The royal governor's powers were augmented, and the governor's council became an appointive, rather than elective, body. Further, the governor

some three thousand troops controlling Boston, the revolutionary momentum shifted from urban radicals to rural farmers who protested in dozens of spontaneous, dramatic showdowns. Some towns found creative ways to get around the Massachusetts Government Act's prohibition on town meetings, and others just ignored the law. Governor Gage's call for elections for a new provincial assembly under his control sparked the formation of a competing unauthorized assembly that met in defiance of his orders. In all Massachusetts counties outside Boston, crowds of thousands of armed men converged to prevent the opening of county courts run by crown-appointed jurists. No judges were physically harmed, but they were forced to resign and made to doff their judicial wigs or run a humiliating gauntlet. By August 1774, farmers and artisans all over Massachusetts had effectively taken full control of their local institutions.

Unfettered by the crown, ordinary citizens throughout New England began serious planning for the showdown everyone assumed would come. Town militias stockpiled gunpowder "in case of invasion." Militia officers repudiated their official chain of command to the governor and stepped

No. X   Engraved for Royal American Magazine.   . Vol. I.

The able Doctor. or America Swallowing the Bitter Draught.

VISUAL ACTIVITY

The Able Doctor, or America Swallowing the Bitter Draught, 1774, Engraved by Paul Revere
Revere's cartoon, a response to the Boston Port Act, shows Lord North forcing tea down the throat of America, depicted as an Indian maiden. The older woman is Britannia (known by her shield), who averts her eyes from the attack. Two British lords hold America down, while two other men to the left, representing France and Spain, look on with amusement and pleasure. Private Collection/Bridgeman Images.

READING THE IMAGE: How does this cartoon rely on widely shared stereotypes of gender and sexual danger to express power relations in the masculine world of politics? What is gained by representing the country of Britain as a woman, in contrast to the male political figures?

CONNECTIONS: According to the Americans, in what sense was Britain forcing them to purchase and drink tea in 1773? Was that sense of coercion still in play in 1774, at the time of this cartoon?

Reactions to the Boston Port Act outside of Massachusetts

As punishment for the destruction of the tea in Boston, Parliament closed Boston's port by naval blockade as of June 1, 1774, until the tea was paid for. News of Parliament's action spurred discussion and action all around the American colonies.

DOCUMENT 1
George Washington Writes to George William Fairfax, 1774

Washington describes the transformation of the Virginia Assembly, shut down by the royal governor, into a new legislative body meeting at a tavern. In one long, breathless sentence he voices his concerns about the Boston Port Act and the threats facing Virginia.

Williamsburg, June 10, 1774 . . . [The Assembly] Members convend themselves at the Raleigh Tavern & enterd into the Inclosd Association which being followed two days after by an Express from Boston accompanied by the Sentiments of some Meetings in our Sister Colonies to the Northwd the proceedings mentiond in the Inclos'd Papers were had thereupon & a general meeting requested of all the late Representatives in this City on the first of August when it is hopd, & expected that some vigorous measures will be effectually adopted to obtain that justice which is denied to our Petitions & Remonstrances; in short the Ministry may rely on it that Americans will never be tax'd without their own consent that the cause of Boston the despotick Measures in respect to it I mean now is and ever will be considerd as the cause of America (not that we approve their cond[uc]t in destroyg the Tea) & that we shall not suffer ourselves to be sacrificed by piecemeal though god only knows what is to become of us, threatned as we are with so many hoverg evils as hang over us at present; having a cruel & blood thirsty Enemy upon our Backs, the Indians, between whom & our Frontier Inhabitants many Skirmishes have happend, & with who(m) a general War is inevitable whilst those from whom we have a right to Seek protection are endeavouring by every piece of Art & despotism to fix the Shackles of Slavry upon us.

Source: George Washington to George William Fairfax 10–15 June 1774, *The Papers of George Washington*, The University Press of Virginia. Copyright © 1995 by the Rector and Visitors of the University of Virginia.

DOCUMENT 2
An Anonymous Philadelphian Implores Boston to Pay for the Tea, 1774

A self-described "friend to the cause of America" argues that paying for the tea is in the best interests of justice and liberty, using repetition for effect.

To the Inhabitants on the Town of BOSTON, and Province of MASSACHUSETTS-BAY.

My Dear BRETHREN,
IN Messi'rs Mills and Hicks's Gazette of the 20th of June, I observed with great concern a paragraph with the signature of "Consideration," calculated to deter you from paying for the tea, a measure at this alarming juncture highly necessary and what every REAL friend to the cause of America must think your indispensible duty. While we contend for liberty, let us not destroy the idea of justice. A trespass has been committed on private property in consequence of the Resolves of your town. Restore to the sufferers the most ample compensation for the injury

up drills of their units. Town after town withheld its tax money from the royal governor and diverted it to military supplies. Governor Gage felt under heavy threat, but he could do little. He wrote London begging for troop reinforcements, and he beefed up fortifications around Boston. But without more soldiers, his options were limited. Seizing the stockpiles of gunpowder was his best move.

The Powder Alarm of September 1 showed just how ready the defiant Americans were to take up arms against Britain. Gage sent troops to a town just outside Boston reported to have a hidden powder storehouse, and in the surprise and scramble of the attack, false news spread that the troops had fired on men defending the powder, killing six. Within twenty-four hours, several thousand armed men from Massachusetts, New Hampshire, and Connecticut streamed on foot to Boston to avenge what they thought was the first bloodshed of war. At this moment, ordinary men became insurgents, willing to kill or be killed in the face of the British clampdown.

they have received—convince your enemies that their property is secure in every Port on the British Continent—Convince them that you do not regard the value of the article destroyed—that you only deny the right of taxation. Let not the annals of your history be sullied by a refusal—pay for the tea—it will rejoice your friends—it will convince your adversaries that the cause you are attach'd to is a righteous and just cause. Convince them that you regard honesty as much as liberty, and that you detest libertinism and licentiousness. . . . Then can you with a degree of confidence call on your friends to stand by and protect you—your enemies, if any there be, you may defy to prejudice you. I beseech you, by every thing you hold dear—I conjure you, as you value a union of the colonies, pay for the tea; it is but justice, pay for it, let nothing retard it; it is an expedient, which ought to have been effected e'er this; we lament that it yet remains undone. . . .

These are the sentiments of the Pennsylvanians, and the anxious prayer of A PHILADELPHIAN.

Source: *The Massachusetts Gazette and the Boston Weekly News-Letter*, 14 July 1774, p. 2. Also at http://www.masshist.org/revolution/image-viewer.php?item_id=691&mode=large&img_step=2&tpc=#page2

DOCUMENT 3
A New Hampshire Town Offers Sympathy and Support to Boston, 1774

Kingston, New Hampshire, was one of hundreds of towns to pledge assistance to Boston.

Sept. 14, 1774

Gentlemen,

The inhabitants of Kingston, in the Province of New Hampshire, see with deep concern the unhappy misunderstanding and disagreement that now subsists between Great Britain and these American Colonies, being fully sensible that the happiness of both countries depend on an union, harmony, and agreement to be established between them on a just, equitable, and permanent foundation. But when we consider the new, arbitrary, and unjust claims of our brethren in Great Britain, to levy taxes upon us at their sovereign will and pleasure, and to make laws to bind us in all cases, whatsoever, we view and consider ourselves and our posterity under the operations of these claims, as absolute slaves: for what is a slave, but one who is bound in all cases whatsoever by the will and command of another. And we look on the late unjust, cruel, hostile, and tyrannical Acts of the British Parliament, respecting the Massachusetts Bay in general, and the Town of Boston in particular, as consequences of these unrighteous claims, and from them clearly see what the whole continent has to expect under their operation.

But when we consider the military forces, both by sea and land, sent in an hostile manner to enforce, with the point of the sword, and mouths of cannon, those acts and claims, we esteem it an high infringement of your rights and privileges, and an insult upon all North America, and are fully persuaded that unless there is a speedy alteration of those measures, a total disaffection will soon take place, and Britain, instead of being our best friend, will be looked upon as an enemy; and then a final separation in all respects will no doubt soon follow, the thoughts of which will fill our minds with trouble, anxiety, and concern.

Source: "Correspondence in 1774 and 1775 between a Committee of the Town of Boston and Contributors of Donations for the Relief of Sufferers by the Boston Port Bill," in *Collections of the Massachusetts Historical Society*, vol. 4, 4th ser. (1858), pp. 74–76.

Questions for Analysis

Recognize Viewpoints: Why does the Philadelphia correspondent urge that the tea must be paid for? How does his position on the destruction of the tea compare to Washington's? To the townsmen of Kingston?

Analyze the Evidence: Both Washington and the townsmen of Kingston invoke fears of slavery and enslavement. What do they mean? What do they not mean?

Ask Historical Questions: Could it be said that the Boston Port Act was the most radicalizing British action in the entire run-up to the American Revolution? Why or why not?

Consider the Context: Which of these three documents most clearly anticipates that a separation from Britain might lie in the future? Why?

The First Continental Congress

Every colony except Georgia sent delegates to Philadelphia in September 1774 to discuss the looming crisis at the **First Continental Congress**. The gathering included notables such as Samuel Adams and John Adams from Massachusetts and George Washington and Patrick Henry from Virginia. A few

Once the error was corrected and the crisis defused, the men returned home peaceably. But Gage could no longer doubt the speed, numbers, and deadly determination of the rebellious subjects.

All this had occurred without orchestration by Boston radicals, Gage reported. But British leaders found it hard to believe, as one put it, that "a tumultuous Rabble, without any Appearance of general Concert, or without any Head to advise, or Leader to conduct" could pull off such effective resistance. Repeatedly in the years to come, the British would seriously underestimate their opponents.

colonies purposely sent men who opposed provoking Britain, such as Pennsylvania's Joseph Galloway, to keep the congress from becoming too radical.

Delegates sought to articulate their liberties as British subjects and the powers Parliament held over them, and they debated possible responses to the Coercive Acts. Some wanted a total ban on trade with Britain to force repeal, while others, especially southerners dependent on tobacco and rice exports, opposed halting trade. Samuel Adams and Patrick Henry were eager for a ringing denunciation of all parliamentary control. The conservative Joseph Galloway proposed a plan (quickly defeated) to create a secondary parliament in America to assist the British Parliament in ruling the colonies.

The congress met for seven weeks and produced a declaration of rights couched in traditional language: "We ask only for peace, liberty and security. We wish no diminution of royal prerogatives, we demand no new rights." But from Britain's point of view, the rights assumed already to exist were radical. Chief among them was the claim that Americans were not represented in Parliament and so each colonial government had the sole right to govern and tax its own people. The one slight concession to Britain was a carefully worded agreement that the colonists would "cheerfully consent" to trade regulations for the larger good of the empire, so long as trade regulation was not a covert means of raising revenue.

To put pressure on Britain, the delegates agreed to a staggered and limited boycott of trade: imports prohibited this year, exports the following, and rice totally exempted (to keep South Carolinians happy). To enforce the boycott, they called for a Continental Association, with chapters in each town variously called committees of public safety or of inspection, to monitor all commerce and punish suspected violators of the boycott (sometimes with a bucket of tar and a bag of feathers). Its work done in a month, the congress disbanded with agreement to reconvene in May.

The committees of public safety, the committees of correspondence, the regrouped colonial assemblies, and the Continental Congress were all political bodies functioning defiantly without any constitutional authority. British officials did not recognize them as legitimate, but many Americans who supported the patriot cause instantly accepted them. A key reason for the stability of such unauthorized governing bodies was that they were composed of many of the same men who had held elective office before.

Britain's severe reaction to Boston's destruction of the tea finally succeeded in making many colonists from New Hampshire to Georgia real-

ize that the problems of British rule went far beyond questions of nonconsensual taxation. The Coercive Acts infringed on liberty and denied self-government; they could not be ignored. With one colony already subordinated to military rule and a British army camped in Boston, the threat of a general war was very real.

REVIEW Why did Parliament pass the Coercive Acts in 1774?

▶ Domestic Insurrections, 1774–1775

Before the Second Continental Congress could meet, violence and bloodshed came to Massachusetts in the towns of Lexington and Concord. Fearing domestic insurrection, General Thomas Gage sent his soldiers there to capture an ammunition depot, but New England farmers mobilized against an intrusive power they feared would enslave them. To the south, a different and inverted version of the same story began to unfold, as thousands of enslaved black men and women seized an unprecedented opportunity to mount a different kind of insurrection—against planter-patriots who looked over their shoulders uneasily whenever they called out for liberty from the British.

Lexington and Concord

During the winter of 1774–75, Americans pressed on with boycotts. Optimists hoped to effect a repeal of the Coercive Acts; pessimists stockpiled arms and ammunition. In Massachusetts, militia units known as minutemen prepared to respond at a minute's notice to any threat from the British troops in Boston.

Thomas Gage realized how desperate the British position was. The people, Gage wrote Lord North, were "numerous, worked up to a fury, and not a Boston rabble but the freeholders and farmers of the country." Gage requested twenty thousand reinforcements. He also strongly advised repeal of the Coercive Acts, but leaders in Britain could not admit failure. Instead, in mid-April 1775, they ordered Gage to arrest the troublemakers immediately, before the Americans got better organized.

Gage quickly planned a surprise attack on a suspected ammunition storage site at Concord, a village eighteen miles west of Boston (Map 6.3). Near midnight on April 18, British soldiers moved

VISUAL ACTIVITY

The British Retreat from Lexington and Concord, April 19, 1775

Two self-trained artists—Ralph Earle, eighteen, and Amos Doolittle, twenty-one—hustled to Concord and Lexington ten days after April 19 to interview witnesses and create engravings for mass production. This scene depicts the British re-treat to Boston, with the redcoats under ambush by American insurgents. On route, the British set fire to several houses. The Granger Collection, New York.

READING THE IMAGE: Who is firing from behind the stone wall? Which side is inflicting the most damage, as depicted in this picture?

CONNECTIONS: In 1774 and 1775, were American militia units up to the task of defending their country against an invasion by Britain?

west across the Charles River. Paul Revere and William Dawes raced ahead to alert the minute-men. When the soldiers got to Lexington, five miles east of Concord, they were met by some seventy armed men. The British commander barked out, "Lay down your arms, you damned rebels, and disperse." The militiamen hesitated and began to comply, but then someone—nobody knows who—fired. Within two minutes, eight Americans were dead and ten were wounded.

The British units continued their march to Concord, any pretense of surprise gone. Three companies of minutemen nervously occupied the town center but offered no challenge to the British as they searched in vain for the ammunition. Finally, at Old North Bridge in Concord, British troops and minutemen exchanged shots, killing two Americans and three British soldiers. As the British returned to Boston, militia units ambushed them, bringing the bloodiest fighting of the day.

MAP ACTIVITY

Map 6.3 Lexington and Concord, April 1775

Two Americans slipped out of Boston to warn of a surprise British attack on Concord. Paul Revere went by boat to Charlestown and then by horse to Lexington, while William Dawes casually rode past British sentries and then galloped at full speed through Lexington to Concord.

READING THE MAP: How did Dawes's route differ from Revere's? What kinds of terrain and potential dangers did each man face during his ride, according to the map?

CONNECTIONS: Why send two men on the same mission? Why not send four or more?

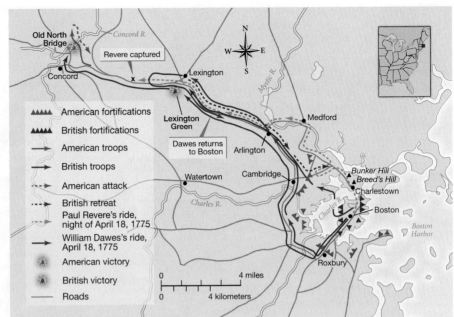

In the end, 273 British soldiers were wounded or dead; the toll for the Americans stood at about 95. It was April 19, 1775, and the war had begun.

Rebelling against Slavery

News of the battles of Lexington and Concord spread within days. In Virginia, Thomas Jefferson observed that "a phrenzy of revenge seems to have seized all ranks of people," causing the royal governor of Virginia, Lord Dunmore, to remove all gunpowder from the Williamsburg powder house to a ship, out of reach of angry Virginians. He also threatened to arm slaves, if necessary, to ward off attacks by colonists. This threat proved effective for several months.

In November 1775, as the crisis deepened, Dunmore issued an official proclamation promising freedom to defecting able-bodied slaves who would fight for the British. Dunmore had no intention of liberating all slaves, and astute blacks noticed that Dunmore neglected to free his own slaves. A Virginia barber named Caesar declared that "he did not know any one foolish enough to believe him [Dunmore], for if he intended to do so, he ought first to set his own free." Within a month some fifteen hundred slaves had joined Dunmore's "Ethiopian Regiment." Camp diseases quickly set in: dysentery, typhoid fever, and smallpox. When Dunmore sailed for England in mid-1776, he took three hundred black survivors with him. But the association of freedom with the British authorities had been established, and throughout the war thousands more southern slaves fled their masters whenever the British army was close enough to offer safe refuge.

In the northern colonies as well, slaves clearly recognized the evolving political struggle with Britain as an ideal moment to bid for freedom. A twenty-one-year-old Boston domestic slave employed biting sarcasm in a 1774 newspaper essay to call attention to the hypocrisy of local slave owners: "How well the Cry for Liberty, and the reverse Disposition for exercise of oppressive Power over others agree,—I humbly think it does not require the Penetration of a Philosopher to Determine." This extraordinary young woman, Phillis Wheatley, had already gained international recognition through a book of poems published in London in 1773. Wheatley's poems spoke of "Fair Freedom" as the "Goddess long desir'd" by Africans enslaved in America. Wheatley's master freed the young poet in 1775.

From north to south, groups of slaves pressed their case. Several Boston blacks offered to fight for the British in exchange for freedom, but General Gage turned them down. In Maryland, a planter complained that blacks impatient for freedom had to be disarmed of about eighty guns along with some swords. In North Carolina, white suspicions about a planned slave uprising led to the arrest of scores of African Americans who were ordered to be whipped by the revolutionary committee of public safety.

By 1783, when the Revolutionary War ended, as many as twenty thousand blacks had voted against slavery with their feet by seeking refuge with the British army. About half failed to achieve the liberation they were seeking, instead succumbing to disease, especially smallpox, in refugee camps. But some eight thousand to ten thousand persisted through the war, and later,

Phillis Wheatley
African-born Phillis became the slave of John Wheatley in Boston at age seven. Remarkably gifted in English, she read the Bible and learned to write elegant poetry and essays. She traveled to London in 1773 and published a book of poems, gaining notice in British literary circles. Once freed, she briefly married and then worked in a Boston boardinghouse. She died in 1784. Corbis.

government to subordinate the colonies into contributing partners in the larger scheme of empire.

American resistance to British policies grew slowly but steadily. In 1765, both loyalist Thomas Hutchinson and patriot Samuel Adams agreed that it was unwise for Britain to assert a right to taxation because Parliament did not adequately represent Americans. As a royal official, Hutchinson was obliged to uphold policy, while Adams protested and made political activists out of thousands in the process.

By 1775, events propelled many Americans to the conclusion that a concerted effort was afoot to deprive them of all their liberties, the most important of which were the right to self-rule and the right to live free of an occupying army. Prepared to die for those liberties, hundreds of minutemen converged on Concord. April 19 marked the start of their rebellion.

Another rebellion under way in 1775 was doomed to be short-circuited. Black Americans who had experienced actual slavery listened to shouts of "Liberty!" from white crowds and appropriated the language of revolution to their own circumstances. Defiance of authority was indeed contagious.

Despite the military conflict at the battles of Lexington and Concord, a war with Britain seemed far from inevitable to colonists outside New England. In the months ahead, American colonial leaders pursued peaceful as well as military solutions to the question of who actually had authority over them. By the end of 1775, however, reconciliation with the crown would be unattainable.

See the Selected Bibliography for this chapter in the Appendix.

under the protection of the British army, left America to start new lives of freedom in Canada's Nova Scotia or Africa's Sierra Leone.

REVIEW   How did enslaved people in the colonies react to the stirrings of revolution?

▶ Conclusion: The Long Road to Revolution

In the aftermath of the Seven Years' War, neither losers nor victors came away satisfied. France lost vast amounts of North American land claims, and Indian land rights were increasingly violated or ignored. Britain's huge war debt and subsequent revenue-generating policies distressed Americans and set the stage for the imperial crisis of the 1760s and 1770s. The years 1763 to 1775 brought repeated attempts by the British

6 Chapter Review

KEY TERMS

Seven Years' War (p. 137)
Pontiac's Rebellion (p. 144)
Sugar (Revenue) Act (p. 145)
Stamp Act (p. 145)
virtual representation (p. 146)
Declaratory Act (p. 151)
Townshend duties (p. 151)
Boston Massacre (p. 153)
committees of correspondence (p. 155)
Tea Act of 1773 (p. 155)
Coercive (Intolerable) Acts (pp. 155–156)
First Continental Congress (p. 159)

REVIEW QUESTIONS

1. How did the Seven Years' War erode relations between colonists and British authorities? (pp. 137–145)

2. Why did the Sugar Act and the Stamp Act draw fierce opposition from colonists? (pp. 145–151)

3. Why did British authorities send troops to occupy Boston in the fall of 1768? (pp. 151–154)

4. Why did Parliament pass the Coercive Acts in 1774? (pp. 154–160)

5. How did enslaved people in the colonies react to the stirrings of revolution? (pp. 160–163)

MAKING CONNECTIONS

1. In the mid-eighteenth century, how did Native Americans influence relations between European nations? Between Britain and the colonies?

2. What other grievances, besides taxation, led colonists by 1775 to openly rebel against Britain?

3. How did the colonists organize to oppose British power so effectively? In your answer, discuss the role of communication in facilitating the colonial resistance, being sure to cite specific examples.

LINKING TO THE PAST

1. In Bacon's Rebellion in Virginia in 1676, back-country farmers protested the rule of a royal governor who did not seem to have the economic interests of many Virginians at heart. Compare the administration of Sir William Berkeley of Virginia with that of Thomas Hutchinson of Massachusetts in the 1770s. Are there more differences than similarities? (See chapter 3.)

2. How does the growing ethnic and religious diversity of the mid-eighteenth-century colonies help explain the evolution of anti-British feeling that culminated in insurrection in 1775? (See chapter 5.)

7 The War for America
1775–1783

CONTENT LEARNING OBJECTIVES

After reading and studying this chapter, you should be able to:

- Define the objectives of the Second Continental Congress.

- Characterize the British and the American armies' strengths and weaknesses during the first year of the Revolutionary War.

- Explain how conflicts between patriots and loyalists played out on the local level.

- Understand how the war proceeded in the North and West, and the roles Native Americans played in the war.

- Consider King George III's southern strategy from 1778 to 1781, including what went wrong for the British, and what were the terms of the peace.

CONTINENTAL ARMY UNIFORM
The Continental army issued dark blue coats for officers' uniforms, using shoulder stripes and facings in varied colors to establish rank. As an officer rose in the ranks, he changed stripes, not coats.
National Museum of American History, Smithsonian Institution, USA/Bridgeman Images.

ROBERT SHURTLIFF WAS A LATECOMER TO THE AMERICAN Revolution, enlisting in the Continental army after the last decisive battle at Yorktown had been fought. The army still needed fresh recruits to counter the British army occupying New York City. The standoff would last nearly two years before the peace treaty was finalized in Paris.

New recruits were scarce in a country exhausted by war. Attracted by cash bounties, beardless boys who had been children in 1775 now stepped forward, Shurtliff among them. Reportedly eighteen, the youth was single, poor, and at loose ends. With a muscular physique and proficiency with a musket, Shurtliff won assignment to an elite light infantry unit, part of Washington's army of 10,000 men stationed north of New York City.

That is, 10,000 men and 1 woman. "Robert Shurtliff" was actually Deborah Sampson, age twenty-three, from Middleborough, Massachusetts. For seventeen months, Sampson masqueraded as a man, marching through woods, skirmishing with the enemy, and enduring the boredom of camp. Understating her age enabled her to blend in with the beardless boys, as did her competence as a soldier. With privacy at a minimum, she faced constant risk of discovery. Why did she run this risk?

A hard-luck childhood had left Sampson both impoverished and unusually plucky. Placed in foster care at age five, Deborah became a servant in a succession of families. Along the way, she learned to plow a field and to read and write, uncommon skills for a female servant. Next she worked as a weaver and then a teacher, low-wage jobs but also ones without supervising bosses. Marriage was the usual next step, but probably the wartime shortage of men kept Deborah "masterless," rare for an eighteenth-century woman. Masterless, but also poor; the cash bounty enticed her to enlist.

When Sampson's true sex was finally discovered, she was discharged immediately. What eventually made Sampson famous was not her war service alone but her success in selling her story to the public. In 1797, she told her life story (a blend of fact and fiction) in a short book and then went on tour reenacting her wartime masquerade. Once again, she was crossing gender boundaries since women normally did not speak from public stages.

Except for her disguised sex, Sampson's Revolutionary War experience was similar to that of most Americans. Disruptions affected everyone's life, whether in military service or on the home front. Wartime shortages caused women to do male jobs. Soldiers fought for ideas, but they also fought to earn money. Hardship was widely endured. And Sampson's quest for personal independence—a freedom from the constraints of being female—was echoed in the general quest for political independence that many Americans identified as a major goal of the war.

Political independence was not everyone's primary goal at first. For more than a year after fighting began, the Continental Congress resisted declaring independence. Some delegates cautiously hoped for reconciliation with Britain. The congress raised an army, financed it, and sought alliances with foreign countries—all the while exploring diplomatic channels for peace.

Once King George III rejected all peace overtures, Americans loudly declared their independence, and the war moved into high gear. In part a classic war with professional armies, the Revolutionary War was also a civil war between committed rebels and loyalists. It had complex ethnic dimensions, pitting Indian tribes allied with the British against others allied with the Americans, and international involvement as well from France and Spain. It also provided an unprecedented opportunity for some enslaved African Americans to win freedom, by joining either the British or the Continental army and state militias, fighting alongside white Americans.

Deborah Sampson
Deborah Sampson opted for this small portrait to illustrate *The Female Review*, a short book about her unusual military career published in 1797. By then a wife and mother, she displays femininity here: long curly hair, necklace, and stylish low-cut gown. Sampson the soldier had used a cloth band to compress her breasts; Sampson the matron wore a satin band to define her bustline. Hulton Archive/Getty Images.

DEBORAH SAMPSON.
Published by H. Mann. 1797.

► The Second Continental Congress

On May 10, 1775, nearly one month after the fighting at Lexington and Concord, the **Second Continental Congress** assembled in Philadelphia. The congress immediately set to work on two crucial but contradictory tasks: to raise and supply an army and to explore reconciliation with Britain. To do the former, they needed soldiers and a commander, they needed money, and they needed to work out a declaration of war. To do the latter, they needed diplomacy to approach the king. But the king was not receptive, and by 1776, as the war progressed and hopes of reconciliation faded, delegates at the congress began to ponder the treasonous act of declaring independence.

Assuming Political and Military Authority

The delegates to the Second Continental Congress were prominent figures at home, but they now had to learn to know and trust one another. Moreover, they did not always agree. The Adams cousins John and Samuel defined the radical end of the spectrum, favoring independence. John Dickinson of Pennsylvania, who in 1767 critiqued British tax policy in *Letters from a Farmer*, was now a moderate, seeking reconciliation with Britain. Benjamin Franklin, fresh off a ship from an eleven-year residence in London, was feared by some to be a British spy. Mutual suspicions flourished easily when the undertaking was so dangerous, opinions were so varied, and a misstep could spell disaster.

Most of the delegates were not yet prepared to break with Britain. Some felt that government without a king was unworkable, while others feared it might be suicidal to lose Britain's protection against its traditional enemies, France and Spain. Colonies that traded actively with Britain feared undermining their economies. Probably the vast majority of ordinary Americans were unable to envision complete independence. From the Stamp Act of 1765 to the Coercive Acts of 1774 (see chapter 6), the constitutional struggle with Britain had focused on the issue of parliamentary power, but almost no one had questioned the legitimacy of the monarchy.

The few men at the Continental Congress who did think that independence was desirable were, not surprisingly, from Massachusetts, the

CHRONOLOGY

1775	• Second Continental Congress convenes. • Battle of Bunker Hill fought. • Olive Branch Petition sent to British king. • Battle of Quebec fought.
1776	• *Common Sense* published. • British evacuate Boston. • Declaration of Independence written. • British take Manhattan.
1777	• British Parliament suspends habeas corpus. • Ambush takes place at Oriskany; Americans hold Fort Stanwix. • British occupy Philadelphia. • British surrender at Saratoga.
1777–1778	• Continental army winters at Valley Forge.
1778	• France signs treaty with America. • British take Savannah, Georgia.
1779	• Militias attack Cherokee west of North Carolina. • Americans destroy Iroquois villages in New York. • Americans take Forts Kaskaskia and Vincennes.
1780	• Philadelphia Ladies Association raises money for soldiers. • British lay siege to Charleston, South Carolina. • French army arrives in Newport, Rhode Island. • British win battle of Camden. • Benedict Arnold exposed as traitor. • Americans win battle of King's Mountain.
1781	• British forces invade Virginia. • French blockade Chesapeake Bay. • Cornwallis surrenders at Yorktown.
1783	• Treaty of Paris ends war.

target of the Coercive Acts and the scene of bloodshed at Lexington and Concord. Even so, those men knew that it was premature to push for a break with Britain. John Adams wrote his wife, Abigail, in June 1775: "America is a great, unwieldy body. Its progress must be slow. It is like a large fleet sailing under convoy. The fleetest sailors must wait for the dullest and slowest."

Yet swift action was needed, for the Massachusetts countryside was under threat of further attack. Even the hesitant moderates in the congress agreed that a military buildup was necessary. Around the country, militia units from New York to Georgia collected arms and trained on village greens in anticipation. On June 14, the congress voted to create the **Continental army**, choosing a Virginian, George Washington,

as commander in chief. This sent the clear message that there was widespread commitment to war beyond New England.

Next the congress drew up a document titled "A Declaration on the Causes and Necessity of Taking Up Arms," which rehearsed familiar arguments about the tyranny of Parliament and the need to defend English liberties. This declaration was first drafted by a young Virginia planter, Thomas Jefferson, a radical on the question of independence. The moderate John Dickinson, fearing that the declaration would offend Britain, was allowed to rewrite it. However, he left intact much of Jefferson's highly charged language about choosing "to die freemen rather than to live slaves." Even a moderate like Dickinson understood the necessity of military defense against an invading army.

VISUAL ACTIVITY

An Exact View of the Late Battle at Charlestown, June 17th 1775
This engraving was for sale within weeks of the battle of Bunker Hill. British and American soldiers in fixed formation fire muskets at one another, while Charlestown is in flames in the background. The Americans, to the left, are dug in along the crest of the hill; British casualties have begun to mount. Who would buy this picture? The Colonial Williamsburg Foundation. Museum Purchase.

READING THE IMAGE: In the end, the British won the battle by taking the hill, but is that the story told in this picture?

CONNECTIONS: In what significant ways did the battle of Bunker Hill differ from the battles of Lexington and Concord two months earlier?

To pay for the military buildup, the congress authorized a currency issue of $2 million. The Continental dollars were merely paper; they were not backed by gold or silver. The delegates somewhat naively expected that the currency would be accepted as valuable on trust as it spread in the population through the hands of soldiers, farmers, munitions suppliers, and beyond.

In just two months, the Second Continental Congress had created an army, declared war, and issued its own currency. It had taken on the major functions of a legitimate government, both military and financial, without any legal basis for its authority, for it had not yet declared independence from the king.

Pursuing Both War and Peace

The second battle of the Revolution occurred on June 17 in Boston. New England militia units had fortified the hilly terrain of the peninsula of Charlestown, which faced the city, and Thomas Gage, still commander in Boston, prepared to attack, aided by the arrival of new troops and three talented generals, William Howe, John Burgoyne, and Henry Clinton.

General William Howe insisted on a bold frontal assault, sending 2,500 soldiers across the water and up Bunker Hill in an intimidating but potentially costly attack. Three bloody assaults were needed before the British took the hill, the third succeeding mainly because the American ammunition supply gave out, and the defenders quickly retreated. The **battle of Bunker Hill** was thus a British victory, but an expensive one. The dead numbered 226 on the British side, with more than 800 wounded; the Americans suffered 140 dead, 271 wounded, and 30 captured. As General Clinton later remarked, "It was a dear bought victory; another such would have ruined us."

Instead of pursuing the fleeing Americans, Howe retreated to Boston, unwilling to risk more raids into the countryside. If the British had had any grasp of the basic instability of the American units around Boston, they might have decisively defeated the Continental army in its infancy. Instead, they lingered in Boston, abandoning it without a fight nine months later.

Howe used the time in Boston to inoculate his army against smallpox because a new epidemic of the deadly disease was spreading in port cities along the Atlantic. Inoculation worked by producing a mild but real (and therefore risky) case of smallpox, followed by lifelong immunity. Howe's instinct was right: During the American Revolution, some 130,000 people on the American continent, most of them Indians, died of smallpox.

A week after Bunker Hill, when General Washington arrived to take charge of the new Continental army, he found enthusiastic but undisciplined troops. Sanitation was an unknown concept, with inadequate latrines fouling the campground. Washington attributed the disarray to the New England custom of letting militia units elect their own officers, which he felt undermined deference. Washington spotted a militia captain, a barber in civilian life, shaving an ordinary soldier, and he moved quickly to impose more hierarchy and authority. "Be easy," he advised his newly appointed officers, "but not too familiar, lest you subject yourself to a want of that respect, which is necessary to support a proper command."

While military plans moved forward, the Second Continental Congress pursued its contradictory objective: reconciliation with Britain. Delegates from the middle colonies (Pennsylvania, Delaware, and New York), whose merchants depended on trade with Britain, urged that channels for negotiation remain open. In July 1775, congressional moderates led by John Dickinson engineered an appeal to the king called the Olive Branch Petition, affirming loyalty to the monarchy and blaming all the troubles on the king's ministers and on Parliament. It proposed that the American colonial assemblies be recognized as individual parliaments under the umbrella of the monarchy. King George III rejected the Olive Branch Petition and heatedly condemned the Americans as traitors.

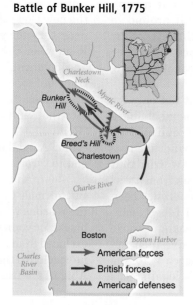

Battle of Bunker Hill, 1775

Charlestown Neck

Bunker Hill

Mystic River

Breed's Hill

Charlestown

Charles River

Boston

Boston Harbor

Charles River Basin

→ American forces

→ British forces

▲▲▲▲ American defenses

Thomas Paine, Abigail Adams, and the Case for Independence

Pressure for independence started to mount in January 1776, when a pamphlet titled *Common Sense* appeared in Philadelphia. Thomas

Paine, its author, was an English artisan and coffeehouse intellectual who had come to America in the fall of 1774. With the encouragement of members of the Second Continental Congress, he wrote *Common Sense* to lay out a lively and compelling case for complete independence.

In simple yet forceful language, Paine elaborated on the absurdities of the British monarchy. Why should one man, by accident of birth, claim extensive power over others? he asked. A king might be foolish or wicked. "One of the strongest natural proofs of the folly of hereditary right in kings," Paine wrote, "is that nature disapproves it; otherwise she would not so frequently turn it into ridicule by giving mankind *an ass for a lion.*" Calling the British king an ass broke through the automatic deference most Americans still had for the monarchy. To replace monarchy, Paine advocated republican government based on the consent of the people. Rulers, according to Paine, were only representatives of the people, and the best form of government relied on frequent elections to achieve the most direct democracy possible.

Paine's pamphlet sold more than 150,000 copies in a matter of weeks. Newspapers reprinted it; men read it aloud in taverns and coffeehouses; John Adams sent a copy to his wife, Abigail, who passed it around to neighbors in Braintree, Massachusetts. New Englanders desired independence, but other colonies, under no immediate threat of violence, remained cautious.

Abigail Adams was impatient not only for independence but also for other legal changes that would revolutionize the new country. In a series of astute letters to her husband, she outlined obstacles and gave advice. She worried that southern slave owners might shrink from a war in the name of liberty: "I have sometimes been ready to think that the passion for Liberty cannot be Equally strong in the Breasts of those who have been accustomed to deprive their fellow Creatures of theirs." And in March 1776, she expressed her hope that women's legal status

Thomas Paine

Thomas Paine's sensational pamphlet *Common Sense* advanced the popular debate on independence. Paine remained a provocative pamphleteer, writing *The Rights of Man* in revolutionary France, followed by *The Age of Reason*, which to many seemed to avow atheism. In 1802, he returned to the United States; although welcomed by Thomas Jefferson, Paine was spurned by nearly everyone else for his irreligiosity. He died in obscurity in 1809. American Antiquarian Society, Worcester, Massachusetts, USA/Bridgeman Images.

would improve under the new government: "In the new Code of Laws which I suppose it will be necessary for you to make I desire you would Remember the Ladies, and be more generous and favourable to them than your ancestors." Her chief concern was husbands' legal dominion over wives: "Do not put such unlimited power into the hands of the Husbands," she advised. "Remember all Men would be tyrants if they could." Abigail Adams anticipated a more radical end to tyranny than did Thomas Paine.

John Adams dismissed his wife's concerns. But to a male politician, Adams privately rehearsed the reasons why women (and men who were free blacks, or young, or propertyless) should remain excluded from political participation. Even though he concluded that nothing should change, at least Abigail's letter had forced him to ponder the exclusion, something few men—or women—did in 1776. Urgent talk of political independence was as radical as most could imagine.

The Declaration of Independence

In addition to Paine's *Common Sense*, another factor hastening independence was the prospect of an alliance with France, Britain's archrival. France was willing to provide military supplies and naval power only if assured that the Americans would separate from Britain. News that the British were negotiating to hire German mercenary soldiers further solidified support for independence. By May 1776, all but four colonies were agitating for a declaration. The holdouts were Pennsylvania, Maryland, New York, and South Carolina, the latter two containing large loyalist populations. An exasperated Virginian wrote to his friend in the congress, "For God's sake, why do you dawdle in the Congress so strangely? Why do you not at once declare yourself a separate independent state?" (See "Making Historical Arguments," page 172.)

In early June, the Virginia delegation introduced a resolution calling for independence. The moderates still commanded enough support to postpone a vote on the measure until July. In the meantime, the congress appointed a committee, with Thomas Jefferson and others, to draft a longer document setting out the case for independence.

On July 2, after intense politicking, all but one state voted for independence; New York abstained. The congress then turned to the document drafted by Jefferson and his committee. Jefferson began with a preamble that articulated philosophical principles about natural rights, equality, the right of revolution, and the consent of the governed as the only true basis for government. He then listed more than two dozen specific grievances against King George. The congress passed over the preamble with little comment and instead wrangled over the list of grievances, especially the issue of slavery. Jefferson had included an impassioned statement blaming the king for slavery, which delegates from Georgia and South Carolina struck out, not wishing to denounce their labor system. But the congress let stand another of Jefferson's grievances, blaming the king for mobilizing "the merciless Indian Savages" into bloody frontier warfare, a reference to Pontiac's Rebellion (see

"Pontiac's Rebellion and the Proclamation of 1763" in chapter 6).

On July 4, the amendments to Jefferson's text were complete, and the congress formally adopted the **Declaration of Independence**, with New York switching from abstention to approval ten days later, making the vote unanimous. In August, the delegates gathered to sign the official parchment copy. Four men, including John Dickinson, declined to sign; several others "signed with regret . . . and with many doubts," according to John Adams. The document was then printed, widely distributed, and read aloud in celebrations everywhere.

Printed copies did not include the signers' names, for they had committed treason, a crime punishable by death. On the day of signing, they indulged in gallows humor. When Benjamin Franklin paused before signing, John Hancock of Massachusetts teased him, "Come, come, sir. We must be unanimous. No pulling different ways. We must all hang together." Franklin replied, "Indeed we must all hang together. Otherwise we shall most assuredly hang separately."

> **REVIEW**   Why were some Americans initially reluctant to pursue independence from Britain?

▶ The First Year of War, 1775–1776

Both sides approached the war for America with uneasiness. The Americans, with inexperienced militias, were opposing the mightiest military power in the world. Also, their country was not unified; many people remained loyal to Britain. The British faced serious obstacles as well. Their disdain for the fighting abilities of the Americans required reassessment in light of the Bunker Hill battle. The logistics of supplying an army with food across three thousand miles of water were daunting. And since the British goal was to regain allegiance, not to destroy and conquer, the army was often constrained in its actions. These patterns—undertrained American troops and British troops strangely unwilling to press their advantage—played out repeatedly in the first year of war.

How Did "New Media" Push Forward the Declaration of Independence?

In a world without public opinion polls, how did the Continental Congress know it had the support of the people? A close study of the way news and opinion circulated in the mid-1770s reveals how revolutionary commitment expressed itself and finally pushed forward the Declaration of Independence. Newspapers, the post office, private letters, and broadsides were vital elements in a new grid of networked communications, all of which functioned both to disseminate information and to boost political activism.

Printers had a hand in all aspects of the communication grid, and they therefore became significant players in educating Americans about the contested issues in the conflict with Britain. One such ardent printer was Isaiah Thomas, editor of the *Massachusetts Spy* in Boston between 1770 and 1775. Just twenty-one when he launched his weekly publication, Thomas was friendly with leaders of Boston's Sons of Liberty, who sometimes met in the *Spy*'s office. His favorable coverage of the radicals soon put him on Thomas Hutchinson's list of enemies. When tensions between town and royal troops spiked in mid-April 1775, Thomas escaped with his printing press under cover of darkness to Worcester, forty-five miles west. From there he set out for nearby Lexington and Concord, to witness the first day of actual war. The *Spy*'s next issue burst with a gripping firsthand account of the fighting, which was reprinted in other newspapers from New Hampshire to Georgia.

Newspapers like the *Spy* formed the backbone of a networked system of communication that emerged in the Revolutionary period. In 1775, some forty newspapers were published in coastal cities. In peaceful times, they were sedate four-page weeklies, carrying advertisements, shipping news, edicts from authorities, and a page or two of news articles picked up from distant papers. Local news rarely appeared: Locals already knew it. But as revolutionary momentum quickened, Boston newspaper editors began to cover electrifying local events, knowing that their publications reached an audience far beyond Boston.

The Boston papers traveled to distant cities by horse free of charge, thanks to a royal postal system that favored newspaper exchanges. While private letters with paid postage were given preferential treatment, the free newspapers went into a secondary satchel, which could be selectively thinned by a postmaster whenever the paid mail got heavy. In 1774, British authorities realized that postmasters had the power to control the flow of information. What if Isaiah Thomas's version of events could not make it to Virginia? British authorities fired the American in charge of the royal postal system, intending to replace him and others with men loyal to Britain who could dispose of seditious newspapers. In response, the Second Continental Congress quickly created its own postal system. Printers lined up to be postmasters, eager to be stationed at the local entry point for incoming news.

Protecting the new postal system was vital. Privacy was essential when writing candidly about treasonous matters, and private letters between political men contained crucial exchanges of information. Equally vital were public letters to the editor written by individual Americans. Although the concept of investigative reporting lay far in the future, letters from well-placed witnesses offered powerful observations on the course of events in various spheres of action.

Printers also produced political broadsides—single sheets for public posting. Boston's committee of correspondence sent broadsides via post riders to communicate with other Massachusetts towns. From its inception in 1772, Boston's committee not only conveyed information but also encouraged towns to reply and engage in debate. A hundred Massachusetts towns developed the practice of holding town meetings, deliberating on proposed resolutions, and sending their opinions to Boston on the tense issues of the day. By 1774, committees of correspondence spread throughout the colo-

The American Military Forces

Americans claimed that the initial months of war were purely defensive, triggered by the British invasion. But the war also quickly became a rebellion, an overthrowing of long-established authority. As both defenders and rebels, many Americans were highly motivated to fight, and the potential manpower that could be mobilized was, in theory, very great.

Local defense in the colonies had long rested with a militia composed of all able-bodied men

Public Reading of the Declaration of Independence, July 8, 1776
This scene of a public reading of the Declaration of Independence in Philadelphia was replicated from Charleston, South Carolina, to Boston, Massachusetts, and at points in between, as when Isaiah Thomas stopped the transit of the printed document to stage a celebration in Worcester, Massachusetts.
The Granger Collection, New York.

Isaiah Thomas got his hands on it and read it to a cheering crowd, who pulled symbols of the monarchy off the courthouse and raised beer mugs to patriotic toasts. The next morning, Thomas learned that his apprentice had run off to join the Continental army, leaving him short-handed. As he had to recognize, the Declaration was transformative at many levels.

Questions for Analysis

Summarize the Argument: What new or changed modes of communication emerged in the 1770s? How did these new capabilities expand the reach and impact of revolutionary ideas and enthusiasm?

Analyze the Evidence: Which of the several elements of networked communications—newspapers, the post office, secure private letters, and committees of correspondence exchanging broadsides and responses—seem to you to provide the most compelling opportunities for creative interaction by ordinary citizens? Why?

Consider the Context: In 1776, very few American newspaper editors were loyalists. Can you suggest some reasons why? What might this fact reveal about the political divisions that existed within the colonies in this period?

nies and prompted local jurisdictions to debate the Coercive Acts. When towns responded with declarations of solidarity for coastal radicals, newspapers printed selections as a demonstration of the state of public opinion.

In early 1776, similar techniques created a groundswell of popular support for a Declaration of Independence. Spurred by their state assembly, ninety Massachusetts towns held town meetings to debate and vote on

independence. Their thoughtful and distinctive justifications, all affirmative, were forwarded to the Continental Congress. Towns in Maryland and Virginia also met to instruct their delegates to vote for independence, as did four of the new state assemblies. The weight of these actions helped push the Declaration to reality.

Swift post riders carried specially printed copies of the Declaration to each state. As the copy destined for Boston passed through Worcester,

over age sixteen. Militias, however, were best suited for local and limited engagements, responding to conflict with Indians or slave rebellions, both relatively infrequent events. In forming the Continental army, the congress set enlistment at one year, which proved inadequate as

the war progressed. Incentives produced longer commitments: a $20 bonus for three years of service, a hundred acres of land for enlistment for the duration of the war—a reward good only if the Americans won the war. Over the course of the war, some 230,000 men enlisted, about

"The Female Combatants," 1776
This British cartoon of January 1776 follows a long tradition of representing countries as female characters: a fancy-dressed matron as Britain and a near-naked Indian maiden as Britain's North American colonies, pummeling each other with fists. The British matron calls out, "I'll force you to Obedience, you Rebellious Slut," while the Indian maiden replies, "Liberty, Liberty forever, Mother, while I exist."
Courtesy of the Lewis Walpole Library, Yale University.

one-quarter of the white male adult population. Women also served in the Continental army, cooking, washing, and nursing the wounded. The British army established a ratio of one woman to every ten men; in the Continental army, the ratio was set at one woman to fifteen men. Close to 20,000 "camp followers," as they were called, served during the war, many of them wives of men in service. Some 12,000 children also tagged along, and babies were born in the camps. Some women helped during battles, supplying drinking water or ammunition to soldiers.

Black Americans at first were excluded from the Continental army. But as manpower needs increased, northern states welcomed free blacks into service; slaves in some states could serve with their masters' permission. About 5,000 black

men served in the Revolutionary War on the rebel side, nearly all from the northern states. Black soldiers sometimes were segregated into separate units, and while some of these men were draftees, others were clearly inspired by ideals of freedom in a war against tyranny. For example, twenty-three blacks gave "Liberty," "Freedom," and "Freeman" as their surnames at the time of enlistment.

Military service helped politicize Americans during the early stages of the war. In early 1776, independence was a risky, potentially treasonous idea. But as the war heated up and recruiters demanded commitment, some Americans discovered that apathy had its dangers as well. Anyone who refused to serve ran the risk of being called a traitor to the cause. Military service became a prime way of demonstrating political allegiance.

The American army was at times raw and inexperienced, and often woefully undermanned. It never had the precision and discipline of European professional armies. But it was never as bad as the British continually assumed. The British would learn that it was a serious mistake to underrate the enemy.

The British Strategy

The American strategy was straightforward—to repulse and defeat an invading army. The British strategy was not as clear. Britain wanted to put down a rebellion and restore monarchical power in the colonies, but the question was how to accomplish this. A decisive defeat of the Continental army was essential but not sufficient to end the rebellion, for the British would still have to contend with an armed and motivated insurgent population. Furthermore, there was no single political nerve center whose capture would spell certain victory. The Continental Congress moved from place to place, staying just out of reach of the British. During the course of the war, the British captured and occupied every major port city, but that brought no serious loss to the Americans, 95 percent of whom lived in the countryside.

Britain's delicate task was to restore the old governments, not to destroy an enemy country. British generals were at first reluctant to ravage the countryside, confiscate food, or burn villages. There were thirteen distinct political entities to capture, pacify, and then restore to the crown, and they stretched in a long line from New Hampshire to Georgia. Clearly, a large land army was required for the job. Without the willingness to seize food from the locals, the British needed hundreds of supply ships—hence their desire to capture the ports. The British strategy also assumed that many Americans remained loyal to the king and would come to the British military's aid.

The overall British plan was a divide-and-conquer approach, focusing first on New York, the state judged to have the greatest number of loyal subjects. New York offered a geographic advantage as well: Control of the Hudson River would allow the British to isolate New England. British armies could descend from Canada and move north from New York City along the Hudson River. Squeezed between a naval blockade on the eastern coast and army raids in the west, Massachusetts could be driven to surrender. New Jersey and Pennsylvania would fall in line, the British thought, because of loyalist strength. Virginia was a problem, like Massachusetts, but the British were confident that the Carolinas would help them isolate and subdue Virginia.

Quebec, New York, and New Jersey

In late 1775, an American expedition was launched to capture the cities of Montreal and Quebec before British reinforcements could arrive (Map 7.1). This offensive was a clear sign that the war was not purely a reaction to the invasion of Massachusetts. A force of New York Continentals commanded by General Richard Montgomery took Montreal easily in September 1775 and then advanced on Quebec. Meanwhile, a second contingent of Continentals led by Colonel Benedict Arnold moved north through Maine to Quebec, a punishing trek through freezing rain with woefully inadequate supplies. Arnold showed heroic determination, but close to half of his men either died or turned back during the march. Arnold and Montgomery jointly attacked Quebec in December but failed to take the city. Worse yet, they encountered smallpox, which killed more men than had the battle for Quebec.

The main action of the first year of the war came not in Canada, however, but in New York. In August 1776, some 45,000 British troops (including 8,000 German mercenaries, called Hessians) under the command of General Howe landed south of New York City. General Washington had anticipated this move and had relocated his army of 20,000 south from

Massachusetts. The **battle of Long Island** in late August pitted the well-trained British "redcoats" (slang referring to their red uniforms) against a very green Continental army. Howe attacked, inflicting many casualties and taking 1,000 prisoners. A British general crowed, "If a good bleeding can bring those Bible-faced Yankees to their senses, the fever of independency should soon abate." Howe failed to press forward, however, perhaps remembering the costly victory of Bunker Hill, and Washington evacuated his troops to Manhattan Island.

Washington knew it would be hard to hold Manhattan, so he withdrew farther north to two forts on either side of the Hudson River. For two months, the armies engaged in limited skirmishing, but in November Howe finally captured Fort Washington and Fort Lee, taking another 3,000 prisoners. Washington retreated quickly across New Jersey into Pennsylvania. Again Howe unaccountably failed to press his advantage. Instead, he parked his German troops in winter quarters along the Delaware River. Perhaps he knew that many of the Continental soldiers' enlistment periods ended on December 31, making him confident that the Americans would not attack him. He was wrong.

On December 25, in an icy rain, Washington stealthily moved his army across the Delaware River and at dawn made a quick capture of the unsuspecting German soldiers. This impressive victory lifted the sagging morale of the patriot side. For the next two weeks, Washington remained on the offensive, capturing supplies in a clever attack on British units at Princeton. Soon he was safe in Morristown, in northern New Jersey, where he settled his army for the winter. Washington finally had time to administer mass smallpox inoculations and see his men through the abbreviated course of the disease.

All in all, in the first year of declared war, the rebellious Americans had a few proud moments but also many worries. The inexperienced Continental army had barely hung on in the New York campaign. Washington had shown exceptional daring and admirable restraint, but what really saved the Americans was the repeated reluctance of the British to follow through militarily when they had the advantage.

REVIEW   Why did the British initially exercise restraint in their efforts to defeat the rebellious colonies?

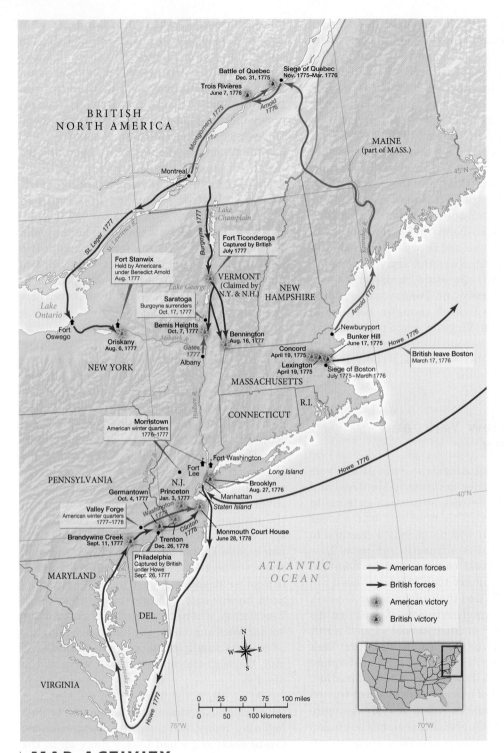

MAP ACTIVITY

Map 7.1   The War in the North, 1775–1778

After battles in Massachusetts in 1775, rebel forces invaded Canada but failed to capture Quebec. The British army landed in New York in 1776, causing turmoil in New Jersey in 1777 and 1778. Burgoyne attempted to isolate New England, but he was stopped at Saratoga in 1777 in the decisive battle of the early war.

READING THE MAP: Which general's troops traveled the farthest in each of these years: 1775, 1776, and 1777? How did the availability of water routes affect British and American strategy?

CONNECTIONS: Why did the French wait until early 1778 to join American forces against the British? What did France hope to gain from participating in the war? (See page 186.)

VISUAL ACTIVITY

British General Sir William Howe

William Howe served as commander in chief in America from 1775 to 1778. A prior deployment during the Seven Years' War gave him warm respect for the New England colonists; he never stopped hoping for reconciliation. He won limited battles but declined to pursue decisive victories. He issued thousands of pardons to individual rebels. Resigning before being fired, he traveled home to defend his reputation. Anne S. K. Brown Military Collection, Brown University.

READING THE IMAGE: What marks Howe as an officer in this picture? What has the artist chosen for the location of the portrait? Is the cannon pointed at his head?

CONNECTIONS: What difference did it make for the outcome of the Revolution that Britain's commander in chief was so hesitant?

▶ The Home Front

Battlefields alone did not determine the outcome of the war. Struggles on the home front were equally important. Men who joined the army often left wives to manage on their own. Some men did not join because they were loyal to Britain and did not welcome war, and many others were undecided about independence. In many communities, both persuasion and force were used to gain the allegiance of the many neutrals. A major factor pushing neutrals to side with the revolution was the harsh British treatment of prisoners of war. Adding to the turbulence of the times was a very shaky wartime economy. The creative financing of the fledgling government brought hardships as well as opportunities, forcing Americans to confront new manifestations of virtue and corruption.

Patriotism at the Local Level

Committees of correspondence, of public safety, and of inspection dominated the political landscape in patriot communities. These committees took on more than customary local governance; they enforced boycotts, picked army draftees, and policed suspected traitors. They sometimes invaded homes to search for contraband goods such as British tea or textiles.

Loyalists were dismayed by the increasing show of power by patriots. A man in Westchester, New York, described his response to intrusions by committees: "Choose your committee or suffer it to be chosen by a half dozen fools in your neighborhood—open your doors to them—let them examine your tea-cannisters and molasses-jugs, and your wives' and daughters' petty coats—bow and cringe and tremble and quake—fall down and worship our sovereign lord the mob. . . . Should any pragmatical committee-gentleman come to my house and give himself airs, I shall show him the door." Oppressive or not, the local committees were rarely challenged. Their persuasive powers convinced many middle-of-the-road citizens that neutrality was not a comfortable option.

Another group new to political life—white women—increasingly demonstrated a capacity for patriotism as wartime hardships dramatically altered their work routines. Many wives whose husbands were away on military or political service took on masculine duties. Their competence to manage farms and make business decisions encouraged some to assert interest in

Families Divide over the Revolution

Generalizing about rebels versus loyalists is a complex historical task. Sometimes categorizing by class, race, and geographic descriptors helps explain the split. But beyond economic interests or cultural politics, sometimes the loyalist-patriot divide cut across families—and cut deeply. These documents reveal people pitted against loved ones over wartime allegiance.

DOCUMENT 1
Patriot Benjamin Franklin and Loyalist Son William Correspond, 1784

Benjamin Franklin, a keen advocate of the Revolution, had a son who stayed loyal to the crown. William was Benjamin's illegitimate son, resulting from a youthful indiscretion. Benjamin raised him and took him to England in 1757 during his extended service as Pennsylvania's colonial agent. William thus acquired connections at court, and in 1762 he was appointed royal governor of New Jersey, a post he held until 1776. When the war began, he was placed under house arrest as a traitor to the patriot cause. Father and son did not communicate for the next nine years, even when William was confined in a Connecticut prison for eight months. During this time, Benjamin took charge of William's oldest son, an illegitimate child born before William's legal marriage. After the war, William moved to England, and in 1784 he wrote to his father, then in Paris, asking for a meeting of reconciliation. He did not apologize for his loyalism.

Dear and honored Father,
Ever since the termination of the unhappy contest between Great Britain and America, I have been anxious to write to you. . . . There are narrow illiberal Minds in all Parties. In that which I took, and on whose Account I have so much suffered, there have not been wanting some who have insinuated that my Conduct has been founded on Collusion with you, that one of us might succeed whichever Party should prevail. . . . The Falsity of such Insinuation in our Case you well know, and I am happy that I can with Confidence appeal not only to you but to my God, that I have uniformly acted from a strong Sense of what I conceived my Duty to my King, and Regard to my Country, required. If I have been mistaken, I cannot help it. It is an Error of Judgment what the maturest Reflection I am capable of cannot rectify; and I verily believe were the same Circumstances to occur again Tomorrow, my Conduct would be exactly similar to what it was heretofore.

The father replied:
Dear Son,
I . . . am glad to find that you desire to revive the affectionate Intercourse, that formerly existed between us. It will be very agreeable to me; indeed nothing has ever hurt me so much and affected me with such keen Sensations, as to find myself deserted in my old age by my only Son; and not only deserted, but to find him taking up Arms against me, in a Cause,

politics as well, as Abigail Adams did while John Adams served in the Continental Congress in Philadelphia. Eliza Wilkinson managed a South Carolina plantation and talked revolutionary politics with women friends. "None were greater politicians than the several knots of ladies who met together," she remarked, alert to the unusual turn female conversations had taken.

Women from prominent Philadelphia families took more direct action, forming the **Ladies Association** to collect money for Continental soldiers. Mrs. Esther DeBerdt Reed, wife of Pennsylvania's governor, published a broadside in 1780 titled "The Sentiments of an American Woman" to defend their female activism: "The time is arrived to display the same sentiments which animated us at the beginning of the Revolution, when we renounced the use of teas [and] when our republican and laborious hands spun the flax."

The Loyalists

Around one-fifth of the American population remained loyal to the crown in 1776, and another two-fifths tried to stay neutral, providing a strong base for the British. In general, **loyalists** believed that social stability depended on a government anchored by monarchy and aristocracy. They feared that democratic tyranny was emergent among the self-styled patriots who appeared to

wherein my good Fame, Fortune and Life were all at Stake. You conceived, you say, that your Duty to your King and regard for your Country requir'd this. I ought not to blame you for differing in Sentiment with me in Public Affairs. We are Men, all subject to errors. Our opinions are not in our own Power; they are form'd and govern'd much by Circumstances, that are often as inexplicable as they are irresistible. Your Situation was such that few would have censured your remaining Neuter, *tho' there are Natural Duties which preceded political ones, and cannot be extinguish'd by them.*

This is a disagreeable Subject. I drop it. And we will endeavor, as you propose mutually to forget what has happened relating to it, as well as we can. I send your Son over to pay his Duty to you. . . . He is greatly esteem'd and belov'd in this Country, and will make his Way anywhere. . . . Wishing you Health, and more happiness than it seems you have lately experienced, I remain your affectionate father, B. Franklin

Source: Courtesy of the American Philosophical Society, http://www.amphilsoc.org.

DOCUMENT 2
Two Oneida Brothers Confront Their Different Allegiances, 1779

Mary Jemison was captured as a girl during the Seven Years' War and adopted into the Seneca tribe of western New York, where she remained for life. When she was eighty, her narrative was taken down and published. In this story from her narrative, she relates how some Oneida warriors siding with the British captured two Indians guiding General Sullivan's 1779 campaign of terror in central New York. One of the captors recognized his own brother.

Envy and revenge glared in the features of the conquering savage, as he advanced to his brother (the prisoner) in all the haughtiness of Indian pride, heightened by a sense of power, and addressed him in the following manner:

"Brother, you have merited death! The hatchet or the war-club shall finish your career! When I begged of you to follow me in the fortunes of war, you was deaf to my cries—you spurned my entreaties!

"Brother! You have merited death and shall have your deserts! When the rebels raised their hatchets to fight their good master, you sharpened your knife, you brightened your rifle and led on our foes to the fields of our fathers! You have merited death and shall die by our hands! When those rebels had drove us from the fields of our fathers to seek out new homes, it was you who could dare to step forth as their pilot, and conduct them even to the doors of our wigwams, to butcher our children and put us to death! No crime can be greater! But though you have merited death and shall die on this spot, my hands shall not be stained in the blood of a brother! *Who will strike?*"

Little Beard, who was standing by, as soon as the speech was ended, struck the prisoner on the head with his tomahawk, and dispatched him at once.

Source: James E. Seaver, *A narrative of the life of Mrs. Mary Jemison, who was taken by the Indians, in the year 1755, when only about twelve years of age, and has continued to reside amongst them to the present time* (1824), chapter VII, Project Gutenberg, http://www.gutenberg.org/ebooks/6960 (accessed August 2, 2013).

Questions for Analysis

Recognize Viewpoints: What did Benjamin Franklin mean by the emphasized words *"Natural Duties"*? Do you think Franklin really believed that his son was entitled to his own political opinions on the Revolutionary War? What may have motivated William's decision to remain loyal to the crown?

Analyze the Evidence: What are the three reasons the Oneida warrior stated to support his contention that his brother merited death?

Consider the Context: To what extent was the American Revolution a civil war, that is, a war between inhabitants of the same country?

be unscrupulous, violent men grabbing power for themselves.

Pockets of loyalism existed everywhere (Map 7.2). The most visible loyalists (called Tories by their enemies) were royal officials, not only governors but also local judges and customs officers. Wealthy merchants gravitated toward loyalism to maintain the trade protections of navigation acts and the British navy. Conservative urban lawyers admired the stability of British law and order. Some colonists chose loyalism simply to oppose traditional adversaries, for example many backcountry Carolina farmers who resented the power of the pro-revolution gentry. Southern slaves had their own resentments against the white slave-owning class and looked to Britain in hope of freedom. Even New England towns at the heart of the turmoil, such as Concord, Massachusetts, had a small and increasingly silenced core of loyalists. On occasion, fathers and sons and even brothers disagreed completely on the war. (See "Analyzing Historical Evidence," above.)

Many Indian tribes chose neutrality at the war's start, seeing the conflict as a civil war between the English and Americans. Eventually, however, they were drawn in, most taking the British side. The powerful Iroquois Confederacy divided: The Mohawk, Cayuga, Seneca, and Onondaga peoples lined up with the British; the

Abigail Adams
Abigail Smith Adams, twenty-two, wears feminine pearls and a lace collar along with a facial expression projecting confidence and maturity not often credited to young women of the 1760s. A decade later, she was running the family's Massachusetts farm while her husband, John, attended the Continental Congress in Philadelphia. Her frequent letters gave him the benefit of her sage advice on politics and the war. © Massachusetts Historical Society, Boston, MA, USA/Bridgeman Images.

Oneida and Tuscarora tribes aided Americans. One young Mohawk leader, Thayendanegea (known also by his English name, Joseph Brant), traveled to England in 1775 to complain to King George about land-hungry New York settlers. "It is very hard when we have let the King's subjects have so much of our lands for so little value," he wrote, "they should want to cheat us in this manner of the small spots we have left for our women and children to live on." Brant pledged Indian support for the king in exchange for protection from encroaching settlers. In the Ohio Country, parts of the Shawnee and Delaware tribes started out pro-American but shifted to the British side by 1779 in the face of repeated betrayals by American settlers and soldiers.

Loyalists were most vocal between 1774 and 1776, when the possibility of a full-scale rebellion against Britain was still uncertain. They challenged the emerging patriot side in pamphlets and newspapers. In 1776 in New York City, 547 loyalists signed and circulated a broadside titled "A Declaration of Dependence" in rebuttal to the congress's July 4 declaration, denouncing the "most unnatural, unprovoked Rebellion that ever disgraced the annals of Time."

Who Is a Traitor?

In June 1775, the Second Continental Congress declared all loyalists to be traitors. Over the next year, state laws defined as treason acts such as provisioning the British army, saying anything that undermined patriot morale, and discouraging men from enlisting in the Continental army. Punishments ranged from house arrest and suspension of voting privileges to confiscation of property and deportation. Sometimes self-appointed committees of Tory hunters bypassed the judicial niceties and terrorized loyalists, raiding their houses or tarring and feathering them.

Were wives of loyalists also traitors? When loyalist families fled the country, their property was typically confiscated. But if the wife stayed, courts usually allowed her to keep one-third of the property, the amount due her if widowed, and confiscated the rest. Yet a wife who fled with her husband might have little choice in the matter. After the Revolution, descendants of refugee loyalists filed several lawsuits to regain property that had entered the family through the mother's inheritance. In one well-publicized Massachusetts case in 1805, the American son of loyalist refugee Anna Martin recovered her dowry property on the grounds that she had no independent will to be a loyalist.

Tarring and feathering, property confiscation, deportation, terrorism—to the loyalists, such denials of liberty of conscience and of freedom to own private property proved that democratic tyranny was more to be feared than the monarchical variety. A Boston loyalist named Mather Byles aptly expressed this point: "They call me a brainless Tory, but tell me . . . which is better—to be ruled by one tyrant three thousand miles away, or by three thousand tyrants not a mile away?" Byles was soon sentenced to deportation.

Throughout the war, probably 7,000 to 8,000 loyalists fled to England, and 28,000 eventually found haven in Canada. Many stayed put while the war's outcome was unknown. In New Jersey, for example, 3,000 Jerseyites felt protected (or scared) enough by the occupying British army in 1776 to swear an oath of allegiance to the king. But then the British drew back to New York City, leaving them at the mercy of local patriot committees. Despite the staunch backing of loyalists in 1776, the British found it difficult to build a winning strategy on their support.

Prisoners of War

The poor handling of loyalists as traitors paled in comparison to the handling of American prisoners of war by the British. Among European military powers, humane treatment of captured soldiers was the custom, including adequate provisions (paid for by the captives' own government) and the possibility of prisoner exchanges. But British leaders refused to see American captives as foot soldiers employed by a sovereign nation. Instead they were traitors, to be treated worse than common criminals.

The 4,000 American prisoners taken in the fall of 1776 were crowded onto two dozen vessels anchored in the river between Manhattan and Brooklyn. The largest ship, the HMS *Jersey*, was a broken-down hull built to house a crew of 400 but now packed with more than 1,100 prisoners. Survivors described the dark, stinking space belowdecks where more than half a dozen men died daily. A twenty-year-old captive seaman described his first view of the hold: "Here was a motley crew, covered with rags and filth; visages pallid with disease, emaciated with hunger and anxiety, . . . and surrounded with the horrors of sickness and death." The Continental Congress sent food to the prisoners, but most was diverted to British use, leaving General Washington fuming.

Treating the captives as criminals potentially triggered the Anglo-American right of habeas corpus, a thirteenth-century British liberty that guaranteed every prisoner the right to challenge his detention before a judge and to learn the charges against him. To remove that possibility, Parliament voted in early 1777 to suspend habeas corpus specifically for "persons taken in the act of high treason" in any of the colonies.

Despite the prison-ship horrors, Washington insisted that captured British soldiers be treated humanely. From the initial group of Hessians taken on Christmas 1776 to the several thousand more soldiers captured in American victories by 1778, America's prisoners of war were gathered in rural encampments. Guarded by local townsmen, the captives typically could cultivate small gardens, move about freely during the day, and

TEUCRO DUCE NIL DESPERANDOM.

Firſt Battalion of PENNSYLVANIA LOYALISTS, commanded by His Excellency Sir WILLIAM HOWE, K. B.

ALL INTREPID ABLE-BODIED

HEROES,

WHO are willing to ſerve His MAJESTY KING GEORGE the Third, in Defence of their Country, Laws and Conſtitution, againſt the arbitrary Uſurpations of a tyrannical Congreſs, have now not only an Opportunity of manifeſting their Spirit, by aſſiſting in reducing to Obedience their too-long deluded Countrymen, but alſo of acquiring the polite Accompliſhments of a Soldier, by ſerving only two Years, or during the preſent Rebellion in America.

Such ſpirited Fellows, who are willing to engage, will be rewarded at the End of the War, beſides their Laurels, with 50 Acres of Land, where every gallant Hero may retire.. . . . .

Each Volunteer will receive, as a Bounty, FIVE DOLLARS, beſides Arms, Cloathing and Accoutrements, and every other Requiſite proper to accommodate a Gentleman Soldier, by applying to Lieutenant Colonel ALLEN, or at Captain KEARNY's Rendezvous, at PATRICK TONRY's, three Doors above Market-ſtreet, in Second-ſtreet.

Loyalist Recruiting Poster, 1777
The British army invites a few good men to restore obedience to their "deluded Countrymen." A five-dollar signing bonus and a promise of free land await each new recruit, who will also be trained in "the polite Accomplishments of a Soldier." Notice the Latin phrase heading the poster, referencing a military leader in the ancient battle of Troy. What subtle message did that send?
The Granger Collection, New York.

even hire themselves out to farmers suffering wartime labor shortages. Officers with money could purchase lodging with local families and mix socially with Americans. Many officers were even allowed to keep their guns as they waited for prisoner exchanges to release them.

Such exchanges were negotiated when the British became desperate to regain valued officers and thus freed American officers. Death was the most common fate of ordinary American soldiers and seamen. More than 15,000 men endured captivity in the prison ships, and two-thirds of them died, a number double those who died in battle (estimated to be around 5,000). News of the horrors of the British death ships increased the revolutionaries' resolve and convinced some neutrals of the necessity of the war.

MAP ACTIVITY

Map 7.2   Loyalist Strength and Rebel Support

The exact number of loyalists can never be known. No one could have made an accurate count at the time, and political allegiance often shifted with the wind. This map shows the regions of loyalist strength on which the British relied—most significantly, the lower Hudson valley and the Carolina Piedmont.

READING THE MAP: Which forces were stronger, those loyal to Britain or those rebelling? (Consider the size of their respective areas, centers of population, and vital port locations.) What areas were contested? If the contested areas ultimately had sided with the British, how would the balance of power have changed?

CONNECTIONS: Who was more likely to be a loyalist and why? How many loyalists left the United States? Where did they go?

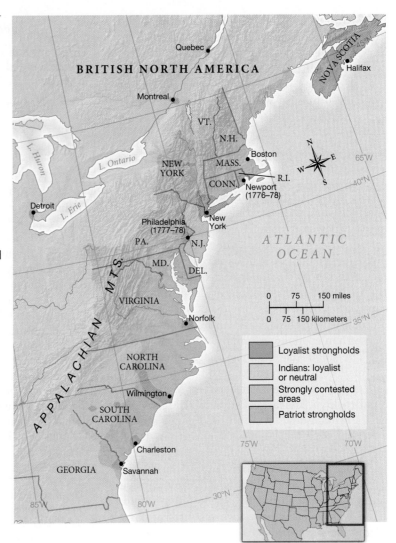

Financial Instability and Corruption

Wars cost money—for arms and ammunition, for food and uniforms, for soldiers' pay, for provisions for prisoners. The Continental Congress printed money, but its value quickly deteriorated because the congress held no precious metals to back the currency. The dollar eventually bottomed out at one-fortieth of its face value. States, too, were printing paper money to pay for wartime expenses, further complicating the economy.

As the currency depreciated, the congress turned to other means to procure supplies and labor. One method was to borrow hard money (gold or silver coins) from wealthy men in exchange for certificates of debt (public securities) promising repayment with interest. The certificates of debt were similar to present-day government bonds. To pay soldiers, the congress issued land-grant certificates, written promises of acreage usually located in frontier areas such as central Maine or eastern Ohio. Both the public securities and the land-grant certificates quickly became forms of negotiable currency, and they too soon depreciated.

Depreciating currency inevitably led to rising prices, as sellers compensated for the falling value of the money. The wartime economy of the late 1770s, with its unreliable currency and price inflation, was extremely demoralizing to Americans everywhere. In 1778, in an effort to impose stability, local committees of public safety began to fix prices on essential goods such as flour. Inevitably, some turned this unstable situation to their advantage. Money that fell fast in value needed to be spent quickly; being in debt was suddenly advantageous because the debt could be repaid in devalued currency. A brisk black market sprang up in prohibited luxury imports, such as tea, sugar, textiles, and wines, even though these items came from Britain. A New Hampshire delegate to the Continental Congress denounced

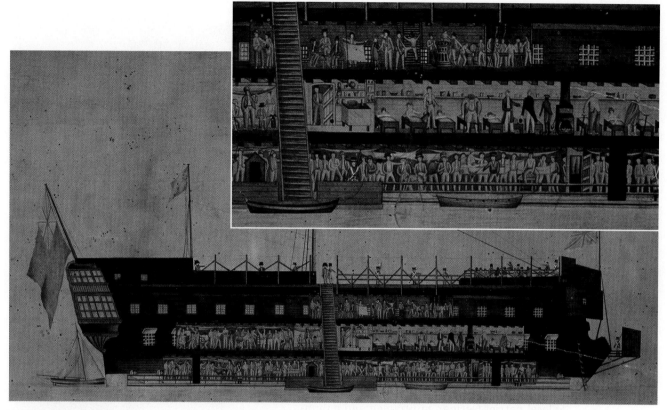

British Prison Ship
A carefully executed cutaway drawing of a prison ship shows scores of American POWs belowdecks being guarded by redcoats. The degree of crowding and of care—note the infirmary on the middle level to the right of the gangplank (see inset)—is represented as more humane than was actually the case. The artist added these words in French beside the drawing: "My God, Have you forgotten me?" Museum of the City of New York/The Art Archive at Art Resource, NY.

the trade: "We are a crooked and perverse generation, longing for the fineries and follies of those Egyptian task masters from whom we have so lately freed ourselves."

REVIEW   How did the patriots promote support for their cause in the colonies?

▶ The Campaigns of 1777–1779: The North and West

In early 1777, the Continental army faced bleak choices. General Washington had skillfully avoided defeat, but the minor victories in New Jersey lent only faint optimism to the American side. Meanwhile, British troops moved south from Quebec, aiming to isolate New England by taking control of the Hudson River. Their presence drew the Continental army up into central New York, turning the Mohawk Valley into a bloody war zone and polarizing the tribes of the ancient Iroquois Confederacy. By 1779, rival tribes in the Ohio Valley were fully involved in the Revolutionary War. Despite an important victory at Saratoga, the increasing involvement of pro-British Indians and the continuing strength of the British forced the American government to look to France for help.

Burgoyne's Army and the Battle of Saratoga

In 1777, British general John Burgoyne, commanding a considerable army, began the northern squeeze on the Hudson River valley. Coming from Canada, he marched south hoping to capture Albany, near the intersection of the Hudson and Mohawk rivers (see Map 7.1). Accompanied by 1,000 "camp followers" (cooks, laundresses, musicians) and some 400 Indian warriors, mostly Mohawks, Burgoyne's army of 7,800 men did not travel light. Food had to be packed in, not only for people but for 400 horses hauling heavy artillery.

In July, Burgoyne captured Fort Ticonderoga with ease. American troops stationed there spotted the approaching British and abandoned the fort without a fight. The British continued to move south, but they lost a month hacking their way through dense forests. Supply lines back to Canada were severely stretched, and soldiers sent out to forage for food were beaten back by local militia units.

The logical second step in isolating New England should have been to advance troops up the Hudson from New York City to meet Burgoyne. American surveillance indicated that General Howe in Manhattan was readying his men for a major move in August 1777. But Howe surprised everyone by sailing south to attack Philadelphia.

To reinforce Burgoyne, British and Hessian troops from Montreal came from the west along the Mohawk River, aided by some thousand Mohawks and Senecas of the Iroquois Confederacy. A hundred miles west of Albany, the British encountered American Continental soldiers at Fort Stanwix and laid siege, causing hundreds of local patriot German militiamen and a number of Oneida Indians to rush to the Continentals' support. On August 6, 1777, Mohawk chief Joseph Brant led his large force of warriors in an ambush on the patriot fighters in a narrow ravine called Oriskany. The result was one of the bloodiest battles of the entire war. Of the 800 local militiamen, nearly 400 were killed and another 50 were wounded in the carnage, while on Brant's side, some 90 warriors died. The defenders of Fort Stanwix ultimately repelled their attackers, who retreated north to Canada. The deadly **battle of Oriskany** and battle of Fort Stanwix were complexly multiethnic, pitting German Americans against Hessian mercenaries, New York patriots against New York loyalists, English Americans against British soldiers, and Indians against Indians. They marked the beginning of the end of the Iroquois Confederacy, ruptured by lethal violence between members of the constituent tribes. By January 1779, the eternal flame of the council fire at Onondaga, which had symbolized the unity of the six confederated tribes of Iroquoia, was extinguished.

The British retreat at Fort Stanwix deprived General Burgoyne of the additional troops he expected. Camped at a small village called Saratoga, he was isolated, with food supplies dwindling and men deserting. His adversary at Albany, General Horatio Gates, began moving his army toward Saratoga. Burgoyne decided to

Chief Joseph Brant
The Mohawk chief Thayendanegea, called Joseph Brant by the Americans, had been educated in English ways at Eleazar Wheelock's New England school (which became Dartmouth College in 1769). In 1775, the thirty-four-year-old Brant traveled to England to negotiate the Mohawk tribe's support for the British. From 1778 to 1780, Brant led his warriors, assisted by loyalist volunteers, in many attacks on frontier settlers in central New York. Library and Archives Canada, accession no. 1981-055-77, C-114468.

attack first, and the British prevailed, but at the great cost of 600 dead or wounded. Three weeks later, an American attack on Burgoyne's forces in the second stage of the **battle of Saratoga** cost the British another 600 men and most of their cannons. General Burgoyne finally surrendered to the American forces on October 17, 1777. It was the first decisive victory for the American Continentals, touching off great celebration throughout the colonies.

General Howe, meanwhile, had succeeded in occupying Philadelphia in September 1777. Figuring that the Saratoga loss was balanced by the capture of Philadelphia, the British government proposed a negotiated settlement—not including independence—to end the war. The American side refused.

Patriot optimism was not well founded. Spirits ran high, but supplies of arms and food ran precariously low. Washington moved his troops into winter quarters at Valley Forge, just west of Philadelphia. Quartered in drafty huts, the men lacked blankets, boots, stockings, and food. Some 2,000 men at Valley Forge died of disease; another 2,000 deserted over the bitter six-month encampment.

Washington blamed the citizenry for lack of support; indeed, evidence of corruption and profiteering was abundant. Army suppliers too often provided defective food, clothing, and gunpowder. One shipment of bedding arrived with blankets one-quarter their customary size. Food supplies arrived rotten. As one Continental officer said, "The people at home are destroying the Army by their conduct much faster than Howe and all his army can possibly do by fighting us."

The War in the West: Indian Country

Between the fall of 1777 and the summer of 1778, the fighting on the Atlantic coast slowed. But in the interior western areas—the Mohawk Valley, the Ohio Valley, and Kentucky—the war of Indians against the American rebels heated up. Native Americans fought to protect their sovereignty, their independence, and their traditional culture, in a near mirror image to the Americans' quest for "life, liberty, and the pursuit of happiness."

The ambush and slaughter at Oriskany in August 1777 marked the beginning of three years of terror for the inhabitants of the Mohawk Valley. Loyalists and Indians engaged in many raids throughout 1778, capturing or killing inhabitants. In retaliation, American militiamen destroyed Joseph Brant's village, killing several children. A month later, Brant's warriors attacked the town of Cherry Valley, killing 16 soldiers and 32 civilians.

The following summer, General Washington authorized a campaign to wreak "total destruction and devastation" on all the Iroquois villages of central New York. Some 4,500 troops commanded by General John Sullivan implemented a campaign of terror in the fall of 1779. Forty Indian towns met with total obliteration; the soldiers torched dwellings, cornfields, and orchards. In a few towns,

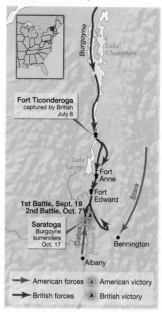

Battle of Saratoga, 1777

Fort Ticonderoga
captured by British
July 6

Burgoyne

Lake Champlain

Lake George

Fort Anne

Fort Edward

Stark

1st Battle, Sept. 19
2nd Battle, Oct. 7

Saratoga
Burgoyne surrenders
Oct. 17

Gates

Hudson R.

Bennington

Albany

→ American forces   ⚔ American victory
→ British forces   ⚔ British victory

women and children were slaughtered, but in most, the inhabitants managed to escape, fleeing to the British at Fort Niagara. Thousands of Indian refugees, sick and starving, camped around the fort in one of the most miserable winters on record.

Much farther to the west, beyond Fort Pitt, another complex story of alliances and betrayals between American militiamen and Indians unfolded. Some 150,000 native people lived between the Appalachian Mountains and the Mississippi River, and by 1779 neutrality was no longer an option. Most sided with the British, but a portion of the Shawnee and Delaware at first sought peace with the Americans. In mid-1778, the Delaware chief White Eyes negotiated a treaty at Fort Pitt, pledging Indian support for the Americans in exchange for supplies and trade goods. But escalating violence undermined the agreement. That fall, when American soldiers killed two friendly Shawnee chiefs, Cornstalk and Red Hawk, the Continental Congress hastened to apologize, as did the governors of Pennsylvania and Virginia, but the soldiers who stood trial for the murders were acquitted. Two months later, White Eyes died under mysterious circumstances, almost certainly murdered by militiamen, who repeatedly had trouble honoring distinctions between allied and enemy Indians.

West of North Carolina (today's Tennessee), militias attacked Cherokee settlements in 1779, destroying thirty-six villages, while Indian raiders repeatedly attacked white settlements such as Boonesborough (in present-day Kentucky) (Map 7.3). In retaliation, a young Virginian named George Rogers Clark led Kentucky militiamen into what is now Illinois, attacking and taking the British fort at Kaskaskia. Clark's men wore native clothing—hunting shirts and breechcloths—but their dress was not a sign of solidarity with the Indians. When they attacked British-held Fort Vincennes in 1779, Clark's troops tomahawked Indian captives and threw their still-live bodies into the river in a gory spectacle witnessed by the redcoats. "To excel them in barbarity is the only way to make war upon Indians," Clark announced.

By 1780, very few Indians remained neutral. Violent raids by Americans drove Indians into the arms of the British at Forts Detroit and Niagara,

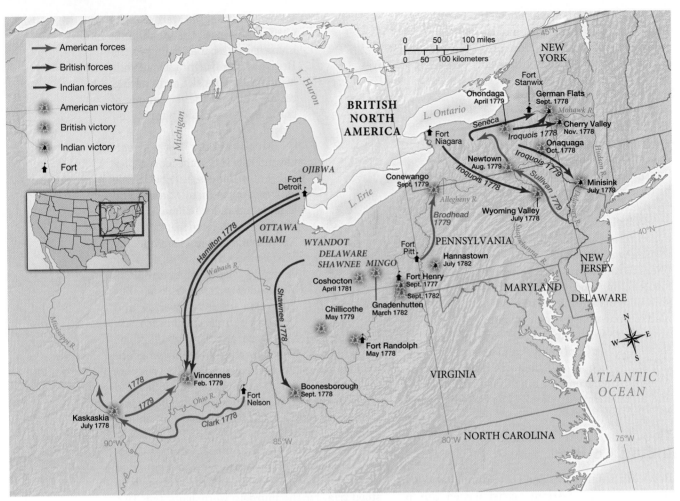

Map 7.3 The Indian War in the West, 1777–1782
Most Indian tribes supported the British. Iroquois Indians attacked New York's Mohawk Valley throughout 1778, causing the Continental army to destroy Iroquois villages throughout central New York. Shawnee and Delaware in western Pennsylvania tangled with American militiamen in 1779, while tribes near Fort Detroit conducted raids on Kentucky settlers. Sporadic frontier fighting continued through 1782.

or into the arms of the Spaniards, west of the Mississippi River. Said one officer on the Sullivan campaign, "Their nests are destroyed but the birds are still on the wing." For those who stayed near their native lands, chaos and confusion prevailed. Rare as it was, Indian support for the American side occasionally emerged out of a strategic sense that the Americans were unstoppable in their westward pressure and that it was better to work out an alliance than to lose in a war. But American treatment of even friendly Indians showed that there was no winning strategy for them.

The French Alliance

On their own, the Americans could not have defeated Britain, especially as pressure from hostile Indians increased. Essential help arrived as a result of the victory at Saratoga, which convinced the French to enter the war; a formal alliance was signed in February 1778. France recognized the United States as an independent nation and promised full military and commercial support. Most crucial was the French navy, which could challenge British supplies and troops at sea and aid the Americans in taking and holding prisoners of war.

Well before 1778, however, the French had been covertly providing cannons, muskets, gunpowder, and highly trained military advisers to the Americans. From the French monarchy's view, the main attraction of an alliance was the opportunity it provided to defeat archrival Britain. A victory would also open pathways to trade and perhaps result in France's acquiring the coveted British West Indies. Even an American defeat would not be a disaster for France if the war lasted many years and drained Britain of men and money.

French support materialized slowly. The navy arrived off the Virginia coast in July 1778 but then sailed south to the West Indies to defend the French sugar-producing islands. French help would prove indispensable to the American cause in 1780 and 1781, but the alliance's first months brought no dramatic changes, and some Americans grumbled that the partnership would prove worthless.

REVIEW Why did the Americans need assistance from the French to ensure victory?

▶ The Southern Strategy and the End of the War

When France joined the war, some British officials favored abandoning the fight. As one troop commander shrewdly observed, "we are far from an anticipated peace, because the bitterness of the rebels is too widespread, and in regions where we are masters the rebellious spirit is still in them. The land is too large, and there are too many people. The more land we win, the weaker our army gets in the field." The commander of the British navy agreed, as did Lord North, the prime minister. But the king was determined to crush the rebellion, and he encouraged a new strategy for victory focusing on the southern colonies, thought to be more reliably loyalist. He had little idea of the depth of anger that would produce deadly guerrilla warfare between loyalists and patriots. The king's plan was brilliant but desperate, and ultimately unsuccessful.

Georgia and South Carolina

The new strategy called for British forces to abandon New England and focus on the South,

VISUAL ACTIVITY

"The Balance of Power," 1780

This English cartoon mocks the alliance of Spain and the Netherlands with France in support of the American war. On the left, the female figure Britannia cannot be moved by all the lightweights on the right. France and Spain embrace while a Dutch boy hops on, saying, "I'll do anything for Money." The forlorn Indian maiden, representing America, wails, "My Ingratitude is Justly punished." The New York Public Library/Art Resource, NY.

READING THE IMAGE: What does this cartoon reveal about British perceptions of the American Revolution?

CONNECTIONS: How did British attitudes toward the colonies contribute to the British defeat in the war?

with its valuable crops and its large slave population, a destabilizing factor that might keep rebellious white southerners in line. Georgia and the Carolinas appeared to hold large numbers of loyalists, providing a base for the British to recapture the southern colonies one by one, before moving north to the more problematic middle colonies and New England.

Georgia, the first target, fell easily at the end of December 1778 (Map 7.4). Most of the Continental army was in the North, keeping an eye on the British occupation of New York; the French were still in the West Indies. A small army of British soldiers occupied Savannah and Augusta, and a new royal governor and loyalist assembly were quickly installed. The British quickly organized twenty loyal militia units, and 1,400 Georgians swore an oath of allegiance to the king. So far, the southern strategy looked as if it might work.

Next came South Carolina. The Continental army put ten regiments into the port city of Charleston to defend it from attack by British troops shipped south from New York under the command of General Clinton, Howe's replacement as commander in chief. For five weeks in early spring 1780, the British laid siege to the city and took it in May 1780, capturing 3,300 American soldiers.

Clinton next announced that slaves owned by rebel masters were welcome to seek refuge with his army, and several thousand escaped to the coastal city. Untrained in formal warfare, they were of use to the British as knowledgeable guides to the countryside and as laborers building defensive fortifications. Escaped slaves with boat-piloting skills were particularly valuable for crucial aid in navigating the inland rivers of the southern colonies.

Clinton returned to New York, leaving the task of pacifying the rest of South Carolina to General Charles Cornwallis and 4,000 troops. A bold commander, Lord Cornwallis quickly chased out the remaining Continentals and established military rule of South Carolina by midsummer. He purged rebels from government office and disarmed rebel militias. Exports of rice, South Carolina's main crop, resumed, and pardons were offered to Carolinians willing to prove their loyalty by taking up arms for the British.

By August, American troops arrived from the North to strike back at Cornwallis. General Gates, the hero of Saratoga, led 3,000 troops, many of them newly recruited militiamen, into battle against Cornwallis at Camden, South Carolina, on August 16 (see Map 7.4). The militiamen panicked at the sight of the approaching British cavalry, however, and fled. When regiment leaders tried to regroup the next day, only 700 soldiers showed up. The battle of Camden was a devastating defeat, and prospects seemed very grim for the Americans.

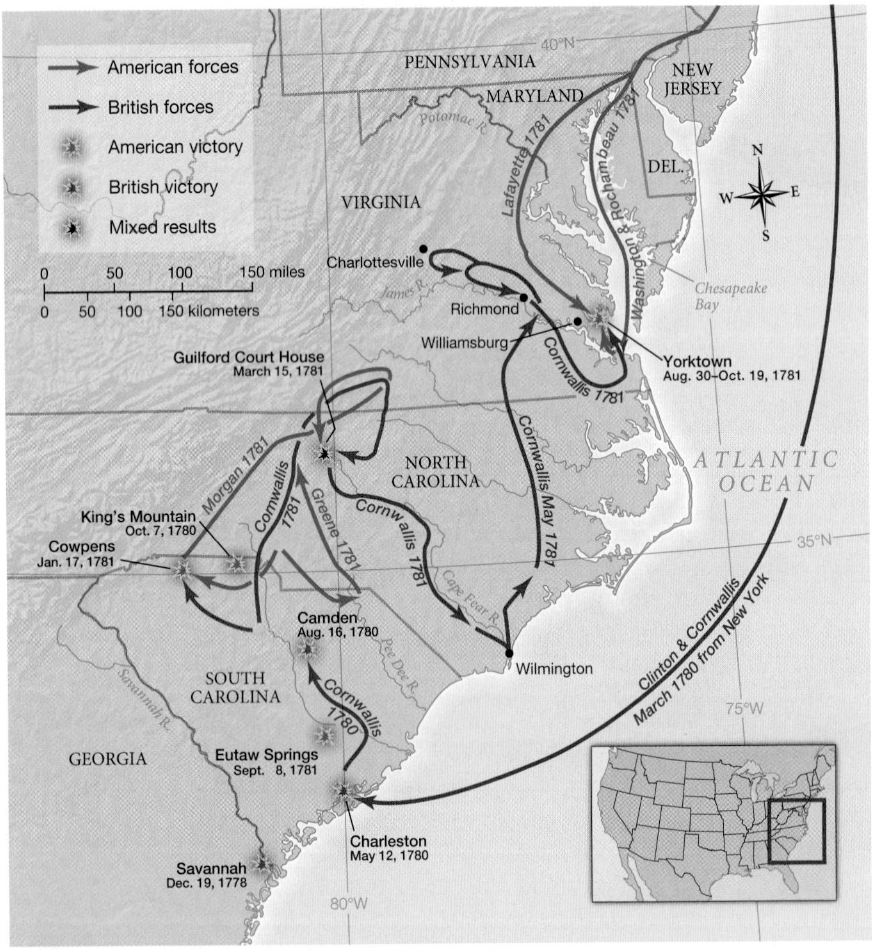

Treason and Guerrilla Warfare

Britain's southern strategy succeeded in 1780 in part because of information about American troop movements secretly conveyed by an American

Map 7.4 The War in the South, 1780–1781
After taking Charleston in May 1780, the British advanced into South and North Carolina, touching off a bloody civil war. An American loss at Camden was followed by victories at King's Mountain and Cowpens. The British next invaded Virginia but got trapped and overpowered at Yorktown in the fall of 1781.

A Shaming Ritual Targeting the Great Traitor
In late 1780, Philadelphians staged a ritual humiliation of Benedict Arnold, represented by a two-faced effigy. Behind him stands the devil, prodding him with a pitchfork and shaking a bag of coins near his ear, reminding all that Arnold sold out for money. To the beat of a fife and drums, soldiers and onlookers march to a bonfire, where the effigy was burned to ashes. Library of Congress, Rare Book and Special Collections Division.

officer, Benedict Arnold. The hero of several American battles, Arnold was a deeply insecure man who never felt he got his due. Sometime in 1779, he opened secret negotiations with General Clinton in New York, trading information for money and hinting that he could deliver far more of value. When General Washington made him commander of West Point, a new fort on the Hudson River sixty miles north of New York City, Arnold's plan crystallized. West Point controlled the Hudson; its capture by the British might well have meant victory in the war.

Arnold's plot to sell a West Point victory to the British was foiled in the fall of 1780 when Americans captured the man carrying plans of the fort's defense from Arnold to Clinton. News of Arnold's treason created shock waves. Arnold represented all of the patriots' worst fears about themselves: greedy self-interest, like that of the war profiteers; the unprincipled abandonment of war aims, like that of turncoat southern Tories; panic, like that of the terrified soldiers at Camden. But instead of demoralizing the Americans, Arnold's treachery revived their commitment to the patriot cause. Vilifying Arnold allowed Americans to stake out a wide distance between themselves and dastardly conduct. It inspired a renewal of patriotism at a particularly low moment.

Shock over Gates's defeat at Camden and Arnold's treason revitalized rebel support in western South Carolina, an area that Cornwallis thought was pacified and loyal. The backcountry of the South soon became the site of guerrilla warfare. In hit-and-run attacks, both sides burned and ravaged not only opponents' property but also the property of anyone claiming to be neutral. Loyalist militia units organized by the British were met by fierce rebel militia units. In South Carolina, some 6,000 men became active partisan fighters, and they entered into at least twenty-six engagements. Guerrilla warfare soon spread to Georgia and North Carolina. Both sides committed atrocities and plundered property, clear deviations from standard military practice.

The British southern strategy depended on sufficient loyalist strength to hold reconquered territory as Cornwallis's army moved north. The backcountry civil war proved this assumption false. The Americans won few major battles in the South, but they ultimately succeeded by harassing the British forces and preventing them from foraging for food. Cornwallis moved the war into North Carolina in the fall of 1780 because the North Carolinians were supplying the South Carolina rebels with arms and men (see Map 7.4). Then news of a massacre of loyalist units by 1,400 frontier riflemen at the battle of King's Mountain, in western South Carolina, sent him hurrying back. The British were stretched too thin to hold even two colonies.

Surrender at Yorktown

By early 1781, the war was going very badly for the British. Their defeat at King's Mountain was quickly followed by a second major defeat at the battle of Cowpens in South Carolina in January 1781. Cornwallis retreated to North Carolina and thence to Virginia, where he captured Williamsburg in June. A raiding party proceeded to Charlottesville, the seat of government, capturing members of the Virginia assembly but not Governor Thomas Jefferson, who escaped the soldiers by a mere ten minutes. (The slaves at Monticello, Jefferson's home, stood their ground and saved his house from plundering, but more than a dozen at two other plantations he owned sought refuge with the British.) These minor victories allowed Cornwallis to imagine he was succeeding in Virginia. His army, now swelled by some 4,000 escaped slaves, marched to Yorktown, near the Chesapeake Bay area. As the general waited for backup troops by ship from British headquarters in New York City, smallpox and typhus began to set in among the black recruits.

At this juncture, the French-American alliance came into play. French regiments commanded by

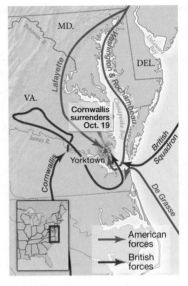

Siege of Yorktown, 1781

the Comte de Rochambeau had joined General Washington in Newport, Rhode Island, in mid-1780, and in early 1781 warships under the Comte de Grasse had sailed from France to the West Indies. Washington, Rochambeau, and de Grasse now fixed their attention on Chesapeake Bay. The French fleet got there ahead of the British troop ships from New York; a five-day naval battle left the French navy in clear control of the Virginia coast. This proved to be the decisive factor in ending the war because the French ships prevented any rescue of Cornwallis's army.

On land, General Cornwallis and his 7,500 troops faced a combined French and American army of 16,000. For twelve days, the Americans and French bombarded the British fortifications at Yorktown; Cornwallis ran low on food and ammunition. He also began to expel the black recruits, some of them sick and dying. A Hessian officer serving under Cornwallis later criticized this British action as disgraceful: "We had used them to good advantage, and set them free, and now, with fear and trembling, they had to face the reward of their cruel masters." The twelve-day siege brought Cornwallis to the realization that neither victory

VISUAL ACTIVITY

Lafayette at Yorktown, with James

In 1781, French officer Lafayette met and borrowed James, slave of a Virginia owner. At the siege of Yorktown, James infiltrated the British command by pretending to be an escaped slave. James fed the British misinformation and brought crucial intelligence back to Lafayette. At the surrender, British leaders spotted James with Lafayette and realized they'd been had. Lafayette was instrumental in obtaining James's freedom in 1786. Lafayette College, Easton, PA. Gift of Helen Fahnstock Hubbard in memory of her husband, John Hubbard, Harvard (class of 1892).

READING THE IMAGE: Lafayette posed for this picture in France in 1783. Do you think James also personally posed for the artist? Why or why not?

CONNECTIONS: Why did many enslaved people side with the British? Why would some (like James) help out the American cause?

nor escape was possible. He surrendered on October 19, 1781.

What began as a promising southern strategy in 1778 had turned into a discouraging defeat. British attacks in the South had energized American resistance, as did the timely exposure of Benedict Arnold's treason. The arrival of the French fleet sealed the fate of Cornwallis at the **battle of Yorktown**, and major military operations came to a halt.

The Losers and the Winners

The surrender at Yorktown spelled the end for the British, but two more years of skirmishes ensued. Frontier areas in Kentucky, Ohio, and Illinois blazed with battles pitting Americans against various Indian tribes. The British army still occupied three coastal cities, including New York, and in response, an augmented Continental army stayed at the ready, north of New York City. Occasional clashes occurred, like the ones in which Deborah Sampson saw action while cross-dressing as a male soldier.

The **Treaty of Paris**, also called the **Peace of Paris**, was two years in the making. (See "Beyond America's Borders," page 192.) Commissioners from America and Britain worked out the ten articles of peace, while a side treaty signed by Britain, France, Spain, and the Netherlands sealed related deals. The first article went to the heart of the matter: "His Britannic Majesty acknowledges the said United States to be free Sovereign and independent States." Other articles set the western boundary at the Mississippi River and guaranteed that creditors on both sides would be paid in sterling money, a provision important to British merchants. Britain agreed to withdraw its troops quickly, but more than a decade later this promise still had not been fully kept. Another agreement prohibited the British from "carrying away any Negroes or other property of the American inhabitants." The treaty was signed on September 3, 1783.

News of the treaty signing was cause for celebration among most Americans, but not among the thousands of self-liberated blacks who had joined the British under promise of freedom. South Carolinian Boston King, a refugee in New York City, recalled that the provision prohibiting evacuation of black refugees "filled us with inexpressible anguish and terror." King and others pressed the British commander in New York, Sir Guy Carleton, to honor pre-treaty British promises. Carleton obliged: For all refugees under British protection for more than a year, he issued certificates of freedom—making them no longer

"property" to be returned. More than 4,000 blacks sailed out of New York for Nova Scotia, Boston King and his family among them. As Carleton coolly explained to a protesting George Washington, "the Negroes in question . . . I found free when I arrived at New York, I had therefore no right, as I thought, to prevent their going to any part of the world they thought proper." British commanders in Savannah and Charleston followed Carleton's lead and aided the exit of perhaps 10,000 blacks from the United States.

The emancipation of slaves had never been a war goal of the British; destabilizing patriot planters and gaining manpower were their initial reasons for promises of freedom. Had the British won the war, they might well have reenslaved insurgent blacks to restore the profitable plantation economy of the South. For their part, blacks viewed British army camps as sites of refuge (not figuring on the devastations of epidemic diseases and food shortages) and had no reason to revere the British monarchy. In fact, some runaways had headed for Indian country instead.

The Treaty of Paris had nothing to say about the Indian participants in the Revolutionary War. As one American told the Shawnee people, "Your Fathers the English have made Peace with us for themselves, but forgot you their Children, who Fought with them, and neglected you like Bastards." Indian lands were assigned to the victors as though they were uninhabited. Some Indian refugees fled west into present-day Missouri and Arkansas, and others, such as Joseph Brant's Mohawks, relocated to Canada. But significant numbers remained within the new United States, occupying their traditional homelands in areas west and north of the Ohio River. For them, the Treaty of Paris brought no peace at all; their longer war against the Americans would extend at least until 1795 and for some until 1813. Their ally, Britain, conceded defeat, but the Indians did not.

With the treaty finally signed, the British began their evacuation of New York, Charleston, and Savannah, a process complicated by the sheer numbers involved—soldiers, fearful loyalists, and refugees from slavery by the thousands. In New York City, more than 27,000 soldiers and 30,000 loyalists sailed on hundreds of ships for England in the late fall of 1783. In a final act of mischief, on the November day when the last ships left, the losing side raised the British flag at the southern tip of Manhattan, cut away the ropes used to hoist it, and greased the flagpole.

REVIEW   Why did the British southern strategy ultimately fail?

European Nations and the Peace of Paris, 1783

News of the decisive British defeat at Yorktown in late 1781 caused Britain's prime minister, Lord North, to stagger as though wounded and exclaim, "Oh, God, it is all over!" But in truth, it was far from over. A full year elapsed before the elements of a formal peace treaty could be worked out, and an additional year passed before the treaty was signed and Britain finally ended its occupation of New York City. The delay occurred in part because several European countries besides Britain had stakes in the war that had nothing to do with the chief American goal of political independence.

France had entered the war mainly to thwart and damage Britain. Certainly the French monarchy had no real sympathy for a democratic revolution in the British colonies. Indeed, for months before the victory at Yorktown, French leaders conferred covertly with the British about a plan to divide the colonies among the key European powers, with Britain to retain New York City and the rice and tobacco colonies of the South, while France and Spain would carve up the rest.

The stubbornness of Britain's George III prevented such a deal. Even after receiving news of the defeat at Yorktown, the delusional king still imagined he could retain all thirteen rebellious colonies. After a series of antiwar votes in Parliament and the resignation of Lord North, George III briefly considered abdicating his throne. Instead, he replaced North with a new minister, Lord Shelburne, who approached the peace talks with the view that independence for America was still up for debate.

Spain's interest in the war stemmed from a secret alliance with France in 1779. The Spanish king wanted to oust the British from Gibraltar, a tiny three-square-mile territory dominated by a massive rock and situated at the southern end of the Iberian Peninsula. From this strategic location, Britain controlled the passage between the Atlantic and the Mediterranean, disrupting Spanish trade. Spain launched a siege that lasted more than three years and tied up scores of British ships and thousands of troops, military assets that were thus not available for the war in America. Another important interest for Spain was control of navigation rights on the Mississippi River. Since 1763, Spain had held the lands west of the river, and it hoped to gain the eastern bank—and thus fully control all navigation of that major river—as a prize for its contribution to defeating Britain.

At various times, Russia, Austria, and Poland had agents in Paris offering to mediate peace talks in order to adjust the balance of power in Europe. None of these countries viewed American independence as a priority. Only Holland offered formal diplomatic recognition of the new country, an act of faith quickly followed up by a sizable loan of money to the new government. No other country was so supportive.

The Continental Congress entrusted three Americans of great distinction to handle the treaty negotiations. Benjamin Franklin, John Adams, and John Jay considered independence as the precondition for the talks to begin, so they were taken aback when the British negotiator showed up with credentials that pointedly addressed them as "the Commissioners of the Colonies." A month later, updated credentials referenced the three as representatives "of the Thirteen United States of America," a far more satisfactory acknowledgment of their new standing. In September 1782, peace talks began in earnest. Shelburne conceded on independence and set his goal as the maintenance of favored trading status with the new country. He saw, perhaps more clearly than did his king, that although

▶ Conclusion: Why the British Lost

The British began the war for America convinced that they could not lose. They had the best-trained army and navy in the world; they were familiar with the landscape from the Seven Years' War; they had the willing warrior-power of most of the native tribes of the backcountry; and they easily captured every port city of consequence in America. A majority of colonists were either neutral or loyal to the crown. Why, then, did the British lose?

One continuing problem the British faced was the uncertainty of supplies. The army depended on a steady stream of supply ships from home, and insecurity about food helps explain their reluctance to pursue the Continental army aggressively. A further obstacle was their continual misuse of loyalist energies. Any plan to repacify the colonies required the cooperation of the loyalists, but the British repeatedly left them to the mercy of vengeful rebels. French aid also helps explain the British defeat. Even before the formal alliance, French artillery and ammunition proved vital to the Continental army. After 1780,

The General P—s, or Peace.

Say what they will, I call this an honourable P—.

I call this a free and Independent P—.

Jack English we confess your exceeding good nature Tho' we have wrangled you out of America you freely make P—, with us.

"The P—s of Paris"
A British broadside of 1783 satirizes the diplomats who negotiated the Peace of Paris. The Indian declares, "I call this a free and Independent P—s" while the Frenchman (far right) gloats that "tho' we have wrangled you out of America you freely make P—s with us." Who does the Indian figure represent? What is the point of view of this cartoon? Library of Congress, LC-DIG-ppmsca-10740.

reason, that Vergennes planned on placing their nation's western boundary some distance east of the Mississippi River, to meet the demands of Spain. So the Americans sidestepped their instructions and negotiated with Britain in secret, producing an acceptable draft treaty in just a few weeks.

By January 1783, France, Britain, and Spain had produced their own treaties, involving deals with lands in India, Africa, and the Mediterranean, and in September of that year all the treaties were officially approved and signed. Franklin wrote to a friend in Massachusetts, "We are now Friends with England and with all Mankind. May we never see another War! for in my Opinion, there never was a good War, or a bad Peace."

Questions for Analysis

Summarize the Argument: What was at stake for France and Spain in the American Revolution? How were those goals reflected in their bargaining positions at the treaty meetings?

Recognize Viewpoints: Compare the views and hopes of King George at the conclusion of the war with those of his ministers, Lord North and Lord Shelburne.

Consider the Context: Many Indian tribes fought boldly with their British allies in the Revolution, so why did they not participate in the treaty making in Paris? Did Britain represent any of the tribes' interests in the diplomatic agreements?

Britain's political dominance over its colonies had now ended, economic dominance might nicely replace it.

The congress also instructed its three diplomats to consult France at every step of the negotiation with Britain, a condition insisted on by the French minister to the United States. But Jay and Adams had deep suspicions of the motives of the French foreign minister, the Count of Vergennes. They feared, with good

the French army fought alongside the Americans, and the French navy made the Yorktown victory possible. Finally, the British abdicated civil power in the colonies in 1775 and 1776, when royal officials fled to safety, and they never really regained it. The basic British goal—to turn back the clock to imperial rule—receded into impossibility as the war dragged on.

The Revolution profoundly disrupted the lives of Americans everywhere. It was a war for independence from Britain, but it was more. It was a war that required men and women to think about politics and the legitimacy of authority. The rhet-

oric employed to justify the revolution against Britain put the words *liberty, tyranny, slavery, independence,* and *equality* into common usage. These words carried far deeper meanings than a mere complaint over taxation without representation. The Revolution unleashed a dynamic of equality and liberty that was largely unintended and unwanted by many of the political leaders of 1776. But that dynamic emerged as a potent force in American life in the decades to come.

See the Selected Bibliography for this chapter in the Appendix.

7 Chapter Review

KEY TERMS

Second Continental Congress (p. 167)
Continental army (p. 168)
battle of Bunker Hill (p. 169)
Common Sense (p. 169)
Declaration of Independence (p. 171)
battle of Long Island (p. 175)
Ladies Association (p. 178)
loyalists (p. 178)
battle of Oriskany (p. 184)
battle of Saratoga (p. 184)
battle of Yorktown (p. 191)
Treaty (Peace) of Paris, 1783 (p. 191)

REVIEW QUESTIONS

1. Why were some Americans initially reluctant to pursue independence from Britain? (pp. 167–171)

2. Why did the British initially exercise restraint in their efforts to defeat the rebellious colonies? (pp. 171–175)

3. How did the patriots promote support for their cause in the colonies? (pp. 177–183)

4. Why did the Americans need assistance from the French to ensure victory? (pp. 183–187)

5. Why did the British southern strategy ultimately fail? (pp. 187–191)

MAKING CONNECTIONS

1. How did the colonists mobilize for war? Discuss specific challenges they faced, noting the unintended consequences of their solutions.

2. Discuss the importance of loyalism for British strategy in the Revolutionary War. In your answer, consider both military and political strategies.

3. How did Native Americans shape the Revolutionary War? What role did African Americans play? What benefits did these two groups hope to gain?

LINKING TO THE PAST

1. Most Indian tribes joined with the French and opposed the British in the Seven Years' War; yet in the American Revolution, most tribes sided with the British and opposed the Americans. What accounts for this apparent shift in alliances? (See chapter 6.)

2. Consider the leading roles of Massachusetts and Virginia in the coming of the American Revolution. With such very different origins and such very different economic, demographic, and religious histories, how could these two so readily join in partnership in the break from British rule? (See chapters 3, 4, and 5.)

8 Building a Republic
1775–1789

CONTENT LEARNING OBJECTIVES

After reading and studying this chapter, you should be able to:

• Articulate the concerns of the Second Continental Congress about sovereignty, representation, taxation, and citizenship. Recognize how these concerns shaped the Articles of Confederation.

• Explain the role state governments played under the Articles of Confederation. Identify how the differing state governments defined citizenship and handled slavery.

• Explain the major issues confronting the new United States to 1788, including how the Articles of Confederation limited the government's ability to solve these problems.

• Understand how the U.S. Constitution was debated and created, and understand the Constitution's position on slavery.

• Distinguish the Federalists and the Antifederalists, and explain their visions for the federal and state governments.

• Follow the process by which the U.S. Constitution was ratified, how its proponents secured ratification, and why some people opposed ratification.

A CHAIR FOR THE NEW NATION
The golden sun on George Washington's chair at the constitutional convention in Philadelphia worried Benjamin Franklin. Was it setting, thus symbolizing failure, or rising, signaling a new beginning for the nation?
Courtesy of Independence National Historic Park.

JAMES MADISON GRADUATED FROM PRINCETON COLLEGE IN New Jersey in 1771, undecided about his next move. Returning to his wealthy father's plantation in Virginia held little appeal. He much preferred the pleasures of books to farming. Fluent in Greek, Latin, French, and mathematics, he enjoyed reading and discussing the great thinkers, both ancient and modern. So he stayed in Princeton as long as he could.

In 1772, he returned home, still adrift. He studied law, but his unimpressive oratorical talents discouraged him. Instead, he swapped reading lists and ideas about political theory by letter with a Princeton classmate. While Madison struggled for direction, the powerful winds before the storm of the American Revolution swirled through the colonies. A trip north to deliver his brother to boarding school put Madison in Philadelphia just as news broke that Britain had shut down the port of Boston. Turbulent protests over the Coercive Acts turned the young man into a committed revolutionary.

Back in Virginia, Madison joined his father on the committee of public safety. He took up musket practice, but he proved a poor shot. Realizing

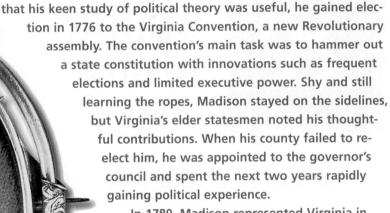

James Madison, by Charles Willson Peale

Philadelphia artist Charles Willson Peale painted this miniature portrait of Madison in 1783, paired with one of Madison's fiancée, Kitty Floyd, the sixteen-year-old daughter of a New York congressman. Meant to be worn like jewelry (note the pin on the right), miniatures were tokens of mutual affection. After Floyd broke off the engagement, Madison waited eleven more years before finding a wife. Library of Congress, 3g04097.

that his keen study of political theory was useful, he gained election in 1776 to the Virginia Convention, a new Revolutionary assembly. The convention's main task was to hammer out a state constitution with innovations such as frequent elections and limited executive power. Shy and still learning the ropes, Madison stayed on the sidelines, but Virginia's elder statesmen noted his thoughtful contributions. When his county failed to re-elect him, he was appointed to the governor's council and spent the next two years rapidly gaining political experience.

In 1780, Madison represented Virginia in the Continental Congress. Twenty-eight, single, and supported by family money, he was free of the burdens that made distant political service difficult for older married men. Three years in Philadelphia acquainted him with a network of leading revolutionaries and a thorny bundle of governance problems arising from the chaotic economy and the precarious war effort. In one crisis, Madison's negotiating skills proved crucial: He broke the deadlock over the ratification of the Articles of Confederation by arranging for the cession of Virginia's vast western lands, soon called the Northwest Territory. But more often, service in the congress frustrated Madison because the central government seemed to lack essential powers, chief among them the power to tax.

Madison returned to the Virginia assembly in 1784. But he did not retreat to a local point of view held by other state politicians. The economic hardships created by heavy state taxation—which in Massachusetts led to a full-fledged rebellion against state government—spurred Madison to pursue means to strengthen the new national government.

Madison helped organize a convention in May 1787, where delegates completely rewrote the structure of the national government, investing it with considerably greater powers. True to form, Madison spent the months before that Philadelphia meeting in feverish study of the great thinkers he had read in college, seeking the best way to constitute a government on republican principles. His lifelong passion for scholarly study, seasoned by a dozen years of energetic political experience, paid off handsomely. The United States Constitution was the result.

By the end of the 1780s, James Madison had had his finger in every kind of political pie on the local, state, confederation, and finally national levels. He even managed to observe the first U.S.-Indian treaty negotiations carried out in 1784. He had transformed himself from a directionless and solitary youth into one of the leading political thinkers of the Revolutionary period. His personal history over the 1780s was deeply entwined with the path of the emerging United States.

▶ The Articles of Confederation

Creating and approving a written plan of government for the new confederation took five years, as delegates and states sought agreement on fundamental principles. With monarchy gone, where would sovereignty lie? What would be the nature of representation? Who would hold the power of taxation? The resulting plan, called the **Articles of Confederation**, proved to be surprisingly difficult to implement, mainly because the thirteen states disagreed over boundaries in the land to the west of the states. Once the Articles were ratified and the active phase of the war had drawn to a close, the congress faded in importance compared with politics in the individual states.

Confederation and Taxation

Only after declaring independence did the Continental Congress turn its attention to creating a written document that would specify what powers the congress had and by what authority it existed. There was widespread agreement on key government powers: pursuing war and peace, conducting foreign relations, regulating trade, and running a postal service. Because the congress's attention was fixed on the war, it took another year of tinkering to reach agreement on the Articles of Confederation, defining the union as a loose confederation of states existing mainly to foster a common defense. Much like the existing Continental Congress, there was no national executive (that is, no president) and no judiciary. The congress, consisting of delegates selected annually by their state legislatures, was the sole governing agency.

Delegates faced term limits of three years, to ensure rotation in office. Anywhere from two to seven delegates could represent each state, with each delegation casting a single vote. Routine decisions required a simple majority of seven states, whereas momentous decisions, such as declaring war, required nine. To approve or amend the Articles required the unanimous consent both of the thirteen state delegations and of the thirteen state legislatures—giving any state a crippling veto power. Most crucially, the Articles gave the national government no power of direct taxation.

Yet taxation was a necessity since all governments require money. To finance the Revolutionary

CHRONOLOGY

1775	• Second Continental Congress opens.
1776	• Declaration of Independence adopted. • Virginia adopts state bill of rights.
1777	• Articles of Confederation sent to states.
1778	• State constitutions completed.
1780	• Pennsylvania institutes gradual emancipation.
1781	• Articles of Confederation ratified. • Executive departments created. • Massachusetts slaves sue for freedom.
1782	• Virginia relaxes state manumission law.
1783	• Newburgh Conspiracy exposed. • Treaty of Paris ends the war. • Massachusetts enfranchises taxpaying free blacks.
1784	• Gradual emancipation laws passed in Rhode Island and Connecticut. • Treaty of Fort Stanwix signed.
1785	• Treaty of Fort McIntosh signed. • Congress calls for large requisition.
1786	• Shays's Rebellion begins.
1787	• Shays's Rebellion crushed. • Northwest Ordinance passed. • Delaware provides manumission law. • Constitutional convention meets in Philadelphia. • *The Federalist Papers* begin to publish.
1788	• U.S. Constitution ratified.
1790	• Maryland provides manumission law.
1799	• Gradual emancipation law passed in New York.
1804	• Gradual emancipation law passed in New Jersey.

VISUAL ACTIVITY

American Flag, ca. 1781

In 1777, Congress authorized a flag with thirteen red and white stripes and thirteen white stars in a field of blue, "representing a new Constellation," a powerful metaphor that anchored the fragile union in the vast heavens. This 1781 variation—one of dozens of flag variations of the day—served as a military banner carried by soldiers in the final winning battle of the Revolutionary War. © Collection of the New-York Historical Society, USA/Bridgeman Images.

READING THE IMAGE: The eagle clutches arrows and a laurel branch in its talons. What do you think these images were meant to represent?

CONNECTIONS: Early American flags marked territory: positions stormed and taken in battle, forts under U.S. control, naval ships at sea, and soon U.S. embassies abroad. Today the flag stands for love of country. Are those two meanings very different, or not? What kind of evidence could you collect to determine when the stars and stripes became an ever-present national symbol of patriotism?

War, the confederation congress issued interest-bearing bonds purchased by French and Dutch bankers as well as middling to wealthy Americans, and revenue was necessary to repay these loans. Other routine government functions required money: Trade regulation required salaried customs officers; a postal system required postmen, horses and wagons, and well-maintained postal roads; the western lands required surveyors; and Indian diplomacy (or war) added further large costs. Article 8 of the confederation document declared that taxes were needed to support "the common defence or general welfare" of the country, yet the congress also had to be sensitive to the rhetoric of the Revolution, which denounced taxation by a nonrepresentative power.

The Articles of Confederation posed a delicate two-step solution. The congress would requisition (that is, request) money to be paid into the common treasury, and each state legislature would then levy taxes within its borders to pay the requisition. The Articles called for state contributions assessed in proportion to the improved property value of the state's land, so that populous states paid more than did sparsely populated states. Requiring that the actual tax bill be passed by the state legislatures preserved the Revolution's principle of taxation only by direct representation. However, no mechanism compelled states to pay.

The lack of authority in the confederation government was exactly what many state leaders wanted in the late 1770s. A league of states with rotating personnel, no executive branch, no power of direct taxation, and a requirement of unanimity for any major change seemed to be a good way to keep government in check. The catch was that ratification itself required unanimous agreement, and that proved difficult to secure.

The Problem of Western Lands

The most serious disagreement delaying ratification of the Articles concerned the absence of any plan for the lands to the west of the thirteen original states. This absence was deliberate: Virginia and Connecticut had old colonial charters that located their western boundaries at the Mississippi River, and six other states also claimed parts of that land. But five states without extensive land claims insisted on redrawing those colonial boundaries to create a national domain to be sold to settlers (Map 8.1). As one Rhode Island delegate put it, "the western world opens an amazing prospect as a national fund; it is equal to our debt."

The eight land-claiming states were ready to sign the Articles of Confederation in 1777 since it protected their interests. Three states without claims—Rhode Island, Pennsylvania, and New Jersey—eventually capitulated and signed, "not from a Conviction of the Equality and Justness of it," said a New Jersey delegate, "but merely from an absolute Necessity there was of complying to save the Continent." But Delaware and Maryland continued to hold out, insisting on a national domain policy. In 1779, the disputants finally compromised: Any land a state volunteered to relinquish would become the national domain. When James Madison and Thomas Jefferson ceded Virginia's huge land claim in 1781, the Articles of Confederation were at last unanimously approved.

The western lands issue demonstrated that powerful interests divided the thirteen new states. The apparent unity of purpose inspired by fighting the war against Britain papered over sizable cracks in the new confederation.

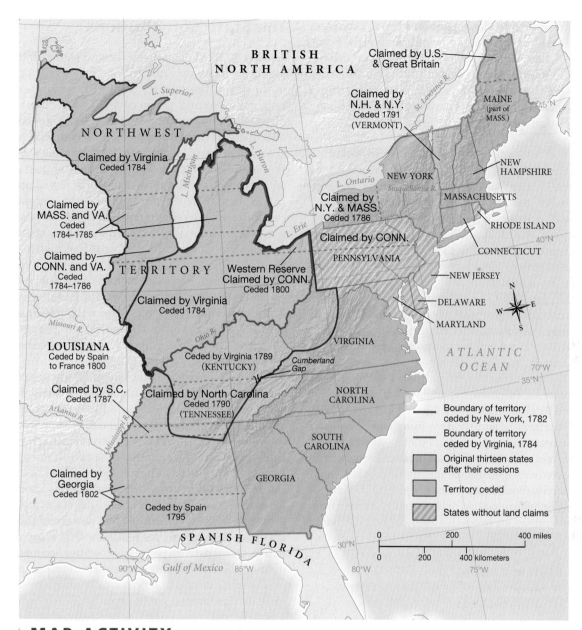

MAP ACTIVITY

Map 8.1 Cession of Western Lands, 1782–1802

The thirteen new states found it hard to ratify the Articles of Confederation without settling their conflicting land claims in the west, a vast area occupied by Indian tribes. The five states objecting to the Articles' silence over western lands policy were Maryland, Delaware, New Jersey, Rhode Island, and Pennsylvania.

READING THE MAP: Which state had the largest claims on western territory?

CONNECTIONS: In what context did the first dispute regarding western lands arise? How was it resolved? Does the map suggest a reason why Pennsylvania, a large state, joined the four much smaller states on this issue?

Running the New Government

No fanfare greeted the long-awaited inauguration of the new government in 1781. The congress continued to sputter along, its problems far from solved by the signing of the Articles. Lack of a quorum—defined as two men from seven states, or fourteen men—often hampered day-to-day activities. The search for the government's official seal stretched out over six years. State legislatures were slow to select delegates, and many politicians preferred to devote their energies to state governments, especially when the congress seemed deadlocked or, worse, irrelevant. Some had difficulty learning the art of formal debate. A Pennsylvanian reflected that "I find there is a great deal of difference between sporting a sentiment in a letter, or over a glass of wine upon politics, and discharging properly the duties of a senator."

It did not help that the congress had no permanent home. During the war, when the British army threatened Philadelphia, the congress relocated to small Pennsylvania towns such as Lancaster and York and then to Baltimore. After hostilities ceased, the congress moved from Trenton to Princeton to Annapolis to New York City. Many delegates were reluctant to travel far from home, especially if they had wives and children. Consequently, some of the most committed delegates were young bachelors, such as James Madison, and men in their fifties and sixties whose families were grown, such as Samuel Adams.

To address the difficulties of an inefficient congress, executive departments of war, finance, and foreign affairs were created in 1781 to handle purely administrative functions. When the department heads were ambitious—as was Robert Morris, a wealthy Philadelphia merchant who served as superintendent of finance—they could exercise considerable executive power. The Articles of Confederation had deliberately refrained from setting up an executive branch, but a modest one was being invented by necessity.

REVIEW   Why was the confederation government's authority so limited?

▶ The Sovereign States

In the first decade of independence, the states were sovereign and all-powerful. Only a few functions, such as declaring war and peace, had been transferred to the confederation government. Familiar and close to home, state governments claimed the allegiance of citizens and became the arena in which the Revolution's innovations would first be tried. Each state implemented a constitution and determined voter qualifications, and many states grappled with the issue of squaring slavery with Revolutionary ideals, with varying outcomes.

The State Constitutions

In May 1776, the congress recommended that all states draw up constitutions based on "the authority of the people." By 1778, ten states had done so, and three more (Connecticut, Massachusetts, and Rhode Island) had adopted and updated their original colonial charters. A shared feature of all the state constitutions was the conviction that government ultimately rests on the consent of the governed. Political writers in the late 1770s embraced the concept of **republicanism** as the underpinning of the new governments. Republicanism meant more than popular elections and representative institutions. For some, republicanism stood for leaders who were autonomous, virtuous citizens putting civic values above private interests. For others, it suggested direct democracy, with nothing standing in the way of the will of the people. For all, it meant government that promoted the people's welfare.

Widespread agreement about the virtues of republicanism went hand in hand with the idea that republics could succeed only in relatively small units, where people could make sure their interests were being served. Eleven states continued the colonial practice of a two-chamber assembly but greatly augmented the powers of the lower house. Pennsylvania and Georgia abolished the more elite upper house altogether, and most states severely limited the powers of the governor. Real power thus resided with the lower houses, responsive to popular majorities because of annual elections and guaranteed rotation in office (term limits). If a representative displeased his constituents, he could be out of office in a matter of months. James Madison learned about such political turnover when he lost reelection to the Virginia assembly in 1777. Ever shy, he attributed the loss to his reluctance to socialize at taverns and glad-hand his constituents in the traditional Virginia style. His series of increasingly significant political posts from 1778 to 1787 all came as a result of appointment, not popular election.

Six of the state constitutions included bills of rights—lists of individual liberties that government could not abridge. Virginia's bill was the first. Passed in June 1776, it asserted that "all men are by nature equally free and independent, and have certain inherent rights, of which, when they enter into a state of society, they cannot by any compact deprive or divest their posterity; namely, the enjoyment of life and liberty, with the means of acquiring and possessing property, and pursuing and obtaining happiness and safety." Along with these inherent rights went more specific rights to freedom of speech, freedom of the press, and trial by jury.

Who Are "the People"?

When the Continental Congress called for state constitutions based on "the authority of the people," and when the Virginia bill of rights granted "all men" certain rights, who was meant by "the people"? Who exactly were the citizens of this new country, and how far would the principle of democratic government extend? Different people answered these questions differently, but in the 1770s certain limits to political participation were widely agreed on.

One limit was defined by property. In nearly every state, voters and political candidates had to meet varying property qualifications. In Maryland, candidates for governor had to be worth the large sum of £5,000, while voters had to own fifty acres of land or £30. In the most democratic state, Pennsylvania, voters and candidates simply needed to be property tax payers, large or small. Only property owners were presumed to possess the necessary independence of mind to make wise political choices. Are not propertyless men, asked John Adams, "too little acquainted with public affairs to form a right judgment, and too dependent upon other men to have a will of their own?" Property qualifications probably disfranchised from one-quarter to one-half of adult white males in all the states. Not all of them took their non-voter status quietly. One Maryland man wondered what was so special about being worth £30, his state's threshold for voting: "Every poor man has a life, a personal liberty, and a right to his earnings; and is in danger of being injured by government in a variety of ways." Others noted that propertyless men were fighting and dying in the Revolutionary War; surely they had legitimate political concerns. A few radical voices challenged the notion that wealth was correlated with good citizenship; maybe the opposite was true. But ideas like this were outside the mainstream. The writers of the new constitutions, themselves men of property, viewed the right to own and preserve property as a central principle of the Revolution.

Another exclusion from voting—women—was so ingrained that few stopped to question it. Yet the logic of allowing propertied females to vote did occur to a handful of well-placed women. Abigail Adams wrote to her husband, John, in 1782, "Even in the freest countrys our property is subject to the controul and disposal of our partners, to whom the Laws have given a sovereign Authority. Deprived of a voice in Legislation, obliged to submit to those Laws which are imposed upon us, is it not sufficient to make us indifferent to the publick Welfare?"

Only three states specified that voters had to be male, so powerful was the unspoken assumption that only men could vote. Yet in New Jersey, small numbers of women began to go to the polls in the 1780s. The state's constitution of 1776 enfranchised all free inhabitants worth more than £50, language that in theory opened the door to free blacks and unmarried women who met the property requirement. (Married women owned no property, for by law their husbands held title to everything.) Little fanfare accompanied this radical shift, and some historians have inferred that the inclusion of unmarried women and blacks was an oversight. Yet other parts of the suffrage clause pertaining to residency and property were extensively debated when the clause was put in the state constitution, and no objections were raised at that time to its gender- and race-free language. Thus other historians have concluded that the law was intentionally inclusive. In 1790, a revised election law used the words *he* or *she* in reference to voters, making woman suffrage explicit. As one New Jersey legislator declared, "Our Constitution gives this right to maids or widows *black* or *white*." However, that legislator was complaining, not bragging, so his words do not mean that egalitarian suffrage was a fact accepted by all.

In 1790, only about 1,000 free black adults of both sexes lived in New Jersey, a state with a population of 184,000. The number of unmarried adult white women was probably also small and comprised mainly widows. In view of the property requirement, the voter blocs enfranchised under this law were minuscule. Still, this highly unusual situation lasted until 1807, when a new state law specifically disfranchised both blacks and women. Henceforth, independence of mind, held essential for voting, was redefined to be sex- and race-specific.

In the 1780s, voting everywhere was class-specific because of property restrictions. John Adams urged the framers of the Massachusetts constitution to stick with traditional property qualifications. If suffrage is brought up for debate, he warned, "there will be no end of it. New claims will arise; women will demand a vote; lads from twelve to twenty-one will think their rights not enough attended to; and every man who has not a farthing, will demand an equal voice with any other."

A Possible Voter in Essex County, New Jersey
Mrs. Annis Boudinot Stockton, widow of a New Jersey politician, frequently entertained members of the Continental Congress. General George Washington became a close friend and long-term correspondent starting in 1781. The politically connected Mrs. Stockton would have been eligible to vote in state elections under New Jersey's unique enfranchisement of property-holding women. She died in 1801, before suffrage was redefined to be the exclusive right of males.
Princeton University Art Museum/Art Resource, NY.

Equality and Slavery

Restrictions on political participation did not mean that propertyless people enjoyed no civil rights and liberties. The various state bills of rights applied to all individuals who were free; unfree people were another matter.

The author of the Virginia bill of rights was George Mason, a planter who owned 118 slaves. When he wrote that "all men are by nature equally free and independent," Mason did not have slaves in mind; he instead was asserting that white Americans were the equals of the British and entitled to equal liberties. Other Virginia legislators, worried about misinterpretations, added a qualifying phrase: that all men "when they enter into a state of society" have inherent rights. As one legislator wrote, with relief, "Slaves, not being constituent members of our society, could never pretend to any benefit from such a maxim."

One month later, the Declaration of Independence used essentially the same phrase about equality, this time without the modifying clause

about entering society. Two state constitutions, Pennsylvania and Massachusetts, also picked it up. In Massachusetts, one town suggested rewording the draft constitution to read "All men, whites and blacks, are born free and equal." The suggestion was not implemented.

Nevertheless, after 1776, the ideals of the Revolution about natural equality and liberty began to erode the institution of slavery. Often, enslaved blacks led the challenge. In 1777, several Massachusetts slaves petitioned for their "natural & unalienable right to that freedom which the great Parent of the Universe hath bestowed equally on all mankind." They modestly asked for freedom for their children at age twenty-one and were turned down. In 1779, similar petitions in Connecticut and New Hampshire met with no success. Seven Massachusetts free men, including the mariner brothers Paul and John Cuffe, refused to pay taxes on the grounds that they could not vote and so were not represented. The Cuffe brothers landed in jail in 1780 for tax evasion, but their petition to the Massachusetts legislature spurred the extension of suffrage to taxpaying free blacks in 1783.

Another way to bring the issue before lawmakers was to sue in court. In 1781, a woman called Elizabeth Freeman (Mum Bett) was the first to win freedom in a Massachusetts court, basing her case on the just-passed state constitution that declared "all men are born free and equal." (See "Experiencing the American Promise," page 204.) Another Massachusetts slave, Quok Walker, charged his master with assault and battery, arguing that he was a free man under that same constitutional phrase. Walker won and was set free, a decision confirmed in an appeal to the state's superior court in 1783. Several similar cases followed, and by 1789 slavery had been effectively abolished in Massachusetts by a series of judicial decisions.

State legislatures acted more slowly. Pennsylvania enacted a **gradual emancipation** law in 1780, providing that infants born to a slave mother on or after March 1, 1780, would be freed at age twenty-eight. Not until 1847 did Pennsylvania fully abolish slavery, but slaves did not wait for such slow implementation. Untold numbers in Pennsylvania simply ran away and asserted their freedom. One estimate holds that more than half of young slave men in Philadelphia joined the ranks of free blacks, and by 1790, free blacks outnumbered slaves in Pennsylvania two to one.

Rhode Island and Connecticut adopted gradual emancipation laws in 1784; New York waited until 1799 and New Jersey until 1804 to enact theirs. These last were the two northern states

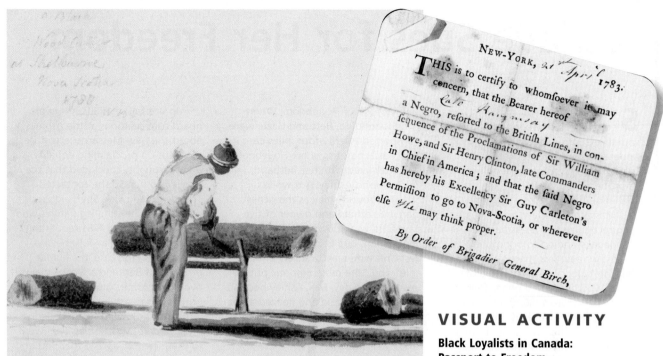

NEW-YORK, 21 April 1783.

THIS is to certify to whomsoever it may concern, that the Bearer hereof *Cato Rammsay* a Negro, resorted to the British Lines, in consequence of the Proclamations of Sir William Howe, and Sir Henry Clinton, late Commanders in Chief in America; and that the said Negro has hereby his Excellency Sir Guy Carleton's Permission to go to Nova-Scotia, or wherever else he may think proper.

By Order of Brigadier General Birch,

VISUAL ACTIVITY

Black Loyalists in Canada: Passport to Freedom

This black woodcutter in Nova Scotia was one of three thousand black loyalists who moved to Canada between 1783 and 1785. The inset shows a passport issued by the British high command to Cato Rammsay, permitting him to leave New York in 1783. Very few of the Nova Scotia refugees were able to acquire land, forcing most to become laborers for whites. Low wages created dissatisfaction, and in 1791–1792 nearly a third left for Sierra Leone in West Africa.
Sketch: Library and Archives Canada, Acc. No. 1970-188-1090, W. H. Coverdale Collection of Canadiana; Passport of Cato Rammsay to emigrate to Nova Scotia, 21 April 1783: Nova Scotia Archives, Gideon White family fonds, MG 1 vol. 948 no. 196 (microfilm no. 14960).

READING THE IMAGE: On what specific grounds did Sir Guy Carleton, British commander in New York City, authorize freedom of passage on this passport?

CONNECTIONS: Thousands of white and black loyalists fled the United States during and after the Revolution. What did they need to start life over in a new location?

---

with the largest number of slaves: New York in 1800 with 20,000 and New Jersey with more than 12,000, whereas in Pennsylvania the number was just 1,700. Gradual emancipation illustrates the tension between radical and conservative implications of republican ideology. Republican government protected people's liberties and property, yet slaves were both people and property. Gradual emancipation balanced the civil rights of blacks and the property rights of their owners by promising delayed freedom.

South of Pennsylvania, in Delaware, Maryland, and Virginia, where slavery was critical to the economy, emancipation bills were rejected. All three states, however, eased legal restrictions and allowed individual

Legal Changes to Slavery, 1777–1804

BRITISH NORTH AMERICA
MAINE (part of MASS.)
L. Ontario
VT. 1777
N.H. 1783
N.Y. 1799
Hudson R.
MASS. 1783
CONN. 1784
R.I. 1784
PA. 1780
N.J. 1804
MD. 1790
DEL. 1787
VA. 1782
ATLANTIC OCEAN
N.C.

Abolished slavery
Gradual emancipation
Individual cases of emancipation

acts of emancipation for adult slaves below the age of forty-five under new manumission laws passed in 1782 (Virginia), 1787 (Delaware), and 1790 (Maryland). By 1790, close to 10,000 newly freed Virginia slaves had formed local free black communities complete with schools and churches.

In the deep South—the Carolinas and Georgia—freedom for slaves was unthinkable among most whites. Yet several thousand slaves had defected to the British during the war, and between 3,000 and 4,000 left with the British at the war's conclusion. Adding northern blacks evacuated from New York City in 1783, the probable total of emancipated blacks who left the United States was between 8,000 and 10,000. Some went to Canada, some to England, and

A Slave Sues for Her Freedom

Stirring language about liberty, equality, and freedom that inspired revolutionaries in the 1770s appeared in many state constitutions in the 1780s. Yet unfree people, held as property, had little recourse to challenge their status.

Massachusetts law, however, had long recognized slaves as persons with legal standing to bring lawsuits against whites. Less than 2 percent of the state's population consisted of slaves, who numbered under four thousand. Before 1780, some thirty Massachusetts slaves had sued for freedom, but their cases had turned on individual circumstances, such as an owner's unfulfilled promise to emancipate. In 1780, a new state constitution boldly declared that "all men are born free and equal," opening the door to lawsuits based on a broad right to freedom. The first such case was brought by Bett, a slave living in the Massachusetts town of Sheffield.

Born of African parents in the early 1740s, Bett and her sister Lizzie grew up as slaves in Claverack, New York, in the wealthy Dutch American family of Pieter Hogeboom. When Hogeboom died, Bett and Lizzie were transported twenty-four miles east into Massachusetts, where Hogeboom's daughter lived with her husband, Colonel John Ashley. A town tax list of 1771 shows Ashley as the richest man in Sheffield and owner of five slaves. He was known as a kind and gentle man, but as one account suggests, his wife was "a shrew untamable" and "the most despotic of mistresses." One day, Mrs. Ashley became enraged with Lizzie and heaved a hot kitchen shovel at her. Bett interceded and sustained a burn on her arm that left a lifelong scar.

On another occasion, in 1773, Bett was, in her own words, "keepin' still and mindin' things" while she served refreshments to a dozen men meeting with Colonel Ashley to draft anti-British resolutions. The first read, "Resolved, That mankind in a state of nature are equal, free, and independent of each other, and have a right to the undisturbed enjoyment of their lives, their liberty and property." Bett well noted the import of their discussion.

In the fall of 1780, Bett overheard conversations at the Ashleys' about the new Massachusetts state constitution proclaiming equality and reasonably concluded that they applied to her. So she contacted Theodore Sedgwick, Sheffield's representative in the state legislature, who filed a writ in April 1781 requesting the recovery of unlawfully held property—in this case, the human property of Bett and a second plaintiff owned by Ashley, a man identified only as Brom. Ashley contested the writ, and the case, officially called *Brom and Bett v. J. Ashley, Esq.*, went to trial. The jury agreed that Bett and Brom were entitled to freedom and ordered Ashley to pay each plaintiff damages as well as court costs. The brief court records do not reveal the legal arguments presented, but Sedgwick descendants later boasted that Theodore Sedgwick invoked the Massachusetts constitution to argue that slavery could not exist in the state.

Bett chose a new name to go with her new status: Elizabeth Freeman. She left Colonel Ashley's and became a paid housekeeper in

some to Sierra Leone on the west coast of Africa. Many hundreds took refuge with the Seminole and Creek Indians, becoming permanent members of their communities in Spanish Florida and western Georgia.

Although all these instances of emancipation were gradual, small, and certainly incomplete, their symbolic importance was enormous. Every state from Pennsylvania north acknowledged that slavery was fundamentally inconsistent with Revolutionary ideology; "all men are created equal" was beginning to acquire real force as a basic principle.

> **REVIEW** What were the limits of citizenship, rights, and freedom within the various states?

▶ The Confederation's Problems

In 1783, the confederation government faced three interrelated concerns: paying down the large war debt, making formal peace with the Indians, and dealing with western settlement. Lacking the power to enforce its tax requisitions, the congress faced added debt pressures when army officers suddenly demanded secure pensions. Revenue from sales of western lands seemed to be a promising solution, but Indian inhabitants of those lands had different ideas.

From 1784 to 1786, the congress struggled mightily with these three issues. Some leaders were gripped by a sense of crisis, fearing that

the Sedgwick family, raising the children when their mother became incapacitated by illness. "Her spirit spurned slavery," a Sedgwick daughter wrote, offering this quotation from Bett as evidence: "Anytime, anytime while I was a slave, if one minute's freedom had been offered to me, and I had been told I must die at the end of that minute, I would have taken it—just to stand one minute on God's earth a free woman—I would."

The Sedgwicks were especially grateful to Freeman for her commanding presence of mind during Shays's Rebellion in 1786. Because Sedgwick represented the legal elite of the county, he was a target of hostile crowd action. Freeman was home alone when insurgents, searching for Sedgwick and for valuables to plunder, demanded entry. Unable to block them, Freeman let the dissidents in but followed them around with a large shovel, threatening to flatten anyone who damaged property. When Freeman died in 1829, she was buried in the Sedgwick family plot, with a gravestone inscription supplied by the Sedgwicks that ended "Good mother, farewell."

Freeman's lawsuit of 1781 inspired others to sue, and in a case in 1783 the judge of the Massachusetts

Elizabeth Freeman in 1811
In freedom, "Mum Bett" found secure employment with the family of her lawyer, Theodore Sedgwick. A Sedgwick son later wrote, "If there could be a practical refutation of the imagined superiority of our race to hers, the life and character of this woman would afford that refutation. She had, when occasion required it, an air of command which conferred a degree of dignity." © Massachusetts Historical Society, Boston, MA, USA/Bridgeman Images.

Supreme Court declared that "slavery is in my judgment as effectively abolished as it can be by the granting of rights and privileges" in the state constitution. It took several more legal challenges and additional time for that news to trickle out, but the erosion of slavery in Massachusetts gradually picked up speed as blacks demanded manumission or wages for work, or simply walked away from their masters. In 1790, the federal census listed 5,369 "other free persons" (that is, nonwhites) in the state and not a single slave.

Questions for Analysis

Consider the Context: What events encouraged the slave Bett to take her master to court to sue for freedom?

Analyzing the Evidence: How would you characterize Mum Bett's status in the Sedgwick household? Was she merely a hired servant, or something more?

Asking Historical Questions: In what way was Elizabeth Freeman's desire for freedom similar to and different from those of white revolutionaries who sought freedom from being "enslaved" by Britain?

the Articles of Confederation were too weak. Others defended the Articles as the best guarantee of liberty because real governance occurred at the state level, closer to the people. A major outbreak of civil disorder in western Massachusetts quickly crystallized the debate and propelled the critics of the Articles into decisive and far-reaching action.

The War Debt and the Newburgh Conspiracy

For nearly two years, the Continental army camped at Newburgh, north of the British-occupied city of New York, awaiting news of a peace treaty. The soldiers were bored, restless, and upset about military payrolls that were far in arrears. An

earlier promise to officers of generous pensions (half pay for life), made in 1780 in a desperate effort to retain them, seemed unlikely to be honored. In December 1782, officers petitioned the congress for immediate back pay for their men so that when peace arrived, no one would go home penniless. The petition darkly hinted that failure to pay the men "may have fatal effects."

Instead of rejecting the petition outright for lack of money, several members of the congress saw an opportunity to pressure the states to approve taxation powers. One of these was Robert Morris, a Philadelphia merchant with a gift for financial dealings. As the congress's superintendent of finance, Morris kept the books and wheedled loans from European bankers using his own substantial fortune as collateral. To forestall

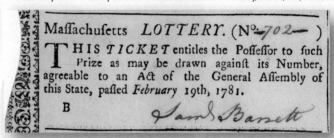

Lucky Man in Massachusetts?
This New Englander posed for a formal portrait around 1790, proudly holding a lottery ticket. Has this man just won the lottery, or is he merely hopeful? State taxes and confederation requisitions often proved hard to collect in the 1780s. Lotteries became a common way to raise supplementary state financing for schools and public works in the earliest years of the Republic. Portrait: American, *Man Holding a (Massachusetts) Lottery Ticket*, ca. 1790. Oil on canvas, 29 5/8 x 24 5/8 in. (75.25 x 62.55 cm). Milwaukee Art Museum, Layton Art Collection, Purchase L1964.1. Photographer credit: Larry Sanders. Lottery ticket: © Massachusetts Historical Society, Boston, MA, USA/Bridgeman Images.

total insolvency, Morris led efforts in 1781 and again in 1786 to amend the Articles to allow collection of a 5 percent impost (an import tax). Each time it failed by one vote, illustrating the difficulties of achieving unanimity. Now the officers' petition offered new prospects to make the case for taxation.

The result was a plot called the **Newburgh Conspiracy**. Morris and several other congressmen encouraged the officers to march the army on the congress to demand its pay. No actual coup was envisioned; both sides shared the goal of wanting to augment the congress's power of taxation. Yet the risks were great, for not everyone would understand that this was a ruse. What if the soldiers, incited by their grievances, could not be held in check?

General George Washington, sympathetic to the plight of unpaid soldiers and officers, had approved the initial petition. But the plotters, knowing of his reputation for integrity, did not inform him of their collusion with congressional leaders. In March 1783, when the general learned of these developments, he delivered an emotional speech to a meeting of five hundred officers, reminding them in stirring language of honor, heroism, and sacrifice. He urged them to put their faith in the congress, and he denounced the plotters as "subversive of all order and discipline." His audience was left speechless and tearful, and the plot was immediately defused.

Morris continued to work to find money to pay the soldiers.

But in the end, a trickle of money from a few states was too little and too late, coming after the army began to disband. For its part, the congress voted to endorse a plan to commute, or transform, the lifetime pension promised the officers into a lump-sum payment of full pay for five years. But no lump sum of money was available. Instead, the officers were issued "commutation certificates," promising future payment with interest, which quickly depreciated in value.

In 1783, the soldiers' pay and officers' pensions added some $5 million to the rising public debt, forcing the congress to press for larger requisitions from the states. The confederation, however, had one new source of enormous untapped wealth: the extensive western territories, attractive to the fast-growing white population but currently inhabited by Indians.

The Treaty of Fort Stanwix

Since the Indians had not participated in the Treaty of Paris of 1783, the confederation government hoped to formalize treaties ending ongoing hostilities between Indians and settlers and securing land cessions. The most pressing problem was the land inhabited by the Iroquois Confederacy, a league of six tribes, now claimed by the states of New York and Massachusetts based on their colonial charters (see Map 8.1).

At issue was the revenue stream that land sales would generate: Which government

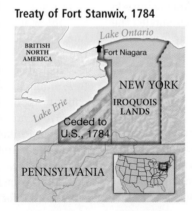

Treaty of Fort Stanwix, 1784

would get it? The congress summoned the Iroquois to a meeting in October 1784 at Fort Stanwix, on the upper Mohawk River. The Articles of Confederation gave the congress (as opposed to individual states) the right to manage diplomacy, war, and "all affairs with the Indians, not members of any of the States." But New York's governor seized on that ambiguous language, claiming that the Iroquois were in fact "members" of his state, and called his own meeting at Fort Stanwix in September. Suspecting that New York might be superseded by the congress, the most important chiefs declined to come and instead sent deputies without authority to negotiate. The Mohawk leader Joseph Brant shrewdly identified the problem of divided authority that afflicted the confederation government: "Here lies some Difficulty in our Minds, that there should be two separate bodies to manage these Affairs." No deal was struck with New York.

Three weeks later, U.S. commissioners opened proceedings at Fort Stanwix with the Seneca chief Cornplanter and Captain Aaron Hill, a Mohawk leader, accompanied by six hundred Iroquois. (James Madison, by chance traveling up the Mohawk River on a trip with a friend, witnessed the opening ceremonies.)

The Americans (accompanied by their own security detail of New Jersey militiamen) demanded a return of prisoners of war; recognition of the confederation's (and not states') authority to negotiate; and an all-important cession of a strip of land from Fort Niagara due south, which established U.S.-held territory adjacent to the border with Canada. This crucial change enclosed the Iroquois land within the United States and made it impossible for the Indians to claim to be between the United States and Canada. When the tribal leaders balked, one of the commissioners sternly replied, "You are mistaken in supposing that, having been excluded from the treaty between the United States and the King of England, you are become a free and independent nation and may make what terms you please. It is not so. You are a subdued people."

In the end, the treaty was signed, gifts were given, and six high-level Indian hostages were kept at the fort awaiting the release of the American prisoners taken during the Revolutionary War, mostly women and children. In addition, a significant side deal sealed the release of much of the Seneca tribe's claim to the Ohio Valley to the United States. This move was a major surprise to the Delaware, Mingo, and

VISUAL ACTIVITY

Cornplanter

Cornplanter, whose Indian name was Kaintwakon ("what one plants"), headed the Seneca delegation at Fort Stanwix in 1784. Raised fully Indian, he was the son of a highborn Seneca woman of the Wolf Clan and a traveling Dutch fur trader he barely knew. During the Revolution, when his father faced capture by Indians, Cornplanter recognized him by his name and released him.

© Collection of the New-York Historical Society, USA/Bridgeman Images.

READING THE IMAGE: Does this portrait, painted in 1796 by an Italian artist in New York City, convey any clue of Cornplanter's mixed-race heritage?

CONNECTIONS: When the U.S. commissioners met with Cornplanter at the Treaty of Fort Stanwix, do you think his mixed-race background might have had any bearing on the outcome of the negotiations? Why or why not?

Shawnee Indians who lived there. In the months to come, tribes not at the meeting tried to disavow the **Treaty of Fort Stanwix** as a document signed under coercion by virtual hostages. But the confederation government ignored those complaints and made plans to survey and develop the disputed lands.

New York's governor astutely figured that the congress's power to implement the treaty terms was limited. The confederation's financial coffers were nearly empty, and its leadership was stretched. So New York quietly began surveying and then selling the very land it had failed to secure by treaty with the Iroquois. As that fact became generally known, it pointed up the weakness of the confederation government. One Connecticut leader wondered, "What is to defend us from the ambition and rapacity of New York, when she has spread over that vast territory, which she claims and holds?"

Land Ordinances and the Northwest Territory

The congress ignored western New York and turned instead to the Ohio Valley to make good on the promise of western expansion. Congressman Thomas Jefferson, charged with drafting a policy, proposed dividing the territory north of the Ohio River and east of the Mississippi—the Northwest Territory—into nine new states with evenly spaced east-west boundaries and townships ten miles square. He even advocated giving, not selling, the land to settlers, because future property taxes on the improved land would be payment enough. Jefferson's aim was to encourage rapid and democratic settlement and to discourage land speculation. Jefferson projected representative governments in the new states; they would not become colonies of the older states. Finally, Jefferson's draft prohibited slavery in the nine new states.

VISUAL ACTIVITY

Jefferson's Map of the Northwest Territory

Thomas Jefferson proposed nine states in his initial plan for the Northwest Territory in 1784. Straight lines and right angles held a strong appeal for him. But such regularity ignored inconvenient geographic features such as rivers and even more inconvenient political facts such as Indian territorial claims. William L. Clements Library, University of Michigan.

READING THE IMAGE: What does this map indicate about Jefferson's vision of the Northwest Territory?

CONNECTIONS: What were the problems with Jefferson's design for the division of the territory? Why did the congress alter it in the land ordinances of 1784, 1785, and 1787?

The congress adopted parts of Jefferson's plan in the Ordinance of 1784: the rectangular grid, the nine states, and the guarantee of self-government and eventual statehood. What the congress found too radical was the proposal to give away the land; it badly needed immediate revenue. The slavery prohibition also failed, by a vote of seven to six states.

A year later, the congress revised the legislation with procedures for mapping and selling the land. The Ordinance of 1785 called for three to five states, divided into townships six miles square, further divided into thirty-six sections of 640 acres, to be subdivided further into family farms (Map 8.2). Reduced to easily mappable squares, the land would be sold at public auction for a minimum of one dollar an acre, with highly desirable land bid up for more. Two further restrictions applied: The minimum purchase was 640 acres, and payment had to be in hard money or in certificates of debt from Revolutionary days. This effectively meant that the land's first

owners would be prosperous speculators. The grid of invariant squares further enhanced speculation, allowing buyers and sellers to operate without ever setting foot on the acreage. The commodification of land had been taken to a new level.

Speculators who held the land for resale avoided direct contact with the most serious obstacle to settlement: the dozens of Indian tribes that claimed the land as their own. The treaty signed at Fort Stanwix in 1784 was followed in 1785 by the Treaty of Fort McIntosh, which similarly coerced partial cessions of land from the Delaware, Wyandot, Chippewa, and Ottawa tribes. Finally, in 1786, a united Indian meeting near Detroit issued an ultimatum: No cession would be valid without the unanimous consent of the tribes. For two more decades, violent Indian wars in Ohio and Indiana would continue to impede white settlement (as discussed in "Ohio Indians in the Northwest" in chapter 9).

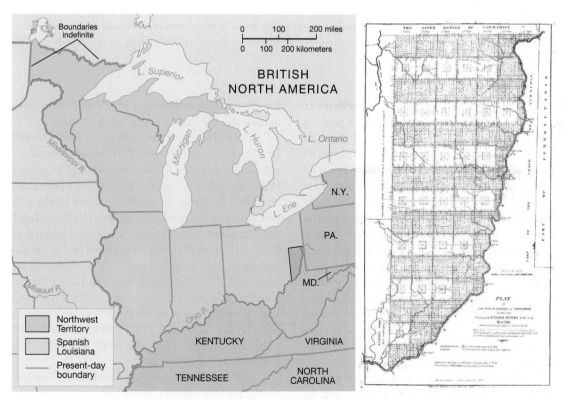

Map 8.2   The Northwest Territory and Ordinance of 1785

Surveyors ventured into the eastern edge of the Northwest Territory in the 1780s and produced this first map (right) showing neat six-mile-square townships, each subdivided into one-mile squares containing sixteen 40-acre farms. Jefferson got his straight lines and right angles after all; compare this map to Jefferson's map of the Northwest Territory. Plat Map © TNGenNet Inc. 2002.

A Newly Cleared Frontier Farm
It took lots of muscle and sweat to turn the densely wooded land of the Northwest Territory into farms. Men with axes and oxen chopped down trees and dragged the logs into piles, to be transformed into log cabins and split-rail fences. Note the smoke: When burned, wood provided the leading energy source for all heat and cooking. The Granger Collection, New York.

A third land act, called the **Northwest Ordinance** of 1787, set forth a three-stage process by which settled territories would advance to statehood. First, the congress would appoint officials for a sparsely populated territory who would adopt a legal code and appoint local magistrates to administer justice. When the male population of voting age and landowning status (fifty acres) reached 5,000, the territory could elect its own legislature and send a nonvoting delegate to the congress. When the population of voting citizens reached 60,000, the territory could write a state constitution and apply for full admission to the Union. At all three territorial stages, the inhabitants were subject to taxation to support the Union, in the same manner as were the original states.

The Northwest Ordinance of 1787 was perhaps the most important legislation passed by the confederation government. It ensured that the new United States, so recently released from colonial dependency, would not itself become a colonial power—at least not with respect to white citizens. The mechanism it established allowed

for the orderly expansion of the United States across the continent in the next century.

Nonwhites were not forgotten or neglected in the 1787 ordinance. The brief document acknowledged the Indian presence and promised that "the utmost good faith shall always be observed towards the Indians; their lands and property shall never be taken from them without their consent; and, in their property, rights, and liberty, they shall never be invaded or disturbed, unless in just and lawful wars authorized by Congress." The 1787 ordinance further pledged that "laws founded in justice and humanity, shall from time to time be made for preventing wrongs being done to them." Such promises indicated noble intentions, but they were not generally honored in the decades to come.

Jefferson's original and remarkable suggestion to prohibit slavery in the Northwest Territory resurfaced in the 1787 ordinance, passing this time with no recorded debate. (See "Analyzing Historical Evidence," page 212.) The prohibition was paired with a fugitive slave provision promising that escaped slaves caught north of the

Ohio River would be returned south. The ordinance thus acknowledged and supported slavery even as it barred it from one region. Still, in the very long run, the stated prohibition of slavery in the Northwest Territory perpetuated the dynamic of gradual emancipation in the North. North-South sectionalism based on slavery was slowly taking shape.

The Requisition of 1785 and Shays's Rebellion, 1786–1787

Without an impost amendment and with public land sales projected but not yet realized, the confederation again requisitioned the states to contribute revenue. In 1785 the amount requested was $3 million, four times larger than the previous year's levy. Of this sum, 30 percent was needed for the government's operating costs, and another 30 percent was earmarked to pay debts owed to foreign lenders, who insisted on payment in gold or silver. The remaining 40 percent was to go to Americans who owned government bonds, the IOUs of the Revolutionary years. A significant slice of that 40 percent represented the interest (but not the principal) owed to army officers for their recently issued "commutation certificates." This was a tax that, if collected, was going to hurt.

At this time, states were struggling under state tax levies. The legislatures of several states without major ports (and the import duties that ports generated) were already pressing higher tax bills onto their farmer citizens in order to retire state debts from the Revolution. New Jersey and Connecticut fit this profile, and both state legislatures voted to ignore the confederation's requisition. In New Hampshire, town meetings voted to refuse to pay, because they could not. In 1786, two hundred armed insurgents surrounded the New Hampshire capitol to protest the taxes but were driven off by an armed militia. The shocked assemblymen backed off from an earlier order to haul delinquent taxpayers into courts. Rhode Island, North Carolina, and Georgia responded to their constituents' protests by issuing abundant amounts of paper money and allowing taxes to be paid in greatly depreciated currency.

Nowhere were the tensions so extreme as in Massachusetts. For four years in a row, a fiscally conservative legislature, dominated by the coastal commercial centers, had passed tough tax laws to pay state creditors who required payment in hard money, not cheap paper. Then in March 1786, the legislature in Boston loaded the federal requisition onto the bill. In June, farmers in southeastern Massachusetts marched on a courthouse in an effort to close it down, and petitions of complaint about oppressive taxation poured in from the western two-thirds of the state. In July 1786, when the legislature adjourned, having yet again ignored their complaints, dissidents held a series of conventions and called for revisions to the state constitution to promote democracy, eliminate the elite upper house, and move the capital farther west in the state.

Still unheard in Boston, the dissidents targeted the county courts, the local symbol of state authority. In the fall of 1786, several thousand armed men shut down courthouses in six counties; sympathetic local militias did not intervene. The insurgents were not predominantly poor or debt-ridden farmers; they included veteran soldiers and officers in the Continental army as well as town leaders. One was a farmer and onetime army captain, Daniel Shays.

The governor of Massachusetts, James Bowdoin, once a protester against British taxes, now characterized the western dissidents as illegal rebels. He vilified Shays as the chief leader, and a Boston newspaper claimed that Shays planned to burn Boston to the ground and overthrow the government. Another former radical, Samuel Adams, took the extreme position that "the man who dares rebel against the laws of a republic ought to suffer death." Those aging revolutionaries were not prepared to believe that representatives in a state legislature could seem to be as oppressive as monarchs. The dissidents challenged the assumption that popularly elected governments would always be fair and just.

Members of the Continental Congress had much to worry about. In nearly every state, the requisition of 1785 spawned some combination of crowd protests, demands for inflationary paper money, and anger at state authorities and alleged money speculators. The Massachusetts insurgency was the worst episode, and it seemed to be spinning out of control. In October, the congress attempted to triple the size of the federal army, but fewer than 100 men enlisted. So Governor Bowdoin raised a private army, gaining the services of some 3,000 men with pay provided by wealthy and fearful Boston merchants.

The Northwest Ordinance and Slavery

An investigation into why the Continental Congress agreed to prohibit slavery in the Northwest Territory turns up remarkably meager surviving evidence.

An early draft of the ordinance prepared by a committee came before Congress in April 1787 but was soon sidelined for lack of a quorum. A second committee appointed on July 9 revised the plan extensively. Its members included two men from Virginia and one each from South Carolina, New York, and Massachusetts. Congress considered this draft on July 11 and again on July 12, with slight revisions. No draft up to this point made any mention of slavery.

On July 13, at the third and final reading, article 6 made its first appearance. The records are silent about the debate, if any, that occurred in response to the article's inclusion. The final document was passed unanimously by the eight states present: Massachusetts, New York, New Jersey, Delaware, Virginia, North Carolina, South Carolina, and Georgia.

DOCUMENT 1
Northwest Ordinance of 1787

The idea to prohibit slavery was borrowed from Thomas Jefferson's failed proposal in the 1784 ordinance. The fugitive slave provision, entirely new to the confederation government, was implanted in the U.S. Constitution ratified in 1788.

Art. 6. There shall be neither slavery nor involuntary servitude in the said territory, otherwise than in the punishment of crimes whereof the party shall have been duly convicted: Provided, always, That any person escaping into the same, from whom labor or service is lawfully claimed in any one of the original States, such fugitive may be lawfully reclaimed and conveyed to the person claiming his or her labor or service as aforesaid.

Source: *Journals of the Continental Congress*, ed. Roscoe R. Hill (Washington, D.C.: Government Printing Office, 1936), 32:339, 343, http://memory.loc.gov /ammem/amlaw/lwjc.html.

DOCUMENT 2
Two Letters by Delegates in Congress

Nathan Dane of Massachusetts served on both drafting committees. Rufus King was a Massachusetts politician. Virginian William Grayson chaired the congress in July 1787. James Monroe of Virginia had headed a 1786 committee to draft the ordinance. Newspapers printed the full ordinance but attracted no discussion of article 6. No further commentary has come to light in private correspondence.

Nathan Dane to Rufus King, New York, July 16, 1787
Dear Sir
. . . We have been much engaged in business for ten or twelve days past for a part of which we have had 8 States. . . . We have been employed about several objects—; the principal ones of which have been the Government inclosed [the Northwest Ordinance] and the Ohio purchase. . . . We tried one day to patch up M[onroe]'s Systems of W.[estern] Govern[men]t. Started new Ideas and committed the whole to Carrington, Dane, R. H. Lee, Smith, & Kean—we met several times and at last agreed on some principles at least Lee, Smith & myself. . . . When I drew the ordinance which passed (in a few words excepted) as I originally formed it, I had no idea the States would agree to the sixth Art. prohibiting Slavery—; as only Massa[chusetts] of the Eastern States was present—; and therefore omitted it in the draft—; but finding the House favourably disposed on this subject, after we had completed the other parts I moved the art[icle]—; which was agreed to without opposition. . . .

William Grayson to James Monroe, New York, August 8, 1787
Dear Sir,
. . . Congress has passed the Ordnance for the government of the Western country, in a manner some thing different from the one which you drew, though I expect the departure is not so essential but that it will meet your approbation. . . . The clause respecting slavery was agreed to by the Southern members for the purpose of preventing Tobacco & Indigo from being made on the N.W. side of the Ohio, as well as for sevl. other political reasons.

Source: *Letters of Delegates to Congress, 1774–1789*, ed. Paul H. Smith (Washington, DC: Library of Congress, 1976), 24:358–59, 394, http://memory.loc.gov/ammem /amlaw/lwdglink.html.

In January 1787, the insurgents learned of the private army marching west from Boston, and 1,500 of them moved swiftly to capture a federal armory in Springfield to obtain weapons. But a militia band loyal to the state government beat them to the weapons facility and met their attack with gunfire; 4 rebels were killed and another 20 wounded. The final and bloodless encounter came at Petersham, where Bowdoin's army surprised the rebels and took several

DOCUMENT 3
Early Residents Petition the U.S. Congress

Territorial population in the early 1790s consisted largely of longtime French settlers in the Illinois country, some of whom owned slaves, and new migrants from Virginia and Kentucky. Several groups sent petitions to the federal government to narrow article 6, arguing that slaves resident before 1787 (and their offspring) should continue as slaves, to preserve slave owners' property rights. This petition of 1796 took aim at the whole article, but the federal government offered no reply.

Your petitioners humbly hope that they will not be thought presumptuous in venturing to disapprove of the article concerning slavery in toto, as contrary not only to the interest, but almost to the existence of the country they inhabit, where laborers can not be procured to assist in cultivating the grounds under one dollar per day. . . . Your petitioners do not wish to increase the number of slaves already in the dominions of the United States; all they hope for or desire is, that they may be permitted to introduce from any of the United States such persons, and such only, as by the laws of such States are slaves therein.

Source: Jacob Piatt Dunn, *Slavery Petitions and Papers* (Indianapolis: Bowen-Merrill, 1894), 6, http://catalog.hathitrust.org /Record /000317559.

DOCUMENT 4
Indenture Record of Jacob, 1805

Indiana's indenture law of 1805 allowed two parties to voluntarily

enter a service contract. One of forty-seven such contracts in Knox County, Indiana, involved Eli Hawkins from South Carolina and his onetime slave Jacob, age sixteen. Before a court clerk they . . .

. . . determined and agreed among themselves . . . that said Jacob shall and will serve the said Eli Hawkins and his assigns for term of Ninety years . . . the said Eli Hawkins and his assigns providing the said Jacob with necessary and sufficient provisions and clothing, washing and lodging, according to his degree and state . . . after the expiration of said term the said Jacob shall be free to all intents and purposes.

Source: Daniel Owen, "Circumvention of Article VI of the Ordinance of 1787," *Indiana Magazine of History* 36 (1940): 115, http://scholarworks.iu.edu/journals /index.php/imh/article/view/7219/8151.

DOCUMENT 5
Territorial and Federal Censuses

Indiana and Illinois together formed the Indiana Territory in 1800. They became separate states in 1816 and 1818. Study the census data below. Does the enumeration of slaves seem surprising? Where would the indentured Jacob be counted?

	Total Population	Free Blacks	Slaves
1800	5,000	163	135
1810	24,500	393	237
1820 Indiana	147,000	1,230	190
Illinois	55,000	457	917

Data source for 1800 and 1810: "Slavery in Indiana Territory," www.in.gov/history/2492.htm. Data source for 1820: Historical Census Browser, http://mapserver.lib.virginia.edu/.

Questions for Analysis

Ask Historical Questions: Did article 6 actually outlaw slavery in the Northwest Territory? Did it mean to? Was there a plan to enforce it? Did it succeed? How does the census data for Indiana and Illinois shape your answers?

Recognize Viewpoints: Who do you think likely wrote article 6? How do you explain its easy passage by a committee largely representing slave states and by a congress dominated by major slave states? Who do you think might have favored or opposed the article? Do you think young Jacob in Document 4 would have considered it a success?

Consider the Context: How do you explain the near-total absence of commentary on article 6 in the 1780s? And the lack of response by the federal government to the petitions? What does the federal government's lack of response to the petitions that opposed the article suggest about the larger political context of the era? Was the federal government at all ready to tackle the problem of slavery?

hundred of them prisoner. In the end, 2 men were executed for rebellion; 16 more sentenced to hang were reprieved at the last moment on the gallows. Some 4,000 men gained leniency by confessing their misconduct and swearing an oath of allegiance to the state. A special Disqualification Act prohibited the penitent rebels from voting, holding public office, serving on juries, working as schoolmasters, or operating taverns for up to three years.

Two Rebel Leaders
A Boston almanac of 1787 portrayed Daniel Shays (on the left) with another rebel leader, Job Shattuck, thought to be ring-leaders in the rebellion against excessive taxation in Massachusetts. It is unlikely the artist ever saw either man. The cannon and drawn swords suggest the men are serious threats. This particular almanac series was pro-Constitution in 1788, so likely this picture is not meant to be sympathetic to the Shaysites. National Portrait Gallery, Smithsonian Institution/Art Resource, NY.

Shays's Rebellion caused leaders throughout the country to worry about the confederation's ability to handle civil disorder. Inflammatory Massachusetts newspapers wrote about bloody mob rule spreading to other states. New York lawyer John Jay wrote to George Washington, "Our affairs seem to lead to some crisis, some revolution—something I cannot foresee or conjecture. I am uneasy and apprehensive; more so than during the war." Benjamin Franklin, in his eighties, shrewdly observed that in 1776 Americans had feared "an excess of power in the rulers" but now the problem was perhaps "a defect of obedience" in the subjects. Among such leaders, the sense of crisis in the confederation had greatly deepened.

REVIEW   What were the most important factors in the failure of the Articles of Confederation?

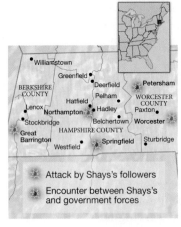

Shays's Rebellion, 1786–1787

* Attack by Shays's followers
* Encounter between Shays's and government forces

▶ The United States Constitution

Shays's Rebellion provoked an odd mixture of fear and hope that the government under the Articles of Confederation was losing its grip on power. A small circle of Virginians decided to try one last time to augment the powers granted to the government by the Articles. Their innocuous call for a meeting to discuss trade regulation led

The Pennsylvania Statehouse
The constitutional convention met in the Assembly Room of the Pennsylvania statehouse in the summer of 1787. Despite the heat, the delegates nailed the windows shut to foil eavesdroppers. The building is now called Independence Hall in honor of the signing of the Declaration of Independence there in 1776; this room has been meticulously restored. Corbis.

within a year to a total reworking of the national government, one with extensive powers and multiple branches based on differing constituencies.

From Annapolis to Philadelphia

The Virginians, led by James Madison, convinced the confederation congress to allow a September 1786 meeting of delegates at Annapolis, Maryland, to try again to revise the trade regulation powers of the Articles. Only five states participated, and the delegates planned a second meeting for Philadelphia in May 1787. The congress reluctantly endorsed the Philadelphia meeting and limited its scope to "the sole and express purpose of revising the Articles of Confederation." But a few leaders, such as Alexander Hamilton of New York, had far more ambitious plans.

The fifty-five men who assembled at Philadelphia in May 1787 for the constitutional convention were generally those who had already concluded that there were serious weaknesses in the Articles of Confederation. Patrick Henry, author of the Virginia Resolves in 1765 and more recently state governor, refused to go to the convention, saying he "smelled a rat." Rhode Island

declined to send delegates. Two men sent by New York's legislature to check the influence of fellow delegate Alexander Hamilton left in dismay in the middle of the convention, leaving Hamilton as the sole representative of the state.

This gathering of white men included no artisans, day laborers, or ordinary farmers. Two-thirds of the delegates were lawyers. Half had been officers in the Continental army. The majority had served in the confederation congress and knew its strengths and weaknesses. Seven men had been governors of their states and knew firsthand the frustrations of thwarted executive power. A few elder statesmen attended, such as Benjamin Franklin and George Washington, but on the whole the delegates were young, like Madison and Hamilton.

The Virginia and New Jersey Plans

The convention worked in secrecy, which enabled the men to freely explore alternatives without fear that their honest opinions would come back to haunt them. The Virginia delegation first laid out a fifteen-point plan that repudiated the principle of a confederation of states. Largely the work of Madison, the **Virginia Plan** set out a three-branch government composed of a two-chamber legislature, a powerful executive, and a judiciary. It practically eliminated the voices of the smaller states by pegging representation in both houses of the congress to population. The theory was that government operated directly on people, not on states. Among the breathtaking powers assigned to the congress were the rights to veto state legislation and to coerce states militarily to obey national laws. To prevent the congress from having absolute power, the executive and judiciary could jointly veto its actions.

In mid-June, delegates from New Jersey, Connecticut, Delaware, and New Hampshire—all small states—unveiled an alternative proposal. The **New Jersey Plan**, as it was called, maintained the existing single-house congress of the Articles of Confederation in which each state had one vote. Acknowledging the need for an executive, it created a plural presidency to be shared by three men elected by the congress from among its membership. Where it sharply departed from the existing government was in the sweeping powers it gave to the new congress: the right to tax, regulate trade, and use force on unruly state governments. In favoring national power over states' rights, it aligned itself with the Virginia Plan. But the New Jersey Plan retained the confederation principle that the national government was to be an assembly of states, not of people.

For two weeks, delegates debated the two plans, focusing on the key issue of representation. The small-state delegates conceded that one house in a two-house legislature could be apportioned by population, but they would never agree that both houses could be. Madison was equally vehement about bypassing representation by state, which he viewed as the fundamental flaw in the Articles.

The debate seemed deadlocked, and for a while the convention was "on the verge of dissolution, scarce held together by the strength of a hair," according to one delegate. Only in mid-July did the so-called Great Compromise break the stalemate and produce the basic structural features of the emerging **United States Constitution**. Proponents of the competing plans agreed on a bicameral legislature. Representation in the lower house, the House of Representatives, would be apportioned by population, and representation in the upper house, the Senate, would come from all the states equally, with each state represented by two independently voting senators.

Representation by population turned out to be an ambiguous concept once it was subjected to rigorous discussion. Who counted? Were slaves, for example, people or property? As people, they would add weight to the southern delegations in the House of Representatives, but as property they would add to the tax burdens of those states. What emerged was the compromise known as the **three-fifths clause**: All free persons plus "three-fifths of all other Persons" constituted the numerical base for the apportionment of representatives.

Using "all other Persons" as a substitute for "slaves" indicates the discomfort delegates felt in acknowledging in the Constitution the existence of slavery. The words *slave* and *slavery* appear nowhere in the document, but slavery figured in two places besides the three-fifths clause. Government power over trade regulation naturally included the slave trade, which the Constitution euphemistically described as "the Migration or Importation of such Persons as any of the States now shall think proper to admit." Another provision contrived to guarantee the return of fugitive slaves using awkward, lawyer-like prose: "No person, held to Service or Labour in one State, under the Laws thereof, escaping into another, shall, in Consequence of any Law or Regulation therein, be discharged from such Service or Labour but shall be delivered up on Claim of the party to whom such Service or Labour may be due." Although slavery was nowhere named, nonetheless it was recognized, protected, and thereby perpetuated by the U.S. Constitution.

Democracy versus Republicanism

The delegates in Philadelphia made a distinction between democracy and republicanism new to the American political vocabulary. Pure democracy was now taken to be a dangerous thing. As a Massachusetts delegate put it, "The evils we experience flow from the excess of democracy." The delegates still favored republican institutions, but they created a government that gave direct voice to the people only in the House and that granted a check on that voice to the Senate, a body of men elected not by direct popular vote but by the state legislatures. Senators served for six years, with no limit on reelection; they were protected from the whims of democratic majorities, and their long terms fostered experience and maturity in office.

Similarly, the presidency evolved into a powerful office out of the reach of direct democracy. The delegates devised an electoral college whose only function was to elect the president and vice president. Each state's legislature would choose the electors, whose number was the sum of representatives and senators for the state, an interesting blending of the two principles of representation. The president thus would owe his office not to the Congress, the states, or the people, but to a temporary assemblage of distinguished citizens who could vote their own judgment on the candidates. His term of office was four years, but he could be reelected without limitation.

The framers had developed a far more complex form of federal government than that provided by the Articles of Confederation. To curb the excesses of democracy, they devised a government with limits and checks on all three of its branches. They set forth a powerful president who could veto legislation passed in Congress, but they gave Congress the power to override presidential vetoes. They set up a national judiciary to settle disputes between states and citizens of different states. They separated the branches of government not only by functions and by reciprocal checks but also by deliberately basing the election of each branch on different universes of voters—voting citizens (the House), state legislators (the Senate), and the electoral college (the presidency).

The convention carefully listed the powers of the president and of Congress. The president could initiate policy, propose legislation, and veto acts of Congress; he could command the military and direct foreign policy; and he could appoint the entire judiciary, subject to Senate approval. Congress held the purse strings: the power to levy taxes, to regulate trade, and to coin money and control the currency. States were expressly forbidden to issue paper money. Two more powers of Congress—to "provide for the common defence and general Welfare" of the country and "to make all laws which shall be necessary and proper" for carrying out its powers—provided elastic language that came closest to Madison's wish to grant sweeping powers to the new government.

While no one was entirely satisfied with every line of the Constitution, only three dissenters refused to sign the document. The Constitution specified a mechanism for ratification that avoided the dilemma faced earlier by the confederation government: Nine states, not all thirteen, had to ratify it, and special ratifying conventions elected only for that purpose, not state legislatures, would make the crucial decision.

> **REVIEW**   Why did the Constitution proposed at the Philadelphia convention include multiple checks on the three branches of government?

▶ Ratification of the Constitution

Had a popular vote been taken on the Constitution in the fall of 1787, it probably would have been rejected. In the three most populous states—Virginia, Massachusetts, and New York—substantial majorities opposed a powerful new national government. North Carolina and Rhode Island refused to call ratifying conventions. Seven of the eight remaining states were easy victories for the Constitution, but securing the approval of the ninth proved difficult. Pro-Constitution forces, called Federalists, had to strategize very shrewdly to defeat anti-Constitution forces, called Antifederalists.

The Federalists

Proponents of the Constitution moved swiftly into action. They first secured agreement from an uneasy confederation congress to defer a vote and instead send the Constitution to the states for their consideration. The pro-Constitution forces next called themselves **Federalists**, a word that implied endorsement of a confederated government. Their opponents thus became known as Antifederalists, a label that made them sound defensive and negative, lacking a program of their own.

To gain momentum, the Federalists targeted the states most likely to ratify quickly. Delaware ratified in early December, before the Antifederalists had even begun to campaign. Pennsylvania, New Jersey, and Georgia followed within a month (Map 8.3). Delaware and New Jersey were small states surrounded by more powerful neighbors; a government that would regulate trade and set taxes according to population was an attractive proposition. Georgia sought the protection that a stronger national government would afford against hostile Indians and Spanish Florida to

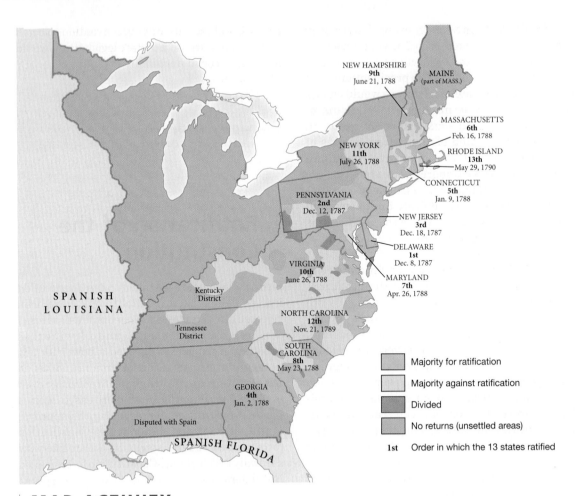

MAP ACTIVITY

Map 8.3   Ratification of the Constitution, 1788–1790

Populated areas cast votes for delegates to state ratification conventions. This map shows Antifederalist strength generally concentrated in backcountry, noncoastal, and non-urban areas, but with significant exceptions (for example, Rhode Island).

READING THE MAP: Where was Federalist strength concentrated? How did the distribution of Federalist and Antifederalist sentiment affect the order of state ratifications of the Constitution?
CONNECTIONS: What objections did Antifederalists have to the new U.S. Constitution? How might their locations have affected their view of the Federalist argument?

the south. "If a weak State with the Indians on its back and the Spaniards on its flank does not see the necessity of a General Government there must I think be wickedness or insanity in the way," said Federalist George Washington.

Another three easy victories came in Connecticut, Maryland, and South Carolina. Again, merchants, lawyers, and urban artisans in general favored the new Constitution, as did large landowners and slaveholders. Antifederalists in these states tended to be rural, western, and noncommercial, men whose access to news was

limited and whose participation in state government was tenuous.

Massachusetts was the first state to give the Federalists serious difficulty. The vote to select the ratification delegates decidedly favored the Antifederalists, whose strength lay in the western areas of the state, home to Shays's Rebellion. One rural delegate from Worcester County voiced widely shared suspicions: "These lawyers and men of learning and money men that talk so finely, and gloss over matters so smoothly, to make us poor illiterate people swallow down the pill, expect to get into Congress themselves; they expect to be the managers of the Constitution and get all the power and all the money into their own hands, and then they will swallow up all us little folks." But another western farmer said he knew "the worth of good government by the want of it," a clear reference to the chaos of the Shaysite rebellion. He urged his fellow farmers to work with the elite leaders; "they are all embarked on the same cause with us, and we must swim or sink together. . . . We shall never have another opportunity." By such arguments and by a vigorous Federalist newspaper campaign, the Antifederalists' initial lead was slowly eroded. In the end, the Federalists won in Massachusetts by a slim margin and only with promises that amendments to the Constitution would be taken up in the First Congress.

By May 1788, eight states had ratified; only one more was needed. North Carolina and Rhode Island were hopeless for the Federalist cause, and New Hampshire seemed nearly as bleak. More worrisome was the failure to win over the largest and most economically critical states, Virginia and New York.

The Antifederalists

The **Antifederalists** were a composite group, united mainly in their desire to block the Constitution. Although much of their strength came from back-country areas long suspicious of eastern elites, many Antifederalist leaders came from the same social background as Federalist leaders; economic class alone did not differentiate them. The Antifederalists also drew strength in states that were already on sure economic footing, such as New York, which could afford to remain independent. Probably the biggest appeal of the Antifederalists' position lay in the long-nurtured fear that distant power might infringe on people's liberties.

But by the time eight states had ratified the Constitution, the Antifederalists faced a difficult task. First, they were no longer defending the status quo now that the momentum lay with the Federalists. Second, it was difficult to defend the confederation government with its admitted flaws. Even so, they remained genuinely fearful that the new government would be too distant from the people and could thus become corrupt or tyrannical. "The difficulty, if not impracticability, of exercising the equal and equitable powers of government by a single legislature over an extent of territory that reaches from the Mississippi to the western lakes, and from them to the Atlantic ocean, is an insuperable objection to the adoption of the new system," wrote Mercy Otis Warren, an Antifederalist woman writing under the name "A Columbia Patriot."

The new government was indeed distant. In the proposed House of Representatives, the only directly democratic element of the Constitution, one member represented some 30,000 people. How could that member really know or communicate with his whole constituency, Antifederalists worried. One Antifederalist essayist contrasted the proposed model with the personal character of state-level representation: "The members of our state legislature are annually elected—they are subject to instructions—they are chosen within small circles—they are sent but a small distance from their respective homes. Their conduct is constantly known to their constituents. They frequently see, and are seen, by the men whose servants they are." They also worried that representatives would always be elites and thus "ignorant of the sentiments of the middling and much more of the lower class of citizens, strangers to their ability, unacquainted with their wants, difficulties, and distress," as one Maryland man worried.

The Federalists generally agreed that the elite would be favored for national elections. Indeed, Federalists wanted power to reside with intelligent, virtuous leaders like themselves. They did not envision a government constituted of every class of people. "Fools and knaves have voice enough in government already," joked one Federalist, without being guaranteed representation in proportion to their total population. Alexander Hamilton claimed that mechanics and laborers preferred to have their social betters represent them. Antifederalists disagreed: "In reality, there will be no part of the people represented, but the rich. . . . It will literally be a government in the hands of the few to oppress and plunder the many." (See "Making Historical Arguments," page 220.)

Antifederalists fretted over many specific features of the Constitution, such as the prohibition on state-issued paper money or the federal power to control the time and place of elections. The most widespread objection was the Constitution's glaring omission of any guarantees of individual liberties in a bill of rights like those contained in many state constitutions.

In the end, a small state—New Hampshire—provided the decisive ninth vote for ratification on June 21, 1788, following an intensive and successful lobbying effort by Federalists.

Was the New United States a Christian Country?

Rebecca Samuel, a Jewish resident of Virginia, conveyed her excitement about the new U.S. Constitution when she wrote her German parents in 1791 that finally "Jew and Gentile are as one" in the realm of politics and citizenship. Other voices were distinctly less approving. An Antifederalist pamphlet warned that the pope could become president; another feared that "a Turk, a Jew, a Roman Catholic, and what is worse than all, a Universalist, may be President."

The document that produced such wildly different reactions was indeed remarkable for the conspicuous absence of religion. The Constitution did not invoke Christianity as a state religion. It made no reference to an almighty being, and it specifically promised, in article 6, section 3, that "no religious test shall ever be required as a qualification to any office or public trust under the United States."

Many Christian leaders were stunned at the Constitution's near silence on religion, a turnabout from most state constitutions. A New Yorker warned that "should the Citizens of America be as irreligious as her Constitution, we will have reason to tremble, lest the Governor

of the universe . . . crush us to atoms." A delegate to North Carolina's ratifying convention predicted that the Constitution was "an invitation for Jews and pagans of every kind to come among us." A concerned Presbyterian minister asked Alexander Hamilton why religion was not in the Constitution. Hamilton reportedly quipped, "Indeed, Doctor, we forgot it."

Measured against the practices of state governments, Hamilton's observation is hardly credible. The men who wrote the state constitutions actively debated qualifications for voting and officeholding. Along with factors like property ownership, race, gender, and age, many also argued for religious qualifications.

Most leaders of the 1780s took for granted that Christianity was the one true faith and the essential foundation of morality. All but two state constitutions assumed the primacy of Protestantism, and one-third of them collected public taxes to support Christian churches. Every state but one required officeholders to take a Christian oath. For example, members of Pennsylvania's legislature swore to "acknowledge the Scripture of the Old and New Testament to be given by divine inspiration."

Governors proclaimed fast days and public thanksgivings in the name of the Holy Trinity. Chaplains led legislatures in Christian prayer. Jurors and witnesses swore Christian oaths. New England states passed Sabbath laws prohibiting all work or travel on Sunday. Blasphemy laws punished people who cursed the Christian God or Jesus.

Although close to half the state constitutions did include freedom of religious conscience as an explicit right, this right promised nothing about political equality. How then did the U.S. Constitution come to be such a break from the immediate past? Had the Constitution's writers really just forgotten about religion?

Not James Madison of Virginia. Madison arrived at the constitutional convention fresh from a hard-fought battle in Virginia to establish religious liberty free from all state interference. Opponents sponsored a bill to support Christian ministers with tax money; Madison instead secured passage in 1786 of the Virginia Statute for Religious Freedom, a document drafted several years earlier by Thomas Jefferson. The statute guaranteed freedom of conscience and prohibited any distinctions in "civil capacities" based on religion. In Jefferson's distinctive formulation, the statute asserted "that our civil rights have no dependence on our religious opinions any more than our opinions in physics or geometry." There could be no religious tests for officeholding thereafter in Virginia and no state funding of ministers.

The Big Holdouts: Virginia and New York

Four states still remained outside the new union, and a glance at a map demonstrated the necessity of pressing the Federalist case in the two largest, Virginia and New York (see Map 8.3). In Virginia, an influential Antifederalist group led by Patrick Henry and George Mason made the outcome uncertain. The Federalists finally

but barely won ratification by proposing twenty specific amendments that the new government would promise to consider.

New York voters tilted toward the Antifederalists out of a sense that a state so large and powerful need not relinquish so much authority to the new federal government. But New York was also home to some of the most persuasive Federalists. Starting in October 1787, Alexander Hamilton collaborated with James Madison and

Touro Synagogue
This 1759 synagogue in Newport, Rhode Island, is the oldest Jewish house of worship still standing in the United States. President Washington visited "the Hebrew Congregation" there in 1790 and wrote: "It is now no more that toleration is spoken of, as if it was by the indulgence of one class of people, that another enjoyed the exercise of their inherent natural rights." © NPS/Alamy Stock Photo.

The Virginia Statute expressed Madison's ideal, but on practical grounds he preferred that the U.S. Constitution say little about religion since state laws reflected a variety of positions. When Antifederalists demanded a bill of rights, Madison drew up a list for the first Congress to consider. Two on his list dealt with religion, but only one was approved: "Congress shall make no law respecting an establishment of religion, or prohibiting the free exercise thereof." In a stroke, Madison placed religious worship and the privileging of any one church beyond Congress's power. His second proposal failed to gain traction: "No State shall violate the equal rights of conscience." Evidently, the states wanted to keep their Christian-only rules that violated dissenters' consciences and kept them out of office.

Gradually, states deleted restrictive laws, but as late as 1840 Jews still could not hold public office in four states. Well into the twentieth century, Sunday laws in some states forced business closings on the Christian Sabbath, creating economic hardship for those whose religion prohibited work on Saturday. The guarantee of freedom of conscience in religion was implanted in various founding documents in the 1770s and 1780s, but it took many years to fulfill Jefferson's and Madison's larger vision of what true religious liberty means: the freedom for religious belief to be independent of civil status.

Questions for Analysis

Summarize the Argument: In what ways was the United States a specifically Christian nation? In what ways was the Constitution designed to be nondenominational?

Analyze the Evidence: What point was Jefferson making when he equated opinions about religion to opinions about physics or geometry as irrelevant factors in determining citizens' civil rights?

Consider the Context: Why do you think so many state constitutions allowed only Protestants to hold political office? What may have motivated the Constitution's departure from those preceding governments?

New York lawyer John Jay on a series of eighty-five essays on the political philosophy of the new Constitution. Published in New York newspapers and later republished as *The Federalist Papers*, the essays brilliantly set out the failures of the Articles of Confederation and offered an analysis of the complex nature of the Federalist position. In one of the most compelling essays, number 10, Madison challenged the Antifederalists' heartfelt conviction that republican government had to be small-scale. Madison argued that a large and diverse population was itself a guarantee of liberty. In a national government, no single faction could ever be large enough to subvert the freedom of other groups. "Extend the sphere, and you take in a greater variety of parties and interests; you make it less probable that a majority of the whole will have a common motive to invade the rights of other citizens," Madison asserted. He called it "a republican

VISUAL ACTIVITY

Mercy Otis Warren

Sister and wife of prominent Massachusetts revolutionaries, Mercy Otis Warren was well positioned to know about revolutionary politics. Abigail and John Adams were close friends until she broke with them in 1788 over her support for antifederalism. At age thirty-five, in 1763, she sat for Boston artist John Singleton Copley wearing a shimmering blue silk gown ornamented with expensive lace. Museum of Fine Arts, Boston, Massachusetts, USA/Bequest of Winslow Warren/ Bridgeman Images.

READING THE IMAGE: How does the artist convey grace and ease as features of feminine beauty? Copley painted two other women in 1763—two from Salem and Mrs. Warren from Barnstable, Massachusetts—each wearing the same blue dress. What might that suggest about Copley's studio practices, about fashion, or about the purpose of family portraits?

CONNECTIONS: What role could upper-class women play in the debate over the Constitution?

"Success to the Tobacco Plant"

As soon as nine states ratified the Constitution, the Federalists staged spectacular victory celebrations intended to demonstrate national unity behind the new government. Philadelphia's parade, on July 4, 1788, mobilized several thousand participants marching under occupational banners representing farmers, brewers, tobacconists, lawyers, and others. This banner was carried by the local sellers of tobacco products, who likely applauded a national government empowered to regulate commerce among the states. Friends of the Thomas Leiper House and the Library Company of Philadelphia.

remedy for the diseases most incident to republican government."

At New York's ratifying convention, Antifederalists predominated, but impassioned debate and lobbying—plus the dramatic news of Virginia's ratification—finally tipped the balance to the Federalists. Even so, the Antifederalists' approval of the document was accompanied by a list of twenty-four individual rights and thirty-three structural changes they hoped to see in the Constitution. New York's ratification ensured the legitimacy of the new government, yet it took another year and a half for Antifederalists in North Carolina to come around. Fiercely independent Rhode Island held out until May 1790, and even then it ratified by only a two-vote margin.

In less than twelve months, the U.S. Constitution was both written and ratified. The Federalists had faced a formidable task, but by building momentum and promising consideration of a bill of rights, they did indeed carry the day.

REVIEW Why did Antifederalists oppose the Constitution?

► Conclusion: The "Republican Remedy"

Thus ended one of the most intellectually tumultuous and creative periods in American history.

The period began in 1775 with a confederation government that could barely be ratified because of its requirement of unanimity, but there was no reaching unanimity on the western lands, an impost, and the proper way to respond to unfair taxation in a republican state. The new Constitution offered a different approach to these problems by loosening the grip of impossible unanimity and by embracing the ideas of a heterogeneous public life and a carefully balanced government that together would prevent any one part of the public from tyrannizing another. The genius of James Madison was to anticipate that diversity of opinion was not only an unavoidable reality but also a hidden strength of the new society beginning to take shape. This is what he meant in Federalist essay number 10 when he spoke of the "republican remedy" for the troubles most likely to befall a government in which the people are the source of authority.

Despite Madison's optimism, political differences remained keen and worrisome to many. The Federalists still hoped for a society in which leaders of exceptional wisdom would discern the best path for public policy. They looked backward to a society of hierarchy, rank, and benevolent rule by an aristocracy of talent, but they created a government with forward-looking checks and balances as a guard against corruption, which they figured would most likely emanate from the people. The Antifederalists also looked backward, but to an old order of small-scale direct democracy and local control, in which virtuous people kept a close eye on potentially corruptible rulers. The Antifederalists feared a national government led by distant, self-interested leaders who needed to be held in check. In the 1790s, these two conceptions of republicanism and of leadership would be tested in real life.

See the Selected Bibliography for this chapter in the Appendix.

8 Chapter Review

REVIEW QUESTIONS

1. Why was the confederation government's authority so limited? (pp. 197–200)

2. What were the limits of citizenship, rights, and freedom within the various states? (pp. 200–204)

3. What were the most important factors in the failure of the Articles of Confederation? (pp. 204–214)

4. Why did the Constitution proposed at the Philadelphia convention include multiple checks on the three branches of government? (pp. 214–217)

5. Why did Antifederalists oppose the Constitution? (pp. 217–223)

MAKING CONNECTIONS

1. Leaders in the new nation held that voting should be restricted to men possessing independence of mind. What did they mean by that? Who did they mean to exclude from voting?

2. Twenty-first-century Americans see a profound tension between the Revolutionary ideals of liberty and equality and the persistence of American slavery. Did Americans in the late eighteenth century see a tension?

3. What proposals were offered to manage the sale and settlement of the Northwest Territory, the confederation's greatest financial asset? How did the Northwest Ordinance of 1787 shape the nation's expansion?

LINKING TO THE PAST

1. Compare and contrast the complaints against taxation connected with the Stamp Act in 1765 and those resulting from the congressional requisition of 1785. What were the principal arguments in each case? In either case, was it simply a matter of people refusing to pay to support government functions? Why do you think anti–Stamp Act activists like Samuel Adams took a negative view of the 1786 tax protests? (See chapter 6.)

2. Thomas Paine's pamphlet *Common Sense*, which sharply criticized the monarchy, was widely circulated and hailed by rebellious colonists in 1776. In light of the colonists' negative view toward monarchical power leading up to the Revolutionary War, how do you explain the powerful presidency that the victorious Americans set up in 1787? (See chapter 7.)

9 The New Nation Takes Form

1789–1800

WASHINGTON'S GIFT TO HIS WIFE
George Washington sat for several official portraits during his presidency, but he commissioned this personal one himself, in 1789, as a gift for his wife. The miniature could be worn as a pendant or pin. Private Collection/Photo © Christie's Images/Bridgeman Images.

ALEXANDER HAMILTON, THE MAN WHO BRILLIANTLY UNIFIED the pro-Constitution Federalists of 1788, headed the Treasury Department in the new government and thereby became the most polarizing figure of the 1790s.

Hamilton grew up on a small West Indies island, the son of an unmarried mother who died when he was eleven. He developed a fierce ambition to overcome his disadvantages and make good. After serving an apprenticeship to a trader, the bright lad made his way to New York City, where he soon gained entry to college. During the American Revolution, he wrote political articles for a newspaper that caught the eye of General George Washington, who was moved to select the nineteen-year-old to be his close aide. In the 1780s, Hamilton practiced law in New York and participated in the constitutional convention in Philadelphia. His shrewd political tactics greatly aided the ratification process.

A Cinderella story characterized Hamilton's private life, too. Handsome and now well connected, he married a wealthy merchant's daughter. He had a magnetic charm that attracted both men and women; at social gatherings, he excelled. Late-night parties, however, never interfered with Hamilton's prodigious capacity for work.

As secretary of the treasury, Hamilton took quick action to build the economy. "If a Government appears to be confident of its own powers, it is the surest way to inspire the same confidence in others," he remarked. He immediately tackled the country's unpaid Revolutionary War debt, producing a complex proposal to fund the debt and pump millions of dollars into the U.S. economy. He drew up a plan for a national banking system to manage the money supply. And he designed a system of government subsidies and tariff policies to promote the development of manufacturing interests.

Hamilton was both visionary and practical, a gifted man with remarkable political intuitions. Yet this magnetic man made enemies; the "founding fathers" of the 1770s and 1780s became competitors and even bitter rivals in the 1790s. Both political philosophy and personality clashes created friction.

Hamilton's charm no longer worked with James Madison, now a representative in Congress and an opponent of all of Hamilton's economic plans. His charm had never worked with John Adams, the new vice president, who privately called him "the bastard brat of a Scotch pedlar" motivated by "disappointed Ambition and unbridled malice and revenge." Years later, when asked why he had deserted Hamilton, Madison coolly replied, "Colonel Hamilton deserted me." Hamilton assumed that government was safest when in the hands of "the rich, the wise, and the good"—by which he meant America's commercial elite. By contrast, agrarian values ran deep with Jefferson and Madison, and they were suspicious of get-rich-quick speculators, financiers, and manufacturing development.

Alexander Hamilton, **by John Trumbull**
Hamilton was confident, handsome, audacious, brilliant, and very hardworking. Ever slender, in marked contrast to the more corpulent leaders of his day, he posed for this portrait in 1792, at the age of thirty-seven and at the height of his power. Everett Collection Historical/Alamy.

The personal and political antagonisms of this first generation of American leaders left their mark on the young country. Leaders generally agreed on Indian policy in the new Republic—peace when possible, war when necessary—but on little else. No one was prepared for the intense and passionate polarization over economic and foreign policy. The disagreements were articulated around particular events and policies: taxation and the public debt, a new treaty with Britain, a rebellion in Haiti, and a near war with France. At their heart, these disagreements sprang from opposing ideologies on the value of democracy, the nature of leadership, and the limits of federal power.

By 1800, the oppositional politics ripening between Hamiltonian and Jeffersonian politicians would begin to crystallize into political parties, the Federalists and the Republicans. To the citizens of that day, this was an unhappy development.

► The Search for Stability

After the struggles of the 1780s, the most urgent task in establishing the new government was to secure stability. Leaders sought ways to heal old divisions, and the first presidential election offered the means to do that in the person of George Washington, who enjoyed widespread veneration. People trusted him to exercise the untested and perhaps elastic powers of the presidency.

Congress had important work as well in initiating the new government. Congress quickly agreed on the Bill of Rights, which answered the concerns of many Antifederalists. Beyond politics, cultural change in the area of gender also enhanced political stability. The private virtue of women was mobilized to bolster the public virtue of male citizens and to enhance political stability. Republicanism was forcing a rethinking of women's relation to the state.

Washington Inaugurates the Government

George Washington was elected president in February 1789 by a unanimous vote of the electoral college. (John Adams got just half as many votes; he became vice president, but his pride was wounded.) Washington perfectly embodied the republican ideal of disinterested, public-spirited leadership. Indeed, he cultivated that image through astute ceremonies such as the dramatic surrender of his sword to the Continental Congress at the end of the war, symbolizing the subservience of military power to the law.

Once in office, Washington calculated his moves, knowing that every step set a precedent and that any misstep could be dangerous for the fragile government. Congress debated a title for Washington, ranging from "His Highness" to "His Majesty, the President"; Washington favored "His High Mightiness." But in the end, republican simplicity prevailed. The final title was simply "President of the United States of America," and the established form of address became "Mr. President," a subdued yet dignified title reserved for property-owning white males.

CHRONOLOGY

1789	• George Washington inaugurated first president. • French Revolution begins. • First Congress meets. • Fort Washington erected in western Ohio.
1790	• Congress approves Hamilton's debt plan. • Judith Sargent Murray publishes "On the Equality of the Sexes." • National capital moved to Philadelphia. • Indians in Ohio defeat General Josiah Harmar.
1791	• States ratify Bill of Rights. • Bank of the United States chartered. • Ohio Indians defeat General Arthur St. Clair. • Congress passes whiskey tax. • Haitian Revolution begins. • Hamilton issues *Report on Manufactures*.
1793	• Anglo-French Wars commence in Europe. • Washington issues Neutrality Proclamation. • Eli Whitney invents cotton gin.
1794	• Whiskey Rebellion protests excise tax. • Battle of Fallen Timbers fought.
1795	• Treaty of Greenville signed. • Jay Treaty approved by Congress.
1796	• John Adams elected president.
1797	• XYZ affair hurts U.S. relationship with France.
1798	• Quasi-War with France erupts. • Alien and Sedition Acts passed. • Virginia and Kentucky Resolutions passed.
1800	• Thomas Jefferson elected president.

Washington's genius in establishing the presidency lay in his capacity for implanting his own reputation for integrity into the office itself. In the political language of the day, he was "virtuous," meaning that he took pains to elevate the public good over private interest and projected honesty and honor over ambition. He remained aloof, resolute, and dignified, to the point of appearing wooden at times. He encouraged pomp and ceremony to create respect for the office, traveling with six horses to pull his coach, hosting formal balls, and surrounding himself with uniformed servants. He even held weekly "levees," as European monarchs did, hour-long audiences granted to distinguished visitors (including women), at which Washington appeared attired in black velvet, with a feathered hat and a polished sword. The president and his guests bowed, avoiding the egalitarian familiarity of a handshake. But he always managed, perhaps just barely, to avoid the extreme of royal splendor.

Washington chose talented and experienced men to preside over the newly created Departments of War, Treasury, and State. For the Department of War, Washington selected General Henry Knox, former secretary of war in the confederation government. For the Treasury—an especially tough job in view of revenue conflicts during the confederation (see "Confederation and Taxation" in chapter 8)—the president appointed Alexander Hamilton, known for his general brilliance and financial astuteness. To lead the State Department, which handled foreign policy, Washington chose Thomas Jefferson, a master diplomat and the current minister to France. For attorney general, Washington picked Edmund Randolph, a Virginian who had attended the constitutional convention but who had turned Antifederalist during ratification. For chief justice of the Supreme Court, Washington designated John Jay, a New York lawyer who had helped to write *The Federalist Papers*.

Soon Washington began to hold regular meetings with these men, thereby establishing the precedent of a presidential cabinet. (Vice President John Adams was not included; his only official duty, to preside over the Senate, he found "a punishment." To his wife he complained, "My country has in its wisdom contrived for me the most insignificant office.")

No one anticipated that two decades of party turbulence would emerge from the brilliant but explosive mix of Washington's first cabinet.

The Bill of Rights

An important piece of business for the First Congress, meeting in 1789, was the passage of the **Bill of Rights**. Seven states had ratified the Constitution with the strong expectation that their concerns about individual liberties and limitations to federal power would be addressed through the amendment process. The Federalists of 1787 had thought an enumeration of rights unnecessary, but in 1789 Congressman James Madison understood that healing the divisions of the 1780s was of prime importance: "It will be a desirable thing to extinguish from the bosom of every member of the community, any apprehensions that there are those among his countrymen who wish to deprive them of the liberty for which they valiantly fought and honorably bled."

Drawing on existing state constitutions with bills of rights, Madison enumerated guarantees of freedom of speech, press, and religion; the right to petition and assemble; and the right to be free from unwarranted searches and seizures. One amendment asserted the right to keep and bear arms in support of a "well-regulated militia," to which Madison added, "but no person religiously scrupulous of bearing arms, shall be compelled to render military service in person." That provision for what a later century would call "conscientious objector" status failed to gain acceptance in Congress.

In September 1789, Congress approved a set of twelve amendments and sent them to the states for approval; by 1791, ten were eventually ratified. The First through Eighth dealt with individual liberties, and the Ninth and Tenth concerned the boundary between federal and state authority.

Still, not everyone was entirely satisfied. State ratifying conventions had submitted some eighty proposed amendments. Congress never considered proposals to change structural features of the new government, and Madison had no intention of reopening debates about the length of the president's term or the power to levy excise taxes. He also had no thought to use the Bill of Rights to address the status of enslaved people. But others capitalized on the

First Amendment's right to petition to force the First Congress into a bitter debate over slavery. (See "Making Historical Arguments," page 230.)

Significantly, no one complained about one striking omission in the Bill of Rights: the right to vote. Only much later was voting seen as a fundamental liberty requiring protection by constitutional amendment—indeed, by four amendments. The Constitution deliberately left the definition of eligible voters to the states because of the existing wide variation in local voting practices. Most of these practices were based on property qualifications, but some touched on religion and, in one unusual case (New Jersey), on sex and race (see "Who Are 'the People'?" in chapter 8).

The Republican Wife and Mother

The exclusion of women from political activity did not mean they had no civic role or responsibility. A flood of periodical articles in the 1790s by both male and female writers reevaluated courtship, marriage, and motherhood in light of republican ideals. Tyrannical power in the ruler, whether king or husband, was declared a thing of the past. Affection, not duty, bound wives to their husbands and citizens to their government. In republican marriages, the writers claimed, women had the capacity to reform the morals and manners of men. One male author promised women that "the solidity and stability of the liberties of your country rest with you; since Liberty is never sure, 'till Virtue reigns triumphant. . . . While you thus keep our country virtuous, you maintain its independence."

Until the 1790s, public virtue was strictly a masculine quality. But another sort of virtue enlarged in importance: sexual chastity, a private asset prized as a feminine quality. Essayists of the 1790s explicitly advised young women to use sexual virtue to increase public virtue in men. "Love and courtship . . . invest a lady with more authority than in any other situation that falls to the lot of human beings," one male essayist proclaimed.

Republican ideals also cast motherhood in a new light. Throughout the 1790s, advocates for female education, still a controversial proposition, argued that education would produce better mothers, who in turn would produce better citizens, a concept historians call republican motherhood. Benjamin Rush, a Pennsylvania physician and educator, called for female education because "our ladies should be qualified . . . in instructing their sons in the principles of liberty and government." A series of essays by Judith Sargent Murray of Massachusetts favored education that would remake women into self-confident, rational beings. Her first essay, published in 1790, was boldly titled "On the Equality of the Sexes."

VISUAL ACTIVITY

A Souvenir Brass Button, 1789

At his inauguration, George Washington wore a suit of plain American fabric, adorned with custom-made buttons engraved with eagles. Similar souvenir buttons, in a variety of sizes, metals, and designs, quickly flooded the market. All carried the same refrain, "Long Live the President," a twist on the traditional British cheer welcoming a new king to his throne. The Granger Collection, New York.

READING THE IMAGE: What is engraved on this brass button in the center circle and around the edge? Two states had not yet ratified the Constitution; are they included on this button?

CONNECTIONS: What was the term of office for presidents under the 1788 Constitution? Could a man serve for life? Do you think the "Long Live" slogan was adopted because it was a habitual ritual for coronation? Or was it a heartfelt wish for a beloved and heroic Washington?

How Did America's First Congress Address the Question of Slavery?

In its opening months, the First Congress had an ambitious agenda. It established executive departments, the judiciary, and a federal postal system. It crafted the Bill of Rights, debated Alexander Hamilton's *Report on Public Credit*, and ratified its first Indian treaty. Tackling slavery was nowhere on its agenda. Congressmen assumed that key North-South compromises embedded in the Constitution had resolved the issue. But they were wrong: An angry debate over slavery burst forth in early 1790.

In mid-February, citizens of Pennsylvania and New York petitioned Congress to "exercise justice and mercy" and to end the "trafficking in the persons of fellow-men"—that is, the slave trade. The petitioners were Quakers, members of a religion with a long-standing moral objection to slavery. The pragmatic James Madison urged the representatives to refer the petitions to a congressional committee, thus keeping them out of public view. Representatives from South Carolina and Georgia instead pressed for

immediate dismissal, citing the Constitution's ban on interference with the slave trade before 1808. Reaching no agreement, Congress postponed discussion for a day.

But the next day brought another petition, not coincidentally. Drawn up by a largely Quaker group called the Pennsylvania Abolition Society, it asked Congress "to discourage every species of traffic in the persons of our fellow-men" and to "countenance the restoration of liberty" to slaves. The petition quoted the Constitution to prove the government's duty to "promote the general welfare, and secure the blessings of liberty" for all. That Benjamin Franklin's signature topped the list of petitioners gave it significant political clout.

This second petition was not just about the Atlantic slave trade, which was indeed protected for twenty years by the Constitution. It called for Congress to legislate on the domestic buying and selling of slaves, about which the Constitution was silent. Further, restoring liberty to slaves required an emancipation

law, again something not barred by the Constitution. No method was specified "for removing this inconsistency from the character of the American people," but the petitioners expressed confidence in a merciful Congress.

The petitions touched off an explosive debate in the House. Several northern representatives tried to use them to reopen the contentious issue; representatives from the deep South were adamantly opposed. A rare moment of contemptuous humor surfaced when a South Carolina member asserted that during ratification, "We took each other, with our mutual bad habits and respective evils, for better, for worse; the Northern States adopted us with our slaves, and we adopted them with their Quakers." No other levity was to be heard. Southerners cited biblical justifications for slavery, argued that slavery civilized slaves, predicted economic collapse if slavery ended, and called the petitioners fanatics. Madison finally got his way: The petitions were referred to a committee, amid mounting concern that newspaper coverage of the debate would create rebelliousness among slaves.

A month later, that committee's report defined a middle road in clarifying the powers of Congress over slavery. As expected, the report affirmed that Congress could not end the slave trade before 1808, but it also concluded that Congress could neither force emancipation nor deny it. And while the report held that Congress had no authority to regulate slave treatment, it urged

---

In a subsequent essay on education, she reassured readers that educated women would retain their "characteristic trait" of sweetness. Murray thus reassured readers that education would not undermine women's compliant natures.

Although women's obligations as wives and mothers were now infused with political meaning, traditional gender relations remained unaltered. The analogy between marriage and civil society worked precisely because of the self-subordination inherent in the term *virtue*.

southern legislatures to pass humanitarian laws regulating the provision of food and housing and the protection of slave women and families. Southern representatives strongly objected to this third pronouncement, touching off yet another bitter public debate in Congress.

In the end, a shorter report was hammered out in debate as the formal reply to the petitioners, in which the key provision read: "The Congress have no authority to interfere in the emancipation of slaves, or in the treatment of them within any of the States; it remaining with the several States alone to provide any regulation therein, which humanity and true policy may require." The final vote on this amended report squeaked by with 29 ayes to 25 nays.

The Quaker groups conceded and ceased filing petitions, but a discouraged Benjamin Franklin made one last attempt to shape public opinion by writing a satirical essay for a Philadelphia newspaper. In it, the elder statesman ridiculed the proslavery speeches by transposing their exact arguments into a bogus document by a purported North African Muslim leader explaining why his country's fifty thousand Christian slaves were better off enslaved than free. It was vintage Franklin—funny, smart, and cutting. It was also Franklin's final public pronouncement; he died suddenly three weeks later, at the age of eighty-four. The congressional report launched against his

Benjamin Franklin
In 1789, a Philadelphia scientific society hired Charles Willson Peale to paint Franklin as a scientist. Franklin was quite ill at the time, so Peale copied the body from an earlier portrait and then visited the bedridden man for many short visits to paint his face. "His pain was so great that he could sit only ¼ hour," reported Peale. Franklin died within a year. DEA Picture Library/Getty Images.

1790 petition stood for more than four decades as the silencing mechanism against any attempt at the federal level to disrupt slavery.

Questions for Analysis

Summarize the Argument: What forces compelled Congress to address the issue of slavery in early 1790, and how did it respond to pressures on both sides of the debate?

Analyze the Evidence: What powers did Congress have over the institution of slavery, according to the Constitution? What power was established, or reinforced, as a result of this debate? What was the South Carolina representative implying when he ironically referred to southern slaves and northern Quakers as "mutual bad habits and respective evils"? Do you think he was talking about slavery as an institution or slaves as people?

Consider the Context: What external factors may have caused the petitions against slavery to surface at this time? Why did some within Congress want to pursue the questions raised by the petitioners while others wanted to drop them? What may have motivated each side?

Men should put the public good first, before selfish desires, just as women must put their husbands and families first, before themselves. Women might gain literacy and knowledge, but only in the service of improved domestic duty. In Federalist America, wives and citizens alike should feel affection for and trust in their rulers; neither should ever rebel.

REVIEW How did political leaders in the 1790s attempt to overcome the divisions of the 1780s?

Republican Womanhood: Judith Sargent Murray

The young woman in this 1772 portrait became known in the 1790s as America's foremost spokeswoman for woman's equality. Judith Sargent Murray published essays under the pen name "Constantia." She argued that women had "natural powers" of mind fully the equal of men's. George Washington and John Adams each bought a copy of her collected essays published in 1798. John Singleton Copley, Portrait of Mrs. John Stevens (Judith Sargent, later Mrs. John Murray). Daniel J. Terra Art Acquisition Endowment Fund 2000.6. Terra Foundation for American Art, Chicago/Art Resource, NY.

► Hamilton's Economic Policies

Compared to the severe financial instability of the 1780s, the 1790s brimmed with opportunity, as seen in improved trade, transportation, and banking. In 1790, the federal government moved from New York City to Philadelphia, a more central location with a substantial mercantile class. There, Alexander Hamilton, secretary of the treasury, embarked on multiple plans to solidify the government's economic base. But controversy ensued. His ambitious plans to fund the national debt, set up a national bank, promote manufacturing through trade laws, and raise revenue via a tax on whiskey mobilized severe opposition.

Agriculture, Transportation, and Banking

Dramatic increases in international grain prices, caused by underproduction in war-stricken Europe, motivated American farmers to boost agricultural production for the export trade. From the Connecticut River valley to the Chesapeake, farmers planted more wheat, generating new jobs for millers, coopers, dockworkers, and shipbuilders.

Cotton production also boomed, spurred by market demand from British textile manufacturers and a mechanical invention. Limited amounts of smooth-seed cotton had long been grown in the coastal areas of the South, but this variety of cotton did not prosper in the drier inland regions. Greenseed cotton grew well inland, but its rough seeds stuck to the cotton fibers and were labor-intensive to remove. In 1793, Yale graduate Eli Whitney devised a machine called a gin that easily separated out the seeds; cotton production soared, giving a boost to transatlantic trade with Britain, whose factories eagerly processed the raw cotton into cloth.

A surge of road building further stimulated the economy. Before 1790, one road connected Maine to Georgia, but with the

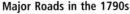

Major Roads in the 1790s

establishment of the U.S. Post Office in 1792, road mileage increased sixfold. Private companies also built toll roads, such as the Lancaster Turnpike west of Philadelphia, the Boston-to-Albany turnpike, and a third road from Virginia to Tennessee. By 1800, a dense network of dirt, gravel, and plank roadways connected towns in southern New England and the Middle Atlantic states, spurring the establishment of commercial stage companies. A trip from New York to Boston took four days; from New York to Philadelphia, less than two (Map 9.1). In 1790, Boston had only three stagecoach companies; by 1800, there were twenty-four.

A third development signaling economic resurgence was the growth of commercial banking. During the 1790s, the number of banks nationwide multiplied tenfold, from three to twenty-nine in 1800. Banks drew in money chiefly through the sale of stock. They then made loans in the form of banknotes, paper currency backed by the gold and silver from stock sales. By issuing two or three times as much money in banknotes as they held in hard money, they were creating new money for the economy.

The U.S. population expanded along with economic development, propelled by large average family size and better than adequate food and land resources. As measured by the first two federal censuses in 1790 and 1800, the population grew from 3.9 million to 5.3 million, an increase of 35 percent.

The Public Debt and Taxes

The upturn in the economy, plus the new taxation powers of the government, suggested that the government might soon repay its wartime debt, amounting to more than $52 million owed to foreign and domestic creditors. But Hamilton had a different plan. He issued a *Report on Public Credit* in January 1790, recommending that the debt be funded—but not repaid immediately—at full value. This meant that old certificates of debt would be rolled over into new bonds, which would earn interest until they were retired several years later. There would still be a public debt, but it would be secure, giving its holders a direct financial stake in the new

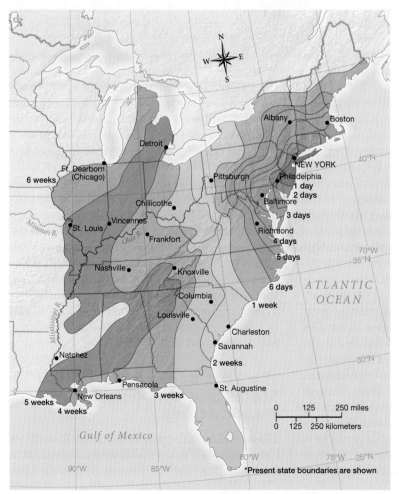

MAP ACTIVITY

Map 9.1   Travel Times from New York City in 1800
Notice that travel out of New York extends over a much greater distance in the first week than in subsequent weeks. River corridors in the West and East speeded up travel—but only going downriver. Also notice that travel by sea (along the coast) was much faster than land travel.

READING THE MAP: Compare this map to the map "Major Roads in the 1790s" and to Map 9.2. What physical and cultural factors account for the slower travel times west of Pittsburgh?

CONNECTIONS: Why did Americans in the 1790s become so interested in traveling long distances? How did travel times affect the U.S. economy?

1790 Census Page

This tally of the first federal census determined representation in Congress and proportional taxation of the states. Notice the five classifications of the population, marking sex, age, race, and status. Can you come up with a reason for each demarcation? Which two states had the largest white population? Which northern states still had slaves? Who were "all other free persons"? Why might any of this matter? U.S. Census Bureau.

The Return for South Carolina having been made since the foregoing Schedule was originally printed, the whole Enumeration is here given complete, except for the N. Western Territory, of which no Return has yet been published.

DISTICTS	Free white Males of 16 years and upwards, including heads of families.	Free white Males under sixteen years.	Free white Females, including heads of families.	All other free persons.	Slaves.	Total.
Vermont	22435	22328	40505	255	16	85539
N. Hampshire	36086	34851	70160	630	158	141885
Maine	24384	24748	46870	538	NONE	96540
Massachusetts	95453	87289	190582	5463	NONE	378787
Rhode Island	16019	15799	32652	3407	948	68825
Connecticut	60523	54403	117448	2808	2764	237946
New York	83700	78122	152320	4654	21324	340120
New Jersey	45251	41416	83287	2762	11423	184139
Pennsylvania	110788	106948	206363	6537	3737	434373
Delaware	11783	12143	22384	3899	8887	59094
Maryland	55915	51339	101395	8043	103036	319728
Virginia	110936	116135	215046	12866	292627	747610
Kentucky	15154	17057	28922	114	12430	73677
N. Carolina	69988	77506	140710	4975	100572	393751
S. Carolina	35576	37722	66880	1801	107094	249073
Georgia	13103	14044	25739	398	29264	82548
	807094	791850	1541263	59150	694280	3893635

Total number of Inhabitants of the United States exclusive of S. Western and N. Territory.	Free white Males of 21 years and upwards.	Free Males under 21 years of age.	Free white Females.	All other persons.	Slaves.	Total.
S. W. territory N. Ditto	6271	10277	15365	361	3417	35691

government. The bonds would circulate, injecting millions of dollars of new money into the economy. "A national debt if not excessive will be to us a national blessing; it will be a powerful cement of our union," Hamilton wrote to a financier. Hamilton's goal was to make the new country creditworthy, not debt-free.

Funding the debt in full was controversial because speculators had already bought up debt certificates cheaply, and Hamilton's report touched off further speculation. Hamilton compounded controversy with his proposal to add to the federal debt another $25 million that some state governments still owed to individuals. During the war, states had obtained supplies by issuing IOUs to farmers, merchants, and moneylenders. Some states, such as Virginia and New York, had paid off these debts entirely. Others, such as Massachusetts, had partially paid them off through heavy taxation of the people. About half the states had made little headway. Hamilton called for the federal government to assume these state debts and combine them with the federal debt, in effect consolidating federal power over the states.

Congressman James Madison strenuously objected to putting windfall profits in the pockets of speculators. He instead proposed a complex scheme to pay both the original holders of the federal debt and the speculators, each at fair fractions of the face value. He also strongly objected to assumption of all the states' debts. A large debt was dangerous, Madison warned, especially because it would lead to high taxation. Secretary of State Jefferson was also fearful of Hamilton's proposals: "No man is more ardently intent to see the public debt soon and sacredly paid off

than I am. This exactly marks the difference between Colonel Hamilton's views and mine, that I would wish the debt paid tomorrow; he wishes it never to be paid, but always to be a thing where with to corrupt and manage the legislature."

A solution to this impasse arrived when Jefferson invited Hamilton and Madison to dinner. Over good food and wine, Hamilton secured the reluctant Madison's promise to restrain his opposition. In return, Hamilton pledged to back efforts to locate the nation's new capital city in the South, along the Potomac River, an outcome that was sure to please Virginians. In early July 1790, Congress voted for the Potomac site, and in late July Congress passed the debt package, assumption and all.

The First Bank of the United States and the *Report on Manufactures*

The second and third major elements of Hamilton's economic plan were his proposal to create a national Bank of the United States and his program to encourage domestic manufacturing. Arguing that banks were the "nurseries of national wealth," Hamilton modeled his bank plan on European central banks that used their government's money to invigorate the economy. According to Hamilton's plan, the central bank was to be capitalized at $10 million, a sum larger than all the hard money in the entire nation. The federal government would hold 20 percent of the bank's stock, making the bank in effect the government's fiscal agent, holding its revenues derived from import duties, land sales, and various other taxes. The other 80 percent of the bank's capital would come from private investors, who could buy stock in the bank with either hard money (silver or gold) or the recently funded and thus sound federal securities. Because of its size and the privilege of being the only national bank, the central bank would help stabilize the economy by exerting prudent control over credit, interest rates, and the value of the currency.

Concerned that a few rich bankers might have undue influence over the economy, Madison tried but failed to stop the plan in Congress. Jefferson advised President Washington that the Constitution did not permit Congress to charter banks. Hamilton countered that Congress had explicit powers to regulate commerce and a broad mandate "to make all laws which shall be necessary and proper for carrying into execution the foregoing powers." Washington sided with Hamilton and signed the Bank of the United States into law in February 1791, giving it a twenty-year charter.

When the bank's privately held stock went on sale in Philadelphia, Boston, and New York City in July, it sold out in a few hours, touching off a lively period of speculative trading by hundreds of urban merchants and artisans. A discouraged Madison reported that in New York "the Coffee House is an eternal buzz with the gamblers." Wide swings in the stock's price pained Jefferson: "The spirit of gaming, once it has seized a subject, is incurable. The tailor who has made thousands in one day, tho' he has lost them the next, can never again be content with the slow and moderate earnings of his needle."

The third component of Hamilton's plan was issued in December 1791 in the **Report on Manufactures**, a proposal to encourage the production of American-made goods. Domestic manufacturing was in its infancy, and Hamilton aimed to mobilize the new powers of the federal government to grant subsidies to manufacturers and to impose moderate tariffs on those same products from overseas. Hamilton's plan targeted manu-

facturing of iron goods, arms and ammunition, coal, textiles, wood products, and glass. Among the blessings of manufacturing, he counted the new employment opportunities that would open to children and unmarried young women, who he assumed were underutilized in agricultural societies. The *Report on Manufactures*, however, was never approved by Congress, and indeed never even voted on. Many confirmed agriculturalists in Congress feared that manufacturing was a curse rather than a blessing. Madison and Jefferson in particular were alarmed by stretching the "general welfare" clause of the Constitution to include public subsidies to private businesses.

The Whiskey Rebellion

Hamilton's plan to restore public credit required new taxation to pay the interest on the large national debt. In deference to the merchant class, Hamilton did not propose a general increase in import duties, nor did he propose land taxes, which would have fallen hardest on the nation's wealthiest landowners. Instead, he convinced Congress in 1791 to pass a 25 percent excise tax on whiskey, to be paid by farmers bringing grain to the distillery and then passed on to whiskey consumers in higher prices. Members of Congress from eastern states favored the tax—especially New Englanders, where the favorite drink was rum. A New Hampshire representative observed that the country would be "drinking down the national debt," an idea he evidently found acceptable. More seriously, Virginia representative James Madison approved, in the hope that the tax might promote "sobriety and thereby prevent disease and untimely deaths."

Not surprisingly, the new excise tax proved unpopular. In 1791, farmers in Kentucky and the western parts of Pennsylvania, Virginia, Maryland, and the Carolinas forcefully conveyed their resentment to Congress. One farmer complained that he had already paid half his grain to the local distillery for distilling his rye, and now the distiller was taking the new whiskey tax out of the farmer's remaining half. "If this is not an oppressive tax, I am at a loss to describe what is so," the farmer wrote. Congress responded with modest modifications to the tax in 1792, but even so, discontent—along with tax evasion—was rampant. In some places, crowds threatened to tar and feather tax collectors. Four counties in Pennsylvania established committees of correspondence and held rallies. Hamilton admitted to Congress that the revenue was far less than anticipated. But rather than abandon the law, he tightened up the prosecution of tax evaders.

VISUAL ACTIVITY

An Exciseman, 1792

This crude cartoon targets the hated figure of the whiskey tax collector, shown making off with two barrels of the drink. An evil imp hooks him by the nose to deliver him to the gallows, where he is roasted over a flaming barrel of whiskey. © Philadelphia History Museum at the Atwater Kent/Bridgeman Images.

READING THE IMAGE: The words above the two small figures on the right read, "Let us tar and feather the rascal." Are they equipped to carry out that threat? What punishment does the tax collector experience in addition to being hanged, according to the picture on the left?

CONNECTIONS: Why might ordinary citizens have targeted the tax collector? Where else could citizens go to complain about excessive federal taxation?

In western Pennsylvania, Hamilton had one ally, a stubborn tax collector named John Neville, who refused to quit even after a group of spirited farmers burned him in effigy. In May 1794, Neville filed charges against seventy-five farmers and distillers for tax evasion. His action touched off the **Whiskey Rebellion**. In July, he and a federal marshal were ambushed in Allegheny County by a forty-man crowd. Neville's house was then burned down by a crowd of five hundred. At the end of July, seven thousand Pennsylvania farmers planned a march—or perhaps an attack, some thought—on Pittsburgh to protest the tax.

In response, President Washington nationalized the Pennsylvania militia and set out, with Hamilton at his side, at the head of thirteen thousand soldiers. A worried Philadelphia newspaper criticized the show of force: "Shall torrents of blood be spilled to support an odious excise system?" But in the end, no blood was spilled. By the time the army arrived in late September, the demonstrators had dispersed. No battles were fought, and no shots were exchanged. Twenty men were rounded up and charged with high treason, but only two were convicted, and Washington soon pardoned both.

Had the federal government overreacted? Thomas Jefferson thought so; he saw the event as a replay of Shays's Rebellion of 1786, when tax protesters had been met with military force (see "The Requisition of 1785 and Shays's Rebellion, 1786–1787" in chapter 8). The rebel farmers agreed; they felt entitled to protest oppressive taxation. Hamilton and Washington, however, thought that laws passed by a republican government must be obeyed. To them, the Whiskey Rebellion presented an opportunity for the new federal government to flex its muscles and stand up to civil disorder.

REVIEW Why were Hamilton's economic policies controversial?

▶ Conflict on America's Borders and Beyond

While the whiskey rebels challenged federal leadership from within the country, disorder threatened the United States from external sources as well. From 1789 onward, serious trouble brewed in four directions. To the southwest, the loosely confederated Creek Indians pushed back against the westward-moving white southern population, giving George Washington an opportunity to test diplomacy. To the northwest, a powerful confederation of Indian tribes in the Ohio Country fiercely resisted white encroachment, resulting in a brutal war. At the same time, conflicts between the major European powers forced Americans to take sides and nearly pulled the country into another war. And to the south, a Caribbean slave rebellion raised fears that racial war would be imported to the United States. Despite these grave prospects, Washington won reelection to the presidency unanimously in the fall of 1792.

Creeks in the Southwest

An urgent task of the new government was to take charge of Indian affairs while avoiding the costs of warfare. Some twenty thousand Indians affiliated with the Creeks occupied lands extending from Georgia into what is now Mississippi, and border skirmishes with land-hungry Georgians were becoming a frequent occurrence. Washington and his secretary of war, Henry Knox, singled out one Creek chief, Alexander McGillivray, and sent a delegation to Georgia for preliminary treaty negotiations.

McGillivray had a mixed-race history that prepared him to be a major cultural broker. His French-Creek mother conferred a legitimate claim to Creek leadership, while his Scottish fur-trading father provided exposure to literacy and numeracy. Fluent in English and near fluent in Spanish, McGillivray spoke several Creek languages and had even studied Greek and Latin. In the 1770s, he worked for the British distributing gifts to various southern tribes; in the 1780s, he gained renown for brokering negotiations with the Spanish in Florida.

The chief reluctantly met with Knox's delegates and spurned the substantial concessions the American negotiators offered, chief among them a guarantee of the Creeks' extensive tribal lands. McGillivray sent the negotiators away, enjoying, as he wrote to a Spanish trader, the spectacle of the self-styled "masters of the new world" having "to bend and supplicate for peace at the feet of a people whom shortly before they despised."

A year later, Secretary Knox reopened diplomatic relations. To coax McGillivray to the treaty table, Knox invited him to New York City to meet with the president. McGillivray arrived in a triumphal procession of various lesser Creek chiefs and was accorded the honors of a head of state.

The negotiations stretched out for a month, resulting in the 1790 Treaty of New York that looked much like Knox's original plan: Creek tribal lands were guaranteed, with a promise of boundary protection by federal troops against land-seeking settlers. The Creeks were assured of annual payments in money and trade goods, including "domestic animals and implements of husbandry"—words that hinted at a future time when the Creeks would become more agricultural and thus less in need of expansive hunting grounds. The Creeks promised to accept the United States alone as its trading partner, shutting out Spain.

Actually, both sides had made promises they could not keep. McGillivray figured that the Creeks' interests were best served by maintaining creative tension between the American and Spanish authorities, and by 1792 he had signed an agreement with the Spanish governor of New Orleans, in which each side offered mutual pledges to protect against encroachments by Georgia settlers. By the time Alexander McGillivray died in 1793, his purported leadership of the Creeks was in serious question, and the Treaty of New York joined the list of treaties never implemented. Its promise of federal protection of Creek boundaries was unrealistic from the start, and its pledge of full respect for Creek sovereignty also was only a promise on paper.

At the very start of the new government, in dealing with the Creeks, Washington and Knox tried to find a different way to approach Indian affairs, one rooted more in British than in

Alexander McGillivray, 1790
Artist John Trumbull approached the Creek delegation in New York City for treaty negotiations and asked them to sit for individual portraits. They "possessed a dignity of manner, form, countenance and expression, worthy of Roman Senators," Trumbull recalled, but all declined. So the artist made five drawings "by stealth." McGillivray here wears an American military coat, a present from President Washington. The New York Public Library/Art Resource, NY.

American experience. But in the end, the demographic imperative of explosive white population growth and westward-moving, land-seeking settlers, together with the economic imperative of land speculation, meant that confrontation with the native population was nearly inevitable. As Washington wrote in 1796, "I believe scarcely any thing short of a Chinese Wall, or line of Troops will restrain Land Jobbers, and the encroachment of Settlers, upon Indian Territory."

Ohio Indians in the Northwest

Tribes of the Ohio Valley were even less willing to negotiate with the new federal government. Left vulnerable by the 1784 Treaty of Fort Stanwix (see "The Treaty of Fort Stanwix" in chapter 8), in which Iroquois tribes in New York had relinquished Ohio lands to the Americans, the Shawnee, Delaware, Miami, and other groups local to Ohio stood their ground. To confuse matters further, British troops still occupied half a dozen forts in the Northwest, protecting an ongoing fur trade between British traders and Indians and thereby sustaining Indians' claims to that land.

Under the terms of the Northwest Ordinance (see "Land Ordinances and the Northwest Territory" in chapter 8), the federal government started to survey and map eastern Ohio, and settlers were eager to buy. So Washington sent units of the U.S. Army into Ohio's western half to subdue the various tribes. Fort Washington, built on the Ohio River in 1789 at the site of present-day Cincinnati, became the command post for three major invasions of Indian country (Map 9.2). The first occurred in the fall of 1790, when General Josiah Harmar marched with 1,400 men into Ohio's northwest region, burning Indian villages. His inexperienced troops were ambushed by Miami and Shawnee Indians led by their chiefs, Little Turtle and Blue Jacket. Harmar lost one-eighth of his soldiers and retreated.

Harmar's defeat spurred enhanced efforts to clear Ohio for permanent American settlement. General Arthur St. Clair, the military governor of the Northwest Territory, had pursued peaceful tactics in the 1780s, signing treaties with Indians for land in eastern Ohio—dubious treaties, as it happened, since the Indian negotiators were not authorized to yield land. In the wake of Harmar's bungled operation, St. Clair geared up for military action, and in the fall of 1791 he and two thousand men (accompanied by two hundred women camp followers) traveled north from Fort Washington along Harmar's route, erecting two

more fortified structures—Fort Jefferson and Fort Hamilton—deep in Indian country. Despite that show of military might, a surprise attack by Indians at the headwaters of the Wabash River left 55 percent of the Americans dead or wounded; only three of the women escaped alive. "The savages seemed not to fear anything we could do," wrote an officer afterward. "The ground was literally covered with the dead." The Indians captured valuable weaponry and scalped and dismembered the dying on the field of battle. With more than nine hundred lives lost, this was the most stunning American loss in the history of the U.S. Indian wars.

Washington doubled the U.S. military presence in Ohio and appointed a new commander, General Anthony Wayne of Pennsylvania, nicknamed "Mad Anthony" for his headstrong, hard-drinking style of leadership. About the Ohio natives, Wayne wrote, "I have always been of the opinion that we never should have a permanent peace with those Indians until they were made to experience our superiority." Throughout 1794, Wayne's army engaged in skirmishes with various tribes. Chief Little Turtle of the Miami tribe advised negotiation; in his view, Wayne's large army looked overpowering. But Blue Jacket of the Shawnees counseled continued warfare, and his view prevailed.

The decisive action came in August 1794 at the battle of Fallen Timbers, near the Maumee River, where a recent tornado had felled many trees. The confederated Indians—mainly Ottawas, Potawatomis, Shawnees, and Delawares numbering around eight hundred—ambushed the Americans but were underarmed, and Wayne's troops made effective use of their guns and bayonets. The Indians withdrew and sought refuge at nearby Fort Miami, still held by the British, but their former allies locked the gate and refused protection. The surviving Indians fled to the woods, their ranks decimated.

Fallen Timbers was a major defeat for the Indians. The Americans had destroyed cornfields and villages on the march north, and with winter approaching, the Indians' confidence was sapped. They reentered negotiations in a much less powerful bargaining position. In 1795, about a thousand Indians representing nearly a dozen tribes met with Wayne and other American emissaries to work out the **Treaty of Greenville**. The Americans offered treaty goods (calico shirts, axes, knives, blankets, kettles, mirrors, ribbons, thimbles, and abundant wine and liquor casks) worth $25,000 and promised additional shipments

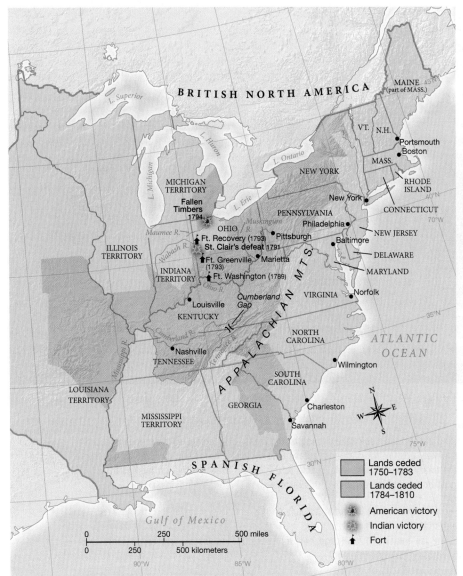

Map 9.2 Western Expansion and Indian Land Cessions to 1810
By the first decade of the nineteenth century, intense Indian wars had resulted in significant cessions of land to the U.S. government by treaty.

READING THE MAP: Locate the Appalachians. The Proclamation Line of 1763 that ran along these mountains forbade colonists to settle west of the line. How well was that purpose met?

CONNECTIONS: How much did the population of the United States grow between 1750 and 1790? How did this growth affect western settlement?

every year. The government's idea was to create a dependency on American goods to keep the Indians friendly. In exchange, the Indians ceded most of Ohio to the Americans; only the northwest part of the territory was reserved solely for the Indians.

The treaty brought temporary peace to the region, but it did not restore a peaceful life to the Indians. The annual allowance from the United States too often came in the form of liquor. "More of us have died since the Treaty of Greenville than we lost by the years of war before, and it is all owing to the introduction of liquor among us," said Chief Little Turtle in 1800. "This liquor

that they introduce into our country is more to be feared than the gun and tomahawk."

France and Britain

While Indian battles engaged the American military in the west, another war overseas to the east was also closely watched. In 1789, monarchy came under attack in France, bringing on a revolution whose democratic ideals inspired Americans in many states to celebrate the victory of the French people. Dozens of pro-French political clubs, called Democratic or Republican Societies, sprang up around the country. Even fashions

VISUAL ACTIVITY

Treaty of Greenville, 1795

This contemporary painting purports to depict the signing of the Treaty of Greenville. An American officer kneels and writes—not a likely posture for drafting a treaty. One Indian gestures emphatically as if to dictate terms, but in fact the treaty was completely favorable to the United States. Although Indians from a dozen Ohio tribes gathered at the signing ceremony, this picture shows very few Indians. © Chicago History Museum, USA/Bridgeman Images.

READING THE IMAGE: How likely is it that the artist actually witnessed the signing of the treaty? Are there clues in the painting that offer evidence?

CONNECTIONS: How did the Jay Treaty of 1795 (page 241) influence the Indians' willingness to capitulate to an unfavorable treaty with the U.S. government?

expressed symbolic solidarity, causing some American women to don sashes and cockades made with ribbons of the French Revolution's red, white, and blue colors. Pro-French headgear for committed women included an elaborate turban, leading one horrified Federalist newspaper editor to chastise the "fiery frenchified dames" thronging Philadelphia's streets. In Charleston, South Carolina, a pro-French pageant in 1793 united two women as partners, one representing France and the other America. The women repudiated their husbands "on account of ill treatment" and "conceived the design of living together in the strictest union and friendship." Most likely, this ceremony was not the country's first same-sex marriage but instead a richly metaphorical piece of street theater in which the spurned husbands represented the French and British monarchs. In addition to these symbolic actions, the growing exchange of political and intellectual ideas across the Atlantic helped plant the seeds of a woman's rights movement in America. (See "Beyond America's Borders," page 244.)

Anti–French Revolution sentiments also ran deep. Vice President John Adams, who lived in France in the 1780s, trembled to think of radicals in France or America. "Too many Frenchmen, after the example of too many Americans, pant for the equality of persons and property," Adams said. "The impracticability of this, God Almighty has decreed, and the advocates for liberty, who attempt it, will surely suffer for it."

Support for the French Revolution remained a matter of personal conviction until 1793, when Britain and France went to war and divided loyalties now framed critical foreign policy debates. Pro-French Americans remembered France's critical help during the American Revolution

and wanted to offer aid now. But those shaken by the report of the guillotining of thousands of French people—including the monarch—as well as those with strong commercial ties to Britain sought ways to stay neutral.

In May 1793, President Washington issued the Neutrality Proclamation, which contained friendly assurances to both sides, in an effort to stay out of European wars. Yet American ships continued to trade between the French West Indies and France. In early 1794, the British expressed their displeasure by capturing more than three hundred of these vessels near the West Indies. Clearly, the president thought, something had to be done to assert American power.

Washington tapped John Jay, the chief justice of the Supreme Court and a man of strong pro-British sentiments, to negotiate commercial relations in the British West Indies and secure compensation for the seized American ships. Jay was also directed to address southerners' demands for reimbursement for the slaves evacuated by the British during the war as well as western settlers' demands to end the British occupation of frontier forts and their continuing involvement in the northwest fur trade.

Jay returned from his diplomatic mission with a treaty that no one could love. First, the **Jay Treaty** completely failed to address the captured cargoes or the lost property in slaves. Second, it granted the British a lenient eighteen months to withdraw from the frontier forts. (Despite that leniency, this provision projecting the end of British presence in the Northwest disheartened the Indians negotiating the Treaty of Greenville in Ohio and loomed as a significant factor in their decision to make peace.) Finally, the treaty called for repayment with interest of the debts that some American planters still owed to British firms dating from the Revolutionary War. In exchange for such generous terms, Jay secured limited trading rights in the West Indies and agreement that some issues—boundary disputes with Canada and the damage and loss claims of shipowners—would be decided later by arbitration commissions.

When newspapers published the terms of the treaty, powerful opposition quickly emerged. Citizens' petitions, newspaper editorials, and public gatherings mobilized public opinion from North to South to a degree not seen before in the early Republic. The debate raised the question of whether citizens could presume to instruct elected officials, or whether they had to accept the judgment of those officials and await the next election to register their displeasure. The negative reactions got ugly. In Massachusetts, disrespectful graffiti ("Damn John Jay!") appeared on walls, and effigies of Jay along with copies of the treaty were ceremoniously burned in noisy street demonstrations. When the Senate passed the treaty in mid-1795 by a vote of 20 to 10, a bare minimum of the two-thirds majority required, and the president signed it, the anti-Treaty opposition among many ordinary citizens refused to evaporate.

The controversy continued well into 1796. Opponents of the Jay Treaty in the House of Representatives called for hearings on the matter, demanding that the president disclose secret diplomatic documents. Washington refused. The House lacked constitutional authority to vote on treaties, but it did have primary power over all spending bills. Anti–Jay Treaty congressmen hoped to hamstring the hated agreement by defunding its key provisions. In the end, the final vote on appropriations for the treaty passed, but only by a 3-vote margin.

The year long struggle over the Jay Treaty revealed an emerging and as yet uncharted role in politics for public opinion, voiced by an aroused citizenry and frequently managed and shaped by newspaper editors and local political clubs. It also brought to the fore a bitter division among elected politicians that emerged along the same lines as the Hamilton-Jefferson split on economic policy.

The Haitian Revolution

In addition to the Indian troubles and the European war across the Atlantic, another bloody conflict to the south polarized and even terrorized many Americans in the 1790s. The French colony of Saint Domingue, in the western third of the large Caribbean island of Hispaniola, became engulfed in revolution starting in 1791. Bloody war raged for more than a decade, resulting in 1804 in the birth of the Republic of Haiti, the first and only independent black state to arise out of a successful slave revolution.

The **Haitian Revolution** was a complex event involving many participants, including the diverse local population and, eventually, three European countries. Some 30,000 whites dominated the island in 1790, running sugar and coffee plantations with close to half a million blacks, two-thirds

of them of African birth. The white French colonists were not the only plantation owners, however. About 28,000 free mixed-race people (*gens de couleur*) owned one-third of the island's plantations and nearly a quarter of the slave labor force. Despite their economic status, these mixed-race planters were barred from political power, but they aspired to it.

The French Revolution of 1789 was the immediate catalyst for rebellion in this already tense society. First, white colonists challenged the white royalist government in an effort to link Saint Domingue with the new revolutionary government in France. Next, the mixed-race planters rebelled in 1791, demanding equal civil rights with the whites. No sooner was this revolt viciously suppressed than another part of the island's population rose up; thousands of slaves armed with machetes and torches wreaked devastation. In 1793, the civil war escalated to include French, Spanish, and British troops fighting the inhabitants and also one another. Led by former slave Toussaint L'Ouverture, slaves and free blacks in alliance with Spain occupied the northern regions of the island, leaving a thousand plantations in ruins and tens of thousands of people dead. Thousands of white and mixed-race planters, along with some of their slaves, fled to Spanish Louisiana and southern cities in the United States.

White Americans followed the revolution in horror through newspapers and refugees' accounts. A few sympathized with the impulse for liberty, but many more feared that violent black insurrection might spread to the United States. Many black American slaves also followed the revolution, for the news of the success of a first-ever massive revolution by slaves traveled quickly in this oral culture.

The Haitian Revolution provoked naked fear of a race war in white southerners. Jefferson, agonizing over the contagion of liberty in 1797, wrote another Virginia slaveholder that "if something is not done, and soon done, we shall be the murderers of our own children . . . ; the revolutionary storm, now sweeping the globe, will be upon us, and happy if we make timely provision to give it an easy passage over our

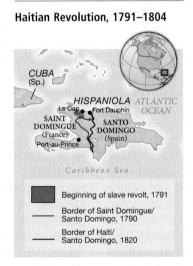

Haitian Revolution, 1791–1804

- Beginning of slave revolt, 1791
- Border of Saint Domingue/ Santo Domingo, 1790
- Border of Haiti/ Santo Domingo, 1820

Toussaint L'Ouverture
Numbers of lithographs and paintings depicted Toussaint L'Ouverture in styles and poses familiar to those of venerated European military leaders. In this image, he looks very much like a black version of Napoleon, a young and successful general who became emperor of France in 1804. The New York Public Library/Art Resource, NY.

land. From the present state of things in Europe and America, the day which brings our combustion must be near at hand; and only a single spark is wanting to make that day to-morrow."

Jefferson's cataclysmic fears were not shared by New Englanders. Timothy Pickering of Massachusetts, in Washington's cabinet since 1795, chastised the inconsistent Jefferson for supporting French revolutionaries while condemning black Haitians fighting for freedom just because they had "a skin not colored like our own." Not that Pickering supported either type of violent revolutionary—he did not. But he and his political allies, soon to be called the Federalists, were far more willing to contemplate trade and diplomatic relations with the emerging black republic of Haiti.

REVIEW   Why did the United States feel vulnerable to international threats in the 1790s?

▶ Federalists and Republicans

By the mid-1790s, polarization over Hamilton's economic program, the French Revolution, Haiti, and most crucially the Jay Treaty had led to two distinct and consistent rival political groups: **Federalists** and **Republicans**. Federalist leaders supported Britain in foreign policy and commercial interests at home, while Republicans rooted for liberty in France and worried about monarchical Federalists at home. The labels did not yet describe full-fledged political parties; such division was still thought to be a sign of failure of the experiment in government. Yet newspapers increasingly backed one group or the other; party lines were being drawn. Washington's decision not to seek a third term led to serious partisan electioneering in the presidential and congressional elections of 1796. Federalist John Adams won the presidency, but party strife accelerated over failed

France, Britain, and Woman's Rights in the 1790s

During the 1770s and 1780s, no one in America wondered publicly about rights for women. Boycotts by the Daughters of Liberty before the Revolution did not challenge gender hierarchy, nor did New Jersey's handful of women voters (see "Who Are 'the People'?" in chapter 8). It took radical ideas from France and Britain to spark new ideas challenging women's subordinate status in American society.

In France between 1789 and 1793, the revolution against monarchy enlarged ideas about citizenship and led some women to call themselves *citoyennes*, female citizens. Women's political clubs, such as the Society of Republican Revolutionary Women in Paris, sent petitions and gave speeches to the National Assembly, demanding education, voting rights, and a curbing of patriarchal powers of men over women. In 1791, Frenchwoman Olympe de Gouges rewrote the male revolutionaries' document *The Declaration of the Rights of Man* into the *Declaration of the Rights of Woman and the Female Citizen*, a manifesto asserting that "all women are born free and remain equal to men in rights." Another prominent woman, Anne Josèphe Théroigne de Méricourt, maintained a political salon (intellectual gathering),

marched around Paris in masculine riding attire, and addressed crowds engaged in violent street actions. Her vision went beyond political rights to the social customs that dictated women's subordination: "It is time for women to break out of the shameful incompetence in which men's ignorance, pride, and injustice have so long held us captive."

Although the male National Assembly never approved voting rights for French women in that era, it did reform French civil and family law in the early 1790s. Marriage was removed from the control of the church, divorce was legalized, and the age of majority for women (when females qualified as adults) was lowered. A far-reaching change in inheritance law required division of a patriarch's estate among all his children, regardless of age, sex, and even legitimacy. By contrast, most American states adopted traditional English family law virtually unchanged.

French feminism traveled across the Channel to Britain and inspired the talented Mary Wollstonecraft. Born into a respectable but downwardly mobile family, Wollstonecraft took work as a governess before establishing herself as a writer in London. There she met the radical Thomas Paine and the philosopher

William Godwin, along with other leading artists and intellectuals. In 1792, she published *A Vindication of the Rights of Woman*, offering a contrast to Paine's 1791 book *The Rights of Man*. Paine wrote about property and politics as fundamental rights and never considered women; Wollstonecraft argued that women also had inherent rights. She spoke forcefully about the intellectual equality of the sexes that would become evident once women could get an equal education. She championed female economic independence and, most radically, suggested that traditional marriage at its worst was legalized prostitution.

Wollstonecraft's book created an immediate sensation in America. Excerpts appeared in periodicals, bookstores stocked the London edition, and by 1795 there were three American reprints. Some women readers were cautious. A sixty-year-old Philadelphian, Elizabeth Drinker, reflected in her diary that Wollstonecraft "speaks my mind" on some issues but not others; "I am not for quite so much independence." A youthful Priscilla Mason delivered a commencement address at her academy, inspired by Wollstonecraft to condemn "the high and mighty lords" (men) who denied women education and professional opportunities. "Happily, a more

diplomacy in France, bringing the country to the brink of war. Pro-war and antiwar antagonism created a major crisis over political free speech, militarism, and fears of sedition and treason.

The Election of 1796

Washington struggled to appear to be above party politics, and in his farewell address he stressed the need to maintain a "unity of government" reflecting a unified body politic. He also urged the country to "steer clear of permanent alliances with any portion of the foreign world." The leading contenders for his position, John Adams of Massachusetts and Thomas Jefferson of Virginia, in theory agreed with him, but around them raged a party contest split along pro-British versus pro-French lines.

FRONTISPIECE.

Publish'd at Philadª Decʳ 1ˢᵗ 1792.

The interest in the rights of woman faded fast, however. The unhappy fate of de Gouges, guillotined in France in 1794, was soon followed by news of Wollstonecraft's death in childbirth in 1797. Soon thereafter, William Godwin, father of her infant daughter, published details of her unconventional personal life: love affairs, two children conceived out of wedlock, and two suicide attempts. "Her licentious practice renders her memory odious to every friend of virtue," declared a prominent American minister in 1801, shutting down nearly all possibility for continued public admiration of Wollstonecraft and her ideas about women.

Questions for Analysis

Summarize the Argument: How do the radical ideas of Mary Wollstonecraft contrast with the more moderate concept of "republican motherhood," which sums up the expectations for American women's contributions to civil society and family life?

Recognize Viewpoints: Why might some have believed that Wollstonecraft's unconventional personal life cast doubt on the value of her ideas about the rights of woman?

Ask Historical Questions: How did the struggle for woman's rights reflect the struggle to define the new American nation?

liberal way of thinking begins to prevail," Mason predicted.

Male readers' responses were also varied. Aaron Burr, a senator from New York, called Wollstonecraft's book "a work of genius." A Fourth of July speaker in New Jersey in 1793 proclaimed that "the Rights of Woman are no longer strange sounds to an American ear" and called for revisions in state law codes. Critics of Wollstonecraft were not in short supply. A New York orator on that same July Fourth rejected Wollstonecraft with the claim that woman's rights really meant a woman's duty "to submit to the control of that government she has voluntarily chosen"—namely, the government of a husband.

Adams and Jefferson were not adept politicians in the modern sense, skilled in the arts of persuasion and intrigue. Bruised by his conflicts with Hamilton, Jefferson had resigned as secretary of state in 1793 and retreated to Monticello, his home in Virginia. Adams's job as vice president kept him closer to the political action, but his personality often put people off. He was temperamental, thin-skinned, and quick to take offense.

The leading Federalists informally caucused and chose Adams as their candidate, with Thomas Pinckney of South Carolina to run with him. The Republicans in Congress settled on Aaron Burr of New York to pair with Jefferson. The Constitution did not anticipate parties and tickets. Instead, each electoral college voter could cast two votes for any two candidates, but on only one ballot. The top

John and Abigail Adams
The artist Gilbert Stuart painted these portraits in 1800; Adams was sixty-five and his wife was fifty-six. A friend once listed Adams's shortcomings as a politician: "He can't dance, drink, game, flatter, promise, dress, swear with gentlemen, and small talk and flirt with the ladies." But luckily, Adams had a secret weapon to keep him resilient: Abigail, his wife, a woman of astute intellect and wisdom. National Gallery of Art, Washington, D.C. Gift of Mrs. Robert Homans.

vote-getter became president, and the next-highest assumed the vice presidency. (This procedural flaw was corrected by the Twelfth Amendment, adopted in 1804.) With only one ballot, careful maneuvering was required to make sure that the chief rivals for the presidency did not land in the top two spots.

A failed effort by Alexander Hamilton to influence the outcome of the election landed the country in just such a position. Hamilton did not trust Adams; he preferred Pinckney, and he tried to influence southern electors to throw their support to the South Carolinian. But his plan backfired: Adams was elected president with 71 electoral votes; Jefferson came in second with 68 and thus became vice president. Pinckney got 59 votes, while Burr trailed with 30.

Adams's inaugural speech pledged neutrality in foreign affairs and respect for the French people, which made Republicans hopeful. To please Federalists, Adams retained three cabinet members from Washington's administration— the secretaries of state, treasury, and war. But the three were Hamilton loyalists, passing off Hamilton's judgments and advice as their own to the unwitting Adams. Vice President Jefferson extended a conciliatory hand to Adams, but the Hamiltonian cabinet ruined the honeymoon. Jefferson's advice was spurned, and he withdrew from active counsel of the president.

The XYZ Affair

From the start, Adams's presidency was in crisis. France retaliated for the British-friendly Jay Treaty by abandoning its 1778 alliance with the United States. French privateers—armed private vessels—started detaining American ships carrying British goods; by March 1797, more than three hundred American vessels had been seized. To avenge these insults, Federalists started murmuring openly about war with France. Adams preferred negotiations and dispatched a three-man commission to France in the fall of 1797. But at the same time, he asked Congress to approve expenditures on increased naval defense.

When the three American commissioners arrived in Paris, French officials would not receive them. Finally, the French minister of foreign affairs, Talleyrand, sent three French agents—unnamed and later known to the American public as X, Y, and Z—to the American commissioners with the information that $250,000 might grease the wheels of diplomacy and that a $12 million loan to the French government would be the price of a peace treaty. Incensed, the commissioners brought news of the bribery attempt to the president.

Americans reacted to the **XYZ affair** with shock and anger. Even staunch pro-French

Republicans began to reevaluate their allegiance. The Federalist-dominated Congress appropriated money for an army of ten thousand soldiers and repealed all prior treaties with France. In 1798, twenty naval warships launched the United States into its first undeclared war, called the Quasi-War by historians to underscore its uncertain legal status. The main scene of action was the Caribbean, where more than one hundred French ships were captured.

There was no home-front unity in this time of undeclared war; antagonism only intensified between Federalists and Republicans. Because the chance of a land invasion by France seemed remote, some Republicans began to fear that the Federalists wanted that enlarged army to threaten domestic dissenters. Adams's cabinet strenuously backed the army buildup, making the president increasingly mistrustful of their advice. He was beginning to suspect that his cabinet was more loyal to Hamilton than to himself.

Party antagonism in the realm of public opinion spiraled out of control. Republican newspapers heaped abuse on Adams. One denounced him as "a person without patriotism, without philosophy, and a mock monarch." Pro-French mobs roamed the streets of Philadelphia, the capital, and Adams, fearing for his personal safety, stocked weapons in his presidential quarters. Federalists, too, went on the offensive. In Newburyport, Massachusetts, they lit a huge bonfire and burned issues of the state's Republican newspapers. Officers in a New York militia unit drank a menacing toast on July 4, 1798: "One and but one party in the United States." A Federalist editor ominously declared that "he who is not for us is against us."

The Alien and Sedition Acts

With tempers so dangerously high and fears that political dissent was akin to treason, Federalist leaders moved to muffle the opposition. In mid-1798, Congress passed the Sedition Act, which not only made conspiracy and revolt illegal but also criminalized any speech or words that defamed the president or Congress. One Federalist warned of the threat that existed "to overturn and ruin the government by publishing the most shameless falsehoods against the representatives of the people." In all, twenty-five men, almost all Republican newspaper editors, were charged with sedition; twelve were convicted. (See "Analyzing Historical Evidence," page 248.)

Congress also passed two Alien Acts. The first extended the waiting period for an alien to achieve citizenship from five to fourteen years and required all aliens to register with the federal government. The second empowered the president in time of war to deport or imprison without trial any foreigner suspected of being a danger to the United States. The clear intent of these laws was to harass French immigrants already in the United States and to discourage others from coming.

Republicans strongly opposed the **Alien and Sedition Acts** on the grounds that the acts conflicted with the Bill of Rights, but they did not have the votes to revoke the acts in Congress, nor could the federal judiciary, dominated by Federalist judges, be counted on to challenge them. Jefferson and Madison turned to the state legislatures, the only other competing political arena, to press their opposition. Each man anonymously drafted a set of resolutions condemning the acts and convinced the legislatures of Virginia and Kentucky to present them to the federal government in late fall 1798. The **Virginia and Kentucky Resolutions** tested the novel argument that state legislatures have the right to judge and even nullify the constitutionality of federal laws, bold claims that held risk that one or both men could be accused of sedition. The resolutions in fact made little dent in the Alien and Sedition Acts, but the idea of a state's right to nullify federal law did not disappear. It would resurface several times in decades to come, most notably in a major tariff dispute in 1832 and in the sectional arguments that led to the Civil War.

Amid all the war hysteria and sedition fears in 1798, President Adams regained his balance. He was uncharacteristically restrained in pursuing opponents under the Sedition Act, and he finally refused to declare war on France, as extreme Federalists wished. No doubt he was beginning to realize how much he had been the dupe of Hamilton. He also shrewdly realized that France was not eager for war and that a peaceful settlement might be close at hand. In January 1799, a peace initiative from France arrived in the form of a letter assuring Adams that diplomatic channels were open again and that new peace commissioners would be welcomed in France. Adams accepted this overture and appointed new negotiators. By late 1799, the Quasi-War with

The Crisis of 1798: Sedition

Republican newspaper editors criticized President John Adams with such venomous insults that civil war appeared possible. Federalists in Congress thus criminalized seditious words as a means to preserve the country. Republicans just redoubled their opposition.

DOCUMENT 1
Abigail Adams Complains of Sedition, 1798

A beleaguered Abigail Adams called repeatedly in letters to her sister for a sedition law to silence Benjamin Bache, editor of the Philadelphia Aurora.

(April 26): . . . Yet dairingly do the vile incendaries keep up in Baches paper the most wicked and base, voilent & caluminiating abuse. . . . But nothing will have an Effect until congress pass a Sedition Bill. . . . (April 28): . . . We are now wonderfully popular except with Bache & Co who in his paper calls the President old, querilous, Bald, blind, cripled, Toothless Adams. . . . (May 10): . . . This Bache is cursing & abusing daily. If that fellow . . . is not surpressd, we shall come to a civil war. . . . (May 26): . . . I wish the Laws of our Country were competant to punish the stirer up of sedition, the writer and Printer of base and unfounded calumny. . . . (June 19): . . . In any other Country Bache & all his papers would have been seazd and ought to be here, but congress are dilly dallying about passing a Bill enabling the President to seize suspisious persons, and their papers.

Source: Excerpts from *New Letters of Abigail Adams, 1788–1801*, edited by Stewart Mitchell. Copyright © 1947 by The American Antiquarian Society. Copyright © renewed 1974 by The American Antiquarian Society. Reprinted by permission of Houghton Mifflin Harcourt Publishing Company. All rights reserved.

DOCUMENT 2
The Sedition Act of 1798

On July 14, Congress made sedition with malicious intent a federal crime.

SECTION 1. . . . if any persons shall unlawfully combine or conspire together, with intent to oppose any measure or measures of the government of the United States . . . , or to intimidate or prevent any person holding . . . office in or under the government of the United States, from undertaking, performing or executing his trust or duty, and if any person or persons, with intent as aforesaid, shall counsel, advise or attempt to procure any insurrection, riot, unlawful assembly. . . , he or they shall be deemed guilty of a high misdemeanor, and on conviction . . . shall be punished by a fine not exceeding five thousand dollars, and by imprisonment during a term not less than six months nor exceeding five years. . . .

SEC. 2. . . . If any person shall write, print, utter or publish . . . , any false, scandalous and malicious writing or writings against the government of the United States, or either house of the Congress of the United States, or the President of the United States, with intent to defame the said government . . . or to bring them . . . into contempt or disrepute; or to excite against them . . . the hatred of the good people of the United States . . . , then such person, being thereof convicted . . . shall be punished by a fine not exceeding two thousand dollars, and by imprisonment not exceeding two years.

Source: Excerpted text from congressional bill, July 14, 1798.

DOCUMENT 3
Matthew Lyon Criticizes John Adams, 1798

Matthew Lyon, congressman from Vermont, criticized Adams and was charged with sedition. Handed a four-

France had subsided, and in 1800 the negotiations resulted in a treaty declaring "a true and sincere friendship" between the United States and France. But he had made enemies inside his own party.

Still, he won candidacy for the 1800 election, handpicked by a small set of Adams loyalists. Adams's Republican opponent was Thomas Jefferson. Faced with this choice, Hamilton supported Jefferson, but without enthusiasm: "If we must have an enemy at the head of government, let it be one whom we can oppose, and for whom we are not responsible."

month sentence and a fine of $1,000, Lyon ran for reelection from his cell—and won.

. . . Whenever I shall, on the part of the Executive, see every consideration of the public welfare swallowed up in a continual grasp for power, in an unbounded thirst for ridiculous pomp, foolish adulation, or selfish avarice; when I shall behold men of real merit daily turned out of office for no other cause but independence of sentiment; when I shall see men of firmness, merit, years, abilities, and experience, discarded on their application for office, for fear they possess that independence; . . . when I shall see the sacred name of religion employed as a State engine to make mankind hate and persecute one another, I shall not be their humble advocate.

Source: Matthew Lyon, Letter in *Spooner's Vermont Journal*, July 31, 1798, pp. 1–2. Courtesy, American Antiquarian Society.

DOCUMENT 4
The Virginia Resolution, December 24, 1798

James Madison drafted the Virginia Resolution and had a trusted ally present it to the Virginia legislature, dominated by Republicans. (Jefferson did the same for Kentucky.) The document denounces the Alien and Sedition Acts and declares that states have the right to "interpose" to stop unconstitutional actions by the federal government.

RESOLVED . . . That this assembly most solemnly declares a warm attachment to the Union of the States, to maintain which it pledges all its powers; and that for this end, it is their duty to watch over and oppose every infraction of those principles which constitute the only basis of that Union, because a faithful observance of them, can alone secure its existence and the public happiness.

That this Assembly doth explicitly and peremptorily declare, that it views the powers of the federal government, as resulting from the compact, to which the states are parties; as limited by the plain sense and intention of the instrument constituting the compact; . . . and that

in case of a deliberate, palpable, and dangerous exercise of other powers, not granted by the said compact, the states who are parties thereto, have the right, and are in duty bound, to interpose for arresting the progress of the evil, and for maintaining within their respective limits, the authorities, rights and liberties appertaining to them. . . .

That the General Assembly doth particularly protest against the palpable and alarming infractions of the Constitution, in the two late cases of the "Alien and Sedition Acts" . . . ; the first of which exercises a power no where delegated to the federal government . . . ; and the other . . . exercises in like manner, a power not delegated by the constitution, but on the contrary, expressly and positively forbidden by one of the amendments thereto; a power, which more than any other, ought to produce universal alarm, because it is levelled against that right of freely examining public characters and measures, and of free communication among the people thereon, which has ever been justly deemed, the only effectual guardian of every other right.

Source: Avalon Project, Yale Law School, 1996. http://www.yale .edu. © 1996–2007 The Avalon Project at Yale Law School.

Questions for Analysis

Analyze the Evidence: Why did the Federalists believe that the Sedition Act was necessary? What exactly was the threat, according to Abigail Adams? What threat is implied by the wording of the act?

Recognize Viewpoints: Does Matthew Lyon's criticism of President Adams rise to the level of threat that the Federalists feared? How do you explain Lyon's guilty verdict? His reelection to Congress?

Ask Historical Questions: What political or personal issues created the deep polarization between Federalists and Republicans that led to the Alien and Sedition Acts?

When the election was finally over, President Jefferson mounted the inaugural platform to announce, "We are all republicans, we are all federalists," an appealing rhetoric of harmony appropriate to an inaugural address. But his formulation perpetuated a denial of the validity of party politics, a denial that ran

deep in the founding generation of political leaders.

REVIEW   How did war between Britain and France intensify the political divisions in the United States?

VISUAL ACTIVITY

Cartoon of the Lyon-Griswold Fight in Congress

Political tensions ran high in 1798. On the floor of Congress, Federalist Roger Griswold called Republican Matthew Lyon a coward. Lyon responded with some well-aimed spit, the first departure from the gentleman's code of honor. Griswold raised his cane to strike Lyon, whereupon Lyon grabbed fire tongs to defend himself. Madison later commented that the two should have dueled, the honorable way to avenge insults. Library of Congress, 3a05342.

READING THE IMAGE: Can you tell which figure is Lyon and which is Griswold? How? How do the other members of Congress react to the brawl, in this satirical cartoon? Are their reactions realistic?

CONNECTIONS: What, if anything, did this fight in Congress have to do with the rise of the Federalist and Republican political parties?

▶ Conclusion: Parties Nonetheless

American political leaders began operating the new government in 1789 with great hopes of unifying the country and overcoming selfish factionalism. The enormous trust in President Washington was the central foundation for those hopes, and Washington did not disappoint, becoming a model Mr. President with a blend of integrity and authority. Stability was further aided by easy passage of the Bill of Rights (to appease Antifederalists) and by attention to cultivating a virtuous citizenry

of upright men supported and rewarded by republican womanhood. Yet the hopes of the honeymoon period soon turned to worries and then fears as major political disagreements flared up.

At the core of the conflict was a group of talented men—Hamilton, Madison, Jefferson, and Adams—so recently allies but now opponents. They diverged over Hamilton's economic program, over relations with the British and the Jay Treaty, over the French and Haitian revolutions, and over preparedness for war abroad and free speech at home. Hamilton was perhaps the driving force in these conflicts, but the antagonism was not about mere personality. Parties were taking shape not around individuals, but around principles, such as ideas about what constituted enlightened leadership, how powerful the federal government should be, who was the best ally in Europe, and when oppositional political speech turned into treason.

In his inaugural address of 1800, Jefferson offered his conciliatory assurance that Americans were at the same time "all republicans" and "all federalists," suggesting that both groups shared two basic ideas—the value of republican government, in which power derived from the people, and the value of the unique federal system of shared governance structured by the Constitution. But by 1800, *Federalist* and *Republican* defined competing philosophies of government. To at least some of his listeners, Jefferson's assertion of harmony across budding party lines could only have seemed bizarre. For the next two decades, these two groups would battle each other, each fearing that the success of the other might bring about the demise of the country.

See the Selected Bibliography for this chapter in the Appendix.

9 Chapter Review

KEY TERMS

Bill of Rights (p. 228)
Report on Public Credit (p. 233)
Report on Manufactures (p. 235)
Whiskey Rebellion (p. 236)
Treaty of Greenville (p. 238)
Jay Treaty (p. 241)
Haitian Revolution (p. 242)
Federalists (p. 243)
Republicans (p. 243)
XYZ affair (p. 246)
Alien and Sedition Acts (p. 247)
Virginia and Kentucky Resolutions (p. 247)

REVIEW QUESTIONS

1. How did political leaders in the 1790s attempt to overcome the divisions of the 1780s? (pp. 227–231)

2. Why were Hamilton's economic policies controversial? (pp. 232–236)

3. Why did the United States feel vulnerable to international threats in the 1790s? (pp. 236–243)

4. How did war between Britain and France intensify the political divisions in the United States? (pp. 243–249)

MAKING CONNECTIONS

1. Why did the Federalist alliance of the late 1780s fracture in the 1790s? Why was this development troubling to the nation? In your answer, cite specific ideological and political developments that hindered cooperation.

2. What provoked the Whiskey Rebellion? How did the government respond? In your answer, discuss the foundations and precedents of the conflict, as well as the significance of the government's response.

3. Americans held that virtue was pivotal to the success of their new nation. What did they mean by *virtue*? How did they hope to ensure that their citizens and their leaders possessed virtue?

4. The domestic politics of the new nation were profoundly influenced by conflicts beyond the nation's borders. Discuss how conflicts abroad contributed to domestic political developments in the 1790s.

LINKING TO THE PAST

1. Americans fought against the French in the Seven Years' War but welcomed them as allies during the Revolutionary War. Did either or both of those earlier experiences with France have any bearing on the sharp division in the 1790s between pro-French and anti-French political leaders in the United States? (See chapters 6 and 7.)

2. Shays's Rebellion appeared to some in 1786 to underscore the need for a stronger national government. Compare the Whiskey Rebellion to Shays's Rebellion. How were they similar, and how were they different? Did the Constitution of 1787 make a difference in the authorities' response to rebellion? (See chapter 8.)

10 Republicans in Power

1800–1824

CONTENT LEARNING OBJECTIVES

After reading and studying this chapter, you should be able to:

• Explain Thomas Jefferson's vision for the United States. Understand how the election of 1800 might be considered a "revolution." Identify the challenges and opportunities that Thomas Jefferson faced once in office.

• Explore the challenges and opportunities that James Madison faced once in office.

• Understand why the United States declared war on Britain in 1812 and identify the major turning points of the war.

• Recognize how the status of white women changed in the early Republic.

• Define the Missouri Compromise and its implications for the future direction of the country.

PATRIOTIC PITCHER, 1800
On this everyday pitcher, a militia officer poses near a cannon, the scene encircled by a toast: "Success to America whose Militia Is better than standing Armies." However, the nation's military preparedness was, in fact, woefully poor in 1800. Kahn Fine Antiques/photo courtesy of Antiques and Fine Arts.

THE NAME TECUMSEH TRANSLATES AS "SHOOTING STAR," A
fitting name for the Shawnee chief who reached meteoric heights of fame among Indians during Thomas Jefferson's presidency. From Canada to Georgia, Tecumseh was by all accounts a charismatic leader. Graceful, eloquent, compelling, astute: Tecumseh was all these and more, a gifted natural commander, equal parts politician and warrior.

The Ohio Country, where Tecumseh was born in 1768, was home to some dozen Indian tribes. During the Revolutionary War, the region became a battleground, and Tecumseh lost his father and two brothers to American fighters. The Revolution's end in 1783 brought no peace to Indian country. The youthful Tecumseh fought at the battle of Fallen Timbers, a major Indian defeat, and stood by as eight treaties ceded much of Ohio to the Americans between 1795 and 1805.

Some resigned Indians looked for ways to accommodate, taking up farming, trade, and intermarriage with white settlers. Others spent their treaty payments on alcohol. Tecumseh's younger brother Tenskwatawa led an embittered life of idleness and drink. But Tecumseh rejected accommodation and instead campaigned for a return to ancient ways. Donning traditional animal-skin clothing, he traveled around the Great Lakes region persuading tribes to join his pan-Indian confederacy. The territorial governor of Indiana, William Henry Harrison, admired and feared Tecumseh, calling him "one of those uncommon geniuses which spring up occasionally to produce revolutions."

Even Tecumseh's dissolute brother was born anew. After a near-death experience in 1805, Tenskwatawa revived and recounted a startling vision of meeting the Master of Life. Renaming himself the Prophet, he urged his many Indian followers to regard whites as children of the Evil Spirit, destined to be destroyed.

President Thomas Jefferson worried about an organized Indian confederacy and its potential for a renewed alliance with the British in Canada. Those worries became a reality during Jefferson's second term in office (1805–1809). Although his first term (1801–1805) brought notable successes, such as the Louisiana Purchase and the Lewis and Clark expedition, his second term was consumed by the threat of war with either Britain or France, in a replay of the late-1790s tensions. When war came in 1812, the enemy was Britain, bolstered by a reenergized Indian-British alliance manifested in battles along the Canadian-U.S. border. Among the causes of the war were insults over international shipping rights and the capture of U.S. vessels, along with unresolved tensions with Indians in the Northwest and Southwest.

In the end, the War of 1812 settled little between the United States and Britain, but it was tragically conclusive for the Indians. Eight hundred warriors led by Tecumseh helped defend Canada against U.S. attacks, but the British did not reciprocate when the Indians were under threat. Tecumseh died on a Canadian battlefield in the fall of 1813. No Indian leader with his star power would emerge again east of the Mississippi.

Tecumseh's briefly unified Indian confederacy had no counterpart in the young Republic's confederation of states, where widespread unity behind a single leader proved impossible to achieve. Republicans did battle with Federalists during the Jefferson and Madison administrations, but then Federalists doomed their party by opposing the War of 1812. The next two presidents, James Monroe and John Quincy Adams, congratulated themselves on the Federalists' demise and Republican unity, but in fact divisions within their own party were extensive. Wives of politicians increasingly inserted themselves into this dissonant mix, managing their husbands' politicking and enabling them to appear above the fray and maintain the fiction of a nonpartisan state. That it was a fiction became sharply apparent in the most serious political crisis of this period, the Missouri Compromise of 1820.

Tecumseh
This 1848 engraving was adapted from an earlier drawing of Tecumseh made in a live sitting by a French fur trader in 1808. The engraver has given Tecumseh a British army officer's uniform, showing that he fought on the British side in the War of 1812. Notice the head covering and the medallion around Tecumseh's neck, marking his Indian identity. Private Collection/Peter Newark Pictures/Bridgeman Images.

► Jefferson's Presidency

The first presidential election of the new century was an all-out partisan battle. A panicky Federalist newspaper in Connecticut predicted that a victory by Thomas Jefferson would produce a bloody civil war and usher in an immoral reign of "murder, robbery, rape, adultery and incest." Apocalyptic fears gripped parts of the South, where a frightful slave uprising seemed a possible consequence of Jefferson's victory. But nothing nearly so dramatic occurred. Jefferson later called his election the "revolution of 1800," referring to his repudiation of Federalist practices and his cutbacks in military spending and taxes. While he cherished a republican simplicity in governance, he inevitably encountered events that required decisive and sometimes expensive government action, including military action overseas to protect American shipping.

Turbulent Times: Election and Rebellion

The election of 1800 (Map 10.1) was historic for procedural reasons: It was the first election to be decided by the House of Representatives. Probably by mistake, Republican voters in the electoral college gave Jefferson and his running mate Senator Aaron Burr of New York an equal number of votes,

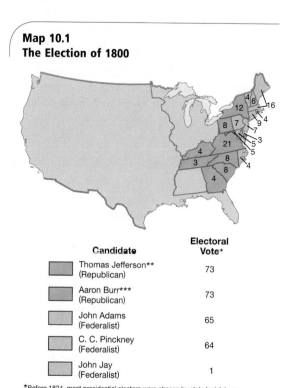

Map 10.1
The Election of 1800

Candidate	Electoral Vote*
Thomas Jefferson** (Republican)	73
Aaron Burr*** (Republican)	73
John Adams (Federalist)	65
C. C. Pinckney (Federalist)	64
John Jay (Federalist)	1

*Before 1824, most presidential electors were chosen by state legislatures rather than by popular vote.
**Chosen president by House of Representatives.
***Chosen vice president by House of Representatives.

CHRONOLOGY

1800	• Thomas Jefferson and Aaron Burr tie in electoral college. • Gabriel's rebellion reported.
1801	• House of Representatives elects Jefferson president. • Barbary War with Tripoli begins.
1803	• *Marbury v. Madison* decided. • United States warned not to ship war goods to Britain or France. • Louisiana Purchase approved by Congress.
1804	• Jefferson meets with Osage Indians.
1804–1806	• Lewis and Clark expedition explores West.
1805	• United States concludes war with Tripoli.
1807	• *Chesapeake* incident leads to Embargo Act. • Embargo Act passes. • United States establishes trade with Comanche Indians.
1808	• James Madison elected president.
1809	• Treaty of Fort Wayne negotiated. • Non-Intercourse Act passes.
1811	• Battle of Tippecanoe fought.
1812	• United States declares war on Great Britain.
1813	• Tecumseh dies at battle of the Thames.
1814	• British attack Washington City. • Treaty of Ghent ends war. • Hartford Convention held.
1815	• Battle of New Orleans fought.
1816	• James Monroe elected president.
1819	• Adams-Onís Treaty negotiated.
1820	• Missouri Compromise approved by Congress.
1823	• Monroe Doctrine asserted.
1825	• John Quincy Adams elected president by House of Representatives.

How Could a Vice President Get Away with Murder?

On July 11, 1804, Vice President Aaron Burr shot Alexander Hamilton, the architect of the Federalist Party, in a duel on the cliffs of Weehawken, New Jersey, across the Hudson River from New York City. The pistol blast tore through a rib, demolished Hamilton's liver, and splintered his spine. Hamilton died the next day in agonizing pain.

How was it that a sitting vice president and a prominent political leader could put themselves at such risk? Two eminent attorneys, skilled in the legal negotiations meant to substitute for violent resolution of disputes, fired .54-caliber weapons at ten paces. Did anyone try to stop them?

Burr challenged Hamilton in late June after learning about a months-old newspaper report that Hamilton "looked upon Mr. Burr to be a dangerous man, and one who ought not be trusted with the reins of government." Burr knew of Hamilton's low opinion of him, but now his private disparagement had made its way into print. Burr felt sure that Hamilton's remark cost him election to the governorship of New York.

Quite possibly, he was right. Suspecting that Jefferson would dump him from the federal ticket in the 1804 election, Burr decided to run for New York's highest office. He needed the support of New York's Federalist leadership, and he appeared to have it—until Hamilton's remark was circulated.

So on June 18, Burr challenged Hamilton to a duel if he did not disavow his comment. For three weeks, the men exchanged letters clarifying the nature of the insult that had aggrieved Burr. Hamilton the lawyer evasively quibbled over words, but at heart, he could neither deny the insult nor spurn the challenge without injury to his own reputation. Both Burr and Hamilton were locked in a highly ritualized procedure meant to uphold a gentleman's code of honor.

Each man had a trusted "second," in accord with the code of dueling, to deliver the letters and to assist at the duel. Only a handful of close friends knew of the challenge, and no one tried to stop it. Hamilton did not tell his wife. He wrote her a tender farewell letter, to be opened in the event of his death. He knew full well the pain dueling brought to loved ones, for three years earlier his nineteen-year-old son Philip had been killed in a duel, fought over heated words exchanged at a New York theater. Even when Hamilton's wife was called to his deathbed, she was first told he had a sudden illness. Women were excluded from the masculine world of dueling.

News of Hamilton's death spread quickly throughout the nation. New York shut down for the funeral, and the city council declared a six-week mourning period. Burr fled to Philadelphia, fearing retribution by crowds of mourners.

Northern newspapers expressed indignation over the illegal duel; not so in the South, where dueling was accepted as an extralegal remedy for insult. Many northern states had recently criminalized dueling, treating a challenge as a misdemeanor and a dueling death as a homicide. Even after death, the loser of an illegal duel could endure a range of penalties—being buried without a coffin, having a stake driven through the body, being strung up in public until the body rotted, or being donated to medical students for dissection. Hamilton's body was spared dishonor. But two ministers in

an outcome possible because of the single balloting to choose both president and vice president. (To fix this problem, the Twelfth Amendment to the Constitution, adopted in 1804, provided for distinct ballots for the two offices.) That meant that the House had to choose between those two men, leaving the Federalist candidate, John Adams, out of the race. The vain and ambitious Burr declined to concede, so the sitting Federalist-dominated House of Representatives, in its waning days in early 1801, got to choose the president.

Some Federalists preferred Burr, believing that his character flaws made him susceptible to Federalist pressure. But the influential Alexander Hamilton, though no friend of Jefferson, recognized that the high-strung Burr would be more dangerous in the presidency. Jefferson was a "contemptible hypocrite" in Hamilton's opinion, but at least he was not corrupt. (In 1804, Burr shot and killed Hamilton in a formal but illegal duel. See "Making Historical Arguments," above.)

Thirty-six ballots and six days later, Jefferson got the votes he needed to win the presidency. This election demonstrated a remarkable feature of the new government: No matter how hard

Pistols from the Burr-Hamilton Duel
These dueling pistols belonged to Hamilton's brother-in-law, who had once fought a non-injury duel with Aaron Burr. Hamilton's son Philip had borrowed them for his own fatal duel in 1799. During a cleaning in 1884, a hidden hair trigger came to light, allowing for a more rapid firing with one-twentieth the force of pull on the trigger. Hamilton gained no advantage from it. Courtesy JPMorgan Chase History Program.

(He dodged that bullet, too.) Hamilton certainly thought Burr a scoundrel, and when that opinion reached print, Burr had cause to defend his honor under the etiquette of dueling. The accuracy of Hamilton's charge was of no account. Dueling redressed questions of honor, not questions of fact.

Dueling held sway in the South for several more decades, but in the North the custom became extremely rare by the 1820s, discouraged by the tragedy of Hamilton's death and by the rise of a legalistic society that now preferred evidence, interrogation, and monetary judgments to avenge injury.

succession refused to administer last rites to him because he was a duelist; one finally relented.

A coroner's jury in New York soon indicted Burr on misdemeanor charges for issuing a challenge, and a grand jury in New Jersey indicted him for murder. By that time, Burr was a fugitive from justice hiding out in South Carolina.

But not for long. Amazingly, he returned to Washington, D.C., in November 1804 to resume presiding over sessions of the Senate, a role he continued to perform until his term ended in March 1805. Federalists

snubbed him, but eleven Republican senators petitioned New Jersey to drop its indictment on the grounds that "civilized nations" do not treat dueling deaths as "common murders." New Jersey did not pursue the murder charge. Burr freely visited New Jersey and New York for three more decades, paying no penalty for killing Hamilton.

Few would doubt that Burr was a scoundrel, albeit a brilliant one. A few years later, he was indicted for treason for a plot to break off part of the United States and start his own country in the Southwest.

Questions for Analysis

Summarize the Argument: For what injury or insult did Burr challenge Hamilton to a duel? Why did Hamilton accept?

Analyze the Evidence: Why might these men, trained as professional lawyers, go outside the law and re-sort to an illegal method to settle their differences?

Consider the Context: How might differences between the North and the South—economic, social, cultural, racial—possibly explain why dueling was a dying custom in the North but continued to be tolerated in the South?

fought the campaign, the leadership of the nation could shift from one group to its rivals in a peaceful transfer of power.

As the country struggled over its white leadership crisis, a twenty-four-year-old blacksmith named Gabriel, the slave of Thomas Prosser, plotted rebellion in Virginia. Inspired by the Haitian Revolution (see "The Haitian Revolution" in chapter 9), Gabriel was said to be organizing a thousand slaves to march on the state capital of Richmond and take the governor, James Monroe, hostage. On the appointed day, however, a few nervous slaves went to the authorities with news

of Gabriel's rebellion, and within days scores of implicated conspirators were jailed and brought to trial.

One of the jailed rebels compared himself to the most venerated icon of the early Republic: "I have nothing more to offer than what General Washington would have had to offer, had he been taken by the British and put to trial by them." Such talk invoking the specter of a black George Washington worried white Virginians, and in the fall of 1800 twenty-seven black men were hanged for allegedly contemplating rebellion. Finally, Jefferson advised Governor Monroe to halt the hangings. "The world at large will forever condemn us if we indulge a principle of revenge," Jefferson wrote.

The Jeffersonian Vision of Republican Simplicity

Once elected, Thomas Jefferson turned his attention to establishing his administration in clear contrast to the Federalists. For his inauguration, the first in the newly established District of Columbia, he dressed in everyday clothing to strike a tone of republican simplicity, and he walked to the Capitol for the modest swearing-in ceremony. As president, he scaled back Federalist building plans for Washington and cut the government budget.

Martha Washington and Abigail Adams had received the wives of government officials at weekly teas, thereby cementing social relations in the governing class. But Jefferson, a longtime widower, disdained female gatherings and avoided the women of Washington City. He abandoned George Washington's practice of holding weekly formal receptions. He preferred small dinner parties with carefully chosen politicos, either all Republicans or all Federalists (and all male). At these intimate dinners, the president exercised influence and strengthened informal relationships that would help him govern.

Jefferson was no Antifederalist; he had supported the Constitution in 1788. But events of the 1790s had caused him to worry about the stretching of powers in the executive branch. Jefferson had watched with distrust as Hamiltonian policies refinanced the public debt, established a national bank, and secured commercial ties with Britain (see "The Public Debt and Taxes" in chapter 9). These policies seemed to Jefferson to promote the interests of greedy speculators and profiteers at the expense of the rest of the country. In Jefferson's vision, the source of true liberty in America was the independent farmer, someone who owned and worked his land both for himself and for the market.

Jefferson set out to dismantle Federalist innovations. He reduced the size of the army by a third, preferring a militia-based defense, and he cut back the navy to six ships. With the consent of Congress, he abolished all federal taxes based on population or whiskey. Government revenue would now derive solely from customs duties and the sale of western land. This strategy benefited the South, where three-fifths of the slaves counted for representation but not for taxation now. By the end of his first term, Jefferson had deeply reduced Hamilton's cherished national debt.

A limited federal government, according to Jefferson, maintained a postal system, federal courts, and coastal lighthouses; it collected customs duties and conducted the census. The president had one private secretary, a young man named Meriwether Lewis, and Jefferson paid him out of his own pocket. The Department of State employed 8 people: Secretary James Madison, 6 clerks, and a messenger. The Treasury Department was by far the largest unit, with 73 revenue commissioners, auditors, and clerks, plus 2 watchmen. The entire payroll of the executive branch amounted to a mere 130 people in 1801.

However, 217 government workers lay beyond Jefferson's command, all judicial and military appointments made by John Adams as his very

***Thomas Jefferson*, by John Trumbull, 1788 (detail)**
This portrait captures Jefferson when he lived in Paris as a diplomat with his daughters and slave Sally Hemings. In 1802, a scandal erupted when a journalist charged that Jefferson had fathered children by Hemings. DNA evidence and historical evidence of Jefferson's whereabouts at the start of Hemings's pregnancies make a powerful case that he did father some and perhaps all of her children. Image copyright © The Metropolitan Museum of Art. Bequest of Cornelia Cruger, 1923 (24.19.1). Image source: Art Resource, NY.

last-minute act in office. Jefferson refused to honor those "midnight judges" whose hires had not yet been fully processed. One disappointed job seeker, William Marbury, sued the new secretary of state, James Madison, for failure to make good on the appointment. This action gave rise to a landmark Supreme Court case, *Marbury v. Madison*, decided in 1803. The Court ruled that although Marbury's commission was valid and the new president should have delivered it, the Court could not compel him to do so. What made the case significant was little noted at the time: The Court found that the grounds of Marbury's suit, resting in the Judiciary Act of 1789, conflicted with the Constitution. For the first time, the Court disallowed a federal law on the grounds that it was unconstitutional.

Dangers Overseas: The Barbary Wars

Jefferson's desire to keep government and the military small met a severe test in the western Mediterranean Sea, where U.S. trading interests ran afoul of several states on the northern coast of Africa. For well over a century, Morocco, Algiers, Tunis, and Tripoli, called the Barbary States by Americans, controlled all Mediterranean shipping traffic by demanding large annual payments (called "tribute") for safe passage. Countries electing not to pay found their ships and crews at risk for seizure. After several years in the 1790s when some hundred American crew members were taken captive and held in slavery, the United States agreed to pay $50,000 a year in tribute.

In May 1801, when the monarch of Tripoli failed to secure a large increase in his tribute, he declared war on the United States. Jefferson considered such payments extortion, and he sent four warships to the Mediterranean to protect U.S. shipping. From 1801 to 1803, U.S. frigates engaged in skirmishes with North African privateers.

Then, in late 1803, the USS *Philadelphia* ran aground near Tripoli's harbor and was captured along with its 300-man crew. In response, in early 1804 a U.S. naval ship commanded by Lieutenant Stephen Decatur sailed into the harbor after dark guided by an Arabic-speaking pilot to fool harbor sentries. Decatur's crew set the *Philadelphia* on fire, rendering it useless to the Tripoli monarch. Later that year, a small force of U.S. ships attacked the harbor and damaged or destroyed nineteen Tripolitan ships and bombarded the city, winning high praise and respect from European governments. Yet the sailors from the *Philadelphia* remained in captivity.

In 1805, William Eaton, an American officer stationed in Tunis, requested a thousand Marines to invade Tripoli, but Secretary of State James Madison rejected the plan. On his own, Eaton assembled a force of four hundred men (mostly Greek and Egyptian mercenaries plus eight Marines) and marched them over five hundred

SAVING THE LIFE OF COMMODORE DECATUR.

Stephen Decatur, Celebrated Hero of the Tripolitan War, 1804
Stephen Decatur, just twenty-five, won soaring praise from the American public for his daring nighttime raid into Tripoli's harbor to burn the USS *Philadelphia*. Decatur's fame grew when, six months later, he led ten men into combat against some fifty Tripolitan sailors. An 1850s artist re-created the dramatic moment when a wounded American took a saber blow for Decatur, who forthwith shot his attacker. *Saving the Life of Commodore Decatur*, Chappel, Alonzo (1828–87)/Private Collection/© Look and Learn/Bridgeman Images.

miles of desert for a surprise attack on Tripoli's second-largest city. Amazingly, he succeeded. The monarch of Tripoli yielded, released the prisoners taken from the *Philadelphia*, and negotiated a treaty in 1805 with the United States.

Periodic attacks by Algiers and Tunis continued to plague American ships during Jefferson's second term of office and into his successor's. This Second Barbary War ended in 1815 when the hero of 1804, Stephen Decatur, now a captain, arrived on the northern coast of Africa with a fleet of twenty-seven ships. By show of force, he engineered three treaties that put an end to the tribute system and provided reparations for damages to U.S. ships. Decatur was widely hailed for restoring honor to the United States.

> REVIEW   How did Jefferson's views of the role of the federal government differ from those of his predecessors?

▶ Opportunities and Challenges in the West

In 1803, an unanticipated opportunity presented itself when France offered to sell its territory west of the Mississippi River to the United States. President Jefferson set aside his usually cautious exercise of federal power and quickly took up the offer. He soon launched four expeditions into the prairie and mountains to explore this huge acquisition of land. The powerful Osage of the Arkansas River valley responded to overtures for an alliance and were soon lavishly welcomed by Jefferson in Washington City, but the even more powerful Comanche of the southern Great Plains stood their ground against all invaders. Meanwhile, the expedition by Lewis and Clark, the longest and northernmost trek of the four launched by Jefferson, mapped U.S. terrain all the way to the Pacific Ocean, giving a boost to expansionist aspirations.

The Louisiana Purchase

In 1763, at the end of the Seven Years' War, a large area west of the United States shifted from France to Spain, but Spain never effectively controlled it (see "The War and Its Consequences" in chapter 6). Centered on the Great Plains, it was home to Indian tribes, most notably the powerful and expansionist Comanche nation. New Orleans was Spain's principal stronghold, a city of French origins and population, strategically sited on the Mississippi River near its outlet to the Gulf of Mexico. Spain profited modestly from trade taxes it imposed on the small flow of agricultural products shipped down the river from American farms in the western parts of Kentucky and Tennessee.

Spanish officials in New Orleans and St. Louis (another city of French origins) worried that their sparse population could not withstand an anticipated westward movement of Americans. At first they hoped for a Spanish-Indian alliance to halt the expected demographic wave, but defending many hundreds of miles along the Mississippi River against Americans on the move was a daunting prospect. Thus, in 1800 Spain struck a secret deal to return this trans-Mississippi territory to France, in the hopes that a French Louisiana would provide a buffer zone between Spain's more valuable holdings in northern Mexico and the land-hungry Americans. The French emperor Napoleon accepted the transfer and agreed to Spain's condition that France could not sell Louisiana to anyone without Spain's permission.

From the U.S. perspective, Spain had proved a weak western neighbor, but France was another story. Jefferson was so alarmed by the rumored transfer that he instructed Robert R. Livingston, America's minister in France, to try to buy New Orleans. When Livingston hinted that the United States might seize it if buying was not an option, the French negotiator asked him to name his price for the entire Louisiana Territory from the Gulf of Mexico north to Canada. Livingston shrewdly stalled and within days accepted the bargain price of $15 million (Map 10.2).

On the verge of war with Britain, France needed both money and friendly neutrality from the United States, and it got both from the quick sale of the Louisiana Territory. In addition, the recent and costly loss of Haiti as a colony made a French presence in New Orleans less feasible as well. But in selling Louisiana to the United States, France had broken its agreement with Spain, which protested that the sale was illegal.

Moreover, there was no clarity on the western border of this land transfer. Spain claimed that the border was about one hundred miles west of the Mississippi River, while in Jefferson's eyes it was some eight hundred miles farther west, defined by the crest of the Rocky Mountains. When Livingston pressured the French negotiator

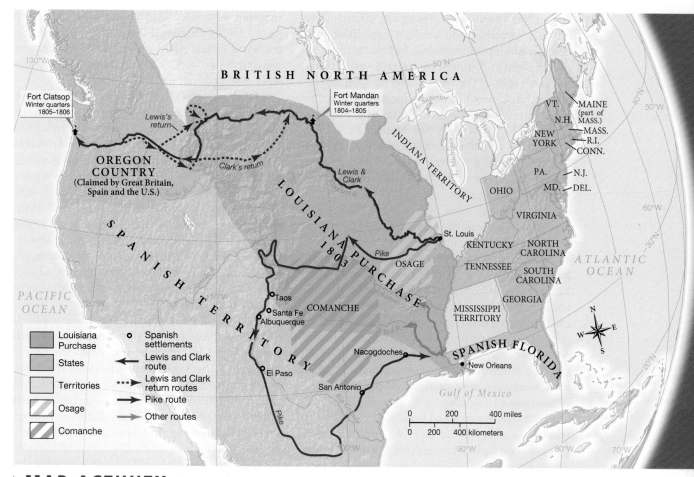

MAP ACTIVITY

Map 10.2 Jefferson's Expeditions in the West, 1804–1806

The Louisiana Purchase of 1803 brought the United States a large territory without clear boundaries. Jefferson sent off four scientific expeditions to take stock of the land's possibilities and to assess the degree of potential antagonism from Indian and Spanish inhabitants.

READING THE MAP: How did the size of the newly acquired territory compare to the land area of the existing American states and territories? What natural features of the land might have suggested boundaries for the Louisiana Purchase? Did those natural features coincide with actual patterns of human habitation already in place?

CONNECTIONS: What political events in Europe created the opportunity for the Jefferson administration to purchase Louisiana? How did the acquisition of Louisiana affect Spain's hold on North America?

to clarify his country's understanding of the boundary, the negotiator replied, "I can give you no direction. You have made a noble bargain for yourself, and I suppose you will make the most of it."

Jefferson gained congressional approval for the **Louisiana Purchase**, but without the votes of Federalist New England, which feared that such a large acquisition of land would be detrimental to Federalist Party strength. In late 1803, the American army took formal control of the Louisiana Territory, and the United States nearly doubled in size—at least on paper.

The Lewis and Clark Expedition

Jefferson quickly launched four government-financed expeditions up the river valleys of the new territory to establish relationships with Indian tribes and to determine Spanish influence and presence. The first set out in 1804 to explore the upper reaches of the Missouri River. Jefferson appointed twenty-eight-year-old Meriwether Lewis, his secretary, to head the expedition and instructed him to investigate Indian cultures, to collect plant and animal specimens, and to chart the geography of the West. Congress wanted the expedition to scout locations for military posts, negotiate fur trade agreements, and identify river routes to the West (see Map 10.2).

For his co-leader, Lewis chose Kentuckian William Clark, a veteran of the 1790s Indian wars. With a crew of forty-five, including expert rivermen, gunsmiths, hunters, interpreters, a cook, and Clark's slave named York, the explorers left St. Louis in the spring of 1804, working their way northwest up the Missouri River. They camped for the winter at a Mandan village in what is now central North Dakota. The Mandan Indians were familiar with British and French traders from Canada, but the black man York created a sensation. Reportedly, the Indians rubbed moistened fingers over the man's skin to see whether the color was painted on.

The following spring, the explorers headed west, accompanied by a sixteen-year-old Shoshoni woman named Sacajawea. Kidnapped by Mandans at about age ten, she had been sold to a French trapper as a slave/wife. Hers was not a unique story among Indian women; such women knew several languages, making them valuable translators and mediators. Further, Sacajawea and her new baby allowed the American expedition to appear peaceful to suspicious tribes. As Lewis wrote in his journal, "No woman ever accompanies a war party of Indians in this quarter."

The **Lewis and Clark expedition** reached the Pacific Ocean at the mouth of the Columbia River in November 1805. When the two leaders returned home the following year, they were greeted as national heroes. They had established favorable relations with dozens of Indian tribes; they had collected invaluable information on the peoples, soils, plants, animals, and geography of the West; and they had inspired a nation of restless explorers and solitary imitators.

Osage and Comanche Indians

The three additional expeditions set forth between 1804 and 1806 to probe the contested southwestern border of the Louisiana Purchase. The first exploring party left from Natchez, Mississippi, and ascended the Red River to the Ouachita River, ending at a hot springs in present-day Arkansas. Two years later, the second group followed the Red River west into eastern Texas, and the third embarked from St. Louis and

traveled west, deep into the Rockies. This third group, led by Zebulon Pike, had gone too far, in the view of the Spaniards: Pike and his men were arrested, taken to northern Mexico, and soon released.

Of the scores of Indian tribes in this lower Great Plains region, two enjoyed reputations for territorial dominance. The Osage ruled the land between the Missouri and the lower Arkansas rivers, while the trading and raiding grounds of the Comanche stretched from the upper Arkansas River to the Rockies and south into Texas, a vast area called Comanchería. Both were formidable tribes that proved equal to the Spaniards. The Osage accomplished this through careful diplomacy and periodic shows of strength, the Comanche by expert horsemanship, a brisk trade in guns and captives, and a readiness to employ deadly force.

In 1804, Jefferson invited Osage tribal leaders to Washington City and greeted them with ceremonies and gifts. He positioned the Osage as equals of the Americans: "The great spirit has given you strength & has given us strength, not that we might hurt one another, but to do each other all the good in our power." Jefferson wanted a trade agreement that would introduce new agricultural tools to the Osage: hoes and ploughs for the men; spinning wheels and looms for the women. These gendered tools signified a departure from the native gender system in which women tended crops while men hunted game. With an agricultural civilization, men would give up the hunt and thus need far less land to sustain their communities. Jefferson expressed his hope that "commerce is the great engine by which we are to coerce them, & not war."

In exchange, the Osage asked for protection against Indian refugees displaced by American settlers east of the Mississippi. Jefferson's Osage alliance soon proved to be quite expensive, driven up by the costs of providing defense, brokering treaties, and giving gifts all around. In 1806, a second ceremonial visit to Washington and other eastern cities by a dozen Osage leaders cost the federal government $10,000.

These promising peace initiatives were short-lived. By 1808, intertribal warfare was on the rise, and the governor of the Louisiana Territory declared that the U.S. government no longer had an obligation to protect the Osage. Jefferson's presidency was waning, and soon the practice of whittling away Indian lands through coercive treaties, so familiar to men like Tecumseh, reasserted itself. Four treaties between 1808 and 1839 shrank the Osage lands, and by the

VISUAL ACTIVITY

Comanche Feats of Horsemanship, 1834

Pennsylvania artist George Catlin toured the Great Plains and captured Comanche equestrian warfare in training. "Every young man," Catlin wrote, learned "to drop his body upon the side of his horse at the instant he is passing, effectually screened from his enemies' weapons. . . . He will hang whilst his horse is at fullest speed, carrying with him his bow and his shield, and also his long lance . . . which he will wield upon his enemy as he passes." Smithsonian American Art Museum, Washington, D.C./Art Resource, NY.

READING THE IMAGE: Is there a riderless horse in this picture? Is this unusual expert riding skill an offensive or defensive posture?

CONNECTIONS: How did the Comanche's formidable presence in the Great Plains affect American westward settlement?

1860s they were relocated to present-day Oklahoma.

By contrast, the Comanche resisted attempts to dominate them. European maps marking Spanish ownership of vast North American lands simply did not correspond to the reality on the ground, and for decades after the Louisiana Purchase of 1803, nothing much changed. In 1807, a newly appointed U.S. Indian agent invited Comanche leaders to Natchitoches in Louisiana where he proclaimed an improbable solidarity with the Comanche: "It is now so long since our Ancestors came from beyond the great Water that we have no remembrance of it. We ourselves are Natives of the Same land that you are, in other words white Indians, we therefore Should feel & live together like brothers & Good Neighbours." Trade relations flourished, with American traders allowed to enter Comanchería to attend local market fairs, selling weapons, cloth, and household metal goods in exchange for horses, bison, and furs. No matter what the map of the United States looked like, on the ground Comanchería remained under the control of the Comanche and thus off-limits to settlement by white Americans until the late nineteenth century (see Map 10.2).

REVIEW   What was the significance of the Louisiana Purchase for the United States?

▶ Jefferson, the Madisons, and the War of 1812

Jefferson easily retained the presidency in the election of 1804, trouncing Federalist Charles Cotesworth Pinckney of South Carolina. A looming problem was the threat of war with both France and Britain that led Jefferson to try a novel tactic, an embargo. His successor, James Madison, continued with a modified embargo, but his much narrower margin of victory over Pinckney in the election of 1808 indicated growing dissatisfaction with the Jefferson-Madison handling of foreign policy.

Madison broke with Jefferson on one very domestic matter: He encouraged his gregarious wife, Dolley Madison, to participate in serious domestic politics. Under her leadership, the White House hosted frequent social events, which fostered political networking. Under his leadership, the country declared war in 1812 on Britain and on Tecumseh's Indian confederacy. The two-year war cost the young nation its White House and its Capitol, but victory was proclaimed at the end nonetheless.

Impressment and Embargo

In 1803, France and Britain went to war, and both repeatedly warned the United States not to ship arms to the other. Britain acted on these threats in 1806, stopping U.S. ships to inspect cargoes for military aid to France and seizing suspected deserters from the British navy, along with many Americans. Ultimately, 2,500 U.S. sailors were "impressed" (taken by force) by the British, who needed them for their war with France. In retaliation against the **impressment** of American sailors, Jefferson convinced Congress to pass a nonimportation law banning particular British-made goods.

Jefferson found one event particularly provoking. In June 1807, the American ship *Chesapeake*, harboring some British deserters, was ordered to stop by the British frigate *Leopard*. When the *Chesapeake* refused, the *Leopard* opened fire, killing three Americans—right at the mouth of the Chesapeake Bay, well within U.S. territory. In response, Congress passed the **Embargo Act of 1807**, prohibiting U.S. ships from traveling to all foreign ports, a measure that brought a swift halt to all overseas trade carried in American vessels. Though a drastic measure, the embargo was meant to forestall war by forcing concessions from the British through economic pressure.

The Embargo Act of 1807 was a disaster. From 1790 to 1807, U.S. exports had increased fivefold, but the embargo brought commerce to a standstill. In New England, the heart of the shipping industry, unemployment rose. Grain plummeted in value, river traffic halted, tobacco rotted in the South, and cotton went unpicked. Protest petitions flooded Washington. The federal government suffered too, for import duties were a significant source of revenue. The Federalist Party, in danger of fading away after its weak showing in the election of 1804, began to revive.

Secretary of State James Madison was chosen by Republican caucuses—informal political groups that orchestrated the selection of candidates. The Federalist caucuses again chose Pinckney. Madison won, but Pinckney secured 47 electoral votes, nearly half of Madison's total. Support for the Federalists remained centered in New England, where the shipping industry suffered heavy losses in the embargo. The

Republicans still held the balance of power nationwide.

Dolley Madison and Social Politics

Although women could not vote and supposedly left politics to men, the female relatives of Washington politicians took on several overtly political functions that greased the wheels of the affairs of state. They networked through dinners, balls, receptions, and the intricate custom of "calling," in which men and women paid brief visits at each other's homes. Webs of friendship and influence in turn facilitated female political lobbying. It was not uncommon for women in this social set to write letters of recommendation for men seeking government work.

Dolley Madison developed elaborate social networks during Jefferson's presidency that were of great benefit during her husband's administration. Called by some the "presidentress," she struck a balance between queenliness and republican openness. She dressed the part in resplendent clothes and opened three elegant rooms in the executive mansion for a weekly open-house party called "Mrs. Madison's crush," or "squeeze." In contrast to George and Martha Washington's stiff, brief receptions, the Madisons' parties went on for hours, with scores or even hundreds of guests milling about, talking, and eating. Members of Congress, cabinet officers, distinguished guests, envoys from foreign countries, and their wives attended with regularity. Mrs. Madison's weekly squeeze was an essential event for gaining political access, trading information, and establishing informal channels that would smooth the governing process.

In 1810 to 1811, the Madisons' house acquired its present name, the White House. The many guests experienced simultaneously the splendor of the executive mansion and the atmosphere of republicanism that made it accessible to so many. Dolley Madison, ever an enormous political asset to her rather shy husband, understood well the symbolic function of the White House to enhance the power and legitimacy of the presidency.

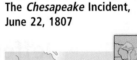

The *Chesapeake* Incident, June 22, 1807

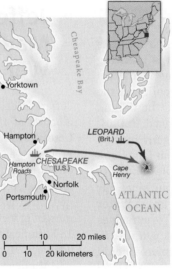

***Dolley Madison*, by Rembrandt Peale**
The "presidentress" of the Madison administration sat for this portrait in 1817 when she was close to fifty and just exiting from the White House. She wears a fashionable satin empire waist dress featuring a low-cut bodice and flowing gown that dropped from the high waistline straight to the ground. Mrs. Madison was noted for her unusual turbans and her unfailing good cheer, as her impish smile conveys. Corbis.

Tecumseh and Tippecanoe

While the Madisons cemented alliances at home, difficulties with Britain and France overseas and with Indians in the old Northwest continued to increase. The Shawnee chief Tecumseh (see pages 253–54) actively solidified his confederacy, while the more northern tribes renewed their ties with supportive British agents in Canada, a potential source of food and weapons. If the United States went to war with Britain, serious repercussions on the frontier would clearly follow.

Shifting demographics put the Indians under pressure. The 1810 census counted some 230,000 Americans in Ohio, while another 40,000 inhabited the territories of Indiana, Illinois, and Michigan. The Indian population of the same area was much smaller, probably about 70,000.

Up to 1805, Indiana's territorial governor, William Henry Harrison, had negotiated a series

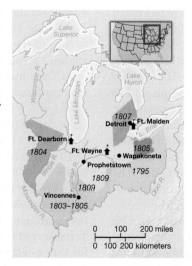

Indian Lands Ceded in the Northwest Territory before 1810

of treaties in a divide-and-conquer strategy aimed at extracting Indian lands for paltry payments.

But with the rise to power of Tecumseh and his brother Tenskwatawa, the Prophet, Harrison's strategy faltered. A fundamental part of Tecumseh's message was the assertion that all Indian lands were held in common by all the tribes. "No tribe has the right to sell [these lands], even to each other, much less to strangers," Tecumseh said. "Sell a country! Why not sell the air, the great sea, as well as the earth? Didn't the Great Spirit make them all for the use of his children?" In 1809, while Tecumseh was away on a recruiting trip, Harrison assembled the leaders of the Potawatomi, Miami, and Delaware tribes to negotiate the Treaty of Fort Wayne. After promising (falsely) that this was the last cession of land the United States would seek, Harrison secured three million acres at about two cents per acre.

When he returned, Tecumseh was furious with both Harrison and the tribal leaders. Leaving his brother in charge at Prophetstown on the Tippecanoe River, the Shawnee chief left to seek alliances with tribes in the South. In November 1811, Harrison decided to attack Prophetstown with a thousand men. The two-hour battle resulted in the deaths of sixty-two Americans and forty Indians before the Prophet's forces fled. The Americans won the **battle of Tippecanoe**, but Tecumseh was now more ready than ever to make war on the United States.

The Indian conflicts in the old Northwest soon merged into the wider conflict with Britain, now known as the War of 1812. Between 1809 and 1812, Madison teetered between declaring either Britain or France America's primary enemy, as attacks by both countries on U.S. ships continued. In 1809, Congress replaced Jefferson's embargo with the Non-Intercourse Act, which prohibited trade only with Britain and France and their colonies, thus opening up other trade routes to alleviate the economic distress of American shippers, farmers, and planters. By 1811, the country was seriously divided and on the verge of war.

The new Congress seated in March 1811 contained several dozen young Republicans from the West and South who would come to be known as the **War Hawks**. Led by thirty-four-year-old Henry Clay from Kentucky and twenty-nine-year-old John C. Calhoun from South Carolina, they welcomed a war with Britain both to justify attacks on the Indians and to bring an end to impressment. Many were also expansionists, looking to occupy Florida and threaten Canada. Clay was elected Speaker of the House, an extraordinary honor for a newcomer, and Calhoun won a seat on the Foreign Relations Committee. The War Hawks approved major defense expenditures, and the army soon quadrupled in size.

In June 1812, Congress declared war on Great Britain in a vote divided along sectional lines: New England and some Middle Atlantic states opposed the war, fearing its effect on commerce, while the South and West strongly favored it. Ironically, Britain had just announced that it would stop the search and seizure of American ships, but the war momentum would not be slowed. The Foreign Relations Committee issued an

Battle of Tippecanoe, 1811

elaborate justification titled *Report on the Causes and Reasons for War*, written mainly by Calhoun and containing extravagant language about Britain's "lust of power," "unbounded... tyranny," and "mad ambition." These were fighting words in a war that was in large measure about insult and honor. (See "Analyzing Historical Evidence," page 268.)

The War Hawks proposed an invasion of Canada, confidently predicting victory in four weeks. Instead, the war lasted two and a half years, and Canada never fell. The northern invasion turned out to be a series of blunders that revealed America's grave unpreparedness for war against the unexpectedly powerful British and Indian forces (Map 10.3). By the fall of 1812, the outlook was grim.

Worse, the New England states were slow to raise troops, and some New England merchants carried on illegal trade with Britain. The fall presidential election pitted Madison against DeWitt Clinton of New York, nominally a Republican but able to attract the Federalist vote. Clinton picked up electoral votes from all of New England, with the exception of Vermont, and from New York, New Jersey, and part of Maryland. Madison won in the electoral college, 128 to 89, but his margin of victory was considerably smaller than in 1808.

In late 1812 and early 1813, the tide began to turn in the Americans' favor. First came some victories at sea. Then the Americans attacked York (now Toronto) and burned it in April 1813. A few months later, Commodore Oliver Hazard Perry defeated the British fleet at the western end of Lake Erie. Emboldened, General Harrison drove an army into Canada from Detroit and in October 1813 defeated the British and Indians at the battle of the Thames, where Tecumseh was killed.

Creek Indians in the South who had allied with Tecumseh's confederacy were also plunged into war. Some 10,000 living in the Mississippi Territory put up a spirited fight against U.S. forces for ten months. But the **Creek War** ended suddenly in March 1814 when a general named Andrew Jackson led 2,500 Tennessee militiamen in a bloody attack called the Battle of Horseshoe Bend. More than 550 Indians were killed, and several hundred more died trying to escape across a river. Later that year, General Jackson extracted from

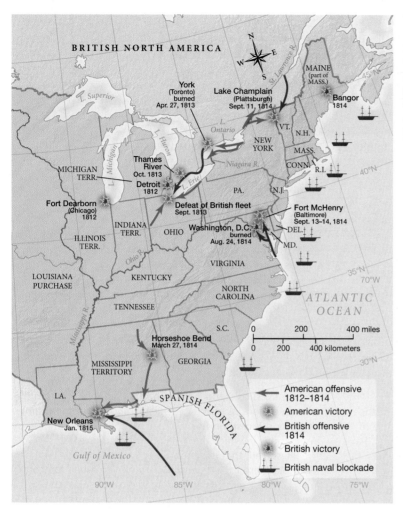

Map 10.3   The War of 1812
During the War of 1812, battles were fought along the Canadian border and in the Chesapeake region. The most important American victory came in New Orleans two weeks after a peace agreement had been signed in England.

the defeated tribe a treaty relinquishing thousands of square miles of their land to the United States.

Washington City Burns: The British Offensive

In August 1814, British ships sailed into Chesapeake Bay, landing 5,000 troops and throwing the capital into a panic. Families evacuated, banks hid their money, and government clerks carted away boxes of important papers. Dolley Madison, with dinner for guests cooking over the fire, fled with her husband's papers, while servants rescued a portrait of George Washington. As the cook related, "When the British did arrive, they ate up the very dinner, and drank the wines, &c., that I had prepared for the President's party." Then the British torched the White House, the Capitol, a newspaper office, and a well-stocked arsenal. Instead of trying to hold the city, the British headed north and attacked Baltimore, but a fierce defense by the Maryland militia thwarted that effort.

In another powerful offensive that same month, British troops marched from Canada into New York State, but a series of mistakes cost them a naval skirmish at Plattsburgh on Lake Champlain, and they retreated to Canada. Five months later, another large British army landed in lower Louisiana and, in early January 1815, encountered General Andrew Jackson and his militia just outside New Orleans. Jackson's forces carried the day. The British suffered between 2,000 and 3,000 casualties, the Americans fewer than 80. Jackson instantly became known as the hero of the **battle of New Orleans**. No one in the United States knew that negotiators in Europe had signed a peace agreement two weeks earlier.

The Treaty of Ghent, signed in December 1814, settled few of the surface issues that had led to war. Neither country could claim victory, and no land changed hands. Instead, the treaty reflected a mutual agreement to give up certain goals. The Americans dropped their plea for an end to impressment, which in any case subsided as soon as Britain and France ended their war

The Nation's First Formal Declaration of War

War fever gripped the United States in the spring of 1812. On June 1, President Madison sent Congress a list of British insults. On June 5, the House voted 79 to 49 to declare war. Two weeks later the Senate did likewise, 19 to 13. No Federalist voted for war, while 81 percent of Republicans supported it.

DOCUMENT 1
Federalist Boston Protests the War

On June 15, 1812, the Boston town meeting approved a lengthy report denouncing the House of Representatives' vote.

. . . Believing, as we do, that an immense majority of the people are invincibly averse from a conflict equally unnecessary, and menacing ruin to themselves and their posterity . . . we cannot but trust that a general expression of the voice of the people would satisfy Congress that those of their Representatives who have voted in favor of war, have not truly represented the wishes of their constituents. . . .

From the commencement of the system of Commercial restrictions [the embargo], the Inhabitants of this Town (inferior we trust to none in ardent patriotism and attachment to the Union) have [deplored] . . . the utter inefficacy, destructive operation, and ultimate tendency of this unprecedented and visionary scheme. They could discern in it nothing but a deliberate sacrifice of their best interests, and a conformity to the views of France . . . and hostility to Britain. . . .

Had the policy of Government been inclined towards resistance to the pretensions of the belligerents, by open war, there could be neither policy, reason, or justice in singling out Great Britain as the exclusive object of hostility. If the object of war is merely to vindicate our honor, why is it not declared against the first aggressor? If the object is defence and success, why is it to be waged against the adversary most able to annoy, and least likely to yield? . . .

Tho' we cannot discern the least reason for this discrimination in favor of France . . . , still in a war with [England] there might have been found some consolation had our country been in any measure prepared. . . . But under the present circumstances, there will be . . . no chance for success, no hope of national glory . . . and in the end an inglorious peace, in which [France will join Britain] to shackle & restrain the commerce of our infant empire, by regulations in which they will find a common interest. . . .

Resolved, that it is the true policy and duty of this nation to adhere to an impartial neutrality; to abandon commercial restrictions; . . . to indemnify itself against the losses to which its commerce is exposed in the present European war. . . . That to abstain from efforts of impotent resentment, blind rage, or desperate policy is not to be deemed submission to any foreign power, but a conformity to necessities imposed on our country by an overruling Providence, for which our courage and patriotism is not responsible. That we should endeavor to ride out the storm which we cannot direct, and that to plunge into the present war would be a wanton and impious rejection of the advantages with which the Almighty has blessed our country.

in 1815. They also gave up any claim to Canada. The British agreed to stop all aid to the Indians. Nothing was said about shipping rights. The most concrete result was a plan for a future commission to determine the exact boundary between the United States and Canada.

Antiwar Federalists in New England could not gloat over the war's ambiguous conclusion because of an ill-timed and seemingly unpatriotic move on their part. The region's leaders had convened a secret meeting in Hartford, Connecticut, in December 1814 to discuss a series of proposals aimed at reducing the South's power and breaking Virginia's lock on the presidency. They proposed abolishing the Constitution's three-fifths clause as a basis of representation; requiring a two-thirds vote instead of a simple majority for imposing embargoes, admitting states, or declaring war; limiting the president to one term; and prohibiting the election of successive presidents from the same state. They even discussed secession from the Union but rejected that path. Coming just as peace was achieved, however, the

Voted, That a suitable number of copies of the foregoing report be printed . . . [and transmitted] to each Town in this Commonwealth.

Source: *A Volume of Records Relating to the Early History of Boston, Containing Boston Town Records, 1796 to 1813* (Boston: Municipal Print Office, 1905), 316–20, http://catalog.hathitrust.org/Record/011718472.

DOCUMENT 2
Congress Declares War

In early June 1812, the House Foreign Relations Committee, chaired by John C. Calhoun, produced a secret seventeen-page "Manifesto" justifying war. It went public on June 18, the day after the formal congressional declaration of war.

The period has now arrived, when the United States must support their character and station among the nations of the earth, or submit to the most shameful degradation. . . . The mad ambition, the lust of power and commercial avarice of Great Britain, arrogating to herself the complete dominion of the ocean, and exercising over it an unbounded and lawless tyranny, have left to neutral nations an alternative only between the base surrender of their rights, and a manly vindication of them.

[The manifesto devotes a dozen pages to maritime provocations by Great Britain stretching back to 1805.]

Under the pretext of impressing British seamen . . . our Citizens are wantonly snatched from their Country . . . ; doomed to an ignominious and slavish bondage; compelled to fight the battles of a foreign Country and often to perish in them. . . . While this practice is continued, it is impossible for the United States to consider themselves an independent Nation. . . .

It is known that symptoms of British hostility towards the United States have never failed to produce corresponding symptoms among those tribes [on the frontiers]. . . . [Furthermore] abundant supplies of the ordinary munitions of war have been afforded by the agents of British commercial companies . . . wherewith they were enabled to commence that system of savage warfare on our frontiers.

. . . From this review of the multiplied wrongs of the British government since the commencement of the present war, it must be evident to the impartial world that the contest which is now forced on the United States, is radically a contest for their sovereignty and independence. . . . The control of our commerce by G. Britain in regulating . . . and expelling it almost from the ocean; the oppressive manner in which these regulations have been carried into effect, by seizing . . . such of our vessels, with their cargoes, as were said to have violated her edicts, often without previous warning . . . ; the impressment of our citizens from on board our own vessels on the high seas . . . are encroachments of that high and dangerous tendency, which could not fail to produce that pernicious effect. . . . The proof which so complete and disgraceful a submission to its [Great Britain's] authority would afford of our degeneracy, could not fail to inspire confidence, and there was no limit to which its usurpations, and our degradation, might not be carried.

Source: House Foreign Relations Committee, *Report, or Manifesto of the Causes and Reasons of War with Great Britain* (Washington, D.C.: A. & G. Way, 1812), 3–4, 10–12, 16–17, https://archive.org/details/cihm_51537.

Questions for Analysis

Recognize Viewpoints: Why do the Boston Federalists oppose the war? Why do Republicans in Congress support it?

Analyze the Evidence: Why does the Boston town meeting liken the problem of British threats to a bad storm that has to be endured? How persuasive are those who argue that "blind rage" and "impotent resentment" will cause only harm to America? Why do the Republicans in Congress think a full-on military response is necessary?

Consider the Context: With all its talk of "independence," does the manifesto suggest that the War of 1812 was a replay of the American Revolution?

Hartford Convention looked very unpatriotic. The Federalist Party never recovered, and within a few years it was reduced to a shadow of its former self, even in New England.

No one really won the War of 1812; however, Americans celebrated as though they had, with parades and fireworks. The war gave rise to a new spirit of nationalism. The paranoia over British tyranny evident in the 1812 declaration of war was laid to rest, replaced by pride in a more equal relationship with the old mother country. Indeed, in 1817 the two countries signed the Rush-Bagot disarmament treaty (named after its two negotiators), which limited each country to a total of four naval vessels, each with just a single cannon, to patrol the vast watery border between them. It was the most successful disarmament treaty for a century to come.

The biggest winners in the War of 1812 were the young men, once called War Hawks, who took up the banner of the Republican Party and carried it in new, expansive directions. These young politicians favored trade, western

VISUAL ACTIVITY

The Taking of the City of Washington in America

This London engraving celebrates Britain's devastating attack on Washington in 1814. Troops fire cannons on the city while other redcoats burn ships and bridges. In the background, huge flames leap from the "Presidential Palace" (so named in a key to the picture). Some soldiers sought trophies of war. Below is James Madison's medicine chest, plundered that night. In 1939, the souvenir was returned to President Franklin D. Roosevelt. Engraving: Library of Congress, LC-DIG-ppmsca-31113; medicine chest: From White House collection, photo courtesy Franklin D. Roosevelt Presidential Library and Museum/NARA.

READING THE IMAGE: How many fires appear in this image? Can you identify the structure meant to be the U.S. Capitol building? Do you think the artist was familiar with the geography or architecture of Washington?

CONNECTIONS: Did the burning of the seat of government mean that Britain really won the war? Who did win the war, in your opinion?

expansion, internal improvements, and the energetic development of new economic markets. The biggest losers of the war were the Indians. Tecumseh was dead, his brother the Prophet was discredited, the prospects of an Indian confederacy were dashed, the Creek's large homeland was seized, and the British protectors were gone.

> **REVIEW**   Why did Congress declare war on Great Britain in 1812?

► Women's Status in the Early Republic

Dolley Madison's pioneering role as "presidentress" showed that elite women could assume an active presence in civic affairs. But, as with the 1790s cultural compromise that endorsed female education to make women into better wives and mothers (see "The Republican Wife and Mother" in chapter 9), Mrs. Madison and her female circle practiced politics to further their husbands' careers. There was little talk of the "rights of woman." Indeed, from 1800 to 1825, key institutions central to the shaping of women's lives—the legal system, marriage, and religion—proved fairly resistant to change. Nonetheless, the trend toward increased commitment to female education that began in the 1780s and 1790s continued in the first decades of the nineteenth century.

Women and the Law

In English common law, wives had no independent legal or political personhood. The legal doctrine of *feme covert* (covered woman) held that a wife's civic life was completely subsumed by her husband's. A wife was obligated to obey her husband; her property was his, her domestic and sexual services were his, and even their children were legally his. Women had no right to keep their wages, to make contracts, or to sue or be sued. American state legislatures generally passed up the opportunity to rewrite the laws of domestic relations even though they redrafted other British laws in light of republican principles. Lawyers never paused to defend, much less to challenge, the assumption that unequal power relations lay at the heart of marriage.

The one aspect of family law that changed in the early Republic was divorce. Before the Revolution, only New England jurisdictions recognized a limited right to divorce; by 1820, every state except South Carolina did so. However, divorce was uncommon and in many states could be obtained only by petition to the state's legislature, a daunting obstacle for many ordinary people. A mutual wish to terminate a marriage was never sufficient grounds for a legal divorce. A New York judge affirmed that "it would be aiming a deadly blow at public morals to decree a dissolution of the marriage contract merely because the parties requested it. Divorces should never be allowed, except for the protection of the innocent party, and for the punishment of the guilty." States upheld the institution of marriage both to protect persons they thought of as naturally dependent (women and children) and to regulate the use and inheritance of property. (Unofficial self-divorce, desertion, and bigamy were remedies that ordinary people sometimes chose to get around the law, but all were socially unacceptable.) Legal enforcement of marriage as an unequal relationship played a major role in maintaining gender inequality in the nineteenth century.

Single adult women could own and convey property, make contracts, initiate lawsuits, and pay taxes. They could not vote (except in New Jersey before 1807), serve on juries, or practice law, so their civil status was limited. Single women's economic status was often limited as well, by custom as much as by law. Job prospects were few and low-paying. Unless they had inherited adequate property or could live with married siblings, single adult women in the early Republic very often were poor.

None of the legal institutions that structured white gender relations applied to black slaves. As property themselves, under the jurisdiction of slave owners, they could not freely consent to any contractual obligations, including marriage.

The protective features of state-sponsored unions were thus denied to black men and women in slavery. But this also meant that slave unions did not establish unequal power relations between partners backed by the force of law, as did marriages among the free.

Women and Church Governance

In most Protestant denominations around 1800, white women made up the majority of congregants. Yet church leadership of most denominations rested in men's hands. There were some exceptions, however. In Baptist congregations in New England, women served along with men on church governance committees, deciding on the admission of new members, voting on hiring ministers, and even debating doctrinal points. Quakers, too, had a history of recognizing women's spiritual talents. Some were accorded the status of minister, capable of leading and speaking in Quaker meetings.

Between 1790 and 1820, a small and highly unusual set of women actively engaged in open preaching. Most were from Freewill Baptist groups centered in New England and upstate New York. Others came from small Methodist sects, and yet others rejected any formal religious affiliation. Probably fewer than a hundred such women existed, but several dozen traveled beyond their local communities, creating converts and controversy. They spoke from the heart, without prepared speeches, often exhibiting trances and claiming to exhort (counsel or warn) rather than to preach.

The best-known exhorting woman was Jemima Wilkinson, who called herself "the Publick Universal Friend." After a near-death experience from a high fever, Wilkinson proclaimed her body no longer female or male but the incarnation of the "Spirit of Light." She dressed in men's clothes, wore her hair in a masculine style, shunned gender-specific pronouns, and preached openly in Rhode Island and Philadelphia. In the early nineteenth century, Wilkinson established a town called New Jerusalem in western New York with some 250 followers. Her fame was sustained by periodic newspaper articles that fed public curiosity about her lifelong cross-dressing and her unfeminine forcefulness.

The decades from 1790 to the 1820s marked a period of unusual confusion, ferment, and creativity in American religion. New denominations blossomed, new styles of religiosity gripped adher-

VISUAL ACTIVITY

Women and the Church: Jemima Wilkinson

In this engraving, Jemima Wilkinson, "the Publick Universal Friend," wears a clerical collar and body-obscuring robe, much as a male minister would wear, in keeping with the claim that the former Jemima was now a person without gender. Wilkinson's hair is swept back from the forehead and curled at the neck in the style of men's powdered wigs of the 1790s. *History and Directory of Yates County* by Stafford C. Cleveland, 1873.

READING THE IMAGE: Was Wilkinson merely masculinized by dress and deportment, or did the "Universal Friend" truly transcend gender?

CONNECTIONS: Why was it so difficult for women to attain religious authority in the early Republic? What allowed a few to rise above social limitations?

The Universal Friend.

ents, and an extensive periodical press devoted to religion popularized all manner of theological and institutional innovations. In such a climate, the age-old tradition of gender subordination came into question here and there among the most radically democratic of the churches. But the presumption of male authority over women was deeply entrenched in American culture. Even denominations that had allowed women to participate in church governance began to pull back, and most churches reinstated patterns of hierarchy along gender lines.

Female Education

First in the North and then in the South, states and localities began investing in public schools to foster an educated citizenry deemed essential in a republic. Young girls attended district schools along with boys, and by 1830, girls had made rapid gains, in many places approaching male literacy rates. Basic literacy and numeracy formed the curriculum taught to white children aged roughly six to eleven. (Far fewer schools addressed the needs of free black children, whether male or female.)

More advanced female education came from a growing number of private academies. Judith Sargent Murray, the Massachusetts author who had called for equality of the sexes around 1790 (see "The Republican Wife and Mother" in chapter 9), predicted in 1800 that "a new era in female history" would emerge because "female academies are everywhere establishing." Some dozen were founded in the 1790s, and by 1830 that number had grown to nearly two hundred. Students of ages twelve to sixteen came from elite families as well as those of middling families with intellectual aspirations, such as ministers' daughters.

The three-year curriculum included both ornamental arts and solid academics. The former strengthened female gentility: drawing, needlework, music, and French conversation. The academic subjects included English grammar, literature, history, the natural sciences, geography, and elocution (the art of effective public speaking). The most ambitious female academies equaled the training offered at male colleges such as Harvard, Yale, Dartmouth, and Princeton, with classes in Latin, rhetoric, theology, moral philosophy, algebra, geometry, and even chemistry and physics.

Two of the best-known female academies were the Troy Female Seminary in New York, founded by Emma Willard in 1821, and the Hartford Seminary in Connecticut, founded by Catharine Beecher in 1822. (See "Experiencing the American Promise," page 274.) Unlike theological seminaries that trained men for the clergy, Troy and Hartford prepared their female students to teach, on the grounds that women made better teachers than did men. Author Harriet Beecher Stowe, educated at her sister's school and then a teacher there, agreed: "If men have more knowledge they have less talent at communicating it. Nor have they the patience, the long-suffering, and gentleness necessary to superintend the formation of character."

The most immediate value of advanced female education lay in the self-cultivation and confidence it provided. Following the model of male colleges, female graduation exercises showcased speeches and recitations performed in front of a mixed-sex audience of family, friends, and local notables. Elocution, a common subject offering in the academies, taught the young women the art of persuasion along with correct pronunciation and the skill of fluent speaking. Academies also took care to promote a pleasing female modesty. Female pedantry or intellectual immodesty triggered the stereotype of the "bluestocking," a British term of hostility for a too-learned woman doomed to fail in the marriage market.

By the mid-1820s, the total annual enrollment at the female academies equaled enrollment at the nearly six dozen male colleges in the United States. Both groups accounted for only about 1 percent of their age cohorts in the country at large, indicating that advanced education was clearly limited to a privileged few. Among the male students, this group disproportionately filled the future rosters of ministers, lawyers, judges, and political leaders. Most female graduates in time married and raised families, but first many of them became teachers at academies and district schools. A large number also became minor authors, contributing essays and poetry to newspapers, editing periodicals, and publishing novels. The new attention to the training of female minds laid the foundation for major changes in the gender system as girl students of the 1810s matured into adult women of the 1830s.

REVIEW How did the civil status of American women and men differ in the early Republic?

▶ Monroe and Adams

Virginians continued their hold on the presidency with the election of James Monroe in 1816 and again in 1820, when Monroe garnered all but one electoral vote. The collapse of the Federalist Party ushered in an apparent period of one-party rule, but politics remained highly partisan. At the state level, increasing political engagement sparked a drive for universal white male suffrage. At the national level, ill feelings were stirred by a sectional crisis in 1820 over the admission of Missouri to the Union, and foreign policy questions involving European claims to Latin America animated sharp disagreements as well. Four candidates vied for the presidency in 1824 in an election decided by the House of Representatives. One-party rule was far from harmonious.

From Property to Democracy

Up to 1820, presidential elections occurred in the electoral college, at a remove from ordinary voters. The excitement generated by state elections, however, created an insistent pressure for greater democratization of presidential elections.

In the 1780s, twelve of the original thirteen states enacted property qualifications based on the time-honored theory that only male freeholders—landowners, as distinct from tenants or servants—had sufficient independence of mind to be entrusted with the vote. Of course, not everyone accepted that restricted idea of the people's role in government (see "Equality and Slavery" in chapter 8). In the 1790s, Vermont became the first state to enfranchise all adult males, and four other states soon broadened suffrage considerably by allowing all male taxpayers to vote. As new states joined the Union, most opted for suffrage for all free white men, which added pressure for eastern states to consider broadening their suffrage laws. Between 1800 and 1830, greater democratization became a contentious issue.

Not everyone favored expanded suffrage; propertied elites tended to defend the status quo. But others managed to get legislatures to call new constitutional conventions in which questions of suffrage, balloting procedures, apportionment, and representation were debated. By 1820, half a dozen states passed suffrage reform, some choosing universal manhood suffrage while others tied the vote to tax status or militia

One Woman's Quest to Provide Higher Education for Women

Talented young men seeking the mental enrichment and career boost of higher education saw their opportunities expand rapidly in the early Republic. By 1830, six dozen colleges offered training in science, history, religion, literature, and philosophy. Not a single one admitted females.

With the spread of district schools and female academies, however, the number of girls trained for advanced study was on the rise. The winning rationale for female education—that mothers molded the character of rising generations—worked well to justify basic schooling. But a highly intellectual woman, negatively termed a "bluestocking," was thought to put her very femininity at risk. Some critics sounded a more practical note: "When girls become scholars, who is to make the puddings and pies?"

The academic aspirations of Emma Hart—born in Connecticut in 1787 as the sixteenth in a farm family of seventeen children—were encouraged by her father, who read Shakespeare at night to his large brood. After attending the local district school and an academy for girls, Emma taught at the district school before moving to Vermont to head the Middlebury Female Academy, founded in 1800. There, she taught sixty adolescents in an underheated building.

Emma ran the academy for two years until she married a Middlebury physician and banker named John Willard in 1809. Marriage for white women usually ended outside employment, so Emma's life now focused on child care and domestic duties. Yet she found time to read books in her husband's well-stocked library, including political philosophy, medical treatises, physiology texts, and Euclid's geometry.

Four years into their marriage, John Willard suffered severe financial losses, leading Emma Willard to open an advanced girls' school in her home. She patterned her courses on those at nearby Middlebury College for men, and her rigorous curriculum soon drew students from all over the Northeast. One satisfied father with political connections persuaded the Willards to relocate to his home state of New York with the promise to help them secure state funding for a school.

Emma drew up a formal proposal in 1819, arguing that advanced female education would both enhance motherhood and supply excellent teachers needed for a projected state-supported school system. Though her proposal was endorsed by Governor DeWitt Clinton, John Adams, and Thomas Jefferson, the New York assembly failed to fund Willard's school. Local citizens in Troy supplied Willard with a building, however, and in 1821 the Troy Female Seminary opened with students coming from many states. Coursework included "masculine" subjects such as Latin, Greek, mathematics, and science in addition to modern languages and literature. Willard taught geometry and trigonometry herself and hired other teachers for classes in astronomy, botany, geology, chemistry, and zoology. She soon forged a cooperative alliance with the neighboring Rensselaer Polytechnic Institute. Just like Harvard and Princeton, her seminary required a course in moral philosophy, taught

service. In the remainder of the states, the defenders of landed property qualifications managed to delay expanded suffrage for two more decades. But it was increasingly hard to persuade the disfranchised that landowners alone had a stake in government. Proponents of the status quo began to argue instead that the "industry and good habits" necessary to achieve a propertied status in life were what gave landowners the right character to vote. Opponents fired back blistering attacks. One delegate to New York's constitutional convention said, "More integrity and more patriotism are generally found in the labouring class of the community than in the higher orders." Owning land was no more predictive of wisdom and good character than it was of a person's height or strength, said another observer.

Both sides of the debate generally agreed that character mattered, and many ideas for ensuring an electorate of proper wisdom came up for discussion. The exclusion of paupers and felons convicted of "infamous crimes" found favor in legislation in many states. Requiring literacy tests and raising the voting age to a figure in the thirties were debated but ultimately discarded.

by Willard herself to the senior class using the same texts employed at the male colleges.

Willard invited the public to weeklong examinations, where students solved algebra problems and geometry proofs on chalkboards and gave twenty-minute discourses on history and philosophy. Educated men were particularly encouraged to question the students, to put to rest any "lurking suspicion, that the learning which a female possesses must be superficial." One minister was astonished, and pleased, to see "Euclid discussed by female lips." By emphasizing geometry, Willard vindicated her claim that women could equal men in logic. But she took pains to make sure her students preserved "feminine delicacy" and avoided "the least indelicacy of language or behavior, such as too much exposure of the person."

More than the rigorous curriculum inspired these young women. Willard was an exemplary role model, beloved by many of her students for her dedication and confidence. One student recalled that her "great distinction seemed to me to be a supreme confidence in herself and, as a consequence, a stubborn faith in the capacity of her own sex." Willard graciously gave much of the credit to her unusually supportive husband: "He entered into the full spirit of my views, with a disinterested zeal for the sex whom, as he had come to believe, his own had unjustly neglected."

Portrait of Emma Willard
Emma Willard, founder of the famed and rigorous Troy Female Seminary, was an exemplary role model to her students. Elizabeth Cady, a student in the 1830s and later an important figure in the woman's rights movement, recalled that Willard had a "profound self respect (a rare quality in a woman) which gave her a dignity truly regal." Her confidence shines through in this portrait. The Granger Collection, New York.

The Troy Female Seminary flourished; it still exists today as the Emma Willard School. From 1821 to 1871, more than 12,000 girls attended; it was larger than most men's colleges. Ministers' daughters received a discount on tuition, and many girls were allowed to defer payment until they were wage-earning teachers. Nearly 5,000 graduates in the first fifty years became teachers, and some 150 directed their own schools scattered across the nation. When the marquis de Lafayette, aging hero of the American Revolution, visited Willard's school in 1824, he pronounced it a "Female University." Willard took pleasure in his recognition of her success.

Questions for Analysis

Summarize the Argument: How did Emma Willard's own life demonstrate the importance of female education for a family's financial security? For a woman's personal sense of competence and independence?

Consider the Context: What factors, large and small, help explain the growth of women's education during the early decades of the nineteenth century?

Ask Historical Questions: What difference might it make for large numbers of females to attain literacy over the course of the first decades of the early Republic?

The exclusion of women required no discussion in the constitutional conventions, so firm was the legal power of *feme covert* mandating the subjugation of married women to their husbands. But in one exceptional moment, at the Virginia constitutional convention in 1829, a delegate wondered aloud why unmarried women older than twenty-one could not vote; he was quickly silenced with the argument that all women lacked the "free agency and intelligence" necessary for wise voting.

Free black men's enfranchisement was another story, generating much discussion at all the conventions. Under existing freehold qualifications, a small number of propertied black men could vote; universal or taxpayer suffrage would inevitably enfranchise many more. Many delegates at the various state conventions spoke against that extension, claiming that blacks as a race lacked prudence, independence, and knowledge. With the exception of New York, which retained the existing property qualification for black voters as it removed it for whites, the general pattern was one of expanded suffrage for whites and a total eclipse of suffrage for blacks.

VISUAL ACTIVITY

"We Owe Allegiance to No Crown"
John Woodside, a Philadelphia sign painter, made his living creating advertisements for hotels and taverns, and he specialized in patriotic banners carried in parades. At some point in his long career from 1815 to 1850, he created this scene of a youthful sailor receiving a laurel wreath, the ancient Greek symbol of victory, from a breezy Miss Liberty (identified by the liberty cap on a stick). Picture Research Consultants & Archives.

READING THE IMAGE: What might the chain at the sailor's feet indicate? What do you think the slogan on the banner means? What do you see in the picture that would help date it? (Hint: Examine the flag. And for the truly curious, consider the history of men's facial hair styles.)

CONNECTIONS: How and why does the painting reference the War of 1812? Regardless of the painting's date, what message do you think Woodside is trying to convey here?

The Missouri Compromise

The politics of race produced the most divisive issue during Monroe's term. In February 1819, Missouri—so recently the territory of the powerful Osage Indians—applied for statehood. Since 1815, four other states had joined the Union (Indiana, Mississippi, Illinois, and Alabama), following the blueprint laid out by the Northwest Ordinance of 1787. But Missouri posed a problem. Although much of its area was on the same latitude as the free state of Illinois, its territorial population included ten thousand slaves brought there by southern planters.

That anomaly—a mostly northern state with the profile of a southern population—led a New York congressman, James Tallmadge Jr., to propose two amendments to the statehood bill. The first stipulated that slaves born in Missouri after statehood would be free at age twenty-five, and the second declared that no new slaves could be imported into the state. Tallmadge's model was New York's gradual emancipation law of 1799 (see "Equality and Slavery" in chapter 8). It did not strip slave owners of their current property, and it allowed them full use of the labor of newborn slaves well into their prime productive years. Still, southern

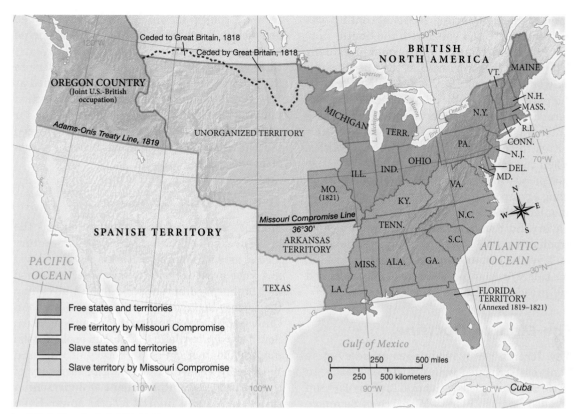

MAP ACTIVITY

Map 10.4   The Missouri Compromise, 1820

After a difficult battle in Congress, Missouri entered the Union in 1821 as part of a package of compromises. Maine was admitted as a free state to balance slavery in Missouri, and a line drawn at latitude 36°30′ put most of the rest of the Louisiana Territory off-limits to slavery in the future.

READING THE MAP: How many free and how many slave states were there prior to the Missouri Compromise? What did the admission of Missouri as a slave state threaten to do?

CONNECTIONS: Who precipitated the crisis over Missouri, what did he propose, and where did the idea come from? Who proposed the Missouri Compromise, and who benefited from it?

congressmen objected because in the long run the amendments would make Missouri a free state, presumably no longer allied with southern economic and political interests. Just as southern economic power rested on slave labor, southern political power drew extra strength from the slave population because of the three-fifths rule. In 1820, the South owed seventeen of its seats in the House of Representatives to its slave population.

Tallmadge's amendments passed in the House by a close and sharply sectional vote of North against South. The ferocious debate led a Georgia representative to observe that the question had started "a fire which all the waters of the ocean could not extinguish. It can be extinguished only in blood." The Senate, with an even number of slave and free states, voted down the amendments, and Missouri statehood was postponed until the next congressional term.

In 1820, a compromise emerged. Maine, once part of Massachusetts, applied for statehood as a free state, balancing against Missouri as a slave state. The Senate further agreed that the southern boundary of Missouri—latitude 36°30′—extended west, would become the permanent line dividing slave from free states, guaranteeing the North a large area where slavery was banned (Map 10.4). The House also approved the **Missouri Compromise**, thanks to expert deal brokering by Kentucky's Henry Clay. The whole package passed because seventeen northern congressmen decided that minimizing sectional conflict was the best course and voted with the South.

President Monroe and former president Jefferson at first worried that the Missouri crisis would reinvigorate the Federalist Party as the party of the North. But even ex-Federalists agreed that the split between free and slave states was too dangerous a fault line to be permitted to become a shaper of national politics. When new parties did develop in the 1830s, they took pains to bridge geography, each party developing a presence in both North and South. Monroe and Jefferson also worried about the future of slavery. Both understood slavery to be deeply problematic, but, as Jefferson said, "We have the wolf by the ear, and we can neither hold him, nor safely let him go. Justice is in one scale, and self-preservation in the other."

The Monroe Doctrine

New foreign policy challenges arose even as Congress struggled with the slavery issue. In 1816, U.S. troops led by General Andrew Jackson invaded Spanish Florida in search of Seminole Indians harboring escaped slaves. Once there, Jackson declared himself the commander of northern Florida, demonstrating his power in 1818 by executing two British men who he claimed were dangerous enemies. In asserting rule over the territory, and surely in executing the two British subjects on Spanish land, Jackson had gone too far. Privately, President Monroe was distressed and pondered court-martialing Jackson, prevented only by Jackson's immense popularity as the hero of the battle of New Orleans. Instead, John Quincy Adams, the secretary of state, negotiated with Spain the Adams-Onís Treaty, which delivered Florida to the United States in 1819 and finally settled the disputed borders of the Louisiana Purchase. In exchange, the Americans agreed to abandon any claim to Texas or Cuba. Southerners viewed this as a large concession, having eyed both places as potential acquisitions for future slave states.

Spain at that moment was preoccupied with its colonies in South America. One after another, Chile, Colombia, Peru, and finally Mexico declared themselves independent in the early 1820s. To discourage Spain and other European countries from reconquering these colonies, Monroe in 1823 formulated a declaration of principles on South America, known in later years as the Monroe Doctrine. The president warned that "the American Continents, by the free and inde- pendent condition which they have assumed and maintain, are henceforth not to be considered as subjects for future colonization by any European power." Any attempt to interfere in the Western Hemisphere would be regarded as "the manifestation of an unfriendly disposition towards the United States." In exchange for noninterference by Europeans, Monroe pledged that the United States would stay out of European struggles.

The Election of 1824

Monroe's nonpartisan administration was the last of its kind, a throwback to eighteenth-century ideals, as was Monroe, with his powdered wig and knee breeches. Monroe's cabinet contained men of sharply different philosophies, all calling themselves Republicans. Secretary of State John Quincy Adams represented the urban Northeast; South Carolinian John C. Calhoun spoke for the planter aristocracy as secretary of war; and William H. Crawford of Georgia, secretary of the treasury, was a proponent of Jeffersonian states' rights and limited federal power. Even before the end of Monroe's first term, these men and others began to maneuver for the election of 1824.

Crucially helping them to maneuver were their wives, who accomplished some of the work of modern campaign managers by courting men—and women—of influence. Louisa Catherine Adams had a weekly party for guests numbering in the hundreds. The somber Adams lacked charm—"I am a man of reserved, cold, austere, and forbidding manners," he once wrote—but his abundantly charming (and hardworking) wife made up for that. She attended to the etiquette of social calls, sometimes making two dozen in a morning, and counted sixty-eight members of Congress as her regular guests. This was smart politics, in case the House of Representatives wound up deciding the 1824 election—which it did.

John Quincy Adams (and Louisa Catherine) was ambitious for the presidency, but so were others. Candidate Henry Clay, Speaker of the House and negotiator of the Treaty of Ghent with Britain in 1814, promoted a new "American System," a package of protective tariffs to encourage manufacturing and federal expenditures for internal improvements such as roads and canals. Treasurer William Crawford was a favorite of Republicans from Virginia and New York, even after he suffered an incapacitating stroke in

General Andrew Jackson
In 1819, Jackson sat for this miniature portrait on ivory made by Anna Claypoole Peale, a member of the artistic Peale family of Philadelphia. At the time, Jackson was in Washington to defend himself against possible congressional charges arising from his unauthorized hangings in Florida. His charming smile and tousled hair do not betray anxiety about the outcome of the proceedings. Yale University Art Gallery.

mid-1824. Calhoun was another serious contender, having served in Congress and in several cabinets. A southern planter, he attracted northern support for his backing of internal improvements and protective tariffs.

The final candidate was an outsider and a latecomer: General Andrew Jackson of Tennessee. Jackson had far less national political experience than the others, but he enjoyed great celebrity from his military career. In 1824, on the anniversary of the battle of New Orleans, the Adamses threw a spectacular ball in his honor, hoping that some of Jackson's charisma would rub off on Adams, who was not yet thinking of Jackson as a rival for office. Not long after, Jackson's supporters put his name forward for the presidency, and voters in the West and South reacted with enthusiasm; Adams was dismayed, and Calhoun dropped out of the race and shifted his attention to winning the vice presidency.

Along with democratizing the vote, eighteen states (out of the full twenty-four) had put the power to choose members of the electoral college directly in the hands of voters, making the 1824 election the first one to have a popular vote tally for the presidency. Jackson proved by far to be the most popular candidate, winning 153,544 votes. Adams was second with 108,740, Clay won 47,136 votes, and the debilitated Crawford garnered 46,618. This was not a large turnout, probably amounting to just over a quarter of adult white males. Nevertheless, the election of 1824 marked a new departure in choosing presidents. Partisanship energized the electorate; apathy and a low voter turnout would not recur until the twentieth century.

In the electoral college, Jackson received 99 votes, Adams 84, Crawford 41, and Clay 37 (Map 10.5). Jackson lacked a majority, so the House of Representatives stepped in for the second time in U.S. history. Each congressional delegation had one vote; according to the Constitution's Twelfth Amendment, passed in 1804, only the top three candidates joined the runoff. Thus Henry Clay was out of the race and in a position to bestow his support on another candidate.

Candidate*	Electoral Vote	Popular Vote	Percent of Popular Vote
John Q. Adams	84	108,740	30.5
Andrew Jackson	99	153,544	43.1
Henry Clay	37	47,136	13.2
W. H. Crawford	41	46,618	13.1

*No distinct political parties

Note: Because no candidate garnered a majority in the electoral college, the election was decided in the House of Representatives. Although Clay was eliminated from the running, as Speaker of the House he influenced the final decision in favor of Adams.

Map 10.5
The Election of 1824

Jackson's supporters later characterized the election of 1824 as the "corrupt bargain." Clay backed Adams, and Adams won by one vote in the House in February 1825. Clay's support made sense on several levels. Despite strong mutual dislike, he and Adams agreed on issues such as federal support to build roads and canals. Moreover, Clay was uneasy with Jackson's volatile temperament and unstated political views and with Crawford's diminished capacity. What made Clay's decision look "corrupt" was that immediately after the election, Adams offered to appoint Clay secretary of state—and Clay accepted.

In fact, there probably was no concrete bargain; Adams's subsequent cabinet appointments demonstrated his lack of political astuteness. But Andrew Jackson felt that the election had been stolen from him, and he wrote bitterly that "the Judas of the West [Clay] has closed the contract and will receive the thirty pieces of silver."

The Adams Administration

John Quincy Adams, like his father, was a one-term president. His career had been built on diplomacy, not electoral politics, and despite his wife's deftness in the art of political influence, his own political horse sense was not well developed. With his cabinet choices, he welcomed his opposition into his inner circle. He asked Crawford to stay on in the Treasury. He retained an openly pro-Jackson postmaster general even though that position controlled thousands of nationwide patronage appointments. He even asked Jackson to become secretary of war. With Calhoun as vice president (elected without opposition by the electoral college) and Clay at the State Department, the whole argumentative crew would have been thrust into the executive branch. Crawford and Jackson had the good sense to decline the appointments.

Adams had lofty ideas for federal action during his presidency, and the plan he put before Congress was sweeping. Adams called for federally built roads, canals, and harbors. He proposed a national university in Washington as well as government-sponsored scientific research. He wanted to build observatories to advance astronomical knowledge and to promote precision in timekeeping, and he backed a decimal-based system of weights and measures. In all these endeavors, Adams believed he was continuing the legacy of Jefferson and Madison, using the powers of government to advance knowledge.

But his opponents feared he was too Hamiltonian, using federal power inappropriately to advance commercial interests.

Whether he was more truly Federalist or Republican was a moot point. Lacking the give-and-take political skills required to gain congressional support, Adams was unable to implement much of his program. He scorned the idea of courting voters to gain support and using the patronage system to enhance his power. He often made appointments (to posts such as customs collectors) to placate enemies rather than to reward friends. A story of a toast offered to the president may well have been mythical, but it came to summarize Adams's precarious hold on leadership. A dignitary raised a glass and said, "May he strike confusion to his foes," to which another voice scornfully chimed in, "as he has already done to his friends."

REVIEW   Why did partisan conflict increase during the administrations of Monroe and Adams?

► Conclusion: Republican Simplicity Becomes Complex

The Jeffersonian Republicans at first tried to undo much of what the Federalists had created in the 1790s, but their promise of a simpler government gave way to the complexities of domestic and foreign issues. The Louisiana Purchase and the Barbary Wars required powerful government responses, and the challenges posed by Britain on the seas finally drew America into declaring war on the onetime mother country. The War of 1812, joined by restive Indian nations fighting with the British, was longer and more costly than anticipated, and it ended inconclusively.

The war elevated to national prominence General Andrew Jackson, whose popularity with voters in the 1824 election surprised traditional politicians and threw the one-party rule of Republicans into a tailspin. John Quincy Adams had barely assumed office in 1825 before the election campaign of 1828 was off and running. Reformed suffrage laws ensured that appeals to the mass of white male voters would be the hallmark of all nineteenth-century elections after

1824. In such a system, Adams and men like him were at a great disadvantage.

Ordinary American women, whether white or free black, had no place in government. Male legislatures maintained women's *feme covert* status, keeping wives dependent on husbands. A few women found a pathway to greater personal autonomy through religion, while many others benefited from expanded female schooling in schools and academies. These substantial gains in education would blossom into a major transformation of gender in the 1830s and 1840s.

Two other developments would prove momentous in later decades. The bitter debate over slavery that surrounded the Missouri Compromise accentuated the serious divisions between northern and southern states—divisions that would only widen in the decades to come. And Jefferson's long embargo and Madison's wartime trade stoppage gave a big boost to American manufacturing by removing competition with British factories. When peace returned in 1815, the years of independent development burst forth into a period of sustained economic growth that continued nearly unabated into the mid-nineteenth century.

See the Selected Bibliography for this chapter in the Appendix.

10 Chapter Review

KEY TERMS

Marbury v. Madison (p. 259)
Louisiana Purchase (p. 261)
Lewis and Clark expedition (p. 262)
impressment (p. 264)
Embargo Act of 1807 (p. 264)
battle of Tippecanoe (p. 266)
War Hawks (p. 266)
Creek War (p. 266)
battle of New Orleans (p. 267)
Hartford Convention (p. 269)
feme covert (p. 270)
Missouri Compromise (p. 277)

REVIEW QUESTIONS

1. How did Jefferson's views of the role of the federal government differ from those of his predecessors? (pp. 255–260)

2. What was the significance of the Louisiana Purchase for the United States? (pp. 260–263)

3. Why did Congress declare war on Great Britain in 1812? (pp. 263–270)

4. How did the civil status of American women and men differ in the early Republic? (pp. 270–273)

5. Why did partisan conflict increase during the administrations of Monroe and Adams? (pp. 273–280)

MAKING CONNECTIONS

1. When Jefferson assumed the presidency following the election of 1800, he expected to transform the national government. Describe President Jefferson's republican vision and his successes and failures in implementing it. Did subsequent Republican presidents advance the same objectives?

2. How did the United States strengthen its control of territory in North America in the early nineteenth century by using diplomatic, military, and political means?

3. Although the United States denied its female citizens equality in public life, some women were able to exert considerable influence. How did they do so?

LINKING TO THE PAST

1. Compare the British-Indian alliance in the Revolutionary War with the British-Indian alliance in the War of 1812. Were there any reasons for men like Tecumseh to think that the alliance might work out better the second time? (See chapter 7.)

2. How do you think the Federalist supporters of the Constitution in 1787–1788 felt about the steady decline in states' property qualifications for male voters that occurred between 1800 and 1824? Did the democratization of voting necessarily undermine the Constitution's restrictions on direct democracy in the federal government? (See chapter 8.)

11 The Expanding Republic
1815–1840

CONTENT LEARNING OBJECTIVES

After reading and studying this chapter, you should be able to:

- Identify several contributing factors to the "market revolution."

- Describe political changes that led to the second party system.

- Identify the Democrats', the Whigs', and Andrew Jackson's political agendas.

- Explain both sides of the controversy over the Indian Removal Act of 1829.

- Explain the Second Great Awakening, and identify the major social reform movements it fueled.

- Identify the issues and challenges that faced Martin Van Buren.

- Explain how slavery emerged as a campaign issue in 1836 and how the panic of 1837 affected the country and Van Buren's administration.

IN 1837, AUDIENCES THROUGHOUT MASSACHUSETTS WITNESSED THE astonishing spectacle of two sisters from a wealthy southern family delivering impassioned speeches about the evils of slavery. Women lecturers were rare in the 1830s, but Sarah and Angelina Grimké were on a mission, channeling a higher power to authorize their outspokenness. Angelina explained that "whilst in the act of speaking I am favored to forget little 'I' entirely & to feel altogether hid behind the great cause I am pleading." In their seventy-nine speaking engagements that year, forty thousand women—and men—came to hear them.

Not much in their family background predicted the sisters' radical break with tradition. They grew up in elite surroundings in Charleston, South Carolina, where their father was chief justice of the state supreme court, yet they somehow managed to develop independent minds and a hatred of slavery. In the 1820s, both sisters moved to Philadelphia and joined the Quakers' Society of Friends.

The abolitionist movement was in its infancy in the 1830s, centered around Boston's William Lloyd Garrison, editor of the *Liberator*, who demanded an immediate end to slavery. In 1835, Angelina Grimké wrote to Garrison, describing herself as a white southern exile from slavery, and Garrison published her letter. Her rare voice of personal testimony caused a stir and propelled her into her new public career.

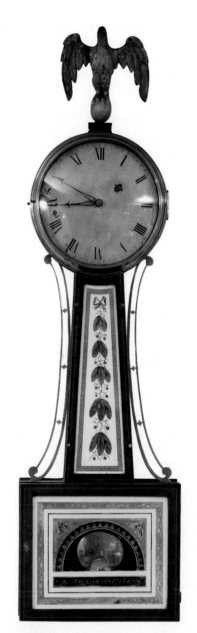

HOUSEHOLD CLOCK
A revolution in household timekeeping devices accompanied the speedup of commerce and transportation in the early Republic. By the mid-1820s, inexpensive, mass-manufactured clocks became commonplace, indicating the increased importance of punctuality. Willard House and Clock Museum.

The sisters' 1837 extended tour of Massachusetts led to a doubling of membership in northern antislavery societies. Newspapers and religious leaders fiercely debated the Grimkés' boldness in presuming to lecture men, and the sisters defended their stand: "Whatever is morally right for a man to do is morally right for a woman to do," Angelina wrote. "I recognize no rights but human rights." Sarah produced a set of essays titled *Letters on the Equality of the Sexes* (1838), the first American treatise asserting women's equality with men.

The Grimké sisters' innovative radicalism was part of a vibrant, contested public life that came alive in the United States of the 1830s. This decade—often summed up as the Age of Jackson, in honor of the larger-than-life president—was a time of rapid economic, political, and social change. Andrew Jackson's bold self-confidence mirrored the new confidence of American society in the years after 1815. An entrepreneurial spirit gripped the country, producing a market revolution of unprecedented scale. Old social hierarchies eroded; ordinary men dreamed of moving high up the ladder of success. Stunning advances in transportation and economic productivity fueled such dreams and propelled thousands to travel west or to cities. Urban growth and technological change fostered the diffusion of a distinctive and lively public culture, spread mainly through the increased circulation of newspapers and also by thousands of public lecturers, like the Grimké sisters, allowing popular opinions to coalesce and intensify.

Expanded communication transformed politics dramatically. Sharp disagreements over the best way to promote individual liberty, economic opportunity, and national prosperity in the new economy defined key differences between presidential parties emerging in the early 1830s, attracting large numbers of white male voters into their ranks. Religion became democratized as well. A nationwide evangelical revival brought its adherents the certainty that salvation was now available to all.

Yet there were downsides. Steamboats blew up, banks and businesses periodically collapsed, alcoholism rates soared, Indians were killed or relocated farther west, and slavery continued to expand. The brash confidence that turned some people into rugged, self-promoting individuals inspired others to think about the human costs of rapid economic expansion and thus about reforming society in dramatic ways. The common denominator was a faith that people and societies could shape their own destinies.

Grimké Sisters
Sarah and Angelina Grimké sat for these portraits around 1840, at ages 48 and 35. Day caps were typical indoor wear for most older women and for Quaker women of all ages. Caps kept hair neat and in place. As important, they signaled modesty, in contrast to fancily coiffed or loose hair, which sent a different signal. Sarah Grimké: Library of Congress, 3a03340; Angelina Grimké: Library of Congress, 3a03341.

► The Market Revolution

The return of peace in 1815 unleashed powerful forces that revolutionized the organization of the economy. Spectacular changes in transportation facilitated the movement of commodities, information, and people, while textile mills and other factories created many new jobs, especially for young unmarried women. Innovations in banking, legal practices, and tariff policies promoted swift economic growth.

This was not yet an industrial revolution, as was beginning in Britain, but rather a market revolution fueled by traditional sources—water, wood, beasts of burden, and human muscle. What was new was the accelerated pace of economic activity and the scale of the distribution of goods. The nature and scale of production and consumption changed Americans' economic behaviors, attitudes, and expectations. The new economy also carried great risk, which periodically resulted in economic crashes.

Improvements in Transportation

Before 1815, transportation in the United States was slow and expensive; it cost as much to ship a crate over thirty miles of domestic roads as it did to send it across the Atlantic Ocean. A stagecoach trip from Boston to New York took four days. But between 1815 and 1840, networks of roads, canals, steamboats, and finally railroads dramatically raised the speed and lowered the cost of travel (Map 11.1).

Improved transportation moved goods into wider markets. It moved passengers, too, allowing young people as well as adults to take up new employment in cities or factory towns. Transportation also facilitated the flow of political information via the U.S. mail with its bargain postal rates for newspapers, periodicals, and books. Enhanced public transport was expensive and produced uneven economic benefits, so presidents from Jefferson to Monroe were reluctant to fund it with federal dollars. Instead, private investors pooled resources and chartered transport companies, receiving significant subsidies and monopoly rights from state governments. Turnpike and roadway mileage increased dramatically after 1815, reducing shipping costs. Stagecoach companies proliferated, and travel time on main routes was cut in half.

Water travel was similarly transformed. In 1807, Robert Fulton's steam-propelled boat, the

CHRONOLOGY

1807	• Robert Fulton sets off steamboat craze.
1816	• Second Bank of the United States chartered.
1817	• American Colonization Society founded.
1819	• Financial panic disrupts economy.
1825	• Erie Canal completed in New York.
1826	• American Temperance Society founded.
1828	• Tariff of Abominations passes. • Andrew Jackson elected president.
1829	• David Walker publishes *An Appeal . . . to the Coloured Citizens of the World*. • Baltimore and Ohio railroad construction begins.
1830	• Indian Removal Act passes.
1830–1831	• Charles Grandison Finney preaches in Rochester, New York.
1831	• William Lloyd Garrison starts *Liberator*.
1832	• Hundreds of Sauk and Fox Indians massacred. • *Worcester v. Georgia* decided. • Jackson vetoes charter renewal of Bank of the United States. • New England Anti-Slavery Society founded.
1833	• South Carolina nullifies federal tariffs. • New York and Philadelphia antislavery societies founded. • New York Female Moral Reform Society founded.
1834	• Female mill workers strike in Lowell, Massachusetts, and again in 1836.
1836	• Martin Van Buren elected president. • American Temperance Union founded.
1837	• Major financial panic disrupts economy.
1838	• Cherokee Trail of Tears migration kills thousands.
1839	• Financial panic recurs.
1840	• William Henry Harrison elected president.

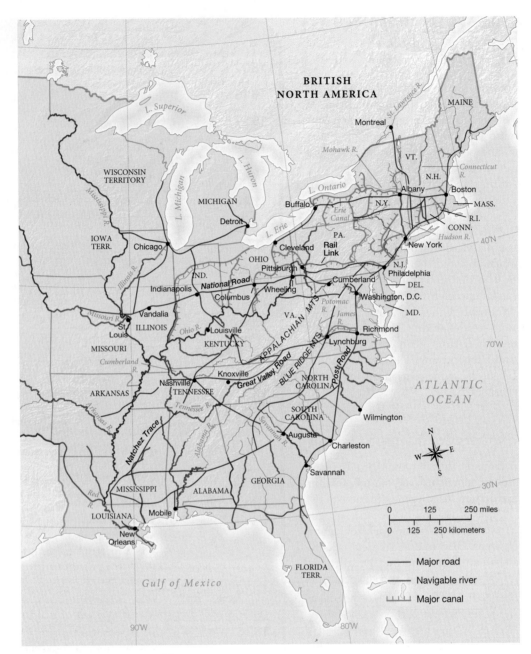

MAP ACTIVITY

Map 11.1 Routes of Transportation in 1840

Transportation advances cut travel times significantly. On the Erie Canal, goods and people could move from New York City to Buffalo in four days, a two-week trip by road. Steamboats cut travel time from New York to New Orleans from four weeks by road to less than two weeks by river.

READING THE MAP: In what parts of the country were canals built most extensively? Were most of them within a single state's borders, or did they encourage interstate travel and shipping?

CONNECTIONS: What impact did the Erie Canal have on the development of New York City? How did improvements in transportation affect urbanization in other parts of the country?

Clermont, churned up the Hudson River from New York City to Albany, touching off a steamboat craze on eastern rivers and the Great Lakes. By the early 1830s, more than seven hundred steamboats were in operation on the Ohio and Mississippi rivers.

Steamboats were not benign advances, however. The urgency to cut travel time led to overstoked furnaces, sudden boiler explosions, and terrible mass fatalities. An investigation of an accident near Cincinnati in 1838, in which 150 passengers were killed, charged: "Such disasters

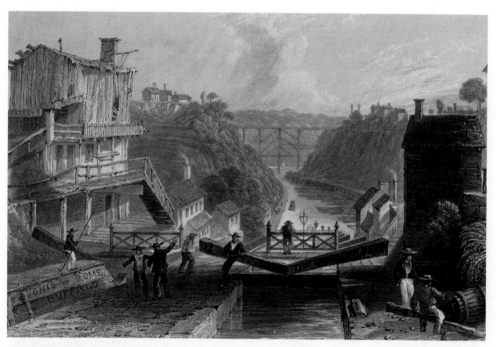

The Erie Canal at Lockport

The Erie Canal, completed in 1825, was impressive not only for its length of 350 miles but also for its elevation, requiring the construction of eighty-three locks. The biggest engineering challenge came at Lockport, twenty miles northeast of Buffalo, where the canal traversed a steep slate escarpment. Work crews—mostly immigrant Irishmen—used gunpowder and grueling physical labor to blast the deep artificial gorge shown here. Department of Rare Books and Special Collections, Rush Rhees Library, University of Rochester.

have their foundation in the present mammoth evil of our country, an inordinate love of gain. We are not satisfied with getting rich, but we must get rich in a day. We are not satisfied with traveling at a speed of ten miles an hour, but we must fly." By the mid-1830s, nearly three thousand Americans had been killed in steamboat accidents, leading to the first federal attempt to regulate safety on vessels used for interstate commerce. Environment costs were also large: Steamboats had to load fuel—"wood up"—every twenty miles or so, resulting in mass deforestation. By the 1830s, the banks of many main rivers were denuded of trees, and forests miles back from the rivers fell to the ax. The smoke from wood-burning steamboats created America's first significant air pollution.

Canals were another major innovation of the transportation revolution. Canal boats powered by mules moved slowly—less than five miles per hour—but the low-friction water enabled one mule to pull a fifty-ton barge. Several states commenced major government-sponsored canal enterprises, the most impressive being the **Erie Canal**, finished in 1825, covering 350 miles between Albany and Buffalo and linking the port of New York City with the entire Great Lakes region. Wheat and flour moved east, household

goods and tools moved west, and passengers went in both directions. By the 1830s, the cost of shipping by canal fell to less than one-tenth of the cost of overland transport, and New York City quickly blossomed into the premier commercial city in the United States.

In the 1830s, private railroad companies heavily subsidized by state legislatures began to give canals competition. The nation's first railroad, the Baltimore and Ohio, laid thirteen miles of track in 1829, and by 1840, three thousand more miles of track materialized nationwide. Rail lines in the 1830s were generally short, on the order of twenty to one hundred miles. They did not yet provide an efficient distribution system for goods, but passengers flocked to experience the marvelous speeds of fifteen to twenty miles per hour. Railroads and other advances in transportation served to unify the country culturally and economically.

Factories, Workingwomen, and Wage Labor

Transportation advances accelerated manufacturing after 1815, creating an ever-expanding market for goods. The two leading industries, textiles and shoes, altered methods of production

VISUAL ACTIVITY

Cotton Textile Mill, 1840

New England textile factories ran on the power of coursing rivers. The linear motion of the river was converted to rotary motion by large waterwheels. A complex series of belts and wheels delivered that motion to the various floors of the factory. This room contains "spinning frames," machines that replaced spinning wheels, turning cleaned cotton into yarn for textile weaving. Cotton textile mill: Mary Evans Picture Library/age fotostock; Shuttle with spindles: Picture Research Consultants & Archives.

READING THE IMAGE: Study the women workers shown here. What do you imagine they might be doing at this power machine? Does this image suggest that the work is stressful or dangerous? What might be the uses of such an image in 1840?

CONNECTIONS: Why was the antebellum textile industry located primarily in New England? Consider the geography and climate that promotes coursing rivers, as well as demographic factors that produce an adequate labor force.

and labor relations. Textile production was greatly spurred by the development of water-driven machinery built near fast-coursing rivers. Shoe manufacturing, still using the power and skill of human hands, involved only a reorganization of production. Both industries pulled young women into wage-earning labor for the first time.

The earliest American textile factory was built in the 1790s by an English immigrant in Pawtucket, Rhode Island. By 1815, nearly 170 spinning mills stood along New England rivers. While British manufacturers hired entire families for mill work, American factory owners innovated by hiring young women, assumed to be cheap to hire because of their limited employment options and their short-term prospects, since most left to get married.

In 1821, a group of Boston entrepreneurs founded the town of Lowell on the Merrimack River, centralizing all aspects of cloth production: combing, shrinking, spinning, weaving, and dyeing. By 1836, the eight **Lowell mills** employed more than five thousand young women, who lived in carefully managed company-owned boardinghouses. Corporation rules at the Lowell mills required church attendance and prohibited drinking and unsupervised court-ship; dorms were locked at 10 p.m. A typical mill worker earned $2 to $3 for a seventy-hour week, more than a seamstress or domestic servant could earn but less than a young man's wages.

Despite the long hours, young women embraced factory work as a means to earn spending money and build savings before marriage; several banks in town held the nest eggs of thousands of workers. Also welcome was the unprecedented, though still limited, personal freedom of living in an all-female social space, away from parents and domestic tasks. In the evening, the women could engage in self-improvement activities, such as attending public lectures. In 1837, 1,500 mill girls crowded Lowell's city hall to hear the Grimké sisters speak about the evils of slavery.

In the mid-1830s, worldwide growth and competition in the cotton market impelled mill owners to speed up work and decrease wages. The workers protested, emboldened by their communal living arrangement and by their relative independence as temporary employees. In 1834 and again in 1836, hundreds of women at Lowell went out on strike. (See "Analyzing Historical Evidence," page 290.) Such strikes spread; in 1834, mill workers in Dover, New Hampshire, denounced their owners for trying to turn them into "slaves." Their assertiveness surprised many, but ultimately the ease of replacing them undermined their bargaining power, and owners in the 1840s began to shift to immigrant families as their primary labor source.

The shoe manufacturing industry centered in eastern New England reorganized production and hired women, including wives, as shoebinders. Male shoemakers still cut the leather and made the soles in shops, but female shoebinders working from home now stitched the upper parts of the shoes. Working from home meant that wives could contribute to family income—unusual for most wives in that period—and still perform their domestic chores.

In the economically turbulent 1830s, shoebinder wages fell. Unlike mill workers, female shoebinders worked in isolation, a serious hindrance to organized protest. In Lynn,

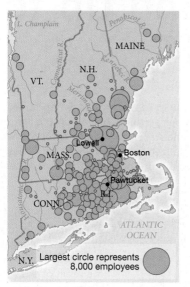

Cotton Textile Industry, ca. 1840

Largest circle represents 8,000 employees

Massachusetts, a major shoe-making center, women used female church networks to organize resistance, communicating via religious newspapers. The Lynn shoebinders who demanded higher wages in 1834 built on a collective sense of themselves as women. "Equal rights should be extended to all—to the weaker sex as well as the stronger," they proclaimed.

In the end, the Lynn shoebinders' protests failed to achieve wage increases. At-home workers all over New England continued to accept low wages, and even in Lynn many women shied away from organized protest, preferring to situate their work in the context of family duty (helping their husbands to finish the shoes) instead of market relations.

Bankers and Lawyers

Entrepreneurs like the Lowell factory owners relied on innovations in the banking system to finance their ventures. Between 1814 and 1816, the number of state-chartered banks in the United States more than doubled from fewer than 90 to 208. By 1830, there were 330, and by 1840 hundreds more. Banks stimulated the economy by making loans to merchants and manufacturers and by enlarging the money supply. Borrowers were issued loans in the form of banknotes—certificates unique to each bank—that were used as money for all transactions. Neither federal nor state governments issued paper money, so banknotes issued by hundreds of individual banks became the country's currency. Constant uncertainty about the true worth of a banknote injected extra risk into the economy. Additionally, the sheer variety of notes in circulation created ideal conditions for counterfeiters to get into the action.

Bankers exercised great power over the economy, deciding who would get loans and what the discount rates would be. The most powerful bankers sat on the board of directors for the **second Bank of the United States**, headquartered in Philadelphia and featuring eighteen branches throughout the country. The twenty-year

Mill Girls Stand Up to Factory Owners, 1834

Lowell's first large "turn out" by mill girls came in February 1834, when factory owners announced a 15 percent wage cut. Newspaper accounts played up the spectacle of young women, thought to be docile, taking to the streets in protest. After four days, the strike fizzled when the inexperienced workers realized that the owners could easily replace them. But lessons were learned, and a later Lowell "turn out," in 1836, was sustained for several months.

DOCUMENT 1
The Lowell Journal Reports the Strike, February 18, 1834

A town newspaper favorable to the factory owners characterized the work stoppage as a delusional farce led by a small number of "wicked and malicious girls."

The Factory Girls.—It has become known, from rumor, that a considerable number of the girls employed in the mills of this town turned out on Friday last, to prevent a reduction in wages. . . . It was proposed, some time since, to make a very small reduction in the wages of all of the hands on the first of March, and notices to that effect were posted in the mills. . . .

Upon this, several wicked and malicious girls . . . undertook to get up a *turn out*, with a view to threaten the agents with an entire stoppage of the works, in order to exact the higher rates of wages. . . . On Friday and Saturday from 800 to 1000 girls revolted under the most laughable delusions, that mischief could invent. The first day, processions were formed of about 700 girls, who listened to sundry stimulative exhortations, . . . and marched through the streets, ankle-deep in mud. . . . Saturday became a day of repentance to many; and they would gladly have returned to their business, but for a pledge, cunningly devised, that each

who did so, should forfeit five dollars to the rebels. The Sabbath afforded opportunity for a little more cool reflection, and on Monday morning, a large concourse attended by a parcel of idle men and boys, heard another speech. . . . The result of the whole matter is, that a few of the ringleaders are refused entrance into the mills, and most of the disaffected, having learned the truth, and becoming sensible of the wicked misrepresentations of which they had nearly been the victims, are returning to their work, ready to take a diminished price, and continue to labor at wages which will give them from one and a half, to two and a half dollars per week, more than their board.—This, to be sure, is not so much as they have had in past times, nor so much as we hope they will soon have again, but it is more than they can get in any other occupation in New England.

Source: The Lowell Journal, February 18, 1834, as reprinted in the New-York Spectator, March 6, 1834. Gale Database, "Nineteenth-Century U.S. Newspapers."

DOCUMENT 2
Anonymous Mill Girls, "Union Is Power"

A position paper, quickly drafted, framed the strikers' goals in terms of "rights" and appealed to the patriotic spirit of the American Revolution to justify their actions.

charter of the first Bank of the United States had expired in 1811, and the second Bank of the United States opened for business in 1816 under another twenty-year charter. The rechartering of this bank would become a major issue in the 1832 presidential campaign.

Lawyer-politicians, too, exercised economic power, by refashioning commercial law to enhance the prospects of private investment. In 1811, states started to rewrite their laws of incorporation (allowing the chartering of businesses by states), and the number of corporations expanded rapidly, from about twenty in 1800 to eighteen

hundred by 1817. Incorporation protected individual investors from being held liable for corporate debts. State lawmakers also wrote laws of eminent domain, empowering states to buy land for roads and canals even from unwilling sellers. In such ways, entrepreneurial lawyers created the legal foundation for an economy that favored ambitious individuals interested in maximizing their own wealth.

Not everyone applauded these developments. Andrew Jackson, himself a skillful lawyer turned politician, spoke for a large and mistrustful segment of the population when he warned about

Our present object is to have union and exertion, and we remain in possession of our own unquestionable rights. We circulate this paper, wishing to obtain the names of all who imbibe the spirit of our patriotic ancestors, who preferred privation to bondage, and parted with all that renders life desirable—and even life itself—to procure independence for their children. The oppressing hand of avarice would enslave us; and to gain their object, they very gravely tell us of the pressure of the times; this we are already sensible of, and deplore it. If any are in want of assistance, the Ladies will be compassionate, and assist them; but we prefer to have the disposing of our charities in our own hands; and as we are free, we would remain in possession of what kind Providence has bestowed upon us, and remain daughters of freemen still.

All who patronize this effort, we wish to have discontinue their labors until terms of reconciliation are made.

Resolved, That we will not go back into the mills to work unless our wages are continued to us as they have been.

Resolved, That none of us will go back unless they receive us all as one.

Source: Printed in *The Man*, February 22, 1834. Published in New York City by G. H. Evans. American Periodicals Series Online.

"We do not estimate our *Liberty* by dollars and cents; consequently it was not the reduction of *wages* alone which caused the excitement, but that *haughty, overbearing disposition*—that *purse proud insolence*, which was becoming more and more apparent—that spirit of tyranny so manifest at present among the *avaricious* and wealthy manufacturers of this and the old country.

"I have only to add, that if the proprietors and agents are not satisfied with alluring us from our homes—from the peaceful abodes of our childhood, under the false promises of a great reward, and then casting us upon the world, . . . merely because we would not be slaves— . . . let them bring down upon us the whole influence of the *rich* and *noble*, the *proud* and the *mighty*, all piled upon the *United States Bank*—steep us in poverty to the very dregs, but we beseech them not to asperse our characters, or *stigmatize* us as *disorderly* persons. Grant us this favor, and give us the privilege of breathing the air of freedom in its *purity*, and we will be content."

Source: *The Man*, March 20, 1834. Published in New York City by G. H. Evans. American Periodicals Series Online.

DOCUMENT 3
A Strike Leader Speaks Out, Mid-March 1834

A month later, one of the leaders explained that the strike was caused not only by reduced wages but also by anger at the insolence of wealthy factory owners. Her remarks were published in The Man, *a New York paper friendly to workingmen's issues.*

The Lowell Girls have been censured in no measured terms by the Federal press of the east, for the "turn out.". . . One of the girls has turned round on her accusers, and while she does not outstep the modesty of her sex, her spirit would do credit to any parentage in these or other days. Hear the yankee girl:

Questions for Analysis

Analyze the Evidence: Does the *Lowell Journal* adequately explain how a few "ring-leaders" could motivate more than eight hundred female workers to engage in street protests?

Recognize Viewpoints: Why do the strikers invoke Revolutionary-era ideals of independence and liberty and the phrase "daughters of freemen"? Do these young women feel subordinate and deferential to the factory owners? Were they in fact subordinates?

Consider the Context: How was the "turn out" of female workers at Lowell an unintended consequence of the market revolution?

the potential abuses of power "which the moneyed interest derives from a paper currency which they are able to control [and] from the multitude of corporations with exclusive privileges which they have succeeded in obtaining in the different states." Jacksonians believed that ending government-granted privileges was the way to maximize individual liberty and economic opportunity.

Booms and Busts

One aspect of the economy that the lawyer-politicians could not control was the threat of financial collapse. The boom years from 1815 to 1818 exhibited a volatility that resulted in the first sharp, large-scale economic downturn in U.S. history. Americans called this downturn a "panic," and the pattern was repeated in the 1830s. Some blamed the panic of 1819 on the second Bank of the United States for failing to control an economic bubble and then contracting the money supply, sending tremors throughout the economy. The crunch was made worse by a financial crisis in Europe in the spring of 1819. Overseas, prices for American cotton, tobacco, and wheat plummeted by more than 50 percent. Thus, when the banks began to call in their outstanding loans, American debtors involved in the commodities trade could not come up with the money. Business and personal bankruptcies skyrocketed. The intricate web of credit and debt relationships meant that almost everyone with even a toehold in the new commercial economy was affected by the panic. Thousands of Americans lost their savings and property, and unemployment estimates suggest that half a million people lost their jobs.

Recovery took several years. Unemployment declined, but bitterness lingered, ready to be stirred up by politicians in the decades to come. The dangers of a system dependent on extensive credit were now clear. In one folksy formulation that circulated around 1820, a farmer compared credit to "a man pissing in his breeches on a cold day to keep his arse warm—very comfortable at first but I dare say . . . you know how it feels afterwards."

By the mid-1820s, the economy was back on track, driven by increases in productivity, consumer demand for goods, and international trade. Despite the panic of 1819, credit financing continued to fuel the system. A network of credit and debt relations grew dense by the 1830s in a system that encouraged speculation and risk taking. A pervasive optimism about continued growth supported the elaborate system, but a single business failure could produce many innocent victims. Well after the panic of 1819, an undercurrent of anxiety about rapid economic change continued to shape the political views of many Americans.

REVIEW   Why did the United States experience a market revolution after 1815?

Second Bank of the United States, Philadelphia
Along with the growth of state banks came a second federal Bank of the United States, chartered by Congress in 1816. It was headquartered in Philadelphia in this imposing Greek Revival building, constructed between 1818 and 1824. The architecture conveyed solidity, security, and timeless permanence. Despite appearances, the bank lost its charter during Andrew Jackson's presidency and ceased to exist. Library Company of Philadelphia, PA, USA/Bridgeman Images.

▶ The Spread of Democracy

Just as the market revolution held out the promise, if not the reality, of economic opportunity for all who worked, the political transformation of the 1830s held out the promise of political opportunity for hundreds of thousands of new voters. During Andrew Jackson's presidency (1829–1837), the second American party system took shape, defined by Jackson's charismatic personality expressed in his efforts to dominate Congress. Not until 1836, however, would the parties have distinct names and consistent programs transcending the particular personalities running for office. Over those years, more men could and did vote, responding to new methods of arousing voter interest.

Popular Politics and Partisan Identity

The election of 1828, pitting Andrew Jackson against John Quincy Adams, was the first presidential contest in which the popular vote determined the outcome. In twenty-two out of twenty-four states, voters—not state legislatures—designated the number of electors committed to a particular candidate. More than a million voters participated, three times the number in 1824 and nearly half the free male population, reflecting the high stakes that voters perceived in the Adams-Jackson rematch. Throughout the 1830s, voter turnout continued to rise and reached 70 percent in some localities, partly because of the disappearance of property qualifications in all but three states and partly because of heightened political interest.

The 1828 election inaugurated new campaign styles. State-level candidates routinely gave speeches at rallies, picnics, and banquets. Adams and Jackson still declined such appearances as undignified, but Henry Clay of Kentucky, campaigning for Adams, earned the nickname "the Barbecue Orator." Campaign rhetoric became more informal and even blunt. The Jackson camp established many Hickory Clubs, trading on Jackson's popular nickname, "Old Hickory," from a common Tennessee tree suggesting resilience and toughness.

Partisan newspapers in ever-larger numbers defined issues and publicized political personalities as never before. Improved printing technology and rising literacy rates fueled a great

TABLE 11.1	THE GROWTH OF NEWSPAPERS, 1820–1840			
	1820	1830	1835	1840
U.S. population (in millions)	9.6	12.8	15.0	17.1
Number of newspapers published	500	800	1,200	1,400
Daily newspapers	42	65	—	138

expansion of newspapers of all kinds (Table 11.1). Party leaders dispensed subsidies and other favors to secure the support of papers, even in remote towns and villages. Political news stories traveled swiftly in the mail, gaining coverage by reprintings in sympathetic newspapers. Presidential campaigns were now coordinated in a national arena.

Politicians at first identified themselves as Jackson or Adams men, honoring the fiction of Republican Party unity. By 1832, however, the terminology had evolved to National Republicans, who favored federal action to promote commercial development, and Democratic Republicans, who promised to be responsive to the will of the majority. Between 1834 and 1836, National Republicans came to be called **Whigs**, while Jackson's party became simply the **Democrats**.

The Election of 1828 and the Character Issue

The campaign of 1828 was the first national election dominated by scandal and character questions. Claims about morality, honor, and discipline became central because voters used them to comprehend the kind of public official each man would make. Jackson and Adams presented two radically different styles of manhood.

John Quincy Adams was vilified by his opponents as an elitist, a bookish academic, and even a monarchist. They attacked his "corrupt bargain" of 1824—the alleged election deal between Adams and Henry Clay (see "The Election of 1824" in chapter 10). Adams's supporters countered by playing on Jackson's fatherless childhood to portray him as the bastard son of a prostitute. Worse, the cloudy circumstances around his marriage to Rachel Donelson Robards in 1791 gave rise to the story that Jackson was a seducer and an adulterer, having married a woman whose divorce from her first husband was not entirely legal. Pro-Adams newspapers howled that Jackson was sinful and impulsive, while portraying Adams as pious, learned, and virtuous.

Editors in favor of Adams played up Jackson's violent temper, as evidenced by his participation in many duels, brawls, and canings. Jackson's supporters used the same stories to project Old Hickory as a tough frontier hero who knew how to command obedience. As for learning, Jackson's rough frontier education gave him a "natural sense," wrote a Boston editor, that "can never be acquired by reading books—it can only be acquired, in perfection, by reading men."

Jackson won a sweeping victory, with 56 percent of the popular vote and 178 electoral votes to Adams's 83 (Map 11.2). Old Hickory took most of the South and West and carried Pennsylvania and New York as well; Adams carried the remainder of the East. Jackson's vice president was John C. Calhoun, who had just served as vice president under Adams but had broken with Adams's policies.

After 1828, national politicians no longer deplored the existence of political parties. They were coming to see that parties mobilized and delivered voters, sharpened candidates' differences, and created party loyalty that surpassed loyalty to individual candidates and elections. Adams and Jackson clearly symbolized the competing ideas of the emerging parties: a moralistic, top-down party (the Whigs) ready to make major decisions to promote economic growth competing against a contentious, energetic party (the Democrats) ready to embrace liberty-loving individualism.

Campaign Poster from 1828
This poster praises Andrew Jackson as a war hero and "man of the people" and reminds readers that Jackson, who won the popular vote in 1824, did not stoop to "bargain for the presidency," as John Quincy Adams presumably had in his dealings with Henry Clay (see "The Election of 1824" in chapter 10). © Collection of the New-York Historical Society, USA/Bridgeman Images.

Jackson's Democratic Agenda

Before the inauguration in March 1829, Rachel Jackson died. Certain that the ugly campaign had hastened his wife's death, the president went into deep mourning, his depression worsened by constant pain from a bullet still lodged in his chest from an 1806 duel and by mercury poisoning from the medicines he took. Aged sixty-two, Jackson carried only 140 pounds on his six-foot-one frame. His adversaries doubted that he would make it to a second term. His supporters, however, went wild at his March 1829 inauguration. Thousands cheered his ten-minute inaugural address, the shortest in history. An open reception at the White House turned into a near riot as well-wishers jammed the premises, used windows as doors, stood on furniture for a better view of the great man, and broke thousands of dollars' worth of china and glasses. During his presidency, Jackson continued to offer unprecedented hospitality to the public. The courteous Jackson, committed to his image as president of the "common man," held audiences with unannounced visitors throughout his two terms.

Candidate	Electoral Vote	Popular Vote	Percent of Popular Vote
Andrew Jackson (Democratic Republican)	178	647,286	56
John Q. Adams (National Republican)	83	508,064	44

Map 11.2
The Election of 1828

Past presidents had tried to lessen party conflict by including men of different factions in their cabinets, but Jackson would have only loyalists, a political tactic followed by most later presidents. For secretary of state, the key job, he tapped New Yorker Martin Van Buren, one of the shrewdest politicians of the day. Throughout the federal government, from postal clerks to ambassadors, Jackson replaced competent civil servants with party loyalists. Jackson's appointment practices were termed a "spoils system" by his opponents, after a Democratic politician coined the affirmative slogan "to the victor belong the spoils."

Jackson's agenda quickly emerged. Fearing that intervention in the economy inevitably favored some groups at the expense of others, Jackson favored a Jeffersonian limited federal government. He therefore opposed federal support of transportation and grants of monopolies and charters that benefited wealthy investors. Like Jefferson, he anticipated the rapid settlement of the country's interior, where land sales would spread economic democracy to settlers. Thus, establishing a federal policy to remove the Indians from this area had high priority. Jackson was freer than previous presidents with the use of the presidential veto power over Congress. In 1830, he vetoed a highway project in Maysville, Kentucky, Henry Clay's home state. The Maysville Road veto articulated Jackson's principled stand that citizens' tax dollars could be spent only on projects of a "general, not local" character. In all, Jackson used the veto twelve times; all previous presidents combined had exercised that right a total of nine times.

> **REVIEW** Why did Andrew Jackson defeat John Quincy Adams so dramatically in the 1828 election?

VISUAL ACTIVITY

Andrew Jackson as "The Great Father"
In 1828, a new process of commercial lithography brought political cartooning to new prominence. Out of some sixty satirical cartoons lampooning Jackson, only one featured his controversial Indian policy. This cropped cartoon lacks the cartoonist's caption, important for understanding the artist's intent. Still, the visual humor of Jackson cradling Indians packs an immediate punch. William L. Clements Library, University of Michigan.

READING THE IMAGE: Examine the body language conveyed in the various characters' poses. Are the Indians depicted as children or as powerless, miniature adults? What is going on in the picture on the wall, and how does it relate to Jackson's Indian removal policy?

CONNECTIONS: Did the Jackson administration protect the Indians? How might Jackson have convinced himself that he was protecting the Indians from certain doom?

▶ Jackson Defines the Democratic Party

In his two terms as president, Andrew Jackson worked to implement his vision of a politics of opportunity for all white men. To open land for white settlement, he favored the relocation of all eastern Indian tribes. He dramatically confronted John C. Calhoun and South Carolina when that state tried to nullify the tariff of 1828. Disapproving of all government-granted privilege, Jackson challenged and defeated the Bank of the United States. In all this, he greatly enhanced the power of the presidency.

Indian Policy and the Trail of Tears

Probably nothing defined Jackson's presidency more than his efforts to solve what he saw as the Indian problem. Thousands of Indians lived in the South and the old Northwest, and many remained in New England and New York. In his first message to Congress in 1829, Jackson, famed for his battles with the Creek and Seminole tribes in the 1810s, declared that removing the

Indians to territory west of the Mississippi was the only way to save them. White civilization destroyed Indian resources and thus doomed the Indians, he claimed: "That this fate surely awaits them if they remain within the limits of the states does not admit of a doubt. Humanity and national honor demand that every effort should be made to avert so great a calamity." Jackson never publicly wavered from this seemingly noble theme, returning to it in his next seven annual messages.

Prior administrations had experimented with different Indian policies. Starting in 1819, Congress funded missionary associations eager to "civilize" native peoples by converting them to Christianity and to whites' agricultural practices. The federal government had also pursued aggressive treaty making with many tribes, dealing with the Indians as foreign nations (see "Creeks in the Southwest" in chapter 9 and "Osage and Comanche Indians " in chapter 10). In contrast, Jackson saw Indians as subjects of the United States (neither foreigners nor citizens) who needed to be relocated to assure their survival. Congress agreed and passed the **Indian Removal Act of 1830**. About 100 million acres of eastern land would be vacated for eventual white settlement under this act authorizing ethnic expulsion (Map 11.3).

The Indian Removal Act generated widespread controversy. Newspapers, public lecturers, and local clubs debated the expulsion law, and public opinion, especially in the North, was heated. "One would think that the guilt of African slavery was enough for the nation to bear, without the additional crime of injustice to the aborigines," one writer declared in 1829. In an unprecedented move, thousands of northern white women signed antiremoval petitions. Between 1830 and 1832, women's petitions rolled into Washington, arguing that sovereign peoples on the road to Christianity were entitled to stay on their land. Jackson ignored the petitions.

For many northern tribes, diminished by years of war, removal was already under way. But not all went quietly. In 1832 in western Illinois, Black Hawk, a leader of the Sauk and Fox Indians who had fought in alliance with Tecumseh in the War of 1812 (see "Jefferson, the Madisons, and the War of 1812" in chapter 10), resisted removal. Volunteer militias attacked and chased the Indians into southern Wisconsin, where, after several skirmishes and a deadly battle (later called the Black Hawk War), Black Hawk was captured and some four hundred of his people were massacred.

The large southern tribes—the Creek, Chickasaw, Choctaw, Seminole, and Cherokee—proved even more resistant to removal. Georgia Cherokees had already taken several assimilationist steps. They had adopted written laws, including, in 1827, a constitution modeled on the U.S. Constitution. Two hundred of the wealthiest Cherokee men had intermarried with whites, adopting white styles of housing, dress, and cotton agriculture, including the ownership of slaves. They developed a written alphabet and published a newspaper and Christian prayer books in their language. These features helped make their cause attractive to the northern white women who petitioned the government on their behalf. Yet most of the

John Ross, Principal Cherokee Chief, 1843
John Ross was elected Principal Chief of the Cherokees from 1828 to 1866. Just one-eighth Cherokee from his maternal line, Ross was raised Cherokee. His mission schooling, bilingual skills, and sharp legal mind provided strong credentials to advance Cherokee interests. Despite a decade of lobbying trips to Washington, Ross could not stop the Cherokee expulsion. His wife, Quatie, died on the Trail of Tears. Library of Congress, LC-DIG-pga-07513.

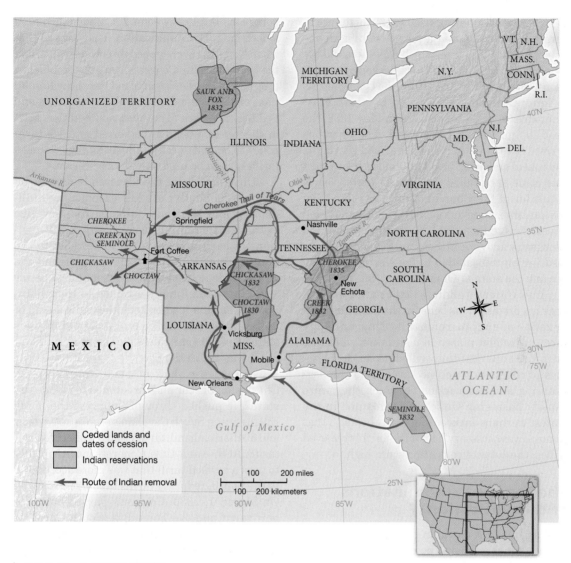

MAP ACTIVITY

Map 11.3   Indian Removal and the Trail of Tears

The federal government under President Andrew Jackson pursued a vigorous policy of Indian removal in the 1830s, forcibly moving tribes west to land known as Indian Territory (present-day Oklahoma). In 1838, as many as a quarter of the Cherokee Indians died on the route known as the Trail of Tears.

READING THE MAP: From which states were most of the Native Americans removed? Through which states did the Trail of Tears go?

CONNECTIONS: Before Jackson's presidency, how did the federal government view Native Americans, and what policy initiatives were undertaken by the government and private groups? How did Jackson change the government's policy toward Native Americans?

seventeen thousand Cherokees maintained cultural continuity with past traditions.

In 1831, when Georgia announced its plans to seize all Cherokee property, the tribal leadership took their case to the U.S. Supreme Court. In *Worcester v. Georgia* (1832), the Court upheld the territorial sovereignty of the Cherokee people, recognizing their existence as "a distinct community, occupying its own territory, in which

the laws of Georgia can have no force." An angry President Jackson ignored the Court and pressed the Cherokee tribe to move west: "If they now refuse to accept the liberal terms offered, they can only be liable for whatever evils and difficulties may arise. I feel conscious of having done my duty to my red children."

The Cherokee tribe remained in Georgia for two more years without significant violence. Then, in 1835, a small, unauthorized faction of the acculturated leaders signed a treaty selling all the tribal lands to the state, which rapidly resold the land to whites. Chief John Ross, backed by several thousand Cherokees, petitioned the U.S. Congress to ignore the bogus treaty to no avail. Most Cherokees refused to move, so in May 1838, the deadline for voluntary removal, federal troops arrived to remove them. Under armed guard, the Cherokees embarked on a 1,200-mile journey west that came to be called the Trail of Tears. Nearly a quarter of the Cherokees died en route from the hardship. Survivors joined the fifteen thousand Creek, twelve thousand Choctaw, five thousand Chickasaw, and several thousand Seminole Indians also forcibly relocated to Indian Territory (which became the state of Oklahoma in 1907).

In his farewell address to the nation in 1837, Jackson professed his belief in the humanitarian benefits of Indian removal: "This unhappy race . . . are now placed in a situation where we may well hope that they will share in the blessings of civilization and be saved from the degradation and destruction to which they were rapidly hastening while they remained in the states." Perhaps Jackson genuinely believed that removal was necessary, but for the forcibly removed tribes, the costs of relocation were high.

The Tariff of Abominations and Nullification

Just as Indian removal in Georgia had pitted a state against a federal power, in the form of a Supreme Court ruling, a second explosive issue also pitted a state against federal regulation. This was the issue of federal tariff policy, strongly opposed by South Carolina.

Federal tariffs as high as 33 percent on imports such as textiles and iron goods had been passed in 1816 and again in 1824 in an effort to shelter new American manufacturers from foreign competition. Some southern congressmen opposed the steep tariffs, fearing they would reduce overseas shipping and thereby hurt cotton exports. In 1828, Congress passed a revised tariff that came to be known as the Tariff of Abominations. A bundle of conflicting duties, some as high as 50 percent, the legislation contained provisions that pleased and angered every economic and sectional interest.

South Carolina in particular suffered from the Tariff of Abominations. Worldwide prices for cotton had declined in the late 1820s, and the falloff in shipping caused by the high tariffs further hurt the South. In 1828, a group of South Carolina

politicians headed by John C. Calhoun advanced a doctrine called nullification. They argued that when Congress overstepped its powers, states had the right to nullify Congress's acts. As precedents, they pointed to the Virginia and Kentucky Resolutions of 1798, intended to invalidate the Alien and Sedition Acts (see "The Alien and Sedition Acts" in chapter 9). Congress had erred in using tariff policy to benefit specific industries, they claimed; tariffs should be used only to raise revenue.

On assuming the presidency in 1829, Jackson ignored the South Carolina statement of nullification and shut out Calhoun, his new vice president, from influence or power. Tariff revisions in early 1832 brought little relief to the South. Sensing futility, Calhoun resigned the vice presidency and became a senator to better serve his state. Finally, strained to their limit, South Carolina leaders took the radical step of declaring federal tariffs null and void in their state as of February 1, 1833. The constitutional crisis was out in the open.

In response, Jackson sent armed ships to Charleston harbor and threatened to invade the state. He pushed through Congress the Force Bill, defining South Carolina's stance as treason and authorizing military action to collect federal tariffs. At the same time, Congress moved quickly to pass a revised tariff that was more acceptable to the South, reducing tariffs to their 1816 level. On March 1, 1833, Congress passed both the new tariff and the Force Bill. South Carolina withdrew its nullification of the old tariff—and then nullified the Force Bill. It was a symbolic gesture since Jackson's show of muscle was no longer necessary.

Yet the question of federal power versus states' rights was far from settled. The implied threat behind nullification was secession, a position articulated in 1832 by some South Carolinians whose concerns went beyond tariff policy. In the 1830s, the political moratorium on discussions of slavery agreed on at the time of the Missouri Compromise (see "The Missouri Compromise" in chapter 10) was coming unglued, and new northern voices opposed to slavery gained increasing attention. If and when a northern-dominated federal government decided to end slavery, the South Carolinians thought, the South should nullify such laws or else remove itself from the Union.

The Bank War and Economic Boom

Along with the tariff and nullification, President Jackson fought another political battle, over the

Bank of the United States. With twenty-nine branches, the bank handled the federal government's deposits, extended credit and loans, and issued banknotes—by 1830, the most stable currency in the country. Jackson, however, thought the bank concentrated undue economic power in the hands of a few.

National Republican (Whig) senators Daniel Webster and Henry Clay decided to force the issue. They convinced the bank to apply for charter renewal in 1832, well before the fall election, even though the existing charter ran until 1836. They fully expected that Congress's renewal would force Jackson to follow through on his rhetoric with a veto, that the unpopular veto would cause Jackson to lose the election, and that the bank would survive on an override vote by a new Congress swept into power on the anti-Jackson tide.

At first, the plan seemed to work. The bank applied for rechartering, Congress voted to renew, and Jackson, angry over being manipulated, issued his veto. But it was a brilliantly written veto, positioning Jackson as the champion of the democratic masses. "Many of our rich men have not been content with equal protection and equal benefits, but have besought us to make them richer by act of Congress," Jackson wrote.

Clay and his supporters found Jackson's economic ideas and his rhetoric of class antagonism so absurd that they distributed thousands of copies of the bank veto as campaign material for their own party. A confident Henry Clay headed his party's ticket for the presidency. But the plan backfired. Jackson's framing of the bank controversy in the language of class conflict resonated with many Americans. Jackson won the election easily, gaining 55 percent of the popular vote and 219 electoral votes to Clay's 49. Jackson's party still controlled Congress, so no override was possible. The second Bank of the United States would cease to exist after 1836.

Jackson wanted to destroy the bank sooner. Calling it a "monster," he ordered the sizable federal deposits to be removed from its vaults and redeposited into Democratic-inclined state banks. In retaliation, the Bank of the United States raised interest rates and called in loans.

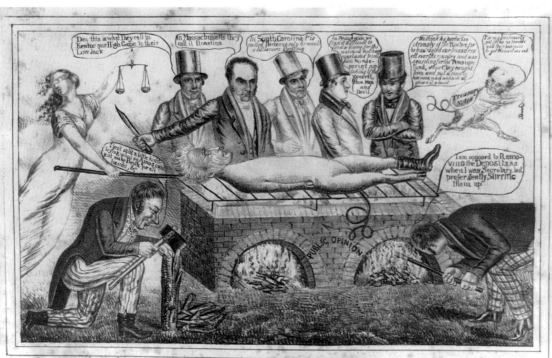

"The Political Barbecue," 1834
Political cartooning became a high art in the 1830s. Here, Pig Jackson roasts on a barbecue grill, fed by the fires of "public opinion" kindled by his decision to take down the Bank of the United States. Political opponents happy to see him get cooked include Henry Clay, Daniel Webster, and Nicholas Biddle, president of the bank. The cartoon is a fantasy: Public opinion generally backed Jackson. Library of Congress, LC-USZ62-9647.

This action caused a brief decline in the economy in 1833 and actually enhanced Jackson's claim that the bank was too powerful for the good of the country.

Unleashed and unregulated, the economy went into high gear in 1834. Just at this moment, an excess of silver from Mexican mines made its way into American banks, giving bankers license to print ever more banknotes. From 1834 to 1837, inflation soared; prices of basic goods rose more than 50 percent. States quickly chartered hundreds of new private banks, each issuing its own banknotes. Entrepreneurs borrowed and invested money, and the webs of credit and debt relationships that were the hallmark of the American economy grew denser yet. The market in western land sales also heated up. In 1834, about 4.5 million acres of the public domain had been sold, the highest annual volume since 1818. By 1836, the total reached an astonishing 20 million acres (Figure 11.1).

In one respect, the economy attained an admirable goal: The national debt disappeared, and from 1835 to 1837, for the only time in American history, the government had a monetary surplus. But much of that surplus consisted of questionable bank currencies—"bloated, diseased" currencies, in Jackson's vivid terminology. While the boom was on, however, few stopped to worry about the consequences if and when the bubble burst.

REVIEW   What were the most significant policies of Andrew Jackson's presidency?

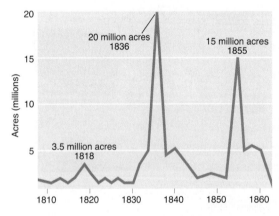

FIGURE 11.1   Western Land Sales, 1810–1860
Land sales peaked in the 1810s, 1830s, and 1850s as Americans rushed to speculate in western land sold by the federal government. The surges in 1818 and 1836 demonstrate the volatile, speculative economy that suddenly collapsed in the panics of 1819 and 1837.

▶ Cultural Shifts, Religion, and Reform

The growing economy, booming by the mid-1830s, transformed social and cultural life. For many families, especially in the commercialized Northeast, standards of living rose, consumption patterns changed, and the nature and location of work were altered. All this had a direct impact on the duties of men and women and on the training of youths for the economy of the future.

Along with economic change came an unprecedented revival of evangelical religion known as the Second Great Awakening. Among the most serious adherents of evangelical Protestantism were men and women of the new merchant classes, whose self-discipline in pursuing market ambitions meshed well with the message of self-discipline in pursuit of spiritual perfection. Not content with individual perfection, many of these people sought to perfect society as well, by defining excessive alcohol consumption, nonmarital sex, and slavery as three major evils of modern life in need of correction. Three social movements championing temperance, moral reform, and abolition gained strength from evangelistic Christianity.

The Family and Separate Spheres

The centerpiece of new ideas about gender relations was the notion that husbands found their status and authority in the new world of work, leaving wives to tend the hearth and home. Sermons, advice books, periodicals, and novels reinforced the idea that men and women inhabited separate spheres and had separate duties. "To woman it belongs . . . to elevate the intellectual character of her household [and] to kindle the fires of mental activity in childhood," wrote Mrs. A. J. Graves in a popular book titled *Advice to American Women*. For men, by contrast, "the absorbing passion for gain, and the pressing demands of business, engross their whole attention." In particular, the home, now said to be the exclusive domain of women, was sentimentalized as the source of intimacy, love, and safety, a refuge from the cruel and competitive world of market relations.

Some new aspects of society gave substance to this formulation of separate spheres. Men's work was undergoing profound change after 1815 and increasingly brought cash to the household, especially in the manufacturing and urban Northeast. Farmers and tradesmen sold products in a market, and bankers, bookkeepers, shoemakers, and canal diggers earned regular salaries or wages. Furthermore, many men now worked away from the home, at an office or a store.

A woman's domestic role was more complicated than the cultural prescriptions indicated. Although the vast majority of married white women did not hold paying jobs, their homes required time-consuming labor. But the advice books treated housework as a loving familial duty, thus rendering it invisible in an economy that evaluated work by how much cash it generated. In reality, many wives contributed to

family income by taking in boarders or sewing for pay. Wives in the poorest classes, including most free black wives, did not have the luxury of husbands earning adequate wages; for them, work as servants or laundresses helped augment family income.

Idealized notions about the feminine home and the masculine workplace gained acceptance in the 1830s because of the cultural ascendancy of the commercialized Northeast, with its domination of book and periodical publishing. Men seeking manhood through work and pay could embrace competition and acquisitiveness, while women established femininity through dutiful service to home and family. This particular formulation of gender difference helped smooth the

VISUAL ACTIVITY

The Caverly Family at Home, 1836

Itinerant amateur artists journeyed the back roads of antebellum America, painting individuals and families in standard repetitive poses. This picture of a New Hampshire family lists the names and ages at the bottom: Azariah, 44; George, 3; Sarah Jane, 7 months; and Eliza, 24. Gift of Stephen C. Clark. Fenimore Art Museum, Cooperstown, New York. Photograph by Richard Walker.

READING THE IMAGE: What do you make of little George's outfit? Are there clues within the picture that this is a male child? How are gender differences established in this image? What might the large age difference between husband and wife suggest?

CONNECTIONS: How did the heightened attention to gender differences correlate with the changing economy and politics of Jacksonian America?

path for the first generation of Americans experiencing the market revolution, and both men and women of the middle classes benefited. Men were set free to pursue wealth, and women gained moral authority within the home. Beyond white families of the middle and upper classes, however, these new gender ideals had limited applicability. And new voices like those of the Grimké sisters challenged whether "virtue" and "duty" had separate masculine and feminine manifestations. Despite their apparent authority in printed material of the period, these gender ideals were never all-pervasive.

The Education and Training of Youths

The market economy required expanded opportunities for training youths of both sexes. By the 1830s, in both the North and the South, state-supported public school systems were the norm, designed to produce pupils of both sexes able, by age twelve to fourteen, to read, write, and participate in marketplace calculations. Literacy rates for white females climbed dramatically, rivaling the rates for white males for the first time. The fact that taxpayers paid for children's education created an incentive to seek an inexpensive teaching force. By the 1830s, school districts replaced male teachers with young females, for, as a Massachusetts report on education put it, "females can be educated cheaper, quicker, and better, and will teach cheaper after they are qualified."

Advanced education continued to expand in the 1830s, with an additional two dozen colleges for men and several more female seminaries offering education on a par with the male colleges. Still, only a very small percentage of young people attended institutions of higher learning. The vast majority of male youths left public school at age fourteen to apprentice in specific trades or to embark on business careers by seeking entry-level clerkships, abundant in the growing urban centers. Young women headed for mill towns or cities in unprecedented numbers, seeking work in the expanding service sector as seamstresses and domestic servants. Changes in patterns of youth employment meant that large numbers of youngsters escaped the watchful eyes of their parents, a cause of great concern for moralists of the era. Advice books published by the hundreds instructed youths in the virtues of hard work and delayed gratification.

The Second Great Awakening

A newly invigorated version of Protestantism gained momentum in the 1820s and 1830s as the economy reshaped gender and age relations.

Women Graduates of Oberlin College, Class of 1855
Oberlin College, founded by abolitionists in the 1830s, admitted men and women of both races. In the early years, black students were all male, and women students were all white. By 1855 black women had integrated the Ladies' Department. Each student wears a dark dress with a detachable lace collar. Note the uniform hairstyles, parted down the middle, with well-oiled locks lustrously coiled over the ears. Oberlin College Archives.

The earliest manifestations of this fervent piety, which historians call the **Second Great Awakening**, appeared in 1801 in Kentucky, when a crowd of ten thousand people camped out on a hillside at Cane Ridge for a revival meeting that lasted several weeks. By the 1810s and 1820s, "camp meetings" had spread to the Atlantic seaboard states, accelerating and intensifying the emotional impact of the revival.

The gatherings attracted women and men hungry for a more immediate access to spiritual peace, one not requiring years of soul-searching. One eyewitness reported that "some of the people were singing, others praying, some crying for mercy. . . . At one time I saw at least five hundred swept down in a moment as if a battery of a thousand guns had been opened upon them, and then immediately followed shrieks and shouts that rent the very heavens."

From 1800 to 1820, church membership doubled in the United States, much of it among the evangelical groups. Methodists, Baptists, and Presbyterians formed the core of the new movement, which attracted women more than men; wives and mothers typically recruited husbands and sons to join them.

A central leader of the Second Great Awakening was a lawyer turned minister named Charles Grandison Finney. Finney lived in western New York, where the completion of the Erie Canal in 1825 fundamentally altered the social and economic landscape overnight. Growth and prosperity came with other, less admirable side effects, such as prostitution, drinking, and gaming. Finney saw New York canal towns as especially ripe for evangelical awakening. In Rochester, he sustained a six-month revival through the winter of 1830–31, generating thousands of converts.

Finney's message, directed primarily at the business classes, argued for a public-spirited outreach to the less-than-perfect to foster their salvation. Evangelicals promoted Sunday schools to bring piety to children; they battled to honor the Sabbath by ending mail delivery, stopping public transport, and closing shops on Sundays. Many women formed missionary societies that distributed millions of Bibles and religious tracts. Through such avenues, evangelical religion offered women expanded spheres of influence. Finney adopted the tactics of Jacksonian-era politicians—publicity, argumentation, rallies, and speeches—to sell his cause. His object, he said, was to get Americans to "vote in the Lord Jesus Christ as the governor of the Universe."

The Temperance Movement and the Campaign for Moral Reform

The evangelical fervor animated vigorous campaigns to eliminate alcohol abuse and eradicate sexual sin. Millions of Americans took the temperance pledge to abstain from strong drink, and thousands became involved in efforts to end prostitution.

Alcohol consumption had risen steadily in the decades up to 1830. All classes imbibed. A lively saloon culture fostered masculine camaraderie along with extensive alcohol consumption among laborers, while in elite homes the after-dinner whiskey or sherry was commonplace. Colleges before 1820 routinely served students a pint of ale with meals, and the military included rum in the daily ration.

Organized opposition to drinking first surfaced in the 1810s among health and religious reformers. In 1826, Lyman Beecher, a Connecticut minister of an "awakened" church, founded the **American Temperance Society**, which warned that drinking led to poverty, idleness, crime, and family violence. Temperance lecturers spread

"Signing the Pledge" in the 1840s
This lithograph celebrates a hard-won moment in the life of a hard-luck family. A temperance worker convinces the father to sign an oath to abstain from alcohol, while his wife exhibits prayerful gratitude. The temperance pledge was a major tool used by anti-alcohol advocates to curb drinking: Could it have really worked? Consider the power of religious oaths in a society infused with religious belief. The Granger Collection, New York.

Who Scorned Temperance and Moral Reform?

The movements to curb alcohol use and stigmatize illicit sexual expression that gained traction in the 1830s were directly linked to new ideals of middle-class domesticity and the intensified religious fervor of the Second Great Awakening. But of course not everyone was won over. Considerable portions of one segment of the population in particular—young single men living away from home—embraced alcohol consumption and free sexual expression as enduring parts of their youthful camaraderie.

Historians of masculinity identify several features of 1830s society that contributed to the emergence of a boisterous subculture of disorderly young men. More than ever before, adolescent boys left their natal farming villages to take entry-level jobs far from home. They moved to commercial hubs and became shop clerks, secretaries, and typesetters. They delayed marriage into their middle twenties, waiting for sufficient economic success to support a family. This delay also extended time free from the responsibilities of family life.

Unlike earlier eras, when apprentices lived with watchful masters in a familial environment, young men now worked for wages and congregated in boardinghouses, often with minimal adult supervision. Long hours of work heightened the appeal of leisure entertainments. Taverns and saloons provided a space for male friends to gather, and in cities, theaters, dance halls, and brothels were additional options. All of these venues served alcohol to patrons, loosening inhibitions and promoting sociability.

Recent discoveries of scores of scurrilous newspapers, stored uncatalogued for years in venerable historical societies or found in attics by surprised descendants, have given historians a direct window into the world of this masculine subculture. This new genre of publications began to appear in the mid-1830s, trumpeting a distinctive oppositional voice to the standard newspapers of the day. They carried names such as the *Owl* and the *Hawk and Buzzard* (suggesting overhead flights that peer into private places); the *Microscope*, the *Gleaner*, the *Paul Pry*, the *Censor*, and the *Whip* (words conveying punishing exposure); and the *Blade*, the *Satirist*, the *Loafer*, the *Flash*, and the *Rake* (humorous self-descriptive labels). Known sites of publication include Boston; Albany, New York; Philadelphia; Baltimore; Washington, D.C.; and the smaller towns of Rochester, New York; and Manchester, New Hampshire. No doubt there were more; this journalistic craze erupted around 1835, generated excitement, and then burned out around 1845. The editors were nearly all youths in their early twenties.

The salacious weeklies combined humor, gossip, and scandal in varying proportions. They featured profiles of well-known sporting men or prostitutes and commentary on the local social, theatrical, and sports scenes. They often devoted much space to reader communications, a feature not found in more traditional newspapers. A recurring "wants to know" column posted dozens of readers' brief gossipy questions: Who was that climbing into Miss B's bedroom window on State Street last Thursday? Who was doing what in a shed on Cooper's alley at 10 p.m. last Saturday? Pickpockets and cheating clerks in stores received scathing treatment, as did unpleasant work supervisors and men who failed to pay their tavern debts. Letters from readers detailed the bawdy social action in their neighborhoods or in nearby towns, naming scoundrels by their initials. The more successful of these papers had wide regional distributions, as shown by their far-flung correspondents.

The editors of these publications piously asserted that they were shaming the licentious by exposing the word, and middle-class drinking began a steep decline. One powerful tool of persuasion was the temperance pledge, which many business owners began to require of employees.

In 1836, leaders of the temperance movement regrouped into a new society, the American Temperance Union, which demanded total abstinence from its adherents. The intensified war against alcohol moved beyond individual moral suasion into the realm of politics as reformers sought to deny taverns liquor licenses. By 1845, temperance advocates had put an impressive dent in alcohol consumption, which diminished to one-quarter of the per capita consumption of 1830.

More controversial than temperance was a social movement called "moral reform," which first aimed at public morals in general but quickly narrowed to a campaign to eradicate sexual sin. In 1833, a group of Finneyite women

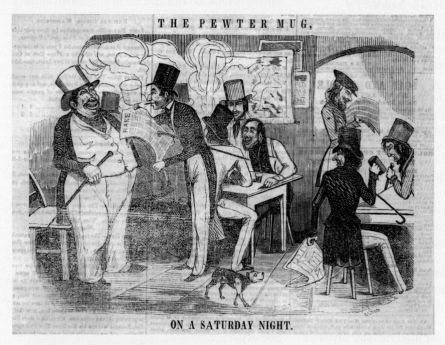

THE PEWTER MUG,

ON A SATURDAY NIGHT.

"The Pewter Mug," 1842
Masculine patrons of a well-known Manhattan saloon called the Pewter Mug blow lots of smoke and lift mugs of alcoholic drinks as they relish reading the latest issue of the *Weekly Rake*. All are wearing the business suit of the day; this is not a working-class bar. This self-celebratory lithograph appeared in the *Weekly Rake*, which offered its readers salacious commentary on sex and the city. American Antiquarian Society, Worcester, Massachusetts, USA/Bridgeman Images.

youth cultivating personal restraint, to a "martial manhood" attracted to service as soldiers, firemen, or policemen, and a working-class "jolly fellow" tavern culture that made a high art of comical and practical jokes.

The raunchy weeklies amplified the presence of hidden enclaves of vice that had long existed in American cities. They provided a guide to the sexual underworld that made that realm visible and navigable to the new throngs of young men on the loose. Their unique interactive quality helped to create and define an oppositional youth culture that thumbed its nose at the moralists, who now grasped, better than ever, how difficult it would be to curb a decade of visible dissolution.

Questions for Analysis

Summarize the Argument: What evidence does the essay provide to explain why an urban sexual underworld came to light in the 1830s? Can you think of additional factors?

Analyze the Evidence: How might the unusual interactive character of the publications discussed in this essay enhance a sense of shared community among the consumers of the newspapers? Are there any parallels to social media of our time? Differences?

Consider the Context: What role did the market revolution and commercial expansion play in the development of this particular subculture of masculinity?

their transgressions. The Boston *Blade*'s masthead proclaimed, "We hold it evident, that truth should be published as villainy stalks abroad, so wide." The New York *Owl* vowed that "the reformation of the rising generation has been our unceasing endeavor." They and everyone else knew such declarations were a joke, especially when the papers detailed exact addresses of brothels and obscene book sellers. Even so, when

editors were hauled into court on obscenity charges, they claimed to be high-minded critics of vice, no more guilty of obscenity than the good ladies agitating in print for moral reform. Skeptical judges sentenced them to jail.

Not all solo young men participated in this subculture, to be sure. Historians have mapped out competing subcultures, from the highly religious or economically ambitious

started the **New York Female Moral Reform Society**. Its members insisted that uncontrolled male sexual expression, manifested in seduction and prostitution, posed a serious threat to society in general and to women in particular. Within five years, more than four thousand auxiliary groups of women had sprung up, mostly in New England, New York, Pennsylvania, and Ohio. (See "Making Historical Arguments," above.)

In its analysis of the causes of licentiousness and its conviction that women had a duty to speak out about unspeakable things, the Moral Reform Society pushed the limits of what even the men in the evangelical movement could tolerate. Yet these women did not regard themselves as radicals. They were simply pursuing the logic of a gender system that defined home protection and morality as women's special sphere and a religious conviction that called for the eradication of sin.

Organizing against Slavery

More radical still was the movement in the 1830s to abolish the sin of slavery. The abolitionist movement had its roots in Great Britain in the late 1700s. Previously, the American Colonization Society, founded in 1817 by Maryland and Virginia planters, promoted gradual individual emancipation of slaves followed by colonization in Africa. By the early 1820s, several thousand ex-slaves had been transported to Liberia on the West African coast. But not surprisingly, newly freed men and women often were not eager to emigrate; their African roots were three or more generations in the past. Colonization was too gradual (and expensive) to have much impact on American slavery.

Around 1830, northern challenges to slavery intensified, beginning in free black communities. In 1829, a Boston printer named David Walker published *An Appeal . . . to the Coloured Citizens of the World*, which condemned racism, invoked the egalitarian language of the Declaration of Independence, and hinted at racial violence if whites did not change their prejudiced ways. In 1830, at the inaugural National Negro Convention meeting in Philadelphia, forty blacks from nine states discussed the racism of American society and proposed emigration to Canada. In 1832 and 1833, a twenty-eight-year-old black woman named Maria Stewart delivered public lectures on slavery and racial prejudice to black audiences in Boston. Her lectures gained wider circulation when they were published in a national publication called the *Liberator*.

The *Liberator*, founded in 1831 in Boston, took antislavery agitation to new heights. Its founder and editor, William Lloyd Garrison, advocated immediate abolition: "On this subject, I do not wish to think, or speak, or write, with moderation. No! No! Tell a man whose house is on fire to give a moderate alarm; tell him to moderately rescue his wife from the hands of the ravisher; tell the mother to gradually extricate her babe from the fire into which it has fallen—but urge me not to use moderation in a cause like the present." In 1832, Garrison's supporters started the New England Anti-Slavery Society.

Similar groups were organized in Philadelphia and New York in 1833. Soon a dozen antislavery newspapers and scores of antislavery lecturers were spreading the word and inspiring the formation of new local societies, which numbered

THE BLACK MAN'S LAMENT.   5

TORN FROM HIS FRIENDS.

***The Black Man's Lament*, 1826**
This colorful yet very violent image appeared in a children's picture book published in London in 1826. The text of the book, titled *The Black Man's Lament; or How to Make Sugar*, consisted of a long poem written by antislavery advocate Amelia Opie. Consider how this image of family separation might affect juvenile readers. What is the significance of the book's subtitle? © Art Media/ HIP/The Image Works.

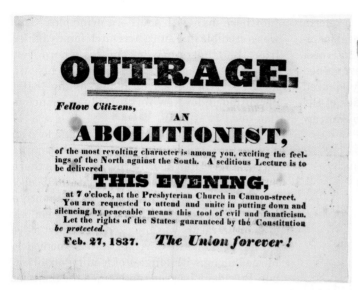

thirteen hundred by 1837. Confined entirely to the North, their membership totaled a quarter of a million men and women.

Many white northerners, even those who opposed slavery, were not prepared to embrace the abolitionist call for emancipation. From 1834 to 1838, there were more than a hundred eruptions of serious mob violence against abolitionists and free blacks. On one occasion, antislavery headquarters in Philadelphia and a black church and orphanage were burned to the ground. In another incident, Illinois abolitionist editor Elijah Lovejoy was killed by a rioting crowd attempting to destroy his printing press. When the Grimké sisters lectured in 1837 (see pages 283–84), some authorities tried to intimidate them and deny them meeting space. The following year, rocks shattered windows when Angelina Grimké gave a speech at a female antislavery convention in Philadelphia. After the women vacated the building, a mob burned the building to the ground.

Despite these dangers, large numbers of northern women played a prominent role in abolition. They formed women's auxiliaries and held fairs to sell handmade crafts to support male lecturers in the field. They circulated antislavery petitions, presented to the U.S. Congress with tens of thousands of signatures. At first women's petitions were framed as respectful memorials to Congress about the evils of slavery, but soon they demanded political action to end slavery in the District of Columbia, under Congress's jurisdiction. By such fervent tactics, antislavery women asserted their claim to be heard on political issues independently of their husbands and fathers.

Garrison particularly welcomed women's activity, despite the potential for danger. The 1837 Massachusetts speaking tour of the Grimké sisters brought out respectful audiences of thousands but also drew intimidation from some quarters. The state leaders of the Congregational Church in Massachusetts banned the sisters from speaking in their churches. While a modest woman deserved deference and protection, church leaders said, immodest women presumptuously instructing men in public forfeited feminine privileges. "When she assumes the place and tone of man as a public reformer, our care and protection of her seem unnecessary; we put ourselves in self-defence against her . . . her character becomes unnatural."

By the late 1830s, the cause of abolition divided the nation as no other issue did. Even among abolitionists, significant divisions emerged. The Grimké sisters, radicalized by the public reaction to their speaking tour, began to write and speak about woman's rights. Angelina Grimké compared the silencing of women to the silencing of slaves: "The denial of our duty to act, is a bold denial of our right to act; and if *we* have no right to act, then may we well be termed 'the white slaves of the North'—for, like our brethren in bonds, we must seal our lips in silence and despair." The Grimkés were opposed by moderate abolitionists who were unwilling to mix the new and controversial issue of woman's rights with their first cause, the rights of blacks.

The many men and women active in reform movements in the 1830s found their initial inspiration in evangelical Protestantism's dual message: Salvation was open to all, and society needed to be perfected. Their activist mentality squared well with the interventionist tendencies of the Whig Party forming in opposition to Andrew Jackson's Democrats.

REVIEW How did evangelical Protestantism contribute to the social reform movements of the 1830s?

▶ Van Buren's One-Term Presidency

By the mid-1830s, a vibrant and tumultuous political culture occupied center stage in American life. Andrew Jackson, too ill to stand for a third term, made way for Martin Van Buren, who faced tough opposition from an array of opposing Whigs and even from slave-owning Jacksonians. Van Buren was a skilled politician, but soon after his inauguration the country faced economic collapse. A shattering panic in 1837, followed by another in 1839, brought the country its worst economic depression yet.

The Politics of Slavery

Sophisticated party organization was the specialty of Martin Van Buren, nicknamed "the Little Magician" for his consummate political skills. First a senator and then governor, the New Yorker became Jackson's secretary of state and then his running mate in 1832, replacing John C. Calhoun. His eight years in the volatile Jackson administration required the full measure of his political deftness as he sought repeatedly to save Jackson from both his enemies and his own obstinacy.

Jackson clearly favored Van Buren for the nomination in 1836, but starting in 1832, the major political parties had developed nominating conventions to choose their candidates. In 1835, Van Buren got the convention nod unanimously, to the dismay of his archrival, Calhoun, who then worked to discredit Van Buren among southern proslavery Democrats. Van Buren spent months assuring them that he was a

"northern man with southern principles." This was a credible line since his Dutch family hailed from the Hudson River counties where New York slavery had once flourished, and his own family had owned slaves as late as the 1810s, permitted under New York's gradual emancipation law.

Calhoun was able to stir up trouble for Van Buren because southerners were becoming increasingly alarmed by the rise of northern antislavery sentiment. When, in late 1835, abolitionists prepared to circulate in the South a million pamphlets condemning slavery, a mailbag of their literature was hijacked at the post office in Charleston, South Carolina, and ceremoniously burned along with effigies of leading abolitionists. President Jackson condemned the theft but issued approval for individual postmasters to exercise their own judgment about whether to allow incendiary materials to reach their destination. Abolitionists saw this as censorship of the mail.

The petitioning tactics of abolitionists escalated sectional tensions. When hundreds of antislavery petitions inundated Congress, proslavery congressmen responded by passing a "gag rule" in 1836. The gag rule prohibited entering the documents into the public record on the grounds that what the abolitionists prayed for was unconstitutional and, further, an assault on the rights of white southerners, as one South Carolina representative put it. Abolitionists like the Grimké sisters considered the gag rule to be an abridgment of free speech. They also argued that, tabled or not, the petitions were effective. "The South already turns pale at the number sent," Angelina Grimké said in a speech exhorting more petitions to be circulated.

Van Buren shrewdly seized on both mail censorship and the gag rule to express his prosouthern sympathies. Abolitionists were "fanatics," he repeatedly claimed, possibly under the influence of "foreign agents" (British abolitionists). He dismissed the issue of abolition in the District of Columbia as "inexpedient" and promised that if he was elected president, he would not allow any interference in southern "domestic institutions."

Elections and Panics

Although the elections of 1824, 1828, and 1832 clearly bore the stamp of Jackson's personality, by 1836 the party apparatus was sufficiently developed to give Van Buren, a backroom politician, a shot at the presidency. Local and state committees existed throughout the country, and more than four hundred newspapers were Democratic partisans.

The Whigs had also built state-level organizations and newspaper loyalty. They had no top contender with nationwide support, so three regional candidates opposed Van Buren. Senator Daniel Webster of Massachusetts could deliver New England, home to reformers, merchants, and manufacturers; Senator Hugh Lawson White of Tennessee attracted proslavery voters still suspicious of the northern Magician; and the aging General William Henry Harrison, now residing in Ohio and remembered for his Indian war heroics in 1811, pulled in the western anti-Indian vote. Not one of the three candidates had the ability to win the presidency, but together they came close to denying Van Buren a majority vote. Van Burenites called the three-Whig strategy a deliberate plot to derail the election and move it to the House of Representatives.

In the end, Van Buren won with 170 electoral votes, while the other three received a total of 113. But Van Buren's victories came from narrow majorities, far below those Jackson had commanded. Although Van Buren had pulled together a national Democratic Party with wins in both the North and the South, he had done it at the cost of committing northern Democrats to the proslavery agenda. And running three candidates had maximized the Whigs' success by drawing Whigs into office at the state level.

When Van Buren took office in March 1837, the financial markets were already quaking; by April, the country was plunged into crisis. The causes of the **panic of 1837** were multiple and far-ranging. Bad harvests in Europe and a large trade imbalance between Britain and the United States caused the Bank of England to start calling in loans to American merchants. Failures in various crop markets and a 30 percent downturn in international cotton prices fed the growing disaster. Cotton merchants in the South could no longer meet their obligations to New York creditors, whose firms began to fail—ninety-eight of them in March and April 1837 alone. Frightened citizens thronged the banks to try to get their money out, and businesses rushed to liquefy their remaining assets to pay off debts. Prices of stocks, bonds, and real estate fell 30 to 40 percent. The familiar events of the panic of 1819 unfolded again, with terrifying rapidity, and the credit market tumbled like a house of cards. Newspapers describing the economic free fall generally used the language of emotional states—excitement, anxiety, terror, panic. Such words focused on human reactions to the crisis rather than on the structural features of the economy that had interacted to amplify the downturn. The vocabulary for understanding the wider economy was still quite limited, making it hard to track the bigger picture of the workings of capitalism. (See "Experiencing the American Promise," page 310.)

Instead, many observers looked to politics, religion, and character flaws to explain the crisis. Some Whig leaders were certain that Jackson's antibank and hard-money policies were responsible for the ruin. New Yorker Philip Hone, a wealthy Whig, called the Jackson administration "the most disastrous in the annals of the country" for its "wicked interference" in banking and monetary matters. Others framed the devastation as retribution for the frenzy of speculation that had gripped the nation. A religious periodical in Boston hoped that Americans would now moderate their greed: "We were getting to think that there was no end to the wealth, and could be no check to the progress of our country; that economy was not needed, that prudence was weakness." In this view, the panic was a wake-up call, a blessing in disguise. Others identified the competitive, profit-maximizing capitalist system as the cause and looked to Britain and France for new socialist ideas calling for the common ownership of the means of production. American socialists, though few in number, were vocal and imaginative, and in the early 1840s several thousand developed utopian alternative communities (as discussed in chapter 12).

The panic of 1837 subsided by 1838, but in 1839 another run on the banks and ripples of business failures deflated the economy, creating a second panic. President Van Buren called a special session of Congress to consider creating an independent treasury system to perform some of the functions of the defunct Bank of the United States. Such a system, funded by government deposits, would deal only in hard money and would exert a powerful moderating influence on inflation and the credit market. But Van Buren encountered strong resistance in Congress, even among Democrats. The treasury system finally won approval in 1840, but by then Van Buren's chances of winning a second term in office were virtually nil.

Going Ahead or *Gone to Smash*: An Entrepreneur Struggles in the 1830s

The spectacular boom of the 1830s gave life to the dream of get-rich-quick entrepreneurship, promising a level of comfort and even affluence previously unimagined. A new slang term, *go-aheadism*, captured the enthusiasm of the day. But this cocky confidence also had a downside, identified by a New York diarist who lamented that *go-aheadism* had made Americans "the most careless, reckless, headlong people on the face of the earth." Soon enough, a rich vocabulary also defined business failure: *gone to smash, fizzled, wiped out, busted, up a tree*, and *GTT*—for "gone to Texas," a location outside the United States (until 1845) and therefore out of reach of U.S. law.

Benjamin Rathbun epitomized both *go-aheadism* and *gone to smash* failure in the turbulent 1830s. A shy man who was never seen to smile, he shrewdly identified Buffalo, New York, as the perfect location for his first business venture, a fancy hotel. Buffalo, a boomtown, linked the Erie Canal with the Great Lakes, where scores of steamboats departed daily for Ohio and Michigan. The town's population doubled from 1830 to 1835, and doubled again, to eighteen thousand inhabitants, by 1840. Fueling this boom were brokerage houses that lined Buffalo's streets,

lending money at high interest rates to borrowers speculating in real estate and business.

The success of the Eagle Hotel enabled Rathbun to become Buffalo's biggest self-made man. In eight years, he built a vast empire of real estate, building construction, banks, stores, and transportation. More than two thousand employees—more than a third of all adult males in Buffalo—were on his payroll. This empire required business acumen, astute management, and a steady influx of borrowed banknotes issued by New York City creditors. Rathbun's trusted younger brother, Lyman, headed financial operations, while Rathbun kept his eye on the big picture: designing the grand architecture of Buffalo (ninety-nine buildings) and cornering the land on the American side of Niagara Falls for profitable resale. Some people believed that Rathbun owned the falls themselves.

Collapse came suddenly in 1836. Rathbun learned that his creditors in New York City had lost faith in him and were selling his IOUs to brokers at a steep discount, a process known as "note shaving." To cover the much higher interest rates charged by the new note holders, the Rathbuns negotiated more loans, supposedly backed by a dozen cosigners from

the Buffalo business community guaranteeing payment if the brothers failed. When Rathbun applied for a $500,000 loan in an attempt to consolidate his debt, the dozen endorsements were revealed to be forgeries. Benjamin Rathbun was convicted of fraud and sentenced to five years' hard labor in state prison; brother Lyman disappeared with trunks full of money—"GTT," many people said.

Rathbun's spectacular failure plunged Buffalo into a severe depression eight months in advance of the panic of 1837. Although deliberate fraud brought him down, his wipeout highlighted the inherent difficulties in an economy of note shaving and discounting, where loans of millions of dollars were granted on the basis of a few signatures. Historians calculate that something like one-fifth of all businessmen in the 1830s *fizzled* or went *up a tree*.

Massive failures in the five years after 1837 led to two striking innovations in business law and loan practices. First, the federal government passed the U.S. Bankruptcy Act of 1841, a controversial and short-term law that enabled failed debtors to wipe debts away legally, paying creditors a fraction of what was owed. Debtors gained release from crushing debt but had to endure the humiliation

---

In 1840, the Whigs settled on William Henry Harrison to oppose Van Buren. The campaign drew on voter involvement as no other presidential campaign ever had. The Whigs borrowed tricks from the Democrats: Harrison was touted as a common man born in a log cabin (in reality, he was born on a Virginia plantation), and campaign parades featured toy log cabins held aloft. His Indian-fighting days, now thirty years behind him, were played up to give him a Jacksonian aura. Whigs staged festive rallies around the country, drumming up mass appeal with candle-

The Eagle Hotel, Buffalo, 1825
Benjamin Rathbun (shown here scowling) bought this three-story building in 1825, doubled it in size, and turned it into the finest hotel west of New York City. The Eagle became the meeting place for all civic and professional groups in early Buffalo. The marquis de Lafayette, French hero of the American Revolution, stayed at the Eagle in 1825 on his U.S. tour. Hotel: Courtesy of the Buffalo History Museum, used by permission. Rathbun: Courtesy of the Buffalo History Museum, used by permission.

of having notices of their bankruptcies printed in the newspapers.

Second, the credit rating industry was born in 1841 when a failed businessman opened the Mercantile Agency in New York City. For a $50 subscription fee, lenders could tap into large books containing confidential information gathered by hundreds of agents around the country who assessed the creditworthiness of local businessmen. Church (and saloon) attendance, family stability, and punctuality were often factors in grading businessmen's reputations for prudence and reliability.

Had it been in existence in 1836, the Mercantile Agency might have unmasked Rathbun's fraud through

semiannual checks on his reputation. The Bankruptcy Act no doubt helped the many debt-saddled Buffalo men who had been caught out by Rathbun's failure. His liquidated estate paid out first to the thousands of workers on his payroll, second to the lawyers, and third to preferred creditors, leaving hundreds of thousands of dollars of debt unpaid.

When Rathbun left prison in 1843, he rejoined his wife, now running a lowly boardinghouse in Buffalo. Soon the Rathbuns moved to New York City, where the onetime proprietor of Buffalo's Eagle Hotel returned to his first occupation. With financial help from cousins, he leased a building for the first in a series of

increasingly seedy hotels that he ran until his death.

Questions for Analysis

Summarize the Argument: What factors led to the Rathbuns' downfall?

Analyze the Evidence: How did the new credit rating agency, established in reaction to the panic of 1837, intend to prevent economic crises?

Consider the Context: What were the causes of the panic of 1837? Did Jackson's war against the Bank of the United States have any connection to the panic?

light parades and song shows, and women participated in rallies as never before. Some 78 percent of eligible voters cast ballots—the highest percentage ever in American history.

Harrison took 53 percent of the popular vote and won a resounding 234 electoral college votes

to Van Buren's 60. A Democratic editor lamented, "We have taught them how to conquer us!"

REVIEW   How did slavery figure as a campaign issue in the election of 1836?

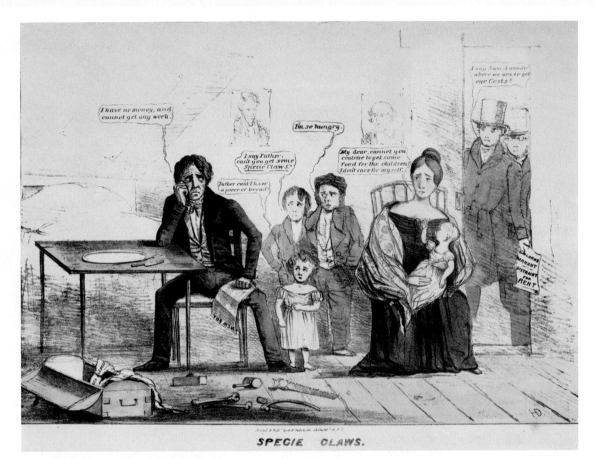

SPECIE CLAWS.

VISUAL ACTIVITY

The Panic of 1837

A sad family with an unemployed father confronts the fallout of the panic of 1837. The wife and children complain of hunger, the house is stripped nearly bare, and rent collectors loom in the doorway. The only support system for the unemployed in 1837 was the local almshouse, where families were split up and living conditions were harsh. Library of Congress, 3g03240.

READING THE IMAGE: What does the clothing worn by family members suggest about their customary economic standing? Can you guess why the artist put sketches of Andrew Jackson and Martin Van Buren on the wall?

CONNECTIONS: What caused the panic of 1837, and why were its consequences suffered by so many people?

▶ Conclusion: The Age of Jackson or the Era of Reform?

Harrison's election closed a decade that had brought the common man and democracy to the forefront of American politics. Economic transformations loom large in explaining the fast-paced changes of the 1830s. Transportation advances put goods and people in circulation, augmenting urban growth and helping to create a national culture, and water-powered manufacturing began to change the face of wage labor.

Trade and banking mushroomed, and western land once occupied by Indians was auctioned off in a landslide of sales. Two periods of economic downturn—including the panic of 1819 and the panics of 1837 and 1839—offered sobering lessons about speculative fever.

Andrew Jackson symbolized this age of opportunity for many. His fame as an aggressive general, Indian fighter, champion of the common man, and defender of slavery attracted growing numbers of voters to the emergent Democratic Party, which championed personal liberty, free competition, and egalitarian opportunity for all white men.

Jackson's constituency was challenged by a small but vocal segment of the population troubled by serious moral problems that Jacksonians preferred to ignore. Inspired by the Second Great Awakening, reformers targeted personal vices (illicit sex and intemperance) and social problems (prostitution, poverty, and slavery) and joined forces with evangelicals and wealthy lawyers and merchants (North and South) who appreciated a national bank and protective tariffs. The Whig Party was the party of activist moralism and state-sponsored entrepreneurship. Whig voters were, of course, male, but thousands of reform-minded women broke new ground by signing political petitions on the issues of Indian removal and slavery. A few exceptional women, like Sarah and Angelina Grimké, captured the national limelight by offering powerful testimony against slavery and in the process pioneered new pathways for women to contribute a moral voice to politics.

National politics in the 1830s were more divisive than at any time since the 1790s. The new party system of Democrats and Whigs reached far deeper into the electorate than had the Federalists and Republicans. Stagecoaches and steamboats carried newspapers from the cities to the backwoods, politicizing voters and creating party loyalty. Politics acquired immediacy and excitement, causing nearly four out of five white men to cast ballots in 1840.

High rates of voter participation would continue into the 1840s and 1850s. Unprecedented urban growth, westward expansion, and early industrialism marked those decades, sustaining the Democrat-Whig split in the electorate. But critiques of slavery, concerns for free labor, and an emerging protest against women's second-class citizenship complicated the political scene of the 1840s, leading to third-party political movements. One of these third parties, called the Republican Party, would achieve dominance in 1860 with the election of an Illinois lawyer, Abraham Lincoln, to the presidency.

See the Selected Bibliography for this chapter in the Appendix.

11 Chapter Review

REVIEW QUESTIONS

1. Why did the United States experience a market revolution after 1815? (pp. 285–292)

2. Why did Andrew Jackson defeat John Quincy Adams so dramatically in the 1828 election? (pp. 293–295)

3. What were the most significant policies of Andrew Jackson's presidency? (pp. 295–300)

4. How did evangelical Protestantism contribute to the social reform movements of the 1830s? (pp. 300–308)

5. How did slavery figure as a campaign issue in the election of 1836? (pp. 308–311)

MAKING CONNECTIONS

1. How did the market revolution that began in the 1810s affect Americans' work and domestic lives? Consider how gender contributed to these developments.

2. Discuss how Jackson benefited from, and contributed to, the vibrant political culture of the 1830s. Cite specific national developments.

3. Describe Andrew Jackson's response to the "Indian problem" during his presidency. How did his policies revise or continue earlier federal policies?

4. Discuss the objectives and strategies of two reform movements of the 1830s and how they relate to larger political and economic trends.

LINKING TO THE PAST

1. How were the economic circumstances and social anxieties that gave rise to the Second Great Awakening similar to, and different from, those that encouraged the First Great Awakening? (See chapter 5.)

2. Compare the development of political parties in the 1790s (Federalists and Republicans) with the second development of parties in the 1830s (Whigs and Democrats). Were the parties of the 1830s in any way the descendants of the two of the 1790s? Or were they completely different? (See chapter 9.)

12

The New West and the Free North

1840–1860

CONTENT LEARNING OBJECTIVES

After reading and studying this chapter, you should be able to:

- Identify the fundamental changes that transformed the American economy from 1840 to 1860.

- Compare and contrast the promises and realities of free labor, including how free-labor proponents explained economic inequality in America.

- Explain how the American nation expanded its boundaries, and define the concept of "manifest destiny."

- Describe the issues that surrounded the debate on the annexation of Texas and Oregon, how the United States provoked war with Mexico, and the consequences of the war.

- Describe the "evangelical temperament," and the reforms evangelical Protestants proposed, and explain how the woman's rights movement evolved from other reform movements.

GOLD NUGGET
Gold! Nuggets like this one scooped from a California river drove easterners crazy with excitement. Only a few of the quarter of a million men who joined the gold rush got rich. CSP_Fireflyphoto/age fotostock.

EARLY IN NOVEMBER 1842, ABRAHAM LINCOLN AND HIS NEW WIFE, Mary, moved into their first home in Springfield, Illinois, a small rented room on the second floor of the Globe Tavern, the nicest place Abraham had ever lived in and the worst place that Mary had ever inhabited. She grew up in Lexington, Kentucky, attended by slaves in the elegant home of her father, a prosperous merchant and banker. In March 1861, the Lincolns moved into the presidential mansion in Washington, D.C.

Abraham Lincoln climbed from the Globe Tavern to the White House by work, ambition, and immense talent—traits he had honed since boyhood. Lincoln and many others celebrated his rise from humble origins as an example of the opportunities in the free-labor economy of the North and West. They attributed his spectacular ascent to his individual qualities and tended to ignore the help he received from Mary and many others.

Born in a Kentucky log cabin in 1809, Lincoln grew up on small, struggling farms as his family migrated west. His father, Thomas Lincoln, who had been born in Virginia, never learned to read and, as his son recalled, "never did more in the way of writing than to bunglingly sign his own name." Lincoln's mother, Nancy, could neither read nor write. In 1816, Thomas Lincoln moved his young family from Kentucky to the Indiana wilderness where Abraham learned the arts of agriculture, but "there was absolutely nothing to excite ambition for education," Lincoln recollected. In contrast, Mary Todd received ten years of schooling in Lexington's best private academies for young women.

In 1830, Thomas Lincoln decided to move farther west and headed to central Illinois. The next spring, when Thomas moved yet again, Abraham set out on his own, a "friendless, uneducated, penniless boy," as he described himself.

By dogged striving, Abraham Lincoln gained an education and the respect of his Illinois neighbors, although a steady income eluded him for years. The newlyweds received help from Mary's father, including eighty acres of land and a yearly allowance of about $1,100 for six years that helped them move out of their room above the Globe Tavern and into their own home. Abraham eventually built a thriving law practice in Springfield, Illinois, and served in the state legislature and in Congress. Mary helped him in many ways, rearing their sons, tending their household, and integrating him into her wealthy and influential extended family in Illinois and Kentucky. Mary also shared Abraham's keen interest in politics and ambition for power. With Mary's support, Abraham became the first president born west of the Appalachian Mountains.

Like Lincoln, millions of Americans believed they could make something of themselves, whatever their origins, so long as they were willing to work. Individuals who were lazy, undisciplined, or foolish had only themselves to blame if they failed, advocates of free-labor ideology declared. Work was a prerequisite for success, not a guarantee. This emphasis on work highlighted the individual efforts of men and tended to slight the many crucial contributions of women and family members to the successes of men like Lincoln. In addition, the rewards of work were skewed toward white men and away from women and free African Americans, as antislavery and woman's rights reformers pointed out. Nonetheless, the promise of such rewards spurred efforts that shaped the contours of America, plowing new fields and building railroads that pushed the boundaries of the nation ever westward to the Pacific Ocean. The nation's economic, political, and geographic expansion raised anew the question of whether slavery should also move west, a question that Lincoln and other Americans confronted repeatedly following the Mexican-American War, yet another outgrowth of the nation's ceaseless westward movement.

▶ Economic and Industrial Evolution

During the 1840s and 1850s, Americans experienced a profound economic transformation. Since 1800, the total output of the U.S. economy had multiplied twelvefold. Four fundamental changes in American society fueled this remarkable economic growth. First, millions of Americans moved from farms to towns and cities, Abraham Lincoln among them. Second, factory workers (primarily in towns and cities) increased to about 20 percent of the labor force by 1860. Third, a shift from water power to steam as a source of energy raised productivity, especially in factories and transportation. Railroads in particular harnessed steam power, speeding transport and cutting costs. Fourth, agricultural productivity nearly doubled during Lincoln's lifetime, spurring the nation's economic growth more than any other factor.

Historians often refer to this cascade of changes as an industrial revolution. However, these changes did not cause an abrupt discontinuity in America's economy or society, which remained overwhelmingly agricultural. Old methods of production continued alongside the new. The changes in the American economy during the 1840s and 1850s might better be termed "industrial evolution."

Agriculture and Land Policy

The foundation of the United States' economic growth lay in agriculture. A French traveler in the United States noted that Americans had "a general feeling of hatred against trees." Although the traveler exaggerated, trees limited agricultural productivity because farmers had to spend much time and energy clearing trees to make fields suitable for cultivation. As farmers pushed westward in a quest for cheap land, they encountered the Midwest's comparatively treeless prairie, where they could spend less time clearing land and more time with a plow and hoe. Rich prairie soils yielded bumper crops, enticing farmers to migrate to the Midwest by the tens of thousands between 1830 and 1860. The populations of Indiana, Illinois, Michigan, Wisconsin, and Iowa exploded tenfold between 1830 and 1860, ten times faster than the growth of the nation as a whole.

Laborsaving improvements in farm implements also boosted agricultural productivity. Inventors tinkered to craft stronger, more efficient plows. In 1837, John Deere made a strong, smooth steel plow that sliced through prairie soil so cleanly

CHRONOLOGY

1830	• *The Book of Mormon* published.
1836	• Battle of the Alamo fought. • Texas declares independence from Mexico.
1837	• Steel plow patented.
1840s	• Practical mechanical reapers created. • Fourierist communities founded.
1841	• First wagon trains head west on Oregon Trail. • Vice President John Tyler becomes president when William Henry Harrison dies.
1844	• James K. Polk elected president. • Samuel F. B. Morse demonstrates telegraph.
1845	• Term *manifest destiny* coined. • Texas enters Union as slave state. • Potato blight spurs Irish immigration.
1846	• Bear Flag Revolt movement raised in California. • Congress declares war on Mexico. • United States and Great Britain divide Oregon Country.
1847	• Mormons settle in Utah.
1848	• Treaty of Guadalupe Hidalgo signed. • Oneida community organized. • Seneca Falls convention held.
1849	• California gold rush begins.
1850	• Utah Territory annexed. • Railroads granted six square miles of land for every mile of track.
1851	• Fort Laramie conference marks beginning of Indian concentration.
1855	• Massachusetts integrates public schools.
1857	• Mormon War reasserts U.S. authority in Utah.
1861	• California connected to nation by telegraph.

that farmers called it the "singing plow." Deere's company produced more than ten thousand plows a year by the late 1850s. Human and animal muscles provided the energy for plowing, but Deere's plows permitted farmers to break more ground and plant more crops.

Improvements in wheat harvesting also increased farmers' productivity. In 1850, most farmers harvested wheat by hand, cutting two or three acres a day. In the 1840s, Cyrus McCormick and others experimented with designs for **mechanical reapers**, and by the 1850s a McCormick reaper that cost between $100 and $150 allowed a farmer to harvest twelve acres a day. Improved reapers and plows, usually powered by horses or oxen, allowed farmers to cultivate more land, doubling the corn and wheat harvests between 1840 and 1860.

Federal land policy made possible the leap in agricultural productivity. Up to 1860, the United States continued to be land-rich and labor-poor. Territorial acquisitions made the nation a great deal richer in land, adding more than a billion acres with the Louisiana Purchase (see "The Louisiana Purchase" in chapter 10) and vast territories following the Mexican-American War. The federal government made most of this land available for purchase to attract settlers and to generate revenue. Millions of ordinary farmers bought federal land for just $1.25 an acre, or $50 for a forty-acre farm that could support a family. Millions of other farmers squatted on unclaimed federal land and carved out farms. By making land available on relatively easy terms, federal land policy boosted the increase in agricultural productivity that fueled the nation's impressive economic growth.

VISUAL ACTIVITY

Mechanical Reaper Advertisement

This advertisement for the mechanical reaper manufactured by the Lagonda Agricultural Works in Ohio illustrates the labor saved—and the labor still required—to harvest wheat. The revolving reel pulled the stalks of wheat toward a cutter and piled the cut grain on a platform. One man pushed the cut wheat onto the ground and another man bound it into sheaves. Library of Congress, LC-DIG-pga-02032.

READING THE IMAGE: What kinds of labor are represented by the two men standing on each side of the oval picture of the reaper? What kinds of labor were saved by the mechanical reaper, and what kinds were required?

CONNECTIONS: How did reapers and other improvements increase agricultural productivity?

Manufacturing and Mechanization

Changes in manufacturing arose from the nation's land-rich, labor-poor economy. In Europe's land-poor, labor-rich economies, meager opportunities in agriculture supplied plenty of factory workers and kept wages low. In the United States, western expansion and government land policies buoyed agriculture, keeping millions of people on the farm—80 percent of the nation's 31 million people lived in rural areas in 1860—and thereby limiting the supply of workers for manufacturing and elevating wages. Because of this relative shortage of workers, American manufacturers searched constantly for ways to save labor.

Mechanization allowed manufacturers to produce more with less labor. In general, factory workers produced twice as much (per unit of labor) as agricultural workers. The practice of manufacturing and then assembling interchangeable parts spread from gun making to other industries and became known as the American system. Standardized parts produced by machine allowed manufacturers to employ unskilled workers, who were much cheaper than highly trained craftsmen. A visitor to a Springfield, Massachusetts, gun factory noted in 1842, for example, that standardized parts made the trained gunsmith's "skill of the eye and hand, [previously] acquired by practice alone, ... no longer indispensable." Factories remained small, however. Even in heavily mechanized industries, factories seldom employed more than twenty or thirty workers.

Manufacturing and agriculture meshed into a dynamic national economy. New England led the nation in manufacturing, shipping goods such as guns, clocks, plows, and axes west and south, while southern and western states sent commodities such as wheat, pork, whiskey, tobacco, and cotton north and east. Between 1840 and 1860, coal production in Pennsylvania, Ohio, and elsewhere multiplied eightfold, cutting prices in half and powering innumerable coal-fired steam engines. Even so, by 1860 coal accounted for less than a fifth of the nation's energy consumption, and, even in manufacturing, muscles provided thirty times more energy than steam did.

American manufacturers specialized in producing for the gigantic domestic market rather than for export. British goods dominated the international market and usually were cheaper and better than American-made products. U.S. manufacturers supported tariffs to minimize British competition, but their best protection from British competitors was to please their American customers, most of them farmers. The burgeoning national economy was accelerated by the growth of railroads, which linked farmers and factories in new ways.

Railroads: Breaking the Bonds of Nature

Railroads captured Americans' imagination because they seemed to break the bonds of nature. When canals and rivers froze in winter or became impassable during summer droughts, trains steamed ahead, averaging more than twenty miles an hour during the 1850s. Above all, railroads gave cities not blessed with canals or navigable rivers a way to compete for rural trade.

In 1850, trains steamed along 9,000 miles of track, almost two-thirds of it in New England and the Middle Atlantic states. By 1860, several railroads spanned the Mississippi River, connecting frontier farmers to the nation's 30,000 miles of track, approximately as much as in all of the rest of the world combined (Map 12.1). In 1857, for example, France had just 3,700 miles of track, while England and Wales had 6,400 miles. The massive expansion of American railroads helped catapult the nation to the world's second-greatest industrial power, after Great Britain.

In addition to speeding transportation, railroads propelled the growth of other industries, such as iron and communications. Iron production grew five times faster than the population during the decades up to 1860, in part to meet railroads' demand. Railroads also stimulated the fledgling telegraph industry. In 1844, Samuel F. B. Morse demonstrated the potential of his telegraph by transmitting an electronic message between Washington, D.C., and Baltimore. By 1861, more than fifty thousand miles of telegraph wire stretched across the continent to the Pacific Ocean, often alongside railroad tracks, accelerating communications of all sorts.

In contrast to government ownership of railroads common in other industrial nations, private corporations built and owned almost all American railroads. But the railroads received massive government aid, especially federal land grants. Up to 1850, the federal government had granted a total of seven million acres of federal land to various turnpike, highway, and canal projects. In 1850, Congress approved a precedent-setting grant to railroads of six square miles of federal land for each mile of track laid. By 1860, Congress had granted railroads more than twenty million acres of federal land, thereby underwriting construction costs and promoting the expansion of

Lackawanna Valley, Pennsylvania
This 1856 portrait of Lackawanna Valley, Pennsylvania—painted by the famous American artist George Innes—depicts the environmental transformation wrought by the railroad. A young man reclines on a hillside overlooking a denuded field littered with tree stumps and cut through by an old dirt road, while contemplating the locomotive pulling a massive train of freight cars away from Scranton, Pennsylvania (to the left of the dirt road leading to the horizon). The giant rail-road roundhouse (center background) and the smokestacks of factories contrast industrial might with the placid orchard (the grove of uniform trees on the right) and the not-yet-cut forest. The painting hints at both the benefits and costs of technological progress in the 1850s. Courtesy National Gallery of Art, Washington, D.C. Gift of Mrs. Huttleston Rogers.

the rail network, the settlement of federal land, and the integration of the domestic market.

The railroad boom of the 1850s signaled the growing industrial might of the American economy. Like other industries, railroads succeeded because they served both farms and cities. But transportation was not revolutionized overnight. Most Americans in 1860 were still far more familiar with horses than with locomotives. Even by 1875, trains carried only about a third of the mail; most of the rest still went by horseback or stagecoach.

The economy of the 1840s and 1850s linked an expanding, westward-moving population in farms and cities with muscles, animals, machines, steam, and railroads. Abraham Lincoln planted corn and split fence rails as a young man before he moved to Springfield, Illinois, and became a successful attorney who defended, among others, railroad corporations. His mobility—westward, from farm to city, from manual to mental labor,

and upward—illustrated the direction of economic change and the opportunities that beckoned enterprising individuals.

REVIEW   Why did the United States become a leading industrial power in the nineteenth century?

▶ Free Labor: Promise and Reality

The nation's impressive economic performance did not reward all Americans equally. Native-born white men tended to do better than immigrants. With few exceptions, women were excluded from opportunities open to men. Tens of thousands of women worked as seamstresses, laundresses,

MAP ACTIVITY

Map 12.1   Railroads in 1860
Railroads were a crucial component of the revolutions in transportation and communications that transformed nineteenth-century America. The railroad system reflected the differences in the economies of the North and South.

READING THE MAP: In which sections of the country was most of the railroad track laid by the middle of the nineteenth century? What cities served as the busiest railroad hubs?
CONNECTIONS: How did the expansion of railroad networks affect the American economy? Why was the U.S. government willing to grant more than twenty million acres of public land to the private corporations that ran the railroads?

domestic servants, factory hands, and teachers but had little opportunity to aspire to higher-paying jobs. In the North and West, slavery was slowly eliminated in the half century after the American Revolution, but most free African Americans were relegated to dead-end jobs as laborers and servants. Discrimination against immigrants, women, and free blacks did not trouble most white men. With certain notable

exceptions, they considered it proper and just, the outcome of the free-labor system that rewarded hard work and, ideally, education.

The Free-Labor Ideal

During the 1840s and 1850s, leaders throughout the North and West emphasized a set of ideas that seemed to explain why the changes under way in their society benefited some people more than others. They referred again and again to the advantages of what they termed *free labor*. (The word *free* referred to laborers who were not slaves. It did not mean laborers who worked for nothing.) By the 1850s, free-labor ideas described a social and economic ideal that accounted for both the successes and the shortcomings of the economy and society taking shape in the North and West.

Spokesmen for the free-labor ideal celebrated hard work, self-reliance, and independence. They proclaimed that the door to success was open not just to those who inherited wealth or status but also to self-made men such as Abraham Lincoln. Free labor, Lincoln argued, was "the just and generous, and prosperous system, which opens the way for all—gives hope to all, and energy, and progress, and improvement of condition to all." Free labor permitted farmers and artisans to enjoy the products of their own labor, and it also benefited wageworkers. "The prudent, penniless beginner in the world," Lincoln asserted, "labors for wages awhile, saves a surplus with which to buy tools or land, for himself; then labors on his own account another while, and at length hires another new beginner to help him." Wage labor, Lincoln claimed, was the first rung on the ladder toward self-employment and eventually hiring others.

The free-labor ideal affirmed an egalitarian vision of human potential. Lincoln and other spokesmen stressed the importance of universal education to permit "heads and hands [to] cooperate as friends." Throughout the North and West, communities supported public schools to make the rudiments of learning available to young children. In rural areas, where the labor of children was more difficult to spare, schools typically enrolled no more than half the school-age children. One farm woman recalled, "I had no books in my house we didn't think about books—papers—We worked—had to live." When available, textbooks and teachers—most of whom were young women—drummed into students the lessons of the free-labor system: self-reliance, discipline, and, above all else, hard work. "Remember that all the ignorance, degradation, and misery in the world is the result of indolence and vice," one textbook intoned. Both in and outside school, free-labor ideology emphasized labor as much as freedom.

Economic Inequality

The free-labor ideal made sense to many Americans, especially in the North and West, who believed it described their own experiences. Money seemed to many the best measure of success. An English visitor observed that he had never "overheard Americans conversing without the word DOLLAR being pronounced." Lincoln frequently referred to his humble beginnings as a hired laborer and implicitly invited his listeners to consider how far he had come. In 1860, his assets of $17,000 easily placed him in the wealthiest 5 percent of the population. A few men became much richer. Most Americans, however, measured success in more modest terms. The average wealth of adult white men in the North in 1860 barely topped $2,000. Nearly half of American men had no wealth at all; about 60 percent owned no land. Because property possessed by married women was normally considered to belong to their husbands, women typically had less wealth than men. Free African Americans had still less; 90 percent of them were propertyless. (See "Beyond America's Borders," page 324.)

Free-labor spokesmen considered these economic inequalities a natural outgrowth of freedom—the inevitable result of some individuals being both luckier and more able and willing to work. These inequalities also demonstrate the gap between the promise and the performance of the free-labor ideal. Economic growth permitted many men to move from being landless squatters to landowning farmers and from being hired laborers to independent, self-employed producers. But many more Americans remained behind, landless and working for wages. Even those who realized their aspirations often had a precarious hold on their independence. Bad debts, market volatility, crop failure, sickness, or death could quickly eliminate a family's gains.

Seeking out new opportunities in pursuit of free-labor ideals created restless social and geographic mobility. While fortunate people such as Abraham Lincoln rose far beyond their social origins, others shared the misfortune of a merchant who, an observer noted, "has been on the sinking list all his life." In search of better prospects, roughly two-thirds of the rural population moved every decade, and population turnover in cities was even greater.

Immigrants and the Free-Labor Ladder

The risks and uncertainties of free labor did not deter millions of immigrants from entering the United States during the 1840s and 1850s. Almost 4.5 million immigrants arrived between 1840 and 1860, six times more than had come during the previous two decades (Figure 12.1).

Nearly three-fourths of the immigrants who arrived in the United States between 1840 and

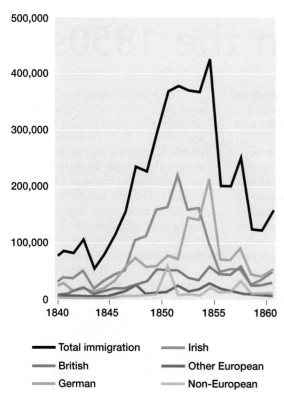

FIGURE 12.1 Antebellum Immigration, 1840–1860

Immigration shot up in the mid-1840s. Between 1848 and 1860, nearly 3.5 million immigrants entered the United States.

- Total immigration
- British
- German
- Irish
- Other European
- Non-European

1860 came from either Germany or Ireland. The majority of the 1.4 million Germans who entered during these years were skilled tradesmen and their families. Roughly a quarter were farmers, many of whom settled in Texas. German Americans were often Protestants and usually occupied the middle stratum of independent producers celebrated by free-labor spokesmen; relatively few worked as wage laborers or domestic servants.

Irish immigrants, in contrast, entered at the bottom of the free-labor ladder and struggled to climb up. Nearly 1.7 million Irish immigrants arrived between 1840 and 1860, nearly all of them desperately poor and often weakened by hunger and disease. Potato blight caused a catastrophic famine in Ireland in 1845 and returned repeatedly in subsequent years. Many Irish people crowded into ships and set out for America, where they congregated in northeastern cities. As one immigrant group declared, "All we want is to get out of Ireland; we must be better anywhere than here."

Roughly three out of four Irish immigrants worked as laborers or domestic servants. Irish men dug canals, loaded ships, laid railroad track, and did odd jobs while Irish women worked in the homes of others—cooking, washing, ironing, minding children, and cleaning house. Almost all Irish immigrants were Catholic, which set them apart from the overwhelmingly Protestant native-born residents. Many natives regarded the Irish as hard-drinking, unruly, half-civilized folk. Job announcements commonly stated, "No Irish need apply." One immigrant recalled that Irish laborers were thought of as "nothing . . . more than dogs . . . despised and kicked about." Despite such prejudices, native residents hired Irish immigrants because they accepted low pay and worked hard.

VISUAL ACTIVITY

A German Immigrant in New York

This 1855 painting depicts a German immigrant in New York City asking directions from an African American man cutting firewood. Like many other German immigrants, the man shown here appears relatively well off. Unlike most Irish immigrants, who arrived without family members, the German immigrant is accompanied by his daughter and son. North Carolina Museum of Art, Raleigh, purchased with funds from the State of North Carolina (52.9.2).

READING THE IMAGE: How does the clothing of the German immigrant compare to that of the black man cutting wood and the white laborer on the right? What racial attitudes are illustrated by the painting?

CONNECTIONS: How did mid-nineteenth-century immigrants compare to native-born Americans?

Global Prosperity in the 1850s

By the 1850s, the U.S. economy had achieved a remarkable economic transformation. In 1801, when president-elect Thomas Jefferson rode horseback the 180 miles from his home in Monticello, Virginia, to Washington, D.C., he and his horse had to swim across several rivers that lacked bridges or ferries. In 1861, when president-elect Abraham Lincoln traveled more than 1,000 miles to Washington from his home in Springfield, Illinois, he did not need to get wet swimming across rivers. He rode the entire way on railroads. The changes that made Lincoln's journey possible created an American economy that produced more goods and services per capita than that of any other country in the world, except one—Great Britain.

In the 1850s, some countries in the world produced more total goods and services than the United States. But since they had much larger populations than the United States, they produced much less per capita. For example, China produced huge quantities of goods and services, roughly four times more than the United States. But since the Chinese population was about twenty times greater than that of the United States, the per capita production of China was only about one-fifth that of the United States.

In other words, if all the goods and services in China and the United States in 1850 had been shared equally by the people who lived in each country, each person in China would have had only one-fifth as much as each person in the United States. Of course, all goods and services were never shared equally in either country (or in any other country for that matter). Rich people had more than poor people; landowners had more than laborers; slave owners had more than slaves; and so on. Still, per capita production can serve as an imperfect but revealing indicator of the general prosperity of a country's economy.

Like China, African countries were about one-fifth as prosperous as the United States. India, Japan, Mexico, and Brazil had somewhat more prosperous economies, with per capita production about one-third that of the United States. European countries such as Russia, Spain, and Italy were about half as prosperous as the United States. Overall, more than 90 percent of the people in the world in 1850 lived in countries whose economies produced half or less (much less, for most people) per capita than did the economy of the United States. In other words, the vast majority of the global population was, in general, much poorer than residents of the United States.

The American economy surpassed even the two largest countries of western continental Europe, France and Germany. Both countries, like the United States, had started to industrialize, making them far more prosperous than most of the world. But they lagged behind the United States in per capita production. Germany's per capita production was about 80 percent of that of the United States; France's was about 90 percent.

Great Britain, the most prosperous country in the world in 1850, surpassed the per capita production of the United States by 30 percent. With a population of 21 million, slightly fewer than the 23 million residents of the United States, Britain produced a whopping 45 percent of the world's manufactured goods.

Many factors contributed to Britain's economic leadership, but three were especially important. First, most people in Britain had moved to towns and cities by 1850. Rural folks made up only 22 percent of Britain's population, compared to 85 percent of the U.S. population. Many urban dwellers worked in industries that, in general, were more productive than agriculture, boosting British output. Second, wages were relatively high in Britain, giving manufacturers a big incentive to replace

In America's labor-poor economy, Irish laborers could earn more in one day than in several weeks in Ireland. In America, one immigrant explained in 1853, there was "plenty of work and plenty of wages plenty to eat and no land lords thats enough what more does a man want." But many immigrants also craved respect and decent working conditions.

Amidst the opportunities for some immigrants and native-born laborers, the free-labor system often did not live up to the optimistic vision outlined by Abraham Lincoln. Many wage laborers could not realistically aspire to become independent, self-sufficient property holders, despite the claims of free-labor proponents.

REVIEW How did the free-labor ideal account for economic inequality?

► The Westward Movement

Beginning in the 1840s, the nation's swelling population, booming economy, and boundless confidence propelled a new era of rapid westward migration. Until then, the overwhelming majority of Americans lived east of the Mississippi River. Under the banner of manifest destiny, Americans encountered Native Americans, who inhabited the plains, deserts, and rugged coasts of the west; the British, who claimed the Oregon Country; and the Mexicans, whose flag flew over the vast expanse of the Southwest. Nevertheless, by 1850 the United States stretched to the Pacific and included the Utah Territory with its Mormon settlement.

lower than in the rest of the world. Low coal prices gave manufacturers a cheap energy source, making it less costly for them to adopt innovative industrial techniques that boosted production—such as steam power. In 1850, coal consumption in Britain was ten times greater than in France and seven times greater than in Germany and the United States. Britain's unique combination of cheap energy, high wages, and a large urban population helped make it the most productive and prosperous country in the world in 1850.

Poverty and Prosperity

The prosperous couple entering the door brings blankets and parcels probably containing food to this poverty-stricken family living in a barren attic. The charity provided by the benevolent couple offered a small measure of temporary relief, but it did not promise a long-term solution to the poor family's plight. The clothing and bodily postures in the painting highlight the contrast between poverty and prosperity in the mid-nineteenth century. The Granger Collection, New York.

Questions for Analysis

Summarize the Argument: In 1850, how did U.S. prosperity compare to that of the rest of the world?

Analyze the Evidence: Why did Britain have the world's leading economy in 1850? What accounted for Britain's success compared to the United States?

Consider the Context: What does the pattern of global prosperity and poverty in 1850 suggest about the motivations for immigration to the United States?

Recognize Viewpoints: To what extent is per capita production a misleading measure of prosperity? Can you think of better measures?

Ask Historical Questions: How did the comparative economic prosperity of the United States influence the experiences and ideas of Americans during the 1850s?

costly labor with machinery. Although machinery required capital outlays to set up and maintain, it was far more efficient and tireless than wageworkers.

Manufacturers in both Britain and the United States had similar incentives to industrialize, but British producers did so first and with far greater effectiveness than did those in the United States, in large measure because Britain had a cheap and nearly inexhaustible source of energy—coal, the third crucial factor in Britain's economic leadership. Britain had a unique endowment of coal resources that could be mined relatively inexpensively, making coal prices much

Frontier settlers took the land and then, with the exception of the Mormons, lobbied their government to acquire the territory they had settled. The human cost of aggressive expansionism was high. The young Mexican nation lost a war and half of its territory. Two centuries of Indian wars, which ended east of the Mississippi during the 1830s, continued for another half century in the West.

Manifest Destiny

Most Americans believed that the superiority of their institutions and white culture bestowed on them a God-given right to spread across the continent. They imagined the West as a howling wilderness, empty and undeveloped. If they recognized Indians and Mexicans at all, they dismissed them as primitives who would have to be redeemed, shoved aside, or exterminated. The West provided young men especially an arena in which to "show their manhood." Most Americans believed that the West needed the civilizing power of the hammer and the plow, the ballot box and the pulpit, which had transformed the East.

In 1845, a New York political journal edited by John L. O'Sullivan coined the term *manifest destiny* to justify white settlers taking the land they coveted. O'Sullivan called on Americans to resist any effort to thwart "the fulfillment of our manifest destiny to overspread the continent allotted by Providence for the free development of our yearly multiplying millions . . . [and] for the development of the great experiment of liberty and federative self-government entrusted to us." Almost overnight, the magic phrase *manifest destiny* swept the nation, providing an ideological shield for conquering the West.

As important as national pride and racial arrogance were to manifest destiny, economic gain made up its core. Land hunger drew hundreds of thousands of Americans westward. Some politicians, moreover, had become convinced that national prosperity depended on capturing the rich trade of the Far East. To trade with Asia, the United States needed the Pacific coast ports that stretched from San Diego to Puget Sound. The United States and Asia must "talk together, and trade together," Missouri senator Thomas Hart Benton declared. "Commerce is a great civilizer." In the 1840s, American economic expansion came wrapped in the rhetoric of uplift and civilization.

Oregon and the Overland Trail

American expansionists and the British competed for the Oregon Country—a vast region bounded on the west by the Pacific Ocean, on the east by the Rocky Mountains, on the south by the forty-second parallel, and on the north by Russian Alaska. In 1818, the United States and Great Britain decided on "joint occupation" that would leave Oregon "free and open" to settlement by both countries. By the 1820s, a handful of American fur traders and "mountain men" roamed the region.

In the late 1830s, settlers began to trickle along the **Oregon Trail**, following a path blazed by the mountain men (Map 12.2). The first wagon trains headed west in 1841, and by 1843 about 1,000 emigrants a year set out from Independence, Missouri. By 1869, when the first transcontinental railroad was completed, approximately 350,000 migrants had traveled west in wagon trains.

Emigrants encountered the Plains Indians, a quarter of a million Native Americans scattered over the area between the Mississippi River and the Rocky Mountains. Some were farmers who lived peaceful, sedentary lives, but a majority—the Sioux, Cheyenne, Shoshoni, and Arapaho of the central plains and the Kiowa, Wichita, and Comanche of the southern plains—were horse-mounted, nomadic, nonagricultural peoples whose warriors symbolized the "savage Indian" in the minds of whites.

Horses, which had been brought to North America by Spaniards in the sixteenth century, permitted the Plains tribes to become highly mobile hunters of buffalo. They came to depend on buffalo for nearly everything—food, clothing, shelter, and fuel. Competition for buffalo led to war between the tribes. Young men were introduced to warfare early, learning to ride ponies at breakneck speed while firing off arrows and, later, rifles with astounding accuracy. "A Comanche on his feet is out of his element," observed western artist George Catlin, "but the moment he lays his hands upon his horse, his *face* even becomes handsome, and he gracefully flies away like a different being."

The Plains Indians struck fear in the hearts of whites on the wagon trains. But Native Americans had far more to fear from whites. Indians killed fewer than four hundred emigrants on the trail between 1840 and 1860, while whites brought alcohol and deadly epidemics. Moreover, white hunters slaughtered buffalo for the international hide market and sometimes just for sport.

The government constructed a chain of forts along the Oregon Trail (see Map 12.2) and adopted a new Indian policy: "concentration." In 1851, government negotiators at the Fort Laramie conference persuaded the Plains Indians to sign

Kee-O-Kuk, the Watchful Fox, Chief of the Tribe, by George Catlin, 1835
In the 1830s, artist George Catlin, convinced that Indian cultures would soon disappear, traveled the West painting Native Americans in their own environments. Keokuk, chief of the Sauk and Fox, struggled with the warrior Black Hawk (see "Indian Policy and the Trail of Tears" in chapter 11) about how to deal with whites. Black Hawk fought American expansion; Keokuk believed that war was fruitless.
Smithsonian American Art Museum, Washington, D.C./Art Resource, NY.

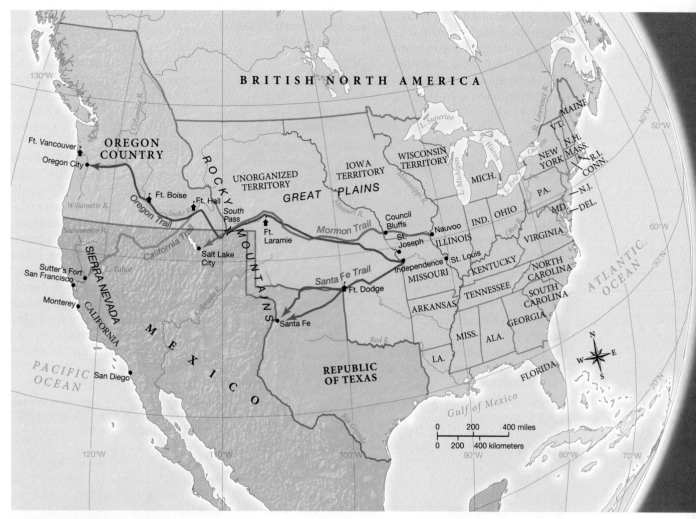

Map 12.2 Major Trails West
In the 1830s, wagon trains began snaking their way to the Southwest and the Pacific coast. Deep ruts, some of which can still be seen today, soon marked the most popular routes.

agreements that cleared a wide corridor for wagon trains by restricting Native Americans to specific areas that whites promised they would never violate. This policy of concentration became the seedbed for the subsequent policy of reservations. But whites would not keep out of Indian territory, and Indians would not easily give up their traditional ways of life. Struggle for control of the West meant warfare for decades to come.

Still, Indians threatened emigrants less than life on the trail did. Emigrants could count on at least six months of grueling travel. With nearly two thousand miles to go and traveling no more than fifteen miles a day, the pioneers endured parching heat, drought, treacherous rivers, disease, physical and emotional exhaustion, and, if the snows closed the mountain passes before

they got through, freezing and starvation. Women faced the ordeal of trailside childbirth. It was said that a person could walk from Missouri to the Pacific stepping only on the graves of those who had died heading west.

Men usually found Oregon "one of the greatest countries in the world." From "the Cascade mountains to the Pacific, the whole country can be cultivated," exclaimed one eager settler. When women reached Oregon, they found that neighbors were scarce and things were in a "primitive state." "I had all I could do to keep from asking George to turn around and bring me back home," one woman wrote to her mother in Missouri. Work seemed unending. "I am a very old woman," declared twenty-nine-year-old Sarah Everett. "My face is thin sunken and wrinkled, my hands bony withered and hard." Another settler observed, "A woman that can not endure almost as much as a horse has no business here." Yet despite the ordeal of the trail and the difficulties of starting from scratch, emigrants kept coming.

The Mormon Exodus

Not every wagon train heading west was bound for the Pacific Slope. One remarkable group of religious emigrants halted near the Great Salt Lake in what was then Mexican territory. After years of persecution in the East, the **Mormons** fled west to find religious freedom and communal security.

In the 1820s, an upstate New York farm boy named Joseph

Plains Indians and Trails West in the 1840s and 1850s

Smith Jr. said that he was visited by an angel who led him to golden tablets buried near his home. With the aid of magic stones, he translated the mysterious language on the tablets to produce *The Book of Mormon*, which he published in 1830. It told the story of an ancient Hebrew civilization in the New World and predicted the appearance of an American prophet who would reestablish Jesus Christ's undefiled kingdom in America. Converts, attracted to the promise of a pure faith in the midst of antebellum America's social turmoil and rampant materialism, flocked to the new Church of Jesus Christ of Latter-Day Saints (the Mormons).

Neighbors branded Mormons heretics and drove Smith and

VISUAL ACTIVITY

Pioneers Heading West

Pioneers headed west in covered wagons, on horseback, and by foot, and all three are captured in this photograph from the harsh Southwest. We do not know the fates of these travelers, but we can hope that they fared better than many who braved the trip. © PVDE/Bridgeman Images.

READING THE IMAGE: Based on this photograph, what were some of the difficulties faced by pioneers traveling west?

CONNECTIONS: How did wagon trains change the western United States?

his followers from New York to Ohio, then to Missouri, and finally in 1839 to Nauvoo, Illinois, where they built a prosperous community. But after Smith sanctioned "plural marriage" (polygamy), non-Mormons arrested Smith and his brother. On June 27, 1844, a mob stormed the jail and shot both men dead.

The embattled church turned to an extraordinary new leader, Brigham Young, who oversaw a great exodus. In 1846, traveling in 3,700 wagons, 12,000 Mormons made their way to Iowa and then, the following year, to their new home beside the Great Salt Lake. Young described the region as a barren waste, "the paradise of the lizard, the cricket and the rattlesnake." Within ten years, however, the Mormons developed an irrigation system that made the desert bloom. Under Young's stern leadership, the Mormons built a thriving community using cooperative labor, not the individualistic and competitive enterprise common among most emigrants.

In 1850, the Mormon kingdom was annexed to the United States as Utah Territory. Shortly afterward, Brigham Young announced that many Mormons practiced polygamy. Although only one Mormon man in five had more than one wife (Young had twenty-three), Young's statement caused an outcry that forced the U.S. government to establish its authority in Utah. In 1857, 2,500 U.S. troops invaded Salt Lake City in what was known as the Mormon War. The bloodless occupation illustrated that most Americans viewed the Mormons as a threat to American morality and institutions.

The Mexican Borderlands

In the Mexican Southwest, westward-moving Anglo-American pioneers confronted northern-moving Spanish-speaking frontiersmen. On this frontier as elsewhere, national cultures, interests, and aspirations collided. Mexico won its independence from Spain in 1821 (Map 12.3), but the young nation was plagued by civil wars, economic crises, quarrels with the Roman Catholic Church, and devastating raids by the Comanche, Apache, and Kiowa. Mexico found it increasingly difficult to defend its sparsely populated northern provinces, especially when faced with a neighbor convinced of its superiority and bent on territorial acquisition.

The American assault began quietly. In the 1820s, Anglo-American traders drifted into Santa Fe, a remote outpost in the northern province of New Mexico. The traders made the long trek southwest along the Santa Fe Trail (see Map 12.2) with wagons crammed with inexpensive American manufactured goods and returned home with Mexican silver, furs, and mules.

The Mexican province of Texas attracted a flood of Americans who had settlement, not long-distance trade, on their minds (see Map 12.3). Wanting to populate and develop its northern territory, the Mexican government granted the American Stephen F. Austin a huge tract of land along the Brazos River. In the 1820s, Austin offered land at only ten cents an acre, and

VISUAL ACTIVITY

Mormon Family
The rest of America found the Mormon practice of polygamy deeply offensive. In 1890, the Mormons officially abandoned plural marriages, but in this photograph from Salt Lake City in the 1850s, a husband, his three wives, and their five children sit for a family portrait.
READING THE IMAGE: How would you describe the family's attitude about their unusual family constellation—at ease and proud or uneasy and embarrassed?
CONNECTIONS: Why would most Americans find the Mormon practice of plural marriage so disturbing?

Map 12.3 Texas and Mexico in the 1830s

As Americans spilled into lightly populated and loosely governed northern Mexico, Texas and then other Mexican provinces became contested territory.

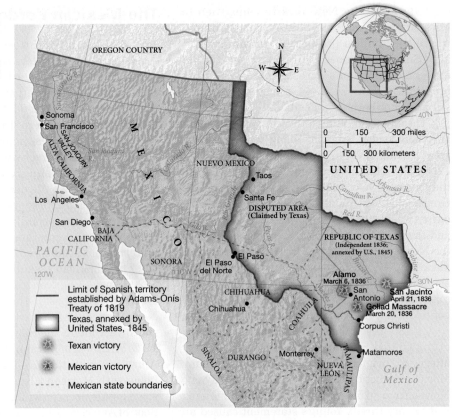

thousands of Americans poured across the border. Most were Southerners who brought cotton and slaves with them.

By the 1830s, the settlers had established a thriving plantation economy in Texas. Americans numbered 35,000, while the *Tejano* (Spanish-speaking) population was less than 8,000. Few Anglo-American settlers were Roman Catholic, spoke Spanish, or cared about assimilating into Mexican culture. Afraid of losing Texas to the new arrivals, the Mexican government in 1830 banned further immigration to Texas from the United States and outlawed the introduction of additional slaves. The Anglo-Americans made it clear that they wanted to be rid of the "despotism of the sword and the priesthood" and to govern themselves.

When the Texan settlers rebelled, General Antonio López de Santa Anna ordered the Mexican army northward. In February 1836, the army arrived

Texas War for Independence, 1836

at the outskirts of San Antonio. Commanded by Colonel William B. Travis from Alabama, the rebels included the Tennessee frontiersman Davy Crockett and the Louisiana adventurer James Bowie, as well as a handful of Tejanos. They took refuge in a former Franciscan mission known as the Alamo. Santa Anna sent wave after wave of his 2,000-man army crashing against the walls until the attackers finally broke through and killed all 187 rebels. A few weeks later, outside the small town of Goliad, Mexican forces captured and executed almost 400 Texans as "pirates and outlaws." In April 1836, at San Jacinto, General Sam Houston's army adopted the massacre of Goliad as a battle cry and crushed Santa Anna's troops in a surprise attack. The Texans had succeeded in establishing the **Lone Star Republic**, and the following year the United States recognized the independence of Texas from Mexico.

Earlier, in 1824, in an effort to increase Mexican migration to

Franciscan Mission in California
When the Spanish moved north from Mexico, Franciscans built missions to serve the settlers and convert the Indians. This scene of Mission Santa Clara in California captures an after-mass gathering of *rancheros* and a family in an oxcart.
Courtesy Bancroft Library, University of California, Berkeley (BANC PIC 19xx.039:16—ALB).

the province of California, the Mexican government granted *ranchos*—huge estates devoted to cattle raising—to new settlers. *Rancheros* ruled over near-feudal empires worked by Indians whose condition sometimes approached that of slaves. In 1834, *rancheros* persuaded the Mexican government to confiscate the Franciscan missions and make their vast lands available to new settlement.

Despite the efforts of the Mexican government, California in 1840 had a population of only 7,000 Mexican settlers. Non-Mexican settlers numbered only 380, but among them were Americans who championed manifest destiny. They sought to convince American emigrants who were traveling the Oregon Trail to head southwest on the California Trail (see Map 12.2). The first overland party arrived in California in 1841. As a New York newspaper observed in 1845, "Let the tide of emigration flow toward California and the American population will soon be sufficiently numerous to play the Texas game." Few Americans in California wanted a war, but many dreamed of living again under the U.S. flag.

In 1846, American settlers in the Sacramento Valley took matters into their own hands. Prodded by John C. Frémont, a former army captain and explorer who had arrived with a party of sixty buckskin-clad frontiersmen spoiling for a fight, the Californians raised an independence movement known as the Bear Flag Revolt. By then, James K. Polk, a champion of aggressive expansion, sat in the White House.

REVIEW   Why did westward migration expand dramatically in the mid-nineteenth century?

► Expansion and the Mexican-American War

Although emigrants acted as the advance guard of American empire, there was nothing automatic about the U.S. annexation of territory in the West. Acquiring territory required political action. In the 1840s, the politics of expansion became entangled with sectionalism and the slavery question. Texas, Oregon, and the Mexican borderlands also thrust the United States into dangerous diplomatic crises with Great Britain and Mexico.

Aggravation between Mexico and the United States escalated to open antagonism in 1845 when the United States annexed Texas. Absorbing territory still claimed by Mexico set the stage for war. But it was President James K. Polk's insistence on having Mexico's other northern provinces that made war certain. The war was not as easy as Polk anticipated, but it ended in American victory and the acquisition of a new American West. The discovery of gold in one of the nation's new territories, California, prompted a massive wave of emigration that nearly destroyed Native American and *Californio* societies.

The Politics of Expansion

Texans had sought admission to the Union almost since winning their independence from Mexico in 1836. Constant border warfare between Mexico and the Republic of Texas in the decade following the revolution underscored the precarious nature of independence. But any suggestion of adding another slave state to the Union outraged most Northerners, who applauded westward expansion but imagined the expansion of liberty, not slavery.

John Tyler, who became president in April 1841 when William Henry Harrison died one month after taking office, understood that Texas was a dangerous issue. Adding to the danger, Great Britain began sniffing around Texas, apparently contemplating adding the young republic to its growing empire. In 1844, Tyler, an ardent expansionist, decided to risk annexing the Lone Star Republic. However, howls of protest erupted across the North. Future Massachusetts senator Charles Sumner deplored the "insidious" plan to annex Texas and carve from it "great slave-holding states." The Senate soundly rejected the annexation treaty.

During the election of 1844, the Whig nominee for president, Henry Clay, in an effort to woo northern voters, came out against annexation of Texas. "Annexation and war with Mexico are identical," he declared. When news of Clay's statement reached Andrew Jackson at his plantation in Tennessee, he chuckled, "Clay [is] a dead political Duck." In Jackson's shrewd judgment, no man who opposed annexation could be elected president.

The Democratic nominee, Tennessean James K. Polk, vigorously backed annexation. To make annexation palatable to Northerners, the Democrats cleverly yoked the annexation of Texas to the annexation of Oregon, thus tapping the desire for expansion in the free states of the North as well as in the slave states of the South. The Democratic platform called for the "reannexation of Texas" and the "reoccupation of Oregon." The statement that the United States was merely reasserting existing rights was poor history but good politics.

When Clay finally recognized the popularity of expansion, he waffled, hinting that he might accept the annexation of Texas after all. His retreat succeeded only in alienating antislavery opinion in the North. James G. Birney, the candidate of the fledging Liberty Party, denounced Clay as "rotten as a stagnant fish pond" and picked up the votes of thousands of disillusioned Clay supporters. In the November election, Polk won a narrow victory.

In his inaugural address on March 4, 1845, Polk underscored his faith in America's manifest destiny. "This heaven-favored land," he proclaimed, enjoyed the "most admirable and wisest system of well-regulated self-government . . . ever devised by human minds." He asked, "Who shall assign limits to the achievements of free minds and free hands under the protection of this glorious Union?"

The nation did not have to wait for Polk's inauguration to see results from his victory. One month after the election, President Tyler announced that the triumph of the Democratic Party provided a mandate for the annexation of Texas "promptly and immediately." In February 1845, after a fierce debate between antislavery and proslavery forces, Congress approved a joint resolution offering the Republic of Texas admission to the United States. Texas entered as the fifteenth slave state.

While Tyler delivered Texas, Polk had promised Oregon, too. Westerners particularly demanded that the new president make good on the Democratic pledge "Fifty-four forty or Fight"— that is, all of Oregon, right up to Alaska (54°40′ was the southern latitude of Russian Alaska). But Polk was close to war with Mexico and could not afford a war with Britain over U.S. claims in Canada. He renewed an old offer to divide Oregon along the forty-ninth parallel. Westerners cried betrayal, but when Britain accepted the compromise, the nation gained an enormous territory peacefully. When the Senate approved the treaty in June 1846, the United States and Mexico were already at war.

Polk and Dallas Banner, 1844
In 1844, Democratic presidential nominee James K. Polk and vice presidential nominee George M. Dallas campaigned under this banner. The extra star spilling over into the red and white stripes symbolizes Polk's vigorous support for annexing the huge slave republic of Texas, which had declared its independence from Mexico eight years earlier.
© David J. & Janice L. Frent Collection/Corbis.

The Mexican-American War, 1846–1848

From the day he entered the White House, Polk craved Mexico's remaining northern provinces: California and New Mexico, land that today makes up California, Nevada, Utah, most of New Mexico and Arizona, and parts of Wyoming and Colorado. Since the 1830s, Indians had attacked Mexican ranches and towns, killing thousands, and the Polk administration invoked Mexico's inability to control its northern provinces to denigrate its claims to them. Polk hoped to buy the territory, but when the Mexicans refused to sell, he concluded that military force would be needed to realize the United States' manifest destiny.

Polk ordered General Zachary Taylor to march his 4,000-man army 150 miles south from its position on the Nueces River, the southern boundary of Texas according to the Mexicans, to the banks of the Rio Grande, the boundary claimed by Texans (Map 12.4). Lieutenant George G. Meade, who would later command troops at Gettysburg, admitted, "I hope for a war and a speedy battle." Viewing the American

advance as aggression, Mexican cavalry on April 25, 1846, attacked a party of American soldiers, killing or wounding 16 and capturing the rest.

On May 11, the president told Congress, "Mexico has passed the boundary of the United States, has invaded our territory, and shed American blood upon American soil." Thus "war exists, and, notwithstanding all our efforts to avoid it, exists by the act of Mexico herself." Congress passed a declaration of war and began raising an army. The U.S. Army was pitifully small, only 8,600 soldiers. Faced with the nation's first foreign war, against a Mexican army that numbered more than 30,000, Polk called for volunteers. More than 30,000 Tennesseans competed for the state's 3,000 allotted positions. Eventually, more than 112,000 white Americans (40 percent were immigrants; blacks were banned) joined the army to fight in Mexico.

Despite the flood of volunteers, the war divided the nation. Northern Whigs in particular condemned the war. The Massachusetts legislature claimed that the war was being fought for the "triple object of extending slavery, of strengthening the slave power, and of obtaining control of the

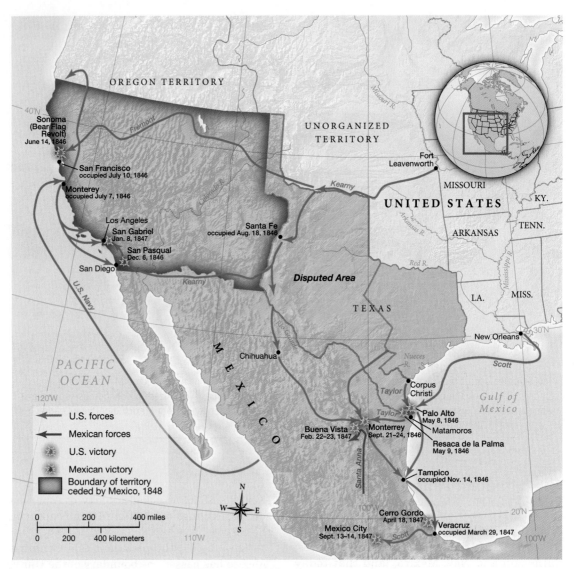

Map 12.4   The Mexican-American War, 1846–1848
American and Mexican soldiers skirmished across much of northern Mexico, but the major battles took place between the Rio Grande and Mexico City.

free states." On January 12, 1848, a gangly fresh-man Whig representative from Illinois rose in the House of Representatives. He likened the president's views to the "half-insane mumbling of a fever dream" and proclaimed Polk a "bewildered, confounded, and miserably perplexed man." Before Abraham Lincoln sat down, he had questioned Polk's intelligence, honesty, and sanity. The president ignored the upstart representative, but antislavery, antiwar Whigs kept up the attack throughout the conflict.

President Polk expected a short war in which U.S. armies would occupy Mexico's northern provinces and defeat the Mexican army in a decisive battle or two, after which Mexico would sue for peace and the United States would keep the territory its armies occupied.

At first, Polk's strategy seemed to work. In May 1846, Zachary Taylor's troops drove south from the Rio Grande and routed the Mexican army, first at Palo Alto, then at Resaca de la Palma (see Map 12.4). "Old Rough and Ready," as Taylor was affectionately known among his troops, became an instant war hero. Polk rewarded Taylor for his victories by making him commander of the Mexican campaign.

A second prong of the campaign centered on Colonel Stephen Watts Kearny, who led a 1,700-man army from Missouri into New Mexico. Without firing a shot, U.S. forces took Santa Fe in August 1846. Kearny then marched to San Diego, where he encountered a major Mexican rebellion against American rule. In January 1847, after several clashes and severe losses, U.S. forces occupied

Batalla del Sacramento, by Julio Michaud y Thomas
Most images of the Mexican-American War were created by artists from the United States, but Mexicans also recorded the war. In this hand-colored lithograph, Mexican artist Julio Michaud y Thomas depicts the February 1847 battle in which 1,100 American troops engaged 3,000 Mexicans on the banks of the Sacramento River near Chihuahua.
Beinecke Rare Book and Manuscript Library, Yale University.

Los Angeles. California and New Mexico were in American hands.

By then, Taylor had driven deep into the interior of Mexico. In September 1846, after house-to-house fighting, he had taken the city of Monterrey. Taylor then pushed his 5,000 troops southwest, where the Mexican hero of the Alamo, General Antonio López de Santa Anna, was concentrating an army of 21,000. On February 23, 1847, Santa Anna's troops attacked Taylor at Buena Vista. The Americans won the day but suffered heavy casualties. The Mexicans suffered even greater losses (some 3,400 dead, wounded, and missing, compared with 650 Americans). During the night, Santa Anna withdrew his battered army.

The series of uninterrupted victories in northern Mexico fed the American troops' sense of invincibility. "No American force has ever thought of being defeated by any amount of Mexican troops," one soldier declared. The Americans worried about other hazards, however. "I can assure you that fighting is the least dangerous & arduous part of a soldier's life," one young man declared. Letters home told of torturous marches across arid wastes alive with tarantulas, scorpions, and rattlesnakes. Others recounted dysentery,

malaria, smallpox, cholera, and yellow fever. Of the 13,000 American soldiers who died (some 50,000 Mexicans perished), fewer than 2,000 fell to Mexican bullets and shells. Disease killed most of the others. Medicine was so primitive that, as one Tennessee man observed, "nearly all who take sick die."

Victory in Mexico

Despite heavy losses on the battlefield, Mexico refused to trade land for peace. One American soldier captured the Mexican mood: "They cannot submit to be deprived of California after the loss of Texas, and nothing but the conquest of their Capital will force them to such a humiliation." President Polk had arrived at the same conclusion. While Taylor occupied the north, Polk ordered General Winfield Scott to land an army on the Gulf coast of Mexico and march 250 miles inland to Mexico City. The plan entailed enormous risk because Scott would have to cut himself off from supplies and lead his men deep into enemy country against a much larger army.

An amphibious landing on March 9, 1847, near Veracruz put some 10,000 American troops ashore. After furious shelling, Veracruz surrendered.

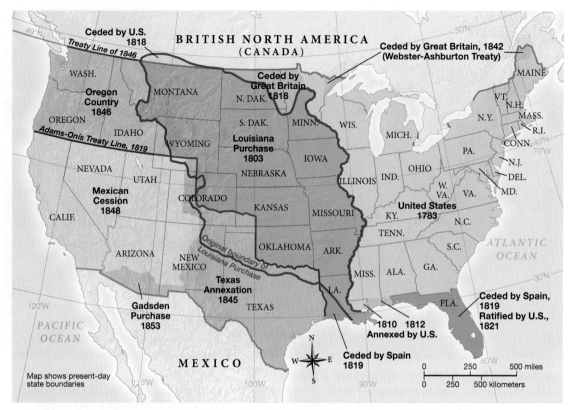

MAP ACTIVITY

Map 12.5 Territorial Expansion by 1860

Less than a century after its founding, the United States spread from the Atlantic seaboard to the Pacific coast. War, purchase, and diplomacy had gained a continent.

READING THE MAP: List the countries from which the United States acquired land. Which nation lost the most land because of U.S. expansion?

CONNECTIONS: Who coined the phrase *manifest destiny*? When? What does it mean? What areas targeted for expansion were the subjects of debate during the presidential campaign of 1844?

In April 1847, after gathering 9,300 wagons, 17,000 pack mules, 500,000 bushels of oats and corn, and 100 pounds of blister ointment, Scott's forces moved westward, following the path blazed more than three centuries earlier by Hernán Cortés to "the halls of Montezuma" (see chapter 2).

After the defeat at Buena Vista, Santa Anna had returned to Mexico City, where he rallied his ragged troops and marched them east to set a trap for Scott in the mountain pass at Cerro Gordo. Knifing through Mexican lines, the Americans almost captured Santa Anna, who fled the field on foot. So complete was the victory that Scott gloated to Taylor, "Mexico no longer has an army." But Santa Anna, ever resilient, again rallied the Mexican army. Some 30,000 troops took up defensive positions on the outskirts of Mexico City and began melting down church bells to cast new cannons.

In August 1847, Scott began his assault on the Mexican capital. The fighting proved the most brutal of the war. Santa Anna backed his army into the city, fighting each step of the way. At the battle of Churubusco, the Mexicans took 4,000 casualties in a single day and the Americans more than 1,000. At the castle of Chapultepec, American troops scaled the walls and fought the Mexican defenders hand to hand. After Chapultepec, Mexico City officials persuaded Santa Anna to evacuate the city to save it from destruction, and on September 14, 1847, Scott rode in triumphantly.

On February 2, 1848, American and Mexican officials signed the **Treaty of Guadalupe Hidalgo** in Mexico City. Mexico agreed to give up all claims to Texas north of the Rio Grande and to cede the provinces of New Mexico and California— more than 500,000 square miles—to the United

States (see Map 12.4). The United States agreed to pay Mexico $15 million and to assume $3.25 million in claims that American citizens had against Mexico. Some Americans clamored for all of Mexico, but the treaty gave the president all he wanted. In March 1848, the Senate ratified the treaty. Polk had his Rio Grande border, his Pacific ports, and all the land that lay between.

The American triumph had enormous consequences. Less than three-quarters of a century after its founding, the United States had achieved its self-proclaimed manifest destiny to stretch from the Atlantic to the Pacific (Map 12.5). It would enter the industrial age with vast new natural resources and a two-ocean economy, while Mexico faced a sharply diminished economic future.

Golden California

Another consequence of the Mexican defeat was that California gold poured into American, not Mexican, pockets. In January 1848, James

Marshall discovered gold in the American River in the foothills of the Sierra Nevada. His discovery set off the **California gold rush**, one of the wildest mining stampedes in the world's history. Between 1849 and 1852, more than 250,000 "forty-niners," as the would-be miners were known, descended on the Golden State. In less than two years, Marshall's discovery transformed California from foreign territory to statehood.

Gold fever quickly spread around the world. A flood of men of various races and nationalities poured into California, where they remade the quiet world of Mexican ranches into a raucous, roaring mining town economy. Only a few struck it rich, and life in the goldfields was nasty, brutish, and often short. The prospectors who filled Hangtown, Hell's Delight, Gouge Eye, and a hundred other crude mining camps faced cholera and scurvy, exorbitant prices for food (eggs cost a dollar apiece), deadly encounters with claim jumpers, and endless backbreaking labor. (See "Analyzing Historical Evidence," page 338.)

Miners, Auburn Ravine, California, 1852
The three white miners on the left of the photograph were separated from the four Chinese miners on the right by more than a sluice box. Whites welcomed Chinese into gold country as hired laborers, not as independent miners like themselves. Fotosearch/Getty Images.

The Gold Rush

The discovery of gold in California stimulated imaginations around the world. But getting to gold country was not easy. Americans in the East could sail 18,000 miles around the tip of South America; or sail to the Atlantic side of the Isthmus of Panama, slog through the jungle to the Pacific, and wait for a ship to San Francisco; or walk overland across the continent. Nothing got easier when they arrived in California. The West presented emigrants with unprecedented challenges and only occasionally fulfillment.

DOCUMENT 1
James Marshall, Account of His Discovery of Gold, 1848

On January 24, 1848, while building a sawmill on the American River for Swiss rancher John Sutter, James Marshall found gold. Marshall gave several accounts of his discovery, but this is probably his first. Marshall never benefited from his discovery and died bitter and penniless.

One morning in January—it was a clear, cold morning; I shall never forget that morning—as I was taking my usual walk along the race after shutting off the water, my eye was caught with the glimpse of something shining in the bottom of the ditch. There was about a foot of water running then. I reached my hand down and picked it up; it made my heart thump, for I was certain it was gold. The piece was about half the size and of the shape of a pea. Then I saw another piece. . . .

When I returned to our cabin for breakfast I showed the two pieces to my men. They were all a good deal excited, and had they not thought that the gold only existed in small quantities they would have abandoned everything and left me to finish my job alone. However, to satisfy them, I told them that as soon as we had the mill finished we would devote a week or two to gold hunting and see what we could make out of it.

. . . We thought it our best policy to keep it as quiet as possible till we should have finished our mill. But there was a great number of disbanded Mormon soldiers in and about the fort, and when they came to hear of it, why it just spread like a wildfire, and soon the whole country was in a bustle. . . .

Source: James W. Marshall, "Marshall's Own Account of the Gold Discovery," *Century Illustrated Magazine*, no. 4 (Feb. 1891): 537–39.

DOCUMENT 2
Sarah Royce, Memoir of the Journey to California in 1849

In 1849, Sarah Royce, with her husband and two-year-old daughter, left New York for California. Her memoir of their journey westward by covered wagon recounts the family's encounters with Indians, cholera, thirst, and hunger. Thirty years later she wrote her memories, and in 1932 her son published them. Here she describes traveling through a desert southwest of Salt Lake City.

By 1853, San Francisco had grown into a raw, booming city of 50,000 that depended as much on gold as did the mining camps inland. Enterprising individuals learned that there was money to be made tending to the needs of miners. Hotels, saloons, restaurants, laundries, brothels, and stores of all kinds exchanged goods and services for miners' gold dust and nuggets. Violent crime was an everyday occurrence. In 1851, the Committee of Vigilance determined to bring order to the city. Members pledged that "no thief, burglar, incendiary or assassin shall escape punishment, either by the quibbles of the law, the insecurity of prisons, the carelessness or corruption of the police, or a laxity of those who pretended to administer justice." Lynchings proved the committee meant business.

Establishing civic order was made more difficult by California's diversity and Anglo bigotry. The Chinese attracted special scrutiny. By 1851, 25,000 Chinese lived in California, and their religion, language, dress, queues (long pigtails), eating habits, and use of opium convinced many Anglos that they were not fit citizens of the Golden State. In 1850, the California legislature passed the Foreign Miners' Tax Law, which levied high taxes on non-Americans to drive them from the goldfields, except as hired laborers working on claims owned by Americans. The Chinese were segregated residentially and occupationally and,

There was no moon yet, but by starlight we had for some time seen, only too plainly, the dead bodies of cattle lying here and there on both sides of the road. As we advanced they increased in numbers, and presently we saw two or three wagons. At first we thought we had overtaken a company but, coming close, no sign of life appeared. . . . Everything indicated a complete break down, and a hasty flight. Some animals were lying nearly in front of a wagon, apparently just as they had dropped down, while loose yokes and chains indicated that part of the teams had been driven on, laden probably with some necessaries of life; for the contents of the wagons were scattered in confusion, the most essential articles alone evidently having been thought worth carrying. . . . It was not a very encouraging scene but our four oxen still kept their feet; we would drive on a little farther, out of this scene of ruin, bait them, rest ourselves, and go on. We did so, but soon found that what we supposed an exceptional misfortune must have been the common fate of many companies; for at still shortening intervals, scenes of ruin similar to that just described kept recurring till we seemed to be but the last, little, feeble struggling band at the rear of a routed Army.

Source: Sarah Royce, *A Frontier Lady* (New Haven, CT: Yale University Press, 1932), 51–53.

DOCUMENT 3
Daniel B. Woods, Life of a California Miner, 1849

Daniel B. Woods, a Philadelphia schoolteacher, reached the diggings in California in 1849. He soon discovered that mining was very hard work, and he suspected that he would never get rich. He poured his frustration and disillusionment into his diary and after sixteen months quit gold country.

July 9th [1849]. To-day we have made $20 each. One of the conclusions at which we are rapidly arriving is that the "chances of our making a fortune in the old mines are about the same as those in favor of our drawing a prize in a lottery." No kind of work is so uncertain.

July 10th. We made three dollars each to-day. This life of severe hardship and exposure has affected my health. Our diet consists of hard bread, flour, which we eat half-cooked, and salt pork, with occasionally a salmon which we purchase of the Indians. Vegetables are not to be procured. Our feet are wet all day, while a hot sun shines down upon our heads, and the very air parches the skin like the hot air of an oven. Our drinking water comes down to us thoroughly impregnated with the mineral substances washed through a thousand cradles above us.

After our days of labor, exhausted and faint, we *retire*—if this word may be applied to the simple act of lying down in our clothes—robbing our feet of their boots to make a pillow of them, and wrapping blankets about us, on a bed of pine boughs, or on the ground, beneath the clear, bright stars of night. . . .

Aug. 23d. After all our preparations and hopes, our toil early and late, toil of the most laborious kind, digging down in the channel of the river till the water was up to our knees, giving ourselves barely time to eat, we have made but $4 each. We sat down on the rocks, and looked at the small ridge of gold in the pan, and at each other. One fell to swearing, another to laughing.

Source: Daniel B. Woods, *Sixteen Months at the Gold Diggings* (New York: Harper & Brothers, 1851), 57–63.

Questions for Analysis

Recognize Viewpoints: What was James Marshall's primary concern after he discovered gold?

Analyze the Evidence: What was Sarah Royce's initial understanding of her nighttime encounter? How well did Sarah Royce's and Daniel Woods's previous experiences prepare them for the gold rush?

Consider the Context: How did the realities of gold rush California fit with the promises of manifest destiny?

along with blacks and Indians, denied public education and the right to testify in court.

Opponents demanded a halt to Chinese immigration, but Chinese leaders in San Francisco fought back. Admitting deep cultural differences, they insisted that "in the important matters we are good men. We honor our parents; we take care of our children; we are industrious and peaceable; we trade much; we are trusted for small and large sums; we pay our debts; and are honest, and of course must tell the truth." Their protestations offered little protection, however, and racial violence grew.

Anglo-American prospectors asserted their dominance over other groups, especially Native Americans and the Californios, Spanish and Mexican settlers who had lived in California for decades. Despite the U.S. government's pledge to protect Mexican and Spanish land titles, Americans took the land of the *rancheros* and through discriminatory legislation pushed Hispanic professionals, merchants, and artisans into the ranks of unskilled labor. Mariano Vallejo, a leading Californio, said of the forty-niners, "The good ones were few and the wicked many." California's Indians would have agreed; for them the gold rush was catastrophic. (See "Making Historical Arguments," page 340.)

The forty-niners created dazzling wealth: In 1852, 81 million ounces of gold, nearly half of the world's production, came from California. However,

Why Was the Gold Rush So Deadly for California's Indians?

By the time of the gold rush, California Indians had already lived with the Spanish and Mexicans for eighty years. The presence of Spanish and Mexican settlers had meant exploitation and a declining Indian population, but the Indians had managed to reach a rough accommodation with the Hispanic newcomers. The arrival of the gold seekers, however, brought demographic disaster. Almost overnight, the Indians experienced near destruction. Approximately 150,000 when the gold rush began, the Indian population dropped to less than 30,000 by 1860. Why did the forty-niners turn California into a killing field?

Most obviously, forty-niner violence killed many Indians. Gold seekers—young, armed, and male—often harbored deep racial prejudices. As one miner said,

California Indians were "about the lowest specimen of humanity found on earth." At the same time, manifest destiny taught that whites were a superior race who advanced civilization, once Indians were out of the way. Largely unpoliced, the early mining frontier placed few restraints on the miners' prejudices and greed. Because California Indians lived in small groups and not in powerful nations whose warriors could fight pitched battles with invaders, wholesale murder was not difficult. "There were so many of these expeditions," remembered one white participant in the campaigns against the Yuki. "We would kill on average fifty or so Indians on a trip." One contemporary described white behavior toward Indians during the gold rush as "one of the last human hunts of

civilization, and the basest and most brutal of them all."

Without ignoring the violence done to Indians, historians have also identified a raft of less obvious but probably even more important causes of the destruction of California's Indian population. Some of these developments were unplanned, even unintended, but they were nevertheless deadly.

The sheer number of forty-niners meant that they pushed hard against the natural resources on which Indians depended. Indians were concentrated in the foothills of the Sierra Nevada, a rich ecosystem that supported one of the densest Indian populations in North America. But the foothills were also where the gold was. As miners poured in, furiously tearing up the land and polluting the rivers, they destroyed the Indians' food supply. Women found it difficult to gather the greens, seeds, and most importantly acorns that sustained their families. Men could no longer fish, and hunting produced fewer and fewer deer. With their hunting and gathering grounds ravaged, Indians faced starvation.

Indians responded in a variety of ways. Many withdrew into the

most miners never struck it rich and eventually took up farming, opened small businesses, or worked for wages for the corporations that took over the mining industry. Other Americans traded furs, hides, and lumber and engaged in whaling and the China trade in tea, silk, and porcelain. Still, as one Californian observed, the state was separated "by thousands of miles of plains, deserts, and almost impossible mountains" from the rest of the Union. Some dreamers imagined a railroad that would someday connect the Golden State with the thriving agriculture and industry of the East. Others imagined a country transformed not by transportation but by progressive individual and institutional reform.

REVIEW   Why did the United States go to war with Mexico?

▶ Reforming Self and Society

While manifest destiny, the Mexican-American War, and the California gold rush transformed the nation's boundaries, many Americans sought personal and social reform. The emphasis on self-discipline and individual effort at the core of the free-labor ideal led Americans to believe that insufficient self-control caused the major social problems of the era. Evangelical Protestants struggled to control individuals' propensity to sin. Temperance advocates exhorted drinkers to control their taste for alcohol. Only about one-third of Americans belonged to a church in 1850, but the influence of evangelical religion reached far beyond church members.

high Sierra, an environment that provided even less food. Others tried to adapt by working in the new economy. One white settler admitted that Indians were at first "saved so much as possible for labour." But conflict with miners soon drove Indian workers out of gold country, and work as ranch hands and farm laborers disappeared with the arrival of white labor and machines. Starvation forced some Indians to turn to livestock raiding, which gave whites another excuse to attack them. Labor for whites, therefore, did not save the Indians.

Close proximity to whites was dangerous, and not just because it invited murder. Malnourishment weakened Indians' resistance to disease, and waves of epidemics of what we now call childhood diseases—measles and chickenpox, particularly—decimated Indian societies. Whites also spread venereal diseases. Sexual violence was common, and syphilis was especially devastating to Indian women, who often died in childbirth, along with their infants. Birthrates plummeted, and soon natural reproduction was insufficient to sustain a population under assault.

Governments also played a role in the destruction of the California Indians. While the federal government made efforts to establish reservations for Indians, the efforts were halfhearted and undermined by state authorities who claimed that Washington wanted to hand over the "finest farming and mineral lands" to people "wholly incapable, by habit or taste, of appreciating its value." The government of California supported whites by authorizing the indenture of Indians, a thinly disguised system of slavery, and it looked the other way when whites kidnapped Indian women and children to make them servants. The first civilian governor of California, Peter Burnett, sanctioned "a war of extermination . . . until the Indian race becomes extinct."

Historians have also argued that profound social and cultural dislocation played a role in reducing the Indian population. The arrival of the forty-niners shattered the traditional family and tribal bonds that had previously sustained Indian life. Working for whites took men away from the villages, discouraging marriage and household formation, and suppressing reproduction. Families suffered further when

impoverishment drove some Indian women into prostitution. Disrupted family structures and dependency on whites undermined the authority of tribal communities and sustaining traditional relationships. Making the right choices allowed a few individual Indians to survive, but Indian communities largely died.

The discovery of gold set forces in motion that caused a demographic catastrophe for Indians. California Indians resisted in many ways, but they were unable to save their homelands, societies, and often themselves.

Questions for Analysis

Summarize the Argument: Why did the forty-niners prove so deadly to the California Indians?

Analyze the Evidence: Why is murder not sufficient to explain the rapid decline of California Indians? What other causes contributed to their demise?

Consider the Context: What was the nature of the California Indians' previous contact with whites? What was different about the arrival of the forty-niners?

The evangelical temperament—a conviction of righteousness coupled with energy, self-discipline, and faith that the world could be improved—animated most reformers. However, a few activists pointed out that certain fundamental injustices lay beyond the reach of individual self-control. Transcendentalists and utopians believed that perfection required rejecting the competitive, individualistic values of mainstream society. Woman's rights activists and abolitionists sought to reverse the subordination of women and to eliminate the enslavement of blacks by changing laws, social institutions, attitudes, and customs. These reformers confronted the daunting challenge of repudiating widespread beliefs in male supremacy and white supremacy and somehow challenging the entrenched institutions that reinforced those views: the family and slavery.

The Pursuit of Perfection: Transcendentalists and Utopians

A group of New England writers who came to be known as transcendentalists believed that individuals should conform neither to the dictates of the materialistic world nor to the dogma of formal religion. Instead, people should look within themselves for truth and guidance. The leading transcendentalist, Ralph Waldo Emerson—an essayist, poet, and lecturer—proclaimed that the power of the solitary individual was nearly limitless. The novelist Herman Melville ridiculed the inward gaze and confident egoism of transcendentalism as "oracular gibberish" and "self-conceit" that represented less an alternative to mainstream values than an extreme form of the rampant individualism of the age.

Unlike transcendentalists who sought to turn inward, a few reformers tried to change the world by organizing utopian communities as alternatives to prevailing social arrangements. Although these communities never attracted more than a few thousand people, the activities of their members demonstrated dissatisfaction with the larger society and efforts to realize their visions of perfection.

Some communities set out to become models of perfection whose success would point the way toward a better life for everyone. During the 1840s, more than two dozen communities organized themselves around the ideas of Charles Fourier. Members of Fourierist phalanxes, as these communities were called, believed that individualism and competition were evils that denied the basic truth that "men ... are brothers and not competitors." Phalanxes aspired to replace competition with harmonious cooperation based on communal ownership of property. But Fourierist communities failed to realize their lofty goals, and few survived more than two or three years.

The **Oneida community** went beyond the Fourierist notion of communalism. John Humphrey Noyes, the charismatic leader of Oneida, believed that American society's commitment to private property made people greedy and selfish. Noyes claimed that the root of private property lay in marriage, in men's conviction that their wives were their exclusive property. Drawing from a substantial inheritance, Noyes organized the Oneida community in New York in 1848 to abolish marital property rights by permitting sexual intercourse between any consenting man and woman in the community. Noyes also required all members to relinquish their economic property to the community. Most of their neighbors considered Oneidans adulterers and blasphemers. Yet the practices that set Oneida apart from its mainstream neighbors strengthened the community, and it survived long after the Civil War.

Woman's Rights Activists

Women participated in the many reform activities that grew out of evangelical churches. Women church members outnumbered men two to one and worked to put their religious ideas into practice by joining peace, temperance, antislavery, and other societies. Involvement in reform organizations gave a few women activists practical experience in such political arts as speaking in public, running a meeting, drafting resolutions, and circulating petitions. The abolitionist Lydia Maria Child pointed out in 1841 that "those who urged women to become missionaries and form tract societies ... have changed the household utensil to a living energetic being and they have no spell to turn it into a broom again."

In 1848, about three hundred reformers led by Elizabeth Cady Stanton and Lucretia Mott gathered at Seneca Falls, New York, for the first national woman's rights convention in the United States. As Stanton recalled, "The general discontent I felt with women's portion as wife, mother, housekeeper, physician, and spiritual guide, [and] the wearied anxious look of the majority of women impressed me with a strong feeling that some active measure should be taken to right the wrongs of society in general, and of women in particular." The **Seneca Falls Declaration of Sentiments** set an ambitious agenda to demand civil liberties for women and to right the wrongs of society. The declaration proclaimed that "the history of mankind is a history of repeated injuries and usurpations on the part of man toward woman, having in direct object the establishment of an absolute tyranny over her." In the style of the Declaration of Independence, the Seneca Falls declaration demanded that women "have immediate admission to all the rights and privileges which belong to them as citizens of the United States," particularly the "inalienable right to the elective franchise."

Nearly two dozen other woman's rights conventions assembled before 1860, repeatedly calling for suffrage and an end to discrimination against women. But women had difficulty receiving a respectful hearing, much less achieving legislative action. Even so, the Seneca Falls declaration served as a pathbreaking manifesto of dissent against male supremacy and of support for woman suffrage that inspired many women to challenge the barriers that limited their opportunities.

Stanton and other activists sought fair pay and expanded employment opportunities for women by appealing to free-labor ideology. Woman's rights advocate Paula Wright Davis urged Americans to stop discriminating against able and enterprising women: "Let [women] ... open a Store, ... learn any of the lighter mechanical Trades, ... study for a Profession, ... be called to the lecture-room, [and] ... the Temperance rostrum ... [and] let

BLOOMERISM—AN AMERICAN CUSTOM.

Bloomers and Woman's Emancipation
This 1851 British cartoon lampoons bloomers, the trouser-like garment worn beneath shortened skirts by two cigar-smoking American women. Bloomers were invented in the United States as an alternative to the uncomfortable, confining, and awkward dresses worn by the "respectable" women on the right. In the 1850s, Elizabeth Cady Stanton and other woman's rights activists wore bloomers and urged all American women to do likewise. The New York Public Library/Art Resource, NY.

her be appointed [to serve in the Post Office]." Some women pioneered in these and many other occupations during the 1840s and 1850s. Woman's rights activists also succeeded in protecting married women's rights to their own wages and property in New York in 1860. But discrimination against women persisted, since most men believed that free-labor ideology required no compromise of male supremacy.

Abolitionists and the American Ideal

During the 1840s and 1850s, abolitionists continued to struggle to draw the nation's attention to the plight of slaves and the need for emancipation. Former slaves Frederick Douglass, Henry Bibb, and Sojourner Truth lectured to reform audiences throughout the North about the cruelties of slavery. Abolitionists published newspapers, held conventions, and petitioned Congress, but they never attracted a mass following among white Americans. Many white Northerners became convinced that slavery was wrong, but they still believed that blacks were inferior. Many other white Northerners shared the common view of white Southerners that slavery was necessary and even desirable. The westward extension of the nation during the 1840s offered abolitionists an opportunity to link their unpopular ideal to a goal that

many white Northerners found much more attractive—limiting the geographic expansion of slavery, an issue that moved to the center of national politics during the 1850s (see "The Wilmot Proviso and the Expansion of Slavery" in chapter 14).

Black leaders rose to prominence in the abolitionist movement during the 1840s and 1850s. African Americans had actively opposed slavery for decades, but a new generation of leaders came to the forefront in these years. Frederick Douglass, Henry Highland Garnet, William Wells Brown, Martin R. Delany, and others became impatient with white abolitionists' appeals to the conscience of the white majority. In 1843, Garnet urged slaves to choose "Liberty or Death" and rise in insurrection against their masters, an idea that alienated almost all white people and had little influence among slaves. To express their own uncompromising ideas, black abolitionists founded their own newspapers and held their own antislavery conventions, although they still cooperated with sympathetic whites.

The commitment of black abolitionists to battling slavery grew out of their own experiences with white supremacy. The 250,000 free African Americans in the North and West constituted less than 2 percent of the total population in 1860. They confronted the humiliations of racial discrimination in nearly every arena of daily life. Only Maine, Massachusetts,

Abolitionist Meeting
This rare daguerreotype portrays an abolitionist meeting in New York in 1850. Frederick Douglass, who had escaped from slavery in Maryland, is seated on the platform next to the woman at the table. One of the nation's most eloquent abolitionists, Douglass also supported equal rights for women. The man behind Douglass is Gerrit Smith, a wealthy and militant abolitionist whose funds supported many reform activities. Digital image courtesy of the Getty's Open Content Program.

New Hampshire, and Vermont—where few African Americans lived—permitted black men to vote; New York imposed a special property-holding requirement on black—but not white—voters, effectively excluding most black men from the franchise. The pervasive racial discrimination both handicapped and energized black abolitionists.

Some cooperated with the efforts of the **American Colonization Society** to send freed slaves and other black Americans to Liberia in West Africa. Others sought to move to Canada, Haiti, or elsewhere. As one African American from Michigan wrote, "It is impracticable, not to say impossible, for the whites and blacks to live together, and upon terms of social and civil equality, under the same government." Most black American leaders refused to embrace emigration and worked against racial prejudice in their own communities, organizing campaigns against segregation, particularly in transportation and education. Their most notable success came in 1855 when Massachusetts integrated its public schools. Elsewhere, white supremacy continued unabated.

Outside the public spotlight, free African Americans in the North and West contributed to the antislavery cause by quietly aiding fugitive slaves. Harriet Tubman escaped from slavery in Maryland in 1849 and repeatedly risked her freedom and her life to return to the South to escort slaves to freedom. When the opportunity arose, free blacks in the North provided fugitive slaves with food, a safe place to rest, and a helping hand. An outgrowth of the antislavery sentiment and opposition to white supremacy that unified nearly all African Americans in the North, this **underground railroad** ran mainly through black neighborhoods, black churches, and black homes.

REVIEW   Why were women especially prominent in many nineteenth-century reform efforts?

▶ Conclusion: Free Labor, Free Men

During the 1840s and 1850s, a cluster of inter-related developments—population growth, steam power, railroads, and the growing mechanization of agriculture and manufacturing—meant greater economic productivity, a burst of output from farms and factories, and prosperity for many. Diplomacy with Great Britain and war with Mexico handed the United States 1.2 million square miles and more than 1,000 miles of Pacific coastline. One prize of manifest destiny, California, almost immediately rewarded its new owners with tons of gold. Most Americans believed that the new territory and vast riches were appropriate rewards for the nation's stunning economic progress and superior institutions.

To Northerners, industrial evolution confirmed the choice they had made to eliminate slavery and promote free labor as the key to independence, equality, and prosperity. Like Abraham Lincoln, millions of Americans could point to their personal experiences as evidence of the practical truth of the free-labor ideal. But millions of others knew that in the free-labor system, poverty and wealth continued to rub shoulders. Free-labor enthusiasts denied that the problems were inherent in the country's social and economic systems. Instead, they argued, most social ills—including poverty and dependency—sprang from individual deficiencies. Consequently, many reformers focused on personal self-control and discipline, on avoiding sin and alcohol. Other reformers agitated for woman's rights and the abolition of slavery. They challenged widespread conceptions of male supremacy and black inferiority, but neither group managed to overcome the prevailing free-labor ideology based on individualism, racial prejudice, and notions of male superiority.

By midcentury, half of the nation had prohibited slavery, and half permitted it. The North and the South were animated by different economic interests, cultural values, and political aims. Each celebrated its regional identity and increasingly disparaged that of the other. Not even the victory over Mexico could bridge the deepening divide between North and South.

See the Selected Bibliography for this chapter in the Appendix.

12 | Chapter Review

KEY TERMS

mechanical reapers (p. 318)
American system (p. 319)
manifest destiny (p. 325)
Oregon Trail (p. 326)
Mormons (p. 328)
Lone Star Republic (p. 330)
Treaty of Guadalupe Hidalgo (p. 336)
California gold rush (p. 337)
Oneida community (p. 342)
Seneca Falls Declaration of Sentiments (p. 342)
American Colonization Society (p. 344)
underground railroad (p. 344)

REVIEW QUESTIONS

1. Why did the United States become a leading industrial power in the nineteenth century? (pp. 317–320)

2. How did the free-labor ideal account for economic inequality? (pp. 320–324)

3. Why did westward migration expand dramatically in the mid-nineteenth century? (pp. 324–331)

4. Why did the United States go to war with Mexico? (pp. 331–340)

5. Why were women especially prominent in many nineteenth-century reform efforts? (pp. 340–344)

MAKING CONNECTIONS

1. Discuss migration to two different regions. What drew the migrants, and how did the U.S. government contribute to their efforts?

2. How did the ideology of manifest destiny contribute to mid-nineteenth-century expansion? Discuss its implications for individual migrants and the nation.

3. How did the Mexican-American War affect national political and economic developments in subsequent decades?

4. How did nineteenth-century reform movements draw on the free-labor ideal to pursue specific reforms?

LINKING TO THE PAST

1. In what ways were the North's economy, society, and political structure during the 1840s and 1850s shaped by the American Revolution and the Constitution? (See chapters 7 and 8.)

2. The nation's mighty push westward in the 1840s and 1850s extended a history of expansion that was as old as the nation itself. How was expansion to the West between 1840 and 1860 similar to and different from expansion between 1800 and 1820? (See chapter 10.)

13 The Slave South
1820–1860

CONTENT LEARNING OBJECTIVES

After reading and studying this chapter, you should be able to:

- Identify the ways slavery, a plantation-based economy, and biracialism distinguished the antebellum South from the North.

- Explain how a plantation was physically organized, and describe the roles of the plantation master and mistress. Define the ideology of paternalism and its role on the plantation.

- Describe the lives led by slaves in the Old South and the elements that contributed to a semi-autonomous slave culture.

- Explain why free blacks posed an ideological dilemma for white Southerners and why their freedom was precarious.

- Identify the "plain folk" of the Old South.

- Explain both how the South became increasingly democratic during the second quarter of the nineteenth century and how planters managed to retain their power.

SLAVE POT
Enslaved African American potters made tens of thousands of ceramic pots to hold water and store food. The most renowned slave potter, Dave, worked in Edgefield District, South Carolina. At a time when teaching slaves to read or write was a crime, Dave often signed his work with a grand flourish. National Museum of American History, Smithsonian Institution, USA/Bridgeman Images.

NAT TURNER WAS BORN A SLAVE IN SOUTHAMPTON COUNTY, VIRGINIA, in October 1800. His parents noticed special marks on his body, which they said were signs that he was "intended for some great purpose." His master said that he learned to read without being taught. As an adolescent, he adopted an austere lifestyle of Christian devotion and fasting. In his twenties, he received visits from the "Spirit," the same spirit, he believed, that had spoken to the ancient prophets. In time, Nat Turner began to interpret these things to mean that God had appointed him an instrument of divine vengeance for the sin of slaveholding.

On the morning of August 22, 1831, he set out with six friends—Hark, Henry, Sam, Nelson, Will, and Jack—to punish slave owners. Turner struck the first blow, an ax to the head of his master, Joseph Travis. The rebels killed all of the white men, women, and children they encountered. By noon, they had visited eleven farms and slaughtered fifty-seven whites. Along the way, they had added fifty or sixty men to their army. Word spread quickly, and soon the militia and hundreds of local whites gathered. They quickly captured or killed all of the rebels except Turner, who hid out for about ten weeks before being captured in nearby woods. Within a week, he was tried, convicted, and executed. By then, forty-five slaves had stood trial, twenty had been convicted and hanged, and

347

Horrid Massacre in Virginia
No contemporary images of Nat Turner are known to exist. This woodcut simply imagines the rebellion as a nightmare in which black brutes took the lives of innocent whites. Although there was never another rebellion as large as Turner's, images of black violence continued to haunt white imaginations.
Library of Congress, 3a33960.

another ten had been banished from Virginia. Frenzied whites had killed another hundred or more blacks—insurgents and innocent bystanders—in their counterattack against the rebellion.

White Virginians blamed the rebellion on outside agitators. In 1829, David Walker, a freeborn black man living in Boston, had published his *An Appeal . . . to the Coloured Citizens of the World*, an invitation to slaves to rise up in bloody revolution, and copies had fallen into the hands of Virginia slaves. Moreover, on January 1, 1831, the Massachusetts abolitionist William Lloyd Garrison had published the first issue of the *Liberator*, his fiery newspaper (see "Organizing against Slavery" in chapter 11).

In the months following the insurrection, the Virginia legislature reaffirmed the state's determination to preserve slavery by passing laws that strengthened the institution and further restricted free blacks. A professor at the College of William and Mary, Thomas R. Dew, published a vigorous defense of slavery that became the bible of Southerners' proslavery arguments. More than ever, the nation was divided along the Mason-Dixon line, the surveyors' mark that in colonial times had established the boundary between Maryland and Pennsylvania but half a century later divided the free North and the slave South.

Black slavery increasingly molded the South into a distinctive region. In the decades after 1820, Southerners, like Northerners, raced westward; but unlike Northerners who spread small farms, manufacturing, and free labor, Southerners spread slavery, cotton, and plantations. Geographic expansion meant that slavery became more vigorous and more profitable than ever, embraced more people, and increased the South's political power. Antebellum Southerners sometimes found themselves at odds with one another—not only slaves and free people but also women and men; Indians, Africans, and Europeans; and aristocrats and common folk. Nevertheless, beneath this diversity, a distinctively southern society and culture were forming. The South became a slave society, and most white Southerners were proud of it.

▶ The Growing Distinctiveness of the South

From the earliest settlements, inhabitants of the southern colonies had shared a great deal with northern colonists. Most whites in both sections were British and Protestant, spoke a common language, and celebrated their victorious revolution against British rule. The creation of the new nation under the Constitution in 1789 forged political ties that bound all Americans. The beginnings of a national economy fostered economic interdependence and communication across regional boundaries. White Americans everywhere praised the prosperous young nation, and they looked forward to its seemingly boundless future.

Despite these national similarities, Southerners and Northerners grew increasingly different. The French political observer Alexis de Tocqueville believed he knew why. "I could easily prove," he asserted in 1831, "that almost all the differences which may be noticed between the character of the Americans in the Southern and Northern states have originated in slavery." And a quarter of a century later, neither Northerners nor Southerners liked developments on the other side of the Mason-Dixon line. "On the subject of slavery," the *Charleston Mercury* declared, "the North and South . . . are not only two Peoples, but they are rival, hostile Peoples." Even more than the cotton-based agriculture that dominated the region, slavery made the South different, and it was the differences between the North and South, not the similarities, that increasingly shaped antebellum American history.

Cotton Kingdom, Slave Empire

In the first half of the nineteenth century, millions of Americans migrated west. In the South, the stampede began after the Creek War of 1813–1814, which divested the Creek Indians of 24 million acres and initiated the government campaign to remove Indian people living east of the Mississippi River to the West. Hard-driving slaveholders seeking virgin acreage for new plantations, ambitious farmers looking for patches of cheap land for small farms, striving herders and drovers pushing their hogs and cattle toward fresh pastures—everyone felt the pull of western land.

But more than anything it was cotton that propelled Southerners westward. South of the

CHRONOLOGY

1808	• External slave trade outlawed.
1810s–1850s	• Suffrage extended throughout South to all adult white males.
1820s–1830s	• Southern legislatures enact slave codes. • Southern legislatures restrict free blacks. • Southern intellectuals fashion systematic defense of slavery.
1822	• Denmark Vesey executed.
1829	• *An Appeal . . . to the Coloured Citizens of the World* published.
1830	• Southern slaves number approximately two million.
1831	• First issue of the *Liberator* published. • Nat Turner leads slave rebellion.
1836	• Arkansas admitted to Union as slave state.
1840	• Cotton accounts for more than 60 percent of nation's exports.
1845	• Texas and Florida admitted to Union as slave states.
1860	• Southern slaves number nearly four million, one-third of South's population.

Mason-Dixon line, climate and geography were ideally suited for the cultivation of cotton. By the 1830s, cotton fields stretched from the Atlantic seaboard to central Texas. Heavy migration led to statehood for Arkansas in 1836 and for Texas and Florida in 1845. Cotton production soared to nearly 5 million bales in 1860, when the South produced three-fourths of the world's supply. The South—especially that tier of states from South Carolina west to Texas called the Lower South—had become the **cotton kingdom** (Map 13.1).

The cotton kingdom was also a slave empire. The South's cotton boom rested on the backs of slaves. As cotton agriculture expanded westward, whites shipped more than a million enslaved

MAP ACTIVITY

Map 13.1   Cotton Kingdom, Slave Empire: 1820 and 1860

As the production of cotton soared, the slave population increased dramatically. Slaves continued to toil in tobacco and rice fields, but in Alabama, Mississippi, and Texas, they increasingly worked on cotton plantations.

READING THE MAP: Where was slavery most prevalent in 1820? In 1860? How did the spread of slavery compare with the spread of cotton?

CONNECTIONS: How much of the world's cotton was produced in the American South in 1860? How did the number of slaves in the American South compare with that in the rest of the world? What does this suggest about the South's cotton kingdom?

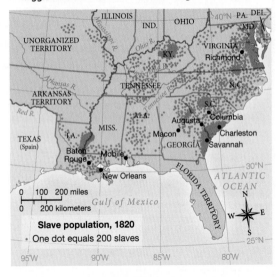

Slave population, 1820
· One dot equals 200 slaves

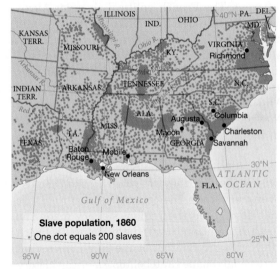

Slave population, 1860
· One dot equals 200 slaves

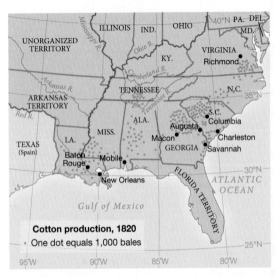

Cotton production, 1820
· One dot equals 1,000 bales

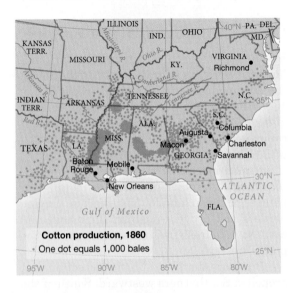

Cotton production, 1860
· One dot equals 1,000 bales

men, women, and children from the Atlantic coast across the continent in what has been called the "Second Middle Passage," a massive deportation that dwarfed the transatlantic slave trade to North America. Victims of this brutal domestic slave trade marched hundreds of miles southwest to the Lower South, where they literally cut new plantations from the forests. Cotton, slaves, and plantations moved west together.

The slave population grew enormously. Southern slaves numbered fewer than 700,000 in 1790, about 2 million in 1830, and almost 4 million by 1860. By 1860, the South contained more slaves than all the other slave societies in the New World combined. The extraordinary growth was not the result of the importation of slaves, which the federal government outlawed

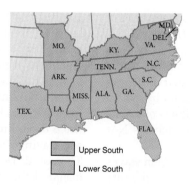

Upper South

Lower South

The Upper and Lower South

in 1808. Instead, the slave population grew through natural reproduction; by midcentury, most U.S. slaves were native-born Southerners.

The South in Black and White

By 1860, one in every three Southerners was black (approximately 4 million blacks to 8 million whites). In the Lower South states of Mississippi and South Carolina, blacks constituted the majority (Figure 13.1). The contrast with the North was striking: In 1860, only one Northerner in seventy-six was black (about 250,000 blacks to 19 million whites).

The presence of large numbers of African Americans had profound consequences for the South. Southern culture—language, food, music, religion, and even accents—was in part shaped

FIGURE 13.1   Black and White Populations in the South, 1860

Blacks represented a much larger fraction of the population in the South than in the North, but considerable variation existed from state to state. Only one Missourian in ten, for example, was black, while Mississippi and South Carolina had black majorities. States in the Upper South were "whiter" than states in the Lower South, despite the Upper South's greater number of free blacks.

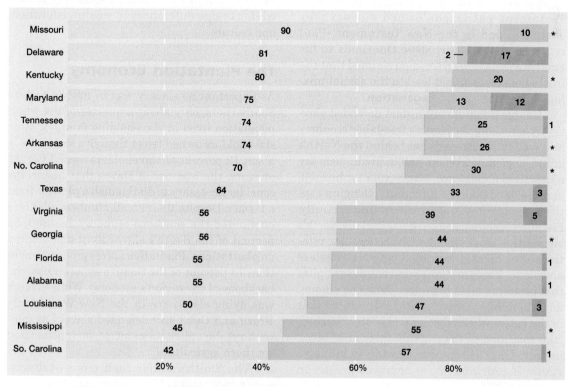

by blacks. But the most direct consequence of the South's biracialism was southern whites' commitment to white supremacy. Northern whites believed in racial superiority, too, but their dedication to white supremacy lacked the intensity and urgency increasingly felt by white Southerners who lived among millions of blacks who had every reason to strike back, as Nat Turner had.

After 1820, attacks on slavery—from slaves and from northern abolitionists—caused white Southerners to make extraordinary efforts to strengthen slavery. State legislatures constructed **slave codes** (laws) that required the total submission of slaves. As the Louisiana code stated, a slave "owes his master . . . a respect without bounds, and an absolute obedience." The laws also underlined the authority of all whites, not just masters. Any white could "correct" slaves who did not stay "in their place."

Intellectuals joined legislators in the campaign to strengthen slavery. The South's academics, writers, and clergy employed every imaginable defense. They argued that slaves were legal property, and wasn't the protection of property the bedrock of American liberty? History also endorsed slavery, they claimed. Weren't the great civilizations—such as those of the Hebrews, Greeks, and Romans—slave societies? They argued that the Bible, properly interpreted, also sanctioned slavery. Old Testament patriarchs owned slaves, they observed, and in the New Testament, Paul returned the runaway slave Onesimus to his master. Proslavery spokesmen claimed that the freeing of slaves would lead to the sexual mixing of the races, or **miscegenation**.

George Fitzhugh of Virginia defended slavery by attacking the North's free-labor economy and society. He claimed that behind the North's grand slogans of freedom and individualism lay a heartless philosophy: "Every man for himself, and the devil take the hindmost." Gouging capitalists exploited wageworkers unmercifully, Fitzhugh declared, and he contrasted the North's vicious free-labor system with the humane relations that he said prevailed between masters and slaves because slaves were valuable capital that masters sought to protect. John C. Calhoun, an influential southern politician, declared that in the states where slavery had been abolished, "the condition of the African, instead of being improved, has become worse," while in the slave states, the Africans "have improved greatly in every respect."

But at the heart of the defense of slavery lay the claim of black inferiority. Black enslavement was both necessary and proper, slavery's defenders argued, because Africans were lesser beings. Rather than exploitative, slavery was a mass civilizing effort that lifted lowly blacks from African barbarism and savagery, taught them disciplined work, and converted them to soul-saving Christianity. According to Virginian Thomas R. Dew, most slaves were grateful. He declared that "the slaves of a good master are his warmest, most constant, and most devoted friends." (See "Analyzing Historical Evidence," page 354.)

African slavery encouraged southern whites to unify around race rather than to divide by class. The grubbiest, most tobacco-stained white man could proudly proclaim his superiority to all blacks and his equality with the most refined southern planter. Georgia attorney Thomas R. R. Cobb observed that every white Southerner "feels that he belongs to an elevated class. It matters not that he is no slaveholder; he is not of the inferior race; he is a freeborn citizen." Consequently, the "poorest meets the richest as an equal; sits at his table with him; salutes him as a neighbor; meets him in every public assembly, and stands on the same social platform." In the South, Cobb boasted, "there is no war of classes." By providing every white Southerner membership in the ruling race, slavery helped whites bridge differences in wealth, education, and culture.

The Plantation Economy

As important as slavery was in unifying white Southerners, only about a quarter of the white population lived in slaveholding families. Most slaveholders owned fewer than five slaves. Only about 12 percent of slaveholders owned twenty or more, the number of slaves that historians consider necessary to distinguish a **planter** from a farmer. Despite their small numbers, planters dominated the southern economy. In 1860, 52 percent of the South's slaves lived and worked on **plantations**. Plantation slaves produced more than 75 percent of the South's export crops, the backbone of the region's economy. While slavery was dying elsewhere in the New World (only Brazil and Cuba still defended slavery at midcentury), slave plantations increasingly dominated southern agriculture.

The South's major cash crops—tobacco, sugar, rice, and cotton—grew on plantations

THE FRUITS OF AMALGAMATION.

VISUAL ACTIVITY

The Fruits of Amalgamation

In this lithograph from 1839, Edward W. Clay of Philadelphia attacked abolitionists by imagining the miscegenation (also known as "amalgamation") that would come from emancipation. He drew a beautiful white woman, her two black children, and her dark-skinned, ridiculously overdressed husband, resting his feet in his wife's lap. American Antiquarian Society, Worcester, Massachusetts, USA/Bridgeman Images.

READING THE IMAGE: What are the races of the servant and the couple at the door, and what do you think the artist is saying?

CONNECTIONS: In the opinion of abolitionists, who was responsible for miscegenation and why?

(Map 13.2). Tobacco, the original plantation crop in North America, had shifted westward in the nineteenth century from the Chesapeake to Tennessee and Kentucky. Large-scale sugar production began in 1795, when Étienne de Boré built a modern sugar mill in what is today New Orleans, and sugar plantations were confined almost entirely to Louisiana. Commercial rice production began in the seventeenth century, and like sugar, rice was confined to a small geographic area, a narrow strip of coast stretching from the Carolinas into Georgia.

But by the nineteenth century, cotton reigned as king of the South's plantation crops. Cotton became commercially significant in the 1790s after the invention of a new cotton gin by Eli Whitney (see "Agriculture, Transportation, and Banking" in chapter 9). Cotton was relatively easy to grow and took little capital to get started—just enough for land, seed, and simple tools. Thus, small farmers as well as planters grew cotton. But planters, whose extensive fields were worked by gangs of slaves, produced three-quarters of the South's cotton, and cotton made planters rich.

Defending Slavery

White Southerners who defended slavery were rationalizing their economic interests and racial privileges, of course, but they also believed what they said about slavery being just, necessary, and godly. Whatever their specific arguments, they agreed with the *Charleston Mercury* that without slavery, the South would become a "most magnificent jungle."

DOCUMENT 1
John C. Calhoun, Speech before the U.S. Senate, 1837

When abolitionists began to denounce slavery as sinful and odious, John C. Calhoun, the South's leading proslavery politician, rose to defend the institution as "a positive good." Calhoun devoted part of his speech to the argument that enslavement benefited the slaves themselves.

Be it good or bad, it [slavery] has grown up with our society and institutions, and is so interwoven with them, that to destroy it would be to destroy us as a people. But let me not be understood as admitting, even by implication, that the existing relations between the two races in the slaveholding States is an evil: far otherwise; I hold it to be a good. . . . I appeal to facts. Never before has the black race of Central Africa, from the dawn of history to the present day, attained a condition so civilized and so improved, not only physically, but morally and intellectually. It came to us in a low, degraded, and savage condition, and in the course of a few generations, it has grown up under the fostering care of our institutions, reviled they have been, to its present comparatively civilized condition. This, with the rapid increase of numbers, is conclusive proof of the general happiness of the race, in spite of all the exaggerated tales to the contrary. . . .

I hold that in the present state of civilization, where two races of different origin, and distinguished by color,

and other physical differences, as well as intellectual, are brought together, the relation now existing in the slave-holding States between the two, is, instead of an evil, a good—a positive good. . . .

I may say with truth, that in few countries so much is left to the share of the laborer, and so little exacted from him, or where there is more kind attention paid to him in sickness or infirmities of age. Compare his condition with the tenants of the poor houses in the more civilized portions of Europe—look at the sick, and the old and infirm slave, on one hand, in the midst of his family and friends, under the kind superintending care of his master and mistress, and compare it with the forlorn and wretched condition of the pauper in the poor house.

Source: John C. Calhoun, "Speech on the Reception of Abolition Petitions, Delivered in the Senate, February 6th, 1837," in *Speeches of John C. Calhoun, Delivered in the House of Representatives and in the Senate of the United States*, edited by Richard K. Cralle (Appleton, 1853), 625–33.

DOCUMENT 2
William Harper, *Memoir on Slavery*, 1837

William Harper—judge, politician, and academic—defended slavery by denouncing abolitionists, particularly the "atrocious philosophy" of "natural equality and inalienable rights" that they used to support their attacks on slavery.

Plantation slavery also enriched the nation. By 1840, cotton accounted for more than 60 percent of American exports. Most of the cotton was shipped to Great Britain, the world's largest manufacturer of cotton textiles. (See "Beyond America's Borders," page 356.) Much of the profit from the sale of cotton overseas returned to planters, but some went to northern middlemen who bought, sold, insured, warehoused, and shipped cotton to the mills in Great Britain. As one New York merchant observed, "Cotton has enriched all through whose hands it has passed."

As middlemen invested their profits in the booming northern economy, industrial development received a burst of much-needed capital. Furthermore, southern plantations benefited northern industry by providing an important market for textiles, agricultural tools, and other manufactured goods.

The economies of the North and South steadily diverged. While the North developed a mixed economy—agriculture, commerce, and manufacturing—the South remained overwhelmingly agricultural. Year after year, planters

All men are born free and equal. Is it not palpably nearer the truth to say that no man was ever born free, and that no two men were ever born equal? . . . Wealth and poverty, fame or obscurity, strength or weakness, knowledge or ignorance, ease or labor, power or subjection, mark the endless diversity in the condition of men. . . .

It is the order of nature and of God, that the being of superior faculties and knowledge, and therefore of superior power, should control and dispose of those who are inferior. It is as much in the order of nature, that men should enslave each other, as that other animals should prey upon each other.

Moralists have denounced the injustice and cruelty which have been practiced towards our aboriginal Indians, by which they have been driven from their native seats and exterminated.

. . . No doubt, much fraud and injustice has been practiced in the circumstances and manner of their removal. Yet who has contended that civilized man had no moral right to possess himself of the country? That he was bound to leave this wide and fertile continent, which is capable of sustaining uncounted myriads of a civilized race, to a few roving and ignorant barbarians? Yet if any thing is certain, it is certain that there were no means by which he could possess the country, without exterminating or enslaving them. Savage and civilized man cannot live together, and the savage can only be tamed by being enslaved or by having slaves.

Source: William Harper, *Memoir on Slavery* (J. S. Burges, 1838).

DOCUMENT 3
Thornton Stringfellow, "The Bible Argument: or, Slavery in the Light of Divine Revelation," 1856

The Reverend Thornton Stringfellow, a Baptist minister from Virginia, defended human bondage based on his reading of the Bible. He makes a case that Jesus himself approved of the relationship between master and slave.

Jesus Christ recognized this institution [slavery] as one that was lawful among men, and regulated its relative duties. . . . I affirm then, first, (and no man denies,) that Jesus Christ has not abolished slavery by a prohibitory command: and second, I affirm, he has introduced no new moral principle which can work its destruction, under the gospel dispensation; and that the principle relied on for this purpose, is a fundamental principle of the Mosaic law, under which slavery was instituted by Jehovah himself. . . .

To the church at Colosse . . . Paul in his letter to them, recognizes the three relations of wives and husbands, parents and children, servants and masters, as relations existing among the members . . . and to the servants and masters he thus writes: "Servants obey in all things your masters, according to the flesh: not with eye service, as men pleasers, but in singleness of heart, fearing God: and whatsoever you do, do it heartily, as to the Lord and not unto men; knowing that of the Lord ye shall receive the reward of the inheritance, for ye serve the Lord Christ. . . . Masters give unto your servants that which is just and equal, knowing that you also have a master in heaven."

Source: *Slavery Defended: The Views of the Old South* by Eric L. McKitrick, editor. Published by Prentice-Hall, 1963. *Cotton Is King and Pro-Slavery Arguments* by Thornton Stringfellow (Pritchard, Abbott & Loomis, 1860), 459–546.

Questions for Analysis

Summarize the Argument: How do the authors' proslavery convictions shape their arguments?

Analyze the Evidence: The authors of these documents build their defenses of slavery on three different kinds of evidence. What are they?

Consider the Context: What did William Harper hope to gain by interjecting Americans' treatment of Indians into his defense of slavery?

funneled the profits they earned from land and slaves back into more land and more slaves. With its capital flowing into agriculture, the South did not develop many factories. By 1860, only 10 percent of the nation's industrial workers lived in the South. Some cotton mills sprang up, but the region that produced 100 percent of the nation's cotton manufactured less than 7 percent of its cotton textiles.

Without significant economic diversification, the South developed fewer cities than the North and West. In 1860, it was the least urban region in the country. Whereas nearly 37 percent of New England's population lived in cities, less than 12 percent of Southerners were urban dwellers. Because the South had so few cities and industrial jobs, it attracted small numbers of European immigrants. Seeking economic opportunity, not competition with slaves (whose labor would keep wages low), immigrants steered northward. In 1860, 13 percent of all Americans were born abroad. But in nine of the fifteen slave states, only 2 percent or less of the population was foreign-born.

Cotton's Global Empire

Long before T-shirts and jeans became our everyday wear, cotton had already changed the world. Before cotton, people wore wool and linen, materials that were expensive, scratchy, and—because they were nearly unwashable—smelly. The world welcomed cotton because it was cheap, comfortable, and washable. But before the world could dress in cotton, planters in the American South, merchants on both sides of the Atlantic, and manufacturers in Britain had to link the plantations of the South with the textile factories of Great Britain. Once they did, the world was never the same.

Before 1793, when Eli Whitney devised a new machine to clean raw cotton, no North American cotton whatsoever reached Britain. Following Whitney's invention, American cotton production exploded almost overnight, and a

"cotton rush" carried cotton, cotton gins, plantations, and slaves westward across land taken from the Indians. U.S. cotton began to arrive in Liverpool in 1795. By 1802, the United States had become the single most important supplier of cotton to Britain, and Britain had become the world's dominant manufacturer of cotton cloth. By the 1850s, the South supplied 77 percent of the 800 million pounds that fed Britain's cotton-hungry textile factories.

Although wool had previously been at the core of late-eighteenth-century English manufacturing and trade, cotton quickly displaced wool in northwestern England's manufacturing districts. Because cotton could not be grown in the cold, rainy climate of Europe, manufacturers had to import every pound. Traders bought the American cotton crop and brought it across the Atlantic to

English mills, where it was spun into yarn, woven into cloth, and shipped to customers around the world. The production of cotton cloth became the world's first mechanized and industrialized business. New machines, new sources of power, and a new labor system revolutionized the making of cotton cloth and made mass production possible.

Cotton was grown by slaves, but it was made into cloth by a new army of wage laborers. The explosion of textile factories in Britain meant that people from the countryside crowded into the cities of Manchester and Liverpool, into housing that was "offensive, dark, damp, and incommodious." For at least twelve hours a day, six days a week, textile workers operated and repaired the machines that turned raw cotton into cloth. The insatiable demand for labor swept

MAP ACTIVITY

Map 13.2 The Agricultural Economy of the South, 1860
Cotton dominated the South's agricultural economy, but the region grew a variety of crops and was largely self-sufficient in foodstuffs.

READING THE MAP: In what type of geographic areas were rice and sugar grown? After cotton, what crop commanded the greatest agricultural area in the South? In which region of the South was this crop predominantly found?

CONNECTIONS: What role did the South play in the U.S. economy in 1860? How did the economy of the South differ from that of the North?

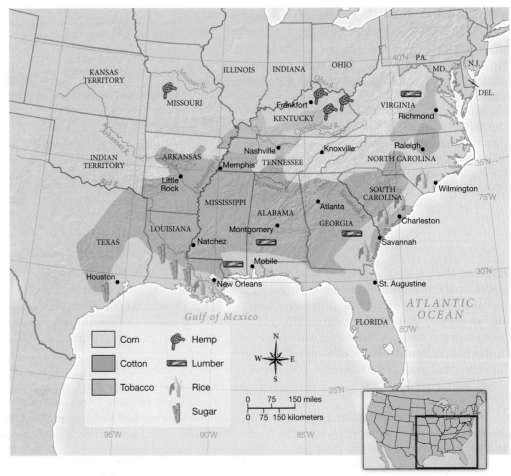

Corn · Hemp · Cotton · Lumber · Tobacco · Rice · Sugar

up huge numbers of women and children. The degree of exploitation was revealed in 1833 when Parliament barred children from working in the spinning mills before the age of nine and required that those between nine and thirteen could work only nine hours a day. An 1833 report observed, "The consequence of this excess of toil is that the growth of the body is checked, and the limbs become weak, and sometimes horribly distorted."

Cotton manufacturing became the center of the British economy and caused extraordinary changes in British society. British factories produced two-thirds of the world's cotton cloth, and Manchester became the most industrialized city in the world. By 1860, nearly 500,000 laborers worked in Britain's cotton industry, where they experienced radically new ways of working and living as well as unprecedented poverty and misery.

Manufacturers elsewhere tried to follow the path that Manchester had blazed. Cotton mills sprang up in France, Germany, Russia, Switzerland, the Netherlands, and Belgium, each hoping to reproduce the success achieved in Britain. In each case, the American South's slave-grown cotton fed the mills. For example, 90 percent of the 192 million pounds used in France came from the United States. Beginning in the 1810s, the United States began building its own cotton factories, and those factories depended entirely on southern cotton. By 1860, cotton textiles were the most important manufacturing industry in the United States in terms of capital invested and workers employed.

Cotton stood at the center of the first modern manufacturing industry and the world's first global economy. When cotton linked two major nineteenth-century developments—the westward expansion of plantation slavery in the United States and the rise of the factory and wage labor in Europe—it created a global web of agriculture, trade, and industrial production. The repercussions from the industrialization of cotton resonated across nations and continents. Mass production put cotton clothes within reach of common people. Because the industrialization of British cotton manufacturing proved to be the first step of what is called the industrial revolution, raw cotton—grown by American slaves—played an essential role in international industrialization.

Questions for Analysis

Analyze the Evidence: What evidence supports the contention that American cotton played an essential role in the industrialization of cotton cloth?

Consider the Context: Why did cotton cloth quickly supplant wool? What were cotton's advantages?

Recognize Viewpoints: How might cotton manufacturers and cotton workers—on both sides of the Atlantic—have viewed the industrialization of cotton cloth differently? Would they have considered it a success? Why or why not?

Northerners claimed that slavery was a backward labor system, and compared with Northerners, Southerners invested less of their capital in industry, transportation, and public education. But few Southerners perceived economic weakness in their region. Indeed, planters' pockets were never fuller than in the 1850s, thanks to the South's near monopoly on cotton,

VISUAL ACTIVITY

Steamboats and Cotton in New Orleans, ca. 1858
Steamboats line up to load bales of cotton. A few years earlier, a visitor had expressed awe: "It must be seen to be believed; and even then, it will require an active mind to comprehend acres of cotton bales standing upon the levee." Corbis.
READING THE IMAGE: Who is absent from this photograph? Whose job would it have been to load the cotton bales on the steamboats?
CONNECTIONS: Why were the South's most significant cities ports?

the hottest commodity in the international marketplace. Planters' decisions to reinvest in cotton ensured the momentum of the plantation economy and the political and social relationships rooted in it.

> **REVIEW** Why did the nineteenth-century southern economy remain primarily agricultural?

▶ Masters and Mistresses in the Big House

Nowhere was the contrast between northern and southern life more vivid than on the plantations of the South. A plantation typically included a "big house," where the plantation owner and his family lived, and a slave quarter. Near the big house were the kitchen, storehouse, smokehouse (for curing and preserving meat), and hen coop. More distant were the barns, toolsheds, artisans' workshops, and overseer's house. Large plantations sometimes had an infirmary and a chapel for slaves. Depending on the crop, there was also a tobacco shed, a rice mill, a sugar refinery, or a cotton gin house. Lavish or plain, plantations everywhere had an underlying similarity (Figure 13.2).

The plantation was the home of masters, mistresses, and slaves. A hierarchy of rigid roles and duties governed their relationships. Presiding was the master, who by law ruled his wife, children, and slaves as dependents under his dominion and protection.

Paternalism and Male Honor

Whereas smaller planters supervised the labor of their slaves themselves, larger planters hired overseers who went to the fields with the slaves, leaving the planters free to concentrate on marketing, finance, and the general affairs of the plantation. Planters also found time to escape to town to discuss cotton prices, to the courthouse and legislature to debate politics, and to the woods to hunt and fish.

Increasingly, planters characterized their mastery in terms of what they called "Christian guardianship" and what historians have called **paternalism**. The concept of paternalism denied that the form of slavery practiced in the South was brutal and exploitative. Instead, paternalism claimed that plantations benefited all. In exchange

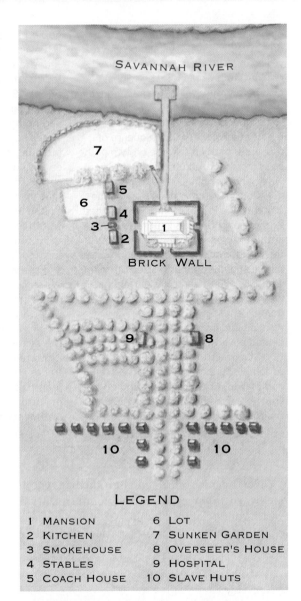

SAVANNAH RIVER

BRICK WALL

LEGEND

1	MANSION	6	LOT
2	KITCHEN	7	SUNKEN GARDEN
3	SMOKEHOUSE	8	OVERSEER'S HOUSE
4	STABLES	9	HOSPITAL
5	COACH HOUSE	10	SLAVE HUTS

FIGURE 13.2 A Southern Plantation
Slavery determined how masters laid out their plantations and where they situated their big houses and slave quarters. This model of the Hermitage, the mansion built in 1830 for Henry McAlpin, a Georgia rice planter, shows the overseer's house poised halfway between the owner's mansion and the slave huts. Data source: *Back of the Big House: The Architecture of Plantation Slavery* by John Michael Vlach. Copyright © 1993 by the University of North Carolina Press. Original illustration property of the Historic American Buildings Survey, a division of the National Park Service.

for the slaves' work and obedience, masters provided basic care and necessary guidance for a childlike, dependent people. In 1814, Thomas Jefferson captured the essence of the advancing ideal: "We should endeavor, with those whom fortune has thrown on our hands, to feed & clothe them well, protect them from ill usage, require such reasonable labor only as is performed voluntarily by freemen, and be led by no repugnancies to abdicate them, and our duties to them." A South Carolina rice planter insisted, "I manage them as my children."

Paternalism was part propaganda and part self-delusion. But it was also economically shrewd. Masters increasingly recognized slaves as valuable assets, particularly after the nation closed its external slave trade in 1808 and the cotton boom stimulated the demand for slaves. The expansion of the slave labor force could come only from natural reproduction. As one slave owner declared in 1849, "It behooves those who own them to make them last as long as possible."

One consequence of paternalism and economic self-interest was a small improvement in slaves' welfare. Diet improved, although nineteenth-century slaves still ate mainly fatty pork and cornmeal. Housing improved, although the cabins still had cracks large enough, slaves said, for cats to slip through. Clothing improved, although slaves seldom received much more than two crude outfits a year and perhaps a pair of cheap shoes. Workdays remained sunup to sundown, but planters often offered a rest period in the heat of the day. Most planters ceased the colonial practice of punishing slaves by branding and mutilation.

Paternalism should not be mistaken for "Ol' Massa's" kindness and goodwill. It encouraged better treatment because it made economic sense to provide at least minimal care for valuable slaves. Nor did paternalism require that planters put aside their whips. They could whip and still claim that they were only fulfilling their responsibilities as guardians of their naturally lazy and at times insubordinate black dependents. State laws gave masters nearly "uncontrolled authority over the body" of the slave, according to one North Carolina judge, and whipping remained planters' basic form of coercion. (See "Making Historical Arguments," page 360.)

Paternalism never won universal acceptance among planters, but by the nineteenth century it had become a kind of communal standard. With its notion that slavery imposed on masters a burden and a duty, paternalism provided slaveholders with a means of rationalizing their rule. But it also provided some slaves with leverage in controlling the conditions of their lives. Slaves learned to manipulate the slaveholder's need to see himself as a good master. To avoid a reputation as a cruel tyrant, planters sometimes negotiated with slaves, rather than just resorting to the whip. Masters sometimes granted slaves small garden plots in which they could work for themselves after working all day in the fields, or they gave slaves a few days off and a dance when they had gathered the last of the cotton.

Virginia statesman Edmund Randolph argued that slavery created in white southern men a "quick and acute sense of personal liberty" and a "disdain for every abridgement of personal independence." Indeed, prickly individualism and aggressive independence became crucial features of the southern concept of honor. Social standing, political advancement, and even self-esteem rested on an honorable reputation. Defending honor became a male passion. Andrew Jackson's mother reportedly told her son, "Never tell a lie, nor take what is not your own, nor sue anybody for slander or assault and battery. *Always settle them cases yourself.*"

Among planters, such advice sometimes led to dueling, a ritual that had arrived from Europe in the eighteenth century. It died out in the North, but in the South, even after legislatures banned it, gentlemen continued to defend their honor with pistols at ten paces. Duels were fought by Andrew Jackson, whose wife one foolish man slandered, as well as by two college students who happened at dinner to reach simultaneously for the last piece of trout.

Southerners also expected an honorable gentleman to be a proper patriarch. Nowhere in America was masculine power more accentuated. Planters allowed no opposition from any of their dependents, black or white. The master's absolute dominion sometimes led to miscegenation. Laws prohibited interracial sex, but as long as slavery gave white men extraordinary power, slave women were forced to submit to the sexual demands of the men who owned them.

In time, as the children of one elite family married the children of another, ties of blood and kinship, as well as ideology and economic interest, linked planters to one another. Aware of what they shared as slaveholders, planters worked together to defend their common interests. The values of the big house—slavery, honor, male domination—washed over the boundaries of plantations and flooded all of southern life.

The Southern Lady and Feminine Virtues

Like their northern counterparts, southern ladies were expected to possess the feminine virtues of piety, purity, chastity, and obedience within the context of marriage, motherhood, and domesticity. Countless toasts praised the southern lady

How Often Were Slaves Whipped?

There is little doubt that the whipping of slaves was widespread and considered acceptable in the South. We know from white sources that whipping was the prescribed method of physical punishment on most antebellum plantations. Masters' instructions to overseers authorized whippings and often established the number of strokes an overseer could administer. Some planters allowed fifteen lashes, some fifty, and some one hundred. But slave owners' instructions, as revealing as they are, tell us more about the severity of beating than about their frequency.

Remembrances of former slaves confirm that whipping was widespread and frequent. In the 1930s, a government program gathered testimony from more than 2,300 elderly African Americans about their experiences as slaves. Their accounts offer grisly evidence of the cruelty of slavery. "You say how did our Master treat his slaves?" asked one woman. "Scandalous, they treated them just like dogs." She was herself whipped "till the blood dripped to the ground." Bert Strong never personally felt the sting of the lash, but he recalled hearing slaves on other farms "hollering when they get beat." He said, "They beat them till it a pity." Beatings occurred often, but how often?

The diary of Bennet H. Barrow, the master of Highland plantation in West Feliciana Parish, Louisiana, provides a rare picture of a master's punishment of his slaves. For a twenty-three-month period in 1840–1841, Barrow meticulously recorded every one of the 160 whippings he administered or ordered, which amounted to one whipping every four and a half days. Barrow's records establish that 60 of the 77 slaves who worked in his fields were whipped in this period, with 80 percent of the males and 70 percent of the females being whipped at least once. Most of the 17 field slaves who escaped being beaten were children and pregnant women.

In most instances, Barrow recorded not only the fact of a whipping but also his reasons for administering it. All sorts of "rascallity" made Barrow reach for his whip. The provocations included family quarrels in the slave quarter, impudence, running away, and failure to keep curfew. But nearly 80 percent of the reasons were related to poor work. Barrow gave beatings for picking "very trashy cotton," for "not picking as well as he can," and for failing to pick the prescribed weight of cotton. One slave claimed to have lost his eyesight and for months refused to work, until Barrow "gave him 25 cuts yesterday morning & ordered him to work Blind or not." Some planters used whips that raised welts, caused blisters, and bruised. Others resorted to rawhide and cowhide whips that broke the skin, caused scarring, and sometimes permanently maimed. Occasionally, slaves were beaten to death.

Whipping was not Barrow's only means of inflicting pain. His diary mentions confining slaves to a plantation jail, putting them in chains, shooting them, breaking a "sword cane" over one slave's head, having slaves mauled by dogs, placing them in stocks, "staking down" slaves for hours, holding their heads under water, and a variety of punishments intended to ridicule and to shame, including making men wear women's clothing and do "women's work," such as the laundry. Still, Barrow's preferred instrument of punishment was the whip.

On the Barrow plantation, as on many others, whipping was public. Victims were often tied to a stake in the quarter, and the other slaves were made to watch. In a real sense, the entire slave population on the plantation experienced a whipping every four and a half days, and all were familiar with its terror and agony.

as the perfect complement to her husband, the commanding patriarch. She was physically weak, "formed only for the less laborious occupations," and thus dependent on male protection. To gain this protection, she exhibited modesty and delicacy, possessed beauty and grace, and cultivated refinement and charm. The lady, southern men said proudly, was an "ornament."

Chivalry—the South's romantic ideal of male-female relationships—glorified the lady while it subordinated her. Chivalry's underlying assumptions about the weakness of women and the protective authority of men resembled the paternalistic defense of slavery. Just as the slaveholder's mastery was written into law, so too were the paramount rights of husbands. Married women lost almost all their property rights to their husbands. Women throughout the nation found divorce difficult, but southern women found it almost impossible.

Was whipping effective? Did it produce a hardworking, efficient, and conscientious labor force? Not according to Barrow's own record. No evidence indicates that whipping changed the slaves' behavior. What Barrow considered bad work continued. Unabated whipping is itself evidence of the failure of punishment to achieve the master's will. Slaves knew the rules, yet they continued to act "badly." And they continued to suffer.

Did Barrow whip as often as other planters whipped? We simply do not know. Still, the Barrow evidence allows us to speculate profitably on the frequency of whipping by large planters. We do know that Barrow did not consider himself a cruel man. He bitterly denounced his neighbor as "the most cruel Master i ever knew of" for castrating three of his slaves. Like most whites, he believed that the lash was essential to get the work done, and he used it no more than he believed absolutely necessary. Still, Barrow's whip fell on someone's back every few days.

Questions for Analysis

Summarize the Argument: What does the evidence from the Barrow plantation tell us about how often slaves were whipped?

Analyze the Evidence: Why must we be cautious about relying on the Barrow evidence to answer the question of how often slaves were whipped?

Consider the Context: How could slaveholders, who increasingly saw themselves as "Christian guardians" to their slaves, have justified whipping them?

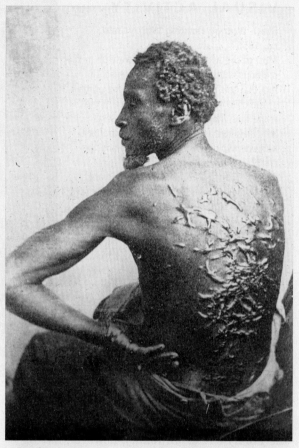

Gordon
This photograph of Gordon, a runaway slave from Baton Rouge, Louisiana, was taken on April 2, 1863. Frederick W. Mercer, an assistant surgeon with the 47th Massachusetts Regiment, examined four hundred other runaways and found many "to be as badly lacerated." Publication of Gordon's photograph in the popular *Harper's Weekly* made him a symbol of slavery's terrible brutality. © Massachusetts Historical Society, Boston, MA/Bridgeman Images.

Daughters of planters confronted chivalry's demands at an early age. At their private boarding schools, they learned to be southern ladies, reading literature, learning languages, and studying the appropriate drawing-room arts. Elite women began courting young and married early. Kate Carney exaggerated only slightly when she despaired in her diary: "Today, I am seventeen, getting quite old, and am not married." Yet marriage meant turning their fates over to their husbands and making enormous efforts to live up to their region's lofty expectations. Caroline Merrick of Louisiana told a friend in 1859, "We owe it to our husbands, children, and friends to represent as nearly as possible the ideal which they hold so dear."

Proslavery advocates claimed that slavery freed white women from drudgery. Surrounded "by her domestics," declared Thomas R. Dew, "she ceases to be a mere beast of burden" and

VISUAL ACTIVITY

Black Woman Holding White Child, ca. 1855

Most of the white children who grew up in the big house had slave nurses, or nannies. The fact that this nannie is included in the portrait of the child indicates her importance in the white household. Library of Congress, 3g05251.

READING THE IMAGE: If she was important, however, why is her face hidden behind the child?

CONNECTIONS: As a female house servant, what other obligations might this nannie have had in the big house?

"becomes the cheering and animating center of the family circle." In reality, however, having servants required the plantation mistress to work long hours. She managed the big house, directly supervising sometimes more than a dozen slaves. One slaveholder remembered that his boyhood home had "two cooks, two washerwomen, one dining room servant, two seamstresses, one house girl, one house boy, one carriage driver, one hostler [stableman], one gardener, [and] one errand boy." And, he added, "they were all under the supervision of my mother." But unlike her husband, the mistress had no overseer. All house servants answered directly to her. She assigned them tasks each morning, directed their work throughout the day, and punished them when she found fault.

Whereas masters used their status as slaveholders as a springboard into public affairs, mistresses' lives were circumscribed by the

Varina Howell Davis, 1849

Elite plantation women often had expensive lockets like this, in which their portraits were painted in miniature on ivory. In 1845, eighteen-year-old Varina Howell married Jefferson Davis, a man twice her age and the future president of the Confederate States of America. National Portrait Gallery, Smithsonian Institution/ Art Resource, NY.

plantation. Masters left when they pleased, but mistresses had heavy responsibilities, and besides they needed chaperones to travel. When they could, they went to church, but women spent most days at home, where they often became lonely. In 1853, Mary Kendall wrote how much she enjoyed her sister's letter: "For about three weeks I did not have the pleasure of seeing one white female face, there being no white family except our own upon the plantation."

As members of slaveholding families, mistresses lived privileged lives. But they also had grounds for discontent. No feature of plantation life generated more anguish among mistresses than miscegenation. Mary Boykin Chesnut of Camden, South Carolina, confided in her diary, "Ours is a monstrous system, a wrong and iniquity. Like the patriarchs of old, our men live all in one house with their wives and their concubines; and the mulattos one sees in every family partly resemble the white children. Any lady is ready to tell you who is the father of all the mulatto children in everybody's household but her own. Those, she seems to think drop from the clouds."

But most planters' wives, including Chesnut, accepted slavery. After all, the privileged life of a mistress rested on slave labor as much as a master's did. Mistresses enjoyed the rewards of their class and race. But these rewards came at a price. Still, the heaviest burdens of slavery fell not on those who lived in the big house, but on those who toiled to support them.

REVIEW   Why did the ideology of paternalism gain currency among planters in the nineteenth century?

▶ Slaves in the Quarter

On most plantations, only a few hundred yards separated the big house and the slave quarter. But the distance was great enough to provide slaves with some privacy. Out of eyesight and earshot of the big house, slaves drew together and built lives of their own. They created families, worshipped God, and developed an African American community and culture. Individually and collectively, slaves found ways to resist their bondage.

Despite the rise of plantations, almost half of the South's slaves lived and worked elsewhere.

Most labored on small farms, where they wielded a hoe alongside another slave or two and perhaps their master. But by 1860, almost half a million slaves (one in eight) did not work in agriculture at all. Some lived in towns and cities, where they worked as domestics, day laborers, bakers, barbers, tailors, and more. Other slaves, far from urban centers, toiled as fishermen, lumbermen, railroad workers, and deckhands on riverboats. Slaves could also be found in most of the South's factories. Nevertheless, a majority of slaves (52 percent) counted plantations as their workplaces and homes.

Work

Whites enslaved blacks for their labor, and all slaves who were capable of productive labor worked. Former slave Carrie Hudson recalled that children who were "knee high to a duck" were sent to the fields to carry water to thirsty workers or to protect ripening crops from hungry birds. Others helped in the slave nursery, caring for children even younger than themselves, or in the big house, where they swept floors or shooed flies in the dining room. When slave boys and girls reached the age of eleven or twelve, masters sent most of them to the fields. After a lifetime of labor, old women left the fields to care for the small children and spin yarn, and old men moved on to mind livestock and clean stables.

The overwhelming majority of plantation slaves worked as field hands. Planters sometimes assigned men and women to separate gangs, the women working at lighter tasks and the men doing the heavy work of clearing and breaking the land. But women also did heavy work. "I had to work hard," Nancy Boudry remembered, and "plow and go and split wood just like a man." The backbreaking labor and the monotonous routines caused one ex-slave to observe that the "history of one day is the history of every day."

A few slaves (about one in ten) became house servants. Nearly all of those (nine out of ten) were women. They cooked, cleaned, babysat, washed clothes, and did the dozens of other tasks the master and mistress required. House servants were constantly on call, with no time that was entirely their own. Since no servant could please constantly, most bore the brunt of white frustration and rage. Ex-slave Jacob Branch of Texas remembered, "My poor mama! Every washday old Missy give her a beating."

Even rarer than house servants were skilled artisans. In the cotton South, no more than one

Slaves Working
Although carefully staged, this photograph of cotton pickers at harvesttime captures the fact that all hands—men, women, and children—were pressed into the fields during this crucial phase of cotton production. Yale Collection of American Literature, Beinecke Rare Book and Manuscript Library.

slave in twenty (almost all men) worked in a skilled trade. Most were blacksmiths and carpenters, but slaves also worked as masons, mechanics, millers, ginsmiths, and shoemakers. Skilled slave fathers took pride in teaching their crafts to their sons. "My pappy was one of the black smiths and worked in the shop," John Mathews remembered. "I had to help my pappy in the shop when I was a child and I learnt how to beat out the iron and make wagon tires, and make plows."

Rarest of all slave occupations was that of slave driver. Probably no more than one male slave in a hundred worked in this capacity. These men were well named, for their primary task was driving other slaves to work harder in the fields. In some drivers' hands, the whip never rested. Ex-slave Jane Johnson of South Carolina called her driver the "meanest man, white or black, I ever see." But other drivers showed all the restraint they could. "Ole Gabe didn't like

that whippin' business," West Turner of Virginia remembered. "When Marsa was there, he would lay it on 'cause he had to. But when old Marsa wasn't lookin', he never would beat them slaves."

Normally, slaves worked from what they called "can to can't," from "can see" in the morning to "can't see" at night. Even with a break at noon for a meal and rest, it made for a long day. For slaves, Lewis Young recalled, "work, work, work, 'twas all they do."

Family and Religion

From dawn to dusk, slaves worked for the master, but at night and all day Sunday and usually Saturday afternoon, slaves were left largely to themselves. Bone tired perhaps, they nonetheless used the time to develop what mattered most to them. Over the generations, they created a community and a culture of their own that sustained them.

Slavery was a severe assault on the slave family. African Americans were bought and sold at public auctions and at private sales. Between 1820 and 1860, while some one million slaves entered the interstate slave trade that fed labor to the booming Cotton South, perhaps twice as many slaves were sold locally. Every slave dreaded the appearance of a slave trader at the gate of the plantation. Falling into the hands of a trader meant separation from family, probably for life, and a new existence under an unknown master.

Though severely battered, the black family survived slavery. Young men and women in the quarter fell in love, married, and set up housekeeping in cabins of their own. But no laws recognized slave marriage, and therefore no master was legally obligated to honor the bond. While plantation records show that some slave marriages were long-lasting, the massive deportation associated with the Second Middle Passage and local sales destroyed hundreds of thousands of slave families.

In 1858, a slave named Abream Scriven wrote to his wife, who lived on a neighboring plantation in South Carolina. "My dear wife," he began, "I take the pleasure of writing you . . . with much regret to inform you I am Sold to man by the name of Peterson, a Treader and Stays in New Orleans." Before he left for Louisiana, Scriven asked his wife to "give my love to my father and mother and tell them good Bye for me. And if we do not meet in this world I hope to meet in heaven. . . . My dear wife for you and my children my pen cannot express the griffe I feel to be parted from you all." He closed with words no master would have permitted in a slave's marriage vows: "I remain your truly husband until Death." The letter makes clear Scriven's love for and commitment to his family; it also demonstrates slavery's massive assault on family life in the quarter.

Masters sometimes permitted slave families to work on their own, "overwork," as it was called. In the evenings and on Sundays, they tilled gardens, raised pigs and fowl, and chopped wood, selling the products in the market for a little pocket change. "Den each fam'ly have some chickens and sell dem and de eggs and maybe go huntin' and sell de hides and git some money," a former Alabama slave remembered. "Den us buy what am Sunday clothes with dat money, sech as hats and pants and shoes and dresses." Slave children remembered the extraordinary efforts their parents made to sustain their families, and they held them in high esteem.

Family outside Cabin, 1862
On a plantation just outside Beaufort, South Carolina, this poor, proud, but unnamed family includes at least four generations. Because of slavery's assault on the family life of slaves, very few blacks could gather as many generations. Library of Congress, LC-DIG-ppmsc-00057.

Religion also provided slaves with a refuge and a reason for living. In the nineteenth century, evangelical Baptists and Methodists had great success in converting slaves from their African beliefs. Planters promoted Christianity in the quarter because they believed that the slaves' salvation was part of the obligation of paternalism; they also hoped that religion would make slaves more obedient. South Carolina slaveholder Charles Colcock Jones, the leading missionary to the slaves, instructed them "to count their Masters 'worthy of all honour,' as those whom God has placed over them in this world." But slaves laughed up their sleeves at such messages. "That old white preacher just was telling us slaves to be good to our masters," one ex-slave said with a chuckle. "We ain't cared a bit about that stuff he was telling us 'cause we wanted to sing, pray, and serve God in our own way."

Meeting in their cabins or secretly in the woods, slaves created an African American Christianity that served their needs, not the masters'. Laws prohibited teaching slaves to read, but a few could read enough to struggle with the Bible. They interpreted the Christian message themselves. Rather than obedience, their faith emphasized justice. Slaves believed that God kept score and that the accounts of this world would be settled in the next. "God is punishing some of them old suckers and their children right now for the way they use to treat us poor colored folks," one ex-slave declared. But the slaves' faith also spoke to their experiences in this world. In the Old Testament, they discovered Moses, who delivered his people from slavery, and in the New Testament, they found Jesus, who offered salvation to all. Jesus' message of equality provided a potent antidote to the planters' claim that blacks were an inferior people whom God condemned to slavery.

Christianity did not entirely drive out traditional African beliefs. Even slaves who were Christians sometimes continued to believe that conjurers, witches, and spirits possessed the power to injure and protect. Moreover, slaves' Christian music, preaching, and rituals reflected the influence of Africa, as did many of their secular activities, such as wood carving, quilt making, dancing, and storytelling. But by the mid-nineteenth century, black Christianity had assumed a central place in slaves' quest for freedom. In the words of one spiritual, "O my Lord delivered Daniel / O why not deliver me too?"

Resistance and Rebellion

Slaves did not suffer slavery passively. They were, as whites said, "troublesome property." Slaves understood that accommodation to what they could not change was the price of survival, but in a hundred ways they protested their bondage. Theoretically, the master was all-powerful and the slave powerless. But sustained by their families, religion, and community, slaves engaged in day-to-day resistance against their enslavers.

The spectrum of slave resistance ranged from mild to extreme. Telling a pointed story by the fireside in a slave cabin was probably the mildest form of protest. But when the weak got the better of the strong, as they did in tales of Br'er Rabbit and Br'er Fox (*Br'er* is a contraction of *Brother*), listeners could enjoy the thrill of a vicarious victory over their masters. Protest in the fields was riskier and included putting rocks in their cotton bags before having them weighed, feigning illness, and pretending to be so thick-headed that they could not understand the simplest instruction. Slaves broke so many hoes that owners outfitted the tools with oversized handles. Slaves so mistreated the work animals that masters switched from horses to mules, which could absorb more abuse. Although slaves worked hard in the master's fields, they also sabotaged his interests.

Running away was a common form of protest, but except along the borders with northern states and with Mexico, escape to freedom was almost impossible. Most runaways could hope only to escape for a few days. They sought temporary respite from hard labor or avoided punishment, and their "lying out," as it was known, usually ended when the runaway, worn-out and ragged, gave up or was finally chased down by slave-hunting dogs.

Although resistance was common, outright rebellion—a violent assault on slavery by large numbers of slaves—was very rare. Conditions gave rebels almost no chance of success. By 1860, whites in the South outnumbered blacks two to one and were heavily armed. Moreover, communication between plantations was difficult, and the South provided little protective wilderness into which rebels could retreat and defend themselves. Rebellion, as Nat Turner's experience showed (see pages 347–48), was virtual suicide.

Despite steady resistance and occasional rebellion, slaves did not have the power to end

"Tearing Up Free Papers," 1838
This engraving portrays every free black's worst nightmare, the loss of his or her freedom papers. Here a white man destroys the only proof that this black woman has that she is legally free. Without documents, every black person was presumed to be a slave. © Boston Athenaeum, USA/Bridgeman Images.

their bondage. Slavery thwarted their hopes and aspirations. It broke some and crippled others. But slavery's destructive power had to contend with the resiliency of the human spirit. Slaves fought back physically, culturally, and spiritually. Not only did they survive bondage, but they also created in the quarter a vibrant African American culture that buoyed them up during long hours in the fields and brought them joy and hope in the few hours they had to themselves.

> **REVIEW** What types of resistance did slaves participate in, and why did slave resistance rarely take the form of rebellion?

▶ The Plain Folk

Most whites in the South did not own slaves, not even one. In 1860, more than six million of the South's eight million whites lived in slaveless households. Some slaveless whites lived in cities and worked as artisans, mechanics, and traders. Others lived in the country and worked as storekeepers, parsons, and schoolteachers. But most "plain folk" were small farmers. Perhaps three out of four were **yeomen**, small farmers who owned their own land. As in the North, farm ownership provided a family with an economic foundation, social respectability, and political standing. Unlike their northern counterparts, however, southern yeomen lived in a region whose economy and society were increasingly dominated by unfree labor.

In an important sense, the South had more than one white yeomanry. The huge southern landscape provided space enough for two yeoman societies, separated roughly along geographic lines. Yeomen throughout the South had much in common, but the life of a small farm family in the cotton belt—the flatlands that spread from South Carolina to Texas—

The Cotton Belt

differed from the life of a family in the upcountry—the area of hills and mountains. And some rural slaveless whites were not yeomen; they owned no land at all and were sometimes desperately poor.

Plantation-Belt Yeomen

Plantation-belt yeomen lived within the orbit of the planter class. Small farms outnumbered plantations in the **plantation belt**, but they were dwarfed in importance. Small farmers grew mainly food crops, particularly corn, but they also produced a few 400-pound bales of cotton each year. Large planters measured their crop in hundreds of bales. Small farmers' cotton tied them to planters. Unable to afford cotton gins or baling presses of their own, they relied on slave owners to gin and bale their cotton. With no link to merchants in the port cities, plantation-belt yeomen also turned to better-connected planters to ship and sell their cotton.

A network of relationships placed small farmers and planters together. Planters hired out surplus slaves to ambitious yeomen who wanted to expand cotton production. They sometimes chose overseers from among the sons of local farm families. Plantation mistresses occasionally nursed ailing neighbors. Family ties could span class lines, making planter and yeoman kin as well as neighbors. Yeomen helped police slaves by riding in slave patrols, which nightly scoured country roads to make certain that no slaves were moving about without permission. On Sundays, plantation dwellers and plain folk came together in church to worship.

Plantation-belt yeomen may have envied, and at times even resented, wealthy slaveholders, but small farmers learned to accommodate. Planters made accommodation easier by going out of their way to behave as good neighbors and avoid direct exploitation of slaveless whites in their community. As a consequence, rather than raging at the oppression of the planter regime, the typical plantation-belt yeoman sought entry into it. He dreamed of adding acreage to his farm, buying a few slaves of his own, and retiring from exhausting field work.

Upcountry of the South

Upcountry Yeomen

By contrast, the hills and mountains of the South resisted the spread of slavery and plantations. In the western parts of Virginia, North Carolina, and South Carolina; in northern Georgia and Alabama; and in eastern Tennessee and Kentucky, the higher elevation, colder climate, rugged terrain, and poor transportation made it difficult for commercial agriculture to make headway. As a result, planters and slaves were scarce. Geographically isolated, the up-country was a yeoman stronghold.

All members of the **upcountry** farm family worked their tasks depending on their sex and age. Husbands labored in the fields, and with their sons they cleared, plowed, planted, and cultivated primarily food crops—corn, wheat, beans, sweet potatoes, and perhaps some fruit. Women and their daughters labored in and about the cabin. One upcountry farmer remembered that his mother "worked in the house cooking, spinning, weaving [and doing] patchwork." Women also tended the vegetable garden, kept a cow and some chickens, preserved food, cleaned their homes, fed their families, and cared for their children. Male and female tasks were equally crucial to the farm's success, but as in other white southern households, the male patriarch ruled the domestic sphere.

The typical upcountry yeoman also grew a little cotton or tobacco, but food production was more important than cash crops. Not much currency changed hands in the upcountry. Barter was common. A yeoman might trade his small cotton or tobacco crop to a country store owner for a little salt, bullets, needles, and nails, or swap extra sweet potatoes for a plow from a blacksmith or for leather from a tanner. Networks of exchange and mutual assistance tied individual homesteads to the larger community. Farm families joined together in logrolling, house and barn raising, and cornhusking.

Even the hills had some plantations and slaves, but the few upcountry folks who owned slaves usually had only two or three. As a result, slaveholders had much less social and economic power, and yeomen had more. But the upcountry did not oppose slavery. As long as plain folk there were free to lead their own lives, they defended slavery and white supremacy just as staunchly as other white Southerners.

Poor Whites

The majority of slaveless white Southerners were hardworking, landholding small farmers, but Northerners held a different image of this group. They believed that slavery had condemned most whites to poverty and backwardness. One antislavery advocate charged that the South harbored three classes: "the slaves on whom devolves all the regular industry, the slaveholders who reap all the fruits, and an idle and lawless rabble who live dispersed over vast plains little removed from absolute barbarism." Critics called this third class a variety of derogatory names: hillbillies, crackers, rednecks, and poor white trash. According to critics, poor whites were not just whites who were poor. They were also supposedly ignorant, diseased, and degenerate.

Contrary to northern opinion, only about one in four nonslaveholding rural white men was landless and very poor. Some worked as tenants, renting land and struggling to make a go of it. Others survived by herding pigs and cattle. And still others worked for meager wages, ditching, mining, logging, and laying track for railroads.

Some poor white men earned reputations for mayhem and violence. One visitor claimed that a "bowie-knife was a universal, and a pistol a not at all unusual companion." Edward Isham, an illiterate roustabout, spent about as much time fighting as he did working. When he was not engaged in ear-biting, eye-gouging free-for-alls, he gambled, drank, stole, had run-ins with the law, and in 1860 murdered a respected slaveholder, for which he was hanged.

Unlike Isham, most poor white men did not engage in ferocious behavior but worked hard and dreamed of becoming yeomen. The Lipscomb family illustrates the possibility of upward mobility. In 1845, Smith and Sally Lipscomb and their children abandoned their worn-out land in South Carolina for Benton County, Alabama. "Benton is a mountainous country but ther is a heep of good levil land to tend in it," Smith wrote back to his brother. Alabama, Smith said, "will be better for the rising generation if not for ourselves but I think it will be the best for us all that live any length of time."

Because the Lipscombs had no money to buy land, they squatted on seven unoccupied acres. With the help of neighbors, they built a 22-by-24-foot cabin, a detached kitchen, and two stables. In the first year, Smith and his sons produced several bales of cotton and enough food for the table. The women worked just as hard in the cabin, and Sally contributed to the family's income by selling homemade shirts and socks. In time, the Lipscombs bought land and joined the Baptist church, completing their transformation to respectable yeomen.

Many poor whites succeeded in climbing the economic ladder, but in the 1850s upward mobility slowed. The cotton boom of that decade caused planters to expand their operations, driving the price of land beyond the reach of poor families. Whether they gained their own land or not, however, poor whites shared common cultural traits with yeoman farmers.

The Culture of the Plain Folk

The lives of most plain folk revolved around farms, family, a handful of neighbors, the local church, and perhaps a country store. Work occupied most hours, but plain folk still found time for pleasure. "Dancing they are all fond of," a visitor to North Carolina discovered, "especially when they can get a fiddle, or bagpipe." But the most popular pastimes of men and boys were fishing and hunting. A traveler in Mississippi recalled that his host sent "two of his sons, little fellows that looked almost too small to shoulder a gun," for food. "One went off towards the river and the other struck into the forest, and in a few hours we were feasting on delicious venison, trout and turtle."

Plain folk did not have much "book learning." Private academies charged fees that yeomen could not afford, and public schools were scarce. "Education is not extended to the masses here as at the North," observed a northern visitor in the 1850s. Although most people managed to pick up the "three R's," approximately one southern white man in five was illiterate in 1860, and the rate for white women was even higher. "People here prefer talking to reading," a Virginian remarked. Telling stories, reciting ballads, and singing hymns were important activities in yeoman culture.

Plain folk spent more hours in revival tents than in classrooms. Preachers spoke day and night to save souls. Baptists and Methodists adopted revivalism most readily and by midcentury had become the South's largest religious groups. By emphasizing free choice and

VISUAL ACTIVITY

Camp Meeting, Mid-Nineteenth Century

Camp meetings, or revivals, were a key feature of southern evangelical Christianity. Many preachers were itinerants who spoke wherever they could draw a crowd. Here an earnest clergyman preaches his message in an open field to an audience that includes both the reverent and the not-so-reverent. Private Collection/Picture Research Consultants & Archives.

READING THE IMAGE: What does the dress of the people in the audience say about their class position?

CONNECTIONS: Why were camp meetings so important to southern Methodists and Baptists?

individual worth, the plain folk's religion was hopeful and affirming. Hymns and spirituals provided guides to right and wrong—praising humility and steadfastness, condemning drunkenness and profanity. Above all, hymns spoke of the eventual release from worldly sorrows and the assurance of eternal salvation.

> **REVIEW** Why did the lives of plantation-belt yeomen and upcountry yeomen diverge?

▶ Black and Free: On the Middle Ground

All white Southerners—slaveholders and slaveless alike—considered themselves superior to all blacks. But not every black Southerner was a slave. In 1860, some 260,000 (approximately 6 percent) of the region's 4.1 million African Americans were free. What is surprising is not that their numbers were small but that they existed at all. According to proslavery thinking, blacks were supposed to be slaves; only whites were supposed to be free. Blacks who were free stood out, and whites made them targets of oppression. But a few found success despite the restrictions placed on them by white Southerners.

Precarious Freedom

The population of **free blacks** swelled after the Revolutionary War, when the natural rights philosophy of the Declaration of Independence, the egalitarian message of evangelical Protestantism, and a depression in the tobacco economy of the Upper South led to a brief flurry of emancipation—the act of freeing from slavery. The soaring numbers of free blacks worried white Southerners, who, because of the cotton boom, wanted more slaves, not more blacks who were free.

In the 1820s and 1830s, state legislatures stemmed the growth of the free black population and shrank the liberty of those blacks who had gained their freedom. New laws denied masters the right to free their slaves. Other laws subjected free blacks to special taxes, prohibited them from interstate travel, denied them the right to have schools and to participate in politics, and required them to carry "freedom papers" to prove they were not slaves. Increasingly, whites subjected free blacks to the same laws as slaves. Free blacks could not testify under oath in a court of law or serve on juries. Free blacks were forbidden to strike whites, even to defend themselves. "Free negroes belong to a degraded caste of society," a South Carolina judge said in 1848. "They are in no respect on a perfect equality with the white man. . . . They ought, by law, to be compelled to demean themselves as inferiors."

Laws confined most free African Americans to poverty and dependence. Typically, free blacks were rural, uneducated, unskilled agricultural laborers and domestic servants who had to scramble to survive. Opportunities of any kind—for work, education, or community—were slim. Planters believed that free blacks set a bad example for slaves, subverting the racial subordination that was the essence of slavery.

Whites feared that free blacks might lead slaves in rebellion. In 1822, whites in Charleston accused Denmark Vesey, a free black carpenter, of conspiring with plantation slaves to slaughter Charleston's white inhabitants. The authorities rounded up scores of suspects, who, prodded by torture and the threat of death, implicated others in a "plot to riot in blood, outrage, and rapine." Although the city fathers never found any weapons and Vesey and most of the accused steadfastly denied the charges of conspiracy, officials hanged thirty-five black men, including Vesey, and banished another thirty-seven blacks from the state.

Achievement despite Restrictions

Despite increasingly harsh laws and stepped-up persecution, free African Americans made the most of the advantages their status offered. Unlike slaves, free blacks could legally marry and pass on their heritage of freedom to their children. Freedom also meant that they could choose occupations and own property. For most, however, these economic rights proved only theoretical, for a majority of the South's free blacks remained propertyless.

Still, some free blacks escaped the poverty and degradation whites thrust on them. Particularly in the South's cities, a free black elite emerged. Consisting of light-skinned African Americans, this group worked at skilled trades, as tailors, carpenters, mechanics, and the like. Their customers were prominent whites—planters, merchants, and judges—who appreciated their able, respectful service. Urban whites enforced many of the restrictive laws only sporadically, allowing free blacks room to maneuver. They operated schools for their children and traveled in and out of their states, despite laws forbidding both activities. They worshipped with whites (in separate seating) and lived scattered about in white neighborhoods, not in ghettos. And some owned slaves. Of the 3,200 black slaveholders (barely 1 percent of the free black population), most owned only a few family members whom they could not legally free. Others owned slaves in large numbers and exploited them for labor.

One such free black slave owner was William Ellison of South Carolina. Born a slave in 1790, Ellison bought his freedom in 1816 and set up business as a cotton gin maker, a trade he had learned as a slave. His business grew with the cotton boom, and by 1835 he was prosperous enough to purchase the home of a former governor of the state. By the time of his death in 1861, he had become a cotton planter, with sixty-three slaves and an 800-acre plantation.

Most free blacks neither became slaveholders nor sought to raise a slave rebellion, as whites accused Denmark Vesey of doing. Rather, most free blacks simply tried to preserve their freedom, which was under increasing attack. Unlike blacks in the North whose freedom was secure, free blacks in the South clung to a precarious freedom by seeking to impress whites with their reliability, economic contributions, and good behavior.

REVIEW Why did many state legislatures pass laws restricting free blacks' rights in the 1820s and 1830s?

▶ The Politics of Slavery

By the mid-nineteenth century, all southern white men—planters and plain folk—and no southern black men, even those who were free, could vote. But even after the South's politics became democratic for white males, political power remained unevenly distributed. The nonslaveholding white majority wielded less political power than their numbers suggested.

The slaveholding white minority wielded more. With a well-developed sense of class interest, slaveholders engaged in party politics, campaigns, and officeholding, and as a result they received significant benefits from state governments. Nonslaveholding whites were concerned mainly with preserving their liberties and keeping their taxes low. They asked government for little of an economic nature, and they received little.

Slaveholders sometimes worried about nonslaveholders' loyalty to slavery, but most whites accepted the planters' argument that the existing social order served *all* Southerners' interests. Slavery rewarded every white man—no matter how poor—with membership in the South's white ruling race. It also provided the means by which nonslaveholders might someday advance into the ranks of the planters. White men in the South argued furiously about many things, but they agreed that they should take land from Indians, promote agriculture, uphold white supremacy and masculine privilege, and defend slavery from its enemies.

The Democratization of the Political Arena

In the first half of the nineteenth century, Southerners eliminated the wealth and property requirements that had once restricted political participation. By the 1850s, every state had extended the right to vote to all adult white males. Most southern states also removed the property requirements for holding state offices. To be sure, undemocratic features lingered. Plantation districts still wielded disproportionate power in several state legislatures. Nevertheless, southern politics took place within an increasingly democratic political structure, as it did elsewhere in the nation.

White male suffrage ushered in an era of vigorous electoral competition in the South. Eager voters rushed to the polls to exercise their new rights. Candidates crisscrossed their electoral districts, treating citizens to barbecues and bands, rum and races, as well as stirring oratory. In the South, it seemed, "everybody talked politics everywhere," even the "illiterate and shoeless."

As politics became aggressively democratic, it also grew fiercely partisan. From the 1830s to the 1850s, Whigs and Democrats battled for the electorate's favor. Both parties presented themselves as the plain white folk's best friend. All candidates declared their allegiance to republican equality and pledged themselves to defend the people's liberty. And each party sought to portray the other as a collection of rich, snobbish, selfish men who had antidemocratic designs up their silk sleeves.

Planter Power

Whether Whig or Democrat, southern officeholders were likely to be slave owners. The power that slaveholders exerted over slaves did not translate directly into political authority over whites, however. In the nineteenth century, political power could only be won at the ballot box, and almost everywhere nonslaveholders were in the majority. Yet year after year, proud and noisily egalitarian common men elected wealthy slaveholders.

By 1860, the percentage of slave owners in state legislatures ranged from 41 percent in Missouri to nearly 86 percent in North Carolina (Table 13.1). Legislators not only tended to own slaves; they also often owned large numbers. The percentage of planters (individuals with twenty or more slaves) in southern legislatures in 1860 ranged from 5.3 percent in Missouri to 55.4 percent in South Carolina. Even in North Carolina, where only 3 percent of the state's white families belonged to the planter class, more than 36 percent of state legislators were planters. Clearly, plain folk did not throw the planters out of office.

Upper-class dominance of southern politics reflected the elite's success in persuading the yeoman majority that what was good for slaveholders was also good for plain folk. In reality, the South had, on the whole, done well by common white men. Most had farms of their own. They participated as equals in a democratic political system. They enjoyed an elevated social status, above all blacks and in theory equal to all other whites. They commanded patriarchal authority over their households. And as long as slavery existed, they could dream of joining the planter class. Slaveless white men found much to celebrate in the slave South.

Most slaveholders took pains to win the plain folk's trust and to nurture their respect. One nonslaveholder told his wealthy neighbor that he had a bright political future because he never thought himself "too good to sit down & talk to a poor man." Mary Boykin Chesnut complained

Legislature	Slaveholders	Planters*
North Carolina	85.8%	36.6%
South Carolina	81.7	55.4
Alabama	76.3	40.8
Mississippi	73.4	49.5
Georgia	71.6	29.0
Virginia	67.3	24.2
Tennessee	66.0	14.0
Louisiana	63.8	23.5
Kentucky	60.6	8.4
Florida	55.4	20.0
Texas	54.1	18.1
Maryland	53.4	19.3
Arkansas	42.0	13.0
Missouri	41.2	5.3

TABLE 13.1   PERCENT OF SLAVEHOLDERS AND PLANTERS IN SOUTHERN LEGISLATURES, 1860

*Planters: Owned 20 or more slaves.

Data source: Ralph A. Wooster, *The People in Power: Courthouse and Statehouse in the Lower South, 1850–1860*, page 40. Copyright © 1975 by Ralph A. Wooster. Courtesy of the University of Tennessee Press.

about the fawning attention her husband, a U.S. senator from South Carolina, showed to poor men, including one who had "mud sticking up through his toes." But smart candidates found ways to convince wary plain folk of their democratic convictions and egalitarian sentiments, whether they were genuine or not. Walter L. Steele, who ran for a seat in the North Carolina legislature in 1846, detested campaigning for votes, but he learned, he said, to speak with a "candied tongue."

Georgia politics illustrate how well planters protected their interests in state legislatures. In 1850, about half of the state's revenues came from taxes on slaves, the principal form of planter wealth. However, the tax rate on slaves was trifling, only about one-fifth the rate on land. Moreover, planters benefited from public spending far more than other groups did. Financing railroads—which carried cotton to market—was the largest state expenditure. The legislature also established low tax rates on land, the principal form of yeoman wealth, which meant that the typical yeoman's annual tax bill was small. Still, relative to their wealth, large slaveholders paid less than did other whites. Relative to their numbers, they got more. Slaveholding legislators protected planters' interests and gave the impression of protecting the small farmers' interests as well.

In addition to politics, slaveholders defended slavery in other ways. In the 1830s, Southerners decided that slavery was too important to debate. "So interwoven is [slavery] with our interest, our manners, our climate and our very being," one man declared in 1833, "that no change can ever possibly be effected without a civil commotion from which the heart of a patriot must turn with horror." Powerful whites dismissed slavery's critics from college faculties, drove them from pulpits, and hounded them from political life. Sometimes antislavery Southerners fell victim to vigilantes and mob violence. One could defend slavery; one could even delicately suggest mild reforms. But no Southerner could any longer safely call slavery evil or advocate its destruction.

In the South, therefore, the rise of the common man occurred alongside the continuing, even growing, power of the planter class. Rather than pitting slaveholders against nonslaveholders, elections remained an effective means of binding the region's whites together. Elections affirmed the sovereignty of white men, whether planter or plain folk, and the subordination of African Americans. Those twin themes played well among white women as well. Though unable to vote, white women supported equality for whites and slavery for blacks. In the antebellum South, the politics of slavery helped knit together all of white society.

> **REVIEW**   How did planters retain political power in a democratic system?

▶ Conclusion: A Slave Society

By the early nineteenth century, northern states had either abolished slavery or put it on the road to extinction, while southern states were building the largest slave society in the New World. Regional differences increased over time, not merely because the South became more and more dominated by slavery, but also because developments in the North rapidly propelled it in a very different direction.

By 1860, one-third of the South's population was enslaved. Bondage saddled blacks with enormous physical and spiritual burdens: hard labor, harsh treatment, broken families, and, most important, the denial of freedom itself. Although degraded and exploited, they were not defeated. Out of African memories and New World realities, blacks created a life-affirming African American culture that sustained and strengthened them. Their families, religion, and community provided defenses against white racism and power. Defined as property, they refused to be reduced to things. Perceived as inferior beings, they rejected the notion that they were natural slaves.

The South was not merely a society with slaves; it had become a slave society. Slavery shaped the region's economy, culture, social structure, and politics. Whites south of the Mason-Dixon line believed that racial slavery was necessary and just. By making all blacks a pariah class, all whites gained a measure of equality and harmony.

Many features of southern life helped to confine class tensions among whites: the wide availability of land, rapid economic mobility, the democratic nature of political life, the patriarchal power among all white men, and, most of all, slavery and white supremacy. All stress along class lines did not disappear, however, and anxious slaveholders continued to worry that yeomen would defect from the proslavery consensus. But during the 1850s, white Southerners' near-universal acceptance of slavery would increasingly unite them in political opposition to their northern neighbors.

See the Selected Bibliography for this chapter in the Appendix.

13 Chapter Review

KEY TERMS

Mason-Dixon line (p. 350)
cotton kingdom (p. 350)
slave codes (p. 352)
miscegenation (p. 352)
planter (p. 352)
plantation (p. 352)
paternalism (p. 358)
chivalry (p. 360)
yeomen (p. 367)
plantation belt (p. 368)
upcountry (p. 368)
free black (p. 370)

REVIEW QUESTIONS

1. Why did the nineteenth-century southern economy remain primarily agricultural? (pp. 349–358)

2. Why did the ideology of paternalism gain currency among planters in the nineteenth century? (pp. 358–363)

3. What types of resistance did slaves participate in, and why did slave resistance rarely take the form of rebellion? (pp. 363–367)

4. Why did the lives of plantation-belt yeomen and upcountry yeomen diverge? (pp. 367–370)

5. Why did many state legislatures pass laws restricting free blacks' rights in the 1820s and 1830s? (pp. 370–371)

6. How did planters retain political power in a democratic system? (pp. 371–373)

MAKING CONNECTIONS

1. How did cotton's profitability shape the region's antebellum development?

2. How did southern white legislators and intellectuals attempt to strengthen the institution of slavery in the 1820s? What prompted them to do this?

3. Discuss the variety of ways in which slaves attempted to resist slavery. What were the short- and long-term effects of their efforts?

4. Despite vigorous political competition in the South, by 1860 legislative power was largely concentrated in the hands of a regional minority— slaveholders. Why were slaveholders politically dominant?

LINKING TO THE PAST

1. Compare and contrast Northerners' defense of free labor and white Southerners' defense of slave labor. (See chapter 12.)

2. How did President Andrew Jackson's Indian removal policies pave the way for the South's cotton empire? (See chapter 11.)

14 The House Divided
1846–1861

After reading and studying this chapter, you should be able to:

- Explain why the question of extending slavery to federal territories was the focus of constitutional debate from 1846 to 1860. Define the Wilmot Proviso, including who supported and opposed it, and why.

- Relate how the debate over the expansion of slavery affected the election of 1848. Explain what led to the Compromise of 1850.

- Determine what destroyed the second American party system in the 1850s, and how the electorate realigned.

- Describe how Kansas was settled and organized, and how it got the name "Bleeding Kansas." Explain the *Dred Scott* decision and how it shaped the perceptions of the North.

- Explain the political rise of Abraham Lincoln.

GRIZZLED, GNARLED, AND FIFTY-NINE YEARS OLD, JOHN BROWN had for decades lived like a nomad, hauling his large family of twenty children back and forth across six states as he tried farming, raising sheep, selling wool, and running a tannery. But failure dogged him. Failure, however, had not budged his conviction that slavery was wrong and ought to be destroyed. In the wake of the fighting that erupted over the future of slavery in Kansas in the 1850s, his beliefs turned violent. On May 24, 1856, he led an eight-man anti-slavery posse in the midnight slaughter of five allegedly proslavery men at Pottawatomie, Kansas. He told Mahala Doyle, whose husband and two oldest sons he killed, that if a man stood between him and what he thought right, he would take that man's life as calmly as he would eat breakfast.

After the killings, Brown slipped out of Kansas and reemerged in the East, where for thirty months he begged money to support his vague plan for military operations against slavery. On the night of October 16, 1859, Brown took his war against slavery into the South. With only twenty-one men, including five African Americans, he invaded Harpers Ferry, Virginia. His band seized the town's armory and rifle works, but the invaders were immediately surrounded. When Brown refused to

JOHN BROWN'S PIKES
In 1859, John Brown brought his abolitionist war to Harpers Ferry, Virginia. He carried with him 950 pikes, which he expected to put into the hands of rebelling slaves. © Chicago History Museum, USA/Bridgeman Images.

surrender, federal troops under Colonel Robert E. Lee charged with bayonets. Although a few of Brown's raiders escaped, federal forces killed
ten of his men (including two of his sons) and captured seven, among
them Brown.

Months before the raid, Brown had claimed, "When I strike, the bees
will begin to swarm." Brown said he would arm slaves and they would
then fight a war of liberation. Brown, however, neglected to inform the
slaves when he had arrived in Harpers Ferry, and the few who knew of
his arrival wanted nothing to do with his enterprise. "It was not a slave
insurrection," Abraham Lincoln observed. "It was an attempt by white
men to get up a revolt among slaves, in which the slaves refused to participate. In fact, it was so absurd that the slaves, with all their ignorance,
saw plainly enough it could not succeed."

White Southerners viewed Brown's raid as proof that Northerners
actively sought to incite slaves in bloody rebellion. Sectional tension
was as old as the Constitution, but hostility had escalated with the outbreak of war with Mexico in May 1846 (see "The Mexican-American
War, 1846–1848" in chapter 12). Only three months after the war
began, national expansion and the slavery issue intersected when
Representative David Wilmot introduced a bill to prohibit slavery in any
territory that might be acquired as a result of the war. After that, the
problem of slavery in the territories became the principal wedge that
divided the nation.

"Mexico is to us the forbidden fruit," South Carolina senator John C.
Calhoun declared at the war's outset. "The penalty of eating it [is] to
subject our institutions to political death." For a decade and a half,
the slavery issue intertwined with the fate of former Mexican
land, poisoning the national political debate. Slavery proved
powerful enough to transform party politics into sectional
politics. Rather than Whigs and Democrats confronting one
another across party lines, Northerners and Southerners
eyed one another hostilely across the Mason-Dixon line.
As the nation lurched from crisis to crisis, southern disaffection and alienation mounted, and support for compromise eroded. The era began with a crisis of union
and ended with the Union in even graver peril. As
Abraham Lincoln predicted in 1858, "A house divided
against itself cannot stand."

John Brown
In this 1859 photograph, John Brown appears respectable, but
contemporaries debated his mental state and moral character,
and the debate still rages. Critics argue that he was a bloody
terrorist, a religious fanatic who believed that he was touched by
God for a great purpose. Admirers see a selfless hero, a shrewd political observer who recognized that only violence would end slavery in
America. Library of Congress, 3a06152.

▶ The Bitter Fruits of War

Victory in the Mexican-American War brought vast new territories in the West into the United States. The gold rush of 1849 transformed the sleepy frontier of California into a booming economy (see "Golden California" in chapter 12). The 1850s witnessed new "rushes," for gold in Colorado and silver in Nevada's Comstock Lode. The phenomenal economic growth of the West demanded the attention of the federal government, but it quickly became clear that Northerners and Southerners had very different visions of the West, particularly the place of slavery in its future. From 1846, when it first appeared that the war with Mexico might mean new territory for the United States, politicians battled over whether to ban slavery from former Mexican land or permit it to expand to the Pacific. In 1850 Congress patched together a plan that Americans hoped would last. This plan for expansion envisioned stability only for the Anglo-Americans, however. Native Americans in the West would soon see their traditional way of life disrupted.

The Wilmot Proviso and the Expansion of Slavery

Most Americans agreed that the Constitution left the issue of slavery to the individual states to decide. Northern states had done away with slavery, while southern states had retained it. But what about slavery in the nation's territories? The Constitution states that "Congress shall have power to . . . make all needful rules and regulations respecting the territory . . . belonging to the United States." The debate about slavery, then, turned toward Congress.

The spark for the national debate appeared in August 1846 when a Democratic representative from Pennsylvania, David Wilmot, proposed that Congress bar slavery from all lands acquired in the war with Mexico. The Mexicans had abolished slavery in their country, and Wilmot declared, "God forbid that we should be the means of planting this institution upon it."

Regardless of party affiliation, Northerners lined up behind the **Wilmot Proviso**. Many supported free soil, by which they meant territory in which slavery would be prohibited, because they wanted to preserve the West for **free labor**, for hardworking, self-reliant free men, not for slaveholders and slaves. But support also came

CHRONOLOGY

1820	• Missouri Compromise forged.
1846	• Wilmot Proviso introduced.
1847	• Wilmot Proviso defeated in Senate. • "Popular sovereignty" compromise offered.
1848	• Free-Soil Party founded. • Zachary Taylor elected president.
1849	• California gold rush begins.
1850	• Taylor dies; Vice President Millard Fillmore becomes president. • Compromise of 1850 becomes law.
1852	• *Uncle Tom's Cabin* published. • Franklin Pierce elected president.
1853	• Gadsden Purchase negotiated.
1854	• American (Know-Nothing) Party emerges. • Kansas-Nebraska Act passes. • Republican Party founded.
1856	• "Bleeding Kansas" pits anti- versus proslavery advocates. • "Sack of Lawrence" orchestrated. • Pottawatomie massacre kills five in Kansas. • James Buchanan elected president.
1857	• *Dred Scott* decision announced. • Congress rejects Lecompton constitution. • Panic of 1857 ripples throughout economy.
1858	• Lincoln and Douglas debate; Douglas wins Senate seat.
1859	• John Brown raids Harpers Ferry.
1860	• Abraham Lincoln elected president. • South Carolina secedes from Union.
1861	• Six other Lower South states secede. • Confederate States of America formed.

from those who were simply anti-South. New slave territories would eventually mean new slave states. Wilmot himself said his proposal would blunt "*the power of slaveholders*" in the national government.

Additional support for free soil came from Northerners who were hostile to blacks and wanted to reserve new land for whites. Wilmot understood what one Indiana man put bluntly: "The American people are emphatically a *Negro-hating* people." Wilmot himself blatantly encouraged racist support when he declared, "I would preserve for free white labor a fair country, a rich inheritance, where the sons of toil, of my own race and own color, can live without the disgrace which association with negro slavery brings upon free labor." It is no wonder that some called the Wilmot Proviso the "White Man's Proviso."

The thought that slavery might be excluded in the territories outraged white Southerners. Like Northerners, they regarded the West as a ladder for economic and social opportunity. They also believed that the exclusion of slavery was a slap in the face to southern veterans of the Mexican-American War. "When the war-worn soldier returns home," one Alabaman asked, "is he to be told that he cannot carry his property to the country won by his blood?" In addition, southern leaders sought to maintain political parity with the North to protect the South's interests, especially slavery. The need seemed especially urgent in the 1840s, when the North's population and wealth were booming. James Henry Hammond of South Carolina predicted that ten new states would be carved from the acquired Mexican land. If free soil won, the North would "ride over us roughshod" in Congress, he claimed. "Our only safety is in *equality* of power."

Foes of slavery's expansion and foes of slavery's exclusion squared off in the nation's capital. Because Northerners had a majority in the House, they easily passed the Wilmot Proviso. In the Senate, however, where slave states outnumbered free states fifteen to fourteen, Southerners defeated it in 1847. Senator John C. Calhoun of South Carolina denied that Congress had the constitutional authority to exclude slavery from the nation's territories. He argued that because

Mexican Cession, 1848

the territories were the "joint and common property" of all the states, Congress could not bar citizens of one state from migrating with their property (including slaves) to the territories. Whereas Wilmot demanded that Congress slam shut the door to slavery, Calhoun called on Congress to hold the door wide open.

Senator Lewis Cass of Michigan offered a compromise through the doctrine of **popular sovereignty**, by which the people who settled the territories would decide for themselves slavery's fate. This solution, Cass argued, sat squarely in the American tradition of democracy and local self-government. Popular sovereignty's most attractive feature was its ambiguity about the precise moment when settlers could determine slavery's fate. Northern advocates believed that the decision on slavery could be made as soon as the first territorial legislature assembled. With free-soil majorities likely because of the North's greater population, they would shut the door to slavery immediately. Southern supporters believed that popular sovereignty guaranteed that slavery would be unrestricted throughout the entire territorial period. Only when settlers in a territory drew up a constitution and applied for statehood could they decide the issue of slavery. By then, slavery would have sunk deep roots. As long as the matter of timing remained vague, popular sovereignty gave hope to both sides.

When Congress ended its session in 1848, no plan had won a majority in both houses. Northerners who demanded no new slave territory anywhere, ever, and Southerners who demanded entry for their slave property into all territories, or else, staked out their extreme positions. Unresolved in Congress, the territorial question naturally became an issue in the presidential election of 1848.

The Election of 1848

When President Polk, worn-out and ailing, chose not to seek reelection, the Democratic convention nominated Lewis Cass of Michigan, the man most closely associated with popular sovereignty.

The Whigs nominated a Mexican-American War hero, General Zachary Taylor, a man who had never voted and who had no known political opinions. The Whigs declined to adopt a party platform, betting that the combination of a military hero and total silence on the slavery issue would unite their divided party. Taylor, who owned more than one hundred slaves on plantations in Mississippi and Louisiana, was hailed by Georgia politician Robert Toombs as a "Southern man, a slaveholder, a cotton planter."

Antislavery Whigs balked. Senator Charles Sumner called for a major political realignment, "one grand Northern party of Freedom." In the summer of 1848, antislavery Whigs and antislavery Democrats founded the Free-Soil Party, nominating a Democrat, Martin Van Buren, for president and a Whig, Charles Francis Adams, for vice president. The platform boldly proclaimed, "Free soil, free speech, free labor, and free men."

The November election dashed the hopes of the Free-Soilers. They did not carry a single state. Taylor won the all-important electoral vote 163 to 127, carrying eight of the fifteen slave states and seven of the fifteen free states (Map 14.1). (Wisconsin had entered the Union earlier in 1848 as the fifteenth free state.) Northern voters were not yet ready for Sumner's "one grand Northern party of Freedom," but the struggle over slavery in the territories had shaken the major parties badly.

Debate and Compromise

Zachary Taylor was very much a mystery when he entered the White House in March 1849. Almost immediately, the slaveholding president shocked the nation by championing a free-soil solution to the Mexican cession. Believing that he could avoid further sectional strife if California and New Mexico skipped the territorial stage, Taylor encouraged the settlers to apply for admission to the Union as states. Predominantly antislavery, the settlers began writing free-state constitutions. "For the first time," Mississippian Jefferson Davis lamented, "we are about permanently to destroy the balance of power between the sections."

Congress convened in December 1849, beginning one of the most contentious and most significant sessions in its history. President Taylor urged Congress to admit California as a free state immediately and to admit New Mexico, which lagged behind a few months, as soon as it applied. Southerners exploded. A North Carolinian declared that Southerners who would "consent to be thus degraded and enslaved, ought to be whipped through their fields by their own negroes."

Into this rancorous scene stepped Senator Henry Clay of Kentucky, the architect of Union-saving compromises in the Missouri and nullification crises (see chapters 10 and 11). Clay offered a series of resolutions meant to answer and balance "all questions in controversy between the free and slave states, growing out of the subject of slavery." Admit California as a free state, he proposed, but organize the rest of the Southwest without restrictions on slavery. Require Texas to abandon its claim to parts of New Mexico, but compensate it by assuming its preannexation debt. Abolish the domestic slave trade in Washington, D.C., but confirm slavery itself in the nation's capital. Affirm Congress's lack of authority to interfere with the interstate slave trade, and enact a more effective fugitive slave law.

Both antislavery advocates and "fire-eaters" (as radical Southerners who urged secession from the Union were called) savaged Clay's plan. Senator Salmon P. Chase of Ohio ridiculed it as "sentiment for the North, substance for the South." Senator Henry S. Foote of Mississippi denounced it as more offensive to the South than the speeches of abolitionists William Lloyd Garrison, Wendell Phillips, and Frederick Douglass combined. The most ominous response came from Calhoun, who

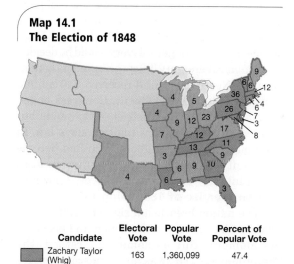

Map 14.1
The Election of 1848

Candidate	Electoral Vote	Popular Vote	Percent of Popular Vote
Zachary Taylor (Whig)	163	1,360,099	47.4
Lewis Cass (Democrat)	127	1,220,544	42.5
Martin Van Buren (Free-Soil)	0	291,263	10.1

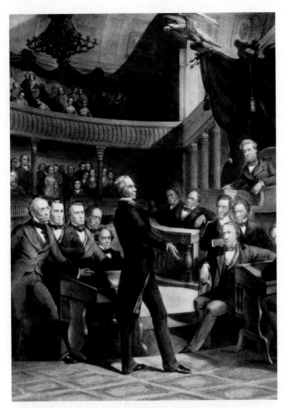

VISUAL ACTIVITY

Henry Clay Offering His California Compromise to the Senate on 5 February 1850
Artist Peter F. Rothermel captures the high intensity of the seventy-three-year-old Kentuckian's last significant political act. Citizens who packed the galleries of the U.S. Senate had come to hear the renowned orator explain that his package of compromises required mutual concessions from both North and South but no sacrifice of "great principle" from either. Friends called his performance the "crowning grace to his public life." The Granger Collection, New York.

READING THE IMAGE: What about the painting suggests that the artist either admired Clay and his effort for compromise or found his effort silly and wrongheaded?

CONNECTIONS: How did Northerners and Southerners respond to Clay's claim that his compromise required no sacrifice of "great principle"?

argued that the fragile political unity of North and South depended on continued equal representation in the Senate, which Clay's plan for a free California destroyed. "As things now stand," he said in February 1850, the South "cannot with safety remain in the Union."

Massachusetts senator Daniel Webster then addressed the Senate. Like Clay, Webster defended compromise. He told Northerners that the South had legitimate complaints, but he told Southerners

that secession from the Union would mean civil war. He argued that the Wilmot Proviso's ban on slavery in the territories was reckless and unnecessary because the harsh climate effectively prohibited the expansion of cotton and slaves into the new American Southwest. Why, then, "taunt" Southerners with the proviso? "I would not take pains uselessly to reaffirm an ordinance of nature, nor to reenact the will of God," Webster declared.

Free-soil forces recoiled from what they saw as Webster's desertion. Senator William H. Seward of New York responded that Webster's and Clay's compromise with slavery was "radically wrong and essentially vicious." He rejected Calhoun's argument that Congress lacked the constitutional authority to exclude slavery from the territories. In any case, Seward said, there was a "higher law than the Constitution"—the law of God—to ensure freedom in all the public domain. Claiming that God was a Free-Soiler did nothing to cool the superheated political atmosphere.

In May 1850, the Senate considered a bill that joined Clay's resolutions into a single comprehensive package. Clay bet that a majority of Congress wanted compromise and that the members would vote for the package, even though it contained provisions they disliked. But the strategy backfired. Free-Soilers and proslavery Southerners voted down the comprehensive plan.

Fortunately for those who favored a settlement, Senator Stephen A. Douglas, a rising Democratic star from Illinois, broke the bill into its parts and skillfully ushered each through Congress. The agreement Douglas won in September 1850 was very much the one Clay had proposed in January. California entered the Union as a free state. New Mexico and Utah became territories where slavery would be decided by popular sovereignty. Texas accepted its boundary with New Mexico and received $10 million from the federal government. Congress ended the slave trade in the District of Columbia but enacted a more stringent fugitive slave law. In September, Millard Fillmore, who had become president when Zachary Taylor died in July, signed into law each bill, collectively known as the **Compromise of 1850** (Map 14.2).

The nation breathed a sigh of relief, for the Compromise preserved the Union and peace for the moment. But as some understood, the Compromise of 1850 was not a true compromise at all. Douglas's parliamentary skill, not a spirit of conciliation, was responsible for the legislative success. The Compromise scarcely touched the

Map 14.2
The Compromise of 1850
The patched-together sectional agreement was both clumsy and unstable. Few Americans—in either North or South—supported all five parts of the Compromise.

Legend:
- Free state or territory
- Slave state
- Opened to slavery by principle of popular sovereignty
- Slave trade ended

deep conflict over slavery. Free-Soiler Salmon Chase observed, "The question of slavery in the territories has been avoided. It has not been settled."

> **REVIEW**   How might the Compromise of 1850 have eased sectional tensions?

The Sectional Balance Undone

The Compromise of 1850 began to come apart almost immediately. Surprisingly, the thread that unraveled it was not slavery in the territories, the crux of the disagreement, but runaway slaves in New England, a part of the settlement that had previously received little attention. The implementation of the Fugitive Slave Act brought the horrors of slavery into the North. Moreover, millions of Northerners who never saw a runaway slave confronted slavery through Harriet Beecher Stowe's *Uncle Tom's Cabin*, a novel that vividly depicts the brutality of the South's "peculiar institution." Congress did its part to undo the Compromise as well. Four years after Congress stitched the sectional compromise together, it ripped the threads out. With the Kansas-Nebraska Act in 1854, it again posed the question of slavery in the territories, the deadliest of all sectional issues.

The Fugitive Slave Act

The issue of runaway slaves was as old as the Constitution, which contained a provision for the return of any "person held to service or labor in one state" who escaped to another. In 1793, a federal law gave muscle to the provision by authorizing slave owners to enter other states to recapture their slave property. Proclaiming the 1793 law a license to kidnap free blacks, northern states in the 1830s began passing "personal liberty laws" that provided fugitives with some protection.

Some northern communities also formed vigilance committees to help runaways. Each year, a few hundred slaves escaped into free states and found friendly northern "conductors" who put them aboard the underground railroad, which was not a railroad at all but a series of secret "stations" (hideouts) on the way to Canada. Harriet Tubman, an escaped slave from Maryland, returned more than a dozen times and guided more than three hundred slaves to freedom in this way.

Furious about northern interference, Southerners in 1850 insisted on the stricter fugitive slave law that was part of the Compromise. According to the **Fugitive Slave Act**, to seize an alleged slave, a slaveholder simply had to appear before a commissioner and swear that the runaway was his. The commissioner earned $10 for every individual returned to slavery but only $5 for those set free. Most galling to Northerners, the law stipulated that all citizens were expected to assist officials in apprehending runaways. That required Northerners to become slave catchers.

Fugitive Ellen Craft in Disguise

In 1848, William and Ellen Craft, a slave couple from Macon, Georgia, executed a daring escape. Light-skinned, Ellen disguised herself as a sickly southern gentleman who was traveling to Philadelphia for medical treatment. She carried her arm in a sling to explain why she couldn't sign travel documents. William acted as her personal servant as they anxiously made their way by train to Savannah, then on to Philadelphia by boat and train. The Crafts told their daring story throughout the North until the Fugitive Slave Law of 1850 drove them to Britain, where adoring crowds greeted them as celebrities. Mary Evans Picture Library/Everett Collection.

In Boston in February 1851, an angry crowd overpowered federal marshals and snatched a runaway named Shadrach from a courtroom, put him on the underground railroad, and whisked him off to Canada. Three years later, when another Boston crowd rushed the courthouse in a failed attempt to rescue runaway Anthony Burns, a guard was shot dead. Martha Russell was among the angry crowd that watched Burns being escorted to the ship that would return him to Virginia. "Did you ever feel every drop of blood in you boiling and seething, throbbing and burning, until it seemed you should suffocate?" she asked. "I have felt all this today. I have seen that poor slave, Anthony Burns, carried back to slavery."

To white Southerners, it seemed that fanatics of the "higher law" creed had whipped Northerners into a frenzy of massive resistance. Actually, the overwhelming majority of fugitives claimed by slaveholders were reenslaved peacefully. But brutal enforcement of the unpopular law had a radicalizing effect in the North, particularly in New England. Textile mill owner Amos A. Lawrence said that "we went to bed one night old fashioned, conservative, Compromise Union Whigs & waked up stark mad abolitionists." He exaggerated, but to Southerners, Northerners had betrayed the Compromise and the Constitution. "The continued existence of the United States as one nation," warned the *Southern Literary Messenger*, "depends upon the full and faithful execution of the Fugitive Slave Bill."

Uncle Tom's Cabin

The spectacle of shackled African Americans being herded south seared the conscience of every Northerner who witnessed such a scene. But even more Northerners were turned against slavery by a novel. Harriet Beecher Stowe, a white Northerner who had never set foot on a plantation, made the South's slaves into flesh-and-blood human beings almost more real than life.

A member of a famous clan of preachers, teachers, and reformers, Stowe despised the slave catchers and wrote to expose the sin of slavery. Published as a book in 1852, *Uncle Tom's Cabin, or Life among the Lowly* became a blockbuster hit, selling 300,000 copies in its first year and more than 2 million copies within ten years. Stowe's characters leaped from the page. Here was the gentle slave Uncle Tom, a Christian saint who forgave those who beat him to death; the courageous slave Eliza, who fled with her child across the frozen Ohio River; and the fiendish overseer Simon Legree, whose Louisiana plantation was a nightmare of torture and death.

Stowe aimed her most powerful blows at slavery's destructive impact on the family. Her character Eliza succeeds in keeping her son from being sold away, but other mothers are not so fortunate. When told that her infant has been sold, Lucy drowns herself. Driven half mad by the sale of a son and daughter, Cassy decides "never again [to] let a child live to grow up!" She gives her third child an opiate and watches as "he slept to death." Northerners shed tears and sang praises to *Uncle Tom's Cabin*.

What Northerners accepted as truth, Southerners denounced as slander. The Virginian George F. Holmes proclaimed Stowe a member of the "Woman's Rights" and "Higher Law" schools and dismissed the novel as a work of "intense fanaticism." The New Orleans *Crescent* called Stowe "part quack and part cutthroat," a fake physician who came with arsenic in one hand and a pistol in the other to treat diseases she had "never witnessed." Although it is impossible to measure precisely the impact of a novel on public opinion, *Uncle Tom's Cabin* clearly helped to crystallize northern sentiment against slavery and to confirm white Southerners' suspicion that they no longer received any sympathy in the free states.

Other writers—ex-slaves who knew life in slave cabins firsthand—also produced stinging indictments of slavery. Solomon Northup's compelling *Twelve Years a Slave* (1853) sold 27,000 copies in two years, and the powerful *Narrative of the Life of Frederick Douglass, as Told by Himself* (1845) eventually sold more than 30,000 copies. But no work touched the North's conscience as did the novel by a free white woman. A decade after its publication, when Stowe visited Abraham Lincoln at the White House, he reportedly said, "So you are the little woman who wrote the book that made this great war."

The Kansas-Nebraska Act

As the 1852 election approached, the Democrats and Whigs sought to close the sectional rifts that had opened within their parties. For their presidential nominee, the Democrats turned to Franklin Pierce of New Hampshire. Pierce's well-known sympathy with southern views on public issues caused his northern critics to include him among the "doughfaces," northern men malleable enough to champion southern causes. The Whigs chose another Mexican-American War hero, General Winfield Scott of Virginia. But the Whigs' northern and southern factions were hopelessly divided, and the Democrat Pierce carried twenty-seven states to Scott's four and won the electoral college vote 254 to 42 (see Map 14.4). The Free-Soil Party lost almost half of the voters who had turned to it in the tumultuous political atmosphere of 1848.

Eager to leave the sectional controversy behind, the new president turned swiftly to foreign expansion. Manifest destiny remained robust. (See

Jar
This small porcelain jar is decorated with a scene from *Uncle Tom's Cabin*. Uncle Tom is tied to a post, and two male slaves beat him at the direction of Simon Legree. Jars like this were commonplace and are evidence of how popular the antislavery novel was among antebellum Northerners. Beinecke Rare Book and Manuscript Library, Yale University.

"Making Historical Arguments," page 384.) Pierce's major objective was Cuba, which was owned by Spain and in which slavery flourished, but when antislavery Northerners blocked Cuba's acquisition to keep more slave territory from entering the Union, Pierce turned to Mexico. In 1853, diplomat James Gadsden negotiated a $10 million purchase of some 30,000 square miles of land in present-day Arizona and New Mexico. The Gadsden Purchase furthered the dream of a transcontinental railroad to California and Pierce's desire for a southern route through Mexican territory. Talk of a railroad ignited rivalries in cities from New Orleans to Chicago as they maneuvered to become the eastern terminus. Inevitably in the 1850s, the contest for a transcontinental railroad became a sectional struggle over slavery.

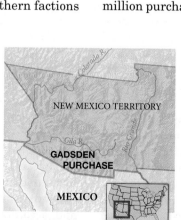

Gadsden Purchase, 1853

Filibusters: Were They the Underside of Manifest Destiny?

Each year, the citizens of Caborca, a small town in the northern state of Sonora, Mexico, celebrate the defeat there in 1857 of a private American army, the "Arizona Colonization Company," under the command of Henry A. Crabb. When the governor of Sonora faced an insurrection, he invited Crabb, a Mississippian who had followed the gold rush to California, to help him repress his enemies in exchange for mining rights and land. Crabb marched his band of sixty-eight heavily armed ex-miners south from Los Angeles, but by the time the Americans arrived, the governor had put down the insurgency, and the Mexicans turned on the invaders. Every American except one died. Crabb's head was preserved in alcohol and placed on display as a symbol of victory.

Henry Crabb was one of thousands of American adventurers, known as "filibusters" (from the Spanish *filibustero*, meaning "freebooter" or "pirate"), who in the mid-nineteenth century joined private armies that invaded foreign countries throughout the Western Hemisphere. In violation of the U.S. Neutrality Act of 1818, these private American armies attacked Canada, Mexico, Ecuador, Honduras, Cuba, and Nicaragua and planned invasions of places as far away as the Hawai'ian kingdom. The federal government usually cracked down on filibusters, fearing that private invasions would jeopardize legitimate diplomatic efforts to promote trade and acquire territory, and they were viewed by many as lawbreakers and rowdy criminals. Filibusters themselves, however, claimed that they were carrying on the work of manifest destiny, extending America's reach beyond Texas, California, and Oregon, the prizes of the 1830s and 1840s.

The Americans who joined rampaging invading armies shared many traits and beliefs with Americans who propelled westward expansion. Filibusters felt proud to be American, were sure of their own racial and national superiority, and tended toward violence. Like the California gold rush, filibustering promised economic opportunity; recruiters promised land, good pay, bonuses, and other rich rewards. Young men saw participation as an exhilarating adventure, a chance to travel to exotic lands, face unknown dangers, and validate their manhood. "Glory or the grave," one participant declared. What is more, filibusters were convinced that their work expanded American freedom. They had no respect for Hispanic peoples and anticipated their redemption through "Anglo-Saxon agency." They marched not under the banner of vicious conquest but of expanding freedom and democracy. A supporter of a successful filibustering expedition in Nicaragua wrote to a San Francisco newspaper: "Call it 'manifest destiny,'. . . call it what you will. . . . Nicaragua is free . . . republican rule has been inaugurated."

Revealingly, John L. O'Sullivan, a radical champion of manifest destiny, also belligerently championed the filibusters. After eagerly endorsing the annexation of Mexican land, he turned his attention to Cuba. O'Sullivan looked forward to ridding Cuba of Spanish colonial rule and expanding American ideals. He vigorously denounced critics of American expansionism as "imbeciles" and "vile toads." While O'Sullivan himself wanted no part in spreading slavery, many who were interested in Cuba served the interests of land- and slave-hungry Southerners.

During the 1850s, filibustering became primarily a southern crusade. One of the most vigorous filibusters to appeal to southern interests was Narciso López, a Venezuelan-born Cuban who dedicated himself to the liberation of Cuba from monarchical Spain. López claimed that Spain was planning to free Cuba's slaves, and he told Southerners that "self-preservation" demanded that they seize the island. In 1851, López and his southern-dominated army

Illinois's Democratic senator Stephen A. Douglas badly wanted the transcontinental railroad for Chicago. Any railroad that ran west from Chicago would pass through a region that Congress in 1830 had designated a "permanent" Indian reserve (see "Indian Policy and the Trail of Tears" in chapter 11). Douglas proposed giving this vast area between the Missouri River and the Rocky Mountains an Indian name, Nebraska, and then throwing the Indians out. Once the region achieved territorial status, whites could survey and sell the land, establish a civil government, and build a railroad.

Nebraska lay within the Louisiana Purchase and, according to the Missouri Compromise of 1820, was closed to slavery (see "The Missouri

Filibustering in Nicaragua
In this image of a pitched battle in Nicaragua in 1856, Costa Ricans on foot fight American filibusters on horseback. Costa Rican soldiers and their Central American allies defeated William Walker's *filibusteros* in 1857. The Pierce administration had already extended diplomatic recognition to Walker's regime, and white Southerners had cheered Walker's attempt to "introduce civilization" in Nicaragua and to develop its resources "with slave labor." *London Illustrated Times*, May 24, 1856.

attacks on Nicaragua, but in 1860 Honduran forces captured and shot him.

By the time filibustering lost steam in the late 1850s, Americans held mixed opinions of filibusters. Some condemned them as criminals and cutthroats, while others celebrated them as heroes, cut from the same cloth as hardy western pioneers. Defenders claimed that Latin American peoples stood in the way of progress and civilization just as much as Indians did. One historian concluded that filibusters were "criminals from manifest destiny's underworld" and another "chapter in the history of American expansionism." A leading proslavery ideologue, George Fitzhugh, defended filibustering through historical comparison: "They who condemn the modern filibuster . . . must also condemn the discoverers and settlers of America, of the East Indies of Holland, and of the Indian and Pacific Oceans."

Questions for Analysis

Summarize the Argument: What is the argument for filibustering as an expression of manifest destiny?

Analyze the Evidence: What specific evidence supports the argument that filibustering was an expression of manifest destiny? Is the evidence persuasive?

Consider the Context: What did filibusters share with pioneers heading west under the banner of manifest destiny? Were there any important differences?

invaded Cuba. The Spaniards crushed the invasion, killing 200 filibusters, shipping 160 prisoners to Spain, executing 50 invaders by firing squad, and publicly garrotting López.

The most successful of all proslavery filibusters was William Walker of Tennessee. In May 1855, Walker and an army of fifty-six men sailed from San Francisco to the west coast of Nicaragua. Two thousand reinforcements and a civil war in Nicaragua gave Walker his victory. He had himself proclaimed president, legalized slavery, and called on Southerners to come raise cotton, sugar, and coffee in "a magnificent country." The U.S. government officially recognized Walker's regime, but his empire survived only until 1857, when a coalition of Central American countries sent him packing. Walker doggedly launched four other

Compromise" in chapter 10). Douglas needed southern votes to pass his Nebraska legislation, but Southerners had no incentive to create another free territory or to help a northern city win the transcontinental railroad. Southerners, however, agreed to help if Congress organized Nebraska according to popular sovereignty. That meant giving slavery a chance in Nebraska Territory and reopening the dangerous issue of slavery expansion.

In January 1854, Douglas introduced his bill to organize Nebraska Territory, leaving to the settlers themselves the decision about slavery. At southern insistence, and even though he knew it would "raise a hell of a storm," Douglas added an explicit repeal of the Missouri

Free state or territory

Slave state or territory

Voters to decide on allowing slavery, Compromise of 1850

Voters to decide on allowing slavery, Kansas-Nebraska Act, 1854

MAP ACTIVITY

Map 14.3 The Kansas-Nebraska Act, 1854
Americans hardly thought twice about dispossessing the Indians of land guaranteed them by treaty, but many worried about the outcome of repealing the Missouri Compromise and opening up the region to slavery.

READING THE MAP: How many slave states and how many free states does the map show? Estimate the percentage of new territory likely to be settled by slaveholders.

CONNECTIONS: Who would be more likely to support changes in government legislation to discontinue the Missouri Compromise—slaveholders or free-soil advocates? Why?

► Realignment of the Party System

Since the early 1830s, Whigs and Democrats had organized and channeled political conflict in the nation. This party system dampened sectionalism and strengthened the Union. To achieve national political power, the Whigs and Democrats had to retain strength in both North and South. Strong northern and southern wings required that each party compromise and find positions acceptable to both sections.

The Kansas-Nebraska controversy shattered this stabilizing political system. In place of two national parties with bisectional strength, the mid-1850s witnessed the development of one party heavily dominated by one section and another party entirely limited to the other section. Rather than "national" parties, the country had what one critic disdainfully called "geographic" parties, a development that thwarted political compromise between the sections.

The Old Parties: Whigs and Democrats

As early as the Mexican-American War, members of the Whig Party had clashed over the future of slavery in annexed Mexican lands. By 1852, the Whig Party could please its proslavery southern wing or its antislavery northern wing but not both. The Whigs' miserable showing in the election of 1852 made it clear that they were no longer a strong national party. By 1856, after more than two decades of contesting the Democrats, they were hardly a party at all (Map 14.4).

The collapse of the Whig Party left the Democrats as the country's only national party. Popular sovereignty provided a doctrine that many Democrats could support. Even so, popular sovereignty very nearly undid the party. When Stephen Douglas applied the doctrine to the part of the Louisiana Purchase where slavery had been barred, he divided northern Democrats and destroyed the dominance of the Democratic Party in the free states. After 1854, the Democrats were a southern-dominated party. Still, gains in the South more than balanced Democratic losses in the North, and during the 1850s Democrats elected two presidents and won majorities in Congress in almost every election.

Compromise. Free-Soilers branded Douglas's plan "a gross violation of a sacred pledge" and an "atrocious plot" to transform free land into a "dreary region of despotism, inhabited by masters and slaves."

Undaunted, Douglas skillfully shepherded the explosive bill through Congress in May 1854. Nine-tenths of the southern members (Whigs and Democrats) and half of the northern Democrats cast votes in favor of the bill. Like Douglas, most northern supporters believed that popular sovereignty would make Nebraska free territory. The **Kansas-Nebraska Act** divided the huge territory in two: Nebraska and Kansas (Map 14.3). With this act, the government pushed the Plains Indians farther west, making way for farmers and railroads.

REVIEW   Why did the Compromise of 1850 fail to achieve sectional peace?

1848

	Candidate	Electoral Vote	Popular Vote	Percent of Popular Vote
	Zachary Taylor (Whig)	163	1,360,099	47.4
	Lewis Cass (Democrat)	127	1,220,544	42.5
	Martin Van Buren (Free-Soil)	0	291,263	10.1

1852

	Candidate	Electoral Vote	Popular Vote	Percent of Popular Vote
	Franklin Pierce (Democrat)	254	1,601,274	50.9
	Winfield Scott (Whig)	42	1,386,580	44.1
	John P. Hale (Free-Soil)	5	155,825	5.0

1856

	Candidate	Electoral Vote	Popular Vote	Percent of Popular Vote
	James Buchanan (Democrat)	174	1,838,169	45.3
	John C. Frémont (Republican)	114	1,341,264	33.1
	Millard Fillmore (American)	8	874,534	21.6

1860

	Candidate	Electoral Vote	Popular Vote	Percent of Popular Vote
	Abraham Lincoln (Republican)	180	1,866,452	39.9
	John C. Breckinridge (Southern Democrat)	72	847,953	18.1
	Stephen A. Douglas (Northern Democrat)	12	1,375,157	29.4
	John Bell (Constitutional Union)	39	590,631	12.6

MAP ACTIVITY

Map 14.4 Political Realignment, 1848–1860

In 1848, slavery and sectionalism began taking their toll on the country's party system. The Whig Party was an early casualty. By 1860, national parties—those that contended for votes in both North and South—had been replaced by regional parties.

READING THE MAP: Which states did the Democrats pick up in 1852 compared to 1848? Which of these states did the Democrats lose in 1856? Compare the general geographic location of the states won by the Republicans in 1856 versus those won in 1860.

CONNECTIONS: In the 1860 election, which party benefited the most from the western and midwestern states added to the Union since 1848? Why do you think these states chose to back this party?

The breakup of the Whigs and the disaffection of many northern Democrats set millions of Americans politically adrift. As they searched for new political harbors, Americans found that the death of the old party system created a multitude of fresh political alternatives.

The New Parties: Know-Nothings and Republicans

Dozens of new political organizations vied for voters' attention. Out of the confusion, two emerged as true contenders. One grew out of the

VISUAL ACTIVITY

Know-Nothing Cartoon

This cartoon underscores the Know-Nothing contention that hard-drinking Irish and German immigrants were stealing elections and polluting American democracy. In addition to the Irishman's whiskey and the German's beer, the artist completes the negative stereotypes by giving the Irishman his shillelagh (club) and the German his pipe. The Granger Collection, New York.

READING THE IMAGE: What is taking place behind the Irishman and German, and how does it spell danger for the Republic?

CONNECTIONS: In what parts of the nation would you suppose the Know-Nothing message had its greatest appeal?

slavery controversy, a coalition of indignant anti-slavery Northerners. The other arose from an entirely different split in American society, between native Protestants and Roman Catholic immigrants.

The wave of immigrants that arrived in America from 1845 to 1855 produced a nasty backlash among Protestant Americans, who feared that the Republic was about to drown in a sea of Roman Catholics from Ireland and Germany (see Figure 12.1, page 323). Nativists (individuals who were anti-immigrant) began to organize, first into secret fraternal societies and then in 1854 into a political party. Recruits swore never to vote for either foreign-born or Roman Catholic candidates and not to reveal any information about the organization. When questioned, they said, "I know nothing." Officially, they were the American Party, but most Americans called them Know-Nothings.

The Know-Nothings enjoyed dazzling success in 1854 and 1855. They captured state legislatures throughout the nation and claimed dozens of seats in Congress. Democrats and Whigs described the Know-Nothings' phenomenal record as a "tornado," a "hurricane," and "a freak of political insanity." But by 1855, an observer might reasonably have concluded that the Know-Nothings had emerged as the successor to the Whigs.

The Know-Nothings were not the only new party making noise, however. One of the new antislavery organizations provoked by the Kansas-Nebraska Act called itself the **Republican Party**. The Republicans attempted to unite all those who opposed the extension of slavery into any territory of the United States.

The Republican creed tapped into the basic beliefs and values of Northerners. Slavery, Republicans believed, degraded the dignity of white labor by associating work with blacks and servility. As evidence, they pointed to the South, where, one Republican claimed, nonslaveholding whites "retire to the outskirts of civilization, where they live a semi-savage life, sinking deeper and more hopelessly into barbarism with every succeeding generation." Republicans warned that the insatiable slaveholders of the South, whom antislavery Northerners called the "Slave Power," were conspiring through their control of the Democratic Party to expand slavery, subvert liberty, and undermine the Constitution.

Only by restricting slavery to the South, Republicans believed, could free labor flourish elsewhere. In the North, one Republican declared in 1854, "every man holds his fortune in his own right arm; and his position in society, in life, is to be tested by his own individual character." Without slavery, western territories would provide vast economic opportunity for free men. Powerful images of liberty and opportunity attracted a wide range of Northerners to the Republican cause.

Women as well as men rushed to the new Republican Party. Indeed, three women helped found the party in Ripon, Wisconsin, in 1854. Although they could not vote and suffered from other legal handicaps, women nevertheless participated in partisan politics by writing campaign literature, marching in parades, giving speeches, and lobbying voters. Women's antislavery fervor attracted them to the Republican Party, and participation in party politics in turn nurtured the woman's rights movement. Susan B. Anthony, who attended Republican meetings throughout the 1850s, found that her political activity made her disfranchisement all the more galling. She and other women in the North worked on behalf of antislavery and woman suffrage and the right of married women to control their own property. (See "Experiencing the American Promise," page 390.)

The Election of 1856

The election of 1856 revealed that the Republicans had become the Democrats' main challenger, and slavery in the territories, not immigration, was the election's principal issue. When the Know-Nothings insisted on a platform that endorsed the Kansas-Nebraska Act, most of the Northerners walked out, and the party came apart. The few Know-Nothings who remained nominated ex-president Millard Fillmore.

The Republican platform focused mostly on "making every territory free." When they labeled slavery a "relic of barbarism," they signaled that they had written off the South. For president, they nominated the soldier and California adventurer John C. Frémont. Frémont lacked political credentials, but his wife, Jessie Frémont, the daughter of Senator Thomas Hart Benton of Missouri, knew the political map well. Though careful to maintain a proper public image, the vivacious young mother and antislavery zealot helped attract voters and draw women into politics. (See "Analyzing Historical Evidence," page 392.)

The Democrats, successful in 1852 in bridging sectional differences by nominating a northern man with southern principles, chose another "doughface," James Buchanan of Pennsylvania. They portrayed the Republicans as extremists ("Black Republican Abolitionists") whose support for the Wilmot Proviso risked pushing the South out of the Union.

The Democratic strategy carried the day for Buchanan, who won 174 electoral votes against Frémont's 114 and Fillmore's 8 (see Map 14.4). But the big news was that the Republicans, campaigning under the banner "Free soil, Free men, Frémont," carried all but five of the states north of the Mason-Dixon line. Sectionalism had fashioned a new party system, one that spelled danger for the Democrats and the nation. Indeed, war had already broken out between proslavery and antislavery forces in the distant Kansas Territory.

REVIEW   Why did the Whig Party disintegrate in the 1850s?

The Realignment of Political Parties

Whig Party

1848	Whig Party divides into two factions over slavery; Whigs adopt no platform and nominate war hero Zachary Taylor, who is elected president.
1852	Whigs nominate war hero General Winfield Scott for president; deep divisions in party result in humiliating loss.
1856	Shattered by sectionalism, Whig Party fields no presidential candidate.

Democratic Party

1848	President Polk declines to run again; Democratic Party nominates Lewis Cass, the man most closely associated with popular sovereignty, but avoids firm platform position on expansion of slavery.
1852	To bridge rift in party, Democrats nominate northern war veteran with southern views, Franklin Pierce, for president; he wins with 50.9 percent of popular vote.
1856	Democrat James Buchanan elected president on ambiguous platform; his prosouthern actions in office alienate northern branch of party.
1860	Democrats split into northern Democrats and southern Democrats; each group fields its own presidential candidate.

Free-Soil Party

1848	Breakaway antislavery Democrats and antislavery Whigs found Free-Soil Party; presidential candidate Martin Van Buren takes 10.1 percent of popular vote, mainly from Whigs.
1852	Support for Free-Soil Party ebbs in wake of Compromise of 1850; Free-Soil presidential candidate John P. Hale wins only 5 percent of popular vote.

American (Know-Nothing) Party

1851	Anti-immigrant American (Know-Nothing) Party formed.
1854–1855	American Party succeeds in state elections and attracts votes from northern and southern Whigs in congressional elections.
1856	Know-Nothing presidential candidate Millard Fillmore wins only Maryland; party subsequently disbands.

Republican Party

1854	Republican Party formed to oppose expansion of slavery in territories; attracts northern Whigs, northern Democrats, and Free-Soilers.
1856	Republican presidential candidate John C. Frémont wins all but five northern states, establishing Republicans as main challenger to Democrats.
1860	Republican Abraham Lincoln wins all northern states except New Jersey and is elected president in four-way race against divided Democrats and southern Constitutional Union Party.

"A Purse of Her Own": Petitioning for the Right to Own Property

In the early Republic, as today, having money and deciding how to spend it was a fundamental aspect of independent adulthood. Yet antebellum married women were denied this privilege, because of the laws of *coverture*, which placed wives under the full legal control of their husbands (see "Women and the Law" in chapter 10). By law, husbands made all the financial decisions in a household. Even money that a wife earned or brought into a marriage from gifts or inheritance was not hers to control as long as she remained married. Ernestine Potowsky Rose of New York City thought that was wrong, and she became the first woman in the United States to take action to change the law.

Born in Poland in 1810, Ernestine Potowsky was the daughter of a rabbi, which meant that her destiny was fixed: an arranged marriage, many children, and a life strictly governed by religious law. Ernestine rejected this fate and left home for London. There, at age nineteen, she married William Rose, a like-minded socialist intellectual. The couple later emigrated to the United States and settled in New York City, where William, a jeweler, started a business.

Ernestine soon learned of a bill presented in 1837 in the New York assembly proposing that married women, "equally with males and unmarried females, possess the rights of *life*, *liberty*, and PROPERTY, and are equally entitled to be protected in all three." But opponents feared that it would undermine a central pillar of marriage: the assumption that husband and wife shared identical interests. Predictably, the bill failed to pass.

The devastating panics of 1837 and 1839 (see "Elections and Panics" in chapter 11), and the resulting bankruptcies, soon changed some traditionalists' minds about wives and property. Men in several state legislatures crafted laws that shielded a wife's inherited property from creditors collecting debts from her husband. Mississippi led the way in 1839, and by 1848 eighteen states had modified property laws in the name of family protection.

In New York, as support for such a law grew, Ernestine Rose mobilized a new constituency of women around the argument that married women should be able to own and control property. She circulated petitions and spoke from public platforms, often joined by Elizabeth Cady Stanton, a young wife from western New York. In April 1848, three months before the Seneca Falls woman's rights convention (see "Woman's Rights Activists" in chapter 12), the New York assembly finally awarded married women sole authority over property they brought to a marriage.

Rose welcomed the new law but recognized its key shortcoming: It made no provision for wages earned by a married woman. Nor did it alter inheritance laws that limited a widow's share of her husband's estate. Speaking at every national woman's rights convention from 1850 to 1860, Rose argued for women's economic independence. In 1853, she itemized the limited belongings allowed to a widow if her husband died without a will: "As to the personal property, after all debts and liabilities are discharged, the widow receives one-half of it; and, in addition, the law allows her, her own wearing apparel, her own ornaments, proper to her station, one bed, with appurtenances for the same, a stove, the Bible, family pictures, and all the school-books; also all spinning wheels and weaving looms, one table, six chairs, ten cups and saucers, one tea-pot, one sugar dish, and six spoons." While her audience laughed appreciatively, Rose questioned whether the spoons would be teaspoons, "since a widow might live on tea only." Spinning wheels, long gone in 1853, needed no elaboration from her to make the law sound pathetically out-of-date.

Of particular concern to Rose was the plight of poor wives. She and Susan B. Anthony encountered

► Freedom under Siege

Events in Kansas Territory in the mid-1850s underscored the Republicans' contention that the slaveholding South presented a profound threat to "free soil, free labor, and free men." Kansas reeled with violence that Republicans argued was southern in origin. Republicans also pointed to the brutal beating by a Southerner of a respected northern senator on the floor of Congress. Even the Supreme Court, in the Republicans' view, reflected the South's drive toward minority rule and tyranny. Then, in 1858, the issues dividing North and South received an extraordinary hearing in a senatorial contest in Illinois, when the

Ernestine Rose
Ernestine Rose, in her mid-forties when this photograph was taken, managed to hold a smile for the several minutes required to capture her image on a photographic plate. Fotosearch/Getty Images.

she earned the money outside the household. Money earned selling eggs or caring for boarders still went directly into the husband's pocket. Perhaps the most significant beneficiaries of this law were women whose husbands were incompetent to support them or who had deserted them. These husbands now had no right to their wives' hard-gained earnings.

The revised New York law made other important changes to coverture. A wife could now sue (or be sued), make legal contracts of her own, and serve as joint guardian of her children, "with equal powers, rights and duties in regard to them." These changes, adopted in many states after 1860, began the long (and still ongoing) process of elevating women to equality with men.

Questions for Analysis

Recognize Viewpoints: What do the laws of coverture reveal about how most men viewed married women in antebellum America?

Analyze the Evidence: Why, according to women activists like Ernestine Rose, did a woman need "a purse of her own"?

Consider the Context: What do you suppose there was about women's condition that drew some northern women to the antislavery campaign?

women trapped in marriages with husbands who failed to support their dependents. Anthony, herself a lifelong single woman, recalled that "as I passed from town to town I was made to feel the great evil of women's utter dependence on man. . . . Woman must have a purse of her own."

Rose's efforts paid off. In 1860, New York amended its law to include a wife's wages as her own, but only if

nation's foremost Democrat debated a resourceful Republican. (See Figure 14.1.)

"Bleeding Kansas"

Three days after the House of Representatives approved the Kansas-Nebraska Act in 1854, Senator William H. Seward of New York boldly challenged the South. "Come on then, Gentlemen of the Slave States," he cried, "since there is no escaping your challenge, I accept it in behalf of the cause of freedom. We will engage in competition for the virgin soil of Kansas, and God give the victory to the side which is stronger in numbers as it is in right." Because of Stephen Douglas, popular sovereignty would determine whether

Women's Politics

Although women could not vote before the Civil War, many women nevertheless participated in public political activity. *Uncle Tom's Cabin*, Harriet Beecher Stowe's searing indictment of slavery, galvanized women's support for the Republican Party's campaign against the extension of slavery. Their struggle on behalf of slaves led many to also join the fight for woman's rights.

DOCUMENT 1
Jessie Benton Frémont's Letter to Elizabeth Blair Lee, 1856

Throughout her life, Jessie Benton Frémont worked to fulfill her domestic roles as wife and mother, even though she found them constraining. She also sought unabashedly to influence politics. During the 1850s, she became one of the principal political analysts and advisers to her husband, John C. Frémont, who ran for president on the Republican ticket. On October 20, 1856, Jessie Frémont wrote to her dear friend Elizabeth Blair Lee, offering a clear-eyed interpretation of the significance of the Republican Party's paper-thin but devastating loss in the October 14 Pennsylvania state election.

I heartily regret the defeat we have met and do not look for things to change for the better. The Democrats will follow up their advantage with the courage of success & our forces are unorganized and just now surprised and inactive. I wish the cause had triumphed. I do wish Mr. Frémont had been the one to administer the bitter dose of subjection to the South for he has the coolness and nerve to do it just as it needs to be done—without passion & without

sympathy—as coldly as a surgeon over a hospital patient would he have cut off their right hand Kansas from the old unhealthy southern body. . . . Tell your Father he must come to us for example & comfort in November for I don't think we will wear any but black feathers this year.

Source: Frémont, Jessie Benton (1824–1902), Mrs. John C. Frémont (undated); Blair and Lee Family Papers; Manuscripts Division, Department of Rare Books and Special Collections, Princeton University Library.

DOCUMENT 2
Harriot K. Hunt's Letter "to . . . [the] Treasurer, and the Assessors, and other Authorities of the city of Boston, and the Citizens generally," 1852

Harriot K. Hunt, a rare female physician who had practiced medicine in Boston since 1835, here protests having to pay taxes when she was prohibited from voting. Women fought for suffrage for principle's sake but also because they wanted a say in matters that were important to them.

Harriot K. Hunt, physician, a native and permanent resident of the city of Boston, and for many years a taxpayer therein, in making payment of her city taxes for the

Kansas became slave or free. Free-state and slave-state settlers each sought a majority at the ballot box, claimed God's blessing, and kept their rifles ready.

Emigrant aid societies sprang up to promote settlement from free states or slave states. Missourians, already bordered on the east by the free state of Illinois and on the north by the free state of Iowa, especially thought it important to secure Kansas for slavery. Thousands of rough frontiersmen, egged on by Missouri senator David Rice Atchison, invaded Kansas. "There are eleven hundred coming over from Platte County to vote," Atchison reported, "and if that ain't enough we

can send five thousand—enough to kill every God-damned abolitionist in the Territory." Not surprisingly, proslavery candidates swept the territorial elections in November 1854. When Kansas's first territorial legislature met, it enacted a raft of proslavery laws, including a statute prohibiting antislavery men from holding office or serving on juries. Ever-pliant President Pierce endorsed the work of the fraudulently elected legislature. Free-soil Kansans did not. They elected their own legislature, which promptly banned both slaves and free blacks from the territory. Organized into two rival governments and armed to the teeth, Kansans verged on civil war.

coming year, begs leave to protest against the injustice and inequality of levying taxes upon women, and at the same time refusing them any voice or vote in the imposition and expenditure of the same. The only classes of male persons required to pay taxes, and not at the same time allowed the privilege of voting, are aliens and minors. The objection in the case of aliens is their supposed want of interest in our institutions and knowledge of them. The objection in the case of minors is the want of sufficient understanding. These objections can not apply to women, natives of the city, all of whose property interests are here, and who have accumulated, by their own sagacity and industry, the very property on which they are taxed. But this is not all; the alien, by going through the forms of naturalization, the minor on coming of age, obtain the right of voting; . . . though so ignorant as not to be able to sign their names, or read the very votes they put into the ballot-boxes. Even drunkards, felons, idiots, and lunatics, if men, may still enjoy that right of voting to which no woman, however large the amount of the taxes she pays, however respectable her character, or useful her life, can ever attain. Wherein, your remonstrant would inquire, is the justice, equality, or wisdom of this?

Source: Elizabeth Cady Stanton, Susan B. Anthony, and Matilda Joslyn Gage, eds., *History of Woman Suffrage*, vol. 1 (New York: Folwer & Wells, 1881), 259.

DOCUMENT 3
Elizabeth Cady Stanton's Letter on Women's Fashions, 1855

Stymied by male politicians who ignored pleas like Hunt's, woman's rights activists pondered how to promote equality in areas of life more directly under their personal control. In a letter to a friend, suffragist leader Elizabeth Cady Stanton explained how women's fashions could be tailored to promote equality.

I fully agree with you that woman is terribly cramped and crippled in her present style of dress . . . it seems that if she would enjoy entire freedom, she should dress just like a man. Why proclaim our sex on the house-tops, seeing that it is a badge of degradation, and deprives us of so many rights and privileges wherever we go? . . . In male attire, we could travel by land or sea; go through all the streets and lanes of our cities and towns by night and day, without a protector; get seven hundred dollars a year for teaching, instead of three, and ten dollars for making a coat, instead of two or three, as we now do. All this we could do without fear of insult, or the least sacrifice of decency or virtue. If nature has not made the sex so clearly defined as to be seen through any disguise, why should we make the difference so striking?

Source: Elizabeth Cady Stanton, Susan B. Anthony, and Matilda Joslyn Gage, eds., *History of Woman Suffrage*, vol. 1 (New York: Fowler & Wells, 1881), 841.

Questions for Analysis

Consider the Context: Jessie Frémont did not interpret the Republican defeat in Pennsylvania in 1856 as a "glorious defeat," as did many other Republicans. Can you suggest possible reasons why she did not? Why might a woman's rights activist have been tougher minded and more realistic?

Summarize the Argument: On what grounds, according to Harriot Hunt, should women be accorded the vote? Do you agree with her argument? Why or why not?

Recognize Viewpoints: What does Elizabeth Cady Stanton's early version of "dressing for success" reveal about how she viewed the challenges faced by women? Do you think other women would have agreed with her suggestions? Why or why not?

Fighting broke out on the morning of May 21, 1856, when several hundred proslavery men raided the town of Lawrence, the center of free-state settlement. Only one man died, but the "Sack of Lawrence," as free-soil forces called it, inflamed northern opinion. Elsewhere in Kansas, news of events in Lawrence provoked John Brown, a free-soil settler, to announce that "it was better that a score of bad men should die than that one man who came here to make Kansas a Free State should be driven out" and to lead the posse that massacred five allegedly proslavery settlers along Pottawatomie Creek (see page 376). After that, guerrilla war engulfed the territory.

Just as **"Bleeding Kansas"** gave the fledgling Republican Party fresh ammunition for its battle against the Slave Power, so too did an event that occurred in the national capital. In May 1856, Senator Charles Sumner of Massachusetts delivered a speech titled "The Crime against Kansas," which included a scalding personal attack on South Carolina senator Andrew P. Butler. Sumner described Butler as a "Don Quixote" who had taken as his mistress "the harlot, slavery."

Preston Brooks, a young South Carolina member of the House and a kinsman of Butler's, felt compelled to defend the honor of his aged relative. On May 22, Brooks entered the Senate, where he

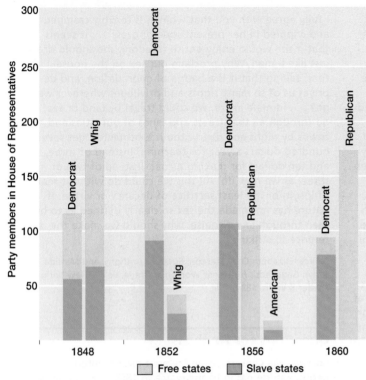

FIGURE 14.1 Changing Political Landscape, 1848–1860
The polarization of American politics between free states and slave states occurred in little more than a decade.

"Bleeding Kansas," 1850s

found Sumner working at his desk. He beat Sumner over the head with his cane until Sumner lay bleeding and unconscious on the floor. Brooks resigned his seat in the House, only to be promptly reelected. In the North, the southern hero became an archvillain. Like "Bleeding Kansas," "Bleeding Sumner" provided the Republican Party with a potent symbol of the South's "twisted and violent civilization."

The *Dred Scott* Decision

Political debate over slavery in the territories became so heated in part because the Constitution lacked precision on the issue. In 1857, in the case of *Dred Scott v. Sandford*, the Supreme Court announced its understanding of the meaning of the Constitution regarding slavery in the territories. The Court's decision demonstrated that it enjoyed no special immunity from the sectional and partisan passions that were convulsing the land.

In 1833, an army doctor bought the slave Dred Scott in St. Louis, Missouri, and took him as his personal servant to Fort Armstrong,

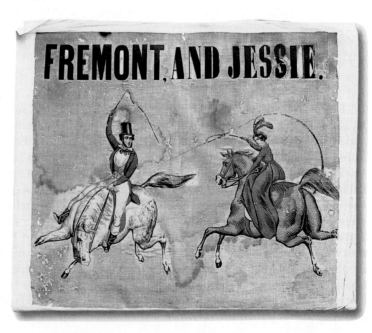

Kansas
Dr. John Doy (seated), an antislavery campaigner in Kansas, was captured, along with thirteen runaway slaves, in January 1859 by proslavery men. Doy's friends pose proudly here after they rescued him in July from a St. Joseph, Missouri, jail.
Private Collection/Peter Newark American Pictures/Bridgeman Images.

Illinois, and then to Fort Snelling in Wisconsin Territory. Back in St. Louis in 1846, Scott, with the help of white friends, sued to prove that he and his family were legally entitled to their freedom. Scott argued that living in Illinois, a free state, and Wisconsin, a free territory, had made his family free and that they remained free even after returning to Missouri, a slave state.

In 1857, Chief Justice Roger B. Taney, who hated Republicans and detested racial equality, wrote the Court's *Dred Scott* decision. First, the Court ruled that Scott could not legally claim violation of his constitutional rights because he was not a citizen of the United States. When the Constitution was written, Taney said, blacks "were regarded as beings of an inferior order . . . so far inferior, that they had no rights which the white man was bound to respect." Second, the laws of Dred Scott's home state, Missouri, determined his status, and thus his travels in free areas did not make him free. Third, Congress's power to make "all needful rules and regulations" for the territories did not include the right to prohibit slavery. The Court explicitly declared

the Missouri Compromise unconstitutional, even though it had already been voided by the Kansas-Nebraska Act.

The Taney Court's extreme proslavery decision outraged Republicans. By denying the federal government the right to exclude slavery in the territories, it cut the legs out from under the Republican Party. Moreover, as the *New York Tribune* lamented, the decision cleared the way for "all our Territories . . . to be ripened into Slave States." Particularly frightening to African Americans in the North was the Court's declaration that free blacks were not citizens and had no rights.

The Republican rebuttal to the *Dred Scott* ruling relied heavily on the dissenting opinion of Justice Benjamin R. Curtis. Scott *was* a citizen of the United States, Curtis argued. At the time of the writing of the Constitution, free black men could vote in five states and participated in the ratification process. Scott *was* free. Because slavery was prohibited in Wisconsin, the "involuntary servitude of a slave, coming into the Territory with his master, should cease to exist." The Missouri Compromise *was* constitutional. The Founders had meant exactly what they said:

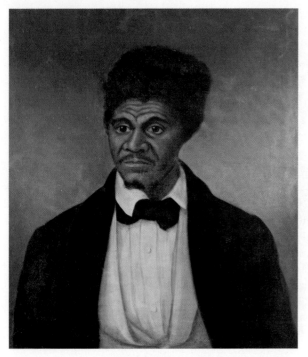

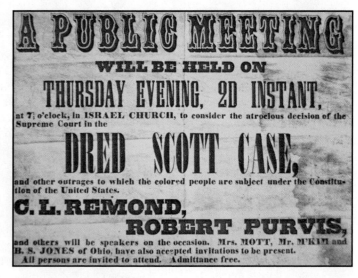

Dred Scott
This portrait of Dred Scott was painted in 1857, the year of the Supreme Court's decision. African Americans in the North were particularly alarmed by the Court's ruling. Although the Court rejected Scott's suit, he gained his freedom in May 1857 when a white man purchased and freed Scott and his family. Portrait: © Collection of the New-York Historical Society, USA/Bridgeman Images; poster: Private Collection/Peter Newark American Pictures/Bridgeman Images.

Congress had the power to make "*all* needful rules and regulations" for the territories, including barring slavery.

Unswayed by Curtis's dissent, the Court, in a seven-to-two decision, validated an extreme statement of the South's territorial rights. John C. Calhoun's claim that Congress had no authority to exclude slavery became the law of the land. White Southerners cheered. One gloated that the *Dred Scott* decision was the "funeral sermon of Black Republicanism . . . crushing and annihilating the anti-slavery platform." Ironically, the *Dred Scott* decision actually strengthened the young Republican Party. Indeed, that "outrageous decision," one Republican argued, was "the best thing that could have happened," for it provided powerful evidence of the Republicans' claim that a hostile Slave Power conspired against northern liberties.

Prairie Republican: Abraham Lincoln

By reigniting the sectional flames, the *Dred Scott* case provided Republican politicians with fresh challenges and fresh opportunities. Abraham Lincoln had long since put behind him his hardscrabble log-cabin beginnings in Kentucky and Indiana. Now living in Springfield, Illinois, he earned good money as a lawyer, but politics was his life. "His ambition was a little engine that knew no rest," observed his law partner, William Herndon. Lincoln had served as a Whig in the Illinois state legislature and in the House of Representatives, but he had not held public office since 1849.

Convinced that slavery was a "monstrous injustice," a "great moral wrong," and an "unqualified evil to the negro, the white man, and the State," Lincoln condemned the Kansas-Nebraska Act of 1854 for giving slavery a new life and in 1856 joined the Republican Party. He accepted that the Constitution permitted slavery in those states where it existed, but he believed that Congress could contain its spread. Penned in, plantation slavery would wither, Lincoln believed, and in time Southerners would end slavery themselves.

Lincoln held what were, for his times, moderate racial views. Although he denounced slavery and defended black humanity, he also viewed black equality as impractical and unachievable. "Negroes have natural rights . . . as other men have," he said, "although they cannot enjoy them here." Insurmountable white prejudice made it impossible to extend full citizenship to blacks in America, he believed. In Lincoln's mind, social stability and black progress required that slavery end and that blacks leave the country.

Lincoln envisioned the western territories as "places for poor people to go to, and better their conditions." But slavery's expansion threatened free men's basic right to succeed. The Kansas-Nebraska Act and the *Dred Scott* decision persuaded him that slaveholders were engaged in a dangerous conspiracy to nationalize slavery. The next step, Lincoln warned, would be "another Supreme Court decision, declaring that the Constitution of the United States does not permit a State to exclude slavery from its limits." Unless the citizens of Illinois woke up, he warned, the Supreme Court would make "Illinois a slave State."

In Lincoln's view, the nation could not "endure, permanently half slave and half free." Either opponents of slavery would arrest its spread and place it on the "course of ultimate extinction," or its advocates would see that it became legal in "*all* the States, *old* as well as *new—North* as well as *South*." Lincoln's convictions that slavery was wrong and that Congress must stop its spread formed the core of the Republican ideology. In 1858, Republicans in Illinois chose him to challenge the nation's premier Democrat, who was seeking reelection to the U.S. Senate.

The Lincoln-Douglas Debates

When Stephen Douglas learned that the Republican Abraham Lincoln would be his opponent for the Senate, he observed: "He is the strong man of the party—full of wit, facts, dates—and the best stump speaker, with his droll ways and dry jokes, in the West. He is as honest as he is shrewd, and if I beat him my victory will be hardly won."

Not only did Douglas have to contend with a formidable foe, but the previous year, the nation's economy had experienced a sharp downturn. Prices had plummeted, thousands of businesses had failed, and many were unemployed. As a Democrat, Douglas had to go before the voters as a member of the party whose policies stood accused of causing the panic of 1857.

Douglas's response to another crisis in 1857, however, helped shore up his standing in Illinois.

Proslavery forces in Kansas met in the town of Lecompton, drafted a proslavery constitution, and applied for statehood. Everyone knew that free-soilers outnumbered proslavery settlers, but President Buchanan instructed Congress to admit Kansas as the sixteenth slave state. Senator Douglas broke with the Democratic administration and denounced the Lecompton constitution; Congress killed the Lecompton bill. (When Kansans reconsidered the Lecompton constitution in an honest election, they rejected it six to one. Kansas entered the Union in 1861 as a free state.) By denouncing the fraudulent proslavery constitution, Douglas declared his independence from the South and, he hoped, made himself acceptable at home.

A relative unknown and a decided underdog in the Illinois election, Lincoln challenged Douglas to debate him face-to-face. The two met in seven communities for what would become a legendary series of debates. To the thousands who stood straining to see and hear, they must have seemed an odd pair. Douglas was five feet four inches tall, broad, and stocky; Lincoln was six feet four, angular, and lean. Douglas was in perpetual motion, darting across the platform, shouting, and jabbing the air; Lincoln stood still and spoke deliberately. Douglas wore the latest fashion and dazzled audiences with his flashy vests. Lincoln wore good suits but managed to look rumpled anyway.

The two men debated the crucial issues of the age—slavery and freedom. Lincoln badgered Douglas with the question of whether he favored the spread of slavery. He tried to force Douglas into the damaging admission that the Supreme Court had repudiated Douglas's own territorial solution, popular sovereignty. At Freeport, Illinois, Douglas admitted that settlers could not now pass legislation barring slavery, but he argued that they could ban slavery just as effectively by not passing protective laws, such as those found in slave states. Southerners condemned Douglas's "Freeport Doctrine" and charged him with trying to steal the victory they had gained with the *Dred Scott* decision. Lincoln chastised his opponent for his "don't care" attitude about slavery, for "blowing out the moral lights around us."

Douglas worked the racial issue. He called Lincoln an abolitionist and an egalitarian enamored of "our colored brethren." Put on the defensive, Lincoln reaffirmed his faith in white rule: "I will say, then, that I am not, nor ever have been, in favor of bringing about in any way the social and political equality of the white and

Lincoln
Alexander Hesler took this photograph in Springfield, Illinois, less than two years after the Lincoln-Douglas debates. Lincoln's law partner, William T. Herndon, observed: "There is the peculiar curve of the lower lip, the lone mole on the right cheek, and a pose of the head so essentially Lincolnian; no other artist has ever caught it." Library of Congress, 3a09621.

black race." But unlike Douglas, who told racist jokes, Lincoln was no negrophobe. He tried to steer the debate back to what he considered the true issue: the morality and future of slavery. "Slavery is wrong," Lincoln repeated, because "a man has the right to the fruits of his own labor."

As Douglas predicted, the election was hard-fought and closely contested. Until the adoption of the Seventeenth Amendment in 1911, citizens voted for state legislators, who in turn selected U.S. senators. Since Democrats won a slight majority in the Illinois legislature, the members returned Douglas to the Senate. But the **Lincoln-Douglas debates** thrust Lincoln, the prairie Republican, into the national spotlight.

> **REVIEW**   Why did the *Dred Scott* decision strengthen northern suspicions of a Slave Power conspiracy?

▶ The Union Collapses

From the Republican perspective, the Kansas-Nebraska Act, the Brooks-Sumner affair, the *Dred Scott* decision, and the Lecompton constitution amounted to irrefutable evidence of the South's aggressive promotion of slavery. White Southerners, of course, saw things differently. They were the ones who were under siege, they declared. They believed that Northerners were itching to use their numerical advantage to attack slavery, and not just in the territories. Republicans had made it clear that they were unwilling to accept the *Dred Scott* ruling as the last word on the issue of slavery expansion. And John Brown's attempt to incite a slave insurrection in Virginia in 1859 proved to Southerners that Northerners would do anything to end slavery.

Talk of leaving the Union had been heard for years, but until the final crisis, Southerners had used secession as a ploy to gain concessions within the Union, not to destroy it. Then the 1850s delivered powerful blows to Southerners' confidence that they could remain in the Union and protect slavery. When the Republican Party won the White House in 1860, many Southerners concluded that they would have to leave.

The Aftermath of John Brown's Raid

For his attack on Harpers Ferry, John Brown stood trial for treason, murder, and incitement of slave insurrection. "To hang a fanatic is to make a martyr of him and fledge another brood of the same sort," cautioned one newspaper, but on December 2, 1859, Virginia executed Brown. In life, he was a ne'er-do-well, but, as the poet Stephen Vincent Benét observed, "he knew how to die." Brown told his wife that he was "determined to make the utmost possible out of a defeat." He told the court: "If it is deemed necessary that I should forfeit my life for the furtherance of the ends of justice, and mingle my blood further with the blood of . . . millions in this slave country whose rights are disregarded by wicked, cruel, and unjust enactments, I say, let it be done."

After Brown's execution, Americans across the land contemplated the meaning of his life and death. Some Northerners celebrated his "splendid martyrdom." Ralph Waldo Emerson likened Brown to Christ when he declared that Brown made "the gallows as glorious as the cross." Most Northerners did not advocate bloody rebellion, however. Like Lincoln, they concluded that Brown's noble antislavery ideals could not "excuse violence, bloodshed, and treason."

Still, when northern churches marked John Brown's hanging with tolling bells, hymns, and prayer vigils, white Southerners contemplated what they had in common with people who "regard John Brown as a martyr and a Christian hero, rather than a murderer and robber." Georgia senator Robert Toombs announced solemnly that Southerners must "never permit this Federal government to pass into the traitorous hands of the black Republican party."

Republican Victory in 1860

When the Democrats converged on Charleston for their convention in April 1860, fire-eating Southerners denounced Stephen Douglas and demanded a platform that included federal protection of slavery in the territories, a goal of extreme proslavery Southerners for years. "Ours are the institutions which are at stake; ours is the property that is to be destroyed; ours is the honor at stake," shouted the Alabaman William Lowndes Yancy. When the delegates approved a platform with popular sovereignty, representatives from the entire Lower South and Arkansas stomped out of the convention. The remaining Democrats adjourned to meet a few weeks later in Baltimore, where they nominated Douglas for president.

When bolting southern Democrats reconvened, they approved a platform with a federal slave code and nominated Vice President John C. Breckinridge of Kentucky. Southern moderates, however, refused to support Breckinridge. They formed the Constitutional Union Party to provide voters with a Unionist choice. Instead of adopting a platform and confronting the slavery question, the Constitutional Union Party merely approved a vague resolution pledging "to recognize no political principle other than *the Constitution . . . the Union . . . and the Enforcement of the Laws.*" For president, they nominated former senator John Bell of Tennessee.

The Republicans smelled victory, but they needed to carry nearly all the free states to win. To make their party more appealing, they expanded their platform beyond antislavery. They hoped that free homesteads, a protective tariff, a transcontinental railroad, and a guarantee of immigrant political rights would provide an agenda broad enough to unify the North.

While reasserting their commitment to stop the spread of slavery, they also denounced John Brown's raid as "among the gravest of crimes" and confirmed the security of slavery in the South.

The foremost Republican, William H. Seward, had made enemies with his radical "higher law" doctrine, which claimed that there was a higher moral law than the Constitution, and with his "irrepressible conflict" speech, in which he declared that North and South were fated to collide. Lincoln, however, since bursting onto the national scene in 1858, had demonstrated his clear purpose, good judgment, and solid Republican credentials. That, and his residence in Illinois, a crucial state, made him attractive to the party. On the third ballot, the delegates chose Lincoln. Defeated by Douglas in a state contest less than two years earlier, Lincoln now stood ready to take him on for the presidency.

The election of 1860 was like none other in American politics. It took place in the midst of the nation's severest crisis. Four major candidates crowded the presidential field. Rather than a four-cornered contest, however, the election broke into two contests, each with two candidates. In the North, Lincoln faced Douglas; in the South, Breckinridge confronted Bell. So outrageous did Southerners consider the Republican Party that they did not even permit Lincoln's name to appear on the ballot in ten of the fifteen slave states.

On November 6, 1860, Lincoln swept all of the eighteen free states except New Jersey, which split its electoral votes between him and Douglas. Although Lincoln received only 39 percent of the popular vote, he won easily in the electoral college with 180 votes, 28 more than he needed for victory (Map 14.5). Lincoln did not win because his opposition was splintered. Even if the votes of his three opponents had been combined, Lincoln still would have won. He won because his votes were concentrated in the free states, which contained a majority of electoral votes. Ominously, however, Breckinridge, running on a southern-rights platform, won the entire Lower South, plus Delaware, Maryland, and North Carolina.

Secession Winter

Anxious Southerners immediately began debating what to do. Although Breckinridge had carried the South, a vote for "southern rights" was not necessarily a vote for secession. Besides,

VISUAL ACTIVITY

***John Brown Going to His Hanging,* by Horace Pippin, 1942**
The grandparents of Horace Pippin, a Pennsylvania artist, were slaves. His grandmother witnessed the hanging of John Brown, and this painting recalls the scene she so often described to him. Pippin used a muted palette to establish the bleak setting, but he also managed to convey its striking intensity. Historically accurate, the painting depicts Brown tied and sitting erect on his coffin, passing resolutely before the silent, staring white men. The black woman in the lower right corner presumably is Pippin's grandmother. Romare Bearden, another African American artist, recalled the central place of John Brown in black memory: "Lincoln and John Brown were as much a part of the actuality of the Afro-American experience, as were the domino games and the hoe cakes for Sunday morning breakfast. I vividly recall the yearly commemorations for John Brown." Courtesy of the Pennsylvania Academy of the Fine Arts, Philadelphia, www.pafa.org. John Lambert Fund.
READING THE IMAGE: What was the artist trying to convey about the tone of John Brown's execution? According to the painting, what were the feelings of those gathered to witness the event?
CONNECTIONS: How did Brown's trial and execution contribute to the growing split between North and South?

slightly more than half of the Southerners who had voted had cast ballots for Douglas and Bell, two stout defenders of the Union. "The people of the South have too much sense to attempt the ruin of the government," Lincoln predicted.

Southern Unionists tried to calm the fears that Lincoln's election triggered. Former congressman Alexander Stephens of Georgia asked what Lincoln had done to justify something as extreme as secession. Had he not promised to respect slavery where it existed? In Stephens's judgment, secession might lead to war, which would loosen the hinges of southern society and possibly even open the door to slave insurrection. "Revolutions are much easier started than controlled," he warned. "I consider slavery much more secure in the Union than out of it."

Candidate	Electoral Vote	Popular Vote	Percent of Popular Vote
Abraham Lincoln (Republican)	180	1,866,452	39.9
John C. Breckinridge (Southern Democrat)	72	847,953	18.1
Stephen A. Douglas (Northern Democrat)	12	1,375,157	29.4
John Bell (Constitutional Union)	39	590,631	12.6

Map 14.5
The Election of 1860

the Union on December 20, 1860. By February 1861, the six other Lower South states followed in South Carolina's footsteps. In general, slaveholders spearheaded secession, while non-slaveholders in the Piedmont and mountain counties, where slaves were relatively few, displayed the greatest attachment to the Union. In February, representatives from South Carolina, Georgia, Florida, Alabama, Mississippi, Louisiana, and Texas met in Montgomery, Alabama, where they created the **Confederate States of America**. Mississippi senator Jefferson Davis became president, and Alexander Stephens of Georgia, who had spoken so eloquently about the dangers of revolution, became vice president. In March 1861, Stephens declared that the Confederacy's "cornerstone" was "the great truth that the negro is not equal to the white man; that slavery, subordination to the superior race, is his natural and moral condition."

Lincoln's election had split the Union. Now secession split the South. Seven slave states seceded during the winter, but the eight slave states of the Upper South rejected secession, at least for the moment. The Upper South had a smaller stake in slavery. Barely half as many white families in the Upper South held slaves (21 percent) as in the Lower South (37 percent). Slaves represented twice as large a percentage of the population in the Lower South (48 percent) as in the Upper South (23 percent). Consequently, whites in the Upper South had fewer fears that Republican ascendancy meant economic catastrophe, social chaos, and racial war. Lincoln would need to do more than just be elected to provoke them into secession.

The nation had to wait until March 4, 1861, when Lincoln took office, to see what he would do. (Presidents-elect waited four months to take office until 1933, when the Twentieth Amendment to the Constitution shifted the inauguration to January 20.) He chose to stay in Springfield after his election and to say nothing. "Lame-duck" president James Buchanan sat in Washington and did nothing. Congress's efforts at cobbling together a peace-saving compromise came to nothing.

Secessionists emphasized the dangers of delay. "Mr. Lincoln and his party assert that this doctrine of equality applies to the negro," former Georgia governor Howell Cobb declared, "and necessarily there can exist no such thing as property in our equals." Lincoln's election without a single electoral vote from the South meant that Southerners were powerless to defend themselves within the Union, Cobb argued. Why wait, he asked, for abolitionists to attack? As for war, there would be none. The Union was a voluntary compact, and Lincoln would not coerce patriotism. If Northerners did resist with force, secessionists argued, one southern woodsman could whip five of Lincoln's greasy mechanics.

For all their differences, southern whites agreed that they had to defend slavery. John Smith Preston of South Carolina spoke for the overwhelming majority when he declared, "The South cannot exist without slavery." They disagreed about whether the mere presence of a Republican in the White House made it necessary to exercise what they considered a legitimate right to secede.

The debate about what to do was briefest in South Carolina, which seceded from

Secession of the Lower South, December 1860–February 1861

Lincoln began his inaugural address with reassurances

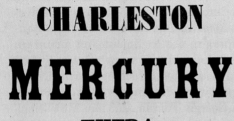

"The Union Is Dissolved"
On December 20, 1860, the *Charleston Mercury* put out this special edition of the paper to celebrate South Carolina's secession from the Union. Six weeks earlier, on hearing the news that Lincoln had won the presidency, the *Mercury* had predicted as much, announcing, "The revolution of 1860 has been initiated." Gilder Lehrman Collection, New York, USA/Bridgeman Images.

to the South. He had "no lawful right" to interfere with slavery where it existed, he declared again, adding for emphasis that he had "no inclination to do so." Conciliatory about slavery, Lincoln proved inflexible about the Union. The Union, he declared, was "perpetual." Secession was "anarchy" and "legally void." The Constitution required him to execute the law "in all the States."

The decision for war or peace rested in the South's hands, Lincoln said. "You can have no conflict, without being yourselves the aggressors. *You* have no oath registered in Heaven to destroy the government, while I shall have the most solemn one to 'preserve, protect, and defend' it."

REVIEW   Why were the states of the Lower and Upper South divided on the question of secession during the winter of 1860–61?

▶ Conclusion: Slavery, Free Labor, and the Failure of Political Compromise

As their economies, societies, and cultures diverged in the nineteenth century, Northerners and Southerners expressed different concepts of the American promise and the place of slavery within it. Their differences crystallized into political form in 1846 when David Wilmot proposed banning slavery in any territory won in the Mexican-American War. "As if by magic," a Boston newspaper observed, "it brought to a head the great question that is about to divide the American people." Discovery of gold and other precious metals in the West added urgency to the controversy over slavery in the territories. Congress attempted to address the issue with the Compromise of 1850, but the Fugitive Slave Act and the publication of *Uncle Tom's Cabin* hardened northern sentiments against slavery and confirmed southern suspicions of northern ill will. The bloody violence that erupted in Kansas in 1856 and the incendiary *Dred Scott* decision in 1857 further eroded hope for a solution to this momentous question.

During the extended crisis of the Union that stretched from 1846 to 1861, the slavery question intertwined with national politics. The traditional Whig and Democratic parties struggled to hold together as new parties, most notably the Republican Party, emerged. Politicians fixed their attention on the expansion of slavery, but from the beginning Americans recognized that the controversy had less to do with slavery in the territories than with the future of slavery in the nation.

For more than seventy years, statesmen had found compromises that accepted slavery and preserved the Union. But as each section grew increasingly committed to its labor system, Americans discovered that accommodation had limits. In 1859, John Brown's militant antislavery pushed white Southerners to the edge. In 1860, Lincoln's election convinced whites in the Lower South that slavery and the society they had built on it were at risk in the Union, and they seceded. But it remained to be seen whether disunion would mean war.

See the Selected Bibliography for this chapter in the Appendix.

14 Chapter Review

KEY TERMS

Wilmot Proviso (p. 377)
free labor (p. 377)
popular sovereignty (p. 378)
Compromise of 1850 (p. 380)
Uncle Tom's Cabin (p. 381)
Fugitive Slave Act (p. 381)
Kansas-Nebraska Act (p. 386)
Republican Party (p. 388)
"Bleeding Kansas" (p. 393)
Dred Scott decision (p. 395)
Lincoln-Douglas debates (p. 398)
Confederate States of America (p. 401)

REVIEW QUESTIONS

1. How might the Compromise of 1850 have eased sectional tensions? (pp. 377–381)

2. Why did the Compromise of 1850 fail to achieve sectional peace? (pp. 381–386)

3. Why did the Whig Party disintegrate in the 1850s? (pp. 386–389)

4. Why did the *Dred Scott* decision strengthen northern suspicions of a Slave Power conspiracy? (pp. 390–398)

5. Why were the states of the Lower and Upper South divided on the question of secession during the winter of 1860–61? (pp. 398–402)

MAKING CONNECTIONS

1. Compromise between slave and free states collapsed with secession. Why did compromise fail at this moment?

2. In the 1850s, many Americans supported popular sovereignty as the best solution to the explosive question of slavery in the western territories. Why was this solution so popular, and why did it ultimately prove inadequate?

3. In the 1840s and 1850s, the United States witnessed the realignment of its long-standing two-party system. Why did the old system fall apart, what emerged to take its place, and how did this process contribute to the coming of the Civil War?

4. Abraham Lincoln believed that he had staked out a moderate position on the question of slavery. Why, then, did some southern states determine that his election necessitated the radical act of secession?

LINKING TO THE PAST

1. How did social and economic developments in the South during the first half of the nineteenth century influence the decisions that southern politicians made in the 1840s and 1850s? (See chapter 13.)

2. How did the policies of the Republican Party reflect the free-labor ideals of the North? (See chapter 12.)

15 The Crucible of War

1861–1865

CONTENT LEARNING OBJECTIVES

After reading and studying this chapter, you should be able to:

- Describe what each side was fighting for and why they each believed they would win.

- Compare the Union's military results in the East and West in 1861 and 1862, and explain the significance of the Union blockade.

- Explain how the Civil War was transformed into a war to end slavery.

- Examine how the war affected Union and Confederate societies and economies, and how African Americans and women took part in the war effort.

- Describe how General Grant accomplished his plan for Union victory from 1863 to 1865 and why the Confederacy collapsed.

UNION PARADE DRUM
Drums signaled soldiers to report for breakfast, roll call, and guard duty, but the most important use of drums was on the battlefield, where they communicated orders from commanding officers to their troops. Photo courtesy Allan Katz Americana, Woodbridge, CT.

ON THE NIGHT OF SEPTEMBER 21, 1862, IN WILMINGTON, North Carolina, twenty-four-year-old William Gould and seven other runaway slaves crowded into a small boat on the Cape Fear River. They rowed hard throughout the night, reaching the Atlantic Ocean by dawn. They made for the Union navy patrolling offshore. At 10:30 that morning, the USS *Cambridge* took the men aboard. Astonishingly, on that same day President Abraham Lincoln revealed his intention to issue a proclamation of emancipation freeing the slaves in the Confederate states. Although Gould was not legally free, the U.S. Navy needed sailors and cared little about the formal status of runaway slaves. Within days, all eight runaways became sailors in the U.S. Navy.

William Gould could read and write, and he began keeping a diary. In some ways, Gould's naval experience looked like that of a white sailor. He found duty on a ship in the blockading squadron both boring and exhilarating, as days of tedious work were occasionally interrupted by a moment of "daring exploit."

But Gould's Civil War experience was shaped by his race. Like most black men in the Union military, he saw service as an opportunity to fight slavery. Gould linked union and freedom, "the holiest of all causes." Gould witnessed a number of ugly racial incidents, however. When a black regiment came aboard, "they were treated verry rough by the crew," he said.

The white sailors "refused to let them eat off the mess pans and called them all kinds of names[;] . . . in all they was treated shamefully."

Still, Gould was proud of his service in the navy and monitored the progress of racial equality during the war. In March 1865, he celebrated the "passage of an amendment of the Con[sti]tution prohibiting slavery througho[ut] the United States." And a month later, he thrilled to the "Glad Tidings that the Stars and Stripe[s] had been planted over the Capital of the D—nd Confederacy by the invincible Grant." He added, the nation must not forget the "Mayrters to the cau[se] of Right and Equality."

Early in the war, black abolitionist Frederick Douglass challenged the friends of freedom to *"be up and doing;—now is your time."* But for the first eighteen months of the war, federal soldiers officially fought only to uphold the Constitution and preserve the nation. Only with the Emancipation Proclamation in 1863 did the northern war effort take on a dual purpose: to save the Union and to free the slaves.

The Crew of the USS *Hunchback*
African Americans served as sailors in the federal military long before they were permitted to become soldiers. They initially served only as coal heavers, cooks, and stewards, but within a year some black sailors joined their ships' gun crews. The *Hunchback* was one of the Union's innovative ironclad ships. National Archives photo no. 111-B-2011.

As the world's first modern war, the Civil War transformed America. It mobilized the entire populations of North and South, harnessed the productive capacities of both economies, and produced battles that fielded 200,000 soldiers and created casualties in the tens of thousands. The carnage lasted four years and cost the nation approximately 750,000 lives. The war helped mold the modern American nation-state, and the federal government emerged with new power and responsibility over national life. It tore families apart and pushed women into new work and roles. But because the war ended slavery, it had truly revolutionary meaning.

Recalling the Civil War years, Frederick Douglass said, "It is something to couple one's name with great occasions." It *was* something—for William Gould and millions of other Americans. Whether they fought for the Confederacy or the Union, whether they labored behind the lines to supply Yankee or rebel soldiers, whether they prayed for the safe return of Northerners or Southerners, all Americans endured the crucible of war. But the war affected no group more than the nearly 4 million African Americans who saw its beginning as slaves and emerged as free people.

▶ "And the War Came"

Abraham Lincoln faced the worst crisis in the history of the nation: disunion. He revealed his strategy to save the Union in his inaugural address on March 4, 1861. He was firm yet conciliatory. First, he denied the right of secession and sought to stop its spread by avoiding any act that would push the skittish Upper South (North Carolina, Virginia, Maryland, Delaware, Kentucky, Tennessee, Missouri, and Arkansas) out of the Union. Second, he sought to reassure the seceding Lower South (South Carolina, Georgia, Florida, Alabama, Mississippi, Louisiana, and Texas) that the Republicans would not abolish slavery. Lincoln believed that Unionists there would assert themselves and overturn the secession decision. Always, Lincoln denied the right of secession and upheld the Union.

His counterpart, Jefferson Davis, fully intended to establish the Confederate States of America as an independent republic. To achieve permanence, Davis had to sustain the secession fever that had carried the Lower South out of the Union. Even if the Lower South held firm, however, the Confederacy would remain weak without additional states. Davis watched for opportunities to add new stars to the Confederate flag.

Neither man sought war; both wanted to achieve their objectives peacefully. As Lincoln later observed, "Both parties deprecated war, but one of them would *make* war rather than let the nation survive, and the other would *accept* war rather than let it perish. And the war came."

Attack on Fort Sumter

Major Robert Anderson and some eighty U.S. soldiers occupied **Fort Sumter**, which was perched on a tiny island at the entrance to Charleston harbor in South Carolina. The fort with its American flag became a hated symbol of the nation that Southerners had abandoned, and they wanted federal troops out. Sumter was also a symbol to Northerners, a beacon affirming federal authority in the seceded states.

Lincoln decided to hold the fort, but Anderson and his men were running dangerously short of food. In early April 1861, Lincoln authorized a peaceful expedition to bring supplies, but not military reinforcements, to the fort. The president understood that in seeking to relieve the fort he risked war, but his plan honored his inaugural promises to defend federal property and to avoid using military force unless first attacked.

CHRONOLOGY

1861
- Fort Sumter attacked.
- Four Upper South states join Confederacy.
- First battle of Bull Run (Manassas) fought.
- First Confiscation Act passes.

1862
- Grant captures Fort Henry and Fort Donelson.
- Battle of Glorieta Pass fought.
- Battle of Pea Ridge fought.
- Battle of Shiloh fought.
- Confederate Congress authorizes draft.
- Homestead Act passes.
- Virginia peninsula campaign waged.
- Second Confiscation Act passes.
- Militia Act passes.
- Battle of Antietam fought.

1863
- Emancipation Proclamation announced.
- National Banking Act passes.
- Congress authorizes draft.
- Vicksburg falls to Union forces.
- Lee defeated at battle of Gettysburg.
- New York City draft riots erupt.

1864
- Grant appointed Union general in chief.
- Wilderness campaign launches.
- Atlanta falls to Union forces.
- Lincoln reelected.
- Savannah falls to Union forces.

1865
- Petersburg and Richmond fall to Union forces.
- Lee surrenders to Grant.
- Lincoln assassinated; Vice President Andrew Johnson becomes president.

Fort Sumter
The Confederate bombardment that began the Civil War on April 12, 1861, lobbed more than 4,000 rounds at Fort Sumter. Shrapnel from thirty-three hours of cannon fire shredded this flag. Union major Robert Anderson surrendered on April 13. When he and his men evacuated the fort the next day, they marched under this tattered banner. When Anderson returned in April 1865, he raised this very flag. Photograph: © Collection of the New-York Historical Society, USA/ Bridgeman Images; flag: United Daughters of the Confederacy.

Masterfully, Lincoln had shifted the fateful decision of war or peace to Jefferson Davis.

On April 9, Davis and his cabinet met to consider the situation in Charleston harbor. Davis argued for military action, but his secretary of state, Robert Toombs of Georgia, replied: "Mr. President, at this time it is suicide, murder, and will lose us every friend at the North. You will wantonly strike a hornet's nest which extends from mountain to ocean, and legions now quiet will swarm out and sting us to death." But Davis ordered Confederate troops in Charleston to take the fort before the relief expedition arrived. Thirty-three hours of bombardment on April 12 and 13 reduced the fort to rubble. Major Anderson's surrender meant that the Confederates had Fort Sumter, but they also had war.

On April 15, when Lincoln called for 75,000 militiamen to serve for ninety days to put down the rebellion, several times that number rushed to defend the flag. Democrats responded as fervently as Republicans. Stephen A. Douglas, the recently defeated Democratic candidate for president, pledged his support and noted, "There can be no neutrals in this war, *only patriots—or traitors.*" But the people of the Upper South found themselves torn.

The Upper South Chooses Sides

The Upper South faced a horrendous choice: either to fight against the Lower South or to fight against the Union. Many who only months earlier had rejected secession now embraced the Confederacy. To vote against southern independence was one thing, to fight fellow Southerners quite another. Thousands felt betrayed, believing that Lincoln had promised to achieve a peaceful reunion by waiting patiently for Unionists to retake power in the seceding states. It was a "politician's war," one man declared, but he conceded that "this is no time now to discuss the causes, but it is the duty of all who regard Southern institutions of value to side with the South, make common cause with the Confederate States and sink or swim with them."

Virginia, Arkansas, Tennessee, and North Carolina joined the Confederacy (Map 15.1). But in the border states of Delaware, Maryland, Kentucky, and Missouri, Unionism triumphed. Only in Delaware, where slaves accounted for less than 2 percent of the population, was the victory easy. In Maryland, Unionism needed a helping hand. Lincoln suspended the writ of habeas corpus, essentially setting aside constitutional guarantees that protect citizens from arbitrary arrest and detention, and he ordered U.S. troops into Baltimore. Maryland's legislature rejected secession.

The struggle turned violent in the West. In Missouri, Unionists won a narrow victory, but southern-sympathizing guerrilla bands roamed the state for the duration of the war, terrorizing civilians and soldiers alike. In Kentucky, Unionists also narrowly defeated secession, but the pro-southern minority claimed otherwise. Throughout the border states, secession divided families. Seven of Kentuckian Henry Clay's grandsons fought: four for the Confederacy and three for the Union.

Lincoln understood that the border states—particularly Kentucky—contained indispensable resources, population, and wealth and also controlled major rivers and railroads. "I think to lose Kentucky is nearly the same as to lose the whole game," Lincoln said. "Kentucky gone, we can not hold Missouri, nor, as I think, Maryland.

Map 15.1
Secession, 1860–1861
After Lincoln's election, the fifteen slave states debated what to do. Seven states quickly left the Union, four left after the firing on Fort Sumter, and four remained loyal to the Union.

Legend:
- Seceded before fall of Fort Sumter
- Seceded after fall of Fort Sumter
- Slave state loyal to Union
- Free state
- Territory
- 1 Order of secession

These all against us, . . . we would as well consent to separation at once."

In the end, only eleven of the fifteen slave states joined the Confederate States of America. Moreover, the four seceding Upper South states contained significant numbers of people who felt little affection for the Confederacy. Dissatisfaction was so rife in the western counties of Virginia that in 1863 citizens there voted to create the separate state of West Virginia, loyal to the Union. Still, the acquisition of four new states greatly strengthened the Confederacy's drive for national independence.

> **REVIEW** Why did the attack on Fort Sumter force the Upper South to choose sides?

▶ The Combatants

Only slaveholders had a direct economic stake in preserving slavery, but most whites in the Confederacy defended the institution, the way of life built on it, and the Confederate nation. The degraded and subjugated status of blacks elevated the status of the poorest whites. One southerner declared, "It is enough that one simply belongs to the superior and ruling race, to secure consideration and respect." Moreover, Yankee "aggression" was no longer a mere threat; it was real and at the South's door.

For Northerners, the South's failure to accept the democratic election of a president and its firing on the nation's flag challenged the rule of law, the authority of the Constitution, and the ability of the people to govern themselves. As an Indiana soldier told his wife, a "good government is the best thing on earth. Property is nothing without it, because it is not protected; a family is nothing without it, because they cannot be educated." Only a Union victory, Lincoln declared, would secure America's promise "to elevate the condition of man."

Northerners and Southerners rallied behind their separate flags, fully convinced that they were in the right and that God was on their side. Yankees took heart from their superior power, but the rebels believed they had advantages that nullified every northern strength. Both sides mobilized swiftly in 1861, and each devised what it believed would be a winning military and diplomatic strategy.

How They Expected to Win

The balance sheet of northern and southern resources reveals enormous advantages for the Union (Figure 15.1). The twenty-three states remaining in the Union had a population of 22.3 million; the eleven Confederate states had a population of only 9.1 million, of whom 3.67 million (40 percent) were slaves. The North's economic advantages were even more

FIGURE 15.1 Resources of the Union and the Confederacy
The Union's enormous statistical advantages failed to convince Confederates that their cause was doomed.

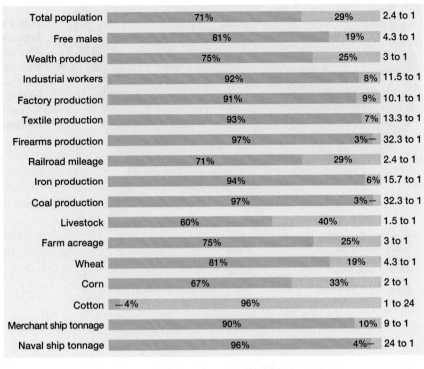

	Union	Confederacy	Ratio
Total population	71%	29%	2.4 to 1
Free males	81%	19%	4.3 to 1
Wealth produced	75%	25%	3 to 1
Industrial workers	92%	8%	11.5 to 1
Factory production	91%	9%	10.1 to 1
Textile production	93%	7%	13.3 to 1
Firearms production	97%	3%—	32.3 to 1
Railroad mileage	71%	29%	2.4 to 1
Iron production	94%	6%	15.7 to 1
Coal production	97%	3%—	32.3 to 1
Livestock	60%	40%	1.5 to 1
Farm acreage	75%	25%	3 to 1
Wheat	81%	19%	4.3 to 1
Corn	67%	33%	2 to 1
Cotton	—4%	96%	1 to 24
Merchant ship tonnage	90%	10%	9 to 1
Naval ship tonnage	96%	4%—	24 to 1

overwhelming. Yet Southerners expected to win—for some good reasons—and they came very close to doing so.

Southerners knew they bucked the military odds, but hadn't the liberty-loving colonists in 1776 also done so? "Britain could not conquer three million," a Louisianan proclaimed, and "the world cannot conquer the South." How could anyone doubt the outcome of a contest between lean, hard, country-born rebel warriors defending family, property, and liberty, and soft, flabby, citified Yankee mechanics waging an unconstitutional war?

The South's confidence also rested on its belief that northern prosperity depended on the South's cotton. Without cotton, New England textile mills would stand idle. Without planters purchasing northern manufactured goods, northern factories would drown in their own unsold surpluses. And without the foreign exchange earned by the overseas sales of cotton, the financial structure of the entire Yankee nation would collapse. A Virginian spoke for most Confederates when he declared that in the South's ability to "withhold the benefits of our trade, we hold a power over the North more powerful than a powerful army in the field."

Cotton would also make Europe a powerful ally of the Confederacy, Southerners reasoned. Of the 900 million pounds of cotton Britain imported annually, more than 700 million pounds came from the American South. If the supply was interrupted, sheer economic need would make Britain (and perhaps France) a Confederate ally. And because the British navy ruled the seas, the North would find Britain a formidable foe.

The Confederacy devised a military strategy to exploit its advantages and minimize its limitations. It recognized that a Union victory required the North to defeat and subjugate the South, but a Confederate victory required only that the South stay at home, blunt invasions, avoid battles that risked annihilating its army, and outlast the North's will to fight. When an opportunity presented itself, the South would strike the invaders. Like the American colonists, the South could win independence by not losing the war.

The Lincoln administration countered with an aggressive strategy designed to take advantage of its superior resources. Lincoln declared a naval blockade of the Confederacy to deny it the ability to sell cotton abroad, giving the South far fewer dollars to pay for war goods. Lincoln also ordered the Union army into Virginia, at the same time planning a march through the Mississippi valley that would cut the Confederacy in two.

Most Americans thought of war in terms of their most recent experience, the Mexican-American War in the 1840s. In Mexico, fighting had taken relatively small numbers of lives and had inflicted only light damage on the countryside. They could not imagine the four ghastly years of bloodletting that lay ahead.

Lincoln and Davis Mobilize

Mobilization required effective political leadership, and at first glance the South appeared to have the advantage. Jefferson Davis brought to the Confederate presidency a distinguished political career, including experience in the U.S. Senate. He was also a West Point graduate, a combat veteran and authentic hero of the Mexican-American War, and a former secretary of war. Dignified and ramrod straight, with "a jaw sawed in steel," Davis appeared to be everything a nation could want in a wartime leader.

By contrast, Abraham Lincoln brought to the White House one lackluster term in the House of Representatives and almost no administrative experience. His sole brush with anything military was as a captain in the militia in the Black Hawk War, a brief struggle in Illinois in 1832 in which whites expelled the last Indians from the state. The lanky, disheveled Illinois lawyer-politician looked anything but military or presidential in his bearing.

Davis, however, proved to be less than he appeared. Although he worked hard, he had no gift for military strategy yet intervened often in military affairs. He was an even less able political leader. Quarrelsome and proud, he had an acid tongue that made enemies the Confederacy could ill afford. In his defense, the Confederacy's intimidating problems might have defeated an even more talented leader.

With Lincoln the North got far more than met the eye. He proved himself a master politician and a superb leader. When forming his cabinet, Lincoln chose the ablest men, no matter that they were often his chief rivals and critics. He appointed Salmon P. Chase secretary of the treasury, knowing that Chase had presidential ambitions. As secretary of state, he chose his chief opponent for the Republican nomination in 1860, William H. Seward. Despite his civilian background, Lincoln displayed an innate understanding of military strategy. No one was more crucial in mapping the Union war plan.

Lincoln and Davis began gathering their armies. Confederates had to build almost everything from scratch, and Northerners had to channel their superior numbers and industrial resources to war. On the eve of the war, the federal army numbered only 16,000 men. One-third of the officers followed the example of the Virginian Robert E. Lee, resigning their commissions and heading south. The U.S. Navy was in better shape. Forty-two ships were in service, and a large merchant marine would in time provide more ships and sailors for the Union cause. Possessing a much weaker navy, the South pinned its hopes on its armies.

The Confederacy made prodigious efforts to build factories to supply its armies with tents, blankets, shoes, and uniforms, but even when factories produced what soldiers needed, southern railroads often could not deliver the goods. And each year, more railroads were captured, destroyed, or left in disrepair. Food production proved less of a problem, but food sometimes rotted before it reached the soldiers. The one bright spot was the Confederacy's Ordnance Bureau, headed by Josiah Gorgas. In April 1864, Gorgas proudly observed: "Where three years ago we were not making a gun, a pistol nor a sabre, no shot nor shell . . . we now make all these in quantities to meet the demands of our large armies."

Recruiting and supplying huge armies required enormous new revenues. At first, the Union and the Confederacy sold war bonds, which essentially were loans from patriotic citizens. In addition, both sides turned to taxes. Eventually, both began printing paper money. Inflation soared, but the Confederacy suffered more because it financed a greater part of its wartime costs through the printing press. Prices in the Union rose by about 80 percent during the war, while inflation in the Confederacy topped 9,000 percent.

Within months of the bombardment of Fort Sumter, both sides found men to fight and ways to supply them. But the underlying strength of the northern economy gave the Union the decided advantage. With their military and industrial muscles beginning to ripple, Northerners became itchy for action that would smash the rebellion. Horace Greeley's *New York Tribune* began to chant: "Forward to Richmond! Forward to Richmond!"

REVIEW   Why did the South believe it could win the war despite numerical disadvantages?

► Battling It Out, 1861–1862

During the first year and a half of the war, armies fought major campaigns in both the East and West. While the eastern campaign was more dramatic, Lincoln had trouble finding a capable general, and the fighting ended in a stalemate. Battles in the West proved more decisive. Union general Ulysses S. Grant won important victories in Kentucky and Tennessee. As Yankee and rebel armies pounded each other on land, the navies fought on the seas and on the rivers of the South. In Europe, Confederate and U.S. diplomats competed for advantage in the corridors of power. All the while, casualty lists on both sides reached appalling lengths.

Stalemate in the Eastern Theater

In the summer of 1861, Lincoln ordered the 35,000 Union troops assembling outside Washington to attack the 20,000 Confederates defending Manassas, a railroad junction in Virginia about thirty miles southwest of Washington. On July 21, the army forded Bull Run, a branch of the Potomac River, and engaged the southern forces (Map 15.2). But fast-moving southern reinforcements blunted the Union attack and then counterattacked. What began as an orderly Union retreat turned into a panicky stampede.

By Civil War standards, the casualties (wounded and dead) at the **battle of Bull Run** (or **Manassas**, as Southerners called the battle) were light, about 2,000 Confederates and 1,600 Federals. The significance of the battle lay in the lessons Northerners and Southerners drew from it. For Southerners, it confirmed the superiority of rebel fighting men and the inevitability of Confederate nationhood. Manassas was *"one of the decisive battles of the world,"* a Georgian proclaimed. It *"has* secured our independence." On the other hand, defeat sobered Northerners. It was a major setback, admitted the *New York Tribune*, but "let us go to work, then, with a will." Within four days of the disaster, the president authorized the enlistment of 1 million men for three years.

Lincoln also found a new general, the young George B. McClellan, whom he appointed commander of the newly named Army of the Potomac. Having graduated from West Point second in his class, the thirty-four-year-old McClellan believed that he was a great soldier and that Lincoln was a dunce, the "original Gorilla." A superb administrator and organizer, McClellan energetically whipped his dispirited soldiers into shape, but for all his energy, McClellan lacked decisiveness.

Lincoln wanted a general who would advance, take risks, and fight, but McClellan went into winter quarters. "If General McClellan does not want to use the army I would like to *borrow* it," Lincoln declared in frustration.

Finally, in May 1862, McClellan launched his long-awaited offensive. He transported his highly polished army, now 130,000 strong, to the mouth of the James River and began slowly moving up the Yorktown peninsula toward Richmond. When he was within six miles of the Confederate capital, General Joseph Johnston hit him like a hammer. In the assault, Johnston was wounded and was replaced by Robert E. Lee, who would become the South's most celebrated general. Lee named his command the Army of Northern Virginia.

The contrast between Lee and McClellan could hardly have been greater. McClellan brimmed with conceit; Lee was courteous and reserved. On the battlefield, McClellan grew timid and irresolute, and Lee became audaciously, even recklessly, aggressive. And Lee had at his side in the peninsula campaign military men of real talent: Thomas J. Jackson, nicknamed "Stonewall" for holding the line at Manassas, and James E. B. ("Jeb") Stuart, a dashing twenty-nine-year-old cavalry commander who rode circles around Yankee troops.

Lee's assault initiated the Seven Days Battle (June 25–July 1) and began McClellan's march back down the peninsula. By the time McClellan reached safety, 30,000 men from both sides had died or been wounded. Although Southerners suffered twice the casualties of Northerners, Lee had saved Richmond. Lincoln fired McClellan and replaced him with General John Pope.

In August, north of Richmond, at the second battle of Bull Run, Lee's smaller army battered Pope's forces and sent them scurrying back to Washington. Lincoln ordered Pope to Minnesota to pacify the Indians and restored McClellan to command. Lincoln had not changed his mind about McClellan's capacity as a warrior, but he had concluded, "There is no man in the Army who can lick these troops of ours into shape half as well as he. . . . If he can't fight himself, he excels in making others ready to fight."

Peninsula Campaign, 1862

Believing that he had the enemy on the run, Lee pushed his army across the Potomac and invaded Maryland. A victory on northern soil would dislodge Maryland from the Union, Lee reasoned, and might even cause Lincoln to sue for peace. On September 17, 1862, McClellan's forces engaged Lee's army at Antietam Creek (see Map 15.2). With "solid shot . . . cracking skulls like eggshells," according to one observer, the armies went after each other. At Miller's Cornfield, the firing was so intense that "every stalk of corn in the . . . field was cut as closely as could have been done with a knife." By nightfall, 6,000 men lay dead or dying on the battlefield, and 17,000 more had been wounded. The **battle of Antietam** would be the bloodiest day of the war and sent the battered Army of Northern Virginia limping back home. McClellan claimed to have saved the North, but Lincoln again removed him from command of the Army of the Potomac and appointed General Ambrose Burnside.

Though bloodied, Lee found an opportunity in December to punish the enemy at Fredericksburg, Virginia, where Burnside's 122,000 Union troops faced 78,500 Confederates dug in behind a stone wall on the heights above the Rappahannock River. Half a mile of open ground separated the armies. "A chicken could not live on that field when we open on it," a Confederate artillery officer predicted. Yet Burnside ordered a frontal assault. When the shooting ceased, the Federals counted nearly 13,000 casualties, the Confederates fewer than 5,000. The battle of Fredericksburg was one of the Union's worst defeats. As 1862 ended, the North seemed no nearer to ending the rebellion than it had been when the war began. Rather than checkmate, military struggle in the East had reached stalemate.

Union Victories in the Western Theater

While most eyes focused on events in the East, the decisive early encounters of the war were taking place between the Appalachian Mountains and the Ozarks (see Map 15.2). Confederates wanted Missouri and Kentucky, states they claimed but did not control. Federals wanted to

The Dead of Antietam
In October 1862, photographer Mathew Brady opened an exhibition that presented the battle of Antietam as the soldiers saw it. A *New York Times* reporter observed, "Mr. Brady has done something to bring to us the terrible reality and earnestness of the war. If he has not brought bodies and laid them in our door-yards and along [our] streets, he has done something very like it." Library of Congress, LC-DIG-cwpbh-03384.

split Arkansas, Louisiana, and Texas from the Confederacy by taking control of the Mississippi River and to occupy Tennessee, one of the Confederacy's main producers of food, mules, and iron—all vital resources.

Before Union forces could march on Tennessee, they needed to secure Missouri to the west. Union troops swept across Missouri to the border of Arkansas, where in March 1862 they encountered a 16,000-man Confederate army, which included three regiments of Indians from the so-called Five Civilized Tribes—the Choctaw, Chickasaw, Creek, Seminole, and Cherokee. The Union victory at the battle of Pea Ridge left Missouri free of Confederate troops, but guerrilla bands led by the notorious William Clarke Quantrill and "Bloody Bill" Anderson burned, tortured, scalped, and murdered Union civilians and soldiers until the final year of the war.

Battle of Glorieta Pass, 1862

Even farther west, Confederate armies sought to fulfill Jefferson Davis's vision of a slaveholding empire stretching all the way to the Pacific. Both sides recognized the immense value of the gold and silver mines of California, Nevada, and Colorado. And both sides bolstered their armies in the Southwest with Mexican Americans. A quick strike by Texas troops took Santa Fe, New Mexico, in the winter of 1861–62. Then in March 1862, a band of Colorado miners ambushed and crushed southern forces at Glorieta Pass, outside Santa Fe, effectively ending dreams of a Confederate empire beyond Texas.

The principal western battles took place in Tennessee, where General Ulysses S. Grant emerged as the key northern commander. Grant, a West Point graduate who served in Mexico, was a thirty-nine-year-old dry-goods clerk in Galena, Illinois, when the war began. Gentle

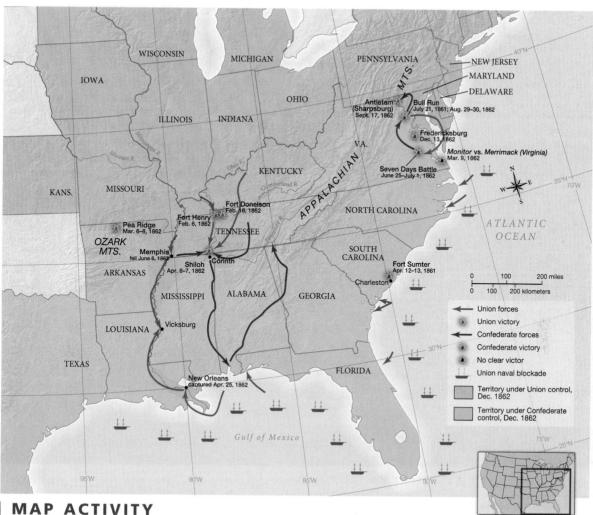

MAP ACTIVITY

Map 15.2   The Civil War, 1861–1862

While most eyes were focused on the eastern theater, especially the ninety-mile stretch of land between Washington, D.C., and the Confederate capital of Richmond, Virginia, Union troops were winning strategic victories in the West.

READING THE MAP: In which states did the Confederacy and the Union each win the most battles during this period? Which side used or followed water routes most for troop movements and attacks?

CONNECTIONS: Which major cities in the South and West fell to Union troops in 1862? Which strategic area did those Confederate losses place in Union hands? How did this outcome affect the later movement of troops and supplies?

at home, he became pugnacious on the battlefield. "The art of war is simple," he said. "Find out where your enemy is, get at him as soon as you can and strike him as hard as you can, and keep moving on." Grant's philosophy of war as attrition would take a huge toll in human life, but it played to the North's superiority in manpower. Later, to critics who wanted the president to sack Grant because of his drinking, Lincoln would say, "*I can't spare this man. He fights.*"

In February 1862, operating in tandem with U.S. Navy gunboats, Grant captured Fort Henry on the Tennessee River and Fort Donelson on the Cumberland (see Map 15.2). Defeat forced the Confederates to withdraw from all of Kentucky and most of Tennessee, but Grant followed.

On April 6, General Albert Sidney Johnston's army surprised Grant at Shiloh Church in Tennessee. Union troops were badly mauled the first day, but Grant remained cool and brought up reinforcements throughout the night. The next morning, the Union army counterattacked, driving the Confederates before it. The **battle of Shiloh** was terribly costly to both sides; there

VISUAL ACTIVITY

Battle of Fredericksburg, 1862

This painting by Private John Richards of the New York Volunteers captures the behind-the-lines Union activity at the battle of Fredericksburg. Long rows of fresh troops await orders to march up the hill to join the fighting under way in the distance. Barely visible, the cavalry charges off into one of the Union's greatest failures. These foot soldiers will follow the cavalry soon. Private Collection/Peter Newark Military Pictures/Bridgeman Images.

READING THE IMAGE: What does the artist portray in the lower left of the painting? What are the lines of wagons hauling?

CONNECTIONS: At Fredericksburg, General Ambrose Burnside joined the list of failed Union generals. What other Union defeats can be attributed, at least in part, to failed Union leadership?

were 20,000 casualties, among them General Johnston. Grant later said that after Shiloh he "gave up all idea of saving the Union except by complete conquest."

Although no one knew it at the time, Shiloh ruined the Confederacy's bid to control the theater of operations in the West. The Yankees quickly captured the strategic town of Corinth, Mississippi; the river city of Memphis; and the South's largest city, New Orleans. By the end of 1862, the far West and most—but not all—of the Mississippi valley lay in Union hands. At the same time, the outcome of the struggle in another theater of war was also becoming clearer.

The Atlantic Theater

When the war began, the U.S. Navy's blockade fleet consisted of about three dozen ships to patrol more than 3,500 miles of southern coastline, and rebel merchant ships were able to slip in and out of southern ports nearly at will. Taking on cargoes in the Caribbean, sleek Confederate blockade runners brought in vital supplies—guns and medicine. But with the U.S. Navy commissioning a new blockader almost weekly, the naval fleet eventually numbered 150 ships on duty, and the Union navy dramatically improved its score.

Unable to build a conventional navy equal to the expanding U.S. fleet, the Confederates experimented with a radical new maritime design: the ironclad warship. At Norfolk, Virginia, the wooden hull of the *Merrimack* was layered with two-inch-thick armor plate. Rechristened *Virginia*, the ship steamed out in March 1862 and sank two wooden federal ships (see Map 15.2). When the *Virginia* returned to finish off the federal blockaders the next morning, it was challenged by the *Monitor*, a federal ironclad of even more radical design, topped with a revolving turret holding two eleven-inch guns. On March 9, the two ships hurled shells at each other for two hours, but the battle ended in a draw.

The Confederacy never found a way to break the **Union blockade** despite exploring many naval innovations, including a new underwater vessel—the submarine. By 1865, the blockaders were intercepting about half of the southern ships attempting to break through. The Union navy, a southern naval officer observed, "shut the Confederacy out from the world, deprived it of supplies, weakened its military and naval strength." The Confederacy was sealed off, with devastating results.

International Diplomacy

What the Confederates could not achieve on the seas, they sought to achieve through international diplomacy. They based their hope for European intervention on King Cotton. In theory, cotton-starved European nations would have no choice but to break the Union blockade

Major Battles of the Civil War, 1861–1862

April 12–13, 1861	Attack on Fort Sumter
July 21, 1861	First battle of Bull Run (Manassas)
February 6, 1862	Battle of Fort Henry
February 16, 1862	Battle of Fort Donelson
March 6–8, 1862	Battle of Pea Ridge
March 9, 1862	Battle of the *Merrimack* (the *Virginia*) and the *Monitor*
March 26, 1862	Battle of Glorieta Pass
April 6–7, 1862	Battle of Shiloh
May–July 1862	McClellan's peninsula campaign
June 6, 1862	Fall of Memphis
June 25–July 1, 1862	Seven Days Battle
August 29–30, 1862	Second battle of Bull Run (Manassas)
September 17, 1862	Battle of Antietam
December 13, 1862	Battle of Fredericksburg

FIGURE 15.2 **Global Comparison: European Cotton Imports, 1860–1870**

In 1860, the South enjoyed a near monopoly in supplying cotton to Europe's textile mills, but the Civil War almost entirely halted its exports. Figures for Europe's importation of cotton from 1861 to 1865 reveal one of the reasons the Confederacy's King Cotton diplomacy failed: Europeans found other sources of cotton. Which countries were most important in filling the void? When the war ended in 1865, cotton production resumed in the South, and exports to Europe again soared. Did the South regain its near monopoly? How would you characterize the United States' competitive position five years after the war?

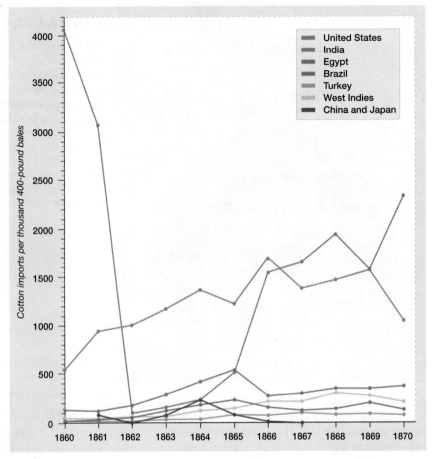

and recognize the Confederacy. Southern hopes were not unreasonable, for at the height of the "cotton famine" in 1862, when 2 million British workers were unemployed, Britain tilted toward recognition. Along with several other European nations, Britain granted the Confederacy "belligerent" status, which enabled it to buy goods and build ships in European ports. But no country challenged the Union blockade or recognized the Confederate States of America as a nation, a bold act that probably would have drawn that country into war.

King Cotton diplomacy failed for several reasons. A bumper cotton crop in 1860 meant that the warehouses of British textile manufacturers bulged with surplus cotton throughout 1861. In 1862, when a cotton shortage did occur, European manufacturers found new sources in India, Egypt, and elsewhere (Figure 15.2). In addition, the development of a brisk trade between the Union and Britain—British war materiel for American grain and flour—helped offset the

decline in textiles and encouraged Britain to remain neutral.

Europe's temptation to intervene disappeared for good in 1862. Union military successes in the West made Britain and France think twice about linking their fates to the struggling Confederacy. Moreover, in September 1862, Lincoln announced a new policy that made an alliance with the Confederacy an alliance with slavery—a commitment the French and British, who had outlawed slavery in their empires and looked forward to its eradication worldwide, were not willing to make. After 1862, the South's cause was linked irrevocably with slavery and reaction, and the Union's cause was linked with freedom and democracy. The Union, not the Confederacy, had won the diplomatic stakes.

REVIEW After a year and a half of fighting, who had the advantage in the war?

► Union *and* Freedom

For a year and a half, Lincoln insisted that the North fought strictly to save the Union and not to abolish slavery. Nevertheless, the war for union became a war for African American freedom. Each month the conflict dragged on, it became clearer that the Confederate war machine depended heavily on slavery. Rebel armies used slaves to build fortifications, haul materiel, tend horses, and perform camp chores. On the southern home front, slaves labored in ironworks and shipyards, and they grew the food that fed both soldiers and civilians. As Frederick Douglass put it, slavery was the "stomach of this rebellion." Slavery undergirded the Confederacy as certainly as it had the Old South. In the field among Union military commanders, in the halls of Congress, and in the White House, the truth gradually came into focus: To defeat the Confederacy, the North would have to destroy slavery. "I am a slow walker," Lincoln said, "but I never walk back." Lincoln's Emancipation Proclamation began the work, and soon African Americans flooded into the Union army, where they fought against the Confederacy and for black freedom.

From Slaves to Contraband

Lincoln detested human bondage, but as president he felt compelled to act prudently in the interests of the Union. He doubted his right under the Constitution to tamper with the "domestic institutions" of any state, even states in rebellion. An astute politician, Lincoln worked within the tight limits of public opinion. The issue of black freedom was particularly explosive in the loyal border states, where slaveholders threatened to jump into the arms of the Confederacy at even the hint of emancipation.

Black freedom also raised alarms in the free states. The Democratic Party gave notice that adding emancipation to the goal of union would make the war strictly a Republican affair. Moreover, many white Northerners were not about to risk their lives to satisfy what they considered abolitionist "fanaticism." "We Won't Fight to Free the Nigger," one popular banner read. They feared that emancipation would propel "two or three million semi-savages" northward, where they would crowd into white neighborhoods, compete for white jobs, and mix with white "sons and daughters." Thus, emancipation threatened to dislodge the loyal slave states from the Union, alienate the Democratic Party, deplete the armies, and perhaps even spark race warfare.

Yet proponents of emancipation pressed Lincoln as relentlessly as did the anti-emancipation forces. Abolitionists argued that by seceding, Southerners had forfeited their right to the protection of the Constitution and that Lincoln could—as the price of their treason—legally confiscate their property in slaves. When Lincoln refused, abolitionists scalded him. Frederick Douglass labeled him "the miserable tool of traitors and rebels."

The Republican-dominated Congress declined to leave slavery policy entirely in President Lincoln's hands. In August 1861, Congress approved the Confiscation Act, which allowed the seizure of any slave employed directly by the Confederate military. It also fulfilled the free-soil dream of prohibiting slavery in the territories and abolished slavery in Washington, D.C. Democrats and border-state representatives voted against even these mild measures.

Slaves, not politicians, became the most insistent force for emancipation. By escaping their masters by the tens of thousands and running away to Union lines, they forced slavery on the North's wartime agenda. Runaways made Northerners answer a crucial question: Were the runaways now free, or were they still slaves who, according to the fugitive slave law, had to be returned to their masters? At first, Yankee military officers sent the fugitives back. But Union armies needed laborers, and at Fort Monroe, Virginia, General Benjamin F. Butler called runaways **contraband of war**, meaning "confiscated property," and put them to work. Congress made Butler's practice national policy in March 1862 when it forbade returning fugitive slaves to their masters. Slaves were still not legally free, but there was a tilt toward emancipation.

Lincoln's policy of noninterference with slavery gradually crumbled. To calm Northerners' racial fears, Lincoln offered colonization, the deportation of African Americans from the United States to Haiti, Panama, or elsewhere. In the summer of 1862, he told a delegation of black visitors that racial prejudice among whites made it impossible for blacks to achieve equality in the United States. One African American responded, "This is our country as much as it is yours, and we will not leave it." Congress voted a small amount of money to underwrite colonization, but practical limitations and stiff black opposition sank the scheme.

While Lincoln was developing his own anti-slavery initiatives, he snuffed out actions that

Human Contraband

These refugees from slavery crossed the Rappahannock River in Virginia in August 1862 to seek sanctuary with a federal army. Most slaves fled with little more than the clothes on their backs, but not all escaped slavery empty-handed. The oxen, horse, wagon, and goods seen here could have been purchased during slavery, "borrowed" from the former master, or gathered during flight. Library of Congress, LC-DIG-cwpb-00218.

he believed would jeopardize northern unity. He was particularly alert to Union commanders who tried to dictate slavery policy from the field. In August 1861, when John C. Frémont, former Republican presidential nominee and now commander of federal troops in Missouri, freed the slaves belonging to Missouri rebels, Lincoln forced the general to revoke his edict. The following May, when General David Hunter freed the slaves in Georgia, South Carolina, and Florida, Lincoln countermanded his order. Events moved so rapidly, however, that Lincoln found it impossible to control federal policy on slavery.

From Contraband to Free People

On August 22, 1862, Lincoln replied to an angry abolitionist who demanded that he attack slavery. "My paramount objective in this struggle *is* to save the Union," Lincoln said, "and is *not* either to save or destroy slavery. If I could save the Union without freeing *any* slave I would do it, and if I could save it by freeing *all* the slaves I would do it; and if I could save it by freeing some and leaving others alone I would also do that." At first glance, Lincoln seemed to restate his old position that union was the North's sole objective. Instead, Lincoln announced that slavery was no longer untouchable and that he would emancipate every slave if doing so would preserve the Union.

By the summer of 1862, events were tumbling rapidly toward emancipation. On July 17, Congress adopted the second Confiscation Act. The first had confiscated slaves employed by the Confederate military; the second declared all slaves of rebel masters "forever free of their servitude." In theory, this breathtaking measure freed most Confederate slaves, for slaveholders formed the backbone of the rebellion. Congress had traveled far since the war began.

Lincoln had too. By July 1862, the president had come to believe that emancipation was "a military necessity, absolutely essential to the preservation of the Union." The lengthening casualty lists had finally brought him around. In September, he announced his preliminary **Emancipation Proclamation** that promised to free *all* the slaves in the seceding states on January 1, 1863. The limitations of the proclamation—it exempted the loyal border states and the Union-occupied areas of the Confederacy—caused some to ridicule the act. The *Times* (London) observed cynically, "Where he has no power Mr. Lincoln will set the negroes free, where he retains power he will consider them as slaves." But Lincoln had no power to free slaves in loyal states, and invading Union armies would liberate slaves in the Confederacy as they advanced.

By presenting emancipation as a "military necessity," Lincoln hoped to disarm his conservative critics. Emancipation would deprive the Confederacy of valuable slave laborers, shorten the war, and thus save lives. Democrats, however, fumed that the "shrieking and howling abolitionist faction" had captured the White House and made it "a nigger war." Democrats gained thirty-four congressional seats in the November 1862 elections. House Democrats quickly proposed a resolution branding emancipation "a high crime

Black Dockworkers, Virginia
Hundreds of thousands of able-bodied free blacks and runaways cleared forests, built roads, erected bridges, constructed fortifications, and transported supplies for the U.S. Army. Their labor became indispensable to the war effort, and as one Northerner remembered, "The truth was we never could get enough of them." These men unloaded Union ships at an unnamed Virginia dock. National Archives photo no. 111-B-400.

against the Constitution." The Republicans, who maintained narrow majorities in both houses of Congress, barely beat it back.

As promised, on New Year's Day 1863, Lincoln issued the final Emancipation Proclamation. In addition to freeing the slaves in the rebel states, the Emancipation Proclamation also committed the federal government to the fullest use of African Americans to defeat the Confederate enemy.

The War of Black Liberation

Even before Lincoln proclaimed emancipation a Union war aim, African Americans in the North had volunteered to fight. Military service, one black volunteer declared, would mean "the elevation of a downtrodden and despised race." But the War Department, doubtful of blacks' abilities and fearful of white reaction to serving side by side with them, refused to make black men soldiers. Instead, the army employed black men as manual laborers; black women sometimes found employment as laundresses and cooks. The navy, however, accepted blacks from the outset, includ-

ing runaway slaves such as William Gould (see pages 405–6).

As Union casualty lists lengthened, Northerners gradually and reluctantly turned to African Americans to fill the army's blue uniforms. With the Militia Act of July 1862, Congress authorized enrolling blacks in "any military or naval service for which they may be found competent." After the Emancipation Proclamation, whites—like it or not—were fighting and dying for black freedom, and few insisted that blacks remain out of harm's way behind the lines. Indeed, whites insisted that blacks share the danger, especially after March 1863, when Congress resorted to the draft to fill the Union army.

The military was far from color-blind. The Union army established segregated black regiments, paid black soldiers $10 per month rather than the $13 it paid whites, refused blacks the opportunity to become commissioned officers, punished blacks as if they were slaves, and assigned blacks to labor battalions rather than to combat units. Still, when the war ended, 179,000 African American men had served in the Union

The Right to Fight: Black Soldiers in the Civil War

"A war undertaken and brazenly carried on for the perpetual enslavement of colored men, calls logically and loudly for colored men to help suppress it," black leader Frederick Douglass declared at the beginning of the Civil War. But it was only in 1863 that the lengthening casualty lists finally convinced the Lincoln administration to begin aggressively recruiting black soldiers.

In February 1863, James Henry Gooding, a twenty-six-year-old seaman from New Bedford, enlisted in the 54th Massachusetts Colored Regiment. Like most black soldiers, Gooding viewed military service as an opportunity to strike blows against slavery. The destruction of slavery, he believed, "depends on the free black men of the North" because "those who are in bonds must have some one to open the door; when the slave sees the white soldier approach, he dares not trust him and why? Because he has heard that *some* have treated him worse than their owners in rebellion. But if the slave sees a black soldier, he knows he has got a friend."

Fighting for the Union also offered a chance to attack white racism. In military service lay "the germs of the elevation of a downtrodden and despised race," Gooding believed, the chance for African Americans "to make themselves a people." Fighting, Gooding said, offered blacks a chance to destroy the "foul aspersion that they were not men."

According to the white commander of the 59th U.S. Colored Infantry, when an ex-slave put on a uniform of army blue, the change was dramatic: "Yesterday a filthy, repulsive 'nigger,' to-day a neatly-attired man; yesterday a slave, to-day a freeman; yesterday a civilian, to-day a soldier." Others noticed the same transformation: "Put a United States uniform on his back and the *chattel* is a man." Black veterans agreed. "This was the biggest thing that ever happened in my life," one ex-soldier remembered. "I felt like a man with a uniform and a gun in my hand." Another said, "I felt freedom in my bones."

Black courage under fire ended skepticism about the capabilities of African American troops. As one white officer observed after a battle, "They seemed like men who were fighting to vindicate their manhood and they did it well." Another remarked, "they have fought their way into the respect of all the army." After the 54th served courageously in South Carolina, Gooding reported: "It is not for us to blow our horn; but when a regiment of white men gave us three cheers as we were passing them, it shows that we did our duty as men should."

Yet discrimination within the Union army continued. When the government refused to pay blacks the same as whites, the 54th refused to accept unequal pay. Gooding wrote to President Lincoln himself to explain his regiment's decision: "Now the main question is, Are we Soldiers, or are we Labourers? . . . Now your Excellency, we have done a Soldier's Duty. Why Can't we have a Soldier's pay?" The 54th's principled stance helped reverse the government's position, and in June 1864 Congress equalized the pay of black and white soldiers.

As Union troops advanced deeper into the Confederacy, former slaves greeted black soldiers as heroes. In March 1865, the white officer of a black regiment in North Carolina reported that black soldiers "stepped like lords & conquerors. The frantic demonstrations of the army. An astounding 71 percent of black men ages eighteen to forty-five in the free states wore Union blue, a participation rate substantially higher than that of white men.

In time, whites allowed blacks to put down their shovels and to shoulder rifles. At the battles of Port Hudson and Milliken's Bend on the Mississippi River and at Fort Wagner in Charleston harbor, black courage under fire finally dispelled notions that African Americans could not fight. More than 38,000 black soldiers died in the Civil War, a mortality rate that was higher than that of white troops. Blacks played a crucial role in the triumph of the Union and the destruction of slavery in the South. (See "Experiencing the American Promise," above.)

From the beginning, African Americans viewed the Civil War as a revolutionary struggle to overthrow slavery and to gain equality for their entire race. "Once let the black man get upon his person the brass letters, U.S.; let him get an eagle on his button, and a musket on his shoulder and bullets in his pocket," Frederick Douglass predicted, "and there is no power on earth which can deny that he has earned the right of citizenship." When black men became soldiers, they and

negro population will never die out of my memory. Their cheers & heartfelt 'God bress ye's' & cries of 'De chains is broke; De chains is broke' mingled sublimely with the lusty shout of our brave soldiery." Hardened and disciplined by their military service, black soldiers drew tremendous strength from their participation in the Union effort. Despite their second-class status, they found army life a great counterweight to the degradation and dependency of slavery.

Eager to shoulder the rights, privileges, and responsibilities of freedom, black veterans often took the lead in the hard struggle for equality after the war. Blacks in the Union army that occupied the South after 1865 assumed a special obligation to protect former slaves. "The fact is," one black chaplain said, "when colored soldiers are about they [whites] are afraid to kick colored women and abuse colored people on the Streets, as they usually do." Black veterans believed that their military service entitled African Americans not only to freedom but also to civil and political rights. Sergeant Henry Maxwell announced: "We want two more boxes besides the cartridge box—the ballot and the jury box." Black men had demonstrated what they could do when permitted to become soldiers; they now demanded the chance to perform as citizens.

James Henry Gooding did not have a chance to participate in the postwar struggle for equal rights.

64th Colored Infantry, Palmyra Bend, Mississippi
The Lincoln administration was slow to accept black soldiers into the Union army, but eventually the valor of black troops eroded white skepticism. Here the 64th Colored Infantry stands in formation in front of their rough winter cabins, with their stacked rifles in the foreground.
Library of Congress, LC-DIG-ppmsca-34152.

Wounded and captured at the battle of Olustee in Florida, he was sent to the infamous Confederate prison Andersonville, where he died on July 19, 1864.

Questions for Analysis

Recognize Viewpoints: Why did the Union resist enrolling black troops?

Analyze the Evidence: What specific benefits or opportunities did black men encounter as a result of military service?

Consider the Context: Why was the right to fight so important to black men? In what ways do you think military service by black men would have been important to the entire black community?

their families gained new confidence and self-esteem. Military service taught them new skills and introduced them to political struggle as they battled for their rights within the army. Wartime experiences stood them in good stead when the war of liberation was over and the battle for equality began. But first there was a rebellion to put down. Victory depended as much on what happened behind the lines as on the battlefields.

REVIEW How did the war for union become a war for black freedom?

▶ The South at War

By seceding, Southerners brought on themselves a firestorm of unimaginable fury. Monstrous losses on the battlefield nearly bled the Confederacy to death. Southerners on the home front also suffered, even at the hands of their own government. Efforts by the Davis administration in Richmond to centralize power in order to fight the war convinced some men and women that the Confederacy had betrayed them. They charged Richmond with tyranny when it impressed goods

VISUAL ACTIVITY

John Wallace Comer, C.S.A., with His Servant, Burrell

Many slaveholders took personal servants with them to war. These slaves cooked, washed, and cleaned for their owners. Owners sometimes dressed their servants in uniforms, as Comer did, which led some observers to conclude erroneously that slaves were members of the Confederate military. Alabama Department of Archives and History, Montgomery, Alabama.

READING THE IMAGE: How would you describe the expressions on the men's faces? Similar? Different? CONNECTIONS: What are the possible ramifications of slaveholders bringing "body servants" to war? How were nonslaveholding soldiers, who did their own chores, likely to have responded?

and slaves and drafted men into the army. War also meant severe economic deprivation. Shortages and inflation hurt everyone, some more than others. By 1863, unequal suffering meant that planters and yeomen who had stood together began to drift apart. Most disturbing of all, slaves became open participants in the destruction of slavery and the Confederacy.

Revolution from Above

As a Confederate general observed, Southerners were engaged in a total war "in which the whole population and the whole production . . . are to be put on a war footing, where every institution is to be made auxiliary to war." Jefferson Davis faced the task of building an army and a navy from almost nothing, supplying them from factories that were scarce and anemic, and paying for it all from a treasury that did not exist. Finding eager soldiers proved easiest. Hundreds of officers defected from the U.S. Army, and hundreds of thousands of eager young rebels volunteered to follow them.

The Confederacy's economy and finances proved tougher problems. Because of the Union blockade, the government had no choice but to build an industrial sector itself. Government-owned clothing and shoe factories, mines, arsenals, and powder works sprang up. The government also harnessed private companies, such as the huge Tredegar Iron Works in Richmond, to the war effort. Paying for the war became the most difficult task. A flood of paper money caused debilitating inflation. By Christmas 1864, a Confederate soldier's monthly pay no longer bought a pair of socks. The Confederacy manufactured much more than most people imagined possible, but it never produced all that the South needed.

Richmond's war-making effort brought unprecedented government intrusion into the private lives of Confederate citizens. In April 1862, the Confederate Congress passed the first conscription (draft) law in American history. All able-bodied white males between the ages of eighteen and thirty-five (later seventeen and fifty) were liable to serve in the rebel army. The government adopted a policy of impressment, which allowed officials to confiscate food, horses, wagons, and whatever else they wanted from private citizens and to pay for them at below-market rates. After March 1863, the Confederacy legally impressed slaves, employing them as military laborers.

Richmond's centralizing efforts ran head-on into the South's traditional values of states' rights and unfettered individualism. Southerners lashed out at what Georgia governor Joseph E. Brown denounced as the "dangerous usurpation by Congress of the reserved right of the States." Richmond and the states struggled for control of money, supplies, and soldiers, with damaging consequences for the war effort.

Hardship Below

Hardships on the home front fell most heavily on the poor. The draft stripped yeoman farms of men, leaving the women and children to grow what they ate. Government agents took 10 percent of harvests as a "tax-in-kind" on agriculture. Like inflation, shortages afflicted the entire population, but the rich lost luxuries while the poor lost necessities. In the spring of 1863, bread riots broke out in a dozen cities and villages across the South. In Richmond, a mob of nearly a thousand hungry women broke into shops and took what they needed.

"Men cannot be expected to fight for the Government that permits their wives & children to starve," one Southerner observed. Although a few wealthy individuals shared their bounty and the Confederate and state governments made efforts at social welfare, every attempt fell short. In late 1864, one desperate farmwife told her husband, "I have always been proud of you, and since your connection with the Confederate army, I have been prouder of you than ever before. I would not have you do anything wrong for the world, but before God, Edward, unless you come home, we must die." When the war ended, one-third of the soldiers had already gone home. A Mississippi deserter explained, "We are poor men and are willing to defend our country but our families [come] first." (See "Analyzing Historical Evidence," page 426.)

Yeomen perceived a profound inequality of sacrifice. They called it "a rich man's war and a poor man's fight." The draft law permitted a man who had money to hire a substitute to take his place. Moreover, the "twenty-Negro law" exempted one white man on every plantation with twenty or more slaves. The government intended this law to provide protection for white women and to see that slaves tended the crops, but yeomen perceived it as rich men evading military service. A Mississippian complained that stay-at-home planters sent their slaves into the fields to grow cotton while in plain view "poor soldiers' wives are plowing with *their own* hands to make a subsistence for themselves and children—while their husbands are suffering, bleeding and dying for their country." In fact, most slaveholders went off to war, but the extreme suffering of common folk and the relative immunity of planters increased class friction.

The Richmond government hoped that the crucible of war would mold a region into a nation. Officials actively promoted Confederate nationalism to "excite in our citizens an ardent and enduring attachment to our Government and its institutions." Clergymen assured their congregations that God had blessed slavery and the new nation. Jefferson Davis claimed that the Confederacy was part of a divine plan and asked citizens to observe national days of fasting and prayer. But these efforts failed to win over thousands of die-hard Unionists, and animosity between yeomen and planters increased. The war also threatened to rip the southern social fabric along its racial seam.

The Disintegration of Slavery

The legal destruction of slavery was the product of presidential proclamation, congressional legislation, and eventually constitutional amendment, but the practical destruction of slavery was the product of war, what Lincoln called war's "friction and abrasion." Slaves took advantage of the upheaval to reach for freedom. Some half a million of the South's 4 million slaves ran away to Union military lines. More than 100,000 runaways took up arms as federal soldiers and sailors and attacked slavery directly. Other men and women stayed in the slave quarter, where they staked their claim to more freedom.

War disrupted slavery in a dozen ways. Almost immediately, it called the master away, leaving the mistress to assume responsibility for the plantation. But mistresses could not maintain traditional standards of slave discipline in wartime, and the balance of power shifted. Slaves got to the fields late, worked indifferently, and quit early. Some slaveholders responded violently; most saw no alternative but to strike bargains—offering gifts or part of the crop—to keep slaves at home and at work. An Alabama complained that she "begged . . . what little is done." Slaveholders had believed that they "knew" their

Home and Country

Christian Marion Epperly and his wife, Mary Epperly, lived in the Blue Ridge Mountains of Virginia. Although neither was an ardent secessionist, Marion entered the Confederate army as a private early in 1862. He hated army life and longed for his wife and children. Mary was equally heartsick without Marion. Despite their limited schooling, the couple's letters reveal how plain folks wrestled with the tangled issues of loyalty and obligation.

DOCUMENT 1
Letter from Chickahominy Creek, Virginia, May 16, 1862

During the peninsula campaign in Virginia, as Union general George B. McClellan was approaching the Confederate capital of Richmond, Marion wrote to Mary from near the action.

I think the people will be bound to suffer for something to eat[;] the grain is all destroid and nearly all the fenses is burnt up from yorktown to Richmond: it looks distressing just to travel along the road: the wheat up waist hi some of it and horses and cattle has eat the most of it to the ground and I think the yankees will make a finish of the ballans [balance] that is left but the[y] cant doo much more damage than our army did[;] our own men killed all the cattle and hogs & sheep that the farmers had[,] even took ther chickens[;] every thing is totally destroid in this part of the State. . . .

I hope and pray this awful war will soon come to a close some way or another[,] any way to get pease in the world wonst more[;] it seems to me I had drather be at home and live on bred and water than to have this war hanging over us but I pray god pease will soon be made[.] I dont think the war can last long.

DOCUMENT 2
Letter from Camp near Bells Bridge, Tennessee, August 15, 1863

By the summer of 1863, Marion's regiment had moved to Tennessee, where he notices increasing war-weariness, desertions, and disillusionment with the Confederacy.

You don't know how glad I would be if I was just thar with you this morning to see the sun rise over the hills in Virginia again[,] for everry thing seames so sad and desolate here this morning; it seames like the absens of dear friends and the present condition of things has brought deep refletion and sadnes upon everry heart, and [men] are growing weary and getting out of heart and leaving the Army everry day. I cant tell wheather it will be for the better or wheather it will make things wors: but I hope it is a way god has provided to bring this war and time of sorrow to an end and to give us pease in our land again: Thoug I believe the south first started on a just course but our own wickedness and disobedians has brought us to what we are and I firmly believe wee will be bound to give up to subjugation[.] I don't think the south will stand much longer, and I am sorrow to say it for wee will be a ruined people while time ma [may] last, but wee ought to submit to any thing to have this awwful war ended.

---

slaves, but they learned that they did not. When the war began, a North Carolina woman praised her slaves as "diligent and respectful." When it ended, she said, "As to the idea of a *faithful servant, it is all a fiction.*" Whites' greatest fear—retaliatory violence—rarely occurred, but slaves gradually undermined white mastery and expanded control over their own lives.

> **REVIEW** How did wartime hardship in the South contribute to class friction?

▶ The North at War

Although little fighting took place on northern soil, almost every family had a son, husband, father, or brother in uniform. Moreover, total war blurred the distinction between home front and battlefield. As in the South, men marched off to fight, but preserving the country was also women's work. For civilians as well as soldiers, for women as well as men, war was transforming.

DOCUMENT 3
Letter from Floyd County, Virginia, August 16, 1863

Mary longs for peace and argues that desertion will end the war.

Oh how much beter satisfied would I be if you was just hear with me this beatiful Sabath morning. I feel as if my troubles on earth would all be over if you was just at home to stay wonst more[,] but god sent it upon us and we will have to bear with it the best we can but I do pray that he may soon end this destressing time some way[.] I would be willing for it to end most any way just so it would end[.] Dear Marion I think if the head men dont soon end this war that the soldiers will for they are runing way from down east by hundreds[;] they was five hundard went through hear last weak and well armed and they say they wont go back any more and I dont blame them for it[.] I wish they would all runaway and these head men would be oblige to fight it out but as long as they can stay at home and speculate off of the poor soulders they dont care how long the war lasts[.] Serious Smith wrote a leter the 9 of this month and he wrote that they had to pay 15 dolars for a bushel of taters . . . how can the poor soulders make out and only get a leven [eleven] dolars a month[?]

DOCUMENT 4
Letter from Outskirts of Dalton, Georgia, March 25, 1864

As his regiment is backing toward Atlanta, trying to fend off Sherman, Marion considers what has gone wrong with the Confederacy.

I dont think it will last much longer if the souldiers doo what they say they will doo[;] they are all verry tired of this war and the way it is carried on[.] I think wee all have stud it about as long as we can unless our leading men dos a heap better than they ever have yet: if they wer God fearing men I would think wee would prosper but so long as they [seek] the Bottom of a Whiskey Barl and frolick around bad places just so long we will hafto fight and suffer. . . . we was all Born in a free land and I think wee ought to stil be free and not be bound down wors than slaves[;] we wonst had a union and was living happy and had all man can wish for[;] now we are cut off from that union and what are wee nothing but a ruend people as long as we shal live . . . dissatisfaction and wickedness all over the south[;] may God show us our errors and put us in the rite way and Bring us Back to our old union again.

Despite his doubts about the Confederacy and continued affection for the Union, Marion left the army without authorization only once, and after a few weeks at home in 1863, he returned to his regiment. Like many disillusioned soldiers, he fought in the rebel army to the very end.

Source: Christian M. Epperly Correspondence, Gilder Lehrman Collection, Pierpont Morgan Library, New York.

Questions for Analysis

Analyze the Evidence: How does Marion contrast his previous life in the Union with life in the Confederacy? What specific differences does he note?

Recognize Viewpoints: How does the Epperlys' perspective on the Confederacy reflect their social position as plain folk in Virginia society?

Consider the Context: Marion makes clear why he had such affection for his home; he is much less clear about why he fought for the Confederacy. What might some of his reasons have been?

The need to build and fuel the Union war machine strengthened the federal government and boosted the economy. The Union sent nearly 2 million men into the military and still increased production in almost every area. But because the rewards and burdens of patriotism were distributed unevenly, the North experienced sharp, even violent, divisions. Workers confronted employers, whites confronted blacks, and Democrats confronted Republicans. Still, Northerners on the home front remained fervently attached to the Union.

The Government and the Economy

When the war began, the United States had no national banking system, no national currency, and no federal income tax. But the secession of eleven slave states cut the Democrats' strength in Congress in half and destroyed their capacity to resist Republican economic programs. The Legal Tender Act of February 1862 created a national currency, paper money that Northerners called "greenbacks." With the passage of the

Union Army Horse Artillery, 1860–1865
Seen here in Virginia, a powerful battery of Union field artillery moved forward to assist infantry units. Each cannon required more than a dozen men and many horses to service it. Assignment to an artillery battery was dangerous for man and beast. Life expectancy for an artillery horse was less than eight months, and it is estimated that 1.5 million horses died in the war. Corbis.

Women and Work at Home and at War

More than a million farm men were called to the military, and farm women added men's chores to their own. "I met more women driving teams on the road and saw more at work in the fields than men," a visitor to Iowa reported in the fall of 1862. Rising production testified to their success in plowing, planting, and harvesting. Rapid mechanization assisted farm women in their new roles. Cyrus McCormick sold 165,000 of his reapers during the war years. The combination of high prices for farm products and increased production ensured that war and prosperity joined hands in the rural North.

In cities, women stepped into jobs vacated by men, particularly in manufacturing, and also into essentially new occupations such as government secretaries and clerks. The number of women working for wages rose 40 percent during the war. As more and more women entered the workforce, employers cut wages. In 1864, New York seamstresses working fourteen-hour days earned only $1.54 a week, not enough "to sustain life," they said. Urban workers resorted increasingly to strikes to wrench decent salaries from their employers, but their protests rarely succeeded.

Most middle-class white women stayed home and contributed to the war effort in traditional ways. They sewed, wrapped bandages, and sold homemade goods at local fairs to raise money to aid the soldiers. Other women expressed their patriotism in an untraditional way. Defying prejudices about female delicacy, thousands of women on both sides volunteered to nurse the wounded. Many northern female volunteers worked through the U.S. Sanitary Commission, a huge civilian organization that bought and distributed clothing, food, and medicine, recruited doctors and nurses, and buried the dead.

Some volunteers went on to become paid military nurses. Dorothea Dix, well known for her efforts to reform insane asylums, was named superintendent of female nurses in April 1861. By 1863, some 3,000 nurses served under her. Most nurses worked in hospitals behind the battle lines, but some, like Clara Barton, who later founded the American Red Cross, worked in battlefield units. Women who served in the war went on to lead the postwar movement to establish training schools for female nurses.

National Banking Act in February 1863, Congress established a system of national banks that by the 1870s had largely replaced the antebellum system of decentralized state banks. Congress also enacted a series of sweeping tax laws.

The Republicans' wartime legislation also aimed at integrating the West into the Union. In May 1862, Congress approved the Homestead Act, which offered 160 acres of public land to settlers who would live and labor on it. The Homestead Act bolstered western loyalty and in time resulted in more than a million new farms. The Pacific Railroad Act in July 1862 provided massive federal assistance for building a transcontinental railroad that ran from Omaha to San Francisco when completed in 1869. Congress further bound East and West by subsidizing the Pony Express mail service and a transcontinental telegraph.

Congress also created the Department of Agriculture and passed the Land-Grant College Act (also known as the Morrill Act after its sponsor, Representative Justin Morrill of Vermont), which set aside public land to support universities that emphasized "agriculture and mechanical arts." The Lincoln administration immeasurably strengthened the North's effort to win the war, but its initiatives also permanently changed the nation.

Politics and Dissent

At first, the bustle of economic and military mobilization seemed to silence politics, but

Women Doing Laundry for Federal Soldiers, ca. 1861
Some northern women were forced by their desperate financial circumstances to wash soldiers' dirty clothes to make a living. Army camps were difficult places for "respectable" women to work. One Union soldier discouraged his wife even from visiting, noting, "It is not a fit place for any woman, for there is all kinds of talk, songs and everything not good for them 2 hear." Corbis.

bipartisan unity did not last. Within a year, Democrats were labeling the Republican administration a "reign of terror" and denouncing as unconstitutional Republican policies expanding federal power, subsidizing private business, and emancipating the slaves. In turn, Republicans were calling Democrats the party of "Dixie, Davis, and the Devil."

When the Republican-dominated Congress enacted the draft law in March 1863, Democrats had another grievance. The law required that all men between the ages of twenty and forty-five enroll and make themselves available for a lottery that would decide who went to war. It also allowed a draftee to hire a substitute or simply to pay a $300 fee and get out of his military obligation. As in the South, common folk could be heard chanting, "A rich man's war and a poor man's fight."

Linking the draft and emancipation, Democrats argued that Republicans employed an unconstitutional means (the draft) to achieve an unconstitutional end (emancipation). In the summer of 1863, antidraft, antiblack mobs went on rampages in northern cities. In July in New York City, Democratic Irish workingmen—crowded into filthy tenements, gouged by inflation, enraged by the draft, and dead set against fighting to free blacks—erupted in four days of rioting. The **New York City draft riots** killed at least 105 people, most of them black.

Lincoln called Democratic opposition to the war "the fire in the rear" and believed that it was even more threatening to national survival than were Confederate armies. The antiwar wing of the Democratic Party, the Peace Democrats—whom some called "Copperheads," after the poisonous snake—found their chief spokesman in Ohio congressman Clement Vallandigham. Vallandigham demanded: "Stop fighting. Make an armistice. . . . Withdraw your army from the seceding States."

In September 1862, in an effort to stifle opposition to the war, Lincoln placed under military arrest any person who discouraged enlistments, resisted the draft, or engaged in "disloyal" practices. Before the war ended, his administration imprisoned nearly 14,000 individuals, most in the border states. The administration's heavy-handed tactics suppressed free speech, but the campaign fell short of a reign of terror, for the majority of the prisoners were not northern Democratic opponents but Confederates, blockade runners, and citizens of foreign countries, and most of those arrested gained quick release. Still, the administration's net captured Vallandigham, who was arrested, convicted of treason, and banished.

REVIEW   Why was the U.S. Congress able to pass such a bold legislative agenda during the war?

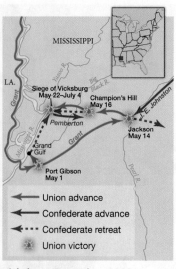

Vicksburg Campaign, 1863

► Grinding Out Victory, 1863–1865

In the early months of 1863, the Union's prospects looked bleak, and the Confederate cause stood at high tide. Then, in July 1863, the tide began to turn. The military man most responsible for this shift was Ulysses S. Grant. Elevated to supreme command in 1864, Grant knit together a powerful war machine that integrated a sophisticated command structure, modern technology, and complex logistics and supply systems. Grant's arithmetic was simple: Killing more of the enemy than he killed of you equaled "the complete over-throw of the rebellion."

The North ground out the victory battle by bloody battle.

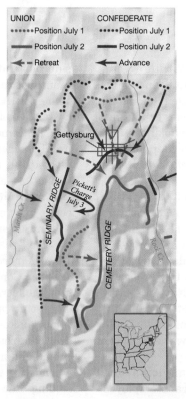

Battle of Gettysburg, July 1–3, 1863

Still, Southerners were not deterred. The fighting escalated in the last two years of the war. As national elections approached in the fall of 1864, Lincoln expected a war-weary North to reject him. Instead, northern voters declared their willingness to continue the war in the defense of the ideals of union and freedom. Lincoln lived to see victory, but only days after Lee surrendered, the president died from an assassin's bullet.

Vicksburg and Gettysburg

Vicksburg, Mississippi, situated on the eastern bank of the Mississippi River, stood between Union forces and complete control of the river. In May 1863, Union forces under Grant laid siege to the city in an effort to starve out the enemy. As the **siege of Vicksburg** dragged on, civilians ate mules and rats to survive. After six weeks, on July 4, 1863, nearly 30,000 rebels marched out of Vicksburg, stacked their arms, and surrendered unconditionally. A Yankee captain wrote home to his wife: "The backbone of the Rebellion is this day broken. The Confederacy is divided. . . . Vicksburg is ours. The Mississippi River is opened, and Gen. Grant is to be our next President."

On the same Fourth of July, word arrived that Union forces had crushed General Lee at Gettysburg, Pennsylvania (Map 15.3). Emboldened by his victory at Chancellorsville in May, Lee and his 75,000-man army had invaded Pennsylvania. On June 28, Union forces under General George G. Meade intercepted the Confederates at the small town of Gettysburg, where Union soldiers occupied the high ground. In three days of furious fighting, the Confederates failed to dislodge the Federals. The **battle of Gettysburg** cost Lee more than one-third of his army—28,000 casualties. "It's all my fault," he lamented. On the night

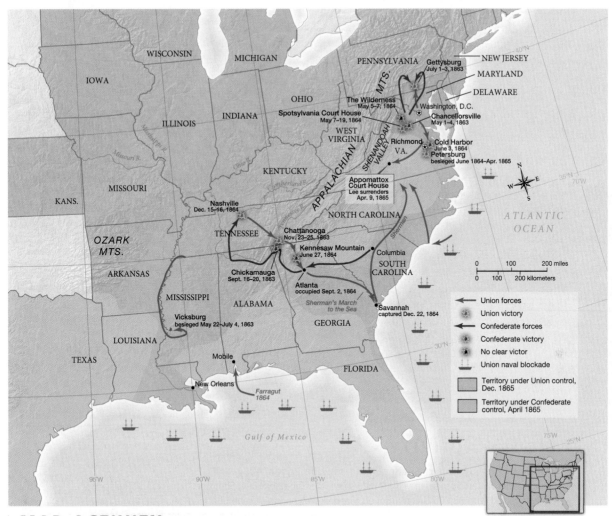

MAP ACTIVITY

Map 15.3 The Civil War, 1863–1865

Ulysses S. Grant's victory at Vicksburg divided the Confederacy at the Mississippi River. William Tecumseh Sherman's march from Chattanooga to Savannah divided it again. In northern Virginia, Robert E. Lee fought fiercely, but Grant's larger, better-supplied armies prevailed.

READING THE MAP: Describe the difference between Union and Confederate naval capacities. Were the battles shown on the map fought primarily in Union-controlled or in Confederate-controlled territory? (Look at the land areas on the map.)

CONNECTIONS: Did former slaves serve in the Civil War? If so, on which side(s), and what did they do?

of July 4, 1863, he marched his battered army back to Virginia.

The twin disasters at Vicksburg and Gettysburg proved to be the turning point of the war. The Confederacy could not replace the nearly 60,000 soldiers who were captured, wounded, or killed. It is hindsight, however, that permits us to see the pair of battles as decisive. At the time, the Confederacy still controlled the heartland of the South, and Lee still had a vicious sting. War-weariness threatened to erode the North's will

to win before Union armies could destroy the Confederacy's ability to go on.

Grant Takes Command

In September 1863, Union general William Rosecrans placed his army in a dangerous situation in Chattanooga, Tennessee, where he had retreated after defeat at the battle of Chickamauga (see Map 15.3). Rebels surrounded

VISUAL ACTIVITY

The Dead Line, by Robert Sneden, Andersonville Prison, 1864
Union soldier Robert Sneden arrived at Andersonville in February 1864. Soon the sixteen-and-a-half acres were crammed with 33,000 Union prisoners. Sneden sketched this scene of a man being shot by a guard while trying to take part of a fence (the "dead line" that prisoners could not cross) for firewood. More than 13,000 prisoners perished at Andersonville. Virginia Historical Society, Richmond, Virginia, USA/Bridgeman Images.
READING THE IMAGE: What does the painting suggest were among the hazards to the health of the prisoners at Andersonville?
CONNECTIONS: How might the state of the Confederate economy have affected conditions at Andersonville?

the disorganized bluecoats and threatened to starve them into submission. Grant, now commander of Union forces between the Mississippi River and the Appalachians, arrived in nearby Chattanooga in October. Within weeks, he opened an effective supply line, broke the siege, and routed the Confederate army. The victory at Chattanooga on November 25 opened the door to Georgia. In March 1864, Lincoln asked Grant to come east to become the general in chief of all Union armies.

In Washington, General Grant implemented his grand strategy for a war of attrition. He ordered a series of simultaneous assaults from Virginia all the way to Louisiana. Two actions proved particularly significant. In one, General

William Tecumseh Sherman, whom Grant appointed his successor to command the western armies, plunged southeast toward Atlanta. In the other, Grant, who took control of the Army of the Potomac, went head-to-head with Lee in Virginia in May and June of 1864.

The fighting between Grant and Lee was particularly savage. At the battle of the Wilderness, where a dense tangle of forest often made it impossible to see more than ten paces, the armies pounded away at each other until approximately 18,000 Yankees and 11,000 rebels had fallen. At Spotsylvania Court House, frenzied men fought hand to hand for eighteen hours in the rain. One veteran remembered men "piled upon each other in some places four layers deep, exhibiting every ghastly phase of mutilation." (See "Making Historical Arguments," page 434.) Spotsylvania cost Grant another 18,000 casualties and Lee 10,000. Grant kept moving and attacked Lee again at Cold Harbor, where he suffered 13,000 additional casualties to Lee's 5,000.

Twice as many Union soldiers as rebel soldiers died in four weeks of fighting in Virginia, but because Lee had only half as many troops as Grant, his losses were equivalent to Grant's. Grant knew that the South could not replace the losses. Moreover, the campaign carried Grant to the outskirts of Petersburg, just south of Richmond, where he abandoned the costly tactic of the frontal assault and began a siege that immobilized both armies and dragged on for nine months.

Simultaneously, Sherman invaded Georgia. Skillful maneuvering, constant skirmishing, and one pitched battle, at Kennesaw Mountain, brought Sherman to Atlanta, which fell on September 2. Intending to "make Georgia howl," Sherman marched out of Atlanta on November 15 with 62,000 battle-hardened veterans, heading for Savannah, 285 miles away on the Atlantic coast. One veteran remembered, "[We] destroyed all we could not eat, stole their niggers, burned their cotton & gins, spilled their sorghum, burned & twisted their R. Roads and raised Hell generally." **Sherman's March to the Sea** aimed at destroying the will of white Southerners to continue the war. A few weeks earlier, General Philip H. Sheridan had carried out his own scorched-earth campaign in the Shenandoah Valley. When Sherman's troops entered an undefended Savannah in mid-December, the general telegraphed Lincoln that he had "a Christmas gift" for him. A month earlier, Union voters had bestowed on the president an even greater gift.

The Election of 1864

In the summer of 1864, with Sherman temporarily checked outside Atlanta and Grant bogged down in the siege of Petersburg, the Democratic Party smelled victory in the fall elections. Lincoln himself concluded, "It seems exceedingly probable that this administration will not be re-elected."

The Democrats were badly divided, however. Peace Democrats insisted on an armistice, while "war" Democrats supported the conflict but opposed Republican means of fighting it. The party tried to paper over the chasm by nominating

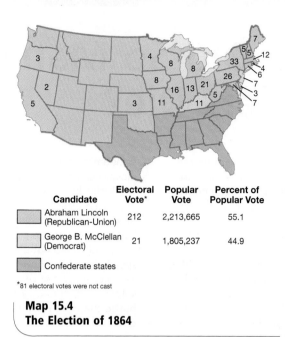

Candidate	Electoral Vote*	Popular Vote	Percent of Popular Vote
Abraham Lincoln (Republican-Union)	212	2,213,665	55.1
George B. McClellan (Democrat)	21	1,805,237	44.9
Confederate states			

*81 electoral votes were not cast

Map 15.4
The Election of 1864

a war candidate, General George McClellan, but adopting a peace platform that demanded that "immediate efforts be made for a cessation of hostilities." Republicans denounced the peace

Major Battles of the Civil War, 1863–1865

May 1–4, 1863	Battle of Chancellorsville
July 1–3, 1863	Battle of Gettysburg
July 4, 1863	Fall of Vicksburg
September 16–20, 1863	Battle of Chickamauga
November 23–25, 1863	Battle of Chattanooga
May 5–7, 1864	Battle of the Wilderness
May 7–19, 1864	Battle of Spotsylvania Court House
June 3, 1864	Battle of Cold Harbor
June 27, 1864	Battle of Kennesaw Mountain
September 2, 1864	Fall of Atlanta
November–December 1864	Sheridan sacks Shenandoah Valley Sherman's March to the Sea
December 15–16, 1864	Battle of Nashville
December 22, 1864	Fall of Savannah
April 2–3, 1865	Fall of Petersburg and Richmond
April 9, 1865	Lee surrenders at Appomattox Court House

Why Did So Many Soldiers Die?

The American Civil War was the bloodiest conflict in American history (Figure 15.3). Precise numbers are hard to determine, but approximately 750,000 soldiers died. Why were the Civil War totals so horrendous?

This question is almost as old as the war itself, and in answering it historians have traditionally pointed to a variety of explanations: the scale and duration of the fighting; military strategy; battlefield technology; and the backward state of medicine. The sheer size of the armies—some battles involved more than 200,000 soldiers—ensured that battlefields would turn red with blood. Moreover, what most Americans expected to be a short war extended for four full years. In addition, armies fought with antiquated Napoleonic strategy. In the generals' eyes, the ideal soldier advanced with his comrades in a compact, close-order formation. But by the 1860s, military technology had made such frontal assaults deadly. Weapons with rifled barrels were replacing smoothbore muskets and cannons, and the new weapons' greater range and accuracy made sitting ducks of charging infantry units. As a result, battles took thousands of lives in a single day. On July 2, 1862, the morning after the battle at Malvern Hill in Virginia, a Union officer surveyed the scene: "Over 5,000 dead and wounded men were on the ground . . . enough were alive and moving to give to the field a singular crawling effect."

When the war began, Union and Confederate medical departments could not cope with skirmishes, much less large-scale battles. They had no ambulance corps to remove the wounded from the scene. They had no field hospitals. Wounded soldiers often lay on battlefields for hours,

sometimes days. Only the shock of massive casualties compelled reform. Gradually, both North and South organized effective ambulance corps, built hospitals, and hired trained surgeons and nurses.

Soldiers did not always count speedy transportation to a hospital as a blessing, however. As one Union soldier said, "I had rather risk a battle than the Hospitals." Field doctors gained a reputation as butchers, but a wounded man's real enemy was medical ignorance. Physicians had almost no knowledge of the cause and transmission of disease or the benefits of antiseptics. Unaware of basic germ theory, surgeons spread infection almost every time they operated. They wore the same bloody smocks for days and washed their hands and their scalpels and saws in buckets of dirty water. Although surgeons used anesthesia (both ether and chloroform), soldiers often did not survive amputations,

not because of the operations but because of the gangrene that inevitably followed. A Union doctor discovered in 1864 that bromine arrested gangrene, but the best that most amputees could hope for was maggots, which ate dead flesh on the stump and thus inhibited the spread of infection. The growing ranks of nurses, including Dorothea Dix and Clara Barton, improved wounded men's odds and alleviated their suffering. Still, during the Civil War, nearly one of every five wounded rebel soldiers died, and one of every six Yankees. A century later, in Vietnam, only one wounded American soldier in four hundred died.

Soldiers who avoided battlefield wounds and hospital infections still faced sickness. Deadly diseases such as dysentery and typhoid swept through crowded army camps, where latrines were often dangerously close to drinking water, and mosquitoes, flies, and body lice were more than nuisances. Pneumonia and malaria also cut down thousands. Quinine from South America proved an effective treatment for malaria, but by the end of the war the going price was $500 an ounce. Civilian relief

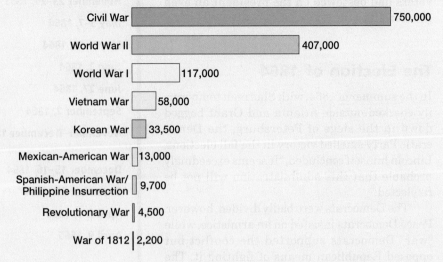

FIGURE 15.3 Civil War Deaths
The loss of life in the Civil War—as many as 750,000—was greater than the losses in all other American wars through the Vietnam War combined.

War	Deaths
Civil War	750,000
World War II	407,000
World War I	117,000
Vietnam War	58,000
Korean War	33,500
Mexican-American War	13,000
Spanish-American War/ Philippine Insurrection	9,700
Revolutionary War	4,500
War of 1812	2,200

Wounded Men at Savage's Station
Misery did not end when the cannons ceased firing. Northern and southern surgeons performed approximately 60,000 amputations with simple instruments such as those included in this surgical kit. The wounded men shown here were but a fraction of those injured or killed during General George McClellan's peninsula campaign in 1862. Photo: Library of Congress, LC-DIG-cwpb-00202; Surgical kit: © Chicago History Museum, USA/Bridgeman Images.

agencies promoted hygiene in army camps and made some headway. Nevertheless, disease killed nearly twice as many soldiers as did combat. Many who died of disease were prisoners of war. Approximately 30,000 Northerners died in Confederate prisons, and approximately 26,000 Southerners died in Union prisons.

Recently, historians have probed another explanation for the death toll, turning to soldiers' cultural attitudes and values to explain why they were willing to die in such great numbers. Some have explored how the nineteenth-century code of masculinity propelled valor on the battlefields, and how patriotism, for

either the Union or the Confederacy, moved soldiers to risk everything. But scholars have focused most especially on how soldiers' religious beliefs about death made it easier for them to negotiate dying. The triumph of evangelical Protestantism in the early nineteenth century meant that Civil War soldiers faced death with calm resignation. They believed in a heaven that promised bodily resurrection and family reunion; the assurance of everlasting life, therefore, made it easier to face death. Culture, then, as well as the scope and length of the war, strategy, technology, and primitive medicine, helps explain the war's tremendous carnage.

Questions for Analysis

Summarize the Argument: What does the author conclude were the major reasons that so many soldiers died in the Civil War?

Analyze the Evidence: In what ways were Civil War strategists fighting the world's first "modern" war? In what ways were they still fighting a traditional war? How do these factors account for the number of dead and wounded soldiers?

Consider the Context: Which economy—the Union's or the Confederacy's—was better able to cope with the loss of manpower to the military, and why?

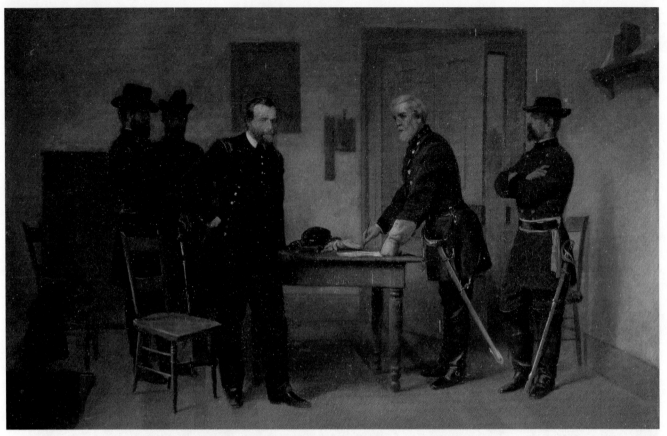

Lee Surrendering to Grant at Appomattox (ca. 1870)
Artist Alonzo Chappel captures the quiet dignity of the moment when Ulysses S. Grant and Robert E. Lee
met in the simple parlor of Wilmer McLean's home in Appomattox Court House, Virginia. After four years
of fighting, Lee surrendered his army, and Grant offered terms even more generous than Lee had hoped
for. Smithsonian American Art Museum, Washington, D.C./Art Resource, NY.

plank as a cut-and-run plan that "virtually proposed to surrender the country to the rebels in
arms against us."

The capture of Atlanta in September turned
the political tide in favor of the Republicans.
Lincoln received 55 percent of the popular vote,
but his electoral margin was a whopping 212 to
McClellan's 21 (Map 15.4). Lincoln's party won
a resounding victory, one that gave him a mandate to continue the war until slavery and the
Confederacy were dead.

The Confederacy Collapses

As 1865 dawned, military disaster littered the
Confederate landscape. With the destruction of
John B. Hood's army at Nashville in December
1864, the interior of the Confederacy lay in Yankee
hands (see Map 15.3). Sherman's troops, resting
momentarily in Savannah, eyed South Carolina

hungrily. Farther north, Grant had Lee's army
pinned down in Petersburg, a few miles from
Richmond.

Some Confederates turned their backs on
the rebellion. News from the battlefield made
it difficult not to conclude that the Yankees had
beaten them. When soldiers' wives begged their
husbands to return home to keep their families
from starving, the stream of deserters grew
dramatically. Still, white Southerners had demonstrated a remarkable endurance for their
cause. Half of the Confederate soldiers had been
killed or wounded or had died of disease, and
ragged, hungry women and children had sacrificed throughout one of the bloodiest wars then
known to history.

The end came with a rush. On February 1,
1865, Sherman's troops stormed out of Savannah
into South Carolina, the "cradle of the Confederacy." In Virginia, Lee abandoned Petersburg on

April 2, and Richmond fell on April 3. Grant pursued Lee until he surrendered on April 9, 1865, at Appomattox Court House, Virginia. Grant offered generous peace terms. He allowed Lee's men to return home and to keep their horses to help "put in a crop to carry themselves and their families through the next winter." With Lee gone, the remaining Confederate armies lost hope and gave up within two weeks. After four years, the war was over.

No one was more relieved than Lincoln, but his celebration was restrained. He told his cabinet that his postwar burdens would weigh almost as heavily as those of wartime. Seeking a distraction, Lincoln attended Ford's Theatre on the evening of Good Friday, April 14, 1865. John Wilkes Booth, an actor with southern sympathies, slipped into the president's box and shot Lincoln, who died the next morning. Vice President Andrew Johnson became president. The man who had led the nation through the war would not lead it during the postwar search for a just peace.

> **REVIEW**   Why were the siege of Vicksburg and the battle of Gettysburg crucial to the outcome of the war?

▶ Conclusion: The Second American Revolution

A transformed nation emerged from the crucible of war. Antebellum America was decentralized politically and loosely integrated economically. To bend the resources of the country to a Union victory, Congress enacted legislation that reshaped the nation's political and economic character. It created a transcontinental railroad and miles of telegraph lines to bind the West to the rest of the nation. The massive changes brought about by the war—the creation of a national government, a national economy, and a national spirit—led one historian to call the American Civil War the "Second American Revolution."

The Civil War also had a profound effect on individual lives. Millions of men put on blue or gray uniforms and fought and suffered for what they passionately believed was right. The war disrupted families, leaving women at home with additional responsibilities and giving others wartime work in factories, offices, and hospitals. It offered blacks new and more effective ways to resist slavery and agitate for equality.

The war devastated the South. Three-fourths of southern white men of military age served in the Confederate army, and half of them became casualties. The war destroyed two-fifths of the South's livestock, wrecked half of the farm machinery, and blackened dozens of cities and towns. The struggle also cost the North a heavy price in lives, but rather than devastating the land, the war set the countryside and cities humming with business activity. The radical shift in power from South to North signaled a new direction in American development: the long decline of agriculture and the rise of industrial capitalism.

Most revolutionary of all, the war ended slavery. Ironically, the South's war to preserve slavery destroyed it. Nearly 200,000 black men, including ex-slave William Gould, dedicated their military service to its eradication. Because slavery was both a labor and a racial system, the institution was entangled in almost every aspect of southern life. Slavery's uprooting inevitably meant fundamental change. But the full meaning of abolition remained unclear in 1865, and the status of ex-slaves would be the principal task of reconstruction.

See the Selected Bibliography for this chapter in the Appendix.

15 Chapter Review

KEY TERMS

Fort Sumter (p. 407)
battle of Bull Run (Manassas) (p. 412)
battle of Antietam (p. 413)
battle of Shiloh (p. 415)
Union blockade (p. 417)
King Cotton diplomacy (p. 418)
contraband of war (p. 419)
Emancipation Proclamation (p. 420)
New York City draft riots (p. 429)
siege of Vicksburg (p. 430)
battle of Gettysburg (p. 430)
Sherman's March to the Sea (p. 433)

REVIEW QUESTIONS

1. Why did the attack on Fort Sumter force the Upper South to choose sides? (pp. 407–409)

2. Why did the South believe it could win the war despite numerical disadvantages? (pp. 409–411)

3. After a year and a half of fighting, who had the advantage in the war? (pp. 412–418)

4. How did the war for union become a war for black freedom? (pp. 419–423)

5. How did wartime hardship in the South contribute to class friction? (pp. 423–426)

6. Why was the U.S. Congress able to pass such a bold legislative agenda during the war? (pp. 426–430)

7. Why were the siege of Vicksburg and the battle of Gettysburg crucial to the outcome of the war? (pp. 430–437)

MAKING CONNECTIONS

1. Despite loathing slavery, Lincoln embraced emancipation as a war objective late and with great caution. Why?

2. The Emancipation Proclamation did not accomplish the destruction of slavery on its own. How did a war over union bring about the end of slavery? In your answer, consider the direct actions of slaves and Union policymakers as well as indirect factors within the Confederacy.

3. In addition to restoring the Union and destroying slavery, what other significant changes did the war produce on the home front and in the nation's capital?

4. Brilliant military strategy alone did not determine the outcome of the war; victory also depended on financial resources, material mobilization, diplomacy, and politics. In light of these considerations, explain why the Confederacy believed it would succeed and why it ultimately failed.

LINKING TO THE PAST

1. Why were white slaveholders surprised by the wartime behavior of slaves? (See chapter 13.)

2. In what ways did the Lincoln administration's wartime policies fulfill the prewar aspirations of Northerners? (See chapters 12 and 14.)

16 Reconstruction
1863–1877

CONTENT LEARNING OBJECTIVES

After reading and studying this chapter, you should be able to:

- Identify the challenges facing reconstruction efforts.

- Describe President Johnson's reconstruction plan and the ways in which it aligned and differed from Lincoln's.

- Recount the significance of the Fourteenth Amendment and why President Johnson advised southern states to reject it. Explain the terms of radical reconstruction and how Johnson's interventions led some in Congress to seek his impeachment.

- Describe the provisions of the Fifteenth Amendment, and explain why some women's rights advocates were dissatisfied with it.

- Describe how congressional reconstruction altered life in the South. Explain why the North abandoned reconstruction, including the role of Grant's troubled presidency and the election of 1877 in this abandonment.

CARPETBAG
A carpetbag was a suitcase made from carpet. "Carpetbagger" was a derogatory name for rootless adventurers, which critics of Republican administrations in the South hurled at white Northerners who moved south during Reconstruction. Elemental Studios/Alamy.

IN 1856, JOHN RAPIER, A FREE BLACK BARBER IN FLORENCE, ALABAMA, urged his four freeborn sons to flee the increasingly repressive and dangerous South. James T. Rapier chose Canada, where he went to live with his uncle in a largely black community and studied Greek and Latin in a log schoolhouse. In a letter to his father, he vowed, "I will endeavor to do my part in solving the problems [of African Americans] in my native land."

The Union victory in the Civil War gave James Rapier the opportunity to redeem his pledge. In 1865, after more than eight years of exile, the twenty-seven-year-old Rapier returned to Alabama, where he presided over the first political gathering of former slaves in the state. He soon discovered, however, that Alabama's whites found it agonizingly difficult to accept defeat and black freedom. They responded to the revolutionary changes under the banner "White Man—Right or Wrong—Still the White Man!"

During the elections of 1868, when Rapier and other Alabama blacks vigorously supported the Republican ticket, the recently organized Ku Klux Klan went on a bloody rampage. A mob of 150 outraged whites scoured Rapier's neighborhood seeking four black politicians they claimed were trying to "Africanize Alabama." They caught and hanged three, but the "nigger carpetbagger from Canada" escaped. After briefly considering fleeing the state, Rapier decided to stay and fight.

In 1872, Rapier won election to the House of Representatives, where he joined six other black congressmen in Washington, D.C. Defeated for reelection in 1874 in a campaign marked by ballot-box stuffing, Rapier turned to cotton farming. But persistent black poverty and unrelenting racial violence convinced him that blacks could never achieve equality and prosperity in the South. He purchased land in Kansas and urged Alabama's blacks to escape with him. In 1883, however, before he could leave Alabama, Rapier died of tuberculosis at the age of forty-five.

Union general Carl Schurz had foreseen many of the troubles Rapier encountered in the postwar South. In 1865, Schurz concluded that the Civil War was "a revolution but half accomplished." Northern victory had freed the slaves, he observed, but it had not changed former slaveholders' minds about blacks' unfitness for freedom. Left to themselves, whites would "introduce some new system of forced labor, not perhaps exactly slavery in its old form but something similar to it." To defend their freedom, Schurz concluded, blacks would need federal protection, land of their own, and voting rights. Until whites "cut loose from the past, it will be a dangerous experiment to put Southern society upon its own legs."

As Schurz understood, the end of the war did not mean peace. Indeed, the nation entered one of its most turbulent eras—Reconstruction. Answers to the era's central questions—about the defeated South's status within the Union and the meaning of freedom for ex-slaves—came not only from Washington, D.C., where the federal government played an active role, but also from the state legislatures and county seats of the South, where blacks eagerly participated in politics. The Fourteenth and Fifteenth Amendments to the Constitution strengthened the claim of African Americans to equal rights. The struggle also took place on the South's farms and plantations, where former slaves sought to become free workers while former slaveholders clung to the Old South. A small band of white women joined in the struggle for racial equality, and soon their crusade broadened to include gender equality. Their attempts to secure voting rights for women were thwarted, however, just as were the efforts of blacks and their allies to secure racial equality. In the contest to determine the consequences of Confederate defeat and emancipation, white Southerners prevailed.

James T. Rapier

In 1874, when Representative James T. Rapier spoke before Congress on behalf of a civil rights bill, he described the humiliation of being denied service at inns all along his route from Montgomery to Washington. Elsewhere in the world, he said, class and religion were invoked to defend discrimination. But in America, "our distinction is color." Alabama Department of Archives and History, Montgomery, Alabama.

► Wartime Reconstruction

Reconstruction did not wait for the end of war. As the odds of a northern victory increased, thinking about reunification quickened. Immediately, a question arose: Who had authority to devise a plan for reconstructing the Union? President Abraham Lincoln firmly believed that reconstruction was a matter of executive responsibility. Congress just as firmly asserted its jurisdiction. Fueling the argument were significant differences about the terms of reconstruction.

In their eagerness to formulate a plan for political reunification, neither Lincoln nor Congress gave much attention to the South's land and labor problems. But as the war rapidly eroded slavery and traditional plantation agriculture, Yankee military commanders in the Union-occupied areas of the Confederacy had no choice but to oversee the emergence of a new labor system. Freedmen's aspirations played little role in the plans that emerged.

"To Bind Up the Nation's Wounds"

As early as 1863, Lincoln began contemplating how "to bind up the nation's wounds" and achieve "a lasting peace." While deep compassion for the enemy guided his thinking about peace, his plan for reconstruction aimed primarily at shortening the war and ending slavery.

Lincoln's Proclamation of Amnesty and Reconstruction in December 1863 set out his terms. He offered a full pardon, restoring property (except slaves) and political rights, to most rebels willing to renounce secession and to accept emancipation. When 10 percent of a state's voting population had taken an oath of allegiance, the state could organize a new government and be readmitted into the Union. Lincoln's plan did not require ex-rebels to extend social or political rights to ex-slaves, nor did it anticipate a program of long-term federal assistance to freedmen. Clearly, the president looked forward to the rapid, forgiving restoration of the broken Union.

Lincoln's easy terms enraged abolitionists such as Wendell Phillips of Boston, who charged that the president "makes the negro's freedom a mere sham." He "is willing that the negro should be free but seeks nothing else for him." Comparing Lincoln to the Union's most passive general, Phillips declared, "What McClellan was

CHRONOLOGY

1863	• Proclamation of Amnesty and Reconstruction pardons most rebels.
1864	• Lincoln refuses to sign Wade-Davis bill.
1865	• Freedmen's Bureau established. • Lincoln assassinated; Andrew Johnson becomes president. • First black codes enacted. • Thirteenth Amendment becomes part of Constitution.
1866	• Congress approves Fourteenth Amendment. • Civil Rights Act passes. • American Equal Rights Association founded. • Ku Klux Klan founded.
1867	• Military Reconstruction Act passes. • Tenure of Office Act passes.
1868	• Impeachment trial of President Johnson held. • Ulysses S. Grant elected president.
1869	• Congress approves Fifteenth Amendment.
1871	• Ku Klux Klan Act passes.
1872	• Liberal Party formed. • President Grant reelected.
1873	• Economic depression sets in. • Slaughterhouse cases decided. • Colfax massacre kills more than eighty blacks.
1874	• Democrats win majority in House of Representatives.
1875	• Civil Rights Act passes.
1876	• United States v. Cruikshank decided.
1877	• Rutherford B. Hayes becomes president; Reconstruction era ends.

Wartime Reconstruction
This cartoon from the presidential campaign of 1864 shows the "Rail Splitter" Abraham Lincoln leveraging the broken nation back together while his running mate, Andrew Johnson, who once was a tailor by trade, stitches the Confederate states securely back into the Union. Optimism that the task of reconstructing the nation after the war would be both quick and easy shines through the cartoon. The Granger Collection, New York.

on the battlefield—'Do as little hurt as possible!'—Lincoln is in civil affairs—'Make as little change as possible!'" Phillips and other northern Radicals called instead for a thorough overhaul of southern society. Their ideas proved to be too drastic for most Republicans during the war years, but Congress agreed that Lincoln's plan was inadequate.

In July 1864, Congress put forward a plan of its own. Congressman Henry Winter Davis of Maryland and Senator Benjamin Wade of Ohio jointly sponsored a bill that demanded that at least half of the voters in a conquered rebel state take the oath of allegiance before reconstruction could begin. The Wade-Davis bill also banned almost all ex-Confederates from participating in the drafting of new state constitutions. Finally, the bill guaranteed the equality of freedmen before the law. Congress's reconstruction would be neither as quick nor as forgiving as Lincoln's. When Lincoln refused to sign the bill and let it

die, Wade and Davis charged the president with usurpation of power.

Undeterred, Lincoln continued to nurture the formation of loyal state governments under his own plan. Four states—Arkansas, Louisiana, Tennessee, and Virginia—fulfilled the president's requirements, but Congress refused to seat representatives from the "Lincoln states." Lincoln admitted that a government based on only 10 percent was not ideal, but he argued, "We shall sooner have the fowl by hatching the egg than by smashing it." Massachusetts senator Charles Sumner responded, "The eggs of crocodiles can produce only crocodiles." In his last public address in April 1865, Lincoln defended his plan but for the first time expressed publicly his endorsement of suffrage for southern blacks, at least "the very intelligent, and . . . those who serve our cause as soldiers." The announcement demonstrated that Lincoln's thinking about reconstruction was still evolving. Four days later, he was dead.

Land and Labor

Of all the problems raised by the North's victory in the war, none proved more critical than the South's transition from slavery to free labor. As federal armies invaded and occupied the Confederacy, hundreds of thousands of slaves became free workers. In addition, Union armies controlled vast territories in the South where legal title to land had become unclear. The Confiscation Acts passed during the war punished "traitors" by taking away their property. The question of what to do with federally occupied land and how to organize labor on it engaged ex-slaves, ex-slaveholders, Union military commanders, and federal government officials long before the war ended.

In the Mississippi valley, occupying federal troops announced a new labor code. It required landholders to give up whipping, sign contracts with ex-slaves, pay wages, and provide food, housing, and medical care. The code required black laborers to enter into contracts, work diligently, and remain subordinate and obedient. Military leaders clearly had no intention of promoting a social or economic revolution. Instead, they sought to restore traditional plantation agriculture with wage labor. The effort resulted in a hybrid system that one contemporary called "compulsory free labor," something that satisfied no one.

Planters complained because the new system fell short of slavery. Blacks could not be "transformed by proclamation," a Louisiana sugar planter declared. Without the right to whip, he argued, the new labor system did not have a chance. Either Union soldiers must "*compel* the negroes to work," or the planters themselves must "be authorized and sustained in using force."

African Americans found the new regime too reminiscent of slavery to be called free labor. Its chief deficiency, they believed, was the failure to provide them with land of their own. Freedmen believed they had a moral right to land because they and their ancestors had worked it without compensation for centuries. "What's the use of being free if you don't own land enough to be buried in?" one man asked. Several wartime developments led freedmen to believe that the federal government planned to undergird black freedom with landownership.

In January 1865, General William Tecumseh Sherman set aside part of the coast south of Charleston for black settlement. By June 1865, some 40,000 freedmen sat on 400,000 acres of "Sherman land." In addition, in March 1865, Congress passed a bill establishing the Bureau

VISUAL ACTIVITY

***The Lord Is My Shepherd,* 1863**
Maine-born Eastman Johnson (1824–1906) did this painting only months after the Emancipation Proclamation. Its title comes from Psalm 23, which begins, "The Lord is my shepherd; I shall not want." The painting captures a humble black man quietly reading his Bible and reminds us of one of the reasons freedmen struggled so hard for literacy. Smithsonian American Art Museum, Washington, D.C./Art Resource, NY.
READING THE IMAGE: What is the artist saying about ex-slaves' capacity to live as free people?
CONNECTIONS: Why did southern whites in the Reconstruction era consider literacy for former slaves less a religious impulse than a dangerous political act?

of Refugees, Freedmen, and Abandoned Lands. The **Freedmen's Bureau**, as it was called, distributed food and clothing to destitute Southerners and eased the transition of blacks from slaves to free persons. Congress also authorized the agency to divide abandoned and confiscated land into 40-acre plots, to rent them to freedmen, and eventually to sell them "with such title as the United States can convey." By June 1865, the Bureau had situated nearly 10,000 black families on a half million acres abandoned by fleeing planters. Other ex-slaves eagerly anticipated farms of their own.

Despite the flurry of activity, wartime reconstruction failed to produce agreement about whether the president or Congress had the authority to devise policy or what proper policy should be.

The Meaning of Freedom

Although the Emancipation Proclamation itself did not free any slaves, it transformed the character of the war. Black people resolutely focused on the possibilities of freedom even before the war ended.

DOCUMENT 1
Letter from John Q. A. Dennis to Edwin M. Stanton, July 26, 1864

John Q. A. Dennis, formerly a slave in Maryland, wrote to ask Secretary of War Edwin M. Stanton for help in reuniting his family.

Boston. Dear Sir I am Glad that I have the Honour to Write you a few line I have been in troble for about four yars my Dear wife was taken from me Nov 19th 1859 and left me with three Children and I being a Slave At the time Could Not do Anny thing for the poor little Children for my master it was took me Carry me some forty mile from them So I Could Not do for them and the man that they live with half feed them and half Cloth them & beat them like dogs & when I was admitted to go to see them it use to brake my heart & Now I say again I am Glad to have the honour to write to you to see if you Can Do Anny thing for me or for my poor little Children I was keap in Slavy untell last Novr 1863. then the Good lord sent the Cornel borne [federal colonel William Birney?] Down their in Marland in worsester Co So as I have been recently freed I have but letle to live on but I am Striveing Dear Sir but what I went too know of you Sir is it possible for me to go & take my Children from those men that keep them in Savery if it is possible will you pleas give me a permit from your hand then I think they would let them go. . . . I want get the little Children out of Slavery. . . .

Source: *Freedom: A Documentary History of Emancipation, 1861–1867,* ser. 1, vol. 1, *The Destruction of Slavery,* 386, edited by Ira Berlin, Joseph P. Reidy, and Leslie S. Rowland. Copyright © 1985.

DOCUMENT 2
Report from the Reverend A. B. Randall, February 28, 1865

A. B. Randall, the white chaplain of a black regiment stationed in Little Rock, Arkansas, affirmed the importance of legal marriage to freed slaves and emphasized their conviction that emancipation was only the first step toward full freedom.

Weddings, just now, are very popular, and abundant among the Colored People. They have just learned, of the Special Order No. 15. of Gen Thomas [Adjutant General Lorenzo Thomas] by which, they may not only be lawfully married, but have their Marriage Certificates, Recorded; in a book furnished by the Government. . . . I have married, during the month, at this Post; Twenty five couples; mostly, those, who have families; & have been living together for years. . . . The Colord People here, generally consider, this war not only; their exodus, from bondage; but the road, to

The African American Quest for Autonomy

Ex-slaves never had any doubt about what they wanted from freedom. They had only to contemplate what they had been denied as slaves. (See "Analyzing Historical Evidence," above.) Slaves had to remain on their plantations; freedom allowed blacks to see what was on the other side of the hill. Slaves had to be at work in the fields by dawn; freedom permitted blacks to sleep through a sunrise. Freedmen also tested the etiquette of racial subordination. "Lizzie's maid passed me today when I was coming from church *without speaking to me,*" huffed one plantation mistress.

To whites, emancipation looked like pure anarchy. Blacks, they said, had reverted to their natural condition: lazy, irresponsible, and wild. Actually, former slaves were experimenting with freedom, but they could not long afford to roam the countryside, neglect work, and casually provoke whites. Soon, most were back at work in whites' kitchens and fields.

But they continued to dream of land and independence. "The way we can best take care of ourselves is to have land," one former slave declared in 1865, "and turn it and till it by our

Responsibility; Competency; and an honorable Citizenship—God grant that their hopes and expectations may be fully realized.

Source: *Freedom: A Documentary History of Emancipation, 1861–1867*, ser. 2, vol. 1, *The Black Military Experience*, 712, edited by Ira Berlin, Joseph P. Reidy, and Leslie S. Rowland. Copyright © 1982.

DOCUMENT 3
Petition "to the Union Convention of Tennessee Assembled in the Capitol at Nashville," January 9, 1865

In January 1865, black Tennesseans petitioned a convention of white Unionists debating the reorganization of state government.

We the undersigned petitioners, American citizens of African descent, natives and residents of Tennessee, and devoted friends of the great National cause, do most respectfully ask a patient hearing of your honorable body in regard to matters deeply affecting the future condition of our unfortunate and long suffering race. . . .

In the contest between the nation and slavery, our unfortunate people have sided, by instinct, with the former. . . . We will work, pray, live, and, if need be, die for the Union, as cheerfully as ever a white patriot died for his country. The color of our skin does not lessen in the least degree, our love either for God or for the land of our birth. . . .

We know the burdens of citizenship, and are ready to bear them. We know the duties of the good citizen, and are ready to perform them cheerfully, and would ask to be put in a position in which we can discharge them more effectually. . . .

This is a democracy—a government of the people. It should aim to make every man, without regard to the color of his skin, the amount of his wealth, or the character of his religious faith, feel personally interested in its welfare. Every man who lives under the Government should feel that it is his property, his treasure, the bulwark and defence of himself and his family. . . .

This is not a Democratic Government if a numerous, law-abiding, industrious, and useful class of citizens, born and bred on the soil, are to be treated as aliens and enemies, as an inferior degraded class, who must have no voice in the Government which they support, protect and defend, with all their heart, soul, mind, and body, both in peace and war. . . .

The possibility that the negro suffrage proposition may shock popular prejudice at first sight, is not a conclusive argument against its wisdom and policy. No proposition ever met with more furious or general opposition than the one to enlist colored soldiers in the United States army. The opponents of the measure exclaimed on all hands that the negro was a coward; that he would not fight; that one white man, with a whip in his hand could put to flight a regiment of them. . . . Yet the colored man has fought so well . . . .

The Government has asked the colored man to fight for its preservation and gladly has he done it. It can afford to trust him with a vote as safely as it trusted him with a bayonet.

Source: *Freedom: A Documentary History of Emancipation, 1861–1867*, ser. 2, vol. 1, *The Black Military Experience*, 811–16, edited by Ira Berlin, Joseph P. Reidy, and Leslie S. Rowland. Copyright © 1982.

Questions for Analysis

Analyze the Evidence: What does John Q. A. Dennis's interpretation of his responsibility as a father say about slavery's ability to destroy slave families?

Consider the Context: Why was legal marriage so important to ex-slaves?

Recognize Viewpoints: According to petitioners to the Union Convention of Tennessee, why was the experience of black soldiers relevant to black voting rights?

own labor." Another group of former slaves in South Carolina declared that they wanted land, "not a Master or owner[,] Neither a driver with his Whip."

Slavery had deliberately kept blacks illiterate, and freedmen emerged from bondage eager to learn to read and write. "I wishes the Childern all in School," one black veteran asserted. "It is beter for them then to be their Surveing a mistes [mistress]." Freemen looked on schools as "first proof of their *independence*."

The restoration of broken families was another persistent black aspiration. Thousands of freedmen took to the roads in 1865 to look for kin who had been sold away or to free those who were being held illegally as slaves. A black soldier from Missouri wrote his daughters that he was coming for them. "I will have you if it cost me my life," he declared. "Your Miss Kitty said that I tried to steal you," he told them. "But I'll let her know that god never intended for a man to steal his own flesh and blood." And he swore that "if she meets me with ten thousand soldiers, she [will] meet her enemy."

Independent worship was another continuing aspiration. African Americans greeted freedom with a mass exodus from white churches, where they had been required to worship when

VISUAL ACTIVITY

Harry Stephens and Family, 1866

The seven members of the Stephens family sit proudly for a photograph just after the Civil War ended. Many black families were not as fortunate as these Virginians. Separated by slavery or war, former slaves desperately sought news of missing family members through newspaper advertisements. G. Gable, *Summer Scene*, 1866. Gilman Collection, Purchase, The Horace W. Goldsmith Foundation Gift, through Joyce and Robert Menschel, 2005 (2005.100.277). Image copyright © The Metropolitan Museum of Art. Image source: Art Resource, NY.

READING THE IMAGE: How does the Stephens family signal that they are free people, not slaves?

CONNECTIONS: How would white Southerners likely respond to the message delivered by this photograph?

slaves. Some joined the newly established southern branches of all-black northern churches, such as the African Methodist Episcopal Church. Others formed black versions of the major southern denominations, Baptists and Methodists.

REVIEW   To what extent did Lincoln's wartime plan for reconstruction reflect the concerns of newly freed slaves?

▶ Presidential Reconstruction

Abraham Lincoln died on April 15, 1865, just hours after John Wilkes Booth shot him at a Washington, D.C., theater. Chief Justice Salmon P. Chase immediately administered the oath of office to Vice President Andrew Johnson of Tennessee. Congress had adjourned in March and would not reconvene until December. Throughout the summer and fall, Johnson drew up and executed a plan of reconstruction without congressional advice.

Congress returned to the capital in December to find that, as far as the president and former Confederates were concerned, reconstruction was completed. Most Republicans, however, thought Johnson's plan made far too few demands of ex-rebels and made a mockery of the sacrifice of Union soldiers. They claimed that Johnson's leniency had acted as midwife to the rebirth of the Old South, that he had achieved political reunification at the cost of black freedom. Republicans in Congress then proceeded to dismantle Johnson's program and substitute a program of their own.

Johnson's Program of Reconciliation

Born in 1808 in Raleigh, North Carolina, Andrew Johnson was the son of illiterate parents. Self-educated and ambitious, Johnson moved to Tennessee, where he worked as a tailor, accumulated a fortune in land, acquired five slaves, and built a career in politics championing the South's common white people and assailing its "illegitimate, swaggering, bastard, scrub aristocracy." The only senator from a Confederate state to remain loyal to the Union, Johnson held the planter class responsible for secession. Less than two weeks before he became president, he announced what he would do to planters if he ever had the chance: "I would arrest them—I would try them—I would convict them and I would hang them."

A Democrat all his life, Johnson occupied the White House only because the Republican Party in 1864 had needed a vice presidential candidate who would appeal to loyal, Union-supporting Democrats. Johnson vigorously defended states' rights (but not secession) and opposed Republican efforts to expand the power of the federal government. A steadfast supporter of slavery, Johnson had owned slaves until 1862, when Tennessee rebels, angry at his Unionism, confiscated them. When he grudgingly accepted emancipation, it was more because he hated planters than sympathized with slaves. "Damn the negroes," he said. "I am fighting those traitorous aristocrats, their masters." The new president harbored unshakable racist convictions. Africans, Johnson said, were "inferior to the white man in point of intellect—better calculated in physical structure to undergo drudgery and hardship."

Like Lincoln, Johnson stressed the rapid restoration of civil government in the South. Like Lincoln, he promised to pardon most, but not all, ex-rebels. Johnson recognized the state governments created by Lincoln but set out his own requirements for restoring the other rebel states to the Union. All that the citizens of a state had to do was to renounce the right of secession, deny that the debts of the Confederacy were legal and binding, and ratify the Thirteenth Amendment abolishing slavery, which became part of the Constitution in December 1865.

Johnson also returned all confiscated and abandoned land to pardoned ex-Confederates, even if it was in the hands of freedmen. Reformers were shocked. Instead of punishing planters as he had promised, Johnson canceled the promising beginnings made by General Sherman and the Freedmen's Bureau to settle blacks on land of their own. As one freedman observed, "Things was hurt by Mr. Lincoln getting killed."

White Southern Resistance and Black Codes

In the summer of 1865, delegates across the South gathered to draw up the new state constitutions required by Johnson's plan of reconstruction. They refused to accept even the president's mild requirements. Refusing to renounce secession, the South Carolina and Georgia conventions merely "repudiated" their secession ordinances, preserving in principle their right to secede. South Carolina and Mississippi refused to disown their Confederate war debts. Mississippi rejected the Thirteenth Amendment, and Alabama rejected it in part. Despite this defiance, Johnson did nothing. White Southerners began to think that by standing up for themselves they could shape the terms of reconstruction.

New state governments across the South adopted a series of laws known as **black codes**, which made a travesty of black freedom. The codes sought to keep ex-slaves subordinate to whites by subjecting them to every sort of discrimination. Several states made it illegal for blacks to own a gun. Mississippi made insulting gestures and language by blacks a criminal offense. The codes barred blacks from jury duty. Not a single southern state granted any black the right to vote.

At the core of the black codes, however, lay the matter of labor. Legislators sought to hustle freedmen back to the plantations. Whites were almost universally opposed to black landownership. Whitelaw Reid, a northern visitor to the South, found that the "man who should sell small tracts to them would be in actual personal danger." South Carolina attempted to limit blacks to either farmwork or domestic service by requiring them to pay annual taxes of $10 to $100 to work in any other occupation. Mississippi declared that blacks who did not possess written evidence of employment could be declared vagrants and be subject to involuntary plantation labor. Under so-called apprenticeship laws, courts bound thousands of black children—orphans and others whose parents they deemed unable to support them—to work for planter "guardians."

Johnson refused to intervene. A staunch defender of states' rights, he believed that citizens of every state should be free to write their own constitutions and laws. Moreover, Johnson was

The Black Codes

Titled *Selling a Freeman to Pay His Fine at Monticello, Florida*, this 1867 drawing from a northern magazine equates black codes with the reinstitution of slavery. The laws stopped short of reenslavement but sharply restricted blacks' freedom. In southern states, certain acts, such as breaking a labor contract, were made criminal offenses, the penalty for which could be involuntary plantation labor for a year. The Granger Collection, New York.

as eager as other white Southerners to restore white supremacy. "White men alone must manage the South," he declared.

Johnson also recognized that his do-nothing response offered him political advantage. A conservative Tennessee Democrat at the head of a northern Republican Party, he had begun to look southward for political allies. Despite tough talk about punishing traitors, he personally pardoned fourteen thousand wealthy or high-ranking ex-Confederates. By pardoning powerful whites, by accepting state governments even when they failed to satisfy his minimal demands, and by acquiescing in the black codes, he won useful southern friends.

In the fall elections of 1865, white Southerners dramatically expressed their mood. To represent them in Congress, they chose former Confederates. Of the eighty senators and representatives they

sent to Washington, fifteen had served in the Confederate army, ten of them as generals. Another sixteen had served in civil and judicial posts in the Confederacy. Nine others had served in the Confederate Congress. One—Alexander Stephens—had been vice president of the Confederacy. As one Georgian remarked, "It looked as though Richmond had moved to Washington."

Expansion of Federal Authority and Black Rights

Southerners had blundered monumentally. They had assumed that what Andrew Johnson was willing to accept, Republicans would accept as well. But southern intransigence compelled even moderates to conclude that ex-rebels were a "generation of vipers," still untrustworthy and dangerous. The black codes became a symbol of southern intentions to "restore all of slavery but its name." "We tell the white men of Mississippi," the *Chicago Tribune* roared, "that the men of the North will convert the State of Mississippi into a frog pond before they will allow such laws to disgrace one foot of the soil in which the bones of our soldiers sleep and over which the flag of freedom waves."

The moderate majority of the Republican Party wanted only assurance that slavery and treason were dead. They did not champion black equality, the confiscation of plantations, or black voting, as did the Radical minority within the party. But southern obstinacy had succeeded in forging unity (at least temporarily) among Republican factions. In December 1865, Republicans refused to seat the southern representatives elected in the fall elections. Rather than accept Johnson's claim that the "work of restoration" was done, Congress challenged his executive power.

Republican senator Lyman Trumbull declared that the president's policy meant that an ex-slave would "be tyrannized over, abused, and virtually reenslaved without some legislation by the nation for his protection." Early in 1866, the moderates produced two bills that strengthened the federal shield. The first, the Freedmen's Bureau bill, prolonged the life of the agency established by the previous Congress. Arguing that the Constitution never contemplated a "system for the support of indigent persons," President Andrew Johnson vetoed the bill. Congress failed by a narrow margin to override the president's veto.

The moderates designed their second measure, what would become the **Civil Rights Act of 1866**, to nullify the black codes by affirming African Americans' rights to "full and equal benefit of all laws and proceedings for the security of person and property as is enjoyed by white citizens." The act boldly required the end of racial discrimination in state laws and represented an extraordinary expansion of black rights and federal authority. The president argued that the civil rights bill amounted to "unconstitutional invasion of states' rights" and vetoed it. In essence, he denied that the federal government possessed the authority to protect the civil rights of African Americans.

In April 1866, an incensed Republican Party again pushed the civil rights bill through Congress and overrode the presidential veto. In July, it passed another Freedmen's Bureau bill and overrode Johnson's veto. For the first time in American history, Congress had overridden presidential vetoes of major legislation. As a worried South Carolinian observed, Johnson had succeeded in uniting the Republicans and probably touched off "a fight this fall such as has never been seen."

REVIEW   When the southern states passed the black codes, how did the U.S. Congress respond?

▶ Congressional Reconstruction

By the summer of 1866, President Andrew Johnson and Congress had dropped their gloves and stood toe-to-toe in a bare-knuckle contest unprecedented in American history. Johnson

VISUAL ACTIVITY

Reconstruction Cartoon

This 1865 cartoon pokes fun at two Richmond ladies as they pass by a Union officer on their way to receive free government rations. One says sourly to the other, "Don't you think that Yankee must feel like shrinking into his boots before such high-toned Southern ladies as we?" The New York Public Library/Art Resource, NY.

READING THE IMAGE: Just a step behind is a smiling black woman. What does her expression say about her impression of the scene taking place in front of her?

CONNECTIONS: What do these white women suggest about the white South's attitude toward defeat and reconstruction?

made it clear that he would not budge on either constitutional issues or policy. Moderate Republicans responded by amending the Constitution. But the obstinacy of Johnson and white Southerners pushed Republican moderates ever closer to the Radicals and to acceptance of additional federal intervention in the South. To end presidential interference, Congress voted to impeach the president for the first time since the nation was formed. Soon after, Congress also debated whether to make voting rights color-blind, while women sought to make voting sex-blind as well.

The Fourteenth Amendment and Escalating Violence

In June 1866, Congress passed the **Fourteenth Amendment** to the Constitution, and two years later the states ratified it. The most important provisions of this complex amendment made all native-born or naturalized persons American citizens and prohibited states from abridging the "privileges and immunities" of citizens, depriving them of "life, liberty, or property without due process of law," and denying them "equal protection of the laws." By making blacks national citizens, the amendment provided a national guarantee of equality before the law. In essence, it protected blacks against violation by southern state governments.

The Fourteenth Amendment also dealt with voting rights. It gave Congress the right to reduce the congressional representation of states that withheld suffrage from some of its adult male population. In other words, white Southerners could either allow black men to vote or see their representation in Washington slashed. Whatever happened, Republicans stood to benefit from the Fourteenth Amendment. If southern whites granted voting rights to freedmen, Republicans would gain valuable black votes. If whites refused, the number of southern Democrats in Congress would plunge.

The Fourteenth Amendment's suffrage provisions ignored the small band of women who had emerged from the war demanding "the ballot for the two disenfranchised classes, negroes and women." Founding the American Equal Rights Association in 1866, Susan B. Anthony and Elizabeth Cady Stanton lobbied for "a government by the people, and the whole people; for the people and the whole people." They felt betrayed when their old antislavery allies refused to work for their goals. "It was the Negro's hour," Frederick Douglass explained.

Senator Charles Sumner suggested that woman suffrage could be "the great question of the future."

The Fourteenth Amendment provided for punishment of any state that excluded voters on the basis of race but not on the basis of sex. The amendment also introduced the word *male* into the Constitution when it referred to a citizen's right to vote. Stanton predicted that "if that word 'male' be inserted, it will take us a century at least to get it out."

Tennessee approved the Fourteenth Amendment in July, and Congress promptly welcomed the state's representatives and senators back. Had President Johnson counseled other southern states to ratify this relatively mild amendment, they might have listened. Instead, Johnson advised Southerners to reject

Elizabeth Cady Stanton and Susan B. Anthony
Stanton, seated, and Anthony, shown in their later years, were lifelong friends and veteran reformers who advocated, among other things, improved working conditions for labor, married women's property rights, liberalization of divorce laws, and women's admission into colleges and trade schools. Their broad agenda led some conservatives to oppose women's political rights because they equated the suffragist cause with radicalism in general.
Library of Congress, 3a02558.

"This Is a White Man's Government" (1868)
This Thomas Nast cartoon lambasts the Democratic Party's recent platform advocating white supremacy. Nast portrays the Democrats as a white Southerner with a knife, a stereotyped Irishman with a club, and a plutocrat lifting a wallet that reads, "capital for votes." They all rest a foot on the back of a prostrate African American soldier. Library of Congress, 3c21735.

the Fourteenth Amendment and to rely on him to trounce the Republicans in the fall congressional elections.

Johnson had decided to make the Fourteenth Amendment the overriding issue of the 1866 elections and to gather its white opponents into a new conservative party, the National Union Party. The president's strategy suffered a setback when whites in several southern cities went on rampages against blacks. Mobs killed thirty-four blacks in New Orleans and forty-six blacks in Memphis. The slaughter shocked Northerners and renewed skepticism about

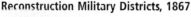

Reconstruction Military Districts, 1867

Johnson's claim that southern whites could be trusted. "Who doubts that the Freedmen's Bureau ought to be abolished forthwith," a New Yorker observed sarcastically, "and the blacks remitted to the paternal care of their old masters, who 'understand the nigger, you know, a great deal better than the Yankees can.'"

The 1866 elections resulted in an overwhelming Republican victory. Johnson had bet that Northerners would not support federal protection of black rights and that a racist backlash would blast the Republican Party. But the war was still fresh in northern minds, and as one Republican explained, southern whites "with all their intelligence were traitors, the blacks with all their ignorance were loyal."

Radical Reconstruction and Military Rule

When Johnson continued to urge Southerners to reject the Fourteenth Amendment, every southern state except Tennessee voted it down. "The last one of the sinful ten," thundered Representative James A. Garfield of Ohio, "has flung back into our teeth the magnanimous offer of a generous nation." After the South rejected the moderates' program, the Radicals seized the initiative.

Each act of defiance by southern whites had boosted the standing of the Radicals within the Republican Party. Except for freedmen themselves, no one did more to make freedom the "mighty moral question of the age." Radicals such as Massachusetts senator Charles Sumner and Pennsylvania representative Thaddeus Stevens united in demanding civil and political equality. Southern states were "like clay in the hands of the potter," Stevens declared in January 1867, and he called on Congress to begin reconstruction all over again.

In March 1867, Congress overturned the Johnson state governments and initiated military rule of the South. The **Military Reconstruction Act** (and three subsequent acts) divided the ten unreconstructed Confederate states into five military districts. Congress placed a Union general in charge of each district and instructed him to "suppress insurrection, disorder, and violence" and to begin political reform. After the military had completed voter registration, which would include black men, voters in each state would elect delegates to conventions that would draw up new state constitutions. Each constitution would guarantee black suffrage. When the voters of each state had approved the constitution and the state legislature had ratified the Fourteenth Amendment, the state could submit its work to Congress. If Congress approved, the state's senators and representatives could be seated, and political reunification would be accomplished.

Radicals proclaimed the provision for black suffrage "a prodigious triumph," for it extended far beyond the limited suffrage provisions of the Fourteenth Amendment. When combined with the disfranchisement of thousands of ex-rebels, it promised to cripple any neo-Confederate resurgence and guarantee Republican state governments in the South.

Despite its bold suffrage provision, the Military Reconstruction Act of 1867 disappointed those who also advocated the confiscation of southern plantations and their redistribution to ex-slaves. Thaddeus Stevens agreed with the freedman who said, "Give us our own land and we take care of ourselves, but without land, the old masters can hire us or starve us, as they please." But most Republicans believed they had provided blacks with what they needed: equal legal rights and the ballot. Besides, confiscation was too radical, even for some Radicals. Confiscating private property, declared the *New York Times*, "strikes at the root of all property rights in both sections. It concerns Massachusetts quite as much as Mississippi." If blacks were to get land, they would have to gain it themselves.

Declaring that he would rather sever his right arm than sign such a formula for "anarchy and chaos," Andrew Johnson vetoed the Military Reconstruction Act, but Congress overrode his veto. With the passage of the Reconstruction Acts of 1867, congressional reconstruction was virtually completed. Congress left whites owning most of the South's land but, in a departure that justified the term *radical reconstruction*, had given black men the ballot.

Impeaching a President

Despite his defeats, Andrew Johnson had no intention of yielding control of reconstruction. In a dozen ways, he sabotaged Congress's will and encouraged southern whites to resist. He issued a flood of pardons, waged war against the Freedmen's Bureau, and replaced Union generals eager to enforce Congress's Reconstruction Acts with conservative officers eager to block them. Johnson claimed that he was merely defending the "violated Constitution." At bottom, however, the president subverted congressional reconstruction to protect southern whites from what he considered the horrors of "Negro domination."

Radicals argued that Johnson's abuse of constitutional powers and his failure to fulfill constitutional obligations to enforce the law were impeachable offenses. According to the Constitution, the House of Representatives can impeach and the Senate can try any federal official for "treason, bribery, or other high crimes and misdemeanors." But moderates interpreted the Constitution to mean violation of criminal statutes. As long as Johnson refrained from breaking the law, impeachment (the process of formal charges of wrongdoing against the president or other federal official) remained stalled.

Then in August 1867, Johnson suspended Secretary of War Edwin M. Stanton from office. As required by the Tenure of Office Act, which demanded the approval of the Senate for the removal of any government official who had been appointed with Senate approval, the president requested the Senate to consent to Stanton's dismissal. When the Senate balked, Johnson removed Stanton anyway. "Is the President crazy, or only drunk?" asked a dumbfounded Republican moderate. "I'm afraid his doings will make us all favor impeachment."

News of Johnson's open defiance of the law convinced every Republican in the House to vote for a resolution impeaching the president. Supreme Court chief justice Salmon Chase presided over the Senate trial, which lasted from March until May 1868. When the vote came, thirty-five senators voted guilty and nineteen not guilty. The impeachment forces fell one vote short of the two-thirds needed to convict.

After his trial, Johnson called a truce, and for the remaining ten months of his term, congressional reconstruction proceeded unhindered by presidential interference. Without interference from Johnson, Congress revisited the suffrage issue.

The Fifteenth Amendment and Women's Demands

In February 1869, Republicans passed the **Fifteenth Amendment** to the Constitution, which prohibited states from depriving any citizen of the right to vote because of "race, color, or previous condition of servitude." The Reconstruction Acts of 1867 already required black suffrage in the South; the Fifteenth Amendment extended black voting nationwide.

Some Republicans, however, found the final wording of the Fifteenth Amendment "lame and halting." Rather than absolutely guaranteeing the right to vote, the amendment merely prohibited exclusion on grounds of race. The distinction would prove to be significant. In time, white Southerners would devise tests of literacy and property and other apparently nonracial measures that would effectively disfranchise blacks yet not violate the Fifteenth Amendment. But an amendment that fully guaranteed the right to vote courted defeat outside the South. Rising antiforeign sentiment—against the Chinese in California and European immigrants in the Northeast—caused states to resist giving up total control of suffrage requirements. In March 1870, after three-fourths of the states had ratified it, the Fifteenth Amendment became part of the Constitution.

Woman suffrage advocates, however, were sorely disappointed with the Fifteenth Amendment's failure to extend voting rights to women. Elizabeth Cady Stanton and Susan B. Anthony condemned the Republicans' "negro first" strategy and pointed out that women remained "the only class of citizens wholly unrepresented in the government." Increasingly, activist women concluded that woman "must not put her trust in man." The Fifteenth Amendment severed the early feminist movement from its abolitionist roots. Over the next several decades, feminists established an independent suffrage crusade that drew millions of women into political life.

Republicans took enough satisfaction in the Fifteenth Amendment to conclude that black suffrage was the "last great point that remained to be settled of the issues of the war" and promptly scratched the "Negro question" from the agenda of national politics. Even that steadfast crusader for equality Wendell Phillips concluded that the black man now held "sufficient shield in his own hands. . . . Whatever he suffers will be largely now, and in future, his own fault." Northerners had no idea of the violent struggles that lay ahead.

> **REVIEW**   Why did Congress impeach President Andrew Johnson?

▶ The Struggle in the South

Northerners believed they had discharged their responsibilities with the Reconstruction Acts and the amendments to the Constitution, but Southerners knew that the battle had just begun. Black suffrage had destroyed traditional southern politics and established the foundation for the rise of the Republican Party. Gathering outsiders and outcasts, southern Republicans won elections, wrote new state constitutions, and formed new state governments.

Challenging the established class for political control was dangerous business. Equally dangerous were the confrontations that took place on southern farms and plantations, where blacks sought to give fuller meaning to their newly won legal and political equality. Ex-masters had their own ideas about the labor system that should replace slavery, and freedom remained contested territory. Southerners fought pitched battles with one another to determine the contours of their new world.

Freedmen, Yankees, and Yeomen

African Americans made up the majority of southern Republicans. After gaining voting rights in 1867, nearly all eligible black men registered to vote as Republicans, grateful to the party that had freed them and granted them the franchise. "It is the hardest thing in the world to keep a negro away from the polls," observed an Alabama white man. Southern blacks did not all have identical political priorities, but they united in their desire for education and equal treatment before the law.

Northern whites who made the South their home after the war were a second element of the South's Republican Party. Conservative white Southerners called them **carpetbaggers**, opportunists who stuffed all their belongings in a single carpet-sided suitcase and headed south to "fatten on our misfortunes." But most Northerners who moved south were young men who looked upon the South as they did the West— as a promising place to make a living. Northerners in the southern Republican Party supported programs that encouraged vigorous economic development along the lines of the northern free-labor model.

What Did the Ku Klux Klan Really Want?

In 1866, six Confederate veterans in Pulaski, Tennessee, founded the Ku Klux Klan for fun and fellowship. By 1868, when congressional recon- struction went into effect, the Klan had spread across the South, and members had turned to more serious matters.

According to former Confederate general and Georgia Democratic poli- tician John B. Gordon, the Klan owed its popularity to the "instinct of self- preservation . . . the sense of insecu- rity and danger, particularly in those neighborhoods where the Negro population largely predominated." Everywhere whites looked, he said, they saw "great crime." Republican politicians marched ignorant freed- men to the polls, where they voted as they were told. Ex-slaves drove overseers from plantations and claimed the land for themselves. Black rapists made white women cower behind barred doors. It was necessary, Gordon declared, "in order to protect our families from outrage and preserve our own lives, to have something that we could regard as a brotherhood—a combination of the best men of the country, to act purely in self- defense."

Behind the Klan's high-minded and self-justifying rhetoric, however, lay another agenda. It was revealed in their actions, not their words. Klansmen embarked on a campaign to reverse history. Garbed in robes and hoods, they engaged in guerrilla warfare against free labor, civil equality, and political democracy. They aimed to terrorize their enemies—ex-slaves and white Republicans—into submission. Changes in four particular areas of southern life proved flash points for Klan violence: racial etiquette, education, labor, and politics.

The Klan punished blacks and whites who broke the Old South's racial code. The Klan considered "impudence" a punishable offense. Asked to define "impudence" before a congressional investigating commit- tee, one white man responded: "Well, it is considered impudence for a negro not to be polite to a white man—not to pull off his hat and bow and scrape to a white man, as was done formerly." Klansmen whipped blacks for speaking disrespectfully,

refusing to yield the sidewalk, and dressing well. Black women who "dress up and fix up like ladies" risked a midnight visit from the Klan. The Klan sought to restore racial sub- ordination in every aspect of private and public life.

Klansmen also took aim at black education. White men found the sight of blacks in classrooms hard to stomach. Schools were easy targets, and scores of them went up in flames. Teachers, male and female, were flogged, or worse. Klansmen drove northern-born teacher Alonzo B. Corliss from North Carolina for "teaching niggers and making them like white men." In Cross Plains, Alabama, the Klan hanged an Irish- born teacher along with four black men. Planters wanted ex-slaves back in the fields, not at desks. In 1869, an Alabama newspaper announced that the burning of a black school should be "a warning for them to stick here- after to 'de shovel and de hoe,' and let their dirty-backed primers go."

Planters also turned to the Klan as part of their effort to preserve plantation agriculture. An Alabama white admitted that in his area the Klan was "intended principally for the negroes who failed to work." Hooded bands "punished Negroes whose landlords had complained of them." Sharecroppers who disputed their share at "settling up time" risked a visit from the night riders. It was dangerous for freedmen to consider changing employers. "If we got out looking for some other place to go," an ex-slave from Texas

Southern whites made up the third element of the South's Republican Party. Approximately one out of four white Southerners voted Republican. The other three condemned the one who did as a traitor to his region and his race and called him a scalawag, a term for runty horses and low-down, good-for-nothing rascals. Yeoman farmers accounted for the major- ity of southern white Republicans. Some were Unionists who emerged from the war with bit- ter memories of Confederate persecution. Others were small farmers who wanted to end state governments' favoritism toward plantation own- ers. Yeomen supported initiatives for public schools and for expanding economic opportunity in the South.

The South's Republican Party, then, was made up of freedmen, Yankees, and yeomen—an improbable coalition. The mix of races, regions, and classes inevitably meant friction as each group maneuvered to define the party. But Reconstruction represented an extraordinary

Two Members of the Ku Klux Klan, about 1868
During Reconstruction, Klansmen wore robes of various designs and colors. Uniform white robes came later. These counterrevolutionary terrorists fought to beat back free labor, democracy, and republicanism and to force the South back into its antebellum channels. Dallas Historical Society, Texas, USA/Bridgeman Images.

was even bloodier, suffering more than one thousand killings in the same year. In Georgia, the Klan murdered three scalawag members of the legislature and drove ten others from their homes. As one Georgia Republican commented after a Klan attack: "We don't call them [D]emocrats, we call them southern murderers."

It proved hard to arrest Klansmen and harder still to convict them. "If a white man kills a colored man in any of the counties of this State," observed a Florida sheriff, "you cannot convict him." Federal intervention—in the Ku Klux Klan Acts of 1870 and 1871—signaled an end to much of the Klan's power but not to counterrevolutionary violence in the South. Other groups continued the terror in the cause of white supremacy.

Questions for Analysis

Summarize the Argument: According to the author, what were the primary goals of the Ku Klux Klan?

Analyze the Evidence: Why did Klansmen believe that their actions were justified? What specific "crimes" did they aim to address? Why do you think they hid their identities?

Consider the Context: How did the Ku Klux Klan serve the counterrevolutionary goals of the South's Democratic Party?

remembered, "them KKK they would tend to Mister negro good and plenty."

Above all, the Klan terrorized Republicans. Klansmen became the military arm of the Democratic Party. They drove blacks from the polls on election day and assaulted Republican officeholders. Klansmen gave Andrew Flowers, a black politician in Chattanooga, a brutal beating and told him that they "did not intend any nigger to hold office in the United States." Jack Dupree, president of the Republican Club in Monroe County, Mississippi, a man known to "speak his mind," had his throat cut and was disemboweled while his wife was forced to watch.

Political violence reached astounding levels. Arkansas experienced nearly three hundred political killings in the three months before the fall elections in 1868. Louisiana

moment in American politics: Blacks and whites joined together in the Republican Party to pursue political change. Formally, of course, only men participated in politics—casting ballots and holding offices—but white and black women also played a part in the political struggle by joining in parades and rallies, attending stump speeches, and even campaigning.

Most whites in the South condemned southern Republicans as illegitimate and felt justified in doing whatever they could to stamp them out.

Violence against blacks—the "white terror"—took brutal institutional form in 1866 with the formation in Tennessee of the **Ku Klux Klan**, a social club of Confederate veterans that quickly developed into a paramilitary organization supporting Democrats. The Klan went on a rampage of whipping, hanging, shooting, burning, and throat-cutting to defeat Republicans and restore white supremacy. (See "Making Historical Arguments," above.) Rapid demobilization of the Union army after the war left only twenty thousand troops to patrol the entire South. Without effective military protection, southern Republicans had to take care of themselves.

Republican Rule

In the fall of 1867, southern states held elections for delegates to state constitutional conventions, as required by the Reconstruction Acts. About 40 percent of the white electorate stayed home because they had been disfranchised or because they had decided to boycott politics. Republicans won three-fourths of the seats. About 15 percent of the Republican delegates to the conventions were Northerners who had moved south, 25 percent were African Americans, and 60 percent were white Southerners. As a British visitor observed, the delegate elections reflected "the mighty revolution that had taken place in America."

The conventions brought together serious, purposeful men who hammered out the legal framework for a new order. The reconstruction constitutions introduced two broad categories of changes in the South: those that reduced aristocratic privilege and increased democratic equality and those that expanded the state's responsibility for the general welfare. In the first

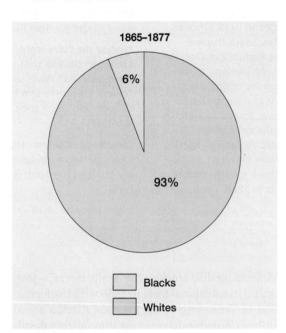

FIGURE 16.1   Southern Congressional Delegations, 1865–1877
The statistics contradict the myth of black domination of congressional representation during Reconstruction.

category, the constitutions adopted universal male suffrage, abolished property qualifications for holding office, and made more offices elective and fewer appointed. In the second category, they enacted prison reform; made the state responsible for caring for orphans, the insane, and the deaf and mute; and exempted debtors' homes from seizure.

To Democrats, however, these progressive constitutions looked like wild revolution. They were blind to the fact that no constitution confiscated and redistributed land, as virtually every former slave wished, or disfranchised ex-rebels wholesale, as most southern Unionists advocated. And Democrats were convinced that the new constitutions initiated "Negro domination." In fact, although 80 percent of Republican voters were black men, only 6 percent of Southerners in Congress during Reconstruction were black (Figure 16.1). The sixteen black men in Congress included exceptional men, such as Representative James T. Rapier of Alabama (see pages 440–41). No state legislature experienced "Negro rule," despite black majorities in the populations of some states.

Southern voters ratified the new constitutions and swept Republicans into power. When the former Confederate states ratified the Fourteenth Amendment, Congress readmitted them. Southern Republicans then turned to a staggering array of problems. Wartime destruction littered the landscape. Making matters worse, racial harassment and reactionary violence dogged Southerners who sought reform. Democrats mocked Republican officeholders as ignorant field hands who had only "agricultural degrees" and "brick yard diplomas," but Republicans began a serious effort to rebuild and reform the region.

Activity focused on three areas—education, civil rights, and economic development. Every state inaugurated a system of public education. Before the Civil War, whites had deliberately kept slaves illiterate, and planter-dominated governments rarely spent tax money to educate the children of yeomen. By 1875, half of Mississippi's and South Carolina's eligible children were attending school. Although schools were underfunded, literacy rates rose sharply. Public schools were racially segregated, but education remained for many blacks a tangible, deeply satisfying benefit of freedom and Republican rule.

Students at a Freedmen's School in Virginia, ca. 1870s
"The people are hungry and thirsty after knowledge," a former slave observed immediately after the Civil War. African American leader Booker T. Washington remembered "a whole race trying to go to school." Students at this Virginia school stand in front of their log-cabin classroom, reading books. For people long forbidden to learn to read and write, literacy symbolized freedom. Photo12/UIG/Getty Images.

State legislatures also attacked racial discrimination and defended civil rights. Republicans especially resisted efforts to segregate blacks from whites in public transportation. Mississippi levied fines and jail terms for owners of railroads and steamboats that pushed blacks into "smoking cars" or to lower decks. But passing color-blind laws was one thing; enforcing them was another. A Mississippian complained: "Education amounts to nothing, good behavior counts for nothing, even money cannot buy for a colored man or woman decent treatment and the comforts that white people claim and can obtain." Despite the laws, segregation—later called Jim Crow—developed at white insistence. Determined to underscore the social inferiority of blacks, whites saw to it that separation by race became a feature

of southern life long before the end of the Reconstruction era.

Republican governments also launched ambitious programs of economic development. They envisioned a South of diversified agriculture, roaring factories, and booming towns. State legislatures chartered scores of banks and industrial companies, appropriated funds to fix ruined levees and drain swamps, and went on a railroad-building binge. These efforts fell far short of solving the South's economic troubles, however. Republican spending to stimulate economic growth also meant rising taxes and enormous debt that siphoned funds from schools and other programs.

The southern Republicans' record, then, was mixed. To their credit, the biracial party adopted

The Slaveholder Exodus

On the eve of the Civil War, southern slaveholders agreed that blacks were inferior, that without total subordination they were dangerous and destructive, and that without coercion they would not work. Voicing nearly universal sentiments, Henry Watson, an Alabama planter, declared that "if emancipation takes place," plantations "will be worth nothing." Mississippi planter James Kirkland asserted that he had rather "be exterminated" than live in the same society "with the slaves if freed." Faced with a Republican victory in the election of 1860, planters led the South out of the Union and fought a ferocious war to keep blacks in bondage.

Yankee victory meant abolition, but slaveholders ended the war much as they began it, still believing that without slavery the South "would be wholly worthless, a barren waste and desolate plain." Robert Barnwell Rhett Sr. of South Carolina reaffirmed the widespread conviction that "it is absurd to suppose that the African will work under a system of voluntary labor. . . . The labor of the negro must be compulsory—he must be a slave."

Three months after Appomattox, an Alabama planter described the scene to his absent partner: "The Yankees have declared the Negroes all free. We have no authority to control them in any way, or even to defend ourselves. . . . Our country and town are filled with idle negroes, crops abandoned in many cases. On some plantations all the negroes have left. . . . The result will be that our whole country north and south will be impoverished and ruined. . . . The loss of our slaves, to a very great extent destroys the value of all other property. . . . All want to sell and get out of the country. Many expect to go to South [America]. . . . The idea is to get away from the free Negro."

Thousands of white Southerners, perhaps as many as ten thousand, fled after the Confederacy fell. They did not flee blindly; planters overwhelmingly chose Brazil. Because "it was the last resting place of slavery," they believed that it offered the best chance of resurrecting antebellum southern society. The ruler of Brazil, Dom Pedro II, personally encouraged Southerners to come settle. But planters had no intention of assimilating into local life. One emigrant remembered that southern planters in Brazil were "tenacious of their ideas, manners, & religion" and "laughed with scorn" at their "adopted land." They had to be, he said, *masters.*

---

an ambitious agenda to change the South. But money was scarce, the Democrats continued their harassment, and factionalism threatened the Republican Party from within. Moreover, corruption infected Republican governments. Nonetheless, the Republican Party made headway in its efforts to purge the South of aristocratic privilege and racist oppression. Republican governments had less success in overthrowing the long-established white oppression of black farm laborers in the rural South.

White Landlords, Black Sharecroppers

Ex-slaves who wished to escape slave labor and ex-masters who wanted to reinstitute old ways clashed repeatedly. Except for having to pay subsistence wages, planters had not been required to offer many concessions to emancipation. They continued to believe that African Americans would not work without coercion. A Tennessee man declared two years after the war ended that blacks were "a trifling set of lazy devils who will never make a living without Masters." Whites moved quickly to restore as much of slavery as they could get away with. (See "Beyond America's Borders," above.)

Ex-slaves resisted every effort to turn back the clock. They argued that if any class could be described as "lazy," it was the planters, who, as one former slave noted, "lived in idleness all their lives on stolen labor." Freedmen believed that land of their own would anchor their economic independence and end planters' interference in their personal lives. They could then, for example, make their own decisions about whether women and children would labor in the fields. Indeed, within months after the war, perhaps one-third of black women abandoned field labor to work on chores in their own cabins just as poor white women did. Black women also negotiated about work ex-mistresses wanted done in the big house. Hundreds of thousands of black children enrolled in school. But without their own land, ex-slaves had little choice but to work on plantations.

Firsthand experience in Brazil pleased some Southerners. Charles G. Gunter of Marengo County, Alabama, loved Brazil's climate, people, land, and government, and he wrote to his son that he expected to soon buy a plantation with "fifty to a hundred slaves." Eight months later, he declared: "Dispose of, give away and settle my affairs as if I were dead to the U.S. I shall never go there again." Now owner of a plot of six thousand acres and "enough negroes to work it," he concluded: "We shall be rich here." His only complaints were "ants and a spirit of democracy among the people—no great evils in comparison with free negro labor, radicalism and taxes."

But many more southern planters were shocked by Brazil. Andrew McCollam of Louisiana quickly concluded that "all is not gold that glitters here." He saw the "finger of decay" everywhere. Even more disturbing was the state of race relations. Everywhere he looked, he found "white men & negro women all together." But in the end it was the shaky status of slavery that ended his experiment as a Brazilian planter. The prevailing impression, he said, was that "slavery would be abolished in less than 20 years, perhaps . . . in ten years." McCollam was captivated by the beauty of the country and said wistfully that if only a hundred good "families from Louisiana could be located here and the institution of slavery insured I should think I had found a new land of promise." With that, he boarded a steamer for Louisiana.

In the end, southern planters failed to re-create antebellum plantation society overseas. By 1870, most émigrés to Brazil had found their way back home, where they joined the vast majority of former slaveholders who had stayed put. Staying put, however, did not signal an acceptance of free black labor. Indeed, for every slaveholder who joined the exodus, several others longed to join him. Many had "the inclination," a Mississippi woman observed in 1866, but "not the means." Since both the returned emigrants and the stay-at-homes shared the same grim prediction for southern plantations with free black labor, they joined together to channel plantation affairs back into familiar antebellum ways.

Questions for Analysis

Summarize the Argument: What drove former slaveholders out of the South after the Civil War, and what specifically attracted them to Brazil?

Recognize Viewpoints: What sustained slaveholders' proslavery ideas through the war, and why didn't the fact of emancipation change their minds about the necessity of slavery?

Consider the Context: What were the consequences of the persistence of proslavery thinking for the South's transition from slavery to free labor during Reconstruction?

Black Woman in Cotton Fields, Thomasville, Georgia
Few images of everyday black women during the Reconstruction era survive. This 1895 photograph poignantly depicts the post–Civil War labor struggle, when white landlords wanted emancipated slaves to continue working in the fields. Freedom allowed some women to escape field labor, but not this Georgian. Her headdress protected her from the fierce heat, and her bare feet reveal the hardships of her life. Courtesy, Georgia Archives, Vanishing Georgia Collection tho096.

Although forced to return to the planters' fields, they resisted efforts to restore slavelike conditions. Instead of working for wages, a South Carolinian observed, "the negroes all seem disposed to rent land," which increased their independence from whites. Out of this tug-of-war between white landlords and black laborers emerged a new system of southern agriculture.

Sharecropping was a compromise that offered something to both ex-masters and ex-slaves but satisfied neither. Under the new system, planters divided their cotton plantations into small farms that freedmen rented,

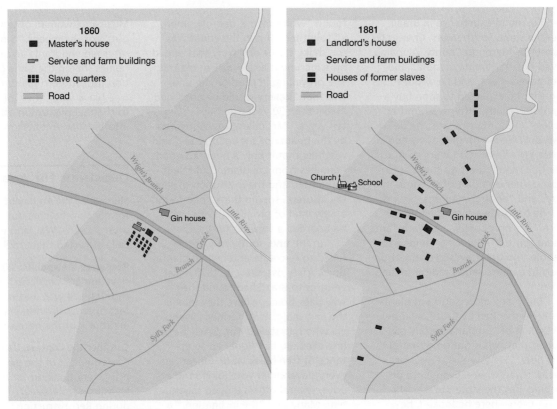

MAP ACTIVITY

Map 16.1   A Southern Plantation in 1860 and 1881

These maps of the Barrow plantation in Georgia illustrate some of the ways in which ex-slaves expressed their freedom. Freedmen and freedwomen deserted the clustered living quarters behind the master's house, scattered over the plantation, built family cabins, and farmed rented land. The former Barrow slaves also worked together to build a school and a church.

READING THE MAP: Compare the number and size of the slave quarters in 1860 with the homes of the former slaves in 1881. How do they differ? Which buildings were prominently located along the road in 1860, and which could be found along the road in 1881?

CONNECTIONS: How might the former master feel about the new configuration of buildings on the plantation in 1881? In what ways did the new system of sharecropping replicate the old system of plantation agriculture? In what ways was it different?

paying with a share of each year's crop, usually half. Sharecropping gave blacks more freedom than the system of wages and labor gangs and released them from day-to-day supervision by whites. Black families abandoned the old slave quarters and built separate cabins for themselves on the patches of land they rented (Map 16.1). Still, most black families remained dependent on white landlords, who had the power to evict them at the end of each growing season. For planters, sharecropping offered a way to resume agricultural production, but it did not allow them to restore the old slave plantation.

Sharecropping introduced the country merchant into the agricultural equation. Landlords supplied sharecroppers with land, mules, seeds, and tools, but blacks also needed credit to obtain essential food and clothing before they harvested their crops. Under an arrangement called a crop lien, a merchant would advance goods to a sharecropper in exchange for a *lien*, or legal claim, on the farmer's future crop. Some merchants charged exorbitant rates of interest, as much as 60 percent, on the goods they sold. At the end of the growing season, after the landlord had taken half of the farmer's crop for rent, the merchant took most of the rest.

"I BEG TO REPEAT THAT THESE FRAUDS ON THE GOVERNMENT SHALL BE PROBED TO THE VERY BOTTOM."

TAMMANY RING. CANAL RING. WHISKEY RING. INDIAN RING PRESS RING. STATE RING COUNTY RING. TOWN RING WARD RING

BELKNAP

FRAUD CLAIMS

BACK PAY GRAB

WHISKEY FRAUDS

BRIBERY

VISUAL ACTIVITY

Grant and Scandal

This anti-Grant cartoon by Thomas Nast, the nation's most celebrated political cartoonist, shows the president falling headfirst into the barrel of fraud and corruption that tainted his administration. During Grant's eight years in the White House, many members of his administration failed him. Sometimes duped, sometimes merely loyal, Grant stubbornly defended wrongdoers, even to the point of perjuring himself to keep an aide out of jail. Picture Research Consultants & Archives.

READING THE IMAGE: How does Nast portray President Grant's role in corruption? According to this cartoon, what caused the problems?

CONNECTIONS: How responsible was President Grant for the corruption that plagued his administration?

Sometimes, the farmer did not earn enough to repay the debt to the merchant, so he would have to borrow more from the merchant and begin the cycle again.

An experiment at first, sharecropping soon dominated the cotton South. Lien merchants forced tenants to plant cotton, which was easy to sell, instead of food crops. The result was excessive production of cotton and falling cotton prices, developments that cost thousands of small white farmers their land and pushed them into the great army of sharecroppers. The new share-cropping system of agriculture took shape just as the political power of Republicans in the South began to buckle under Democratic pressure.

REVIEW   How did politics and economic concerns shape reconstruction in the South?

▶ Reconstruction Collapses

By 1870, after a decade of war and reconstruction, Northerners wanted to put "the southern problem" behind them. Practical business-minded men came to dominate the Republican Party, replacing the band of reformers and idealists who had been prominent in the 1860s. Civil War hero Ulysses S. Grant succeeded Andrew Johnson as president in 1869 and quickly became an issue himself, proving that brilliance on the battlefield does not necessarily translate into accomplishment in the White House. As north-ern commitment to defend black freedom eroded, southern commitment to white supremacy inten-sified. Without northern protection, southern Republicans were no match for the Democrats' economic coercion, political fraud, and bloody violence. One by one, Republican state governments fell in the South. The election of 1876 both confirmed and completed the collapse of reconstruction.

Grant's Troubled Presidency

In 1868, the Republican Party's presidential nomination went to Ulysses S. Grant, the North's favorite general. His Democratic opponent, Horatio Seymour of New York, ran on a platform that blasted reconstruction as "a flagrant usurpation of power . . . unconstitutional, revolutionary, and void." The Republicans answered by "waving the bloody shirt"—that is, they reminded voters that the Democrats were "the party of rebellion." Despite a reign of terror in the South, costing hundreds of Republicans their lives, Grant gained a narrow 309,000-vote margin in the popular vote and a substantial victory (214 votes to 80) in the electoral college (Map 16.2).

Grant was not as good a president as he was a general. The talents he had demonstrated on the battlefield—decisiveness, clarity, and resolution—were less obvious in the White House. Grant sought both justice for blacks and sectional reconciliation. But he surrounded himself with fumbling kinfolk and old friends from his army days and made a string of dubious appointments that led to a series of damaging scandals. Charges

of corruption tainted his vice president, Schuyler Colfax, and brought down two of his cabinet officers. Though never personally implicated in any scandal, Grant was aggravatingly naive and blind to the rot that filled his administration. Republican congressman James A. Garfield declared: "His imperturbability is amazing. I am in doubt whether to call it greatness or stupidity."

In 1872, anti-Grant Republicans bolted and launched the Liberal Party. To clean up the graft and corruption, Liberals proposed ending the spoils system, by which victorious parties rewarded loyal workers with public office, and replacing it with a nonpartisan civil service commission that would oversee competitive examinations for appointment to office (as discussed in chapter 18). Liberals also demanded that the federal government remove its troops from the South and restore "home rule" (southern white control). Democrats liked the Liberals' southern policy and endorsed the Liberal presidential candidate, Horace Greeley, the longtime editor of the *New York Tribune*. The nation, however, still felt enormous affection for the man who had saved the Union and reelected Grant with 56 percent of the popular vote.

Northern Resolve Withers

Although Grant genuinely wanted to see blacks' civil and political rights protected, he understood that most Northerners had grown weary of reconstruction and were increasingly willing to let southern whites manage their own affairs. Citizens wanted to shift their attention to other issues, especially after the nation slipped into a devastating economic depression in 1873. More than eighteen thousand businesses collapsed, leaving more than a million workers on the streets. Northern businessmen wanted to invest in the South but believed that recurrent federal intrusion was itself a major cause of instability in the region. Republican leaders began to question the wisdom of their party's alliance with the South's lower classes—its small farmers and sharecroppers. One member of Grant's administration proposed allying with the "thinking and influential native southerners . . . the intelligent, well-to-do, and controlling class."

Congress, too, wanted to leave reconstruction behind, but southern Republicans made that difficult. When the South's Republicans begged for federal protection from increasing Klan violence, Congress enacted three laws in 1870 and 1871 that were intended to break the back of

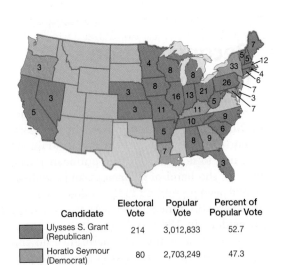

Candidate	Electoral Vote	Popular Vote	Percent of Popular Vote
Ulysses S. Grant (Republican)	214	3,012,833	52.7
Horatio Seymour (Democrat)	80	2,703,249	47.3
Nonvoting states (Reconstruction)			

Map 16.2
The Election of 1868

white terrorism. The severest of the three, the Ku Klux Klan Act (1871), made interference with voting rights a felony. Federal marshals arrested thousands of Klansmen and came close to destroying the Klan, but they did not end all terrorism against blacks. Congress also passed the Civil Rights Act of 1875, which boldly outlawed racial discrimination in transportation, public accommodations, and juries. But federal authorities never enforced the law aggressively, and segregation remained the rule throughout the South.

By the early 1870s, the Republican Party had lost its leading champions of African American rights to death or defeat at the polls. Other Republicans concluded that the quest for black equality was mistaken or hopelessly naive. In May 1872, Congress restored the right of officeholding to all but three hundred ex-rebels. Many Republicans had come to believe that traditional white leaders offered the best hope for honesty, order, and prosperity in the South.

Underlying the North's abandonment of reconstruction was unyielding racial prejudice. Northerners had learned to accept black freedom during the war, but deep-seated prejudice prevented many from accepting black equality. Even the actions they took on behalf of blacks often served partisan political advantage. Northerners generally supported Indiana senator Thomas A. Hendricks's harsh declaration that "this is a white man's Government, made by the white man for the white man."

The U.S. Supreme Court also did its part to undermine reconstruction. The Court issued a series of decisions that significantly weakened the federal government's ability to protect black Southerners. In the *Slaughterhouse* cases (1873), the Court distinguished between national and state citizenship and ruled that the Fourteenth Amendment protected only those rights that stemmed from the federal government, such as voting in federal elections and interstate travel. Since the Court decided that most rights derived from the states, it sharply curtailed the federal government's authority to defend black citizens. Even more devastating, the *United States v. Cruikshank* ruling (1876) said that the reconstruction amendments gave Congress the power to legislate against discrimination only by states, not by individuals. The "suppression of ordinary crime," such as assault, remained a state responsibility. The Supreme Court did not declare reconstruction unconstitutional but eroded its legal foundation.

The mood of the North found political expression in the election of 1874, when for the first

"White Man's Country"
This silk ribbon from the 1868 presidential campaign between Republican Ulysses S. Grant and his Democratic opponent, New York governor Horatio Seymour, openly declares the Democrats' goal of white supremacy. During the campaign, Democratic vice presidential nominee Francis P. Blair Jr. promised that a Seymour victory would restore "white people" to power by declaring the reconstruction governments in the South "null and void." David J. & Janice L. Frent Collection/Corbis.

time in eighteen years the Democrats gained control of the House of Representatives. As one Republican observed, the people had grown tired of the "negro question, with all its complications, and the reconstruction of Southern States, with all its interminable embroilments." Reconstruction had come apart. Rather than defend reconstruction from its southern enemies, Northerners steadily backed away from the challenge. By the early 1870s, southern Republicans faced the forces of reaction largely on their own.

White Supremacy Triumphs

Reconstruction was a massive humiliation to most white Southerners. Republican rule meant intolerable insults: Black militiamen patrolled town streets, black laborers negotiated contracts with former masters, black maids stood up to former mistresses, black voters cast ballots, and black legislators such as James T. Rapier enacted laws. Whites fought back by extolling the "great Confederate cause," or Lost Cause. They celebrated their soldiers, "the noblest band of men who ever fought," and by making an idol of Robert E. Lee, the embodiment of the southern gentleman.

But the most important way white Southerners responded to reconstruction was their assault on Republican governments in the

South. These Republican governments attracted more hatred than did any other political regimes in American history. The northern retreat from reconstruction permitted southern Democrats to set things right. Taking the name **Redeemers**, Democrats in the South promised to replace "bayonet rule" (a few federal troops continued to be stationed in the South) with "home rule." They promised that honest, thrifty Democrats would supplant corrupt tax-and-spend Republicans. Above all, Redeemers swore to save southern civilization from a descent into "African barbarism." As one man put it, "We must render this either a white man's government, or convert the land into a Negro man's cemetery."

Southern Democrats adopted a multipronged strategy to overthrow Republican governments. First, they sought to polarize the parties around race. They went about gathering all the South's white voters into the Democratic Party, leaving the Republicans to depend on blacks, who made up a minority of the population in almost every southern state. To dislodge whites from the Republican Party, Democrats fanned the flames of racism. A South Carolina Democrat crowed that his party appealed to the "proud Caucasian race, whose sovereignty on earth God has proclaimed." Ostracism also proved effective. Local newspapers published the names of whites who kept company with blacks. So complete was the ostracism that one of its victims said, "No white

man can live in the South in the future and act with any other than the Democratic party unless he is willing and prepared to live a life of social isolation."

Democrats also exploited the severe economic plight of small white farmers by blaming it on Republican financial policy. Government spending soared during Reconstruction, and small farmers saw their tax burden skyrocket. "This is tax time," a South Carolinian reported. "We are nearly all on our head about them. They are so high & so little money to pay with" that farmers were "selling every egg and chicken they can get." In 1871, Mississippi reported that one-seventh of the state's land—3.3 million acres—had been forfeited for nonpayment of taxes. The small farmers' economic distress had a racial dimension. Because few freedmen succeeded in acquiring land, they rarely paid taxes. In Georgia in 1874, blacks made up 45 percent of the population but paid only 2 percent of the taxes. From the perspective of a small white farmer, Republican rule meant that he was paying more taxes and paying them to aid blacks.

If racial pride, social isolation, and financial hardship proved insufficient to drive yeomen from the Republican Party, Democrats turned to terrorism. "Night riders" targeted white Republicans as well as blacks for murder and assassination. Whether white or black, a "dead Radical is very harmless," South

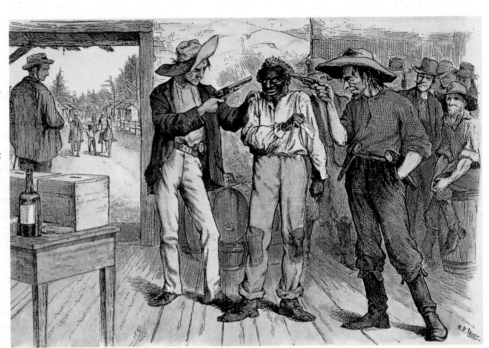

"Of Course He Wants to Vote the Democratic Ticket"
This Republican cartoon from the October 21, 1876, issue of *Harper's Weekly* comments sarcastically on the possibility of honest elections in the South. The caption reads: "You're free as air, ain't you? Say you are or I'll blow yer black head off." The cartoon demonstrates not only some Northerners' concern that violence would deliver the election to the Democrats but also the perception that white Southerners were crude, drunken, ignorant brutes. The Granger Collection, New York.

Carolina Democratic leader Martin Gary told his followers.

But the primary victims of white violence were black Republicans. Violence escalated to an unprecedented ferocity on Easter Sunday in 1873 in tiny Colfax, Louisiana. The black majority in the area had made Colfax a Republican stronghold until 1872, when Democrats turned to intimidation and fraud to win the local election. Republicans refused to accept the result and occupied the courthouse in the middle of the town. After three weeks, 165 white men attacked. They overran the Republicans' defenses and set the courthouse on fire. When the blacks tried to surrender, the whites murdered them. At least 81 black men were slaughtered that day. Although the federal government indicted the attackers, the Supreme Court ruled that it did not have the right to prosecute. And since local whites would not prosecute neighbors who killed blacks, the defendants in the Colfax massacre went free.

Even before adopting the all-out white supremacist tactics of the 1870s, Democrats had taken control of the governments of Virginia, Tennessee, and North Carolina. The new campaign brought fresh gains. The Redeemers retook Georgia in 1871, Texas in 1873, and Arkansas and Alabama in 1874. As the state election approached in Mississippi in 1876, Governor Adelbert Ames appealed to Washington for federal troops to control the violence, only to hear from the attorney general that the "whole public are tired of these annual autumnal outbreaks in the South." Abandoned, Mississippi Republicans succumbed to the Democratic onslaught in the fall elections. By 1876, only three Republican state governments survived in the South (Map 16.3).

An Election and a Compromise

The year 1876 witnessed one of the most tumultuous elections in American history. The election took place in November, but not until March 2 of the following year did the nation know who would be inaugurated president on March 4. Sixteen years after Lincoln's election, Americans feared that a presidential election would again precipitate civil war.

MAP ACTIVITY

Map 16.3 The Reconstruction of the South

Myth has it that Republican rule of the former Confederacy was not only harsh but long. In most states, however, conservative southern whites stormed back into power in months or just a few years. By the election of 1876, Republican governments could be found in only three states, and they soon fell.

READING THE MAP: List in chronological order the readmission of the former Confederate states to the Union. Which states reestablished conservative governments most quickly?

CONNECTIONS: What did the former Confederate states need to do to be readmitted to the Union? How did reestablished conservative governments react to Reconstruction?

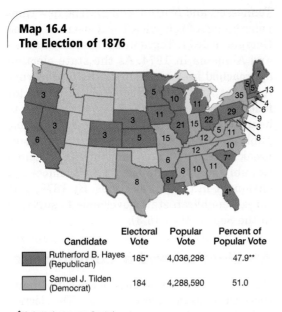

Map 16.4
The Election of 1876

Candidate	Electoral Vote	Popular Vote	Percent of Popular Vote
Rutherford B. Hayes (Republican)	185*	4,036,298	47.9**
Samuel J. Tilden (Democrat)	184	4,288,590	51.0

*19 electoral votes were disputed.

**Percentages do not total 100 because some popular votes went to other parties.

The Democrats nominated New York's governor, Samuel J. Tilden, who immediately targeted the corruption of the Grant administration and the "despotism" of Republican reconstruction. The Republicans put forward Rutherford B. Hayes, governor of Ohio. Privately, Hayes considered "bayonet rule" a mistake but concluded that waving the bloody shirt remained the Republicans' best political strategy.

On election day, Tilden tallied 4,288,590 votes to Hayes's 4,036,298. But in the all-important electoral college, Tilden fell one vote short of the majority required for victory. The electoral votes of three states—South Carolina, Louisiana, and Florida, the only remaining Republican governments in the South—remained in doubt because both Republicans and Democrats in those states claimed victory. To win, Tilden needed only one of the nineteen contested votes. Hayes had to have all of them.

Congress had to decide who had actually won the elections in the three southern states and thus who would be president. The Constitution provided no guidance for this situation. Moreover, Democrats controlled the House, and Republicans controlled the Senate. Congress created a special electoral commission to arbitrate the disputed returns. All of the commissioners voted their party affiliation, giving every state to the Republican Hayes and putting him over the top in electoral votes (Map 16.4).

Some outraged Democrats vowed to resist Hayes's victory. Rumors flew of an impending coup and renewed civil war. But the impasse was broken when negotiations behind the scenes resulted in an informal understanding known as the **Compromise of 1877**. In exchange for a Democratic promise not to block Hayes's inauguration and to deal fairly with the freedmen, Hayes vowed to refrain from using the army to uphold the remaining Republican regimes in the South and to provide the South with substantial federal subsidies for railroads.

Stubborn Tilden supporters bemoaned the "stolen election" and damned "His Fraudulency," Rutherford B. Hayes. Old-guard Radicals such as William Lloyd Garrison denounced Hayes's bargain as a "policy of compromise, of credulity, of weakness, of subserviency, of surrender." But the nation as a whole celebrated, for the country had weathered a grave crisis. The last three Republican state governments in the South fell quickly once Hayes abandoned them and withdrew the U.S. Army. Reconstruction came to an end.

REVIEW   Why did northern support for Reconstruction collapse?

▶ Conclusion: "A Revolution but Half Accomplished"

In 1865, when General Carl Schurz visited the South, he discovered "a revolution but half accomplished." White Southerners resisted the passage from slavery to free labor, from white racial despotism to equal justice, and from white political monopoly to biracial democracy. The old elite wanted to get "things back as near to slavery as possible," Schurz reported, while African Americans such as James T. Rapier and some whites were eager to exploit the revolutionary implications of defeat and emancipation.

Although the northern-dominated Republican Congress refused to provide for blacks' economic welfare, it employed constitutional amendments to require ex-Confederates to accept legal equality and share political power with black men. Congress was not willing to extend such power to women, however. Conservative southern whites fought ferociously to recover their power and privilege. When Democrats regained control of politics, whites used both state power and private violence to wipe out many of the gains of Reconstruction, leading one observer to conclude that the North had won the war but the South had won the peace.

The Redeemer counterrevolution, however, did not mean a return to slavery. Northern victory in the Civil War ensured that ex-slaves no longer faced the auction block and could send their children to school, worship in their own churches, and work independently on their own rented farms. Sharecropping, with all its hardships, provided more autonomy and economic welfare than bondage had. It was limited freedom, to be sure, but it was not slavery.

The Civil War and emancipation set in motion the most profound upheaval in the nation's history. War destroyed the largest slave society in the New World and gave birth to a modern nation-state. The world of masters and slaves gave way to that of landlords and sharecroppers. Washington increased its role in national affairs, and the victorious North set the nation's compass toward the expansion of industrial capitalism and the final conquest of the West.

Despite massive changes, however, the Civil War remained only a "half accomplished" revolution. By not fulfilling the promises the nation seemed to hold out to black Americans at war's end, Reconstruction represents a tragedy of enormous proportions. The failure to protect blacks and guarantee their rights had enduring consequences. It was the failure of the first reconstruction that made the modern civil rights movement necessary.

See the Selected Bibliography for this chapter in the Appendix.

16 Chapter Review

KEY TERMS

Freedmen's Bureau (p. 443)
black codes (p. 447)
Civil Rights Act of 1866 (p. 449)
Fourteenth Amendment (p. 450)
Military Reconstruction Act (p. 451)
Fifteenth Amendment (p. 452)
carpetbagger (p. 453)
scalawag (p. 454)
Ku Klux Klan (p. 455)
sharecropping (p. 459)
Redeemers (p. 464)
Compromise of 1877 (p. 466)

REVIEW QUESTIONS

1. To what extent did Lincoln's wartime plan for reconstruction reflect the concerns of newly freed slaves? (pp. 441–446)

2. When the southern states passed the black codes, how did the U.S. Congress respond? (pp. 446–449)

3. Why did Congress impeach President Andrew Johnson? (pp. 449–453)

4. How did politics and economic concerns shape reconstruction in the South? (pp. 453–461)

5. Why did northern support for reconstruction collapse? (pp. 461–466)

MAKING CONNECTIONS

1. Why and how did the federal government retreat from defending African Americans' civil rights in the 1870s?

2. Why was distributing plantation land to former slaves such a controversial policy? Why did Congress reject redistribution as a general policy?

3. After emancipation, how did ex-slaves exercise their new freedoms, and how did white Southerners attempt to limit them?

4. How did the identification of the Republican Party with reconstruction policy affect the party's political fortunes in the 1870s?

LINKING TO THE PAST

1. In what ways did the attitudes and actions of President Johnson increase northern resolve to reconstruct the South and the South's resolve to resist reconstruction?

2. White women, abolitionists, and blacks all had hopes for a brighter future that were in some ways dashed during the turmoil of reconstruction. What specific goals of these groups slipped away? What political allies abandoned their causes, and why?

17 The Contested West
1865–1900

CONTENT LEARNING OBJECTIVES

After reading and studying this chapter, you should be able to:

- Explain federal policies toward Native Americans during the last decades of the nineteenth century. Describe how Native Americans resisted these policies and how the government quashed these acts of resistance.

- Recount how the late-nineteenth-century frenzy for gold and silver in the West transformed the region and explain how the development of the western mining industry mirrored the processes of industrialization in other parts of the country.

- Identify who worked and settled in the West and why they were drawn there.

- Describe the ways in which farming became increasingly commercialized and ranching became increasingly industrialized.

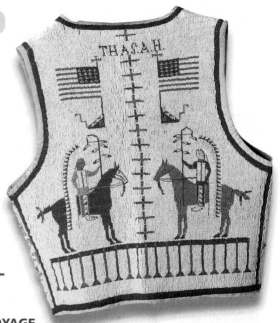

LAKOTA VEST
This late-nineteenth-century Lakota vest displays the American flag, which was a common design in Indian bead art and testifies to the great changes that took place in the American West. Private Collection, photograph American Hurrah Archive, NYC.

TO CELEBRATE THE 400TH ANNIVERSARY OF COLUMBUS'S VOYAGE to the New World, Chicago hosted the World's Columbian Exposition in 1893, creating a magical White City on the shores of Lake Michigan. Among the organizations vying to hold meetings at the fair was the American Historical Association, whose members gathered on a warm July evening to hear Frederick Jackson Turner deliver his landmark essay "The Significance of the Frontier in American History." Turner began by noting that the 1890 census no longer discerned a clear frontier line. His tone was elegiac: "The existence of an area of free land, its continuous recession, and the advance of settlement westward," he observed, "explained American development."

Of course, *west* has always been a comparative term in American history. Until the gold rush focused attention on California, the West for settlers lay beyond the Appalachians. But by the second half of the nineteenth century, the West stretched from Canada to Mexico, from the Mississippi River to the Pacific Ocean.

Turner, who originally studied the old frontier east of the Mississippi, viewed the West as a process as much as a place. The availability of land provided a "safety valve," releasing social tensions and providing opportunities for social mobility that worked to Americanize Americans. Turner's West demanded strength and nerve, fostered invention and adaptation, and produced self-confident, individualistic Americans. His frontier thesis underscored the exceptionalism of America's history, highlighting its difference from the rest of the world. His "frontier thesis" would earn him a professorship at Harvard and a permanent place in American history.

Yet the historians who applauded Turner in Chicago had short memories. That afternoon, many had crossed the midway to attend Buffalo Bill Cody's Wild West extravaganza—a cowboys-and-Indians shoot-'em-up. The historians cheering in the stands that hot afternoon no doubt dismissed Buffalo Bill's history as amateur, but he made a point that Turner's thesis ignored: The West was neither free nor open. It was the story of a fierce and violent contest for land and resources.

In the decades following the Civil War, the United States pursued empire in the American West in Indian wars that lasted until 1890. Pushed off their land and onto reservations, Native Americans resisted as they faced waves of miners and settlers as well as the degradation of the environment by railroads, mines, barbed wire, and mechanized agriculture. The pastoral agrarianism Turner celebrated in his frontier thesis clashed with the urban, industrial West emerging on the Comstock Lode in Nevada and in the commercial farms of California.

Buffalo Bill's mythic West, with its heroic cowboys and noble savages, also obscured the complex reality of the West as a fiercely contested terrain. Competing groups of Anglos, Hispanics, former slaves, Chinese, and a host of others arrived seeking the promise of land and riches, while the Indians struggled to preserve their cultural identities. Turner's rugged white "frontiersman" masked racial diversity and failed to acknowledge the role of women in community building.

Yet in the waning decade of the nineteenth century, as history blurred with nostalgia, Turner's evocation of the frontier as a crucible for American identity hit a nerve in a population facing rapid changes. A major depression started even before the Columbian Exposition opened its doors. Americans worried about the economy, immigration, and urban industrialism found in Turner's message a new cause for concern. Would America continue to be America now that the frontier was closed? Were the problems confronting the United States at the turn of the twentieth century—the exploitation of land and labor, the consolidation of capital, and vicious ethnic and racial rivalries—destined to play out under western skies?

VISUAL ACTIVITY

Buffalo Bill Poster

William (Buffalo Bill) Cody used colorful posters to publicize his Wild West show during the 1880s and 1890s. This poster from 1899 shows Indians attacking a wagon train and a village of tepees in the background. By the 1870s, the era of the wagon train had ended with the coming of the transcontinental railroads. The mythic West that Cody (featured on the right) re-created, was already part of the past. Library of Congress, LC-DIG-ppmsca-13514.

READING THE IMAGE: How does Buffalo Bill contribute to the "myth of the old West" in this poster?

CONNECTIONS: What would Frederick Jackson Turner and the historians who gathered in Chicago have thought of the history of expansion depicted in Buffalo Bill's Wild West show?

BUFFALO BILL'S WILD WEST AND CONGRESS OF ROUGH RIDERS OF THE WORLD.

A CONGRESS OF AMERICAN INDIANS. REPRESENTING VARIOUS TRIBES, CHARACTERS AND PECULIARITIES OF THE WILY DUSKY WARRIORS IN SCENES FROM ACTUAL LIFE GIVING THEIR WEIRD WAR DANCES AND PICTURESQUE STYLE OF HORSEMANSHIP.

COL. W. F. CODY
BUFFALO BILL
WILL APPEAR
AT EVERY PERFORMANCE

► Conquest and Empire in the West

While the European powers expanded their authority and wealth through imperialism and colonialism in far-flung empires abroad, the United States focused its attention on its own western lands. From the U.S. Army attack on the remainder of the Comanche empire to the conquest of the Black Hills, whites pushed Indians aside as they moved West. As posited by Frederick Jackson Turner, American exceptionalism stressed how the history of the United States differed from that of European nations, citing America's western frontier as a cause. Yet expansion in the trans-Mississippi West involved the conquest, displacement, and rule over native peoples—a process best understood in the global context of imperialism and colonialism. (See "Beyond America's Borders," page 472.)

The U.S. government, through trickery and conquest, pushed tribes off their lands (Map 17.1) and onto designated Indian territories or reservations. The Indian wars depleted the Native American population and handed most Indian land to white settlers. The decimation of the bison herds pushed the Plains Indians onto reservations, where they lived as wards of the state. Thus did the United States, committed to an imperialist, expansionist ideology, colonize the West.

Indian Removal and the Reservation System

Manifest destiny—the belief that the United States had a "God-given" right to aggressively spread the values of white civilization and expand the nation from ocean to ocean—dictated U.S. policy toward Indians and other nations. In the name of manifest destiny, Americans forced the removal of the Five Civilized Tribes of the South (the Cherokee, Choctaw, Chickasaw, Creek, and Seminole peoples) to Oklahoma in the 1830s; colonized Texas and won its independence from Mexico in 1836; conquered California, Arizona, New Mexico, and parts of Utah and Colorado in the Mexican-American War of 1846–1848; invaded Oregon in the mid-1840s; and paid Mexico for land in Arizona and New Mexico in the Gadsden Purchase of 1854.

By midcentury, western lands no longer seemed inexhaustible. Hordes of settlers crossed the Great Plains on their way to the goldfields of California or the rich farmland of Washington

CHRONOLOGY

1851	• First Treaty of Fort Laramie negotiated.
1862	• Homestead Act passes. • Great Sioux Uprising (Santee Uprising) kills 1,000 settlers.
1864	• Sand Creek massacre kills several hundred Indians.
1867	• Treaty of Medicine Lodge negotiated.
1868	• Washita massacre led by Custer. • Second Treaty of Fort Laramie negotiated.
1869	• First transcontinental railroad completed.
1870s	• Hunters begin to decimate bison herds.
1873	• "Big Bonanza" discovered on Comstock Lode.
1874	• Gold discovered in Black Hills.
1876	• Battle of the Little Big Horn destroys Custer's army.
1877	• Chief Joseph surrenders.
1879	• Carlisle Indian School opens. • Exodusters move to Kansas.
1881	• Sitting Bull surrenders.
1882	• Chinese Exclusion Act passes.
1886	• Geronimo surrenders.
1886–1887	• Severe blizzards decimate cattle.
1887	• Dawes Allotment Act passes.
1889	• Ghost Dance spreads. • Two million acres in Oklahoma opened for settlement.
1890	• Sitting Bull killed. • Massacre at Wounded Knee kills several hundred Indians.
1893	• Last land rush occurs in Oklahoma Territory. • Frederick Jackson Turner presents "frontier thesis."

Imperialism, Colonialism, and the Treatment of the Sioux and the Zulu

Viewed through the lens of colonialism, the British war with the Zulu in South Africa offers a compelling contrast to the war of the United States against the Lakota Sioux. The Zulu, like the Sioux, came to power as a result of devastating intertribal warfare. In the area that is today the KwaZulu-Natal province of the Republic of South Africa, the Zulu king Shaka united his empire by 1826 with an army of more than twenty thousand. Like the Sioux, the Zulu earned a formidable reputation as brave warriors who fought to protect their land from white encroachment.

In 1806, the British seized the Cape of Good Hope to secure shipping interests, leading to conflicts with Dutch-speaking settlers known as the Boers, who had inhabited the southern tip of Africa since the seventeenth century. Clashes between Britons and Boers eventually resulted in the Great Trek, the migration of nearly twelve thousand Boers northeastward beginning in 1835. There they claimed land and established the South African Republic (the Transvaal) in 1853 and the Orange Free State in 1854, both independent of British rule. But the Great Trek brought the Boers into Zululand, where they met with bloody resistance.

The Zulu lived in a highly complex society, with regiments of warriors arranged by age and bound to local chiefs under the supreme command of the Zulu king. During his harsh reign, King Shaka inspected his regiments after each battle and put cowards to death on the spot. Young men could not start their own households without the local chief's permission, thus ensuring an ample stock of warriors and making the Zulu army, in the words of one English observer, "a celibate, man-slaying machine." The Boer settlers repeatedly faced the wrath of the Zulu, who slaughtered the first trekkers to arrive in Zululand and raided Boer settlements to steal cattle.

The British entered the fray in 1879, sparking the Anglo-Zulu War, which a recent historian has condemned as being "as unnecessary as it was unjust." Sir Theophilus Shepstone, British secretary for native affairs, hinted at Britain's motive when he wrote in 1878, "Had [its] 30,000 warriors been in time changed to labourers working for wages, Zululand would have been a prosperous peaceful country instead of what it is now, a source of perpetual danger to itself and its neighbors."

With aims of both placating the Boers and securing a source of labor for British economic expansion—made paramount by the discovery of diamonds in the region—British troops invaded Zululand. Leading soldiers armed with the latest rifles and artillery, Lieutenant Commander Lord Chelmsford—with a confidence reminiscent of that of George Armstrong Custer—expected to subdue the Zulu easily. But in January 1879, at the battle of Isandlwana, the Zulu army of more than 25,000 surprised a British encampment. In less than two hours,

Zululand and Cape Colony, 1878

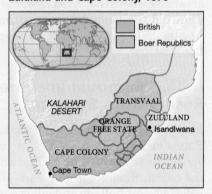

and Oregon. In their path stood a solid wall of Indian land. To solve this "Indian problem," the U.S. government took Indian lands with the promise to pay annuities in return and put the Indians on lands reserved for their use—**reservations**. In 1851, some ten thousand Plains Indians came together at Fort Laramie in Wyoming to negotiate a treaty that ceded a wide swath of their land to allow passage to the West. In return, the government promised that the remaining Indian land would remain inviolate.

The Indians who "touched the pen" to the 1851 Treaty of Fort Laramie hoped to preserve their land and culture in the face of the white onslaught. Settlers and miners cut down trees, polluted streams, and killed off the bison. Whites brought alcohol, guns, and something even more deadly—disease. Between 1780 and 1870, the population of the Plains tribes declined by half. "If I could see this thing, if I knew where it came from, I would go there and fight it," a Cheyenne warrior anguished. Disease shifted the power

Zulu Warriors
Chief Ngoza (center) poses with Zulu men in full war dress. Their distinctive cowhide shields date to the reign of King Shaka. Each warrior also carried two or three throwing spears and an *ikwa*, or flat-bladed stabbing spear used in close combat. Zulu warriors marched at the double and could cover up to fifty miles a day. Campbell Collections of the University of KwaZulu-Natal.

into sedentary, God-fearing farmers, may seem less exploitative if no less ruthless in its cultural imperialism.

Both the Little Big Horn and Isandlwana became legends that spawned a romantic image of the "noble savage": fierce in battle, honored in defeat. Describing this myth, historian James Gump, who has chronicled the subjugation of the Sioux and the Zulu, observed, "Each western culture simultaneously dehumanized and glamorized the Sioux and Zulu." Gump noted that the noble savage mythology was "a product of the racist ideologies of the late nineteenth century as well as the guilt and compassion associated with the bloody costs of empire building." The imperial powers of Britain and the United States defeated indigenous rivals and came to dominate their lands (and, in the case of the Zulu, their labor) in the global expansion that marked the nineteenth century.

more than 4,000 Zulu and British were killed. Only a handful of British soldiers managed to escape, and Chelmsford lost 1,300 officers and men.

When news of Isandlwana reached London, commentators compared the massacre to Custer's defeat at the Battle of the Little Big Horn and noted that native forces armed with spears had defeated a modern army.

The British immediately launched unconditional war against the Zulu. In the ensuing battles, neither side took prisoners. The Zulu beat the British twice more, but after seven months the British finally routed the

Zulu army and abandoned Zululand to its fate—partition, starvation, and civil war.

Historians would later compare the British victory to the U.S. Army's defeat of the Sioux in the American West, but the Zulu and Sioux met different economic fates. As Shepstone hinted in 1878, the British goal had been to subdue the Zulu and turn them into cheap labor. Compared to the naked economic exploitation of the Zulu, the U.S. policy toward the Sioux, with its forced assimilation on reservations and its misguided attempts to turn the nomadic tribes

Questions for Analysis

Summarize the Argument: How was the British war with the Zulu both similar to and different from the American war with the Sioux?

Ask Historical Questions: Compare the fate of the defeated Zulu with that of the Lakota Sioux.

Recognize Viewpoints: Policy toward indigenous peoples in the United States and Great Britain in the nineteenth century differed. What distinguished them?

from Woodland agrarian tribes, whose proximity to whites meant they died at high rates, to the Lakota (Western) Sioux, who fled the contagion by pursuing an equestrian nomadic existence that displaced weaker tribes in the western plains.

In the Southwest, the Navajo people, in a removal similar to that of the Cherokee in the 1830s, endured a forced march called the "Long Walk" from their homeland to the desolate Bosque Redondo Reservation in New Mexico in 1864.

"This ground we were brought on, it is not productive," complained the Navajo leader Barboncito. "All the stock we brought here have nearly all died."

Poverty and starvation stalked the reservations. Confined by armed force, the Indians eked out an existence on stingy government rations. Styled as stepping-stones to "civilization," Indian reservations closely resembled colonial societies where native populations, ruled by outside bureaucrats, saw their culture assaulted, their religious

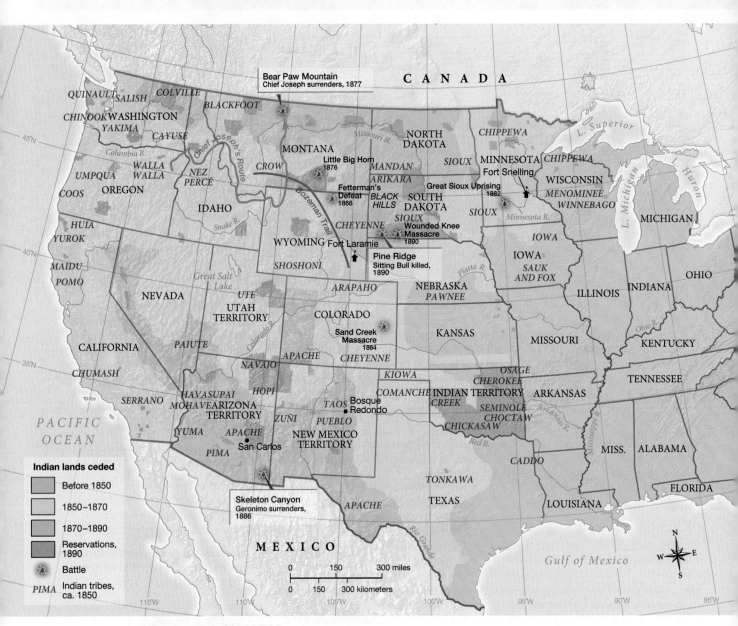

MAP ACTIVITY

Map 17.1   The Loss of Indian Lands, 1850–1890

By 1890, western Indians were isolated on small, scattered reservations. Native Americans had struggled to retain their land in major battles, from the Great Sioux Uprising in Minnesota in 1862 to the massacre at Wounded Knee, South Dakota, in 1890.

READING THE MAP: Where was the largest reservation located in 1890? Which states on this map show no reservations in 1890? Compare this map to Map 17.3.

CONNECTIONS: Why did the federal government force Native Americans onto reservations? What developments prompted these changes?

practices outlawed, their children sent away to school, and their way of life attacked in the name of progress.

To Americans raised on theories of racial superiority, the Indians constituted, in the words of one Colorado militia major, "an obstacle to civilization . . . [and] should be exterminated." This attitude pervaded the military. As a result, the massacre of Native American men, women, and children became commonplace in the West. In November 1864 at Sand Creek in Colorado Territory, Colonel John M. Chivington and his

Colorado militia descended on a village of Cheyenne, mostly women and children. Their leader, Black Kettle, raised a white flag and an American flag to signal surrender, but the charging cavalry ignored his signal and butchered 270 Indians. Chivington watched as his men scalped and mutilated their victims and later justified the killing of Indian children with the terse remark, "Nits make lice." The city of Denver treated Chivington and his men as heroes, but a congressional inquiry eventually castigated the soldiers for their "fiendish malignity" and condemned the "savage cruelty" of the massacre. Four years later, Black Kettle, who had survived Sand Creek, died in another massacre when George Armstrong Custer slaughtered more than one hundred people on the banks of the Washita River in Oklahoma.

The Decimation of the Great Bison Herds

After the Civil War, the accelerating pace of industrial expansion brought about the near extinction of the American bison (buffalo). By 1850, the dynamic ecology of the Great Plains, with its droughts, fires, and blizzards, along with the demands of Indian buffalo-robe traders as well as whites and their cattle, had driven the bison herds onto the far western plains.

In the 1870s, industrial demand for heavy leather belting used in machinery and the development of larger, more accurate rifles combined to hasten the slaughter of the bison. The nation's transcontinental railroad systems cut the range in two and divided the dwindling herds. For the Sioux and other nomadic tribes of the plains, the buffalo constituted a way of life—a source of food, fuel, and shelter and a central part of religion and ritual. Railroad owners, however, considered bison a nuisance—at best a cheap source of meat for their workers and a target for sport.

Although the army took credit for the conquest of the Plains Indians, the decimation of the great bison herds was largely responsible for the Indians' fate. With their food supply gone, Indians had to choose between starvation and the reservation. "A cold wind blew across the prairie when the last buffalo fell," the great Sioux leader Sitting Bull lamented, "a death wind for my people."

On the southern plains in 1867, more than five thousand warring Comanches, Kiowas, and Southern Arapahos gathered at Medicine Lodge Creek in Kansas to negotiate the Treaty of Medicine Lodge, hoping to preserve limited land

HARPER'S WEEKLY.
JOURNAL OF CIVILIZATION
Vol. XVIII.—No. 937.]   NEW YORK, SATURDAY, DECEMBER 12, 1874.   [WITH A SUPPLEMENT. PRICE TEN CENTS.

SLAUGHTERED FOR THE HIDE.—[See Page 1025.]

VISUAL ACTIVITY

"Slaughtered for the Hide"

In 1874, *Harper's Weekly* featured this illustration of a buffalo-hide hunter skinning a carcass on the southwestern plains. City father Colonel Richard Dodge wrote of the carnage, "The air was foul with sickening stench, and the vast plain, which only a short twelve-month before teemed with animal life, was a dead, solitary, putrid desert." Library of Congress, 3b03485.

READING THE IMAGE: What virtues and stereotypes of the West does this magazine cover express?

CONNECTIONS: How did the slaughter of buffalo affect the lives of Plains Indians?

and hunting by moving the tribe to a reservation. Three years after the treaty became law, hide hunters poured into the region; within a decade, they had nearly exterminated the southern bison herds. Luther Standing Bear recounted the sight and stench: "I saw the bodies of hundreds of dead buffalo lying about, just wasting, and the odor was terrible. . . . They were letting our food lie on the plains to rot." Once an estimated 40 million bison roamed the West; by 1895, fewer than 1,000 remained. With the buffalo gone, the Indians faced starvation and reluctantly moved onto the reservations.

Indian Wars and the Collapse of Comanchería

The Indian wars in the West marked the last resistance of a Native American population devastated by disease and demoralized by the federal government's reservation policy. The Dakota Sioux in Minnesota went to war in 1862. For years, under the leadership of Chief Little Crow, the Dakota—also known as the Santee—had pursued a policy of accommodation, ceding land in return for the promise of annuities. But with his people on the verge of starvation (the local Indian agent told the hungry Dakota, "Go and eat grass"), Little Crow led his angry warriors in a desperate campaign against the intruders, killing more than 1,000 settlers. American troops quelled the Great Sioux Uprising (also called the Santee Uprising) and marched 1,700 Sioux to Fort Snelling, where 400 Indians were put on trial for murder and 38 died in the largest mass execution in American history.

Further west, the great Indian empire of **Comanchería** had once stretched from the Canadian plains to Mexico. By 1865, after two decades of what one historian has labeled "ethnic cleansing," fewer than five thousand Comanches remained in west Texas and Oklahoma. Through decades of dealings with the Spanish and French, the Comanche had built a complex empire based on trade in horses, hides, guns, and captives. Expert riders, the Comanche waged war in the saddle, giving the U.S. Cavalry reason to hate and fear them.

After the Civil War, President Ulysses S. Grant faced the prospect of protracted Indian war. Reluctant to spend more money and sacrifice more lives, Grant adopted a "peace policy" designed to segregate and control the Indians while opening up land to white settlers. This policy won the support of both friends of the Indians and those who coveted the Indians' land. The army herded the Indians onto reservations (see Map 17.1), where the U.S. Bureau of Indian Affairs hired agents who, in the words of Paiute Sarah Winnemucca, did "nothing but fill their pockets." In 1871, Congress determined to no longer deal with Indians as sovereign nations but to eliminate treaties and treat Indians as wards of the state. Grant's peace policy in the West gave way to all-out warfare as the U.S. Army dispatched 3,000 soldiers to wipe out the remains of Comanchería. Raiding parties of Comanche virtually obliterated white settlements in west Texas. To defeat the Indians, the army adopted the practice of burning and destroying everything in its path, using the tactics that General William Tecumseh Sherman had perfected in his march through Georgia during the Civil War. At the decisive battle of Palo Duro Canyon in 1874, only three Comanche warriors died in battle, but U.S. soldiers took the Indians' camp; burned more than 200 tepees, hundreds of robes and blankets, and thousands of pounds of winter supplies; and shot more than 1,000 horses. Coupled with the decimation of the bison, the army's scorched-earth policy led to the final collapse of the Comanche people. The surviving Indians of Comanchería, now numbering fewer than 1,500, reluctantly retreated to the reservation at Fort Sill.

The Fight for the Black Hills

On the northern plains, the fever for gold fueled the conflict between Indians and Euro-Americans. In 1866, the Cheyenne united with the Sioux in Wyoming to protect their hunting grounds in the Powder River valley, which were threatened by the construction of the Bozeman Trail connecting Fort Laramie with the goldfields in Montana. Captain William Fetterman, who had boasted that with eighty men he could ride through the Sioux nation, died along with all of his troops at the hands of the Sioux. The Indians' impressive victories led to the second Treaty of Fort Laramie in 1868, in which the United States agreed to abandon the Bozeman Trail and guaranteed the Indians control of the **Black Hills**, land sacred to the Lakota Sioux.

The government's fork-tongued promises induced some of the tribes to accept the treaty. The great Sioux chief Red Cloud led many of his people onto the reservation. Red Cloud soon regretted his decision. "Think of it!" he told a visitor to the Pine Ridge Reservation. "I, who used to own . . . country so extensive that I could not ride through it in a week . . . must tell Washington when I am hungry. I must beg for that which I own." On a visit to Washington, D.C., in 1870, Red Cloud told the secretary of the interior, "We are melting like snow on the hillside, while you are grown like spring grass. . . . When the white man comes in my country he leaves a trail of blood behind him." As leadership of the Sioux passed to a new generation, younger chiefs, among them Crazy Horse and Sitting Bull, refused to sign the treaty and called for armed resistance. Crazy Horse later declared that he wanted no part of the "piecemeal penning" of his people.

In 1874, the discovery of gold in the Black Hills led the government to break its promise to Red Cloud. Miners began pouring into the Dakotas, and the Northern Pacific Railroad made plans to lay track. At first, the government offered to purchase the Black Hills. But the Lakota Sioux refused to sell. The army responded by issuing an ultimatum ordering all Lakota Sioux and Northern Cheyenne bands onto the Pine Ridge Reservation and threatening to hunt down those who refused.

In the summer of 1876, the army launched a three-pronged attack led by Lieutenant Colonel George Armstrong Custer, General George Crook, and Colonel John Gibbon. Crazy Horse stopped Crook at the Battle of the Rosebud. Custer, leading the second prong of the army's offensive, divided his troops and ordered an attack. On June 25, he spotted signs of the Indians' camp. Crying "Hurrah boys, we've got them," he led 265 men of the Seventh Cavalry into the largest gathering of Indians ever assembled on the Great Plains (more than 8,000), camped along the banks of the Greasy Grass River. Indian warriors led by Sitting Bull and Crazy Horse set upon Custer and his men and quickly annihilated them. "It took us about as long as a hungry man to eat his dinner," the Cheyenne chief Two Moons recalled. (See "Analyzing Historical Evidence," page 478.)

"Custer's Last Stand," or the **Battle of the Little Big Horn**, soon became part of national mythology. But it proved to be the last stand for the Sioux. The nomadic bands that had massed at the Little Big Horn scattered, and the army hunted them down. "Wherever we went," wrote the Oglala holy man Black Elk, "the soldiers came to kill us." In 1877, Crazy Horse was captured and killed. Four years later, Sitting Bull surrendered. The government took the Black Hills and confined the Lakota to the reservation. The Sioux never accepted the loss of the Black Hills. In 1923, they filed suit, demanding the return of the land illegally taken from them. After a protracted court battle lasting nearly sixty years, the U.S. Supreme Court ruled in 1980 that the government had illegally violated the Treaty of Fort Laramie. Declaring "a more ripe and rank case of dishonorable dealings will never, in all probability, be found in our history," the Court awarded the tribes $122.5 million. The Sioux refused the settlement and continue to press for the return of the Black Hills.

> **REVIEW**   How did the slaughter of the bison contribute to the Plains Indians' removal to reservations?

► Forced Assimilation and Indian Resistance

Imperialistic attitudes of whites toward Indians continued to evolve in the late nineteenth century. To "civilize" the Indians, the U.S. government sought to force assimilation on their children. Reservations became increasingly unpopular among whites who coveted Indian land and among friends of the Indians appalled by the conditions on the reservations. A new policy of allotment gained favor. It promised to put Indians on parcels of land, forcing them into farming, and then to redistribute the remaining land to settlers. In the face of this ongoing assault on their way of life, Indians actively resisted, contested, and adapted to colonial rule.

Indian Schools and the War on Indian Culture

Indian schools constituted the cultural battleground of the Indian wars in the West, their avowed purpose being, in the words of one of their fervent supporters, "To kill the Indian . . . and save the man." In 1877, Congress appropriated funds for Indian education, reasoning, in the words of one congressman, that it was less expensive to educate Indians than to kill them. That education effort focused on Native American boys and girls, from toddlers to teenagers. Virginia's Hampton Institute, created in 1868 to school newly freed slaves, accepted its first Indian students in 1878. Although many Indian schools operated on the reservations, authorities much preferred boarding facilities that isolated students from the "contamination" of tribal values.

Many Native American parents resisted sending their children away. When all else failed, the military kidnapped the children and sent them off to school. An agent at the Mescalero Apache Agency in Arizona Territory reported in

Custer's Last Stand

Crazy Horse at the Little Big Horn, by Amos Bad Heart Bull The Granger Collection, New York.

Only one American soldier survived the Battle of the Little Big Horn. Yet many Indians remembered the battle and depicted it in illustrations. In this pictograph, Amos Bad Heart Bull, an Oglala Sioux from the Pine Ridge Reservation, dramatized the battle at the river the Indians called the Greasy Grass. Although the artist was only seven years old in 1876 when the battle occurred, he based his pictures on the recollections of his uncle and other Oglala elders. Crazy Horse ritually prepared for battle by painting hailstones on his body, wearing a small stone tied behind one ear, and placing a

single eagle feather in his hair. Featured at the center of the pictograph, he can be identified by his unique war paint. According to one Arapaho warrior who fought beside him, Crazy Horse "was the bravest man he ever saw."

Even at the time, Indian and white participants interpreted events differently. One of the soldiers cut off from Custer's group feared for his life as he heard "wild victory dances" coming from the Lakota camp. But what he heard, according to a Cheyenne warrior named Wooden Leg, were the songs of the Lakota and Cheyenne, mourning their sons, husbands, and

fathers. The soldier, who huddled on Reno Hill praying throughout the night, not only survived but lived to 1950, making him the only white survivor of "Custer's Last Stand."

Many of the battle depictions by whites were little more than romantic idealism, with Custer on horse back leading a valiant charge. In this 1889 lithograph of the battle (page 479), Custer and his men are shown dismounted, firing at Indians on horseback. A much more accurate portrayal than many of the others in circulation at the time, the lithograph shows how badly Custer was outnumbered when he divided his

1886 that "it became necessary to visit the camps unexpectedly with a detachment of police, and seize such children as were proper and take them away to school, willing or unwilling." The parents put up a struggle. "Some hurried their children off to the mountains or hid them away in camp, and the police had to chase and capture them

like so many wild rabbits," the agent observed. "This unusual proceeding created quite an outcry. The men were sullen and muttering, the women loud in their lamentations and the children almost out of their wits with fright."

Once at school, the children were stripped and scrubbed, their clothing and belongings

The Battle of the Little Big Horn, 1889 Private Collection, Bridgeman Images.

forces and led one contingent into the largest gathering of Indians ever to meet on the plains.

Popular portrayals of the battle proliferated. Buffalo Bill Cody staged a reenactment of the battle as a centerpiece in his Wild West show. At least one poster from the 1880s shows a Custer who looks remarkably like Buffalo Bill. Both men were famous for their long blond hair. Remarkably, Custer did not lose his scalp, as did most of his men. By all accounts, Custer's body was not mutilated (except for one fingertip and a pierced eardrum). Why did the Indians not take his scalp as a trophy? In large part, the

answer has changed as Custer's fortunes with historians and the public have waxed and waned. At the time of his death and for decades after, Custer was viewed as a hero and martyr. Writers explained that his Indian foes respected the man they called Phuska, or Long Hair, and refused to take his scalp. A century later, Custer's reputation sank to a low ebb as historians began to focus on the Indians' experience in the West. One author speculated that Custer, who was balding by 1879, was spared because from a warrior's point of view his scalp made a poor trophy.

Questions for Analysis

Analyze the Evidence: Compare the portrayals of Custer's Last Stand. What strikes you about the Indian version in relationship to the Anglo lithograph?

Recognize Viewpoints: Who is the center of the focus for the Indians? Who for the Anglos? How does this reflect the two sides' different interpretations of this dramatic encounter?

Consider the Context: In what ways does the comparison of the depictions of the Battle of the Little Big Horn point to conflicting interpretations of the larger history of the American West?

confiscated, and their hair hacked off and doused with kerosene to kill lice. Issued stiff new uniforms, shoes, and what Luther Standing Bear recalled as the "torture" of woolen long underwear, the children often lost not only their possessions but also their names. Children were asked to stand at the blackboard, take a pointer, and select

a proper English name, recalled Standing Bear, who immediately became Luther.

The **Carlisle Indian School** in Pennsylvania, founded in 1879, became the model for later institutions. To encourage assimilation, Carlisle pioneered the "outing system"—sending students to live with white families during summer

The Assimilation of Sioux Students at Carlisle Indian School
This pair of before and after photographs of Wounded Yellow Robe, Timber Yellow Robe, and Henry Standing Bear reveals the distinct turn away from tribal culture upon their enrollment in Carlisle Indian School in 1883. The forced assimilation policy at such schools set out to divest the Indians of any remnant of their former lives. Archives and Special Collections, Dickinson College.

vacations. The policy reflected the school's slogan: "To civilize the Indian, get him into civilization. To keep him civilized, let him stay." The curriculum featured agricultural and manual arts for boys and domestic skills for girls, training designed to eliminate Indians' dependence on government support.

Merrill Gates, a member of the Board of Indian Commissioners, summed up the goal of Indian education: "To get the Indian out of the blanket and into trousers,—and trousers with a pocket in them, *and with a pocket that aches to be filled with dollars!*" Gates's faith in the "civilizing" power of the dollar reflected the unabashed materialism of the age. But the cultural annihilation that Gates cheerfully predicted did not prove so easy.

Despite whites' efforts, Indians continued being Indians. Even in the "iron routine" of the "civilizing machine" at boarding school, Zitkala-Sa recounted how Indians retained their tribal loyalties and Indian identities. Luther Standing Bear, whose father enrolled him at Carlisle to learn white ways, confessed, "Though my hair had been cut and I wore civilian clothes, I never forsook the blanket." Students continued to speak tribal languages and attend tribal dances even though the punishment was whipping with a leather belt. The schools themselves ultimately subverted their goal by creating generations of Indians who shared a common language, English,

and would later create a pan-Indian reform movement in the Progressive Era.

The Dawes Act and Indian Land Allotment

In the 1880s, the practice of rounding up and herding Indians onto reservations lost momentum in favor of allotment—a new policy designed to encourage assimilation through farming and the ownership of private property. Americans vowing to avenge Custer's defeat urged the government to get tough with the Indians. Reservations, they argued, took up too much good land that white settlers coveted and forced Americans to support "lazy" reservation Indians. At the same time, people sympathetic to the Indians were appalled at the desperate poverty on the reservations and feared for the Indians' survival. Helen Hunt Jackson, in her classic work *A Century of Dishonor* (1881), convinced many readers that the Indians had been treated unfairly. "Our Indian policy," the *New York Times* concluded, "is usually spoliation behind the mask of benevolence."

The Indian Rights Association, a group of mainly white easterners formed in 1882, campaigned for the dismantling of the reservations, now viewed as obstacles to progress. To "cease to treat the Indian as a red man and treat him as a man" meant putting an end to tribal communalism and fostering individualism.

"Selfishness," declared Senator Henry Dawes of Massachusetts, "is at the bottom of civilization." Dawes called for "allotment in severalty"—the institution of private property.

In 1887, Congress passed the **Dawes Allotment Act**, which divided up reservations and allotted parcels of land to individual Indians as private property. Each unmarried Indian man and woman as well as married men and children (married women were excluded) became eligible to receive 160 acres of land from reservation property. Indians who took allotments earned U.S. citizenship. This fostering of individualism through land distribution ultimately dealt a crippling blow to traditional tribal culture.

To protect Indians from land speculators, the government held most of the allotted land in trust—Indians could not sell it for twenty-five years. Since Indian land far surpassed the acreage needed for allotments, the government reserved the right to sell the "surplus" to white settlers. Many Indians sold their allotments and moved to urban areas, where they lost touch with tribal ways.

The Dawes Act effectively reduced Indian land from 138 million acres to a scant 48 million. The legislation, in the words of one critic, worked "to despoil the Indians of their lands and to make them vagabonds on the face of the earth." By 1890, the United States controlled 97.5 percent of the territory formerly occupied by Native Americans.

Indian Resistance and Survival

Faced with the extinction of their entire way of life, different groups of Indians responded in different ways. In the 1870s, Comanche and Kiowa raiding parties frustrated the U.S. Army by brazenly using the reservations as a seasonal supply base during the winter months. When spring came, they resumed their nomadic hunting as long as there were buffalo to hunt.

Some tribes, including the Crow and Shoshoni, chose to fight alongside the army against their old enemies, the Sioux. The Crow chief Plenty Coups explained why he allied with the United States: "Not because we loved the white man . . . or because we hated the Sioux . . . but because we plainly saw that this course was the only one which might save our beautiful country for us." The Crow and Shoshoni got to stay in their homelands and avoided the fate of other tribes shipped to reservations far away.

Indians who refused to stay on reservations risked being hunted down. The Nez Percé war is perhaps the most harrowing example of the army's policy. In 1863, the government dictated a treaty drastically reducing Nez Percé land. Most of the chiefs refused to sign the treaty and did not move to the reservation. When the army cracked down in 1877, some eight hundred Nez Percé people, many of them women and children, fled across the mountains of Idaho, Wyoming, and Montana, heading for the safety of Canada. After a 1,300-mile trek, 50 miles from freedom, they stopped in the Bear Paw Mountains to rest in the snow. The army caught up with them and attacked. Fewer than three hundred of the Indians eluded the army and made it to Canada. Yellow Wolf recalled the plight of those trapped: "Children crying with cold. No fire. There could be no light. Everywhere the crying, the death wail." After a five-day siege, the Nez Percé leader, Chief Joseph, surrendered. His speech, reported by a white soldier, would become famous. "I am tired of fighting," he said as he surrendered his rifle. "Our chiefs are killed. It is cold and we have no blankets. The little children are freezing to death. . . . I am tired. My heart is sick and sad. From where the sun now stands, I will fight no more forever."

In the Southwest, the Apaches resorted to armed resistance. They roamed the Sonoran Desert of southern Arizona and northern Mexico, perfecting a hit-and-run guerrilla warfare that terrorized white settlers and bedeviled the army in the 1870s and 1880s. General George Crook combined a policy of dogged pursuit with judicious diplomacy. Crook relied on Indian scouts to track the raiding parties, recruiting nearly two hundred Apaches, Navajos, and Paiutes. By 1882, Crook had succeeded in persuading most of the Apaches to settle on the San Carlos Reservation in Arizona Territory. A desolate piece of desert inhabited by scorpions and rattlesnakes, San Carlos, in the words of one Apache, was "the worst place in all the great territory stolen from the Apaches."

Geronimo, a respected shaman (medicine man) of the Chiricahua Apache, refused to stay at San Carlos and repeatedly led raiding parties in the early 1880s. His warriors attacked ranches to obtain ammunition and horses. Among Geronimo's band was Lozen, a woman who rode with the warriors, armed with a rifle and a cartridge belt. Lozen's brother, a great chief, described her as being as "strong as a man, braver than most, and cunning in strategy." In the spring of 1885, Geronimo and his followers, including Lozen, went on a ten-month offensive, moving from the Apache sanctuary in the Sierra Madre

Chief Joseph
Chief Joseph came to symbolize the heroic resistance of the Nez Percé. General Nelson Miles promised the Nez Percé that they could return to their homeland if they surrendered. But instead the Nez Percé were shipped off to Indian Territory (Oklahoma). In 1879, Chief Joseph traveled to Washington, D.C., to speak for his people. "Let me be a free man," he pleaded, "free to think and talk and act for myself—and I will obey every law." National Anthropological Archives, Smithsonian Institution (INV 01008900).

to raid and burn ranches and towns on both sides of the Mexican border. General Crook caught up with Geronimo in the fall and persuaded him to return to San Carlos, only to have him slip away on the way back to the reservation. Chagrined,

Crook resigned his post. General Nelson Miles, Crook's replacement, adopted a policy of hunt and destroy.

Geronimo's band of thirty-three Apaches, including women and children, eluded Miles's troops for more than five months. The pursuit left Miles's cavalry ragged. Over time, Lieutenant Leonard Wood had discarded his horse and was reduced to wearing nothing "but a pair of canton flannel drawers, and an old blouse, a pair of moccasins and a hat without a crown." Eventually, Miles's scouts cornered Geronimo in 1886 at Skeleton Canyon where he agreed to march north and negotiate a settlement. "We have not slept for six months," he admitted, "and we are worn out." Although fewer than three dozen Apaches had been considered "hostile," when General Miles induced them to surrender, the government rounded up nearly five hundred Apaches and sent them as prisoners to the South. By 1889, more than a quarter of them had died, some as a result of illnesses contracted in the damp lowland climate of Florida and Alabama and some by suicide. Their plight roused public opinion, and in 1892 they were moved to Fort Sill in Oklahoma and later to New Mexico.

Geronimo lived to become something of a celebrity. He appeared at the St. Louis Exposition in 1904 and rode in President Theodore Roosevelt's inaugural parade in 1905. In a newspaper interview, he confessed, "I want to go to my old home before I die. . . . Want to go back to the mountains again. I asked the Great White Father to allow me to go back, but he said no." None of the Apaches were permitted to return to Arizona; when Geronimo died in 1909, he was buried in Oklahoma.

On the plains, many tribes turned to a non-violent form of resistance—a compelling new religion called the **Ghost Dance**. The Paiute shaman Wovoka, drawing on a cult that had developed in the 1870s, combined elements of Christianity and traditional Indian religion to found the Ghost Dance religion in 1889. Wovoka claimed that he had received a vision in which the Great Spirit spoke through him to all Indians, prophesying that if they would unite in the Ghost Dance ritual, whites would be destroyed in an apocalypse and the buffalo would return. His religion, born of despair and with a message of hope, spread like wildfire over the plains. The Ghost Dance was performed in Idaho, Montana, Utah, Wyoming, Colorado, Nebraska, Kansas, the Dakotas, and Indian Territory by tribes as diverse as the Sioux, Arapaho, Cheyenne, Pawnee, and Shoshoni. Dancers often went into hypnotic trances, dancing until they dropped from exhaustion.

Ghost Dancers, ca. 1893
Arapaho women participate in the Ghost Dance. Tribes performed variations of the dance, but generally dancers formed a circle and danced until they reached a trancelike state. Whites feared the dancers and demanded that the army dispatch troops. The result was the killing of Sitting Bull and the massacre at Wounded Knee. © TopFoto/The Image Works.

The Ghost Dance was nonviolent, but it frightened whites, especially when the Sioux taught that wearing a white ghost shirt made Indians immune to soldiers' bullets. Soon whites began to fear an uprising. "Indians are dancing in the snow and are wild and crazy," wrote the Bureau of Indian Affairs agent at the Pine Ridge Reservation in South Dakota. Frantic, he pleaded for reinforcements. "We are at the mercy of these dancers. We need protection, and we need it now." President Benjamin Harrison dispatched several thousand federal troops to Sioux country to handle any outbreak.

In December 1890, when Sitting Bull attempted to join the Ghost Dance, he was killed by Indian police as they tried to arrest him at his cabin on the Standing Rock Reservation. His people, fleeing the scene, joined with a larger group of Miniconjou Sioux, who were apprehended by the Seventh Cavalry, Custer's old regiment, near Wounded Knee Creek, South Dakota. As the Indians laid down their arms, a soldier attempted to take a rifle from a deaf Miniconjou man and the gun went off. The soldiers opened fire. In the ensuing melee, more than two hundred Indian men, women, and children were mowed down in minutes by the army's brutally efficient Hotchkiss rapid-fire guns. Settler Jules Sandoz surveyed the scene the day after the massacre at **Wounded Knee**. "Here in ten minutes an entire community was as the buffalo that bleached on the plains," he wrote. "There was something loose in the world that hated joy and happiness as it hated brightness and color, reducing everything to drab agony and gray."

It had taken Euro-Americans 250 years to wrest control of the eastern half of the United States from the Indians. It took them only 40 years to take the western half. The subjugation of the American Indians marked the first chapter in a national mission of empire that would anticipate overseas imperialistic adventures in Asia, Latin America, the Caribbean, and the Pacific islands.

REVIEW   In what ways did different Indian groups defy and resist colonial rule?

▶ Mining the West

Mining stood at the center of the quest by the United States for empire in the West. The California gold rush of 1849 touched off the frenzy. The four decades following witnessed equally frenetic rushes for gold and other metals, most notably on the **Comstock Lode** in Nevada and later in New Mexico, Colorado, the Dakotas, Montana, Idaho, Arizona, and Utah (Map 17.2). At first glance, the mining West may seem much different from the East, but by the 1870s the term *urban industrialism* described Virginia City, Nevada, as accurately as it did Pittsburgh or Cleveland. A close look at life on the Comstock Lode indicates some of the patterns and paradoxes of western mining. The diversity of peoples drawn to the West by the promise of mining riches and land made the region the most cosmopolitan in the nation, as well as the most contested. And although mining was often a tale of boom and bust, it was also a story of community building.

Life on the Comstock Lode

By 1859, refugees from California's played-out goldfields flocked to the Washoe basin in Nevada. While searching for gold, Washoe miners stumbled on the richest vein of silver ore on the continent—the legendary Comstock Lode, named for prospector Henry Comstock.

To exploit even potentially valuable silver claims required capital and expensive technology well beyond the means of the prospector. An active San Francisco stock market sprang up to finance operations on the Comstock. Shrewd businessmen soon recognized that the easiest way to get rich was to sell their claims or to form mining companies and sell shares of stock. The most unscrupulous mined the wallets of gullible investors by selling shares in bogus mines. Speculation, misrepresentation, and outright thievery ran rampant. In twenty years, more than $300 million poured from the earth in Nevada alone, most of it going to speculators in San Francisco.

The promise of gold and silver drew thousands to the mines of the West. As Mark Twain observed in Virginia City's *Territorial Enterprise*, "All the peoples of the earth had representative adventures in the Silverland." Irish, Chinese, Germans, English, Scots, Welsh, Canadians, Mexicans, Italians, Scandinavians, French, Swiss, Chileans, and other South and Central Americans came to share in the bonanza. With them came a sprinkling of Russians, Poles, Greeks, Japanese, Spaniards,

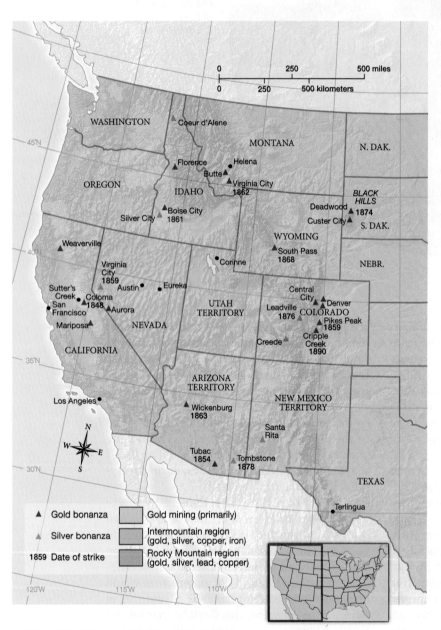

Map 17.2 Western Mining, 1848–1890
Rich deposits of gold, silver, copper, lead, and iron larded the mountains of the West. Miners from all over the world flocked to the region. Few struck it rich, but many stayed on as paid workers in the increasingly mechanized corporate mines.

Mining on the Comstock
This photo of a miner at work shows the dangers faced on the Comstock Lode. Without a hard hat or miner's light, he is working with timbers to shore up the mine shaft. After the discovery of the "Big Bonanza" in 1873, eight years after this picture was taken, silver mines honeycombed the hills of Nevada. National Archives, photo no. 77-KS-1-15.

Hungarians, Portuguese, Turks, Pacific Islanders, and Moroccans, as well as other North Americans, African Americans, and American Indians. This polyglot population, typical of mining boomtowns, made Virginia City in the 1870s more cosmopolitan than New York or Boston. In the part of Utah Territory that eventually became Nevada, as many as 30 percent of the people came from outside the United States, compared to 25 percent in New York and 21 percent in Massachusetts.

Irish immigrants formed the largest ethnic group in the mining district. In Virginia City, fully one-third of the population claimed at least one parent from Ireland. Irish women constituted the largest group of women on the Comstock. As servants, boardinghouse owners, and washerwomen, they made up a significant part of the workforce. In contrast, the Chinese community, numbering 642 in 1870, remained overwhelmingly male. Virulent anti-Chinese sentiment barred the men from work in the mines, but despite this, the mining community came to depend on Chinese labor.

The discovery of precious metals on the Comstock spelled disaster for the Indians. No sooner had the miners struck pay dirt than they demanded that army troops "hunt Indians" and establish forts to protect transportation to and from the diggings. This sudden and dramatic intrusion left Nevada's native tribes—the Northern Paiute and Bannock Shoshoni—exiles in their own land. At first they resisted, but over time they adapted and preserved their culture and identity despite the havoc wreaked by western mining and settlement.

In 1873, Comstock miners uncovered a new vein of ore, a veritable cavern of gold and silver. This "Big Bonanza" speeded the transition from small-scale industry to corporate oligopoly, creating a radically new social and economic environment. The Comstock became a laboratory for new mining technology. Huge stamping mills pulverized rock with pistonlike hammers driven by steam engines. Enormous Cornish pumps sucked water from the mine shafts, and huge ventilators circulated air in the underground chambers. No backwoods mining camp, Virginia City was an industrial center with more than 1,200 stamping mills working on average a ton of ore every day. Almost 400 men worked in milling, nearly 300 labored in manufacturing industries, and roughly 3,000 toiled in the mines. The Gould and Curry mine covered sixty acres. Most of the miners who came to the Comstock ended up as laborers for the big companies.

New technology eliminated some of the dangers of mining but often created new ones. In the hard-rock mines of the West, accidents in the 1870s disabled one out of every thirty miners and killed one in eighty. Ross Moudy, who worked as a miner in Cripple Creek, Colorado, recalled how a stockholder visiting the mine nearly fell to his death. The terrified visitor told the miner next to him that "instead of being paid $3 a day, they ought to have all the gold they could take out." On the Comstock Lode, because of the difficulty of obtaining skilled labor, the richness of the ore, and the need for a stable workforce, labor unions formed early and held considerable bargaining power. Comstock miners commanded $4 a day, the highest wage in the mining West.

The mining towns of the "Wild West" are often portrayed as lawless outposts, filled with saloons and rough gambling dens and populated almost exclusively by men. The truth is more complex, as Virginia City's development attests. An established urban community built to serve an industrial giant, Virginia City in its first decade boasted churches, schools, theaters, an opera house, and hundreds of families. By 1870, women composed 30 percent of the population, and 75 percent of the women listed their occupation in the census as housekeeper. Mary McNair Mathews, a widow from Buffalo, New York, who lived on the Comstock in the 1870s, worked as a teacher, nurse, seamstress, laundress, and lodging-house operator. She later published a book on her adventures.

By 1875, Virginia City boasted a population of 25,000 people, making it one of the largest cities between St. Louis and San Francisco. The city, dubbed the "Queen of the Comstock," hosted American presidents as well as legions of lesser dignitaries. Virginia City represented, in the words of a recent chronicler, "the distilled essence of America's newly established course—urban, industrial, acquisitive, and materialistic, on the move, 'a living polyglot' of cultures that collided and converged."

The Diverse Peoples of the West

The West of the late nineteenth century was a polyglot place, as much so as the big cities of the East. The sheer number of peoples who mingled in the West produced a complex blend of racism and prejudice. One historian has noted, not entirely facetiously, that there were at least eight oppressed "races" in the West—Indians, Latinos, Chinese, Japanese, blacks, Mormons, strikers, and radicals.

African Americans who ventured out to the territories faced hostile settlers determined to keep the West "for whites only." In response, they formed all-black communities such as Nicodemus, Kansas. That settlement, founded by thirty black Kentuckians in 1877, grew to a community of seven hundred by 1880. Isolated and often separated by great distances, small black settlements grew up throughout the West, in Nevada, Utah, and the Pacific Northwest, as well as in Kansas. Black soldiers who served in the West during the Indian wars often stayed on as settlers. Called buffalo soldiers because Native Americans thought their hair resembled that of the bison, these black troops numbered up to 25,000. In the face of discrimination, poor treatment, and harsh conditions, the buffalo soldiers served with distinction and boasted the lowest desertion rate in the army.

Hispanic peoples had lived in Texas and the Southwest since Juan de Oñate led pioneer settlers up the Rio Grande in 1598. Hispanics had occupied the Pacific coast since San Diego was founded in 1769. Overnight, they were reduced to a "minority" after the United States annexed

Texas in 1845 and took land stretching to California after the Mexican-American War ended in 1848. At first, the Hispanic owners of large *ranchos* in California, New Mexico, and Texas greeted conquest as an economic opportunity. But racial prejudice soon ended their optimism. *Californios* (Mexican residents of California), who had been granted American citizenship by the Treaty of Guadalupe Hidalgo (1848), faced discrimination by Anglos who sought to keep them out of California's mines and commerce. Whites illegally squatted on *rancho* land while protracted litigation over Spanish and Mexican land grants forced the Californios into court. Although the U.S. Supreme Court eventually validated most of their claims, it took so long—seventeen years on average—that many Californios sold their property to pay taxes and legal bills.

Swindles, trickery, and intimidation dispossessed scores of Californios. Many ended up segregated in urban barrios (neighborhoods) in their own homeland. Their percentage of California's population declined from 82 percent in 1850 to 19 percent in 1880 as Anglos migrated to the state. In New Mexico and Texas, Mexicans remained a majority of the population but became increasingly impoverished as Anglos dominated business and took the best jobs. Skirmishes between Hispanics and whites in northern New Mexico over the fencing of the open range lasted for decades. Groups of Hispanics with names such as *Las Manos Negras* (the Black Hands) cut fences and burned barns. In Texas, violence along the Rio Grande pitted *Tejanos* (Mexican residents of Texas) against the Texas Rangers, who saw their role as "keeping Mexicans in their place."

Mormons, too, faced prejudice and hostility. The followers of Joseph Smith, the founder and prophet of the Church of Jesus Christ of Latter-Day Saints, fled west to Utah Territory in 1844 to avoid religious persecution. They believed they had a divine right to the land, and their messianic militancy made others distrust them. The Mormon practice of polygamy (church leader Brigham Young had twenty-three wives) also came under attack. To counter the criticism of polygamy, the Utah territorial legislature gave women the right to vote in 1870, the first universal woman suffrage act in the nation. (Wyoming had granted suffrage to white women in 1869.) Although women's rights advocates argued that the newly enfranchised women would "do away with the horrible institution of polygamy," it remained in force. Not until 1890 did the church hierarchy yield to pressure and renounce

VISUAL ACTIVITY

Vaqueros in a Horse Corral, 1877
In this exciting scene, artist James Walker captures the skill of Hispanic *vaqueros* lassoing horses in a Texas corral. As Anglo settlers gradually displaced Hispanic landholders across the West, the domain of the rancho gradually declined, as did a way of life. Private Collection/Peter Newark Pictures/Bridgeman Images.
READING THE IMAGE: What about the painting tells you that these are Hispanic cowboys and not Anglo cowboys?
CONNECTIONS: In another twenty years, what would these vaqueros likely be doing for a living?

polygamy. The fierce controversy over polygamy postponed statehood for Utah until 1896.

The Chinese suffered the most brutal treatment of all the newcomers at the hands of employers and other laborers. Drawn by the promise of gold, more than 20,000 Chinese had joined the rush to California by 1852. Miners determined to keep "California for Americans" succeeded in passing prohibitive foreign license laws to keep the Chinese out of the mines. But Chinese immigration continued. In the 1860s, when white workers moved on to find riches in the bonanza mines of Nevada, Chinese laborers took jobs abandoned by the whites. Railroad magnate Charles Crocker hired Chinese gangs to work on the Central Pacific, reasoning that "the race that built the Great Wall" could lay tracks across the treacherous Sierra Nevada. Some 10,000 Chinese, representing 90 percent of Crocker's workforce, completed America's first transcontinental railroad in 1869.

By 1870, more than 63,000 Chinese immigrants lived in America, 77 percent of them in California. A 1790 federal statute that limited naturalization to "white persons" was modified after the Civil War to extend naturalization to blacks ("persons of African descent"). But the Chinese and other Asians continued to be denied access to citizenship. As perpetual aliens, they constituted a reserve army of transnational laborers that many saw as a threat to American labor.

In 1876, the Workingmen's Party formed to fight for Chinese exclusion. Racial and cultural animosities stood at the heart of anti-Chinese agitation. Denis Kearney, the fiery San Francisco leader of the movement, made clear this racist bent when he urged legislation to "expel every one of the moon-eyed lepers." Nor was California alone in its anti-immigrant nativism. As the country confronted growing ethnic and racial diversity with the rising tide of global immigration in the decades following the Civil War, many questioned the principle of racial equality at the same time they argued against the assimilation of "nonwhite" groups. In this climate, Congress passed the **Chinese Exclusion Act** in 1882, effectively barring Chinese immigration and setting a precedent for further immigration restrictions.

The Chinese Exclusion Act led to a sharp drop in the Chinese population—from 105,465 in 1880 to 89,863 in 1900—because Chinese immigrants, overwhelmingly male, did not have families to sustain their population. Eventually, Japanese immigrants, including women as well as men, replaced the Chinese, particularly in

agriculture. As "nonwhite" immigrants, they could not become naturalized citizens, but their children born in the United States claimed the rights of citizenship. Japanese parents, seeking to own land, purchased it in their children's names. Although anti-Asian prejudice remained strong in California and elsewhere in the West, Asian immigrants formed an important part of the economic fabric of the western United States.

> **REVIEW** What role did mining play in shaping the society and economy of the American West?

Chinese Railroad Worker, ca. 1867
This photograph of a lone Chinese laborer carrying a shoulder pole illustrates the magnitude of the task workers faced in the Sierra Nevada. This worker stands in front of what would become Tunnel no. 8, one of the innumerable tunnels carved by hand through the granite. Six years of backbreaking work culminated in the epic achievement of the Central Pacific Railroad. Library of Congress, 1s00553.

▶ Land Fever

In the three decades following 1870, more land was settled than in all the previous history of the country. Americans by the hundreds of thousands packed up and moved west, goaded if not by the hope of striking gold, then by the promise of owning land to farm or ranch. The agrarian West shared with the mining West a persistent restlessness, an equally pervasive addiction to speculation, and a penchant for exploiting natural resources and labor.

Two factors stimulated the land rush in the trans-Mississippi West. The **Homestead Act of 1862** promised 160 acres free to any citizen or prospective citizen, male or female, who settled on the land for five years. Even more important, transcontinental railroads opened up new areas and actively recruited settlers. After the completion of the **first transcontinental railroad** in 1869, homesteaders abandoned the covered wagon, and by the 1880s rampant railroad overbuilding meant that settlers could choose from four competing rail lines and make the trip west in a matter of days.

Although the country was rich in land and resources, not all who wanted to own land achieved their goal. During the transition from the family farm to large commercial farming, small farms and ranches gave way to vast spreads worked by migrant labor or paid farmworkers and cowhands. Just as industry corporatized and consolidated in the East, the period from 1870 to 1900 witnessed corporate consolidation in mining, ranching, and agriculture.

Moving West: Homesteaders and Speculators

A Missouri homesteader remembered packing as her family pulled up stakes and headed west to Oklahoma in 1890. "We were going to God's Country," she wrote. "You had to work hard on that rocky country in Missouri. I was glad to be leaving it. . . . We were going to a new land and get rich."

Settlers who headed west in search of "God's Country" faced hardship, loneliness, and deprivation. To carve a farm from the raw prairie of Iowa, the plains of Nebraska, or the forests of the Pacific Northwest took more than fortitude and backbreaking toil. It took luck. Blizzards, tornadoes, grasshoppers, hailstorms, drought, prairie fires, accidental death, and disease were only a few of the catastrophes that could befall even the best farmer. Homesteaders on free land still needed as much as $1,000 for a house, a team of farm animals, a well, fencing, and seed. Poor farmers called "sodbusters" did without even these basics, living in houses made from sod (blocks of

Midwestern Settlement before 1862

DAKOTA TERRITORY

MINN.   WIS.

Western extent of settlement before Homestead Act of 1862

NEBRASKA TERRITORY

IOWA

KANSAS

MISSOURI

INDIAN TERRITORY

ARKANSAS

TEXAS

grass-covered earth) or dugouts carved into hillsides and using muscle instead of machinery. (See "Making Historical Arguments," page 490.)

"Father made a dugout and covered it with willows and grass," one Kansas girl recounted. When it rained, the dugout flooded, and "we carried the water out in buckets, then waded around in the mud until it dried." Rain wasn't the only problem. "Sometimes the bull snakes would get in the roof and now and then one would lose his hold and fall down on the bed. . . . Mother would grab the hoe . . . and after the fight was over Mr. Bull Snake was dragged outside."

For women on the frontier, obtaining simple daily necessities such as water and fuel meant backbreaking labor. Out on the plains, where water was scarce, women often had to trudge to the nearest creek or spring. "A yoke was made to place across [Mother's] shoulders, so as to carry at each end a bucket of water," one daughter recollected, "and then water was brought a half mile from spring to house." Gathering fuel was another heavy chore. Without ready sources of coal or firewood, the most prevalent fuel was "chips"—chunks of dried cattle and buffalo dung, found in abundance on the plains.

VISUAL ACTIVITY

Norwegian Immigrant and Sod House
Norwegian immigrant Beret Olesdater sits in front of her sod house in Lac qui Parle, Minnesota, in 1896. On the plains, where trees were scarce, settlers carved dugouts into a hillside or built huts like the one here, carved from blocks of sod. Minnesota Historical Society/Corbis.

READING THE IMAGE: What do the woman's dress and the expression on her face tell us about the life of women on the plains?

CONNECTIONS: What expectations did homesteaders have for their lives on the plains, and how did this compare to the realities they faced?

Did Westerners Really Build It All by Themselves?

The myth of the American West goes something like this: In the mid-nineteenth century, torrents of gutsy pioneers began pouring into the vast empty space beyond the Mississippi. Abundant free land offered opportunity to anyone ambitious enough to claim it and tough enough to work it. Far from everything, entirely on his own, a man could rely only on his own will, grit, and muscle. In time, strong, self-reliant, can-do Americans made the harsh environment bloom and produce. The West offered limitless possibilities, as long as government kept out of the way.

While the myth is not wrong about the courage and endurance of the pioneer, it ignores a number of significant facts. The plains and prairies were not empty. Pioneer women were as important as men in conquering the West. And the celebration of self-reliance and individual responsibility ignores the heavy debt that pioneers owed the federal government for helping them settle and develop the West.

In countless ways, westerners depended on the government for access to the West's bountiful resources—land, minerals, grass, timber, and water. Through purchases, treaties, annexations, and war, the federal government acquired the land that would become the American West. Washington oversaw the territorial governments that controlled most of the West, sometimes well into the twentieth century. Federally appointed governors and judges meant political dependence, but they also provided access to federal funds for development. Government business brought jobs, contracts, and subsidies. And the federal presence offered access to policymakers. When westerners decided that Asian laborers were undesirable, Congress passed the 1882 Exclusion Act suspending Chinese immigration. When citizens objected to Mormon marriage practices, a federal law banned polygamy. Territorial status gave the national government increased power in the West, but westerners found that dependency had its rewards.

Westerners cheered when the U.S. Army swept away the Indians and Anglo law dispossessed the Hispanic inhabitants of the region, clearing the way for land-seeking settlers. The U.S. Geological Survey explored and mapped the region, and the General Land Office surveyed, sold, and registered the property it laid out. The federal government maintained public order until Congress judged settlers ready to take over their own affairs. Congress passed hundreds of laws granting Americans easy access to the public domain. The 1862 Homestead Act, for example, helped 1.4 million homesteaders gain land titles. The federal government's actions sometimes undercut its democratic land policy, but its open-handed distribution of public land drew countless numbers of settlers westward.

Farms without the means to transport crops to market were not worth much, and the second half

Despite the hardships, some homesteaders succeeded in building comfortable lives. The dugout made way for the sod hut—a more substantial dwelling; the log cabin yielded to a white clapboard home with a porch and a rocking chair. For others, the promise of the West failed to materialize. Already by the 1870s, much of the best land had been taken. Too often, homesteaders found that only the least desirable tracts were left—poor land, far from markets, transportation, and society. "There is plenty of land for sale in California," one migrant complained in 1870, but "the majority of the available lands are held by speculators, at prices far beyond the reach of a poor man." The railroads, flush from land grants provided by the state and federal governments, owned huge swaths of land in the West and actively recruited buyers. Altogether, the land grants totaled approximately 180 million acres—an area almost one-tenth the size of the United States (Map 17.3). The vast majority of farmland sold for a profit.

As land grew scarce on the prairie in the 1870s, farmers began to push farther west, moving into western Kansas, Nebraska, and eastern Colorado—the region called the Great American Desert by settlers who had passed over it on their way to California and Oregon. Many agricultural experts warned that the semiarid land (where less than twenty inches of rain fell annually) would not support a farm on the 160 acres allotted to homesteaders. But their words of caution were drowned out by the extravagant claims of western promoters, many employed by the railroads to sell off land grants. "Rain follows the plow" became the slogan of

of the nineteenth century became the great era of federal support for transportation. The federal government built roads, established stage and wagon lines, strung telegraph wires, and, most important, offered huge grants of public land to subsidize the construction of railroads. Federal initiatives built the communication and transportation networks that integrated the products of western farms into the markets of the nation and the world.

The mining industry also depended on the federal bounty. When the gold rush exploded in California in 1849, the federal government raced just to keep up. But by the time Comstock Lode was discovered in 1859, federal law took control and framed the western mining enterprise. Federal laws helped mining companies beat back miner unions and collective bargaining. Mine owners won their fierce struggle with mine workers when the courts enforced the notion of individual responsibility and let mining corporations escape liability for injured miners. In 1874, when gold was discovered in the Black Hills, Congress promptly repealed the 1868 treaty that had granted the land to the Sioux, thereby opening new gold

country to American citizens. Like farmers, miners celebrated their independence from government oversight while simultaneously reaping the benefits of government intervention.

Cattle ranchers also owed a debt to the federal government. The prosperous western cattle industry depended on cattle grazing on public lands and being shipped east on federally subsidized railroads. When nasty disputes between cattle owners threatened to disrupt the industry, Congress established the Bureau of Animal Husbandry to keep the peace. To protect ranchers from competition, Congress passed laws that banned foreign land purchases in the West. To protect vulnerable cattle, the U.S. Biological Survey and the Forest Service waged war on wolves and mountain lions, and to guard grazing land they took aim at elk, antelope, and prairie dogs. By 1884, with the crucial support of the government, 20 million cattle grazed the American West.

The last of the western territories became states early in the twentieth century, but statehood did not end the West's dependence on the federal government. Indeed, as the government undertook massive water projects, created subsidies

for agriculture, opened scores of national parks, and increased its efforts to secure the nation's borders, Uncle Sam continued to expand his footprint. Today, the government makes resources available for private appropriation, investment, and development, as it did in the nineteenth century, and farmers, ranchers, miners, and lumber producers continue to need help in solving their problems.

Questions for Analysis

Summarize the Argument: How did the federal government assist in the settlement and development of the West, and who were the major beneficiaries?

Analyze the Evidence: Does the evidence for federal assistance add up to a persuasive argument that the federal government played a crucial, even indispensable, role in the settlement and development of the West?

Consider the Context: What do you suppose were the origins of the myth of the American West? Can you identify other American beliefs and values that might have contributed to the myth? Why do you suppose the myth has been so persistent?

western boosters, who insisted that cultivation would alter the climate of the region and bring more rainfall. Instead, drought followed the plow. Droughts were a cyclical fact of life on the Great Plains. Plowed up, the dry topsoil blew away in the wind. A period of relatively good rainfall in the early 1880s encouraged farming; then a protracted drought in the late 1880s and early 1890s forced thousands of starving farmers to leave, some in wagons carrying the slogan "In God we trusted, in Kansas we busted."

Fever for fertile land set off a series of spectacular land runs in Oklahoma. When two million acres of land in former Indian Territory opened for settlement in 1889, thousands of homesteaders massed on the border. At the opening pistol shot, "with a shout and a yell the swift

riders shot out, then followed the light buggies or wagons," a reporter wrote. "Above all, a great cloud of dust hover[ed] like smoke over a battlefield." By nightfall, Oklahoma boasted two tent cities with more than ten thousand residents. In the last frenzied land rush on Oklahoma's Cherokee strip in 1893, several settlers were killed in the stampede, and nervous men guarded their claims with rifles. As public land grew scarce, the hunger for land grew fiercer for both farmers and ranchers.

Barbed wire, invented in 1874, revolutionized the cattle business and sounded the death knell for the open range. As the largest ranches in Texas began to fence, nasty fights broke out between big ranchers and "fence cutters," who resented the end of the open range. One old-timer observed, "Those persons, Mexicans and Americans,

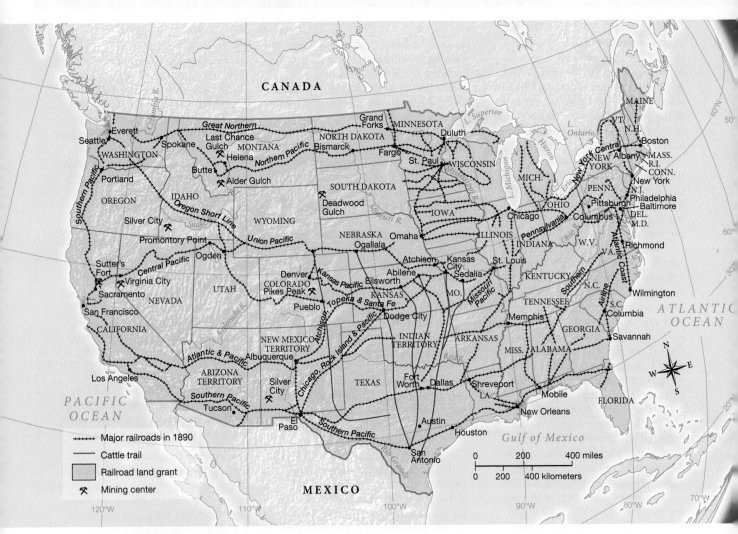

MAP ACTIVITY

Map 17.3   Federal Land Grants to Railroads and the Development of the West, 1850–1900
Railroads received more than 180 million acres, an area as large as Texas. Built well ahead of demand, the western railroads courted settlers, often onto land not fit for farming.

READING THE MAP: Which mining cities and towns were located directly on railroad lines? Which towns were located at the junction of more than one railroad line or branch?
CONNECTIONS: In what ways did the growth of the railroads affect the population of the West? What western goods and products did the railroads help bring east and to ports for shipping around the world?

without land but who had cattle were put out of business by fencing." Fencing forced small-time ranchers who owned land but could not afford to buy barbed wire or sink wells to sell out for the best price they could get. The displaced ranchers, many of them Mexicans, ended up as wageworkers on the huge spreads owned by Anglos or by European syndicates.

On the range, the cowboy gave way to the cattle king and, like the miner, became a wage laborer. Many cowboys were African Americans (as many as five thousand in Texas alone). Writers of western literature chose to ignore the presence

of black cowboys like Deadwood Dick (Nat Love), who was portrayed as a white man in the dime novels of the era.

By 1886, cattle overcrowded the range. Severe blizzards during the winter of 1886–87 decimated the herds. "A whole generation of cowmen," wrote one chronicler, "went dead broke." Fencing worsened the situation. During blizzards, cattle stayed alive by keeping on the move. But when they ran up against barbed wire fences, they froze to death. In the aftermath of the "Great Die Up," new labor-intensive forms of cattle ranching replaced the open-range model.

Tenants, Sharecroppers, and Migrants

In the post–Civil War period, as agriculture became a big business tied by the railroads to national and global markets, an increasing number of laborers worked land that they would never own. In the southern United States, farmers labored under particularly heavy burdens. The Civil War wiped out much of the region's capital, which had been invested in slaves, and crippled the plantation economy. "The colored folks stayed with the old boss man and farmed and worked on the plantations," a black Alabama sharecropper observed bitterly. "They were still slaves, but they were free slaves." Some freedpeople did manage to pull together enough resources to go west. In 1879, more than fifteen thousand black Exodusters, as the black settlers were known, moved from Mississippi and Louisiana to take up land in Kansas.

California's Mexican cowboys, or *vaqueros*, commanded decent wages throughout the Southwest. But by 1880, as the coming of the railroads ended the long cattle drives and as large feedlots began to replace the open range, the value of their skills declined. Many vaqueros ended up as migrant laborers, often on land their families had once owned. Similarly, in Texas, Tejanos found themselves displaced. After the heyday of cattle ranching ended in the late 1880s, cotton production rose in the southeastern regions of the state. Ranchers turned their pastures into sharecroppers' plots and hired displaced cowboys, most of them Mexicans, as seasonal laborers for as little as seventy-five cents a day, thereby creating a growing army of agricultural wageworkers.

Land monopoly and large-scale farming fostered tenancy and migratory labor on the West Coast. By the 1870s, less than 1 percent of California's population owned half the state's available agricultural land. The rigid economics of large-scale commercial agriculture and the seasonal nature of the crops spawned a ragged army of migratory agricultural laborers. Derisively labeled "blanket men" or "bindle stiffs," these transients worked the fields in the growing season and wintered in the flophouses of San Francisco. After passage of the Chinese Exclusion Act of 1882, Mexicans, Filipinos, and Japanese immigrants filled the demand for migratory workers.

Commercial Farming and Industrial Cowboys

In the late nineteenth century, the population of the United States remained overwhelmingly rural. The 1870 census showed that nearly 80

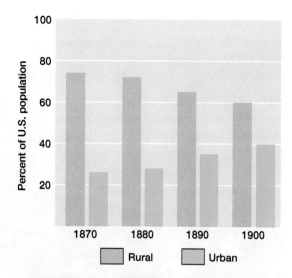

FIGURE 17.1 Changes in Rural and Urban Populations, 1870–1900
Between 1870 and 1900, both the number of urban dwellers and the number of farms increased, even as the number of rural inhabitants fell. Mechanization made it possible to farm with fewer hands, fueling the exodus from farm to city throughout the second half of the nineteenth century.

percent of the nation's people lived on farms and in villages of fewer than 8,000 inhabitants. By 1900, the figure had dropped to 60 percent (Figure 17.1). At the same time, the number of farms rose. Rapid growth in the West increased the number of farms from 2 million in 1860 to more than 5.7 million in 1900.

New technology and farming techniques revolutionized American farm life. Mechanized farm machinery halved the time and labor cost of production and made it possible to cultivate vast tracts of land. Meanwhile, urbanization provided farmers with expanding markets for their produce, and railroads carried crops to markets thousands of miles away. Even before the start of the twentieth century, American agriculture had entered the era of what would come to be called agribusiness—farming as a big business—with the advent of huge commercial farms.

As farming moved onto the prairies and plains, mechanization took command. Steel plows, reapers, mowers, harrows, seed drills, combines, and threshers replaced human muscle. Horse-drawn implements gave way to steam-powered machinery. By 1880, a single combine could do the work of twenty men, vastly increasing the acreage a farmer could cultivate. Mechanization spurred the growth of bonanza wheat farms,

Farm Family, 1890s
In the 1880s, when the Great Plains witnessed the triumph of wheat, wheat farming became agribusiness on a massive scale. Here a proud Nebraska family stands atop its new wheat harvester. Very soon, horse-drawn harvesters like this would be replaced with steam-powered machinery. © AS400 DB/Corbis.

some more than 100,000 acres, in California and the Red River Valley of North Dakota and Minnesota. This agricultural revolution meant that Americans raised more than four times the corn, five times the hay, and seven times the wheat and oats they had before the Civil War.

Like cotton farmers in the South, western grain and livestock farmers increasingly depended on foreign markets for their livelihood. A fall in global market prices meant that a farmer's entire harvest went to pay off debts. In the depression that followed the panic of 1893, many heavily mortgaged farmers lost their land to creditors. As a Texas cotton farmer complained, "By the time the World Gets their Liveing out of the Farmer as we have to Feed the World, we the Farmer has nothing Left but a Bear Hard Liveing." Commercial farming, along with mining, represented another way in which the West developed its own brand of industrialism. The far West's industrial economy sprang initially from California gold and the vast territory that came under American control following the Mexican-American War. In the ensuing rush on land and resources, environmental factors interacted with economic

and social forces to produce enterprises as vast in scale and scope as anything found in the East.

Two German immigrants, Henry Miller and Charles Lux, pioneered the West's mix of agriculture and industrialism. Beginning as meat wholesalers, Miller and Lux quickly expanded their business to encompass cattle, land, and land reclamation projects such as dams and irrigation systems. With a labor force of migrant workers, a highly coordinated corporate system, and large sums of investment capital, the firm of Miller & Lux became one of America's industrial behemoths. Eventually, these "industrial cowboys" grazed a herd of 100,000 cattle on 1.25 million acres of company land in California, Oregon, and Nevada and employed more than 1,200 migrant laborers on their corporate ranches. Miller & Lux dealt with the labor problem by offering free meals to migratory workers, thus keeping wages low while winning goodwill among an army of unemployed who competed for the work. When the company's Chinese cooks rebelled at washing all the dishes, the migrant laborers were forced to eat off dirty plates. By the 1890s, more than 800 migrants a year followed what came to be known as the "Dirty Plate Route" on Miller & Lux ranches throughout California.

Since the days of Thomas Jefferson, agrarian life had been linked with the highest ideals of a democratic society. Agrarianism had been transformed. The farmer was no longer a self-sufficient yeoman but often a businessman or a wage laborer tied to a global market. And even as farm production soared, industrialization outstripped it. More and more farmers left the fields for urban factories or found work in the "factories in the fields" of the new industrialized agribusinesses. Now that the future seemed to lie not with small farmers but with industrial enterprises, was democracy itself at risk? This question would ignite a farmers' revolt in the 1880s and dominate political debate in the 1890s.

Territorial Government

The federal government practiced a policy of benign neglect when it came to territorial government. A governor, a secretary, a few judges, an attorney, and a marshal held jurisdiction. In Nevada Territory, that meant a handful of officials governed an area the size of New England. Originally a part of the larger Utah Territory, Nevada, propelled by mining interests, moved on the fast track to statehood, entering the Union in 1864.

More typical were the territories extant in 1870—New Mexico, Utah, Washington, Colorado, Dakota, Arizona, Idaho, Montana, and Wyoming. These areas remained territories for inordinately long periods ranging from twenty-three to sixty-two years. While awaiting statehood, they were subject to territorial governors, who won their posts due to party loyalty and who were largely underpaid, uninformed, often unqualified, and largely ignored by Washington. Wages rarely arrived on schedule, leading one cynic to observe, "Only the rich, or those having 'no visible means of support,' can afford to accept office." John C. Frémont, governor of Arizona Territory, complained he could not inspect the Grand Canyon because he was too poor to own a horse.

Western governors with fewer scruples accepted money from local interests—mine owners and big ranchers or lumber companies. Nearly all territorial appointees tried to maintain business connections in the East or take advantage of speculative opportunities in the West. Corruption ran rampant. Yet the distance from the nation's capital meant that few charges of corrupt dealings were investigated. Gun-toting westerners served as another deterrent. One judge sent to New Mexico Territory in 1871 to investigate fraud "stayed three days, made up his mind that it would be dangerous to do any investigating, . . . and returned to his home without action."

Underfunded and overlooked victims of cronyism and prey to special interests, territorial governments mirrored the self-serving political and economic values of the era.

> **REVIEW** How did the fight for land and resources unfold in the West?

▶ Conclusion: The West in the Gilded Age

In 1871, author Mark Twain published *Roughing It*, a chronicle of his days spent in mining towns in California and Nevada. There he found the same corrupt politics, vulgar display, and mania for speculation that he later skewered in *The Gilded Age* (1873), his biting satire of greed and corruption in the nation's capital. Far from being an antidote to the tawdry values of the East—an innocent idyll out of place and time—the American West, with its get-rich-quick ethos, addiction to gambling and speculation, and virulent racism, helped set the tone for the Gilded Age.

Twain's view countered that of Frederick Jackson Turner and perhaps better suited a West that witnessed the reckless overbuilding of railroads; the consolidation of business in mining and ranching; the rise of commercial farming; corruption and a penchant for government handouts; racial animosity; the exploitation of labor and natural resources, which led to the decimation of the great bison herds, the pollution of rivers with mining wastes, and the overgrazing of the plains; and the beginnings of an imperial policy that would provide a template for U.S. adventures abroad. Turner, intent on promoting what was unique about the frontier, failed to note that the same issues that came to dominate debate east of the Mississippi—the growing power of big business, the exploitation of land and labor, corruption in politics, and ethnic and racial tensions exacerbated by colonial expansion and unparalleled immigration—took center stage in the West at the end of the nineteenth century.

See the Selected Bibliography for this chapter in the Appendix.

17 Chapter Review

KEY TERMS

reservations (p. 472)
Comanchería (p. 476)
Black Hills (p. 476)
Battle of the Little Big Horn (p. 477)
Carlisle Indian School (p. 479)
Dawes Allotment Act (p. 481)
Ghost Dance (p. 482)
Wounded Knee (p. 483)
Comstock Lode (p. 484)
Chinese Exclusion Act (p. 488)
Homestead Act of 1862 (p. 488)
first transcontinental railroad (p. 488)

REVIEW QUESTIONS

1. How did the slaughter of the bison contribute to the Plains Indians' removal to reservations? (pp. 471–477)

2. In what ways did different Indian groups defy and resist colonial rule? (pp. 477–483)

3. What role did mining play in shaping the society and economy of the American West? (pp. 484–488)

4. How did the fight for land and resources unfold in the West? (pp. 488–495)

MAKING CONNECTIONS

1. Westward migration brought settlers into conflict with Native Americans. What was the U.S. government's policy toward Indians in the West, and how did it evolve over time?

2. How did innovations in business and technology transform mining and agriculture in the West?

3. In competition for work and land in the American West, why did Anglo-American settlers usually have the upper hand over settlers from other countries? How did legal developments contribute to this circumstance?

4. What role did railroads play in western settlement, industrialization, and agriculture? How did railroads affect Indian populations in the West?

LINKING TO THE PAST

1. In what ways were the goals of migrants to the West similar to those of the Northerners who moved to the South after the Civil War? How did they differ? (See chapter 16.)

2. How did the racism of the West compare with the racist attitudes against African Americans in the Reconstruction South? (See chapter 16.)

18 Railroads, Business, and Politics in the Gilded Age

1865–1900

CONTENT LEARNING OBJECTIVES

After reading and studying this chapter, you should be able to:

• Describe the ways in which industries were transformed in the late nineteenth century, including the railroad, steel, and oil industries.

• Explain the factors that led to business mergers and the rise of corporations and explain the role of finance capitalism. Describe the ideas of social Darwinism and the gospel of wealth.

• Describe how regional sectionalism, race, and gender affected political culture in the late nineteenth century.

• Describe the issues and personalities that drove national party politics during the Gilded Age and explain why the Republican Party divided into factions.

• Identify the key economic issues of the Gilded Age and how those issues led to party realignment in the 1890s.

CAMPAIGN PINS
Presidential campaign pins from 1884 depict James G. Blaine thumbing his nose at rival Grover Cleveland. The gilt pins symbolize the lavish wealth and corruption and political strife of the Gilded Age.
David J. & Janice L. Frent Collection/Corbis.

ONE NIGHT OVER DINNER, MARK TWAIN AND CHARLES Dudley Warner teased their wives about the sentimental novels they read. When the two women challenged them to write something better, they set to work. Warner supplied the melodrama while Twain "hurled in the facts." The result, *The Gilded Age* (1873), was a runaway best seller, a savage satire of the "get-rich-quick" era that would forever carry the book's title.

Twain left no one unscathed in the novel—political hacks, Washington lobbyists, Wall Street financiers, small-town boosters, and the "great putty-hearted public." Underneath the glitter of the Gilded Age lurked vulgarity, crass materialism, and political corruption. In Twain's satire, Congress is for sale to the highest bidder:

Why the matter is simple enough. A Congressional appropriation costs money. . . . A majority of the House Committee, say $10,000 apiece—$40,000; a majority of the Senate Committee, the same each—say $40,000; a little extra to one or two chairmen of one or two such committees, say $10,000 each—$20,000; and there's $100,000 of the money gone, to begin with. Then, seven male lobbyists, at $3,000 each—$21,000; one female lobbyist, $3,000; a high moral Congressman or Senator here and there—the high moral ones cost more, because they give tone to a measure—say ten of these at $3,000 each, is $30,000; then a lot of small fry country members who won't vote for anything whatever without pay—say twenty at $500 apiece, is $10,000 altogether; lot of jimcracks for Congressmen's wives and children . . . well, those things cost in a lump, say $10,000 . . . and then comes your printed documents. . . . Well, never mind the details, the total in clean numbers foots up $118,254.42 thus far!

The Gilded Age seemed to tarnish many who lived under its reign. No one knew that better than Twain, who, even as he attacked it as an "era of incredible rottenness," fell prey to its enticements. Born Samuel Langhorne Clemens, he grew up in a rough Mississippi River town, where he became a riverboat pilot. Taking the pen name Mark Twain, he wrote and played to packed houses as an itinerant humorist. But his work was judged too vulgar for the genteel tastes of the time. Boston banned his masterpiece, *The Adventures of Huckleberry Finn*, when it appeared in 1884. Huck Finn's creator eventually stormed the citadels of polite society and hobnobbed with the wealthy. Succumbing to the money fever of his age, he plunged into a scheme in the hope of making millions. By the 1890s, he faced bankruptcy. Twain's tale was common in an age when the promise of wealth led as many to ruin as to riches. Wall Street panics in both 1873 and 1893 plunged the country into depression.

The rush to build railroads and other industries and the corrupt interplay of business and politics formed the key themes in the Gilded Age. The runaway growth of the railroads and the surge in new inventions and technologies like electricity, the telephone, and the telegraph encouraged the rise of big business and led to an age of industrial capitalism.

Such rapid growth had alarming social and political implications. Economic issues increasingly shaped party politics. Social Darwinism, with its insistence on the "survival of the fittest," supported the power of the wealthy, while the poor and middle classes championed antimonopoly measures to restore competition, currency reform to ease debt, and civil service to end corruption. As always, race, class, and gender influenced politics and policy.

The hopes and fears of the Gilded Age were most evident in the public's attitude toward the business moguls of the day. Men like Jay Gould, Andrew Carnegie, and John D. Rockefeller sparked the popular imagination as the heroes and villains of industrialization. And as concern grew over the power of big business and the growing chasm between rich and poor, many Americans, women as well as men, looked to the government for solutions.

▶ Railroads and the Rise of New Industries

In the years following the Civil War, the American economy underwent a transformation. Where once wealth had been measured in tangible assets—property, livestock, buildings—the economy now ran on money and the new devices of business—paper currency, securities, and anonymous corporate entities. Wall Street, the heart of the country's financial system, increasingly affected Main Street. Driving the transition was the building of a transcontinental railroad system, which radically altered the scale and scope of American industry. Old industries like iron transformed into modern industries such as the behemoth U.S. Steel. Discovery and invention stimulated new industries, from oil refining to electric light and power. The overbuilding of the railroad in the decades after the Civil War played a key role in transforming the American economy, as business came to rely on huge government subsidies, "friends" in Congress, and complicated financial transactions.

Jay Gould in railroads, Andrew Carnegie in steel, and John D. Rockefeller in oil pioneered new strategies to seize markets and consolidate power. With keen senses of self-interest, these tycoons set the tone in the get-rich-quick era of freewheeling capitalism that came to be called the **Gilded Age**.

Railroads: America's First Big Business

The military conquest of America's inland empire and the dispossession of Native Americans (see chapter 17) was fed by an elaborate new railroad system in the West built on speculation and government giveaways. Between 1870 and 1880, the amount of track in the country doubled, and it nearly doubled again in the following decade. By 1900, the nation boasted more than 193,000 miles of railroad track—more than in all of Europe and Russia combined (Map 18.1). The railroads had become America's first big business. Credit fueled the railroad boom. Privately owned but publicly financed, and subsidized by enormous land grants from the federal government and the states, the railroads epitomized the insidious nexus of business and politics in the Gilded Age.

CHRONOLOGY

1869	• First transcontinental railroad completed. • National Woman Suffrage Association founded.
1870	• John D. Rockefeller incorporates Standard Oil Company.
1872	• Andrew Carnegie builds world's largest steel plant.
1873	• Wall Street panic leads to major economic depression.
1874	• Woman's Christian Temperance Union founded.
1876	• Alexander Graham Bell demonstrates telephone.
1877	• Rutherford B. Hayes sworn in as president. • *Munn v. Illinois* decided.
1880	• James A. Garfield elected president.
1881	• Garfield assassinated; Vice President Chester A. Arthur becomes president.
1882	• John D. Rockefeller develops the trust.
1883	• Pendleton Civil Service Act enacted.
1884	• Grover Cleveland elected president.
1886	• *Wabash v. Illinois* decided.
1887	• Interstate Commerce Act enacted.
1888	• Benjamin Harrison elected president.
1890	• McKinley tariff passes. • General Federation of Women's Clubs founded. • Sherman Antitrust Act enacted.
1892	• Ida B. Wells launches antilynching campaign.
1893	• Wall Street panic touches off national depression.
1895	• J. P. Morgan bails out U.S. Treasury.
1901	• U.S. Steel incorporated and capitalized at $1.4 billion.

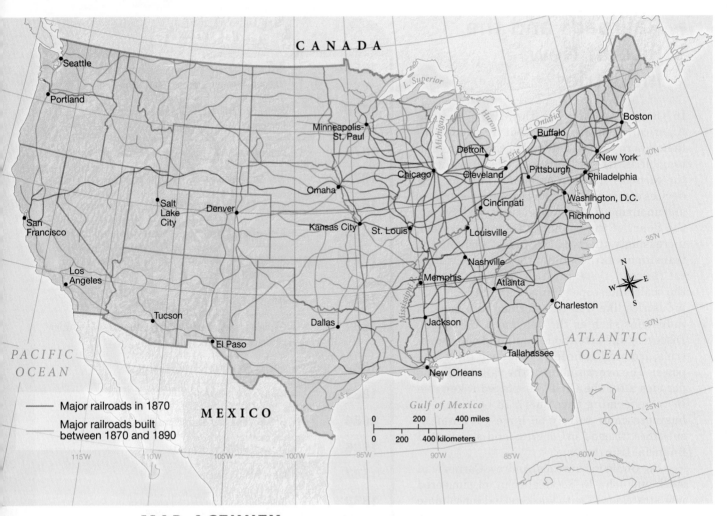

MAP ACTIVITY

Map 18.1   Railroad Expansion, 1870–1890

Railroad mileage nearly quadrupled between 1870 and 1890, with the greatest growth occurring in the trans-Mississippi West. The western lines were completed in the 1880s. Fueled by speculation and built ahead of demand, the western railroads made fortunes for individual speculators. But they rarely paid for themselves and speeded the demise of Native Americans.

READING THE MAP: Where were most of the railroad lines located in 1870? What was the end point of the only western route? By 1890, how many railroads reached the West Coast?

CONNECTIONS: Why were so many rails laid between 1870 and 1890? How did the railroads affect the nation's economy?

To understand how the railroads came to dominate American life, there is no better place to start than with the career of Jay Gould, the era's most notorious speculator. Jason "Jay" Gould bought his first railroad before he turned twenty-five. It was only sixty-two miles long, in bad repair, and on the brink of failure, but within two years he sold it at a profit of $130,000.

The secretive Gould operated in the stock market like a shark, looking for vulnerable railroads, buying enough stock to take control, and threatening to undercut his competitors until they bought him out at a high profit. The railroads that fell into his hands often went bankrupt. Gould's genius lay not in providing transportation, but in cleverly buying and selling railroad stock on Wall Street. Gould soon realized that a corporate failure could still mean financial success. His strategy of expansion and consolidation encouraged overbuilding even as it stimulated a new national market.

JUSTICE IN THE WEB.

The first transcontinental railway had been completed in 1869 at Promontory Summit, Utah. In the 1880s, Gould moved to put together a second transcontinental railroad. To defend their interests, his competitors had little choice but to adopt his strategy of expansion. The railroads built ahead of demand, regardless of the social and environmental costs. Soon more railroads trailed into the West—by 1893, Kansas alone had at least six competing lines.

The railroad moguls put up little of their own money to build the roads and instead relied on the largesse of government and the sale of railroad bonds and stock. Bondholders were creditors who required repayment at a specific time. Stockholders bought a share in the company and received dividends if the company prospered. Thus, railroad moguls received money from these sales of financial interests but did not need to pay out until later. If the railroad failed, a receiver was appointed to determine how many pennies on the dollar shareholders would receive. The owners, astutely using the market, came out ahead. Novelist Charles Dudley Warner described how wrecking a railroad could yield profits:

> [They fasten upon] some railway that is prosperous, . . . and has a surplus. They contrive to buy . . . a controlling interest in it. . . . Then they absorb its surplus; they let it run down so that it pays no dividends, and by-and-by cannot even pay its interest; then they squeeze the bondholders, who may be glad to accept anything that is offered out of the wreck, and perhaps they throw the property into the hands of a receiver, or consolidate it with some other road at a value far greater than it cost them in stealing it. Having one way or another sucked it dry, they look around for another road.

With help from railroad growth and speculation, the New York Stock Exchange expanded. The volume of stock increased sixfold between 1869 and 1901. The line between investment and speculation blurred, causing many Americans to question whether the manipulation of speculators fueled the boom and bust cycles that led to panic and depression in 1873 and again twenty years later. The dramatic growth of the railroads created the country's first big business. Before the Civil War, even the largest textile mill in New England employed no more than 800 workers. By contrast, the Pennsylvania Railroad by the 1870s boasted a payroll of more than 55,000 workers. Capitalized at more than $400 million, the Pennsylvania Railroad constituted the largest private enterprise in the world.

The big business of railroads bestowed enormous riches on a handful of tycoons. Both Gould and his competitor "Commodore" Cornelius Vanderbilt amassed fortunes estimated at $100 million. Such staggering wealth eclipsed the power and influence of upper-class Americans from previous generations and created an abyss between the nation's rich and poor. In its wake, it left a legacy of lavish spending for an elite

Charles Crocker, the Big Four, and the Race for Riches

In 1861, four Sacramento store owners—Collis P. Huntington and his partner Mark Hopkins (hardware), Leland Stanford (groceries), and Charles Crocker (dry goods)—created the Central Pacific Railroad of California. A year later, Congress passed the Pacific Railroad Act authorizing a transcontinental railroad and granting right of way to the Union Pacific to build west from Omaha and the Central Pacific to build east from Sacramento. The government provided both companies with a lavish package of loans, bonds, cash payments, and massive grants of public land. Obscure California storekeepers had secured one of the biggest government contracts in history. In time, they would take at least $200 million from the enterprise, in today's dollars, billions.

"None of us knew anything about railroad building," Crocker admitted, "but at the same time [we] were enterprising men." The Big Four, as they became known, quickly settled into their respective roles. Stanford would manage relationships with the state of California, Huntington would take care of lobbying in Washington, Hopkins would keep the books, and Charles Crocker would supervise construction.

Crocker, who was born in Troy, New York, in 1822, came west with the forty-niners. Prospecting had gained him nothing, but with railroads, the energetic, red-faced 250-pound man knew he was on to something. As construction chief of the Central Pacific, Crocker's first problem was a labor shortage. While the Union Pacific employed Irish immigrants, Crocker turned instead to Chinese emigrant workers. Some ten thousand Chinese pushed the Central Pacific across, and sometimes through, the Sierra Nevada, chiseling railroad tunnels through solid granite by hand. Crocker paid his workers barely a dollar a day. (In contrast, the Irish got three.) When the Chinese went on strike for a few more pennies, Crocker cut off their supply of food and observed that "they really began to suffer." The strike quickly collapsed. Once the crews were on the other side of the mountains, the cry became "a mile a day!" Construction subsidies depended on miles of track laid, and Crocker pushed his men hard. On May 10, 1869, after some six years, the two railroads met at Promontory Summit, Utah.

Years later, Crocker declared, "We built that road for the profits we could make in building it." Uninterested in moving people and goods, the Big Four were instead experts at lining their own pockets, and their deception knew few limits. They organized a sham construction company, Charles Crocker & Company, and paid construction costs from

crop of ultrarich heirs. (See "Experiencing the American Promise," above.)

The Republican Party, firmly entrenched in Washington after the Civil War, worked closely with business interests, subsidizing the transcontinental railroad system. Significant amounts of money changed hands to move bills through Congress. Along with "friends," often on the railroads' payrolls, lobbyists worked to craft legislation favorable to railroad interests. Friends of the railroads in state legislatures and Congress lavished the new western roads with land grants of a staggering 100 million acres (mostly owned by the Indians) and $64 million in tax incentives and direct aid. States and local communities joined the railroad boom, betting that only those towns and villages along the tracks would grow and flourish. A revolution in communication accompanied and supported the growth of the railroads. The telegraph, developed by Samuel F. B. Morse, marched across the continent alongside the railroad. By transmitting coded messages along electrical wire, the telegraph formed the "nervous system" of the new industrial order. Telegraph service quickly replaced Pony Express mail carriers in the West and transformed business by providing instantaneous communication. Again Jay Gould took the lead. In 1879, through stock manipulation, he seized control of Western Union, the company that monopolized the telegraph industry.

The railroads soon fell on hard times. Already by the 1870s, lack of planning led to overbuilding. Across the nation, railroads competed fiercely for business. Manufacturers in areas served by competing railroads could get substantially reduced shipping rates in return for promises of steady business. Because railroad owners lost money through this kind of competition, they tried to set up agreements, or "pools," to divide government funds to themselves. A suit against the Central Pacific charged that of the $240 million the company received in government subsidies, only $19 million was actually spent on construction. We will never know whether the accusation was accurate because Huntington burned the Central Pacific's books on the eve of a congressional investigation. The Big Four forged maps and surveys, tricked inspectors, and laid miles of bad track. They bought newspapermen, created phony stockholders, and lied to banks when they borrowed. They bullied ranchers off their lands and may have even condoned murder. The business of bribing politicians was never-ending. Huntington spent five years in Washington, D.C., carrying a leather satchel crammed with cash on his rounds. "There are more hungry men in Congress this session than I have ever known before," he once complained. While working furiously to get rich, the Big Four also built a railroad.

Late in his career, Crocker mused: "One man works hard all his life and ends up a pauper. Another man, no smarter, makes twenty million dollars. Luck has a hell of a lot to do with it." Luck no doubt played a part, but ruthless disregard for the law, cruel exploitation of labor, and unremitting greed were also significant. One rival described Crocker as "a living, breathing, waddling monument of the triumph of vulgarity, viciousness and dishonesty." Crocker did not see himself like that, of course. Questioned later about the fraud and corruption, he replied, "I knew nothing about that. I was building the road." By the time Crocker died in 1888, with a fortune estimated at $40 million, he had turned to philanthropy, endowing art galleries, museums, and cathedrals that can still be seen in San Francisco today.

Building the Iron Horse—the transcontinental railroad—was one of the greatest triumphs of the Gilded Age. Railroads remade America on a massive scale and defined modern capitalism in the Gilded Age. But the country paid a heavy price. It was, after all, the people's money that was stolen and the people's government and political system that were corrupted and polluted. We still don't know all of the costs. We don't know, for example, how many Chinese workers died making the Central Pacific, although one estimate is 1,500.

Moreover, building railroads just to make a profit from government aid eventually brought about national economic ruin. Overbuilding produced a railroad bubble, which burst in 1873 with devastating consequences. The Big Four, however, not only survived the depression but gobbled up most of the track in California. Until their deaths, they continued to pioneer new ways to put government money into the pockets of private business.

Questions for Analysis

Analyze the Evidence: Since none of the Big Four went to jail, what is the evidence for concluding that they were crooks?

Recognize Viewpoints: How do you suppose the Big Four would have defended themselves? What arguments could they use to explain their actions?

Consider the Context: How did the behavior of the Big Four compare with the values and behavior of other business titans in the Gilded Age? How did these men reflect the larger cultural and political trends of the period?

---

up territory and set rates. But these informal gentlemen's agreements invariably failed because men like Gould, intent on undercutting all competitors, refused to play by the rules.

The public's alarm at the control wielded by the new railroad magnates and the tactics they employed came to light in the Crédit Mobilier scandal of 1872. Crédit Mobilier, a fiscal enterprise set up by partners including Thomas Durant, an executive of the Union Pacific Railroad, would provide sole bids on construction work. Using money procured from investors and government bonds, the work was then subcontracted out, leaving profits in the hands of the financiers. With profits booming, senators clambered to profit as well. Charles Dana's *New York Sun* described the Crédit Mobilier moneymaking scheme as "The King of Frauds" and attempted to document the way the railroads controlled their friends in government with lavish gifts of stock. Although the press never got the financial dealings straight, the scandal and resulting investigation implicated the Union Pacific Railroad, the vice president, and numerous congressmen. The real revelation was how little the key players knew about how railroads were built or operated. The promoters knew little about building the roads; the investors had an even shakier grasp on what they were investing in; and the politicians who subsidized the roads, instead of overseeing them, remained vague on specifics and failed to provide governmental oversight. All that was clear was that the Union Pacific had sold stock below market prices to its friends. In the end, no one was punished and no money returned.

The Crédit Mobilier scandal increased public suspicion of the corrupt relationship between business and government and led to a strong antipathy toward speculators and a movement to end monopoly.

Andrew Carnegie, Steel, and Vertical Integration

If Jay Gould was the man Americans loved to hate, Andrew Carnegie became one of America's heroes. Unlike Gould, Carnegie turned his back on speculation and worked to build something enduring—Carnegie Steel, the biggest steel business in the world during the Gilded Age.

The growth of the steel industry proceeded directly from railroad building. The first railroads ran on iron rails, which cracked and broke with alarming frequency. Steel, both stronger and more flexible than iron, remained too expensive for use in rails until Englishman Henry Bessemer developed a way to make steel more cheaply. Andrew Carnegie, among the first to champion the new "King Steel," came to dominate the emerging industry.

Carnegie, a Scottish immigrant, landed in New York in 1848 at the age of twelve. He rose from a job cleaning bobbins in a textile factory to become one of the richest men in America. Before he died, he gave away more than $300 million, most notably to public libraries. His generosity, combined with his own rise from poverty, burnished his public image.

While Carnegie was a teenager, his skill as a telegraph operator caught the attention of Tom Scott, superintendent of the Pennsylvania Railroad. Scott hired Carnegie, soon promoted him, and lent him the money for his first foray into Wall Street investment. As a result of this crony capitalism, Carnegie became a millionaire before his thirtieth birthday. At that point, Carnegie turned away from speculation. "My preference was always manufacturing," he wrote. "I wished to make something tangible." By applying the lessons of cost accounting and efficiency that he had learned with the Pennsylvania Railroad, Carnegie turned steel into the nation's first manufacturing big business.

In 1872, Andrew Carnegie built the world's largest, most up-to-date steel mill in Braddock, Pennsylvania. At that time, steelmakers produced about 70 tons a week. Within two decades, Carnegie's blast furnaces poured out an incredible 10,000 tons a week. His formula for success was simple: "Cut the prices, scoop the market, run the mills full; watch the costs and profits will take care of themselves." Carnegie pioneered a system of business organization called vertical integration in which all aspects of the business were under Carnegie's control—from the mining of iron ore, to its transport on the Great Lakes, to the production of steel. As one observer noted,

Andrew Carnegie
A millionaire by his twenties, Carnegie, here in 1905 after he had retired, urged his fellow plutocrats to act as stewards of the people and to spend their money for the good of society. Before he died in 1919, he gave away an estimated $300 million to charitable causes. Library of Congress, 3b35116.

"There was never a price, profit, or royalty paid to any outsider."

The great productivity Carnegie encouraged came at a high price. He deliberately pitted his managers against one another, firing the losers and rewarding the winners with a share in the company. Workers achieved the output Carnegie demanded by enduring low wages, dangerous working conditions, and twelve-hour days six days a week. One worker, observing the contradiction between Carnegie's generous endowment of public libraries and his labor policy, observed, "After working twelve hours, how can a man go to a library?"

By 1900, Andrew Carnegie had become the best-known manufacturer in the nation, and the age of iron had yielded to an age of steel (Figure 18.1). Steel from Carnegie's mills supported the elevated trains in New York and Chicago, formed the skeleton of the Washington Monument, supported the first steel bridge to span the Mississippi, and girded America's first skyscrapers. As a captain of industry, Carnegie's only rival was the titan of the oil industry, John D. Rockefeller.

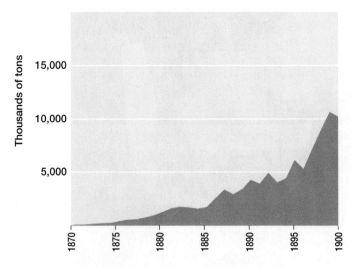

FIGURE 18.1   Iron and Steel Production, 1870–1900
Iron and steel production in the United States grew from nearly none in 1870 to 10 million tons a year by 1900. The secrets to such a great increase were the use of the Bessemer process and vertical integration, pioneered by Andrew Carnegie. By 1900, Carnegie's mills alone produced more steel than all of Great Britain's. With corporate consolidation after 1900, the rate of growth in steel proved even more spectacular.

John D. Rockefeller, Standard Oil, and the Trust

In the days before the automobile and gasoline, crude oil was refined into lubricating oil for machinery and kerosene for lamps, the major source of lighting in the nineteenth century. The amount of capital needed to buy or build an oil refinery in the 1860s and 1870s remained relatively low—roughly what it cost to lay one mile of railroad track. As a result, the new petroleum industry experienced riotous competition. Ultimately, John D. Rockefeller and his Standard Oil Company succeeded in controlling nine-tenths of the oil-refining business.

Rockefeller grew up the son of a shrewd Yankee who peddled quack cures for cancer. Under his father's rough tutelage, Rockefeller learned how to drive a hard bargain. In 1865, at the age of twenty-five, he controlled the largest oil refinery in Cleveland. Like a growing number of business owners, Rockefeller abandoned partnership or single proprietorship to embrace the corporation as the business structure best suited to maximize profit and minimize personal liability. In 1870, he incorporated his oil business, founding the Standard Oil Company.

As the largest refiner in Cleveland, Rockefeller demanded illegal rebates from the railroads in exchange for his steady business. The secret rebates enabled Rockefeller to drive out his competitors through predatory pricing. The railroads needed Rockefeller's business so badly that they gave him a share of the rates that his competitors paid. A Pennsylvania Railroad official later confessed that Rockefeller extracted such huge rebates that the railroad, which could not risk losing his business, sometimes ended up paying him to transport Standard's oil. Rebates enabled Rockefeller to undercut his competitors and pressure competing refiners to sell out or face ruin.

To gain legal standing for Standard Oil's secret deals, Rockefeller in 1882 pioneered a new form of corporate structure—the **trust**. The trust differed markedly from Carnegie's vertical approach in steel. Rockefeller used horizontal integration to control not the entire process, but only an aspect of oil production—refining. Several trustees held stock in various refinery companies "in trust" for Standard's stockholders. This elaborate stock swap allowed the trustees to coordinate policy among the refineries by gobbling up all the small, competing refineries. Often buyers did not know they were actually selling out to Standard. By the end of the century, Rockefeller enjoyed a virtual monopoly of the oil-refining business. The Standard Oil trust, valued at more than $70 million, paved the way for trusts in sugar, whiskey, matches, and many other products.

When the federal government responded to public pressure to outlaw the trust in 1890, Standard Oil changed tactics and reorganized as a holding company. Instead of stockholders in competing companies acting through trustees to set prices and determine territories, the holding company simply brought competing companies under one central administration. Now one business, not an assortment of individual refineries, Standard Oil controlled competition without violating antitrust laws that forbade competing companies from forming "combinations in restraint of trade." By the 1890s, Standard Oil ruled more than 90 percent of the oil business, employed 100,000 people, and was the biggest,

VISUAL ACTIVITY

"What a Funny Little Government"
The power wielded by John D. Rockefeller and his Standard Oil Company is satirized here by cartoonist Horace Taylor. Rockefeller is pictured holding the White House and the Treasury Department in the palm of his hand, while in the background the U.S. Capitol has been converted into an oil refinery. © Collection of the New-York Historical Society, USA/Bridgeman Images.

READING THE IMAGE: According to Horace Taylor, what kind of relationship did John D. Rockefeller have with the federal government? What did the public think of it?

CONNECTIONS: How much influence did industrialists such as Rockefeller exert over the national government in the late nineteenth century?

richest, most feared, and most admired business organization in the world.

John D. Rockefeller enjoyed enormous success in business, but he was not well liked by the public. Editor and journalist Ida M. Tarbell's "History of the Standard Oil Company," which ran in serial form in *McClure's Magazine* (1902–1905), largely shaped the public's harsh view of Rockefeller. Her history chronicled the illegal methods Rockefeller had used to take over the oil industry. By the time Tarbell finished her story, Rockefeller slept with a loaded revolver by his bed. Standard Oil and the man who created it had become the symbol of heartless monopoly.

New Inventions: The Telephone and the Telegraph

The second half of the nineteenth century was an age of invention. Men like Thomas Alva Edison and Alexander Graham Bell became folk heroes. But no matter how dramatic the inventors or

the inventions, the new electric and telephone industries pioneered by Edison and Bell soon eclipsed their inventors and fell under the control of bankers and industrialists.

Alexander Graham Bell came to America from Scotland at the age of twenty-four with a passion to find a way to teach the deaf to speak (his wife and mother were deaf). Instead, he developed a way to transmit voice over wire— the telephone. Bell's invention astounded the world when he demonstrated it at the Philadelphia Centennial Exposition in 1876. In 1880, Bell's company, American Bell, pioneered "long lines" (long-distance telephone service), creating American Telephone and Telegraph (AT&T) as a subsidiary. In 1900, AT&T developed a complicated structure that enabled Americans to communicate not only locally but also across the country. And unlike a telegraph message, the telephone connected both parties immediately and privately. Bell's invention proved a boon to business, contributing to speed and

Ida M. Tarbell, Scourge of Standard Oil
Tarbell served as managing editor of the popular *McClure's Magazine*, where her "History of the Standard Oil Company" ran in serial form for three years. Her revelations of the ruthless railroad rebates John D. Rockefeller used to control the oil-refining business came from Tarbell's deep research but also from her experience growing up in the Pennsylvania oil fields, where she witnessed how Standard Oil forced out its competitors.
Tarbell: Library of Congress, 3b01876; magazine: The Ida M. Tarbell Collection, Special Collections, Pelletier Library, Allegheny College.

efficiency. The number of telephones soared, reaching 310,000 in 1895 and more than 1.5 million in 1900.

Even more than Alexander Graham Bell, inventor Thomas Alva Edison embodied the old-fashioned virtues of Yankee ingenuity and rugged individualism that Americans most admired. A self-educated dynamo, he worked twenty hours a day in his laboratory in Menlo Park, New Jersey, vowing to turn out "a minor invention every ten days and a big thing every six months or so." He almost made good on his promise. At the height of his career, he averaged a patent every eleven days and invented such "big things" as the phonograph, the motion picture camera, and the filament for the incandescent lightbulb.

Edison, in competition with George W. Westinghouse, pioneered the use of electricity as an energy source. By the late nineteenth century, electricity had become a part of American urban life. It powered trolley cars and lighted factories, homes, and office buildings. Indeed, electricity became so prevalent in urban life that it symbolized the city, whose bright lights contrasted with rural America, left largely in the dark.

The day of the inventor quietly yielded to the heyday of the corporation. In 1892, the electric industry consolidated. Reflecting a nationwide trend in business, Edison General Electric dropped

Notable American Inventions, 1865–1899

1865	Railroad sleeping car
1867	Typewriter
1868	Railroad refrigerator car
1870	Stock ticker
1874	Barbed wire
1876	Telephone
1877	Phonograph
1879	Incandescent lightbulb
1880	Cigarette rolling machine
1882	Electric fan
1885	Adding machine
1886	Coca-Cola
1888	Kodak camera
1890	Electric chair
1891	Zipper
1895	Safety razor
1896	Electric stove
1899	Tape recorder

Alexander Graham Bell

Alexander Graham Bell sits at the New York end of the first long-distance telephone call to Chicago on October 18, 1892. Years earlier, Bell went to the Roosevelts for financial backing of his new invention. He hooked up a telephone so that young Theodore could talk from his desk to a room down the hall. Teddy concluded that while the device had potential as a toy, it had no real future. The Granger Collection, New York.

the name of its inventor, becoming simply General Electric (GE). For years, an embittered Edison refused to set foot inside a GE building. GE, a prime example of the trend toward business consolidation, soon dominated the market.

> **REVIEW** When, why, and how did the transcontinental railroad system develop, and what was its impact on American business?

▶ From Competition to Consolidation

Even as Rockefeller and Carnegie built their empires, the era of the "robber barons," as they were dubbed by their detractors, was drawing to a close. Increasingly, businesses replaced partnerships and sole proprietorships with the anonymous corporate structure that would come to dominate the twentieth century. At the same time, mergers led to the creation of huge new corporations.

Banks and financiers played key roles in this consolidation, so much so that the decades at the turn of the twentieth century can be characterized as a period of **finance capitalism**—investment sponsored by banks and bankers. When the depression that followed the panic of 1893 bankrupted many businesses, bankers stepped in to bring order and to reorganize major industries. During these years, a new social philosophy developed that helped to justify consolidation and to inhibit state or federal regulation of business. A conservative Supreme Court further frustrated attempts to control business by consistently declaring unconstitutional legislation designed to regulate railroads or to outlaw trusts and monopolies.

J. P. Morgan and Finance Capitalism

John Pierpont Morgan, the preeminent finance capitalist of the late nineteenth century, loathed competition and sought whenever possible to eliminate it by substituting consolidation and central control. Morgan's passion for order made him the architect of business mergers. At the turn of the twentieth century, he dominated American banking, exerting an influence so powerful that his critics charged he controlled a vast "money trust" even more insidious than Rockefeller's Standard Oil.

Morgan acted as a power broker in the reorganization of the railroads and the creation of industrial giants such as General Electric. When the railroads collapsed, Morgan took over and eliminated competition by creating what he called "a community of interest." By the time he finished "Morganizing" the railroads, a handful of directors controlled two-thirds of the nation's track. Morgan's directors were bankers, not railroad men, and they saw the roads as little more than "a set of books." Their conservative approach aimed at short-term profit and discouraged the technological and organizational innovation necessary to run the railroads effectively.

In 1898, Morgan moved into the steel industry, directly challenging Andrew Carnegie. The pugnacious Carnegie cabled his partners in the summer of 1900: "Action essential: crisis has arrived . . . have no fear as to the result; victory certain." The press trumpeted news of the impending fight between the feisty Scot and the haughty Wall Street banker. But for all his belligerence, the sixty-six-year-old Carnegie yearned to retire to Scotland. Morgan, who disdained haggling, agreed to pay Carnegie's asking price, $480 million (the equivalent of about $10 billion in today's currency). According to legend, when Carnegie later teased Morgan, saying that he should have asked $100 million more, Morgan replied, "You would have got it if you had."

Morgan's acquisition of Carnegie Steel signaled the passing of the old entrepreneurial order personified by Andrew Carnegie and the arrival of a new anonymous corporate world. Morgan quickly moved to pull together Carnegie's chief competitors to form a huge new corporation, United States Steel, known today as USX. Created in 1901 and capitalized at $1.4 billion, U.S. Steel was the largest corporation in the world.

Even more than Carnegie or Rockefeller, Morgan left his stamp on the twentieth century and formed the model for corporate consolidation that economists and social scientists justified with a new social theory later called social Darwinism.

VISUAL ACTIVITY

Homestead Steelworks

The Homestead steelworks, outside Pittsburgh, is pictured shortly after J. P. Morgan created U.S. Steel, the precursor of today's USX. Try to count the smokestacks in the picture. Air pollution on this scale posed a threat to the health of citizens and made for a dismal landscape. Workers complained that trees would not grow in Homestead. The Granger Collection, New York.

READING THE IMAGE: What does the photo tell you about the purpose of Homestead? What does it say about the lives of the Homestead workers?

CONNECTIONS: How did the Homestead steelworks reflect Gilded Age values and interests?

Social Darwinism: Did Wealthy Industrialists Practice What They Preached?

Darwinism, with its emphasis on tooth-and-claw competition, seemed ideally suited to the get-rich-quick mentality of the Gilded Age. By placing the theory of evolution in an economic context, social Darwinism argued against government intervention in business while at the same time insisting that reforms to ameliorate the evils of urban industrialism would only slow evolutionary progress. Most of the wealthy industrialists of the day probably never read Charles Darwin or the exponents of social Darwinism. Nevertheless, the catchphrases of social Darwinism peppered the rhetoric of business in the Gilded Age.

Andrew Carnegie, alone among the American business moguls, not only championed social Darwinism but also avidly read the works of its primary exponent, the British social philosopher Herbert Spencer. Significantly, Spencer, not Darwin, coined the catchphrase "survival of the fittest." Carnegie spoke of his indebtedness to Spencer in terms usually reserved for religious conversion: "Before Spencer, all for me had been darkness, after him, all had become light—and right." In his autobiography, Carnegie wrote, "I had found the truth of evolution. 'All is well since all grows better' became my motto, my true source of comfort."

Not content to worship Spencer from afar, Carnegie assiduously worked to make his acquaintance and then would not rest until he had convinced the reluctant Spencer to come to America. In Pittsburgh, Carnegie promised, Spencer could best view his evolutionary theories at work in the world of industry. Clearly, Carnegie viewed his steelworks as the apex of America's new industrial order, a testimony to the playing out of evolutionary theory in the economic world.

In 1882, Spencer undertook an American tour. Carnegie personally invited him to Pittsburgh, squiring him through the Braddock steel mills.

But Spencer failed to appreciate Carnegie's achievement. The heat, noise, and pollution of Pittsburgh reduced Spencer to near collapse, and he could only choke out, "Six months' residence here would justify suicide." Carnegie must have been devastated.

How well Carnegie actually understood the principles of social Darwinism is debatable. In his 1900 essay "Popular Illusions about Trusts," Carnegie spoke of the "law of evolution that moves from the heterogeneous to the homogeneous," citing Spencer as his source. Spencer, however, had written of the movement "from an indefinite incoherent homogeneity to a definite coherent heterogeneity." Instead of acknowledging that the history of human evolution moved from the simple to the more complex, Carnegie seemed to insist that evolution moved from the complex to the simple. This confusion of the most basic evolutionary theory calls into question Carnegie's grasp

Social Darwinism, Laissez-Faire, and the Supreme Court

John D. Rockefeller Jr., the son of the founder of Standard Oil, once remarked to his Baptist Bible class that the Standard Oil Company, like the American Beauty rose, resulted from "pruning the early buds that grew up around it." The elimination of competition, he declared, was "merely the working out of a law of nature and a law of God." The comparison of the business world to the natural world resembled the theory of evolution formulated by the British naturalist Charles Darwin. In his monumental work *On the Origin of Species* (1859), Darwin theorized that in the struggle for survival, adaptation to the environment triggered among species a natural selection process that led to evolution. Herbert Spencer in Britain and William Graham Sumner in the United States developed the theory of **social Darwinism**. The social Darwinists insisted that societal progress came about as a result of relentless competition in which the strong survived and the weak died out.

In social terms, the idea of the "survival of the fittest," coined by Spencer, had profound significance, as Sumner, a professor of political economy at Yale University, made clear in his book *What Social Classes Owe to Each Other* (1883). "The drunkard in the gutter is just where he ought to be, according to the fitness and tendency of things," Sumner insisted. Conversely, "millionaires are the product of natural selection," and although "they get high wages and live in

Herbert Spencer

Herbert Spencer became a hero to industrialist Andrew Carnegie, who judged his steel business the apotheosis of survival of the fittest. But on a visit in 1882, the sage of social Darwinism proved a great disappointment to Carnegie. Hulton Archive/ Getty Images.

America's foremost social Darwinist. Ironically, Sumner, who often sounded like an apologist for the rich, aroused the wrath of the very group he championed. The problem was that strict social Darwinists like Sumner insisted absolutely that the government ought not to meddle in the economy. The purity of Sumner's commitment to laissez-faire led him to adamantly oppose the protective tariffs the pro-business Republicans enacted to inflate the prices of manufactured goods produced abroad so that U.S. businesses could compete against foreign rivals. Sumner outspokenly attacked the tariff and firmly advocated free trade from his chair in political economy at Yale University. In 1890, the same year Congress passed the McKinley tariff, Sumner's fulminations against this highest tariff in the nation's history so outraged Yale's wealthy alumni that they mounted a campaign (unsuccessful) to have him fired.

Inconsistency never seemed to trouble Carnegie, who did not acknowledge a contradiction between his worship of Spencer and his strong support for the tariff. The comparison of Carnegie's position and Sumner's underscores the reality that although in theory laissez-faire constrained the government from playing an active role in business affairs, in practice industrialists fought for government favors—whether tariffs, land grants, or subsidies—that worked to their benefit. Only when legislatures proposed taxes or regulation did business leaders cry foul and invoke the "natural laws" of social Darwinism and its corollary, laissez-faire.

Questions for Analysis

Summarize the Argument: Andrew Carnegie championed Spencer and his ideas, but did he actually understand the principles of social Darwinism as Spencer enunciated them?

Analyze the Evidence: How does William Graham Sumner's trouble at Yale point to the inconsistency of wealthy proponents of social Darwinism?

Consider the Context: How did wealthy industrialists benefit from social Darwinism in the Gilded Age?

of Spencer's ideas or indeed of Darwin's. Other business leaders too busy making money to read no doubt understood even less about the working of evolutionary theory and social Darwinism, which they so often claimed as their own.

The distance between preachment and practice is boldly evident in the example of William Graham Sumner,

luxury," Sumner claimed, "the bargain is a good one for society."

Social Darwinists equated wealth and power with "fitness" and believed that any efforts by the rich to aid the poor would only tamper with the laws of nature and slow down evolution. Social Darwinism acted to curb social reform while glorifying great wealth. In an age when Rockefeller and Carnegie amassed hundreds of millions of dollars (billions in today's currency) and the average worker earned $500 a year, social Darwinism justified economic inequality. (See "Making Historical Arguments," above.)

Carnegie softened some of the harshness of social Darwinism in his essay "The Gospel of Wealth," published in 1889. The millionaire, Carnegie wrote, acted as a "mere trustee and

agent for his poorer brethren, bringing to their service his superior wisdom, experience, and ability to administer, doing for them better than they could or would do for themselves." Carnegie preached philanthropy and urged the rich to "live unostentatious lives" and "administer surplus wealth for the good of the people." His **gospel of wealth** earned much praise but won few converts. Most millionaires followed the lead of Morgan, who contributed to charity but hoarded private treasures in his marble library.

With its emphasis on the free play of competition and the survival of the fittest, social Darwinism encouraged the economic theory of laissez-faire (French for "let it alone"). Business leaders argued that government should not meddle in economic affairs, except to protect private property (or support high tariffs and government subsidies). A conservative Supreme Court agreed. During the 1880s and 1890s, the Court increasingly reinterpreted the Constitution, judging corporations to be "persons" in order to protect business from taxation, regulation, labor organization, and antitrust legislation.

Only in the arena of politics did Americans tackle the social issues raised by corporate capitalism.

> **REVIEW**   Why did the ideas of social Darwinism appeal to many Americans in the late nineteenth century?

▶ Politics and Culture

For many Americans, politics provided a source of identity, a means of livelihood, and a ready form of entertainment. No wonder voter turnout averaged a hefty 77 percent (compared to roughly 57.5 percent in the 2012 presidential election). A variety of factors contributed to the complicated interplay of politics and culture. Patronage provided an economic incentive for voter participation, but ethnicity, religion, sectional loyalty, race, and gender all influenced the political life of the period.

Political Participation and Party Loyalty

Political parties in power doled out federal, state, and local government jobs to their loyal supporters. With hundreds of thousands of jobs to be filled, the choice of party affiliation could mean the difference between a paycheck and an empty pocket. Money greased the wheels of this system of patronage, dubbed the **spoils system** from the adage "To the victor go the spoils." With their livelihoods tied to their party identity, government employees had a powerful incentive to vote in great numbers.

Political affiliation provided a sense of group identity for many voters proud of their loyalty to the Democrats or the Republicans. Democrats, who traced the party's roots back to Thomas Jefferson, called theirs "the party of the fathers." The Republican Party, founded in the 1850s, still claimed strong loyalties in the North as a result of its alignment with the Union during the Civil War. Republicans proved particularly adept at evoking Civil War loyalty, using a tactic called "waving the bloody shirt."

Religion and ethnicity also played a significant role in politics. In the North, Protestants from the old-line denominations, particularly Presbyterians and Methodists, flocked to the Republican Party, which championed a series of moral reforms, including local laws requiring businesses to close on Sunday in observance of the Sabbath. In the cities, the Democratic Party courted immigrants and working-class Catholic and Jewish voters and charged, rightly, that Republican moral crusades often masked attacks on immigrant culture.

Sectionalism and the New South

After the end of Reconstruction, most white voters in the former Confederate states remained loyal Democrats, creating the so-called solid South that lasted for the next seventy years. Labeling the Republican Party the agent of "Negro rule," Democrats urged white southerners to "vote the way you shot." Yet the South proved far from solid for the Democrats on the state and local levels, leading to shifting political alliances and to third-party movements that challenged Democratic attempts to define politics along race lines and maintain the Democrats as the white man's party.

The South's economy, devastated by the war, foundered at the same time the North experienced an unprecedented industrial boom. Soon an influential group of southerners called for a New South modeled on the industrial North. Henry Grady, the ebullient young editor of the *Atlanta Constitution*, used his paper's influence to exhort the South to use its natural advantages—cheap labor and abundant natural resources—to go head-to-head in competition with northern industry. And even as southern Democrats took back control of state governments, they embraced northern promoters who promised prosperity and profits.

The railroads came first, opening up the region for industrial development. Southern railroad mileage grew fourfold from 1865 to 1890. The number of cotton spindles also soared as textile mill owners abandoned New England in search of the cheap labor and proximity to raw materials promised in the South. By 1900, the South had become the nation's leading producer of cloth, and more than 100,000 southerners, many of them women and children, worked in the region's textile mills.

The New South prided itself most on its iron and steel industry, which grew up in the area surrounding Birmingham, Alabama. During this period, the smokestack replaced the white-pillared plantation as the symbol of the New South. Andrew Carnegie toured the region in 1889 and observed, "The South is Pennsylvania's most formidable industrial enemy." But southern industry remained controlled by northern investors, who had no intention of letting the South beat the North at its own game. Elaborate mechanisms rigged the price of southern steel, inflating it, as one northern insider confessed, "for the purpose of protecting the Pittsburgh mills and in turn the Pittsburgh steel users." Similarly, in the lumber and mining industries, investors in the North and abroad, not southerners, reaped the lion's share of the profits.

In only one industry did the South truly dominate—tobacco. Capitalizing on the invention of a machine for rolling cigarettes, the American Tobacco Company, founded by the Duke family of North Carolina, eventually dominated the industry. As cigarettes replaced chewing tobacco in popularity at the turn of the twentieth century, a booming market developed for Duke's "ready mades." Soon the company sold 400,000 cigarettes a day.

In practical terms, the industrialized New South proved an illusion. Much of the South remained agricultural, caught in the grip of the insidious crop lien system (see "White Landlords, Black Sharecroppers" in chapter 16). White southern farmers, desperate to get out of debt, sometimes joined African Americans to pursue mutual political goals. Between 1865 and 1900, voters in every southern state experimented with political alliances that crossed the color line and threatened the status quo.

Gender, Race, and Politics

Gender—society's notion of what constitutes acceptable masculine or feminine behavior—influenced politics throughout the nineteenth century. From the early days of the Republic, citizenship had been defined in male terms. Citizenship and its prerogatives (voting and officeholding) served as a badge of manliness and rested on its corollary, patriarchy—the power and authority men exerted over their wives and families. With the advent of universal (white) male suffrage in the early nineteenth century, gender eclipsed class as the defining feature of citizenship; men's dominance over women provided the common thread that knit all white men together politically. The concept of separate spheres dictated political participation for men only. Once the public sphere of political participation became equated with manhood, women found themselves increasingly restricted to the private sphere of the home.

Women were not alone in their limited access to the public sphere. Blacks continued to face discrimination well after Reconstruction, especially in the New South. Segregation, commonly practiced through **Jim Crow** laws (see "Progressivism for White Men Only" in chapter 21), prevented ex-slaves from riding in the same train

Bonsack Machine and Operator, ca. 1880s
James Bonsack invented the first cigarette rolling machine in 1880, but it was James Buchanan Duke who used it to mechanize cigarette manufacturing. Until then, a worker could hand roll a few hundred cigarettes a day; the Bonsack machine turned out that many each minute. By 1888, machines had entirely replaced hand rollers. Courtesy of the North Carolina Department of Cultural Resources.

Ida B. Wells and Her Campaign to Stop Lynching

Ida B. Wells fearlessly crusaded to stop lynching in the South by researching and reporting lynchings in detail and by comparing coverage from black and white sources.

DOCUMENT 1
Ida B. Wells, Editorial Protesting the Lynching of Friends in Memphis, 1892

The lynching in 1892 of three friends who ran a grocery store outside of Memphis touched Wells deeply. She wrote an outraged editorial in the Free Press. *Later she would repeat the details in her first pamphlet,* Southern Horrors: Lynch Law in All Its Phases *(1892).*

On March 9, 1892, there were lynched in this same city three of the best specimens of young since-the-war Afro-American manhood. They were peaceful, law-abiding citizens and energetic business men. . . . They owned a flourishing grocery business in a thickly populated suburb of Memphis, and a white man named Barrett had one on the opposite corner. After a personal difficulty which Barrett sought by going into the "People's Grocery" drawing a pistol and was thrashed by Calvin McDowell, he (Barrett) threatened to "clean them out." These men were a mile beyond the city limits and the police protection; hearing that Barrett's crowd was coming to attack them Saturday night, they mustered forces and prepared to defend themselves against the attack.

When Barrett came he led a posse of officers, twelve in number, who afterward claimed to be hunting a man for whom they had a warrant. That twelve men in citizen's clothes should think it necessary to go in the night to hunt one man who had never before been arrested, or made any record as a criminal has never been explained. When they entered the back door the young men thought the threatened attack was on, and fired into them. Three of the officers were wounded, and when the defending party found it was officers of the law upon whom they had fired, they ceased and got away.

Thirty-one men were arrested and thrown in jail as "conspirators," although they all declared more than once they did not know they were firing on officers. Excitement was at fever heat until the morning papers, two days after, announced that the wounded deputy sheriffs were out of danger. This hindered rather than helped the plans of the whites. There was no law on the statute books which would execute an Afro-American for wounding a white man, but the "unwritten law" did. Three of these men, the president, the manager and the clerk of the grocery—"the leaders of the conspiracy"—were secretly taken from jail and lynched in a shockingly brutal manner. "The Negroes are getting too independent," they say, "we must teach them a lesson."

What lesson? The lesson of subordination. "Kill the leaders and it will cow the Negro who dares to shoot a white man, even in self-defense."

Source: *Southern Horrors and Other Writings*, edited by Jacqueline Jones Royster (Boston: Bedford/St. Martin's, 1997), 64–65.

cars as whites, from eating in the same restaurants, or from using the same toilet facilities.

Amid the turmoil of the post-Reconstruction South, some groups struck cross-racial alliances. In Virginia, the "Readjusters," a coalition of blacks and whites determined to "readjust" (lower) the state debt and spend more money on public education, captured state offices from 1879 to 1883. Groups like the Readjusters believed universal political rights could be extended to black males while maintaining racial segregation in the private sphere. Democrats fought back by arguing that black voting would lead to racial mixing, and many whites returned to the Democratic fold to protect "white womanhood."

The notion that black men threatened white southern womanhood reached its most vicious form in the practice of lynching—the killing and mutilation of black men by white mobs. By 1892, the practice had become so prevalent that a courageous black editor, Ida B. Wells, launched an antilynching movement. That year, a white mob lynched a friend of Wells's whose grocery store competed too successfully with a white-owned store. Wells shrewdly concluded that lynching served "as an excuse to get rid of Negroes who were acquiring wealth and property and thus keep the race terrorized." (See "Analyzing Historical Evidence," above.) She began to collect data on lynching and discovered that in the decade between 1882 and 1892, lynching rose in the South by an overwhelming 200 percent, with more than 241 black people killed. The vast increase in lynching testified to the retreat of

DOCUMENT 2
Ida B. Wells, On Lack of Justice and Due Process for Accused Blacks, 1894

In her 1894 pamphlet The Red Record, *Wells insisted that lynching assumed all black men were guilty, thus denying them the constitutional right to defend themselves in front of a judge and jury.*

In lynching, opportunity is not given the Negro to defend himself against the unsupported accusations of white men and women. The word of the accuser is held to be true and the excited blood-thirsty mob demands that the rule of law be reserved and instead of proving the accused to be guilty, the victim of their hate and revenge must prove himself innocent. No evidence he can offer will satisfy the mob; he is bound hand and foot and swung into eternity. Then to excuse its infamy, the mob almost invariably reports the monstrous falsehood that its victim made a full confession before he was hanged.

Source: Royster, *Southern Horrors*, 153.

DOCUMENT 3
Ida B. Wells, On Mob Rule in New Orleans, 1900

In her last pamphlet, Mob Rule in New Orleans, *Wells describes the riot that occurred when a black man, Robert Charles, attacked by a police officer with a billy club, retaliated. This led to a duel that then brought on further violence.*

During the entire time the mob held the city in its hands and went about holding up street cars and searching them, taking from them colored men to assault, shoot and kill, chasing colored men upon the public square, through alleys and into houses of anybody who would take them in, breaking into the homes of defenseless colored men and women and beating aged and decrepit men and women to death, the police and the legally-constituted authorities showed plainly where their sympathies were, for in no case reported through the daily papers does there appear the arrest, trial and conviction of one of the mob for any of the brutalities which occurred. The ringleaders of the mob were at no time disguised. Men were chased, beaten and killed by white brutes, who boasted of their crimes, and the murderers still walk the streets of New Orleans, well known and absolutely exempt from prosecution. Not only were they exempt from prosecution by the police while the town was in the hands of the mob, but even now that law and order is supposed to resume control, these men, well known, are not now, nor ever will be, called to account for the unspeakable brutalities of that terrible week. On the other hand, the colored men who were beaten by the police and dragged into the station for purposes of intimidation were quickly called before the courts and fined or sent to jail upon the statement of the police.

Source: Royster, *Southern Horrors,* 181–82.

Questions for Analysis

Analyze the Evidence: In her campaign to end lynching, how does Wells seek to generate sympathy for the victims and to build an outraged antilynching coalition that will end the practice?

Recognize Viewpoints: How did the white people involved in lynching defend their actions?

Consider the Context: In addition to lynching, what else did white southerners do to keep African Americans in subordinate positions?

---

the federal government following Reconstruction and to white southerners' determination to maintain supremacy through terrorism and intimidation.

Wells articulated lynching as a problem of gender as well as race. She insisted that the myth of black attacks on white southern women masked the reality that mob violence had more to do with economics and the shifting social structure of the South than with rape. She demonstrated in a sophisticated way how the southern patriarchal system, having lost its control over blacks with the end of slavery, used its control over white women to circumscribe the liberty of black men.

Wells's outspoken stance immediately resulted in reprisal. While she was traveling in the North, vandals ransacked her office in Tennessee and destroyed her printing equipment. Yet the warning that she would be killed on sight if she ever returned to Memphis only stiffened her resolve. As she wrote in her autobiography, *Crusade for Justice* (1928), "Having lost my paper, had a price put on my life and been made an exile . . . , I felt that I owed it to myself and to my race to tell the whole truth now that I was where I could do so freely."

Lynching did not end during Wells's lifetime, but her forceful voice brought the issue to national and international prominence. At Wells's funeral in 1931, black leader W. E. B. Du Bois eulogized Wells as the woman who "began the awakening of the conscience of the nation." Wells's determined campaign against lynching provided just one

Ida B. Wells
Ida B. Wells began her antilynching campaign in 1892 after a friend's murder led her to examine lynching in the South. Through lectures and pamphlets, she brought the horror of lynching to national and international audiences and became a founding member of the National Association for the Advancement of Colored People (NAACP). Special Collections Research Center, University of Chicago Library.

example of women's political activism during the Gilded Age. The suffrage and temperance movements, along with the growing popularity of women's clubs, dramatized how women refused to be relegated to a separate sphere that kept them out of politics.

Women's Activism

In 1869, Elizabeth Cady Stanton and Susan B. Anthony formed the National Woman Suffrage Association (NWSA), the first independent women's rights organization in the United States, to fight for the vote for women. But women found ways to act politically long before they voted and cleverly used their moral authority as wives and mothers to move from the domestic sphere into the realm of politics.

The extraordinary activity of women's clubs in the period following the Civil War provides just one example. Women's clubs proliferated beginning in the 1860s. Newspaper reporter Jane Cunningham Croly (pen name Jennie June) founded the Sorosis Club in New York City in 1868, after the New York Press Club denied entry to women journalists wishing to attend a banquet honoring the British author Charles Dickens. In 1890, Croly brought state

and local clubs together under the umbrella of the General Federation of Women's Clubs (GFWC). Not wishing to alienate southern women, the GFWC barred black women's clubs from joining, despite vehement objections. Women's clubs soon abandoned literary pursuits to devote themselves to "civic usefulness," endorsing an end to child labor, supporting the eight-hour workday, and helping pass pure food and drug legislation.

The temperance movement (the movement to end drunkenness) attracted by far the largest number of organized women in the late nineteenth century. By the late 1860s and the 1870s, the liquor business was flourishing, with about one saloon for every fifty males over the age of fifteen. During the winter of 1873–74, temperance women adopted a radical new tactic. Armed with Bibles and singing hymns, they marched on taverns and saloons and refused to leave until the proprietors signed a pledge to quit selling liquor. Known as the Woman's Crusade, the movement spread like a prairie fire through small towns in Ohio, Indiana, Michigan, and Illinois and soon moved east into New York, New England, and Pennsylvania. Before it was over, more than 100,000 women had marched in more than 450 cities and towns.

"Woman's Holy War"
This political cartoon styles the temperance campaign as "Woman's Holy War" and shows a woman knight in armor (demurely seated sidesaddle on her charger), wielding a battle-ax and trampling on barrels of liquor. The image of temperance women as ax-wielding Amazons proved a popular satiric image. The cartoon appeared in 1874, the year the Woman's Christian Temperance Union formed. Picture Research Consultants & Archives.

The women's tactics may have been new, but the temperance movement dated back to the 1820s. Originally, the movement was led by Protestant men who organized clubs to pledge voluntary abstinence from liquor. By the 1850s, temperance advocates won significant victories when states, starting with Maine, passed laws to prohibit the sale of liquor. The Woman's Crusade dramatically brought the issue of temperance back into the national spotlight and, in 1874, led to the formation of a new organization, the **Woman's Christian Temperance Union (WCTU)**. Composed entirely of women, the WCTU advocated total abstinence from alcohol.

Temperance provided women with a respectable outlet for their increasing resentment of women's inferior status and their growing recognition of women's capabilities. In its first five years, the WCTU relied on education and moral suasion, but when Frances Willard became president in 1879, she politicized the organization (see chapter 20). When the women of the WCTU joined with the Prohibition Party (formed in 1869 by a group of evangelical clergymen), one wag observed, "Politics is a man's game, an' women, childhern, and prohyibitionists do well to keep out iv it." By sharing power with women, the prohibitionist men violated the old political rules and risked attacks on their honor and manhood.

Even though women found ways to affect the political process, especially in third parties, it remained true that politics, particularly presidential politics, remained an exclusively male prerogative.

> **REVIEW**   How did race and gender influence politics?

▶ Presidential Politics

The presidents of the Gilded Age, from Rutherford B. Hayes (1877–1881) to William McKinley (1897–1901), are largely forgotten men, primarily because so little was expected of them. The dominant creed of laissez-faire, coupled with the dictates of social Darwinism, warned the presidents and the government to leave business alone (except when they were working in its interests). Still, presidents in the Gilded Age grappled with corruption and party strife, and they struggled toward the creation of new political ethics designed to replace patronage with a civil service system that promised to award jobs on the basis of merit, not party loyalty.

Corruption and Party Strife

The political corruption and party factionalism that characterized the administration of Ulysses S. Grant (1869–1877) (see "Grant's Troubled Presidency" in chapter 16) continued to trouble the nation in the 1880s. The spoils system remained the driving force in party politics at all levels of government. Pro-business Republicans generally held a firm grip on the White House, while Democrats had better luck in Congress. Both parties relied on patronage to cement party loyalty.

A small but determined group of reformers championed a new ethics that would preclude politicians from getting rich from public office. The selection of U.S. senators particularly concerned them. Under the Constitution, senators were selected by state legislatures, not directly elected by the voters. Powerful business interests often contrived to control state legislatures and through them U.S. senators. As journalist Henry Demarest Lloyd quipped, Standard Oil "had done everything to the Pennsylvania legislature except to refine it." In this climate, a constitutional amendment calling for the direct election of senators faced stiff opposition from entrenched interests.

Republican president Rutherford B. Hayes tried to steer a middle course between spoilsmen and reformers. Hayes proved a hardworking, well-informed executive who wanted peace, prosperity, and an end to party strife. Yet the Republican Party remained divided into factions led by strong party bosses who boasted that they could make or break any president.

Foremost among the Republican Senate bosses stood Roscoe Conkling of New York. He and his followers, who fiercely supported the patronage system, were known as "Stalwarts." Conkling's rival, Senator James G. Blaine of Maine, led the "Half Breeds," who were less openly corrupt yet still tainted by their involvement in the Crédit Mobilier scandal. A third group, called the "Mugwumps," consisted of reformers from Massachusetts and New York who deplored the spoils system and advocated civil service reform.

President Hayes's middle course pleased no one, and he soon managed to alienate all factions of his party. Few were surprised when he announced that he would not seek reelection in 1880. To avoid choosing among its factions, the Republican Party in 1880 nominated a dark-horse candidate, Representative James A. Garfield of Ohio. To foster party unity, they picked Stalwart Chester A. Arthur as the vice presidential candidate. The Democrats made an attempt to overcome sectionalism by selecting former Union general Winfield Scott Hancock. Hancock garnered only lukewarm support, receiving just 155 electoral votes to Garfield's 214, although the popular vote was less lopsided.

Garfield's Assassination and Civil Service Reform

"My God," Garfield swore after only a few months in office, "what is there in this place that a man should ever want to get into it?" Garfield, like Hayes, faced the difficult task of remaining independent while pacifying the party bosses and placating the reformers. On July 2, 1881, less

VISUAL ACTIVITY

Civil Service Exams

In this 1890 photograph, prospective police officers in Chicago take the written civil service exam. With the rise of a written exam, issues of class and status meant that many men, particularly immigrants and their sons, needed education and not simply connections to make the grade.
© Chicago History Museum, USA/Bridgeman Images.

READING THE IMAGE: What types of people are sitting for the civil service exam? Would you expect to see women or people of color?

CONNECTIONS: Who pressed for civil service reform, and what were the repercussions for those who held government positions?

than four months after taking office, Garfield was shot and died two months later. His assailant, Charles Julius Guiteau, though clearly insane, turned out to be a disappointed office seeker, motivated by political partisanship. He told the police officer who arrested him, "I did it; I will go to jail for it: Arthur is president, and I am a Stalwart."

The press almost universally condemned Republican factionalism for creating the political climate that produced Guiteau. Attacks on the spoils system increased, and both parties claimed credit for passage of the Pendleton Civil Service Act of 1883, which established a permanent Civil Service Commission consisting of three members appointed by the president. Some fourteen thousand jobs came under a merit system that required examinations for office and made it impossible to remove jobholders for political reasons. The new law also prohibited federal jobholders from contributing to political campaigns, thus drying up the major source of the party bosses' revenue. Businesses soon stepped in as the nation's chief political contributors. Ironically, **civil service reform** gave business an even greater influence in political life.

Reform and Scandal: The Campaign of 1884

James G. Blaine assumed leadership of the Republican Party and at long last captured the presidential nomination in 1884. A magnetic Irish American, Blaine inspired such devotion that his supporters called themselves Blainiacs. But Mugwump reformers bolted the party and embraced the Democrats' presidential nominee, Governor Grover Cleveland of New York. The burly, beer-drinking Cleveland distinguished himself from a generation of politicians by the simple motto "A public office is a public trust." First as mayor of Buffalo and later as governor of New York, he built a reputation for honesty, economy, and administrative efficiency. The Democrats, who had not won the presidency since 1856, had high hopes for his candidacy, especially after the Mugwumps threw their support to Cleveland, announcing, "The paramount issue this year is moral rather than political."

They soon regretted their words. In July, Cleveland's hometown paper, the *Buffalo Telegraph*, dropped the bombshell that the candidate had fathered an illegitimate child in an affair with a local widow. Cleveland, a bachelor, stoically accepted responsibility for the child.

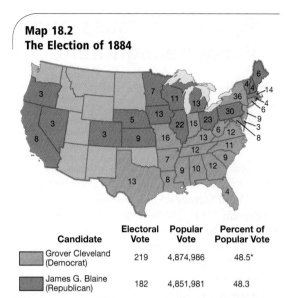

Map 18.2
The Election of 1884

Candidate	Electoral Vote	Popular Vote	Percent of Popular Vote
Grover Cleveland (Democrat)	219	4,874,986	48.5*
James G. Blaine (Republican)	182	4,851,981	48.3

*Percentages do not total 100 because some popular votes went to other parties.

Crushed by the scandal, the Mugwumps lost much of their enthusiasm. At public rallies, Blaine's partisans taunted Cleveland, chanting, "Ma, Ma, where's my Pa?"

Blaine set a new campaign style by launching a whirlwind national tour. On a last-minute stop in New York City, the exhausted candidate committed a misstep that may have cost him the election. He overlooked a remark by a supporter, a local clergyman who cast a slur on Catholic voters by styling the Democrats as the party of "Rum, Romanism, and Rebellion." Linking drinking (rum) and Catholicism (Romanism) offended Irish Catholic voters, whom Blaine had counted on to desert the Democratic Party and support him because of his Irish background.

With less than a week to go until the election, Blaine had no chance to recover from the negative publicity. He lost New York State by fewer than 1,200 votes and with it the election. In the final tally, Cleveland defeated Blaine by a scant 23,005 votes nationwide but won with 219 electoral votes to Blaine's 182 (Map 18.2), ending twenty-four years of Republican control of the presidency. Cleveland's followers had the last word. To the chorus of "Ma, Ma, where's my Pa?" they retorted, "Going to the White House, ha, ha, ha."

REVIEW   How did the question of civil service reform contribute to divisions within the Republican Party?

▶ Economic Issues and Party Realignment

Four years later, in the election of 1888, fickle voters turned Cleveland out, electing Republican Benjamin Harrison, the grandson of President William Henry Harrison. Then, in the only instance in American history when a president once defeated at the polls returned to office, the voters brought Cleveland back in the election of 1892. What factors account for such a surprising turnaround? The 1880s witnessed a remarkable political realignment as a set of economic concerns replaced appeals to Civil War sectional loyalties. The tariff, federal regulation of the railroads and trusts, and the campaign for free silver restructured American politics. Then a Wall Street panic in 1893 set off a major depression that further fed political unrest.

The Tariff and the Politics of Protection

The tariff became a potent political issue in the 1880s. The concept of a protective tariff to raise the price of imported goods and stimulate American industry dated back to the founding days of the Republic. Republicans turned the tariff to political ends in 1861 by enacting a measure that both raised revenues for the Civil War and rewarded their industrial supporters, who wanted protection from foreign competition. After the war, the pro-business Republicans continued to raise the tariff. Manufactured goods such as steel and textiles, and some agricultural products, including sugar and wool, benefited from protection. Most farm products, notably wheat and cotton, did not. By the 1880s, the tariff produced more than $2.1 billion in revenue. Not only did the high tariff pay off the nation's Civil War debt and fund pensions for Union soldiers, but it also created a huge surplus that sat idly in the Treasury's vaults while the government argued about how (or even whether) to spend it.

To many Americans, particularly southern and midwestern farmers who sold their crops in a world market but had to buy goods priced artificially high because of the protective tariff, the answer was simple: Reduce the tariff. But the Republican Party seized on the tariff question to forge a new national coalition. "Fold up the bloody shirt and lay it away," Blaine advised a colleague in 1880. "It's of no use to us. You want to shift the main issue to protection." By

encouraging an alliance among industrialists, labor, and western producers of raw materials—groups seen to benefit from the tariff—Blaine hoped to solidify the North, Midwest, and West against the solidly Democratic South. Although the tactic failed for Blaine in the presidential election of 1884, it worked for the Republicans four years later.

Cleveland, who had straddled the tariff issue in the election of 1884, startled the nation in 1887 by calling for tariff reform. The president attacked the tariff as a tax levied on American consumers by powerful industries. And he pointed out that high tariffs impeded the expansion of American markets abroad at a time when American industries needed to expand. The Republicans countered by arguing that "tariff tinkering" would only unsettle prosperous industries, drive down wages, and shrink the farmers' home market. Republican Benjamin Harrison, who supported the high tariff, ousted Cleveland from the White House in 1888, carrying all the western and northern states except Connecticut and New Jersey.

Back in power, the Republicans brazenly passed the highest tariff in the nation's history in 1890. The new tariff, sponsored by Republican representative William McKinley of Ohio, stirred up a hornet's nest of protest across the United States. The American people had elected Harrison to preserve protection but not to enact a higher tariff. Democrats condemned the McKinley tariff and labeled the Republican Congress that passed it the "Billion Dollar Congress" for its carnival of spending, which depleted the nation's surplus by enacting a series of pork barrel programs shamelessly designed to bring federal money to congressmen's constituencies. In the congressional election of 1890, angry voters swept the hapless Republicans, including tariff sponsor McKinley, out of office. Two years later, Harrison himself was defeated, and Grover Cleveland returned to the White House. Such were the changes in the political winds whipped up by the tariff issue.

Controversy over the tariff masked deeper divisions in American society. Conflict between workers and farmers on the one side and bankers and corporate giants on the other erupted throughout the 1880s and came to a head in the 1890s. Both sides in the tariff debate spoke to concerns over class conflict when they insisted that their respective plans, whether McKinley's high tariff or Cleveland's tariff reform, would bring prosperity and harmony. For their part, many working people shared the sentiment voiced by one labor leader that the tariff was "only a scheme devised by the old parties to throw dust in the eyes of laboring men."

Railroads, Trusts, and the Federal Government

American voters may have divided on the tariff, but increasingly they agreed on the need for federal regulation of the railroads and federal legislation to curb the power of the "trusts" (a term loosely applied to all large business combinations). As early as the 1870s, angry farmers in the Midwest who suffered from the unfair shipping practices of the railroads organized to fight for railroad regulation. The Patrons of Husbandry, or the Grange, founded in 1867 as a social and educational organization for farmers, soon became an independent political movement. By electing Grangers to state office, farmers made it possible for several midwestern states to pass laws in the 1870s and 1880s regulating the railroads. At first, the Supreme Court ruled in favor of state regulation (*Munn v. Illinois*, 1877). But in 1886, the Court reversed itself, ruling that because railroads crossed state boundaries, they fell outside state jurisdiction (*Wabash v. Illinois*). With more than three-fourths of railroads crossing state lines, the Supreme Court's decision effectively quashed the states' attempts at railroad regulation.

Anger at the *Wabash* decision finally led to the first federal law regulating the railroads, the Interstate Commerce Act, passed in 1887 during Cleveland's first administration. The act established the nation's first federal regulatory agency, the **Interstate Commerce Commission (ICC)**, to oversee the railroad industry. Railroad lobbyists worked furiously behind the scenes to make the new agency palatable to business leaders, many of whom felt a federal agency would be more lenient than state regulators. In its early years, the ICC was never strong enough to pose a serious threat to the railroads. For example, it could not end rebates to big shippers. In its early decades, the ICC proved more important as a precedent than effective as a watchdog.

Concern over the growing power of the trusts led Congress to pass the **Sherman Antitrust Act** in 1890. The act outlawed pools and trusts, ruling that businesses could no longer enter into agreements to restrict competition. It did nothing to restrict huge holding companies such as Standard Oil, however, and proved to be a weak sword against the trusts. In the following decade, the government successfully struck down only

six trusts but used the law four times against labor by outlawing unions as a "conspiracy in restraint of trade." In 1895, the conservative Supreme Court dealt the antitrust law a crippling blow in *United States v. E. C. Knight Company*. In its decision, the Court ruled that "manufacture" did not constitute "trade." This semantic quibble drastically narrowed the law, in this case allowing the American Sugar Refining Company, which had bought out a number of other sugar companies (including E. C. Knight) and controlled 98 percent of the production of sugar, to continue its virtual monopoly. Yet the Court insisted the law could be used against labor unions.

Both the ICC and the Sherman Antitrust Act testified to the nation's concern about corporate abuses of power and to a growing willingness to use federal measures to intervene on behalf of the public interest. As corporate capitalism became more and more powerful, public pressure toward government intervention grew. Yet not until the twentieth century would more active presidents sharpen and use these weapons effectively against the large corporations.

The Fight for Free Silver

While the tariff and regulation of the trusts gained many backers, the silver issue stirred passions like no other issue of the day. On one side stood those who believed that gold constituted the only honest money. Many who supported the gold standard were eastern creditors who did not wish to be paid in devalued dollars. On the opposite side stood a coalition of western silver barons and poor farmers from the West and South who called for **free silver**. Farmers from the West and South hoped to increase the money supply with silver dollars and create inflation, which would give them some debt relief by enabling them to pay off their creditors with cheaper dollars. The mining interests, who had seen the silver bonanza in the West drive down the price of the precious metal, wanted the government to buy silver and mint silver dollars.

During the depression following the panic of 1873, critics of hard money organized the Greenback Labor Party, an alliance of farmers and urban wage laborers. The Greenbackers favored issuing paper currency not tied to the gold supply, citing the precedent of the greenbacks issued during the Civil War. The government had the right to define what constituted legal tender, the Greenbackers reasoned: "Paper is equally money, when . . . issued according to law."

Greenback Labor Party Seal
The Greenback Labor Party, active in the 1870s, pushed for an inflationary currency that would give farmers and workers more money in circulation to help pay off debts. Its party seal is progressive for the era, focusing on the family by picturing a girl child and not a man or boy—a sign of how important women were in the organization. The Granger Collection, New York.

They proposed that the nation's currency be based on its wealth—land, labor, and capital—and not simply on its reserves of gold. The Greenback Labor Party captured more than a million votes and elected fourteen members to Congress in 1878. Although conservatives considered the Greenbackers dangerous cranks, their views eventually prevailed in the 1930s, when the country abandoned the gold standard.

After the Greenback Labor Party collapsed, proponents of free silver came to dominate the monetary debate in the 1890s. Advocates of free silver pointed out that until 1873 the country had enjoyed a system of bimetallism—the minting of both silver and gold into coins. In that year, at the behest of those who favored gold, the Republican Congress had voted to stop buying and minting silver, an act silver supporters denounced as the "crime of '73." By sharply contracting the money supply at a time when the nation's economy was burgeoning, the Republicans had enriched bankers and investors at the expense of cotton and wheat farmers and industrial wage-workers. In 1878 and again in 1890, with the Sherman Silver Purchase Act, Congress took steps to ease the tight money policy and appease advocates of silver by passing legislation requiring the government to buy silver and issue silver certificates. Though good for the mining interests, the laws did little to promote the inflation desired

by farmers. Soon monetary reformers began to call for "the free and unlimited coinage of silver," a plan whereby nearly all the silver mined in the West would be minted into coins circulated at the rate of sixteen ounces of silver—equal in value to one ounce of gold.

By the 1890s, the silver issue crossed party lines. The Democrats hoped to use it to achieve a union between western and southern voters. Unfortunately for them, Democratic president Grover Cleveland supported the gold standard as vehemently as any Republican. After a panic on Wall Street in the spring of 1893, Cleveland called a special session of Congress and bullied the legislature into repealing the Silver Purchase Act because he believed it threatened economic confidence. Repeal proved disastrous for Cleveland. It did nothing to bring prosperity and dangerously divided the country. Angry farmers warned Cleveland not to travel west of the Mississippi River if he valued his life.

Panic and Depression

President Cleveland had scarcely begun his second term in 1893 when the country plunged into the worst depression it had yet seen. In the face of economic disaster, Cleveland clung to the economic orthodoxy of the gold standard. In the winter of 1894–95, the president walked the floor of the White House, sleepless over the prospect that the United States might go bankrupt. Individuals and investors, rushing to trade in their banknotes for gold, strained the country's monetary system. The Treasury's gold reserves dipped so low that unless they could be buttressed, the unthinkable might happen: The U.S. Treasury might not be able to meet its obligations.

At this juncture, J. P. Morgan stepped in. A group of bankers pledged to purchase millions in U.S. government bonds, paying in gold. Cleveland knew that such a scheme would unleash a thunder of protest, yet to save the gold standard, the president had no choice. But if President Cleveland's action managed to salvage the gold standard, it did not save the country from hardship. In the winter of 1894–95, people faced unemployment, cold, and hunger. Cleveland, a firm believer in limited government, insisted that nothing could be done to help: "I do not believe that the power and duty of the General Government ought to be extended to the relief of individual suffering which is in no manner properly related to the public service or benefit." Nor did it occur to Cleveland that his great faith in the gold standard prolonged the depression, favored creditors over debtors, and caused immense hardship for millions of Americans.

> **REVIEW**   What role did economic issues play in party realignment?

► Conclusion: Business Dominates an Era

The gold deal between J. P. Morgan and Grover Cleveland underscored a dangerous reality: The federal government was so weak that its solvency depended on a private banker. This lopsided power relationship signaled the dominance of business in the era Mark Twain satirically but accurately characterized as the Gilded Age. Birthed by the railroads, the new economy spawned greed, corruption, and vulgarity on a grand scale. Speculators like Jay Gould not only built but also wrecked railroads to turn paper profits; the get-rich-quick ethic of the gold rush infused the whole continent; and business boasted openly of buying politicians, who in turn lined their pockets at the public's expense.

Nevertheless, the Gilded Age was not without its share of solid achievements. Where dusty roads and cattle trails once sprawled across the continent, steel rails now bound the country together, creating a national market that enabled America to make the leap into the industrial age. Factories and refineries poured out American steel and oil at unprecedented rates. Businessmen like Carnegie, Rockefeller, and Morgan developed new strategies to consolidate American industry. New inventions, including the telephone and electric light and power, transformed Americans' everyday lives.

By the end of the nineteenth century, the United States had achieved industrial maturity. It boasted the largest, most innovative, most productive economy in the world. The rise of Gilded Age industry came at a cost, however. The rampant railway building changed the nature of politics in the United States, entwining the state and the corporations and making a mockery of a free market economy. And as one historian speculated, had railroad magnates waited to build western railroads to meet demand, their restraint might have resulted in less waste, less environmental degradation, and less human suffering for Native Americans and whites alike.

The effects of American industry worried many Americans and gave rise to the era's political turmoil. Race and gender profoundly influenced American politics, leading to new political alliances. Fearless activist Ida B. Wells fought racism in its most brutal form—lynching. Women's organizations championed causes, notably suffrage and temperance, and challenged prevailing views of woman's proper sphere. Reformers fought corruption by instituting civil service. And new issues—the tariff, the regulation of the trusts, and currency reform—restructured the nation's politics.

The Gilded Age witnessed a nation transformed. Fueled by railroad building and expanding industry, cities grew exponentially, bulging at the seams with new inhabitants from around the globe and bristling with new bridges, subways, and skyscrapers. The frenzied growth of urban America brought wealth and opportunity, but also the exploitation of labor, racism toward newcomers, and social upheaval that lent a new urgency to calls for social reform.

See the Selected Bibliography for this chapter in the Appendix.

18 Chapter Review

REVIEW QUESTIONS

1. When, why, and how did the transcontinental railroad system develop, and what was its impact on American business? (pp. 499–508)

2. Why did the ideas of social Darwinism appeal to many Americans in the late nineteenth century? (pp. 508–512)

3. How did race and gender influence politics? (pp. 512–517)

4. How did the question of civil service reform contribute to divisions within the Republican Party? (pp. 517–519)

5. What role did economic issues play in party realignment? (pp. 520–523)

MAKING CONNECTIONS

1. What were some of the key technology and business innovations in the late nineteenth century? How did they aid the maturation of American industry?

2. By the 1870s, what new issues displaced slavery as the defining question of American politics, and how did they shape new regional, economic, and racial alliances and rivalries?

3. How did the activism of women denied the vote contribute to Gilded Age electoral politics? Be sure to cite specific examples of political action.

4. Citing specific policies and court decisions, discuss how government helped augment the power of big business in the late nineteenth century.

LINKING TO THE PAST

1. In what ways did the military conquest of the trans-Mississippi West, with its dislocation of Native Americans, play a significant role in the industrial boom of the Gilded Age? (See chapter 17.)

2. In what ways did the rampant get-rich-quick mentality of western miners and land speculators help set the tone for the Gilded Age? Is the West the herald of the Gilded Age, or must we look to New York and Washington? (See chapter 17.)

19 The City and Its Workers

1870–1900

After reading and studying this chapter, you should be able to:

- Identify the factors that led to rapid urbanization during the late nineteenth century. Describe how the social geography of the city changed and the reactions to those changes.

- Describe the diversity of American labor, including the role of women and children in the workforce.

- Understand why workers organized and how management responded to labor's demands. Analyze the impact of the Great Strike of 1877, the Knights of Labor, the American Federation of Labor, and the Haymarket bombing.

- Describe how notions of domesticity and everyday amusements reflected class divisions.

- Identify the nature of city government in the late nineteenth century and the growth of city amenities. Explain Americans' ambivalence toward cities.

BROOKLYN BRIDGE FAN
This commemorative fan celebrates the opening of the bridge on May 24, 1883. It took fourteen years and cost the lives of twenty-seven men to complete the bridge.
© Museum of the City of New York, USA/Bridgeman Images.

"A TOWN THAT CRAWLED NOW STANDS ERECT, AND WE WHOSE backs were bent above the hearths know how it got its spine," boasted a steelworker surveying New York City. Where once wooden buildings stood rooted in the mire of unpaved streets, cities of stone and steel sprang up in the last decades of the nineteenth century. The labor of millions of workers, many of them immigrants, laid the foundations for urban America.

No symbol better represented the new urban landscape than the Brooklyn Bridge, opened in May 1883. The great bridge soared over the East River in a single mile-long span. Building the Brooklyn Bridge took fourteen years and cost the lives of twenty-seven men. To sink the foundation in the riverbed, laborers tunneled through the mud and worked in boxes that were open at the bottom and pressurized to keep the water out. Before long, workers experienced the malady they called "bends" because it left them doubled over in pain when they rose to the surface. (Scientists later learned that nitrogen bubbles trapped in the bloodstream caused the bends, which could be prevented by allowing for decompression.) The first death occurred when the foundation reached a depth of seventy-one feet. A German immigrant complained that he did not feel well. He collapsed and died on his way home. Eight days later, another man dropped dead, and the entire workforce went out on strike. Terrified workers demanded a higher wage for fewer hours of work.

A scrawny sixteen-year-old from Ireland, Frank Harris, remembered the fearful experience of going to work on the bridge a few days after landing in America:

The six of us were working naked to the waist in the small iron chamber with the temperature of about 80 degrees Fahrenheit: In five minutes the sweat was pouring from us, and all the while we were standing in icy water that was only kept from rising by the terrific pressure. No wonder the headaches were blinding.

By his fifth day, Harris quit. Many immigrant workers walked off the job, often as many as a hundred a week. But a ready supply of immigrants meant that new workers took up the digging, where they could earn in a day more than they made in a week in Ireland or Italy.

Begun in 1869, the bridge was the dream of builder John Roebling, who died in a freak accident almost as soon as construction began. Washington Roebling took over as chief engineer after his father's death, routinely working twelve- to fourteen-hour days, six days a week. Soon he too fell victim to the bends. He directed the completion of the bridge through a telescope from his bedroom window in Brooklyn Heights. His wife, Emily Warren Roebling, acted as site superintendent and general engineer of the project.

At the end of the nineteenth century, the Brooklyn Bridge stood as a symbol of many things: the industrial might of the United States; the labor of the nation's immigrants; the ingenuity and genius of its engineers and inventors; the rise of iron and steel; and, most of all, the ascendancy of urban America. Poised on the brink of the twentieth century, the nation was shifting from a rural, agricultural society to an urban, industrial nation. The gap between rich and poor widened. In the burgeoning cities, tensions erupted into conflict as workers squared off to organize into labor unions and to demand safer working conditions, shorter hours, and better pay, sometimes with violent and bloody results. The explosive growth of the cities fostered political corruption as unscrupulous bosses and entrepreneurs cashed in on the building boom. Immigrants, political bosses, middle-class managers, poor laborers, and the very rich populated the nation's cities, crowding the streets, laboring in the stores and factories, and taking their leisure at the new ballparks, amusement parks, dance halls, and municipal parks. As the new century dawned, the city and its workers moved to center stage in American life.

VISUAL ACTIVITY

Workers on the Brooklyn Bridge

Illustrations show workers tunneling under the East River to lay the foundations for the Brooklyn Bridge. A cylindrical airlock took them down more than seventy feet. "What with the flaming lights, the deep shadows, the confusing noise of hammer, drills, and chains, the half-naked forms flitting about," wrote one reporter, the scene resembled hell. Library of Congress, 3c24944.

READING THE IMAGE: What would you guess about the age and the physical condition of the workers pictured?

CONNECTIONS: Who did the work of building America's new industrial infrastructure? How were they rewarded?

▶ The Rise of the City

"We cannot all live in cities, yet nearly all seem determined to do so," New York editor Horace Greeley complained. The last three decades of the nineteenth century witnessed an urban explosion. Cities and towns grew more than twice as rapidly as the total population. By 1900, the United States boasted three cities with more than a million inhabitants—New York, Chicago, and Philadelphia.

Patterns of **global migration** contributed to the rise of the city. In the port cities of the East Coast, more than fourteen million people arrived, many from southern and eastern Europe, and huddled together in dense urban ghettos. The word *slum* entered the American vocabulary along with a growing concern over the rising tide of newcomers. In the city, the widening gap between rich and poor became not just financial but physical. Changes in the city landscape brought about by advances in transportation and technology accentuated the great divide in wealth at the same time they put physical distance between rich and poor.

The Urban Explosion: A Global Migration

The United States grew up in the country and moved to the city, or so it seemed by the end of the nineteenth century. Between 1870 and 1900, eleven million people moved into cities. Burgeoning industrial centers such as Pittsburgh, Chicago, New York, and Cleveland acted as giant magnets, attracting workers from the countryside. But rural Americans were not the only ones migrating to cities. Millions of immigrants moved from their native countries to America. Worldwide in scope, the movement from rural areas to urban industrial centers attracted millions of immigrants to American shores.

By the 1870s, the world could be conceptualized as three interconnected geographic regions (Map 19.1). At the center stood an industrial core that encompassed the eastern United States and western Europe. Surrounding this industrial core lay a vast agricultural domain from the Canadian wheat fields to the hinterlands of northern China. Capitalist development in the late nineteenth century shattered traditional patterns of economic activity in this rural periphery. As old patterns broke down, these rural areas exported, along with other raw materials, new recruits for the industrial labor force.

CHRONOLOGY

1869	• Knights of Labor founded. • Cincinnati mounts first paid baseball team.
1871	• Boss Tweed's rule in New York City ends. • Chicago's Great Fire breaks out.
1873	• Panic on Wall Street touches off depression.
1877	• Great Railroad Strike paralyzes nation.
1880s	• Immigration from southern and eastern Europe rises.
1882	• Chinese Exclusion Act enacted.
1883	• Brooklyn Bridge opens.
1886	• American Federation of Labor founded. • Haymarket bombing occurs in Chicago.
1890	• Jacob Riis publishes *How the Other Half Lives*.
1890s	• African American migration from the South begins.
1892	• Ellis Island opens.
1893	• World's Columbian Exposition opens in Chicago. • Panic on Wall Street touches off major economic depression.
1895	• Boston Public Library opens in Copley Square.
1896	• President Grover Cleveland vetoes immigrant literacy test.
1897	• Steeplechase Park opens on Coney Island. • Nation's first subway system opens in Boston.

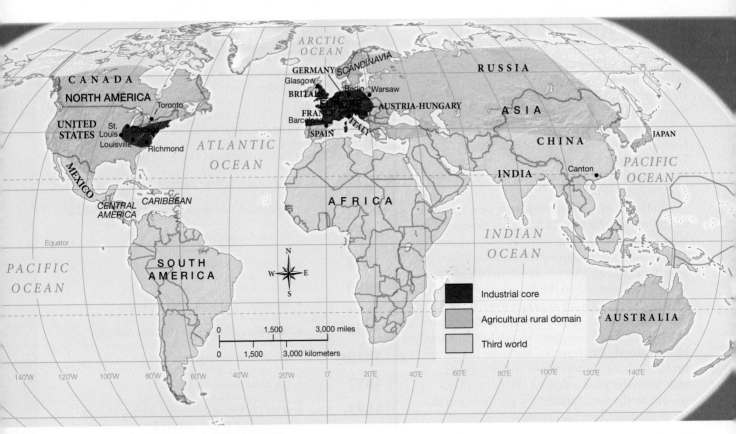

MAP ACTIVITY

Map 19.1   Economic Regions of the World, 1890

The global nature of the world economy at the turn of the twentieth century is indicated by three interconnected geographic regions. At the center stands the industrial core—western Europe and the northeastern United States. The second region—the agricultural periphery—supplied immigrant laborers to the industries in the core. Beyond these two regions lay a vast area tied economically to the industrial core by colonialism.

READING THE MAP: What types of economic regions were contained in the United States in this period? Which continents held most of the industrial core? Which held most of the agricultural rural domain? Which held the greatest portion of the third world?

CONNECTIONS: Which of these three regions provided the bulk of immigrant workers to the United States? What major changes prompted the global migration at the end of the nineteenth century?

Beyond this second circle lay an even larger third world. Colonial ties between this part of the world and the industrial core strengthened in the late nineteenth century, but most of the people living there stayed put. They worked on plantations and railroads, and in mines and ports, as part of a huge export network managed by foreign powers that staked out spheres of influence and colonies in this vast region.

In the 1870s, railroad expansion and low steamship fares gave the world's peoples a new-found mobility, enabling industrialists to draw on a global population for cheap labor. When Andrew Carnegie opened his first steel mill in 1872, his superintendent hired workers he called "buckwheats"—young American boys just off the farm. By the 1890s, however, Carnegie's workforce was liberally sprinkled with other rural boys, Hungarians and Slavs who had migrated to the United States, willing to work for low wages.

Altogether, more than 25 million immigrants came to the United States between 1850 and 1920. They came from all directions: east from Asia, south from Canada, north from Latin America, and west from Europe (Map 19.2). Part of a worldwide migration, emigrants traveled to South America and Australia as well as to the United States. Yet more than 70 percent of all European emigrants chose North America as their destination.

Historically, the largest number of immigrants to the United States came from the British Isles

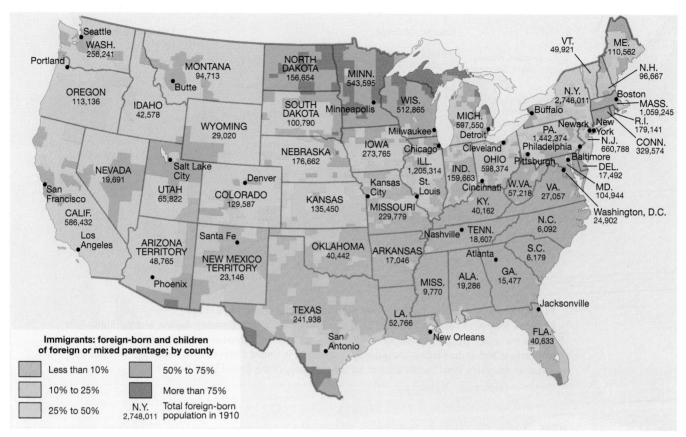

MAP ACTIVITY

Map 19.2   The Impact of Immigration, to 1910

Immigration flowed in all directions—south from Canada, north from Mexico and Latin America, east from Asia, and west from Europe.

READING THE MAP: Which states had the highest percentages of immigrants? Which cities attracted the most immigrants? Which cities attracted the fewest?

CONNECTIONS: Why did most immigrants gravitate toward the cities? Why do you think the South drew such a low percentage of immigrants?

and from German-speaking lands (Figure 19.1). The vast majority of immigrants were white; Asians accounted for fewer than one million immigrants, and other people of color numbered even fewer. Yet ingrained racial prejudices increasingly influenced the country's perception of immigration patterns. One of the classic formulations of the history of European immigration divided immigrants into two distinct waves that have been called the "old" and the "new" immigration. According to this theory, before 1880 the majority of immigrants came from northern and western Europe, with Germans, Irish, English, and Scandinavians making up approximately 85 percent of the newcomers. After 1880, the pattern shifted, with more and more ships carrying passengers from southern and eastern Europe. Italians, Hungarians, eastern European Jews, Turks, Armenians, Poles, Russians, and other

Slavic peoples accounted for more than 80 percent of all immigrants by 1896 (Figure 19.2). Implicit in the distinction was an invidious comparison between "old" pioneer settlers and "new" unskilled laborers. Yet this sweeping generalization spoke more to perception than to reality. In fact, many of the earlier immigrants from Ireland, Germany, and Scandinavia came not as settlers or farmers, but as wageworkers, and they were met with much the same disdain as the Italians and Slavs who followed them.

During good financial times, the need for cheap, unskilled labor for America's industries stimulated demand for immigrant workers. In 1873 and again in 1893, when the United States experienced economic depressions, immigration slowed, only to pick up again when prosperity returned. Steamship companies courted immigrants—a highly profitable, self-loading cargo.

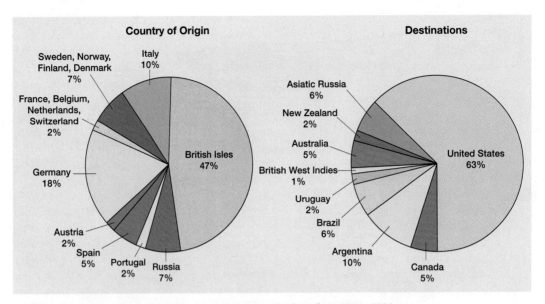

FIGURE 19.1 **Global Comparison: European Emigration, 1870–1890**
European emigration between 1870 and 1890 shows that people from Germany, Austria, and the British Isles formed the largest group of out-migrants. After 1890, the origin of European emigrants tilted south and east, with Italians and eastern Europeans growing in number. The United States took in nearly two-thirds of the European emigrants. What factors account for the popularity of the United States?

By the 1880s, the price of a ticket from Liverpool had dropped to less than $25. Would-be immigrants eager for information about the United States relied on letters from friends and relatives, advertisements, and word of mouth—sources that were not always dependable or truthful. As one Italian immigrant recalled, "News was colored, success magnified, comforts and advantages exaggerated beyond all proportions." Even photographs proved deceptive: Workers dressed in their Sunday best looked more prosperous than they actually were to relatives in the old country, where only the

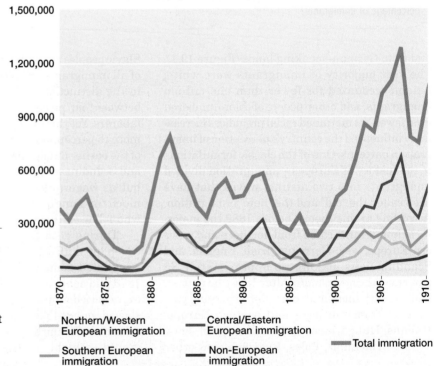

FIGURE 19.2 **European Emigration, 1870–1910**
Before 1880, more than 85 percent of U.S. immigrants came from northern and western Europe—Germany, Ireland, England, and the Scandinavian countries. After 1880, 80 percent of the "new" immigrants came from Italy, Turkey, Hungary, Armenia, Poland, Russia, and other Slavic countries.

Northern/Western European immigration
Central/Eastern European immigration
Southern European immigration
Non-European immigration
Total immigration

very wealthy wore white collars or silk dresses. No wonder people left for the United States believing, as one Italian immigrant observed, "that if they were ever fortunate enough to reach America, they would fall into a pile of manure and get up brushing the diamonds out of their hair."

Most of the newcomers stayed in the nation's cities. By 1900, almost two-thirds of the country's immigrant population resided in cities. (See "Making Historical Arguments," page 532.) Many of the immigrants were too poor to move on. (The average laborer immigrating to the United States carried only about $21.50.) Although the foreign-born rarely outnumbered the native-born population, taken together immigrants and their American-born children did constitute a majority in some areas, particularly in the nation's largest cities: Philadelphia, 55 percent; Boston, 66 percent; Chicago, 75 percent; and New York City, an amazing 80 percent in 1900.

Not all the newcomers came to stay. Perhaps eight million European immigrants—most of them young men—worked for a year or a season and then returned to their homelands. Immigration officers called these immigrants, many of them Italians, "birds of passage" because they followed a regular pattern of migration to and from the United States. By 1900, almost 75 percent of the new immigrants were young, single men. Willing to accept conditions other workers regarded as intolerable, these young migrants showed little interest in labor unions. They organized only when the dream of returning home faded, as it did for millions who ultimately remained in the United States.

Women generally had less access to funds for travel and faced tighter family control. Because the traditional sexual division of labor relied on women's unpaid domestic labor and care of the very young and the very old, women most often came to the United States as wives, mothers, or daughters, not as single wage laborers. Only among the Irish, where the great potato famine presented the grim choice of starve or leave, did women immigrants outnumber men by a small margin from 1871 to 1891.

Jews from eastern Europe and Russia most often came with their families and came to stay. Fear of conscription into the Russian army motivated many young men to leave Russia. In addition, beginning in the 1880s, a wave of violent pogroms, or persecutions, in Russia and Poland prompted the departure of more than a million Jews in the next two decades. Mary Antin, a Jew leaving Poland for America, recalled her excitement: "So, at last I was going to America! Really going at last! The boundaries burst. The arch of heaven soared. . . . America! America!" Most of the Jewish immigrants settled in the port cities of the East, creating distinct ethnic enclaves, like Hester Street in the heart of New York City's Lower East Side, which rang with the calls of pushcart peddlers and vendors hawking their wares, from pickles to feather beds.

Racism and the Cry for Immigration Restriction

Ethnic diversity and racism played a role in dividing skilled workers (those with a craft or

Pushcart Peddlers in Little Italy
This photo shows banana sellers working from a pushcart in a street in New York's Little Italy. Italian immigrants constituted the majority of banana importers at the turn of the twentieth century. Library of Congress, 3c31516.

What Happened to Urban Workers' Standard of Living during the Gilded Age?

A relatively small number of factory owners and financiers enjoyed higher living standards during the Gilded Age. But what happened to the standard of living of urban workers, who made up 85 percent of city residents?

Since nearly all urban workers came from rural areas, a good way to assess what happened to their living standards is to compare them with those of farmers in the same period. Consider, for example, urban workers' earnings, hours, and conditions of work; housing, food, and domestic labor.

Factory workers typically labored ten to twelve hours a day six days a week, for wages that averaged $500 to $750 a year. In a good year, the average farm family produced crops worth as much as $1,000. But since family members provided most farm labor (outside the southern states), they typically received room and board as compensation rather than cash wages. Even the low wages received by factory workers put some cash in their pockets, giving them choices about spending that farmers seldom had.

Factory hands worked long hours at grueling and often dangerous tasks. Farmwork, however, had its own dangers and typically began before dawn and lasted until after dark, as long as or longer than factory workdays. Farmwork was more varied and self-directed than factory work, which typically was monotonous, repetitive, and closely supervised by a boss. But urban workers left the job behind when they walked out the factory gate, unlike farmers, whose responsibilities never ended.

Neither urban workers nor farmers enjoyed much economic security. Factory workers could be laid off or fired at any time for any reason. During the severe depressions in 1873 and 1893, unemployment sapped workers' ability to support their families, causing extreme poverty and even starvation in many cities. Farmers' ability to keep their heads above water depended on the uncertainties of weather, insect pests, and crop diseases. But they also suffered from declining agricultural prices during the era that made their cash crops worth less and less. Farmers protected their families from the starvation that stalked cities in hard times by growing food crops for their own consumption.

Squalid tenements that commonly housed immigrants in New York City made up only about 5 percent of urban housing in most other cities. The vast majority of urban working people resided in single-family cottages that resembled small versions of farmhouses. Like farmhouses, workers' homes lacked running water and toilets. By the end of the century, all farms and the great majority of urban households still used either a chamber pot or an outdoor privy that drained into a ditch or street. After dark, light came from a flame supplied by a candle or kerosene in both the city and country. In the summer, disease-carrying insects readily flew into urban and rural houses since all windows lacked screens. Insects feasted on human and vegetable waste as well as on the droppings of horses that powered urban transportation. In 1870, for example, Boston's 250,000 residents shared the city with 50,000 horses, each of them depositing 30 to 50 pounds of manure and about a gallon of urine on city streets every day, making the filth, stench, and toxicity of urban streets and households much worse than in the countryside.

Both urban workers and farmers enjoyed ample diets compared to their British or European counterparts. For the most part, however, urban working people had access to a greater variety of food choices than farmers, especially after canned foods became rela-

specialized ability) from the globe-hopping proletariat of unskilled workers (those who supplied muscle or tended machines). Skilled workers, frequently members of older immigrant groups, criticized the newcomers. One Irish worker complained, "There should be a law . . . to keep all the Italians from comin' in and takin' the bread out of the mouths of honest people."

The Irish worker's resentment brings into focus the impact racism had on America's immigrant laborers. Throughout the nineteenth century and into the twentieth, members of the educated elite as well as the uneducated viewed ethnic and even religious differences as racial characteristics, referring to the Polish or the Jewish "race." Americans judged immigrants of southern and eastern European "races" as infe-

Pittsburgh Family
This family in Pittsburgh, Pennsylvania, around the turn of the century illustrates housing common among urban workers across the nation. At first glance, it might appear that the children are gathered outside a barn or shed on a farm, rather than in the yard outside their home in the city. Their mother's clothing resembles that common among farm women, but their father is dressed unmistakably as a city man. Archives Service Center, University of Pittsburgh.

tively common toward the end of the century. Workingmen could also buy at a local saloon a five-cent beer that was served with a free lunch of sausage, cheese, beans, bread, and sauerkraut, a lunch-hour perk not available to farmers. Still, workers' need to buy food made their families' welfare dependent on their wages—no work, no wages, no food—a formula that farmers were able to avoid.

Women did the taxing, never-ending domestic labor in both urban and rural households: cooking, cleaning, washing, tending children, gardening, and more. Today, for example, when water flows from a faucet by gravity, it is easy to forget how much water weighs. During the Gilded Age, urban and rural women carried nearly every drop of water used for washing, cooking, cleaning, and drinking. A typical woman toted heavy buckets of water eight to ten times a day from a well or cistern into the house, and then carried most of it out again, hauling in a year's time some 36 tons of water—200 pounds a day—almost 150 miles.

Overall, the living standards of urban working people resembled those of farm families in many ways, despite some important differences in wages, working conditions, and unhealthy waste disposal. In general, however, when compared with the rural lives that many urban workers left behind, it is clear that urban working people did not share the dramatic improvement in living standards that was enjoyed by the Gilded Age plutocrats.

Questions for Analysis

Summarize the Argument: How did the living standards of urban working people compare with those of farmers? With those of factory owners and financiers?

Analyze the Evidence: What role did wages and working conditions play in the living standards of urban working people?

Consider the Context: Given what happened to the living standards of urban working people in the Gilded Age, what motivations did they have to leave farms and move to cities?

rior. Each wave of newcomers was deemed somehow inferior to the established residents. The Irish who criticized the Italians so harshly had themselves been stigmatized as a lesser "race" a generation earlier.

Immigrants not only brought their own religious and racial prejudices to the United States but also absorbed the popular prejudices of American culture. Social Darwinism, with its strongly racist overtones, decreed that whites stood at the top of the evolutionary ladder. But who was "white"? Skin color supposedly served as a marker for the "new" immigrants—"swarthy" Italians; dark-haired, olive-skinned Jews. But even blond, blue-eyed Poles were not considered "white." The social construction of race is nowhere more apparent than in the testimony of an Irish dockworker, who boasted that he hired only "white men," a category that he insisted excluded "Poles and Italians." For the new immigrants, Americanization and assimilation would prove inextricably part of becoming "white."

For African Americans, the cities of the North promised not just economic opportunity but an escape from institutionalized segregation and persecution. Throughout the South, Jim Crow laws—restrictions that segregated blacks—became common in the decades following Reconstruction. Intimidation and lynching terrorized blacks. "To die from the bite of frost is far more glorious than at the hands of a mob," proclaimed the *Defender*, Chicago's largest African American newspaper. In the 1890s, many blacks moved north, settling for the most part in the growing cities. Racism relegated them to poor jobs and substandard living conditions, but by 1900, New York, Philadelphia, and Chicago had the largest black communities in the nation. Although the most significant African American migration out of the South would occur during and after World War I, the great exodus was already under way.

On the West Coast, Asian immigrants became scapegoats of the changing economy. Hard times in the 1870s made them a target for disgruntled workers, who dismissed them as "coolie" labor. Contract laborers recruited by employers, or later by prosperous members of their own race or ethnicity, represented the antithesis of free labor to the workers who competed with them. In the West, the issue became racialized, and while the Chinese were by no means the only contract laborers, the Sinophobia that produced the scapegoat of the "coolie" permeated the labor movement. Prohibited from owning land, the Chinese migrated to the cities. In 1870, San Francisco housed a Chinese population estimated at 12,022, and it continued to grow until passage of the Chinese Exclusion Act in 1882 (see "The Diverse Peoples of the West" in chapter 17). For the first time in the nation's history, U.S. law excluded an immigrant group on the basis of race.

Some Chinese managed to come to America using a loophole in the exclusion law that allowed relatives to join their families. Meanwhile the number of Japanese immigrants rapidly grew until pressure to keep out all Asians led in 1910 to the creation of an immigration station at Angel Island in San Francisco Bay, where immigrants were quarantined until judged fit to enter the United States.

On the East Coast, the volume of immigration from Europe in the last two decades of the century proved unprecedented. In 1888 alone, more than half a million Europeans landed in America, 75 percent of them in New York City. The Statue of Liberty, erected in 1886 as a gift from the people of France, stood sentinel in the harbor.

A young Jewish woman named Emma Lazarus penned the verse inscribed on Lady Liberty's base:

> Give me your tired, your poor,
> Your huddled masses yearning to breathe
> free,
> The wretched refuse of your teeming shore.
> Send these, the homeless, tempest-tost to me,
> I lift my lamp beside the golden door!

Lazarus's poem stood as both a promise and a warning. With increasing immigration, some Americans soon would question whether the country really wanted the "huddled masses" or the "wretched refuse" of the world.

The tide of immigrants to New York City soon swamped the immigration office in lower Manhattan. After the federal government took over immigration in 1890, it built a facility on **Ellis Island**, in New York harbor, which opened in 1892. After fire gutted the wooden building, a new brick edifice replaced it in 1900. Able to process 5,000 immigrants a day, it was already inadequate by the time it opened. Its overcrowded halls became the gateway to the United States for millions.

To many Americans the new southern and eastern European immigrants appeared backward, uneducated, and outlandish in appearance—impossible to assimilate. "These people are not Americans," editorialized the popular journal *Public Opinion*, "they are the very scum and offal of Europe." Terence V. Powderly, head of the broadly inclusive Knights of Labor, complained that the newcomers "herded together like animals and lived like beasts." Blue-blooded Yankees led by Senator Henry Cabot Lodge of Massachusetts formed an unlikely alliance with leaders of organized labor—who feared that immigrants would drive down wages—to press for immigration restrictions. In 1896, Congress approved a literacy test for immigrants, but President Grover Cleveland promptly vetoed it. "It is said," the president reminded Congress, "that the quality of recent immigration is undesirable. The time is quite within recent memory when the same thing was said of immigrants who, with their descendants, are now numbered among our best citizens."

Immigrant Mothers and Children
Like many other immigrants, these mothers and children in New York City lived in crowded, run-down apartments. Packed together on the rude bench, the small children cling to their mothers in the presence of the photographer, Lewis Hine, who was documenting living conditions among the poor. Presumably the men in these families were at work when the photographer visited their home. Science & Society Picture Library/Getty Images.

The Social Geography of the City

During the Gilded Age, the social geography of the city changed enormously. Cleveland, Ohio, provides a good example. In the 1870s, Cleveland was a small city in both population and area. Oil magnate John D. Rockefeller could, and often did, walk from his large brick house on Euclid Avenue to his office downtown. On his way, he passed the small homes of his clerks and other middle-class families. Behind these homes ran miles of alleys crowded with the dwellings of Cleveland's working class. Farther out, on the shores of Lake Erie, close to the factories and foundries, clustered the shanties of the city's poorest laborers.

Within two decades, the Cleveland that Rockefeller knew no longer existed. The coming of mass transit transformed the walking city. In its place emerged a central business district surrounded by concentric rings of residences organized by ethnicity and income. First the horsecar in the 1870s and then the electric streetcar in the 1880s made it possible for those who could afford the five-cent fare to work downtown and flee after work to the "cool green rim" of the city. Social segregation—the separation of rich and poor, and of ethnic and old-stock Americans—became one of the major social changes engendered by the rise of the industrial metropolis.

Race and ethnicity affected the way cities evolved. Newcomers to the nation's cities faced hostility and, not surprisingly, sought out their kin and countryfolk as they struggled to get ahead. Distinct ethnic neighborhoods often formed around a synagogue or church. African Americans typically experienced the greatest residential segregation, but every large city had its distinct ethnic neighborhoods—Little Italy, Chinatown, Bohemia Flats, Germantown—where English was rarely spoken.

Poverty, crowding, dirt, and disease constituted the daily reality of New York City's immigrant poor—a plight documented by photojournalist Jacob Riis in his best-selling book *How the Other Half Lives* (1890). By taking his camera into the hovels of the poor, Riis opened the nation's eyes to the filthy, overcrowded conditions in the city's slums (see chapter 21, "Analyzing Historical Evidence," page 600).

However, Riis's book, like his photographs, presented a world of black and white. There were many layers to the population Riis labeled "the other half"—distinctions deepened by ethnicity,

VISUAL ACTIVITY

The Arrival of the Electric Streetcar

The electric streetcar was part of the transformation of the cityscape in the late nineteenth century. This shiny new streetcar stands in front of Cincinnati's City Hall in 1890. Corbis.

READING THE IMAGE: What other type of transportation is pictured here, and what do you see that suggests the electric streetcar would be cleaner for the immediate environment?

CONNECTIONS: What did the coming of mass transit mean to the social geography of the city?

religion, race, and gender. *How the Other Half Lives* must be read more as a reformer's call to action than as an entirely accurate portrayal of the varied and complex lives of "the other half." But it served its purpose. Tenement reform and city playgrounds grew out of Riis's exposé.

While Riis's audience shivered at his revelations about the "other half," many middle-class Americans worried equally about the excesses of the wealthy. They feared the class antagonism fueled by the growing chasm between rich and poor and shared Riis's view that "the real danger to society comes not only from the tenements, but from the ill-spent wealth which reared them."

The excesses of the Gilded Age's newly minted millionaires were nowhere more visible than in the lifestyle of the Vanderbilts. Cornelius "Commodore" Vanderbilt, the uncouth ferryman who built the New York Central Railroad, died in 1877. Today he still holds first place among the richest men in America (when adjusted for inflation). He left his son William $90 million.

William doubled the sum, and his two sons proceeded to spend it on Fifth Avenue mansions and "cottages" in Newport, Rhode Island, that sought to rival the palaces of Europe. Alva Vanderbilt, looked down on by the old-money matrons of New York, launched herself into New York society in 1883 with a costume party so opulent that her detractors had to cave in and accept her invitation. Alice Vanderbilt, her sister, topped all the guests by appearing as that miraculous new invention, the electric light, resplendent in a white satin evening dress studded with diamonds. The *New York World* speculated that Alva's party cost more than a quarter of a million dollars, more than $5 million in today's dollars.

Such ostentatious displays of wealth became especially alarming when they were coupled with disdain for the well-being of ordinary people. When a reporter in 1882 asked William Vanderbilt whether he considered the public good when running his railroads, he shot back, "The public be damned." The fear that America had become a plutocracy—a society ruled by the rich—gained credence from the fact that the wealthiest 1 percent of the population owned more than half the real and personal property in the country. As the new century dawned, reformers would form a progressive movement to address the problems of urban industrialism and the substandard living and working conditions it produced.

REVIEW　Why did American cities experience explosive growth in the late nineteenth century?

▶ At Work in Industrial America

The number of industrial wageworkers in the United States exploded in the second half of the nineteenth century, more than tripling from 5.3 million in 1860 to 17.4 million in 1900. These workers toiled in a variety of settings. Many skilled workers and artisans still earned a living in small workshops. But with the rise of corporate capitalism, large factories, mills, and mines increasingly dotted the landscape. Sweatshops and the contracting out of piecework, including finishing garments by hand, provided work experiences different from those of factory operatives and industrial workers. Pick-and-shovel labor constituted the lowest-paid labor, while managers, as well as women "typewriters" and salesclerks, formed a new white-collar segment of America's workforce. Children also worked in growing numbers in mills and mines across the country.

America's Diverse Workers

Common laborers formed the backbone of the American labor force. They built the railroads and subways, tunneled under New York's East River to anchor the Brooklyn Bridge, and helped lay the foundation of industrial America. These "human machines" generally came from the most recent immigrant groups. Initially, the Irish wielded the picks and shovels that built American cities, but by the turn of the century, as the Irish bettered their lot, Slavs and Italians took up their tools.

At the opposite end of labor's hierarchy stood skilled craftsmen like iron puddler James J. Davis, a Welsh immigrant who worked in the Pennsylvania mills. Using brains along with brawn, puddlers earned good wages—Davis drew up to $7 a day at a time when streetcar fare was 3 cents—when there was work. But most industry and manufacturing work in the nineteenth century remained seasonal; few workers could count on year-round pay. In addition, two major depressions twenty years apart, beginning in 1873 and 1893, brought unemployment and hardship. With no social safety net, even the best worker could not guarantee security for his family. "The fear of ending in the poor-house is one of the terrors that dog a man through life," Davis confessed.

Employers attempted to replace people with machines, breaking down skilled work into ever-smaller tasks that could be performed by unskilled factory operatives. New England's textile mills provide a classic example. Mary, a weaver at the mills in Fall River, Massachusetts, went to work in the 1880s at the age of twelve. Mechanization of the looms had reduced the job of the weaver to watching for breaks in the thread. "At first the noise is fierce, and you have to breathe the cotton all the time, but you get used to it," Mary told a reporter from the *Independent* magazine. "When the bobbin flies out and a girl gets hurt, you can't hear her shout—not if she just screams, you can't. She's got to wait, 'till you see her. . . . Lots of us is deaf."

During the 1880s, the number of foreign-born mill workers almost doubled. At Fall River, Mary and her Scots-Irish family resented the new immigrants. "The Polaks learn weavin' quick," she remarked, using a common derogatory term to identify a rival group. "They just as soon live on nothin' and work like that. But it won't do 'em much good for all they'll make out of it." Employers encouraged racial and ethnic antagonism because it inhibited labor organization.

Mechanization transformed the garment industry as well. The introduction of the foot-pedaled sewing machine in the 1850s and the use of mechanical cloth-cutting knives drove out independent tailors, who were replaced by pieceworkers. Sadie Frowne, a sixteen-year-old Polish Jew, worked in a Brooklyn **sweatshop** in the 1890s. Frowne sewed for eleven hours a day in a 20-by-14-foot room containing fourteen machines. "The machines go like mad all day, because the faster you work the more money you get," she recalled. She earned about $4.50 a week and, by rigid economy, tried to save $2. Young and single, Frowne typified the

Women at Work
Women workers labor under bright lights in this tenement hat shop in New York City. Often sweatshop workers labored in dim tenements belonging to the contractor who hired them. Garment workers frequently worked with highly combustible fabric in unsafe buildings. The Granger Collection, New York.

woman wage earner in the late nineteenth century. In 1890, the average workingwoman was twenty-two and had been working since the age of fifteen, laboring twelve hours a day six days a week and earning less than $6 a week.

The Family Economy: Women and Children

In 1900, the typical male worker in manufacturing earned $500 a year, about $12,000 in today's dollars. Many working-class families, whether native-born or immigrant, lived in or near poverty, their economic survival dependent on the contributions of all family members, regardless of sex or age. "Father," asked one young immigrant girl, "does everybody in America live like this? Go to work early, come home late, eat and go to sleep? And the next day again work, eat, and sleep?" Most workers did. The **family economy** meant that everyone contributed to maintain even the most meager household.

In the cities, boys as young as six years old plied their trades as bootblacks and newsboys. Often working under an adult contractor, these children earned as little as fifty cents a day. Many of them were homeless—orphaned or cast off by their families. "We wuz six, and we ain't got no father," a child of twelve told reporter Jacob Riis. "Some of us had to go."

Child labor increased each decade after 1870. The percentage of children under fifteen engaged in paid labor did not drop until after World War I. The 1900 census estimated that 1,750,178 children ages ten to fifteen were employed, an increase of more than a million over thirty years. Children in this age range constituted more than 18 percent of the industrial labor force.

Women working for wages in nonagricultural occupations more than doubled in number between 1870 and 1900 (Figure 19.3). Yet white married women, even among the working class, rarely worked for wages outside the home. In 1890, only 3 percent were employed. Black women, married and unmarried, worked out of the home for wages in much greater numbers. The 1890 census showed that 25 percent of married African American women were employed, often as domestics in the houses of white families.

White-Collar Workers: Managers, "Typewriters," and Salesclerks

In the late nineteenth century, a managerial revolution created a new class of white-collar workers who worked in offices and stores. As skilled workers saw their crafts replaced by mechanization, some moved into management positions. "The middle class is becoming a salaried class," a writer for the *Independent* magazine

Bootblacks
The faces and hands of the two bootblacks shown here on a New York City street in 1896 testify to their grimy trade. Boys as young as six worked as bootblacks and newsboys, often for contractors who took a cut of their meager earnings. When families could no longer afford to feed their children, young boys often headed out on their own. Library of Congress, 3a49659.

observed, "and is rapidly losing the economic and moral independence of former days." As large business organizations consolidated, corporate development separated management from ownership, and the job of directing the firm became the province of salaried executives and managers, the majority of whom were white men drawn from the 8 percent of Americans who held high school diplomas.

Until late in the century, when engineering schools began to supply recruits, many skilled workers moved from the shop floor to positions of considerable responsibility. Captain William "Billy" Jones, son of a Welsh immigrant, grew up in the heat of the blast furnaces, where he worked as an apprentice at the age of ten. Jones, by all accounts the best steelman in the business, took as his motto "Good wages and good workmen." In 1872 Andrew Carnegie hired Jones as general superintendent of his new Pittsburgh steelworks. Although Carnegie constantly tried to force down workers' pay, Jones resisted, and he succeeded in shortening the shift from twelve to eight hours by convincing Carnegie that shorter hours reduced absenteeism and accidents. Jones demanded and received "a hell of a big salary"—$25,000, the same as the president of the United States.

The new white-collar workforce also included women **"typewriters"** and salesclerks. In the decades after the Civil War, as businesses became larger and more far-flung, the need for more elaborate and exact records, as well as the greater volume of correspondence, led to the hiring of more office workers. The adding machine, the cash register, and the typewriter came into general use in the 1880s. Employers seeking literate workers soon turned to nimble-fingered women.

FIGURE 19.3 Women and Work, 1870–1890
In 1870, close to 1.5 million women worked in nonagricultural occupations. By 1890, that number had more than doubled to 3.7 million. More and more women sought work in manufacturing and mechanical industries, although domestic service still constituted the largest employment arena for women.

Chart: Women (in thousands), y-axis from 500 to 5,000; x-axis years 1870, 1880, 1890. Legend: Domestic and personal service; Manufacturing and mechanical industries; Trade and transportation.

Office Machine Sales Booth
Mechanization of office work involved far more than the typewriter. Shown here is the Edison Company sales booth at a trade show in Madison Square Garden featuring "business phonographs" to play advertising messages, "numbering machines" to stamp consecutive numbers on office invoices, and "Daus' Tip Top," a device that made copies of hand-written or typed documents. Women clerks (on the right) used the machines to entice male customers to mechanize their own offices. © Museum of the City of New York, USA/Bridgeman Images.

Educated men had many other career choices, but for middle-class white women, secretarial work constituted one of the very few areas where they could put their literacy to use for wages.

Sylvie Thygeson was typical of the young women who went to work as secretaries. Thygeson grew up in an Illinois prairie town and went to work as a country schoolteacher after graduating high school in 1884. Realizing that teaching school did not pay a living wage, she mastered typing and stenography and found work as a secretary to help support her family. According to her account, she made "a fabulous sum of money" (possibly $25 a month). Nevertheless, she gave up her job after a few years when she met and married her husband.

But by the 1890s, secretarial work was the overwhelming choice of native-born, single white women, who constituted more than 90 percent of the female clerical force. Not only considered more genteel than factory work or domestic labor, office work also meant more money for shorter hours. In 1883, Boston's clerical workers on average made more than $6 a week, compared with less than $5 for women working in manufacturing.

As a new consumer culture came to dominate American urban life in the late nineteenth century, department stores offered another employment opportunity for women in the cities. Boasting ornate facades, large plate-glass display windows, and marble and brass fixtures, stores such as Macy's in New York, Wanamaker's in Philadelphia, and Marshall Field in Chicago stood as monuments to the material promise of the era. Within these palaces of consumption, cash girls, stock clerks, and wrappers earned as little as $3 a week, while at the top of the scale, buyers like Belle Cushman of the fancy goods department at Macy's earned $25 a week, an unusually high salary for a woman in the 1870s. Salesclerks counted themselves a cut above factory workers. Their work was neither dirty nor dangerous, and even when they earned less than factory workers, they felt a sense of superiority.

> **REVIEW** How did business expansion and consolidation change workers' occupations in the late nineteenth century?

▶ Workers Organize

By the late nineteenth century, industrial workers were losing ground in the workplace. In the fierce competition to reduce prices and cut costs, industrialists invested heavily in new machinery that replaced skilled workers with unskilled labor. The erosion of skills and the redefinition of labor as mere "machine tending" left the worker with a growing sense of individual helplessness that spurred collective action. The 1870s and 1880s witnessed the emergence of two labor unions—the Knights of Labor and the American Federation of Labor. In 1877, in the midst of a depression, labor flexed its muscle in the Great Railroad Strike. But unionism would suffer a major setback after the mysterious Haymarket bombing in 1886.

The Great Railroad Strike of 1877

Economic depression following the panic of 1873 threw as many as three million people out of work. Those who were lucky enough to keep their jobs watched as pay cuts eroded wages until they could no longer feed their families. In the summer of 1877, the Baltimore and Ohio (B&O) Railroad announced a 10 percent wage cut at the same time it declared a 10 percent dividend to its stockholders. Angry brakemen in West Virginia, whose wages had already fallen from $70 to $30 a month, walked out on strike. One B&O worker described the hardship that drove him to take such desperate action: "We eat our hard bread and tainted meat two days old on the sooty cars up the road, and when we come home, find our wives complaining that they cannot even buy hominy and molasses for food."

The West Virginia brakemen's strike touched off the **Great Railroad Strike** of 1877, a nationwide uprising that spread rapidly to Pittsburgh and Chicago, St. Louis and San Francisco (Map 19.3). Within a few days, nearly 100,000 railroad workers had walked off the job. An estimated 500,000 sympathetic railway workers soon joined the strikers. In Reading, Pennsylvania,

---

Map 19.3 The Great Railroad Strike of 1877
Starting in West Virginia and Pennsylvania, the strike spread as far north as Albany, New York, and as far west as San Francisco, bringing rail traffic to a standstill. Called the Great Uprising, the strike heralded the beginning of a new era of working-class protest and trade union organization.

🔆 Strike activity

Destruction from the Great Railroad Strike of 1877
Pictures of the devastation caused in Pittsburgh during the strike shocked many Americans. When militiamen fired on striking workers, killing more than twenty strikers, the mob retaliated by destroying a two-mile area along the track, reducing it to a smoldering rubble. Property damage totaled $2 million. In the aftermath, the curious came out to view the destruction. Carnegie Library of Pittsburgh.

militiamen refused to fire on the strikers, saying, "We may be militiamen, but we are workmen first." Rail traffic ground to a halt; the nation lay paralyzed.

Violence erupted as the strike spread. In Pittsburgh, militia brought in from Philadelphia fired on the crowds, killing more than twenty people. Angry workers retaliated by reducing an area two miles long beside the tracks to rubble. Before the day ended, the militia shot twenty workers and the railroad sustained more than $2 million in property damage.

Within eight days, the governors of nine states, acting at the prompting of the railroad owners and managers, defined the strike as an "insurrection" and called for federal troops. President Rutherford B. Hayes, after hesitating briefly, called out the army. By the time the troops arrived, the violence had run its course. Federal

troops did not shoot a single striker in 1877. But they struck a blow against labor by acting as strikebreakers—opening rail traffic, protecting nonstriking "scab" train crews, and maintaining peace along the line. In three weeks, the strike was over.

Middle-class Americans initially sympathized with the conditions that led to the strike. But they quickly condemned the strikers for the violence and property damage that occurred. The *New York Times* editorialized about the "dangerous classes," and the *Independent* magazine offered the following advice on how to deal with "rioters": "If the club of a policeman, knocking out the brains of the rioter, will answer then well and good; but if it does not promptly meet the exigency, then bullets and bayonets . . . constitutes the one remedy and one duty of the hour."

"The strikes have been put down by force," President Hayes noted in his diary on August 5. "But now for the real remedy. Can't something be done by education of the strikers, by judicious control of the capitalists, by wise general policy to end or diminish the evil? The railroad strikers, as a rule, are good men, sober, intelligent, and industrious." While Hayes acknowledged the workers' grievances, most businessmen condemned the idea of labor unions as agents of class warfare. For their part, workers quickly recognized that they held little power individually and flocked to join unions. As labor leader Samuel Gompers noted, the nation's first national strike dramatized the frustration and unity of the workers and served as an alarm bell to labor "that sounded a ringing message of hope to us all."

The Knights of Labor and the American Federation of Labor

The **Knights of Labor**, the first mass organization of America's working class, proved the chief beneficiary of labor's newfound consciousness. The Noble and Holy Order of the Knights of Labor had been founded in 1869 as a secret society of workers who envisioned a "universal brotherhood" of all workers, from common laborers to master craftsmen. Secrecy and ritual served to bind Knights together at the same time that they discouraged company spies and protected members from reprisals.

Although the Knights played no active role in the 1877 railroad strike, membership swelled as a result of the growing interest in labor organizing that followed the strike. In 1878, the Knights abandoned secrecy and launched an ambitious campaign to organize workers. (See "Analyzing Historical Evidence," page 544.)

The Knights attempted to bridge the boundaries of ethnicity, gender, ideology, race, and occupation. Leonora Barry served as general investigator for women's work from 1886 to 1890, helping the Knights recruit teachers, waitresses, housewives, and domestics along with factory and sweatshop workers. Women composed perhaps 20 percent of the membership. The Knights also recruited more than 95,000 black workers. That the Knights of Labor often fell short of its goals to unify the working class proved less surprising than the scope of its efforts.

Under the direction of Grand Master Workman Terence V. Powderly, the Knights became the dominant force in labor during the 1880s. The organization advocated a kind of workers' democracy that embraced reforms including public ownership of the railroads, an income tax, equal pay for women workers, and the abolition of child labor. It called for one big union to create a cooperative commonwealth that would supplant the wage system and remove class distinctions. Only the "parasitic" members of society—gamblers, stockbrokers, lawyers, bankers, and liquor dealers—were denied membership.

The Knights of Labor was not without rivals. Many skilled workers belonged to craft unions organized by trade. Among the largest and richest of these unions stood the Amalgamated Association of Iron and Steel Workers, founded in 1876 and counting twenty thousand skilled workers as members. Trade unionists spurned the broad reform goals of the Knights and focused on workplace issues. Samuel Gompers founded the Organized Trades and Labor Unions in 1881 and reorganized it in 1886 into the **American Federation of Labor (AFL)**, which coordinated the activities of craft unions throughout the United States. His plan was simple: Organize skilled workers such as machinists and locomotive engineers—those with the most bargaining power—and use strikes to gain immediate objectives such as higher pay and better working conditions. Gompers at first drew few converts. The AFL had only 138,000 members in 1886, compared with 730,000 for the Knights of Labor. But events soon brought down the Knights, and Gompers's brand of unionism came to prevail.

Haymarket and the Specter of Labor Radicalism

While the AFL and the Knights of Labor competed for members, more radical labor groups, including socialists and anarchists, believed that reform was futile and called instead for social revolution. Both the socialists and the anarchists, sensitive to criticism that they preferred revolution in theory to improvements here and now, rallied around the popular issue of the eight-hour day.

Since the 1840s, labor had sought to end the twelve-hour workday, which was standard in industry and manufacturing. By the mid-1880s, it seemed clear to many workers that labor shared too little in the new prosperity of the decade, and pressure mounted for the eight-hour day. Labor championed the popular issue and launched major rallies in cities across the nation. Supporters of the movement set May 1, 1886, as the date for a nationwide general strike in support of the eight-hour workday.

The Songs of the Knights of Labor

From the 1870s, the Knights of Labor knew the power of song to knit together a movement. The Knights reported joyous singing scattered throughout its meetings. Glee clubs, bands, and quartets made up significant components of the local unions, uniting workers across the bounds of literacy. Songbooks, broadsides, and clippings testify to the role music played in union building and solidarity. The Knights' first songbook appeared in 1886. In the lyrics are found the values and virtues of fraternalism and the significance of the Order. Songs focused on corruption, greed, hypocrisy, tyranny, and workers' need to unite to bring things right. These early songs form a part of America's legacy of social protest.

DOCUMENT 1
"Storm the Fort"

This rousing anthem, written in 1882 by Thomas W. "Old Beeswax" Taylor and sung during the Homestead lockout, became the trademark song of the Knights of Labor. It lays out the Knights' vision of a new economic landscape in which the producers have replaced the idle rich and created a new political and social order.

Chorus
Toiling millions now are waking,
See them marching on:
All the tyrants now are shaking,
Ere their power is gone.

Chorus
Storm the fort ye Knights of Labor,
Battle for your cause;
Equal rights for every neighbor
Down with tyrant laws!

Lazy drones steal all the honey
From hard labor's hives;
Bankers control the nation's money
And destroy our lives.

Chorus
Do not load the workman's shoulder
With an unjust debt;
Do not let the rich bondholder
Live by blood and sweat.

Chorus
Why should those who fought for freedom
Wear old slavery's chains?
Working men will quickly break them
When they use their brains.

Source: Robert Weir, *Beyond Labor's Veil: The Culture of the Knights of Labor* (University Park: Pennsylvania State University Press, 1996), 103.

DOCUMENT 2
"The Noble Knights of Labor"

The Knights celebrated its history in song, going back to its founding in 1869 and celebrating Uriah Stephens, the Order's first leader. By using song as oral history, the Knights kept its origins alive.

In the year of sixty-nine they commenced to fall in line,
The great Knights, the noble Knights of Labor.
Like the good old Knights of old, they cannot be bought or sold.
U.S. Stephens was the man this great order once began
The great Knights, the noble Knights of Labor.
And he started what they say is the strongest band today
The great Knights, the noble Knights of Labor.
Bless the mind that gave them birth, they're the finest men on Earth.

Source: Philip S. Foner, *American Labor Songs of the Nineteenth Century* (Urbana: University of Illinois Press, 1975), 148.

DOCUMENT 3
"The Knights of Labor Song"

Kansas Knight Francis Goodwin penned this rousing song. Exhorting workers to organize, the Knights of Labor sang of vanquishing its foes and achieving justice. The song underlines the radical vision of the Knights, who wanted, in the words of a recent historian, "not just a larger piece of the pie, but a new recipe for a different kind of pie."

Ye valiant Knights of Labor, rise,
Unfurl your banners to the skies,
And go to work and organize.
    Until the world is won.
See the lordly nabobs* quake,
See the politicians shake,
Labor now is wide awake.
    Justice will be done.

*The rich.

Source: Weir, *Beyond Labor's Veil*, 111–12.

DOCUMENT 4
"Organize the Hosts of Labor"

Will Minnick, a coal miner from Iowa, wrote in this song about the universality of the Knights' cause. Note that he includes industrial laborers, miners, and farmers as brother toilers who will organize and depose the nonproducing owners.

Organize the hosts of labor
    In one common brotherhood
He who drives the locomotive
    And the one who turns the sod.

Those who dig the dusky diamonds,
    And produce the shining gold.
Those in factory and in workshop,
    Bring them to the shepherd's fold. . . .

Give them through united effort,
    Organize and drill with care
In the tactics of our Order
    Knighthood teaches everywhere.

Moving on in one direction,
    Labor's cause to guard and guide

By the wise and wholesome council
    Each assembly shall provide.

Source: Weir, *Beyond Labor's Veil*, 112–13.

DOCUMENT 5
"Only the Working Class"

The Knights of Labor employed Leonora Barry to organize women workers. At its peak, there were 50,000 female Knights. But male attitudes toward manliness and the fraternal ties that bound workers clashed with the women's belief in class over gender solidarity. An Ontario "sister" argued in the following lines that women made good Knights and had a key role to play in the struggle to liberate the working class.

It is not any woman's part
    We often hear folks say,
And it will mar our womanhood
    To mingle in the fray.
I fear I will never understand,
    Or realize it quite,
How a woman's fame can suffer
    In struggling for the right.

Source: Weir, *Beyond Labor's Veil*, 184.

Questions for Analysis

Consider the Context: How did the Knights of Labor address the vast disparity of wealth in the Gilded Age?

Recognize Viewpoints: Who is the enemy the Knights want to overthrow? What specific goals or perspectives are addressed in the song lyrics?

Analyze the Evidence: In what ways is the vision of the Knights of Labor political and social as well as economic? What role do women play in the Knights?

All factions of the labor movement came together in Chicago on May Day. A group of labor radicals led by anarchist Albert Parsons, a *Mayflower* descendant, and August Spies, a German socialist, spearheaded the eight-hour movement in Chicago. Chicago's Knights of Labor rallied to the cause even though Powderly and the union's national leadership, worried about the increasing activism of the rank and file, refused to endorse the movement for shorter hours. Gompers was also on hand to lead the city's trade unionists, although he privately urged the AFL assemblies not to participate in the general strike.

The cautious labor leaders in their frock coats and starched shirts stood in sharp contrast to the dispossessed workers out on strike across town at Chicago's huge McCormick reaper works. There strikers watched helplessly as the company brought in strikebreakers to take their jobs and marched the "scabs" to work under the protection of the Chicago police and security guards supplied by the Pinkerton Detective Agency. Cyrus McCormick Jr., son of the inventor of the mechanical reaper, viewed labor organization as a threat to his power as well as to his profits; he was determined to smash the union.

During the May Day rally, 45,000 workers paraded peacefully down Michigan Avenue in support of the eight-hour day. Many sang what had become the movement's anthem:

> We want to feel the sunshine;
> We want to smell the flowers,
> We're sure that God has willed it,
> And we mean to have eight hours.
> Eight hours for work, eight hours for rest,
> Eight hours for what we will!

Trouble came two days later, when strikers attacked strikebreakers outside the McCormick works and police opened fire, killing or wounding six men. Angry radicals urged workers to "arm yourselves and appear in full force" at a rally in Haymarket Square.

On the evening of May 4, the turnout at Haymarket was disappointing. No more than two or three thousand gathered in the drizzle to hear Spies, Parsons, and the other speakers. Mayor Carter Harrison, known as a friend of labor, mingled conspicuously in the crowd, pronounced the meeting peaceable, and went home to bed. Sometime later, police captain John "Blackjack" Bonfield marched his men into the crowd, by now fewer than three hundred people, and demanded that it disperse.

VISUAL ACTIVITY

"The Chicago Riot"
Inflammatory pamphlets published in the wake of the Haymarket bombing aimed to scare the public. In this charged atmosphere, the anarchist speakers at the rally were tried and convicted for the bombing even though witnesses testified that none of them had thrown the bomb. Even today, the identity of the bomb thrower remains uncertain. © Chicago History Museum, USA/ Bridgeman Images.
READING THE IMAGE: What does the cover suggest about the views of the author of the pamphlet?
CONNECTIONS: In what ways does this pamphlet reflect the public climate following the Haymarket bombing?

Suddenly, someone threw a bomb into the police ranks. After a moment of stunned silence, the police drew their revolvers. "Fire and kill all you can," shouted a police lieutenant. When the melee ended, seven policemen and an unknown number of others lay dead. An additional sixty policemen and thirty or forty civilians suffered injuries.

News of the "Haymarket riot" provoked a nationwide convulsion of fear, followed by blind rage directed at anarchists, labor unions, strikers, immigrants, and the working class in general. Eight men, including Parsons and Spies, went on trial in Chicago. "Convict these men," thundered the state's attorney, Julius S. Grinnell, "make examples of them, hang them, and you save our institutions." Although the state could not link any of the defendants to the **Haymarket bombing**, the jury nevertheless found them all guilty. Four men were hanged, one committed suicide, and three received prison sentences.

The bomb blast at Haymarket had lasting repercussions. To commemorate the death of the Haymarket martyrs, labor made May 1 an annual international celebration of the worker. But the Haymarket bomb, in the eyes of one observer, proved "a godsend to all enemies of the labor movement." It effectively scotched the eight-hour-day movement and dealt a blow to the Knights of Labor. With the labor movement everywhere under attack, many skilled workers turned to the AFL. Gompers's narrow economic strategy made sense at the time and enabled one segment of the workforce—the skilled—to organize effectively and achieve tangible gains.

REVIEW   Why did membership in the Knights of Labor rise in the late 1870s and decline in the 1890s?

▶ At Home and at Play

The growth of urban industrialism not only dramatically altered the workplace but also transformed home and family life, and it gave rise to new forms of commercialized leisure. Industrialization redefined the very concepts of work and home. Increasingly, men went out to work for wages, while most white married women stayed home, either working in the home without pay—cleaning, cooking, and rearing children—or supervising paid domestic servants who did the housework.

Domesticity and "Domestics"

The separation of the workplace and the home that marked the shift to industrial society led to a new ideology, one that sentimentalized the home and women's role in it. The cultural idea that dictated a woman's place was in the home, where she would create a haven for her family, began to develop in the early 1800s. It has been called the **cult of domesticity**, a phrase used to prescribe an ideal of middle-class, white womanhood that dominated the period from 1820 to the end of the nineteenth century.

The cult of domesticity and the elaboration of the middle-class home led to a major change in patterns of hiring household help. The live-in servant, or domestic, became a fixture in the North, replacing the hired girl of the previous century. In American cities by 1870, 15 to 30 percent of all households included live-in domestic servants, more than 90 percent of them women. Earlier in the mid-nineteenth century, native-born women increasingly took up other work and left domestic service to immigrants. In the East, the maid was so often Irish that "Bridget" became a generic term for female domestics. The South continued to rely on poorly paid black female "help."

Servants by all accounts resented the long hours and lack of privacy. "She is liable to be rung up at all hours," one study of domestics reported. "Her very meals are not secure from interruption, and even her sleep is not sacred." Domestic service became the occupation of last resort, a "hard and lonely life" in the words of one female servant.

For women of the white middle class, domestics were a boon, freeing them from household drudgery and giving them more time to spend with their children, to pursue club work, or to work for reforms. Thus, while domestic service supported the cult of domesticity, it created for those women who could afford it opportunities that expanded their horizons outside the home. They became involved in women's clubs as well as the temperance and suffrage movements.

Cheap Amusements

Growing class divisions manifested themselves in patterns of leisure as well as in work and home life. The poor and working class took their leisure, when they had any, not in the crowded tenements that housed their families but increasingly in the cities' new dance halls, music houses, ballparks, and amusement arcades, which by the 1890s formed a familiar part of the urban landscape.

Young workingwomen no longer met prospective husbands only through their families. Fleeing crowded tenements, the young sought each other's company in dance halls and other commercial retreats. Young workingwomen counted on being "treated" by men, a transaction

VISUAL ACTIVITY

Beach Scene at Coney Island

Coney Island became a symbol of commercialized leisure and mechanical excitement at the turn of the century. This fanciful rendering of Coney Island captures men and women frolicking in the waves. Notice the modest woolen bathing outfits. Men box and play ball, a woman flies on a parachute, and a uniformed policeman wades into the fray, while the Ferris wheel dominates onshore. Library of Congress, var.2117.

READING THE IMAGE: What does the scene present as the mood at Coney Island, and what does it tell us about who visited Coney Island and who didn't?

CONNECTIONS: Many reformers worried about the moral temptations mass leisure afforded city workers. Why?

that often implied sexual payback. Their behavior sometimes blurred the line between respectability and promiscuity. The dance halls became a favorite target of reformers who feared they lured teenage girls into prostitution.

For men, baseball became a national pastime in the 1870s—then, as now, one force in urban life capable of uniting a city across class lines. Cincinnati mounted the first entirely paid team, the Red Stockings, in 1869. Soon professional teams proliferated in cities across the nation, and Mark Twain hailed baseball as "the very symbol, the outward and visible expression, of the drive and push and rush and struggle of the raging, tearing, booming nineteenth century."

The increasing commercialization of entertainment in the late-nineteenth-century city was best seen at Coney Island. A two-mile stretch of sand nine miles from Manhattan by trolley or steamship, Coney Island in the 1890s was transformed into the site of some of the largest and most elaborate amusement parks in the country. Promoter George Tilyou built Steeplechase Park in 1897, advertising "10 hours of fun for 10 cents." With its mechanical thrills and fun-house laughs, the amusement park

encouraged behavior that one schoolteacher aptly described as "everyone with the brakes off." By 1900, as many as a million New Yorkers flocked to Coney Island on any given weekend, making the amusement park the unofficial capital of a new mass culture.

> REVIEW   How did urban industrialism shape home life and the world of leisure?

▶ City Growth and City Government

Private enterprise, not city planners, built the cities of the United States. With a few notable exceptions, cities simply mushroomed, formed by the dictates of profit and the exigencies of local politics. With the rise of the city came the need for public facilities, transportation, and services that would tax the imaginations of America's architects and engineers and set the scene for the rough-and-tumble of big-city government, politics, and bossism.

Chicago Street
This lantern slide depicts State Street, a major commercial thoroughfare in Chicago about 1890. The modern skyscraper (center right) contrasts with the dirt road and horse-pulled wagons. The number of horses and people in the photo is about the same. Notice that rules of the road familiar today did not exist; wagons traveled any part of the road in any direction. Pedestrians crowded along the sidewalk, avoiding the danger and dirt of the street. Imagno/Getty Images.

Building Cities of Stone and Steel

Skyscrapers and mighty bridges dominated the imagination and the urban landscape. Less imposing but no less significant were the paved streets, the parks and public libraries, and the subways and sewers. In the late nineteenth century, Americans rushed to embrace new technology of all kinds, making their cities the most modern in the world.

Structural steel made enormous advances in building possible. A decade after the completion of the Brooklyn Bridge, engineers used the new technology to construct the Williamsburg Bridge. More prosaic and utilitarian than its neighbor, the new bridge was never as acclaimed,

but it was longer by four feet and completed in half the time. It became the model for future building as the age of steel supplanted the age of stone and iron.

Chicago, not New York, gave birth to the modern skyscraper. Rising from the ashes of the Great Fire of 1871, which destroyed three square miles and left eighteen thousand people homeless, Chicago offered a generation of skilled architects and engineers the chance to experiment. Commercial architecture became an art form at the hands of a skilled group of architects who together constituted the "Chicago school." Employing the dictum "Form follows function," they built startlingly modern structures.

Across the United States, municipal governments undertook public works on a scale never before seen. They paved streets, built sewers and water mains, replaced gas lamps with electric lights, ran trolley tracks on the old horsecar lines, and dug underground to build subways, tearing down the unsightly elevated tracks that had clogged city streets. Boston completed the nation's first subway system in 1897, and New York and Philadelphia soon followed.

Cities became more beautiful with the creation of urban public parks to complement the new buildings that quickly filled city lots. Much of the credit for America's greatest parks goes to one man—landscape architect Frederick Law Olmsted. New York City's Central Park, completed in 1873, became the first landscaped public park in the United States. Olmsted and his partner, Calvert Vaux, directed the planting of more than five million trees, shrubs, and vines to transform the eight hundred acres between 59th and 110th streets into an oasis for urban dwellers. "We want a place," he wrote, where people "may stroll for an hour, seeing, hearing, and feeling nothing of the bustle and jar of the streets."

American cities did not overlook the mind in their efforts at improvement. They created a comprehensive free public school system that educated everyone from the children of the middle class to the sons and daughters of immigrant workers. Yet the exploding urban population strained the system and led to crowded and inadequate facilities. In 1899, more than 544,000 pupils attended school in New York's five boroughs. Municipalities across the United States provided free secondary school education for all who wished to attend, even though only 8 percent of Americans completed high school.

To educate those who couldn't go to school, American cities created the most extensive free public library system in the world. In 1895, the Boston Public Library opened its bronze doors in its new Copley Square location under the inscription "Free to All." Designed in the style of a Renaissance palazzo, with more than 700,000 books on the shelves ready to be checked out, the library earned the description "a palace of the people."

Despite the Boston Public Library's legend "Free to All," the poor did not share equally in the advantages of city life. The parks, the libraries, and even the subways and sewers benefited some city dwellers more than others. Few library cards were held by Boston's laborers, who worked six days a week and found the library closed on Sunday. And in the 1890s, there was nothing central about New York's Central Park. It was a four-mile walk from the tenements of Hester Street to the park's entrance at 59th Street and Fifth Avenue. Then, as now, the comfortable, not the indigent, reaped a disproportionate share of the benefits in the nation's big cities.

Any story of the American city, it seems, must be a tale of two cities—or, given the cities' great diversity, a tale of many cities within each metropolis. At the turn of the twentieth century, a central paradox emerged: The enduring monuments of America's cities—the bridges, skyscrapers, parks, and libraries—stood as the undeniable achievements of the same system of municipal government that reformers dismissed as boss-ridden, criminal, and corrupt.

City Government and the "Bosses"

The physical growth of the cities required the expansion of public services and the creation of entirely new facilities: streets, subways, elevated trains, bridges, docks, sewers, and public utilities. There was work to be done and money to be made. The professional politician—the colorful big-city boss—became a phenomenon of urban growth and **bossism** a national phenomenon. Though corrupt and often criminal, the boss saw to the building of the city and provided needed social services for the new residents in return for their political support. Yet not even the big-city boss could be said to rule the unruly city. The governing of America's cities resembled more a tug-of-war than boss rule.

The most notorious of all the city bosses was William Marcy "Boss" Tweed of New York. At midcentury, Boss Tweed's Democratic Party "machine" held sway. A machine was really no more than a political party organized at the grassroots level. Its purpose was to win elections and reward its followers, often with jobs on the city's payroll. New York's citywide Democratic machine, Tammany Hall, commanded an army of party functionaries. They formed a shadow government more powerful than the city's elected officials.

As chairman of the Tammany general committee, Tweed kept the Democratic Party together and ran the city through the use of bribery and graft. "As long as I count the votes," he shamelessly boasted, "what are you going to do about it?" The excesses of the Tweed ring soon led to a clamor for reform and cries of "Throw the rascals out." Tweed's rule ended in 1871. Eventually, he was tried and convicted, and later died in jail. New York was not the only city to experience bossism and corruption. The British visitor James Bryce concluded in 1888, "There is no denying that the government of cities is the one conspicuous failure of the United States." More than 80 percent of the nation's thirty largest cities experienced some form of boss rule in the decades around the turn of the twentieth century. However, infighting among powerful ward bosses often meant that no single boss enjoyed exclusive power in the big cities.

Urban reformers and proponents of good government (derisively called "goo goos" by their rivals) challenged machine rule and sometimes succeeded in electing reform mayors. But the reformers rarely managed to stay in office for long. Their detractors called them "mornin' glories," observing that they "looked lovely in the mornin' and withered up in a short time." The bosses enjoyed continued success largely because the urban political machine helped the cities' immigrants and poor, who remained the bosses' staunchest allies. "What tells in holding your district," a Tammany ward boss observed, "is to go right down among the poor and help them in the different ways they need help. It's philanthropy, but it's politics, too—mighty good politics."

The big-city boss, through the skillful orchestration of rewards, exerted powerful leverage and lined up support for his party from a broad range of constituents, from the urban poor to wealthy industrialists. In 1902, when journalist Lincoln Steffens began "The Shame of the Cities," a series of articles exposing city corruption, he found that business leaders who fastidiously refused to mingle socially with the bosses nevertheless struck deals with them. "He is a self-righteous fraud, this big businessman," Steffens concluded. "I found him buying boodlers [bribers] in St. Louis, defending grafters in Minneapolis, originating corruption in Pittsburgh, sharing with bosses in Philadelphia, deploring reform in Chicago, and beating good government with corruption funds in New York."

For all the color and flamboyance of the big-city boss, he was simply one of many actors in the drama of municipal government. Old-stock aristocrats, new professionals, saloonkeepers, pushcart peddlers, and politicians all fought for their interests in the hurly-burly of city government. They didn't much like each other, and they sometimes fought savagely. But they learned to live with one another. Compromise and accommodation—not boss rule—best characterized big-city government by the turn of the twentieth century, although the cities' reputation for corruption left an indelible mark on the consciousness of the American public.

White City or City of Sin?

Americans have always been of two minds about the city. They like to boast of its skyscrapers and bridges, its culture and sophistication, and they pride themselves on its bigness and bustle. At the same time, they fear it as the city of sin, the home of immigrant slums, the center of vice and crime. Nowhere did the divided view of the American city take form more graphically than in Chicago in 1893. In that year, Chicago hosted the **World's Columbian Exposition**, the grandest world's fair in the nation's history. (See "Beyond America's Borders," page 552.) The fairground, only five miles down the shore of Lake Michigan from downtown Chicago, offered a lesson in what Americans on the eve of the twentieth century imagined a city might be. Christened the "White City," it seemed light-years away from Chicago, with its stockyards, slums, and bustling terminals. Frederick Law Olmsted and architect Daniel Burnham supervised the transformation of a swampy wasteland into a pristine paradise of lagoons, fountains, wooded islands, gardens, and imposing white buildings.

"Sell the cookstove if necessary and come," novelist Hamlin Garland wrote to his parents on the farm. And come they did, in spite of the panic and depression that broke out only weeks after the fair opened in May 1893. In six months, fairgoers purchased more than 27 million tickets, turning a profit of nearly a half million dollars for promoters. Visitors from home and abroad strolled the elaborate grounds and visited the exhibits—everything from a model of the Brooklyn Bridge carved in soap to the latest goods and inventions. Half carnival, half culture, the great fair offered something for everyone. On the Midway Plaisance, crowds thrilled to the massive wheel built by Mr. Ferris and watched agog as Little Egypt danced the hootchy-kootchy.

In October, the fair closed its doors in the midst of the worst depression the country had yet seen. During that winter, Chicago's unemployed and homeless took over the grounds, vandalized the buildings, and frightened the city's

The World's Columbian Exposition and Nineteenth-Century World's Fairs

The 1893 World's Columbian Exposition in Chicago, like the other great world's fairs of the nineteenth and twentieth centuries, represented a unique outgrowth of industrial capitalism and a testament to the expanding global market economy. The Chicago fair, named to celebrate the 400th anniversary of Columbus's arrival in the New World (the organizers missed the deadline by a year), offered a cornucopia of international exhibits, testifying to growing international influences ranging from cultural to technological exchange.

Great cities vied to host the fairs, as much to promote commercial growth as to demonstrate cultural refinement. Each successive fair sought to outdo its predecessor. Chicago's fair followed on the great success of the 1889 Universal Exposition in Paris, crowned by the 900-foot steel tower constructed by Alexandre-Gustave Eiffel. How could Chicago, a prairie upstart, top that?

The answer was to create from scratch an ideal White City with monumental architecture, landscaped grounds, and the world's first Ferris wheel. The White City celebrated the classicism of the French Beaux Arts school, with massive geometric styling and elaborate detailing borrowed from Greek, Roman, and Renaissance architecture. Prairie architects Louis Sullivan and Frank Lloyd Wright later complained the fair was a "virus" that held back modern architecture for decades.

But beneath its Renaissance facade, the White City acted as an enormous emporium dedicated to the unabashed materialism of the Gilded Age. Fairgoers could view virtually every kind of manufactured product in the world inside the imposing Manufactures and Liberal Arts Building. As suited an industrial age, manufactured products and heavy machinery drew the largest crowds. Displays introduced visitors to the latest innovations, many the result of international influences. For five cents, fairgoers could put two hard rubber tubes into their ears and listen for the first time to a gramophone playing the popular tune "The Cat Came Back." The invention, the work of a German immigrant, Emile Berliner, signaled the beginning of the recorded music industry. Later Thomas Edison claimed credit for a similar invention, calling it the phonograph.

Such international influences were evident throughout the Columbian Exposition. At the Tiffany pavilion, Louis Comfort Tiffany displayed jewelry and objects influenced by Japanese art forms. The Colt firearms factory, known throughout the world for its revolver, was already international in scope, having opened a factory in England in 1851. At the fair, Colt debuted its new automatic weapon, the machine gun—soon to play a major role on the world stage in both the Boxer uprising in China and the Spanish-American War.

All manner of foodstuffs tempted fairgoers—teas from India, whiskey from Ireland, and pastries and other confectionaries from Germany and France. American products such as Shredded Wheat, Aunt Jemima syrup, and Juicy Fruit gum debuted at the fair, where they competed for ribbons, like Pabst Blue Ribbon Beer. And the fair introduced two new foods—carbonated soda and the hamburger—destined to become America's best-known contributions to international cuisine.

By displaying technology in action, the White City tamed it and made it accessible to American and world consumers. The fair helped promote electric light and power, with its 90,000 electric lights, 5,100 arc lamps, electric fountains, an electric elevated railroad, and electric launches plying the lagoons. Fairgoers visited the Bell Telephone Company exhibit, marveled at General Electric's huge dynamo (electric generator), and gazed into the future at the all-electric home and model demonstration kitchen.

Consumer culture received its first major expression and celebration at the fair. Not only did this world's fair anticipate the mass

"All Nations Are Welcome"

Uncle Sam, flanked by the city of Chicago, welcomes representatives carrying the flags of many nations to the World's Columbian Exposition in 1893. In the background are the fairgrounds on the shores of Lake Michigan. More than one hundred nations participated in the fair by sending exhibits and mounting pavilions to showcase their cultures and products. © Chicago History Museum, USA/Bridgeman Images.

marketing, packaging, and advertising of the twentieth century, but the vast array of products on display also cultivated the urge to consume. Thousands of concessionaires with products for sale sent a message that tied enjoyment inextricably to spending money and purchasing goods, both domestic and foreign. The Columbian Exposition encouraged the rise of a new middle-class consumer culture and made a powerful statement about the possibilities of urban life in an industrial age. As G. Brown Goode, head of the Smithsonian Institution, observed, the Columbian Exposition was in many ways "an illustrated encyclopedia of civilization."

Questions for Analysis

Summarize the Argument: To what extent was the Columbian Exposition simultaneously a commercial venture, a cultural display, and entertainment?

Consider the Context: How did the Columbian Exposition and the White City reflect changes in late-nineteenth-century America? How did the international flavor of the White City compare with the reality of global migration into America's fast-growing cities?

Ask Historical Questions: What role did the fair play in popularizing new technologies?

Chicago's White City
This painting by H. D. Nichols captures the monumental architecture of the White City built for the World's Columbian Exposition in 1893. In the foreground, the central Court of Honor features a Frederick MacMonnies fountain, with Christopher Columbus at the prow of his ship. In the distance is Daniel Chester French's sixty-foot gilded statue *Republic*. The awe-inspiring exposition drew millions of visitors from America and abroad. © Chicago History Museum, USA/Bridgeman Images.

comfortable citizens out of their wits. When reporters asked Daniel Burnham, its chief architect, what should be done with the moldering remains of the White City, he responded, "It should be torched." And it was. In July 1894, in a clash between federal troops and striking railway workers, incendiaries set fires that leveled the fairgrounds.

In the end, the White City remained what it had always been, a dreamscape. Buildings that looked like marble were actually constructed of staff, a plaster substance that began to crumble even before fire destroyed the fairgrounds. Perhaps it was not so strange, after all, that the legacy of the White City could be found on Coney Island, where two new amusement parks, Luna and Dreamland, sought to combine, albeit in a more tawdry form, the beauty of the White City and the thrill of the Midway Plaisance. More enduring than the White City itself was what it represented: the emergent industrial might of the United States, at home and abroad, with its inventions, manufactured goods, and growing consumer culture.

REVIEW   How did municipal governments respond to the challenges of urban expansion?

▶ Conclusion: Who Built the Cities?

As great a role as industrialists, financiers, and engineers played in building the nation's cities, common workers—most of them immigrants—provided the muscle. The unprecedented growth of urban, industrial America resulted from the labor of millions of men, women, and children who toiled in workshops and factories, in sweatshops and mines, and on railroads and construction sites across America.

America's cities in the late nineteenth century teemed with life. Townhouses and tenements jostled for space with skyscrapers and great department stores, while parks, ball fields, amusement arcades, and public libraries provided the city masses with recreation and entertainment. Municipal governments, straining to build the new cities, experienced the rough-and-tumble of machine politics as bosses and their constituents looked to profit from city growth.

For America's workers, urban industrialism along with the rise of big business and corporate consolidation drastically changed the workplace. Industrialists replaced skilled workers with new machines that could be operated by cheaper unskilled labor. And during hard times, employers did not hesitate to cut workers' already meager wages. As the Great Railroad Strike of 1877 demonstrated, when labor united, it could bring the nation to attention. Organization held out the best hope for the workers; first the Knights of Labor and later the AFL won converts among the nation's working class.

The rise of urban industrialism challenged the American promise, which for decades had been dominated by Jeffersonian agrarian ideals. Could such a promise exist in the changing world of cities, tenements, immigrants, and huge corporations? In the great depression that came in the 1890s, mounting anger and frustration would lead farmers and workers to join forces and create a grassroots movement to fight for change under the banner of a new People's Party.

See the Selected Bibliography for this chapter in the Appendix.

KEY TERMS

global migration (p. 527)
Ellis Island (p. 534)
sweatshop (p. 537)
family economy (p. 538)
"typewriters" (p. 539)
Great Railroad Strike (p. 541)
Knights of Labor (p. 543)
American Federation of Labor (AFL) (p. 543)
Haymarket bombing (p. 547)
cult of domesticity (p. 547)
bossism (p. 550)
World's Columbian Exposition (p. 551)

MAKING CONNECTIONS

1. Americans expressed both wonder and concern at the nation's mushrooming cities. Why did cities provoke such divergent responses?

2. Why did patterns of immigration to the United States in the late nineteenth century change? How did Americans respond to the immigrants?

3. How did urban industrialization affect Americans' lives outside of work?

4. When workers began to embrace organization in the late 1870s, what did they hope to accomplish? Were they successful? Why or why not?

REVIEW QUESTIONS

1. Why did American cities experience explosive growth in the late nineteenth century? (pp. 527–537)

2. How did business expansion and consolidation change workers' occupations in the late nineteenth century? (pp. 537–541)

3. Why did membership in the Knights of Labor rise in the late 1870s and decline in the 1890s? (pp. 541–547)

4. How did urban industrialism shape home life and the world of leisure? (pp. 547–548)

5. How did municipal governments respond to the challenges of urban expansion? (pp. 548–554)

LINKING TO THE PAST

1. Compare the lives of migrant workers and industrial cowboys in the West to workers in the nation's cities. What are the major similarities? (See chapter 17.)

2. You have already looked at the development of America's industries in the nineteenth century from the vantage point of moguls such as Andrew Carnegie and John D. Rockefeller. How does your view of industrialism change when the focus is shifted to the nation's workers? (See chapter 18.)

20 Dissent, Depression, and War

1890–1900

CONTENT LEARNING OBJECTIVES

After studying this chapter, you should be able to:

- Identify the economic and social ills American farmers and laborers faced at the turn of the century and how Farmers' Alliances and the Populist movement aimed to address some of these problems.

- Explain the factors that led to the labor wars of the 1890s.

- Characterize the political activism of American women during the last decades of the nineteenth century.

- Describe the political climate during the depression of 1893 and identify the defining issues of the election of 1896.

- Explain American expansionism in the late nineteenth century, how the United States emerged as a world power, and the resulting debate over American imperialism.

PEOPLE'S PARTY BANNER
This 1892 Populist convention banner promises to elect "Honest Men." The bison mascot was a poor choice for the new party, for just as the great herds were decimated, the People's Party was defeated in 1896. Nebraska State Historical Society, no. 7294-32, copy and reuse restrictions apply.

FRANCES WILLARD TRAVELED TO ST. LOUIS IN FEBRUARY 1892 WITH high hopes. Political change was in the air, and Willard was there to help fashion a new reform party. As head of the Woman's Christian Temperance Union (WCTU), an organization with members in every state and territory in the nation, Willard wielded considerable clout. At her invitation, twenty-eight of the country's leading reformers met in Chicago to draft a set of principles to bring to St. Louis. No American woman before her had played such a central role in a political movement. At the height of her power, Willard took her place among the leaders onstage in St. Louis.

Exposition Music Hall presented a colorful spectacle. "The banners of the different states rose above the delegates throughout the hall, fluttering like the flags over an army encamped," wrote one reporter. The fiery orator Ignatius Donnelly attacked the money kings of Wall Street. Terence V. Powderly, head of the Knights of Labor, called on workers to join hands with farmers against the "nonproducing classes." And Frances Willard took the podium, urging the crowd to outlaw liquor and give women the vote.

Frances Willard

Frances Willard, the forward-thinking leader of the Woman's Christian Temperance Union, learned to ride a bicycle at age fifty-three. Willard brought her progressive ideas to the 1892 People's Party convention, where she shared a place on the platform with the new party's leaders. Courtesy of the Frances E. Willard Memorial Library and Archives.

Delegates hammered out a series of demands, breathtaking in their scope. They tackled the tough questions of the day—the regulation of business, the need for banking and currency reform, the right of labor to organize and bargain collectively, and the role of the federal government in regulating business, curbing monopoly, and giving the people greater voice. But the new party was determined to stick to economic issues and resisted endorsing either temperance or woman suffrage. As a member of the platform committee, Willard fought for both and complained of the "crooked methods . . . employed to scuttle these planks."

The convention ended its work amid a chorus of cheers. According to one eyewitness, "Hats, paper, handkerchiefs, etc., were thrown into the air; . . . cheer after cheer thundered and reverberated through the vast hall reaching the outside of the building where thousands who had been waiting the outcome joined in the applause till for blocks in every direction the exultation made the din indescribable."

What was all the shouting about? The crowd, fed up with the Democrats and the Republicans, celebrated the birth of a new political party, officially named the People's Party. The St. Louis gathering marked an early milestone in one of the most turbulent decades in U.S. history. An agrarian revolt, labor strikes, a severe depression, and a war shook the 1890s. As the decade opened, Americans flocked to organizations including the Farmers' Alliance, the American Federation of Labor, the Woman's Christian Temperance Union, and the National Woman's Suffrage Association. Their political alliance gave birth to the People's (or Populist) Party. In a decade of unrest and uncertainty, the Populists countered laissez-faire economics by insisting that the federal government play a more active role to ensure economic fairness in industrial America.

This challenge to the status quo culminated in 1896 in one of the most hotly contested presidential elections in the nation's history. At the close of the tumultuous decade, the Spanish-American War brought the country together, with Americans rallying to support the troops. American imperialism and overseas expansion raised questions about the nation's role on the world stage as the United States stood poised to enter the twentieth century.

▶ The Farmers Unite

Hard times in the 1880s and 1890s created a groundswell of agrarian revolt. A bitter farmer wrote from Minnesota, "I settled on this Land in good Faith Built House and Barn. Broken up Part of the Land. Spent years of hard Labor in grubbing fencing and Improving." About to lose his farm to foreclosure, he lamented, "Are they going to drive us out like trespassers . . . and give us away to the Corporations?"

Farm prices fell decade after decade, even as American farmers' share of the world market grew. In parts of Kansas, corn sold for as little as ten cents a bushel, and angry farmers burned their crops for fuel rather than sell them on the market. At the same time, consumer prices soared (Figure 20.1). In Kansas alone, almost half the farms had fallen into the hands of the banks by 1894 through foreclosure. Farmers soon banded together into Farmers' Alliances that gave birth to a broad political movement.

The Farmers' Alliance

At the heart of the farmers' problems stood a banking system dominated by eastern commercial banks committed to the gold standard, a railroad rate system both capricious and unfair, and rampant speculation that drove up the price of land. In the West, farmers rankled under a system that allowed railroads to charge them exorbitant freight rates while granting rebates to large shippers (see "Railroads, Trusts, and the Federal Government" in chapter 18). The practice of charging higher rates for short hauls than for long hauls meant that grain elevators could ship their wheat from Chicago to New York and across the Atlantic for less than a Dakota farmer paid to send his crop to mills in Minneapolis. In the South, lack of currency and credit drove farmers to the stopgap credit system of the crop lien. To pay for seed and supplies, farmers pledged their crops as collateral to local creditors (furnishing merchants). Determined to do something, farmers banded together to fight for change.

Farm protest was not new. In the 1870s, farmers had supported the Grange and the Greenback Labor Party. As the farmers' situation grew more desperate, they organized, forming regional alliances. The first **Farmers' Alliance** came together in Lampasas County, Texas, to fight "landsharks and horse thieves." In frontier farmhouses in Texas, in log cabins in the back-

CHRONOLOGY

1884	• Frances Willard calls for woman suffrage.
1890	• National American Woman Suffrage Association formed. • Wyoming only state allowing women to vote in national elections. • Southern Farmers' Alliance numbers three million members.
1892	• People's (Populist) Party founded. • Homestead lockout ends in violence.
1893	• Stock market crash touches off economic depression. • President Grover Cleveland nixes attempt to annex Hawai'i.
1894	• Miners strike in Cripple Creek, Colorado. • Coxey's army marches to Washington, D.C. • Pullman boycott crushed.
1895	• Cleveland enforces Monroe Doctrine in border dispute between British Guiana and Venezuela.
1896	• Democrats and Populists support William Jennings Bryan for president. • William McKinley elected president.
1898	• USS *Maine* explodes in Havana harbor. • Congress declares war on Spain. • Admiral George Dewey destroys Spanish fleet in Manila Bay. • U.S. troops defeat Spanish forces in Cuba. • Treaty of Paris ends war with Spain. • United States annexes Hawai'i.
1899–1900	• Secretary of State John Hay enunciates Open Door policy. • Boxer uprising takes place in China.
1901	• Boxer Protocol imposed on Chinese government.

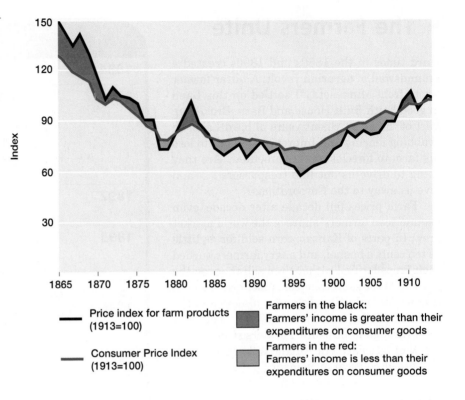

FIGURE 20.1 Consumer Prices and Farm Income, 1865–1910
Around 1870, consumer prices and farm income were about equal. During the 1880s and 1890s, however, farmers suffered great hardships as prices for their crops steadily declined and the cost of consumer goods continued to rise.

Price index for farm products (1913=100)

Consumer Price Index (1913=100)

Farmers in the black: Farmers' income is greater than their expenditures on consumer goods

Farmers in the red: Farmers' income is less than their expenditures on consumer goods

woods of Arkansas, and in the rural parishes of Louisiana, separate groups of farmers formed similar alliances for self-help.

As the movement grew in the 1880s, farmers' groups consolidated into two regional alliances: the Northwestern Farmers' Alliance, active in Kansas, Nebraska, and other midwestern Granger states; and the more radical Southern Farmers' Alliance. Traveling lecturers preached the Alliance message. Worn-out men and care-worn women did not need to be convinced that something was wrong. By 1890, the Southern Farmers' Alliance alone counted more than three million members.

Radical in its inclusiveness, the Southern Alliance reached out to African Americans, women, and industrial workers. Through cooperation with the Colored Farmers' Alliance, an African American group founded in Texas in the 1880s, blacks and whites attempted to make common cause. As Georgia's Tom Watson, a Southern Alliance stalwart, pointed out, "The colored tenant is in the same boat as the white tenant, . . . and . . . the accident of color can make no difference in the interests of farmers, croppers, and laborers." The Alliance reached out to industrial workers as well as farmers. During a major strike against Jay Gould's Texas and Pacific Railroad in 1886, the Alliance vocally sided with the workers and rushed food and supplies to the strikers. Women as well as

men rallied to the Alliance banner. "I am going to work for prohibition, the Alliance, and for Jesus as long as I live," swore one woman.

At the heart of the Alliance movement stood a series of farmers' cooperatives. By "bulking" their cotton—that is, selling it together—farmers could negotiate a better price. And by setting up trade stores and exchanges, they sought to escape the grasp of the merchant/creditor. Through the cooperatives, the Farmers' Alliance promised to change the way farmers lived. "We are going to get out of debt and be free and independent people once more," exulted one Georgia farmer. But the Alliance faced insurmountable difficulties in running successful cooperatives. Opposition by merchants, bankers, wholesalers, and manufacturers made it impossible for the cooperatives to get credit. As the cooperative movement died, the Farmers' Alliance moved into politics.

The Populist Movement

In the earliest days of the Alliance movement, a leader of the Southern Farmers' Alliance insisted, "The Alliance is a strictly white man's nonpolitical, secret business association." But by 1892, it was none of those things. Advocates of a third party carried the day at the convention of laborers, farmers, and common folk in 1892 in St. Louis, where the Farmers' Alliance gave birth to the

The Farmers' Alliance and the Populist Party
Isaac Ware, from Southwest Custer County, Nebraska, proudly holds a copy of the *Alliance Independent*, a newspaper published in Lincoln, Nebraska. In 1892, before this picture was taken, Farmers' Alliance members came together in St. Louis to form the People's or Populist Party. Small local newspapers sprouted up all across the West and South to carry the message. Nebraska State Historical Society, no. 11188, copy and reuse restrictions apply.

People's Party (Populist Party) and launched the Populist movement. The same spirit of religious revival that animated the Farmers' Alliance infused the People's Party. Convinced that the money and banking systems worked to the advantage of the wealthy few, Populists demanded economic democracy. To help farmers get the credit they needed at reasonable rates, southern farmers hit on the ingenious idea of a subtreasury—a plan that would allow farmers to store their nonperishable crops until prices rose and to receive commodity credit from the federal government to obtain needed supplies. To the western farmer, the Populists promised land reform, championing a plan to claim excessive land granted to railroads or sold to foreign investors. The Populists' boldest proposal called for government ownership of the railroads and the telegraph system to put an end to discriminatory rates.

The Populists solidly supported free silver, in the hope of increasing the nation's tight money

Mary Elizabeth Lease
This photograph of Mary Elizabeth Lease, taken in 1895 at the height of her activities as a Populist leader in Kansas, reflects her reputation as a hell-raiser who supposedly exhorted Kansas farmers to "raise less corn and more hell." In the eyes of her detractors, she was "a lantern-jawed, google-eyed nightmare." Kansas State Historical Society.

supply. To empower the common people, the Populist platform called for the direct election of senators and for other electoral reforms, including the secret ballot and the right to initiate legislation, to recall elected officials, and to submit issues to the people by means of a referendum. In support of labor, the Populists supported the eight-hour workday.

The sweeping array of reforms enacted in the Populist platform changed the agenda of politics for decades to come. More than just a response to hard times, Populism presented an alternative vision of American economic democracy.

> **REVIEW**   Why did American farmers organize alliances in the late nineteenth century?

▶ The Labor Wars

While farmers united to fight for change, industrial laborers fought their own battles in a series of bloody strikes historians have called the "labor wars." Industrial workers took a stand in the 1890s. At issue was the right of workers to organize and to speak through unions, to bargain collectively, and to fight for better working conditions, higher wages, shorter hours, and greater worker control in the face of increased mechanization. Three major conflicts—the lockout of steelworkers in Homestead, Pennsylvania, in 1892; the miners' strike in Cripple Creek, Colorado, in 1894; and the Pullman boycott that same year—raised fundamental questions about the rights of labor and the sanctity of private property.

The Homestead Lockout

In 1892, steelworkers in Pennsylvania squared off against Andrew Carnegie in a decisive struggle over the right to organize in the Homestead steel mills. Carnegie resolved to crush the Amalgamated Iron and Steel Workers, one of the largest and richest craft unions in the American Federation of Labor (AFL). When the Amalgamated attempted to renew its contract at Carnegie's Homestead mill, its leaders were told that since "the vast majority of our employees are Non union, the Firm has decided that the minority must give place to the majority." While it was true that only 800 skilled workers belonged to the elite Amalgamated, the union had long enjoyed the support of the plant's 3,000 non-union workers. Slavs, who did much of the unskilled work,

made common cause with the Welsh, Scottish, and Irish skilled workers who belonged to the union.

Carnegie, who often praised labor unions, preferred not to be directly involved in the union busting, so that spring he sailed to Scotland and left Henry Clay Frick, the toughest antilabor man in the industry, in charge. By summer, a strike looked inevitable. Frick prepared by erecting a fifteen-foot fence around the Homestead plant and topping it with barbed wire. Workers aptly dubbed it "Fort Frick." Frick then hired 316 mercenaries from the Pinkerton National Detective Agency at the rate of $5 per day, more than double the wage of the average Homestead worker.

On June 28, the **Homestead lockout** began when Frick locked the doors of the mills and prepared to bring in strikebreakers. Hugh O'Donnell, the young Irishman who led the union, vowed to prevent "scabs" from entering the plant. On July 6 at 4 a.m., a lookout spotted two barges moving up the Monongahela River in the fog. Frick was attempting to smuggle his Pinkertons into Homestead.

Workers sounded the alarm, and within minutes a crowd of more than a thousand, hastily armed with rifles, hoes, and fence posts, rushed to the riverbank. When the scabs attempted to come ashore, gunfire broke out, and more than a dozen Pinkertons and some thirty strikers fell, killed or wounded. The Pinkertons retreated to the barges. For twelve hours, the workers, joined by their family members, threw everything they had at the barges, from fireworks to dynamite. Finally, the Pinkertons hoisted a white flag and arranged with O'Donnell to surrender. With three workers dead and scores wounded, the crowd, numbering perhaps ten thousand, was in no mood for conciliation. As the hated "Pinks" came up the hill, they were forced to run a gantlet of screaming, cursing men, women, and children. When a young guard dropped to his knees, weeping for mercy, a woman used her umbrella to poke out his eye. One Pinkerton had been killed in the siege on the barges. In the grim rout that followed their surrender, not one avoided injury. The workers took control of the plant and elected a council to run the community. At first, public opinion favored their cause. A congressman castigated Carnegie for "skulking in his castle in Scotland." Populists, meeting in St. Louis, condemned the use of "hireling armies."

The action of the Homestead workers struck at the heart of the capitalist system, pitting the

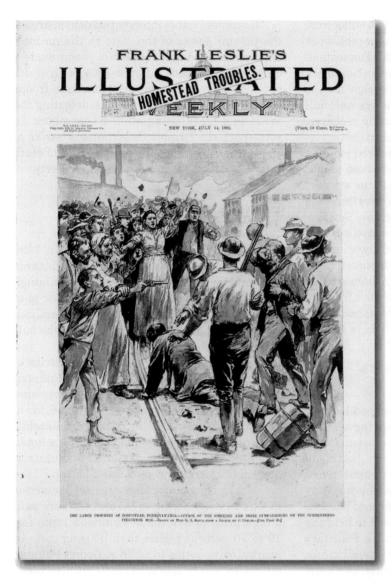

FRANK LESLIE'S
ILLUSTRATED
WEEKLY

HOMESTEAD TROUBLES.

NEW YORK, JULY 14, 1892.

THE LABOR TROUBLES AT HOMESTEAD, PENNSYLVANIA—ATTACK OF THE STRIKERS AND THEIR SYMPATHIZERS ON THE SURRENDERED PINKERTON MEN.

Homestead Workers Attack the Pinkertons

The nation's attention was riveted on labor strife at the Homestead steel mill in the summer of 1892. *Frank Leslie's Illustrated Weekly* ran a cover story on the violence that Pinkerton agents faced from an armed crowd of men, women, and children who were enraged that Frick had hired the Pinkertons to bring in strikebreakers. Beaten and overwhelmed by the strikers, the Pinkertons surrendered. The New York Society Library.

workers' right to their jobs against the rights of private property. The workers' insistence that "we are not destroying the property of the company—merely protecting our rights" did not prove as compelling to the courts and the state as the property rights of the owners. Four days after the confrontation, Pennsylvania's governor, who sympathized with the workers, nonetheless yielded to pressure from Frick and ordered eight thousand National Guard troops into Homestead to protect Carnegie's property. The workers, thinking they had nothing to fear from the militia, welcomed the troops with a brass band. But the troops' occupation not only protected Carnegie's property but also enabled Frick to reopen the mills and bring in strikebreakers. "We have been deceived," one worker complained bitterly. "We have stood idly by and let the town be occupied by soldiers who come here, not as our protectors,

but as the protectors of non-union men. . . . If we undertake to resist the seizure of our jobs, we will be shot down like dogs."

Then, in a misguided effort to ignite a general uprising, Alexander Berkman, a Russian immigrant and anarchist, attempted to assassinate Frick. Berkman bungled his attempt. Shot twice and stabbed with a dagger, Frick survived and showed considerable courage, allowing a doctor to remove the bullets but refusing to leave his desk until the day's work was completed. "I do not think that I shall die," Frick remarked coolly, "but whether I do or not, the Company will pursue the same policy and it will win."

After the assassination attempt, public opinion turned against the workers. Berkman was quickly tried and sentenced to prison. Although the Amalgamated and the AFL denounced his action, the incident linked anarchism and unionism. O'Donnell later wrote, "The bullet from Berkman's pistol, failing in its foul intent, went straight through the heart of the Homestead strike." The Homestead mill reopened in November, and the men returned to work, except for the union leaders, now blacklisted in every steel mill in the country. With the owners firmly in charge, the company slashed wages, reinstated the twelve-hour day, and eliminated five hundred jobs.

The workers at Homestead had been taught a lesson. They would never again, in the words of the National Guard commander, "believe the works are theirs quite as much as Carnegie's." Another forty-five years would pass before steelworkers, unskilled as well as skilled, successfully unionized. In the meantime, Carnegie's production tripled, even in the midst of a depression. "Ashamed to tell you profits these days," Carnegie wrote a friend in 1899. And no wonder: Carnegie's profits had grown from $4 million in 1892 to $40 million in 1900.

The Cripple Creek Miners' Strike of 1894

Less than a year after the Homestead lockout, a panic on Wall Street in the spring of 1893 touched off a bitter economic depression. In the West, silver mines fell on hard times, leading to the **Cripple Creek miners' strike of 1894**. When mine owners moved to lengthen the workday from eight to ten hours, the newly formed Western Federation of Miners (WFM) vowed to hold the line in Cripple Creek, Colorado. In February 1894, the WFM threatened to strike all mines running more than eight-hour shifts. The mine owners divided: Some quickly settled with the WFM; others continued to demand ten hours, provoking a strike.

The striking miners received help from many quarters. Working miners paid $15 a month to a strike fund, and miners in neighboring districts sent substantial contributions. The miners enjoyed the support and assistance of local businesses and grocers, who provided credit to the strikers. With these advantages, the Cripple Creek strikers could afford to hold out for their demands.

Even more significant, Governor Davis H. Waite, a Populist elected in 1892, had strong ties to the miners and refused to use the power of the state against the strikers. Governor Waite asked the strikers to lay down their arms and demanded that the mine owners disperse their hired deputies. The miners agreed to arbitration and selected Waite as their sole arbitrator. By May, the recalcitrant mine owners capitulated, and the union won an eight-hour day.

Governor Waite's intervention demonstrated the pivotal power of the state in the nation's labor wars. Having a Populist in power made a difference. A decade later, in 1904, with Waite out of office, mine owners relied on state troops to take back control of the mines, defeating the WFM and blacklisting all of its members. In retrospect, the Cripple Creek miners' strike of 1894 proved the exception to the rule of state intervention on the side of private property.

Eugene V. Debs and the Pullman Strike

The economic depression that began in 1893 swelled the ranks of the unemployed to three million, almost half of the working population. "A fearful crisis is upon us," wrote a labor publication. Nowhere were workers more demoralized than in the model town of Pullman, on the outskirts of Chicago.

In the wake of the Great Railroad Strike of 1877, George M. Pullman, the builder of Pullman railroad cars, moved his plant and workers nine miles south of Chicago and built a model town. The town of Pullman boasted parks, fountains, playgrounds, an auditorium, a library, a hotel, shops, and markets, along with 1,800 units of housing. Noticeably absent was a saloon.

The housing in Pullman was clearly superior to that in neighboring areas, but workers paid a high price to live there. Pullman's rents ran 10 to 20 percent higher than housing costs in nearby communities. In addition, George Pullman refused to "sell an acre under any circumstances." As long as he controlled the town absolutely, he held the powerful whip of eviction over his employees and could quickly get rid of "troublemakers." Although observers at first praised the beauty and orderliness of the town, critics by the 1890s compared Pullman's model town to a "gilded cage" for workers.

The depression brought hard times to Pullman. Workers saw their wages slashed five times between May and December 1893, with cuts totaling at least 28 percent. At the same time, Pullman refused to lower the rents in his model town, insisting that "the renting of the dwellings and the employment of workmen at Pullman are in no way tied together." When workers went to the bank to cash their paychecks, they found that the rent had been taken out. One worker discovered only forty-seven cents in his pay envelope for two weeks' work. When the bank teller asked him whether he wanted to apply it to his back rent, he retorted,

"If Mr. Pullman needs that forty-seven cents worse than I do, let him have it." At the same time, Pullman continued to pay his stockholders an 8 percent dividend, and the company accumulated a $25 million surplus.

At the heart of the labor problems at Pullman lay not only economic inequity but also the company's attempt to control the work process, substituting piecework for day wages and undermining skilled craftsworkers. During the spring of 1894, Pullman's desperate workers, seeking help, flocked to the ranks of the American Railway Union (ARU), led by the charismatic Eugene V. Debs. The ARU, unlike the skilled craft unions of the AFL, pledged to organize all railway workers—from engineers to engine wipers.

George Pullman responded to union organization at his plant by firing three of the union's leaders the day after they protested wage cuts. Angry men and women walked off the job in disgust. What began as a spontaneous protest in May 1894 quickly blossomed into a strike that involved more than 90 percent of Pullman's 3,300 workers. Pullman countered by shutting down the plant. In June, the Pullman strikers appealed to the ARU to come to their aid. Debs pleaded with the workers to find another solution. But when George Pullman refused arbitration, the ARU membership voted to boycott all Pullman cars. Beginning on June 29, switchmen across the United States refused to handle any train that carried Pullman cars.

The conflict escalated quickly. The General Managers Association (GMA), an organization of managers from twenty-four different railroads, acted in concert to quash the **Pullman boycott**. They recruited strikebreakers and fired all the protesting switchmen. Their tactics set off a chain reaction. Entire train crews walked off the job in a show of solidarity with the Pullman workers. By July 2, rail lines from New York to California lay paralyzed. Even the GMA was forced to concede that the railroads had been "fought to a standstill."

The boycott remained surprisingly peaceful. In contrast to the Great Railroad Strike of 1877, no major riots broke out, and no serious property damage occurred. Debs fired off telegrams to all parts of the country advising his followers to avoid violence and respect law and order. But the nation's newspapers, fed press releases by the GMA, distorted the issues and misrepresented the strike. Across the country, papers ran headlines like "Wild Riot in Chicago" and "Mob Is in Control." (See "Analyzing Historical Evidence," page 566.)

In Washington, Attorney General Richard B. Olney, a lawyer with strong ties to the rail-

A Pullman Craftsworker
Pullman Palace cars were known for their luxurious details. Here, a painter working in the 1890s applies elaborate decoration to the exterior of a Pullman car. The Pullman workers' strike in 1894 stemmed in part from the company's efforts to undermine the status of craftsworkers by reducing them to low-paid piecework. The fight to control the workplace contributed to the labor wars of the 1890s. © Chicago History Museum, USA/Bridgeman Images.

roads, was determined to put down the strike. In his way stood the governor of Illinois, John Peter Altgeld, who, observing that the boycott remained peaceful, refused to call out troops. To get around Altgeld, Olney convinced President Grover Cleveland that federal troops had to

The Press and the Pullman Strike: Framing Class Conflict

Newspaper coverage of the 1894 Pullman strike and the subsequent American Railway Union boycott provides a window into the way the press framed class conflict in the United States in the 1890s. The *Chicago Times*, for example, clearly supported the workers and the union. By contrast, the *Chicago Tribune* and most other Chicago newspapers sided with George M. Pullman and the General Managers Association. Nellie Bly, the era's most colorful investigative reporter, wrote a personal account of her experience with the striking workers for the *New York World*.

DOCUMENT 1
Chicago Tribune, May 12, 1894

PULLMAN MEN OUT
Discharges the Cause

Two thousand employees in the Pullman car works struck yesterday, leaving 800 others at their posts. This was not enough to keep the works going, so a notice was posted on the big gates at 6 o'clock . . . saying: "These shops closed until further notice."

Mr. Pullman said last night he could not tell when work would be resumed. The American Railway Union, which has been proselytizing for a week among the workmen, announces that it will support the strikers . . . [intimating] that the trainmen on the railways on which are organized branches of the union might refuse to handle any of the Pullman rolling stock.

DOCUMENT 2
Chicago Times, May 12, 1894

PULLMAN MEN OUT
Firing Three Men Starts It

Almost the entire force of men employed in the Pullman shops went on strike yesterday. Out of the 4,800 men and women employed in the various departments there were probably not over 800 at work at 6 o'clock last evening. The immediate cause of the strike was the discharge or laying off of three men in the iron machine shop. The real but remote cause is the question of wages over which the men have long been dissatisfied and on account of which they had practically resolved to strike a month ago. . . .

The position of the company is that no increase in wages is possible. . . . President George M. Pullman told the committee that the company was doing business at a loss even at the reduced wages paid the men and offered to show his books in support of his assertion.

DOCUMENT 3
Chicago Times, May 15, 1894

SKIMS OFF THE FAT
Pullman Company Declares a Dividend Today

Full Pockets Swallow $600,000 While Honest Labor Is Starving

Today the Pullman Company will declare a quarterly dividend of 2 per cent on its capital stock of $30,000,000 and President George M. Pullman is authority for the statement that his company owes no man a cent. This despite the assertion of Mr. Pullman that the works have been run at a loss for eight months. Six hundred thousand dollars to shareholders, while starvation threatens the workmen.

DOCUMENT 4
Chicago Tribune, July 1, 1894

MOBS BENT ON RUIN
Men Who Attempt to Work Are Terrorized and Beaten

Continued and menacing lawlessness marked the progress yesterday of Dictator Debs and those who obey his orders in their efforts at coercing the railroads of the country into obeying the mandates of the American Railway Union. . . . At Blue Island, anarchy reigned. The Mayor and police force of that town could do nothing to repress the riotous strikers and they did their own sweet will. . . .

DOCUMENT 5
Chicago Tribune, July 7, 1894

YARDS FIRE SWEPT
Rioters Prevent Firemen from Saving the Property

From Brighton Park to Sixty-First Street the yards of the Pan-Handle road were last night put to the torch by the rioters. Between 600 and 700 freight cars have been destroyed, many of them loaded. Miles and miles of costly track are in a snarled tangle of heat-twisted rails. Not less than $750,000—possibly a whole $1,000,000 of property—has been sacrificed to the caprice of a mob of drunken Anarchists and rebels.

DOCUMENT 6
Chicago Times, July 7, 1894

MEN NOT AWED BY SOLDIERS
Railway Union Is Confident of Winning against Armed Capital

Despite the presence of United States troops and the mobilization of five regiments of state militia, despite threats of martial law and total extermination of the strikers by bullet and bayonet, the great strike inaugurated by the American Railway Union holds three-fourths of the roads running out of Chicago in its strong fetters, and last night traffic was more fully paralyzed than at any time since the inception of the tie-up. . . .

If the soldiers are sent to this district, bloodshed and perhaps death will follow today, for this is the most lawless element in the city, as is shown by their riotous work yesterday. . . . But the perpetrators are not American Railway Union men. The people engaged in this outrageous work of destruction are not strikers, most of them are not even grown men. The persons who set the fires yesterday on the authority of the firemen and police are young hoodlums . . . and the

police on the scene apparently didn't care to or would not make arrests.

DOCUMENT 7
New York World, July 14, 1894

CHEERS FOR NELLIE BLY
Nellie Bly Covers the Strike

I found in my mail this morning an earnest request from the Pullman A. R. U. for me to be present at a meeting which was to be held in the Turner Hall, Kensington. . . .

So I took my nerves in hand and my place before the table near where the speakers sat. I don't intend to repeat what I said, but I told them several truths. They were especially amused when I told them that I had come to Chicago very bitterly set against the strikers; that so far as I understood the question, I thought the inhabitants of the model town of Pullman hadn't a reason on earth to complain. With this belief I visited the town, intending in my articles to denounce the riotous and bloodthirsty strikers. Before I had been half a day in Pullman I was the most bitter striker in the town.

That is true. I've [flip]flopped, as they call it, and I am brave enough to confess it. If ever men and women had cause to strike, those men and women are in Pullman. I also said to these men, sitting so quietly and peaceably before me, hungry for a word of sympathy or a word of hope, that if any of them wished to make any statements to me I would be glad to have them do so. After the meeting I was besieged. If I attempted to tell half the tales of wrong I've listened to I could fill an entire copy of *The World*.

Questions for Analysis

Recognize Viewpoints: How do the *Tribune* and the *Times* articles differ in their portrayal of events and actors in the strike? Which version of the strike do you think most middle-class readers, who tended to be sympathetic to the strikers but fearful of violence, would have found more compelling?

Consider the Context: What economic and social conditions led workers to strike in the 1890s?

Ask Historical Questions: Do you think readers found Nellie Bly's article persuasive? Why or why not?

intervene to protect the rails. To further cripple the boycott, two conservative Chicago judges issued an injunction so sweeping that it prohibited Debs from speaking in public. By issuing the injunction, the court made the boycott a crime punishable by a jail sentence for contempt of court, a civil process that did not require a jury trial. Even the conservative *Chicago Tribune* judged the injunction "a menace to liberty . . . a weapon ever ready for the capitalist." Furious, Debs risked jail by refusing to honor it.

Olney's strategy worked. President Grover Cleveland called out the army. On July 5, nearly 8,000 troops marched into Chicago. Violence immediately erupted. In one day, troops killed 25 workers and wounded more than 60. In the face of bullets and bayonets, the strikers held firm. "Troops cannot move trains," Debs reminded his followers, a fact that was borne out as the railroads remained paralyzed despite the military intervention. But if the army could not put down the boycott, the injunction did. Debs was arrested and imprisoned for contempt of court. With its leader in jail, its headquarters raided and ransacked, and its members demoralized, the ARU collapsed along with the boycott. Pullman reopened his factory, hiring new workers to replace many of the strikers and leaving 1,600 without jobs.

In the aftermath of the strike, a special commission investigated the events at Pullman, taking testimony from 107 witnesses, from the lowliest workers to George M. Pullman himself. Stubborn and self-righteous, Pullman spoke for the business orthodoxy of his era, steadfastly affirming the right of business to safeguard its interests through confederacies such as the GMA and at the same time denying labor's right to organize. "If we were to receive these men as representatives of the union," he stated, "they could probably force us to pay any wages which they saw fit."

From his jail cell, Eugene Debs reviewed the events of the Pullman strike. With the courts and the government ready to side with industrialists in defense of private property, strikes seemed futile, and unions remained helpless. Workers would have to take control of the state itself. Debs went into jail a trade unionist and came out six months later a socialist. At first, he turned to the Populist Party, but after its demise he formed the Socialist Party in 1900 and ran for president five times.

> **REVIEW**   What led to the labor wars of the 1890s?

▶ Women's Activism

"Do everything," Frances Willard urged her followers in 1881. The new president of the Woman's Christian Temperance Union (WCTU) meant what she said. The WCTU followed a trajectory that was common for women in the late nineteenth century. As women organized to deal with issues that touched their homes and families, they moved into politics, lending new urgency to the cause of woman suffrage. Urban industrialism dislocated women's lives no less than men's. Like men, women sought political change and organized to promote issues central to their lives, campaigning for temperance and woman suffrage.

Frances Willard and the Woman's Christian Temperance Union

A visionary leader, Frances Willard spoke for a group left almost entirely out of the U.S. electoral process. In 1890, only one state, Wyoming, allowed women to vote in national elections. But lack of the franchise did not mean that women were apolitical. The WCTU demonstrated the breadth of women's political activity in the late nineteenth century.

Women supported the temperance movement because they felt particularly vulnerable to the effects of drunkenness. Dependent on men's wages, married women and their children suffered when money went for drink. The drunken, abusive husband epitomized the evils of a nation in which women remained second-class citizens. The WCTU, composed entirely of women, viewed all women's interests as essentially the same and therefore did not hesitate to use the singular *woman* to emphasize gender solidarity. Although mostly white and middle-class, WCTU members resolved to speak for their entire sex.

When Willard became president in 1879, she radically changed the direction of the organization. Social action replaced prayer as women's answer to the threat of drunkenness. Viewing alcoholism as a disease rather than a sin and poverty as a cause rather than a result of drink, the WCTU became involved in labor issues, joining with the Knights of Labor to press for better working conditions for women workers. Describing workers in a textile mill, a WCTU member wrote in the organization's *Union Signal* magazine, "It is dreadful to see these girls, stripped almost to the skin . . . and running like racehorses from the beginning to the end of the day." She concluded, "The hard slavish work is drawing the girls into the saloon."

VISUAL ACTIVITY

Woman's Christian Temperance Union Postcard
The WCTU distributed postcards like this to attack the liquor trade. Such cards are typical in their portrayal of saloon backers as traitors to the nation. Notice the man trampling on the American flag as he casts his ballot—a sly allusion to the need for woman suffrage. The History Center on Main Street, Mansfield, PA.
READING THE IMAGE: What do the images that surround the top slogan tell us about the abuses of alcohol?
CONNECTIONS: Why was temperance primarily a woman's movement?

Willard capitalized on the cult of domesticity as a shrewd political tactic. Using "home protection" as her watchword, she argued as early as 1884 that women needed the vote to protect home and family. By the 1890s, the WCTU's grassroots network of local unions included 200,000 dues-paying members and had spread to all but the most isolated rural areas of the country.

Willard worked to create a broad reform coalition in the 1890s, embracing the Knights of Labor, the People's Party, and the Prohibition Party. Until her death in 1898, she led, if not a women's rights movement, then the first organized mass movement of women united around a women's issue. By 1900, thanks largely to the WCTU, women could claim a generation of experience in political action—speaking, lobbying, organizing, drafting legislation, and running private charitable institutions. As Willard observed, "All this work has tended more toward the liberation of women than it has toward the extinction of the saloon."

Elizabeth Cady Stanton, Susan B. Anthony, and the Movement for Woman Suffrage

Unlike the WCTU, the organized movement for woman suffrage remained small and relatively weak in the late nineteenth century. In 1869, Elizabeth Cady Stanton and her ally, Susan B. Anthony, launched the National Woman Suffrage Association (NWSA), demanding the vote for women (see "Women's Activism" in chapter 18). A more conservative group, the American Woman Suffrage Association (AWSA), formed the same year. Composed of men as well as women, the AWSA believed that women should stick with the Republican Party and make suffrage the Sixteenth Amendment. Their optimism proved misplaced.

By 1890, the split had healed, and the newly united **National American Woman Suffrage Association (NAWSA)** launched campaigns on the state level to gain the vote for women. Twenty years had made a great change. Woman suffrage, though not yet generally supported, was no longer considered a crackpot idea, thanks in part to the WCTU's support of the "home protection" ballot. The NAWSA honored Elizabeth Cady Stanton by electing her its first president, but Susan B. Anthony, who took the helm in 1892, emerged as the leading figure in the new united organization.

Stanton and Anthony, both in their seventies, were coming to the end of their public careers. Since the days of the Seneca Falls woman's rights convention, they had worked for reforms for their sex, including property rights, custody rights, and the right to education and gainful employment. But the prize of woman suffrage still eluded

Woman's Suffrage Campaigners
Two respectably attired middle-class suffragists from Long Island, New York, drove this cart to Boston to campaign for woman's suffrage. The boys standing behind the cart suggest the ridicule suffragists often encountered. One suffragist said driving the cart allowed them to stop frequently to explain their cause "to farmers and people in small towns." Buyenlarge/Getty Images.

them. Suffragists won victories in Colorado in 1893 and Idaho in 1896. One more state joined the suffrage column in 1896 when Utah entered the Union. But women suffered a bitter defeat in a California referendum on woman suffrage that same year. Never losing faith, Anthony remarked in her last public appearance, in 1906, "Failure is impossible."

> **REVIEW** How did women's temperance activism contribute to the cause of woman suffrage?

▶ Depression Politics

The depression that began in the spring of 1893 and lasted for more than four years put nearly half of the labor force out of work, a higher percentage than during the Great Depression of the 1930s. The human cost of the depression was staggering. "I Take my pen in hand to let you know that we are Starving to death," a Kansas farm woman wrote to the governor in 1894. "Last cent gone," wrote a young widow in her diary. "Children went to work without their breakfasts."

Following the harsh dictates of social Darwinism and laissez-faire, the majority of America's elected officials believed that it was inappropriate for the government to intervene. But the scope of the depression made it impossible for churches and local agencies to supply sufficient relief, and increasingly Americans called on the federal government to take action. Armies of the unemployed marched on Washington to demand relief, and the Populist Party experienced a surge of support as the election of 1896 approached.

Coxey's Army

Masses of unemployed Americans marched to Washington, D.C., in the spring of 1894 to call attention to their plight and to urge Congress to enact a public works program to end unemployment. Jacob S. Coxey of Massilon, Ohio, led the most publicized contingent. Convinced that men could be put to work building badly needed roads for the nation, Coxey proposed a scheme to finance public works through non-interest-bearing bonds. "What I am after," he maintained, "is to try to put this country in a condition so that no man who wants work shall be obliged to remain idle." His plan won support from the AFL and the Populists.

Starting out from Ohio with one hundred men, **Coxey's army**, as it was dubbed, swelled as it marched east through the spring snows of the Alleghenies. In Pennsylvania, Coxey recruited several hundred from the ranks of those left unemployed by the Homestead lockout.

On May 1, Coxey's army arrived in Washington. When Coxey defiantly marched his men onto the Capitol grounds, police set upon the demonstrators with nightsticks, cracking skulls and arresting Coxey and his lieutenants. Coxey went to jail for twenty days and was fined $5 for "walking on the grass." But other armies of the unemployed, totaling possibly as many as five thousand people, were still on their way. The more daring contingents commandeered entire trains, stirring fears of revolution. Journalists who covered the march did little to quiet the nation's fears. They delighted in military terminology, describing themselves as "war correspondents." To boost newspaper sales, they gave to the episode a tone of urgency and heightened the sense of a nation imperiled.

By August, the leaderless, tattered armies dissolved. Although the "On to Washington" movement proved ineffective in forcing federal relief legislation, Coxey's army dramatized the plight of the unemployed and acted, in the words of one participant, as a "living, moving object lesson." Like the Populists, Coxey's army called into question the underlying values of the new industrial order and demonstrated how ordinary citizens turned to means outside the regular party system to influence politics in the 1890s.

The People's Party and the Election of 1896

Even before the depression of 1893, the Populists had railed against the status quo. "We meet in the midst of a nation brought to the verge of moral, political, and material ruin," Ignatius Donnelly had declared in his keynote address at the creation of the People's Party in St. Louis in 1892. "The fruits of the toil of millions are boldly stolen to build up colossal fortunes for a few. . . . From the same prolific womb of governmental injustice we breed the two great classes—tramps and millionaires."

The fiery rhetoric frightened many who saw in the People's Party a call not to reform but to revolution. Throughout the country, the press denounced the Populists as "cranks, lunatics, and idiots." When one self-righteous editor

Coxey's Army
A contingent of Coxey's army stops to rest on its way to Washington, D.C. A "petition in boots," Coxey's followers were well dressed. Music was an important component of the march, including the anthem "Marching with Coxey." Band members are pictured on the right with their instruments. Despite their peaceful pose, the marchers stirred the fears of many Americans, who predicted an uprising of the unemployed. Courtesy of the Ohio Historical Connection, AL01139.

dismissed them as "calamity howlers," Populist governor Lorenzo Lewelling of Kansas shot back, "If that is so I want to continue to howl until those conditions are improved."

The People's Party captured more than a million votes in the presidential election of 1892, a respectable showing for a new party (Map 20.1). But increasingly, sectional and racial animosities threatened its unity. Realizing that race prejudice obscured the common economic interests of black and white farmers, Populist Tom Watson of Georgia openly courted African Americans, appearing on platforms with black speakers and promising "to wipe out the color line." When angry Georgia whites threatened to lynch a black Populist preacher, Watson rallied two thousand gun-toting Populists to the man's defense. Although many Populists remained racist in their attitudes toward African Americans, the spectacle of white Georgians riding through the night to protect a black man from lynching was symbolic of the enormous changes the Populist Party promised in the South.

As the presidential election of 1896 approached, the depression intensified cries for reform not only from the Populists but also throughout the electorate. Depression worsened the tight money problem caused by the deflationary pressures of the gold standard. Once again, proponents of free silver stirred rebellion in the ranks of both the Democratic and the Republican parties. When the Republicans nominated Ohio governor William McKinley on a platform pledging the preservation of the gold standard, western advocates of free silver representing miners and farmers walked out of the convention. Open rebellion also split the Democratic Party as vast segments in the West and South repudiated President Grover Cleveland because of his support for gold. In South Carolina, Benjamin Tillman won his race for Congress by promising, "Send me to Washington and I'll stick my pitchfork into [Cleveland's] old ribs!"

The spirit of revolt animated the Democratic National Convention in Chicago in the summer of 1896. William Jennings Bryan of Nebraska, the thirty-six-year-old "boy orator from the Platte," whipped the convention into a frenzy calling passionately for free silver with a ringing exhortation: "Do not crucify mankind upon a cross of gold." Pandemonium broke loose as delegates stampeded to nominate Bryan, the youngest candidate ever to run for the presidency.

The juggernaut of free silver rolled out of Chicago and on to St. Louis, where the People's

Candidate	Electoral Vote	Popular Vote	Percent of Popular Vote
Grover Cleveland (Democrat)	277	5,555,426	46.1
Benjamin Harrison (Republican)	145	5,182,690	43.0
James B. Weaver (People's)	22	1,029,846	8.5

Map 20.1
The Election of 1892

Party met a week after the Democrats adjourned. Many western Populists urged the party to ally with the Democrats and endorse Bryan. A major obstacle in the path of fusion, however, was Bryan's running mate, Arthur M. Sewall. A Maine railway director and bank president, Sewall, who had been placed on the ticket to appease conservative Democrats, embodied everything the Populists detested. Moreover, die-hard southern Populists wanted no part of fusion. Southern Democrats had resorted to fraud and violence to steal elections from the Populists in southern states, and support for a Democratic ticket proved hard to swallow.

Populists struggled to work out a compromise. To show that they remained true to their principles, delegates first voted to support all the planks of the 1892 platform, added to it a call for public works projects for the unemployed, and only narrowly defeated a plank for woman suffrage. To deal with the problem of fusion, the convention selected the vice presidential candidate first. The nomination of Tom Watson undercut opposition to Bryan's candidacy. And although Bryan quickly sent a telegram to protest that he would not drop Sewall as his running mate, mysteriously his message never reached the convention floor. Fusion triumphed. Bryan won nomination by a lopsided vote. The Populists did not know it, but their cheers for Bryan signaled the death knell for the People's Party.

Few contests in the nation's history have been as fiercely fought as the presidential election of 1896. On one side stood Republican William McKinley, backed by the wealthy

Candidate	Electoral Vote	Popular Vote	Percent of Popular Vote
William McKinley (Republican)	271	7,104,779	51.1
William J. Bryan (Democrat-People's)	176	6,502,925	47.7

Map 20.2
The Election of 1896

industrialist and party boss Mark Hanna. Hanna played on the business community's fears of Populism to raise a Republican war chest more than double the amount of any previous campaign. On the other side, William Jennings Bryan, with few assets beyond his silver tongue, struggled to make up in energy and eloquence what his party lacked in campaign funds. He crisscrossed the country in a whirlwind tour, by his own reckoning visiting twenty-seven states and speaking to more than five million Americans.

On election day, four out of five voters went to the polls in an unprecedented turnout. The silver states of the Rocky Mountains lined up solidly for Bryan. The Northeast went for McKinley. The Midwest tipped the balance. In the end, the election hinged on between 100 and 1,000 votes in several key states, including Wisconsin, Iowa, and Minnesota. Although McKinley won twenty-three states to Bryan's twenty-two, the electoral vote showed a lopsided 271 to 176 in McKinley's favor (Map 20.2).

The biggest losers in 1896 turned out to be the Populists. On the national level, they polled fewer than 300,000 votes, a million less than in 1894. In the clamor to support Bryan, Populists in the South, determined to beat McKinley at any cost, swallowed their differences and drifted back to the Democratic Party.

REVIEW   Why was the People's Party unable to translate national support into victory in the 1896 election?

VISUAL ACTIVITY

"Swallowed!"
This cartoon from 1900 shows William Jennings Bryan as a python swallowing the Democratic Party's donkey mascot. Bryan, who ran unsuccessfully for president in 1896, won the Democratic nomination again in 1900 and in 1908. Ironically, it was not the Democratic Party so much as the Populist Party that Bryan swallowed. By nominating the Democrat Bryan on its ticket in 1896, the Populist Party lost its identity. The Granger Collection, New York.
READING THE IMAGE: Does the image of a Populist Bryan swallowing the Democratic Party accurately reflect what happened in 1896? What happened to the Populists after 1896?
CONNECTIONS: What issues did the Populists support?

Regime Change in Hawai'i

Queen Lili'uokalani came to the throne in Hawai'i in 1891 determined to take back power for her monarchy and her people. As a member of Hawai'i's native royalty, or *ali'i*, she had received a first-rate education in missionary school. As a young woman, she converted to Christianity, adopted the English name Lydia, and married the white (*haole*) governor of Maui. Yet she maintained a reverence for traditional Hawai'ian ways and resented the treatment of her people by the white minority. Her brother, King Kalakaua, had proven a weak leader, coerced by the white elite into signing the "Bayonet Constitution," which put the government squarely in the hands of the whites. Determined to rule, not simply to reign, Lili'uokalani moved ahead with plans to wrest power from the minority she referred to as Hawai'i's "guests."

American missionaries first came to Hawai'i in 1820. Some intermarried with their Christian converts, creating a group of *hapa haole* (half whites), as well as a growing number of children born in Hawai'i to white parents. The temptations of wealth led many missionaries, like Amos Starr Cooke, to acquire land and take up sugar planting. In 1851, he founded Castle & Cooke, which became one of the world's largest sugar producers. By the end of the century, missionaries and planters had blended into one ruling class and gained control of extensive tracts of land. Thanks to the "Bayonet Constitution," they controlled the islands, even though native Hawai'ians and the Japanese and Chinese laborers imported to work on the sugar plantations outnumbered them ten to one.

Sugar became a booming business in Hawai'i as a result of favorable reciprocity treaties with the United States. But hard times came to the islands with the passage of the McKinley tariff in 1890. The tariff wiped out the advantage Hawai'ian sugar had enjoyed in the American market, with devastating results. Within two years, the value of Hawai'ian sugar exports plummeted from $13 million to $8 million.

One way to avoid the tariff was by incorporating Hawai'i into the United States through annexation. Foremost among those who championed this scheme was Lorrin Thurston, the thirty-five-year-old grandson of American missionaries. Thurston, born in Hawai'i and educated in the United States, was zealous in his belief that Hawai'i should be ruled by white Americans and their children. In 1892, he traveled to Washington, D.C., where he won the support of Republican secretary of state James G. Blaine. Thurston returned to Hawai'i knowing that annexation had friends in Washington.

Queen Lili'uokalani picked Saturday, January 14, 1893, as the day to promulgate her new constitution. Her aim was to return Hawai'i to Hawai'ians by allowing only those with native ancestry the right to vote. Learning of her intentions, Thurston quickly hatched a plot to overthrow the monarchy. Late that night, he called on John L. Stevens, the American minister to Hawai'i. Laying out his plan, he urged Stevens, a staunch annexationist, to support the overthrow of the queen and to pledge U.S. support for Thurston's actions. Without hesitating, Stevens promised to land Marines from the USS *Boston* "to protect American lives and property."

Two days later, 162 American Marines and sailors marched into Honolulu armed with carbines, howitzers (small cannons), and Gatling guns. The next day, Thurston and 17 of his confederates seized control of a government building and proclaimed themselves a "provisional government." Minister Stevens promptly recognized the revolutionaries as the legitimate government of Hawai'i.

▶ The United States and the World

Throughout much of the second half of the nineteenth century, U.S. interest in foreign policy took a backseat to territorial expansion in the American West. The United States fought the Indian wars while European nations carved empires in Asia, Africa, Latin America, and the Pacific.

At the turn of the twentieth century, the United States pursued a foreign policy consisting of two currents—isolationism and expansionism. Although the determination to remain detached from European politics had been a hallmark of U.S. foreign policy since the nation's founding, Americans simultaneously believed in manifest destiny—the "obvious" right to expand the nation from ocean to ocean. With its own inland empire secured, the United States looked outward. Determined to protect its sphere of influence in the Western Hemisphere and to expand its trading in Asia, the nation turned away from isolationism and toward a more active role on the world stage that led to intervention in China's Boxer uprising and war with Spain.

Markets and Missionaries

The depression of the 1890s provided a powerful impetus to American commercial expansion. As

To avoid bloodshed, Queen Lili'uokalani agreed to step aside. But in a masterstroke, she composed a letter addressed not to her enemies in the provisional government, but to the U.S. government. Protesting her overthrow, she yielded her authority "until such time as the Government of the United States, shall, upon the facts being presented to it, undo the action of its representatives and reinstate me in the authority which I claim as the constitutional sovereign of the Hawai'ian Islands." The action now shifted to Washington, where Grover Cleveland, a Democrat skeptical of America's adventures abroad, quickly squelched plans for annexation and supported the Hawai'ian queen. The provisional government, however, enjoyed the support of Republicans in Congress and refused to step down, biding its time, waiting for the Republicans to take back the White House.

In 1898, as the taste for empire swept the United States in the wake of the Spanish-American War, President William McKinley quietly signed a treaty annexing Hawai'i. His action pleased not only Hawai'i's sugar growers but also American expansionists, who judged Hawai'i strategically important in expanding U.S. trade with China.

"Hawai'i is ours," Grover Cleveland wrote sadly. "As I look back upon the first steps in this miserable business, and as I contemplate the

Queen Lili'uokalani (1838–1917)
An accomplished woman who straddled two cultures, Lydia Kamakaeha Dominis, or Queen Lili'uokalani, spoke English as easily as her native Hawai'ian, was fluent in French and German as well, and traveled widely. Although Lili'uokalani never regained her throne, in 1993, Congress passed and President Bill Clinton signed a resolution offering an apology to native Hawai'ians for the overthrow of their queen. Bettmann/Corbis.

means used to complete the outrage, I am ashamed of the whole affair."

Questions for Analysis

Summarize the Argument: How did the government of Queen Lili'uokalani come to be overthrown in 1893?

Consider the Context: How did economic issues on the mainland affect the status of Hawai'i?

Recognize Viewpoints: What role did party politics play in the annexation of Hawai'i?

---

markets weakened at home, American businesses looked abroad for profits. As the depression deepened, one diplomat warned that Americans "must turn [their] eyes abroad, or they will soon look inward upon discontent."

Exports constituted a small but significant percentage of the profits of American business in the 1890s (Figure 20.2). And where American interests led, businessmen expected the government's power and influence to follow to protect their investments. Companies like Standard Oil actively sought to use the U.S. government as their agent, often putting foreign service employees on the payroll. "Our ambassadors and ministers and consuls," wrote John D. Rockefeller

appreciatively, "have aided to push our way into new markets and to the utmost corners of the world."

America's foreign policy often appeared little more than a sidelight to business development. In Hawai'i (first called the Sandwich Islands), American sugar interests fomented a rebellion in 1893, toppling the increasingly independent Queen Lili'uokalani. (See "Beyond America's Borders," above.) They pushed Congress to annex the islands to avoid the high McKinley tariff on sugar. When President Cleveland learned that Hawai'ians opposed annexation, he withdrew the proposal from Congress. But expansionists still coveted the islands and looked for an opportunity to push through annexation.

Business interests alone did not account for the new expansionism that seized the nation during the 1890s. As Alfred Thayer Mahan, leader of a growing group of American expansionists, confessed, "Even when material interests are the original exciting cause, it is the sentiment to which they give rise, the moral tone which emotion takes that constitutes the greater force." Much of that moral tone was set by American missionaries intent on spreading the gospel of Christianity to the "heathen." No area on the globe constituted a greater challenge than China.

An 1858 agreement, the Tianjin (Tientsin) treaty, admitted foreign missionaries to China. Although Christians converted only 100,000 in a population of 400 million, the Chinese nevertheless resented the interference of missionaries in village life. Opposition to foreign missionaries took the form of antiforeign secret societies, most notably the Boxers, whose Chinese name translated to "Righteous Harmonious Fist." In 1899, the Boxers hunted down and killed Chinese Christians and missionaries in northwestern Shandong Province. With the tacit support of China's Dowager Empress, the Boxers, shouting "Uphold the Ch'ing Dynasty, Exterminate the Foreigners," marched on the cities. Their rampage eventually led to the massacre of some 30,000 Chinese converts and 250 foreign nuns, priests, and missionaries.

As the Boxers spread terror throughout northern China, some 800 Americans and Europeans sought refuge in the foreign diplomatic buildings in Peking (today's Beijing). Along with missionaries from the countryside came thousands of their Chinese converts. Unable to escape and cut off from outside aid and communication, the Americans and Europeans in Beijing mounted a defense to face the Boxer onslaught. One American described the scene as 20,000 Boxers stormed the walls in June 1900:

> Their yells were deafening, while the roar of gongs, drums, and horns sounded like thunder. . . . They waved their swords and stamped on the ground with their feet. They wore red turbans, sashes, and garters over blue cloth. . . . They were now only twenty yards from our gate. Three or four volleys from the Lebel rifles of our marines left more than fifty dead on the ground.

For two months the little group held out under siege, eating mule and horse meat and losing 76 men in battle. Sarah Conger, wife of the U.S. ambassador, wrote wearily, "[The siege] was exciting at first, but night after night of this firing, horn-blowing, and yelling, and the whizzing of bullets has hardened us to it."

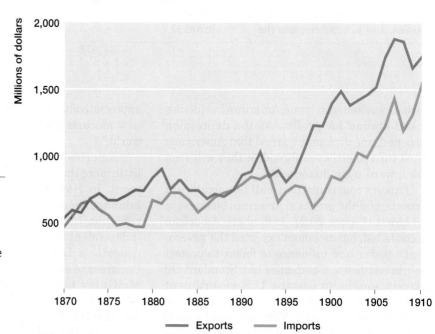

FIGURE 20.2   Expansion in U.S. Trade, 1870–1910
Between 1870 and 1910, American exports more than tripled. Imports generally rose, but they were held in check by the high protective tariffs championed by Republican presidents from Ulysses S. Grant to William Howard Taft. A decline in imports is particularly noticeable after the passage of the prohibitive McKinley tariff in 1890.

In August 1900, 2,500 U.S. troops joined an international force sent to rescue the foreigners and put down the uprising in the Chinese capital. The European powers imposed the humiliating Boxer Protocol in 1901, giving themselves the right to maintain military forces in Beijing and requiring the Chinese government to pay an exorbitant indemnity of $333 million.

In the aftermath of the **Boxer uprising**, missionaries voiced no concern at the paradox of bringing Christianity to China at gunpoint. "It is worth any cost in money, worth any cost in bloodshed," argued one bishop, "if we can make millions of Chinese true and intelligent Christians." Merchants and missionaries alike shared such moralistic reasoning. Indeed, they worked hand in hand; trade and Christianity marched into Asia together. "Missionaries," admitted the American clergyman Charles Denby, "are the pioneers of trade and commerce. . . . The missionary, inspired by holy zeal, goes everywhere and by degrees foreign commerce and trade follow."

The Monroe Doctrine and the Open Door Policy

The emergence of the United States as a world power pitted the nation against other colonial powers, particularly Germany and Japan, which posed a threat to the twin pillars of America's expansionist foreign policy. The first, the **Monroe Doctrine**, came to be interpreted as establishing the Western Hemisphere as an American "sphere of influence" and warned European powers to stay away or risk war. The second, the Open Door, dealt with maintaining market access to China.

American diplomacy actively worked to buttress the Monroe Doctrine, with its assertion of American hegemony (domination) in the Western Hemisphere. In the 1880s, Republican secretary of state James G. Blaine promoted hemispheric peace and trade through Pan-American cooperation but, at the same time, used American troops to intervene in Latin American border disputes. In 1895, President Cleveland risked war with Great Britain to enforce the Monroe Doctrine when a conflict developed between Venezuela and British Guiana. After American saber rattling, the British backed down and accepted U.S. mediation in the area despite their territorial claims in Guiana.

In Central America, American business triumphed in a bloodless takeover that saw French

VISUAL ACTIVITY

American Soldiers at the Chinese Imperial Palace
After helping suppress the Boxer uprising, these American soldiers stood alongside the road to the Chinese Imperial Palace to celebrate the conclusion of the fighting and the imposition of the Boxer Protocol. Strolling along the center of the road is a Christian missionary with his family, suggesting the triumph over the anti-Christian Boxers. Corbis.
READING THE IMAGE: How did this ceremony display the consequences of the suppression of the Boxer crisis?
CONNECTIONS: How did the suppression of the Boxer uprising reflect American foreign policy?

and British interests routed. The United Fruit Company of Boston virtually dominated the Central American nations of Costa Rica and Guatemala, while an importer from New Orleans turned Honduras into a "banana republic" (a country run by U.S. business interests). Thus, by 1895, the United States, through business as well as diplomacy, had successfully achieved hegemony in Latin America and the Caribbean, forcing even the British to concur that "the infinite resources [of the United States] combined with its isolated position render it master of the situation and practically invulnerable as against any or all other powers."

At the same time that American foreign policy warned European powers to stay out of the Western Hemisphere, the United States competed for trade in the Eastern Hemisphere. As American interests in China grew, the United States became more aggressive in defending its presence in Asia and the Pacific. In 1889, it risked war with Germany to guarantee the U.S. Navy access to Pago Pago in the Samoan Islands,

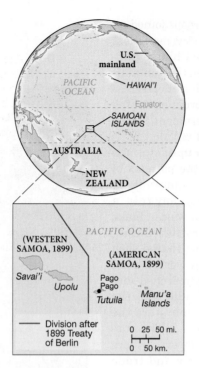

The Samoan Islands, 1889

a port for refueling on the way to Asia. Germany, seeking dominance over the islands, sent warships to the region. But before fighting broke out, a typhoon destroyed the German and American ships. The potential combatants later divided the islands amicably in the 1899 Treaty of Berlin.

In the 1890s, China, weakened by years of internal warfare, was partitioned into spheres of influence by Britain, Japan, Germany, France, and Russia. Concerned about the integrity of China and no less about American trade, Secretary of State John Hay in 1899–1900 wrote a series of notes calling for an "open door" policy that would ensure trade access to all and maintain Chinese sovereignty. The notes were greeted by the major powers with polite evasion. Nevertheless, Hay skillfully managed to maneuver them into doing his bidding, and in 1900 he boldly announced the Open Door as international policy. The United States, by insisting on the **Open Door policy**, managed to secure access to Chinese markets, expanding its economic power while avoiding the problems of maintaining a far-flung colonial empire on the Asian mainland. But as the Spanish-American War soon demonstrated, Americans found it hard to resist the temptations of overseas empire.

"A Splendid Little War"

The **Spanish-American War** began as a humanitarian effort to free Cuba from Spain's colonial grasp and ended with the United States itself acquiring territory overseas and fighting a dirty guerrilla war with Filipino nationalists who, like the Cubans, sought independence. Behind the contradiction stood the twin pillars of American foreign policy: The Monroe Doctrine made Spain's presence in Cuba unacceptable; and U.S. determination to keep open the door to Asia made the Philippines attractive. Precedent for the nation's imperial adventures also came from the recent Indian wars in the American West, which provided a template for the subjugation of native peoples in the name of civilization.

Looking back on the Spanish-American War of 1898, Secretary of State John Hay judged it "a splendid little war; begun with the highest motives, carried on with magnificent intelligence and spirit, favored by that fortune which loves the brave." At the close of a decade marred by bitter depression, social unrest, and political upheaval, the war offered Americans a chance to wave the flag and march in unison. War fever proved as infectious as the tune of a John Philip Sousa march. Few argued the merits of the conflict until it was over and the time came to divide the spoils.

The war began with moral outrage over the treatment of Cuban revolutionaries, who had launched a fight for independence against the Spanish colonial regime in 1895. In an attempt to isolate the guerrillas, the Spanish general Valeriano Weyler herded Cubans into crowded and unsanitary concentration camps, where thousands died of hunger, disease, and exposure. Starvation soon spread to the cities. By 1898, fully a quarter of the island's population had perished in the Cuban revolution.

As the Cuban rebellion dragged on, pressure for American intervention mounted. American newspapers fueled public outrage at Spain. A fierce circulation war raged in New

York City between William Randolph Hearst's *Journal* and Joseph Pulitzer's *World*. Their competition provoked what came to be called **yellow journalism**, named for the colored ink used in a popular comic strip. The Cuban war provided a wealth of dramatic copy. Newspapers fed the American people a daily diet of "Butcher" Weyler and Spanish atrocities. Hearst sent artist Frederic Remington to document the horror, and when Remington wired home, "There is no trouble here. There will be no war," Hearst shot back, "You furnish the pictures and I'll furnish the war."

American interests in Cuba were, in the words of the U.S. minister to Spain, more than "merely theoretical or sentimental." American business had more than $50 million invested in Cuban sugar, and American trade with Cuba, a brisk $100 million a year before the rebellion, had dropped to near zero. Nevertheless, the business community balked, wary of a war with Spain. When industrialist Mark Hanna, the Republican kingmaker and senator from Ohio, urged restraint, a hotheaded Theodore Roosevelt exploded, "We will have this war for the freedom of Cuba, Senator Hanna, in spite of the timidity of commercial interests."

To expansionists like Roosevelt, more than Cuban independence was at stake. As assistant secretary of the navy, Roosevelt took the helm in the absence of his boss and, in the summer of 1897, audaciously ordered the U.S. fleet to be ready to steam to Manila in the Philippines. In the event of conflict with Spain, Roosevelt put the navy in a position to capture the islands and gain a stepping-stone to China.

President McKinley moved slowly toward intervention. In a show of American force, he dispatched the battleship *Maine* to Cuba. On the night of February 15, 1898, a mysterious explosion destroyed the *Maine*, killing 267 crew members. The source of the explosion remained unclear, but inflammatory stories in the press enraged Americans. (See "Making Historical Arguments," page 580.) Rallying to the cry "Remember the *Maine*," Congress declared war on Spain. In a surge of patriotism, more than a million men rushed to enlist. War brought with it a unity of purpose and national harmony that ended a decade of political dissent and strife. "In April,

Did Terrorists Sink the *Maine*?

At 9:40 p.m. on the evening of February 15, 1898, the U.S. battleship *Maine* blew up in Havana harbor. "The shock threw us backward," reported one eyewitness. "From the deck forward of amidships shot a streak of fire as high as the tall buildings on Broadway. Then the glare of light widened out like a funnel at the top, and down through this bright circle fell showers of wreckage and mangled sailors." In all, 267 sailors drowned or burned to death in one of the worst naval catastrophes to occur during peacetime.

Captain Charles Dwight Sigsbee, the last man to leave the burning ship, filed a terse report saying that the *Maine* had blown up and "urging [that] public opinion should be suspended until further report." But the yellow press, led by William Randolph Hearst's *New York Journal*, ran banner headlines proclaiming, "The War Ship *Maine* Was Split in Two by an Enemy's Secret Infernal Machine!"

Public opinion quickly divided between those who suspected foul play and those who believed the explosion had been an accident. Foremost among the accident theorists was the Spanish government, along with U.S. business interests who hoped to avoid war. The "jingoes," as proponents of war were called, rushed to blame Spain.

Even before the details were known, Assistant Secretary of the Navy Theodore Roosevelt wrote, "The *Maine* was sunk by an act of dirty treachery on the part of the Spaniards I believe; though we shall never find out definitely, and officially it will go down as an accident."

In less than a week, the navy formed a court of inquiry, and divers inspected the wreckage. The panel reported on March 25, 1898, that a mine had exploded under the bottom of the ship, igniting gunpowder in the forward magazine. The panel could not determine whether the mine had been planted by the Spanish government or by recalcitrant followers of Valeriano Weyler. The infamous Weyler had been ousted after the American press dubbed him "the Butcher" for his harsh treatment of the Cubans.

As time passed, however, more people came to view the explosion of the *Maine* as an accident. European experts concluded that the *Maine* had exploded accidentally, from a fire in the coal bunker adjacent to the reserve gunpowder. Perhaps poor design, not treachery, had sunk the *Maine*.

In 1910, New York congressman William Sultzer put it succinctly: "The day after the ship was sunk, you could hardly find an American who did not believe that she had

been foully done to death by a treacherous enemy. Today you can hardly find an American who believes Spain had anything to do with it." The *Maine* still lay in the mud of Havana harbor, a sunken tomb containing the remains of many sailors. The Cuban government asked for the removal of the wreck, and veterans demanded a decent burial for the sailors. So in March 1910, Congress voted to raise the *Maine* and reinvestigate.

The "Final Report on Removing the Wreck of Battleship *Maine* from the Harbor of Habana, Cuba" appeared in April 1913. This report confirmed that the original naval inquiry was in error, but it ruled out the accident theory by concluding that the nature of the initial explosion indicated a homemade bomb—once again casting suspicion on Weyler's fanatic followers. Following the investigation and removal of human remains, the wreckage of the *Maine* was towed out to sea and, with full funeral honors, sunk in six hundred fathoms of water.

Controversy over the *Maine* proved harder to sink. In the Vietnam era, when faith in the "military establishment" plummeted, Admiral Hyman Rickover launched yet another investigation. Viewing the 1913 "Final Report" as a cover-up, he complained that the ship had been sunk so deep "that there will be no chance of the true facts being revealed." Rickover, a maverick who held the naval brass in low esteem, blamed "the warlike atmosphere in Congress and the press, and the natural tendency to look for reasons

everywhere over this good fair land, flags were flying," wrote Kansas editor William Allen White. "At the stations, crowds gathered to hurrah for the soldiers, and to throw hats into the air, and to unfurl flags."

Five days after McKinley signed the war resolution, a U.S. Navy squadron destroyed the Spanish fleet in Manila Bay (Map 20.3).

The stunning victory caught most Americans by surprise. Few had ever heard of the Philippines. Even McKinley confessed that he could not locate the archipelago on the map. Nevertheless, he dispatched U.S. troops to secure the islands.

The war in Cuba ended almost as quickly as it began. The first troops landed on June 22,

for the loss that did not reflect on the Navy." Judging the sinking an accident, Rickover warned, "We must make sure that those in 'high places' do not without more careful consideration of the consequences, exert our prestige and might."

Two decades later, the pendulum swung back. A 1995 study of the *Maine* published by the Smithsonian Institution concluded that zealot followers of General Weyler sank the battleship: "They had the opportunity, the means, and the motivation, and they blew up the *Maine* with a small low-strength mine they made themselves." According to this theory, the terrorists' homemade bomb burst the *Maine*'s hull, triggering a massive explosion. And in 1998, *National Geographic* employed computer models to show that an external explosion (bomb) was capable of sinking the *Maine*.

Questions for Analysis

Summarize the Argument: How have explanations for the sinking of the *Maine* changed over time? Has the evidence changed, or have interpretations of the evidence shifted?

Analyze the Evidence: Why were jingoists so quick to blame Spain for the sinking of the *Maine*?

Consider the Context: In 1995, the Smithsonian panel judged the sinking of the *Maine* a result of terrorism perpetrated by followers of the deposed General Weyler. Was their use of the word *terrorism* as inflammatory then as it is today?

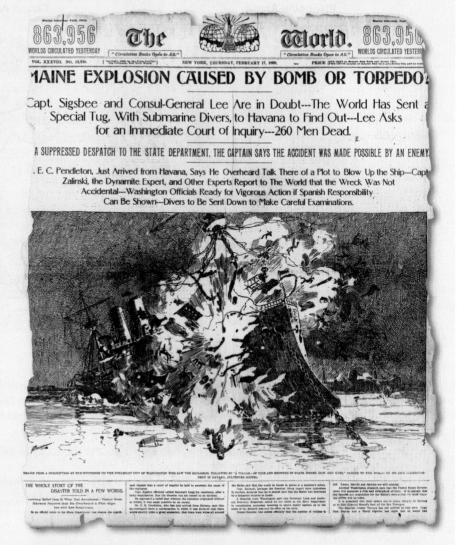

"Maine Explosion Caused by Bomb or Torpedo?"
The front page of the *New York World* two days after the blast trumpeted the news and graphically portrayed the destruction of the ship. The text insisted the explosion was not accidental, even though there was no evidence to back up the assertion. The extent of the destruction and the deaths of 267 sailors fueled war fever. © Collection of the New-York Historical Society, USA/Bridgeman Images.

and after a handful of battles the Spanish forces surrendered on July 17. The war lasted just long enough to elevate Theodore Roosevelt to the status of bona fide war hero. Roosevelt resigned his navy post and formed the Rough Riders, a regiment composed of a sprinkling of Ivy League polo players and a number of western cowboys Roosevelt befriended during his stint as a cattle rancher in the Dakotas. The Rough Riders' charge up Kettle Hill and Roosevelt's role in the decisive battle of San Juan Hill made front-page news. Overnight, Roosevelt became the most famous man in America. By the time he sailed home from Cuba, a coalition of independent Republicans was already plotting his political future.

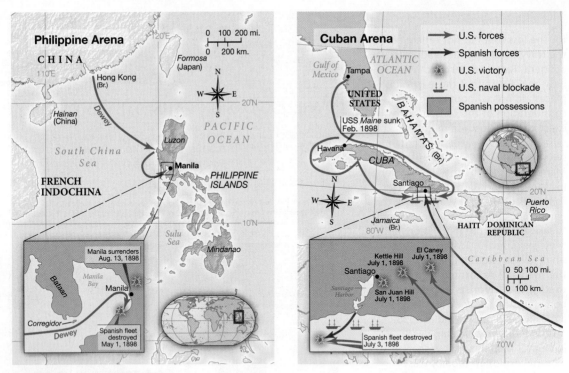

MAP ACTIVITY

Map 20.3   The Spanish-American War, 1898
The Spanish-American War was fought in two theaters, the Philippine Islands and Cuba. Five days after President William McKinley called for a declaration of war, Admiral George Dewey captured Manila. The war lasted only eight months. Troops landed in Cuba in mid-June and by mid-July had destroyed the Spanish fleet.

READING THE MAP: Which countries held imperial control over countries and territories immediately surrounding the Philippine Islands and Cuba?
CONNECTIONS: What role did American newspapers play in the start of the war? How did the results of the war serve American aims in both Asia and the Western Hemisphere?

The Debate over American Imperialism

After a few brief campaigns in Cuba and Puerto Rico brought the Spanish-American War to an end, the American people woke up in possession of an empire that stretched halfway around the globe. As part of the spoils of war, the United States acquired Cuba, Puerto Rico, Guam, and the Philippines. And Republicans quickly moved to annex Hawai'i in July 1898.

Contemptuous of the Cubans, whom General William Shafter declared "no more fit for self-government than gun-powder is for hell," the U.S. government imposed a Cuban constitution and refused to give up military control of the island until the Cubans accepted the so-called Platt Amendment—a series of provisions that granted the United States the right to intervene to protect Cuba's "independence," as well as the power to oversee Cuban debt so that European creditors would not find an excuse for intervention. For good measure, the United States gave itself a ninety-nine-year lease on a naval base at Guantánamo. In return, McKinley promised to implement an extensive sanitation program to clean up the island, making it more attractive to American investors.

In the formal Treaty of Paris (1898), Spain ceded the Philippines to the United States along with the former Spanish colonies of Puerto Rico and Guam (Map 20.4). Empire did not come cheap. When Spain initially balked at these terms, the United States agreed to pay an indemnity of $20 million for the islands. Nor was the cost measured in money alone. Filipino revolutionaries under Emilio Aguinaldo, who had greeted U.S. troops as liberators, bitterly

Emilio Aguinaldo and His Soldiers
Emilio Aguinaldo (on horseback) led these and many other Filipino soldiers during their long and bloody insurrection against American takeover of the Philippines. Aguinaldo and his men fought courageously for independence from Spanish rule, officially proclaiming their "right to be free and independent." When the Spanish-American War ended, they felt betrayed by Americans' refusal to recognize Philippine independence. Bettmann/Corbis.

fought the new masters. It would take seven years and 4,000 American dead—almost ten times the number killed in Cuba—not to mention an estimated 20,000 Filipino casualties, to defeat Aguinaldo and secure American control of the Philippines.

At home, a vocal minority, mostly Democrats and former Populists, resisted the country's foray into overseas empire, judging it unwise, immoral, and unconstitutional. William Jennings Bryan, who enlisted in the army but never saw action, concluded that American expansionism only distracted the nation from problems at home. Pointing to the central paradox of the war, Representative Bourke Cockran of New York admonished, "We who have been the destroyers of oppression are asked now to become its agents." But the expansionists won the day. As Senator Knute Nelson of Minnesota assured his colleagues, "We come as ministering angels, not as despots." Fresh from its conquest of Native Americans in the West, the nation largely embraced the heady mixture of racism and missionary zeal that fueled American adventurism abroad. The *Washington Post* trumpeted, "The taste of empire is in the mouth of the people," thrilled at the prospect of "an imperial policy, the Republic renascent, taking her place with the armed nations."

> **REVIEW**   Why did the United States largely abandon its isolationist foreign policy in the 1890s?

► Conclusion: Rallying around the Flag

A decade of domestic strife ended amid the blare of martial music and the waving of flags. The Spanish-American War drowned out the calls for social reform that had fueled the Populist politics of the 1890s. During that decade, angry farmers facing hard times looked to the Farmers' Alliances to fight for their vision of economic democracy, workers staged bloody battles across

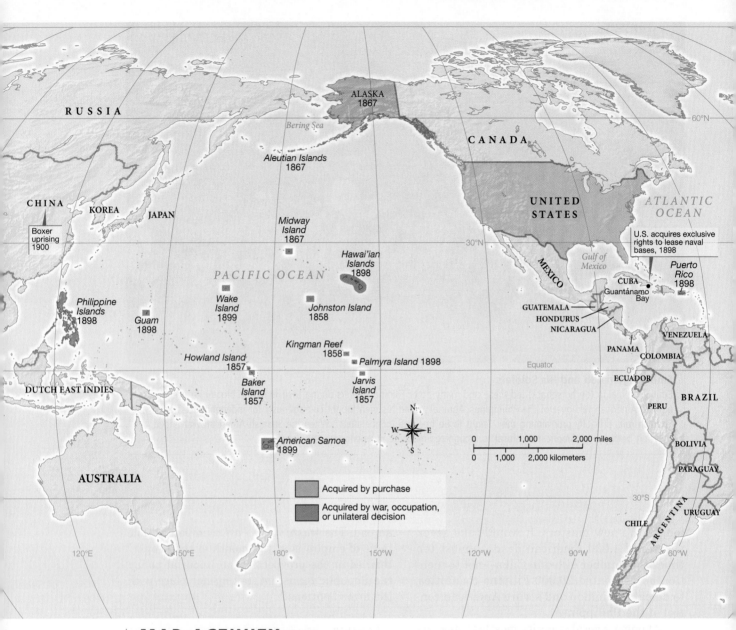

MAP ACTIVITY

Map 20.4   U.S. Overseas Expansion through 1900

The United States extended its interests abroad with a series of territorial acquisitions. Although Cuba was granted independence, the Platt Amendment kept the new nation firmly under U.S. control. In the wake of the Spanish-American War, the United States woke up to find that it held an empire extending halfway around the globe.

READING THE MAP: Does the map indicate that more territory was acquired by purchase or by war, occupation, or unilateral decision? How many purchases of land outside the continental United States did the government make?
CONNECTIONS: What foreign policy developments occurred in the 1890s? How did American political leaders react to them? Where was U.S. expansion headed, and why?

the country to assert their rights, and women like Frances Willard preached temperance and suffrage. Together they formed a new People's Party to fight for change.

The bitter depression that began in 1893 led to increased labor strife. The Pullman boycott brutally dramatized the power of property and the conservatism of the laissez-faire state. But workers' willingness to confront capitalism on the streets of Chicago, Homestead, Cripple Creek, and a host of other sites across America eloquently testified to labor's growing determination, unity, and strength.

As the depression deepened, the sight of Coxey's army of unemployed marching on Washington to demand federal intervention in the economy signaled a growing shift in the public mind against the stand-pat politics of laissez-faire. The call for the government to take action to better the lives of workers, farmers, and the dispossessed manifested itself in the fiercely fought presidential campaign of William Jennings Bryan in 1896. With the outbreak of the Spanish-American War in 1898, the decade ended on a harmonious note with patriotic Americans rallying around the flag. But even though Americans basked in patriotism and contemplated empire, old grievances had not been laid to rest. The People's Party had been beaten, but the Populist spirit lived on in the demands for greater government involvement in the economy, expanded opportunities for direct democracy, and a more equitable balance of profits and power between the people and the big corporations. A new generation of progressive reformers championed the unfinished reform agenda in the first decades of the twentieth century.

See the Selected Bibliography for this chapter in the Appendix.

20 | Chapter Review

KEY TERMS

Farmers' Alliance (p. 559)

People's Party (Populist Party) (p. 561)

Homestead lockout (p. 562)

Cripple Creek miners' strike of 1894 (p. 564)

Pullman boycott (p. 565)

National American Woman Suffrage Association (NAWSA) (p. 569)

Coxey's army (p. 571)

Boxer uprising (p. 577)

Monroe Doctrine (p. 577)

Open Door policy (p. 578)

Spanish-American War (p. 578)

yellow journalism (p. 579)

REVIEW QUESTIONS

1. Why did American farmers organize alliances in the late nineteenth century? (pp. 559–562)

2. What led to the labor wars of the 1890s? (pp. 562–568)

3. How did women's temperance activism contribute to the cause of woman suffrage? (pp. 568–570)

4. Why was the People's Party unable to translate national support into victory in the 1896 election? (pp. 570–573)

5. Why did the United States largely abandon its isolationist foreign policy in the 1890s? (pp. 574–583)

MAKING CONNECTIONS

1. Why did so many farmers and urban workers look to the government to help advance their visions of economic justice?

2. What circumstances gave rise to labor protests in the 1890s? How did they differ from those triggering earlier strikes?

3. How did women's activism in the late nineteenth century help advance the cause of woman suffrage?

LINKING TO THE PAST

1. How did the conquest of Native Americans in the West foreshadow U.S. expansion abroad? In what ways did the assumptions of racial superiority evident in U.S. Indian policy affect the treatment of Cubans and Filipinos? (See chapter 17.)

2. Why in the midst of burgeoning growth did the United States experience a major depression in the 1890s? Draw on your knowledge of the development of U.S. industries such as the railroads. (See chapter 18.)

21 Progressivism from the Grass Roots to the White House

1890–1916

CONTENT LEARNING OBJECTIVES

After reading and studying this chapter, you should be able to:

- Explain how and why grassroots progressivism arose near the start of the twentieth century and why proponents like Jane Addams and Hull House served as spearheads for reform.

- Identify how President Theodore Roosevelt put his progressive activism to work with big business, conservation, and international affairs and how successor William Howard Taft stalled the progressive reforms Roosevelt had begun.

- Explain why progressives led an insurgent campaign during the election of 1912 and the factors that led to Woodrow Wilson's victory.

- Describe how Wilson sought to enact his "New Freedom" once in office, and explain how he became a reluctant progressive.

- Understand the limits of progressive reform, and identify the organizations that offered more radical visions of America's future.

IN THE SUMMER OF 1889, JANE ADDAMS LEASED TWO FLOORS OF A dilapidated mansion on Chicago's West Side. Her immigrant neighbors must have wondered why this well-dressed woman, who surely could afford better housing, chose to live on South Halsted Street. Yet the house, built by Charles Hull, precisely suited Addams's needs.

For Addams, personal action marked the first step in her search for solutions to the social problems created by urban industrialism. She wanted to help her immigrant neighbors, and she wanted to offer meaningful work to educated women like herself. Addams's emphasis on the reciprocal relationship between the social classes made Hull House different from other philanthropic enterprises. She wished to do things with, not just for, Chicago's poor.

In the next decade, Hull House expanded from two rented floors in the old brick mansion to some thirteen buildings housing a remarkable variety of activities. Addams provided public baths, opened a restaurant for working women too tired to cook after their long shifts, and sponsored a nursery and kindergarten. Hull House offered classes, lectures, art exhibits, musical instruction, and college extension courses. It boasted a

PROGRESSIVE PARTY SOUVENIR BANDANA
This red bandana is a campaign souvenir from 1912, the year Theodore Roosevelt's followers broke with Republicans to form the Progressive Party. Roosevelt challenged laissez-faire liberalism and argued for government action for social justice. David J. & Janice L. Frent Collection/Corbis.

gymnasium, a theater, a manual training workshop, a labor museum, and the first public playground in Chicago.

From the first, Hull House attracted an extraordinary set of reformers who pioneered the scientific investigation of urban ills. Armed with statistics, they launched campaigns to improve housing, end child labor, fund playgrounds, and lobby for laws to protect workers.

Addams quickly learned that it was impossible to deal with urban problems without becoming involved in politics. Piles of decaying garbage overflowed South Halsted Street's wooden trash bins, breeding flies and disease. To rectify the problem, Addams got herself appointed garbage inspector. Out on the streets at six in the morning, she rode atop the garbage wagon to make sure it made its rounds. Eventually, her struggle to aid the urban poor led her on to the state capitol and to Washington, D.C.

Under Addams's leadership, Hull House became a "spearhead for reform," part of a broader movement that contemporaries called progressivism. The transition from personal action to political activism that Addams personified became one of the hallmarks of this reform period, which lasted from the 1890s to World War I.

Classical liberalism, which opposed the tyranny of centralized government, did not address the enormous power of Gilded Age business giants. As the gap between rich and poor widened in the 1890s, progressive reformers demonstrated a willingness to use the government to counterbalance the power of private interests and, in doing so, redefined liberalism in the twentieth century.

Faith in activism united an otherwise diverse group of progressive reformers. A sense of Christian mission inspired some. Others, fearing social upheaval, sought to remove some of the worst evils of urban industrialism—tenements, child labor, and harsh working conditions. A belief in technical expertise and scientific management infused progressivism and made the cult of efficiency part of the movement.

Progressives shared a growing concern about the power of wealthy individuals and a distrust of the trusts, but they were not immune to the prejudices of their era. Although they called for greater democracy, many progressives sought to restrict the rights of African Americans, Asians, and even the women who formed the backbone of the movement.

Uplift and efficiency, social justice and social control, direct democracy and discrimination all came together in the Progressive Era at every level of politics and in the presidencies of Theodore Roosevelt and Woodrow Wilson. While in office, Roosevelt advocated conservation, pushed through antitrust reforms, and championed the nation as a world power. Roosevelt's successor, William Taft, failed to follow in Roosevelt's footsteps, and the resulting split in the Republican Party paved the way for Wilson's victory in 1912. A reluctant progressive, Wilson eventually presided over reforms in banking, business, and labor.

Jane Addams

Jane Addams was twenty-nine years old when she founded Hull House on South Halsted Street in Chicago. Her desire to live among the poor and her insistence that settlement house work benefited educated women such as her as well as her immigrant neighbors marked the distance from philanthropy to progressive reform. Her autobiographical *Twenty Years at Hull-House* was published in 1910. Photo: Jane Addams Memorial Collection (JAMC_8000_0005_0014), Special Collections, University of Illinois at Chicago, photographer: Max Platz; book: Newberry Library, Chicago, Illinois, USA/Bridgeman Images.

▶ Grassroots Progressivism

Much of progressive reform began at the grass-roots level and percolated upward into local, state, and eventually national politics as reformers attacked the social problems fostered by urban industrialism. Although **progressivism** flourished in many different settings across the country, urban problems inspired the progressives' greatest efforts. In their zeal to "civilize the city," reformers founded settlement houses, professed a new Christian social gospel, and campaigned against vice and crime in the name of "social purity." Allying with the working class, women progressives sought to better the lot of sweatshop garment workers and to end child labor. These local reform efforts often ended up being debated in state legislatures and in the U.S. Congress.

Civilizing the City

Progressives attacked the problems of the city on many fronts. **Settlement houses**, which began in England, spread in the United States. By 1893, the needs of poor urban neighborhoods that had motivated Jane Addams led Lillian Wald to recruit several other nurses to move to New York City's Lower East Side "to live in the neighborhood as nurses, identify ourselves with it socially, and . . . contribute to it our citizenship." Wald's Henry Street settlement pioneered public health nursing.

Women, particularly college-educated women like Addams and Wald, formed the backbone of the settlement house movement. Settlement houses gave college-educated women eager to use their knowledge a place to put their talents to work in the service of society and to champion progressive reform. (See "Experiencing the American Promise," page 590.) Such reformers believed that only by living among the poor could they help bridge the growing class divide. Settlements like Hull House grew in number from six in 1891 to more than four hundred in 1911. In the process, settlement house women created a new profession—social work.

For their part, churches confronted urban social problems by enunciating a new **social gospel**, one that saw its mission as not simply to reform individuals but to reform society. The social gospel offered a powerful corrective to social Darwinism and the gospel of wealth, which fostered the belief that riches somehow signaled divine favor. Charles M. Sheldon's popular book *In His Steps* (1898)

CHRONOLOGY

1889	• Jane Addams opens Hull House.
1896	• *Plessy v. Ferguson* decided.
1900	• Socialist Party founded.
1901	• William McKinley assassinated; Theodore Roosevelt becomes president.
1902	• Antitrust lawsuit filed against Northern Securities Company. • Roosevelt mediates anthracite coal strike.
1903	• Women's Trade Union League founded. • Panama Canal construction begins.
1904	• Roosevelt Corollary to Monroe Doctrine announced.
1905	• Industrial Workers of the World founded.
1906	• Pure Food and Drug Act and Meat Inspection Act enacted. • Atlanta race riot kills several hundred blacks. • Hepburn Act enacted.
1907	• Panic on Wall Street causes economic downturn. • "Gentlemen's Agreement" made with Japan.
1908	• *Muller v. Oregon* decided. • William Howard Taft elected president.
1909	• Garment workers strike. • National Association for the Advancement of Colored People formed.
1911	• Triangle Shirtwaist Company fire kills workers.
1912	• Roosevelt runs for president on Progressive Party ticket. • Woodrow Wilson elected president.
1913	• Suffragists march in Washington, D.C. • Federal Reserve Act enacted.
1914	• Federal Trade Commission created. • Clayton Antitrust Act enacted.
1916	• Margaret Sanger opens first U.S. birth control clinic.

Making the Workplace Safer: Alice Hamilton Explores the Dangerous Trades

Nothing in Alice Hamilton's middle-class, midwestern upbringing hinted at the leading role she would play in the progressive movement as a pioneer in the field of occupational health and safety. Yet at an early age, she resolved to become a doctor because, as she wrote, "as a doctor I could go anywhere I pleased—to the far-off lands or to city slums—and be quite sure that I could be of use anywhere."

This desire to be of use prompted Hamilton to earn a medical degree at the University of Michigan and to study bacteriology in Germany and at Johns Hopkins University. In September 1897, she fulfilled a longtime dream by moving into Hull House, where she, like most of the residents, worked a day job (at Northwestern University's Medical School) and participated in settlement activities in the evenings and on weekends. Hamilton soon focused on the area of public health, particularly the link between occupation and illness.

Through her work, Hamilton came to believe that the poor health of many immigrants resulted from unsafe conditions and noxious chemicals, especially lead dust, in the industrial workplace. Employers insisted that lead poisoning resulted from workers' failure to wash their hands before they ate, or they blamed workers' ill health on alcoholism, but Hamilton disagreed. As she noted, the United States was far behind Europe in the field of industrial toxicology and in the regulation of dangers in the workplace. "The employers [here] could, if they wished, shut their eyes to the dangers their workmen faced," Hamilton observed, "for nobody held them responsible, while the workers [largely immigrants] accepted the risks with fatalistic submissiveness as part of the price one must pay for being poor."

In 1910, at the age of thirty-two, Hamilton was appointed to the newly created Occupational Disease Commission of Illinois, the first investigative body of its kind in the United States. For the next decade, she relied primarily on "shoe leather epidemiology" to explore the dangerous trades. With her assistants, she visited factories, read hospital records, and interviewed workers in their homes to discover instances of lead poisoning. "No young doctor," she wrote, "can hope for work as exciting and rewarding." Lead poisoning builds up slowly in the body, leading to colic and convulsions. Lead harms the nervous system, causing paralysis and wrist drop, a condition in which the hands and fingers cannot be extended. In cases of chronic lead poisoning, victims suffer from weight loss, constipation, high blood pressure, anemia, abdominal pain, fatigue, and premature senility. One of Hamilton's case studies tells the grim story.

A Hungarian, thirty-six years old, worked for seven years grinding lead paint. During this time he had three attacks of colic, with vomiting and headache. I saw him in the hospital, a skeleton of a man, looking almost twice his age, his limbs soft and flabby, his muscles wasted. He was extremely emaciated, his color was a dirty grayish yellow, his eyes dull and expressionless. He lay in an apathetic condition, rousing when spoken to and answering rationally but slowly, with often an appreciable delay, then sinking back into apathy.

In 1911, Hamilton prepared a report making clear the connection between occupation and illness, lead-

---

called on men and women to Christianize capitalism by asking the question "What would Jesus do?"

Ministers also played an active role in the social purity movement, the campaign to attack vice. To end the "social evil," as reformers delicately referred to prostitution, the social purity movement brought together ministers who wished to stamp out sin, doctors concerned about the spread of venereal disease, and women reformers. Advanced progressives linked prostitution to poverty and championed higher wages for women working in industrial or other jobs.

Attacks on alcohol went hand in hand with the push for social purity. The Anti-Saloon League, formed in 1895 under the leadership of Protestant clergy, added to the efforts of the Woman's Christian Temperance Union in campaigning to end the sale of liquor. Reformers pointed to links between drinking, prostitution, wife and child abuse, unemployment, and industrial accidents. The powerful liquor lobby fought back, spending liberally in election campaigns, fueling the charge that liquor corrupted the political process.

Alice Hamilton

This picture of Alice Hamilton was taken the year she graduated from the University of Michigan Medical School in 1893. A resident of Hull House, she pioneered the field of occupational health and safety. Schlesinger Library, Radcliffe Institute, Harvard University.

began a program in industrial hygiene in 1916, Hamilton became the first woman invited to join the faculty. Until her retirement in 1935, she alternated a semester of teaching at Harvard with her field work "exploring the dangerous trades." In her long retirement (she lived to be 101), she continued to blend her commitment to social justice and civil rights, political activism, and concern for the poorest workers. Hamilton died on September 22, 1970, three months before Congress passed the Occupational Safety and Health Act, institutionalizing the reforms she had fought for her whole life.

Questions for Analysis

Analyze the Evidence: What evidence persuaded Hamilton that hazardous working conditions caused illness among workers?

Recognize Viewpoints: How did the viewpoint of Hamilton toward lead poisoning compare with that of workers and employers? What accounts for the differences in viewpoints?

Ask Historical Questions: How did working as a volunteer and for government agencies contribute to Hamilton's investigations of industrial diseases?

ing to needed reforms in Illinois. In 1913, the U.S. commissioner of labor asked her to undertake a national study. "I had, as a Federal agent," she wrote, "no right to enter any establishment—that depended on the courtesy of the employer. I must discover for myself where the plants were, and the method of investigation to be followed. . . . Nobody would keep tabs on me, I should not even receive a salary." Using her intelligence and charm,

she was rarely denied entry, and her experience at Hull House led her directly to the workers in their homes when she wanted the facts. Her powers of persuasion prompted several employers to institute reforms in their plants to cut down on lead dust.

By 1915, Hamilton had become the foremost American authority on lead poisoning and one of a handful of prominent specialists in industrial disease. When the Harvard Medical School

An element of nativism (dislike of foreigners) ran through the movement for prohibition, as it did in a number of progressive reforms. The Irish, the Italians, and the Germans were among the groups stigmatized by temperance reformers for their drinking. Progressives campaigned to enforce the Sunday closing of taverns, stores, and other commercial establishments and pushed for state legislation to outlaw the sale of liquor. By 1912, seven states were "dry."

Progressives' efforts to civilize the city demonstrated their willingness to take action; their

belief that environment, not heredity alone, determined human behavior; and their optimism that conditions could be corrected through government action without radically altering America's economy or institutions. All of these attitudes characterized the progressive movement.

Progressives and the Working Class

Day-to-day contact with their neighbors made settlement house workers particularly sympathetic

Garment Workers on Strike
These two young women, both of them probably immigrants, walked the picket line during the successful "uprising of the twenty thousand" garment workers in 1909. The women's hats and dresses display their needlework skills and their respectability. The glowering men in the background suggest the conventional middle-class opposition to the working women's strike. Library of Congress, LC-DIG-ggbain-04505.

to labor. When Mary Kenney O'Sullivan complained that her bookbinders' union met in a dirty, noisy saloon, Jane Addams invited them to meet at Hull House. And during the Pullman strike in 1894 (see chapter 20, "Analyzing Historical Evidence," page 566), Hull House residents organized strike relief. "Hull-House has been so unionized," grumbled one Chicago businessman, "that it has lost its usefulness and become a detriment and harm to the community." But to the working class, the support of middle-class reformers marked a significant gain.

Attempts to forge a cross-class alliance became institutionalized in 1903 with the creation of the Women's Trade Union League (WTUL). The WTUL brought together women workers and middle-class "allies." Its goal was to organize working women into unions under the auspices of the American Federation of Labor (AFL). Although the alliance between working women, primarily immigrants and daughters of immigrants, and their middle-class allies was not without tension, the WTUL helped working women achieve significant gains.

The WTUL's most notable success came in 1909 in the "uprising of the twenty thousand," when hundreds of women employees of the Triangle Shirtwaist Company in New York City went on strike to protest low wages, dangerous working conditions, and management's refusal to recognize their union, the International Ladies' Garment Workers Union. In support, an estimated twenty thousand garment workers, most of them teenage girls and many of them Jewish and Italian immigrants, stayed out on strike through the winter, picketing in the bitter cold. Police and hired thugs harassed the picketing strikers, beating them up and arresting more than six hundred of them for "street walking" (prostitution). When WTUL allies, including J. P. Morgan's daughter Anne, joined the picket line, the harassment quickly stopped. By the time the strike ended in February 1910, the workers had won important demands in many shops. The solidarity shown by the women workers proved to be the strike's greatest achievement. As Clara Lemlich, one of the strike's leaders, exclaimed, "They used to say that you couldn't even organize women. They wouldn't come to union meetings. They were 'temporary' workers. Well we showed them!"

But for all its success, the uprising of the twenty thousand failed fundamentally to change conditions for women workers, as the tragic Triangle fire dramatized in 1911. A little over a year after the shirtwaist makers' strike ended, fire alarms sounded at the Triangle Shirtwaist factory. The ramshackle building, full of lint and

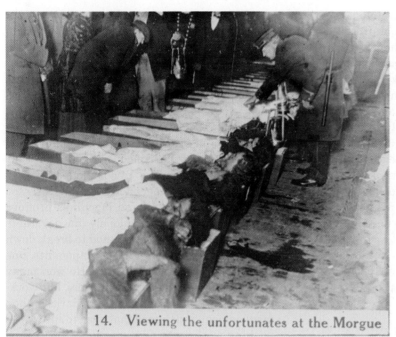

14.   Viewing the unfortunates at the Morgue

VISUAL ACTIVITY

Identifying the Dead

After the Triangle fire on March 26, 1911, New York City set up a makeshift morgue at the end of Manhattan's Charities Pier. There, the remains of more than a hundred young women and two dozen young men were laid out in coffins for their friends and relatives to identify. Often small personal items provided the only clues to the victim's identity. Hadwin Collection, Kheel Center, Cornell University, Ithaca, NY.

READING THE IMAGE: As you look at the picture, can you tell which Triangle victims would be easily identified and which would not?

CONNECTIONS: Why was the Triangle fire such an important turning point in U.S. labor history?

combustible cloth, burned to rubble in half an hour. A WTUL member described the scene below on the street: "Two young girls whom I knew to be working in the vicinity came rushing toward me, tears were running from their eyes and they were white and shaking as they caught me by the arm. 'Oh,' shrieked one of them, 'they are jumping. Jumping from ten stories up! They are going through the air like bundles of clothes.'"

The terrified Triangle workers had little choice but to jump. Flames blocked one exit, and the other door had been locked to prevent workers from pilfering. The flimsy, rusted fire escape collapsed under the weight of fleeing workers, killing dozens. Trapped, 54 workers on the top floors jumped to their deaths. Of 500 workers, 146 died and scores of others were injured. The owners of the Triangle firm went to trial for negligence, but they avoided conviction when authorities determined that a careless smoker had started the fire. The Triangle Shirtwaist Company reopened in another firetrap within a matter of weeks.

Outrage and a sense of futility overwhelmed Rose Schneiderman, a leading WTUL organizer, who made a bitter speech at the memorial service for the dead Triangle workers. "I would be a traitor to those poor burned bodies if I came here to talk good fellowship," she told her audience. "We have tried you good people of the public and we have found you wanting. . . . I know from my experience it is up to the working people to save themselves . . . by a strong working class movement." The

Triangle fire severely tested the bonds of the cross-class alliance. Schneiderman and other WTUL leaders determined that organizing and striking were no longer enough, particularly when the AFL paid so little attention to women workers. Increasingly, the WTUL turned its efforts to lobbying for protective legislation—laws that would limit hours and regulate women's working conditions.

The National Consumers League (NCL) also fostered cross-class alliance and advocated for protective legislation. When Florence Kelley took over the leadership of the NCL in 1899, she urged middle-class women to boycott stores and exert pressure for decent wages and working conditions for women employees. Frustrated by the reluctance of the private sector to reform, the NCL promoted protective legislation to better the working conditions for women.

Advocates of protective legislation had won a major victory in 1908 when the U.S. Supreme Court, in *Muller v. Oregon*, reversed its previous rulings and upheld an Oregon law that limited to ten the number of hours women could work in a day. A mass of sociological evidence put together by Florence Kelley of the NCL and Josephine Goldmark of the WTUL convinced the Court that long hours endangered women and therefore the entire human race. The Court's ruling set a precedent, but one that separated the well-being of women workers from that of men by arguing that women's reproductive role justified special treatment. Later generations of women fighting for equality would question the effectiveness of this strategy and argue that it ultimately closed good jobs to women. The WTUL, however, greeted protective legislation as a first step in the attempt to ensure the safety of all workers.

Reform also fueled the fight for woman suffrage. For women like Jane Addams, involvement in social reform led inevitably to support for woman suffrage. These new suffragists emphasized the reforms that could be accomplished if women had the vote. Addams insisted that in an urban, industrial society, a good housekeeper could not be sure the food she fed her family, or the water and milk they drank, were pure unless she could vote.

> **REVIEW**   What types of people were drawn to the progressive movement, and why?

▶ Progressivism: Theory and Practice

Progressivism emphasized action and experimentation. Dismissing the view that humans should leave progress to the dictates of natural selection, a new group of reform Darwinists argued that evolution could be advanced more rapidly if men and women used their intellects to improve society. In their zeal for action, progressives often showed an unchecked admiration for speed and efficiency that promoted scientific management and a new cult to improve productivity. These varied strands of progressive theory found practical application in state and local politics, where reformers challenged traditional laissez-faire government.

Reform Darwinism and Social Engineering

The active, interventionist approach of the progressives directly challenged social Darwinism, with its insistence on survival of the fittest. A new group of sociologists argued that progress could be advanced more rapidly if people used their intellects to alter their environment. The best statement of this **reform Darwinism** came from sociologist Lester Frank Ward in his book *Dynamic Sociology* (1883). Ward insisted the "blind natural forces in society must give way to human foresight." This theory condemned the laissez-faire approach, insisting that the liberal state should play a more active role in solving social problems.

Efficiency and *expertise* became progressives' watchwords. In *Drift and Mastery* (1914), journalist and critic Walter Lippmann called for skilled "technocrats" to use scientific techniques to control social change. Unlike the Populists, who advocated a greater voice for the masses, progressives, for all their interest in social justice, insisted that experts be put in charge. At its extreme, the application of expertise and social engineering took the form of scientific management.

Frederick Winslow Taylor pioneered "systematized shop management" in 1911. Obsessed with making humans and machines produce more and faster, he meticulously timed workers with a stopwatch and attempted to break down their work into its simplest components, one repetitive action after another. He won many converts among corporate managers, but workers hated the monotony of systematized shop management and argued that it led to speedup—pushing workers to produce more in less time and for less pay. Nevertheless, many progressives applauded the increased productivity and efficiency of Taylor's system.

Progressive Government: City and State

Progressivism burst forth at every level of government in 1900, but nowhere more forcefully than in Cleveland with the election of Democrat Thomas Loftin Johnson as mayor. A self-made millionaire by age forty, Johnson moved to Cleveland in 1899, where he began his career in politics. During his mayoral campaign, he pledged to reduce the streetcar fare from five cents to three cents. His election touched off a seven-year war between Johnson and the streetcar moguls. To get his three-cent fare, Johnson had Cleveland buy the streetcar system, a tactic of municipal ownership progressives called "gas and water socialism." Reelected four times, Johnson fought for fair taxation and championed greater democracy through the use of the initiative and referendum to let voters introduce legislation, and the recall to get rid of elected officials and judges. Under his administration, Cleveland became, in the words of journalist Lincoln Steffens, the "best governed city in America."

In Wisconsin, Republican Robert M. La Follette converted to the progressive cause early in the 1900s. La Follette capitalized on the grassroots movement for reform to launch his long political career as governor (1901–1905)

Tom Johnson Collage
Tom Johnson's greatest achievement as mayor of Cleveland is memorialized in this collage, which shows incidents from his successful fight to get a three-cent streetcar fare for Cleveland. To get this low fare, Johnson finally instituted municipal ownership of the transit system. In the picture on the bottom right, he takes the controls of the city's first streetcar in 1906. Library of Congress, 3b16023.

and U.S. senator (1906–1925). La Follette brought scientists and professors into his administration and used the university, just down the street from the statehouse in Madison, as a resource. As governor, La Follette lowered railroad rates, raised railroad taxes, improved education, preached conservation, established factory regulation and workers' compensation, instituted the first direct primary in the country, and inaugurated the first state income tax. Under his leadership, Wisconsin earned the title "laboratory of democracy." A fiery orator, "Fighting Bob" La Follette united his supporters around issues that transcended party loyalties. Democrats and Republicans like Tom Johnson and Robert La Follette crossed party lines to work for reform.

West of the Rockies, progressivism arrived somewhat later and found a champion in Republican Hiram Johnson, who served as governor of California from 1911 to 1917 and later as U.S. senator. The Southern Pacific Railroad had dominated California politics since the 1870s. As governor, Johnson promised to "kick the Southern Pacific out of politics" and "return the government to the people," winning support from progressive voters. During Johnson's governorship, California adopted the direct primary; supported initiative, referendum, and recall; strengthened the state's railroad commission; and enacted an employer's liability law.

REVIEW   How did progressives justify their demand for more activist government?

▶ Progressivism Finds a President: Theodore Roosevelt

On September 6, 1901, President William McKinley was shot by Leon Czolgosz, an anarchist, while attending the Pan-American Exposition in Buffalo, New York. Eight days later, McKinley died. When news of the assassination reached Republican boss Mark Hanna, he is said to have growled, "Now that damned cowboy is president." He was speaking of Vice President Theodore Roosevelt, the colorful hero of San Juan Hill, who had indeed cattle ranched in the Dakotas in the 1880s.

Roosevelt immediately reassured the shocked nation that he intended "to continue absolutely unbroken" the policies of McKinley. But Roosevelt was as different from McKinley as the nineteenth century from the twentieth. An activist and a moralist, imbued with the progressive spirit, Roosevelt would turn the Executive Mansion, which he insisted on calling the White House,

Theodore Roosevelt
Aptly described by a contemporary observer as "a steam engine in trousers," Theodore Roosevelt, at forty-two, was the youngest president ever to occupy the White House. He brought to the office energy, intellect, and activism in equal measure. Roosevelt boasted that he used the presidency as a "bully pulpit"—a forum from which he advocated reforms ranging from trust-busting to conservation. Library of Congress, LC-DIG-ppmsca-37304.

into a "bully pulpit." Under his leadership, he achieved major reforms, advocated conservation and antitrust lawsuits, and championed the nation's emergence as a world power. In the process, Roosevelt would work to shift the nation's center of power from Wall Street to Washington.

After serving nearly two full terms as president, Roosevelt left office at the height of his powers. Any man would have found it difficult to follow in his footsteps, but his handpicked successor, William Howard Taft, proved poorly suited to the task. Taft's presidency was marked by vigorous trust-busting but would end with a progressive stalemate and a bitter break with Roosevelt that ultimately caused a schism in the Republican Party.

The Square Deal

At age forty-two, Theodore Roosevelt became the youngest man ever to move into the White House. A patrician by birth and an activist by temperament, Roosevelt brought to the job enormous talent and energy. Early in his career, he had determined that the path to power did not lie in the good government leagues formed by his well-bred New York friends. "If it is the muckers that govern," he wrote, "then I want to see if I cannot hold my own with them." He served his political apprenticeship under a Republican ward boss in a grubby meeting hall above a saloon on Morton Street. Roosevelt's rise in politics was swift and sure. He went from the New York assembly at the age of twenty-three to the presidency with time out as a cowboy in the Dakotas, police commissioner of New York City, assistant secretary of the navy, and a colonel of the Rough Riders. Elected governor of New York in 1898, he alienated the Republican boss, who finagled to get him "kicked upstairs" as a candidate for the vice presidency in 1900. The party bosses reasoned Roosevelt could do little harm as vice president. But one bullet proved the error of their logic.

Once president, Roosevelt would harness his explosive energy to strengthen the power of the federal government, putting business on notice that it could no longer count on a laissez-faire government to give it free rein. In Roosevelt's eyes, self-interested capitalists like John D. Rockefeller, whose Standard Oil trust monopolized the refinery business, constituted "the most dangerous members of the criminal class—the criminals of great wealth." The "absolutely vital question" facing the country, Roosevelt wrote to a friend in 1901, was "whether or not the government has the power to control the trusts." The Sherman Antitrust Act of 1890 had been badly weakened by a conservative Supreme Court and by attorneys general more willing to use it against labor unions than against monopolies. To determine whether the law had any teeth left, Roosevelt, in one of his first acts as president, ordered his attorney general to begin a secret antitrust investigation of the Northern Securities Company, a behemoth that monopolized railroad traffic in the Northwest.

Just five months after Roosevelt took office, Wall Street rocked with the news that the government had filed an antitrust suit against Northern Securities. As one newspaper editor sarcastically observed, "Wall Street is paralyzed at the thought that a President of the United States would sink so low as to try to enforce the law." Roosevelt's thunderbolt put Wall Street on notice that the new president expected to be treated as an equal and was willing to use government as a weapon to curb business excesses. Roosevelt later recounted how J. P. Morgan had come to him, one Harvard man to another, to suggest that "if we have done anything wrong, send your man to my man and they can fix it up." Roosevelt's attorney general responded, "We don't want to fix it up, we want to stop it." Roosevelt chortled over the exchange, noting, "This is a most illuminating illustration of the Wall Street point of view. Mr. Morgan could not help regarding me as a big rival operator." And indeed he was. Perhaps sensing the new mood, the Supreme Court, in a significant turnaround, upheld the Sherman Act and called for the dissolution of Northern Securities in 1904.

"Hurrah for Teddy the Trustbuster," cheered the papers. Roosevelt went on to use the Sherman Act against forty-three trusts, including such giants as American Tobacco, Du Pont, and Standard Oil. Always the moralist, he insisted on a "rule of reason." He would punish "bad" trusts (those that broke the law) and leave "good" ones alone. In practice, he preferred regulation to antitrust suits. In 1903, he pressured Congress to pass the Elkins Act, outlawing railroad rebates. And he created the new cabinet-level Department of Commerce and Labor with the subsidiary Bureau of Corporations to act as a corporate watchdog.

In his handling of the anthracite coal strike in 1902, Roosevelt again demonstrated his willingness to assert the authority of the presidency, this time to mediate between labor and management. In May, 147,000 coal miners in Pennsylvania went on strike. The United Mine Workers (UMW) demanded a reduction in the workday from twelve to ten hours, an equitable system of weighing each miner's output, and a 10 percent wage increase, along with recognition of the union. When asked about the appalling conditions in

the mines that led to the strike, George Baer, the mine operators' spokesman, scoffed, "The miners don't suffer, why they can't even speak English."

Realist author Stephen Crane had already investigated mining life for "In the Depths of a Coal Mine." There he found a vicious circle. Children worked as "breaker boys" separating out pieces of slate from streams of coal speeding by on conveyor belts. Paid 55 cents a day, the boys moved up to become miners, but "having survived gas, the floods, the 'squeezes' of falling rocks, the cars shooting through little tunnels, the precarious elevators," they had little to look forward to: "When old and decrepit, he finally returns to the breaker where he started as a child."

The strike dragged on through the summer and into the fall. Hoarding and profiteering more than doubled the price of coal. As winter approached, coal shortages touched off near riots in the nation's big cities. At this juncture, Roosevelt stepped in. Instead of sending in troops, he determined to mediate. His unprecedented intervention served notice that government counted itself an independent force in business and labor disputes. At the same time, it gave unionism a boost by granting the UMW a place at the table.

At the meeting, Baer and the mine owners refused to talk with the union representative— a move that angered the attorney general and insulted the president. Beside himself with rage over the "woodenheaded obstinacy and stupidity" of management, Roosevelt threatened to seize the mines and run them with federal troops. This quickly brought management to the table. In the end, the miners won a reduction in hours and a wage increase, but the owners succeeded in preventing formal recognition of the UMW.

Taken together, Roosevelt's actions in the Northern Securities case and the anthracite coal strike marked a dramatic departure from the presidential passivity of the Gilded Age. Roosevelt's actions demonstrated conclusively that government intended to act as a countervailing force to the power of the big corporations. Pleased with his role in the anthracite strike, Roosevelt announced that all he had tried to do was give labor and capital a "square deal."

The phrase "Square Deal" became Roosevelt's campaign slogan in the 1904 election. Roosevelt easily defeated the Democrats, who abandoned their former candidate, William Jennings Bryan, to support Judge Alton B. Parker, a "safe" choice they hoped would lure business votes away from Roosevelt. In the months before the election, the president prudently toned down his criticism of big business. Roosevelt swept into office with

Breaker Boys
Coal mines employed thousands of young boys to pick out rocks and other impurities from mined coal. The breaker boys here at a Pennsylvania coal company keep their eyes on the endless conveyor belt of coal for twelve hours a day, while supervisors stand behind them ready to kick them or whack them with a rod to keep them on task. Library of Congress, LC-DIG-nclc-01127.

the largest popular majority—57.9 percent—any candidate had polled up to that time.

Roosevelt the Reformer

"Tomorrow I shall come into my office in my own right," Roosevelt is said to have remarked on the eve of his election. "Then watch out for me!" Roosevelt's stunning victory gave him a mandate for reform. He would need all the popularity and political savvy he could muster, however, to guide his reform measures through Congress. The Senate remained controlled by a staunchly conservative Republican "Old Guard," with many senators on the payrolls of the corporations Roosevelt sought to curb. The *New York Times* suggested that "a millionaire could buy a Senate seat, just as he would buy an opera box, a yacht, or any other luxury."

Roosevelt's pet project remained railroad regulation. The Elkins Act prohibiting rebates had not worked. Roosevelt determined that the only solution lay in giving the Interstate Commerce Commission (ICC) real power to set rates and prevent discriminatory practices. But the right to determine the price of goods or services was an age-old prerogative of private enterprise, and

one that business had no intention of yielding to government.

The Hepburn Act of 1906 marked the crowning legislative achievement of Roosevelt's presidency. It gave the ICC the power to set rates subject to court review. Committed progressives like La Follette judged the law a defeat for reform. Die-hard conservatives branded it a "piece of populism." Both sides exaggerated. The law left the courts too much power and failed to provide adequate means for the ICC to determine rates, but its passage proved a landmark in federal control of private industry. For the first time, a government commission had the power to investigate private business records and to set rates.

Always an apt reader of the public temper, Roosevelt witnessed a growing appetite for reform. Revelations of corporate and political wrongdoing as well as social injustice filled the papers and boosted the sales of popular magazines. Roosevelt counted many of the new investigative journalists among his friends. (See "Analyzing Historical Evidence," page 600.) But he warned them against going too far, citing the allegorical character in *Pilgrim's Progress* who was too busy raking muck to notice higher things. Roosevelt's criticism gave the American vocabulary a new word, *muckraker*, which journalists soon appropriated as a title of honor.

Muckraking, as Roosevelt well knew, provided enormous help in securing progressive legislation. In the spring of 1906, publicity generated by the muckrakers about poisons in patent medicines goaded the Senate, with Roosevelt's backing, into passing a pure food and drug bill. Opponents in the House of Representatives hoped to keep the legislation locked up in committee. There it would have died, were it not for the publication of Upton Sinclair's novel *The Jungle* (1906), with its sensational account of filthy conditions in meatpacking plants. Roosevelt, who read the book over breakfast, was sickened. He immediately invited Sinclair to the White House. Sinclair wanted socialism; Roosevelt wanted food inspection. But thanks to the publicity generated by *The Jungle*, a massive public outcry led to the passage of the Pure Food and Drug Act and the Meat Inspection Act in 1906.

In the waning years of his administration, Roosevelt allied with the more progressive elements of the Republican Party. In speech after speech, he attacked "malefactors of great wealth." Styling himself a "radical," he claimed credit for leading the "ultra conservative" party of McKinley to a position of "progressive conservatism and conservative radicalism."

When an economic panic developed in the fall of 1907, business interests quickly blamed the president. Once again, J. P. Morgan stepped in to avert disaster, this time switching funds from one bank to another to prop up weak institutions. For his services, Morgan dispatched his lieutenants to Washington, where they told Roosevelt that the sale of the Tennessee Coal and Iron Company would aid the economy "but little benefit" U.S. Steel. Willing to take the word of a gentleman, Roosevelt tacitly agreed not to institute antitrust proceedings against U.S. Steel over the acquisition. Roosevelt's promise would give rise to the charge that he acted as a tool of the Morgan interests.

The charge of collusion between business and government underscored the extent to which corporate leaders like Morgan found federal regulation preferable to unbridled competition or harsher state measures. During the Progressive Era, enlightened business leaders cooperated with government in the hope of avoiding antitrust prosecution. Convinced that regulation and not trust-busting offered the best way to deal with big business, Roosevelt never acknowledged that his regulatory policies fostered an alliance between business and government that today is called corporate liberalism.

Roosevelt and Conservation

In the area of conservation, Roosevelt proved indisputably ahead of his time. When he took office, some 43 million acres of forestland remained as government reserves. He more than quadrupled that number to 194 million acres. To conserve natural resources, he fought western cattle barons, lumber kings, mining interests, and powerful leaders in Congress, including Speaker of the House Joseph Cannon, who vowed to spend "not one cent for scenery."

As the first president to have lived and worked in the West, Roosevelt came to the White House convinced of the need for better management of the nation's rivers and forests as well as the preservation of wildlife and wilderness. During his presidency, he placed the nation's conservation policy in the hands of scientifically trained experts like his chief forester, Gifford Pinchot. Pinchot preached conservation—the efficient use of natural resources. Willing to permit grazing, lumbering, and the development of hydroelectric power, conservationists fought private interests only when they felt business acted irresponsibly or threatened to monopolize water and electric power. Preservationists like John Muir, founder of the Sierra Club, believed that the wilderness needed to be protected. Roosevelt, a fervent Darwinian naturalist and an (overly) enthusiastic game hunter, a conservationist who built big dams and a preservationist who saved the redwoods, aimed to have it both ways. (See "Making Historical Arguments," page 604.)

In 1907, Congress attempted to put the brakes on Roosevelt's conservation program by passing a law limiting his power to create forest reserves in six western states. In the days leading up to the law's enactment, Roosevelt feverishly created twenty-one new reserves and enlarged eleven more, saving 16 million acres from development. Once again, Roosevelt had outwitted his adversaries. "Opponents of the forest service turned handsprings in their wrath," he wrote, "but the threats . . . were really only a tribute to the efficiency of our action." Worried that private utilities were gobbling up waterpower sites and creating a monopoly of hydroelectric power, he connived with Pinchot to withdraw 2,565 power sites from private use by designating them "ranger stations." Firm in his commitment to wild America, Roosevelt proved willing to stretch the law when it served his ends. His legacy is more than 234 million acres of American wilderness saved for posterity (Map 21.1).

The Flash and the Birth of Photojournalism

Photography changed the way Americans viewed their world. By the 1890s, any amateur could purchase the Kodak camera that George Eastman marketed with the slogan "You push the button, we do the rest." As the poet Oliver Wendell Holmes observed, the camera became not just "the mirror of reality" but "the mirror with a memory."

Yet for Jacob Riis, a progressive reformer wishing to document the grim horrors of tenement life, photography was useless because it required daylight or careful studio lighting. He could only crudely sketch the dim hovels, the criminal nightlife, and the windowless tenement rooms of New York. Then came the breakthrough: "One morning scanning my newspaper at my breakfast table, I put it down with an outcry. . . . There it was, the thing I had been looking for all these years. . . . A way had been discovered to take pictures by flashlight."

Riis set out to shine light in the dark corners of New York. "Our party carried terror wherever it went," Riis recalled. "The spectacle of strange men invading a house in the midnight hours armed with [flash] pistols which they shot off recklessly was hardly reassuring." But the

Five Cents a Spot Widener Library, Harvard University.

results were a huge step forward for photojournalism.

Riis's book *How the Other Half Lives* (1890) made photographic history. Along with Riis's text and engravings of his drawings, it contained reproductions of seventeen photographs taken with his camera and flash. By looking at a line drawing side by side with the corresponding photograph, we can compare the impact of the two mediums.

The Big Stick

Roosevelt's activism extended to his foreign policy. A fierce proponent of America's interests abroad, he relied on executive power to pursue a vigorous foreign policy, sometimes stretching the powers of the presidency beyond legal limits. In his relations with the European powers, he relied on military strength and diplomacy, a combination he aptly described with the aphorism "Speak softly but carry a big stick."

A strong supporter of the Monroe Doctrine, Roosevelt jealously guarded the U.S. sphere of influence in the Western Hemisphere. His proprietary attitude toward the Caribbean became evident in the case of the Panama Canal. Roosevelt had long been a supporter of a canal linking the Caribbean and the Pacific. By enabling ships to move quickly from the Atlantic to the Pacific, a canal would trim 8,000 miles from a coast-to-coast voyage and effectively double the U.S. Navy's power. Having decided on a route across the Panamanian isthmus (a narrow strip of land connecting North and South America), then part of Colombia, Roosevelt in 1902 offered the Colombian government a one-time sum of $10

DOCUMENT 1

In his early work, Riis had to rely on his own sketches of the conditions he encountered in New York's tenements. Riis is a careful draughtsman, but how much detail can you see in the line drawing (page 600)?

DOCUMENT 2

On a police raid to evict tenement lodgers, Riis describes the room as "not thirteen feet either way," in which "slept twelve men and women, two or three in bunks in a sort of alcove, the rest on the floor." Note how the flash catches the sleepy faces and tired bodies, the crowding, dirt, and disorder (below). Once Riis adopted the flash, he was able to show more graphically life in the tenements. What details are visible in the photograph that are missing in the line drawing?

DOCUMENT 3

Riis took his camera into Baxter Street Court and recorded these observations: "I counted the other day the little ones up to ten years old in a . . . tenement that for a yard has a . . . space in the center with sides fourteen or fifteen feet long, just enough for a row of ill-smelling closets [toilets] . . . and a hydrant. There was about as much light in the 'yard' as in the average cellar. . . . I counted one hundred twenty eight [children] in forty families." Riis's pioneering photojournalism shocked the nation and led not only to tenement reform but also to the development of city playgrounds, neighborhood parks, and child labor laws.

Five Cents a Spot Library of Congress, 3a18572.

Questions for Analysis

Summarize the Argument: How significant is the advent of flash photography? Compare the drawn image with the photograph. Why is the photo so much more dramatic?

Analyze the Evidence: Would you agree that Riis's photographs are "a mirror of reality," or did he interpret and frame the "reality" he photographed?

Ask Historical Questions: How do you think photography affected Americans' views of their society?

---

million and an annual rent of $250,000. When the government in Bogotá refused to accept the offer, Roosevelt became incensed at what he called the "homicidal corruptionists" in Colombia for trying to "blackmail" the United States. At the prompting of a group of New York investors, the Panamanians staged an uprising in 1903, and with unseemly haste the U.S. government recognized the new government within twenty-four hours. The Panamanians promptly accepted the $10 million, and the building got under way. The canal would take eleven years and $375 million to complete; it opened in 1914 (Map 21.2).

In the wake of the Panama affair, a confrontation with Germany over Venezuela, and yet another default on a European debt, this time in the Dominican Republic, Roosevelt grew concerned that financial instability in Latin America would lead European powers to interfere. In 1904, he announced the **Roosevelt Corollary** to the Monroe Doctrine, in which he declared the United States had a right to act as "an international police power" in the Western Hemisphere. Roosevelt stated the United States would not intervene in Latin America as long as nations there conducted their affairs with "decency," but

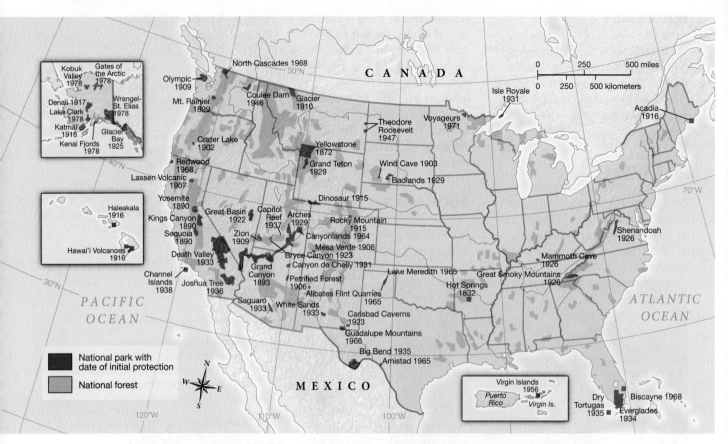

MAP ACTIVITY

Map 21.1 National Parks and Forests

The national park system in the West began with Yellowstone in 1872. Grand Canyon, Yosemite, Kings Canyon, and Sequoia followed in the 1890s. During his presidency, Theodore Roosevelt added six parks—Crater Lake, Wind Cave, Petrified Forest, Lassen Volcanic, Mesa Verde, and Zion.

READING THE MAP: Collectively, do national parks or national forests encompass more land? According to the map, how many national parks were created before 1910? How many were created after 1910?

CONNECTIONS: How do conservation and preservation differ? Why did Roosevelt believe that saving land in the West was important? What principles guided the national land use policy of the Roosevelt administration?

it would step in to stop "brutal wrongdoing." The Roosevelt Corollary served notice to the European powers to keep out.

In Asia, Roosevelt inherited the Open Door policy initiated by Secretary of State John Hay in 1899, designed to ensure U.S. commercial entry into China. As European powers raced to secure Chinese trade and territory, Roosevelt was tempted to use force to gain economic or possibly territorial concessions. Realizing that Americans would

The Roosevelt Corollary in Action

not support an aggressive Asian policy, the president sensibly held back.

In his relations with Europe, Roosevelt sought to establish the United States as a rising force in world affairs. When tensions flared between France and Germany in Morocco in 1905, Roosevelt mediated at a conference in Algeciras, Spain, where he worked to maintain a balance of power that helped neutralize German ambitions. His skillful mediation gained

him a reputation as an astute player on the world stage and demonstrated the nation's new presence in world affairs.

Roosevelt earned the Nobel Peace Prize in 1906 for his role in negotiating an end to the Russo-Japanese War, which had broken out when the Japanese invaded Chinese Manchuria, threatening Russia's sphere of influence in the area. Once again, Roosevelt sought to maintain a balance of power, in this case working to curb Japanese expansionism. Roosevelt admired the Japanese, judging them "the most dashing fighters in the world," but he did not want Japan to become too strong in Asia.

When good relations with Japan were jeopardized by discriminatory legislation in California calling for segregated public schools for Asians, Roosevelt smoothed over the incident and negotiated the "Gentlemen's Agreement" in 1907, which allowed the Japanese to save face by voluntarily restricting immigration to the United States. To demonstrate America's naval power and to counter Japan's growing bellicosity, Roosevelt dispatched the Great White Fleet, sixteen of the navy's most up-to-date battleships, on a "goodwill mission" around the world. U.S. relations with Japan improved, and in the 1908 Root-Takahira agreement the two nations pledged to maintain the Open Door and support the status quo in the Pacific.

Roosevelt's show of American force constituted a classic example of his dictum "Speak softly but carry a big stick."

The Troubled Presidency of William Howard Taft

Roosevelt promised on the eve of his election in 1904 that he would not seek another term. So he retired from the presidency in 1909 at age fifty and removed himself from the political scene by going on safari in Africa. He turned the White House over to his handpicked successor, William Howard Taft, a lawyer who had served as governor-general of the Philippines. Affectionately known as "Big Bill," Taft had served as Roosevelt's right-hand man in the cabinet. In the presidential election of 1908, Taft soundly defeated the perennial Democratic candidate William Jennings Bryan.

A genial man with a talent for law, Taft had no experience in elective office, no feel for politics, and no nerve for controversy. His ambitious wife coveted the office and urged him to seek it. He would have been better off listening to his mother, who warned, "Roosevelt is a good fighter and enjoys it, but the malice of politics would make you miserable." Sadly for Taft, his wife suffered a stroke in his first months in office, leaving him grieving and without his strongest ally.

Progressives and Conservation: Should Hetch Hetchy Be Dammed or Saved?

In 1890, President Benjamin Harrison signed into law an act setting aside two million acres in California's Yosemite Valley and designating Yosemite a national park. For naturalist John Muir, the founder of the Sierra Club, the act marked a victory in his crusade to guarantee that "incomparable Yosemite" would be preserved for posterity. But Muir's fight was not yet over.

The growing city of San Francisco needed water and power, and Mayor James Phelan soon sought to obtain water rights in Hetch Hetchy, a spectacular mountain valley within Yosemite's borders. There, the Tuolumne River could easily be dammed and the valley flooded to create a reservoir large enough to ensure the city's water supply for one hundred years.

When Muir heard of the plan, he sprang into action to save Hetch Hetchy. "That any one would try to destroy such a place seems incredible," he wrote, describing the valley as "one of Nature's rarest and most precious mountain temples." All of Yosemite National Park, he argued, should remain sacrosanct. In 1903, the secretary of the interior concurred, denying San Francisco supervisors commercial use of Hetch Hetchy on the grounds that it lay within the national park.

But the San Francisco earthquake and resulting fire in 1906 created a groundswell of sympathy for the devastated city. In this climate, San Francisco renewed its efforts to obtain Hetch Hetchy and, in 1907, succeeded in gaining authorization to proceed with plans to dam the river and flood the valley.

Given President Theodore Roosevelt's commitment to conservation, how could his administration have agreed to the destruction of the Hetch Hetchy valley? Historians traditionally have styled the struggle as one that pitted conservationists against preservationists. Roosevelt's chief forester, Gifford Pinchot, represented the forces of conservation, or managed use. To him, the battle was not over preservation but over public versus private control of water and power. Roosevelt somewhat reluctantly agreed, although he softened the blow by designating a redwood sanctuary north of San Francisco a national monument in 1907 and naming it Muir Woods.

California progressives, who swept into office with the election of Hiram Johnson as governor in 1910, argued that if Congress did not grant the city of San Francisco the right to control Hetch Hetchy, the powerful Pacific Gas and Electric Company

(PG&E) would monopolize the city's light and power industry. These progressives dismissed Muir and his followers as "nature fakers" and judged them little more than dupes in the machinations of PG&E.

For their part, Muir and the preservationists, although they fought for the integrity of the national parks, did not champion the preservation of wilderness for its own sake. The urban professional men and women who joined the Sierra Club saw nature as a retreat and restorative for city dwellers. The club hosted an annual camping trip to popularize Yosemite and spoke in glowing terms of plans to build new roads and hotels that would make the "healing power of Nature" accessible to "thousands of tired, nerve-shaken, over-civilized people." As historian Robert Righter has pointed out, the battle over Hetch Hetchy represented not so much conservation versus preservation, or managed use versus wilderness, as it did the victory of water and power over tourism and recreation.

Nevertheless, the engineers and irrigation men who dammed Hetch Hetchy demonstrated a breathtaking arrogance. Speaking for them, Franklin Lane, interior secretary under Woodrow Wilson, proclaimed, "The mountains are our enemy. We must pierce them and make them serve. The sinful rivers we must curb." Lane and the conservationists won the day. In 1913, Congress passed the Raker Act authorizing the building of the O'Shaughnessy Dam, completed a decade later. To build the dam, the Hetch Hetchy valley was first denuded of its trees and then flooded under two hundred feet of water. Muir did not live to see the destruction of Hetch Hetchy. He died in 1914, cursing the "dark

Once in office, Taft proved a perfect tool in the hands of Republicans who yearned for a return to the days of a less active executive. A lawyer by training and instinct, Taft believed that it was up to the courts, not the president, to arbitrate social issues. Roosevelt had carried presidential power to a new level, often flouting the separation of powers and showing thinly veiled contempt for Congress and the courts. He believed that the president had the legal right

damn-dam-damnation." But his fight to save Hetch Hetchy galvanized the preservation movement and led to the passage of the National Park Service Act in 1916, creating a federal agency to protect the nation's parks.

The last chapter in the battle over Hetch Hetchy may yet be written. In 1987, President Ronald Reagan's secretary of the interior, Donald Hodel, shocked San Francisco by suggesting the removal of the O'Shaughnessy Dam and the restoration of the Hetch Hetchy valley. Although it is unlikely that the dam will be demolished (it supplies San Francisco not only with water but also with revenue from electric power), advocates for the restoration of the Hetch Hetchy valley continue to rally to the cause. As Ken Browner of the Sierra Club wrote, "Waiting in Yosemite National Park, under water, is a potential masterpiece of restoration" and a chance "to correct the biggest environmental mistake ever committed against the National Park System."

Questions for Analysis

Summarize the Argument: What does the damming of Hetch Hetchy tell us about the Progressive Era's conservation policies in the West?

Analyze the Evidence: How did the goals of conservationists and preservationists differ? Were preservationists like Muir determined to keep the wild places wild? What were the priorities of the conservationists?

Consider the Context: Given President Theodore Roosevelt's progressive conservation policies overall, are critics like Muir right in accusing him of failing to preserve the wilderness?

Roosevelt and Muir in Yosemite
This 1903 photograph shows President Theodore Roosevelt on a camping trip in Yosemite National Park with John Muir. Muir later clashed with Chief Forester Gifford Pinchot over the flooding of the Hetch Hetchy valley in Yosemite to give San Francisco the right to dam the valley to supply water and power. Pinchot never bothered to visit the valley he condemned to a watery grave. Theodore Roosevelt Collection, Houghton Library, Harvard University.

to act as steward of the people, and to do anything necessary "unless the Constitution or the laws explicitly forbid him to do it." Taft found such presidential activism difficult to condone. Although he pursued the trusts vigorously, he acted more like a judge than a steward. Wary of the progressive insurgents in Congress, Taft relied increasingly on conservatives in the Republican Party. As a progressive senator lamented, "Taft is a ponderous and amiable man

THE WORLD'S CONSTABLE.

VISUAL ACTIVITY

"The World's Constable"

In this political cartoon from 1905, President Theodore Roosevelt, dressed as a constable, wields the club of "The New Diplomacy" in one hand with "Arbitration" tucked under his arm. The Roosevelt Corollary to the Monroe Doctrine made the United States the Western Hemisphere's policeman, a role Roosevelt relished. The Granger Collection, New York.

READING THE IMAGE: How does this political cartoon visually represent Roosevelt's foreign policy? Does it appear to be supportive or critical of his policies? How does it treat the other peoples of the world?

CONNECTIONS: What aspects of Roosevelt's foreign policy ideas and actions are depicted in the cartoon?

completely surrounded by men who know exactly what they want."

Taft's troubles began on the eve of his inaugural, when he called a special session of Congress to deal with the tariff. Roosevelt had been too politically astute to tackle the troublesome tariff issue, even though he knew that rates needed to be lowered. Ida Tarbell, who lent her meticulous research skills to the tariff debate, concluded, "At a time when wealth is rolling up as never before, a vast number of hard-working people . . . are really having a more difficult time making ends meet than they have ever had before." Tarbell's articles proved a revelation to many, who had never understood the relationship between the tariff and the price of a pair of shoes.

Taft struggled to transform growing public sentiment against the tariff into legislation. But

Taft blundered into the fray. The Payne-Aldrich bill that emerged was amended in the Senate so that it actually raised the tariff, benefiting big business and the trusts at the expense of consumers. As if paralyzed, Taft neither fought for changes nor vetoed the measure. On a tour of the Midwest in 1909, he was greeted with jeers when he claimed, "I think the Payne bill is the best bill that the Republican Party ever passed." In the eyes of a growing number of Americans, Taft's praise of the tariff made him either a fool or a liar.

Taft's legalism soon got him into hot water in the area of conservation. He undid Roosevelt's work to preserve hydroelectric power sites when he learned that they had been improperly designated as ranger stations. And when Gifford Pinchot publicly denounced Taft's secretary of the interior as a tool of western land-grabbers,

VOL. LXVIII. No. 1768.   PUCK BUILDING, New York, January 18th, 1911.   PRICE TEN CENTS.

THE LOST SKI.

William Howard Taft
In this 1911 *Puck* cartoon, the hapless William Howard Taft veers out of control, losing power in the House of Representatives as he skis down the nomination slide for 1912. Taft had little aptitude for politics and quickly lost the support of progressives in his party. Library of Congress, LC-DIG-ppmsca-27702.

Taft fired Pinchot, touching off a storm of controversy that damaged Taft and alienated Roosevelt. When Roosevelt returned from Africa, Pinchot was among the first to greet him with a half dozen letters from progressives complaining of Taft's leadership.

In June 1910, Roosevelt returned to the United States, where he received a hero's welcome and attracted a stream of visitors and reporters seeking his advice and opinions. Hurt, Taft kept his distance. By late summer, Roosevelt had taken sides with the progressive insurgents in his party. "Taft is utterly hopeless as a leader," Roosevelt confided to his son as he set out on a speaking tour of the West. Reading the mood of the country, Roosevelt began to sound more and more like a candidate.

With the Republican Party divided, the Democrats swept the congressional elections of 1910. Branding the Payne-Aldrich tariff "the mother of trusts," they captured a majority in the House of Representatives and won several key governorships. The revitalized Democratic Party could look to new leaders, among them the progressive governor of New Jersey, Woodrow Wilson.

The new Democratic majority in the House, working with progressive Republicans in the Senate, achieved a number of key reforms, including legislation to regulate railroad safety, to create the Children's Bureau in the Department of Labor, and to establish an eight-hour day for federal workers and miners. Two significant constitutional amendments—the Sixteenth Amendment, which provided for a modest graduated income tax, and the Seventeenth Amendment, which called for the direct election of senators (formerly chosen by state legislatures)—went to the states, where they would win ratification in 1913. While Congress rode the high tide of

Taft's "Dollar Diplomacy"

progressive reform, Taft sat on the sidelines.

In foreign policy, Taft continued Roosevelt's policy of extending U.S. influence abroad, but here, too, Taft had a difficult time following Roosevelt. Taft's "dollar diplomacy" championed commercial goals rather than the strategic aims Roosevelt had pursued. Taft naively assumed he could substitute "dollars for bullets." In the Caribbean, he provoked anti-American feeling by dispatching U.S. Marines to Nicaragua and the Dominican Republic in 1912 pursuant to the Roosevelt Corollary. In Asia, he openly avowed his intent to promote "active intervention to secure for . . . our capitalists opportunity for profitable investment." Lacking Roosevelt's understanding of power politics, Taft failed to recognize that an aggressive commercial policy could not exist without the willingness to use military might to back it up.

Taft faced the limits of dollar diplomacy when revolution broke out in Mexico in 1911. Under pressure to protect American investments, he mobilized troops along the border. In the end, however, with no popular support for a war with Mexico, he had to fall back on diplomatic pressure to salvage American interests.

Taft's greatest dream was to encourage world peace through the use of a world court and arbitration. He unsuccessfully sponsored a series of arbitration treaties that Roosevelt, who prized national honor more than international law, vehemently opposed as weak and cowardly. By 1910, Roosevelt had become a vocal critic of Taft's foreign policy.

The final breach between Taft and Roosevelt came in 1911, when Taft's attorney general filed an antitrust suit against U.S. Steel. In its brief against the corporation, the government cited Roosevelt's agreement with the Morgan interests in the 1907 acquisition of Tennessee Coal and Iron. The incident greatly embarrassed Roosevelt. Either he had been hoodwinked or he had colluded with Morgan. Neither idea pleased him. Thoroughly enraged, he lambasted Taft's "archaic" antitrust policy and hinted that he might be persuaded to run for president again.

REVIEW How did Theodore Roosevelt advance the progressive agenda?

▶ Woodrow Wilson and Progressivism at High Tide

Disillusionment with Taft resulted in a split in the Republican Party and the creation of a new Progressive Party that rallied to Theodore Roosevelt. In the election of 1912, four candidates styled themselves "progressives," but it was Democrat Woodrow Wilson, with a minority of the popular vote, who won the presidency. He would continue Roosevelt's presidential power and help enact progressive legislation.

Progressive Insurgency and the Election of 1912

Convinced that Taft was inept, in February 1912, Roosevelt declared his candidacy for the Republican nomination, announcing, "My hat is in the ring." Taft, with uncharacteristic strength, refused to step aside. Roosevelt took advantage of newly passed primary election laws and ran in thirteen states, winning 278 delegates to Taft's 48. But at the Chicago convention, Taft's bosses refused to seat the Roosevelt delegates. Fistfights broke out on the convention floor as Taft won nomination on the first ballot. Crying robbery, Roosevelt's supporters bolted the party.

Seven weeks later, in the same Chicago auditorium, the hastily organized Progressive Party met to nominate Roosevelt. Full of reforming zeal, the delegates chose Roosevelt and Hiram Johnson to head the new party. Jane Addams seconded Roosevelt's nomination. "I have been fighting for progressive principles for thirty years," she told the enthusiastic crowd. "This is the first time there has been a chance to make them effective. This is the biggest day of my life." The new party lustily approved the most ambitious platform since that of the Populists. Planks called for woman suffrage, presidential primaries, conservation of natural resources, an end to child labor, workers' compensation, a living wage for both men and women workers, social security, health insurance, and a federal income tax.

Roosevelt arrived in Chicago to accept the nomination and announced that he felt "as fit as a bull moose," giving the new party a nickname and a mascot. With characteristic vigor, he launched his campaign with the exhortation, "We stand at Armageddon and do battle for the Lord!" But for all the excitement and the cheering, the new Progressive Party was doomed, and

Woodrow Wilson
Woodrow Wilson, the Democrats' presidential nominee in 1912, speaks to an outdoor campaign rally in New York City. Note the absence of a microphone. Wilson, a former professor of political science and president of Princeton University and recently elected governor of New Jersey, gave carefully phrased, logical, and clear speeches in a somewhat professorial style that contrasted with the charisma and bombast of the Bull Moose candidate, Theodore Roosevelt. Corbis.

the candidate knew it. Privately he confessed to a friend, "I am under no illusion about it. It is a forlorn hope." The people may have supported the party, but the politicians, even progressives such as La Follette, refused to support the new party. The Democrats, delighted at the split in the Republican ranks, nominated Woodrow Wilson, the governor of New Jersey. After only eighteen months in office, the former professor of political science and president of Princeton University found himself running for president of the United States.

Voters in 1912 could choose among four candidates who claimed to be progressives. Taft, Roosevelt, and Wilson each embraced the label, and even the Socialist candidate, Eugene V. Debs, styled himself a progressive. That the term *progressive* could stretch to cover these diverse candidates underscored major disagreements in progressive thinking about the relationship between business and government. Taft, in spite of his trust-busting, was generally viewed as the candidate of the Republican Old Guard. Debs urged voters to support the Socialist Party as the true spirit of the working class. The real contest for the presidency came down to a fight between Roosevelt and Wilson and the two political philosophies summed up in their respective campaign slogans: "**The New Nationalism**" and "**The New Freedom**."

The New Nationalism expressed Roosevelt's belief in federal planning and regulation. He accepted the inevitability of big business but demanded that government act as "a steward of the people" to regulate the giant corporations. Wilson, schooled in the Democratic principles of limited government and states' rights, set a markedly different course with his New Freedom. Wilson promised to use antitrust legislation to get rid of big corporations and to give small businesses and farmers better opportunities in the marketplace.

The energy and enthusiasm of the Bull Moosers made the race seem closer than it was. In the end, the Republican vote split, while the Democrats remained united. No candidate claimed a majority in the race. Wilson captured a bare 42 percent of the popular vote. Roosevelt and his Bull Moose Party won 27 percent, an unprecedented tally for a new party. Taft came in third with 23 percent. The Socialist Party, led by Debs, captured a surprising 6 percent (Map 21.3). The Republican Party moved in a conservative direction, while the Progressive Party essentially collapsed after Roosevelt's defeat. It had always been, in the words of one astute observer, "a house divided against itself and already mortgaged."

Wilson's Reforms: Tariff, Banking, and the Trusts

Born in Virginia and raised in Georgia, Woodrow Wilson became the first southerner elected president since 1844 and only the second Democrat to occupy the White House since Reconstruction.

Candidate	Electoral Vote	Popular Vote	Percent of Popular Vote
Woodrow Wilson (Democrat)	435	6,293,454	41.9
Theodore Roosevelt (Progressive)	88	4,119,538	27.4
William H. Taft (Republican)	8	3,484,980	23.2
Eugene V. Debs (Socialist)	0	900,672	6.1

Map 21.3
The Election of 1912

A believer in states' rights, Wilson nevertheless promised legislation to break the hold of the trusts. This lean, ascetic scholar was, as one biographer conceded, a man whose "political convictions were never as fixed as his ambition." Building on the base built by Roosevelt in strengthening presidential power, Wilson exerted leadership to achieve banking reform and worked through his party in Congress to accomplish the Democratic agenda. Before he was finished, Wilson lent his support to many of the Progressive Party's social reforms.

With the Democrats thoroughly in control of Congress, Wilson immediately called for tariff reform. "The object of the tariff," Wilson told Congress, "must be effective competition." The Democratic House of Representatives hastily passed the Underwood tariff, which lowered rates by 15 percent. To compensate for lost revenue, the House approved a moderate federal income tax made possible by the ratification of the Sixteenth Amendment a month earlier. In the Senate, lobbyists for industries quietly went to work to get the tariff raised, but Wilson rallied public opinion by attacking the "industrious and insidious lobby." In the harsh glare of publicity, the Senate passed the Underwood tariff.

Wilson next turned his attention to banking. The panic of 1907 led the government to turn once again to J. P. Morgan to avoid economic catastrophe. But by the time Wilson came to office, Morgan's legendary power had come under close scrutiny. In 1913, a Senate committee investigated the "money trust," calling Morgan himself to testify. The committee uncovered an alarming concentration of banking power. J. P. Morgan and Company and its affiliates held 341 directorships in 112 corporations, controlling assets of more than $22 million (billions in today's dollars). The sensational findings led to reform.

The Federal Reserve Act of 1913 marked the most significant piece of domestic legislation of Wilson's presidency. It established a national banking system composed of twelve regional banks, privately controlled but regulated and supervised by the Federal Reserve Board, appointed by the president. It gave the United States its first efficient banking and currency system and, at the same time, provided for a greater degree of government control over banking. The new system made currency more elastic and credit adequate for the needs of business and agriculture.

Wilson, flush with success, tackled the trust issue next. When Congress reconvened in January 1914, he supported the introduction and passage of the Clayton Antitrust Act to outlaw "unfair competition"—practices such as price discrimination and interlocking directorates (directors from one corporation sitting on the board of another). In the midst of the successful fight for the Clayton Act, Wilson changed course and threw his support behind the creation of the Federal Trade Commission (FTC), precisely the kind of federal regulatory agency that Roosevelt had advocated in his New Nationalism. The FTC, created in 1914, had not only wide investigatory powers but also the authority to prosecute corporations for "unfair trade practices" and to enforce its judgments by issuing "cease and desist" orders. Despite his campaign promises, Wilson's antitrust program worked to regulate rather than to break up big business.

Wilson, Reluctant Progressive

By the fall of 1914, Wilson declared that the progressive movement had fulfilled its mission and that the country needed "a time of healing." Progressives watched in dismay as Wilson repeatedly obstructed or obstinately refused to endorse further reforms. He failed to support labor's demand for an end to court injunctions against labor unions. He twice threatened to veto legislation providing farm credits for nonperishable crops. He refused to support child labor legislation or woman suffrage. Wilson used the rhetoric of the

New Freedom to justify his actions, claiming that his administration would condone "special privileges to none." But, in fact, his stance often reflected the interests of his small-business constituency.

In the face of Wilson's obstinacy, reform might have ended in 1913 had not politics intruded. In the congressional elections of 1914, the Republican Party, no longer split by Roosevelt's Bull Moose faction, won substantial gains. Democratic strategists recognized that Wilson needed to pick up support in the Midwest and the West by capturing votes from former Bull Moose progressives. Wilson responded belatedly by lending his support to reform in the months leading up to the election of 1916. In a sharp about-face, he cultivated union labor, farmers, and social reformers. To please labor, he appointed progressive Louis Brandeis to the Supreme Court. To woo farmers, he threw his support behind legislation to obtain rural credits. And he won praise from labor by supporting workers' compensation and the Keating-Owen child labor law (1916), which outlawed the regular employment of children younger than sixteen. When a railroad strike threatened in the months before the election, Wilson ordered Congress to establish an eight-hour day on the railroads. He had moved a long way from his New Freedom of 1912, and, as Wilson noted, the Democrats had "come very near to carrying out the platform of the Progressive Party." Wilson's shift toward reform, along with his claim that he had kept the United States out of the war in Europe (as discussed in chapter 22), helped him win reelection in 1916.

> **REVIEW**   How and why did Woodrow Wilson's reform program evolve during his first term?

▶ The Limits of Progressive Reform

While progressivism called for a more active role for the liberal state, at heart it was a movement that sought reforms designed to preserve American institutions and stem the tide of more radical change. Its basic conservatism can be seen by comparing it with the more radical movements of socialism, radical labor, and birth control—and by looking at the groups progressive reform left behind, including women, Asians, and African Americans.

Radical Alternatives

The year 1900 marked the birth of the Social Democratic Party in America, later called simply the **Socialist Party**. Like the progressives, the socialists were middle-class and native-born. They had broken with the older, more militant Socialist Labor Party precisely because of its dogmatic approach and immigrant constituency. The new group of socialists proved eager to appeal to a broad mass of disaffected Americans.

The Socialist Party chose as its presidential standard-bearer Eugene V. Debs, whose experience in the Pullman strike of 1894 (see "Eugene V. Debs and the Pullman Strike" in chapter 20) convinced him that "there is no hope for the toiling masses of my countrymen, except by the pathways mapped out by Socialism." Debs would run for president five times, in every election (except 1916) from 1900 to 1920. The socialism Debs advocated preached cooperation over competition and urged men and women to liberate themselves from "the barbarism of private ownership and wage slavery." In the 1912 election, Debs indicted both old parties as dedicated to the preservation of capitalism and the continuation of the wage system. Styling the Socialist Party the "revolutionary party of the working class," he urged voters to rally to his standard. Debs's best showing came in 1912, when his 6 percent of the popular vote totaled more than 900,000 votes.

Further to the left and more radical than the socialists stood the **Industrial Workers of the World (IWW)**, nicknamed the Wobblies. In 1905, Debs, along with Western Federation of Miners leader William Dudley "Big Bill" Haywood, created the IWW, "one big union" dedicated to organizing the most destitute segment of the workforce, the unskilled workers disdained by Samuel Gompers's AFL: western miners, migrant farmworkers, lumbermen, and immigrant textile workers. Haywood, a craggy-faced miner with one eye (he had lost the other in a childhood accident), was a charismatic leader and a proletarian intellectual. Seeing workers on the lowest rung of the social ladder as the victims of violent repression, the IWW advocated direct action, sabotage, and the general strike—tactics designed to trigger a workers' uprising and overthrow the capitalist state. The IWW claimed it had as many as 100,000 members. Although membership fluctuated greatly, the influence of the IWW extended far beyond its numbers (as discussed in chapter 22).

VISUAL ACTIVITY

Margaret Sanger's Brownsville Birth Control Clinic

Margaret Sanger opened the first birth control clinic in the United States in the Brownsville section of Brooklyn in 1916. Before police shut it down, more than 400 women visited the clinic. Sanger located her clinic in the heart of an immigrant neighborhood to prove that Italian Catholics and Russian Jews wanted birth control as much as their middle- and upper-class Protestant counterparts. Sophia Smith Collection, Smith College. READING THE IMAGE: From this photo, what can you surmise about the women who sought birth control at Sanger's clinic in 1916? Why do so many of them have baby carriages? CONNECTIONS: Why did Sanger consider birth control a radical cause?

In contrast to political radicals like Debs and Haywood, Margaret Sanger promoted the **birth control movement** as a means of social change. Sanger, a nurse who had worked among the poor on New York's Lower East Side, coined the term *birth control* in 1915 and launched a movement with broad social implications. Sanger and her followers saw birth control not only as a sexual and medical reform but also as a means to alter social and political power relationships and to alleviate human misery. By having fewer babies, the working class could constrict the size of the workforce and make possible higher wages and at the same time refuse to provide "cannon fodder" for the world's armies.

The desire for family limitation was widespread, and in this sense birth control was nothing new. The birthrate in the United States had been falling consistently throughout the nineteenth century. The average number of children per family dropped from 7.0 in 1800 to 3.6 by 1900. But the open advocacy of contraception, the use of artificial means to prevent pregnancy, struck many people as both new and shocking. And it was illegal. Anthony Comstock, New York City's commissioner of vice, promoted laws in the 1870s making it a felony not only to sell contraceptive devices like condoms and cervical caps but also to publish information on how to prevent pregnancy.

When Sanger used her militant feminist paper, the *Woman Rebel*, to promote birth control, the Post Office confiscated Sanger's publication and brought charges of obscenity against her. Facing arrest, she fled to Europe, only to return in 1916 as something of a national celebrity. In her absence, birth control had become linked with free speech and had been taken up as a liberal cause. Under public pressure, the government dropped the charges against Sanger, who undertook a nationwide tour to publicize the birth control cause.

Sanger then took direct action, opening the nation's first birth control clinic in the Brownsville section of Brooklyn in October 1916. Located in the heart of a Jewish and Italian immigrant neighborhood, the clinic attracted 464 clients. On the tenth day, police shut down the clinic and threw Sanger in jail. By then, she had become a national figure, and the cause she championed had gained legitimacy, if not legality. Sanger soon reopened her clinic. After World War I, the birth control movement would become much less radical. Altering her tactics to suit the conservative temper of the times, Sanger sought support from medical doctors. She even jumped aboard the popular fad of eugenics, a racist genetic theory that warned against allowing the "unfit" to reproduce. But in its infancy, birth control was part of a radical vision for reforming the world that made common cause with the socialists and the IWW in challenging the limits of progressive reform.

Woman Suffrage Parade

Suffragettes staged a grand parade in Washington, D.C., in 1913, demanding, among other reforms, a constitutional amendment to enfranchise women, as depicted on the float shown here. Angry crowds tried unsuccessfully to break up the parade. The parade illustrated both the strong, organized support for woman suffrage and the implacable opposition. Schlesinger Library, Radcliffe Institute, Harvard University/Bridgeman Images.

Progressivism for White Men Only

The day before President Woodrow Wilson's inauguration in March 1913, the largest mass march to that date in the nation's history took place as more than five thousand demonstrators took to the streets in Washington to demand the vote for women. A rowdy crowd on hand to celebrate the Democrats' triumph attacked the marchers. Men spat at the suffragists and threw lighted cigarettes and matches at their clothing. "If my wife were where you are," a burly cop told one suffragist, "I'd break her head." But for all the marching, Wilson pointedly ignored woman suffrage in his inaugural address the next day.

The march served as a reminder that the political gains of progressivism were not spread equally throughout the population. As the twentieth century dawned, women still could not vote in most states, although they had won major victories in the West. Increasingly, however, woman suffrage had become an international movement.

Alice Paul, a Quaker social worker who had visited England and participated in suffrage activism there, returned to the United States in 1910 in time to plan the mass march on the eve of Wilson's inauguration and to lobby for a federal amendment to give women the vote. Paul's dramatic tactics alienated many in the National American Woman Suffrage Association. In 1916, Paul founded the militant National Woman's Party, which became the radical voice of the suffrage movement.

Women weren't the only group left out in progressive reform. Progressivism, as it was practiced in the West and South, was tainted with racism by seeking to limit the rights of Asians and African Americans. Anti-Asian bigotry in the West led to a renewal of the Chinese Exclusion Act in 1902. At first, California governor Hiram Johnson stood against the strong anti-Asian prejudice of his state. But in 1913, he caved in to popular pressure and signed the Alien Land Law, which barred Japanese immigrants from purchasing land in California.

South of the Mason-Dixon line, the progressives' racism targeted African Americans. Progressives preached the disfranchisement of black voters as a "reform." During the bitter electoral fights that had pitted Populists against Democrats in the 1890s, the party of white supremacy held its power by votes purchased or coerced from African Americans. Southern progressives proposed to reform the electoral system by eliminating black voters. Beginning in 1890 with Mississippi, southern states curtailed the African American vote through devices such as poll taxes (fees required for voting) and literacy tests.

The Progressive Era also witnessed the rise of Jim Crow laws to segregate public facilities. The new railroads precipitated segregation in the South where it had rarely existed before, at least on paper. Soon, separate railcars, separate waiting rooms, separate bathrooms, and separate dining facilities for blacks sprang up across the South. In courtrooms in Mississippi, blacks were required to swear on a separate Bible.

In the face of this growing repression, Booker T. Washington, the preeminent black leader of the day, urged caution and restraint. A former slave, Washington opened the Tuskegee Institute in Alabama in 1881 to teach vocational skills to African Americans. He emphasized education and economic progress for his race and urged African Americans to put aside issues of political and social equality. In an 1895 speech in Atlanta that came to be known as the Atlanta Compromise, he stated, "In all things that are purely social we can be as separate as the fingers, yet one as the hand in all things essential to mutual progress." Washington's accommodationist policy appealed to whites and elevated "the wizard of Tuskegee" to the role of national spokesman for African Americans.

VISUAL ACTIVITY

Booker T. Washington and Theodore Roosevelt Dine at the White House

Theodore Roosevelt invited Booker T. Washington to the White House in 1901, stirring up a hornet's nest of controversy that continued into the election of 1904. The Republican campaign piece pictured shows Roosevelt and a light-skinned Washington sitting under a portrait of Abraham Lincoln. Democrats' campaign buttons pictured Washington with darker skin and implied that Roosevelt had "painted the White House black" and favored "race mingling." David J. & Janice L. Frent Collection/Corbis.

READING THE IMAGE: In this Republican image of the famous meeting of Booker T. Washington and Theodore Roosevelt at the White House, what role does skin color play in the depiction?

CONNECTIONS: Why did African Americans in the South continue to ally with the Republican Party?

DINNER GIVEN AT THE WHITE HOUSE BY PRESIDENT ROOSEVELT TO BOOKER T. WASHINGTON, OCTOBER 17th, 1901

The year after Washington proclaimed the Atlanta Compromise, the Supreme Court upheld the legality of racial segregation, affirming in *Plessy v. Ferguson* (1896) the constitutionality of the doctrine of "separate but equal." Blacks could be segregated in separate schools, restrooms, and other facilities as long as the facilities were "equal" to those provided for whites. Of course, facilities for blacks rarely proved equal.

Woodrow Wilson brought to the White House southern attitudes toward race and racial segregation. He instituted segregation in the federal workforce, especially the Post Office, and approved segregated drinking fountains and restrooms in the nation's capital. When critics attacked the policy, Wilson insisted that segregation was "in the interest of the Negro."

In 1906, a major race riot in Atlanta called into question Booker T. Washington's strategy of uplift and accommodation. For three days in September, the streets of Atlanta ran red with blood as angry white mobs chased and cornered any blacks they happened upon. An estimated 250 African Americans died in the riots—members of Atlanta's black middle class along with the poor and derelict. Professor William Crogman of Clark College noted the central irony of the riot: "Here we have worked and prayed and tried to make good men and women of our colored population," he observed, "and at our very doorstep the whites kill these good men." The riot caused many African Americans to question Washington's strategy of gradualism and accommodation.

Foremost among Washington's critics stood W. E. B. Du Bois, a Harvard graduate who urged African Americans to fight for civil rights and racial justice. In *The Souls of Black Folk* (1903), Du Bois attacked the "Tuskegee Machine," comparing Washington to a political boss who used his influence to silence his critics and reward his followers. Du Bois founded the Niagara movement in 1905, calling for universal male suffrage, civil rights, and leadership composed of a black intellectual elite. The Atlanta riot only bolstered his resolve. In 1909, the Niagara movement helped found the National Association for the Advancement of Colored People (NAACP), a coalition of blacks and whites that sought legal and political rights for African Americans through the courts. In the decades that followed, the NAACP came to represent the future for African Americans, while Booker T. Washington, who died in 1915, represented the past.

REVIEW   How did race, class, and gender shape the limits of progressive reform?

▶ Conclusion: The Transformation of the Liberal State

Progressivism's goal was to reform the existing system—by government intervention if necessary—but without uprooting any of the traditional American political, economic, or social institutions. As Theodore Roosevelt, the bellwether of the movement, insisted, "The only true conservative is the man who resolutely sets his face toward the future." Roosevelt was such a man, and progressivism was such a movement. But although progressivism was never radical, progressives' willingness to use the power of government to regulate business and achieve a measure of social justice redefined liberalism in the twentieth century, tying it to the expanded power of the state.

Progressivism contained many paradoxes. A diverse coalition of individuals and interests, the progressive movement began at the grass roots but left as its legacy a stronger presidency and unprecedented federal involvement in the economy and social welfare. A movement that believed in social justice, progressivism often promoted social control. And while progressives called for greater democracy, they fostered elitism with their worship of experts and efficiency, and they often failed to champion equality for women and minorities.

Whatever its inconsistencies and limitations, progressivism took action to deal with the problems posed by urban industrialism. Progressivism saw grassroots activists address social problems on the local and state levels and search for national solutions. By increasing the power of the presidency and expanding the power of the state, progressives worked to bring about greater social justice and to achieve a better balance between government and business. Jane Addams and Theodore Roosevelt could lay equal claim to the movement that redefined liberalism and launched the liberal state of the twentieth century. War on a global scale would provide progressivism with yet another challenge even before it had completed its ambitious agenda.

See the Selected Bibliography for this chapter in the Appendix.

21 Chapter Review

REVIEW QUESTIONS

1. What types of people were drawn to the progressive movement, and why? (pp. 589–594)

2. How did progressives justify their demand for more activist government? (pp. 594–595)

3. How did Theodore Roosevelt advance the progressive agenda? (pp. 596–608)

4. How and why did Woodrow Wilson's reform program evolve during his first term? (pp. 608–611)

5. How did race, class, and gender shape the limits of progressive reform? (pp. 611–615)

MAKING CONNECTIONS

1. Roosevelt's foreign policy was summed up in the dictum "Speak softly but carry a big stick." Using two examples, describe how this policy worked.

2. Compare the legislative programs of Roosevelt and Wilson and the evolution of their policies over time.

3. What movements lay outside progressive reform? Why did progressivism coincide with the restriction of minority rights?

LINKING TO THE PAST

1. In what ways did Populism and progressivism differ? In what ways were they similar? (See chapter 20.)

2. During the Gilded Age, industrial capitalism concentrated power in the hands of corporations. How did Roosevelt respond to this problem? How did his approach differ from that of the Gilded Age presidents? Was his strategy effective? (See chapter 18.)

22 World War I: The Progressive Crusade at Home and Abroad

1914–1920

CONTENT LEARNING OBJECTIVES

After reading and studying this chapter, you should be able to:

• Explain the origins of World War I, and why Woodrow Wilson advocated U.S. neutrality. List the events that prompted the United States to enter the war.

• Describe how America geared up domestically and militarily to fight a foreign war.

• Recognize how the war transformed policy at home and understand how women's rights activists used U.S. involvement to secure woman suffrage.

• Explain Wilson's vision for a postwar world, and how that vision was compromised at Versailles. Chronicle the fate of the Paris peace treaty in the U.S. Senate, and explain why it faced so much opposition.

• Understand what threats democracy faced in the immediate postwar period.

GAS MASK
Both the Germans and Allies used poison gas during the First World War. Despite this gas mask's crude appearance, it proved highly effective. But many of those who were gassed and survived were left disabled. Collection of Colonel Stuart S. Corning Jr./ Picture Research Consultants & Archives.

GEORGE "BROWNIE" BROWNE WAS ONE OF TWO MILLION SOLDIERS who crossed the Atlantic during World War I to serve in the American Expeditionary Force in France. The twenty-three-year-old civil engineer from Waterbury, Connecticut, volunteered in July 1917, three months after the United States entered the war, serving with the 117th Engineers Regiment, 42nd Division. Two-thirds of the "doughboys" (American soldiers in Europe) saw action during the war, and few white troops saw more than Brownie did.

When the 42nd arrived at the front, veteran French troops taught Brownie's regiment of engineers how to build and maintain trenches, barbed-wire entanglements, and artillery and machine-gun positions. Although Brownie came under German fire each day, he wrote Martha Johnson, his girlfriend back home, "the longer I'm here the more spirit I have to 'stick it out' for the good of humanity and the U.S. which is the same thing."

Training ended in the spring of 1918 when the Germans launched a massive offensive in the Champagne region. The German bombardment made the night "as light as daytime, and the ground . . . was a mass of flames and whistling steel from the bursting shells." One doughboy from the 42nd remembered, "Dead bodies were all around me. Americans, French, Hun [Germans] in all phases and positions of death." Another declared that soon "the odor was something fierce. We had to put on our gas masks to keep from getting sick." Eight days of combat cost the 42nd nearly 6,500 dead, wounded, and missing, 20 percent of the division.

After only ten days' rest, Brownie and his unit joined in the first major American offensive, an attack against German defenses at Saint-Mihiel. On September 12, 3,000 American artillery launched more than a million rounds against German positions. This time the engineers preceded the advancing infantry, cutting through or blasting any barbed wire that remained. The battle cost the 42nd another 1,200 casualties, but Brownie was not among them.

At the end of September, the 42nd shifted to the Meuse-Argonne region, where it participated in the most brutal American fighting of the war. And it was there that Brownie's war ended. The Germans fired thousands of poison gas shells, and the gas, "so thick you could cut it with a knife," felled Brownie. When the war ended on November 11, 1918, he was recovering from his respiratory wounds at a camp behind the lines. Discharged from the army in February 1919, Brownie returned home, where he and Martha married. Like the rest of the country, they were eager to get on with their lives.

President Woodrow Wilson had never expected to lead the United States into the Great War, as the Europeans called it. When war erupted in 1914, he declared America's absolute neutrality. But trade and principle entangled the United States in Europe's troubles and gradually drew the nation into the conflict. Wilson claimed that America's participation would serve grand purposes and uplift both the United States and the entire world.

At home, the war helped progressives finally achieve their goals of national prohibition and woman suffrage, but it also promoted a vicious attack on Americans' civil liberties. Hyperpatriotism meant intolerance, repression, and vigilante violence. In 1919, Wilson sailed for Europe to secure a just peace. Unable to dictate terms to the victors, he accepted disappointing compromises. Upon his return to the United States, he met a crushing defeat that marked the end of Wilsonian internationalism abroad. Crackdowns on dissenters, immigrants, racial and ethnic minorities, and unions also signaled the end of the Progressive Era at home.

George "Brownie" Browne
Training at Fort Slocum, New York, Brownie complained about the army's red tape, bad food, shortage of equipment, inexperienced officers, lack of sleep, and physical exhaustion. Still, he enjoyed the camaraderie of the camp and was, as this photograph reveals, a happy soldier. When his unit arrived at Saint-Nazaire in October 1917, Brownie was proud to be one of the first doughboys in France. Courtesy of Janet W. Hansen.

► Woodrow Wilson and the World

Shortly after winning election to the presidency in 1912, Woodrow Wilson confided to a friend: "It would be an irony of fate if my administration had to deal with foreign affairs." Indeed, Wilson had focused his life and career on domestic concerns; in his campaign for the presidency, Wilson had hardly mentioned the world abroad.

Wilson, however, could not avoid the world and the rising tide of militarism, nationalism, and violence that beat against American shores. Economic interests compelled the nation outward. Moreover, Wilson was drawn abroad by his own progressive political principles. He believed that the United States had a moral duty to champion national self-determination, peaceful free trade, and political democracy. "We have no selfish ends to serve," he proclaimed. "We desire no conquest, no dominion. . . . We are but one of the champions of the rights of mankind." Yet as president, Wilson was as ready as any American president to apply military solutions to problems of foreign policy. This readiness led Wilson and the United States into military conflict in Mexico and then in Europe.

Taming the Americas

When he took office, Wilson sought to distinguish his foreign policy from that of his Republican predecessors. To Wilson, Theodore Roosevelt's "big stick" and William Howard Taft's "dollar diplomacy" appeared as crude flexing of military and economic muscle. To signal a new direction, Wilson appointed William Jennings Bryan, a pacifist, as secretary of state.

But Wilson and Bryan, like Roosevelt and Taft, also believed that the Monroe Doctrine gave the United States special rights and responsibilities in the Western Hemisphere. Issued in 1823 to warn Europeans not to attempt to colonize the Americas again, the doctrine had become a cloak for U.S. domination. Wilson thus authorized U.S. military intervention in Nicaragua, Haiti, and the Dominican Republic, paving the way for U.S. banks and corporations to take financial control. All the while, Wilson believed that U.S. actions were promoting order and democracy. "I am going to teach the South American Republics to elect good men!" he declared (Map 22.1).

Wilson's most serious involvement in Latin America came in Mexico. When General Victoriano Huerta seized power by violent means in 1913,

CHRONOLOGY

1914	• U.S. Marines occupy Veracruz, Mexico. • Archduke Franz Ferdinand assassinated. • Austria-Hungary declares war on Serbia. • Germany attacks Russia and France. • Great Britain declares war on Germany.
1915	• German U-boat sinks *Lusitania*.
1916	• Pancho Villa attacks Americans in Mexico and New Mexico. • Wilson reelected.
1917	• Zimmermann telegram intercepted. • United States declares war on Germany. • Committee on Public Information created. • Selective Service Act enacted. • Espionage Act and Trading with the Enemy Act enacted.
1918	• Wilson gives Fourteen Points speech. • Russia arranges separate peace with Germany. • Sedition Act enacted. • U.S. Marines see first major combat. • Armistice signed ending World War I.
1919	• Paris peace conference begins. • Treaty of Versailles signed. • Wave of labor strikes occurs.
1920	• American Civil Liberties Union founded. • Prohibition begins. • Palmer raids ordered. • Senate votes against ratification of Treaty of Versailles. • American women get the vote. • Warren G. Harding elected president.

Map 22.1   U.S. Involvement in Latin America and the Caribbean, 1895–1941

Victory against Spain in 1898 made Puerto Rico an American possession and Cuba a protectorate. The United States later gained control of the Panama Canal Zone. The nation protected its expanding economic interests with military force by propping up friendly, though not necessarily democratic, governments.

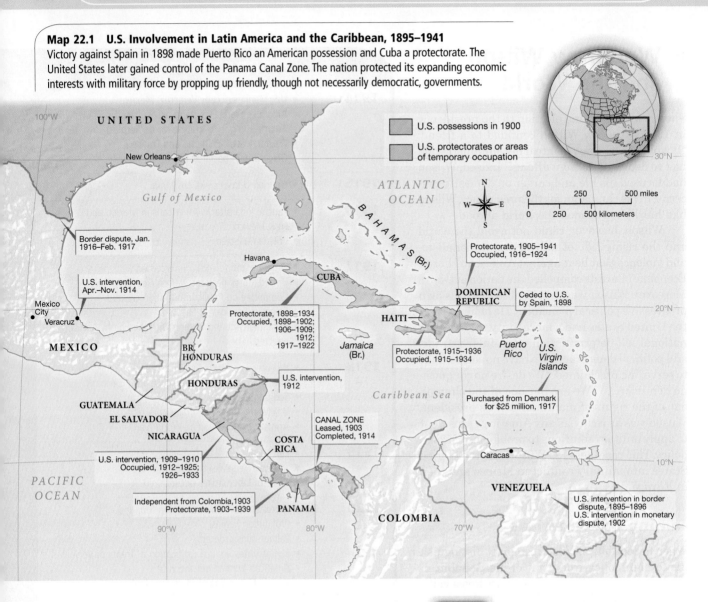

U.S. Intervention in Mexico, 1916–1917

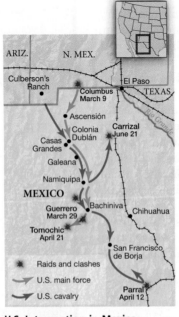

most European nations promptly recognized Mexico's new government, but Wilson refused, declaring that he would not support a "government of butchers." In April 1914, Wilson sent 800 Marines to seize the port of Veracruz to prevent the unloading of a large shipment of arms for Huerta. Huerta fled to Spain, and the United States welcomed a more compliant government.

But a rebellion erupted among desperately poor farmers who believed that the new government, aided by U.S. business interests, had betrayed the revolution's promise to help the common people. In January 1916, the rebel army, commanded by Francisco "Pancho" Villa, seized a train carrying gold to Texas from an American-owned mine in Mexico and killed the 17 American engineers aboard. In March, Villa's men crossed the border for a predawn raid on Columbus, New Mexico, where they killed 18 Americans. Wilson promptly dispatched 12,000 troops, led by Major General John J. Pershing. But Villa avoided capture, and in January 1917

Wilson recalled Pershing so that he might prepare the army for the possibility of fighting in the Great War.

The European Crisis

Before 1914, Europe had enjoyed decades of peace, but just beneath the surface lay the potentially destructive forces of nationalism and imperialism. The consolidation of the German and Italian states into unified nations and the similar ambition of Russia to create a Pan-Slavic union initiated new rivalries throughout Europe. As the conviction spread that colonial possessions were a mark of national greatness, competition expanded onto the world stage. Most ominously, Germany's efforts under Kaiser Wilhelm II to challenge Great Britain's world supremacy by creating industrial muscle at home, an empire abroad, and a mighty navy threatened the balance of power and thus the peace.

European nations sought to avoid an explosion by developing a complex web of military and diplomatic alliances. By 1914, Germany, Austria-Hungary, and Italy (the **Triple Alliance**) stood opposed to Great Britain, France, and Russia (the **Triple Entente**, also known as "the Allies"). But in their effort to prevent war through a balance of power, Europeans had actually magnified the possibility of large-scale conflict (Map 22.2). Treaties, some of them secret, obligated members of the alliances to come to the aid of another member if attacked.

The fatal sequence began on June 28, 1914, in the city of Sarajevo, when a Bosnian Serb terrorist assassinated Archduke Franz Ferdinand, heir to the Austro-Hungarian throne. On July 18, Austria-Hungary declared war on Serbia. The elaborate alliance system meant that the war could not remain local. Russia announced that it would back the Serbs. Compelled by treaty to support Austria-Hungary, Germany on August 3 attacked Russia and France. In response, on August 4, Great Britain, upholding its pact with France, declared war on Germany. Within weeks, Europe was engulfed in war. The conflict became a world war when Japan, seeing an opportunity to rid itself of European competition in China, joined the cause against Germany.

The evenly matched alliances would fight a disastrous war lasting more than four years, at a cost of 8.5 million soldiers' lives. A war that started with a solitary murder proved impossible to stop. Britain's foreign secretary, Edward Grey, lamented: "The lamps are going out all over Europe. We shall not see them lit again in our lifetime."

The Ordeal of American Neutrality

Woodrow Wilson promptly announced that because the war engaged no vital American interest and involved no significant principle, the United States would remain neutral. Neutrality entitled the United States to trade safely with all nations at war, he declared. Unfettered trade, Wilson believed, was not only a right under international law but also a necessity because in 1913 the U.S. economy had slipped into a recession that wartime disruption of European trade could drastically worsen.

Although Wilson proclaimed neutrality, his sympathies, like those of many Americans, lay with Great Britain and France. Americans gratefully remembered crucial French assistance in the American Revolution and shared with the British a language, a culture, and a commitment to liberty. Germany, by contrast, was a monarchy with strong militaristic traditions. Still, Wilson insisted on neutrality, in part because he feared the conflict's effects on the United States as a nation of immigrants. As he told the German ambassador, "We definitely have to be neutral, since otherwise our mixed populations would wage war on each other."

Britain's powerful fleet controlled the seas and quickly set up an economic blockade of Germany. The United States vigorously protested, but Britain refused to give up its naval advantage. The blockade actually had little economic impact on the United States. Between 1914 and the spring of 1917, while trade with Germany evaporated, war-related exports to Britain—food, clothing, steel, and munitions—escalated by some 400 percent, enough to pull the American economy out of its slump. Although the British blockade violated American neutrality, the Wilson administration gradually acquiesced, thus beginning the fateful process of alienation from Germany.

Germany retaliated with a submarine blockade of British ports. German *Unterseebooten*, or U-boats, threatened notions of "civilized" warfare.

Map. 22.2   European Alliances after the Outbreak of World War I
With Germany and Austria-Hungary wedged between their Entente rivals and all parties fully armed, Europe
was poised for war when Archduke Franz Ferdinand of Austria-Hungary was assassinated in Sarajevo in
June 1914.

Unlike surface warships that could harmlessly stop freighters and prevent them from entering a war zone, submarines relied on sinking their quarry. And once they sank a ship, the tiny U-boats could not pick up survivors. Nevertheless, in February 1915, Germany announced that it intended to sink on sight enemy ships en route to the British Isles. On May 7, 1915, a German U-boat torpedoed the British passenger liner *Lusitania*, killing 1,198 passengers, 128 of them U.S. citizens.

American newspapers featured drawings of drowning women and children, and some demanded war. Calmer voices pointed out that Germany had warned prospective passengers and that the *Lusitania* carried millions of rounds

of ammunition and so was a legitimate target. Secretary of State Bryan resisted the hysteria and declared that a ship carrying war materiel "should not rely on passengers to protect her from attack—it would be like putting women and children in front of an army." He counseled Wilson to warn American citizens that they traveled on ships of belligerent countries at their own risk.

Wilson sought a middle course that would retain his commitment to peace and neutrality without condoning German attacks on passenger ships. On May 10, 1915, he announced that any further destruction of ships would be regarded as "deliberately unfriendly" and might lead the United States to break diplomatic relations with Germany. Wilson essentially demanded that Germany abandon unrestricted submarine warfare. Bryan resigned, predicting that the president had placed the United States on a collision course with Germany. Wilson replaced Bryan with Robert Lansing, who believed that Germany's anti-democratic character and goal of "world dominance" meant that it "must not be permitted to win this war."

After Germany apologized for the civilian deaths on the *Lusitania*, tensions subsided. And in 1916, Germany went further, promising no more submarine attacks without warning and without provisions for the safety of civilians. Wilson's supporters celebrated the success of his middle-of-the-road strategy.

Wilson's diplomacy proved helpful in his bid for reelection in 1916. In the contest against Republican Charles Evans Hughes, the Democratic Party ran Wilson under the slogan "He kept us out of war." Wilson felt uneasy with the claim, protesting that "they talk of me as though I were a god. Any little German lieutenant can push us into the war at any time by some calculated outrage." But the Democrats' case for Wilson's neutrality appealed to enough of those in favor of peace to eke out a majority. Wilson won, but only by the razor-thin margins of 600,000 popular and 23 electoral votes.

The United States Enters the War

Step by step, the United States backed away from "absolute neutrality." The consequence of protesting the German blockade of Great Britain but accepting the British blockade of Germany was that by 1916 the United States was supplying the Allies with 40 percent of their war materiel. When France and Britain ran short of money to pay for U.S. goods and asked for loans, Wilson argued that "loans by American bankers to any foreign government which is at war are inconsistent with the true spirit of neutrality." But rather than jeopardize

Sinking of the *Lusitania*, 1915

America's wartime prosperity, Wilson allowed billions of dollars in loans that kept American goods flowing to Britain and France.

In January 1917, Germany decided that it could no longer afford to allow neutral shipping to reach Great Britain while Britain's blockade gradually starved Germany. It announced that its navy would resume unrestricted submarine warfare and sink without warning any ship, enemy or neutral, found in the waters off Great Britain. Germany understood that the decision would probably bring the United States into the war but gambled that its submarines would strangle the British economy and allow German armies to win a military victory in France before American troops arrived in Europe.

Resisting demands for war, Wilson continued to hope for a negotiated peace and only broke off diplomatic relations with Germany. Then, on February 25, 1917, British authorities informed Wilson of a secret telegram sent by the German foreign secretary, Arthur Zimmermann, to the German minister in Mexico. It promised that in the event of war between Germany and the United States, Germany would see that Mexico regained its "lost provinces" of Texas, New Mexico, and Arizona if Mexico would declare war against the United States. Wilson angrily responded to the Zimmermann telegram by asking Congress to approve a policy of "armed neutrality" that would allow merchant ships to fight back against attackers.

In March, German submarines sank five American vessels off Britain, killing 66 Americans. On April 2, the president asked Congress to issue a declaration of war. He accused Germany of "warfare against all mankind." Still, he called for a "war without hate" and declared that America fought only to "vindicate the principles of peace and justice." He promised a world made "safe for democracy." On April 6, 1917, by majorities of 373 to 50 in the House and 82 to 6 in the Senate, Congress voted to declare war.

Wilson feared what war would do at home. He said despairingly, "Once lead this people into war, and they'll forget there ever was such a thing as tolerance. To fight you must be brutal

"Chums"

This American war poster from 1918 depicts the devil seated with his arm around Germany's Kaiser Wilhelm, a devil-like figure himself, who holds a bloody sword. The devil is congratulating Wilhelm for sinking the *Lusitania* three years earlier. The poster left no doubt that America was on the side of the angels and did the right thing by going to war. Library of Congress, 3g07819.

and ruthless, and the spirit of ruthless brutality will infect Congress, the courts, the policeman on the beat, the man in the street."

> **REVIEW**   Why did President Wilson fail to maintain U.S. neutrality during World War I?

▶ "Over There"

American soldiers joined the fighting just after the Russians withdrew from the war, leaving France as the primary battleground. Americans sailed for France eager to do their part in making the world safe for democracy. Some doughboys, including George Browne, maintained their idealism to the end. Although black soldiers eventually won respect under the French command, they faced discrimination under American commanders. The majority of American soldiers found little that was noble in rats, lice, and poison gas and—despite the progressives' hopes—little to elevate the human soul in a landscape of utter destruction and death.

The Call to Arms

When America entered the war, Britain and France were nearly exhausted after almost three years of conflict. Millions of soldiers had perished; food and morale were dangerously low. Another Allied power, Russia, was in turmoil. In March 1917, a revolution had forced Czar Nicholas II to abdicate, and a year later, in a separate peace with Germany, the **Bolshevik** revolutionary government withdrew Russia from the war. Peace with Russia allowed Germany to withdraw hundreds of thousands of its soldiers from the eastern front and to deploy them against the Allies on the western front in France.

On May 18, 1917, Wilson signed a sweeping Selective Service Act, authorizing a draft of all young men into the armed forces. Conscription transformed a tiny volunteer armed force of 80,000 men into a vast army and navy. Draft boards eventually inducted 2.8 million men into the armed services, in addition to the 2 million, including George Browne, who volunteered.

Among the 4.8 million men under arms, 370,000 were black Americans. During training, black recruits suffered the same prejudices that they encountered in civilian life. One base in Virginia that trained blacks as cargo handlers

USS *Recruit*, ca. 1917
Shortly after the United States declared war on Germany in April 1917, the government instituted a military draft. But efforts to sign up volunteers continued. This photograph shows the USS *Recruit*, a wooden battle-ship constructed in Manhattan by the navy as a recruiting tool. When the war ended, 2.8 million men had been drafted and another 2 million men volunteered. Library of Congress, LC-DIG-ggbain-24411.

quartered black recruits in tents without floors or stoves and provided no changes of clothes, no blankets for the winter, and no facilities for bathing. Only after several deaths from disease and exposure did the authorities move to make conditions even tolerable. (See "Making Historical Arguments," page 626.)

Training camps sought to transform raw white recruits into fighting men. Progressives in the government were also determined that the camps turn out soldiers with the highest moral and civic values. To provide recruits with "invisible armor," YMCA workers and veterans of the settlement house and playground movements led them in games, singing, and college extension courses. The army asked soldiers to stop thinking about sex, explaining that a "man who is thinking below the belt is not efficient." Wilson's choice to command the army on the battlefields of France, Major General John "Black Jack" Pershing, was as morally upright as he was militarily uncompromising. Described by one observer as "lean, clean, keen," he gave progressives perfect confidence.

The War in France

At the front, the **American Expeditionary Force (AEF)** discovered a desperate situation. The war had degenerated into a stalemate of armies dug into hundreds of miles of trenches that stretched across France. Huddling in the mud among the corpses and rats, soldiers were separated from the enemy by only a few hundred yards of "no-man's-land." When ordered "over the top," troops raced desperately toward the enemy's trenches, only to be entangled in barbed wire, enveloped in poison gas, and mowed down by machine guns. The three-day battle of the Somme in 1916 cost the French and British forces 600,000 dead and wounded and the Germans 500,000. The deadliest battle of the war allowed the Allies to advance their trenches only a few meaningless miles.

Still, U.S. troops saw almost no combat in 1917. Troops continued to train and used much of their free time to explore places that most of them could otherwise never hope to see. True to the crusader image, American officials allowed

What Did African Americans Want from World War I, and What Did They Get?

When the United States entered the First World War, some black leaders remembered the crucial role that black soldiers had played in the Civil War. They rejoiced that military service would once again offer blacks a chance to demonstrate their patriotism and fitness for full citizenship. Others, however, believed that black Americans had already long ago demonstrated their worth.

The National Association for the Advancement of Colored People (NAACP) declared that black Americans would support the war but added, "Absolute loyalty in arms and civil duties need not for a moment lead us to abate our just complaints and just demands." W. E. B. Du Bois, the NAACP's most outspoken member, urged blacks to "close ranks" in support of the war effort—until the nation had won the war. The enemy of the moment, Du Bois insisted, was German "military despotism," which unchecked, "spells death to the aspirations of Negroes and all darker races for equality, freedom, and democracy."

While African Americans remained skeptical about President Wilson's claim that the United States was fighting to make the world safe for democracy, most nevertheless

followed Du Bois's advice. On the first day of registration for military service, more than 70,000 black men signed in at their draft boards. By war's end, 370,000 blacks had been inducted, some 31 percent of the total number of blacks registered. The figure for whites was 26 percent.

During training, black recruits discovered that they were rigidly segregated, usually assigned to labor battalions, and faced crude abuse and miserable living conditions. When black soldiers arrived in Europe, white commanders made a point of maintaining American racial standards. A report from the headquarters of the American commander, General John J. Pershing, advised the French that their failure to draw the color line threatened Franco-American relations. Among other things, the French allowed black soldiers to serve alongside whites. They should resist the urge, the report declared, to accept blacks as equals or to thank them for their efforts, for fear of "spoiling the Negroes."

Seeking to take advantage of the situation, German propagandists raised some difficult questions. One leaflet distributed to black troops reminded them that they lacked the rights whites enjoyed, were

segregated, and sometimes lynched. "Why, then, fight the Germans," the leaflet asked, "only for the benefit of the Wall Street robbers and to protect the millions they have loaned to the British, French, and Italians?" Why, indeed?

Black soldiers wanted to prove a point. While at first they worked mainly as laborers, before long they had their chance to fight. In February 1918, General Pershing received an urgent call from the French for help on the front lines. Determined not to lose control over the white troops he valued more, Pershing sent black regiments from the 92nd Division. At the front, they were integrated into units of the French army. The black 369th Regiment spent 191 days in battle—longer than any other American outfit. The 369th won the most medals of any American combat unit, more than one hundred Croix de Guerre, crosses given by the French for gallantry in war. Black soldiers recognized the irony of having to serve with the French to gain respect.

When the battle-scarred survivors of the 92nd Division returned home, they marched proudly past cheering crowds in Manhattan and Chicago. African American spokesmen proclaimed a new era for black

only uplifting tourism. The temptations of Paris were off-limits. French premier Georges Clemenceau's offer to supply American troops with licensed prostitutes was declined with the half-serious remark that if Wilson found out he would stop the war.

Sightseeing ended abruptly in March 1918 when a million German soldiers punched a hole in the Allied lines. Pershing finally committed

the AEF to combat. In May and June, at Cantigny and then at Château-Thierry, the eager but green Americans checked the German advance with a series of assaults (Map 22.3). Then they headed toward the forest stronghold of Belleau Wood, moving against streams of retreating Allied soldiers who cried defeat: "La guerre est finie!" (The war is over!). A French officer commanded the Americans to retreat with them,

Black Troops Return from War
This photograph captures the joy and pride felt by African American troops when they arrived in New York City after the war. The ship carried the famous 369th New York Infantry, black soldiers who served valiantly with the French and never fought alongside American troops. National Archives, photo no. 165-WW-127(42).

Americans. In May 1919, Du Bois argued that it was time for African Americans to collect what was due them. "We return *from fighting*," Du Bois declared. "We *return fighting*. Make way for Democracy. We saved it in France, and by the Great Jehovah, we will save it in the U.S.A., or know the reason why."

Reasons soon presented themselves. Segregation remained entrenched, and nothing black soldiers did in France persuaded white Americans that race relations should change. Defenders of second-class citizenship for blacks continued to hold power in Congress and in the White House. Postwar recession left blacks "the last hired, the first fired." Whites scapegoated blacks for their

troubles and launched race riots across the nation. The willingness of blacks to stand their ground demonstrated a new resolve, but it also meant more suffering from escalating violence.

Even the armed services failed to continue to offer new opportunities. Until the late 1940s, after the next world war, the American military remained not only segregated but almost devoid of black officers. Discrimination extended even beyond the ultimate sacrifice. When organizers of a trip to France for parents of soldiers lost in the First World War announced that the ship would be segregated, black mothers felt honor bound to decline the offer to visit the cemeteries where their sons lay.

Questions for Analysis

Summarize the Argument: What does the author argue that African Americans sought with their participation in the fighting in France during World War I, and what in fact did they gain?

Analyze the Evidence: Why were African Americans so wrong in their expectations? What frustrations did they face during their service, and what policies prevented them from achieving their goals after the war?

Consider the Context: Who else in America saw in the war an opportunity for reform and regeneration? Which of these struggles were successful, and which were disappointed?

but the American commander replied sharply, "Retreat, hell. We just got here." After charging through a wheat field against withering machine-gun fire, the Marines plunged into hand-to-hand combat. Victory came hard, but a German report praised the enemy's spirit, noting that "the Americans' nerves are not yet worn out." Indeed, it was German morale that was on the verge of cracking.

In the summer of 1918, the Allies launched a massive counteroffensive that would end the war. A quarter of a million U.S. troops joined in the rout of German forces along the Marne River. In September, more than a million Americans took part in the assault that threw the Germans back from positions along the Meuse River. In four brutal days, the AEF sustained 45,000 casualties. In November, a revolt

VISUAL ACTIVITY

Life in the Trenches

One U.S. soldier in a rat-infested trench watches for danger, while three others sit or lie in exhausted sleep. This trench is dry for the moment, but with the rains came mud so deep that wounded men drowned in it. Barbed wire, machine-gun nests, and mortars backed by heavy artillery protected the trenches. Trenches with millions of combatants stretched from French ports on the English Channel all the way to Switzerland. Such holes were miserable, but a decent shave with a Gillette safety razor and a friendly game of checkers offered doughboys temporary relief. Inevitably, however, the whistles would blow, sending the young men rushing toward enemy lines. Photo: © The Print Collector/Heritage/The Image Works; shaving kit and checkers set: Collection of Colonel Stuart S. Corning Jr./Picture Research Consultants & Archives.

READING THE IMAGE: What do these images suggest about the reality of life for American soldiers during World War I?

CONNECTIONS: How do you suppose the photograph of the trench compares with the doughboys' expectations of military service in France?

against the German government sent Kaiser Wilhelm II fleeing to Holland. On November 11, 1918, a delegation from the newly established German republic met with the French high command to sign an armistice that brought the fighting to an end.

The adventure of the AEF was brief, bloody, and victorious. When Germany had resumed unrestricted U-boat warfare in 1917, it had been gambling that it could defeat Britain and France before the Americans could raise and train an army and ship it to France. The German military had miscalculated badly. By the end, 112,000 AEF soldiers perished from wounds and disease, while another 230,000 Americans, including George Browne, suffered casualties but survived. Only the Civil War, which lasted much longer, had cost more American lives. European nations, however, suffered much greater losses: 2.2 million Germans, 1.9 million Russians, 1.4 million French, and 900,000 Britons (Figure 22.1). Where they had fought, the landscape was as blasted and barren as the moon.

REVIEW How did the AEF contribute to the defeat of Germany?

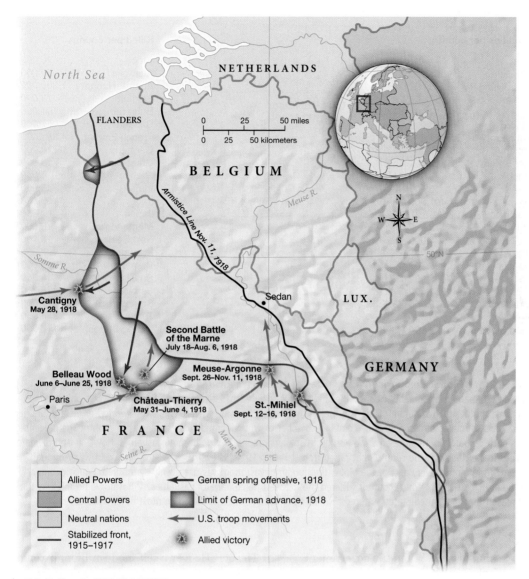

MAP ACTIVITY

Map 22.3   The American Expeditionary Force, 1918
In the last year of the war, the AEF joined the French army on the western front to respond to the final German offensive and pursue the retreating enemy until surrender.

READING THE MAP: Across which rivers did the Germans advance in 1918? Where did the armistice line of November 11, 1918, lie in relation to the stabilized front of 1915–1917? Through which countries did the armistice line run?

CONNECTIONS: What events paved the way for the AEF to join the combat effort in 1918? What characteristic(s) differentiated American troops from other Allied forces and helped them achieve victory?

▶ The Crusade for Democracy at Home

Many progressives hoped that the war would improve the quality of American life as well as free Europe from tyranny and militarism. Mobilization helped propel the crusades for woman suffrage and prohibition to success. Progressives enthusiastically channeled industrial and agricultural production into the vast war effort. Labor shortages caused by workers entering the military provided new opportunities for women in the booming wartime economy. With labor at a premium, unionized workers gained higher pay and shorter hours. To instill loyalty in Americans whose ancestry was rooted in the belligerent nations, Wilson launched a campaign to foster patriotism. But fanning patriotism

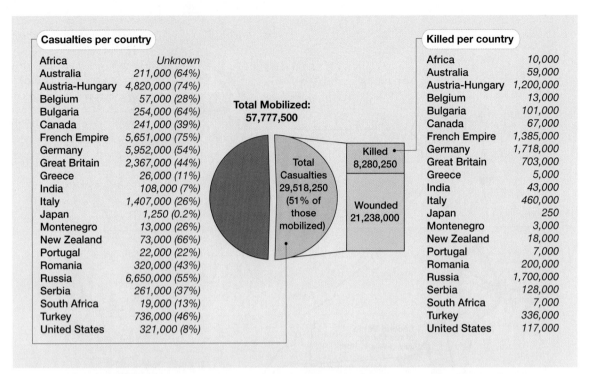

Casualties per country		Killed per country	
Africa	*Unknown*	Africa	*10,000*
Australia	*211,000 (64%)*	Australia	*59,000*
Austria-Hungary	*4,820,000 (74%)*	Austria-Hungary	*1,200,000*
Belgium	*57,000 (28%)*	Belgium	*13,000*
Bulgaria	*254,000 (64%)*	Bulgaria	*101,000*
Canada	*241,000 (39%)*	Canada	*67,000*
French Empire	*5,651,000 (75%)*	French Empire	*1,385,000*
Germany	*5,952,000 (54%)*	Germany	*1,718,000*
Great Britain	*2,367,000 (44%)*	Great Britain	*703,000*
Greece	*26,000 (11%)*	Greece	*5,000*
India	*108,000 (7%)*	India	*43,000*
Italy	*1,407,000 (26%)*	Italy	*460,000*
Japan	*1,250 (0.2%)*	Japan	*250*
Montenegro	*13,000 (26%)*	Montenegro	*3,000*
New Zealand	*73,000 (66%)*	New Zealand	*18,000*
Portugal	*22,000 (22%)*	Portugal	*7,000*
Romania	*320,000 (43%)*	Romania	*200,000*
Russia	*6,650,000 (55%)*	Russia	*1,700,000*
Serbia	*261,000 (37%)*	Serbia	*128,000*
South Africa	*19,000 (13%)*	South Africa	*7,000*
Turkey	*736,000 (46%)*	Turkey	*336,000*
United States	*321,000 (8%)*	United States	*117,000*

Total Mobilized: 57,777,500

Total Casualties 29,518,250 (51% of those mobilized)

Killed 8,280,250

Wounded 21,238,000

FIGURE 22.1   Global Comparison: Casualties of the First World War
Historians disagree about the number of casualties in World War I. Record keeping in many countries was only rudimentary. Moreover, the destructive nature of the war meant that countless soldiers were wholly obliterated or instantly buried. This chart shows estimates of casualties (the combined number of wounded and killed soldiers) per country. The percentage listed with each casualty figure represents the portion of soldiers mobilized who became casualties. However approximate, these figures make clear that the conflict that raged from 1914 to 1918 was a truly catastrophic world war. Although soldiers came from almost every part of the globe, the human devastation was not evenly distributed. Which country suffered the most casualties? Which country suffered the greatest percentage of casualties? What do you think was the principal reason that the United States suffered a smaller percentage of casualties than most other nations?

led to suppressing dissent. When the government launched a harsh assault on civil liberties, mobs gained license to attack those whom they considered disloyal. As Wilson feared, democracy took a beating at home when the nation undertook its crusade for democracy abroad.

The Progressive Stake in the War

Progressives embraced the idea that the war could be an agent of national improvement. The Wilson administration, realizing that the federal government would have to assert greater control to mobilize the nation's human and physical resources, created new agencies to manage the war effort. Bernard Baruch, a Wall Street stockbroker, headed the War Industries Board, charged with stimulating and directing industrial production. Baruch brought industrial management and labor together into a team that produced everything from boots to bullets and made U.S. troops the best-equipped soldiers in the world.

Herbert Hoover, a self-made millionaire engineer, headed the Food Administration. He led remarkably successful "Hooverizing" campaigns for "meatless" Mondays and "wheatless" Wednesdays and other ways of conserving resources. Guaranteed high prices, the American heartland not only supplied the needs of U.S. citizens and armed forces but also became the breadbasket of America's allies.

Wartime agencies multiplied: The Railroad Administration directed railroad traffic, the Fuel Administration coordinated the coal industry and other fuel suppliers, the Shipping Board organized the merchant marine, and the National War Labor Policies Board resolved labor disputes. Their successes gave most progressives reason to believe that, indeed, war and reform marched together. Still, skeptics like Wisconsin senator Robert La Follette declared that Wilson's promises of permanent peace and democracy were a case of "the blind leading the blind."

Industrial leaders found that wartime agencies enforced efficiency, which helped corporate

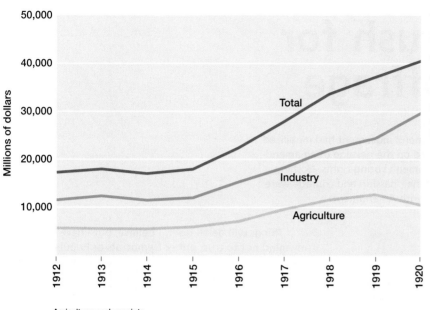

FIGURE 22.2   Industrial Wages, 1912–1920
With help from unions and progressive reformers, wageworkers gradually improved their economic condition. The entry of millions of young men into the armed forces during World War I caused labor shortages and led to a rapid surge in industrial wages.

Agriculture: cash receipts.
Industry: includes mining, electric power, manufacturing, construction, and communications.

profits triple. Some working people also had cause to celebrate. Mobilization meant high prices for farmers and plentiful jobs at high wages in the new war industries (Figure 22.2). Because increased industrial production required peaceful labor relations, the National War Labor Policies Board enacted the eight-hour day, a living minimum wage, and collective bargaining rights in some industries. The American Federation of Labor (AFL) saw its membership soar from 2.7 million to more than 5 million.

The war also provided a huge boost to the crusade to ban alcohol. By 1917, prohibitionists had convinced nineteen states to go dry. Liquor's opponents now argued that banning alcohol would make the cause of democracy powerful and pure. At the same time, shutting down the distilleries would save millions of bushels of grain that could feed the United States and its allies. "Shall the many have food or the few drink?" the drys asked. Prohibition received an additional boost because many of the breweries had German names—Schlitz, Pabst, and Anheuser-Busch. In December 1917, Congress passed the **Eighteenth Amendment**, which banned the manufacture, transportation, and sale of alcohol. After swift ratification by the states, the prohibition amendment went into effect on January 1, 1920.

Women, War, and the Battle for Suffrage

Women had made real strides during the Progressive Era, and war presented new opportunities. More

than 25,000 women served in France. About half were nurses. The others drove ambulances; ran canteens for the Salvation Army, Red Cross, and YMCA; worked with French civilians in devastated areas; and acted as telephone operators and war correspondents. Like men who joined the war effort, they believed that they were taking part in a great national venture. "I am more than willing to live as a soldier and know of the hardships I would have to undergo," one canteen worker declared when applying to go overseas, "but I want to help my country. . . . I want . . . to do the *real* work." And like men, women struggled against disillusionment in France. One woman explained: "Over in America, we thought we knew something about the war . . . but when you get here the difference is [like the one between] studying the laws of electricity and being struck by lightning."

Nora Saltonstall, daughter of a prominent Massachusetts family, was one of the American women who volunteered with the Red Cross and sailed for France. Attached to a mobile surgical hospital that followed closely behind the French armies, she became a driver, chauffeuring personnel, transporting the wounded, and hauling supplies. Soon she was driving on muddy, shell-pocked roads in the dark without lights. Her life, she said, consisted of "choked carburetors, broken springs, long hours on the road, food snatched when you can get it, and sleep." She "hated the war," but she told her mother, "I love my job." She was proud of "doing something necessary here."

At home, long-standing barriers against hiring women fell when millions of workingmen

The Final Push for Woman Suffrage

By the early twentieth century, the women's movement had mobilized millions, who increasingly concentrated on the passage of an amendment to the U.S. Constitution to ensure women's voting rights. Nothing came easily to the suffragists, but in 1920 their passion and courage were rewarded by the ratification of the Nineteenth Amendment.

DOCUMENT 1
Politicking for Suffrage

While radical suffragists chained themselves to the White House fence and went on hunger strikes, other women followed more traditional political channels—methodically gathering petitions, lobbying legislators, building alliances, and rounding up votes. Mary Garrett Hay, vice president of the National American Woman Suffrage Association (NAWSA), reports her efforts with New York state legislators.

New York City, N.Y.
March 13th, 1919
Mrs. Maud Wood Park
1626 Rhode Island Avenue
Washington, D.C.

Dear Mrs. Park,
. . . I kept in very close touch on the telephone and telegraph wire with New York Congressmen and they reported to me, really twice a day what was going on, as far as Speaker, Floor Leader and Suffrage Committee was concerned. I can do more in the House than in the Senate, and I have asked Mr. Hays on the long distance telephone to try and see that things are perfectly straight for our Cause there.

Things will be all right, I believe, but I have made up my mind not to trust either Democrats or Republicans, until the Suffrage Amendment is passed; however, I do not say this to the men[,] only to you, and I shall keep my eyes and ears open and busy, and on the job all I can.

Source: *Women and Social Movements in the United States, 1600–2000,* "How Did Suffragists Lobby to Obtain Congressional Approval of a Woman Suffrage Amendment to the U.S. Constitution, 1917–1920?" Document #10. Courtesy of the Schlesinger Library, Radcliffe Institute, Harvard University (Cambridge, MA).

DOCUMENT 2
The President Intervenes

Although some people urged suffragists to muffle their demands during the war so that the nation could concentrate on victory, Carrie Chapman Catt, president of the NAWSA since 1915, pressed on, recognizing that the war offered a special opportunity. Catt prodded President Woodrow Wilson quietly but persistently, and on September 30, 1918, Wilson finally intervened directly, urging the Senate to pass the Nineteenth Amendment. His argument on behalf of democracy mirrored precisely that of radical suffragists who were protesting in front of the White House.

became soldiers and few new immigrant workers crossed the Atlantic. Tens of thousands of women found work in defense plants as welders, metalworkers, and heavy machine operators and with the railroads. A black woman, a domestic before the war, celebrated her job as a laborer in a railroad yard: "We . . . do not have to work as hard as at housework which requires us to be on duty from six o'clock in the morning until nine or ten at night, with might[y] little time off and at very poor wages." Other women found white-collar work. Between 1910 and 1920, the number of women clerks doubled. Before the war ended, more than a

million women had found work in war industries. One women's rights advocate exaggerated when she declared, "At last . . . women are coming into the labor and festival of life on equal terms with men," but women had made real economic strides.

The most dramatic advance for women came in the political arena. Adopting a state-by-state approach before the war, suffragists had achieved some success (Map 22.4). More commonly, voting rights for women met strong hostility and defeat. After 1910, suffrage leaders added a federal campaign to amend the Constitution to the traditional state-by-state strategy for suffrage.

[The Senate's] adoption is, in my judgment, clearly necessary to the successful prosecution of the war and the successful realization of the objects for which the war is being fought.

. . . If we be indeed democrats and wish to lead the world to democracy, we can ask other peoples to accept in proof of our sincerity and our ability to lead them whither they wish to be led, nothing less persuasive and convincing than our actions.

. . . They are looking to the great, powerful, famous democracy of the West to lead them to a new day for which they have so long waited; and they think, in their logical simplicity, that democracy means that women shall play their part in affairs alongside men and upon an equal footing with them.

. . . We have made partners of the women in this war. Shall we admit them only to a partnership of suffering and sacrifice and toil and not to a partnership of privilege and right?

This war could not have been fought, either by the other nations engaged or by America, if it had not been for the services of the women—services rendered in every sphere. . . .

. . . I tell you plainly that this measure which I urge upon you is vital to the winning of the war and to the energies alike of preparation and of battle.

. . . And not to winning the war only. It is vital to the right solution of the great problems which we must settle, and settle immediately, when the war is over. We shall need in our vision of affairs, as we have never needed them before, the sympathy and insight and clear moral instinct of the women of the world. . . . We shall need their moral sense to preserve what is right and fine and worthy in our system of life as well as to discover just what it is that ought to be purified and reformed. Without their counsellings we shall be only half wise.

Source: "Appeal of President Wilson to the Senate of the United States to Submit the Federal Amendment for Woman Suffrage Delivered in Person Sept. 20, 1918," in *History of Woman Suffrage*, vol. 5, 1900–1920, ed. Ida Husted Harper (New York: NAWSA, 1922), 760–63.

DOCUMENT 3
Reflections on Victory

Catt celebrates the passage of the Nineteenth Amendment in this letter to her staff at the NAWSA on Thanksgiving Day 1920. She reflects on the long road to victory and considers the satisfactions of the journey.

I have kept Thanksgiving sacred to reflections upon the long trail behind us, and the triumph which was its inevitable conclusion. John Adams said long after the Revolution that only about one third of the people were for it, a third being against it, and the remaining third utterly indifferent. Perhaps this proportion applies to all movements. At least a third of the women were for our cause at the end. . . . As I look back over the years . . . I realize that the greatest thing in the long campaign for us was not its crowning victory, but the discipline it gave us all. . . . It was a great crusade, the world has seen none more wonderful. . . . My admiration, love and reverence go out to that band which fought and won a revolution . . . with congratulations that we were permitted to establish a new and good thing in the world.

Source: Carrie Chapman Catt to NAWSA Office Staff, Thanksgiving Day 1920, in *Women's Suffrage in America: An Eyewitness History*, ed. Elizabeth Frost and Kathryn Cullen-DuPont (New York: Facts on File, 1992), 335–36.

Questions for Analysis

Analyze the Evidence: What, according to Woodrow Wilson, would America's rejection of the Nineteenth Amendment have jeopardized?

Consider the Context: How did the First World War further the cause of woman suffrage in the United States?

Ask Historical Questions: Compare the strategies adopted by suffragists and by African Americans seeking reform during World War I. Which was more effective, and why?

The radical wing of the suffragists, led by Alice Paul, picketed the White House, where the marchers unfurled banners that proclaimed "America Is Not a Democracy. Twenty Million Women Are Denied the Right to Vote." They chained themselves to fences and went to jail, where many engaged in hunger strikes. "They seem bent on making their cause as obnoxious as possible," Woodrow Wilson declared. His wife, Edith, detested the idea of "masculinized" voting women. But membership in the mainstream organization, the National American Woman Suffrage Association (NAWSA), led by Carrie Chapman Catt, soared to some two million. Seeing the handwriting on the wall, the Republican and Progressive parties endorsed woman suffrage in 1916.

In 1918, Wilson finally gave his support to suffrage, calling the amendment "vital to the winning of the war." He conceded that it would be wrong not to reward the wartime "partnership of suffering and sacrifice" with a "partnership of privilege and right." By linking their cause to the wartime emphasis on national unity, the advocates of woman suffrage finally triumphed. In 1919, Congress passed the **Nineteenth Amendment**, granting women the vote, and by August 1920 the required two-thirds of the states had ratified it. (See "Analyzing Historical Evidence," above.)

MAP ACTIVITY

Map 22.4   Women's Voting Rights before the Nineteenth Amendment

The long campaign for women's voting rights reversed the pioneer epic that moved from east to west. From its first successes in the new democratic West, suffrage rolled eastward toward the entrenched, male-dominated public life of the Northeast and South.

READING THE MAP: What was the first state to grant woman suffrage? How many states extended full voting rights to women before 1914? How many extended these rights during World War I (1914–1918)?

CONNECTIONS: Suffragists redirected their focus during the war. What strategies did they use then?

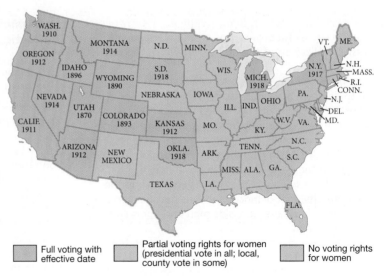

Full voting with effective date

Partial voting rights for women (presidential vote in all; local, county vote in some)

No voting rights for women

Rally around the Flag—or Else

When Congress committed the nation to war, only a handful of peace advocates resisted the tide of patriotism. A group of professional women, led by settlement house leader Jane Addams and economics professor Emily Greene Balch, denounced what Addams described as "the pathetic belief in the regenerative results of war." After America entered the conflict, advocates for peace were labeled cowards and traitors.

To suppress criticism of the war, Wilson stirred up patriotic fervor. In 1917, the president created the Committee on Public Information under the direction of George Creel, a journalist who became the nation's cheerleader for war. Creel sent "Four-Minute Men," a squad of 75,000 volunteers, around the country to give brief pep talks that celebrated successes on the battlefields and in the factories. Posters, pamphlets, and cartoons depicted brave American soldiers and sailors defending freedom and democracy against the evil "Huns," the derogatory nickname applied to German soldiers.

America rallied around Creel's campaign. The film industry cranked out pro-war melodramas and taught audiences to hiss at the German kaiser. Colleges and universities generated war propaganda in the guise of scholarship. When Professor James McKeen Cattell of Columbia University urged that America seek peace with Germany short of victory, university president Nicholas Murray Butler fired him on the grounds that "what had been folly is now treason."

A firestorm of anti-German passion erupted. Across the nation, "100% American" campaigns enlisted ordinary people to sniff out disloyalty.

German, the most widely taught foreign language in 1914, practically disappeared from the nation's schools. Targeting German-born Americans, the *Saturday Evening Post* declared that it was time to rid the country of "the scum of the melting pot." Anti-German action reached its extreme with the lynching of Robert Prager, a German-born baker with socialist leanings. Persuaded by the defense lawyer who praised what he called a "patriotic murder," the jury at the trial of the killers took only twenty-five minutes to acquit.

As hysteria increased, the campaign reached absurd levels. Menus across the nation changed German toast to French toast and sauerkraut to liberty cabbage. In Milwaukee, vigilantes mounted a machine gun outside the Pabst Theater to prevent the staging of Schiller's *Wilhelm Tell*, a powerful protest against tyranny. The fiancée of one of the war's leading critics, caught dancing on the dunes of Cape Cod, was held on suspicion of signaling to German submarines.

The Wilson administration's zeal in suppressing dissent contrasted sharply with its war aims of defending democracy. In the name of self-defense, the Espionage Act (June 1917), the Trading with the Enemy Act (October 1917), and the Sedition Act (May 1918) gave the government sweeping powers to punish any opinion or activity it considered "disloyal, profane, scurrilous, or abusive." When Postmaster General Albert Burleson blocked mailing privileges for dissenting publications, dozens of journals were forced to close down. Of the 1,500 individuals eventually charged with sedition, all but a dozen had merely spoken words the government found objectionable.

One of them was Eugene V. Debs, the leader of the Socialist Party, who was convicted under the Espionage Act and sentenced to ten years. In a speech on June 16, 1918, Debs declared that the United States was not fighting a noble war to make the world safe for democracy but had joined greedy European imperialists seeking to conquer the globe. The government claimed that Debs had crossed the line between legitimate dissent and criminal speech. From the Atlanta penitentiary, Debs argued that he was just telling the truth, like hundreds of his friends who were also in jail.

The president hoped that national commitment to the war would silence partisan politics, but his Republican rivals used the war as a weapon against the Democrats. The trick was to oppose Wilson's conduct of the war but not the war itself. Republicans outshouted Wilson on the nation's need to mobilize for war but then complained that Wilson's War Industries Board was a tyrannical agency that crushed free enterprise. As the war progressed, Republicans gathered power against the Democrats, who had narrowly reelected Wilson in 1916.

In 1918, Republicans gained a narrow majority in both the House and the Senate. The end of Democratic control of Congress not only halted further domestic reform but also meant that the United States would advance toward military victory in Europe with political power divided between a Democratic president and a Republican Congress likely to challenge Wilson's plans for international cooperation.

REVIEW   How did progressive ideals fare during wartime?

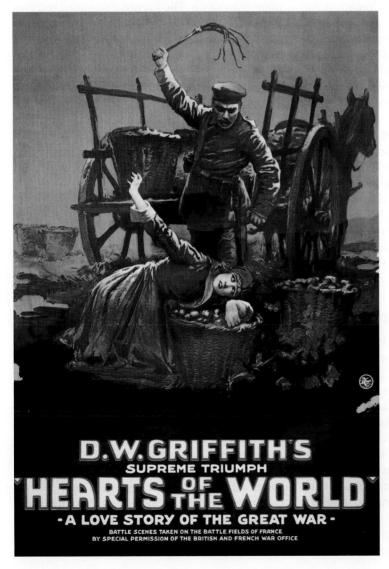

D. W. Griffith's *Hearts of the World*, 1918
Hollywood joined in the government's efforts to stir up rage against the Germans. In this poster announcing the 1918 film by D. W. Griffith, a German soldier is about to whip a defenseless farm woman (played by Lillian Gish). First Lady Edith Wilson, who sought to moderate the hate campaign, wrote to Griffith pleading with him to cut or soften the violent scene. Everett Collection.

► A Compromised Peace

Wilson decided to reaffirm his noble war ideals by announcing his peace aims before the end of hostilities. He hoped the victorious Allies would adopt his plan for international democracy, but he was sorely disappointed. America's allies understood that Wilson's principles jeopardized their own postwar plans for the acquisition of enemy territory, new colonial empires, and reparations. Wilson also faced strong opposition at home from those who feared that his enthusiasm for international cooperation would undermine American sovereignty.

Wilson's Fourteen Points

On January 8, 1918, ten months before the armistice in Europe, President Wilson revealed to Congress his **Fourteen Points**, his blueprint for a new democratic world order. The first five points affirmed basic liberal ideals: an end to secret treaties, freedom of the seas, removal of economic barriers to free trade, reduction of weapons of war, and recognition of the rights of colonized peoples. The next eight points supported the right to self-determination of European peoples who had been dominated by Germany or its allies. Wilson's fourteenth point called for a "general association of nations"—a **League of Nations**—to provide "mutual guarantees of political independence and territorial integrity to great and small states alike." A League of Nations reflected Wilson's lifelong dream of a "parliament of man." Only such an organization of "peace-loving nations," he believed, could justify the war and secure a lasting peace.

The Paris Peace Conference

From January 18 to June 28, 1919, the eyes of the world focused on Paris. Wilson, inspired by his mission, decided to head the U.S. delegation. He said he owed it to the American soldiers. "It is now my duty," he announced, "to play my full part in making good what they gave their life's blood to obtain." A dubious British diplomat retorted that Wilson was drawn to Paris "as a debutante is entranced by the prospect of her first ball." The decision to leave the country at a time when his political opponents challenged his leadership was risky enough, but his stubborn refusal to include prominent Republicans

in the delegation proved foolhardy and eventually cost him his dream of a new world order.

After four terrible years of war, the common people of Europe almost worshipped Wilson, believing that he would create a safer, more decent world. When the peace conference convened at Louis XIV's magnificent palace at Versailles, however, Wilson encountered a different reception. To the Allied leaders, Wilson appeared a naive and impractical moralist. His desire to gather former enemies within a new international democratic order showed how little he understood hard European realities. Georges Clemenceau, premier of France, claimed that Wilson "believed you could do everything by formulas" and "empty theory." Disparaging the Fourteen Points, he added, "God himself was content with ten commandments."

The Allies wanted to fasten blame for the war on Germany, totally disarm it, and make it pay so dearly that it would never threaten its neighbors again. The French demanded retribution in the form of territory containing Germany's richest mineral resources. The British made it clear that they were not about to give up the powerful weapon of naval blockade for the vague principle of freedom of the seas.

The Allies forced Wilson to make drastic compromises. In return for France's moderating its territorial claims, he agreed to support Article 231 of the peace treaty, assigning war guilt to Germany. Though saved from permanently losing Rhineland territory to the French, Germany was outraged at being singled out as the instigator of the war and being saddled with more than $33 billion in damages. Many Germans felt that their nation had been betrayed. After agreeing to an armistice in the belief that peace terms would be based in Wilson's generous Fourteen Points, they faced hardship and humiliation instead.

Wilson had better success in establishing the principle of self-determination. But from the beginning, Secretary of State Robert Lansing knew that the president's concept of self-determination was "simply loaded with dynamite." Lansing wondered, "What unit has he in mind? Does he mean a race, a territorial area, or a community?" Even Wilson was vague about what self-determination actually meant. "When I gave utterance to those words," he admitted, "I said them without the knowledge that nationalities existed, which are coming to us day after day." Lansing suspected that the notion "will raise hopes which can never be realized. It will, I fear, cost thousands of lives. In the end it is bound to be discredited, to be called the dream of an idealist who failed to realize the danger until it was too late."

Yet partly on the basis of self-determination, the conference redrew the map of Europe and parts of the rest of the world. Portions of Austria-Hungary were ceded to Italy, Poland, and Romania, and the remainder was reassembled into Austria, Hungary, Czechoslovakia, and Yugoslavia—independent republics whose boundaries were drawn with attention to concentrations of major ethnic groups. More arbitrarily, the Ottoman empire was carved up into small mandates (including Palestine) run by local leaders but under the control of France and Great Britain. The conference reserved the mandate system for those

regions it deemed insufficiently "civilized" to have full independence. Thus, the reconstructed nations—each beset with ethnic and nationalist rivalries—faced the challenge of making a new democratic government work (Map 22.5). Many of today's bitterest disputes—in the Balkans and Iraq, between Greece and Turkey, between Arabs and Jews—have roots in the decisions made in Paris in 1919.

Wilson hoped that self-determination would also dictate the fate of Germany's colonies in Asia and Africa. But the Allies, who had taken over the colonies during the war, went no further than allowing the League of Nations a mandate to administer them. Technically, the mandate system rejected imperialism, but in reality it allowed the Allies to maintain control. Thus,

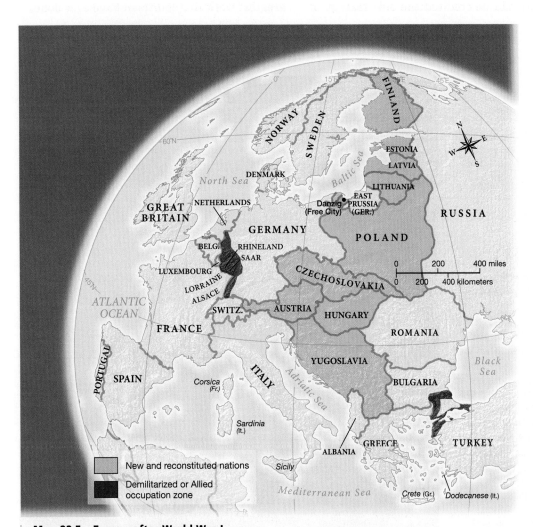

Map 22.5 Europe after World War I
The post–World War I settlement redrew boundaries to create new nations based on ethnic groupings. Within defeated Germany and Russia, this outcome left bitter peoples who resolved to recover the territory taken from them.

while denying Germany its colonies, the Allies retained and added to their own empires.

The cause of democratic equality suffered another setback when the peace conference rejected Japan's call for a statement of racial equality in the treaty. Wilson's belief in the superiority of whites, as well as his apprehension about how white Americans would respond to such a declaration, led him to oppose the clause. To soothe hurt feelings, Wilson agreed to grant Japan a mandate over the Shantung Peninsula in northern China, which had formerly been controlled by Germany. The gesture mollified Japan's moderate leaders, but the military faction preparing to take over the country used bitterness toward racist Western colonialism to build support for expanding Japanese power throughout Asia.

Closest to Wilson's heart was finding a new way to manage international relations. In Wilson's view, war had discredited the old strategy of balance of power. Instead, he proposed a League of Nations that would provide collective security. The league would establish rules of international conduct and resolve conflicts between nations through rational and peaceful means. When the Allies agreed to the league, Wilson was overjoyed. He believed that the league would rectify the errors his colleagues had forced on him in Paris.

To some Europeans and Americans, the **Versailles treaty** came as a bitter disappointment. Wilson's admirers were shocked that the president dealt in compromise like any other politician. But without Wilson's presence, the treaty that was signed on June 28, 1919, surely would have been more vindictive. Wilson returned home in July 1919 consoled that, despite his frustrations, he had gained what he most wanted—a League of Nations. In Wilson's judgment, "We have completed in the least time possible the greatest work that four men have ever done."

VISUAL ACTIVITY

The Signing of Peace in the Hall of Mirrors, Versailles, 28th June 1919, **by Sir William Orpen**

Set in the dazzling Hall of Mirrors at Versailles, built for Louis XIV as a symbol of his power, this painting captures the moment when the treaty was signed in June 1919. The leaders in charge of putting the world back together after the Great War are gathered at the table. Wilson is seated fifth from the left, dignified but seemingly isolated, while the French premier Georges Clemenceau and the British prime minister David Lloyd George are huddled together at Wilson's left. Imperial War Museum, London, UK/Bridgeman Images.

READING THE IMAGE: What might have been the artist's message in depicting Wilson, Clemenceau, and Lloyd George as he did?

CONNECTIONS: Diplomats and politicians hammered out the treaty. How did Americans back home respond to the work of Wilson and the other world leaders at Versailles?

The Fight for the Treaty

The tumultuous reception Wilson received when he arrived home persuaded him, probably correctly, that the American people supported the treaty. When the president submitted the treaty to the Senate in July 1919, he warned that failure to ratify it would "break the heart of the world." By then, however, criticism of the treaty was mounting, especially from Americans convinced that their countries of ethnic origin—Ireland, Italy, and Germany—had not been given fair treatment. Others worried that the president's concessions at Versailles had jeopardized the treaty's capacity to provide a workable plan for rebuilding Europe and to guarantee world peace.

In the Senate, Republican "irreconcilables" condemned the treaty for entangling the United States in world affairs. A larger group of Republicans did not object to American participation in world politics but feared that membership in the League of Nations would jeopardize the nation's ability to act independently. No Republican, in any case, was eager to hand Wilson and the Democrats a foreign policy victory with the 1920 presidential election little more than a year away.

At the center of Republican opposition was Wilson's archenemy, Senator Henry Cabot Lodge of Massachusetts. Lodge was no isolationist, but he thought that much of the Fourteen Points was a "general bleat about virtue being better than vice." Lodge expected the United States' economic and military power to propel the nation into a major role in world affairs. But he insisted that membership in the League of Nations, which would require collective action to maintain peace, threatened the nation's independence in foreign relations.

With Lodge as its chairman, the Senate Foreign Relations Committee produced several amendments, or "reservations," that sought to limit the consequences of American membership in the league. For example, several reservations required approval of both the House and the Senate before the United States could participate in league-sponsored economic sanctions or military action.

It gradually became clear that ratification of the treaty depended on acceptance of the Lodge reservations. Democratic senators, who overwhelmingly supported the treaty, urged Wilson to accept Lodge's terms, arguing that they left the essentials of the treaty intact. Wilson, however, insisted that the reservations cut "the very heart out of the treaty."

Wilson decided to take his case directly to the people. On September 3, 1919, still exhausted

Cartoon about the League of Nations, 1919
This cartoon captures President Wilson's deep commitment to and personal sense of responsibility for the League of Nations. The failure of the United States to join the league broke Wilson's heart. The Granger Collection, New York.

from the peace conference, he set out by train on the most ambitious speaking tour ever undertaken by a president. On September 25 in Pueblo, Colorado, Wilson collapsed and had to return to Washington. There, he suffered a massive stroke that partially paralyzed him. From his bedroom, Wilson sent messages instructing Democrats in the Senate to hold firm against any and all reservations. Wilson commanded enough loyalty to ensure a vote against the Lodge reservations. But when the treaty without reservations came before the Senate in March 1920, the combined opposition of the Republican irreconcilables and reservationists left Wilson six votes short of the two-thirds majority needed for passage.

The nations of Europe organized the League of Nations at Geneva, Switzerland. Although Woodrow Wilson received the Nobel Peace Prize in 1920 for his central role in creating the league, the United States never became a member. Whether American membership could have prevented the world war that would begin in Europe in 1939 is highly unlikely, but the United States' failure to join certainly weakened the league from the start. In refusing to accept relatively minor compromises with Senate moderates, Wilson lost his treaty and American membership in the league.

REVIEW   Why did the Senate fail to ratify the Versailles treaty?

▶ Democracy at Risk

The defeat of Wilson's plan for international democracy proved the crowning blow to progressives who had hoped that the war could boost reform at home. When the war ended, Americans wanted to demobilize swiftly. In the process, servicemen, defense workers, and farmers lost their war-related jobs. The volatile combination—of unemployed veterans returning home, a stalled economy, and leftover wartime patriotism looking for a new cause—threatened to explode. Wartime anti-German passion was quickly succeeded by the Red scare, an antiradical campaign broad enough to ensnare unionists, socialists, dissenters, and African Americans and Mexicans who had committed no offense but to seek an escape from rural poverty as they moved north.

Economic Hardship and Labor Upheaval

Americans demanded that the nation return to a peacetime economy. The government abruptly abandoned its wartime economic controls and canceled war contracts. In a matter of months, 3 million soldiers mustered out of the military and flooded the job market just as war production ceased. Unemployment soared. At the same time, consumers went on a postwar spending spree that drove inflation skyward. In 1919 alone, prices rose 75 percent over prewar levels.

VISUAL ACTIVITY

Returning Veterans and Work
After the war, the federal government promoted returning veterans for employment. This poster reminds prospective employers of the U.S. Marines' accomplishments in France by listing their battles—Cantigny, Château-Thierry, St.-Mihiel, Argonne, Marne. But the government had little to offer veterans beyond posters. Library of Congress, 3g07712.
READING THE IMAGE: What relationship does the poster assume exists between fighting in France and employment in America?
CONNECTIONS: Why did the government believe it needed to actively promote veterans for jobs back home?

PUT FIGHTING BLOOD IN YOUR BUSINESS · HERE'S HIS RECORD! DOES HE GET A JOB?
—ARTHUR WOODS, ASSISTANT TO THE SECRETARY OF WAR
NEEDS WITH THE U.S. EMPLOYMENT SERVICE
CROSS CO-OPERATING WITH THE DEPARTMENT OF WAR
THE DEPARTMENT OF LABOR

Most of the gains workers had made during the war evaporated. Freed from government controls, business turned against the eight-hour day and attacked labor unions. With inflation eating up their paychecks, workers fought back. The year 1919 witnessed nearly 3,600 strikes involving 4 million workers. The most spectacular strike occurred in February 1919 in Seattle, where shipyard workers had been put out of work by demobilization. When a coalition of the radical Industrial Workers of the World (IWW, known as Wobblies) and the moderate American Federation of Labor (AFL) called a general strike, the largest work stoppage in American history shut down the city. Newspapers claimed that the walkout was "a Bolshevik effort to start a revolution." The suppression of the Seattle general strike by city officials cost the AFL many of its wartime gains and contributed to the destruction of the IWW soon afterward.

A strike by Boston policemen in the fall of 1919 underscored postwar hostility toward labor militancy. Although the police were paid less than pick-and-shovel laborers, they won little sympathy. Once the officers stopped walking their beats, looters sacked the city. Massachusetts governor Calvin Coolidge called in the National Guard to restore order and broke the Boston police strike. The public welcomed Coolidge's anti-union assurance that "there is no right to strike against the public safety by anybody, anywhere, any time."

Labor strife climaxed in the grim steel strike of 1919. Faced with the industry's plan to revert to seven-day weeks, twelve-hour days, and weekly wages of about $20, Samuel Gompers, head of the AFL, called for a strike. In September, 350,000 workers in fifteen states walked out. The steel industry hired 30,000 strikebreakers and convinced the public that the strikers were radicals bent on subverting democracy and capitalism. In January 1920, after 18 striking workers were killed, the strike collapsed. That devastating defeat initiated a sharp decline in the fortunes of the labor movement, a trend that would continue for almost twenty years.

The Red Scare

Suppression of labor strikes was one response to the widespread fear of internal subversion that swept the nation in 1919. The **Red scare** ("Red" referred to the color of the Bolshevik flag) exceeded even the assault on civil liberties during the war. It had homegrown causes: the postwar recession, labor unrest, terrorist acts, and the difficulties of reintegrating millions of returning veterans. But unsettling events abroad also added to Americans' anxieties.

Two epidemics swept the globe in 1918. One was Spanish influenza, which brought on a lethal accumulation of fluid in the lungs. A nurse near the front lines in France observed that victims "run a high temperature, so high that we can't believe it's true. . . . It is accompanied by vomiting and dysentery. When they die, as about half of them do, they turn a ghastly dark gray and are taken out at once and cremated." Before the flu virus had run its course, 40 million people had died worldwide, including some 700,000 Americans.

The other epidemic was Russian bolshevism, which seemed to most Americans equally contagious and deadly. Bolshevism became even more menacing in March 1919, when the new Soviet leaders created the Comintern, a worldwide association of Communists sworn to revolution in capitalist countries. (See "Beyond America's Borders," page 642.) A Communist revolution in the United States was extremely unlikely, but edgy Americans, faced with a flurry of terrorist acts, believed otherwise. Dozens of prominent individuals had received bombs through the mail. On September 16, 1920, a wagon filled with dynamite and iron exploded on Wall Street, killing 38 and maiming 143 others. Authorities never caught the terrorists, and the successful attack on America's financial capital fed the nation's anger and fear.

Even before the Wall Street bombing, the government had initiated a hunt for domestic revolutionaries. Led by Attorney General A. Mitchell Palmer, who believed that "there could be no nice distinctions drawn between the theoretical ideals of the radicals and their actual violations of our national laws," the campaign targeted men and women for their ideas, not their illegal acts. In January 1920, Palmer ordered a series of raids that netted 6,000 alleged subversives. Finding no revolutionary conspiracies, Palmer nevertheless ordered 500 noncitizen suspects deported.

His action came in the wake of a campaign against the most notorious radical alien, Russian-born Emma Goldman. Before the war, Goldman's passionate support of labor strikes, women's rights, and birth control had made her a symbol of radicalism. In 1919, after she spent time in prison for denouncing military conscription, J. Edgar Hoover, the director of the Justice Department's Radical Division, ordered her deported. One observer remarked, "With

Bolshevism

In March 1917, revolutionaries overthrew the Russian czar, whose hereditary rule was the target of peasants and urban workers seeking a more democratic government. But Marxist radicals, who called themselves Bolsheviks, were not satisfied with the regime change. In November, the Bolsheviks seized control of Russia and made their leader, Vladimir Ilyich Lenin, ruler. Lenin scoffed at the idea that the Allies were fighting for democracy and insisted that greedy capitalists were waging war for international dominance. In March 1918, he shocked Woodrow Wilson and the Allies by signing a separate peace with Germany and withdrawing Russia from the war. Still locked in the desperate struggle with Germany, the Allies cried betrayal.

The Bolshevik regime dedicated itself to ending capitalism in Russia (known as the Soviet Union after 1922) and to instituting what it called a "dictatorship of the proletariat." In theory, workers—agricultural and industrial—would control the economy and exercise political power. But very quickly a gap opened between the workers and party leaders, who instituted a top-down apparatus that institutionalized the bloody repression of their opponents.

Prodded by British leader Winston Churchill, who declared that "the Bolshevik infant should be strangled in its cradle," Britain and France urged the United States to join them in sending troops to Russia in support of Russian democrats opposing the new revolutionary regime. Several prominent Americans spoke out against American intervention. Senator William Borah of Idaho declared: "The Russian people have the same right to establish a Socialist state as we have to establish a republic." But Wilson concluded that the Bolsheviks were a dictatorial party that had come to power through a violent coup that denied Russians political choice, and in September 1918 he ordered 14,000 U.S. troops to join British and French forces in Russia. U.S., British, and French troops fought to overthrow Lenin and annul the Bolshevik Revolution, but the Bolsheviks (by now calling themselves Communists) prevailed. U.S. troops withdrew from Russia in June 1919, after the loss of more than 200 American lives.

The Bolshevik regime also committed itself to overthrowing capitalist and imperialist regimes around the world. Clearly, Lenin's imagined future was at odds with Wilson's proposed liberal new world order. Wilson withheld U.S. diplomatic recognition of the Soviet Union (a policy that persisted until 1934) and joined the Allies in an economic boycott to bring down the Bolshevik government. Unbowed, Lenin promised that his party would "incite rebellion among all the peoples now oppressed," and revolutionary agitation became central to Soviet foreign policy. Just after the armistice, Communist revolutions erupted in Bavaria and Hungary. Though short-lived, the Communist regimes there sent shock waves throughout the West. In 1919, moreover, a Russian official bragged that monies being sent to Europe to foment Bolshevik rebellion were "nothing compared to the funds transmitted to New York for the purpose of spreading bolshevism in the United States." American attention shifted from revolutionaries in Europe to revolutionaries at home. The Red scare was on.

Attorney General A. Mitchell Palmer perceived a "blaze of Revolution sweeping over every American institution of law and order . . . licking the altars of churches . . . crawling into the sacred corners of American homes." In 1919, the U.S. government launched an all-out attack on the Communist ("Red") menace. In the same year, disgruntled socialists founded the American Communist Party, but it attracted only a handful of members, who spent most of their time arguing the fine points of doctrine, not manufacturing

Prohibition coming in and Emma Goldman goin' out, 'twill be a dull country."

The effort to rid the country of alien radicals was matched by efforts to crush troublesome citizens. Law enforcement officials and vigilante groups joined hands against so-called Reds. In November 1919 in the rugged lumber town of Centralia, Washington, a menacing crowd gathered in front of the IWW hall. Nervous Wobblies inside opened fire, killing three people. Three IWW members were arrested and later convicted of murder, but another, ex-soldier Wesley Everett, was carried off by the mob, which castrated him, hung him from a bridge, and then riddled his body with bullets. His death was officially ruled a suicide.

Public institutions joined the attack on civil liberties. Local libraries removed dissenting books. Schools fired unorthodox teachers. Police shut down radical newspapers. State legislatures refused to seat elected representatives who professed socialist ideas. And in 1919, Congress removed its lone socialist representative, Victor Berger, on the pretext that he was a threat to national safety.

That same year, the Supreme Court provided a formula for restricting free speech. In upholding the conviction of socialist Charles Schenck for publishing a pamphlet urging resistance to

bombs. However, a few radicals did resort to bombs, and they prompted near panic in some quarters. Even mild dissenters faced bullying and threats. Workers seeking better wages and conditions, women and African Americans demanding equal rights, and anyone else pushing for change found the government hurling the epithet "Red" at them. Before the hysteria subsided, the nation witnessed beatings, jailings, and deportations.

The Bolshevik Revolution had endless consequences. In the Soviet Union, it initiated a brutal reign of terror that lasted for more than seven decades. In international politics, it set up a polarity that lasted nearly as long. In a very real sense, the Cold War, which set the United States and the Soviet Union at each other's throats after World War II, began in 1917. America's abortive military intervention against the Bolshevik regime and the Bolsheviks' call for worldwide revolution convulsed relations from the very beginning. In the United States, the rabid antiradicalism of the Red scare threatened traditional American values. Commitment to the protection of dissent succumbed to irrational anticommunism. Even mild reform became tarred with the brush of bolshevism. Although the Red scare quickly withered, the habit of crushing dissent in the name of security would live on. Years later, in the 1950s, when Americans' anxiety mounted and their confidence waned once again, witch-hunts

Vladimir Ilyich Lenin
After the Bolshevik success in Russia in 1917, Lenin became the face of the Communist revolution. His call for workers everywhere to rise against the ruling classes and end capitalism and imperialism sent chills down spines throughout much of western Europe and the United States. Rather than viewing Lenin as a bloodthirsty monster, however, this dramatic portrait presents him as the courageous hero of the people's revolution. AP Photo.

against radicalism reemerged to undermine American democracy.

Questions for Analysis

Consider the Context: Why did U.S.-Bolshevik relations get off to such a rocky start? Were harsh relations the result of certain policy decisions or inherent in the clashing value systems?

Ask Historical Questions: In the United States, is there an inevitable tension between national security and free expression? Why or why not?

Analyze the Evidence: How did Lenin's and Wilson's aspirations for the post–World War I world differ? How did the differences in their goals contribute to growing tensions?

---

the draft during wartime (*Schenck v. United States*), the Court established a "clear and present danger" test. Such utterances as Schenck's during a time of national peril, Justice Oliver Wendell Holmes wrote, were equivalent to shouting "Fire!" in a crowded theater.

In 1920, the assault on civil liberties provoked the creation of the American Civil Liberties Union (ACLU), which was dedicated to defending an individual's constitutional rights. One of the ACLU's founders, Roger Baldwin, declared, "So long as we have enough people in this country willing to fight for their rights, we'll be called a democracy." The ACLU championed the targets

of Attorney General Palmer's campaign—politically radical immigrants, trade unionists, socialists and Communists, and antiwar activists who still languished in jail.

The Red scare eventually collapsed because of its excesses. In particular, the antiradical campaign lost credibility after Palmer warned that radicals were planning to celebrate the Bolshevik Revolution with a nationwide wave of violence on May 1, 1920. Officials called out state militias, mobilized bomb squads, and even placed machine-gun nests at major city intersections. When May 1 came and went without a single disturbance, the public mood turned from fear to scorn.

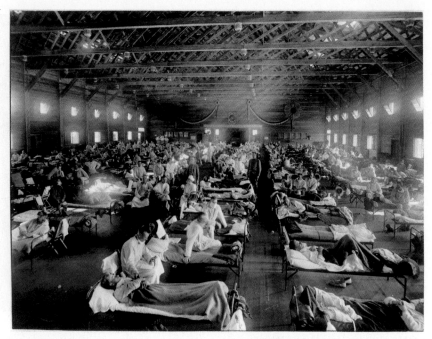

Emergency Hospital
Despite its name, the Spanish flu was first observed in 1918 in Kansas. Army camps, with their close troop quarters, proved perfect incubators. This emergency hospital at Camp Funston, Kansas, is filled with some of the flu's early victims. Crowded troopships quickly spread the virus to Europe. Civilians were not immune. In October 1918 in Philadelphia, more than 4,500 people died in a single week. National Museum of Health and Medicine (NCP 001603).

The Great Migrations of African Americans and Mexicans

Before the Red scare lost steam, the government raised alarms about the loyalty of African Americans. A Justice Department investigation concluded that Reds were fomenting racial unrest among blacks. Although the report was wrong about Bolshevik influence, it was correct in noticing a new stirring among African Americans.

In 1900, nine of every ten blacks still lived in the South, where poverty, disfranchisement, segregation, and violence dominated their lives. A majority of black men worked as dirt-poor tenants or sharecroppers, while many black women worked in the homes of whites as domestics. Whites remained committed to keeping blacks down. "If we own a good farm or horse, or cow, or bird-dog, or yoke of oxen," a black sharecropper in Mississippi observed in 1913, "we are harassed until we are bound to sell, give away, or run away, before we can have any peace in our lives."

The First World War provided African Americans with the opportunity to escape the South's cotton fields and kitchens. When war channeled almost 5 million American workers into military service and nearly ended European immigration, northern industrialists turned to black labor. Black men found work in northern steel mills, shipyards, munitions plants, railroad yards, automobile factories, and mines. From 1915 to 1920, a half million blacks (approximately 10 percent of the South's black population) boarded trains bound for Philadelphia, Detroit, Cleveland, Chicago, St. Louis, and other industrial cities.

Thousands of migrants wrote home to tell family and friends about their experiences in the North. One man announced proudly that he had recently been promoted to "first assistant to the head carpenter." He added, "I should have been here twenty years ago. I just begin to feel like a man. . . . My children are going to the same school with the whites and I don't have to [h]umble to no one. I have registered—will vote the next election and there ain't any 'yes sir'—it's all yes and no and Sam and Bill."

But the North was not the promised land. Black men stood on the lowest rungs of the labor ladder. Jobs of any kind proved scarce for black women, and most worked as domestic servants as they did in the South. The existing black middle class sometimes shunned the less educated, less sophisticated rural southerners crowding into northern cities. Many whites, fearful of losing jobs and status, lashed out against the new migrants. Savage race riots ripped through two dozen northern cities. The worst occurred in July 1917 when a mob of whites invaded a section of East St. Louis, Illinois, and murdered 39 people. In 1918, the nation witnessed 96 lynchings of blacks, some of them decorated war veterans still in uniform.

Still, most black migrants stayed in the North and encouraged friends and family to follow. By 1940, more than one million blacks had left the South, profoundly changing their own lives and the course of the nation's history. Black enclaves

If You are a Stranger in the City

If you want a job   If you want a place to live
If you are having trouble with your employer
If you want information or advice of any kind
CALL UPON

The CHICAGO LEAGUE ON URBAN
CONDITIONS AMONG NEGROES
3719 South State Street

Telephone Douglas 9098   T. ARNOLD HILL, Executive Secretary

No charges—no fees. We want to help YOU

SELF-HELP

1. Do not loaf. Get a job at once.
2. Do not live in crowded rooms. Others can be obtained.
3. Do not carry on loud conversations in street cars and public places.
4. Do not keep your children out of school.
5. Do not send for your family until you get a job.
6. Do not think you can hold your job unless you are industrious, sober, efficient and prompt.

Cleanliness and fresh air are necessary for good health. In case of sickness send immediately for a good physician. Become an active member in some church as soon as you reach the city.

Issued by

VISUAL ACTIVITY

African Americans Migrate North

Wearing their Sunday best and carrying the rest of what they owned in two suitcases, this southern family waits to board a northern-bound train in 1912. In Chicago, the League on Urban Conditions among Negroes, which became the Urban League, sought to ease the transition of southern blacks to life in the North by distributing cards such as the one shown here (front and back).

Photo: Schomburg Center, NYPL/Art Resource, NY; cards: Arthur and Graham Aldis papers (APF_0001_0006a-01 a/b), Special Collections, The University Library, University of Illinois at Chicago.

READING THE IMAGE: This photograph captures the migration of a family. How many generations are represented?

CONNECTIONS: Why do you suppose the "Self-Help" card emphasizes hard work, cleanliness, and quiet?

such as Harlem in New York and the South Side of Chicago, "cities within cities," emerged in the North. These assertive communities provided a foundation for black protest and political organization in the years ahead.

At nearly the same time, another migration was under way in the American Southwest. Between 1910 and 1920, the Mexican-born population in the United States soared from 222,000 to 478,000. Mexican immigration resulted from developments on both sides of the border. When Mexicans revolted against dictator Porfirio Díaz in 1910, initiating a ten-year civil war, migrants flooded northward. In the United States, the Chinese Exclusion Act of 1882 and later the disruption of World War I cut off the supply of cheap foreign labor and caused western employers in the expanding rail, mining, construction, and agricultural industries to look south to Mexico for workers.

Like immigrants from Europe and black migrants from the South, Mexicans in the American Southwest dreamed of a better life. And like the others, they found both opportunity and disappointment. Wages were better than in Mexico, but life in the fields, mines, and factories was hard, and living conditions—in boxcars, labor camps, or urban barrios—were dismal. Signs warning "No Mexicans Allowed" increased

Mexican Women Arriving in El Paso, 1911
These Mexican women, carrying bundles and wearing traditional shawls, try to get their bearings upon arriving in El Paso, Texas—the Ellis Island for Mexican immigrants. They were part of the first modern wave of Mexican immigration to the United States. Women like them found work in the fields, canneries, and restaurants of the Southwest, as well as at home taking in sewing, laundry, and boarders. New Mexico State University Library, Archives and Special Collections.

Postwar Politics and the Election of 1920

A thousand miles away in Washington, D.C., President Woodrow Wilson, bedridden and paralyzed, ignored the mountain of domestic troubles—labor strikes, the Red scare, race riots, immigration backlash—and insisted that the 1920 election would be a "solemn referendum" on the League of Nations. Dutifully, the Democratic nominees for president, James M. Cox of Ohio, and for vice president, Franklin Delano Roosevelt of New York, campaigned on Wilson's international ideals. The Republican Party chose the handsome, gregarious Warren Gamaliel Harding, senator from Ohio.

Harding found the winning formula when he declared that "America's present need is not heroics, but healing; not nostrums [questionable remedies] but normalcy." But what was "normalcy"? Harding explained: "By 'normalcy' I don't mean the old order but a regular steady order of things. I mean normal procedure, the natural way, without excess." Eager to put wartime crusades and postwar strife behind them, voters responded by giving Harding the largest presidential victory ever: 60.5 percent of the popular vote and 404 out of 531 electoral votes (Map 22.6). Harding's election lifted the national pall, signaling a new, more easygoing era.

REVIEW   How did the Red scare contribute to the erosion of civil liberties after the war?

rather than declined. Mexicans were considered excellent prospects for manual labor but not for citizenship. By 1920, ethnic Mexicans made up about three-fourths of California's farm laborers.

Among Mexican Americans, some of whom had lived in the Southwest for more than a century, *los recién llegados* (the recent arrivals) encountered mixed reactions. One Mexican American expressed this ambivalence: "We are all Mexicans anyway because the gueros [Anglos] treat us all alike." But he also called for immigration quotas because the recent arrivals drove down wages and incited white prejudice that affected all ethnic Mexicans.

Despite friction, large-scale immigration into the Southwest meant a resurgence of the Mexican cultural presence, which became the basis for greater solidarity and political action for the ethnic Mexican population. In 1929 in Texas, Mexican Americans formed the League of United Latin American Citizens.

Candidate	Electoral Vote	Popular Vote	Percent of Popular Vote
Warren G. Harding (Republican)	404	16,143,407	60.5
James M. Cox (Democrat)	127	9,130,328	34.2
Eugene V. Debs (Socialist)	0	919,799	3.4

Map 22.6
The Election of 1920

▶ Conclusion: Troubled Crusade

America's experience in World War I was exceptional. For much of the world, the Great War produced great destruction—blackened fields, ruined factories, and millions of casualties. But in the United States, war and prosperity marched hand in hand. America emerged from the war with the strongest economy in the world and a position of international preeminence.

Still, the nation paid a heavy price both at home and abroad. American soldiers and sailors encountered unprecedented horrors—submarines, poison gas, machine guns—and more than 100,000 died. But rather than redeeming the sacrifice of George Browne and others as Woodrow Wilson promised, the peace that followed the armistice tarnished it.

At home, rather than permanently improving working conditions, advancing public health, and spreading educational opportunity, as progressives had hoped, the war threatened to undermine the achievements of the previous two decades. Moreover, rather than promoting democracy, the war bred fear, intolerance, and repression that led to a crackdown on dissent and a demand for conformity. Reformers could count only woman suffrage as a permanent victory.

Woodrow Wilson had promised more than anyone could deliver. Progressive hopes of extending democracy and liberal reform nationally and internationally were dashed. In 1920, a bruised and disillusioned society stumbled into a new decade. The era coming to an end had called on Americans to crusade and sacrifice. The new era promised peace, prosperity, and a good time.

See the Selected Bibliography for this chapter in the Appendix.

22 Chapter Review

KEY TERMS

Triple Alliance (p. 621)
Triple Entente (p. 621)
Lusitania (p. 622)
Bolshevik (p. 624)
American Expeditionary Force (AEF) (p. 625)
Eighteenth Amendment (prohibition) (p. 631)
Nineteenth Amendment (woman suffrage) (p. 633)
Fourteen Points (p. 636)
League of Nations (p. 636)
Versailles treaty (p. 638)
Red scare (p. 641)
Schenck v. United States (p. 643)

REVIEW QUESTIONS

1. Why did President Wilson fail to maintain U.S. neutrality during World War I? (pp. 619–624)

2. How did the AEF contribute to the defeat of Germany? (pp. 624–628)

3. How did progressive ideals fare during wartime? (pp. 629–635)

4. Why did the Senate fail to ratify the Versailles treaty? (pp. 636–640)

5. How did the Red scare contribute to the erosion of civil liberties after the war? (pp. 640–646)

MAKING CONNECTIONS

1. Why did the United States at first resist intervening in World War I? Why did it later retreat from this policy and send troops?

2. How did World War I contribute to progressive-influenced domestic developments? Did they endure in peacetime?

3. After the war, what factors drove the conservative reaction in American politics, most vividly in the labor upheaval and Red scare that swept the nation? How did they shape the postwar political spectrum?

4. What drove African American and Mexican migration north? How did the war facilitate these changes? How was this migration significant?

LINKING TO THE PAST

1. How did America's experience in World War I compare with its experience during the Spanish-American War, its previous war abroad? Discuss the decision to go to war in each case, the military aspects, and the outcome. (See chapter 20.)

2. How did the experience of America's workers during World War I compare with their experience in the previous three decades? Consider the composition of the workforce, wages, conditions, and labor's efforts to organize. (See chapters 20 and 21.)

23 From New Era to Great Depression

1920–1932

CONTENT LEARNING OBJECTIVES

After reading and studying this chapter, you should be able to:

- Determine how business and industry contributed to a "New Era" and the growth of mass consumer and popular culture in the 1920s.

- Describe the effectiveness of prohibition in the 1920s.

- Explain how the "new woman" and the "New Negro" challenged social norms. Explain how some artists and intellectuals rejected America's mass culture.

- Evaluate ways in which social changes met with resistance, particularly in rural areas, and how this affected the presidential election of 1928.

- Describe the various factors that contributed to the Great Crash of 1929. Explain President Hoover's response and why it proved to be inadequate.

- Describe how the Great Depression affected the lives of ordinary Americans.

AMERICANS IN THE 1920S CHEERED HENRY FORD AS AN AUTHENTIC American hero. When the decade began, he had already produced six million automobiles; by 1927, the figure reached fifteen million. In 1920, a Ford car cost $845; in 1928, the price was less than $300, within range of most of the country's skilled workingmen. Henry Ford put America on wheels, and in the eyes of most Americans he was an honest man who made an honest car: basic, inexpensive, and reliable.

Born in 1863 on a farm in Dearborn, Michigan, Ford at sixteen fled rural life for Detroit, where he became a journeyman machinist. In 1893, he put together one of the first successful gasoline-driven carriages in the United States. His ambition, he said, was to "make something in quantity." The product he chose reflected American restlessness. "Everybody wants to be someplace he ain't," Ford declared. "As soon as he gets there he wants to go right back." In 1903, Ford gathered twelve workers in a 250-by-50-foot shed and created the Ford Motor Company.

Ford's early cars were custom-made one at a time. By 1914, his cars were being built along a continuously moving assembly line. Workers bolted on parts brought to them by cranes and conveyor belts. In 1920, one car rolled off the Ford assembly line every minute; in 1925, one appeared every ten seconds. Ford made only one kind of car, the Model T, which became synonymous with mass production. Throughout the rapid expansion

MODEL T FORD
When Henry Ford introduced the Model T in 1908, Americans thought of automobiles as toys of the rich. But by the 1920s, millions of Americans owned Fords, and their lives were never the same. Division of Work & Industry, National Museum of American History, Smithsonian Institution.

of the automotive industry, the Ford Motor Company remained the industry leader, peaking in 1925, when it outsold all its rivals combined (Map 23.1).

When Ford began his rise, progressive critics condemned the industrial giants of the nineteenth century as "robber barons" who lived in luxury while reducing their workers to wage slaves. Ford, however, identified with the common folk and saw himself as the benefactor of average Americans. But like the age in which he lived, Ford was more complex and more contradictory than this simple image suggests.

A man of genius whose compelling vision of modern mass production led the way in the 1920s, Ford was also cranky, tightfisted, and mean-spirited. He hated Jews and Catholics, bankers and doctors, and liquor and tobacco, and his money allowed him to act on his prejudices. His automobile plants made him a billionaire, but their regimented assembly lines reduced workers to near robots. On the cutting edge of modern technology, Ford nevertheless remained nostalgic about rural values. He sought to revive the past in Greenfield Village, where he relocated buildings from a bygone era, including his parents' farmhouse. His museum contrasted sharply with the roaring Ford assembly plant at River Rouge. Yet if Americans remained true to their agrarian past and managed to be modern and scientific at the same time, Ford insisted, all would be well.

Tension between traditional values and modern conditions lay at the heart of the conflicted 1920s. For the first time, more Americans lived in urban than in rural areas, and cities seemed to harbor everything rural people opposed. While millions admired urban America's sophisticated new style and consumer products, others condemned postwar society for its loose morals and vulgar materialism. The Ku Klux Klan and other champions of an older America resorted to violence as well as words when they chastised the era's "new woman," "New Negro," and surging immigrant populations. Those who sought to dam the tide of change proposed prohibition, Protestantism, and patriotism.

The public, disillusioned with the outcome of World War I, turned away from the Christian moralism and idealism of the Progressive Era. In the 1920s, Ford and businessmen like him replaced political reformers such as Theodore Roosevelt and Woodrow Wilson as the models of progress. The U.S. Chamber of Commerce crowed, "The American businessman is the most influential person in the nation." The fortunes of the era rose, then in 1929 crashed, according to the values and practices of the business community. When prosperity collapsed, the nation entered the most serious economic depression of all time.

MAP ACTIVITY

Map 23.1 Auto Manufacturing

By the mid-1920s, the massive coal and steel industries of the Midwest had made that region the center of the new automobile industry. A major road-building program by the federal government carried the thousands of new cars produced each day to every corner of the country.

READING THE MAP: How many states had factories involved with the manufacture of automobiles? In what regions was auto manufacturing concentrated?

CONNECTIONS: On what related industries did auto manufacturing depend? How did the integration of the automobile into everyday life affect American society?

Number of factories producing auto parts, materials, and vehicles

　8–20　　21–50　　51–100　　More than 100　　—— Major roads

▶ The New Era

Once Woodrow Wilson left the White House, energy flowed away from government activism and civic reform and toward private economic endeavor. The rise of a freewheeling economy and a heightened sense of individualism caused Secretary of Commerce Herbert Hoover to declare that America had entered a "New Era," one of many labels used to describe the complex 1920s. Some terms focus on the decade's high-spirited energy and cultural change: Roaring Twenties, Jazz Age, Flaming Youth. Others echo the rising importance of money—Dollar Decade, Golden Twenties—or reflect the sinister side of gangster profiteering—Lawless Decade. Still others emphasize the lonely confusion of the Lost Generation and the stress and anxiety of the Aspirin Age.

America in the twenties was many things, but President Calvin Coolidge got at an essential truth when he declared: "The business of America is business." Politicians and diplomats proclaimed business the heart of American civilization as they promoted its products at home and abroad. Average men and women bought into the idea that business and its wonderful goods were what made America great, as they snatched up the flood of new consumer items American factories sent forth. Nothing caught Americans' fancy more powerfully than the automobile.

A Business Government

Republicans controlled the White House from 1921 to 1933. The first of the three Republican presidents was Warren Gamaliel Harding, the Ohio senator who in his 1920 campaign called for a "return to normalcy," by which he meant the end of public crusades and a return to private pursuits. Harding appointed a few men of real stature to his cabinet. Herbert Hoover, for example, the former head of the wartime Food Administration, became secretary of commerce. But wealth and friendship also counted: Andrew Mellon, one of the richest men in America, became secretary of the treasury, and Harding handed out jobs to his friends, members of his old "Ohio gang." This curious combination of merit and cronyism made for a disjointed administration.

When Harding was elected in 1920 (see chapter 22, Map 22.6), the unemployment rate hit 20 percent, the highest ever up to that point. The bankruptcy rate of farmers increased tenfold. Harding pushed measures to regain national prosperity—high tariffs to protect American

CHRONOLOGY

1920	• Prohibition begins. • Women get the vote. • Warren G. Harding elected president.
1921	• Sheppard-Towner Act enacted. • Congress restricts immigration.
1922	• Teapot Dome scandal breaks. • Five-Power Naval Treaty signed.
1923	• Equal Rights Amendment defeated in Congress. • Harding dies; Vice President Calvin Coolidge becomes president.
1924	• Dawes Plan effected. • Coolidge elected president. • Johnson-Reed Act enacted. • Indian Citizenship Act enacted.
1925	• Scopes trial held.
1927	• Charles Lindbergh flies nonstop across Atlantic. • Nicola Sacco and Bartolomeo Vanzetti executed.
1928	• Kellogg-Briand pact signed. • Herbert Hoover elected president.
1929	• St. Valentine's Day murders occur. • Agricultural Marketing Act enacted. • *Middletown* published. • Stock market collapses.
1930	• Congress authorizes $420 million for public works projects. • Hawley-Smoot tariff passed.
1931	• Scottsboro Boys arrested. • Harlan County, Kentucky, coal miners strike.
1932	• River Rouge factory demonstration takes place. • Reconstruction Finance Corporation established. • National Farmers' Holiday Association formed.

businesses, price supports for agriculture, and the dismantling of wartime government control over industry in favor of unregulated private business. "Never before, here or anywhere else," the U.S. Chamber of Commerce said proudly, "has a government been so completely fused with business."

Harding's policies to boost American enterprise made him very popular, but ultimately his small-town congeniality and trusting ways did him in. Some of his friends in the Ohio gang were up to their necks in lawbreaking. Three of Harding's appointees would go to jail. Interior Secretary Albert Fall was convicted of accepting bribes of more than $400,000 for leasing oil reserves on public land in Teapot Dome, Wyoming, and "**Teapot Dome**" became a synonym for political corruption.

On August 2, 1923, when Harding died from a heart attack, Vice President Calvin Coolidge became president. Coolidge, who once said that "the man who builds a factory builds a temple, the man who works there worships there," continued and extended Harding's policies of promoting business and limiting government. Secretary of the Treasury Andrew Mellon reduced the government's control over the economy and cut taxes for corporations and wealthy individuals. New rules for the Federal Trade Commission severely restricted its power to regulate business. Secretary of Commerce Herbert Hoover hedged government authority by encouraging trade associations that ideally would keep business honest and efficient through voluntary cooperation.

Coolidge found an ally in the Supreme Court. For years, the Court had opposed federal regulation of hours, wages, and working conditions on the grounds that such legislation was the proper concern of the states. In the 1920s, the Court found ways to curtail a state's ability to regulate business. It ruled against closed shops—businesses where only union members could be employed—while confirming the right of owners to form exclusive trade associations. In 1923, the Court declared unconstitutional the District of Columbia's minimum-wage law for women, asserting that the law interfered with the freedom of employer and employee to make labor contracts. The Court and the president attacked government intrusion in the free market, even when the prohibition of government regulation threatened the welfare of workers.

The election of 1924 confirmed the defeat of the progressive principle that the state should take a leading role in ensuring the general welfare. To oppose Coolidge, the Democrats nominated John W. Davis, a corporate lawyer whose conservative views differed little from Republican principles. Only the Progressive Party and its presidential nominee, Senator Robert La Follette of Wisconsin, offered a genuine alternative. When La Follette championed labor unions, regulation of business, and protection of civil liberties, Republicans coined the slogan "Coolidge or Chaos." Voters chose Coolidge in a landslide. Coolidge was right when he declared, "This is a business country, and it wants a business government." What was true

VISUAL ACTIVITY

Teapot Dome Scandal, 1924
This cartoon shows Washington officials madly racing down the road to the White House in a desperate attempt to outrun the steamroller of scandal. Teapot Dome was only one example of the rampant corruption that tainted the Harding administration. The Granger Collection, New York.
READING THE IMAGE: How does the artist portray the fleeing politicians—as dignified public servants or something else?
CONNECTIONS: Why didn't Teapot Dome and the other scandals doom Republican chances in the elections of 1924?

of the government's relationship to business at home was also true abroad.

Promoting Prosperity and Peace Abroad

After orchestrating the Senate's successful effort to block U.S. membership in the League of Nations, Henry Cabot Lodge boasted, "We have torn Wilsonism up by the roots." But repudiation of Wilsonian internationalism and rejection of collective security through the League of Nations did not mean that the United States retreated into isolationism. The United States emerged from World War I with its economy intact and enjoyed a decade of stunning growth. New York replaced London as the center of world finance, and the United States became the world's chief creditor. Economic involvement in the world and the continuing chaos in Europe made withdrawal impossible.

One of the Republicans' most ambitious foreign policy initiatives was the Washington Disarmament Conference, which convened in 1921 to establish a global balance of naval power. Secretary of State Charles Evans Hughes shaped the **Five-Power Naval Treaty of 1922** committing Britain, France, Japan, Italy, and the United States to a proportional reduction of naval forces. The treaty led to the scrapping of more than two million tons of warships, by far the world's greatest success in disarmament. By fostering international peace, Hughes also helped make the world a safer place for American trade.

A second major effort on behalf of world peace came in 1928, when Secretary of State Frank Kellogg joined French foreign minister Aristide Briand to produce the Kellogg-Briand pact. Nearly fifty nations signed the solemn pledge to renounce war and settle international disputes peacefully.

But Republican administrations preferred private-sector diplomacy to state action. With the blessing of the White House, a team of American financiers led by Charles Dawes swung into action when Germany suspended its war reparation payments in 1923. Impoverished, Germany was staggering under the massive bill of $33 billion presented by the victorious Allies in the Versailles treaty. When Germany failed to meet its annual payment, France occupied Germany's industrial Ruhr Valley, creating the worst international crisis since the war. In 1924, the Dawes Plan halved Germany's annual reparation payments, initiated fresh American loans to Germany, and caused the French to retreat from the Ruhr. Although the United States failed

to join the League of Nations, it continued to exercise significant economic and diplomatic influence abroad. These Republican successes overseas helped fuel prosperity at home.

Automobiles, Mass Production, and Assembly-Line Progress

The automobile industry emerged as the largest single manufacturing industry in the nation. Henry Ford shrewdly located his company in Detroit, knowing that key materials for his automobiles were manufactured in nearby states (see Map 23.1). Keystone of the American economy, the automobile industry not only employed hundreds of thousands of workers directly but also brought whole industries into being—filling stations, garages, fast-food restaurants, and "guest cottages" (motels). The need for tires, glass, steel, highways, oil, and refined gasoline for automobiles provided millions of related jobs. By 1929, one American in four found employment directly or indirectly in the automobile industry. "Give us our daily bread" was no longer addressed to the Almighty, one commentator quipped, but to Detroit.

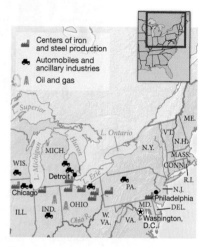

Detroit and the Automobile Industry in the 1920s

Automobiles changed where people lived, what work they did, how they spent their leisure, even how they thought. Hundreds of small towns decayed because the automobile enabled rural people to bypass them in favor of more distant cities and towns. In cities, streetcars began to disappear as workers moved to the suburbs and commuted to work along crowded highways. Nothing shaped modern America more than the automobile, and efficient mass production made the automobile revolution possible.

Mass production by the assembly-line technique became standard in almost every factory, from automobiles to meatpacking to cigarettes. To improve efficiency, corporations reduced assembly-line work to the simplest, most repetitive tasks. Changes on the assembly line and in management, along with technological advances, significantly boosted overall efficiency. Between 1922 and 1929, productivity in manufacturing increased 32 percent. Average wages, however, increased only 8 percent.

VISUAL ACTIVITY

Auto Assembly Line

This photograph of an automobile assembly line in Detroit in 1923 makes clear that workers stayed in one place while work came to them. Efficiency increased, but so, too, did boredom. Library of Congress, 4a27966.

READING THE IMAGE: What are the specific jobs of these two assembly-line workers?

CONNECTIONS: What else, besides automobiles, was mass-produced in the 1920s?

Industries also developed programs for workers that came to be called **welfare capitalism**. Some businesses improved safety and sanitation inside factories. They also instituted paid vacations and pension plans. Welfare capitalism encouraged loyalty to the company and discouraged traditional labor unions. One labor organizer in the steel industry bemoaned the success of welfare capitalism. "So many workmen here had been lulled to sleep by the company union, the welfare plans, the social organizations fostered by the employer," he declared, "that they had come to look upon the employer as their protector, and had believed vigorous trade union organization unnecessary for their welfare."

Consumer Culture

Mass production fueled corporate profits and national economic prosperity. During the 1920s, per capita income increased by a third, the cost of living stayed the same, and unemployment remained low. But the rewards of the economic boom were not evenly distributed. Americans who labored with their hands inched ahead, while white-collar workers enjoyed significantly more money and more leisure time to spend it. Mass production of a broad range of new products—automobiles, radios, refrigerators, electric irons, washing machines—produced a consumer goods revolution.

In this new era of abundance, more people than ever conceived of the American dream in terms of the things they could acquire. *Middletown* (1929), a study of the inhabitants of Muncie, Indiana, revealed that Muncie had become, above all, "a culture in which everything hinges on money." Moreover, faced with technological and organizational change beyond their comprehension, many citizens had lost confidence in their ability to play an effective role in civic affairs. More and more they became passive consumers, deferring to the supposed expertise of leaders in politics and economics.

The rapidly expanding business of advertising stimulated the desire for new products and attacked the traditional values of thrift and saving. Advertising linked material goods to the fulfillment of every spiritual and emotional need. Americans increasingly defined and measured their social status, and indeed their personal worth, on the yardstick of material possessions. Happiness itself rode on owning a car and choosing the right cigarettes and toothpaste. (See "Analyzing Historical Evidence," page 656.)

By the 1920s, the United States had achieved the physical capacity to satisfy Americans' material wants (Figure 23.1). The economic problem shifted from production to consumption: Who would buy the goods flying off American assembly lines? One solution was to expand America's markets in foreign countries, and government and business joined in that effort. Another solution to the problem of consumption was to expand the market at home.

Henry Ford realized early on that "mass production requires mass consumption." He understood that automobile workers not only produced cars but would also buy them if they made enough money. "One's own employees ought to be one's own best customers," Ford said. In 1914, he raised wages in his factories to $5 a day, more than twice the going rate. High wages made for workers who were more loyal and more exploitable, and high wages returned as profits when workers bought Fords.

Many people's incomes, however, were too puny to satisfy the growing desire for consumer goods. The solution was installment buying—a little money down, a payment each month—which allowed people to purchase expensive items they could not otherwise afford or to purchase items before saving the necessary money. As one newspaper announced, "The first responsibility of an American to his country is no longer that of a citizen, but of a consumer." During the 1920s, America's motto became spend, not save. Old values—"Use it up, wear it out, make it do or do without"—seemed about as pertinent as a horse and buggy. American culture had shifted.

REVIEW   How did the spread of the automobile transform the United States?

FIGURE 23.1   Production of Consumer Goods, 1921–1929
Transportation, communications, and entertainment changed the lives of consumers in the 1920s. Laborsaving devices for the home were popular, but the vastly greater sales of automobiles and radios showed that consumerism was powerful in moving people's attention beyond their homes.

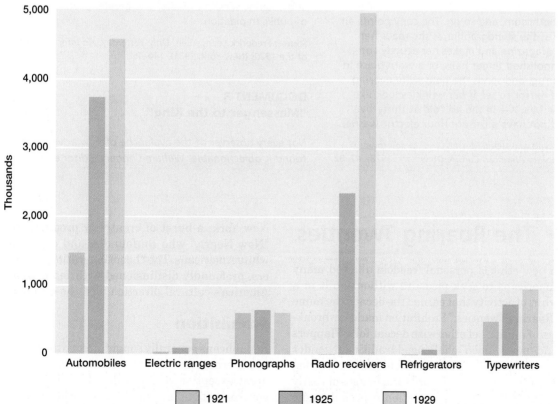

Advertising in a Consumer Age

Just as American business changed dramatically in the early decades of the twentieth century, so, too, did advertising. Businesses in the New Era sought to attract customers in new and different ways. Before the 1920s, advertising had focused on production. Even small businesses presented themselves as powerful and efficient producers of consumer goods such as stoves and furniture. But beginning in the consumer society of the 1920s, companies sought to teach Americans to judge themselves and others not by what they produced, but by what they bought.

DOCUMENT 1
The Art of Making People Uneasy

In their study of Muncie, Indiana, sociologists Robert and Helen Merrell Lynd found that "advertising is to a business what fertilizer is to a farm" and examined the ways that large-scale advertising—in popular magazines, movies, radio, and elsewhere—was rapidly changing ideas about "what things are essential to living."

Advertising is concentrating increasingly upon a type of copy aiming to make the reader emotionally uneasy, to bludgeon him with the fact that decent people don't live the way *he* does; *decent* people ride on balloon tires, have a second bathroom, and so on. The copy points an accusing finger at the stenographer as she reads her *Motion Picture Magazine* and makes her acutely conscious of her unpolished finger nails, or a worn place in the living room rug, and sends the housewife peering anxiously in the mirror to see if *her* wrinkles look like those that made Mrs. X— in the ad "old at thirty-five" because she did not have a Leisure Hour electric washer.

Source: Robert S. Lynd and Helen Merrell Lynd, *Middletown: A Study in Contemporary American Culture* (New York: 1928), 47, 82.

DOCUMENT 2
Unmasking Advertising

Frederick Lewis Allen, a journalist and historian, was an acute observer of contemporary life. In his enormously popular Only Yesterday, *published only two years after the 1920s ended, he contemplates an advertising campaign based on anxiety about bad breath.*

By far the most famous of these dramatic advertisements of the Post-war Decade was the long series in which the awful results of halitosis were set forth through the depiction of a gallery of unfortunates whose closest friends would not tell them. "Often a bridesmaid but never a bride. . . . Edna's case was really a pathetic one." . . . "Why did she leave him that way?" . . . "*That's* why you're a failure," . . . and then that devilishly ingenious display which capitalized on the fears aroused by earlier tragedies in the series: the picture of a girl looking at a Listerine advertisement and saying to herself, "This *can't* apply to me!" Useless for the American Medical Association to insist that Listerine was "not a true deodorant," that it simply covered one smell with another. Just as useless as for the Life Extension Institute to find "one out of twenty with pyorrhea [gum disease], rather than Mr. Forhan's [a mouth product] famous four-out-of-five." . . . Halitosis had the power of dramatic advertising behind it, and Listerine swept to greater and greater profits on a tide of public trepidation.

Source: Frederick Lewis Allen, *Only Yesterday: An Informal History of the 1920s* (New York: 1931), 144–45.

DOCUMENT 3
"Messenger to the King"

Not every observer of the avalanche of new advertising found it objectionable. William Chenery, editor and

▶ The Roaring Twenties

A new ethic of personal freedom allowed many Americans to seek pleasure without guilt in a whirl of activity that earned the decade the name "Roaring Twenties." Prohibition made lawbreakers of millions of otherwise decent folk. Flappers and "new women" challenged traditional gender boundaries. Other Americans enjoyed the Roaring Twenties through the words and images of vastly expanded mass communication, especially radio and movies. In America's big cities, particularly New York, a burst of creativity produced the "New Negro," who confounded and disturbed white Americans. The "Lost Generation" of writers, profoundly disillusioned with mainstream America's cultural direction, fled the country.

Prohibition

Republicans generally sought to curb the powers of government, but the twenties witnessed a great exception to this rule when the federal government implemented one of the last reforms of the Progressive Era: the Eighteenth Amendment,

Ad for Breath Freshener
The message is clear: Bad breath could be keeping you on the sidelines while your friends are dancing! Buy Listerine and join in the fun! AS400 DB/Corbis.

publisher of Collier's, *a national magazine, sang advertising's praises in this 1930 article in his magazine.*

Advertising, essentially, is the awakening of human desire. There is no stronger force in this new world of ours.

The successful advertisement makes you crave new things. The motive is frankly commercial but the consequences reach far beyond trade. . . . The byproducts of the [advertiser's] efforts have had prodigious effects upon our opinions, our standards of taste, our habits, and even upon our picture of a good life.

We arise in the morning and we bathe. Why? Merely because soap makers have taught us the importance of cleanliness. . . .

Beards and even mustaches have gone out of fashion because razor manufacturers persuaded us to shave.

We clean our teeth because toothpaste manufacturers have made us believe in the importance of oral hygiene. They have saved us from more aches than the dentists could cure.

Our breakfast habits are the results of the teaching of food manufacturers. The old heavy American breakfast has gone the way of the hoop skirt. Our health is better. Advertising did it.

The clothes we wear, the houses we live in, the furniture we use, our very conception of a home is the product of advertising. . . .

If journalism is the little sister of literature, advertising began certainly as the Cinderella of selling. Now it is the great motive force in our commercial life. It is the life blood of public demand. Our material civilization has been made possible by it.

Source: William Chenery, "Messenger to the King," *Collier's*, May 3, 1930.

Questions for Analysis

Analyze the Evidence: According to the critics—Frederick Lewis Allen and the Lynds—what is the most pernicious feature of modern advertising?

Recognize Viewpoints: How might William Chenery's job have helped shape his positive opinion of advertising? How might the other writers included here dispute his argument?

Consider the Context: How did the rise of mass production translate into the rise of mass advertising and mass consumption?

---

which banned the manufacture and sale of alcohol and took effect in January 1920 (see "The Progressive Stake in the War" in chapter 22). Drying up the rivers of liquor that Americans consumed, supporters of **prohibition** claimed, would eliminate crime, boost production, and lift the nation's morality. Prohibition would destroy the saloon, which according to a leading "dry" was the "most fiendish, corrupt and hell-soaked institution that ever crawled out of the slime of the eternal pit." Instead, prohibition initiated a fourteen-year orgy of lawbreaking unparalleled in the nation's history.

The Treasury Department agents charged with enforcing prohibition faced a staggering task. Although they smashed more than 172,000 illegal stills in 1925 alone, loopholes in the law almost guaranteed failure. Sacramental wine was permitted, allowing fake clergy to party with bogus congregations. Farmers were allowed to ferment their own "fruit juices." Doctors and dentists could prescribe liquor for medicinal purposes.

In 1929, a Treasury agent in Indiana reported intense local resistance to enforcement of prohibition. "Conditions in most important cities

Prohibition

In 1921, New York City deputy police commissioner John A. Leach watches as agents pour bootleg liquor that they have confiscated down the sewer. Successes like this were common during prohibition, but not even the criminalization of liquor could permanently defeat "Satan in a bottle." Library of Congress, 3c23257.

very bad," he declared. "Lax and corrupt public officials great handicap . . . prevalence of drinking among minor boys and the . . . middle or better classes of adults." The "speakeasy," an illegal nightclub, became a common feature of the urban landscape. Speakeasies' dance floors led to the sexual integration of the formerly all-male drinking culture, changing American social life forever. Detroit, probably America's wettest city, was home to more than 20,000 illegal drinking establishments, making the alcohol business the city's second-largest industry, behind automobile manufacturing.

Eventually, serious criminals took over the liquor trade. During the first four years of prohibition, Chicago witnessed more than two hundred gang-related killings as rival mobs struggled for control of the lucrative liquor trade. The most notorious event came on St. Valentine's Day 1929, when Alphonse "Big Al" Capone's Italian-dominated mob machine-gunned seven members of a rival Irish gang. Capone's bootlegging empire brought in $95 million a year, when a chicken dinner cost 5 cents. Federal authorities finally sent Capone to prison for income tax evasion. "I violate the Prohibition law—sure," he told a reporter. "Who doesn't? The only difference is, I take more chances than the man who drinks a cocktail before dinner."

Americans overwhelmingly favored the repeal of the Eighteenth Amendment, the "noble experiment," as Herbert Hoover called prohibition. In 1931, a panel of distinguished experts reported that the experiment had failed. The social and political costs of prohibition outweighed the benefits. Prohibition fueled criminal activity, corrupted the police, demoralized the judiciary, and caused ordinary citizens to disrespect the law. In 1933, the nation ended prohibition, making the Eighteenth Amendment the only constitutional amendment to be repealed.

The New Woman

Of all the changes in American life in the 1920s, none sparked more heated debate than the alternatives offered to the traditional roles of women. Increasing numbers of women worked and went to college, defying older gender norms. Even mainstream magazines such as the *Saturday Evening Post* began publishing stories about young, college-educated women who drank gin cocktails, smoked cigarettes, and wore skimpy dresses and dangly necklaces. Before the Great War, the **new woman** dwelt in New York City's bohemian Greenwich Village, but afterward the mass media brought her into middle-class America's living rooms.

When the Nineteenth Amendment, ratified in 1920, granted women the vote, feminists felt liberated and expected women to reshape the political landscape. A Kansas woman declared, "I went to bed last night a *slave*[;] I awoke this morning a *free woman*." Women began pressuring

Congress to pass laws that especially concerned women, including measures to protect women in factories and grant federal aid to schools. Black women lobbied particularly for federal courts to assume jurisdiction over the crime of lynching. But women's only significant national legislative success came in 1921 when Congress enacted the Sheppard-Towner Act, which extended federal assistance to states seeking to reduce high infant mortality rates.

A number of factors helped thwart women's political influence. Male domination of both political parties, the rarity of female candidates, and lack of experience in voting, especially among recent immigrants, kept many women away from the polls. In some places, male-run election machines actually disfranchised women, despite the Nineteenth Amendment. In the South, poll taxes, literacy tests, and outright terrorism continued to decimate the vote of African Americans, men and women alike.

Most important, rather than forming a solid voting bloc, feminists divided. Some argued for women's right to special protection; others demanded equal protection. The radical National Woman's Party fought for an Equal Rights Amendment that stated flatly: "Men and women shall have equal rights throughout the United States." The more moderate League of Women Voters feared that the amendment's wording threatened state laws that provided women special protection, such as preventing them from working on certain machines. Put before Congress in 1923, the Equal Rights Amendment went down to defeat, and radical women were forced to work for the causes of birth control, legal equality for minorities, and the end of child labor through other means.

Economically, more women worked for pay—approximately one in four by 1930—but they clustered in "women's jobs." The proportion of women working as secretaries, stenographers, and typists skyrocketed. Women almost monopolized the occupations of librarian, nurse, elementary school teacher, and telephone operator. Women also represented 40 percent of salesclerks by 1930. More female white-collar workers meant that fewer women were interested in protective legislation for women; new women wanted salaries and opportunities equal to men's.

Increased earnings gave working women more buying power in the new consumer culture. A stereotype soon emerged of the flapper, so called because of the short-lived fad of wearing unbuckled galoshes. The flapper had short "bobbed" hair and wore lipstick and rouge. She spent freely on the latest styles—dresses with short skirts, drop waists, bare arms, and no petticoats—and she danced all night to wild jazz. As F. Scott Fitzgerald described her in his novel *This Side of Paradise* (1920), she was "lovely and expensive and about nineteen."

The new woman both reflected and propelled the modern birth control movement. Margaret Sanger, the crusading pioneer for contraception during the Progressive Era (see "Radical Alternatives" in chapter 21), restated her principal conviction in 1920: "No woman can call herself free until she can choose consciously

---

VISUAL ACTIVITY

"The Girls' Rebellion"
The August 1924 cover of *Redbook*, a popular women's magazine, portrays the kind of postadolescent girl who was making respectable families frantic. Flappers scandalized their middle-class parents by flouting the old moral code. This young woman sports the "badges of flapperhood," including what one critic called an "intoxication of rouge." Fictionalized, emotion-packed stories such as this brought the new woman into every woman's home. Picture Research Consultants & Archives.

READING THE IMAGE: In addition to the rouge, what else identifies this young woman as a flapper?
CONNECTIONS: In addition to flappers, what other developments in the 1920s challenged America's traditional values?

25 Cents
THE RED BOOK MAGAZINE
August 1924
"The Girls' Rebellion"
A startling and revealing story of "the younger generation" that everyone should read

Was There a Sexual Revolution in the 1920s?

"Cigarette in hand, shimmying to the music of the masses, the New Woman and the New Morality have made their theatric debut upon the modern scene," lamented one commentator in 1926. The *Atlantic* magazine declared that a moral chasm had opened between the generations, and the old and young in America "were as far apart in point of view, codes, and standards as if they belonged to different races." Charlotte Perkins Gilman represented many older feminists who were disappointed with the outcome of recent advances for women: "It is sickening to see so many of the newly freed abusing that freedom in a mere imitation of masculine weakness and vice." Older Americans wholeheartedly

Heroes and Heroines
Two kinds of women look up adoringly at two kinds of 1920s heroes. A wholesome image is seen on the left in a 1927 cover of *People's Popular Monthly* magazine. The outdoor girl, smartly turned out in her raccoon coat and pennant, flatters a naive college football hero. On the right, Vilma Banky kneels imploringly before the hypnotic gaze of the movies' greatest heartthrob, Rudolph Valentino. Magazine: Picture Research Consultants & Archives; poster: Mary Evans/FEATURE PICTURES INC/Ronald Grant/Everett Collection.

whether she will or will not be a mother." Shifting strategy in the twenties, Sanger courted the conservative American Medical Association and linked birth control with the eugenics movement, which advocated limiting reproduction among "undesirable" groups. Thus, she made contraception a respectable subject for discussion.

Flapper style and values spread from coast to coast through films, novels, magazines, and

agreed that the younger generation was in full-fledged revolt against traditional standards of morality, and that America was in danger of going to hell in a handbasket.

Critics had, it seemed, plenty of evidence. Between newspapers, movies, and magazines, even the small towns of America were "literally saturated with sex," one observer complained. Flappers and college coeds claimed the privileges of men, smoking cigarettes, drinking from hip flasks, and staying out all night. When eight hundred college women met to discuss life on campus and what "nice girls" should do, they concluded, "Learn temperance in petting, not abstinence." Anxious observers counseled intervention. The Ohio legislature debated whether to prohibit any "female over fourteen years of age" from wearing a "skirt which does not reach to that part of the foot known as the instep." The *Ladies' Home Journal* urged "legal prohibition" of jazz dancing.

But were the concerned observers correct? Was there really a sexual revolution in the 1920s? The principal movers of the new morality were youths, and without a doubt, young middle-class men and women felt freer than ever to openly express their feelings about sex. But we must separate the new candor from actual sexual behavior. Although solid evidence is difficult to come by, correspondence, diaries, and other personal documents; physicians' records; divorce proceedings; advice literature; and a few early sex surveys provide important clues.

A good place to begin the investigation is where youth congregated: college campuses. Campus life included a self-conscious ethos of experimentation and innovation, but as students demolished old rules, they also created new ones. One

major innovation was "dating"—that is, going out unsupervised rather than receiving callers at home or meeting at church socials. Dating was encouraged by the automobile, that "house of prostitution on wheels," as one juvenile judge in Indiana labeled it. Dating led to a second innovation: "petting," or any sexual activity short of intercourse. One examination of coed behavior at the end of the 1920s found that 92 percent of women admitted engaging in petting.

Like dating, petting represented a significant change in female behavior. But it was not a total rejection of traditional morality because it took place within the search for the ideal marriage partner. There was also a modest increase in premarital sexual intercourse, made possible by the widespread acceptance of contraceptives. But sexual intercourse usually took place between partners who assumed they would marry. The new woman of the 1920s, though freer sexually, continued to focus on romance, marriage, and family.

Did the new sexual behavior mark a drastic change from the past? Evidence of sexual habits before World War I is even more difficult to come by than for the 1920s, but it appears that changes in attitudes and behaviors had been under way for decades. Nineteenth-century Victorian notions of sexless women who felt little or no passion had been eroding since at least the 1890s. A small survey of the sexual practices of middle-class women in the 1890s conducted by Dr. Clelia Duel Mosher, a physician at Stanford University, found that women were enthusiastic about sex and often found satisfaction. The primary ideologues of the sexual revolution, Havelock Ellis, who celebrated female passion, and Sigmund Freud, who stressed the

centrality of sex in human endeavor, reached large American audiences before World War I.

Changes in sexual morality, therefore, were evolutionary rather than revolutionary. Still, liberal attitudes and behaviors had their greatest impact in the 1920s. American culture was being remade, and young people, especially women, were on the cutting edge. Now equal at the polling booth, women were also growing more economically independent. Changes in women's political and economic lives were reflected in their sexual attitudes and behaviors. In place of the idea that women were naturally pure, the new morality proclaimed the equality of desire. Only the boldest women publicly rejected a "double standard" (the notion that the sexual behavior of women should be more circumscribed than that of men), but many jettisoned notions of female submission, obedience, and endless childbearing. Charges that the giddy flapper and her partner were bringing down American civilization were overblown, but young women certainly were changing the culture.

Questions for Analysis

Summarize the Argument: What is the evidence for the contention that changes in sexual behavior in the 1920s were more evolutionary than revolutionary?

Analyze the Evidence: How did changes in women's political and economic lives affect their sexual behaviors?

Consider the Context: What was the relationship of the emergence of the "new woman" in the 1920s and the sexual habits of young women?

advertisements. New women challenged American convictions about separate spheres for women and men, the double standard of sexual conduct, and Victorian ideas of proper female appearance and behavior. (See "Making Historical Arguments," above.) Although only a minority of American women became flappers, all women, even those who remained at home, heard about girls gone wild and felt the great changes of the era.

The New Negro

The 1920s witnessed the emergence not only of the "new woman" but also of the "New Negro." African Americans who challenged the caste system that confined dark-skinned Americans to the lowest levels of society confronted whites who insisted that race relations would not change. As cheers for black soldiers faded after their return from World War I, African Americans faced grim days of economic hardship and race riots.

The prominent African American intellectual W. E. B. Du Bois and the National Association for the Advancement of Colored People (NAACP) aggressively pursued the passage of a federal antilynching law to counter mob violence against blacks in the South. At the same time, however, many disillusioned poor urban blacks turned to the new leadership of the Jamaican-born visionary Marcus Garvey, who urged African Americans to rediscover the heritage of Africa, take pride in their own achievements, and maintain racial purity by avoiding miscegenation. In 1917, Garvey launched the Universal Negro Improvement Association (UNIA) to help African Americans gain economic and political independence entirely outside white society. In 1919, the UNIA created its own shipping company, the Black Star Line, to support the "Back to Africa" movement among black Americans. In 1927, the federal government pinned charges of illegal practices on Garvey and deported him to Jamaica. Nevertheless, the issues Garvey raised about racial pride, black identity, and the search for equality persisted, and his legacy remains at the center of black nationalist thought.

Still, most African Americans maintained hope in the American promise. In New York City, hope and talent came together. The city's black population jumped 115 percent (from 152,000 to 327,000) in the 1920s. In Harlem in uptown Manhattan, an extraordinary mix of black artists, sculptors, novelists, musicians, and poets set out to create a distinctive African American culture that drew on their identities as Americans and Africans. As scholar Alain Locke put it in 1925, they introduced to the world the "**New Negro**," who rose from the ashes of slavery and segregation to proclaim African Americans' creative genius.

The emergence of the New Negro came to be known as the Harlem Renaissance. Building on the independence and pride displayed by black soldiers during the war, black artists sought to defeat the fresh onslaught of racial discrimination and violence with poems, paintings, and plays. "We younger Negro artists . . . intend to express our individual dark-skinned selves without fear or shame," poet Langston Hughes said of the Harlem Renaissance. "If white people are pleased, we are glad. If they are not, it doesn't matter. We know we are beautiful. And ugly, too."

The Harlem Renaissance produced dazzling talent. Black writer James Weldon Johnson, who in 1903 had written the Negro national anthem, "Lift Every Voice," wrote *God's Trombones* (1927), in which he expressed the wisdom and beauty of black folktales from the South. The poetry of Langston Hughes, Claude McKay, and Countee Cullen celebrated the vitality of life in Harlem. Zora Neale Hurston's novel *Their Eyes Were Watching God* (1937) explored the complex passions of black people in a southern community. Black painters, led by Aaron Douglas, linked African art, which had recently inspired European modernist artists, to the concept of the New Negro.

Despite such vibrancy, Harlem for most whites remained a separate black ghetto known only for its lively nightlife. Fashionable whites crowded into Harlem's segregated nightclubs, the most famous of which was the Cotton Club, where they believed they could hear "real" jazz, a relatively new musical form, in its "natural" surroundings. The vigor of the Harlem Renaissance left a powerful legacy for black Americans, but the creative burst did little in the short run to dissolve the prejudice of white society. (See "Experiencing the American Promise," page 664.)

Entertainment for the Masses

In the 1920s, popular culture, like consumer goods, was mass-produced and mass-consumed. The proliferation of movies, radios, music, and sports meant that Americans found plenty to do, and in doing the same things, they helped create a national culture.

Nothing offered escapist delights like the movies. Hollywood, California, discovered the successful formula of combining opulence, sex, and adventure. Admission was cheap, and by 1929 the movies were drawing more than 80 million people in a single week. Hollywood created "movie stars," glamorous beings whose every move was tracked by fan magazines. Rudolph Valentino, described as "catnip to women," and Clara Bow, the "It Girl" (everyone knew what *it* was), became household names. Most loved of all was the comic Charlie Chaplin, whose famous character, the wistful Little Tramp, showed an endearing inability to cope with the rules and complexities of modern life.

Duke Ellington Leads His Jazz Band
From 1927 to 1931, the Duke Ellington Orchestra was the house band at the Cotton Club in Harlem, where black performers played for white audiences. The photograph captures something of the energy and exuberance that helped make Ellington America's greatest jazz composer and bandleader.
© Bettmann/Corbis.

Americans also found heroes in sports. Baseball solidified its place as the national pastime in the 1920s. It remained essentially a game played by and for the working class. In George Herman "Babe" Ruth, baseball had the most cherished free spirit of the time. The rowdy escapades of the "Sultan of Swat" demonstrated that sports offered a way to break out of the ordinariness of everyday life. By "his sheer exuberance," one sportswriter declared, Ruth "has lightened the cares of the world."

The public also fell in love with a young boxer from the grim mining districts of Colorado. As a teenager, Jack Dempsey had made his living hanging around saloons betting he could beat anyone in the house. When he took the heavyweight crown just after World War I, he was revered as the people's champ, a stand-in for the average American who felt increasingly confined by bureaucracy and machine-made culture. In Philadelphia in 1926, a crowd of 125,000 fans saw challenger Gene Tunney pummel and defeat the people's champ.

Football, essentially a college sport, held greater sway with the upper classes. The most famous coach, Knute Rockne of Notre Dame, celebrated football for its life lessons of hard work and teamwork. Let the professors make learning as exciting as football, Rockne advised, and the problem of getting young people to learn would disappear. But in keeping with the times,

football moved toward a more commercial spectacle. Harold "Red" Grange, "the Galloping Ghost," led the way by going from stardom at the University of Illinois to the Chicago Bears in the new professional football league.

The decade's hero worship reached its zenith in the celebration of Charles Lindbergh, a young pilot who set out on May 20, 1927, to become the first person to fly solo nonstop across the Atlantic. Newspapers tagged Lindbergh "the Lone Eagle"— the perfect hero for an age that celebrated individual accomplishment. "Charles Lindbergh," one journalist proclaimed, "is the stuff out of which have been made the pioneers that opened up the wilderness. His are the qualities which we, as a people, must nourish." Lindbergh realized, however, that technical and organizational complexity was fast reducing chances for solitary achievement. Consequently, he titled his book about the flight *We* (1927) to include the machine that had made it all possible.

Another machine—the radio—became crucial to mass culture in the 1920s. The nation's first licensed radio station, KDKA in Pittsburgh, began broadcasting in 1920, and soon American airwaves buzzed with news, sermons, soap operas, sports, comedy, and music. Because they could now reach prospective customers in their own homes, advertisers bankrolled radio's rapid growth. Between 1922 and 1929, the number of radio stations in the United States increased from 30 to 606. In

The Quest for Home Ownership in Segregated Detroit

Owning a place of one's own has always been important in America. In the nineteenth century, with the rise of industry and cities, the goal of a family farm gave way to the goal of a single-family house. Home ownership has been widely realized today, with a little less than two-thirds of Americans (with the assistance of mortgage companies) owning their own homes.

In the 1920s, decent housing was in short supply in Detroit, America's great boomtown, as thousands poured in to work in Henry Ford's automobile factories. Arriving before World War I, blue-collar German, Irish, and Polish immigrants found homes in working-class neighborhoods scattered around the city center. The property owners resolved to keep their neighborhoods all-white by channeling the great migration of southern blacks into Black Bottom, the downtown ghetto. Although the U.S. Supreme Court had struck down a law mandating segregated housing in 1917, inventive white homeowners created other means to draw racial boundaries. Real estate agents refused to show blacks houses in white neighborhoods. Banks turned down blacks for mortgages. Whites signed restrictive covenants, promising not to sell their homes to blacks. If a black family managed to slip through their defenses, whites resorted to violence.

Dr. Ossian Sweet, a black physician, arrived in Detroit in 1921. He set up his medical practice in Black Bottom and prospered. He soon had the down payment for a home, but he refused to settle his wife and baby daughter in the congested, rat-infested ghetto. In 1925, Sweet bought a substantial bungalow at 2905 Garland Avenue, several blocks inside a working-class white neighborhood. His brother said later, "He wasn't looking for trouble. He just wanted to bring up his little girl in good surroundings." Sweet understood the danger; whites had recently run other black professionals out of their Detroit neighborhoods. "Well, we have decided we are not going to run," Sweet told a friend. "We're not going to look for any trouble, but we're going to be prepared to protect ourselves if trouble arises." When Gladys and Ossian Sweet moved into their home on September 8, 1925, nine friends and family members accompanied them. The moving van that brought their furniture also carried a shotgun, two rifles, six pistols, and four hundred rounds of ammunition.

Hundreds of white men quickly filled the streets, greatly outnumbering the few police who hoped to keep the peace. Shouting that they would send the "niggers" back where they belonged, the mob began throwing rocks, breaking windows, and advancing. Suddenly, gunfire erupted from the second story of the Sweet house, and two white men were shot; one was killed. The police kept the mob away long enough for a paddy wagon to haul the eleven blacks to the police station, where they were all indicted for murder.

Asked why he wanted to move to a white neighborhood, where there was likely to be trouble, Sweet said, "Because I bought the house, and it was my house, and I felt I had a right to live in it." The NAACP, which saw the case as an opportunity to strike a legal blow in favor of self-defense against racial violence, hired Clarence Darrow to defend the accused. Darrow was the most celebrated defense lawyer in the country and fresh from the Scopes trial in Tennessee (see page 668). Darrow told the jury that the facts were simple: "When they defended their home, they were arrested and charged with murder." He reminded the all-white jury that "every man's home is his castle, which even the king may not enter. Every man has a right to kill to defend himself or his family, or others, either in defense of the home, or in defense of themselves." A split jury caused the judge to declare a mistrial. A second trial ended in not guilty verdicts for all the defendants.

just seven years, homes with radios jumped from 60,000 to a staggering 10.25 million.

The Lost Generation

Some writers and artists felt alienated from America's mass-culture society, which they found shallow, anti-intellectual, and materialistic. Silly movie stars disgusted them. They believed that business culture blighted American life. In their minds, Henry Ford made a poor hero. Young, white, and mostly college educated, these expatriates, as they came to be called, felt embittered by the war and renounced the progressives who had promoted it as a crusade. For them, Europe—not Hollywood or Harlem—seemed the place to seek their potential.

The American-born writer Gertrude Stein, long established in Paris, remarked famously

Dr. Ossian Sweet and His House

Dr. Ossian Sweet's substantial two-story brick home is listed on the National Register of Historic Places. In September 1925, Sweet tried to move his family into the then all-white Detroit suburb where the house is located. Residents reacted violently, determined to uphold "the present high standards of the neighborhood." Dr. Sweet: Courtesy of the Burton Historical Collection, Detroit Public Library; house: Michigan State Historic Preservation Office.

Over the next several decades, blacks succeeded in breaking out of the inner cities and moving into the suburbs, where today more than one-third of African Americans live. But breaching city boundaries did not mean leaving residential segregation behind. Of all the nation's segregated cities, none was more segregated than Detroit. As late as 1963, Martin Luther King Jr. declared: "I have a dream this afternoon that one day right here in Detroit Negroes will be able to buy a house or rent a house anywhere their money will carry them." As for Sweet, he moved back into his home on Garland Avenue in 1928, but without his wife and daughter, both of whom had died of tuberculosis, perhaps contracted while in jail. He stayed in the bungalow for more than twenty-five years, and when he left, the neighborhood around him was still largely white.

Questions for Analysis

Recognize Viewpoints: Why did whites in Sweet's neighborhood oppose his living there?

Analyze the Evidence: Why was Clarence Darrow's defense so effective before an all-white jury?

Consider the Context: What does the case of Ossian Sweet reveal about the aspirations of middle-class black Americans during the 1920s?

as the young exiles gathered around her, "They are the lost generation." Most of the expatriates, however, believed to the contrary that they had finally found themselves. The Lost Generation helped launch the most creative period in American art and literature in the twentieth century. The novelist whose spare, clean style best exemplified the expatriate efforts to make art mirror basic reality was Ernest Hemingway. Admirers found the terse language and hard lessons of his novel *The Sun Also Rises* (1926) to be perfect expressions of a world stripped of illusions.

Many writers who remained in America were exiles in spirit. Before the war, intellectuals had eagerly joined progressive reform movements. Afterward, they were more likely critics of American cultural vulgarity. Novelist Sinclair

Lewis in *Main Street* (1920) and *Babbitt* (1922) satirized his native Midwest as a cultural wasteland. Humorists such as James Thurber created outlandish characters to poke fun at American stupidity and inhibitions. And southern writers, led by William Faulkner, explored the South's grim class and race heritage. Worries about alienation surfaced as well. F. Scott Fitzgerald spoke sadly in *This Side of Paradise* (1920) of a disillusioned generation "grown up to find all Gods dead, all wars fought, all faiths in man shaken."

REVIEW   How did the new freedoms of the 1920s challenge older conceptions of gender and race?

▶ Resistance to Change

Large areas of the country did not share in the wealth of the 1920s. By the end of the decade, 40 percent of the nation's farmers were landless, and 90 percent of rural homes lacked indoor plumbing, gas, or electricity. Rural America's traditional distrust of urban America turned to despair in the 1920s when the census reported that the majority of the population had shifted to the city (Map 23.2). Once the "backbone of the republic," rural Americans had become poor country cousins. Urban domination over the nation's political and cultural life and sharply rising economic disparity drove rural Americans in often ugly, reactionary directions.

MAP ACTIVITY

Map 23.2   The Shift from Rural to Urban Population, 1920–1930

The movement of whites and Hispanics toward urban and agricultural opportunity made Florida, the West, and the Southwest the regions of fastest population growth. By contrast, large numbers of blacks left the rural South to find a better life in the North. Almost all migrating blacks went from the countryside to cities in distant parts of the nation, while white and Hispanic migrants tended to move shorter distances toward familiar places.

READING THE MAP: Which states had the strongest growth? To which cities did southern blacks predominantly migrate?

CONNECTIONS: What conditions in the countryside made the migration to urban areas appealing to many rural Americans? In what social and cultural ways did rural America view itself as different from urban America?

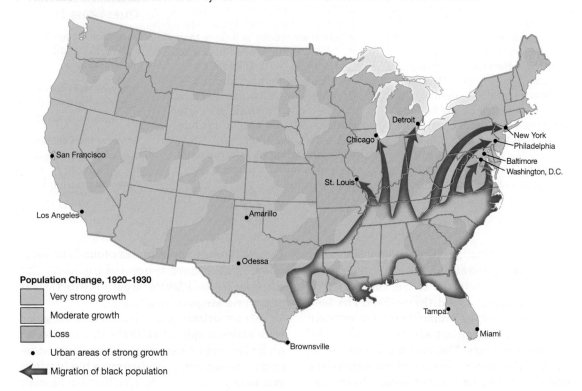

Population Change, 1920–1930

- Very strong growth
- Moderate growth
- Loss
- • Urban areas of strong growth
- ◀ Migration of black population

Cities seemed to stand for everything rural areas stood against. Rural America imagined itself as solidly Anglo-Saxon (despite the presence of millions of African Americans in the South and Mexican Americans, Native Americans, and Asian Americans in the West), and the cities seemed to be filled with undesirable immigrants. Rural America was the home of old-time Protestant religion, and the cities teemed with Catholics, Jews, liberal Protestants, and atheists. Rural America championed old-fashioned moral standards—abstinence and self-denial—while the cities spawned every imaginable vice. In the 1920s, frustrated rural people sought to recapture their country by helping to push through prohibition, dam the flow of immigrants, revive the Ku Klux Klan, defend the Bible as literal truth, and defeat an urban Roman Catholic for president.

Rejecting the Undesirables

Before the war, when about a million immigrants arrived each year, some Americans warned that unassimilable foreigners were drowning the nation. War against Germany and its allies expanded nativist and antiradical sentiment. After the war, large-scale immigration resumed (another 800,000 immigrants arrived in 1921) at a moment when industrialists no longer needed new factory laborers. Returning veterans, as well as African American and Mexican migration, had relieved labor shortages. Moreover, union leaders feared that millions of poor immigrants would undercut their efforts to organize American workers. Rural America's God-fearing Protestants were particularly alarmed that most of the immigrants were Catholic or Jewish. In 1921, Congress responded by severely restricting immigration.

Three years later, Congress very nearly slammed the door shut. The **Johnson-Reed Act** of 1924 limited the number of immigrants to no more than 161,000 a year and established quotas for each European nation. The act revealed the fear and bigotry that fueled anti-immigration legislation. While it cut immigration by more than 80 percent, it squeezed some nationalities far more than others. Backers of Johnson-Reed, who declared that America had become the "garbage can and the dumping ground of the world," manipulated quotas to ensure entry only to "good" immigrants from western Europe. The law, for example, allowed Great Britain 62,458 entries, but Russia could send only 1,992. Johnson-Reed effectively reversed the trend toward immigration from southern and eastern Europe, which by 1914 had amounted to 75 percent of the yearly total.

The 1924 law also reaffirmed the 1880s legislation barring Chinese immigrants and added Japanese and other Asians to the list of the excluded. But it left open immigration from the Western Hemisphere because farmers in the Southwest demanded continued access to cheap agricultural labor. During the 1920s, some 500,000 Mexicans crossed the border legally. In addition, Congress in 1924 passed the Indian Citizenship Act, which extended suffrage and citizenship to all American Indians.

Rural Americans, who had most likely never laid eyes on a Polish packinghouse worker, a Slovak coal miner, an Armenian sewing machine operator, or a Chinese laundry worker, strongly supported immigration restriction, as did industrialists and labor leaders. The laws of the 1920s marked the end of the era symbolized by the Statue of Liberty's open-armed welcome to Europe's "huddled masses yearning to breathe free."

Antiforeign hysteria climaxed in the trial of two anarchist immigrants from Italy, Nicola Sacco and Bartolomeo Vanzetti. Arrested in 1920 for robbery and murder in South Braintree, Massachusetts, the men were sentenced to death by a judge who openly referred to them as "anarchist bastards." In response to doubts about the fairness of the verdict, a blue-ribbon review committee found the trial judge guilty of a "grave breach of official decorum" but refused to recommend a motion for retrial. When Massachusetts executed Sacco and Vanzetti on August 23, 1927, fifty thousand American mourners followed the caskets, convinced that the men had died because they were immigrants and radicals, not because they were murderers.

The Rebirth of the Ku Klux Klan

The nation's sour antiforeign mood struck a responsive chord in members of the secret society the **Ku Klux Klan**. The Klan first appeared in the South during Reconstruction to thwart black freedom and expired with the reestablishment of white supremacy (see chapter 16). In 1915, the Klan was reborn at Stone Mountain, Georgia, but when the new Klan extended its targets beyond black Americans, it quickly spread beyond the South. Under a banner proclaiming "100 percent Americanism," the Klan promised to defend family, morality, and traditional American values against the threats posed by blacks, immigrants, radicals, feminists, Catholics, and Jews.

Sacco and Vanzetti
Murder suspects Bartolomeo Vanzetti (left) and Nicola Sacco (right) talk with Sacco's wife, Rosina, while waiting in the prisoners' dock. Even today, the 1927 executions symbolize for some the shortcomings of American justice. AS400 DB/Corbis.

Building on the frustrations of rural America, the Klan in the 1920s spread throughout the nation, almost controlling Indiana and influencing politics in Illinois, California, Oregon, Texas, Louisiana, Oklahoma, and Kansas. In 1926, Klan imperial wizard Hiram Wesley Evans described the assault of modernity: "One by one all our traditional moral standards went by the boards or were so disregarded that they ceased to be binding," he explained. "The sacredness of our Sabbath, of our homes, of chastity, and finally even of our right to teach our own children in schools [represented] fundamental facts and truth torn away from us."

Eventually, social changes, along with lawless excess, crippled the Klan. Immigration restrictions eased the worry about invading foreigners, and sensational wrongdoing by Klan leaders cost it the support of traditional moralists. Grand Dragon David Stephenson of Indiana, for example, went to jail for the kidnapping and rape of a woman who subsequently committed suicide. Yet the social grievances, economic problems, and religious anxieties of the countryside and small towns remained alive, ready to be ignited.

The Scopes Trial

In 1925 in a Tennessee courtroom, old-time religion and the new spirit of science went head-to-head. The confrontation occurred after several southern states passed legislation against the teaching of Charles Darwin's theory of evolution in the public schools. Scientists and civil liberties organizations clamored for a challenge to the law, and John Scopes, a young biology teacher in Dayton, Tennessee, offered to test his state's ban on teaching evolution. When Scopes came to trial, Clarence Darrow, a brilliant defense lawyer from Chicago, volunteered to defend him. Darrow, an avowed agnostic, took on the prosecution's William Jennings Bryan, three-time Democratic nominee for president, fervent fundamentalist, and symbol of rural America.

The **Scopes trial** quickly degenerated into a media circus. The first trial to be covered live on radio, it attracted a nationwide audience. When, under relentless questioning by Darrow, Bryan declared on the witness stand that he did indeed believe that the world had been created in six days and that Jonah had lived in the belly of a whale, his humiliation in the eyes of most urban observers was complete. Nevertheless, the Tennessee court upheld the law and punished Scopes with a $100 fine. Although fundamentalism won the battle, it lost the war. Baltimore journalist H. L. Mencken had the last word in a merciless obituary for Bryan, who died just a week after the trial ended. Portraying the "monkey trial" as a battle between the country and the city, Mencken flayed Bryan as a "charlatan, a mountebank, a zany without shame or dignity," motivated solely by "hatred of the city men who had laughed at him for so long."

As Mencken's acid prose indicated, Bryan's humiliation was not purely a victory of reason and science. It also revealed the disdain urban people felt for country people and the values they clung to. The Ku Klux Klan revival and the Scopes trial dramatized and inflamed divisions between city and country, intellectuals and the uneducated, the privileged and the poor, the scoffers and the faithful.

Al Smith and the Election of 1928

The presidential election of 1928 brought many of the developments of the 1920s—prohibition, immigration, religion, and the clash of rural and urban values—into sharp focus. Republicans emphasized the economic success of their party's pro-business government and turned to Herbert Hoover, the energetic secretary of commerce and leading public symbol of 1920s prosperity. But because both parties generally agreed that the American economy was basically sound, the campaign turned on social issues that divided Americans.

The Democrats nominated four-time governor of New York Alfred E. Smith. Smith adopted "The Sidewalk of New York" as a campaign theme song and seemed to represent all that rural Americans feared and resented. A child of immigrants, Smith got his start in politics with the help of New York City's Irish-dominated Tammany Hall political machine, to many the epitome of big-city corruption. He denounced immigration quotas, signed New York State's anti-Klan bill, and opposed prohibition, believing that it was a nativist attack on immigrant customs. When Smith supposedly asked reporters, "Wouldn't you like to have your foot on the rail and blow the foam off some suds?" prohibition forces dubbed him "Alcohol Al." But Smith's greatest vulnerability in the heartland was his religion. He was the first Catholic to run for president. A Methodist bishop in Virginia denounced Roman Catholicism as "the Mother of ignorance, superstition, intolerance and sin" and begged Protestants not to vote for a candidate who represented "the kind of dirty people that you find today on the sidewalks of New York."

Hoover, who neatly combined the images of morality, efficiency, service, and prosperity, won the election by a landslide (Map 23.3). He received nearly 58 percent of the vote and gained 444 electoral votes to Smith's 87. The only bright spot for Democrats was the nation's cities, which voted Democratic, indicating the rising strength of ethnic minorities, including Smith's fellow Catholics.

REVIEW   How did some Americans resist cultural change?

▶ The Great Crash

At his inauguration in 1929, Hoover told the American people, "Given a chance to go forward with the policies of the last eight years, we shall soon with the help of God be in sight of the day when poverty will be banished from this nation." Those words came back to haunt Hoover when eight months later the prosperity he touted collapsed in the stock market crash of 1929. The nation ended nearly three decades of barely interrupted economic growth. Like much of the world, the United States fell into the most serious economic depression of all time. Hoover's reputation was among the first casualties, along with the reverence for business that had been the hallmark of the New Era.

Herbert Hoover: The Great Engineer

When Hoover became president in 1929, he seemed the perfect choice to lead a prosperous business nation. His rise from poor Iowa orphan to one of the world's most celebrated mining engineers by the time he was thirty personified America's

Map 23.3
The Election of 1928

Candidate	Electoral Vote	Popular Vote	Percent of Popular Vote
Herbert Hoover (Republican)	444	21,391,381	57.4
Alfred E. Smith (Democrat)	87	15,016,443	40.3
Norman Thomas (Socialist)	0	881,951	2.3

rags-to-riches ideal. His success in managing efforts to feed civilian victims of the fighting during World War I won him acclaim as "the Great Humanitarian" and led Woodrow Wilson to name him head of the Food Administration once the United States entered the war. Hoover's reputation soared even higher as secretary of commerce in the Harding and Coolidge administrations.

Hoover belonged to the progressive wing of his party. "The time when the employer could ride roughshod over his labor[ers] is disappearing with the doctrine of 'laissez-faire' on which it is founded," he declared in 1909. He urged a limited business-government partnership that would manage the sweeping changes Americans were experiencing. Hoover brought a reform agenda to the White House: "We want to see a nation built of home owners and farm owners. We want to see their savings protected. We want to see them in steady jobs. We want to see more and more of them insured against death and accident, unemployment and old age. We want them all secure."

But Hoover also had ideological and political liabilities. Principles that appeared strengths in the prosperous 1920s—individual self-reliance, industrial self-management, and a limited federal government—became straitjackets when economic catastrophe struck. Moreover, Hoover had never held an elected public office, had a poor political touch, and was too thin-skinned to be an effective politician. Even so, most Americans considered him "a sort of superman" able to solve any problem. Prophetically, he confided to a friend his fear that "if some unprecedented calamity should come upon the nation . . . I would be sacrificed to the unreasoning disappointment of a people who expected too much." The distorted national economy set the stage for the calamity Hoover so feared.

The Distorted Economy

In the spring of 1929, the United States enjoyed a fragile prosperity. Although America had become the world's leading economy, it had done little to help rebuild Europe's shattered economy after World War I. Instead, the Republican administrations demanded that Allied nations repay their war loans, creating a tangled web of debts and reparations that sapped Europe's economic

VISUAL ACTIVITY

Hoover Campaign Poster
This poster effectively illustrates Herbert Hoover's 1928 campaign message: Republican administrations in the 1920s had produced middle-class prosperity, complete with a house in the suburbs and the latest automobile. David J. & Janice L. Frent Collection/Corbis.
READING THE IMAGE: What in the poster reminds voters that Hoover as secretary of commerce had helped create prosperity by promoting industry?
CONNECTIONS: How does the spirit of the poster compare with the actual campaign against the Democrat (and Catholic) Al Smith?

VOTE FOR HERBERT HOOVER and CHARLES CURTIS for the Prosperity of your Country and the Happiness and your home....

vitality. Moreover, to boost American business, the United States enacted tariffs that prevented other nations from selling their goods to Americans. Fewer sales meant that foreign nations had less money to buy American goods. American banks propped up the nation's export trade by extending credit to foreign customers, deepening their debt.

America's domestic economy was also in trouble. Wealth was badly distributed. Farmers continued to suffer from low prices and chronic indebtedness; the average income of farm families was only $240 per year. The wages of industrial workers, though rising during the decade, failed to keep up with productivity and corporate profits. Overall, nearly two-thirds of all American families lived on less than the $2,000 per year that economists estimated would "supply only basic necessities." In sharp contrast, the wealthiest 1 percent of the population received 15 percent of the nation's income—the amount received by the poorest 42 percent. The Coolidge administration worsened the deepening inequality by cutting taxes on the wealthy.

By 1929, the inequality of wealth produced a serious problem in consumption. The rich, brilliantly portrayed in F. Scott Fitzgerald's novel *The Great Gatsby* (1925), spent lavishly, but they could absorb only a tiny fraction of the nation's output. For a time, the new device of installment buying—buying on credit—kept consumer demand up. By the end of the decade, four out of five cars and two out of three radios were bought on credit.

Signs of economic trouble began to appear at mid-decade. New construction slowed down. Automobile sales faltered. Companies began cutting back production and laying off workers. Between 1921 and 1928, as investment and loan opportunities faded, five thousand banks failed, wiping out the life savings of hundreds of thousands.

The Crash of 1929

Even as the economy faltered, Americans remained upbeat. Hoping for even bigger slices of the economic pie, Americans speculated wildly in the stock market on Wall Street. Between 1924 and 1929, the values of stocks listed on the New York Stock Exchange increased by more than 400 percent. Buying stocks on margin—that is, putting up only part of the money at the time of purchase—accelerated. Some people got rich this way, but those who bought on credit could finance their loans only if their stocks increased in value.

A Yale economist assured doubters that stock prices had reached "a permanently high plateau." Former president Calvin Coolidge declared that, at current prices, stocks were a bargain. But President Hoover observed, "The only trouble with capitalism is capitalists. They're too damned greedy."

Finally, in the autumn of 1929, the market hesitated. Investors nervously began to sell their overvalued stocks. The dip quickly became a panic on October 24, the day that came to be known as Black Thursday. More panic selling came on Black Tuesday, October 29, the day the market suffered a greater fall than ever before. In the next six months, the stock market lost six-sevenths of its total value.

It was once thought that the crash alone caused the Great Depression. It did not. In 1929, the national and international economies were already riddled with severe problems. But the dramatic losses in the stock market crash and the fear of risking what was left acted as a great brake on economic activity. The collapse on Wall Street shattered the New Era's confidence that America would enjoy perpetually expanding prosperity.

Hoover and the Limits of Individualism

When the bubble broke, Americans expressed relief that Hoover resided in the White House. Not surprisingly for a man who had been such an active secretary of commerce, Hoover acted quickly to arrest the decline. In November 1929, to keep the stock market collapse from ravaging the entire economy, Hoover called a White House conference of business and labor leaders. He urged them to join in a voluntary plan for recovery: Businesses would maintain production and keep their workers on the job; labor would accept existing wages, hours, and conditions. Within a few months, however, the bargain fell apart. As demand for their products declined, industrialists cut production, sliced wages, and laid off workers. Poorly paid or unemployed workers could not buy much, and their decreased spending led to further cuts in production and further loss of jobs. Thus began the terrible spiral of economic decline.

To deal with the problems of rural America, Hoover got Congress to pass the Agricultural Marketing Act in 1929. The act created the Farm Board, which used its budget of $500 million to buy up agricultural surpluses and thus, it was hoped, raise prices. But prices continued to fall. To help end the decline, Hoover joined conservatives in urging protective tariffs on agricultural goods, and the Hawley-Smoot tariff of 1930 established the highest rates in history. The same year, Congress also authorized $420 million for public works projects to give the unemployed jobs and create more purchasing power. In three years, the Hoover administration nearly doubled federal public works expenditures.

But with each year of Hoover's term, the economy weakened. Tariffs did not end the suffering of farmers because foreign nations retaliated with increased tariffs of their own that crippled American farmers' ability to sell abroad. In 1932, Hoover hoped to help hard-pressed industry with the **Reconstruction Finance Corporation (RFC)**, a federal agency empowered to lend government funds to endangered banks and corporations. The theory was trickle-down economics: Pump money into the economy at the top, and in the long run the people at the bottom would benefit. Or, as one wag put it, "Feed the sparrows by feeding the horses." In the end, very little of what critics of the RFC called a "millionaires' dole" trickled down to the poor.

Meanwhile, hundreds of thousands of workers lost their jobs each month. By 1932, an astounding one-quarter of the American workforce—nearly thirteen million people—were unemployed. There was no direct federal assistance, and state services and private charities were swamped. The depression that began in 1929 devastated much of the world, but no other industrialized nation provided such feeble support to the jobless. Cries grew louder for the federal government to give hurting people relief.

Hoover was no do-nothing president, but there were limits to his conception of the government's proper role in fighting the economic disaster. He compared direct federal aid to the needy to the "dole" in Britain, which he thought destroyed the moral fiber of the chronically unemployed. "Prosperity cannot be restored by raids on the public Treasury," Hoover declared. Besides, he said, the poor could rely on their neighbors to protect them "from hunger and cold." In 1931, he allowed the Red Cross to distribute government-owned agricultural surpluses to the hungry. In 1932, he relaxed his principles further to offer small federal loans, not gifts, to the states to help them in their relief efforts. But Hoover's restricted notions of legitimate government action

proved vastly inadequate to address the problems of restarting the economy and ending human suffering.

REVIEW Why did the American economy collapse in 1929?

▶ Life in the Depression

In 1930, suffering on a massive scale set in. Men and women hollow-eyed with hunger grew increasingly bewildered and angry in the face of cruel contradictions. They saw agricultural surpluses pile up in the countryside and knew that their children were going to bed hungry. They saw factories standing idle, yet they knew that they and millions of others were willing to work. The gap between the American people and leaders who failed to resolve these contradictions widened as the depression deepened. By 1932, America's economic problems had created a dangerous social and political crisis.

The Human Toll

Statistics only hint at the human tragedy of the Great Depression. When Hoover took office in 1929, the American economy stood at its peak. When he left in 1933, it had reached its twentieth-century low (Figure 23.2). In 1929, national income was $88 billion. By 1933, it had declined to $40 billion. In 1929, unemployment was 3.1 percent, or 1.5 million workers. By 1933, unemployment stood at 25 percent, almost 13 million workers. In Cleveland, Ohio, 50 percent of the workforce was jobless, and in Toledo, 80 percent. By 1932, more than 9,000 banks had shut their doors, wiping out millions of savings accounts.

Jobless, homeless victims wandered in search of work, and the tramp, or hobo, became one of the most visible figures of the decade. Riding the rails or hitchhiking, a million vagabonds moved southward and westward looking for seasonal agricultural work. Other unemployed men and women, sick or less hopeful, huddled in doorways, overcome, one man remembered, by "helpless despair and submission." Scavengers haunted alleys behind restaurants in search of food. One writer told

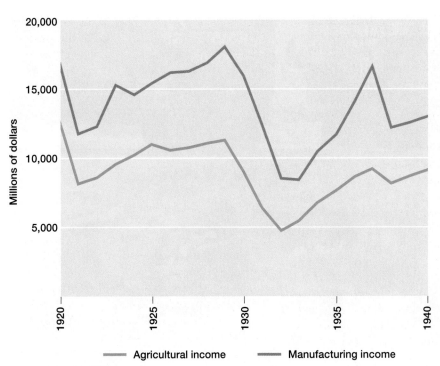

FIGURE 23.2 **Manufacturing and Agricultural Income, 1920–1940**
After economic collapse, recovery in the 1930s began under New Deal auspices.

of an elderly woman who always took off her glasses to avoid seeing the maggots crawling over the garbage she ate. In 1931, four New York City hospitals reported ninety-five deaths from starvation. "I don't want to steal," a Pennsylvania man wrote to the governor, "but I won't let my wife and boy cry for something to eat. . . . How long is this going to keep up? I cannot stand it any longer."

Rural poverty was most acute. Tenant farmers and sharecroppers, mainly in the South, came to symbolize how poverty crushed the human spirit. Eight and a half million people, three million of them black, crowded into cabins without plumbing, electricity, or running water. They subsisted—just barely—on salt pork, cornmeal, molasses, beans, peas, and whatever they could hunt or fish. When economist John Maynard Keynes was asked whether anything like this degradation had existed before, he replied, "Yes, it was called the Dark Ages and it lasted four hundred years."

There was no federal assistance to meet this human catastrophe, only a patchwork of strapped charities and destitute state and local agencies. For a family of four without any income, the best the city of Philadelphia could do was provide $5.50 per week. That was not enough to live on but better than Detroit, which allot-ted 60 cents a week before the city ran out of money altogether.

The deepening crisis roused old fears and caused some Americans to look for scapegoats. Among the most thoroughly scapegoated were Mexican Americans. During the 1920s, cheap agricultural labor from Mexico flowed legally across the U.S. border, welcomed by the large farmers. In the 1930s, however, the public denounced the newcomers as dangerous aliens who took jobs from Americans. Government officials, most prominently those in Los Angeles County, targeted Mexican residents for deportation regardless of citizenship status. As many as half a million Mexicans and Mexican Americans were deported or fled to Mexico.

The depression deeply affected the American family. Young people postponed marriage. When they did marry, they produced few children. White women, who generally worked in low-paying service areas, did not lose their jobs as often as men who worked in steel, automobile, and other heavy industries. Idle husbands suffered a loss of self-esteem. "Before the depression," one unemployed man reported, "I wore the pants in this family, and rightly so." Jobless, he lost "self-respect" and also "the respect of my children, and I am afraid that I am losing my wife." Employers discriminated against

Hoboes, 1920s
Out-of-work men gather around a fire in front of the train that may have brought them to this unnamed place in the Midwest. With no work at home, many decided to "ride the rails" for free in search of a job. Hoboing was dangerous because of accidents and the violence of the railroad security staffs, nicknamed "bulls." The Granger Collection, New York.

married women workers, but necessity continued to drive women into the marketplace. As a result, by 1940 some 25 percent more women were employed for wages than in 1930.

Denial and Escape

President Hoover assured the American nation that economic recovery was on its way, but the president's optimism was contradicted by makeshift shantytowns, called "Hoovervilles," that sprang up on the edges of America's cities. Newspapers used as cover by those sleeping on the streets were "Hoover blankets." An empty pocket turned inside out was a "Hoover flag," and jackrabbits caught for food were "Hoover hogs." Bitter jokes circulated about the increasingly unpopular president. One told of Hoover asking for a nickel to telephone a friend. Flipping him a dime, an aide said, "Here, call them both."

While Hoover practiced denial, other Americans sought refuge from reality at the movies. Throughout the depression, between 60 million and 75 million people (nearly two-thirds of the nation) scraped together enough change to fill the movie palaces every week. Box office hits such as *42nd Street* and *Gold Diggers of 1933* capitalized on the hope that prosperity lay just around the corner. But a few filmmakers grappled with realities rather than escape them. *The Public Enemy* (1931) taught hard lessons about gangsters' ill-gotten gains. Indeed, under the new production code of 1930, designed to protect public morals, all movies had to find some way to show that crime did not pay.

Despite Hollywood's efforts to keep Americans on the right side of the law, crime increased. In the countryside, the plight of people who had lost their farms to bank foreclosures led to the romantic idea that bank robbers were only getting back what banks had stolen from the poor. Woody Guthrie, the populist folksinger from Oklahoma, captured the public's tolerance for outlaws in his tribute to a murderous bank robber with a choirboy face, "The Ballad of Pretty Boy Floyd." Guthrie sang that there were two kinds of robbers, those who used guns and those who used pens, and he observed that robbers with guns, like

Pretty Boy Floyd, never drove families from their homes. Named Public Enemy No. 1, Floyd was shot and killed by police in 1934. His funeral in Oklahoma was attended by between 20,000 and 40,000 people, many of whom viewed Floyd as a tragic figure, a victim of the hard times.

Working-Class Militancy

The nation's working class bore the brunt of the economic collapse. By 1931, William Green, head of the American Federation of Labor (AFL), had turned militant. "I warn the people who are exploiting the workers," he shouted, "that they can drive them only so far before they will turn on them and destroy them. They are taking no account of the history of nations in which governments have been overturned. Revolutions grow out of the depths of hunger."

The American people were slow to anger, but on March 7, 1932, several thousand unemployed autoworkers massed at the gates of Henry Ford's River Rouge factory in Dearborn, Michigan, to demand work. Pelted with rocks, Ford's private security forces responded with gunfire, killing four demonstrators. Forty thousand outraged citizens turned out for the unemployed men's funerals.

Harlan County Coal Strike, 1931

Farmers mounted uprisings of their own. When Congress refused to guarantee farm prices, several thousand farmers created the National Farmers' Holiday Association in 1932, so named because its members planned to take a "holiday" from shipping crops to market. Farm militants also resorted to what they called "penny sales." When banks foreclosed and put farms up for auction, neighbors warned others not to bid, bought the foreclosed property for a few pennies, and returned it to the bankrupt owners. Militancy won farmers little in the way of long-term solutions, but one individual observed that "the biggest and finest crop of revolutions you ever saw is sprouting all over the country right now."

Even those who had proved their patriotism by serving in World War I rose up in protest against the government. In 1932, tens of thousands of unemployed veterans traveled to Washington, D.C., to petition Congress for the immediate payment of the pension (known as a "bonus") that Congress had promised them in 1924. Hoover feared that the veterans would spark a riot and ordered the U.S. Army to evict the **Bonus Marchers** from their camp on the outskirts of the city. Tanks destroyed the squatters' encampments while five hundred soldiers wielding bayonets and tear gas sent the protesters fleeing. The spectacle of the army driving peaceful, petitioning veterans from the nation's capital further undermined public support for the beleaguered Hoover.

The Great Depression—the massive failure of capitalism—catapulted the Communist Party to its greatest size and influence in American history. Some 100,000 Americans—workers, intellectuals, college students—joined the Communist Party in the belief that only an overthrow of the capitalist system could save the victims of the depression. In 1931, the party, through its National Miners Union, moved into Harlan County, Kentucky, to support a strike by brutalized coal miners. Mine owners unleashed thugs against the strikers and eventually beat the miners down. But the Communist Party gained a reputation as the most dedicated and fearless champion of the union cause.

The left also led the fight against racism. While both major parties refused to challenge segregation in the South, the Socialist Party, led by Norman Thomas, attacked the system of sharecropping that left many African Americans in near servitude. The Communist Party also took action. When nine young black men in Scottsboro, Alabama (the **Scottsboro Boys**), were arrested on trumped-up rape charges in 1931, a team of lawyers sent by the party saved the defendants from the electric chair.

Radicals on the left often sparked action, but protests by moderate workers and farmers occurred on a far greater scale. Breadlines, soup kitchens, foreclosures, unemployment, government violence, and cold despair drove patriotic men and women to question American capitalism. "I am as conservative as any man could be," a Wisconsin farmer explained, "but any economic

Scottsboro Boys
Nine black youths, ranging in age from thirteen to twenty-one, were convicted of the rape of two white women and sentenced to death by an all-white jury in March 1931. None was executed, and eventually the state dropped the charges against the youngest four and granted paroles to the others. The last Scottsboro Boy left jail in 1950. © Bettmann/Corbis.

system that has in its power to set me and my wife in the streets, at my age—what can I see but red?"

REVIEW   How did the depression reshape American politics?

▶ Conclusion: Dazzle and Despair

In the aftermath of World War I, America turned its back on progressive crusades and embraced conservative Republican politics, the growing influence of corporate leaders, and business values. Changes in the nation's economy—Henry Ford's automobile revolution, mass production,

advertising—propelled fundamental change throughout society. Living standards rose, economic opportunity increased, and Americans threw themselves into private pleasures—gobbling up the latest household goods and fashions, attending baseball and football games and boxing matches, gathering around the radio, and going to the movies. As big cities came to dominate American life, the culture of youth and flappers became the leading edge of what one observer called a "revolution in manners and morals." At home in Harlem and abroad in Paris, American literature, art, and music flourished.

For many Americans, however, none of the glamour and vitality had much meaning. Instead of seeking thrills at the speakeasies, plunging into speculation on Wall Street, or escaping abroad, the vast majority struggled to earn a decent living. Blue-collar America did not participate fully in white-collar prosperity. Rural America was almost entirely left out of the Roaring Twenties. Country folk, deeply suspicious and profoundly discontented, championed prohibition, revived the Klan, attacked immigration, and defended old-time Protestant religion.

The crash of 1929 and the depression that followed starkly revealed the economy's crises of international trade and consumption. Hard times swept high living off the front pages of the nation's newspapers. Different images emerged: hoboes hopping freight trains, strikers confronting police, malnourished sharecroppers staring blankly into the distance, empty apartment buildings alongside cardboard shantytowns, and mountains of food rotting in the sun while guards with shotguns chased away the hungry.

The depression hurt everyone, but the poor were hurt most. As farmers and workers sank into aching hardship, businessmen rallied around Herbert Hoover to proclaim that private enterprise would get the country moving again. But things fell apart, and Hoover faced increasingly radical opposition. Membership in the Socialist and Communist parties surged, and more and more Americans contemplated desperate measures. By 1932, the depression had nearly brought the nation to its knees. America faced its greatest crisis since the Civil War, and citizens demanded new leaders who would save them from the "Hoover Depression."

See the Selected Bibliography for this chapter in the Appendix.

23 Chapter Review

KEY TERMS

Teapot Dome (p. 652)
Five-Power Naval Treaty of 1922 (p. 653)
welfare capitalism (p. 654)
prohibition (p. 657)
new woman (p. 658)
New Negro (p. 662)
Johnson-Reed Act (p. 667)
Ku Klux Klan (p. 667)
Scopes trial (p. 668)
Reconstruction Finance Corporation (RFC) (p. 672)
Bonus Marchers (p. 675)
Scottsboro Boys (p. 675)

REVIEW QUESTIONS

1. How did the spread of the automobile transform the United States? (pp. 651–655)

2. How did the new freedoms of the 1920s challenge older conceptions of gender and race? (pp. 656–666)

3. How did some Americans resist cultural change? (pp. 666–669)

4. Why did the American economy collapse in 1929? (pp. 669–672)

5. How did the depression reshape American politics? (pp. 672–676)

MAKING CONNECTIONS

1. What drove popular opinion in the 1920s to unrestrained confidence in American business? How did it influence Republicans' approach to governance and the development of the American economy in the 1920s?

2. Americans' encounters with the wealth and increased personal freedom characteristic of the 1920s varied greatly. Why did some embrace the era's changes, while others resisted them?

3. How did shifting government policy contribute to both the boom of the 1920s and the bust of 1929?

4. How did Americans attempt to lessen the impact of the Great Depression?

LINKING TO THE PAST

1. How did America's experience in World War I—both at home and abroad—help shape the 1920s? (See chapter 22.)

2. How did attitudes toward government in the Progressive Era differ from those in the 1920s? (See chapter 21.)

24 The New Deal Experiment

1932–1939

CONTENT LEARNING OBJECTIVES

After reading and studying this chapter, you should be able to:

- Explain which issues shaped the presidential campaign of 1932 and how the candidates' strategies differed. Determine the significance of Roosevelt's victory.

- Analyze which factors united New Deal reformers and what kinds of policies they endorsed. Describe the initial reforms enacted during Roosevelt's first one hundred days in office.

- Recount why critics resisted the New Deal.

- Explain how the Second New Deal moved the country toward a welfare state and describe the kinds of programs reformers proposed. Evaluate why some Americans were left out of the New Deal.

- Identify the final phase of the New Deal and why it ultimately reached a deadlock.

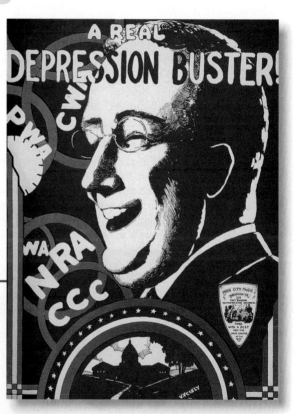

NEW DEAL PRESIDENTIAL CAMPAIGN POSTER
This 1936 poster proclaims President Franklin D. Roosevelt "A Real Depression Buster," without mentioning his name. The acronyms on the poster refer to the New Deal programs that exemplified Roosevelt's commitment to an activist government. David J. & Janice L. Frent Collection/ Corbis.

IN MARCH 1936, FLORENCE OWENS PILED HER SEVEN children into her old Hudson. They had been picking beets in southern California, near the Mexican border, but the harvest was over now. Owens headed north, where she hoped to find work picking lettuce. About halfway there, her car broke down. She coasted into a labor camp of more than two thousand migrant workers who were hungry and out of work. They had been attracted by advertisements of work in the pea fields, only to find the crop ruined by a heavy frost. Owens set up a lean-to shelter and prepared food for her family while two of her sons worked on the car. They ate half-frozen peas from the field and small birds the children killed. Owens recalled later, "I started to cook dinner for my kids, and all the little kids around the camp came in. 'Can I have a bite? . . .' And they was hungry, them people was."

Florence Owens was born in 1903 in Oklahoma, then Indian Territory. Both of Florence's parents were Cherokee. When she was seventeen, Florence married Cleo Owens, a farmer who moved his growing family to California, where he worked in sawmills. Cleo died of tuberculosis in 1931, leaving Florence a widow with six young children.

Florence began to work as a farm laborer in California's Central Valley to support herself and her children. She picked cotton, earning about $2 a day. "I'd leave home before daylight and come in after dark," she explained. "We just existed!" To survive, she worked nights as a waitress, making "50-cents a day and the leftovers." Sometimes, she remembered, "I'd carry home two water buckets full" of leftovers to feed her children.

Like tens of thousands of other migrant laborers, Owens followed the crops, planting, cultivating, and harvesting as jobs opened up in the fields along the West Coast from California to Oregon and Washington. Joining Owens and other migrants—many of whom were Mexicans and Filipinos—were Okie refugees from the Dust Bowl, the large swath of Great Plains states that suffered drought, failed crops, and foreclosed mortgages during the 1930s.

Soon after Florence Owens fed her children at the pea pickers' camp, a car pulled up, and a woman with a camera got out and began to take photographs of Owens. The woman was Dorothea Lange, a photographer employed by a New Deal agency to document conditions among farmworkers in California. Lange snapped six photos of Owens, and climbed back in her car and headed to Berkeley. Owens and her family, their car now repaired, drove off to look for work in the lettuce fields.

Lange's last photograph of Owens, subsequently known as *Migrant Mother*, became an icon of the desperation among Americans that President Franklin Roosevelt's New Deal sought to alleviate. While *Migrant Mother* became Dorothea Lange's most famous photograph, Florence Owens continued to work in the fields, "ragged, hungry, and broke," as a San Francisco newspaper noted.

Unlike Owens, her children, and other migrant workers, many Americans received government help from Roosevelt's New Deal initiatives to provide relief for the needy, to speed economic recovery, and to reform basic economic and governmental institutions. Roosevelt's New Deal elicited bitter opposition from critics on the right and the left, and it failed to satisfy fully its own goals of relief, recovery, and reform. But within the Democratic Party, the New Deal energized a powerful political coalition that helped millions of Americans withstand the privations of the Great Depression. In the process, the federal government became a major presence in the daily lives of most American citizens.

Florence Owens and Children
This classic photograph of migrant farm laborer Florence Owens and her children was taken in 1936 in the labor camp of a pea field in California by New Deal photographer Dorothea Lange. The photo depicts the privations common among working people during the depression, but it also evokes a mother's leadership, dignity, and affection, qualities that helped shelter her family from poverty and joblessness. Library of Congress, 8b29516.

▶ Franklin D. Roosevelt: A Patrician in Government

Unlike the millions of impoverished Americans, Franklin Roosevelt came from a wealthy and privileged background that contributed to his optimism, self-confidence, and vitality. He drew on these personal qualities in his political career to bridge the economic, social, and cultural chasm that separated him from the struggles of ordinary people like Florence Owens. During the twelve years he served as president (1933–1945), many elites came to hate him as a traitor to his class, while millions more Americans in his New Deal coalition, especially the hardworking poor and dispossessed, revered him because he cared about them and their problems.

The Making of a Politician

Born in 1882, Franklin Delano Roosevelt grew up on his father's leafy estate at Hyde Park on the Hudson River, north of New York City. Roosevelt prepared for a career in politics, hoping to follow in the political footsteps of his fifth cousin, Theodore Roosevelt. In 1905 Franklin married his distant cousin, Eleanor Roosevelt, and Theodore Roosevelt—the current president of the United States and Eleanor's uncle—gave the bride away. Unlike cousin Teddy, Franklin Roosevelt sought his political fortune in the Democratic Party. In 1920, he catapulted to the second spot on the national Democratic ticket as the vice presidential candidate of presidential nominee James M. Cox. Although Cox lost the election (see "Postwar Politics and the Election of 1920" in chapter 22), Roosevelt's energetic campaigning convinced Democratic leaders that he had a bright future.

In the summer of 1921, at the age of thirty-nine, Roosevelt caught polio, which paralyzed both his legs. For the rest of his life, he wore heavy steel braces, and he could walk a few steps only by leaning on another person. Tireless physical therapy helped him regain his vitality and intense desire for high political office, although he carefully avoided being photographed in the wheelchair he used routinely.

After his polio attack, Roosevelt frequented a polio therapy facility at Warm Springs, Georgia. There, he got to know southern Democrats, which helped make him a rare political creature: a New Yorker from the Democratic Party's urban and

CHRONOLOGY

1933	• Franklin D. Roosevelt becomes president. • Roosevelt's "Hundred Days" launches the New Deal. • Roosevelt declares four-day "bank holiday." • Federal Emergency Relief Administration created.
1934	• Securities and Exchange Commission created. • Upton Sinclair loses California governorship bid. • American Liberty League founded. • Dr. Francis Townsend devises Old Age Revolving Pension scheme. • Indian Reorganization Act enacted.
1935	• Works Progress Administration created. • Wagner Act enacted. • Committee for Industrial Organization founded. • Social Security Act enacted. • Father Charles Coughlin begins National Union for Social Justice.
1936	• Franklin Roosevelt reelected by a landslide.
1937	• Sit-down strike organized at General Motors plant in Flint, Michigan. • Roosevelt's court-packing legislation defeated. • Economic recession deepens.
1938	• Second Agricultural Adjustment Act enacted. • Fair Labor Standards Act enacted. • Congress rejects antilynching bill.

immigrant wing who got along with whites from the party's entrenched southern wing.

By 1928, Roosevelt had recovered sufficiently to campaign for governor of New York, and he squeaked out a victory. As governor of the nation's most populous state, Roosevelt showcased his activist policies, which became a dress rehearsal for his presidency.

As the Great Depression spread hard times throughout the nation, Governor Roosevelt believed that government should intervene to protect citizens from economic hardships rather than wait for the law of supply and demand to improve the economy. According to the laissez-faire views of many conservatives—especially Republicans, but also numerous Democrats—the depression simply represented market forces separating strong survivors from weak losers. Unlike Roosevelt, conservatives believed that government help for the needy sapped individual initiative and impeded the self-correcting forces of the market by rewarding people for losing the economic struggle to survive. Roosevelt lacked a full-fledged counterargument to these conservative claims, but he sympathized with the plight of poor people. "To these unfortunate citizens," he proclaimed, "aid must be extended by governments, not as a matter of charity but as a matter of social duty. . . . [No one should go] unfed, unclothed, or unsheltered."

To his supporters, Roosevelt seemed to be a leader determined to attack the economic crisis without deviating from democracy—unlike the fascist parties gaining strength in Europe—or from capitalism—unlike the Communists in power in the Soviet Union. Roosevelt's ideas about how to revive the economy were vague. A prominent journalist described Roosevelt in 1931 as "a kind of amiable boy scout . . . who, without any important qualifications for the office, would very much like to be president." Roosevelt's many supporters appreciated his energy and his conviction that government should do something to help Americans climb out of the economic abyss, and they propelled him into the front ranks of the national Democratic Party.

The Election of 1932

Democrats knew that Herbert Hoover's unpopularity gave them a historic opportunity to recapture the White House in 1932. Since Abraham Lincoln's election, Republicans had occupied the White House three-fourths of the time, a trend Democrats hoped to reverse. Democrats, however, had to overcome warring factions that divided the party by region, religion, culture, and commitment to the status quo. The southern, native-born, white, rural, Protestant, conservative wing of the Democratic Party found

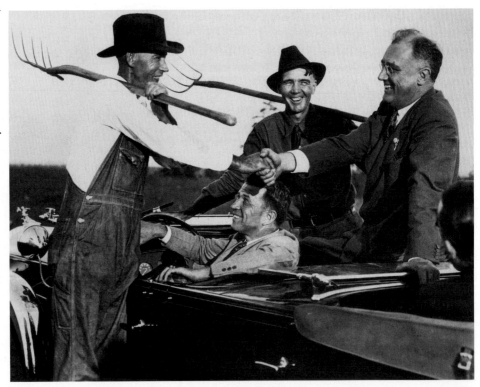

VISUAL ACTIVITY

Roosevelt Campaigning
This photo of Franklin Roosevelt on the campaign trail in rural Georgia in October 1932 displays the candidate's support for ordinary Americans. The carefully posed photo illustrates Roosevelt's attempt to reach across the class divide that separated his patrician upbringing and lifestyle from the experience of the vast majority of Americans who lacked his privileges. Hulton-Deutsch/Corbis.
READING THE IMAGE: How does the photo contrast the lives of rural people with that of the presidential candidate? What is the significance of Roosevelt sitting atop the seat back in the car to shake hands?
CONNECTIONS: Why was it important in the 1932 election for the presidential candidates to seek the support of rural Americans?

little common ground with the northern, immigrant, urban, disproportionately Catholic, liberal wing. Eastern-establishment Democratic dignitaries shared few goals with angry farmers and factory workers. Still, this unruly coalition managed to agree on Franklin Roosevelt as its presidential candidate.

In his acceptance speech, Roosevelt vowed to help "the forgotten man at the bottom of the pyramid" with "bold, persistent experimentation." Highlighting his differences with Hoover and the Republicans, he pledged "a new deal for the American people." Few details about what Roosevelt meant by "a new deal" emerged in the presidential campaign. He declared that "the people of America want more than anything else . . . two things: work . . . and a reasonable measure of security . . . for themselves and for their wives and children." Voters decided that whatever Roosevelt's new deal might be, it was better than reelecting Hoover.

Roosevelt won the 1932 presidential election in a historic landslide. He received 57 percent of the nation's votes, the first time a Democrat had won a majority of the popular vote since 1852 (Map 24.1). He amassed 472 electoral votes to Hoover's 59, carrying state after state that had voted Republican for years (Map 24.2). Roosevelt's coattails swept Democrats into control of Congress by large margins. The popular mandate for change was loud and clear.

Roosevelt's victory represented the emergence of what came to be known as the **New Deal**

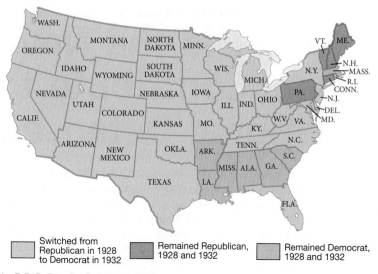

Switched from Republican in 1928 to Democrat in 1932	Remained Republican, 1928 and 1932	Remained Democrat, 1928 and 1932

MAP ACTIVITY

Map 24.2   Electoral Shift, 1928–1932

The Democratic victory in 1932 signaled the rise of a New Deal coalition within which women and minorities, many of them new voters, made the Democrats the majority party for the first time in the twentieth century.

READING THE MAP: How many states voted Democratic in 1928? How many states voted Republican in 1932? How many states shifted from Republican to Democratic between 1928 and 1932?

CONNECTIONS: What factions within the Democratic Party opposed Franklin Roosevelt's candidacy in 1932, and why did they do so? To what do you attribute his landslide victory?

coalition. Attracting support from farmers, factory workers, immigrants, city folk, African Americans, women, and progressive intellectuals, Roosevelt launched a realignment of the nation's political loyalties. The New Deal coalition dominated American politics throughout Roosevelt's presidency and remained powerful long after his death in 1945. United less by their ideologies or support for specific policies, voters in the New Deal coalition instead expressed faith in Roosevelt's promise of a government that would somehow change things for the better. Nobody, including Roosevelt, knew exactly what the New Deal would change or whether the changes would revive the nation's ailing economy and improve Americans' lives. But as he said during the presidential campaign, "It is high time to admit with courage that we are in the midst of an emergency at least equal to that of war. Let us mobilize to meet it." Roosevelt and many others knew that the future of American capitalism and democracy was at stake.

Candidate	Electoral Vote	Popular Vote	Percent of Popular Vote
Franklin D. Roosevelt (Democrat)	472	22,821,857	57.4
Herbert C. Hoover (Republican)	59	15,761,841	39.7
Norman Thomas (Socialist)	0	881,951	2.2
William Z. Foster (Communist)	0	102,991	0.3

Map 24.1
The Election of 1932

REVIEW   Why did Franklin D. Roosevelt win the 1932 presidential election by such a large margin?

How Did the New Deal Contribute to National Defense?

The New Deal strengthened the nation by providing relief and employment. In the 1930s, most New Dealers and most Americans believed the biggest threats to the nation were domestic poverty and unemployment, not foreign nations. In contrast, Germany, Japan, and the Soviet Union aggressively built up their military might during this period. Germany, for example, multplied its military spending by a factor of thirty-eight; the Soviet Union, by a factor of twenty. An American congressional leader expressed the common view: "Why should we build up our Navy . . . when it will have nothing to do after we have built it. . . . No wars [are going on] now and no war is in sight." Consequently, American military spending barely doubled during the 1930s.

Americans' complacency about foreign threats worried military planners, who believed that Japan in particular posed a dangerous military challenge to American interests. During the 1930s, Japanese military spending multiplied by nine, with the vast majority before 1937 going to the Japanese navy; the Japanese army got a larger share after 1937 when military conquests in Asia required more soldiers. According to American military planners, the U.S.

Navy—not the army—needed to be rebuilt and modernized to counter the threat from Japan.

After World War I, the United States drastically shrank its military. By 1930, American armed forces numbered about 230,000 soldiers and sailors, less than half the size of Italy's military, even though the U.S. population was three times larger than Italy's. International treaties signed after World War I limited the size of the navies of the major powers to prevent a naval arms race that might lead to war. Both German and Japanese navies exceeded their treaty limits, but during the 1920s the U.S. fleet numbered only about 75 percent of the ships permitted by treaty. Congress and Republican presidents during the 1920s had no desire to build expensive warships, especially after the Great Depression struck. Most Americans agreed, sharing the view of a British leader in 1931 that "war was never more remote, nor peace more secure."

Unlike his predecessors, President Roosevelt had long advocated naval power, a view strengthened by his service as assistant secretary of the navy during the Wilson administration. Soon after his election, a battleship captain privately wrote Roosevelt, "Take

good care of Uncle Sam's Navy! We have long been in need of a friend . . . in the White House." Lacking congressional support for rebuilding the fleet, Roosevelt and his advisers attached a provision for building thirty-two new warships (including aircraft carriers, cruisers, destroyers, and submarines) by siphoning $238 million from the $3.3 billion appropriated in June 1933 for the National Industrial Recovery Act (NIRA). Roosevelt and many New Dealers justified the expenditure as a public works program that would combat unemployment and preserve the skilled workforce at the nation's largest private shipyards.

Secretary of Labor Frances Perkins explained that "the Navy is part of the public works project, and the purpose of the [NIRA] is not to build ships but to give employment." When many more millions were earmarked from Public Works Administration (PWA) funds for naval aircraft and renovation of shore stations, Harold Ickes, the head of the PWA, fumed, "I hate to see $70 million go into one battleship when we are having difficulty keeping our people from starving." Roosevelt's supporters—who included the navy, private shipyards, and congressional advocates of naval power—argued that PWA funds were better spent to "get some kind of decent Navy than . . . to rake leaves." However, Ickes and other critics continued to denounce Roosevelt's sweetheart deal with the navy. "The Navy has more Public Works money tied up than any one else," Ickes thundered, adding, "There isn't enough money in the United States Treasury to satisfy the Navy."

▶ Launching the New Deal

At noon on March 4, 1933, Americans gathered around their radios to hear the inaugural address of the newly elected president. Roosevelt began by asserting his "firm belief that the only thing we have to fear is fear itself—nameless, unreasoning, unjustified terror which paralyzes needed efforts to convert retreat into advance." He promised "direct, vigorous action," and the first months of his administration, termed "the Hundred Days," fulfilled that promise in a whirlwind of government initiatives that launched the New Deal.

Roosevelt and his advisers had three interrelated objectives: to provide relief to the destitute, especially the one out of four Americans

Big Guns

Roosevelt loved to tour navy ships both in port and at sea. Here the commander in chief—the Big Gun, so to speak—posed under the big guns of a battleship that he believed were needed in much larger numbers to defend the nation. The photograph promoted Roosevelt's campaign to assert presidential leadership in order to overcome isolationist sentiment, rebuild the navy, and protect the nation's interests around the world. Bettmann/Corbis.

Naval rearmament masquerading as public works was only the beginning of New Deal support for naval shipbuilding. In March 1934, Roosevelt signed the Vinson-Trammell Naval Act, named for its congressional sponsors. The act authorized the navy to build an additional 102 warships that would bring the navy up to treaty limits. The Naval Expansion Act four years later provided for a 20 percent expansion of the fleet beyond treaty limits and up to 3,000 aircraft. Overall, between 1933 and 1939, the New Deal increased the number of aircraft carriers and cruisers by 40 percent and modern destroyers by 1,500 percent. Although the fleet expanded enormously beyond 1939 levels during World War II, the New Deal built the navy into a powerful force for national defense that became more crucial than ever after 1939 as war clouds gathered in Europe and the Pacific.

Questions for Analysis

Summarize the Argument: How did the New Deal contribute to national defense?

Analyze the Evidence: What New Deal measures authorized naval rearmament? How did critics respond to these measures?

Consider the Context: How did New Deal domestic programs influence naval rearmament?

who were unemployed; to foster the economic recovery of farms and businesses, thereby creating jobs and reducing the need for relief; and to reform the government and economy in ways that would reduce the risk of devastating consequences in future economic slumps and thereby strengthen capitalism. The New Deal never fully achieved these goals of relief, recovery, and reform. But by aiming for them, Roosevelt's experimental programs enormously expanded government's role in the nation's economy and society. (See "Making Historical Arguments, above.)

The New Dealers

To design and implement the New Deal, Roosevelt needed ideas and people. He convened a "Brains Trust" of economists and other leaders to offer suggestions and advice about the problems facing the nation. No New Dealers were more important than the president and his wife, Eleanor. The gregarious president radiated charm and good cheer, giving the New Deal's bureaucratic regulations a benevolent human face. Eleanor Roosevelt became the New Deal's unofficial ambassador. She served, she said, as "the eyes and ears of the New Deal," traveling throughout the nation meeting Americans of all colors and creeds. A North Carolina women's rights activist recalled, "One of my greatest pleasures was meeting Mrs. Roosevelt. . . . She was so free of prejudice . . . and she was always willing to take a stand, and there were stands to take about blacks and women."

As Roosevelt's programs swung into action, the millions of beneficiaries of the New Deal became grassroots New Dealers who expressed their appreciation by voting Democratic on election day. In this way, the New Deal created a durable political coalition of Democrats that reelected Roosevelt in 1936, 1940, and 1944.

Four guiding ideas shaped New Deal policies. First, Roosevelt and his advisers sought capitalist solutions to the economic crisis. They had no desire to eliminate private property or impose socialist programs, such as public ownership of productive resources. Instead, they hoped to save the capitalist economy by remedying its flaws.

Second, Roosevelt's Brains Trust persuaded him that the greatest flaw of America's capitalist economy was **underconsumption**, the root cause of the current economic paralysis. Underconsumption, New Dealers argued, resulted from the gigantic productive success of capitalism. Factories and farms produced more than they could sell to consumers, causing factories to lay off workers and farmers to lose money on bumper crops. Workers without wages and farmers without profits shrank consumption and choked the economy. Somehow, the balance between consumption and production needed to be restored.

Third, New Dealers believed that the immense size and economic power of American corporations needed to be counterbalanced by government and by organization among workers and small producers. Unlike progressive trustbusters, New Dealers did not seek to splinter big businesses. Roosevelt and his advisers hoped to counterbalance big economic institutions with government programs focused on protecting individuals and the public interest.

Fourth, New Dealers believed that government must somehow moderate the imbalance of wealth created by American capitalism. Wealth concentrated in a few hands reduced consumption by most Americans and thereby contributed to the current economic gridlock. Government needed to find a way to permit ordinary working people to share more fully in the fruits of the economy. "Our task now," Roosevelt declared during the presidential campaign, "is . . . meeting the problem of underconsumption, . . . adjusting production to consumption, . . . [and] distributing wealth and products more equitably."

Banking and Finance Reform

Roosevelt wasted no time making good on his inaugural pledge for "action now." As he took the oath of office on March 4, the nation's banking system was on the brink of collapse. Roosevelt immediately devised a plan to shore up banks and restore depositors' confidence. Working round the clock, New Dealers drafted the Emergency Banking Act, propped up the private banking system with federal funds, and subjected banks to federal regulation and oversight. To secure the confidence of depositors, Congress passed the Glass-Steagall Banking Act, setting up the **Federal Deposit Insurance Corporation (FDIC)**, which guaranteed bank customers that the federal government would reimburse them for deposits if their banks failed. In addition, the act required the separation of commercial banks (which accept deposits and make loans to individuals and small businesses) and investment banks (which make speculative investments with their funds), in an effort to insulate the finances of Main Street America from the risky speculations of Wall Street wheeler-dealers.

On Sunday night, March 12, while the banks were still closed, Roosevelt broadcast the first of a series of **fireside chats**. Speaking in a friendly, informal manner, he explained the new banking legislation that, he said, made it "safer to keep your money in a reopened bank than under the mattress." With such plain talk, Roosevelt translated complex matters into common sense. This and subsequent fireside chats forged a direct connection—via radio—between Roosevelt and millions of Americans, a connection felt by a man from Paris, Texas, who wrote to Roosevelt, "You are the one & only President that ever helped a Working Class of People. . . . Please help us some way I Pray to God for relief."

The banking legislation and fireside chat worked. Within a few days, most of the nation's major banks reopened, and they remained solvent as reassured depositors switched funds from their mattresses to their bank accounts (Figure 24.1). One New Dealer boasted, "Capitalism was saved in eight days." The rescue of the banking system took much longer to succeed, though.

In his inaugural address, Roosevelt criticized financiers for their greed and incompetence. To prevent the fraud, corruption, and insider trading that had tainted Wall Street and contributed to the crash of 1929, New Dealers created the Securities and Exchange Commission (SEC) in 1934 to oversee financial markets by licensing investment dealers, monitoring all stock transactions, and requiring corporate officers to make full disclosures about their companies. To head the SEC, Roosevelt appointed an ambitious Wall Street financier, Joseph P. Kennedy (father of the future president John F. Kennedy), who had a shady reputation for stock manipulation. Under Kennedy's leadership, the SEC helped clean up and regulate Wall Street, which slowly recovered.

Relief and Conservation Programs

Patching the nation's financial structure provided little relief for the hungry and unemployed. A poor man from Nebraska asked Eleanor Roosevelt "if the folk who was borned here in America . . . are this Forgotten Man, the President had in mind, [and] if we are this Forgotten Man then we are still Forgotten." The federal government had never assumed responsibility for needy people, except in moments of natural disaster or emergencies such as the Civil War. Instead, churches, private charities, county and municipal governments, and occasionally states assumed the burden of poor relief, usually with meager payments. The depression necessitated unprecedented federal relief efforts, according to New Dealers. As a New Yorker who still had a job wrote the government, "We work, ten hours a day for six days. In the grime and dirt of a nation [for] . . . low pay [making us] . . . slaves—slaves of the depression!"

The Federal Emergency Relief Administration (FERA), established in May 1933, supported four million to five million households with $20 or $30 a month. FERA also created jobs for the unemployed on thousands of public works projects, organized into the Civil Works Administration (CWA), which put paychecks worth more than $800 million into the hands of previously jobless workers. Earning wages between 40 and 60 cents an hour, laborers renovated schools, dug sewers, and rebuilt roads and bridges.

Fireside Chat
President Roosevelt explained New Deal programs to ordinary Americans in his frequent radio broadcasts. Despite the depression, radio ownership grew during the 1930s from 35 percent to 82 percent of the population. Roosevelt's fireside chats assured millions of listeners, like the northern California farmer and his daughter shown here, that Washington cared about their plight and was trying to relieve it. Everett Collection.

The most popular work relief program was the **Civilian Conservation Corps (CCC)**, established in March 1933. It offered unemployed young men a chance to earn wages while working to conserve natural resources, a long-standing interest of Roosevelt. Women were excluded from working in the CCC until Eleanor Roosevelt demanded that a token number of young women be hired. By the end of the program in 1942, three million CCC workers had left a legacy of vast new recreation areas, along with roads that made those areas accessible to millions of Americans. Just as important, the CCC, CWA, and other work relief efforts replaced the stigma of welfare with the dignity of jobs. As one woman said about her husband's work relief job, "We aren't on relief anymore. My husband is working for the Government."

The New Deal's most ambitious and controversial natural resources development project was the Tennessee Valley Authority (TVA), created in May 1933 to build dams along the

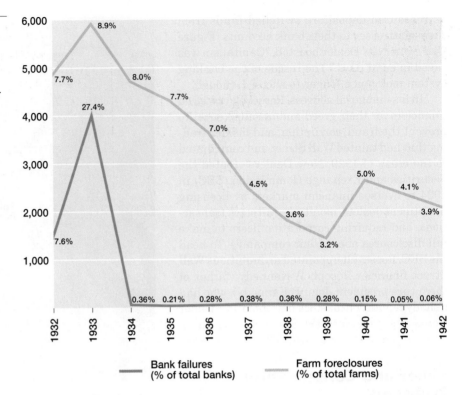

FIGURE 24.1 **Bank Failures and Farm Foreclosures, 1932–1942**
New Deal legislation to stabilize the economy had its most immediate and striking effect in preventing banks, along with their depositors, from going under and farmers from losing their land.

Tennessee River to supply impoverished rural communities with cheap electricity (Map 24.3). The TVA set out to demonstrate that a partnership between the federal government and local residents could overcome the barriers of state governments and private enterprises to make efficient use of abundant natural resources and break the ancient cycle of poverty. The TVA

Civilian Conservation Corps (CCC)
The New Deal's CCC gave work and wages to some 3 million young men to build roads, improve parks, and undertake other conservation projects. These CCC workers in Oregon, like their counterparts elsewhere in the nation, earned about $30 a month, $25 of which was sent directly to their parents. Corbis.

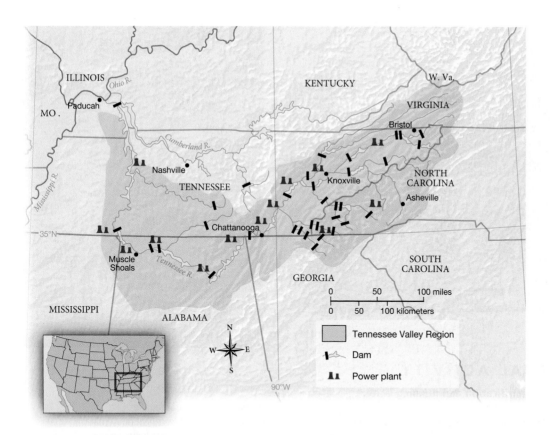

MAP ACTIVITY

Map 24.3   The Tennessee Valley Authority
The New Deal created the Tennessee Valley Authority to modernize a vast impoverished region with hydro-electric power dams and, at the same time, to reclaim eroded land and preserve old folkways.

READING THE MAP: How many states were affected by the TVA? How many miles of rivers (approximately) were affected?
CONNECTIONS: What kinds of benefits—economic as well as social and cultural—did TVA programs bring to the region? How might the lives of a poor farming family in Alabama or Tennessee have changed after the mid-1930s owing to these programs?

improved the lives of millions in the region with electric power, flood protection, soil reclamation, and jobs, although it raised the hackles of many Americans who thought it trespassed unforgivably on free enterprise.

New sources of hydroelectric power helped the New Deal bring the wonders of electricity to country folk, fulfilling an old progressive dream. When Roosevelt became president, 90 percent of rural Americans lacked electricity. Private electric companies refused to build transmission lines into the sparsely settled countryside when they had a profitable market in more accessible and densely populated urban areas. Beginning in 1935, the Rural Electrification Administration (REA) made low-cost loans available to local cooperatives for power plants and transmission lines to serve rural communities. Within ten

years, the REA delivered electricity to nine out of ten farms, giving rural Americans access for the first time to modern conveniences that urban people had enjoyed for decades.

Agricultural Initiatives

Farmers had been mired in a depression since the end of World War I. New Dealers diagnosed the farmers' plight as a classic case of overproduction and underconsumption. Following age-old practices, farmers tried to compensate for low crop prices by growing more crops. Of course, producing more crops pushed prices lower still. Farm families' income sank to $167 a year, barely one-tenth of the national average in 1932.

New Dealers sought to cut agricultural production, thereby raising crop prices and farmers'

VISUAL ACTIVITY

Rural Electrification and Running Water

New Deal programs brought electricity and running water for the first time to many rural families, like those shown here in east-central Tennessee. The Tennessee Valley Authority and Rural Electrification Administration helped families in this and many other villages replace kerosene lamps with electric lights and to have access to clean, safe water. Pump: Franklin D. Roosevelt Presidential Library and Museum/NARA; poster: USDA, National Agricultural Library, Special Collections.

READING THE IMAGE: Where can you see evidence of New Deal benefits in this photo? What difference did electricity and running water make in the lives of people like the children depicted here at the pump?

CONNECTIONS: Why did New Deal programs devote so much attention to improving the lives of rural Americans?

income. With more money in their pockets, farm families—who made up one-third of all Americans—would then buy more goods and lift consumption in the entire economy. To reduce production, the **Agricultural Adjustment Act (AAA)** passed in May 1933 authorized the "domestic allotment plan," which paid farmers not to grow crops. Individual farmers who agreed not to plant crops on a portion of their fields (their "allotment") would receive a government payment compensating them for the crops they did not plant. While millions of Americans like Florence Owens and her children went to bed hungry, farmers slaughtered livestock and destroyed crops to qualify for their allotment payments.

With the formation of the Commodity Credit Corporation, the federal government allowed farmers to hold their harvested crops off the market and wait for a higher price. New Dealers also sponsored the Farm Credit Act (FCA) to provide long-term credit on mortgaged farm property, allowing debt-ridden farmers to avoid foreclosures that were driving thousands off their land (see Figure 24.1).

Crop allotments, commodity loans, and mortgage credit made farmers major beneficiaries of the New Deal. Crop prices rose impressively, farm income jumped 50 percent by 1936, and FCA loans financed 40 percent of farm mortgage debt by the end of the decade. These gains were distributed fairly equally among farmers in the corn, hog, and wheat region of the Midwest. In the South's cotton belt, however, landlords controlled the distribution of New Deal agricultural benefits and shamelessly rewarded themselves while denying benefits to many sharecroppers and tenant farmers—blacks and whites—by taking the land they worked out of production and assigning it to the allotment program. As the president of the Oklahoma Tenant Farmers' Union explained, large farmers who got "Triple-A" payments often used the money to buy tractors and then "forced their tenants and [share]croppers off the land," causing these "Americans to be starved and dispossessed of their homes in our land of plenty."

Industrial Recovery

Unlike farmers, industrialists cut production with the onset of the depression. Between 1929 and 1933, industrial production fell more than 40 percent in an effort to balance low demand with low supply and thereby maintain prices. But falling industrial production meant that millions of working people lost their jobs. Unlike farmers, most working people needed jobs to eat. Mass unemployment also reduced consumer demand for industrial products, contributing to a downward spiral in both production and jobs, with no end in sight. Industries responded by reducing wages for employees who still had jobs, further reducing demand—a trend made worse by competition among industrial producers. New Dealers struggled to find a way to break this cycle of unemployment and underconsumption— a way consistent with corporate profits and capitalism.

The New Deal's National Industrial Recovery Act opted for a government-sponsored form of industrial self-government through the **National Recovery Administration (NRA)**, established in June 1933. The NRA encouraged industrialists to agree on rules, known as "codes," to define fair working conditions, to set prices, and to minimize competition. The idea behind codes was to stabilize existing industries and maintain their workforces. Industry after industry wrote elaborate codes addressing detailed features of production, pricing, and competition. In exchange for the relaxation of federal antitrust regulations that prohibited such business agreements, the participating businesses promised to recognize the right of working people to organize and engage in collective bargaining. To encourage consumers to patronize businesses with NRA codes, posters with the NRA's Blue Eagle appeared in shop windows throughout the nation.

New Dealers hoped that NRA codes would yield businesses with a social conscience, ensuring fair treatment of workers and consumers as well as promotion of the general economic welfare. Instead, NRA codes tended to strengthen conventional business practices. Large corporations wrote codes that served primarily their own interests rather than the needs of workers or the welfare of the national economy. (See "Experiencing the American Promise," page 692.)

The failure of codes to cover domestic workers or agricultural laborers like Florence Owens led one woman to complain to Roosevelt that the NRA "never mentioned the robbery of the Housewives" by the privations caused by the depression.

Many business leaders criticized NRA codes as heavy-handed government regulation of private enterprise. In reality, compliance with NRA codes was voluntary, and government enforcement efforts were weak to nonexistent. The NRA did little to reduce unemployment, raise consumption, or relieve the depression. In effect, it represented a peace offering to business leaders by Roosevelt and his advisers, conveying the message that the New Deal did not intend to wage war against profits or private enterprise. The peace offering failed, however. Most corporate leaders became bitter opponents of Roosevelt and the New Deal.

> **REVIEW**   How did the New Dealers try to steer the nation toward recovery from the Great Depression?

▶ Challenges to the New Deal

The first New Deal initiatives engendered fierce criticism and political opposition. From the right, Republicans and businesspeople charged that New Deal programs were too radical, undermining private property, economic stability, and democracy. Critics on the left faulted the New Deal for its failure to allay the human suffering caused by the depression and for its timidity in attacking corporate power and greed.

Resistance to Business Reform

New Deal programs rescued capitalism, but business leaders lambasted Roosevelt, even though their economic prospects improved more than those of most other Americans during the depression. Republicans and business leaders denounced New Deal efforts to regulate or reform what they considered their private enterprises.

Textile Workers Strike for Better Wages and Working Conditions

"The 'Stretch-out System' is the cause of the whole trouble," a textile worker declared in 1930, echoing the sentiments of thousands of other mill workers. The "stretch-out" was the term coined by mill workers for the cost-cutting efficiencies implemented by mill owners that led to layoffs and poor working conditions for textile workers during the 1920s and 1930s. Textile manufacturers drastically increased the workload of their employees to cut labor costs and raise productivity. A mill worker who tended thirty looms in 1920 was responsible for ninety or more looms by 1929—if she or he still had a job. Layoffs of mill hands in the midst of the Great Depression contributed to further deterioration in wages and working conditions. So many people were desperate for work, no matter what the wage, that manufacturers were able to cut wages in half. The result, as one textile worker wrote Roosevelt, was that "the ones who are Still at Work are Being Treated as Bad or Worse tha[n] the Slaves were in Slavery times."

Like so many other textile workers who faced the tough choice of working with the stretch-out or not working at all, Icy Norman was relieved to find work in 1929 at Burlington Mills in Piedmont Heights, North Carolina, where the supervisor happened to be a friend of her deceased father's. He hired Norman to wind thread onto bobbins for weaving. At first, she earned only 15 cents a day, but as she became more skilled, her wages rose to $10 a week, a little over 15 cents an hour. "After I got used to being in there," Norman recalled, "I really loved my work. . . . I got pleasure out of it and it made me happy to do my job." Still, as one mill worker wrote to Roosevelt, "every textile worker in the South would walk out of the mill today if they were not afraid of starvation."

In September 1934, hundreds of thousands of textile workers throughout the nation overcame their fears and walked out of the mills in the largest strike in American history. Strikers shut down mills from Maine to Alabama. More than half of all textile workers nationwide and about two-thirds of mill hands in the southern heartland of the textile industry walked out, including Icy Norman. Loosely organized by the Textile Workers' Union, the strikers demanded better working conditions and wages through enforcement of the textile code established by the New Deal's National Recovery Administration (NRA).

Like other NRA codes, the textile code was written and administered by the leading textile manufacturers.

It provided for a maximum forty-hour workweek, a minimum weekly wage of $12 for southern mill hands, and the right of workers to organize unions. Textile workers celebrated the passage of the NRA in June 1933. "It seemed too good to be true," one textile worker observed. Mill hands told a New Dealer, "We trust in the Supreme Being and Franklin Roosevelt. . . . [We] know that the President will see that [we] have work and proper wages; and that the stretchout will be abandoned."

But their faith was misplaced, and the code was widely ignored. When workers complained that mill owners continued the stretch-out, cutting wages and firing any mill hands they suspected of union sympathies, their grievances were heard by the textile manufacturers who headed the NRA code authority. In the year before the strike, the textile code authority received nearly 4,000 complaints, investigated 96, and resolved just 1 in favor of a worker. Boiling with frustration over the failure of the textile code, more than 400,000 mill hands went on strike. Seeking to realize what they viewed as the unfulfilled promises of the New Deal's NRA, they aimed to organize a union to bargain with mill owners to improve wages and working conditions.

By 1935, two major business organizations, the National Association of Manufacturers and the Chamber of Commerce, had become openly anti–New Deal. Their critiques were amplified by the American Liberty League, founded in 1934, which blamed the New Deal for betraying basic constitutional guarantees of freedom and individualism. A League spokesman declared, "This administration has copied the autocratic tactics of fascism, Hitlerism and communism at their worst."

Economists who favored rational planning in the public interest and labor leaders who sought to influence wages and working conditions by organizing unions attacked the New Deal from the left. In their view, the NRA stifled enterprise by permitting monopolistic practices.

Striking Mill Workers Jeer Strikebreakers
Textile workers on strike against the Cannon Textile Mills in North Carolina in September 1934 shouted taunts and curses at employees who refused to honor the strikers' picket line. Why do you think strikers and strikebreakers wore different styles of clothing? Although thousands of women joined the strike, no women appear among the strikers shown here. Why might that be? Bettmann/Corbis.

The strike lasted three weeks and led to numerous violent confrontations with police and the National Guard. It ended because of the combination of the mill owners' intransigence, the Textile Workers' Union's lack of resources, the mill workers' increasingly desperate financial situation, and Roosevelt's focus on the need for industrial peace to achieve economic recovery.

The mill hands achieved virtually nothing as a result of the strike. Mill owners continued to flout the textile codes, the stretch-out continued without interruption, and working conditions did not improve. Angry mill owners fired and blacklisted strike leaders, succeeding in their efforts to crush workers' organizations.

Icy Norman went back to work after the strike ended, and since she was not a union activist, she managed to keep her job until she retired in 1976, after forty-seven years at Burlington Mills. For her efforts, the company rewarded her with a free visit to a local hairdresser, a tour of the Burlington executive suite, and a farewell handshake.

Questions for Analysis

Summarize the Argument: Why did the textile strike occur? Why did it fail? How did the New Deal affect industrial workers differently than farmers?

Analyze the Evidence: How did the NRA codes thwart textile workers' goals of improved working conditions, better wages, and union organization?

Recognize Viewpoints: How did the goals of the textile mill owners differ from those of workers and New Deal officials?

They pointed out that industrial trade associations twisted NRA codes to suit their aims, thwarted competition, and engaged in price gouging. Labor leaders especially resented the NRA's willingness to allow businesses to form company-controlled unions while blocking workers from organizing genuine grassroots unions to bargain for themselves.

The Supreme Court stepped into this cross fire of criticisms in May 1935 and declared that the NRA unconstitutionally conferred powers reserved to Congress on an administrative agency. The NRA codes soon lost the little authority they had. The failure of the NRA demonstrated the depth of many Americans' resistance to economic planning and the stubborn refusal of business

Major Legislation of the New Deal's First Hundred Days

	Name of Act	Basic Provisions
March 9, 1933	Emergency Banking Act	Provides for reopening stable banks and authorizing the Reconstruction Finance Corporation to supply funds.
March 31, 1933	Civilian Conservation Corps Act	Provides jobs for unemployed young men.
May 12, 1933	Agricultural Adjustment Act	Provides funds to pay farmers for not growing crops.
May 12, 1933	Federal Emergency Relief Act	Provides relief funds for the destitute.
May 18, 1933	Tennessee Valley Authority Act	Creates the TVA to bring electric power and conservation to the area.
June 16, 1933	National Industrial Recovery Act	Specifies cooperation among business, government, and labor in setting fair prices and working conditions.
June 16, 1933	Glass-Steagall Banking Act	Creates the Federal Deposit Insurance Corporation (FDIC) to insure bank deposits.

owned their land. One black sharecropper explained why only $75 a year from New Deal agricultural subsidies trickled down to her: "De landlord is landlord, de politicians is landlord, de judge is landlord, de shurf [sheriff] is landlord, ever'body is landlord, en we [sharecroppers] ain' got nothin'!" Like the NRA, the AAA tended to help most those who least needed help. Roosevelt's political dependence on southern Democrats caused him to avoid confronting economic and racial inequities in the South.

Displaced tenants often joined the army of migrant workers like Florence Owens who straggled across rural America during the 1930s, some to flee Great Plains dust storms. Many migrants came from Mexico to work Texas cotton, Michigan beans, Idaho sugar beets, and California crops of all kinds. But since the number of people willing to take agricultural jobs usually exceeded the number of jobs available, wages fell and native-born white migrants fought to reserve even these low-wage jobs for themselves. Hundreds of thousands of "Okies" streamed out of the Dust Bowl of Oklahoma, Kansas, Texas, and Colorado, where chronic drought and harmful agricultural practices blasted crops and hopes. Parched, poor, and windblown, Okies—like the Joad family immortalized in John Steinbeck's novel *The Grapes of Wrath* (1939)—migrated to the lush fields and orchards of California, congregating in labor camps and hoping to find work and a future. But migrant laborers seldom found steady or secure work. As one Okie said, "When they need us they call us migrants, and when we've picked their crop, we're bums and we got to get out."

leaders to yield to government regulations or reforms.

Casualties in the Countryside

The AAA weathered critical battering by champions of the old order better than the NRA. Allotment checks for keeping land fallow and crop prices high created loyalty among farmers with enough acreage to participate. As a white farmer in North Carolina declared, "I stand for the New Deal and Roosevelt . . . , the AAA . . . and crop control."

Protests stirred, however, among those who did not qualify for allotments. The Southern Farm Tenants Union argued passionately that the AAA enriched large farmers while it impoverished small farmers who rented rather than

Politics on the Fringes

Politically, the New Deal's staunchest opponents were in the Republican Party—organized, well-heeled, mainstream, and determined to challenge Roosevelt at every turn. But the New Deal also faced challenges from the political fringes, fueled by the hardship of the depression and the hope for a cure-all.

Socialists and Communists accused the New Deal of being the handmaiden of business elites and of rescuing capitalism from its self-inflicted crisis. Socialist author Upton Sinclair ran for governor of California in 1934 on a plan that the state take ownership of idle factories and unused land and then give them to cooperatives of working people, a first step toward putting the needs of people above profits. Sinclair lost the election, ending the most serious socialist electoral challenge to the New Deal.

Evicted Sharecroppers
The New Deal's Agricultural Adjustment Administration that maintained farm prices by reducing acreage in production often resulted in the eviction of tenant farmers when the land they worked was left idle. These African American share-croppers protested AAA policies that caused cotton farmers to evict them from their homes. They were among the many rural laborers whose lives were made worse by New Deal agricultural policies. Bettmann/Corbis.

Some intellectuals and artists sought to advance the cause of more radical change by joining left-wing organizations, including the American Communist Party. At its high point in the 1930s, the party had only about thirty thousand members, the large majority of them immigrants, especially Scandinavians in the upper Midwest and eastern European Jews in major cities. Individual Communists worked to organize labor unions, protect the civil rights of black people, and help the destitute, but the party preached the overthrow of "bourgeois democracy" and the destruction of capitalism in favor of Soviet-style communism. Such talk attracted few followers among the nation's millions of poor and unemployed. They

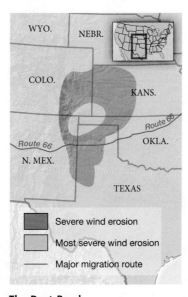

The Dust Bowl

wanted jobs and economic security within American capitalism and democracy, not violent revolution to establish a dictatorship of the Communist Party.

More powerful radical challenges to the New Deal sprouted from homegrown roots. Many Americans felt overlooked by New Deal programs that concentrated on finance, agriculture, and industry but did little to produce jobs or aid the poor. The merciless reality of the depression also continued to erode the security of people who still had jobs but worried constantly that they, too, might be pushed into the legions of the unemployed and penniless.

A Catholic priest in Detroit named Charles Coughlin spoke to and for many worried Americans in his weekly radio broadcasts, which reached a nationwide audience of 40 million. Father Coughlin expressed outrage at the suffering and inequities that he blamed on Communists, bankers, and "predatory capitalists" who, he claimed, appealing to widespread anti-Semitic sentiments, were mostly Jews. At first, Coughlin championed the New Deal, proclaiming, "I will never change my philosophy that the New Deal is Christ's deal." When Coughlin became frustrated by Roosevelt's refusal to grant him influence, he turned against the New Deal and in 1935 founded the National Union for Social Justice, or Union Party, to challenge Roosevelt in the 1936 presidential election.

Dr. Francis Townsend, of Long Beach, California, also criticized the timidity of the New Deal. Angry that many of his retired patients lived in misery, Townsend proposed in 1934 the creation of the Old Age Revolving Pension, which would pay every American over age sixty a pension of $200 a month. To receive the pension, senior citizens had to agree to spend the entire amount within thirty days, thereby stimulating the economy.

Townsend organized pension clubs and petitioned the federal government to enact his scheme. When the major political parties ignored his impractical plan, Townsend merged his forces with Coughlin's Union Party in time for the 1936 election.

A more formidable challenge to the New Deal came from the powerful southern wing of the Democratic Party. Huey Long, son of a backcountry Louisiana farmer, was elected governor of the state in 1928 with his slogan "Every man a king, but no one wears a crown." Unlike nearly all other southern white politicians who harped on white supremacy, Long championed the poor over the rich, country people over city folk, and the humble over elites. As governor, "the Kingfish"— as he liked to call himself—delivered on his promises to provide jobs and build roads, schools, and hospitals, but he also behaved ruthlessly to achieve his goals. Long delighted his supporters, who elected him to the U.S. Senate in 1932, where he introduced a sweeping "soak the rich" tax bill that would outlaw personal incomes of more than $1 million and inheritances of more than $5 million. When the Senate rejected his proposal, Long decided to run for president, mobilizing more than five million Americans behind his "Share Our Wealth" plan. "Is that right," Long asked, "when . . . more [is] owned by 12 men than . . . by 120,000,000 people? . . . They own the banks, they own the steel mills, they own the railroads, they own the bonds, they own the mortgages, they own the stores, and they have chained the country from one end to the other." Like Townsend's scheme, Long's program promised far more than it could deliver. The Share Our Wealth campaign died when Long was assassinated in 1935, but his constituency and the wide appeal of a more equitable distribution of wealth persisted.

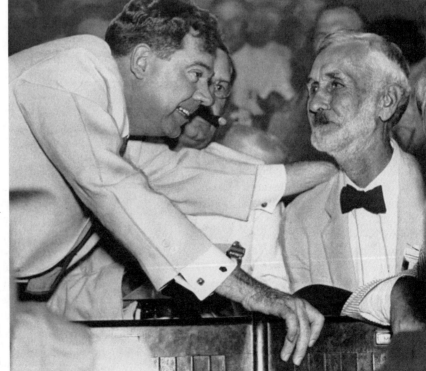

Huey Long
Huey Long, U.S. senator and former governor of Louisiana, pressured delegates at the 1932 Democratic convention into supporting Franklin Roosevelt, as depicted here. After Roosevelt's election, Long challenged the president from the left with his Share Our Wealth plan and, until he was assassinated in 1935, campaigned to replace Roosevelt on the Democratic ticket in the next presidential election. NY Daily News via Getty Images.

The challenges to the New Deal from both right and left stirred Democrats to solidify their winning coalition. In the midterm congressional elections of 1934—normally a time when a president loses support—voters gave New Dealers a landslide victory. Democrats increased their majority in the House of Representatives and gained a two-thirds majority in the Senate.

REVIEW   Why did groups at both ends of the political spectrum criticize the New Deal?

▶ Toward a Welfare State

The popular mandate for the New Deal revealed by the congressional elections persuaded Roosevelt to press ahead with bold new efforts to achieve relief, recovery, and reform. Despite the initiatives of the Hundred Days, the depression still strangled the economy. In 1935, Roosevelt capitalized on his congressional majorities to enact major new programs that signaled the emergence of an American welfare state.

Taken together, these New Deal efforts stretched a safety net under the lives of ordinary Americans, including such landmark initiatives as Social Security, which provided modest pensions for the elderly, and the Wagner Act, which encouraged the organization of labor unions. Although many citizens remained unprotected, New Deal programs helped millions with jobs, relief, and government support. Knitting together the safety net was the idea that, when individual Americans suffered because of forces beyond their control, the federal government had the responsibility to support and protect them. The safety net of welfare programs tied the political loyalty of working people to the New Deal and the Democratic Party. As a North Carolina mill worker said, "Mr. Roosevelt is the only man we ever had in the White House who would understand that my boss is a sonofabitch."

Relief for the Unemployed

First and foremost, Americans still needed jobs. Since the private economy left eight million people jobless by 1935, Roosevelt and his advisers launched a massive work relief program. Roosevelt believed that direct government handouts crippled recipients with "spiritual and moral disintegration . . . destructive to the human spirit." Jobs, by contrast, bolstered individuals' "self-respect, . . . self-reliance and courage and determination." With a congressional appropriation of nearly $5 billion—more than all government revenues in 1934—the New Deal created the **Works Progress Administration (WPA)** to give unemployed Americans government-funded jobs on public works projects. The WPA put millions of jobless citizens to work on roads, bridges, parks, public buildings, and more. In addition, Congress passed, over Roosevelt's veto, the bonus long sought by Bonus Marchers, giving veterans an average of $580 and further stimulating the economy.

By 1936, WPA funds provided jobs for 7 percent of the nation's labor force. In effect, the WPA made the federal government the employer of last resort, creating useful jobs when the capitalist economy failed to do so. In hiring, WPA officials tended to discriminate in favor of white men and against women and racial minorities. Still, the WPA made major contributions to both relief and recovery, putting thirteen million men and women to work earning paychecks worth $10 billion. (See "Analyzing Historical Evidence," page 698.)

About three out of four WPA jobs involved construction and renovation of the nation's physical infrastructure. WPA workers built 572,000 miles of roads, 78,000 bridges, 67,000 miles of city streets, 40,000 public buildings, and much else. In addition, the WPA gave jobs to thousands of artists, musicians, actors, journalists, poets, and novelists. The WPA also organized sewing rooms for jobless women, giving them work and wages. These sewing rooms produced more than 100 million pieces of clothing that were donated to the needy. Throughout the nation, WPA projects displayed tangible evidence of the New Deal's commitment to public welfare.

Empowering Labor

During the Great Depression, factory workers who managed to keep their jobs worried constantly about being laid off while their wages and working hours were cut. When workers tried to organize labor unions to protect themselves, municipal and state governments usually sided with employers. Since the Gilded Age, state and federal governments had been far more effective at busting unions than at busting trusts. The New Deal dramatically reversed the federal government's stance toward unions. With legislation and political support, the New Deal

Americans Encounter the New Deal

Americans in all walks of life encountered New Deal measures in their daily lives. In 1938 and 1939, the Federal Writers Project, a part of the WPA, interviewed thousands of ordinary citizens throughout the nation, and many expressed their opinions about the New Deal. A sample of their views of the depression, Franklin Roosevelt, the WPA, and the CIO, as well as of political and economic power, can be found in the following excerpts from three interviews.

DOCUMENT 1
Charles Fusco, On the Value of Relief Work during the Depression, December 6, 1938

An Italian American machinist in a munitions plant in Hampden, Connecticut, explained the value of the relief work provided by the WPA.

I can get a job today even if we got a depression. I don't mean that I wasn't on relief when things got tough because there was a time when everything was shut down and I had to get on relief for a job. It isn't so long ago I was working on WPA. Believe me it was a big help. But it wasn't the kind of a job I should have had because this town is Republican and I am a Republican and I was a good worker for the party—making voters and helping a lot of people out. . . . Getting jobs for them. When it came my turn that I needed help the politicians told me that I had to go on relief—well, when I did I was handed a shovel and pick. . . . Roosevelt is a damn good man. . . . You know there shouldn't be a depression in this country . . . the Democrats are in power and the Republicans won't let loose with the money. Well I say that the money men started this thing and I believe the government should make laws to force these capitalists to bring back prosperity. They can do it if they wanted to.

Source: Interview with Charles Fusco. Manuscript. U.S. Works Progress Administration, Federal Writers Project. From Library of Congress, *Folklore Project, Life Histories, 1936–39*, GIF. http://www.loc.gov/resource/wpalh0.09030115/seq-1#seq-1 (accessed December 3, 2013).

DOCUMENT 2
Myron Buxton, The Benefits of WPA Projects, July 25, 1939

A native-born draftsman and assistant to an engineer working on WPA building projects in Newburyport, Massachusetts, illuminated the WPA's benefits to the community and to the individual workers.

One reason people here don't like WPA is because they don't understand it's not all bums and drunks and aliens! Nobody ever explains to them that they'd never have had the new High School they're so goddam proud of if it hadn't been for WPA. They don't stop to figure that new brick sidewalks wouldn't be there, the shade trees wouldn't be all dressed up to look at along High Street and all around town, if it weren't for WPA projects. To most in this town, and I guess it's not much

encouraged an unprecedented wave of union organizing among the nation's working people. When the head of the United Mine Workers, John L. Lewis, told coal miners that "the President wants you to join a union," he exaggerated only a little. New Dealers believed that unions would counterbalance the organized might of big corporations by defending working people, maintaining wages, and replacing the bloody violence that often accompanied strikes with economic peace and commercial stability.

Violent battles on the nation's streets and docks showed the determination of militant labor leaders to organize unions that would protect jobs as well as wages. In 1934, striking workers in Toledo, Minneapolis, San Francisco, and elsewhere were beaten and shot by police and the National Guard. In Congress, labor leaders lobbied for the National Labor Relations Act, a bill sponsored by Senator Robert Wagner of New York that authorized the federal government to intervene in labor disputes and supervise the organization of labor unions. The **Wagner Act**, as it came to be called, guaranteed industrial workers the right to organize unions, putting the might of federal law behind the appeals of labor leaders. If the majority of workers at a company voted for a union, the union became the sole bargaining agent for the entire workplace, and the employer was required to negotiate with the elected union

different in this, than any other New England place, WPA's just a racket, set up to give a bunch of loafers and drunks steady pay to indulge in their vices! They don't stop to consider that on WPA are men and women who have traveled places and seen things, been educated and found their jobs folded up and nothing to replace them with. . . . The working guy in this country never had such a swell chance to get a toe-hold as he's had in the last four years! The louder the Republicans yell, the more of a toe-hold you can figure the ordinary guy's got!

Source: Seymour D. Buck. Interview with Myron Buxton. Manuscript. U.S. Works Progress Administration, Federal Writers Project. From Library of Congress, *Folklore Project, Life Histories, 1936–39*, GIF. http://www.loc.gov/resource/wpalh1.14030415/#seq-1 (accessed December 3, 2013).

DOCUMENT 3
Jim Cole, Overcoming Racism in the Unions, May 18, 1939

An African American packinghouse worker near Chicago, Illinois, explained how the CIO united workers from different racial and ethnic backgrounds when other unions turned them away.

I'm working in the Beef Kill section. Butcher on the chain. Been in the place twenty years, I believe. You got to have a certain amount of skill to do the job I'm doing. Long ago, I wanted to join the AFL union, the Amalgamated Butchers and Meat Cutters, they called it and wouldn't take me. Wouldn't let me in the union. Never said it to my face, but reason of it was plain. Negro. That's it. Just didn't want a Negro man to have what he should. That's wrong. You know that's wrong. Long about 1937 the CIO come. Well, I tell you, we Negroes was glad to see it come. Well, you know, sometimes the bosses, or either the company stooges try to keep the white boys from joining the union. They say, "you don't want to belong to a black man's organization. That's all the CIO is." Don't fool nobody, but they got to lie, spread lyin' words around. There's a many different people, talkin' different speech, can't understand English very well, we have to have us union interpreters for lots of our members, but that don't make no mind, they all friends in the union, even if they can't say nothin' except "Brother," an' shake hands. Well, my own local, we elected our officers and it's the same all over. We try to get every people represented. President of the local, he's Negro. First V[ice] President, he's Polish. Second V. President, he's Irish. Other officers, Scotchman, Lithuanian, Negro, German. . . . I don't care if the union don't do another lick of work raisin' our pay, or settling grievances about anything, I'll always believe they done the greatest thing in the world gettin' everybody who works in the yards together, and breakin' up the hate and bad feelings that used to be held against the Negro.

Source: Betty Burke. Interview with Jim Cole. Manuscript. U.S. Works Progress Administration, Federal Writers Project. From Library of Congress, *Folklore Project, Life Histories, 1936–39*, GIF. http://www.loc.gov/resource/wpalh0.07050602/seq-1#seq-1 (accessed December 3, 2013).

Questions for Analysis

Analyze the Evidence: What did Fusco, Buxton, and Cole see as successes and shortcomings of the New Deal? According to these men, how did New Deal programs influence the lives of ordinary American citizens?

Consider the Context: Who did these men identify as opponents of New Deal measures, and why?

Recognize Viewpoints: What attitudes did these men believe other Americans had about the WPA, the CIO, and the New Deal in general?

leaders. Roosevelt signed the Wagner Act in July 1935, for the first time providing federal support for labor organization—the most important New Deal reform of the industrial order.

The achievements that flowed from the Wagner Act and renewed labor militancy were impressive. When Roosevelt became president in 1933, union membership—composed almost entirely of skilled workers in trade unions affiliated with the American Federation of Labor (AFL)—stood at three million. With the support of the Wagner Act, union membership expanded to fourteen million by 1945. By then, 30 percent of the workforce was unionized, the highest in American history.

Most of the new union members were factory workers and unskilled laborers, many of them immigrants, women, and African Americans. For decades, established AFL unions had no desire to organize factory and unskilled workers. In 1935, under the aggressive leadership of the mine workers' John L. Lewis and the head of the Amalgamated Clothing Workers, Sidney Hillman, a coalition of unskilled workers formed the **Committee for Industrial Organization (CIO)**; later the Congress of Industrial Organizations. The CIO, helped by the Wagner Act, mobilized organizing drives in major industries, including the bitterly anti-union automobile and steel industries.

VISUAL ACTIVITY

City Activities Mural

During the 1930s, artists—many of them employed by New Deal agencies—painted thousands of murals depicting the variety of American life. These murals often appeared in public buildings. The mural shown here, by Missouri-born artist Thomas Hart Benton, illustrates the seductive pleasures and the spirit found in American cities. The Metropolitan Museum of Art. Gift of AXA Equitable, 2012 (2012.478a-j). © The Metropolitan Museum of Art. Image source: Art Resource, NY.

READING THE IMAGE: What features of urban experience does Benton emphasize in this mural? What ideas and attitudes, if any, link the people shown here?

CONNECTIONS: To what extent does the mural highlight activities distinct to U.S. cities, compared with urban life in Europe, Africa, or Asia?

The bloody struggle by the CIO-affiliated United Auto Workers (UAW) to organize workers at General Motors climaxed in January 1937. Striking workers occupied the main assembly plant in Flint, Michigan, in a sit-down strike that slashed the plant's production of 15,000 cars a week to a mere 150. Stymied, General Motors eventually surrendered and agreed to make the UAW the sole bargaining agent for all the company's workers and to refrain from interfering with union activity. The UAW expanded its campaign until, after much violence, the entire industry was unionized by 1941.

The CIO hoped to ride organizing success in auto plants to victory in the steel mills. But after unionizing the giant U.S. Steel, the CIO ran up against determined opposition from smaller steel firms. Following a police attack that killed ten strikers at Republic Steel outside Chicago in May 1937, the battered steelworkers halted their organizing campaign. In steel and other major industries, such as the stridently anti-union southern textile mills, organizing efforts stalled until after 1941, when military mobilization created labor shortages that gave workers greater bargaining power.

Social Security and Tax Reform

The single most important feature of the New Deal's emerging welfare state was **Social Security**. An ambitious, far-reaching, and permanent reform, Social Security was designed to provide a modest income to relieve the poverty of elderly people.

Only about 15 percent of older Americans had private pension plans, and during the depression corporations and banks often failed to pay the meager pensions they had promised. Corporations routinely fired or demoted employees to avoid or reduce pension payments. Prompted by the popular but impractical panaceas of Dr. Townsend, Father Coughlin, and Huey Long, Roosevelt told Congress that "it is our plain duty to provide for that security upon which welfare depends . . . and undertake the great task of furthering the security of the citizen and his family through social insurance."

The political struggle for Social Security highlighted class differences among Americans. Support for the measure came from a coalition of advocacy groups for the elderly and the poor, traditional progressives, leftists, social workers, and labor unions. Arrayed against them were economic conservatives, including the American Liberty League, the National Association of Manufacturers, the Chamber of Commerce, and the American Medical Association. Enact the Social Security system, these conservatives and other Republicans warned, and the government will ruin private property, destroy initiative, and reduce proud individuals to spineless loafers.

The large New Deal majority in Congress passed the Social Security Act in August 1935. The act provided that contributions from workers and their employers would fund pensions for the elderly, giving contributing workers a personal stake in the system and making it politically invulnerable. When eligible workers reached retirement age, they were not subject to a means test to prove that they were needy. Instead, they had earned benefits based on their contributions and years of work. Social Security also created unemployment insurance that provided modest benefits for workers who lost their jobs.

Not all workers benefited from the Social Security Act. It excluded domestic and agricultural workers like Florence Owens, thereby making ineligible about half of all African Americans and more than half of all employed women—about five million people in all. The law also excluded employees of religious and nonprofit organizations, such as schools and hospitals, thereby rendering even more women and minorities ineligible.

VISUAL ACTIVITY

Women's Emergency Brigade Supports Sit-Down Strikers
General Motors cut wages and employment in half during the depression, causing a wave of strikes by autoworkers. During the famous sit-down strike in Flint, Michigan, in 1937, the wives of striking workers organized the Emergency Brigade, shown here, to support the strikers. The photo does not show the thousands of armed police and National Guardsmen who surrounded the plant. Bettmann/Corbis.
READING THE IMAGE: Why do you think the woman leading the Emergency Brigade carried an American flag? What kind of support did the Women's Emergency Brigade appear to provide to the striking autoworkers, according to the photo?
CONNECTIONS: In what ways did the New Deal support labor unions?

Social Security provided states with multi-million-dollar grants to help them support dependent children, blind people, and public health services. After the Supreme Court upheld Social Security in 1937, the program was expanded to include benefits for dependent survivors of deceased recipients. Although the first Social Security check (for $41.30) was not issued until 1940, the system gave millions of working people the assurance that, when they became too old to work, they would receive a modest income from the federal government. This safety net protected many ordinary working people from fears of a penniless and insecure old age.

Fervent opposition to Social Security struck New Dealers as evidence that the rich had learned little from the depression. Roosevelt had long felt contempt for the moneyed elite who ignored the suffering of the poor. He looked for a way to redistribute wealth that would weaken conservative opposition, advance the cause of social equity, and defuse political challenges from Huey Long and Father Coughlin. Roosevelt charged in 1935 that large fortunes put "great and undesirable concentration of control in [the hands of] relatively few individuals." He urged a graduated tax on corporations, an inheritance tax, and an increase in maximum personal income taxes. Congress endorsed Roosevelt's basic principle by taxing those with higher incomes at a somewhat higher rate.

Neglected Americans and the New Deal

The patchwork of New Deal reforms erected a two-tier welfare state. In the top tier, farmers and organized workers in major industries were the greatest beneficiaries of New Deal initiatives. In the bottom tier, millions of neglected Americans—women, children, and old folks, along with the unorganized, unskilled, uneducated, and unemployed—often fell through the New Deal safety net. Many working people remained more or less untouched by New Deal benefits. The average unemployment rate for the 1930s stayed high—17 percent. Workers in industries that resisted unions received little help from the Wagner Act or the WPA. Tens of thousands of women in southern textile mills, for example, commonly received wages of less than ten cents an hour and were fired if they protested. Domestic workers, almost all of them women, and agricultural workers—many of them African, Hispanic, or Asian Americans—were neither unionized nor eligible for Social Security.

The New Deal neglected few citizens more than African Americans. About half of black Americans in cities were jobless, more than double the unemployment rate among whites. In the rural South, where the vast majority of African Americans lived, conditions were worse, given the New Deal agricultural policies such as the AAA that favored landowners, who often pushed blacks off the land they farmed. Only 11 of more than 10,000 WPA supervisors in the South were black, even though African Americans accounted for a third of the region's population. Disfranchisement by intimidation and legal subterfuge prevented southern blacks from protesting their plight at the ballot box. Protesters risked vicious retaliation from local whites. Bitter critics charged that the New Deal's NRA stood for "Negro Run Around" or "Negroes Ruined Again."

Roosevelt responded to such criticisms with great caution since New Deal reforms required the political support of powerful conservative, segregationist, southern white Democrats who would be alienated by programs that aided blacks. A white Georgia relief worker expressed the common view that "any Nigger who gets over $8 a week is a spoiled Nigger, that's all." Stymied by the political clout of entrenched white racism, New Dealers still attracted support from black voters. Roosevelt's overtures to African Americans prompted northern black voters in the 1934 congressional elections to shift from the Republican to the Democratic Party, helping elect New Deal Democrats.

Eleanor Roosevelt sponsored the appointment of Mary McLeod Bethune—the energetic cofounder of the National Council of Negro Women—as head of the Division of Negro Affairs in the National Youth Administration. The highest-ranking black official in Roosevelt's administration, Bethune used her position to guide a small number of black professionals and civil rights activists to posts within New Deal agencies. Ultimately, about one in four African Americans got access to New Deal relief programs.

Despite these gains, by 1940 African Americans still suffered severe handicaps. Most of the thirteen million black workers toiled at low-paying menial jobs, unprotected by the New Deal safety net. Segregated and unequal schools were the norm, and only 1 percent of black students earned college degrees. In southern states, vigilante violence against blacks went unpunished. For these problems of black Americans, the New Deal offered few remedies.

Hispanic Americans fared no better. About a million Mexican Americans lived in the United States in the 1930s, most of them first- or

Antilynching Protesters
These Howard University students protested the New Deal's refusal to support antilynching legislation by standing outside the Washington, D.C., building of the Daughters of the American Revolution in 1935 with nooses around their necks and placards naming recent lynching victims. Roosevelt and his advisers never made federal antilynching laws a priority since they feared alienating white southerners whose votes were needed to pass other New Deal measures. Corbis.

second-generation immigrants who worked crops throughout the West. During the depression, field workers saw their low wages plunge lower still to about a dime an hour. Ten thousand Mexican American pecan shellers in San Antonio, Texas, earned only a nickel an hour. To preserve scarce jobs for U.S. citizens, the federal government choked off immigration from Mexico, while state and local officials deported tens of thousands of Mexican Americans, many with their American-born children. New Deal programs throughout the West often discriminated against Hispanics and other people of color. A New Deal study concluded that "the Mexican is . . . segregated from the rest of the community as effectively as the Negro . . . [by] poverty and low wages."

Asian Americans had similar experiences. Asian immigrants were still excluded from U.S. citizenship and in many states were not permitted to own land. By 1930, more than half of Japanese Americans had been born in the United States, but they were still liable to discrimination. One young Asian American expressed the frustration felt by many others: "I am a fruit-stand worker. I would much rather it were doctor

or lawyer . . . but my aspirations [were] frustrated long ago by circumstances. . . . I am only what I am, a professional carrot washer."

Native Americans also suffered neglect from New Deal agencies. As a group, they remained the poorest of the poor. Since the Dawes Act of 1887 (see "The Dawes Act and Indian Land Allotment" in chapter 17), the federal government had encouraged Native Americans to assimilate—to abandon their Indian identities and adopt the cultural norms of the majority society. Under the leadership of the New Deal's commissioner of Indian affairs, John Collier, the New Deal's Indian Reorganization Act (IRA) of 1934 largely reversed that policy. Collier claimed that "the most interesting and important fact about Indians" was that they "do not expect much, often they expect nothing at all; yet they are able to be happy." Given such views, the IRA provided little economic aid to Native Americans, but it did restore their right to own land communally and to have greater control over their own affairs. The IRA brought little immediate benefit to Native Americans, but it provided an important foundation for Indians' economic, cultural, and political resurgence a generation later.

Mexican Migrant Farmworkers
These Mexican immigrants are harvesting sugar beets in 1937 in northwestern Minnesota. Between 1910 and 1940, when refugees from the Mexican revolution poured across the American border, the Hispanic-American Alliance and other such organizations sought to protect Mexican Americans' rights against nativist fears and hostility. The alliance steadfastly emphasized Mexican Americans' desire to receive permanent legal status in the United States. Library of Congress, 8a28739.

Voicing common experiences among Americans neglected by the New Deal, singer and songwriter Woody Guthrie traveled the nation for eight years during the 1930s and heard other rambling men tell him "the story of their life": "how the home went to pieces, how . . . the crops got to where they wouldn't bring nothing, work in factories would kill a dog . . . and—always, always [you] have to fight and argue and cuss and swear . . . to try to get a nickel more out of the rich bosses."

REVIEW What features of a welfare state did the New Deal create, and why?

▶ The New Deal from Victory to Deadlock

To accelerate the sputtering economic recovery, Roosevelt shifted the emphasis of the New Deal in the mid-1930s. Instead of seeking cooperation from conservative business leaders, he decided to rely on the growing New Deal coalition to enact reforms over the strident opposition of the Supreme Court, Republicans, and corporate interests. Roosevelt's conservative opponents reacted to the massing of New Deal forces by intensifying their opposition to the welfare state.

While he continued to lose conservatives' support, Roosevelt added new allies on the left in farm states and big cities. Throughout Roosevelt's first term, socialists and Communists denounced the slow pace of change and accused the New Deal of failing to serve the interests of the workers who produced the nation's wealth. But in 1935, the Soviet Union, worried about the threat of fascism in Europe, instructed Communists throughout the world to join hands with non-Communist progressives in a "Popular Front" to advance the fortunes of the working class. Many radicals soon switched from opposing the New Deal to supporting its relief programs and support for labor unions.

Roosevelt won reelection in 1936 in a landslide and soon concluded that the economy was improving. He reduced government spending in 1937, triggering a sharp recession that undermined economic recovery and prolonged the depression.

The Election of 1936

Roosevelt believed that the presidential election of 1936 would test his leadership and progressive ideals. The depression still had a stranglehold on the economy. Conservative leaders believed that the New Deal's failure to lift the nation out of the depression indicated that Americans were ready for a change. Left-wing critics insisted that the New Deal had missed the opportunity to displace capitalism with a socialist economy and that voters would embrace candidates who recommended more radical remedies.

Republicans turned to Kansas governor Alfred (Alf) Landon as their presidential nominee, a moderate who stressed mainstream Republican proposals to achieve a balanced federal budget and less government bureaucracy. Landon recommended that the perils of sickness and old age should be eased by old-fashioned neighborliness instead of a government program like Social Security.

Roosevelt put his faith in the growing New Deal coalition, whose members shared his conviction that the New Deal promised to liberate the nation from the long era of privilege and wealth for a few and "economic slavery" for the rest. He proclaimed that "the forces of selfishness and lust for power met their match" in his first term as president, and he hoped it would be said about his second term that "these forces met their master."

Roosevelt triumphed spectacularly. He won 60.8 percent of the popular vote, making it the widest margin of victory in a presidential election to date. Third parties—including the Socialist and Communist parties—fell pitifully short of the support they expected and never again mounted a significant challenge to the New Deal. Congressional results were equally lopsided, with Democrats outnumbering Republicans more than three to one in both houses. In his inaugural address, Roosevelt announced, "I see one third of a nation ill-housed, ill-clad, [and] ill-nourished," and he promised to devote his second term to alleviating their hardship.

Court Packing

In the afterglow of his reelection triumph, Roosevelt pondered how to remove the remaining obstacles to New Deal reforms. He decided to target the Supreme Court. Conservative justices appointed by Republican presidents had invalidated eleven New Deal measures as unconstitutional interferences with free enterprise. Now, Social Security, the Wagner Act, the Securities and Exchange Commission, and other New Deal innovations were about to be considered by the justices.

To ensure that the Supreme Court did not dismantle the New Deal, Roosevelt proposed a **court-packing plan** that added one new justice for each existing judge who had served for ten years and was over the age of seventy. In effect, the proposed law would give Roosevelt the power to pack the Court with up to six New Dealers who could outvote the elderly, conservative, Republican justices.

But the president had not reckoned with Americans' deeply rooted deference to the independent authority of the Supreme Court. More than two-thirds of Americans believed that the Court should be free from political interference. Even New Deal supporters were disturbed by the court-packing scheme. The suggestion that individuals over age seventy had diminished mental capacity offended many elderly members of Congress, which defeated Roosevelt's plan in 1937.

Supreme Court justices still got the message. The four most conservative of the elderly justices—the "four horsemen of reaction," according to one New Dealer—retired. Roosevelt eventually named eight justices to the Court—more than any other president—ultimately giving New Deal laws safe passage through the Court.

Reaction and Recession

Emboldened by their defeat of the court-packing plan, Republicans and southern Democrats rallied around their common conservatism to obstruct additional reforms. Former president Herbert Hoover proclaimed that the New Deal was the "repudiation of Democracy" and that "the Republican Party alone [was] the guardian of . . . the charter of freedom." Democrats' arguments over whether the New Deal needed to be expanded—and if so, how—undermined the consensus among reformers and sparked antagonism between Congress and the White House. The ominous rise of belligerent regimes in Germany, Italy, and Japan also slowed reform as some Americans began to worry more about defending the nation than changing it.

Roosevelt himself favored slowing the pace of the New Deal. He believed that existing New Deal measures had steadily boosted the economy and

Distributing Surplus Food to the Needy
When bountiful harvests produced surplus crops that would depress prices if they were sent to market, the New Deal arranged to distribute some of the surplus to needy Americans. Here, farmworkers in east-central Arizona near the New Mexico border line up to receive a ration of potatoes authorized by the New Deal agent checking the box of index cards. Library of Congress, 1a34185.

largely eliminated the depression crisis. In fact, the gross national product in 1937 briefly equaled the 1929 level before dropping lower for the rest of the decade. Unemployment declined to 14 percent in 1937 but quickly spiked upward and stayed higher until 1940. Roosevelt's unwarranted optimism about the economic recovery persuaded him that additional deficit spending by the federal government was no longer necessary.

Roosevelt's optimism failed to consider the stubborn realities of unemployment and poverty, and the reduction in deficit spending reversed the improving economy. Even at the high-water mark of recovery in the summer of 1937, seven million people lacked jobs. In the next few months, national income and production slipped so steeply that almost two-thirds of the economic gains since 1933 were lost by June 1938.

This economic reversal hurt the New Deal politically. Conservatives argued that this recession proved that New Deal measures produced only an illusion of progress. The way to weather the recession was to tax and spend less as well as to wait for the natural laws of supply and demand to restore prosperity. Many New Dealers insisted instead that the continuing depression demanded that Roosevelt revive federal spending and redouble efforts to stimulate the economy. In 1938, Congress heeded such pleas and enacted a massive new program of federal spending.

The recession scare of 1937–1938 taught the president the lesson that economic growth had to be carefully nurtured. The English economist John Maynard Keynes argued that only government intervention could pump enough money into the economy to restore prosperity, a concept that became known as Keynesian economics. Roosevelt never had the inclination or time to master Keynesian thought. But in a commonsense

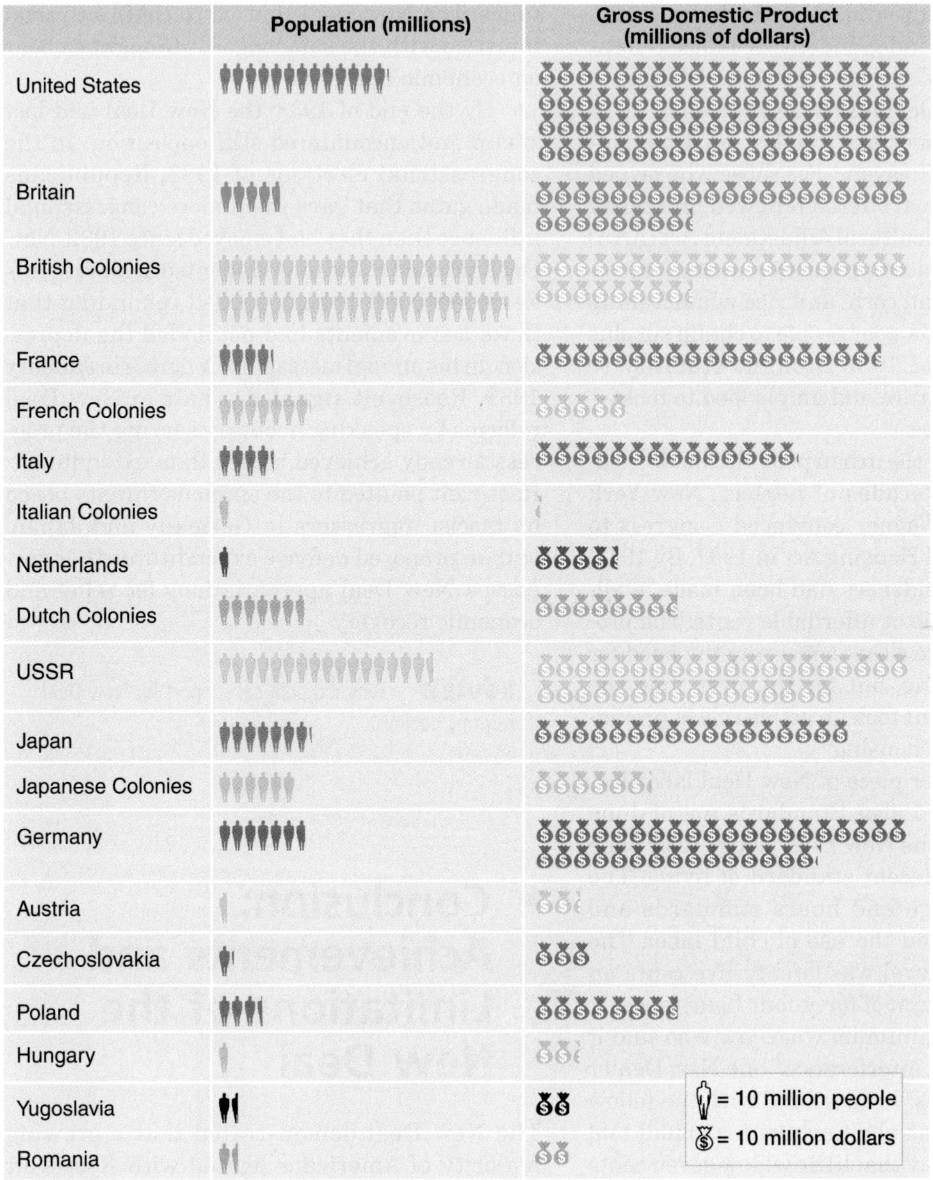

	Population (millions)	Gross Domestic Product (millions of dollars)
United States		
Britain		
British Colonies		
France		
French Colonies		
Italy		
Italian Colonies		
Netherlands		
Dutch Colonies		
USSR		
Japan		
Japanese Colonies		
Germany		
Austria		
Czechoslovakia		
Poland		
Hungary		
Yugoslavia		
Romania		

= 10 million people
= 10 million dollars

FIGURE 24.2 Global Comparison: National Populations and Economies, ca. 1938
Throughout the Great Depression, the United States remained more productive than any other nation in the world. By 1938, the United States produced more than twice as much as its closest competitors, Germany and the USSR. If Germany had gained control of the other European nations listed here, it would have become the biggest economy in the world. What do these data suggest about the relationship between population and product?

way, he understood that escape from the depression required a plan for large-scale spending to alleviate distress and stimulate economic growth (Figure 24.2).

The Last of the New Deal Reforms

From the moment he was sworn in, Roosevelt sought to expand the powers of the presidency. He believed that the president needed more authority to meet emergencies such as the depression and to administer the sprawling federal bureaucracy. Combined with a Democratic majority in Congress, a now-friendly Supreme Court, and the revival of deficit spending, the newly empowered White House seemed to be in a good

position to move ahead with a revitalized New Deal.

Resistance to further reform was also on the rise, however. Conservatives argued that the New Deal had pressed government centralization too far. Even the New Deal's friends became weary of one emergency program after another while economic woes continued to shadow New Deal achievements. By the midpoint of Roosevelt's second term, restive members of Congress balked at new initiatives. But enough support remained for one last burst of reform.

Agriculture still had strong claims on New Deal attention in the face of drought, declining crop prices, and impoverished sharecroppers and tenants. In 1937, the Agriculture Department created the Farm Security Administration (FSA) to provide housing and loans to help tenant farmers become independent. A black tenant farmer in North Carolina who received an FSA loan told a New Deal interviewer, "I wake up in the night sometimes and think I must be half-dead and gone to heaven." For those who owned farms, the New Deal offered renewed prosperity with a second Agricultural Adjustment Act (AAA) in 1938, which placed production quotas on cotton, tobacco, wheat, corn, and rice while issuing food stamps to allow poor people to obtain surplus food. The AAA of 1938 brought stability to American agriculture and ample food to most—but not all—tables.

Advocates for the urban poor also made modest gains after decades of neglect. New York senator Robert Wagner convinced Congress to pass the National Housing Act in 1937. By 1941, some 160,000 residences had been made available to poor people at affordable rents. The program did not come close to meeting the need for affordable housing, but for the first time the federal government took an active role in providing decent urban housing.

The last major piece of New Deal labor legislation, the Fair Labor Standards Act of June 1938, reiterated the New Deal pledge to provide workers with a decent standard of living. The new law set wage and hours standards and at long last curbed the use of child labor. The minimum-wage level was twenty-five cents an hour for a maximum of forty-four hours a week. To critics of the minimum wage law who said it was "government interference," one New Dealer responded, "It was. It interfered with the fellow running that pecan shelling plant . . . [and] told him he couldn't pay that little widow seven cents an hour." To attract enough conservative votes, the act exempted domestic help and farm laborers—relegating most women and African Americans to lower wages. Enforcement of the minimum-wage standards was weak and haphazard. Nevertheless, the Fair Labor Standards Act slowly advanced Roosevelt's inaugural promise to improve the living standards of the poorest Americans.

The final New Deal reform effort failed to make much headway against the hidebound system of racial injustice. Although Roosevelt denounced lynching as murder, he would not jeopardize his vital base of southern political support by demanding antilynching legislation, and Congress voted down attempts to make lynching a federal crime. Laws to eliminate the poll tax—used to deny blacks the opportunity to vote—encountered the same overwhelming resistance. The New Deal refused to confront racial injustice with the same vigor it brought to bear on economic hardship.

By the end of 1938, the New Deal had lost steam and encountered stiff opposition. In the congressional elections of 1938, Republicans made gains that gave them more congressional influence than they had enjoyed since 1932. New Dealers could claim unprecedented achievements since 1933, but nobody needed reminding that those achievements had not ended the depression. In his annual message to Congress in January 1939, Roosevelt signaled a halt to New Deal reforms by speaking about preserving the progress already achieved rather than extending it. Roosevelt pointed to the ominous threats posed by fascist aggressors in Germany and Japan, and he proposed defense expenditures that surpassed New Deal appropriations for relief and economic recovery.

REVIEW Why did political support for New Deal reforms decline?

► Conclusion: Achievements and Limitations of the New Deal

The New Deal demonstrated that a growing majority of Americans agreed with Roosevelt that the federal government should help those in need. Through programs that sought relief, recovery, and reform, the New Deal vastly expanded the size and influence of the federal government and changed the way many Americans viewed Washington. New Dealers achieved significant victories, such as Social Security, labor's right to organize, and guarantees that farm prices would be maintained through controls on production and marketing. New Deal measures marked the emergence of a welfare state, but its limits left millions of needy Americans like Florence Owens and her children with little aid.

Full-scale relief, recovery, and reform eluded the New Deal. Even though millions of Americans benefited from New Deal initiatives, both relief and recovery were limited and temporary. In 1940, the depression still plagued the economy. Perhaps the most impressive achievement of the

New Deal was what did not happen. Although authoritarian governments and anticapitalist policies were common outside the United States during the 1930s, they were shunned by the New Deal. The greatest economic crisis the nation had ever faced did not cause Americans to abandon democracy, as happened in Germany, where Adolf Hitler seized dictatorial power. Nor did the nation turn to radical alternatives such as socialism or communism.

Republicans and other conservatives claimed that the New Deal amounted to a form of socialism that threatened democracy and capitalism. But rather than attack capitalism, Franklin Roosevelt sought to save it. And he succeeded. That success also marked the limits of the New Deal's achievements. Franklin Roosevelt believed that a shift of authority toward the federal government would allow capitalist enterprises to be balanced by the nation's democratic tradition. The New Deal stopped far short of challenging capitalism either by undermining private property or by imposing strict national planning.

New Dealers repeatedly described their programs as a kind of warfare against the depression of the 1930s. In the next decade, the Roosevelt administration had to turn from the economic crisis at home to participate in a worldwide conflagration to defeat the enemies of democracy abroad.

Nonetheless, many New Deal reforms continued for decades to structure the basic institutions of banking, the stock market, union organizations, agricultural markets, Social Security, minimum-wage standards, and more. Opponents of these measures and of the basic New Deal notion of an activist government remained powerful, especially in the Republican Party. They claimed that government was the problem, not the solution—a slogan that Republicans championed during and after the 1980s and that led, with the cooperation of some Democrats, to the dismantling of a number of New Deal programs, including the regulation of banking. The deregulation of banking played a large role in the financial meltdown that began in 2008.

See the Selected Bibliography for this chapter in the Appendix.

24 Chapter Review

KEY TERMS

New Deal coalition (p. 683)
underconsumption (p. 686)
Federal Deposit Insurance Corporation (FDIC) (p. 686)
fireside chats (p. 686)
Civilian Conservation Corps (CCC) (p. 687)
Agricultural Adjustment Act (AAA) (p. 690)
National Recovery Administration (NRA) (p. 691)
Works Progress Administration (WPA) (p. 697)
Wagner Act (p. 698)
Committee for Industrial Organization (p. 699)
Social Security (p. 700)
court-packing plan (p. 705)

REVIEW QUESTIONS

1. Why did Franklin D. Roosevelt win the 1932 presidential election by such a large margin? (pp. 681–683)

2. How did the New Dealers try to steer the nation toward recovery from the Great Depression? (pp. 684–691)

3. Why did groups at both ends of the political spectrum criticize the New Deal? (pp. 691–697)

4. What features of a welfare state did the New Deal create, and why? (pp. 697–704)

5. Why did political support for New Deal reforms decline? (pp. 704–708)

MAKING CONNECTIONS

1. How did Roosevelt build an effective interregional political coalition for the Democratic Party? How did the coalition shape the policies of the New Deal?

2. How effective were reform efforts targeting rural and industrial America?

3. Were any of Roosevelt's critics able to influence the New Deal? If so, how?

4. Who was in need of New Deal assistance but did not receive it? Why?

LINKING TO THE PAST

1. To what degree did the New Deal reflect a continuation of the progressive movement of the late nineteenth and early twentieth centuries? In what ways did the New Deal depart from progressive ideals? In general, how new was the New Deal? (See chapters 21 and 22.)

2. How did the New Deal coalition compare to the long-standing political coalition that had elected Republicans to the presidency since 1920? What accounted for the differences and similarities? (See chapter 23.)

25 The United States and the Second World War

1939–1945

CONTENT LEARNING OBJECTIVES

After reading and studying this chapter, you should be able to:

- Describe the foreign policy dilemmas that confronted the United States during the interwar years.

- Explain which events led to the onset of war and why the United States became involved. Describe the United States' war mobilization efforts.

- Outline the crucial military and diplomatic events of 1941 through 1943, demonstrating how the United States turned the tide in the Pacific and explaining its prime military objectives in the European theater.

- Analyze the impact of the war on American society, including the effects it had on women and families, African Americans, and the 1944 presidential campaign.

- Assess which military and diplomatic events during 1943 to 1945 contributed to Allied victory in Europe and over Japan.

GI MAIL
Soldiers who engaged in deadly combat also stayed in touch with family and friends. The soldier who drew on this envelope emphasized that Uncle Sam was crushing the leaders of Germany and Japan. National Museum of American History, Smithsonian Institution, USA/Bridgeman Images.

ON A SUN-DRENCHED FLORIDA AFTERNOON IN 1927, TWELVE-YEAR-OLD Paul Tibbets clambered into the front seat of the open cockpit of a biplane for his first airplane ride. While the pilot brought the plane in low over the Hialeah racetrack in Miami, Florida, Tibbets pitched Baby Ruth candy bars tethered to small paper parachutes to racing fans in the grandstands below. After repeating this stunt, sales of Baby Ruths soared, and Tibbets was hooked on flying.

In 1937, Tibbets joined the Army Air Corps and became a military pilot. Shortly after the Japanese attack on Pearl Harbor in December 1941 immediately overcame American isolationism and brought the United States into World War II, Tibbets flew antisubmarine patrols against German U-boats lurking along the East Coast. When heavily armored B-17 Flying Fortress bombers became available early in 1942, he took a squadron of the new planes to England. In August 1942, he led the first American daytime bombing raid on German-occupied Europe, releasing on railroad yards in northern France the first of some 700,000 tons of explosives dropped by American bombers during the air war in Europe.

After numerous raids over Europe, Tibbets was reassigned to the North African campaign. After eight months of combat missions, Tibbets returned to the United States and was ordered to test the new B-29 Super Fortress being built in Wichita, Kansas. The B-29 was much bigger than the B-17 and could fly higher and faster, making it ideal for the campaign against Japan. Tibbets's mastery of the B-29 caused him to be singled out in September 1944 to command a top-secret unit training for a special mission.

The mission was to be ready to drop on Japan a bomb so powerful that it might end the war. No such bomb yet existed, but American scientists and engineers were working around the clock to build one. In May 1945, Tibbets and his men went to Tinian Island in the Pacific, where they trained for their secret mission by flying raids over Japanese cities and dropping ordinary bombs. The atomic bomb arrived on Tinian on July 26, just ten days after a successful test explosion in the New Mexico desert. Nicknamed "Little Boy," the bomb packed the equivalent of 40 million pounds of TNT, or 200,000 of the 200-pound bombs Tibbets and other American airmen had dropped on Europe.

On August 6, 1945, Tibbets, his crew, and their atomic payload took off in the B-29 bomber *Enola Gay* and headed for Japan. Less than seven hours later, over the city of Hiroshima, Tibbets and his men released Little Boy from the *Enola Gay*'s bomb bay. Three days later, airmen from Tibbets's command dropped a second atomic bomb on Nagasaki, and within five days Japan surrendered.

Paul Tibbets's experiences traced an arc followed by millions of Americans during World War II. Like Tibbets, Americans joined their allies to fight the Axis powers in Europe and Asia. Like his *Enola Gay* crewmen—who hailed from New York, Texas, California, New Jersey, New Mexico, Maryland, North Carolina, Pennsylvania, Michigan, and Nevada—Americans from all regions united to help defeat the fascist aggressors in Asia and Europe. American industries mobilized to produce advanced bombers along with enough other military equipment to supply the American armed forces and their allies. At enormous cost in human life and suffering—including millions of civilians killed in military actions and millions more exterminated in the Holocaust of the Nazis' racist death camps—the war resulted in employment and prosperity to most Americans at home, ending the depression, providing new opportunities for women and African Americans, and ushering the nation into the postwar world as a triumphant economic and atomic superpower.

Colonel Paul Tibbets
Before taking off to drop the world's first atomic bomb on Hiroshima, Tibbets posed on the tarmac next to his customized B-29 Super Fortress bomber, named *Enola Gay* in honor of his mother. A crew of eleven handpicked airmen accompanied Tibbets on the top-secret mission. Bettmann/Corbis.

▶ Peacetime Dilemmas

The First World War left a dangerous and ultimately deadly legacy. The victors—especially Britain, France, and the United States—sought to avoid future wars at almost any cost. The defeated nation, Germany, aspired to reassert its power and avenge its losses by means of renewed warfare. Italy and Japan felt humiliated by the Versailles peace settlement and saw war as a legitimate way to increase their global power. Japan invaded the northern Chinese province of Manchuria in 1931 with ambitions to expand throughout Asia. Italy, led by the fascist Benito Mussolini since 1922, hungered for an empire in Africa. In Germany, National Socialist Adolf Hitler rose to power in 1933 in a quest to dominate Europe and the world. These aggressive, militaristic, antidemocratic regimes seemed a smaller threat to most people in the United States during the 1930s than did the economic crisis at home. Shielded from external threats by the Atlantic and Pacific oceans, Americans hoped to avoid entanglement in foreign woes and to concentrate on climbing out of the nation's economic abyss.

Roosevelt and Reluctant Isolation

Like most Americans during the 1930s, Franklin Roosevelt believed that the nation's highest priority was to attack the domestic causes and consequences of the depression. But unlike most Americans, Roosevelt had long advocated an active role for the United States in international affairs.

The depression forced Roosevelt to retreat from his previous internationalism. He came to believe that energetic involvement in foreign affairs diverted resources and political support from domestic recovery. Once in office, Roosevelt sought to combine domestic economic recovery with a low-profile foreign policy that encouraged free trade and disarmament.

Roosevelt's pursuit of international amity was constrained by economic circumstances and American popular opinion. After an opinion poll demonstrated popular support for recognizing the Soviet Union—an international pariah since the Bolshevik Revolution in 1917—Roosevelt established formal diplomatic relations in 1933. But when the League of Nations condemned Japanese and German aggression, Roosevelt did not support the league's attempts to keep the peace because he feared jeopardizing isolationists' support for New Deal measures in Congress. America watched

CHRONOLOGY

1935–1937	• Neutrality acts passed.
1936	• Nazi Germany occupies Rhineland. • Italian armies conquer Ethiopia. • Spanish civil war begins.
1937	• Japanese troops capture Nanjing.
1938	• Hitler annexes Austria.
1939	• German troops occupy Czechoslovakia. • Nazi-Soviet nonaggression pact formed. • Germany's attack on Poland begins World War II.
1940	• Germany invades Denmark, Norway, France, Belgium, Luxembourg, and the Netherlands. • British and French troops evacuate from Dunkirk. • Battle of Britain fought. • Tripartite Pact formed.
1941	• Lend-Lease Act passes. • Germany invades Soviet Union. • Japanese attack Pearl Harbor.
1942	• Japanese Americans moved to internment camps. • Japan captures the Philippines. • Congress of Racial Equality founded. • Battles of Coral Sea and Midway fought. • Manhattan Project begins. • U.S. forces invade North Africa.
1943	• Allied leaders demand unconditional surrender of Axis powers. • U.S. and British forces invade Sicily.
1944	• D Day executed.
1945	• Yalta Conference held. • Roosevelt dies; Vice President Harry Truman becomes president. • Germany surrenders. • United States joins United Nations. • United States drops atomic bombs on Hiroshima and Nagasaki. • Japan surrenders, ending World War II.

Americans All

The good neighbor policy emphasized the common interests of the United States and its Latin American neighbors. One consequence of the policy is illustrated by this World War II poster, which asserts the shared goal of Uncle Sam and sombrero-wearing Latin Americans to defeat the Axis powers. Above all, the United States sought to prevent Latin American nations from allying with Germany or Japan. National Archives photo no. 513803.

from the sidelines when Japan withdrew from the league and ignored the limitations on its navy imposed after World War I. The United States also looked the other way when Hitler rearmed Germany and recalled its representative to the league in 1933. Roosevelt worried that German and Japanese actions threatened world peace, but he reassured Americans that the nation would not "use its armed forces for the settlement of any [international] dispute anywhere."

The Good Neighbor Policy

In 1933, Roosevelt announced that the United States would pursue "the policy of the good neighbor" in international relations, which meant that no nation had the right to intervene in the internal or external affairs of another. He emphasized that this policy applied specifically to Latin America, where U.S. military forces had often intervened. The **good neighbor policy** did not indicate a U.S. retreat from empire in Latin America, though. Instead, it declared that, unlike in past decades, the United States would not depend on military force to exercise its influence in the region. Roosevelt refrained from sending troops to defend the interests of American corporations when Mexico nationalized American oil properties and revolution boiled over in Nicaragua, Guatemala, and Cuba during the 1930s. In 1934, Roosevelt withdrew American Marines from Haiti, where they had been stationed since 1916. While Roosevelt's hands-off policy honored the principle of national self-determination, it also permitted the rise of dictators in Nicaragua, Cuba, and elsewhere, who exploited and terrorized their nations with private support from U.S. businesses.

Military nonintervention also did not prevent the United States from exerting its economic influence in Latin America. In 1934, Congress gave the president the power to reduce tariffs on goods imported into the United States from nations that agreed to lower their own tariffs on U.S. exports. By 1940, twenty-two nations had agreed to such reciprocal tariff reductions, helping to double U.S. exports to Latin America, contributing to the New Deal's goal of boosting the domestic economy through free trade, and planting seeds of friendship and hemispheric solidarity.

The Price of Noninvolvement

In Europe, fascist governments in Italy and Germany threatened military aggression. Britain and France made only verbal protests. Emboldened, Hitler plotted to avenge defeat in World War I by recapturing territories with German inhabitants, all the while accusing Jews of polluting the purity of the Aryan master race. The virulent anti-Semitism of Hitler and his Nazi Party unified non-Jewish Germans and attracted sympathizers among many other Europeans, even in France and Britain.

In Japan, a stridently militaristic government planned to follow the invasion of Manchuria in 1931 with conquests extending throughout Southeast Asia. The Manchurian invasion bogged down in a long and vicious war when Chinese Nationalists rallied around their leader, Jiang Jieshi (Chiang Kai-shek), to fight against the Japanese. Preparations for new Japanese conquests continued, however. In 1936, Japan openly violated naval limitation treaties and began to build a battle-ready fleet to seek naval superiority in the Pacific.

In the United States, the hostilities in Asia and Europe reinforced isolationist sentiments. Popular disillusionment with the failure of Woodrow Wilson's idealistic goals caused many Americans to question the nation's participation in World War I. In 1933, Gerald Nye, a Republican from North Dakota, chaired a Senate committee that concluded that greedy "merchants of death"—American weapons makers, bankers, and financiers—dragged the nation into the war to line their own pockets. International tensions and the Nye committee report prompted Congress to pass a series of **neutrality acts** between 1935 and 1937 designed to avoid entanglement in foreign wars. The neutrality acts prohibited making loans and selling arms to nations at war.

By 1937, the growing conflicts overseas caused some Americans to call for a total embargo on all trade with warring countries. The Neutrality Act of 1937 attempted to reconcile the nation's desire for both peace and foreign trade with a "cash-and-carry" policy that required warring nations to pay cash for nonmilitary goods and to transport them in their own ships. This policy benefited the nation's economy, but it also helped foreign aggressors by supplying them with goods and thereby undermining peace.

The desire for peace in France, Britain, and the United States led Germany, Italy, and Japan to launch offensives on the assumption that the Western democracies lacked the will to oppose them. In March 1936, Nazi troops marched into the industry-rich Rhineland on Germany's western border, in blatant violation of the Treaty of Versailles. One month later, Italian armies completed their conquest of Ethiopia, projecting fascist power into Africa. In December 1937, Japanese invaders captured Nanjing (Nanking) and celebrated their triumph in the "Rape of Nanking," a deadly rampage that killed 200,000 Chinese civilians.

In Spain, a bitter civil war broke out in July 1936 when the Nationalists—fascist rebels led by General Francisco Franco—attacked the democratically elected Republican government. Both Germany and Italy reinforced Franco, while the Soviet Union provided much less aid to the Republican Loyalists. The Spanish civil war did not cause European democracies or the U.S. government to help the Loyalists, but more than 3,000

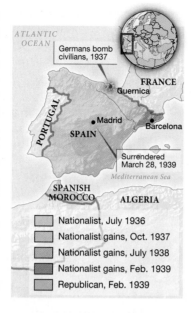

Spanish Civil War, 1936–1939

individual Americans enlisted in the Russian-sponsored Abraham Lincoln Brigade to fight alongside the Republicans. Abandoned by the Western nations, the Republican Loyalists were defeated in 1939, and Franco built a fascist bulwark in Spain.

Hostilities in Europe, Africa, and Asia alarmed Roosevelt and some Americans. The president sought to persuade most Americans to moderate their isolationism and find a way to support the victims of fascist aggression. He warned that an "epidemic of world lawlessness is spreading" and pointed out that "mere isolation or neutrality" offered no remedy. The popularity of isolationist sentiment caused Roosevelt to remark, "It's a terrible thing to look over your shoulder when you are trying to lead and find no one there." Roosevelt understood that he needed to maneuver carefully if the United States were to help prevent fascist aggressors from conquering Europe and Asia, leaving the United States an isolated island of democracy.

REVIEW   Why did isolationism during the 1930s concern Roosevelt?

▶ The Onset of War

Between 1939 and 1941, fascist victories overseas eventually eroded American isolationism. At first, U.S. intervention was limited to providing material support to the enemies of Germany and Japan, principally Britain, China, and the Soviet Union. But Japan's surprise attack on Pearl Harbor eliminated that restraint, and the nation began to mobilize for an all-out assault on foreign foes.

Nazi Aggression and War in Europe

Under the spell of isolationism, Americans passively watched Hitler's relentless campaign to dominate Europe (Map 25.1). In 1938, Hitler incorporated Austria into Germany and turned his attention to the Sudetenland, which had been granted to Czechoslovakia by the World War I peace settlement. Hoping to avoid war, British

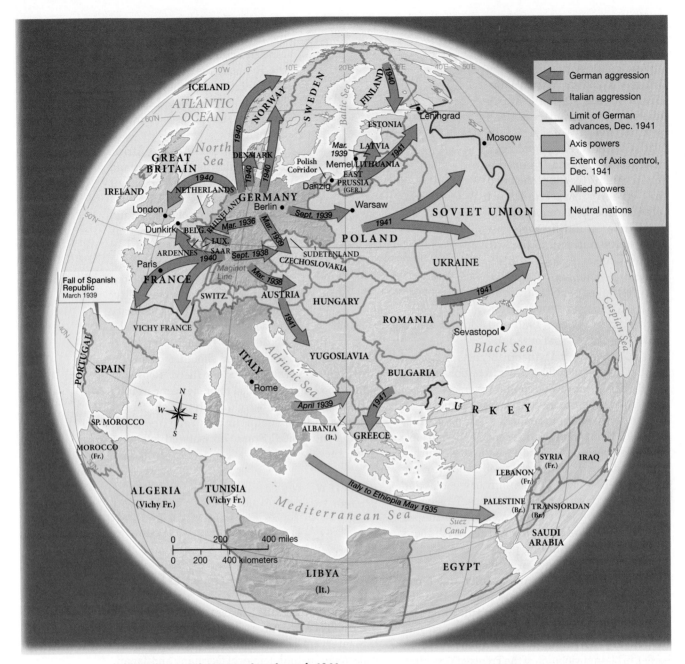

Map 25.1 Axis Aggression through 1941
Through a series of surprise strikes before 1942, Mussolini sought to re-create the Roman empire in the Mediterranean while Hitler aimed to annex Austria and reclaim German territories occupied by France after World War I. World War II broke out when the German dictator attacked Poland.

prime minister Neville Chamberlain offered Hitler terms of appeasement that would give the Sudetenland to Germany if Hitler agreed to leave the rest of Czechoslovakia alone. Hitler accepted the terms but did not keep his promise. By 1939, Hitler had annexed Czechoslovakia and demanded that Poland return the German territory it had gained after World War I. Recognizing that **appeasement** of Hitler had failed, Britain and France assured Poland that they would go to war

with Germany if Hitler attacked. In turn, Hitler negotiated with his bitter enemy, Soviet premier Joseph Stalin, offering him concessions to prevent the Soviet Union from joining Britain and France in opposing a German attack on Poland. Despite the enduring hatred between fascist Germany and the Communist Soviet Union, the two powers signed the Nazi-Soviet treaty of nonaggression in August 1939, exposing Poland to an onslaught by both the German and Soviet armies.

Nazi Invasion of Czechoslovakia
Adolf Hitler's invasion of Czechoslovakia in October 1938 was greeted with wild enthusiasm by Nazi Party members and sympathizers. Here, grim-faced Nazis (the men in white shirts) come face-to-face with their Führer while they grasp each other's belts to protect Hitler from the crowd of civilians exuberantly saluting him in celebration of his new conquest. AP Photo.

At dawn on September 1, 1939, Hitler unleashed his *blitzkrieg* (literally, "lightning war") on Poland. "Act brutally!" Hitler exhorted his generals. "Send [every] man, woman, and child of Polish descent and language to their deaths, pitilessly and remorselessly." The attack triggered Soviet attacks on eastern Poland and declarations of war from France and Britain two days later, igniting a conflagration that raced around the globe. In September 1939, Germany seemed invincible, causing many people to fear that all of Europe would soon share Poland's fate.

After the Nazis overran Poland, Hitler soon launched a westward blitzkrieg. In the first six months of 1940, German forces smashed through Denmark, Norway, the Netherlands, Belgium, and France. The speed of the German attack trapped more than 300,000 British and French soldiers, who retreated to the port of Dunkirk, where an improvised armada of British vessels ferried them to safety across the English Channel. By mid-June 1940, France had surrendered the largest army in the world, signed an armistice that gave Germany control of nearly two-thirds of the countryside, and installed a collaborationist government at Vichy. With an empire that stretched across Europe from Poland to France, Hitler seemed poised to attack Britain.

The new British prime minister, Winston Churchill, vowed that Britain, unlike France, would never surrender to Hitler. "We shall fight on the seas and oceans [and] . . . in the air," he proclaimed, "whatever the cost may be, we shall fight on the beaches, . . . and in the fields and in the streets." Churchill's defiance stiffened British resolve against Hitler's attack, which began in mid-June 1940 when wave after wave of German bombers targeted British military installations and cities, killing tens of thousands of civilians. The outgunned Royal Air Force fought as doggedly as Churchill had predicted and finally won the Battle of Britain by November, clearing German bombers from British skies and handing Hitler his first defeat. Churchill praised the valiant British pilots, declaring that "never . . . was so much owed by so many to so few." Advance knowledge of German plans aided British pilots, who had access to the new technology of radar and to decoded top-secret German military communications. Battered and exhausted by German attacks, Britain needed American help to continue to fight, as Churchill repeatedly wrote Roosevelt in private.

From Neutrality to the Arsenal of Democracy

Most Americans condemned German aggression and favored Britain and France, but isolationism remained powerful. Roosevelt feared that if

Congress did not repeal the arms embargo mandated by the Neutrality Act of 1937, France and Britain would soon succumb to the Nazi onslaught. "What worries me," Roosevelt wrote a friend, "is that public opinion . . . is patting itself on the back every morning and thanking God for the Atlantic Ocean (and the Pacific Ocean)" and underestimating "the serious implications" of the European war "for our own future." Congress agreed in November 1939 to allow belligerent nations to buy arms, as well as nonmilitary supplies, on a cash-and-carry basis.

In practice, the revised neutrality law permitted Britain and France to purchase American war materiel and carry it across the Atlantic in their own ships, thereby shielding American vessels from attack by German submarines lurking in the Atlantic. Roosevelt searched for a way to aid Britain short of entering a formal alliance or declaring war against Germany. Churchill pleaded for American destroyers, aircraft, and munitions, but he had no money to buy them under the prevailing cash-and-carry neutrality law. By late summer in 1940, as the Battle of Britain raged, Roosevelt concocted a scheme to deliver fifty old destroyers to Britain in exchange for American access to British bases in the Western Hemisphere, the first steps toward building a firm Anglo-American alliance against Hitler.

While German Luftwaffe (air force) pilots bombed Britain, Roosevelt decided to run for an unprecedented third term as president in 1940. But the presidential election, which Roosevelt won handily, provided no clear mandate for American involvement in the European war. The Republican candidate, Wendell Willkie, ridiculed by New Dealers as a "simple, barefoot Wall Street lawyer," attacked Roosevelt as a warmonger. Willkie's accusations caused the president to promise voters, "Your boys are not going to be sent into any foreign wars," a pledge counterbalanced by his repeated warnings about the threats to America posed by Nazi aggression.

Once reelected, Roosevelt maneuvered to support Britain in every way short of war. In a fireside chat shortly after Christmas 1940, he proclaimed that it was incumbent on the United States to become "the great arsenal of democracy" and send "every ounce and every ton of munitions and supplies that we can possibly spare to help the defenders who are in the front lines."

In January 1941, Roosevelt proposed the **Lend-Lease Act**, which allowed the British to obtain arms from the United States without paying cash but with the promise to reimburse the United States when the war ended. The purpose of Lend-Lease, Roosevelt proclaimed, was to defend democracy and human rights throughout the world, specifically the Four Freedoms: "freedom of speech and expression . . . freedom of every person to worship God in his own way . . . freedom from want . . . [and] freedom from fear." Isolationist opponents accused Roosevelt of concocting a "Triple A foreign policy" that would lead to war and "plow under every fourth American boy." Fiercely debated but approved by Congress, Lend-Lease started a flow of support to Britain that totaled more than $50 billion during the war, far more than all federal expenditures combined since Roosevelt had become president in 1933.

Stymied in his plans for an invasion of England, Hitler turned his massive army eastward and on June 22, 1941, sprang a surprise attack on the Soviet Union, his ally in the 1939 Nazi-Soviet nonaggression pact. Neither Roosevelt nor Churchill had any love for Joseph Stalin or communism, but they both welcomed the Soviet Union to the anti-Nazi cause. Both Western leaders understood that Hitler's attack on Russia would provide relief for the hard-pressed British. Roosevelt quickly persuaded Congress to extend Lend-Lease to the Soviet Union, beginning the shipment of millions of tons of trucks, jeeps, and other equipment that, in all, supplied about 10 percent of Russian war materiel.

As Hitler's Wehrmacht raced across the Russian plains and Nazi U-boats tried to choke off supplies to Britain and the Soviet Union, Roosevelt met with Churchill aboard a ship near Newfoundland to cement the Anglo-American alliance. In August 1941, the two leaders issued the Atlantic Charter, pledging the two nations to freedom of the seas and free trade as well as the right of national self-determination.

Japan Attacks America

Although the likelihood of war with Germany preoccupied Roosevelt, Hitler exercised a measure of restraint in directly provoking America. Japanese ambitions in Asia clashed more openly with American interests and commitments, especially in China and the Philippines. And unlike Hitler, the Japanese high command planned to attack the United States in order to pursue Japan's aspirations to rule an Asian empire it termed the

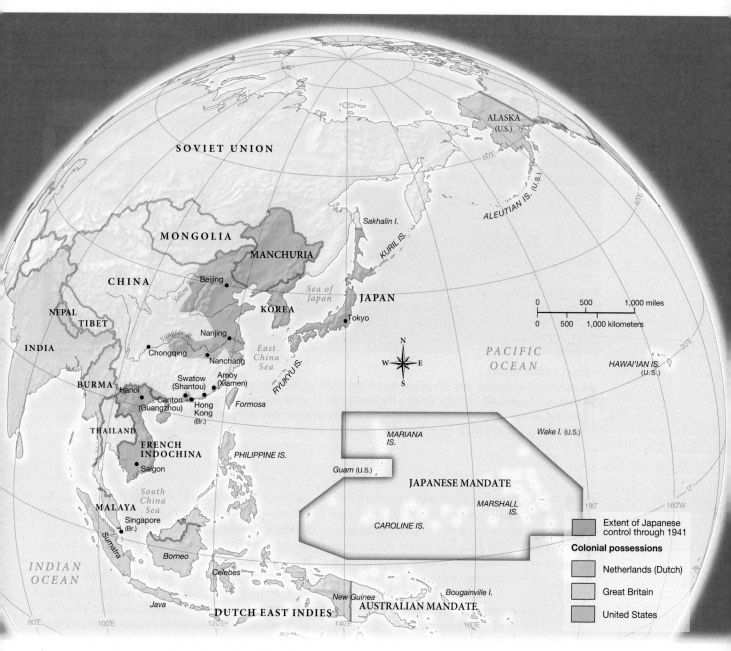

Map 25.2 Japanese Aggression through 1941
Beginning with the invasion of Manchuria in 1931, Japan sought to extend its imperialist control over most of East Asia. Japanese aggression was driven by the need for raw materials for the country's expanding industries and by the military government's devotion to martial honor.

Greater East Asia Co-Prosperity Sphere. Appealing to widespread Asian bitterness toward such white colonial powers as the British in India and Burma, the French in Indochina (now Vietnam), and the Dutch in the East Indies (now Indonesia), the Japanese campaigned to preserve "Asia for the Asians." Japan's invasion of China—which had lasted for ten years by 1941—proved that its true goal was Asia for the Japanese (Map 25.2). Japan coveted the raw materials available from China and Southeast Asia, and it ignored American demands to stop its campaign of aggression.

In 1940, Japan signaled a new phase of its imperial designs by entering a defensive alliance with Germany and Italy—the Tripartite Pact. To thwart Japanese plans to invade the Dutch East

Pearl Harbor Attack
A Japanese photographer took this picture just as the attack on Pearl Harbor began. A torpedo has exploded into the American battleship *West Virginia*, causing the huge plume of water and smoke. Other ships have already been torpedoed and are listing. Two Japanese aircraft can be seen in the upper right quadrant of the picture while Japanese submarines are invisible beneath the surface of the water. U.S. Naval History and Heritage Command Photograph.

Indies, in July 1941 Roosevelt announced a trade embargo that denied Japan access to oil, scrap iron, and other goods essential for its war machines. Roosevelt hoped the embargo would strengthen factions within Japan that opposed the militarists.

Instead, the American embargo played into the hands of Japanese militarists headed by General Hideki Tojo, who seized control of the government in October 1941 and persuaded other leaders, including Emperor Hirohito, that swift destruction of American naval bases in the Pacific would leave Japan free to follow its destiny. On December 7, 1941, 183 aircraft lifted off six Japanese carriers and attacked the U.S. Pacific Fleet at Pearl Harbor on the Hawai'ian island of Oahu. The devastating surprise attack sank all of the fleet's battleships, killed more than 2,400 Americans, and almost crippled U.S. war-making capacity in the Pacific. Luckily for the United States, Japanese pilots failed to destroy oil storage facilities at Pearl Harbor or any of the nation's aircraft carriers, which happened to be at sea during the attack.

The Japanese scored a stunning tactical victory at Pearl Harbor, but in the long run the attack proved a colossal blunder. The victory made many Japanese commanders overconfident about their military prowess. Worse for the Japanese, Americans instantly united in their desire to fight and avenge the attack. Roosevelt vowed that "this form of treachery shall never endanger us again." On December 8, Congress endorsed the president's call for a declaration of war. Both Hitler and Mussolini declared war against America on December 11, bringing the United States into all-out war with the Axis powers in both Europe and Asia.

REVIEW   How did Roosevelt attempt to balance American isolationism with the military aggression of Germany and Japan in the late 1930s and early 1940s?

Bombing of Pearl Harbor, December 7, 1941

Oahu
Maui
Pearl Harbor
Hawai'i

East Loch
Ford Island
U.S. Naval Air Station
Pearl Harbor

Sunk
Damaged
Undamaged

▶ Mobilizing for War

The time had come, Roosevelt announced, for the prescriptions of "Dr. New Deal" to be replaced by the stronger medicines of "Dr. Win-the-War." Military and civilian leaders rushed to secure the nation against possible attacks, causing Americans with Japanese ancestry to be stigmatized and sent to internment camps. Roosevelt and his advisers lost no time enlisting millions of Americans in the armed forces to bring the isolationist-era military to fighting strength for a two-front war. The war emergency also required economic mobilization unparalleled in the nation's history. As Dr. Win-the-War, Roosevelt set aside the New Deal goal of reform and plunged headlong into transforming the American economy into the world's greatest military machine, thereby achieving full employment and economic recovery, goals that had eluded the New Deal.

Home-Front Security

Shortly after declaring war against the United States, Hitler dispatched German submarines to hunt American ships along the Atlantic coast, where Paul Tibbets and other American pilots tried to destroy them. The U-boats had devastating success for about eight months, sinking hundreds of U.S. ships and threatening to disrupt the Lend-Lease lifeline to Britain and the Soviet Union. But by mid-1942, the U.S. Navy had chased German submarines into the mid-Atlantic.

Within the continental United States, Americans remained sheltered from the chaos and destruction the war brought to hundreds of millions in Europe and Asia. Nevertheless, the government worried constantly about espionage and internal subversion. Posters warned Americans that "Loose lips sink ships" and "Enemy agents are always near; if you don't talk, they won't hear." The campaign for patriotic vigilance focused on German and Japanese foes, but Americans of Japanese descent became targets of official and popular persecution because of Pearl Harbor and long-standing racial prejudice against people of Asian descent.

About 320,000 people of Japanese ancestry lived in U.S. territory in 1941, two-thirds of them in Hawai'i, where they largely escaped wartime persecution because they were essential and valued members of society. On the mainland, however, Japanese Americans were a tiny minority—even along the West Coast, where most of them worked on farms and in small businesses. Although an official military survey concluded that Japanese Americans posed no danger, popular hostility fueled a campaign to round up all mainland Japanese Americans—two-thirds of them U.S. citizens. "A Jap's a Jap. . . . It makes no difference whether he is an American citizen or not," one official declared.

The Road to War: The United States and World War II

1931 Japan invades Manchuria.

1933 Franklin D. Roosevelt becomes U.S. president. Adolf Hitler becomes German chancellor.

1935–1937 Congress passes series of neutrality acts to protect United States from involvement in world conflicts.

1936 **March.** Nazi troops invade Rhineland, violating Treaty of Versailles.

July. Civil war breaks out in Spain.

Mussolini's fascist Italian regime conquers Ethiopia.

November. Roosevelt reelected president.

1937 **December.** Japanese troops capture Nanjing, China.

1938 Hitler annexes Austria.

September 29. Hitler accepts offer of "appeasement" in Munich from British prime minister Neville Chamberlain.

1939 **March.** Hitler invades Czechoslovakia.

August. Hitler and Stalin sign Nazi-Soviet nonaggression pact.

September 1. Germany invades Poland, beginning World War II. United States and Britain conclude cash-and-carry agreement for arms sales.

1940 **Spring.** German blitzkrieg smashes through Denmark, Norway, Belgium, Luxembourg, Netherlands, and northern France.

Japan signs Tripartite Pact with Germany and Italy.

May–June. German armies flank Maginot Line. British and French evacuated from Dunkirk. France surrenders to Germany.

Summer/Fall. Germany conducts bombing campaign against England.

November. Roosevelt wins third term as president. Royal Air Force wins Battle of Britain.

1941 **March.** Congress approves Lend-Lease Act, making arms available to Britain.

June 22. Hitler invades Soviet Union.

August. Roosevelt and Churchill issue Atlantic Charter.

October. Militarists led by Hideki Tojo take over Japan.

December 7. Japanese bomb Pearl Harbor. United States declares war on Japan.

December 11. Germany and Italy declare war on United States.

Japanese Internment

Determined that the bombing of Pearl Harbor would not be followed by more sneak attacks, military and political leaders on the West Coast targeted persons of Japanese descent—aliens and citizens alike—as potential saboteurs.

DOCUMENT 1
General John DeWitt, Final Recommendations of the Commanding General, Western Defense Command and Fourth Army, Submitted to the Secretary of War, 1942

Early in 1942, General John DeWitt, commander of the Western Defense Command, persuaded President Franklin Roosevelt to round up Japanese living in the United States and confine them to relocation camps for the duration of the war. DeWitt's recommendation expressed concern for military security and appealed to racist conceptions long used to curb Asian immigration. Japanese Americans and their supporters fought the internment order in the courts as a violation of fundamental constitutional rights, an argument rejected during the war by the U.S. Supreme Court.

February 14, 1942
Memorandum for the Secretary of War

Subject: Evacuation of Japanese and Other Subversive Persons from the Pacific Coast. . .
Brief Estimate of the Situation.
1) . . . The following are possible and probable enemy activities: . . .
(a) Naval attack on shipping on coastal waters;
(b) Naval attack on coastal cities and vital installations;
(c) Air raids on vital installations, particularly within two hundred miles of the coast;
(d) Sabotage of vital installations throughout the Western Defense Command. . . .

Hostile Naval and air raids will be assisted by enemy agents signaling from the coastline and the vicinity thereof; and by supplying and otherwise assisting enemy vessels and by sabotage. . . .

In the war in which we are now engaged racial affinities are not severed by migration. The Japanese race is an enemy race and while many second and third generation Japanese born on United States soil, possessed of United States citizenship, have become "Americanized," the racial strains are undiluted. To conclude otherwise is to expect that children born of white parents on Japanese soil sever all racial affinity and become loyal Japanese subjects, ready to fight and, if necessary, to die for Japan in a war against the nation of their parents. . . .

It, therefore, follows that along the vital Pacific Coast over 112,000 potential enemies, of Japanese extraction, are at large today. There are indications that these are organized and ready for concerted action at a favorable opportunity. The very fact that no sabotage has taken place to date is a disturbing and confirming indication that such action will be taken.

Source: *Final Recommendations*, report by General John Lesesne DeWitt to the United States Secretary of War, February 14, 1942.

On February 19, 1942, Roosevelt issued Executive Order 9066, which authorized sending all Americans of Japanese descent to ten makeshift **internment camps** located in remote areas of the West and South (Map 25.3). Allowed little time to sell or secure their properties, Japanese Americans lost homes and businesses worth about $400 million and lived out the war penned in by barbed wire and armed guards. (See "Analyzing Historical Evidence," above.) Although several thousand Japanese Americans served with distinction in the U.S. armed forces and no case of subversion by a Japanese American was ever uncovered, the Supreme Court, in its 1944 *Korematsu* decision, upheld Executive Order 9066's blatant violation of constitutional rights as justified by "military necessity."

Building a Citizen Army

In 1940, Roosevelt encouraged Congress to pass the **Selective Service Act** to register men of military age who would be subject to a draft if the need arose. More than 6,000 local draft boards registered more than 30 million men and, when the war came, rapidly inducted them into military service. In all, more than 16 million men and women served in uniform during the war, two-thirds of them draftees, mostly young men. Women were barred from combat duty, but they worked at nearly every noncombatant task, eroding traditional barriers to women's military service.

The Selective Service Act prohibited discrimination "on account of race or color," and

DOCUMENT 2
Charles Kikuchi, Prison Camp Diary, 1941–1942

Charles Kikuchi, a student at the University of California at Berkeley, sought in his prison camp diary to make sense of the internment and to judge where it would lead.

December 7, 1941
Berkeley, California

Pearl Harbor. We are at war! Jesus Christ, the Japs bombed Hawai'i and the entire fleet has been sunk. I just can't believe it. I don't know what in the hell is going to happen to us, but we will all be called into the Army right away.

. . . The next five years will determine the future of the Nisei [Japanese American citizens]. They are now at the crossroads. Will they be able to take it or will they go under? If we are ever going to prove our Americanism, this is the time. The Anti-Jap feeling is bound to rise to hysterical heights, and it is most likely that the Nisei will be included as Japs. I wanted to go to San Francisco tonight, but Pierre says I am crazy. He says it's best we stick on campus. In any event, we can't remain on the fence, and a positive approach must be taken if we are to have a place in fulfilling the Promise of America. I think the U.S. is in danger of going Fascist too, or maybe Socialist. . . .

I don't know what to think or do. Everybody is in a daze.
April 30, 1942, Berkeley

Today is the day that we are going to get kicked out of Berkeley. It certainly is degrading. . . .

I'm supposed to see my family at Tanforan as Jack told me to give the same family number. I wonder how it is going to be living with them as I haven't done this for years and years? I should have gone over to San Francisco and evacuated with them, but I had a last final to take. I understand that we are going to live in the horse stalls. I hope that the Army has the courtesy to remove the manure first. . . .

July 14, 1942

Marie, Ann, Mitch, Jimmy, Jack, and myself got into a long discussion about how much democracy meant to us as individuals. Mitch says that he would even go in the army and die for it, in spite of the fact that he knew he would be kept down. Marie said that although democracy was not perfect, it was the only system that offered any hope for a future, if we could fulfill its destinies. Jack was a little more skeptical. He even suggested that we [could] be in such grave danger that we would then realize that we were losing something. Where this point was he could not say. I said that this was what happened in France and they lost all. Jimmy suggested that the colored races of the world had reason to feel despair and mistrust the white man because of the past experiences. . . .

In reviewing the four months here, the chief value I got out of this forced evacuation was the strengthening of the family bonds. I never knew my family before this and this was the first chance that I have had to really get acquainted.

Source: Excerpts (pp. 43, 51, 183, 252) from *The Kikuchi Diary: Chronicle from an American Concentration Camp*, edited by John Modell. Copyright © 1973 by the Board of Trustees of the University of Illinois.

Questions for Analysis

Analyze the Evidence: How does Charles Kikuchi's diary describe the meaning of internment for the detainees?

Consider the Context: What explains General DeWitt's insistence on evacuating the Japanese after he received the report of military investigators that no acts of sabotage had occurred?

Recognize Viewpoints: How did the internment camp experience influence the detainees' attitudes about their identity as Americans of Japanese descent?

Ask Historical Questions: How did Americans and the American government treat minority citizens during World War II?

▲ WRA relocation camp

☐ States with more than 1,000 internees

Map 25.3 Western Relocation Authority Centers

Responding to prejudice and fear of sabotage, President Roosevelt authorized the relocation of all Americans of Japanese descent in 1942. Taken from their homes in the cities and farmland of the far West, more than 120,000 Japanese Americans were confined in camps scattered as far east as the Mississippi River.

VISUAL ACTIVITY

Japanese Internment

This photo shows Japanese Americans who were rounded up and confined to the horse barns and race-track at Santa Anita, California, before being shipped out to internment camps throughout the western states. The imprisoned people on the left are saying good-bye to their friends seen waving from the windows of the train shown on the right, which was taking them to internment camps. Corbis.

READING THE IMAGE: Why were these women, men, and children surrounded by high barbed-wire fences? What kinds of connections does the photo depict among the Japanese Americans at Santa Anita?

CONNECTIONS: How did World War II influence racial discrimination and civil rights in the United States?

almost a million African American men and women donned uniforms, as did half a million Mexican Americans, 25,000 Native Americans, and 13,000 Chinese Americans. The racial insults and discrimination suffered by all people of color made some soldiers ask, as a Mexican American GI did on his way to the European front, "Why fight for America when you have not been treated as an American?" Only black Americans were trained in segregated camps, confined in segregated barracks, and assigned to segregated units.

Most black Americans were consigned to manual labor, and relatively few served in combat until late in 1944, when the need for military manpower in Europe intensified. Then, as General George Patton told black soldiers in a tank unit in Normandy, "I don't care what color you are, so long as you go up there and kill those Kraut sonsabitches."

Homosexuals also served in the armed forces, although in much smaller numbers than black Americans. Allowed to serve as long as their sexual preferences remained covert, gay Americans, like other minorities, sought to demonstrate their worth under fire. "I was super-patriotic," a gay combat veteran recalled. Another gay GI remarked, "Who in the hell is going to worry about [homosexuality]" in the midst of the life-or-death realities of war?

African American Machine Gunners

Soldiers William Adam Leake and Adam Parham, shown here in May 1944, were among the first African American combat troops in the Pacific theater. They and thousands of other black soldiers fought in the Bougainville campaign, which continued until August 1945, to retake the Japanese-occupied portions of the Solomon Islands, just north of Australia. The Granger Collection, New York.

Conversion to a War Economy

In 1940, the American economy remained mired in the depression. Nearly one worker in seven was still unemployed, factories operated far below their productive capacity, and the total federal budget was less than $10 billion. Shortly after the attack on Pearl Harbor, Roosevelt announced the goal of converting the economy to produce "overwhelming . . . , crushing superiority of equipment in any theater of the world war." Factories were converted to assembling tanks and airplanes, and production soared to record levels. By the end of the war, jobs exceeded workers, plants operated at full capacity, and the federal budget topped $100 billion.

To organize and oversee this tidal wave of military production, Roosevelt called upon business leaders to come to Washington and, for the token payment of a dollar a year, head new government agencies such as the War Production Board, which set production priorities and pushed for maximum output. Contracts flowed to large corporations, often on a basis that guaranteed their profits. During the first half of 1942, the government issued contracts worth more than the entire gross national product in 1941.

Booming wartime employment swelled union membership. To speed production, the government asked unions to pledge not to strike. Despite the relentless pace of work, union members mostly kept their no-strike pledge, with the important exception of members of the United Mine Workers, who walked out of the coal mines in 1943, demanding a pay hike and earning the enmity of many Americans.

Overall, conversion to war production achieved Roosevelt's ambitious goal of "crushing superiority" in military goods. At a total cost of $304 billion (equivalent to about $4 trillion today) during the war, the nation produced an avalanche of military equipment, more than double the combined production of Germany, Japan, and Italy (Figure 25.1). This outpouring of military goods supplied not only U.S. forces but also America's allies, giving tangible meaning to Roosevelt's pledge to make America the "arsenal of democracy."

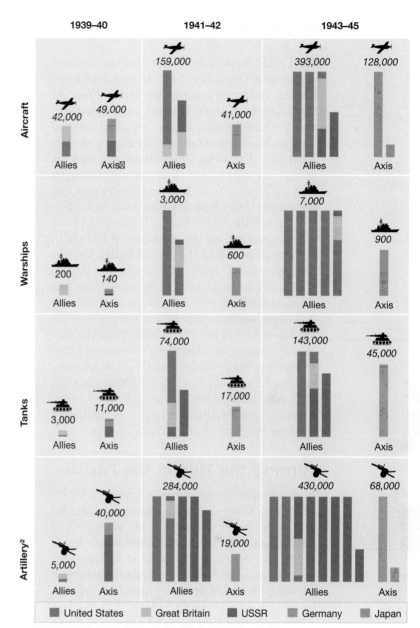

FIGURE 25.1   Global Comparison: Weapons Production by the Axis and Allied Powers during World War II
U.S. weapons dominated the air and the sea during World War II. Together, the three Allied powers produced about three times as many aircraft and five to eight times as many warships as the two Axis powers. The Soviet Union led the other Allies in the production of tanks and artillery. What does the chronology of weapons production suggest about the kind of warfare emphasized by each belligerent nation and the course of the war?

REVIEW   How did the Roosevelt administration mobilize the human and industrial resources necessary to fight a two-front war?

► Fighting Back

The United States confronted a daunting military challenge in December 1941. The attack on Pearl Harbor destroyed much of its Pacific Fleet. In the Atlantic, Hitler's U-boats sank American ships, while German armies occupied most of western Europe and relentlessly advanced eastward into the Soviet Union. Roosevelt and his military advisers believed that defeating Germany took top priority. To achieve that victory required preventing Hitler from defeating America's allies, Britain and the Soviet Union. If they fell, Hitler would command all the resources of Europe in a probable assault on the United States. To fight back effectively against Germany and Japan, the United States had to coordinate military and political strategy with its allies and muster all its human and economic assets. Victory over the Japanese fleet at the Battle of Midway, the successful elimination of Germany's menace to Allied shipping in the prolonged Battle of the Atlantic, and the Allied assault on North Africa and then Italy established Allied naval superiority in the Atlantic and Pacific and began to challenge German domination of southern Europe.

Turning the Tide in the Pacific

In the Pacific theater, Japan's leading military strategist, Admiral Isoroku Yamamoto, believed that if his forces did not quickly conquer and secure the territories they targeted, Japan would eventually lose the war because of America's far greater resources. Swiftly, the Japanese assaulted American airfields in the Philippines and captured U.S. outposts on Guam and Wake Island. After capturing Singapore and Burma, Japan sought to complete its domination of the southern Pacific with an attack in January 1942 on the American stronghold in the Philippines (see Map 25.5). American defenders surrendered to the Japanese in May. The Japanese victors sent captured American and Filipino soldiers on the infamous Bataan Death March to a concentration camp, causing thousands to die. By the summer of 1942, the Japanese had conquered the Dutch East Indies and were poised to strike Australia and New Zealand.

In the spring of 1942, U.S. forces launched a major two-pronged counteroffensive that military officials hoped would reverse Japanese advances. Forces led by General Douglas MacArthur, commander of the U.S. armed forces in the Pacific theater, moved north from Australia and eventually attacked the Japanese in the Philippines. Far more decisively, Admiral Chester W. Nimitz sailed his battle fleet west from Hawai'i to retake Japanese-held islands in the southern and mid-Pacific. On May 7–8, 1942, in the Coral Sea just north of Australia, the American fleet and carrier-based warplanes defeated a Japanese armada that was sailing around the coast of New Guinea.

Nimitz then learned from an intelligence intercept that the Japanese were massing an invasion force aimed at Midway Island, an outpost guarding the Hawai'ian Islands. Nimitz maneuvered his carriers and cruisers to surprise the Japanese at the Battle of Midway. In a furious battle that raged on June 3–6, American ships and planes delivered a devastating blow to the Japanese navy. The **Battle of Midway** reversed the balance of naval power in the Pacific and put the Japanese at a disadvantage for the rest of the war. Japan managed to build only six more large aircraft carriers during the war, while the United States launched dozens, proving the wisdom of Yamamoto's prediction. But the Japanese still occupied and defended the many places they had conquered.

The Campaign in Europe

After Pearl Harbor, Hitler's eastern-front armies marched ever deeper into the Soviet Union while his western-front forces prepared to invade Britain. As in World War I, the Germans attempted to starve the British into submission by destroying their seaborne lifeline. In 1941 and 1942, they sank Allied ships faster than new ones could be built. Overall, the U-boat campaign sank 4,700 merchant vessels and almost 200 warships and killed 40,000 Allied seamen.

Until mid-1943, the outcome of the war in the Atlantic remained in doubt. Then, newly invented radar detectors and production of sufficient destroyer escorts for merchant vessels allowed the Allies to prey upon the lurking U-boats. After suffering a 75 percent casualty rate among U-boat crews, Hitler withdrew German submarines from the North Atlantic in late May 1943, allowing thousands of American supply ships to cross the Atlantic unimpeded. Winning the Battle of the Atlantic allowed the United States to continue to supply its British and Soviet allies for the duration of the war and to reduce the imminent threat of a German invasion of Britain.

The most important strategic questions confronting the United States and its allies were

Flamethrower in Combat in the Solomon Islands
American soldiers used flamethrowers in both the Pacific and European theaters. They
were especially effective against enemy soldiers dug into bunkers that were difficult to
penetrate by rifle or machine-gun fire. The Marine shown here, fighting in the Solomon
Islands in 1943, carried on his back canisters of jellied gasoline and compressed air
that were combined and projected through the gunlike machine. Soldiers: National Archives
photo no. 111-SC-233458; flamethrower: National Museum of American History, Smithsonian Institution, USA/
Bridgeman Images.

when and where to open a second front against
the Nazis. Stalin demanded that America and
Britain mount an immediate and massive assault
across the English Channel into western France
to force Hitler to divert his armies from the
eastern front and relieve the pressure on the
Soviet Union. Churchill and Roosevelt instead
delayed opening a second front, allowing the
Germans and the Soviets to slug it out. This
drawn-out conflict weakened both the Nazis and
the Communists and made an eventual Allied
attack on western France more likely to succeed.
Churchill and Roosevelt decided to strike first

in North Africa to help secure Allied control of
the Mediterranean.

In October and November 1942, British forces
at El-Alamein in Egypt halted German general
Erwin Rommel's drive to capture the Suez Canal,
Britain's lifeline to the oil of the Middle East and
to British colonies in India and South Asia (see
Map 25.4). In November, an American army under
General Dwight D. Eisenhower landed far to the
west, in French Morocco. Propelled by American
tank units commanded by General George Patton,
the Allied armies defeated the Germans in North
Africa in May 1943. The North African campaign

VISUAL ACTIVITY

North African Campaign
The Allied campaign to clear Axis forces from North Africa involved highly mobile tanks on both sides. Here relatively fast-moving American M-10 tank destroyers—widely used during World War II—roll through a Tunisian village in 1943. The open tops gave crewmen excellent visibility to spot enemy forces but also made them vulnerable to attack. Corbis.
READING THE IMAGE: The soldiers do not appear to be interested in the village they are passing through. Why not? What relationship do the soldiers appear to assume the civilian villagers have with the Germans?
CONNECTIONS: How did the use of tanks contribute to the Allies' strategic goals in the North African campaign?

pushed the Germans out of Africa, made the Mediterranean safe for Allied shipping, and opened the door for an Allied invasion of Italy.

In January 1943, while the North African campaign was still under way, Roosevelt and Churchill met in Casablanca and announced that they would accept nothing less than the "unconditional surrender" of the Axis powers, ruling out peace negotiations. They concluded that they should capitalize on their success in North Africa and strike against Italy, consigning the Soviet Union to continue to bear the brunt of the Nazi war machine.

In July 1943, American and British forces landed in Sicily. Soon afterward, Mussolini was deposed in Italy, ending the reign of Italian fascism. Quickly, the Allies invaded the mainland, and the Italian government surrendered unconditionally. The Germans responded by rushing reinforcements to Italy, turning the Allies' Italian campaign into a series of battles to liberate Italy from German occupation.

German troops dug into strong fortifications and fought to defend every inch of Italy's rugged terrain. Allied forces continued to battle against stubborn German defenses for the remainder of the war, making the Italian campaign the war's deadliest for American infantrymen. One soldier wrote that his buddies "died like butchered swine."

REVIEW How did the United States seek to counter the Japanese in the Pacific and the Germans in Europe?

▶ The Wartime Home Front

The war effort mobilized Americans as never before. Factories churned out ever more bombs, bullets, tanks, ships, and airplanes, which workers rushed to assemble, leaving their farms and small towns and congregating in cities. Women took jobs with wrenches and welding torches, boosting the nation's workforce and violating traditional notions that a woman's place was in the home rather than on the assembly line. Despite rationing and shortages, unprecedented government expenditures for war production brought prosperity to many Americans after years of depression-era poverty. Although Americans in uniform risked their lives on battlefields in Europe and Asia, Americans on the U.S. mainland enjoyed complete immunity from foreign attack—in sharp contrast to their Soviet and British allies. The wartime ideology that contrasted Allied support for human rights with Axis tyranny provided justification for the many sacrifices Americans were required to make in support of the military effort. It also established a standard of basic human equality that became a potent weapon in the campaign for equal rights at home and in condemning atrocities such as the Holocaust perpetrated by the Nazis.

Women and Families, Guns and Butter

Millions of American women gladly took their places on assembly lines in defense industries. At the start of the war, about a quarter of adult women worked outside the home, but few women worked in factories, except for textile mills and sewing industries. But wartime mobilization of the economy and the enlistment of millions of men in the armed forces left factories begging for women workers.

Government advertisements urged women to take industrial jobs by assuring them that their household chores had prepared them for work on the "Victory Line." One billboard proclaimed, "If you've sewed buttons, or made buttonholes, on a [sewing] machine, you can learn to do spot welding on airplane parts." Millions of women responded. Advertisers often referred to a woman who worked in a war industry as "Rosie the Riveter," a popular wartime term. By the end of the war, women working outside the home numbered 50 percent more than in

VISUAL ACTIVITY

Riveting Rosies
Dora Miles (left) and Dorothy Johnson (right) were among the millions of women (nicknamed "Rosie the Riveter") who flocked to work in war industries at jobs formerly held by men. Like many other women war workers, Miles and Johnson helped build airplanes. Here they are depicted riveting the frame of an aircraft at a plant in Long Beach, California. Library of Congress, 8e01288.

READING THE IMAGE: How does the work Miles and Johnson are doing compare to the conventional work routines of women before the war? What does the photo suggest about the relationship between Miles (driving the rivet into a hole) and Johnson (smashing the end of the rivet snug against the airframe)?

CONNECTIONS: What contributions did American women make to the war effort?

1939. Contributing to the war effort also paid off in wages. A Kentucky woman remembered her job at a munitions plant, where she earned "the fabulous sum of $32 a week. To us it was an absolute miracle. Before that we made nothing." Although men were paid an average of $54 for comparable wartime work, women accepted the pay differential and welcomed their chance to earn wages and help win the war at the same time.

The majority of married women remained at home, occupied with domestic chores and child care. But they, too, supported the war effort, planting Victory Gardens, saving tin cans and newspapers for recycling into war materiel, and buying war bonds. Many families scrimped to cope with the 30 percent inflation during the war, but men and women in manufacturing industries enjoyed wages that grew twice as fast as inflation.

The war influenced how all families spent their earnings. Buying a new washing machine or car was out of the question since factories that formerly built them now made military goods. Many other consumer goods—such as tires, gasoline, shoes, and meat—were rationed at home to meet military needs overseas. But most Americans readily found things to buy, including movie tickets, cosmetics, and music recordings.

The wartime prosperity and abundance enjoyed by most Americans contrasted with the experiences of their hard-pressed allies. Personal consumption fell by 22 percent in Britain, and food output plummeted to just one-third of prewar levels in the Soviet Union, creating widespread hunger and even starvation. Few went hungry in the United States as farm output grew 25 percent annually during the war, providing a cornucopia of food for export to the Allies.

The Double V Campaign

Fighting against Nazi Germany and its ideology of Aryan racial supremacy, Americans confronted extensive racial prejudice in their own country. The *Pittsburgh Courier*, a leading black newspaper, asserted that the wartime emergency called for a **Double V campaign** seeking "victory over our enemies at home and victory over our enemies on the battlefields abroad." As a Mississippi-born African American combat veteran of the Pacific theater recalled, "We had two wars to fight: prejudice . . . and those Japs."

In 1941, black organizations demanded that the federal government require companies receiving defense contracts to integrate their workforces. A. Philip Randolph, head of the Brotherhood of Sleeping Car Porters, promised that 100,000 African American marchers would descend on Washington if the president did not eliminate discrimination in defense industries. Roosevelt decided to risk offending his white allies in the South and in unions, and he issued Executive Order 8802 in mid-1941. It authorized the Committee on Fair Employment Practices to investigate and prevent racial discrimination in employment.

Progress came slowly, however. In 1940, nine out of ten black Americans lived below the federal poverty line, and those who worked earned an average of just 39 percent of whites' wages. In search of better jobs and living conditions, 5.5 million black Americans migrated from the South to centers of industrial production in the North and West, making a majority of African Americans city dwellers for the first time in U.S. history. Severe labor shortages and government fair employment standards opened assembly-line jobs in defense plants to African Americans, causing black unemployment to drop by 80 percent during the war. But more jobs did not mean equal pay for blacks. The average income of black families rose during the war, but by the end of the conflict it still stood at only half of what white families earned.

Blacks' migration to defense jobs intensified racial antagonisms, which boiled over in the hot summer of 1943, when 242 race riots erupted in 47 cities. The worst mayhem occurred in Detroit, where a long-simmering conflict between whites and blacks over racially segregated housing ignited into a race war. In two days of violence, twenty-five blacks and nine whites were killed, and scores more were injured.

Racial violence created the impetus for the Double V campaign, officially supported by the National Association for the Advancement of Colored People (NAACP), which asserted black Americans' demands for the rights and privileges enjoyed by all other Americans—demands reinforced by the Allies' wartime ideology of freedom and democracy. While the NAACP focused on court challenges to segregation, a new organization founded in 1942, the Congress of Racial Equality, organized picketing and sit-ins against racially segregated restaurants and theaters. Still, the Double V campaign achieved only limited success against racial discrimination during the war.

Wartime Politics and the 1944 Election

Americans rallied around the war effort in unprecedented unity. In June 1944, Congress recognized the sacrifices made by millions of veterans and unanimously passed the landmark **GI Bill of Rights**, which gave military veterans government funds for education, housing, and health care, as well as providing loans to start businesses and buy homes. The GI Bill put the financial resources of the federal government behind the abstract goals of freedom and democracy for which veterans were fighting, and it empowered millions of GIs to better themselves and their families after the war.

After twelve turbulent years in the White House, Roosevelt was exhausted and gravely ill with heart disease, but he was determined to remain president until the war ended. His poor health made the selection of a vice presidential candidate unusually important. Convinced that many Americans had soured on liberal reform, Roosevelt chose Senator Harry S. Truman of

Principal German concentration and extermination camp

The Holocaust, 1933–1945

Missouri as his running mate. A reliable party man from a southern border state, Truman satisfied urban Democratic leaders while not worrying white southerners who were nervous about challenges to racial segregation.

The Republicans, confident of a strong conservative upsurge in the nation, nominated as their presidential candidate the governor of New York, Thomas E. Dewey, who had made his reputation as a tough crime fighter. In the 1944 presidential campaign, Roosevelt's failing health alarmed many observers, but his frailty was outweighed by Americans' unwillingness to change presidents in the midst of the war and by Dewey's failure to persuade most voters that the New Deal was a creeping socialist menace. Voters gave Roosevelt a 53.5 percent majority, his narrowest presidential victory, ensuring his continued leadership as Dr. Win-the-War.

Reaction to the Holocaust

Since the 1930s, the Nazis had persecuted Jews in Germany and every German-occupied terri-

Mass Execution of Jewish Women and Children
On October 14, 1942, Jewish women and children from the village of Mizocz in present-day Ukraine were herded into a ravine, forced to undress and lie facedown, and then shot at point-blank range by German officials. To centralize such executions, the Nazis built death camps, where they systematically slaughtered millions of Jews and other "undesirables." United States Holocaust Memorial Museum.

Nazi Anti-Semitism and the Atomic Bomb

During the 1930s, Jewish physicists fled Adolf Hitler's fanatical anti-Semitic persecutions and came to the United States, where they played a leading role in the research and development of the atomic bomb. In this way, Nazi anti-Semitism contributed to making the United States the first atomic power.

One of Germany's greatest scientists, Albert Einstein, won the Nobel Prize for physics in 1921. Among other things, Einstein's work demonstrated that the nuclei of atoms of physical matter stored almost inconceivable quantities of energy. A fellow scientist praised Einstein's discoveries as "the greatest achievements in the history of human thought." But Einstein was a Jew, and his ideas were ridiculed by German anti-Semites. A German physicist who had won the Nobel Prize in 1905 attacked Einstein for his "Jewish nonsense," which was "hostile to the German spirit." Einstein wrote to a friend, "Anti-Semitism is strong here [in Berlin] and political reaction is violent." Einstein's associates warned him that the anti-Semites had targeted him for assassination.

In his manifesto, *Mein Kampf*, Hitler proclaimed that Jews were "a foreign people," "inferior beings,"

the "personification of the devil," "a race of dialectical liars," "parasites," and "eternal bloodsuckers," who had the "clear aim of ruining the . . . white race." Hitler's rantings attracted a huge audience in Germany, and his personal Nazi army, which numbered 400,000 by 1933, terrorized and murdered anyone who got in the way.

In January 1933, just weeks before Franklin Roosevelt's inauguration as president of the United States, Hitler became chancellor of Germany on a tidal wave of popular support for his Nazi Party. Within months, he abolished freedom of speech and assembly, outlawed all political opposition, and exercised absolute dictatorial power. On April 7, Hitler announced the Law for the Restoration of the Professional Civil Service, which stipulated that "civil servants of non-Aryan descent must retire." A non-Aryan was defined as any person "descended from non-Aryan, especially Jewish, parents or grandparents." The law meant that scientists of Jewish descent who worked for state institutions, including universities, no longer had jobs. About 1,600 intellectuals in Germany immediately lost their livelihood and their future in Hitler's Reich. Among them were about a

quarter of the physicists in Germany, including Einstein and ten other Nobel Prize winners. The Nazis' anti-Semitism laws forced many leading scientists to leave Germany. Between 1933 and 1941, Einstein and about 100 other Jewish physicists joined hundreds of Jewish intellectuals in an exodus from Nazi Germany to the safety of the United States.

The refugee physicists scrambled to find positions at American universities and research institutes that would allow them to continue their studies. The accelerating pace of research in physics during the 1930s raised the possibility that a way might exist to release the phenomenal energy bottled up in atomic nuclei, perhaps even to create a superbomb. Einstein and other scientists considered that possibility remote. But many worried that if scientists loyal to Germany discovered a way to harness nuclear energy, Hitler would have the power to spread Nazi terror throughout the world. The refugee physicists asked Einstein to write a letter to President Roosevelt explaining the military and political threats posed by the latest research in nuclear physics.

In early October 1939, as Hitler's blitzkrieg swept through Poland,

tory, causing many Jews to seek asylum beyond Hitler's reach. (See "Beyond America's Borders," above.) Thousands of Jews sought to immigrate to the United States, but 82 percent of Americans opposed admitting them, and they were turned away. In 1942, numerous reports reached the United States that Hitler was sending Jews, Gypsies, religious and political dissenters, homosexuals, and others to concentration camps, where old people, children, and others deemed too weak

to work were systematically killed and cremated, while the able-bodied were put to work at slave labor until they died of starvation and abuse. Other camps were devoted almost exclusively to murdering and cremating Jews. Despite reports of the brutal slave labor and death camps, U.S. officials refused to grant asylum to Jewish refugees. Most Americans, including top officials, believed that reports were exaggerated. Only 152,000 of Europe's millions of Jews managed

Roosevelt received Einstein's letter and immediately grasped the central point, exclaiming, "What you are after is to see that the Nazis don't blow us up." Roosevelt quickly convened a small group of distinguished American scientists, who convinced the president to mount an all-out effort to learn whether an atomic bomb could be built and, if so, to build it. Only weeks before the Japanese attack on Pearl Harbor, Roosevelt decided to launch the Manhattan Project, the top-secret atomic bomb program.

Leading scientists from the United States and Britain responded to the government's appeal: "No matter what you do with the rest of your life, nothing will be as important to the future of the World as your work on this Project right now." Many of the most creative, productive, and irreplaceable scientists involved in the Manhattan Project were physicists who had fled Nazi Germany. Their efforts had brought the possibility of an atomic bomb to Roosevelt's attention. Having personally experienced Nazi anti-Semitism, they understood what was at stake—a world in which either Hitler had the atomic bomb or his enemies did.

In the end, Hitler's scientists failed to develop an atomic bomb, and Germany surrendered before the American bomb was ready to be used. But the Manhattan Project succeeded, as Paul Tibbets proved over Hiroshima, Japan, on August 6, 1945. After the war, Leo Szilard, a leader

Einstein Becomes a U.S. Citizen
Nazi anti-Semitism caused Albert Einstein to renounce his German citizenship, immigrate to the United States, and—in the 1940 naturalization ceremony recorded in this photo—officially become an American citizen. He is joined here by his secretary, Helen Dukas (right), and his stepdaughter, Margot Einstein (left). American Stock Archive/Getty Images.

among the refugee physicists, remarked, "If Congress knew the true history of the atomic energy project . . . it would create a special medal to be given to meddling foreigners for distinguished services."

Questions for Analysis

Summarize the Argument: How did German anti-Semitism contribute to the United States' willingness to build and employ the atomic bomb?

Analyze the Evidence: Why did Jewish physicists leave Germany for the United States?

Consider the Context: Why were German Jewish scientists accepted into American society at a time when Japanese Americans were isolated in internment camps?

Ask Historical Questions: In what ways were the United States' development and use of the atomic bomb "important to the future of the World"?

to gain refuge in the United States before America's entry into the war. Afterward, the number of Jewish refugees dropped to just 2,400 by 1944.

Desperate to stem the killing, the World Jewish Congress appealed to the Allies to bomb the death camps and the railroad tracks leading to them in order to hamper the killing and block further shipments of victims. Intent on achieving military victory as soon as possible, the Allies repeatedly turned down such bombing requests, arguing that the air forces could not spare resources from their military missions.

The nightmare of the **Holocaust** was all too real. When Russian troops arrived at Auschwitz in Poland in January 1945, they found emaciated prisoners, skeletal corpses, gas chambers, pits filled with human ashes, and loot the Nazis had stripped from the dead, including hair, gold fillings, and false teeth. At last, the truth about the Holocaust began to be known beyond the

Germans who had perpetrated and tolerated these atrocities and the men, women, and children who had succumbed to the genocide. By then, it was too late for the 11 million civilian victims—mostly Jews—of the Nazis' crimes against humanity.

> **REVIEW** How did the war influence American society?

▶ Toward Unconditional Surrender

By February 1943, Soviet defenders had finally defeated the massive German offensive against Stalingrad, turning the tide of the war in Europe. After gargantuan sacrifices in fighting that had lasted for eighteen months, the Red Army forced Hitler's Wehrmacht to turn back toward the west. In the Pacific, the Allies had halted the expansion of the Japanese empire but now had the deadly task of dislodging Japanese defenders from the outposts they still occupied. Allied military planners devised a strategy to annihilate Axis resistance by taking advantage of America's industrial superiority. A secret plan to develop a superbomb harnessing atomic power came to fruition too late to use against Germany. But when the atomic bomb devastated the cities of Hiroshima and Nagasaki, Japan finally surrendered, canceling the planned assault on the Japanese homeland by hundreds of thousands of American soldiers and sailors and their allies.

From Bombing Raids to Berlin

While the Allied campaigns in North Africa and Italy were under way, British and American pilots flew bombing missions from England to German-occupied territories and to Germany itself as an airborne substitute for the delayed second front on the ground. During night raids, British bombers targeted general areas, hoping to hit civilians, create terror, and undermine morale. Beginning with Paul Tibbets's flight in August 1942, American pilots flew heavily armored B-17s from English airfields in daytime raids on industrial targets vital for the German war machine.

German air defenses took a fearsome toll on Allied pilots and aircraft. In 1943, two-thirds of American airmen did not survive to complete their twenty-five-mission tours of duty. In all, 85,000 American airmen were killed in the skies over Europe. Many others were shot down and held as prisoners of war. In February 1944, the arrival of America's durable and deadly P-51 Mustang fighter gave Allied bombers superior protection. The Mustangs slowly began to sweep the Luftwaffe from the skies, allowing bombers to penetrate deep into Germany and pound civilian and military targets around the clock.

In November 1943, Churchill, Roosevelt, and Stalin met in Tehran to discuss wartime strategy and the second front. Roosevelt conceded to Stalin that the Soviet Union would exercise de facto control of the Eastern European countries that the Red Army occupied as it rolled back the still-potent German Wehrmacht. Stalin agreed to enter the war against Japan once Germany finally surrendered, in effect promising to open a second front in the Pacific theater. Roosevelt and Churchill promised that they would at last launch a massive second-front assault in northern France, code-named Overlord, scheduled for May 1944.

General Eisenhower was assigned overall command of Allied forces, and mountains of military supplies were stockpiled in England. The huge deployment of Hitler's armies in the east, which were trying to halt the Red Army's westward offensive, left too few German troops to stop the millions of Allied soldiers waiting to attack France. More decisive, years of Allied air raids had decimated the German Luftwaffe, which could send aloft only 300 fighter planes against 12,000 Allied aircraft.

After frustrating delays caused by stormy weather, Eisenhower launched the largest amphibious assault in world history on **D Day**, June 6, 1944 (Map 25.4). Allied soldiers finally succeeded in securing the beachhead. An officer told his men, "The only people on this beach are the dead and those that are going to die—now let's get the hell out of here." And they did, finally surmounting the cliffs that loomed over the beach and destroying the German defenses. One GI who made the landing recalled the soldiers "were exhausted and we were exultant. We had survived D Day!"

Within a week, a flood of soldiers, tanks, and other military equipment propelled Allied forces toward Germany. On August 25, the Allies liberated Paris from four years of Nazi occupation. As the giant pincers of the Allied and Soviet armies closed on Germany in December 1944, Hitler

MAP ACTIVITY

Map 25.4   The European Theater of World War II, 1942–1945

The Russian reversal of the German offensive at Stalingrad and Leningrad, combined with Allied landings in North Africa and Normandy, trapped Germany in a closing vise of Allied armies on all sides.

READING THE MAP: By November 1942, which nations or parts of nations in the European theater were under Axis control? Which had been absorbed by the Axis powers before the war? Which nations remained neutral? Which ones were affiliated with the Allies?

CONNECTIONS: What were the three fronts in the European theater? When did the Allies initiate actions on each front, and why did Churchill, Stalin, and Roosevelt disagree on the timing of the opening of these fronts?

ordered a counterattack to capture the Allies' essential supply port at Antwerp, Belgium. In the Battle of the Bulge (December 16, 1944, to January 31, 1945), as the Allies termed it, German forces drove fifty-five miles into Allied lines before being stopped at Bastogne. The battle caused nearly 90,000 American casualties, more than in any other battle of the war. An American lieutenant recalled the macabre scene of "all the bodies . . . frozen stiff . . . many dead Americans and Germans . . . [many with] the ring finger . . . cut off in order to get the ring." The battle cost the Nazis hundreds of tanks and more than 100,000 men, fatally depleting Hitler's reserves.

In February 1945, while Allied armies relentlessly pushed German forces backward, Churchill, Stalin, and Roosevelt met secretly at the Yalta Conference (named for the Russian resort town where it was held) to discuss their plans for the postwar world. Roosevelt managed to secure Stalin's promise to permit votes of self-determination in the Eastern European countries occupied by the Red Army. The Allies pledged to support Jiang Jieshi (Chiang Kaishek) as the leader of China. The Soviet Union obtained a role in the postwar governments of Korea and Manchuria in exchange for entering the war against Japan after the defeat of Germany.

The "Big Three" also agreed on the creation of a new international peacekeeping organization, the United Nations (UN). All nations would have a place in the UN General Assembly, but the Security Council would wield decisive power, and its permanent representatives from the Allied powers—China, France, Great Britain, the Soviet Union, and the United States—would possess a veto over UN actions. The Senate ratified the United Nations Charter in July 1945 by a vote of 89 to 2, reflecting the triumph of internationalism during the nation's mobilization for war.

While Allied armies sped toward Berlin, Allied warplanes dropped more bombs after D Day than in all the previous European bombing raids combined. By April 11, Allied armies reached the banks of the Elbe River and paused while the Soviets smashed into Berlin. The Red Army captured Berlin on May 2. Hitler had committed suicide on April 30, and the provisional German government surrendered unconditionally on May 7. The war in Europe was finally over, with the sacrifice of 135,576 American soldiers, nearly 250,000 British troops, and 9 million Russian combatants. (See "Making Historical Arguments," page 738.)

Roosevelt did not live to witness the end of the war. On April 12, he suffered a fatal stroke. Americans grieved for the man who had led them through years of depression and world war, and they worried about his untested successor, Vice President Harry Truman.

The Defeat of Japan

After punishing defeats in the Coral Sea and at Midway, Japan had to fend off Allied naval and air attacks. In 1943, British and American forces, along with Indian and Chinese allies, launched an offensive against Japanese outposts in southern Asia, pushing through Burma and into China, where Jiang's armies continued to resist conquest. In the Pacific, Americans and their allies attacked Japanese strongholds by sea, air, and land, moving island by island toward the Japanese homeland (Map 25.5).

The island-hopping campaign began in August 1942, when American Marines landed on Guadalcanal in the southern Pacific. For the next six months, a savage battle raged for control of the strategic area. Finally, during the night of February 8, 1943, Japanese forces withdrew. The terrible losses on both sides indicated to the Marines how costly it would be to defeat Japan. After the battle, Joseph Steinbacher, a twenty-one-year-old from Alabama, sailed from San Francisco to New Guinea, where, he recalled, "all the cannon fodder waited to be assigned" to replace the killed and wounded.

In mid-1943, Allied forces launched offensives in New Guinea and the Solomon Islands that gradually secured the South Pacific. In the Central Pacific, amphibious forces conquered the Gilbert and Marshall islands, which served as forward bases for air assaults on the Japanese home islands. As the Allies attacked island after island, Japanese soldiers were ordered to refuse to surrender no matter how hopeless their plight.

While the island-hopping campaign kept pressure on Japanese forces, the Allies invaded the Philippines in the fall of 1944. In the four-day Battle of Leyte Gulf, one of the greatest naval battles in world history, the American fleet crushed the Japanese armada, clearing the way for Allied victory in the Philippines. While the Philippine campaign was under way, American forces captured two crucial islands—Iwo Jima and Okinawa—from which they planned to launch an attack on the Japanese homeland. To defend Okinawa, Japanese leaders ordered thousands

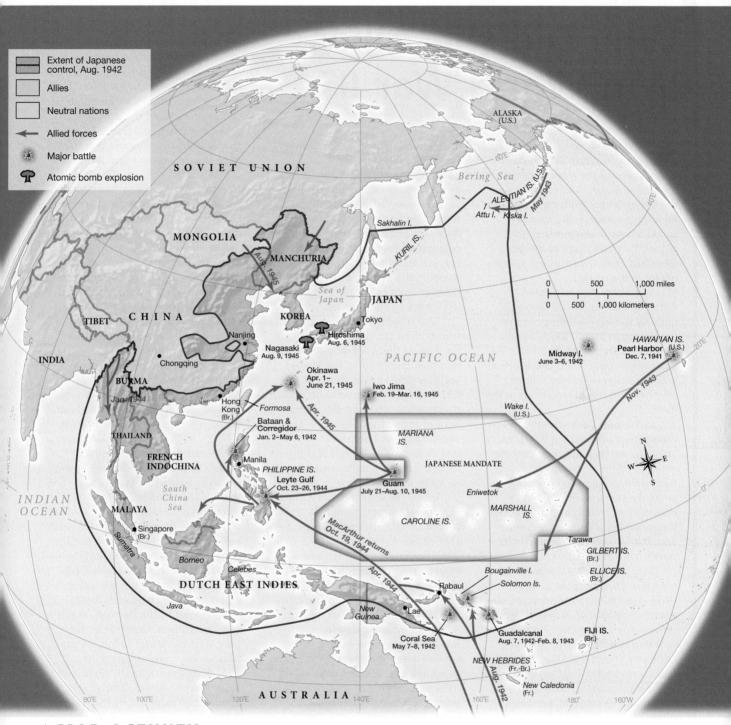

MAP ACTIVITY

Map 25.5 The Pacific Theater of World War II, 1941–1945

To drive the Japanese from their far-flung empire, the Allies launched two combined naval and military offensives—one to recapture the Philippines and then attack Japanese forces in China, the other to hop from island to island in the Central Pacific toward the Japanese mainland.

READING THE MAP: What was the extent of Japanese control up until August 1942? Which nations in the Pacific theater sided with the Allies? Which nations remained neutral?

CONNECTIONS: Describe the economic and military motivations behind Japanese domination of the region. How and when did they achieve this dominance? Judging from this map, what strategic and geographic concerns might have prompted Truman and his advisers to consider using the atomic bomb against Japan?

Why Did the Allies Win World War II?

An indispensable factor in Allied victory in World War II was the alliance among the major powers: the United States, Great Britain, and the Soviet Union. Fighting alone, none of the Allies could have prevailed against Nazi Germany. Together, they were able to defeat what had been the strongest military power in the world.

The major Axis nations—Germany and Japan—did almost nothing to help each other. In the Pacific, Japan fought alone against the United States and its other allies, especially Australia and China. Britain and the Soviet Union contributed relatively little to Allied efforts in the Pacific.

In Europe, Germany enjoyed the support of Hungary, Romania, Bulgaria, and Italy, but none of these nations had the resources and industrial might to field a fully modern army. The Germans conscripted tens of thousands of men from the territories they occupied as their armies swept east, but such coerced recruits made poorly motivated soldiers.

In contrast, the Allies had a single galvanizing purpose: to defeat Hitler. The United States devoted only about 15 percent of its war effort to defeat Japan; the remaining 85 percent was directed against Germany. Little else united the Allies. Political and ideological differences between the capitalist democracies and a Communist dictatorship produced suspicion and mistrust. Nonetheless, the Allies collaborated to force the unconditional surrender of Germany. Three militarily significant consequences of the wartime alliance stand out as decisive ingredients of Allied victory: American material support for Britain and the Soviet Union; American and British bombing campaigns and the D Day invasion of Europe; and the Red Army's success in stopping the eastward advance of the German army at Stalingrad, then driving it back to Berlin.

The flood of military supplies that poured out of American factories during the war made Allied victory possible. In total, the United States produced two-thirds of all Allied military equipment. In addition to shipping hundreds of millions of tons of supplies to Britain and stockpiling equipment for the D Day invasion, the United States sent more than half a million military vehicles to the Soviet Union, accounting for the bulk of the Red Army's motorized transportation. By 1944, American refineries supplied 90 percent of the Allies' high-octane gasoline, prompting Stalin to raise a toast at the Tehran conference "to the American auto industry and the American oil industry." American food shipments provided the equivalent of one meal a day for each Russian soldier. The American canned meat Spam was distributed so widely that Soviet troops called it "The Second Front," a sarcastic reference to the Americans' delay in opening a second front in western Europe.

The British and American bombing campaign against German targets in western Europe served as a crucial second-front surrogate until D Day, and it eventually allowed Allied pilots to rule the skies. The bombing campaign reduced the production of tanks, airplanes, and trucks by more than a third and diverted two-thirds of Germany's aircraft and three-quarters of its antiaircraft weapons from supporting the infantry on the eastern front to protecting German cities from Allied air attacks. Furthermore, improvements in Allied fighter planes allowed British and American pilots to decimate the Luftwaffe. Although the German civilian population and Allied air crews suffered huge casualties as a result of the air campaign, it decisively aided the Soviets' battle against the Germans on the eastern front.

But neither the bombing campaign nor the mountains of American supplies would have won the war if the Soviet Union had not stopped the seemingly unstoppable advance of the German Wehrmacht in the east. Within six months of Hitler's surprise attack on the Soviet Union in June 1941, Stalin's army had lost 4 million soldiers and nearly all its tanks and airplanes, and German armies threatened Moscow. U.S. military officials expected Stalin to capitulate within two or three months. Instead, the Red Army regrouped and managed to halt the Germans' eastward advance by early 1943.

Reversal of the German assault required colossal sacrifices by the people of the Soviet Union. As the German army swept east during 1941, Russians frantically dismantled more than 1,500 industrial plants about to be captured by the Nazis, shipped them east of the Ural Mountains, and reassembled them

Soviet Counterattack on the Eastern Front
This photo depicts Russian soldiers, following a Red Army tank, participating in the massive Soviet counterattack in mid-1942 to push back the Nazi onslaught while snow is still on the ground. German soldiers firing from somewhere behind the smoke have killed two of the Russians as their comrades trudge doggedly ahead. The photo suggests the brutal, inch-by-inch, farmhouse-by-farmhouse fighting on the eastern front. Bettmann/Corbis.

there. They also built new plants and soon began producing thousands of new tanks, aircraft, and artillery to rearm the Soviet military. Through sheer hard work, the productivity of Soviet war industries more than doubled during the war. Meanwhile, food production plummeted, allowing the average Russian only one-fourth the amount of food available to the average German. Soviet casualties dwarfed the losses of the other Allies. For every American killed during the war, forty-five Soviets died. No contribution to Allied victory was more important than the monumental success of the Soviet Union on the eastern front.

Questions for Analysis

Summarize the Argument: How did the Allies help one another defeat the Axis powers?

Analyze the Evidence: How did American war production contribute to Allied victory? To what extent was the Allied bombing campaign an effective substitute for the second front? Why was the eastern front so important to Allied victory?

Consider the Context: How did the war aims of the Allies shape their military strategy? How did the military strategy of the Axis powers reflect their war aims?

VISUAL ACTIVITY

The Allied War Effort

The Russian poster shown here illustrates the combined efforts of the Allies, declaring, "We won't let the evil enemy escape the noose. He will not evade it." Museum of World War II, Natick, MA, www.museumofworldwarii.com.

READING THE IMAGE: What does the depiction of Hitler on the Russian poster suggest about his leadership and character?

CONNECTIONS: What does the poster suggest about the importance of the alliance among the major Allied powers?

of suicide pilots, known as *kamikaze*, to crash their bomb-laden planes into Allied ships. But instead of destroying the American fleet, they demolished the last vestige of the Japanese air force. By June 1945, the Japanese were nearly defenseless on the sea and in the air. Still, their leaders prepared to fight to the death for their homeland.

Joseph Steinbacher and other GIs who had suffered "horrendous" casualties in the Philippines were now told by their commanding officer, "Men, in a few short months we are going to invade [Japan]. . . . We will be going in on the first wave

and are expecting ninety percent casualties the first day. . . . For the few of us left alive the war will be over." Steinbacher later recalled his mental attitude at that moment: "I know that I am now a walking dead man and will not have a snowball's chance in hell of making it through the last great battle to conquer the home islands of Japan."

Atomic Warfare

In mid-July 1945, as Allied forces prepared for the final assault on Japan, American scientists tested a secret weapon at an isolated desert site near Los Alamos, New Mexico. In 1942, Roosevelt had authorized the top-secret **Manhattan Project** to find a way to convert nuclear energy into a superbomb before the Germans added such a weapon to their arsenal. More than 100,000 Americans, led by scientists, engineers, and military officers at Los Alamos, worked frantically to win the race for an atomic bomb. Germany surrendered two and a half months before the test on July 16, 1945, when scientists first witnessed an atomic explosion that sent a mushroom cloud of debris eight miles into the atmosphere. After watching the successful test of the bomb, J. Robert Oppenheimer, the head scientist at Los Alamos, remarked soberly, "Lots of boys not grown up yet will owe their life to it."

President Truman saw no reason not to use the atomic bomb against Japan if doing so would save American lives. Despite numerous defeats, Japan still had more than 6 million reserves at home for a last-ditch defense against the anticipated Allied assault, which U.S. military advisers estimated would kill at least 250,000 Americans. But first Truman issued an ultimatum: Japan must surrender unconditionally or face utter ruin. When the Japanese failed to respond by the deadline, Truman ordered that an atomic bomb be dropped on a Japanese city. The bomb that Colonel Paul Tibbets and his crew released over Hiroshima on August 6 leveled the city and incinerated about 80,000 people, and many thousands more died later from injuries and radiation. Three days later, after the Japanese government still refused to surrender, the second atomic bomb killed nearly as many civilians at Nagasaki.

With American assurance that the emperor could retain his throne after the Allies took over, Japan surrendered on August 14. On a troopship departing from Europe for what would have been the final assault on Japan, an American soldier spoke for millions of others when he heard the wonderful news that the killing was over: "We are going to grow to adulthood after all."

While all Americans welcomed peace, some worried about the consequences of unleashing atomic power. Almost every American believed that the atomic bomb had brought peace in 1945, but nobody knew what it would bring in the future.

REVIEW   Why did Truman elect to use the atomic bomb against Japan?

Major Campaigns and Battles of World War II, 1939–1945

September 1, 1939	Germany attacks Poland.
September 3, 1939	Britain and France declare war on Germany.
April 1940	Germany attacks Denmark and Norway.
May 1940	Germany invades Netherlands, Belgium, Luxembourg, and France.
June 1940	Italy joins Germany in war against Allies.
June–November 1940	Battle of Britain.
June 22, 1941	Germany invades Soviet Union.
December 7, 1941	Japan attacks Pearl Harbor.
December 8, 1941	U.S. Congress declares war on Japan.
December 11, 1941	Germany and Italy declare war on United States.
January 2–May 6, 1942	Battles of Bataan and Corregidor.
May 7–8, 1942	Battle of the Coral Sea.
June 3–6, 1942	Battle of Midway.
August 1942–February 1943	Battle of Guadalcanal.
August 21, 1942–January 31, 1943	Battle of Stalingrad.
October 23–November 5, 1942	British halt Germans at Battle of El-Alamein.
November 1942–May 1943	Allies mount North African campaign.
July 10, 1943	Allies begin Italian invasion through Sicily.
June 4, 1944	Allies liberate Rome from German occupation.
June 6, 1944	D Day—Allied forces invade Normandy.
August 25, 1944	Allies liberate Paris.
September 12, 1944	Allies enter Germany.
October 23–26, 1944	Battle of Leyte Gulf.
December 16, 1944–January 31, 1945	Battle of the Bulge.
February 19–March 16, 1945	Battle of Iwo Jima.
April 1–June 21, 1945	Battle of Okinawa.
May 2, 1945	Soviet forces capture Berlin.
August 6, 1945	United States drops atomic bomb on Hiroshima.
August 9, 1945	United States drops atomic bomb on Nagasaki.

Hiroshima
This photo shows part of Hiroshima shortly after the atomic bomb dropped from the *Enola Gay*, leveling the densely populated city. Deadly radiation from the bomb maimed and killed Japanese civilians for years afterward. Bettmann/Corbis.

▶ Conclusion: Allied Victory and America's Emergence as a Superpower

At a cost of 405,399 American lives, the nation united with its allies to crush the Axis aggressors into unconditional surrender. Almost all Americans believed they had won a "good war" against totalitarian evil. The Allies saved Asia and Europe from enslavement and finally halted the Nazis' genocidal campaign against Jews and many others whom the Nazis considered inferior. To secure human rights and protect the world against future wars, the Roosevelt administration took the lead in creating the United Nations.

Wartime production lifted the nation out of the Great Depression. The gross national product soared to four times what it had been when Roosevelt became president in 1933. Jobs in defense industries eliminated chronic unemployment, provided wages for millions of women workers and African American migrants from southern farms, and boosted Americans' prosperity. Ahead stretched the challenge of maintaining that prosperity while reintegrating millions of uniformed men and women, with help from the benefits of the GI Bill.

By the end of the war, the United States had emerged as a global superpower. Wartime mobilization made the American economy the strongest in the world, buttressed by the military clout of the nation's nuclear monopoly. Although the war left much of the world a rubble-strewn wasteland, the American mainland had enjoyed immunity from attack. The Japanese occupation of China had left 50 million people without homes and millions more dead, maimed, and orphaned. The German offensive against the Soviet Union had killed more than 20 million Russian soldiers and civilians. Germany and Japan lay in ruins, their economies and societies as shattered as their military forces. But in the gruesome balance sheet of war, the Axis powers had inflicted far more grief, misery, and destruction on the global victims of their aggression than they had suffered in return.

As the dominant Western nation in the postwar world, the United States asserted its leadership in the reconstruction of Europe while occupying Japan and overseeing its economic and political recovery. America soon confronted new challenges in the tense aftermath of the war, as the Soviets seized political control of Eastern Europe, a Communist revolution swept China, and national liberation movements emerged in the colonial empires of Britain and France. The forces unleashed by World War II would shape the United States and the rest of the world for decades to come. Before the ashes of World War II had cooled, America's wartime alliance with the Soviet Union fractured, igniting a Cold War between the superpowers. To resist global communism, the United States became, in effect, the policeman of the free world, repudiating the pre–World War II legacy of isolationism.

See the Selected Bibliography for this chapter in the Appendix.

25 Chapter Review

KEY TERMS

good neighbor policy (p. 714)
neutrality acts (p. 715)
appeasement (p. 716)
Lend-Lease Act (p. 718)
internment camps (p. 722)
Selective Service Act (p. 722)
Battle of Midway (p. 726)
Double V campaign (p. 730)
GI Bill of Rights (p. 731)
Holocaust (p. 733)
D Day (p. 734)
Manhattan Project (p. 741)

REVIEW QUESTIONS

1. Why did isolationism during the 1930s concern Roosevelt? (pp. 713–715)

2. How did Roosevelt attempt to balance American isolationism with the military aggression of Germany and Japan in the late 1930s and early 1940s? (pp. 715–720)

3. How did the Roosevelt administration mobilize the human and industrial resources necessary to fight a two-front war? (pp. 721–725)

4. How did the United States seek to counter the Japanese in the Pacific and the Germans in Europe? (pp. 726–728)

5. How did the war influence American society? (pp. 728–734)

6. Why did Truman elect to use the atomic bomb against Japan? (pp. 734–741)

MAKING CONNECTIONS

1. Did isolationism bolster or undermine national security and national economic interests? Discuss Roosevelt's evolving answer to this question.

2. Who benefited most from the wartime economy? What financial limitations did various members of society face, and why?

3. How did the United States play a decisive role in the Allies' victory?

4. How did minorities' contributions to the war effort draw attention to domestic racism? What were the political implications of these developments?

LINKING TO THE PAST

1. How did America's involvement in World War II differ from its participation in World War I? Consider diplomacy, allies and enemies, wartime military and economic policies, and social and cultural changes. (See chapter 22.)

2. Why did World War II succeed in creating the full economic recovery that remained elusive during the New Deal? Consider specifically the scope and limits of New Deal economic reforms and how they changed, if at all, during World War II. (See chapter 24.)

26 Cold War Politics in the Truman Years

1945–1953

After reading and studying this chapter, you should be able to:

- Explain the origins of the Cold War, and describe where and how the containment policy was implemented.
- Describe President Truman's Fair Deal domestic agenda, and explain its accomplishments and failures.
- Explain why the United States went to war in Korea and how military objectives changed. Identify the war's costs and consequences.

COLD WAR COMIC BOOK
After World War II, fear of communism pervaded American politics and popular culture. This comic book series showed the United States winning victories over the Soviet Union with nuclear weapons. Image Courtesy of The Advertising Archives.

HEADS TURNED WHEN CONGRESSWOMAN HELEN Gahagan Douglas walked through the U.S. Capitol. She was one of only ten female representatives in the 435-seat body, and she also drew attention as an attractive former Broadway star and opera singer. Douglas served in Congress from 1945 to 1951 when the fate of the New Deal hung in the balance and the nation charted an unprecedented course in foreign policy.

Born in 1900, Helen Gahagan grew up in Brooklyn, New York, and left college early for the stage. She quickly won fame on Broadway, starring in show after show until she fell in love with one of her leading men, Melvyn Douglas. They married in 1931, and she followed him to Hollywood, where he hoped to advance his movie career and where she bore two children.

Helen Gahagan Douglas admired Franklin D. Roosevelt's leadership during the depression, and the Douglases joined Hollywood's liberal political circles. Douglas visited migrant camps where she saw "faces stamped with poverty and despair." Her work on behalf of poor migrant farmworkers led her to testify before Congress and become a friend of the Roosevelts. In 1944, she won election to Congress, representing not the posh Hollywood district where she lived but a multiracial district in downtown Los Angeles, which cemented her dedication to progressive politics.

Like many liberals, Douglas was devastated by Roosevelt's death and unsure of his successor. "Who was Harry Truman anyway?" she asked. A compromise choice for the vice presidency, this "accidental president" lacked the charisma and political skills with which Roosevelt had transformed foreign and domestic policy, won four presidential elections, and forged a Democratic Party coalition that dominated national politics. Besides confronting domestic problems that the New Deal had not solved—how to avoid another depression without the war to fuel the economy—Truman faced new international challenges that threatened to undermine the nation's security.

By 1947, a new term described the hostility that had emerged between the United States and its wartime ally, the Soviet Union: Cold War. Truman and his advisers insisted that the Soviet Union posed a major threat to the United States, and they gradually shaped a policy to contain Soviet power wherever it threatened to spread. As a member of the House Foreign Affairs Committee, Douglas urged cooperation with the Soviet Union and initially opposed aid to Greece and Turkey, the first step in the new containment policy. Yet thereafter, Douglas was Truman's loyal ally, supporting the Marshall Plan, the creation of the North Atlantic Treaty Organization, and the war in Korea. The containment policy achieved its goals in Europe, but communism spread in Asia, and at home a wave of anti-Communist hysteria—a second Red scare—harmed many Americans and stifled dissent and debate.

Douglas's earlier links with leftist groups and her advocacy of civil rights and social welfare programs made her and other liberals easy targets for conservative politicians exploiting the anti-Communist fervor that accompanied the Cold War. Running for the U.S. Senate in 1950, she faced Republican Richard M. Nixon, who had gained national attention for his efforts to expose Communists in government. Nixon's campaign labeled Douglas as "pink right down to her underwear" and sent thousands of voters the anonymous message, "I think you should know Helen Douglas is a Communist." Douglas's political career ended in defeat, just as much of Truman's domestic agenda fell victim to the Red scare.

Helen Gahagan Douglas in Congress
Long accustomed as an actress to appearing before an audience, the congresswoman from California was a popular campaigner for Democratic candidates and a charismatic speaker. When soaring prices threatened ordinary Americans' budgets in 1948, she brought a basket of groceries to the House of Representatives to plead for the continuance of government price controls. Bettmann/Corbis.

▶ From the Grand Alliance to Containment

With Japan's surrender in August 1945, Americans besieged the government to bring their loved ones home. They looked forward to the end of international crises and the dismantling of the large military establishment. Postwar realities quickly shattered these hopes. The wartime alliance of the United States, Great Britain, and the Soviet Union crumbled, giving birth to a Cold War. The United States began to develop the means for containing the spread of Soviet power around the globe, including a military buildup and an enormous aid program for Europe, known as the Marshall Plan.

The Cold War Begins

"The guys who came out of World War II were idealistic," reported Harold Russell, a young paratrooper who had lost both hands in a training accident. "We felt the day had come when the wars were all over." But such hopes were quickly dashed. Once the Allies had overcome a common enemy, the prewar mistrust and antagonism between the Soviet Union and the West resurfaced over their very different visions of the postwar world.

The Western Allies' delay in opening a second front in Western Europe aroused Soviet suspicions during the war. The Soviet Union had made supreme wartime sacrifices, losing more than twenty million citizens and vast portions of its agricultural and industrial capacity. Soviet leader Joseph Stalin wanted to make Germany pay for Soviet economic reconstruction and to expand Soviet influence in the world. Above all, he wanted friendly governments on the Soviet Union's borders in Eastern Europe, through which his nation had been attacked twice in the past twenty-five years. A ruthless dictator, Stalin also wanted to maintain his own power.

In contrast to the Soviet devastation, American losses were light, and the United States emerged from the war as the most powerful nation on the planet, with a vastly expanded economy and a monopoly on atomic weapons. That sheer power, along with U.S. economic interests and a belief in the superiority of American institutions and intentions,

CHRONOLOGY

1945	• Roosevelt dies; Truman becomes president.
1946	• Postwar labor unrest affects major industries. • President's Committee on Civil Rights created. • George F. Kennan drafts containment policy. • United States grants independence to Philippines. • Employment Act passes. • Republicans gain control of Congress.
1947	• National Security Act passes. • Truman announces Truman Doctrine. • United States sends aid to Greece and Turkey. • Truman establishes loyalty program. • *Mendez v. Westminster* decided.
1948	• Marshall Plan approved. • Truman orders desegregation of military. • American GI Forum founded. • United States recognizes Israel. • Truman elected president.
1948–1949	• Berlin crisis precipitates airlift drops.
1949	• Communists take over China. • North Atlantic Treaty Organization formed. • Soviet Union explodes atomic bomb. • Truman approves hydrogen bomb.
1950	• Senator Joseph McCarthy claims U.S. government harbors Communists. • Korean War begins.
1951	• Truman fires General Douglas MacArthur. • U.S. occupation of Japan ends.
1952	• Dwight D. Eisenhower elected president.
1953	• Korean War ends.

all affected how American leaders approached the Soviet Union.

With the depression still fresh in their minds, American officials believed that a healthy economy depended on opportunities abroad. American companies needed access to raw materials, markets for their goods, and security for their investments overseas, needs best met in countries with similar economic and political systems. As President Harry S. Truman put it in 1947, "The American system can survive in America only if it becomes a world system." Yet leaders and citizens alike regarded their foreign policy not as a self-interested campaign for economic advantage, but as the means to preserve national security and bring freedom, democracy, and capitalism to the rest of the world. Laura Briggs, a woman from Idaho, spoke for many Americans who believed "it was our destiny to prove that we were the children of God and that our way was right for the world."

Recent history also shaped postwar foreign policy. Americans believed that World War II might have been avoided had Britain and France resisted rather than appeased Hitler's initial aggression. Navy Secretary James V. Forrestal opposed trying to "buy [the Soviets'] understanding and sympathy. We tried that once with Hitler." The man with ultimate responsibility for U.S. policy was a keen student of history but had little international experience beyond his service in World War I. Harry S. Truman expected Soviet-American cooperation, as long as the Soviet Union conformed to U.S. plans for the postwar world. Proud of his ability to make quick decisions, Truman was determined to take a firm hand if the Soviets tried to expand, confident that America's nuclear monopoly gave him the upper hand.

The **Cold War** first emerged over clashing Soviet and American interests in Eastern Europe. Stalin insisted that wartime agreements gave him a free hand in the countries defeated or liberated by the Red Army, just as the United States was unilaterally reconstructing governments in Italy and Japan. The Soviet dictator used harsh methods to install Communist governments in neighboring Poland and Bulgaria but initially tolerated non-Communist governments in Hungary and Czechoslovakia. In early 1946, he responded to Western pressure and removed troops from Iran on the Soviet Union's southwest border, allowing U.S. access to the rich oil fields there.

Stalin saw hypocrisy when U.S. officials demanded democratic elections in Eastern Europe while supporting dictatorships friendly to U.S. interests in Latin America. But the Western Allies were unwilling to match tough words with military force against the largest army in the world. Their sharp protests failed to prevent the Soviet Union from establishing satellite countries throughout Eastern Europe (Map 26.1).

In 1946, the wartime Allies contended over Germany's future. Both sides wanted to demilitarize Germany, but U.S. policymakers sought rapid industrial revival there to foster European economic recovery. By contrast, the Soviet Union wanted Germany weak both militarily and economically, and Stalin demanded heavy reparations from Germany to help rebuild the devastated Soviet economy. Unable to settle their differences, the Allies divided Germany. The Soviet Union installed a puppet Communist government in the eastern section, and Britain, France, and the United States began to unify their occupation zones, eventually establishing the Federal Republic of Germany—West Germany—in 1949.

The war of words escalated early in 1946. Boasting of the superiority of the Soviet system, Stalin told a Moscow audience in February that capitalism inevitably produced war. One month later, Truman sat beside Winston Churchill, the former prime minister, who denounced Soviet interference in Eastern Europe. "From Stettin in the Baltic to Trieste in the Adriatic, an **iron curtain** has descended across the Continent," Churchill said. (See "Analyzing Historical Evidence," page 750.) Stalin saw Churchill's proposal for joint British-American action to combat Soviet aggression as "a call to war against the USSR."

In February 1946, George F. Kennan, a career diplomat and expert on Russia, wrote a comprehensive rationale for what came to be called the policy of **containment**. Downplaying the influence of Communist ideology, he instead stressed Soviet insecurity and Stalin's need to maintain authority at home as the prime forces behind efforts to expand Soviet power abroad. Kennan believed that the Soviet Union would retreat if the United States would respond with "unalterable counterforce." This approach, he predicted, would eventually end in "either the breakup or the gradual mellowing of Soviet power."

Not all public figures agreed. In September 1946, Secretary of Commerce Henry A. Wallace urged greater understanding of the Soviets' national security concerns, insisting that "we

MAP ACTIVITY

Map 26.1   The Division of Europe after World War II
The "iron curtain," a term coined by Winston Churchill to refer to the Soviet grip on Eastern Europe, divided the continent for nearly fifty years. Communist governments controlled the countries along the Soviet Union's western border, except for Finland, which remained neutral.

READING THE MAP: Is the division of Europe among NATO, Communist, and neutral countries about equal? Why would the location of Berlin pose a problem for the Western Allies?

CONNECTIONS: When was NATO founded, and what was its purpose? How did the postwar division of Europe compare with the wartime alliances?

have no more business in the political affairs of Eastern Europe than Russia has in the political affairs of Latin America." State Department officials were furious at Wallace for challenging the administration's hard line against the Soviet Union, and Truman fired Wallace.

The Truman Doctrine and the Marshall Plan

In 1947, the United States began to implement the doctrine of containment that would guide

foreign policy for the next four decades. It was not an easy transition; Americans approved of taking a hard line against the Soviet Union but wanted to keep their soldiers and tax dollars at home. In addition to selling containment to the public, Truman had to gain the support of a Republican-controlled Congress, which included those staunchly opposed to a strong U.S. presence in Europe.

Crises in two Mediterranean countries triggered the implementation of containment. In February 1947, Britain informed the United States

The Emerging Cold War

Early in 1946, Soviet and Western leaders began to charge each other with hostile actions that endangered world peace. Within the United States, disagreement arose about how to deal with the Soviet Union. A close reading of early Cold War speeches helps us to understand what public officials saw as the primary threats to their nations' security and how they viewed the interests and motives of other nations.

DOCUMENT 1
Joseph Stalin, Address on the Strengths of the Soviet Social System, Moscow, February 9, 1946

In early 1946, Premier Joseph Stalin called on the Soviet people to support his program for economic development. Leaders in the West viewed his comments about communism and capitalism and his boasts about the strength of the Red Army as a threat to peace.

The [Second World War] arose as the inevitable result of the development of the world economic and political forces on the basis of monopoly capitalism. . . .

. . . The uneven development of the capitalist countries leads in time to sharp disturbances in their relations, and the group of countries which consider themselves inadequately provided with raw materials and export markets try usually to change this situation and to change the position in their favor by means of armed force. As a result of these factors, the capitalist world is split into two hostile camps and war follows. . . . The Soviet social system has proved to be more capable of life and more stable than a non-Soviet social system. . . .

. . . The Red Army heroically withstood all the adversities of the war, routed completely the armies of our enemies and emerged victoriously from the war. This is recognized by everybody—friend and foe.

[Stalin talks about his new Five-Year Plan.] Special attention will be focused on expanding the production of goods for mass consumption, on raising the standard of life of the working people by consistent and systematic reduction of the costs of all goods, and on wide-scale construction of all kinds of scientific research institutes to enable science to develop its forces. I have no doubt that if we render the necessary assistance to our scientists they will be able not only to overtake but also in the very near future to surpass the achievements of science outside the boundaries of our country.

Source: Excerpts from Joseph Stalin, "New Five-Year Plan for Russia," *Vital Speeches of the Day*, February 9, 1946, pp. 300–304.

DOCUMENT 2
Winston Churchill, "Iron Curtain" Speech, Westminster College, Fulton, Missouri, March 5, 1946

With Truman beside him, Winston Churchill, former prime minister of Great Britain, assessed Soviet actions in harsh terms. In response, Stalin equated Churchill with Hitler, a "firebrand of war."

. . . I have a strong admiration and regard for the valiant Russian people and for my war-time comrade, Marshal Stalin. . . . We understand the Russians need to be secure on her western frontiers from all renewal of German aggression. . . . It is my duty, however, to place before you certain facts. . . .

From Stettin in the Baltic to Trieste in the Adriatic, an iron curtain has descended across the Continent. Behind that line lie all the capitals of the ancient states of central and eastern Europe. Warsaw, Berlin, Prague, Vienna, Budapest, Belgrade, Bucharest and Sofia, all these famous cities and

that its crippled economy could no longer sustain military assistance to Greece, where the autocratic government faced economic disaster and a leftist uprising, and to Turkey, which was trying to resist Soviet pressures. Unaware that the Soviet Union had deliberately avoided aiding the Greek Communists, Truman promptly sought congressional authority to send both countries military and economic aid. Meeting with congressional leaders, Undersecretary of State Dean Acheson predicted that if Greece and Turkey fell, communism would soon consume three-fourths of the world. After a stunned silence, Michigan senator Arthur Vandenberg, the Republican foreign policy leader, warned that to get approval, Truman would have to "scare hell out of the country."

Truman did just that. He warned that if Greece fell to the rebels, "confusion and disorder might well spread throughout the entire Middle East" and then create instability in

the populations around them lie in the Soviet sphere and all are subject in one form or another, not only to Soviet influence but to a very high and increasing measure of control from Moscow. . . . The Communist parties, which were very small in all these eastern states of Europe, have been raised to preeminence and power far beyond their numbers and are seeking everywhere to obtain totalitarian control. Police governments are prevailing in nearly every case. . . .

. . . In a great number of countries, far from the Russian frontiers and throughout the world, Communist fifth columns are established and work in complete unity and absolute obedience to the directions they receive from the Communist center.

I do not believe that Soviet Russia desires war. What they desire is the fruits of war and the indefinite expansion of their power and doctrines. . . . Our difficulties and dangers will not be removed by . . . mere waiting to see what happens; nor will they be relieved by a policy of appeasement. . . . I am convinced that there is nothing [the Russians] admire so much as strength, and there is nothing for which they have less respect than for military weakness.

Source: Reproduced with permission of Curtis Brown, London on behalf of the Estate of Sir Winston Churchill. Copyright © Winston S. Churchill.

DOCUMENT 3
Henry A. Wallace, Address on the Folly of the U.S. "Get Tough with Russia" Policy, Madison Square Garden, New York, September 12, 1946

Throughout 1946, Henry A. Wallace, Truman's secretary of commerce, urged the president to take a more conciliatory approach toward the Soviet Union, a position reflected in his speech to leftist and liberal groups.

We cannot rest in the assurance that we invented the atom bomb—and therefore that this agent of destruction will work best for us. He who trusts in the atom bomb will sooner or later perish by the atom bomb—or something worse. . . .

To achieve lasting peace, we must study in detail just how the Russian character was formed—by invasions of Tartars, Mongols, Germans, Poles, Swedes, and French; by the czarist rule based on ignorance, fear and force; by the

intervention of the British, French and Americans in Russian affairs from 1919 to 1921; by the geography of the huge Russian land mass situated strategically between Europe and Asia; and by the vitality derived from the rich Russian soil and the strenuous Russian climate. Add to all this the tremendous emotional power which Marxism and Leninism gives to the Russian leaders—and then we can realize that we are reckoning with a force which cannot be handled successfully by a "Get tough with Russia" policy. "Getting tough" never bought anything real and lasting—whether for schoolyard bullies or businessmen or world powers. The tougher we get, the tougher the Russians will get. . . .

We should recognize that we have no more business in the political affairs of Eastern Europe than Russia has in the political affairs of Latin America, Western Europe and the United States. . . . We have to recognize that the Balkans are closer to Russia than to us—and that Russia cannot permit either England or the United States to dominate the politics of that area. . . .

. . . Under friendly peaceful competition the Russian world and the American world will gradually become more alike. The Russians will be forced to grant more and more of the personal freedoms; and we shall become more and more absorbed with the problems of social-economic justice.

Source: Courtesy of Henry A. Wallace Papers. University of Iowa Libraries, Iowa City, Iowa.

Questions for Analysis

Consider the Context: What lessons did these three leaders draw from World War II? How were these lessons shaped by the thirty-year history of relationships between the Soviet Union and the West?

Recognize Viewpoints: What differences did these men see between the political and economic systems of the Soviet Union and those of the United States and Western Europe? How did their predictions about these systems differ?

Analyze the Evidence: What motives did these three men ascribe to Soviet actions? How do Churchill's and Wallace's proposals for the Western response to the Soviet Union differ?

Europe. According to what came to be called the **Truman Doctrine**, the United States must not only resist Soviet military power but also "support free peoples who are resisting attempted subjugation by armed minorities or by outside pressures." The president failed to convince Helen Gahagan Douglas and some of her congressional colleagues, who wanted the United States to work through the United Nations and opposed propping up the authoritarian Greek

government. But the administration won the day, setting a precedent for forty years of Cold War interventions that would aid any kind of government if the only alternative appeared to be communism.

A much larger assistance program for Europe followed aid to Greece and Turkey. In May 1947, Acheson described a war-ravaged Western Europe, with "factories destroyed, fields impoverished, transportation systems wrecked, populations scattered and on the borderline of starvation." American citizens were sending generous amounts of private aid, but Europe needed large-scale assistance to keep desperate citizens from turning to socialism or communism.

In March 1948, Congress approved such assistance, which came to be called the **Marshall Plan**, after Secretary of State George C. Marshall, who proposed what a British official called "a lifeline to a sinking man." Over the next five years, the United States spent $13 billion ($117 billion in 2010 dollars) to restore the economies of sixteen Western European nations. Marshall invited all European nations and the Soviet Union to cooperate in a request for aid, but the Soviets objected to the American insistence on free trade and financial disclosure. As U.S. officials had expected, the Soviets rejected the offer and ordered their Eastern European satellites to do the same.

Humanitarian impulses as well as the goal of keeping Western Europe free of communism drove the adoption of this enormous aid program. The Marshall Plan also helped boost the U.S. economy; the European recipients used the aid to buy American products, and Europe's economic recovery created new markets and opportunities for American investment. By insisting that the recipient nations work together, the Marshall Plan marked the first step toward the European Union. (See "Making Historical Arguments," page 754.)

While Congress was debating the Marshall Plan, in February 1948 the Soviets brutally installed a Communist regime in Czechoslovakia, the last democracy left in Eastern Europe. Next, Stalin threatened Western access to Berlin. That former capital of Germany lay within

Berlin Divided, 1948

Soviet-controlled East Germany, but all four Allies jointly occupied it. As the Western Allies moved to organize West Germany as a separate nation, the Soviets retaliated by blocking roads and rail lines between West Germany and the Western-held sections of Berlin, cutting off food, fuel, and other essentials to two million inhabitants (see Map 26.1).

"We stay in Berlin, period," Truman vowed. To avoid a confrontation with Soviet troops, for nearly a year U.S. and British pilots airlifted 2.3 million tons of goods to sustain the West Berliners. Stalin hesitated to shoot down these cargo planes, and in 1949 he lifted the blockade. The city was then divided into East Berlin, under Soviet control, and West Berlin, which became part of West Germany.

Building a National Security State

During the Truman years, advocates of the new containment policy fashioned a six-pronged defense strategy: (1) development of atomic weapons, (2) strengthening traditional military power, (3) military alliances with other nations, (4) military and economic aid to friendly nations, (5) an espionage network and secret means to subvert Communist expansion, and (6) a propaganda offensive to win friends around the world.

In September 1949, the Soviet Union detonated its own atomic bomb, ending the U.S. monopoly on atomic weapons. Truman then approved the development of a hydrogen bomb—equivalent to five hundred atomic bombs—rejecting the counterarguments of several scientists who had worked on the atomic bomb and of George Kennan, who

The Berlin Airlift
At the peak of the Berlin airlift in 1948, U.S. or British planes landed every three minutes twenty-four hours a day. These children, on top of a mountain of wartime rubble, may have been watching for air force pilot Gail S. Halvorsen, who, after meeting hungry schoolchildren, began to drop candy and gum as his plane approached the landing strip. picture-alliance/dpa/AP Images.

warned of an endless arms race. The "superbomb" was ready by 1954, but the U.S. advantage was brief. In November 1955, the Soviets exploded their own hydrogen bomb.

From the 1950s through the 1980s, deterrence formed the basis of American nuclear strategy. To deter a Soviet attack, the United States strove to maintain a nuclear force more powerful than that of the Soviets. Because the Russians pursued a similar policy, the superpowers became locked in an ever-escalating nuclear arms race amassing weapons that could destroy the earth many times over. Albert Einstein, whose mathematical discoveries had laid the foundations for nuclear weapons, commented grimly that the war that came after World War III would "be fought with sticks and stones."

Implementing the second component of containment, the United States beefed up its conventional military power to deter Soviet threats that might not warrant nuclear retaliation. The National Security Act of 1947 united the military branches under a single secretary of defense and created the National Security Council (NSC) to advise the president. During the Berlin crisis in 1948, Congress hiked military appropriations and enacted a peacetime draft. In addition, Congress granted permanent status to the women's military branches, though it limited the number of women, the jobs they could do, and the rank they could attain. With 1.5 million men and women in uniform in 1950, the military strength of the United States had quadrupled since the 1930s, and defense expenditures claimed one-third of the federal budget.

Collective security, the third prong of containment strategy, marked a sharp reversal of the nation's traditional foreign policy. In 1949, the United States joined Canada and Western European nations in its first peacetime military alliance, the **North Atlantic Treaty Organization (NATO)**, designed to counter a Soviet threat to Western Europe (see Map 26.1). For the first time in its history, the United States pledged to go to war if one of its allies was attacked.

The fourth element of defense strategy provided foreign assistance programs to strengthen friendly countries, such as aid to Greece and Turkey and the Marshall Plan. In addition, in 1949 Congress approved $1 billion of military aid to its NATO allies, and the government began economic assistance to nations in other parts of the world.

The fifth ingredient of containment improved the government's capacity to thwart communism through espionage and covert activities. The National Security Act of 1947 created the **Central Intelligence Agency (CIA)** to gather information and to perform any activities "related to intelligence affecting the national security" that the NSC might authorize. Such functions included propaganda, sabotage, economic warfare, and support for "anti-communist elements in threatened countries of the free world." In 1948, secret CIA operations helped defeat Italy's Communist Party. Subsequently, CIA agents would intervene even more actively, helping to topple legitimate foreign governments and violating the rights of U.S. citizens.

Finally, the U.S. government created cultural exchanges and propaganda to win "hearts and minds" throughout the world. The Voice of America, established during World War II to broadcast U.S. propaganda abroad, expanded, and the State Department sent books, exhibits, jazz musicians, and other performers to foreign countries as "cultural ambassadors."

By 1950, the United States had abandoned age-old tenets of foreign policy. Isolationism and neutrality gave way to a peacetime military alliance and efforts to control events far beyond U.S. borders. Short of war, the United States could not

Cold War Spying

"Intelligence," the gathering of information about the enemy, took on new importance with the Cold War and creation of the Central Intelligence Agency (CIA) in 1947. While much intelligence work took place in Washington, where analysts combed through Communist newspapers, official reports, and speeches, secret agents gathered information behind the iron curtain with bugs and devices such as these cameras hidden in cigarette packs. Jack Naylor Collection/Picture Research Consultants & Archives.

Why Did the United States Launch the European Recovery Program?

When Secretary of State George Marshall proposed a program of massive economic aid to Europe in June 1947, the United States was still recovering from World War II, the national debt had skyrocketed, and most Americans ranked foreign events low among their concerns. The Truman administration insisted that $17 billion was needed over the next four years and asked specifically for $6.8 billion for the first 15 months, a staggering amount when the total annual federal budget was around $40 billion. The $13 billion that was ultimately spent amounted to more than $100 billion in current dollars. So why did the administration believe it was necessary to launch such an enormous program, and why did Congress consent?

The objective conditions in Europe were plain for anyone to see. World War II had left behind utter devastation. Thirty percent of Britain's housing stock lay in rubble, and three-fourths of Berlin's buildings were uninhabitable. Destroyed roads, railroads, and bridges littered the landscape. Thirteen million people had been displaced from their homes, and millions of Europeans subsisted on the borderline of starvation. Then, in January 1947, a brutal winter descended, freezing to a stop what factories and railroads had survived the war and destroying three million acres of wheat. The snowmelt from that winter produced ravaging floods.

When Marshall proposed what came to be called the European Recovery Program (ERP), he declared, "Our policy is directed not against any country or doctrine but against hunger, poverty, desperation and chaos." Indeed, the U.S. government had already sent millions of dollars of aid and huge loans to individual countries, and the American people sent some $2 billion of private aid in the six years following World War II. British foreign secretary Ernest Bevin spoke of the Marshall Plan as "generosity beyond my belief."

But motives beyond humanitarianism were also at work. With the Soviet Union in control of Eastern Europe, U.S. policymakers feared the spread of communism to Western nations. In most of Europe, Communist parties enjoyed popular support, in part because Communists had led the resistance to Nazism. After the war, they were elected to coalition governments in several Western countries, including Italy, where a Communist coalition had won 40 percent of the vote, and France. U.S. leaders feared that persistent economic desperation could send Western European countries into the arms of the Soviets without a shot being fired.

If U.S. policy leaders were alarmed by the security threat posed by a Soviet-dominated Europe, they also recognized how closely European recovery was tied to the health of the American economy. A prosperous and stable continent meant markets for American products and investment opportunities for American businesses. But in the postwar years, European nations were importing much more from the United States than they could export, resulting in a mounting "dollar gap." If not contained, this dollar deficit would leave Europeans without the means to trade with the United States. Marshall Plan advocates also pointed out that American businesses would benefit in the short run because Europeans would use the assistance to purchase American goods—ranging from milk to tractors to industrial equipment—carried on American ships and loaded by American dockworkers.

Finally, the ERP helped to solve the problem of how to promote German reindustrialization, deemed necessary for the recovery of the rest of Western Europe, while also containing Germany's ability to wage war. To this end, the United States required nations receiving aid to take the initiative, cooperate with one another, and lower trade restrictions among themselves. Encouraged by Marshall Plan aid, European leaders knit their countries together, eventually leading to the creation of the European Union in 1993.

The multitude of interests that lay behind the Marshall Plan proposal gave the Truman administration a broad platform on which to appeal for congressional support. It launched a full-scale publicity campaign of ads, brochures, and speakers to appeal to every segment of the American public. Marshall himself compared his strenuous speaking tour to "running for the Senate or the presidency." Truman allowed the program to be popularly named after the revered, nonpartisan general, making it more palatable to Republicans who controlled Congress.

"We Build a New Europe"

In 1950, the ERP launched a poster contest on the subject "Intra-European Cooperation for a Better Standard of Living" and received more than 10,000 submissions from artists throughout Europe. One of the finalists, "We Build a New Europe," submitted by Austrian Kurt Krapeik, shows the wartime devastation in a burned tree and the promise of recovery in new shoots. The European nations, represented by flags, fit tightly together in the nest, which is being supplied by doves, symbols of peace. Library of Congress, 3b49410.

themselves to resist the aggression of Russia over their territories." A CIA report asserted in April 1947 that "the greatest danger to the security of the United States is the possibility of economic collapse in western Europe and the consequent accession to power of Communist elements." Created to serve strategic interests, the Marshall Plan simultaneously helped the U.S. economy and highlighted values of generosity and humanitarianism.

The Soviet Union made its own contributions to the enactment of the Marshall Plan. Not wanting to be judged responsible for the division of Europe, U.S. officials had extended the invitation to develop a recovery plan to every European nation. Foreign ministers from the Soviet Union, Britain, and France met to discuss a response, but Stalin balked at sharing economic information with other participants, and he wanted German industry used for reparations rather than for European recovery. The Soviet representative walked out of the meeting, and Stalin ordered the Eastern European satellites not to participate. Consequently, no U.S. aid would be going to Communist countries. Further solidifying public and congressional support for the

Marshall Plan, the iron curtain moved westward in February 1948, when Communists in Czechoslovakia staged a coup and took over the government.

In the end, security interests carried the day. Senator Arthur Vandenberg, a leading Republican spokesman on foreign policy and an advocate for the Marshall Plan opened the debate on the ERP bill with the warning, "The exposed frontiers of hazard move almost hourly to the west." Other members of Congress echoed their support for the Marshall Plan in terms that emphasized the Soviet threat, such as Oklahoma senator Elmer Thomas's argument that European aid would "enable the free countries of Europe to prepare

Questions for Analysis

Summarize the Argument: What does the author conclude were the U.S. government's primary motivations for launching the ERP?

Analyze the Evidence: What specific risks did the U.S. government hope to avoid by implementing the ERP? What conditions enabled the ERP to gain the support of the Republican-controlled Congress?

Consider the Context: How did external events that occurred during the period between Marshall's proposal for European aid in June 1947 and its enactment into law in April 1948 influence the passage of the ERP? What specific events were significant in the passage of the ERP?

Louis Armstrong in Düsseldorf
As one of its Cold War weapons, the United States sent representatives of American culture abroad. Jazz was especially popular around the world, and the State Department sponsored tours by black jazz artists in part to counter the image of the United States as a racist nation. Louis Armstrong, the great trumpet player, singer, and jazz innovator, is shown here captivating a German crowd in 1952. AP Photo/Albert Gillhausen.

stop the descent of the iron curtain, but it aggressively and successfully promoted economic recovery and a military shield for the rest of Europe.

Superpower Rivalry around the Globe

Efforts to implement containment moved beyond Europe. In Africa, Asia, and the Middle East, World War II accelerated a tide of national liberation movements against war-weakened imperial powers. By 1960, forty countries had won their independence. These nations, along with Latin America, came to be referred to collectively as the third world.

Like Woodrow Wilson during World War I, Roosevelt and Truman promoted the ideal of self-determination. The United States granted independence to the Philippines in 1946 and applauded the British withdrawal from India. As the Cold War intensified, however, the ideal of self-determination gave way to concern when new governments supplanting the old empires failed to emulate the American model. U.S. policymakers encouraged democracy and capitalism in emerging nations and sought to preserve opportunities for American trade, while U.S. corporations coveted the vast oil reserves in the Middle East. Yet leaders of many liberation

movements, impressed with Russia's rapid economic growth, adopted socialist or Communist ideas. Although few of these movements had formal ties with the Soviet Union, American leaders saw them as a threatening extension of Soviet power. Seeking to hold communism at bay by fostering economic development and political stability, in 1949 the Truman administration began a small program of aid to developing nations.

Meanwhile civil war raged in China, where the Communists, led by Mao Zedong (Mao Tse-tung), fought the official Nationalist government under Jiang Jieshi (Chiang Kai-shek). While the Communists gained popular support for their land reforms, Jiang's corrupt, incompetent government alienated much of the population, and his military forces had been devastated by the Japanese. Failing to achieve a settlement between Jiang and Mao, the United States provided $3 billion in aid to the Nationalists. Yet, recognizing the ineptness of Jiang's government, Truman refused to divert further resources from Europe to China.

In October 1949, Mao established the People's Republic of China (PRC), and the Nationalists fled to the island of Taiwan. Fearing a U.S.-supported invasion to recapture China for the Nationalists, Mao signed a mutual defense treaty with the Soviet Union. The United States refused to recognize the PRC, blocked its admission to the United Nations, and supported the Nationalist government in Taiwan. Only a massive U.S. military commitment could have stopped the Chinese Communists, yet some Republicans charged that Truman and "pro-Communists in the State Department" had "lost" China. China became a political albatross for the Democrats, who resolved never again to be vulnerable to charges of being soft on communism.

With China in turmoil, U.S. policy shifted to helping Japan rapidly reindustrialize. In a short time, the Japanese economy was flourishing, and the official military occupation ended when the two nations signed a peace treaty and a mutual security pact in September 1951. Like West Germany, Japan now sat squarely within the American orbit, ready to serve as an economic hub in a vital area.

The one place where Cold War considerations did not control American policy was Palestine. In 1943, then-senator Harry Truman spoke passionately about Nazi Germany's annihilation of the Jews, asserting, "This is not a Jewish problem, it is an American problem—and we must . . . face it squarely and honorably." As president, he made good on his words. Jews had been migrating to Palestine, their biblical homeland, since the nineteenth century, resulting in tension and hostilities with the Palestinian Arabs. After World War II, as hundreds of thousands of European Jews sought refuge and a national homeland in Palestine, fighting and terrorism escalated on both sides.

Truman's foreign policy experts sought American-Arab friendship to contain Soviet influence in the Middle East and to secure access to Arabian oil. Uncharacteristically defying his advisers, the president responded instead to pleas from Jewish organizations, his moral commitment to Holocaust survivors, and his interest in the American Jewish vote. When Jews in Palestine declared the state of Israel in May 1948, Truman quickly recognized the new country and made its defense the cornerstone of U.S. policy in the Middle East.

Israel, 1948

REVIEW　What factors contributed to the emergence of the Cold War?

▶ Truman and the Fair Deal at Home

Referring to the Civil War general who coined the phrase "War is hell," Truman said in December 1945, "Sherman was wrong. I'm telling you I find peace is hell." Challenged by crises abroad, Truman also faced shortages, strikes, and inflation as the economy shifted to peacetime production. At the same time, he tried to expand the New Deal with his own Fair Deal agenda of initiatives in civil rights, housing, education, and health care—efforts hindered by the wave of anti-Communist hysteria sweeping the country. In sharp contrast to the bipartisan support Truman won for his foreign policy, he achieved few domestic reforms.

Reconverting to a Peacetime Economy

Despite scarcities and deprivations, World War II had brought most Americans a higher standard of living than ever before. Economic experts as well as ordinary citizens worried about sustaining that standard and providing jobs for millions of returning soldiers. To that end, Truman asked Congress for a twenty-one-point program of social and economic reforms. He wanted the government to continue regulating the economy while it adjusted to peacetime production, and he sought government programs to provide basic essentials such as housing and health care to those in need. "Not even President Roosevelt ever asked for as much at one sitting," exploded Republican leader Joseph W. Martin Jr.

Congress approved just one of Truman's key proposals—full-employment legislation—and then only after watering it down. The Employment Act of 1946 called on the federal government "to promote maximum employment, production, and purchasing power," thereby formalizing government's responsibility for maintaining a healthy economy. It created the Council of Economic Advisors to assist the president, but it authorized no new powers to translate the government's obligations into effective action.

Inflation, not unemployment, turned out to be the biggest problem. Consumers had $30 billion in wartime savings to spend, but shortages of meat, automobiles, housing, and other items persisted, thereby driving up prices. With a basket of groceries to dramatize rising costs, Helen Gahagan Douglas urged Congress to maintain price and rent controls. Those efforts, however, fell to pressures from business groups and others determined to trim government powers.

Labor relations were another thorn in Truman's side. Organized labor emerged from the war with its 14.5 million members making up 35 percent of the nonagricultural workforce. Yet union members feared the erosion of wartime gains and turned to the weapon they had surrendered during the war. Five million workers went out on strike in 1946, affecting nearly every major industry. Shortly before voting to strike, a former Marine and his coworkers calculated that an executive had spent more on a party than they would earn in a whole year at the steel mill. "That sort of stuff made us realize, hell we had to bite the bullet. . . . The bosses sure didn't give a damn for us." Although most Americans approved of unions in principle, they became fed up with strikes and blamed unions for shortages and rising prices. When the strikes subsided, workers had won wage increases of about 20 percent, but the loss of overtime pay and rising

prices left their purchasing power only slightly higher than in 1942.

Women workers fared even worse. Polls indicated that 68 to 85 percent wanted to keep their wartime jobs, but most who remained in the workforce had to settle for relatively low-paying jobs in light industry or the service sector (Figure 26.1). Displaced from her shipyard work, Marie Schreiber took a cashier's job, lamenting, "You were back to women's wages, you know . . . practically in half." With the backing of women's organizations and union women, Congresswoman Douglas sponsored bills to require equal pay for equal work, provide child care for employed mothers, and create a government commission to study women's status. But at a time when women were viewed primarily as wives and mothers and opposition to further expansion of federal powers was strong, these initiatives got nowhere.

By 1947, the economy had stabilized, avoiding the postwar depression that so many had feared. Wartime profits enabled businesses to expand. Consumers could now spend their wartime savings on items that had lain beyond their reach during the depression and war. Defense spending and foreign aid that enabled war-stricken countries to purchase American products also stimulated the economy. A soaring birthrate further sustained consumer demand. Although prosperity was far from universal, the United States entered into a remarkable economic boom that lasted through the 1960s (see "New Work and Living Patterns in an Economy of Abundance" in chapter 27).

Another economic boost came from the only large welfare measure passed after the New Deal. The Servicemen's Readjustment Act (GI Bill), enacted in 1944, offered 16 million veterans job training and education; unemployment compensation until they found jobs; and low-interest loans to purchase homes, farms, and small businesses. By 1948, some 1.3 million veterans had bought houses with government loans. Helping 2.2 million ex-soldiers attend college, the subsidies sparked a boom in higher education. A drugstore clerk before his military service, Don Condren was able to get an engineering degree and buy his first house. "I think the GI Bill gave the whole country an upward boost economically," he said.

Yet the impact of the GI Bill was uneven. As wives and daughters of veterans, women benefited indirectly from the GI subsidies, but few women qualified for the employment and educational preferences available to some 15 million men. Moreover, GI programs were administered at the state and local levels, which

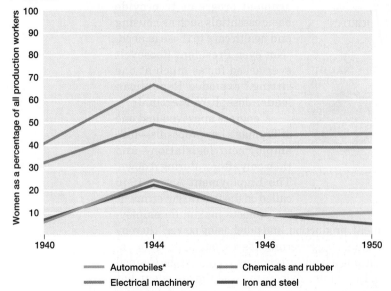

FIGURE 26.1 Women Workers in Selected Industries, 1940–1950 Women demolished the idea that some jobs were "men's work" during World War II, but they failed to maintain their gains in the manufacturing sector after the war.

Women as a percentage of all production workers

- Automobiles*
- Chemicals and rubber
- Electrical machinery
- Iron and steel

*During World War II, this industry did not produce cars, but rather military transportation such as jeeps, tanks, aircraft, etc.

VISUAL ACTIVITY

Women's Role in Peacetime

Like many manufacturers during World War II, Proctor Electric Company, which had shifted its focus from making appliances to producing bomb fuses, cartridges, and airplane wing flaps, hoped to profit after the war from pent-up consumer demand. Even before the company had fully reconverted its plants, ads tempted consumers with products soon to come, as in this 1946 ad. Picture Research Consultants & Archives.

READING THE IMAGE: Why do you think a woman is featured in this ad? Considering the scene in the background, what message is conveyed about women's employment during and after the war?

CONNECTIONS: How did the shortage of consumer goods affect the postwar economy? What role did consumer goods play in the economic revival?

resulted in routine racial and ethnic discrimination, especially in the South. Southern universities remained segregated, and historically black colleges could not accommodate all who wanted to attend. Black veterans were shuttled into menial labor. One decorated veteran reported "My color bars me from most decent jobs, and if, instead of accepting menial work, I collect my $20 a week readjustment allowance, I am classified as a 'lazy nigger.'" Thousands of black veterans did benefit, but the GI Bill did not help all ex-soldiers equally.

Blacks and Mexican Americans Push for Their Civil Rights

"I spent four years in the army to free a bunch of Frenchmen and Dutchmen," an African American corporal declared, "and I'm hanged if I'm going to let the Alabama version of the Germans kick me around when I get home." Black veterans along with civilians resolved not to return to the racial injustices of prewar America. The migration of two million African Americans to northern and western cities meant that they could now vote and participate in ongoing struggles to end discrimination in housing and education. Pursuing civil rights through the courts and Congress, the National Association for the Advancement of Colored People (NAACP) counted half a million members.

In the postwar years, individual African Americans broke through the color barrier, achieving several "firsts." Jackie Robinson integrated major league baseball, playing for the Brooklyn Dodgers and braving abuse from fans and players to win the Rookie of the Year Award in 1947. In 1950, Ralph J. Bunche received the Nobel Peace Prize for his United Nations work, and Gwendolyn Brooks won the Pulitzer Prize for poetry. Some organizations, such as the American Medical Association in 1949, opened their doors to black members. Still, little had changed for most African Americans, especially in the South, where violence greeted their attempts to assert their rights. Armed white men prevented Medgar Evers (who would become a key civil rights leader in the 1960s) and four other veterans from voting in Mississippi. A mob lynched Isaac Nixon for voting in Georgia, and an all-white jury acquitted the men accused of his murder. Segregation and economic discrimination were widespread in the North as well.

The Cold War heightened U.S. leaders' sensitivity to racial issues, as the superpowers vied for the allegiance of newly independent nations with nonwhite populations, and Soviet propaganda repeatedly highlighted racial injustice in the United States. Secretary of State Dean Acheson noted that systematic segregation and discrimination endangered "our moral leadership of the free and democratic nations of the world."

Integration of the Military
Truman's 1948 executive order integrating the armed services met steely resistance from parts of the military and took years to implement fully. The pressures of the Korean War forced the military to use African Americans where personnel were needed, placing black and white soldiers, such as these Marines, side by side. In 1954, the army dissolved its last all-black unit. Official Marine Corps Photo #A171810.

"My very stomach turned over when I learned that Negro soldiers just back from overseas were being dumped out of army trucks in Mississippi and beaten," wrote Truman. Risking support from southern white voters, Truman spoke more boldly on civil rights than any previous president had. In 1946, he created the President's Committee on Civil Rights, and in February 1948 he asked Congress to enact the committee's comprehensive recommendations. The first president to address the NAACP, Truman asserted that all Americans should have equal rights to housing, education, employment, and the ballot.

As with much of his domestic program, Truman failed to act aggressively on his bold words. Congress rejected his proposals for national civil rights legislation, although some non-southern states did pass laws against discrimination in employment and public accommodations. Running for reelection in 1948 and hoping to appeal to northern black and liberal voters, Truman issued an executive order to desegregate the armed services, but it lay unimplemented until the Korean War, when the cost of segregation to military efficiency became apparent. Then officers gradually integrated their ranks, and by 1953 nearly all African Americans served in mixed units. Although actual accomplishments fell far short of Truman's proposals,

desegregation of the military and the administration's support of civil rights cases in the Supreme Court contributed to far-reaching changes.

Discussion of race and civil rights usually focused on African Americans, but Mexican Americans fought similar injustices. In 1929, they had formed the League of United Latin American Citizens (LULAC) to combat discrimination and segregation in the Southwest. Like black soldiers, Mexican American veterans believed, as one insisted, that "we had earned our credentials as American citizens." Problems with getting their veterans' benefits spurred the formation of the American GI Forum in 1948 in Corpus Christi, Texas. Dr. Héctor Peréz García, president of the local LULAC and a Bronze Star combat surgeon, led the GI Forum, which became a national force for battling discrimination and electing sympathetic officials.

"Education is our freedom," read the GI Forum's motto, yet Mexican American children were routinely segregated in public schools. In 1945, with the help of LULAC, parents filed a class action suit in southern California, challenging school districts that barred their children from white schools. In the resulting decision, *Mendez v. Westminster* (1947), a federal court for the first time struck down school segregation. NAACP lawyer Thurgood Marshall filed a

supporting brief in the case, which foreshadowed the landmark *Brown v. Board of Education* decision of 1954 (see "African Americans Challenge the Supreme Court and the President" in chapter 27). Efforts to gain equal education, challenges to employment discrimination, and campaigns for political representation all demonstrated a growing mobilization of Mexican Americans in the Southwest.

The Fair Deal Flounders

Republicans capitalized on public frustrations with strikes and shortages in the 1946 congressional elections, accusing the Truman administration of "confusion, corruption, and communism." Helen Gahagan Douglas kept her seat, but the Republicans captured control of Congress for the first time in fourteen years. Many had campaigned against the New Deal, and in the Eightieth Congress they weakened some reform programs and enacted tax cuts favoring higher-income groups.

Organized labor took the most severe blow when Congress passed the **Taft-Hartley Act** over Truman's veto in 1947. Called a "slave labor" law by unions, the measure amended the Wagner Act (see "Empowering Labor" in chapter 24), putting restraints on unions that reduced their power to bargain with employers and made it more difficult to organize workers. States could now pass "right-to-work" laws, which banned the practice of requiring all workers to join a union once a majority had voted for it. Many states, especially in the South and West, rushed to enact such laws, encouraging industries to relocate there. Taft-Hartley maintained the New Deal

principle of government protection for collective bargaining, but it tipped the balance of power more in favor of management.

In the 1948 elections, Truman faced not only a resurgent Republican Party headed by New York governor Thomas E. Dewey but also two revolts within his own party. On the left, Henry A. Wallace, whose foreign policy views had cost him his cabinet seat, led the new Progressive Party. On the right, South Carolina governor J. Strom Thurmond headed the States' Rights Party—the Dixiecrats—formed by southern Democrats who walked out of the 1948 Democratic Party convention when it passed a liberal civil rights plank.

Truman launched a vigorous campaign, yet his prospects were so bleak that on election night the *Chicago Daily Tribune* printed its next day's issue with the headline "Dewey Defeats Truman." But even though the Dixiecrats won four southern states, Truman took 303 electoral votes to Dewey's 189, and his party regained control of Congress (Map 26.2). Truman's unexpected victory attested to the broad support for his foreign policy and the enduring popularity of New Deal reform.

While most New Deal programs survived Republican attacks, Truman failed to enact his Fair Deal agenda. Congress made modest improvements in Social Security and raised the minimum wage, but it passed only one significant reform measure. The **Housing Act of 1949** authorized 810,000 units of government-constructed housing over the next six years and represented a landmark commitment by the government to address the housing needs of the poor. Yet it fell far short of actual need, and slum clearance frequently displaced the poor without providing alternatives.

VISUAL ACTIVITY

Truman's 1948 Victory

Although large crowds turned out for Truman's coast-to-coast "whistle-stop" campaign, most experts thought he had little chance to win the election, given the defections from his party on both the left and right. Polls predicted that Dewey would win about 50 percent of the popular vote and Truman around 45 percent, but the last one was taken two weeks before election day. W. Eugene Smith/Getty Images.

READING THE IMAGE: The *Chicago Daily Tribune* was one of Truman's harshest critics, but its incorrect headline resulted primarily from a printers' strike that required it to go to press earlier than normal. Truman retorted, "Ain't the way I heard it," and here gloats over the error before a crowd of supporters. What made the victory especially satisfying?

CONNECTIONS: Truman was under attack by Republicans and could not get his Fair Deal through Congress. Why do you think Americans responded so well to his campaign? In what ways have presidential campaigns changed since Truman's time?

With southern Democrats posing a primary obstacle, Congress rejected Truman's proposals for civil rights, a powerful medical lobby blocked plans for a universal health care program, and

Candidate	Electoral Vote	Popular Vote	Percent of Popular Vote
Harry S. Truman (Democrat)	303	24,105,695	49.5
Thomas E. Dewey (Republican)	189	21,969,170	45.1
J. Strom Thurmond (States' Rights)	39	1,169,021	2.4
Henry A. Wallace (Progressive)	0	1,156,103	2.4

Map 26.2
The Election of 1948

conflicts over race and religion thwarted federal aid to education. Truman's efforts to revise immigration policy were mixed. The McCarran-Walter Act of 1952 ended the outright ban on immigration and citizenship for Japanese and other Asians, but it authorized the government to bar suspected Communists and homosexuals and maintained the discriminatory quota system established in the 1920s.

Truman's concentration on foreign policy rather than domestic proposals contributed to the failure of his Fair Deal. By late 1950, the Korean War embroiled the president in controversy and depleted his power as a legislative leader (see pages 766–69). Truman's failure to make good on his domestic proposals set the United States apart from most European nations, which by the 1950s had in place comprehensive health, housing, and employment security programs to underwrite the material well-being of their populations.

The Domestic Chill: McCarthyism

Truman's domestic agenda also suffered from a wave of anticommunism that weakened

"YOU READ BOOKS, EH?"

VISUAL ACTIVITY

The Red Scare

A celebrated editorial cartoonist for the *Washington Post*, Herbert Lawrence Block was a frequent critic of McCarthyism. In this 1949 cartoon, he addressed the intimidation of teachers, which occurred across the country in public schools and universities. Public officials demanded that teachers take loyalty oaths, grilled them about their past and present political associations, and fired those who refused to cooperate. A 1949 Herblock Cartoon, © The Herb Block Foundation.

READING THE IMAGE: What is the effect of portraying a female teacher and nine hefty male investigators? What does the man with scissors appear to be doing, and how does this ridicule the Red scare? Do you think it was coincidental that the artist included a portrait of Thomas Jefferson, who inspired the Bill of Rights?

CONNECTIONS: How did the Red scare affect the prospects of Truman's domestic agenda?

liberals. "Red-baiting" (attempting to link individuals or ideas with communism) and official retaliation against leftist critics of the government had flourished during the Red scare at the end of World War I (see "The Red Scare" in chapter 22), and Republicans had attacked the New Deal as a plot of radicals. A second Red scare followed World War II, born of partisan politics, foreign policy setbacks, and disclosures of Soviet espionage.

Republicans jumped on events such as the Soviet takeover of Eastern Europe and the Communist triumph in China to accuse Democrats of fostering internal subversion. Wisconsin senator Joseph R. McCarthy avowed that "the Communists within our borders have been more responsible for the success of Communism abroad than Soviet Russia." McCarthy's charges—such as the allegation that retired general George C. Marshall belonged to a Communist conspiracy—were reckless and often ludicrous, but the press covered him avidly, and *McCarthyism* became a term synonymous with the anti-Communist crusade.

Revelations of Soviet espionage lent credibility to fears of internal communism. A number of ex-Communists, including Whittaker Chambers and Elizabeth Bentley, testified that they and others had provided secret documents to the Soviets. Most alarming of all, in 1950 a British physicist working on the atomic bomb project confessed that he was a spy and implicated several Americans, including Ethel and Julius Rosenberg. The Rosenbergs pleaded not guilty but were convicted of conspiracy to commit espionage and electrocuted in 1953.

Records opened in the 1990s showed that the Soviet Union did receive secret documents from Americans that probably hastened its development of nuclear weapons by a year or two. Yet the vast majority of individuals hunted down in the Red scare had done nothing more than at one time joining the Communist Party, associating with Communists, or supporting radical causes. And nearly all the accusations related to activities that had taken place long before the Cold War had made the Soviet Union an enemy.

The hunt for subversives was conducted by both Congress and the executive branch. Stung by charges of communism in the 1946 midterm elections, Truman issued Executive Order 9835 in March 1947, establishing loyalty review boards to investigate every federal employee. "A nightmare from which there [was] no awakening" was how State Department employee Esther Brunauer described it when she and her husband, a chemist in the navy, both lost their jobs because he had joined a Communist youth organization in the 1920s and associated with suspected radicals. Government investigators allowed anonymous informers to make charges and placed the burden of proof on the accused. More than two thousand civil service employees lost their jobs, and another

An Immigrant Scientist Encounters the Anti-Communist Crusade

Qian Xuesen (Tsien Hsue-shen), whose name means "study to be wise," was born to a privileged family in Hangzhou, China, in 1911 and graduated at the top of his class from Jiaotong University in Shanghai, China's best engineering school. Deciding that aviation was the wave of the future and aware of how far behind his country lagged in flight, Qian looked abroad to further his education. In 1935, with his country torn by Japanese aggression and internal opposition to the Nationalist government, he accepted an American-sponsored scholarship and quickly earned a master's degree in aeronautical engineering from the Massachusetts Institute of Technology (MIT). One year later, he moved to the California Institute of Technology (Caltech) in Pasadena, where he earned a Ph.D.

At Caltech, Qian joined a group of scientists working on questions about flight and contributed to the development of theoretical aerodynamics and jet propulsion, which eventually provided a foundation for America's space program. School officials were so impressed with Qian's work that they helped him get a visa extension, and in 1942 the government gave him security clearance so that he could work on secret military

projects. Qian served on the air force's Scientific Advisory Board, and after World War II he went on a U.S. mission to interview Nazi scientists in Germany. He spent a year on the faculty at MIT and then traveled home to China amid the turmoil of a civil war between the Communists, led by Mao Zedong (Mao Tse-tung), and the Nationalist government of Jiang Jieshi (Chiang Kai-shek). There Qian spent time with his father, gave motivational speeches to large audiences of students, and married a woman he had known in childhood, an opera singer and the daughter of one of Jiang Jieshi's generals.

In 1949, he returned to Caltech to direct the Jet Propulsion Center, teach, and continue his lifelong passion for scientific research. With satisfying work and a close circle of colleagues whom he entertained with classical music and elaborate dinners, Qian seemed to have all he could want. He applied for U.S. citizenship, but one year later, after the Communists had taken control of China, the U.S. government revoked Qian's security clearance. The FBI interrogated him about a group he had socialized with in the 1930s, which the FBI said was a cell of the Communist Party. Qian denied any participation in Communist activities,

but the proud, angry, and humiliated scientist concluded that, given the "cloud of suspicion . . . the only gentlemanly thing left to do is to depart." The promise of a brilliant career shattered, he resisted Caltech officials who begged him to remain; instead, he readied a shipment of his belongings to send on to China. The government seized the shipment and accused Qian of taking secret documents. Although the claim was later refuted, the Immigration and Naturalization Service arrested him. He was released after two weeks, but for the next five years the government refused to let him go, kept him and his family under constant surveillance, and barred his research. Although Caltech administrators worked furiously to clear his name, some of his associates began to avoid him, fearing that they, too, would be caught up in the hunt for Communists. Finally, in 1955, he was deported as part of a prisoner of war exchange following the Korean War.

Qian disembarked in China with his wife and two children to a hero's reception and a career that would eventually earn him the title of "father of Chinese rocketry." Denied the full use of his talents by the United States, he organized and led China's

ten thousand resigned as Truman's loyalty program continued into the mid-1950s. Hundreds of homosexuals resigned or were fired over charges of "sexual perversion," which anti-Communist crusaders said could subject them to blackmail. Years later, Truman said privately that the loyalty program had been a mistake.

Congressional committees, such as the **House Un-American Activities Committee (HUAC),** also investigated individuals' political associations. When those under scrutiny refused to name

names, investigators charged that silence was tantamount to confession, and these "unfriendly witnesses" lost their jobs and suffered public ostracism. In 1947, HUAC investigated radical activity in Hollywood. Some actors and directors cooperated, but ten refused, citing their First Amendment rights. The "Hollywood Ten" served jail sentences for contempt of Congress—a punishment that Helen Gahagan Douglas fought—and then found themselves blacklisted in the movie industry. Popular crooner Frank Sinatra,

Qian Xuesen

Qian Xuesen, the Chinese rocket scientist, teaches a class at the California Institute of Technology in 1955, shortly before his deportation back to China. Students who worked with him were "awestruck" by his brilliance. They recalled that he generously mentored those whose mental powers matched his, but was impatient and harsh toward those he deemed intellectually incapable. Bettmann/Corbis.

we forced him to go." The Red scare dashed Qian's belief that America promised an opportunity for any talented individual to live a free and prosperous life. It also delivered a brilliant scientist to the nation's enemy.

Questions for Analysis

Consider the Context: How did the timing of events in Qian's case correlate with domestic and international developments related to the Cold War and McCarthyism? How were other people and ideas silenced during the Red scare?

Analyze the Evidence: What does Qian's case reveal about the power of individual agency? Could he have done anything differently to avoid the surveillance and subsequent deportation?

Ask Historical Questions: What caused Qian's status to change from that of trusted government adviser to that of suspected subversive?

rocketry program, developing its ballistic missiles and satellites. Like anyone who hoped to have a successful career in China, he became a trusted Communist Party official. Though the extremely private scientist said little about his experiences in the United States, he refused to return in 1979 to accept Caltech's Distinguished Alumni Award. Qian had lost faith in the U.S. government but maintained affection for the American people and sent both his children to study at American universities. He died in China in 2009 at the age of ninety-eight.

Questions linger about Qian's associations and intentions in the United States. A 1999 congressional report maintained that he had been a spy, but his supporters claimed that the report lacked evidence. Every one of his Caltech colleagues vouched for his integrity, and some went to great lengths to defend him against government charges. Dan A. Kimball, who was secretary of the navy in the early 1950s, later said that Qian's deportation "was the stupidest thing this country ever did. He was no more a Communist than I was—and

a defender of the Hollywood Ten, wondered if someone called for "a square deal for the underdog, will they call you a Commie?"

The Truman administration went after the Communist Party directly, prosecuting its leaders under a 1940 law that made it a crime to "advocate the overthrow and destruction of the [government] by force and violence." Although civil libertarians argued that the guilty verdicts violated First Amendment freedoms of speech, press, and association, the Supreme Court ruled

in 1951 that the Communist threat overrode constitutional guarantees.

The domestic Cold War spread beyond the nation's capital. State and local governments investigated citizens, demanded loyalty oaths, fired employees suspected of disloyalty, banned books from public libraries, and more. College professors and public school teachers lost their jobs in New York, California, and elsewhere. (See "Experiencing the American Promise," above.) Because the Communist Party had helped organize unions and championed racial justice, labor and civil rights activists fell prey to McCarthyism as well. African American activist Jack O'Dell remembered that segregationists pinned the tag of Communist on "anybody who supported the right of blacks to have civil rights."

McCarthyism caused untold harm to thousands of innocent individuals. Anti-Communist crusaders humiliated and discredited law-abiding citizens, hounded them from their jobs, and in some cases even sent them to prison. The anti-Communist crusade violated fundamental constitutional rights of freedom of speech and association and stifled the expression of dissenting ideas or unpopular causes.

> **REVIEW**   Why did Truman have limited success in implementing his domestic agenda?

▶ The Cold War Becomes Hot: Korea

The Cold War erupted into a shooting war in June 1950 when troops from Communist North Korea invaded South Korea. For the first time, Americans went into battle to implement containment. Confirming the global reach of the Truman Doctrine, U.S. involvement in Korea also marked the militarization of American foreign policy. The United States, in concert with the United Nations, ultimately held the line in Korea, but at a great cost in lives, dollars, and domestic unity.

MAP ACTIVITY

Map 26.3   The Korean War, 1950–1953
Although each side had plunged deep into enemy territory, the war ended in 1953 with the dividing line between North and South Korea nearly where it had been before the fighting began.

READING THE MAP: How far south did the North Korean forces progress at the height of their invasion? How far north did the UN forces get? What countries border Korea, and what was the significance of these particular countries' presence so close to the territory in dispute?

CONNECTIONS: What dangers did the forays of MacArthur's forces to within forty miles of the Korean-Chinese border pose? Why did Truman forbid MacArthur to approach that border? What political considerations on the home front influenced Truman's policy and military strategy regarding Korea?

Korea and the Military Implementation of Containment

The **Korean War** grew out of the artificial division of Korea after World War II. Having expelled the Japanese, the United States and the Soviet Union created two occupation zones separated by the thirty-eighth parallel (Map 26.3). With Moscow and Washington unable to agree on unification, the United Nations sponsored elections in South Korea in July 1948. The American-favored candidate, Syngman Rhee, was elected president, and the United States withdrew most of its troops. In the fall of 1948, the Soviets established the People's Republic of North Korea under Kim Il-sung and also withdrew. Although unsure whether Rhee's repressive government could sustain popular support, U.S. officials appreciated his anticommunism and provided economic and military aid to South Korea.

Skirmishes between North and South Korean troops at the thirty-eighth parallel began in 1948. Then, in June 1950, 90,000 North Koreans swept into South Korea. Truman's advisers assumed

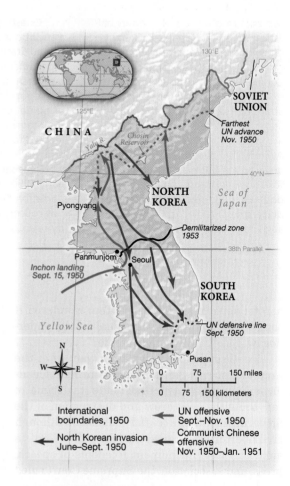

On the Defensive in Korea
After UN troops approached the Yalu River, the Chinese entered the Korean War, throwing UN forces on the defensive and pushing deep into the South. In this photo, taken in April 1951, infantrymen are protecting a pontoon bridge so that UN trucks and tanks on the other side can escape the advancing Chinese army. Eventually, UN forces recaptured this territory. AP Photo/James Martenhoff.

that the Soviet Union or China had instigated the attack (an assumption later proved incorrect), and the president quickly decided to intervene, viewing Korea as "the Greece of the Far East." With the Soviet Union absent from the Security Council, the United States obtained UN sponsorship of a collective effort to repel the attack. Authorized to appoint a commander for the UN force, Truman named World War II hero General Douglas MacArthur.

Sixteen nations sent troops to Korea, but the United States furnished most of the personnel and weapons, deploying almost 1.8 million troops and dictating strategy. By dispatching troops without asking Congress for a declaration of war, Truman violated the spirit if not the letter of the Constitution and contributed to the expansion of executive power that would characterize the Cold War.

The first American soldiers rushed to Korea unprepared and ill equipped: "I didn't even know how to dig a foxhole," recalled a nineteen-year-old army reservist, who was told by his sergeant to "Make it like a grave." As a result, U.S. forces suffered severe defeats early in the war. The North Koreans took the capital of Seoul and drove deep into South Korea, forcing UN troops to retreat to Pusan. Then, in September 1950, General MacArthur launched a bold counteroffensive at Inchon, 180 miles behind North Korean lines. By October, UN and South Korean forces had retaken Seoul

and pushed the North Koreans back to the thirty-eighth parallel. Now Truman had to decide whether to invade North Korea and seek to unify the country.

From Containment to Rollback to Containment

"Troops could not be expected . . . to march up to a surveyor's line and stop," remarked Secretary of State Dean Acheson, reflecting support for transforming the military objective from containment to elimination of the enemy and unification of Korea. Thus, for the only time during the Cold War, the United States tried to roll back communism by force. With UN approval, on September 27, 1950, Truman authorized MacArthur to cross the thirty-eighth parallel. Concerned about possible intervention by China, the president directed him to keep UN troops away from the Korean-Chinese border. Disregarding the order, MacArthur sent them to within forty miles of China, whereupon 300,000 Chinese soldiers crossed into Korea. With Chinese help, the North Koreans recaptured Seoul.

After three months of grueling battle, UN forces fought their way back to the thirty-eighth parallel. At that point, Truman decided to seek a negotiated settlement. MacArthur was furious when the goal of the war reverted to containment, which to him represented defeat. Taking his case

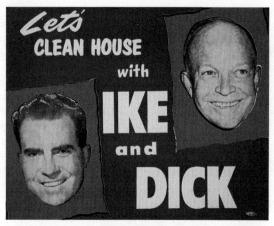

The 1952 Republican Ticket
This 1952 campaign poster shows Republican presidential nominee Dwight D. Eisenhower with his running mate Richard Nixon. The slogan refers to scandals involving Truman associates, but not Truman himself, and his failure to end the Korean War. David J. & Janice L. Frent Collection/Corbis.

to the public, he challenged both the president's authority to conduct foreign policy and the principle of civilian control of the military. Fed up with MacArthur's insubordination, Truman fired him in April 1951. Many Americans sided with MacArthur, reflecting their frustration with containment. Why should Americans die simply to preserve the status quo? Why not destroy the enemy once and for all? Those siding with MacArthur assumed that the United States was all-powerful and blamed the stalemate in Korea on the government's ineptitude or willingness to shelter subversives.

When Congress investigated MacArthur's dismissal, all of the top military leaders supported the president. According to the chairman of the Joint Chiefs of Staff, MacArthur wanted to wage "the wrong war, at the wrong place, at the wrong time, with the wrong enemy." Yet Truman never recovered from the political fallout. Nor was he able to end the war. Negotiations began in July 1951, but peace talks dragged on for two years while 12,000 more U.S. soldiers died.

Korea, Communism, and the 1952 Election

Popular discontent with Truman's war boosted Republicans in the 1952 election. Their presidential nominee, General Dwight D. Eisenhower, was a popular hero. As supreme commander in Europe, he won widespread acclaim for leading the Allied armies to victory over Germany in

World War II, and in 1950 Truman appointed Eisenhower the first supreme commander of NATO forces.

Although Eisenhower believed that professional soldiers should stay out of politics, he found compelling reasons to run in 1952. He largely agreed with Truman's foreign policy, but he deplored the Democrats' propensity to solve domestic problems with costly new federal programs. He also disliked the foreign policy views of leading Republican presidential contender Senator Robert A. Taft, who attacked containment and sought to cut defense spending. Eisenhower defeated Taft for the nomination, but the old guard prevailed on the party platform. It excoriated containment as "negative, futile, and immoral" and charged the Truman administration with shielding "traitors to the Nation in high places." By choosing thirty-nine-year-old Senator Richard M. Nixon for his running mate, Eisenhower helped to appease the right wing of the party.

Richard Milhous Nixon grew up in southern California, worked his way through college and law school, served in the navy, and briefly practiced law before winning election to Congress in 1946. Nixon quickly made a name for himself as a member of HUAC and a key anti-Communist, moving to the Senate with his victory over Helen Gahagan Douglas in 1950.

With his public approval ratings plummeting, Truman decided not to run for reelection. The Democrats nominated Adlai E. Stevenson, the popular governor of Illinois, but he could neither escape the domestic fallout from the Korean War nor match Eisenhower's widespread appeal. Shortly before the election, Eisenhower announced dramatically, "I shall go to Korea," and voters registered their confidence in his ability to end the war. Cutting sharply into traditional Democratic territory, Eisenhower won several southern states and garnered 55 percent of the popular vote overall. His coattails carried a narrow Republican majority to Congress.

An Armistice and the War's Costs

Eisenhower made good on his pledge to end the Korean War. In July 1953, the two sides reached an armistice that left Korea divided, again roughly at the thirty-eighth parallel, with North and South separated by a two-and-a-half-mile-wide demilitarized zone (see Map 26.3). The war fulfilled the objective of containment, since the United States had backed up its promise to help nations that were resisting communism. Both

Truman and Eisenhower managed to contain what amounted to a world war—involving twenty nations altogether—within a single country and to avoid the use of nuclear weapons.

Yet the war took the lives of 36,000 Americans and wounded more than 100,000. Thousands of U.S. soldiers suffered as prisoners of war. South Korea lost more than a million people to war-related causes, and 1.8 million North Koreans and Chinese were killed or wounded.

Korea had an enormous effect on defense policy and spending. In April 1950, just before the war began, the National Security Council completed a top-secret report, known as **NSC 68**, on the United States' military strength, warning that national survival required a massive military buildup. The Korean War brought about nearly all of the military expansion called for in NSC 68, vastly increasing U.S. capacity to act as a global power. Military spending shot up from $14 billion in 1950 to $50 billion in 1953 and remained above $40 billion thereafter. By 1952, defense spending claimed nearly 70 percent of the federal budget, and the size of the armed forces had tripled.

To General Matthew Ridgway, MacArthur's successor as commander of the UN forces, Korea taught the lesson that U.S. forces should never again fight a land war in Asia. Eisenhower concurred. Nevertheless, during the Korean War the Truman administration had expanded its role in Asia by increasing aid to the French, who were fighting to hang on to their colonial empire in Indochina. As U.S. Marines retreated from a battle against Chinese soldiers in 1950, they sang, prophetically, "We're Harry's police force on call, / So put back your pack on, / The next step is Saigon."

REVIEW   How did U.S. Cold War policy lead to the Korean War?

▶ Conclusion: The Cold War's Costs and Consequences

Hoping for continued U.S.-Soviet cooperation rather than unilateral American intervention to resolve foreign crises, Helen Gahagan Douglas initially opposed the implementation of containment. By 1948, however, she was squarely behind Truman's decision to fight communism throughout the world, a decision that marked the most momentous foreign policy initiative in the nation's history.

More than any development in the postwar world, the Cold War defined American politics and society for decades to come. It transformed the federal government, shifting its priorities from domestic to external affairs, greatly expanding its budget, and substantially increasing the power of the president. Military spending helped transform the nation itself, as defense contracts promoted economic and population booms in the West and Southwest. The nuclear arms race put the people of the world at risk, consumed resources that might have been used to improve living standards, and skewed the economy toward dependence on military projects.

In sharp contrast to foreign policy, the domestic policies of the postwar years reflected continuity with the 1930s. Douglas had come to Congress hoping to expand the New Deal, to help find "a way by which all people can live out their lives in dignity and decency." She avidly supported Truman's proposals for new programs in education, health, and civil rights, but a majority of her colleagues did not. Consequently, the poor and minorities suffered even while a majority of Americans enjoyed a higher standard of living in an economy boosted by Cold War spending and the reconstruction of Western Europe and Japan.

Another cost of the early Cold War years was the anti-Communist hysteria that swept the nation, denying Douglas a Senate seat, intimidating radicals and liberals, and narrowing the range of ideas acceptable for political discussion. Partisan politics and Truman's warnings about the Communist menace fueled McCarthyism, along with popular frustrations over the failure of containment to produce clear-cut victories. The Korean War, which ended in stalemate rather than the defeat of communism, exacerbated feelings of frustration. It would be a major challenge of the Eisenhower administration to restore national unity and confidence.

See the Selected Bibliography for this chapter in the Appendix.

26 Chapter Review

KEY TERMS

Cold War (p. 748)
iron curtain (p. 748)
containment (p. 748)
Truman Doctrine (p. 751)
Marshall Plan (p. 752)
North Atlantic Treaty Organization (NATO) (p. 753)
Central Intelligence Agency (CIA) (p. 753)
Taft-Hartley Act (p. 761)
Housing Act of 1949 (p. 761)
House Un-American Activities Committee (HUAC) (p. 764)
Korean War (p. 766)
NSC 68 (p. 769)

REVIEW QUESTIONS

1. What factors contributed to the emergence of the Cold War? (pp. 747–757)

2. Why did Truman have limited success in implementing his domestic agenda? (pp. 757–766)

3. How did U.S. Cold War policy lead to the Korean War? (pp. 766–769)

MAKING CONNECTIONS

1. What was the containment policy, and how successful was it up to 1953? Discuss the views of both the supporters and the critics of the policy.

2. How did returning American soldiers change postwar domestic life in the areas of education and civil rights? Discuss how wartime experiences influenced their demands.

3. Why did anti-Communist hysteria sweep the country in the early 1950s? How did it shape domestic politics? Be sure to consider the influence of developments abroad and at home.

LINKING TO THE PAST

1. What events and decisions during World War II contributed to the rise of the Cold War in the late 1940s? (See chapter 25.)

2. What did the anti-Communist hysteria of the late 1940s and the 1950s have in common with the Red scare that followed World War I, and how did these two phenomena differ? (See chapter 22.)

27 The Politics and Culture of Abundance
1952–1960

CONTENT LEARNING OBJECTIVES

After reading and studying this chapter, you should be able to:

- Explain the major issues of the Eisenhower administration and how Eisenhower's approach represented the politics of the "Middle Way."

- Describe how the Eisenhower administration practiced containment and explain how the "New Look" in foreign policy influenced its handling of world events.

- Explain the factors that led to an economy of abundance and how that abundance influenced Americans' lives.

- Analyze how the economy of abundance influenced consumption, religion, gender roles, and the media.

- Explain the origins of the modern civil rights movement and the strategies activists used to end racial segregation.

1959 CADILLAC
The automobile reflected 1950s prosperity and generated one of every six jobs. This Cadillac was manufactured by General Motors, the biggest and richest corporation in the world. Bill Philpot/Alamy Stock Photo.

TRAILED BY REPORTERS, VICE PRESIDENT RICHARD M. NIXON LED Soviet premier Nikita Khrushchev through the American National Exhibition in Moscow in July 1959. The display of American consumer goods was part of a cultural exchange that reflected a slight thaw in the Cold War after Khrushchev replaced Stalin. In Moscow, both Khrushchev and Nixon seized on the propaganda potential of the moment. As they examined the display, they exchanged a slugfest of words and gestures that reporters dubbed the kitchen debate.

Showing off a new color television set, Nixon said that the Soviet Union "may be ahead of us . . . in the thrust of your rockets," but he insisted that the United States outstripped the Soviets in consumer goods. Nixon linked capitalism with democracy, asserting that the array of products represented "what freedom means to us . . . our right to choose." Moreover, Nixon boasted that "any steelworker could buy this house," as the two leaders walked through a model of a six-room ranch-style home. Khrushchev retorted that in the Soviet Union "you are entitled to housing," whereas in the United States the homeless slept on the pavement.

Nixon declared that the household appliances were "designed to make things easier for our women." Khrushchev disparaged "the capitalist attitude

771

The Kitchen Debate
Soviet premier Nikita Khrushchev (left) and Vice President Richard M. Nixon (center) debate the merits of their nations' different economies at the American National Exhibition held in Moscow in 1959. "You are a lawyer for capitalism and I am a lawyer for communism," Khrushchev told Nixon as each tried to outdo the other. AP Photo.

toward women," maintaining that the Soviets appreciated women's contributions to the economy, not their domesticity. Nixon got Khrushchev to agree that it was "far better to be talking about washing machines than machines of war," yet Cold War tensions surfaced when Khrushchev later blustered, "We too are giants. You want to threaten— we will answer threats with threats."

In fact, the Eisenhower administration (1953–1961) had begun with threats, and the two nations engaged in an intense arms race throughout the decade and beyond. During the 1952 campaign, Republicans had vowed to roll back communism and liberate "enslaved" peoples under Soviet rule. In practice, President Dwight D. Eisenhower pursued a containment policy much like that of his predecessor, Harry S. Truman, though Eisenhower relied more on nuclear weapons and on Central Intelligence Agency (CIA) secret operations against left-leaning governments. Yet as Nixon's visit to Moscow demonstrated, Eisenhower seized on political changes in the Soviet Union to reduce tensions in Soviet-American relations.

Continuity with the Truman administration also characterized domestic policy. Although Eisenhower favored corporations with tax cuts and resisted strong federal efforts in health care, education, and race relations, he did not try to demolish the New Deal. He even extended the reach of the federal government with a massive highway program.

Although poverty clung stubbornly to one of every five Americans, the Moscow display testified to the unheard-of material gains savored by many in the postwar era. Cold War weapons production spurred the economy, whose vitality stimulated suburban development, contributed to the growth of the South and Southwest (the Sun Belt), and enabled millions of Americans to buy a host of new products. As new homes, television sets, and household appliances transformed living patterns, Americans took part in a consumer culture that celebrated the family and traditional gender roles, even as more and more married women took jobs outside the home. Challenging the dominant norms were dissenting writers known as the Beats and an emerging youth culture.

The Cold War and the economic boom helped African Americans mount the most dramatic challenge of the 1950s, a struggle against the system of segregation and disfranchisement that had replaced slavery. Large numbers of African Americans took direct action against the institutions of injustice, developing the organizations, leadership, and strategies to mount a civil rights movement of unprecedented size and influence.

▶ Eisenhower and the Politics of the "Middle Way"

Moderation was the guiding principle of Eisenhower's domestic agenda and leadership style. In 1953, he pledged a "middle way between untrammeled freedom of the individual and the demands for the welfare of the whole Nation," promising that his administration would "avoid government by bureaucracy as carefully as it avoids neglect of the helpless." Eisenhower generally resisted expanding the federal government's power, he acted reluctantly when the Supreme Court ordered schools to desegregate, and his administration terminated the federal trusteeship of dozens of Indian tribes. As a moderate Republican, however, Eisenhower supported the continuation of New Deal programs, and in some cases, such as in the creation of a national highway system, he expanded federal action. Nicknamed "Ike," the confident war hero remained popular, but he was not able to lift his party to national dominance.

Modern Republicanism

In contrast to the old guard conservatives in his party who criticized containment and wanted to repeal much of the New Deal, Dwight D. Eisenhower preached "modern Republicanism." This meant resisting additional federal intervention in economic and social life, but not turning the clock back to the 1920s. "Should any political party attempt to abolish social security and eliminate labor laws and farm programs," he wrote privately in 1954, "you would not hear of that party again in our political history." Democratic control of Congress after the elections of 1954 further contributed to Eisenhower's moderate approach.

The new president attempted to distance himself from the anti-Communist fervor that had plagued the Truman administration, even as he intensified Truman's loyalty program, allowing federal executives to dismiss thousands of employees on grounds of loyalty, security, or "suitability." Reflecting his inclination to avoid controversial issues, Eisenhower refused to denounce Senator Joseph McCarthy publicly. But, in 1954, McCarthy began to destroy himself when he hurled reckless charges of communism against military personnel during televised hearings. When the army's lawyer demanded of

CHRONOLOGY

1952	• Dwight D. Eisenhower elected president.
1953	• CIA organizes coup against Iranian government.
1954	• CIA organizes coup against Guatemalan government. • Geneva accords end French presence in Vietnam. • United States begins aid to South Vietnam. • Operation Wetback begins. • *Hernandez v. Texas* decided. • *Brown v. Board of Education* decided. • Senate condemns Senator Joseph McCarthy.
1955	• Eisenhower and Khrushchev meet in Geneva.
1955–1956	• Montgomery, Alabama, bus boycott carried out.
1956	• Interstate Highway and Defense System Act becomes law. • Eisenhower reelected.
1957	• Southern Christian Leadership Conference (SCLC) founded. • Soviets launch *Sputnik*. • Civil Rights Act of 1957 passes.
1958	• National Aeronautics and Space Administration (NASA) established. • National Defense Education Act passes.
1959	• Nixon and Khrushchev engage in kitchen debate.
1960	• Soviets shoot down U.S. U-2 spy plane. • One-quarter of Americans live in suburbs. • Thirty-five percent of women work outside the home.

McCarthy, "Have you left no sense of decency?" those in the hearing room applauded. A Senate vote in 1954 to condemn him marked the end of his influence but not the end of harassing dissenters on the left.

Eisenhower sometimes echoed conservative Republicans' conviction that government was best left to the states and economic decisions to private business. Yet he signed laws bringing ten million more workers under Social Security, increasing the minimum wage, and creating a new Department of Health, Education, and Welfare. And when the spread of polio neared epidemic proportions, Eisenhower obtained funds from Congress to distribute a vaccine, even though conservatives wanted the states to bear that responsibility.

Eisenhower's greatest domestic initiative was the **Interstate Highway and Defense System Act of 1956** (Map 27.1). Promoted as essential to national defense and an impetus to economic growth, the act authorized construction of a national highway system, with the federal government paying most of the costs through increased fuel and vehicle taxes. The new highways accelerated the mobility of people and goods, spurred suburban expansion, and benefited the trucking, construction, and automobile industries that had lobbied hard for the law. Eventually, the monumental highway project exacted unforeseen costs in the form of air pollution, energy consumption, declining railroads and mass transportation, and decay of central cities.

In other areas, Eisenhower restrained federal activity in favor of state governments and private enterprise. His large tax cuts directed most benefits to business and the wealthy, and he resisted federal aid to primary and secondary education as well as strong White House leadership on behalf of civil rights. Eisenhower opposed national health insurance, preferring the growing practice of private insurance provided by employers. Although Democrats sought to keep nuclear power in government hands, Eisenhower signed legislation authorizing the private manufacture and sale of nuclear energy. The first commercial nuclear power plant opened in 1958 in northwest Pennsylvania.

Termination and Relocation of Native Americans

Eisenhower's efforts to limit the federal government were consistent with a new direction in Indian policy, which reversed the New Deal emphasis on strengthening tribal governments and preserving Indian culture (see "Neglected Americans and the New Deal" in chapter 24). After World War II, when some 25,000 Indians had left their homes for military service and another 40,000 for work in defense industries, policymakers began to favor assimilating Native Americans and ending their special relationships with the government.

To some officials, who reflected Cold War emphasis on conformity to dominant American values, the communal practices of Indians resembled socialism and stifled individual initiative. Eisenhower's commissioner of Indian affairs, Glenn Emmons, did not believe that tribal lands could produce income sufficient to eliminate poverty, but he also revealed the bias of policymakers when he insisted that Indians wanted to "work and live like Americans." Moreover, Indians still held rights to water, land, minerals, and other resources that were increasingly attractive to state governments and private entrepreneurs.

By 1960, the government had implemented a three-part program of compensation, termination, and relocation. In 1946, Congress established

The Polio Vaccine

Building on the work of other scientists, Dr. Jonas Salk, a researcher at the University of Michigan and the University of Pittsburgh, was the first to develop a successful polio vaccine. In this 1953 photo, he injects a girl during the trials that established the drug's success. Salk became a national hero when the vaccine became available to millions of children in 1955. Hulton Archive/Getty Images.

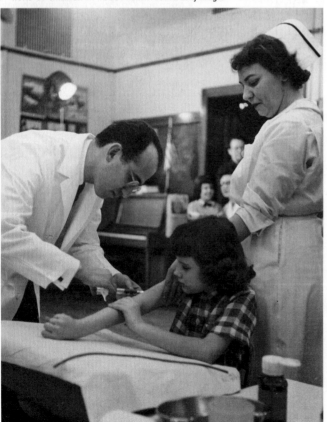

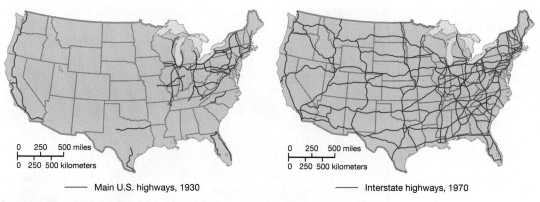

——— Main U.S. highways, 1930   ——— Interstate highways, 1970

MAP ACTIVITY

Map 27.1   The Interstate Highway System, 1930 and 1970

Built with federal funds authorized in the Interstate Highway and Defense System Act of 1956, superhighways soon crisscrossed the nation. Trucking, construction, gasoline, and travel were among the industries that prospered, but railroads suffered from the subsidized competition.

READING THE MAP: What regions of the United States had main highways in 1930? What regions did not? How had the situation changed by 1970?

CONNECTIONS: What impact did the growth of the interstate highway system have on migration patterns in the United States? What benefits did the new interstate highways bring to Americans and at what costs?

---

the Indian Claims Commission to hear outstanding claims by Native Americans for land taken by the government. When it closed in 1978, the commission had settled 285 cases, with compensation exceeding $800 million. Yet the awards were based on land values at the time the land was taken and did not include interest.

The second policy, termination, also originated in the Truman administration when Commissioner Dillon S. Myer asserted that his Bureau of Indian Affairs should do "nothing for Indians which Indians can do for themselves." Beginning in 1953, Eisenhower signed bills transferring jurisdiction over tribal land to state and local governments and ending the trusteeship relationship between Indians and the federal government. The loss of federal hospitals, schools, and other special arrangements devastated Indian tribes. As had happened after passage of the Dawes Act in 1887 (see "The Dawes Act and Indian Land Allotment" in chapter 17), corporate interests and individuals took advantage of the opportunity to purchase Indian land cheaply. The government abandoned termination in the 1960s after some 13,000 Indians

and more than one million acres of their land had been affected.

The Indian Relocation Program, the third piece of Native American policy, began in 1948 and involved more than 100,000 Native Americans by 1973. The government encouraged Indians to move to cities, where relocation centers were supposed to help with housing, job training, and medical care. Even though Indians were moved far from their reservations, about one-third returned.

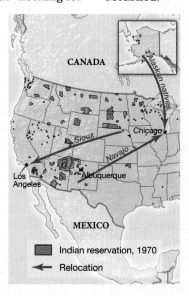

Major Indian Relocations, 1950–1970

Indian reservation, 1970
Relocation

Most who stayed in cities faced racism, unemployment, poor housing, and the loss of their traditional culture. "I wish we had never left home," said one woman whose husband was out of work and drinking heavily. "It's dirty and noisy, and people all around, crowded. . . . It seems like I never see the sky or trees." Reflecting long-standing disagreements among Indians themselves, some who overcame these obstacles applauded the program. But most urban Indians remained poor, and even many who had welcomed relocation worried that "we would lose our identity as Indian people, lose our culture and our [way] of living." Within

VISUAL ACTIVITY

Indian Relocation

As part of its new emphasis on assimilation, the Bureau of Indian Affairs urged Native Americans to move from their reservations to cities, and the percentage of Indians in urban areas grew from 13.4 in 1950 to 44 in 1970. Jack Riddle/Getty Images.

READING THE IMAGE: In 1955, Native Americans who had relocated to Denver formed an intertribal organization, the Denver White Buffalo Council of American Indians, to help Indians survive economically and adjust to their new environment. This 1959 photo captures a weekly gathering of the council. What does it suggest about other goals of the organization?

CONNECTIONS: How did Indian relocation fit into larger goals of the Eisenhower administration?

two decades, a national pan-Indian movement—a by-product of this urbanization—emerged to resist assimilation and to demand much more for Indians (as discussed in "Native American Protest" in chapter 28).

The 1956 Election and the Second Term

Eisenhower easily defeated Adlai Stevenson in 1956, doubling his victory margin of 1952. Yet Democrats kept control of Congress, and in the midterm elections two years later, they all but wiped out the Republican Party, gaining a 64–34 majority in the Senate and a 282–135 advantage in the House. Although Ike captured voters' hearts, a majority of Americans remained wedded to the programs and policies of the Democrats.

Eisenhower faced more serious leadership challenges in his second term. When the economy plunged into a recession in late 1957, he fought with Congress over the budget and vetoed bills to expand housing, urban development, and public works projects. The president and Congress did agree on the first, though largely symbolic, civil rights law in a century and on a larger federal role in education, largely in the interest of national security (as discussed on pages 795 and 782).

In the end, the first Republican administration after the New Deal left the functions of the federal government intact, though it tipped policy benefits somewhat toward corporate interests. Even with two recessions, unparalleled prosperity graced the Eisenhower years, and inflation was kept low. Eisenhower celebrated what he called the "wide diffusion of wealth and incomes" across the United States, yet amid the remarkable abundance were some forty million impoverished Americans. Rural deprivation was particularly pronounced, as was poverty among the elderly, African Americans, and other minorities.

REVIEW   How did Eisenhower's domestic policies reflect his moderate political vision?

▶ Liberation Rhetoric and the Practice of Containment

At his first inauguration, Eisenhower warned that "forces of good and evil are massed and armed and opposed as rarely before in history." Like Truman, he saw communism as a threat to the nation's security and economic interests, and he wanted to keep the United States the most powerful country in the world. Eisenhower's foreign policy differed, however, in three areas: its rhetoric, its means, and—after Stalin's death in 1953—its movement toward accommodation with the Soviet Union.

Although some Republicans, such as Secretary of State John Foster Dulles, deplored containment as "negative, futile, and immoral," the Eisenhower administration did not attempt to roll back communism with force. Nuclear weapons and CIA secret operations took on a more prominent role in defense strategy, and the United States intervened at the margins of Communist power in Asia, Latin America, and the Middle East. Toward the end of his presidency, Eisenhower sought to ease tensions between the superpowers.

The "New Look" in Foreign Policy

Eisenhower was determined to control military expenditures in order to balance the budget and cut taxes. Reflecting American confidence in technology and opposition to a large peacetime army, Eisenhower's "New Look" in defense strategy concentrated U.S. military strength in nuclear weapons and missiles to deliver them. Instead of maintaining large ground forces of its own, the United States would arm friendly nations and back them up with an ominous nuclear arsenal, providing, according to one defense official, "more bang for the buck." Dulles believed that America's willingness to "go to the brink" of war with its intimidating nuclear weapons—a strategy called brinksmanship—would block any Soviet efforts to expand.

Nuclear weapons could not stop a Soviet nuclear attack, but in response to one, they could inflict enormous destruction. This certainty of "massive retaliation" was meant to deter the Soviets from launching an attack. Because the Soviet Union could respond similarly to an American first strike, this nuclear standoff became known as **mutually assured destruction**, or **MAD**. As leaders of both nations pursued an ever-escalating arms race, the United States stayed on top of the Soviet Union in nuclear warheads and delivery missiles.

Nuclear weapons could not roll back the iron curtain. When a revolt against the Soviet-controlled government began in Hungary in 1956, Dulles's liberation rhetoric proved to be empty. A radio plea from Hungarian freedom fighters cried, "SOS! They just brought us a rumor that the American troops will be here within one or two hours." But help did not come. Eisenhower was unwilling to risk U.S. soldiers and possible nuclear war, and

---

Missiles in the Nuclear Age
By the 1950s, both the United States and the Soviet Union were arming missiles with nuclear weapons, and the U.S. Air Force began to deploy those missiles in Europe before it developed the capability to strike Moscow from a launching site in the United States. This photograph shows the first Thor ballistic missile arriving at an RAF base in Norfolk, England, in 1958. © Mary Evans/The Image Works.

Soviet troops soon suppressed the insurrection, killing or wounding thousands of Hungarians.

Applying Containment to Vietnam

A major challenge to the containment policy came in Southeast Asia. During World War II, Ho Chi Minh and his nationalist coalition, the Vietminh, fought both the occupying Japanese forces and the French colonial rulers. In 1945, the Vietminh declared Vietnam's independence from France, and when France fought back, the area plunged into war. Because Ho declared himself a Communist, the Truman administration quietly began to provide aid to the French. American principles of national self-determination took a backseat to the battle against communism.

Eisenhower viewed communism in Vietnam much as Truman had regarded it in Greece and Turkey. In what became called the **domino theory**, Eisenhower explained, "You have a row of dominoes, you knock over the first one, and what will happen to the last one is the certainty that it will go over very quickly." A Communist victory in Southeast Asia, he warned, could trigger the fall of Japan, Taiwan, and the Philippines. By 1954, the United States was paying 75 percent of the cost of France's war, but Eisenhower resisted a larger role. When the French asked for American troops and planes to avert almost certain defeat in the battle for Dien Bien Phu, Eisenhower, remembering the Korean War, refused.

Dien Bien Phu fell to the Vietminh in May 1954, and two months later in Geneva a truce was signed. The Geneva accords recognized Vietnam's independence and temporarily partitioned it at the seventeenth parallel, separating the Vietminh in the north from the puppet government established by the French in the south. Within two years, the Vietnamese people were to vote in elections for a unified government. Some officials warned against U.S. involvement in Vietnam, envisioning "nothing but grief in store for us if we remained in that area." Eisenhower and Dulles nonetheless moved to prop up the dominoes with a new alliance and put the CIA to work infiltrating and destabilizing North

Geneva Accords, 1954

Vietnam. Fearing a Communist victory in the elections mandated by the Geneva accords, they supported South Vietnamese prime minister Ngo Dinh Diem's refusal to hold the vote.

Between 1955 and 1961, the United States provided $800 million to the South Vietnamese army (ARVN). Yet the ARVN proved grossly unprepared for the guerrilla warfare that began in the late 1950s. With help from Ho Chi Minh's government in Hanoi, Vietminh rebels in the south stepped up their attacks on the Diem government. The insurgents gained support from the largely Buddhist peasants, who were outraged by the repressive regime of the Catholic, Westernized Diem. Unwilling to abandon containment, Eisenhower left his successor with a deteriorating situation and a firm commitment to defend South Vietnam against communism.

Interventions in Latin America and the Middle East

While supporting friendly governments in Asia, the Eisenhower administration sought to topple unfriendly ones in Latin America and the Middle East. Officials saw internal civil wars in terms of the Cold War conflict between the superpowers and often viewed nationalist movements as Communist challenges to democracy. They also acted against governments that threatened U.S. economic interests. The Eisenhower administration took this course of action out of sight of Congress and the public, making the CIA an important arm of foreign policy.

Guatemala's government, under the popularly elected president Jacobo Arbenz, was not Soviet controlled, but it accepted support from the small local Communist Party. In 1953, Arbenz moved to help landless, poverty-stricken peasants by nationalizing land owned, but not cultivated, by the United Fruit Company, a U.S. corporation whose annual profits were twice the size of Guatemala's budget. United Fruit refused Arbenz's offer to compensate the company at the value of the land it had declared for tax purposes. Then, equating Arbenz's reformist government with the spread of communism, the CIA provided pilots and other support to an opposition army that overthrew the elected government and installed a military dictatorship in 1954. United Fruit kept its land, and Guatemala succumbed to destructive civil wars that lasted through the 1990s.

In 1959, when Cubans' desire for political and economic autonomy erupted into a revolution led by Fidel Castro, a CIA agent promised "to take care of Castro just like we took care of Arbenz." American companies controlled major Cuban resources, and decisions made in Washington directly influenced the lives of the Cuban people. The 1959 **Cuban revolution** drove out the U.S.-supported dictator Fulgencio Batista and led the CIA to warn Eisenhower that "Communists and other extreme radicals appear to have penetrated the Castro movement." When the United States denied Castro's requests for loans, he turned to the Soviet Union. And when U.S. companies refused Castro's offer to purchase their Cuban holdings at their assessed value, he began to nationalize their property. Many anti-Castro Cubans fled to the United States and reported his atrocities. (See "Experiencing the American Promise," page 780.) Before leaving office, Eisenhower broke off diplomatic relations with Cuba and authorized the CIA to train Cuban exiles for an invasion to overthrow the Castro government.

In the Middle East, the CIA intervened in Iran to oust an elected government, support an unpopular dictatorship, and maintain Western access to Iranian oil (see Map 30.3). In 1951, the Iranian parliament, led by Prime Minister Mohammed Mossadegh, nationalized the country's oil fields and refineries, which had been held primarily by a British company and from which Iran received less than 20 percent of profits. Britain strongly objected to the takeover and eventually sought help from the United States.

Advisers convinced Eisenhower that Mossadegh, whom *Time* magazine had called "the Iranian George Washington," left Iran vulnerable to communism, and the president wanted to keep oil-rich areas "under the control of people who are friendly." With Eisenhower's authorization, CIA agents instigated a coup, bribing army officers and financing demonstrations in the streets. In August 1953, Iranian army officers captured Mossadegh and reestablished the authority of the shah, Mohammad Reza Pahlavi, known for favoring Western interests and the Iranian wealthy classes. U.S. companies received a 40 percent share of Iran's oil concessions. But resentment over the intervention would poison U.S.-Iranian relations into the twenty-first century.

The CIA Helps Restore the Shah of Iran
Iranian prime minister Mohammed Mossadegh's commitment to democracy threatened the authority of Shah Reza Pahlavi, and his nationalization of Iran's oil alarmed U.S. officials. In 1953, President Eisenhower authorized the CIA to organize a coup against Mossadegh, which its agents did by paying bribes to military and political leaders and staging street demonstrations. Here demonstrators rally in support of the shah. AP Photo/Aziz Rashki.

Operation Pedro Pan: Young Political Refugees Take Flight

Six-year-old María was awakened before dawn one summer day in Cuba in 1962. Her parents drove her to the Havana airport, with one suitcase and her favorite doll. A paper pinned to her gingham dress gave her name and the phone number of family friends in Miami who were to meet her. She traveled with a six-year-old boy whose father in Miami had obtained the visa waivers the children would need to enter the United States. María, excited but anxious, had never been away from her parents before; she would not see them for four months.

On a different flight that summer, ten-year-old Carlos flew to Miami with his older brother, leaving behind a father they would never see again. Because of their age difference, the boys were separated on arrival and sent to different refugee camps in rural Florida. A family acquaintance—a Cuban lawyer working as a janitor in Miami—helped them gain temporary placement with foster families just ten blocks apart. A few months later, they were transferred to a juvenile delinquent facility that provided only one meal a day. Finally, a Cuban uncle arrived and took them with him to a small midwestern town where no one spoke Spanish. After three years of traumatic

separation, their mother fled Cuba and joined them.

María and Carlos were just two of more than fourteen thousand unaccompanied children, ages six to eighteen, whose lives were dramatically changed by the Cold War. They left Cuba as part of a special U.S. government–facilitated program called Operation Pedro Pan, which functioned from December 1960 to October 1962. With little money, no knowledge of English, and often no friends or relatives to receive them, the children faced daunting loneliness and possibly neglect. What drove the parents of these children to take such an extraordinary step?

The U.S. government had already made unusual accommodation for the large exodus of adults fleeing Cuba after Fidel Castro came to power in 1959. Assuming that the refugees would return as soon as Castro's government fell, the United States relaxed immigration restrictions for Cubans, allowed refugees to work, and authorized millions of dollars in relief and resettlement funds for people "subjected to the captivity of Communist despotism." The U.S. government felt an obligation to shelter Cubans who had worked in the government or military of deposed dictator Fulgencio Batista, who had been a close U.S.

ally. Many other Cubans who fled after the revolution had worked for U.S.-owned businesses. Still others were wealthy landowners, business owners, and professionals. By the fall of 1962, 248,000 Cubans had chosen to flee communism, furnishing the United States with a powerful symbolic statement of Cold War politics.

An even more potent symbol was Operation Pedro Pan, with its implication that Castro's Cuba had to be truly terrible for parents to part with their children, even though they expected to see their children soon. Cuban parents who opposed Castro feared not for their children's lives, but for their minds. Public schools in Cuba reportedly taught an escalating rhetoric of revolution, while private schools were shut down. Compulsory military service for boys and summer programs relocating teenagers to jobs teaching literacy in the rural countryside threatened parental rights to determine their children's activities. Relatively prosperous Cuban families did not benefit from Castro's reforms, which focused on improving health and education for the impoverished masses. Their fears of socialized child rearing were reinforced by a program of disinformation allegedly broadcast from a CIA radio station, which warned parents that

Elsewhere in the Middle East, Eisenhower continued Truman's support of Israel but also pursued friendships with Arab nations to secure access to oil and build a bulwark against communism. U.S. officials demanded that smaller nations take the American side in the Cold War, even when those nations preferred neutrality.

In 1955, as part of this effort to win Arab allies, Secretary of State Dulles began talks with Egypt about American support to build the Aswan Dam on the Nile River. The following year, Egypt's leader, Gamal Abdel Nasser, sought arms from Communist Czechoslovakia, formed a military alliance with other Arab nations, and recognized

OPERATION PEDRO PAN GROUP, INC.

Mel Martinez

Melquiades R. (Mel) Martinez left Cuba for the United States in 1962 at the age of fifteen and lived in youth camps and with foster families for six years until his parents arrived. In 2004, he became the first Cuban American elected to the U.S. Senate, where he parted ways with other conservative Republicans to work with Democrats on immigration reform. AP Photo/Lynne Sladky.

Florida in the U.S. Senate. María de los Angeles Torres and Carlos Eire, two among the thousands, grew up to become university professors in the United States. But some of the children, now grown, have questioned whether coming to America was worth the trauma they endured and have speculated that Cold War politics might have shaped the operation more than humanitarian concerns.

Questions for Analysis

Analyze the Evidence: What motivated adults to leave Cuba after the Castro revolution, and what motivated parents to send their children out of Cuba?

Recognize Viewpoints: What were the propaganda benefits to the United States in Operation Pedro Pan?

Ask Historical Questions: In what other ways did anticommunism shape relationships between the United States and Latin American countries?

"the Revolutionary Government will take [your children] away from you when they turn five and will keep them until they are eighteen." Rumors of Communist indoctrination ran rampant.

Fear of communism gripped the United States in the 1950s, and the Pedro Pan exodus both demonstrated and heightened that fear. The belief that Communists brainwashed children and turned them against their parents led some Cuban parents to try to save their children by sending them to a country that celebrated freedom. As with the adult refugees who had fled Cuba for the United States, parents of the Pedro Pan children believed that the trip would be temporary, until the fall of Castro's regime. Most children reunited with their parents in the United States, and some had prominent careers, such as Mel Martinez, who represented

the People's Republic of China. In retaliation, Dulles called off the deal for the dam.

In July 1956, Nasser responded by seizing the Suez Canal, then owned by Britain and France but scheduled to revert to Egypt within seven years. In response to the seizure, Israel, whose forces had been skirmishing with Egyptian troops along their common border since 1948, attacked Egypt, with help from Britain and France. Eisenhower opposed the intervention, recognizing that the Egyptians had claimed their own territory and that Nasser "embodie[d] the emotional demands of the people ... for independence." Calling on the United Nations to arrange a truce, he pressured Britain and France to pull back, forcing Israel to retreat.

Despite staying out of the Suez crisis, Eisenhower made it clear in a January 1957 speech that the United States would actively combat communism in the Middle East. In March, Congress approved aid to any Middle Eastern nation "requesting assistance against armed aggression from any country controlled by international communism." The president invoked this **Eisenhower Doctrine** to send aid to Jordan in 1957 and troops to Lebanon in 1958 to counter anti-Western pressures on those governments.

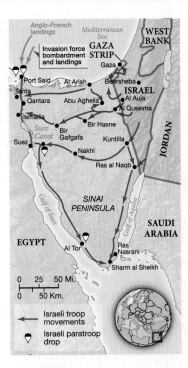

The Suez Crisis, 1956

The Nuclear Arms Race

While Eisenhower moved against perceived Communist inroads abroad, he also sought to reduce superpower tensions. After Stalin's death in 1953, Nikita Khrushchev emerged as a more moderate leader. Like Eisenhower, who remarked privately that the arms race would lead "at worst to atomic warfare, at best to robbing every people and nation on earth of the fruits of their own toil," Khrushchev wanted to reduce defense spending and the threat of nuclear devastation. Eisenhower and Khrushchev met in Geneva in 1955 at the first summit conference since the end of World War II. Although the meeting produced no new agreements, it symbolized what Eisenhower called "a new spirit of conciliation and cooperation."

In August 1957, the Soviets test-fired their first intercontinental ballistic missile (ICBM) and, two months later, beat the United States into space by launching *Sputnik*, the first man-made satellite to circle the earth. The United States launched a successful satellite of its own in January 1958, but *Sputnik* raised fears that the Soviets led not only in missile development and space exploration but also in science and education. In response, Eisenhower established the National Aeronautics and Space Administration (NASA) with a huge budget increase for space exploration. He also signed the National Defense Education Act, providing support for students in math, foreign languages, and science and technology.

Eisenhower assured the public that the United States possessed nuclear superiority. In fact, during his presidency, the stockpile of nuclear weapons more than quadrupled. With ICBMs at home and in Britain, the United States was prepared to deploy more in Italy and Turkey. In 1960 the United States launched the first Polaris submarine carrying nuclear missiles. Yet nuclear weapons could not guarantee security for either superpower because they both possessed sufficient capacity to devastate each other. Most Americans did not follow Civil Defense Administration recommendations to construct home bomb shelters, but they did realize how precarious their lives had become. A new organization, the Committee for a Sane Nuclear Policy, called the nuclear arms race "a danger unlike any danger that has ever existed."

In the midst of the arms race, the superpowers continued to talk, and by 1960, the two sides were close to a ban on nuclear testing. But just before a planned summit in Paris, a Soviet missile shot down an American U-2 spy plane over Soviet territory. The State Department first denied that U.S. planes had been violating Soviet airspace, but the Soviets produced the pilot and the photos taken on his flight. Eisenhower and Khrushchev met briefly, but the U-2 incident dashed all prospects for a nuclear arms agreement.

As Eisenhower left office, he warned about the growing influence of the **military-industrial complex**. Eisenhower had struggled against persistent pressures from defense contractors who, in tandem with the military, sought more dollars for newer, more powerful weapons systems. In his farewell address, he warned that the "conjunction of an immense military establishment and a large arms industry ... exercised a total influence ... in every city, every state house, every office of the federal government," but his administration had done little to curtail the defense industry's power. The Cold War had created a warfare state.

REVIEW   Where and how did Eisenhower practice containment?

VISUAL ACTIVITY

The Age of Nuclear Anxiety

As schools routinely held drills to prepare for possible Soviet attacks, children directly experienced the anxiety and insecurity of the 1950s nuclear arms race. The federal government distributed this pamphlet about how to protect oneself from an atomic attack. Photo: American Stock Archive/Getty Images; pamphlet: Lynn Museum and Historical Society.

READING THE IMAGE: How effective do you think the strategy pictured here would be in a nuclear attack? Why would the government suggest that civilians could protect themselves?

CONNECTIONS: In what other ways did the Cold War shape the everyday lives of Americans?

▶ New Work and Living Patterns in an Economy of Abundance

Stimulated by Cold War spending and technological advances, economic productivity increased enormously in the 1950s. A multitude of new items came on the market, and consumption became the order of the day. Millions of Americans enjoyed new homes in the suburbs, and higher education enrollments skyrocketed. Although every section of the nation enjoyed the new abundance, the Southwest and South—the Sun Belt—especially boomed in production, commerce, and population.

Work itself was changing. Fewer people labored on farms, service sector employment overtook manufacturing jobs, women's employment grew, and union membership soared. Not all Americans benefited from these changes; forty million lived in poverty. Most Americans, however, enjoyed a higher standard of living, prompting economist John Kenneth Galbraith to call the United States "the affluent society."

Technology Transforms Agriculture and Industry

Between 1940 and 1960, agricultural output mushroomed even while the number of farmworkers declined by almost one-third. Farmers achieved unprecedented productivity through greater crop specialization, intensive use of fertilizers, and, above all, mechanization. A single mechanical cotton picker replaced fifty people and cut the cost of harvesting a bale of cotton from $40 to $5.

The decline of family farms and the growth of large commercial farming, or agribusiness, were both causes and consequences of mechanization. Benefiting handsomely from federal price supports begun in the New Deal, larger farmers could afford technological improvements, while smaller producers lacked capital to purchase the

What Role Did the Government Play in the Prosperity of the Post–World War II Years?

Most observers of the past regard the twenty-five years following World War II as a golden age of economic growth and prosperity in the United States. Success was measured both by national economic statistics and by the material circumstances of individuals' lives. *Life* magazine gushed that Americans' shopping carts "became cornucopias filled with an abundance that no other country in the world has ever known." Between 1950 and 1960 alone, the gross national product increased by more than one-third, median family income grew by 30 percent, and two million factory jobs were created. The percentage of people who lived in poverty fell from around one-third at the end of the war to 15 percent in 1966.

Many factors contributed to the astonishing advance. The baby boom spurred population growth and increased the demand for commercial products. American companies faced limited competition from abroad as other nations such as Germany and Japan recovered from the war's devastation. Relative stability in the Middle East gave U.S. industry and commerce access to cheap oil, especially critical for the auto industry that boasted the largest U.S. corporation and depended on products from a host of other industries. The application of new technologies increased productivity in industry and agriculture alike. Above all, federal government activities, unnoticed and overt, worked in myriad ways to sustain and increase demand for the products of the American economy.

The government stimulated business enterprise in the name of national security both during and after the war. It sold facilities built for military purposes during World War II to private interests, and its wartime-sponsored research produced advances in areas such as plastics, aviation, and computing. Defense spending, especially after the start of the Korean War, supported many corporations and employed millions of workers. The government's foreign aid programs helped U.S. manufacturers to sell products abroad. And the Interstate Highway and Defense System Act of 1956, prompted in part by security considerations as its name suggests, stimulated a raft of industries from construction to fast food restaurants.

machinery necessary to compete. Consequently, average farm size more than doubled between 1940 and 1964, and the number of farms fell by more than 40 percent.

Many small farmers who hung on constituted a core of rural poverty. Southern landowners replaced sharecroppers and tenants with machines. Hundreds of thousands of African Americans moved to cities, where racial discrimination and a lack of jobs mired many in urban poverty. A Mississippi mother reported that most of her relatives headed for Chicago when they realized that "it was going to be machines now that harvest the crops." Worrying that "it might be worse up there" for her children, she agonized, "I'm afraid to leave and I'm afraid to stay."

New technologies also transformed industrial production. Between 1945 and 1960 the number of labor-hours needed to manufacture a car fell by 50 percent. Technology revolutionized industries such as electronics, chemicals, and air transportation. It also promoted the growth of television, plastics, computers, and other newer industries. American businesses enjoyed access to cheap oil, ample markets abroad, and little foreign competition. Even with Eisenhower's conservative fiscal policies, government spending reached $80 billion annually and created new jobs. (See "Making Historical Arguments," above.)

The strength of labor unions contributed to prosperity by putting money into the hands of people who would spend it. Real earnings for production workers shot up 40 percent. A steelworker's son remembered, "In 1946, we did not have a car, a television set, or a refrigerator. By 1952 we had all those things." In most industrial nations, government programs underwrote their citizens' security, but the United States developed a mixed system in which company-funded programs won by unions provided for retirement,

Federal contributions to the production of "human capital" for economic expansion were also linked to national defense. The GI Bill provided college or technical education for nearly eight million veterans by the late 1950s, and the federal government sent millions of dollars to universities for defense-related research, reaching $1.57 billion a year by the late 1960s.

Housing, a key industry in the postwar economic boom, benefited from government action in several ways. Homeowners may have associated government housing programs with public projects erected for the poor, but they themselves relied heavily on federally backed low-interest mortgages through the Federal Housing Association and the GI Bill of Rights. These government programs that enabled ordinary Americans to buy homes promoted the construction industry, which in turn expanded demand for everything from cement mixers to electric appliances, and created jobs for carpenters, electricians, plumbers, and others. A California suburban developer remarked, "If it weren't for the government, the boom would end overnight."

The tax code also contributed to a thriving economy by shifting money into the hands of those who were most likely to spend it. Until the 1960s, the wealthy paid income tax rates as high as 90 percent, and corporate taxes were 52 percent. This progressive tax system helped to moderate somewhat a sharply unequal distribution of national income: The top 20 percent of families saw their share of income drop from over 50 percent in the 1930s to 45 percent in 1957, while the bottom 40 percent saw their portion rise from 12 to 16 percent. The tax code also underwrote purchasing power by allowing deductions for employers who provided health care and pensions to their employees. In addition, the government subsidized homeowners by allowing them to claim income tax deductions for interest they paid on housing loans, thereby contributing to the booming housing industry.

Finally, the New Deal welfare state sustained a market for American products, even when the economy slipped into recession. Congress amended Social Security to extend unemployment insurance and old-age pensions to new segments of the population and increased benefits under both Truman and Eisenhower.

By 1960, more than five million families received $10.7 million in benefits. Government support for labor unions meant that some eighteen million workers earned higher wages than they were likely to have received without collective bargaining. Many of these workers also enjoyed guaranteed cost-of-living increases, company pensions, and health insurance. All of these programs not only improved Americans' material lives but also, by sustaining consumer demand, helped to keep the economy humming.

Questions for Analysis

Summarize the Argument: According to the author, what is a major explanation for the success of the American economy in the 1950s?

Analyze the Evidence: What examples are given to demonstrate the role of the federal government in promoting economic prosperity?

Consider the Context: What factors aside from government action contributed to the higher standard of living enjoyed by most Americans in the 1950s?

health care, paid vacations, supplementary unemployment benefits, and more. This system, often called a private welfare state, resulted in wide disparities among workers, disadvantaging those who did not belong to strong unions and those with irregular employment.

While the number of organized workers continued to grow, union membership peaked at 27.4 percent of all workers in 1957. Technological advances eliminated jobs in heavy industry. "You are going to have trouble collecting union dues from all of these machines," commented a Ford manager to union leader Walter Reuther. Moreover, the economy as a whole was shifting from production to service. Beginning in 1957, white-collar jobs outnumbered blue-collar jobs, as more workers distributed goods, performed services, provided education, and carried out government work. Unions made some headway in these fields, especially among government employees, but most service industries resisted unionization.

The growing clerical and service occupations swelled the demand for female workers, who held nearly one-third of all jobs by the end of the 1950s. The vast majority of them worked in offices, light manufacturing, domestic service, teaching, and nursing; because these occupations engaged primarily women, wages were relatively low. In 1960, the average female full-time worker earned just 60 percent of the average male worker's wages. At the bottom of the employment ladder, black women took home only 42 percent of what white men earned.

Burgeoning Suburbs and Declining Cities

Although suburbs had existed since the nineteenth century, nothing symbolized the affluent society more than their tremendous expansion in the 1950s. Eleven million new homes went up in the suburbs, and by 1960 one in four

Technology Transforms Agriculture
The years from 1945 to 1970 saw a second agricultural revolution in the United States. In 1940, one farmer could feed 10.7 people; by 1970, the ratio was one to 75.8. This photo of a Minnesota grain field in 1949 illustrates both the mechanization of agriculture and the rise of large commercial farming. Jack Fletcher/National Geographic Creative/Corbis.

Americans lived there. As Nixon boasted to Khrushchev during the kitchen debate, the suburban homes were accessible to families with modest incomes. Builder William J. Levitt adapted the factory assembly line to home construction, erecting nearly identical units so that workers moved from house to house performing one specific job. In 1949, families could purchase

The New Suburbs
William J. Levitt adapted the factory assembly-line process to home building, planning nearly identical units so that individual workers could move from house to house performing the same single operation. This photograph reflects a typical Levittown street in 1954. Bettmann/Corbis.

VISUAL ACTIVITY

Air-Conditioning

The first air-conditioning system was installed in factories, but room air-conditioning began to appear in homes in the 1930s and spread rapidly in the 1950s. Fewer than one million homes had room air conditioners in 1950, but nearly eight million did in 1960, and more than half of all homes had some form of air-conditioning by 1975, as its status changed from a luxury to a necessity. Picture Research Consultants & Archives.

READING THE IMAGE: What does this ad promise consumers? What negative effects of air-conditioning does it leave out?

CONNECTIONS: How was air-conditioning related to the rise of the Sun Belt? What other factors contributed to its growth?

mass-produced houses in his 17,000-home development, called Levittown, on Long Island, New York, for just under $8,000 each ($80,000 in 2016 dollars). Similar developments, as well as more luxurious ones, quickly went up throughout the country. The government subsidized home ownership by guaranteeing low-interest mortgages and by making interest on mortgages tax deductible. Government-funded interstate highways running through metropolitan areas also encouraged suburban development.

By the 1960s, suburbs came under attack for bulldozing the natural environment, creating groundwater contamination, and disrupting wildlife patterns. Social critic Lewis Mumford disparaged suburbia as "a multitude of uniform, unidentifiable houses in a treeless communal wasteland, inhabited by people of the same class, the same income, the same age group." Yet most families were thrilled to be able to own new homes. "It was a miracle to them," one man said of his working-class parents who moved to Levittown.

The suburbs did help polarize society, especially along racial lines. Each Levittown homeowner signed a contract pledging not to rent or sell to a non-Caucasian. The Supreme Court declared such covenants unenforceable in 1948, but suburban America remained severely segregated. Although some African Americans joined the suburban migration, most moved to cities in

search of economic opportunity, doubling their numbers in major cities during the 1950s. But those cities were already in decline, losing not only population but also commerce, industry, and jobs to the suburbs or to southern and western states. "Detroit is in the doldrums," commented social worker Mary Jorgensen in 1952.

The Rise of the Sun Belt

No regions experienced the postwar economic and population booms more intensely than the South and Southwest (Map 27.2). California overtook New York as the most populous state. Sports franchises followed fans: In 1958, the Brooklyn Dodgers moved to Los Angeles, joined by the Minneapolis Lakers three years later.

A pleasant natural environment attracted new residents to the **Sun Belt**, but no magnet proved stronger than economic opportunity. As railroads had fueled western growth in the nineteenth century, so the automobile and airplane spurred the post–World War II surge. Air-conditioning cooled nearly eight million homes by 1960, and it facilitated industrial development and tourism. "Can you conceive a Walt Disney World in central Florida without its air-conditioned hotels?" asked a journalist.

So important was the defense industry to the South and Southwest that the area was later referred to as the "Gun Belt." The aerospace industry boomed in such cities as Los Angeles and Dallas–Fort Worth, and military bases helped underwrite prosperity in San Diego and San Antonio. Although defense dollars benefited other regions—military bases and aerospace plants were numerous in the Northwest—the Sun Belt captured the lion's share of Cold War spending.

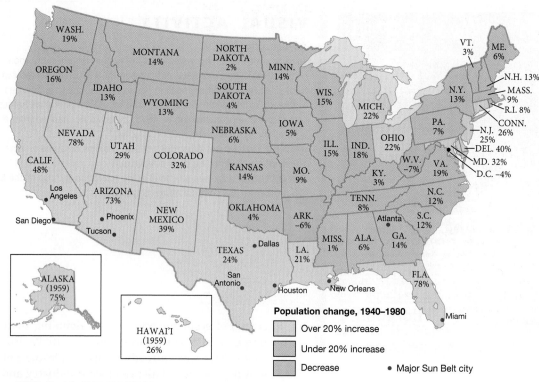

MAP ACTIVITY

Map 27.2   The Rise of the Sun Belt, 1940–1980

The growth of defense industries, a non-unionized labor force, and the spread of air-conditioning all helped spur economic development and population growth in the Southwest and the South. This made the Sun Belt the fastest-growing region of the country between 1940 and 1980.

READING THE MAP: Which states experienced population growth of more than 20 percent? Which states experienced the largest population growth?

CONNECTIONS: What stimulated the population boom in the Southwest? What role did the Cold War play in this expansion? What developments made the Southwest diverse in the composition of its population?

By the 1960s, nearly one of every three California workers held a defense-related job.

The surging populations and industries soon threatened the environment. Providing sufficient water and power to cities and to agribusiness meant building dams and reservoirs on free-flowing rivers. Native Americans lost fishing sites on the Columbia River, and dams on the Upper Missouri displaced nine hundred Indian families. Sprawling suburban settlement without efficient public transportation contributed to blankets of smog over Los Angeles and other cities.

The high-technology basis of economic development drew well-educated, highly skilled workers to the West, but economic promise also attracted the poor. "We see opportunity all around us here. . . . We smell freedom here, and maybe soon we can taste it," commented a black mother in California. Between 1945 and 1960, more than

one-third of African Americans leaving the South moved west.

The Mexican American population also grew, especially in California and Texas. To supply California's vast agribusiness industry, the government continued the *bracero* program begun in 1942, under which Mexicans were permitted to enter the United States to work for a limited period. Until the program ended in 1964, more than 100,000 Mexicans entered the United States each year to labor in the fields—and many of them stayed, legally or illegally. But permanent Mexican immigration was not as welcome as Mexicans' low-wage labor. In 1954, the government launched a series of raids called "Operation Wetback," sending more than a million Mexicans back across the border.

At the same time, Mexican American citizens gained a victory in their ongoing struggle for

civil rights in *Hernandez v. Texas*. In this 1954 case, the Supreme Court ruled unanimously that Mexican Americans constituted a distinct group and that their systematic exclusion from juries violated the Fourteenth Amendment guarantee of equal protection. Legal scholar Ian Haney-Lopez called *Hernandez* "huge for the Mexican American community. They now had the highest court in the land saying it's unconstitutional to treat Mexicans as if they're an inferior race."

Free of the discrimination faced by minorities, white Americans enjoyed the fullest prosperity in the West. In April 1950, when California developers opened Lakewood, a 17,500-home development in Los Angeles County, thirty thousand people lined up to buy houses at prices averaging $87,500 in 2016 dollars. Many of the new homeowners were veterans, blue-collar and lower-level white-collar workers whose defense-based jobs at aerospace corporations enabled them to fulfill the American dream of the 1950s. A huge shopping mall, Lakewood Center, offered myriad products of the consumer culture, and the workers' children lived within commuting distance from community colleges and six state universities.

The Democratization of Higher Education

California's university system exemplified a spectacular transformation of higher education. Between 1940 and 1960, college enrollments in the United States more than doubled, and more than 40 percent of young Americans attended college by the mid-1960s. The federal government subsidized the education of more than two million veterans, and the Cold War sent millions of federal dollars to universities for defense-related research. State governments vastly expanded the number of public colleges and universities, while municipalities began to build two-year community colleges.

All Americans did not benefit equally from the democratization of higher education. Although their college enrollments surged from 37,000 in 1941 to 90,000 in 1961, African Americans constituted only about 5 percent of all college students. For a time the educational gap between white men and women grew, even though women's enrollments increased. In 1940, women had earned 40 percent of undergraduate degrees, but as veterans flocked to college campuses, women's proportion fell to 25 percent, rising to just 33 percent by 1960. Women were more likely than men to drop out of college after marriage, taking jobs to keep their husbands in school. Reflecting gender norms of the 1950s, most white college women agreed that "it is natural for a woman to be satisfied with her husband's success and not crave personal achievement."

REVIEW   What fueled the prosperity of the 1950s?

▶ The Culture of Abundance

Prosperity in the 1950s intensified the transformation of the nation into a consumer society, changing the way Americans lived and shifting the traditional work ethic toward an ethic of consumption. The new medium of television both reflected and stimulated a consumer culture. People married at earlier ages, the birthrate soared, and dominant values celebrated family life and traditional gender roles. Undercurrents of rebellion, especially among young people, and women's increasing employment defied some of the dominant norms but did not greatly disrupt the complacency of the 1950s.

Consumption Rules the Day

Scorned by Khrushchev during the kitchen debate as unnecessary gadgets, consumer items flooded American society in the 1950s. Although the purchase and display of consumer goods was not new (see "Consumer Culture" in chapter 23), at midcentury consumption had become a reigning value, vital for economic prosperity and essential to individuals' identity and status. In place of the traditional emphasis on work and savings, the consumer culture encouraged satisfaction and happiness through the acquisition of new products.

The consumer culture rested on a firm material base. Between 1950 and 1960, both the gross national product (the value of all goods and services produced) and median family income grew by 25 percent in constant dollars (Figure 27.1). Economists claimed that 60 percent of Americans enjoyed middle-class incomes in 1960. By then, four-fifths of all families owned a television set, nearly all had a refrigerator, and most owned at least one car. The number of shopping centers quadrupled between 1957 and 1963.

Several forces spurred this unparalleled abundance. A population surge—from 152 million to 180 million during the 1950s—expanded demand for products and boosted industries ranging from housing to baby goods. Consumer borrowing also fueled the economic boom, as people made purchases on installment plans and began to use credit cards. Increasingly Americans enjoyed their possessions while they paid for them instead of saving their money for future purchases.

Although the sheer need to support themselves and their families motivated most women's employment, a desire to secure some of the new abundance sent growing numbers of women to work. As one woman remarked, "My Joe can't put five kids through college . . . and the washer had to be replaced, and Ann was ashamed to bring friends home because the living room furniture was such a mess, so I went to work." The standards for family happiness imposed by the consumer culture increasingly required a second income.

The Revival of Domesticity and Religion

Despite married women's growing employment, a dominant ideology celebrated traditional family

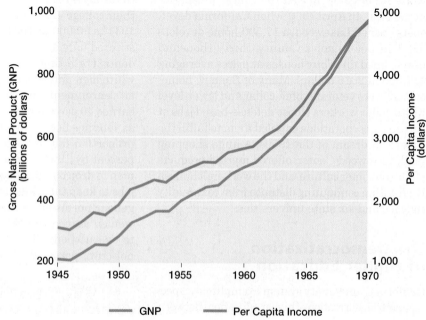

FIGURE 27.1 The Postwar Economic Boom: GNP and Per Capita Income, 1945–1970
American dominance of the worldwide market, innovative technologies that led to new industries such as computers and plastics, population growth, and increases in worker productivity all contributed to the enormous economic growth of the United States after World War II.

life and conventional gender roles. Both popular culture and public figures defined the ideal family as a male breadwinner, a full-time homemaker, and three or four children. Writer and feminist Betty Friedan gave a name to the idealization of women's domestic roles in her 1963 book *The Feminine Mystique*. Friedan criticized health professionals, scholars, advertisers, and public officials for assuming that biological differences dictated different roles for men and women. According to this feminine mystique that they promulgated, women should find fulfillment in devotion to their homes, families, and serving others. Not many women directly challenged these ideas, but writer Edith Stern maintained that "many arguments about the joys of housewifery have been advanced, largely by those who have never had to work at it."

Although the glorification of domesticity clashed with women's increasing employment, many Americans' lives did embody the family ideal. Postwar prosperity enabled people to marry earlier and to have more children. In the midst of a general downward trend over the century, the American birthrate soared between 1945 and 1965, peaking in 1957 with 4.3 million births and producing the **baby boom** generation. Experts like Dr. Benjamin Spock encouraged mothers to devote even more attention to child rearing, while they also urged fathers to cultivate family "togetherness" by spending more time with their children.

Interest in religion also surged in the 1950s. From 1940 to 1960, membership in churches and synagogues rose from 50 to 63 percent of all Americans. Polls reported that 95 percent of the population believed in God. Evangelism took on new life, most notably in the nationwide crusades of Baptist minister Billy Graham. Congress linked religion more closely to the state by adding "under God" to the pledge of allegiance and by requiring that "In God We Trust" be printed on all currency.

Evangelist Billy Graham Preaches in New York City
Billy Graham, a young Baptist minister from North Carolina, captivated mass audiences, urging them to find salvation in Jesus Christ and to uphold Christian moral standards. Americans flocked to his crusades even as he implicitly condemned their avid participation in consumerism as "materialistic, worldly, secular, greedy, and covetous." Here in 1957, he exhorts a crowd of 40,000 at the Polo Grounds stadium in New York City. AP Photo.

Religion helped to calm anxieties in the nuclear age, while ministers such as Graham made the Cold War a holy war, labeling communism "a great sinister anti-Christian movement masterminded by Satan." Some critics questioned the depth of the religious revival, attributing the growth in church membership to a desire for conformity and a need for social outlets. One commentator noted that 53 percent of Americans could not name a single book of the Christian New Testament.

Television Transforms Culture and Politics

Just as family life and religion offered a respite from Cold War anxieties, so too did the new medium of television. By 1960, nearly 90 percent of American homes boasted a television set, and the average viewer spent more than five hours each day watching it. Audiences were especially attracted to situation comedies, which projected the family ideal and the feminine mystique into millions of homes. On TV, married women did not have paying jobs and they deferred to their husbands, though they often got the upper hand through subtle manipulation.

Television also began to affect politics. Eisenhower's 1952 presidential campaign used TV ads for the first time, although he was not happy that "an old soldier should come to this." By 1960, television played a key role in election campaigns. Reflecting on his narrow victory, president-elect John F. Kennedy remarked, "We wouldn't have had a prayer without that gadget." In addition, money played a much larger role in elections because candidates needed to pay for expensive TV ads. The ability to appeal directly to voters in their living rooms put a premium on personal attractiveness and encouraged candidates to build their own campaign organizations, relying less on political parties. The declining strength of parties and the growing power of money in elections were not new trends, but TV accelerated them.

Unlike government-financed television in Europe, private enterprise paid for American TV. What NBC called a "selling machine in every living room" became the major vehicle for fostering consumption, and advertisers did not hesitate to interfere with shows that might jeopardize the sale of their products. In 1961, Newton Minow, chairman of the Federal Communications Commission, called television a "vast wasteland." While acknowledging some of TV's achievements, particularly documentaries and drama, Minow depicted it as "a procession of game shows, . . . formula comedies about totally unbelievable families, blood and thunder, mayhem, violence, sadism, murder, . . . and cartoons." But viewers kept tuning in. In little more than a decade, television came to dominate Americans' leisure time, influence their consumption patterns, and shape their perceptions of the nation's leadership.

Countercurrents

Pockets of dissent underlay the conventionality of the 1950s. Some intellectuals took exception to the materialism and conformity of the era. In *The Lonely Crowd* (1950), sociologist David Riesman lamented a shift from the "inner-directed" to the "other-directed" individual, as Americans replaced independent thinking with an eagerness to adapt to external standards of behavior and belief. Sharing that distaste for the importance of "belonging," William H. Whyte Jr., in his popular book *The Organization Man* (1956), blamed the modern corporation for making employees tailor themselves to the group. Vance Packard's 1959 best seller, *The Status Seekers*, decried "the vigorous merchandising of goods as status-symbols."

Implicit in much of the critique of consumer culture was concern about the loss of traditional masculinity. Consumption was associated with women and their presumed greater susceptibility to manipulation. Men, required to conform to get ahead, moved further away from the masculine ideals of individualism and aggressiveness. Moreover, the increase in married women's employment compromised the male ideal of breadwinner. Into this gender confusion came *Playboy*, which began publication in 1953 and quickly gained a circulation of one million. The new magazine idealized masculine independence in the form of bachelorhood and assaulted the middle-class norms of domesticity and respectability. By associating the sophisticated bachelor with good wine, music, furnishings, and the like, the magazine made consumption more masculine while promoting sexual freedom, at least for men.

In fact, two books published by Alfred Kinsey and other researchers at Indiana University— *Sexual Behavior in the Human Male* (1948) and *Sexual Behavior in the Human Female* (1953)— disclosed that Americans' sexual behavior often departed from the postwar family ideal. Large numbers of men and women reported that they had engaged in premarital sex and adultery; one-third of the men and one-seventh of the women reported homosexual experiences. Although Kinsey's sampling procedures later cast doubt

The most blatant revolt against conventionality came from the self-proclaimed Beat generation, a small group of mostly male literary figures based in New York City and San Francisco. Rejecting nearly everything in mainstream culture—patriotism, consumerism, technology, conventional family life, discipline—writers such as Allen Ginsberg and Jack Kerouac celebrated spontaneity and absolute personal freedom, including drug consumption and freewheeling sex. The Beats shocked "square" Americans, but both they and their lifestyles would provide a model for a new movement of youthful dissidents in the 1960s.

Bold new styles in the visual arts also showed the 1950s to be more than a decade of bland conformity. In New York City, "action painting" or "abstract expressionism" flowered, rejecting the idea that painting should represent recognizable forms. Jackson Pollock and other abstract expressionists poured, dripped, and threw paint on canvases or substituted sticks and other implements for brushes. The new form of painting so captivated and redirected the Western art world that New York replaced Paris as its center.

REVIEW   Why did American consumption expand so dramatically in the 1950s, and what aspects of society and culture did it influence?

on his ability to generalize across the population, the books became best sellers.

Less direct challenges to mainstream standards appeared in the everyday behavior of young Americans. "Roll over Beethoven and tell Tchaikovsky the news!" belted out Chuck Berry in his 1956 hit record celebrating **rock and roll**, a new form of music that combined country with black rhythm and blues. White teenagers lionized Elvis Presley, who shocked their parents with his tight pants, hip-rolling gestures, and sensuous rock-and-roll music. "Before there was Elvis . . . I started going crazy for 'race music,'" recalled a white man of his teenage years. His recollection underscored African Americans' contributions to rock and roll, as well as the rebelliousness expressed by white youths' attraction to black music.

▶ The Emergence of a Civil Rights Movement

Building on the civil rights initiatives begun during World War II, African Americans posed the most dramatic challenge to the status quo of the 1950s as they sought to overcome discrimination and segregation. Every southern state mandated rigid segregation in public settings ranging from schools to cemeteries. Voting laws and practices in the South disfranchised the vast majority of African Americans. Employment discrimination kept blacks at the bottom throughout the country. Schools, restaurants, and other public spaces were often as segregated, though usually not by law, in the North as in the South.

Although black protest was as old as American racism, in the 1950s grassroots movements arose that attracted national attention and the support of white liberals. Pressed by civil rights groups, the Supreme Court delivered significant institutional reforms, but the most important changes occurred among blacks themselves. Ordinary African Americans in substantial numbers sought their own liberation, building a movement that would transform race relations in the United States.

African Americans Challenge the Supreme Court and the President

Several factors spurred black protest in the 1950s. Between 1940 and 1960, more than three million African Americans moved from the South into areas where they had a political voice. Black leaders emphasized how racist practices at home tarnished the U.S. image abroad and handicapped the United States in its competition with the Soviet Union. The very system of segregation meant that African Americans controlled certain organizational resources, such as churches, colleges, and newspapers, where leadership skills could be honed and networks developed.

The legal strategy of the major civil rights organization, the National Association for the Advancement of Colored People (NAACP), reached its crowning achievement with the Supreme Court decision *Brown v. Board of Education* in 1954, which consolidated five separate suits. Oliver Brown, a World War II veteran in Topeka, Kansas, filed suit because his daughter had to pass by a white school near their home to attend a black school more than a mile away. In Virginia, sixteen-year-old Barbara Johns initiated a student strike over wretched conditions in her black high school, leading to another of the suits joined in *Brown*. The NAACP's lead lawyer, future Supreme Court justice Thurgood Marshall, urged the Court to overturn the "separate but equal" precedent established in *Plessy v. Ferguson* in 1896 (see "Progressivism for White Men Only" in chapter 21). A unanimous Court, headed by Chief Justice Earl Warren, agreed, declaring that "separate educational facilities are inherently unequal" and thus violated the Fourteenth Amendment.

Ultimate responsibility for enforcement of the decision lay with President Eisenhower, but he refused to endorse *Brown*. He also kept silent in 1955 when whites murdered Emmett Till, a fourteen-year-old black boy who had allegedly whistled at a white woman in Mississippi. Reflecting his own prejudice, his preference for limited federal intervention in the states, and a leadership style that favored consensus and gradual progress, Eisenhower kept his distance from civil rights issues. Such inaction fortified southern resistance.

In September 1957, Governor Orval Faubus sent Arkansas National Guard troops to block the enrollment of nine black students in Little Rock's Central High School. Later, he allowed them to enter but withdrew the National Guard, leaving the students to face an angry white mob. "During those years when we desperately needed approval from our peers," Melba Patillo Beals remembered, "we were victims of the most harsh rejection imaginable." As television cameras transmitted the ugly scene, Eisenhower was forced to send regular army troops to Little Rock, the first federal military intervention in the South since Reconstruction. Paratroopers escorted the "Little Rock Nine" into the school, but resistance to integration continued across the South. (See "Analyzing Historical Evidence," page 796.)

School segregation outside the South was not usually sanctioned by law, but northern school districts separated black and white students by manipulating neighborhood boundaries and with other devices. Even before *Brown*, black parents in dozens of northern cities challenged the assignment of their children to inferior "colored" schools. While these protests reaped some successes, the structure of residential segregation, often supported by official action, made school segregation a reality for African Americans in both the North and South.

Eisenhower ordered the integration of public facilities in Washington, D.C., and on military bases, and he supported the first federal civil rights legislation since Reconstruction. Yet the Civil Rights Acts of 1957 and 1960 were little more than symbolic. Baseball star Jackie Robinson spoke for many African Americans when he wired Eisenhower in 1957, "We disagree that half a loaf is better than none. Have waited this long for a bill with meaning—can wait a little longer." Eisenhower appointed the first black professional to his White House staff, but E. Frederick Morrow confided in his diary, "I feel ridiculous . . . trying to defend the administration's record on civil rights."

Montgomery and Mass Protest

What set the civil rights movement of the 1950s and 1960s apart from earlier acts of black protest was its widespread presence in the South, the large number of people involved, their willingness to confront white institutions directly, and the use of nonviolent protest and civil disobedience to bring about change. The Congress of Racial Equality and other groups had experimented with these tactics in the 1940s, organizing to integrate movie theaters, restaurants, and swimming pools in northern cities. In the South, the first sustained protest to claim national

VISUAL ACTIVITY

Civil Rights Activism in the North

While southern civil rights activism gained national attention in the 1950s, black protest had a long history in the North. African Americans and their allies battled job discrimination and segregation in schools, housing, and public accommodations. Here demonstrators march outside the Stork Club in New York City in 1951, protesting its refusal to serve the world-famous dancer, singer, and actress Josephine Baker. FPG/ Getty Images.

READING THE IMAGE: Who sponsored this demonstration? What do the people in the photo tell you about the racial makeup of the protest? How does one of the signs capitalize on Cold War rhetoric?

CONNECTIONS: How did this kind of protest in the North differ from that in the South?

The *Brown* Decision

Responding to lawsuits argued by NAACP lawyers, *Brown v. Board of Education* was the culmination of a series of Supreme Court rulings that chipped away at an earlier Court's decision in *Plessy v. Ferguson* (1896) permitting "separate but equal" public facilities.

DOCUMENT 1
Brown v. Board of Education, May 1954

In 1954, Chief Justice Earl Warren delivered the unanimous opinion of the Supreme Court, declaring racial segregation in public education unconstitutional and explaining why.

It is doubtful that any child may reasonably be expected to succeed in life if he is denied the opportunity of an education. Such an opportunity, if the state has undertaken to provide it, is a right that must be made available to all on equal terms. . . .

We come then to the question presented: Does segregation of children in public schools solely on the basis of race, even though the physical facilities and other "tangible" factors may be equal, deprive the children of the minority group of equal educational opportunities?

We believe that it does. . . . In *McLaurin* [a 1950 case], the Court, in requiring that a Negro admitted to a white graduate school be treated like all other students, again resorted to intangible considerations: ". . . his ability to study, to engage in discussions and exchange views with other students, and, in general, to learn his profession." Such considerations apply with added force to children in grade and high schools. To separate them from others of similar age and qualifications solely because of their race generates a feeling of inferiority as to their status in the community that may affect their hearts and minds in a way unlikely ever to be undone.

We conclude that in the field of public education the doctrine of "separate but equal" has no place. Separate educational facilities are inherently unequal.

Source: *Brown v. Board of Education*, 347 U.S. 483 (1954).

DOCUMENT 2
Southern Manifesto on Integration, March 1956

The Brown *decision outraged many southern whites. In 1956, more than one hundred members of Congress signed a manifesto pledging resistance to the ruling.*

We regard the decision of the Supreme Court in the school cases as a clear abuse of judicial power. It climaxes a trend in the Federal judiciary undertaking to legislate . . . and to encroach upon the reserved rights of the states and the people.

The original Constitution does not mention education. Neither does the Fourteenth Amendment nor any amendment. . . . The Supreme Court of the United States, with no legal basis for such action, undertook to exercise their naked judicial power and substituted their personal political and social ideas for the established law of the land.

This unwarranted exercise of power by the court, contrary to the Constitution, is creating chaos and confusion in the states principally affected. It is destroying the amicable relations between the white and negro races that have been created through ninety years of patient effort by the good people of both races. . . .

We pledge ourselves to use all lawful means to bring about a reversal of this decision which is contrary to the Constitution and to prevent the use of force in its implementation.

Source: "Southern Manifesto on Integration," *Congressional Record*, 84th Congress, 2nd Session, vol. 102, pt. 4 (Washington, D.C.: Governmental Printing Office, 1956), 4459–60.

---

attention began in Montgomery, Alabama, on December 1, 1955.

That day, police arrested Rosa Parks for violating a local segregation ordinance. Riding a crowded bus home from work, she refused to give up her seat in the white section so that a man could sit down. She resisted not because she was physically tired, she recalled; rather she was "tired of giving in." The bus driver called the police, who promptly arrested her. Parks had long been active in the local NAACP, headed by E. D. Nixon. They had already talked

In the face of white hostility, black children carried the burden of implementing the Brown *decision, as these accounts testify.*

DOCUMENT 3
A High School Boy in Oak Ridge, Tennessee, 1957

I like it a whole lot better than the colored school. You have a chance to learn more and you have more sports. I play forward or guard on the basketball team, only I don't get to participate in all games. Some teams don't mind my playing. Some teams object not because of the fellows on the team, but because of the people in their community. Mostly it's the fans or the board of education that decides against me. . . . The same situation occurs in baseball. I'm catcher, but the first game I didn't get to participate in. A farm club of the major league wrote the coach that they were interested in seeing me play so maybe I'll get to play the next time.

Source: Dorothy Sterling, *Tender Warriors* (New York: Hill and Wang, 1958), 83. Copyright © 1958 by Hill and Wang.

DOCUMENT 4
A High School Girl in the Deep South, May 1966

The first day a news reporter rode the bus with us. All around us were state troopers. In front of them were federal marshals. When we got to town there were lines of people and cars all along the road. A man without a badge or anything got on the bus and started beating up the newspaper reporter. . . . When we got to the school the students were all around looking through the windows. The mayor said we couldn't come there because the school was already filled to capacity. We turned around and the students started yelling and clapping. When we went back [after obtaining a court order] there were no students there at all. [The white students did not return, so the six black students finished the year by themselves.] The shocking thing was during the graduation ceremonies. All six of the students got together to make a speech. After we finished, I looked around and saw three teachers crying. The principal

had tears in his eyes and he got up to make a little speech about us. He said at first he didn't think he would enjoy being around us. You could see in his face that he was really touched.

Source: *In Their Own Words: A Student Appraisal of What Happened after School Desegregation* (Washington, D.C.: Department of Health, Education, and Welfare, Office of Education, 1966), 17–18.

DOCUMENT 5
A High School Girl in the Deep South, May 1966

I chose to go because I felt that I could get a better education here. I knew that the [black] school that I was then attending wasn't giving me exactly what I should have had. . . . As far as the Science Department was concerned, it just didn't have the chemicals we needed and I just decided to change. When I went over the students there weren't very friendly and when I graduated they still weren't. They didn't want us there and they made that plain, but we went there anyway and we stuck it out.

Source: *In Their Own Words: A Student Appraisal of What Happened after School Desegregation* (Washington, D.C.: Department of Health, Education, and Welfare, Office of Education, 1966), 44.

Questions for Analysis

Recognize Viewpoints: What reasons did the Supreme Court give in favor of desegregation? What reasons did black students give for wanting to attend integrated schools? How do these reasons differ?

Analyze the Evidence: On what grounds did signers of the "Southern Manifesto" argue that the Supreme Court decision violated the Constitution?

Consider the Context: Why did President Eisenhower initially resist desegregation, and what steps did he eventually take to support integration?

about challenging bus segregation. So had the Women's Political Council (WPC), led by Jo Ann Robinson, an English professor at Alabama State, who had once been humiliated by a bus driver when she accidentally sat in the white section.

When word came that Parks would fight her arrest, WPC leaders mobilized teachers and students to distribute fliers urging blacks to boycott the buses. E. D. Nixon called a mass meeting at a black church, where those assembled founded the Montgomery Improvement Association

(MIA). The MIA arranged volunteer car pools and marshaled most of the black community to sustain the yearlong **Montgomery bus boycott**.

Elected to head the MIA was twenty-six-year-old Martin Luther King Jr., a young Baptist pastor with a doctorate in theology from Boston University. A captivating speaker, King addressed mass meetings at churches throughout the bus boycott, inspiring blacks' courage and commitment by linking racial justice to Christianity. He promised, "If you will protest courageously and yet with dignity and Christian love . . . historians will have to pause and say, 'There lived a great people—a black people—who injected a new meaning and dignity into the veins of civilization.'"

Montgomery blacks summoned their courage and determination in abundance. An older woman insisted, "I'm not walking for myself, I'm walking for my children and my grandchildren." Boycotters walked miles or carpooled to get to work, contributed their meager financial resources, and stood up to intimidation and police harassment. Authorities arrested several leaders, and whites firebombed King's house. Yet the movement persisted until November 1956, when the Supreme Court declared unconstitutional Alabama's laws requiring bus segregation.

King's face on the cover of *Time* magazine in February 1957 marked his rapid rise to national and international fame. In January, black clergy from across the South had chosen King to head the Southern Christian Leadership Conference (SCLC), newly established to coordinate local protests against segregation and disfranchisement. The prominence of King and other ministers obscured the substantial numbers and critical importance of black women in the movement. King's fame and the media's focus on the South also hid the national scope of racial injustice and the struggles for racial equality in the North that both encouraged and benefited from the black freedom struggle in the South.

REVIEW What were the goals and strategies of civil rights activists in the 1950s?

▶ Conclusion: Peace and Prosperity Mask Unmet Challenges

At the American exhibit in Moscow in 1959, the consumer goods that Nixon proudly displayed to Khrushchev and the Cold War competition that crackled through their dialogue reflected two dominant themes of the 1950s: American prosperity and the superpowers' success in keeping their antagonism within the bounds of peace. The tremendous economic growth of the 1950s, which raised the standard of living for most Americans, resulted in part from Cold War defense spending.

Prosperity changed the very landscape of the United States. Suburban housing developments sprang up, interstate highways cut up cities and connected the country, farms declined in number but grew in size, and population and industry moved south and west. Daily habits and even values shifted as the economy became more service oriented and the appearance of television and a host of new products intensified the growth of a consumer culture.

The prosperity, however, masked a number of developments and problems that Americans would soon face head-on: rising resistance to racial injustice, a 20 percent poverty rate, married women's movement into the labor force, and the emergence of a youth rebellion. Although defense spending and housing, highway, and education subsidies helped to sustain the economic boom, in general Eisenhower tried to curb domestic programs and let private enterprise have its way. His administration maintained the welfare state inherited from the New Deal but resisted the expansion of federal programs.

In global affairs, Eisenhower exercised restraint on large issues, recognizing the limits of U.S. power. In the name of deterrence, he promoted the development of more destructive atomic weapons, but he withstood pressures for even larger defense budgets. Still, Eisenhower shared Truman's assumption that the United States must fight communism everywhere, and when movements in Iran, Guatemala, Cuba, and Vietnam seemed too radical, too friendly to communism, or too inimical to American economic interests, he tried to undermine them, often with secret operations. Eisenhower presided over eight years of peace and prosperity, but his foreign policy inspired anti-Americanism and forged commitments and interventions that plagued future generations. As Eisenhower's successors took on the struggle against communism and grappled with the domestic challenges of race, poverty, and urban decay that he had avoided, the tranquility and consensus of the 1950s would give way to turbulence and conflict in the 1960s.

See the Selected Bibliography for this chapter in the Appendix.

27 Chapter Review

REVIEW QUESTIONS

1. How did Eisenhower's domestic policies reflect his moderate political vision? (pp. 773–776)

2. Where and how did Eisenhower practice containment? (pp. 777–782)

3. What fueled the prosperity of the 1950s? (pp. 783–789)

4. Why did American consumption expand so dramatically in the 1950s, and what aspects of society and culture did it influence? (pp. 790–793)

5. What were the goals and strategies of civil rights activists in the 1950s? (pp. 794–798)

MAKING CONNECTIONS

1. How did Eisenhower's "modern Republicanism" address the New Deal legacy?

2. What economic and demographic changes contributed to the growth of suburbs and the Sun Belt? Consider both Americans who participated in these trends and those who did not.

3. What developments in American society in the 1950s were at odds with prevailing norms and values?

4. Explain how new policies and court decisions regarding minorities came about and their impact, for better and for worse.

LINKING TO THE PAST

1. How did the policies of termination and relocation differ from the New Deal's policy toward Indians? (See chapter 24.)

2. What developments stemming from World War II influenced U.S. foreign policy in such areas as Vietnam and Latin America? (See chapter 25.)

28

Reform, Rebellion, and Reaction

1960–1974

CONTENT LEARNING OBJECTIVES

After reading and studying this chapter, you should be able to:

- Identify the ways in which liberalism was manifested in President Johnson's Great Society.

- Identify the strategies civil rights activists used during the 1960s and describe Washington's response. Explain the rise of the black power movement and its influence on American society.

- Explain how the civil rights movement inspired protest movements among other groups, including Native Americans, Chicanos, students, and gays and lesbians.

- Define the origins of the feminist movement and identify its various strategies and criticisms of society. Explain feminism's achievements and the backlash it provoked.

- Describe the ways in which liberalism persisted during the Nixon administration.

PROTEST BANNER
In the 1960s, Americans carried banners to broadcast a variety of political positions. This pennant represents the black freedom struggle, which inspired a host of other movements. Collection of Mark Hooper.

ON AUGUST 31, 1962, FORTY-FIVE-YEAR-OLD FANNIE LOU HAMER boarded a bus carrying eighteen African Americans to the county seat in Indianola, Mississippi, where they intended to register to vote. Blacks constituted a majority of Sunflower County's population but only 1.2 percent of registered voters. Before civil rights activists arrived in Ruleville to start a voter registration drive, Hamer recalled, "I didn't know that a Negro could register and vote." The poverty, exploitation, and political disfranchisement she experienced typified the lives of most blacks in the rural South. The daughter of sharecroppers, Hamer began work in the cotton fields at age six, attending school in a one-room shack from December to March and only until she was twelve. After marrying Perry Hamer, she moved onto a plantation where she worked in the fields, did domestic work for the owner, and recorded the cotton that sharecroppers harvested.

At the Indianola County courthouse, Hamer passed through a hostile, white, gun-carrying crowd. Refusing to be intimidated, she registered to vote on her third attempt, attended a civil rights leadership workshop, and began to mobilize others to vote. In 1963, she and other activists were arrested in Winona, Mississippi, and beaten so brutally that Hamer went from jail to the hospital.

Fannie Lou Hamer's courage and determination made her a prominent figure in the black freedom struggle, which shook the nation's conscience, provided a protest model for other groups, and pressured the government. After John F. Kennedy was assassinated in November 1963, Lyndon B. Johnson launched the Great Society—a multitude of efforts to promote racial justice, education, medical care, urban development, environmental and economic health, and more. Those who struggled for racial justice made great sacrifices, but by the end of the decade American law had caught up with the American ideal of equality.

Yet strong civil rights legislation and pathbreaking Supreme Court decisions could not alone mitigate the deplorable economic conditions of African Americans nationwide, on which Hamer and others increasingly focused after 1965. Nor were liberal politicians reliable supporters, as Hamer found out in 1964 when President Johnson's allies rebuffed black Mississippi Democrats' efforts to be represented at the Democratic National Convention. By 1966, a minority of African American activists were demanding black power; the movement soon splintered, while white support sharply declined. The war in Vietnam stifled liberal reform, while a growing conservative movement denounced the challenge to American traditions and institutions mounted by blacks, students, and others.

Though disillusioned and often frustrated, Fannie Lou Hamer remained an activist until her death in 1977, participating in new social movements stimulated by the black freedom struggle. In 1969, she supported students at Mississippi Valley State College who demanded black studies courses and a voice in campus decisions. In 1972, she attended the first conference of the National Women's Political Caucus, established to challenge sex discrimination in politics and government.

Feminists and other groups, including ethnic minorities, environmentalists, and gays and lesbians, carried the tide of reform into the 1970s. They pushed Richard M. Nixon's Republican administration to sustain the liberalism of the 1960s, with its emphasis on a strong government role in regulating the economy, guaranteeing the welfare and rights of all individuals, and improving the quality of life. Despite its conservative rhetoric, the Nixon administration implemented affirmative action and adopted innovative measures in environmental regulation, equality for women, and justice for Native Americans. The years between 1960 and 1974 witnessed the greatest efforts to reconcile America's promise with reality since the New Deal.

Mississippi Freedom Democratic Party Rally
Fannie Lou Hamer (left) and other activists rally at the 1964 Democratic National Convention, supporting the Mississippi Freedom Democratic Party (MFDP) in its challenge to the all-white delegation sent by the state party. Next to Hamer is Eleanor Holmes Norton, a civil rights lawyer, and Ella Baker (far right), who helped organize the Southern Christian Leadership Conference. In the straw hat is Stokely Carmichael, leader of the Student Nonviolent Coordinating Committee. © George Ballis/Take Stock/The Image Works.

▶ Liberalism at High Tide

At the Democratic National Convention in 1960, John F. Kennedy proclaimed "a New Frontier" that would confront "unsolved problems of peace and war, unconquered pockets of ignorance and prejudice, unanswered questions of poverty and surplus." Four years later, Lyndon B. Johnson invoked the ideal of a "Great Society, [which] rests on abundance and liberty for all [and] demands an end to poverty and racial injustice." Acting under the liberal faith that government should use its power to solve social and economic problems, end injustice, and promote the welfare of all citizens, the Democratic administrations of the 1960s won legislation on civil rights, poverty, education, medical care, housing, consumer safeguards, and environmental protection. These measures, along with momentous Supreme Court decisions, responded to demands for rights from African Americans and other groups and addressed problems arising from rapid economic growth.

The Unrealized Promise of Kennedy's New Frontier

John F. Kennedy grew up in privilege, the child of an Irish Catholic businessman who became a New Deal official and the U.S. ambassador to Britain. Helped by a distinguished World War II navy record, Kennedy won election to the House of Representatives in 1946 and the Senate in 1952. With a powerful political machine, his family's fortune, and a dynamic personal appeal, Kennedy won the Democratic presidential nomination in 1960. He stunned many Democrats by choosing as his running mate Lyndon B. Johnson of Texas, whom liberals disparaged as a typical southern conservative.

In the general election, Kennedy narrowly defeated his Republican opponent, Vice President Richard M. Nixon, by a 118,550-vote margin (Map 28.1). African American voters contributed to his victory, Johnson helped carry the South, and Kennedy also benefited from the nation's first televised presidential debates, at which he appeared cool and confident beside a nervous and pale Nixon.

At forty-three, Kennedy was the youngest man ever to be elected president and the first Roman Catholic. His administration projected energy, idealism, and glamour, while the press kept from the public his serious health problems and extramarital affairs. At his inauguration,

CHRONOLOGY

1960	• John F. Kennedy elected president. • Student Nonviolent Coordinating Committee (SNCC) founded. • Students for a Democratic Society (SDS) established.
1961	• Freedom Rides challenge segregation.
1962	• United Farm Workers founded.
1963	• President's Commission on the Status of Women issues report. • Equal Pay Act passes. • *Baker v. Carr* decided. • *Abington School District v. Schempp* decided. • March on Washington draws 250,000 participants. • President Kennedy assassinated; Lyndon B. Johnson becomes president.
1964	• Civil Rights Act passes. • Mississippi Freedom Summer Project conducts voter registration drives.
1964–1966	• Congress passes most of Johnson's Great Society domestic programs.
1965	• Voting Rights Act passes.
1965–1968	• Riots erupt in major cities.
1966	• Black Panther Party for Self-Defense founded. • *Miranda v. Arizona* decided. • National Organization for Women (NOW) founded.
1967	• *Loving v. Virginia* decision strikes down state laws against interracial marriages.
1968	• Martin Luther King Jr. assassinated. • American Indian Movement (AIM) launched. • Richard M. Nixon elected president.
1969	• Stonewall riots erupt.
1970	• Environmental Protection Agency (EPA) established. • Clean Air Act passed.
1972	• Title IX bans sex discrimination in education. • "Trail of Broken Treaties" caravan protests in Washington, D.C.
1973	• *Roe v. Wade* decided.

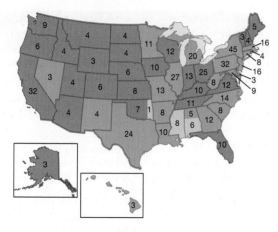

Candidate	Electoral Vote	Popular Vote	Percent of Popular Vote
John F. Kennedy (Democrat)	303	34,227,096	49.9
Richard M. Nixon (Republican)	219	34,108,546	49.6
Harry F. Byrd (Independent)	15	501,643	0

Map 28.1
The Election of 1960

Kennedy called on Americans to serve the common good. "Ask not what your country can do for you," he implored, "ask what you can do for your country." That idealism inspired many, but Kennedy failed to persuade Congress to expand the welfare state with federal education and health care programs. Moreover, he resisted leadership on behalf of racial justice until civil rights activists gave him no choice.

Moved by the desperate conditions he observed while campaigning in Appalachia, Kennedy pushed poverty onto the national agenda. In 1962, he read Michael Harrington's *The Other America*, which identified more than one in five Americans "maimed in body and spirit, existing at levels beneath those necessary for human decency." By 1962, Kennedy had won support for a $2 billion urban renewal program, providing incentives to businesses to locate in economically depressed areas and job training for the unemployed. In the summer of 1963, he asked aides to plan a full-scale attack on poverty.

With economic growth a key objective, Kennedy called for an enormous tax cut in 1963, which he promised would increase demand and create jobs. Passed in February 1964, the law contributed to an economic boom, as unemployment fell to 4.1 percent and the gross national product shot up. Some liberal critics of the tax cut, however, noted that it favored the well-off and argued instead for increased spending on social programs.

Kennedy's domestic efforts were in their infancy when an assassin's bullets struck him

The Kennedy Appeal
The freshness and glamour of the Kennedy administration are apparent in this photo of the candidate and his wife riding through New York City a few weeks before his election in 1960. The couple's second child was born between his election and inauguration, further contributing to his youthful image.
Frank Hurley/NY Daily News Archive via Getty Images.

down on November 22, 1963. Within minutes of the shooting—which occurred as Kennedy's motorcade passed through Dallas, Texas—radio and television broadcast the unfolding horror to the nation. Stunned Americans struggled to understand what had happened. Soon after the assassination, police arrested Lee Harvey Oswald and concluded that he had fired the shots from a nearby building. Two days later, while officers were transferring Oswald from one jail to another, a local nightclub operator killed him. Suspicions arose that Oswald was murdered to cover up a conspiracy by ultraconservatives who hated Kennedy or by Communists who supported Castro's Cuba (see "Meeting the 'Hour of Maximum Danger'" in chapter 29). To get at the truth, President Johnson appointed a commission headed by Chief Justice Earl Warren, which concluded that both Oswald and his assassin had acted alone.

Kennedy's domestic record had been unremarkable in his first two years, but his attention to taxes, civil rights, and poverty in 1963 suggested an important shift. Whether Kennedy could have persuaded Congress to enact his proposals remained in question. Journalist James Reston commented, "What was killed was not only the president but the promise. . . . We saw him only as a rising sun."

Johnson Fulfills the Kennedy Promise

Lyndon B. Johnson assumed the presidency with a wealth of political experience. A self-made man from the Texas Hill Country, he had won election in 1937 to the House of Representatives and in 1948 to the Senate, where he served skillfully as Senate majority leader. His modest upbringing, his admiration for Franklin Roosevelt, and his ambition to outdo the New Deal president all spurred his commitment to reform. Equally compelling were external pressures generated by the black freedom struggle and the host of movements it helped inspire.

Lacking Kennedy's sophistication, Johnson excelled behind the scenes, where he could entice, maneuver, or threaten legislators to support his objectives. His persuasive power, the famous "Johnson treatment," became legendary. In his ability to achieve his legislative goals, Johnson had few peers in American history.

Johnson entreated Congress to act so that "John Fitzgerald Kennedy did not live or die in vain." He pushed through Kennedy's tax cut bill by February 1964. More remarkable was passage of the **Civil Rights Act of 1964**, which made discrimination in employment, education, and public accommodations illegal. The strongest such measure since Reconstruction required every ounce of Johnson's political skill to pry sufficient votes from Republicans to overcome opposition by southern Democrats. Republican senator Everett Dirksen's aide reported that Johnson "never left him alone for thirty minutes." In proportion to their numbers in Congress, more Republicans voted for the measure than Democrats.

Antipoverty legislation followed fast on the heels of the Civil Rights Act. Johnson announced "an unconditional war on poverty" in his January 1964 State of the Union message, and in August Congress passed the Economic Opportunity Act. The law authorized ten new programs, allocating $800 million—about 1 percent of the federal budget—for the first year. Many provisions targeted children and youths, including Head Start for preschoolers, work-study grants for college students, and the Job Corps for unemployed young people. The Volunteers in Service to America (VISTA) program paid modest wages to those working with the disadvantaged, and a legal services program provided lawyers for the poor.

The most novel and controversial part of the law, the Community Action Program (CAP), required "maximum feasible participation" of the poor themselves in antipoverty projects. Poor people began to organize to make welfare agencies, school

The "Johnson Treatment"

Abe Fortas, a distinguished lawyer who had argued a major criminal rights case, *Gideon v. Wainwright* (1963), before the Supreme Court, was a close friend of and adviser to President Johnson. This photograph of the president and Fortas taken in July 1965 illustrates how Johnson used his body as well as his voice to bend people to his will. LBJ Library photo by Yoichi Okamoto.

boards, police departments, and housing authorities more accountable to the people they served. When local Democratic officials complained, Johnson backed off from pushing genuine representation for the poor. Still, CAP gave people usually excluded from government an opportunity to act on their own behalf and develop leadership skills. A Mississippi sharecropper was elated to attend a CAP literacy program that enabled him "to help my younger children when they start school."

Policymaking for a Great Society

As the 1964 election approached, Johnson projected stability and security in the midst of a booming economy. Few voters wanted to risk the dramatic change promised by his Republican opponent, Arizona senator Barry M. Goldwater, who attacked the welfare state and entertained the use of nuclear weapons in Vietnam. Johnson achieved a record-breaking 61 percent of the popular vote, and Democrats won resounding majorities in the House (295–140) and Senate (68–32). Still, Goldwater's considerable grassroots support marked a growing movement on the right (see "Emergence

of a Grassroots Movement" in chapter 30) and a threat to Democratic control of the South.

"I want to see a whole bunch of coonskins on the wall," Johnson told his aides, using a hunting analogy to stress his ambitious legislative goals for what he called the "Great Society." The large Democratic majorities in Congress, his own political skills, and pressure from the black freedom struggle and other movements enabled Johnson to obtain legislation on discrimination, poverty, education, medical care, housing, consumer and environmental protection, and more. Reporters called the legislation of the Eighty-ninth Congress (1965–1966) "a political miracle."

The Economic Opportunity Act of 1964 was the opening shot in the War on Poverty. Congress doubled the program's funding in 1965, enacted new economic development measures for depressed regions, and authorized more than $1 billion to improve the nation's slums. Direct aid included a new food stamp program, giving poor people greater choice in obtaining food, and rent supplements that provided alternatives to public housing. Moreover, a movement of welfare mothers, the National Welfare Rights Organization, assisted by antipoverty lawyers, pushed administrators of Aid to Families with Dependent Children (AFDC) to ease restrictions on welfare recipients. The number of families receiving assistance jumped from less than one million in 1960 to three million by 1972, benefiting 90 percent of those eligible.

Central to Johnson's War on Poverty were efforts to equip the poor with the skills necessary to find jobs. His Elementary and Secondary Education Act of 1965 marked a turning point by involving the federal government in K–12 education. The measure sent federal dollars to local school districts and provided equipment and supplies to private and parochial schools serving the poor. That same year, Congress passed the Higher Education Act, vastly expanding federal assistance to colleges and universities for buildings, programs, scholarships, and loans.

The federal government's responsibility for health care marked an even greater watershed. Faced with a powerful medical lobby that opposed national health insurance as "socialized medicine," Johnson

Medicare Becomes Law
President Lyndon Johnson traveled to the Truman Presidential Library in Independence, Missouri, to sign the law establishing Medicare and Medicaid, recognizing that President Harry Truman had first tried to enact universal health care two decades earlier. Here, Lady Bird Johnson, Vice President Hubert Humphrey, and Bess Truman look on while Johnson presents Truman with a pen he used to sign the bill. LBJ Library photo.

focused on the elderly, who constituted a large portion of the nation's poor. Congress responded with the **Medicare** program, providing the elderly with universal medical insurance financed largely through Social Security taxes. A separate program, **Medicaid**, authorized federal grants to supplement state-paid medical care for poor people. By the twenty-first century, these two programs covered 87 million Americans, nearly 30 percent of the population.

Whereas programs such as Medicare fulfilled New Deal promises, the Great Society's civil rights legislation represented a break with the past. Racial minorities were neglected or discriminated against in many New Deal programs; by contrast, the Civil Rights Act of 1964 made discrimination in employment, education, and public accommodations illegal. The **Voting Rights Act of 1965** banned literacy tests and other practices used to disqualify black voters and authorized federal intervention to ensure access to the voting booth.

Another form of bias fell with the **Immigration and Nationality Act of 1965**, which abolished quotas based on national origins that discriminated against non–Western European immigrants. The law maintained caps on the total number of immigrants and, for the first time, included the Western Hemisphere in those limits; preference was now given to immediate relatives of U.S. citizens and to those with desirable skills. The measure's unanticipated consequences triggered a surge of immigration in the 1980s and thereafter (see "The Internationalization of the United States" in chapter 31).

Great Society benefits reached well beyond victims of discrimination and the poor. Medicare covered the elderly, regardless of income. A groundswell of consumer activism won legislation making cars safer and raising standards for the food, drug, and cosmetics industries. Johnson insisted that the Great Society meet "not just the needs of the body but the desire for beauty and hunger for community." In 1965, he sent Congress the first presidential message on the environment, obtaining measures to control water and air pollution and to preserve the natural beauty of the American landscape. In addition, the National Arts and Humanities Act of 1965 funded artists, musicians, writers, and scholars and brought their work to public audiences.

The flood of reform legislation dwindled after 1966, when Democratic majorities in Congress diminished and a backlash against government programs arose. The Vietnam War dealt the largest blow to Johnson's ambitions, diverting his attention, spawning an antiwar movement that crippled his leadership, and devouring tax dollars that might have been used for reform (see "The Widening War at Home" in chapter 29).

In 1968, Johnson pried out of Congress one more civil rights law, which banned discrimination in housing and jury service. He also signed the National Housing Act of 1968, which authorized an enormous increase in low-income housing—1.7 million units over three years—and put construction and ownership in private hands.

Assessing the Great Society

The reduction in poverty in the 1960s was considerable. The number of poor Americans fell from more than 20 percent of the population in 1959 to around 13 percent in 1968. Those who in Johnson's words "live on the outskirts of hope" saw new opportunities. To Rosemary Bray, what turned her family of longtime welfare recipients into taxpaying workers "was the promise of the civil rights movement and the war on poverty." A Mexican American who learned to be a sheet metal worker through a jobs program reported, "[My children] will finish high school and maybe go to college. . . . I see my family and I know the chains are broken."

Certain groups, especially the aged, fared better than others. Many male-headed families rose out of poverty, but impoverishment among female-headed families actually increased. Whites escaped poverty faster than racial and ethnic minorities. Great Society programs contributed to a burgeoning black middle class, yet one in three African Americans remained poverty-stricken (Figure 28.1).

Conservative critics charged that Great Society programs discouraged initiative by giving the poor "handouts." Liberal critics claimed that focusing on training and education wrongly blamed the poor themselves rather than an economic system that could not provide enough adequately paying jobs. In contrast to the New Deal, the Great Society avoided structural reform of the economy and spurned public works projects as a means of providing jobs for the disadvantaged.

Some critics insisted that ending poverty required raising taxes in order to create jobs, overhaul welfare systems, and rebuild slums. Great Society programs did invest more heavily in the public sector, but the Great Society was funded from economic growth rather than from

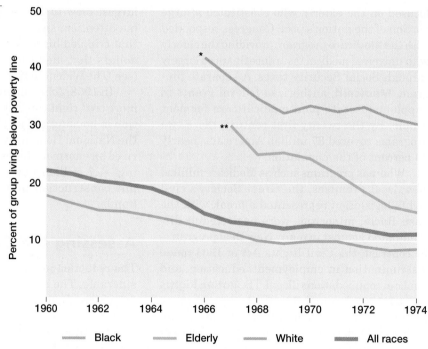

FIGURE 28.1   Poverty in the United States, 1960–1974
The short-term effects of economic growth and the Great Society's attack on poverty are seen here. Which groups experienced the sharpest decline in poverty, and what might account for the differences?

*Statistics on blacks for years 1960–1965 not available.
**Statistics on the elderly for years 1960–1966 not available.

new taxes on the rich or middle class. There was no significant redistribution of income, despite large increases in subsidies for food, housing, and medical care. Economic prosperity allowed spending for the poor to rise and improved the lives of millions, but that spending never approached the amounts necessary to claim victory in the War on Poverty.

The Judicial Revolution

A key element of liberalism's ascendancy emerged in the Supreme Court under Chief Justice Earl Warren (1953–1969). In contrast to the federal courts of the Progressive Era and New Deal, which blocked reform, the **Warren Court** often moved ahead of Congress and public opinion. Expanding the Constitution's promise of equality and individual rights, the Court's decisions supported an activist government to prevent injustice and provided new protections to disadvantaged groups and accused criminals.

Following the pathbreaking *Brown v. Board of Education* school desegregation decision of 1954 (see "African Americans Challenge the

Supreme Court and the President" in chapter 27), the Court struck down southern states' maneuvers to avoid integration and defended protesters' rights to freedom of assembly and speech. In addition, a unanimous Court in *Loving v. Virginia* (1967) invalidated state laws banning interracial marriage, calling marriage one of the "basic civil rights of man."

Chief Justice Warren considered *Baker v. Carr* (1963) his most important decision. The case grew out of a complaint that inequitably drawn Tennessee electoral districts gave sparsely populated rural districts far more representatives than densely populated urban areas. Using the Fourteenth Amendment guarantee of "equal protection of the laws," the Court established the principle of "one person, one vote" for state legislatures and for the House of Representatives. As states redrew electoral districts, legislatures became more responsive to metropolitan interests.

The Warren Court also reformed the criminal justice system, overturning a series of convictions on the grounds that the accused had been deprived of "life, liberty, or property, without due process of law," guaranteed in the Fourteenth Amendment.

Reforms of the Great Society, 1964–1968

1964

Tax Reduction Act	Provides $10 billion in tax cuts in 1964 and 1965.
Civil Rights Act of 1964	Bans discrimination in public accommodations, public education, and employment and extends protections to American Indians on reservations.
Economic Opportunity Act	Creates programs for the disadvantaged, including Head Start, VISTA, the Job Corps, and CAP.

1965

Elementary and Secondary Education Act	Provides $1.3 billion in aid to elementary and secondary schools.
Medical Care Act	Provides health insurance (Medicare) for all citizens age sixty-five and over and health care for the poor through a joint federal-state program (Medicaid).
Voting Rights Act	Bans literacy tests and other voting restrictions and authorizes the federal government to act directly to enable African Americans to register and vote.
Executive Order 11246	Bans discrimination on the basis of race, religion, and national origin by employers awarded government contracts and requires them to "take affirmative action to ensure equal opportunity."
Department of Housing and Urban Development	Provides programs to improve housing and neighborhoods in urban areas.
National Arts and Humanities Act	Creates National Endowment for the Arts (NEA) and Humanities (NEH) to support the work of artists, musicians, writers, and scholars.
Water Quality Act	Requires states to set and enforce water quality standards.
Immigration and Nationality Act	Abolishes fifty-year-old discriminatory quotas based on national origins and sets equal limits for all countries.
Air Quality Act	Imposes air pollution standards for motor vehicles.
Higher Education Act	Expands federal assistance to colleges and universities.

1966

National Traffic and Motor Vehicle Safety Act	Establishes federal safety standards.
Model Cities Act	Authorizes more than $1 billion to ameliorate the nation's slums.

1967

Executive Order 11375	Extends an earlier executive order banning discrimination and requiring affirmative action by federal contractors to cover women.

1968

Civil Rights Act of 1968	Bans discrimination in housing and jury service.
National Housing Act	Subsidizes the private construction of 1.7 million units of low-income housing.

In decisions that dramatically altered law enforcement practices, the Court declared that states, as well as the federal government, were subject to the Bill of Rights. *Gideon v. Wainwright* (1963) ruled that when an accused criminal could not afford to hire a lawyer, the state had to provide one. *Miranda v. Arizona* (1966) required police officers to inform suspects of their rights upon arrest. The Court also overturned convictions based on evidence obtained by unlawful arrest, by electronic surveillance, or without a search warrant. Critics accused the justices of "handcuffing the police" and letting criminals go free; liberals argued that these rulings promoted equal treatment in the criminal justice system.

The Court's decisions on religion provoked even greater outrage. *Abington School District v. Schempp* (1963) ruled that requiring Bible reading and prayer in public schools violated the First Amendment principle of separation of church and state. Later judgments banned official prayer in public schools even if students were not required to participate. The Court's supporters declared that these decisions protected the rights of non-Christians and atheists and left students perfectly free to pray on their own, but the decisions infuriated many Christians. Billboards demanding "Impeach Earl Warren" spoke for critics of the Court, who joined a larger backlash mounting against Great Society liberalism.

> **REVIEW** How did the Kennedy and Johnson administrations exemplify a liberal vision of the federal government?

▶ The Second Reconstruction

As much as Supreme Court decisions, the black freedom struggle distinguished the liberalism of the 1960s from that of the New Deal. Before the Great Society reforms—and, in fact, contributing to them—African Americans had mobilized a movement that struck down legal separation and discrimination in the South and secured their voting rights. Whereas the first Reconstruction reflected the power of northern Republicans in the aftermath of the Civil War, the second Reconstruction depended heavily on the courage and determination of black people themselves to stand up to racist violence.

Civil rights activism that focused on the South and on legal rights won widespread acceptance in most of the country. But when African Americans stepped up protests against racial injustice outside the South and challenged the economic deprivation that equal rights left untouched, a strong backlash developed as the movement itself lost cohesion.

The Flowering of the Black Freedom Struggle

The Montgomery bus boycott of 1955–1956 gave racial issues national visibility and produced a leader in Martin Luther King Jr. In the 1960s, protest expanded dramatically, as blacks directly confronted the people and institutions that segregated and discriminated against them: retail establishments, public parks and libraries, buses and depots, voting registrars, and police forces.

Massive direct action in the South began in February 1960, when four African American college students in Greensboro, North Carolina, requested service at the whites-only Woolworth's lunch counter. Within days, hundreds of young people joined them, and others launched sit-ins in thirty-one southern cities. From Southern Christian Leadership Conference headquarters, Ella Baker telephoned her young contacts at black colleges: "What are you going to do? It's time to move."

In April, Baker helped protesters form a new organization, the Student Nonviolent Coordinating Committee (SNCC). Embracing King's civil disobedience and nonviolence principles, activists would confront their oppressors and stand up for their rights, but they would not respond if attacked. In the words of SNCC leader James Lawson, "Nonviolence nurtures the atmosphere in which reconciliation and justice become actual possibilities." SNCC, however, rejected the top-down leadership of King and the established civil rights organizations, adopting a structure that fostered decision making and leadership development at the grassroots level.

The activists' optimism and commitment to nonviolence soon underwent severe tests. Although some cities quietly met student demands, more typically activists encountered violence. Hostile whites poured food over demonstrators, burned them with cigarettes, called them "niggers," and pelted them with rocks. Local police attacked protesters with dogs, clubs, fire hoses, and tear gas, and they arrested thousands of demonstrators.

Another wave of protest occurred in May 1961, when the Congress of Racial Equality (CORE) organized Freedom Rides to implement Court orders for integrated transportation. When a group of six whites and seven blacks reached Alabama, whites bombed their bus and beat them with baseball bats so fiercely that an observer "couldn't see their faces through the blood." CORE leader James Farmer rebuffed President Kennedy's pleas for a cooling-off period, noting that blacks had been "cooling off for 150 years. If we cool off anymore, we'll be in a deep freeze." Finally, after a huge mob attacked the Freedom Riders in Montgomery, Alabama, Attorney General Robert Kennedy dispatched federal marshals to restore order. Nonetheless, Freedom Riders arriving in Jackson, Mississippi, were promptly arrested, and several hundred spent weeks in jail. All told, more than four hundred blacks and whites participated in the Freedom Rides.

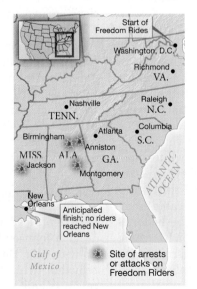

Civil Rights Freedom Rides, May 1961

In the summer of 1962, SNCC and other groups began the Voter Education Project to register black voters in southern states. They, too, met violence. Whites bombed black churches, threw tenant farmers out of their homes, and beat and jailed activists like Fannie Lou Hamer. In June 1963, a white man gunned down Mississippi NAACP leader Medgar Evers in front of his house. Similar violence met King's 1963 campaign in Birmingham, Alabama, to integrate public facilities and open jobs to blacks. The police attacked demonstrators, including children, with dogs, cattle prods, and fire hoses—brutalities that television broadcast around the world.

The largest demonstration drew 250,000 blacks and whites to the nation's capital in August 1963 in the March on Washington for Jobs and Freedom, inspired by the strategy of A. Philip Randolph in 1941 (see "The Double V Campaign" in chapter 25). Speaking from the Lincoln Memorial, King put his indelible stamp on the day. "I have a dream," he repeated again and again, imagining the day "when

What Difference Did the Voting Rights Act Make?

In May 1966, in Birmingham, Alabama, where some of the most violent actions against civil rights protesters had taken place, Willie Bolden voted for the first time. "It made me think I was sort of somebody," the eighty-one-year-old grandson of slaves said. Ardies Mauldin, the first African American voter registered in Selma, Alabama, under the Voting Rights Act of 1965 (VRA), reflected that "people . . . look more like citizens now." Fannie Lou Hamer reported that when blacks had no political voice, she got "hate stares" from whites. "Those same people now call me Mrs. Hamer." A sense of personal respect and dignity was just one of the trans-formations generated by African Americans' struggle for the most basic right of citizenship.

That effort did not end with the passage of the VRA. As NAACP leader Roy Wilkins warned, "Legislation is not self-implementing." The law suspended the literacy tests that had been used to disqualify blacks but not whites, and it brought electoral operations in most southern states under federal control. The Justice Department had to approve in advance any changes in state pro-cedures that could disadvantage black voters, and the attorney general was empowered to send federal agents to observe registration and election processes and even to register voters in areas of continued white resistance.

Civil rights activists organized more than two hundred voter registration drives between 1966 and 1968, resulting in dramatic increases in the numbers of blacks registered. Across the South, the proportion of African Americans on voter rolls jumped from 43 percent in 1964 to 62 percent in 1968. In Mississippi during that time, the total leaped from just 6.7 percent to 68 percent.

Black voting had an immediate effect on political representation. In the first ten years of the VRA, the number of black elected officials in the South grew from 72 to 1,588; while no African American sat in a southern state legislature in 1965, 95 did in 1975. Just seven years after whites bludgeoned civil rights activists during the voting rights campaign in Selma, Alabama, black candidates won half the seats on the city's council. Barbara Jordan of Texas and Andrew Young of Georgia won election to the House of Representatives in 1972, becoming the first African Americans from the

all of God's children . . . will be able to join hands and sing . . . 'Free at last, free at last; thank God Almighty, we are free at last.'"

The euphoria of the March on Washington faded as activists returned to face continued violence in the South. In 1964, the Mississippi Freedom Summer Project mobilized more than a thousand northern black and white college students to conduct voter registration drives. Resistance was fierce, and by the end of the summer, only twelve hundred new voters had been allowed to register. Southern whites had killed several activists, beaten eighty, arrested more than a thousand, and burned thirty-five black churches. Hidden resistance came from the federal government itself, as the Federal Bureau of Investigation (FBI) spied on King and expanded its activities to "expose, disrupt, mis-direct, discredit, or otherwise neutralize" black protest.

Still, the movement persisted. In March 1965, Alabama state troopers used such violent force to turn back a voting rights march from Selma to the state capital, Montgomery, that the inci-dent earned the name "Bloody Sunday" and compelled President Johnson to call up the Alabama National Guard to protect the march-ers. Battered and hospitalized on Bloody Sunday, John Lewis, chairman of SNCC (and later a congressman from Georgia), called the Voting Rights Act, which passed that October, "every bit as momentous as the Emancipation Proclamation." Referring to the Selma march, he said, "we all felt we'd had a part in it."

The Response in Washington

Civil rights leaders would have to wear sneakers, Lyndon Johnson said, if they were going to keep up with him. But both Kennedy and Johnson, reluctant to alienate southern voters and their congressional representatives, tended to move only when events gave them little choice. In June 1963, Kennedy finally made good on his promise

South to sit in Congress since Reconstruction. In 1973, Atlanta, Georgia, elected its first black mayor, Maynard Jackson. Black electoral success was not limited to the South. Nationwide the number of black elected officials rose from around 1,500 in 1965 to more than 10,000 on the fiftieth anniversary of the Voting Rights Act. Black representation in Congress inched up to 45 out of 535 voting members.

Electoral success translated into tangible benefits. Fred Reese, who was elected to the Selma city council, said in 1975, "We've got black police-men, black secretaries, and we can use the public restrooms. The word 'nigger' is almost out of existence." In Atlanta, Maynard Jackson ap-pointed a black police chief and in-creased African Americans' share of city jobs from 42 to 51 percent. Black local officials also awarded more contracts to minority businesses. When African Americans took office, their constituents saw improvements in public facilities, police protection, roads, trash collection, and other basic services. Referring to Unita

Blackwell's accomplishments as mayor of Mayersville, Mississippi, one resident noted, "She brought in the water tower. Mostly it was the pumps then. . . . Sewage, too." Another resident pointed to "old folks' houses and paved streets." Even when they were heavily outnumbered by whites, black officials could at least introduce issues of concern that whites had ignored, and they gained access to information about behind-the-scenes government. An African American member of a city council in Florida pointed out that "no matter what happened [my white colleagues] knew I was listening to everything that went on."

In the twenty-first century, African Americans still struggled for full equality. The election of a black president was a milestone, but African Americans were still underrepresented among elected officials. Only three blacks have served as governor (one in the South), and just four have been elected to the U.S. Senate since Reconstruction. The Supreme Court

in 2013 limited the reach of the VRA, and more than a dozen states passed voter ID laws and other measures making voting more difficult, especially for the elderly and the poor. Georgia representa-tive John Lewis, who was bloodied and sent to the hospital during the Selma voting rights drive, said in response to voter ID laws, "Our struggle is not a struggle that lasts one day . . . or one session of Congress. . . . Our struggle is the struggle of a lifetime."

Questions for Analysis

Summarize the Argument: What kinds of psychological and material benefits does the author argue were derived from the VRA?

Analyze the Evidence: In what specific ways did the VRA change African Americans' lives?

Consider the Context: How important was the VRA in contrast to other gains of the black freedom struggle?

---

to seek strong antidiscrimination legislation. Pointing to the injustice suffered by blacks, Kennedy asked white Americans, "Who among us would then be content with the counsels of patience and delay?" Johnson took up Kennedy's commitment with passion, as scenes of violence against peaceful demonstrators appalled televi-sion viewers across the world. The resulting public support, the "Johnson treatment," and the president's appeal to memories of the martyred Kennedy all produced the most important civil rights law since Reconstruction.

The Civil Rights Act of 1964 guaranteed access for all Americans to public accommoda-tions, public education, employment, and voting, and it extended constitutional protections to Indians on reservations. Title VII of the measure, banning discrimination in employment, not only attacked racial discrimination but also outlawed discrimination against women. Because Title VII applied to every aspect of employment, including wages, hiring, and promotion, it represented a

giant step toward equal employment opportunity for white women as well as for racial minorities.

Responding to voter registration drives in the South, Johnson demanded legislation to remove "every remaining obstacle to the right and the opportunity to vote." In August 1965, he signed the Voting Rights Act, empowering the federal government to intervene directly to enable African Americans to register and vote, thereby launching a major transformation in southern politics. Black voting rates shot up dramatically (Map 28.2). In turn, the number of African Americans holding political office in the South increased from a handful in 1964 to more than a thousand by 1972. Such gains translated into tangible benefits as black officials upgraded public facilities, police protection, and other basic services for their constituents. (See "Making Historical Arguments," above.)

Johnson also declared the need to realize "not just equality as a right and theory, but equality as fact and result." To this end, he issued an

VISUAL ACTIVITY

Selma March

The fifty-four-mile voting rights march from Selma, Alabama, to the state capital, Montgomery, gained national attention because of the violent reaction to the marchers from onlookers and state officials. The protest helped get the 1965 Voting Rights Act through Congress, a measure that eventually re-wrote politics in the South. © Bruce Davidson/Magnum Photos.

READING THE IMAGE: Why do you think the young boy lowered the flag to cover his body? What do the presence of the priest in the background and the signs behind him reflect about the breadth of the black freedom struggle?

CONNECTIONS: How was this protest like and different from other civil rights protests during the 1960s?

executive order in 1965 requiring employers holding government contracts (affecting about one-third of the labor force) to take affirmative action to ensure equal opportunity. Extended to cover women in 1967, the affirmative action program aimed to counter the effects of centuries of discrimination by requiring employers to act vigorously to align their labor forces with the available pool of qualified candidates. Most corporations came to see affirmative action as a good employment practice that could make them more successful in "today's increasingly global marketplace."

In 1968, Johnson maneuvered one final bill through Congress. While those in other regions often applauded the gains made by the black freedom struggle in the South, whites were just as likely to resist claims for racial justice in their own locations. In 1963, California voters rejected a law passed by the legislature banning discrimination in housing. And when Martin Luther King Jr. launched a campaign against de facto segregation in Chicago in 1966, thousands of whites jeered and threw stones at demonstrators. Johnson's efforts to get a federal open-housing law succeeded only in the wake of King's assassination in 1968. The Civil Rights Act of 1968 banned racial discrimination in housing and jury selection, and it authorized federal intervention when states failed to protect civil rights workers from violence.

Black Power and Urban Rebellions

By 1966, black protest engulfed the entire nation, demanding not just legal equality but also economic justice and abandoning passive resistance as a basic principle. These developments were not completely new. African Americans had waged campaigns for decent jobs, housing, and education outside the South since the 1930s. Some African Americans had always armed themselves in self-defense, and many protesters doubted that their passive response to violent attacks would change the hearts of racists. Still, the black freedom struggle began to appear more threatening to the white majority.

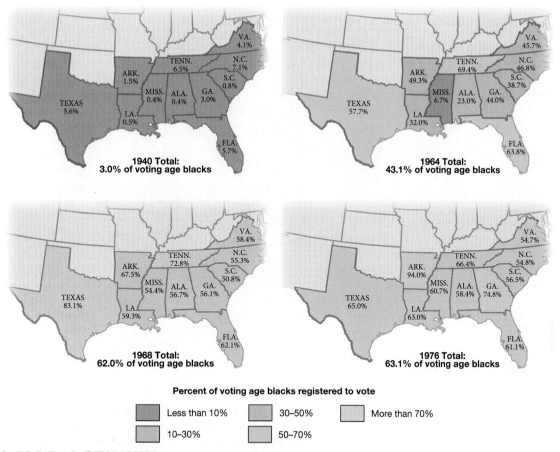

Percent of voting age blacks registered to vote

Less than 10%   30–50%   More than 70%

10–30%   50–70%

MAP ACTIVITY

Map 28.2   The Rise of the African American Vote, 1940–1976

Voting rates of southern blacks increased gradually in the 1940s and 1950s but shot up dramatically in the deep South after the Voting Rights Act of 1965 provided for federal agents to enforce African Americans' right to vote.

READING THE MAP: When did the biggest change in African American voter registration occur in the South? In 1968, which states had the highest and which had the lowest voter registration rates?

CONNECTIONS: What role did African American voters play in the 1960 election? What were the targets of two major voting drives in the 1960s?

The new emphases resulted from a combination of heightened activism and unrealized promise. Legal equality could not quickly ameliorate African American poverty, and black rage at oppressive conditions erupted in waves of urban uprisings from 1965 to 1968 (Map 28.3). In a situation where virtually all-white police forces patrolled black neighborhoods, incidents between police and local blacks typically sparked the riots and resulted in looting, destruction of property, injuries, and deaths. The worst riots occurred in Watts (Los Angeles) in August 1965, Newark and Detroit in July 1967, and the nation's capital in April 1968, but violence visited hundreds of cities, and African Americans suffered most of the casualties.

In the North, Malcolm X posed a powerful challenge to the ethos of nonviolence. Calling for black pride and autonomy, separation from the "corrupt [white] society," and self-defense against white violence, Malcolm X attracted a large following, especially in urban ghettos. At a June 1966 rally in Greenwood, Mississippi, SNCC chairman Stokely Carmichael gave the ideas espoused by Malcolm X a new name when he shouted, "We want black power." Carmichael rejected integration and assimilation because they implied white superiority. African Americans were encouraged to develop independent businesses and control their own schools, communities, and political organizations. The phrase "Black is beautiful" emphasized pride in African

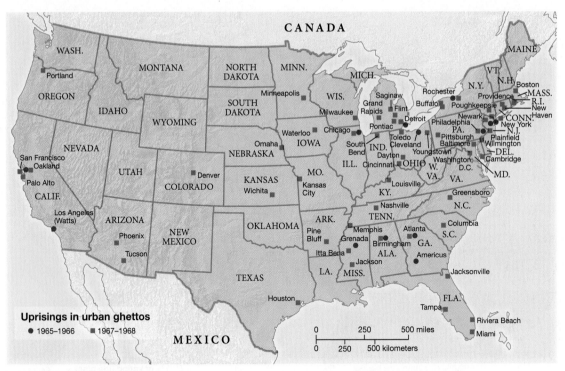

MAP ACTIVITY

Map 28.3 Urban Uprisings, 1965–1968

When a white police officer in the Watts district of Los Angeles struck a twenty-one-year-old African American, whom he had just pulled over for driving drunk, one onlooker shouted, "We've got no rights at all—it's just like Selma." The altercation sparked a five-day uprising, during which young blacks set fires, looted, and attacked police and firefighters. When the riot ended, 34 people were dead, more than 3,000 were arrested, and scores of businesses had been wiped out. Similar but smaller-scale violence erupted in dozens of cities across the nation during the next three summers.

READING THE MAP: In what regions and cities of the United States were the 1960s uprisings concentrated? What years saw the greatest unrest?

CONNECTIONS: What were some of the causes of racial unrest in America's cities during this period? Whom did whites generally hold responsible for the violence, and why?

American culture and connections to dark-skinned people around the world who were claiming their independence from colonial domination. Black power quickly became the rallying cry in SNCC and CORE as well as other organizations such as the Black Panther Party for Self-Defense, organized to combat police brutality.

The press paid inordinate attention to the **black power movement**, and civil rights activism met with a severe backlash from whites. Although the urban riots of the mid-1960s erupted spontaneously, triggered by specific incidents of alleged police mistreatment, horrified whites blamed black power militants. By 1966, 85 percent of the white population—up from 34 percent two years earlier—thought that African Americans were pressing for too much too quickly.

Martin Luther King Jr. agreed with black power advocates about the need for economic justice and "a radical reconstruction of society," yet he clung to nonviolence and integration as the means to this end. In 1968, the thirty-nine-year-old leader went to Memphis to support striking municipal sanitation workers. There, on April 4, he was murdered by an escaped white convict.

Although black power organizations captured the headlines, they failed to gain the massive support from African Americans that King and other leaders had attracted. Nor could they alleviate the poverty and racism entrenched in the entire country. Black radicals were harassed by the FBI and jailed; some encounters left both black militants and police dead. Yet black power's emphasis on racial pride and its

Black Power
Black Panthers in San Francisco organized a number of community centers where they provided free breakfasts to poor children, distributed party literature, organized protests, and operated "liberation schools." Here adults and children give the black power salute outside the Panther school in the Fillmore district in 1969. Such shows of militancy struck fear into many whites. Bettmann/Corbis.

critique of American institutions resonated loudly and helped shape the protest activities of other groups.

> **REVIEW**   How and why did the civil rights movement change in the mid-1960s?

▶ A Multitude of Movements

The civil rights movement's undeniable moral claims helped make protest more respectable, while its successes encouraged other groups with grievances. Native Americans, Latinos, college students, women, gay men and lesbians, and others drew on the black freedom struggle for inspiration and models of activism. Many of these groups engaged in direct-action protests, expressed their own cultural nationalism, and challenged dominant institutions and values. Their grievances gained attention in the political arena, and they expanded justice and opportunity for many of their constituents.

Native American Protest

The cry "red power" reflected the influence of black radicalism on young Native Americans, whose activism took on fresh militancy and goals in the 1960s. The termination and relocation programs of the 1950s, contrary to their intent, stirred a sense of Indian identity across tribal lines and a determination to preserve traditional culture. Native Americans demonstrated and occupied land and public buildings, claiming rights to natural resources and territory they had owned collectively before European settlement.

In 1969, Native American militants captured world attention when several dozen seized Alcatraz Island, an abandoned federal prison in San Francisco Bay, claiming their right of "first discovery" of this land. For nineteen months, they used the occupation to publicize injustices against Indians, promote pan-Indian cooperation, and celebrate traditional cultures. One of the organizers, Dr. LaNada Boyer, the first Native American to attend the University of California, Berkeley, said of Alcatraz, "We were able to reestablish our identity as Indian people, as a culture, as political entities."

In Minneapolis in 1968, two Chippewa Indians, Dennis Banks and George Mitchell, founded the **American Indian Movement (AIM)** to attack problems in cities, where about 300,000 Indians lived. AIM sought to protect Indians from police harassment, secure antipoverty funds, and establish "survival schools" to teach Indian history and values. The movement's appeal quickly spread and filled many Indians with a new sense of purpose.

Native Americans Occupy Alcatraz Island
From November 1969 to June 1971, groups of Native Americans occupied Alcatraz Island in San Francisco Bay. Calling themselves "Indians of All Tribes" to reflect their diversity, they demanded the deed to the island and the creation of an Indian university, museum, and cultural center. Although failing to achieve their goals, they brought attention to the Native American cause and spurred further activism. Ralph Crane/Getty Images.

more than one hundred Sioux Indians in 1890 (see "Indian Resistance and Survival" in chapter 17).

Although these dramatic occupations failed to achieve their specific goals, Indians won the end of relocation and termination policies, greater tribal sovereignty and control over community services, protection of Indian religious practices, and a measure of respect and pride. A number of laws and court decisions restored rights to ancestral lands and compensated tribes for land seized in violation of treaties.

Latino Struggles for Justice

The fastest-growing minority group in the 1960s was Latino, or Hispanic American, an extraordinarily varied population encompassing people of Mexican, Puerto Rican, Caribbean, and other Latin American origins. (The term *Latino* stresses their common bonds as a minority group in the United States. The older, less political term *Hispanic* also includes people with origins in Spain.) People of Puerto Rican and Caribbean descent populated East Coast cities, but more than half of the nation's Latino population—including some six million Mexican Americans—lived in the Southwest. In addition, thousands illegally crossed the border between Mexico and the United States yearly in search of economic opportunity and security from violence.

Political organization of Mexican Americans dated back to the League of United Latin American Citizens (LULAC), founded in 1929, which fought segregation and discrimination through litigation (see "Blacks and Mexican Americans Push for Their Civil Rights" in chapter 26). In the 1960s, however, young Mexican Americans increasingly rejected traditional politics in favor of direct action. One symbol of this generational challenge was young activists' adoption of the term *Chicano* (from *mejicano*, the Spanish word for "Mexican").

The **Chicano movement** drew national attention to California, where Cesar Chavez and Dolores Huerta organized a movement to overcome the exploitation of migrant agricultural workers. As the child of migrant farmworkers, Chavez lived in soggy tents, saw his parents cheated by labor contractors, changed schools frequently, and encountered indifference and discrimination. One teacher, he recalled, "hung a sign on me that said, 'I am a clown, I speak Spanish.'" After serving in World War II, Chavez began to organize voter registration drives among Mexican Americans.

In contrast to Chavez, Dolores Huerta grew up in an integrated neighborhood and avoided the farmworkers' grinding poverty but witnessed

Lakota activist and author Mary Crow Dog wrote that AIM's visit to her South Dakota reservation "loosened a sort of earthquake inside me." AIM leaders helped organize the "Trail of Broken Treaties" caravan to the nation's capital in 1972, when activists occupied the Bureau of Indian Affairs to express their outrage at the bureau's policies and interference in Indians' lives. In 1973, a much longer siege occurred on the Lakota Sioux reservation in South Dakota. Conflicts there between AIM militants and older tribal leaders led AIM to take over for seventy-two days the village of Wounded Knee, where U.S. troops had massacred

Cesar Chavez and Dolores Huerta
Under posters showing Senator Robert Kennedy and Mahatma Gandhi, Chavez and Huerta confer in 1968 during the United Farm Workers' struggle with grape growers for better wages and working conditions. Chavez, like Martin Luther King Jr., had studied the ideas of Gandhi, who used civil disobedience and nonviolence to gain independence for India. People across the country, including Robert Kennedy, supported the UFW's grape boycott. Arthur Schatz/Getty Images.

subtle forms of discrimination. Once, a high school teacher challenged her authorship of an essay because it was so well written. Believing that collective action was the key to progress, she and Chavez founded the United Farm Workers (UFW) union in 1962. To gain leverage for striking workers, the UFW mounted a nationwide boycott of California grapes, winning support from millions of Americans and gaining a wage increase for the workers in 1970. Although the UFW struggled and lost membership during the 1970s, it helped politicize Mexican Americans and improve farmworkers' lives.

Other Chicanos pressed the Equal Employment Opportunity Commission (EEOC) to act against job discrimination against Mexican Americans. After LULAC, the American GI Forum (see "Blacks and Mexican Americans Push for Their Civil Rights" in chapter 26), and other groups picketed government offices, President Johnson responded in 1967 by appointing Vicente T. Ximenes as the first Mexican American EEOC commissioner and creating a special committee on Mexican American issues.

Claiming "brown power," Chicanos organized to end discrimination in education, gain political power, and combat police brutality. In Denver, Rodolfo "Corky" Gonzales set up "freedom schools" where Chicano children learned Spanish and Mexican American history. The nationalist strains of Chicano protest were evident in La Raza Unida (the United Race), a political party founded in 1970 based on cultural pride and brotherhood. Along with blacks and Native Americans, Chicanos continued to be disproportionately impoverished, but they gradually won more political offices, more effective enforcement of antidiscrimination legislation, and greater respect for their culture.

Student Rebellion, the New Left, and the Counterculture

Although materially and legally more secure than their African American, Indian, and Latino counterparts, white youths also expressed dissent, participating in the black freedom struggle, student protests, the antiwar movement, and the new feminist movement. Challenging establishment institutions, young activists were part of a larger international phenomenon of student movements around the globe.

The central organization of white student protest was Students for a Democratic Society (SDS), whose 1962 statement of purpose asserted, "We are people of this generation, bred in at least modest comfort, housed now in universities, looking uncomfortably at the world we inherit." The idealistic students criticized the complacency of their elders, the remoteness of decision makers, and the powerlessness and alienation generated by a bureaucratic society. SDS aimed to mobilize a "New Left" around the goals of civil rights, peace, and universal economic security. Other forms of student activism soon followed.

The first large-scale white student protest arose at the University of California, Berkeley, in 1964, when university officials banned students from setting up tables to recruit support for various causes. Led by whites returning from civil rights work in the South, the "free speech" movement occupied the administration building,

Student Protest

Although only a minority of college students participated in the rebellions of the 1960s, a sizable number at all kinds of colleges challenged traditional authority, criticized established institutions, and demanded a voice in decision making.

DOCUMENT 1
Edward Schwartz, Student Power, October 1967

Student activist Edward Schwartz wrote this statement to represent the views of the National Student Association, the largest college student organization in the 1960s.

Let this principle apply—he who must obey the rule should make it.

Students should make the rules governing dormitory hours, boy-girl visitation, student unions, student fees, clubs, newspapers, and the like. Faculty and administrators should advise—attempt to persuade, even. Yet the student should bear the burden of choice.

Students and faculty should co-decide curricular policy.

Students, faculty, and administration should co-decide admissions policy, overall college policy affecting the community, even areas like university investment. . . . Student power should not be argued on legal grounds. It is not a legal principle. It is an educational principle.

Student power is threatening to those who wield power now, but this is understandable. A student should threaten his administrators outside of class, just as bright students threaten professors inside of class.

Student power ultimately challenges everyone in the university—the students who must decide; the faculty and administrators who must rethink their own view of community relations in order to persuade.

People who say that student power means anarchy imply really that students are rabble who have no ability to form community and to adhere to decisions made by community. Student power is not the negation of rules—it is the creation of a new process for the enactment of rules. Student power is not the elimination of authority, it is the development of a democratic standard of authority.

Source: Excerpt from "He Who Must Obey the Rule Should Make It," from *The University Crisis Reader*, vol. 1, *The Liberal University under Attack* by Immanuel Wallerstein and Paul Starr, eds., pp. 482–84. Copyright © 1971 by Random House, Inc.

DOCUMENT 2
SDS Explanation of the Columbia Strike, September 1968

One of the longest, most violent student protests occurred in New York City at Columbia University in spring 1968. A key issue was the university's expansion through buying up land in neighboring Harlem and evicting black tenants. Members of the Columbia chapter of SDS rationalize their actions below.

When we seized five buildings at Columbia University, we engaged the force of wealth, privilege, property—and the force of state violence that always accompanies them—with little more than our own ideals, our fears, and a vague sense of outrage at the injustices of our society. Martin Luther King had just been shot, his name demeaned by Columbia officials who refused to grant a decent wage to Puerto Rican workers, and who had recently grabbed part of Harlem for a student gym. . . .

and more than seven hundred students were arrested before the California Board of Regents overturned the new restrictions.

Hundreds of student rallies and building occupations followed on campuses across the country, especially after 1965, when opposition to the Vietnam War mounted and students protested against universities' ties with the military (see "The Widening War at Home" in chapter 29). Students also challenged the collegiate environment. Women at the University of Chicago, for example, charged in 1969 that all universities "discriminate against women, impede their full intellectual development, deny them places on the faculty, exploit talented women and mistreat women students." At Howard University, African American students called for a "Black Awareness Research Institute," demanding that academic departments "place more emphasis on how these disciplines may be used to effect the liberation of black people." Across the country, students won curricular reforms such as black studies and women's studies programs, more financial aid for minority and poor students, independence from paternalistic rules, and a larger voice in campus decision making. (See "Analyzing Historical Evidence," above.)

For years Columbia Trustees had evicted tenants from their homes, taken land through city deals, and fired workers for trying to form a union. For years they had trained officers for Vietnam who, as ROTC literature indicates, killed Vietnamese peasants in their own country. In secret work for the IDA [Institute for Defense Analysis] and the CIA, in chemical-biological war research for the Department of War, the Trustees implicated their own University in genocide. They had consistently . . . lied to their own constituents and published CIA books under the guise of independent scholarship. . . . Columbia, standing at the top of a hill, looked down on Harlem. . . . People who survived in Harlem had been evicted by the Trustees from Morningside or still paid rent to Columbia. . . . We walked to our classrooms across land that had been privatized; we studied in buildings that had once been homes in a city that is underhoused; and we listened to the apologies for Cold War and capital in our classes.

Columbia professors often claim that the University is a neutral institution. . . . A University could not, even if it wanted, choose to be really value-free. It can choose good values; it can choose bad values; or it can remain ignorant of the values on which it acts. . . . A social institution should at least articulate its own perspective, so that its own values may be consciously applied or modified. It is a typical fallacy of American teaching, that to remain silent on crucial issues is to be objective with your own constituents. Actually a "neutral" institution is far more manipulative than a University committed to avowed goals and tasks.

Source: Excerpt from "The Columbia Statement," Columbia SDS, from *The University Crisis Reader*, vol. 1, *The Liberal University under Attack* by Immanuel Wallerstein and Paul Starr, eds., pp. 23–47. Copyright © 1971 by Random House, Inc.

DOCUMENT 3
Counterthrust on Student Power, Spring 1967

While the majority of students simply avoided involvement in campus rebellions, some actively criticized the protesters. A leaflet titled "Student Power Is a Farce" reflected the views of Counterthrust, a conservative group at Wayne State University in Michigan.

Our University is being treated to the insanity of Left-Wing students demanding the run of the University. . . . Wayne students are told by the Left that "student power" merely means more democracy on campus. This is an outright lie! Student power is a Left-Wing catchword symbolizing campus militancy and radicalism. In actuality, the Left-Wing, spearheaded by the SDS, want to radically alter the university community. . . .

The Leftists charge a sinister plot by private enterprise to train students for jobs at taxpayers' expense. Evidently it never occurred to the SDS that private enterprise is also the biggest single taxpayer for schools. But, of course, that would require a little thought on the part of the SDS which they have already demonstrated they are incapable of. . . .

The byword of student power-union advocates is Radicalism. . . . Fraternities and student Governments will have no place in student power-unions since both are considered allies of the status quo and thus useless. . . . As responsible Wayne students, we cannot allow our University to be used by Leftists for their narrow purposes. We were invited to this campus by the Michigan Taxpayer to receive an education. Let us honor that invitation.

Source: Excerpt from "Student Power Is a Farce," Counterthrust, from *The University Crisis Reader*, vol. 1, *The Liberal University under Attack* by Immanuel Wallerstein and Paul Starr, eds., pp. 487–88. Copyright © 1971 by Random House, Inc.

Questions for Analysis

Recognize Viewpoints: How do the three statements differ in terms of the issues they address? What do the differences reveal about the authors' motivations for writing?

Ask Historical Questions: To what extent do your own campus policies and practices suggest that student protests during the 1960s and 1970s made a difference?

Consider the Context: In what ways did student protests differ from other protest movements of the 1960s?

Student protest sometimes blended into a cultural revolution against nearly every conventional standard of behavior. Drawing on the ideas of the Beats of the 1950s (see "Countercurrents" in chapter 27), the so-called hippies rejected mainstream values such as consumerism, order, and sexual restraint. Seeking personal rather than political change, they advocated "Do your own thing" and drew attention with their long hair, wildly colorful clothing, and drug use. Across the country, thousands of radicals established communes in cities or on farms, where they renounced private property and shared everything.

Rock and folk music defined both the counterculture and the political left. Music during the 1960s often carried insurgent political and social messages that reflected radical youth culture. "Eve of Destruction," a top hit of 1965, reminded young men of draft age at a time when the voting age was twenty-one, "You're old enough to kill but not for votin'." The 1969 Woodstock Music Festival, attended by 400,000 young people, epitomized the centrality of music to the youth rebellion. Hippies faded away in the 1970s, but many elements of the counterculture—rock music, jeans, and long hair, as well as new social attitudes—filtered into the mainstream. More

Birth Control
In the 1960s, the advent of the birth control pill, court decisions lifting restrictions on contraception, the rise of feminism, and demands for greater sexual freedom all threw birth control into the political spotlight. In July 1968, Pope Paul VI issued an encyclical condemning artificial birth control, which prompted this demonstration in front of New York's St. Patrick's Cathedral. Bettmann/Corbis.

tolerant approaches to sexual behaviors spawned what came to be called the "sexual revolution," with help from the birth control pill, which became available in the 1960s. Self-fulfillment became a dominant concern of many Americans, and questioning of authority became more widespread.

Gay Men and Lesbians Organize

More permissive sexual norms did not stretch easily to include tolerance of homosexuality. Gay men and lesbians escaped discrimination and ridicule only by concealing their very identities. Those who couldn't or wouldn't found themselves fired from jobs, arrested for their sexual activities, deprived of their children, or accused of being "perverted." Despite this, some gays and lesbians began to organize.

An early expression of gay activism challenged the government's aggressive efforts to keep homosexuals out of civil service. In October 1965, picketers outside the White House held signs calling discrimination against homosexuals "as immoral as discrimination against Negroes and Jews." Not until ten years later, however, did the Civil Service Commission formally end its antigay policy.

A turning point in gay activism came in 1969 when police raided a gay bar, the Stonewall Inn, in New York City's Greenwich Village, and gay men and lesbians fought back. "Suddenly, they were not submissive anymore," a police officer remarked. Energized by the defiance shown at the Stonewall riots, gay men and lesbians organized a host of new groups, such as the Gay Liberation Front and the National Gay and Lesbian Task Force.

In 1972, Ann Arbor, Michigan, passed the first antidiscrimination ordinance, and two years later Elaine Noble's election to the Massachusetts legislature marked the first time an openly gay candidate won state office. In 1973, gay activists persuaded the American Psychiatric Association to withdraw its designation of homosexuality as a mental disease. It would take decades for these initial gains to improve conditions for most homosexuals, but by the mid-1970s gay men and lesbians had a movement through which they could claim equal rights and express pride in their identities.

> **REVIEW** What other movements emerged in the 1960s, and how were they influenced by the black freedom struggle?

▶ The New Wave of Feminism

On August 26, 1970, the fiftieth anniversary of woman suffrage, tens of thousands of women across the country—from radical women in jeans to conservatively dressed suburbanites, peace activists, and politicians—took to the streets. They carried signs reading "Sisterhood Is Powerful" and "Don't Cook Dinner—Starve a Rat Today." Some of the banners opposed the war in Vietnam, others demanded racial justice, but women's own liberation stood at the forefront.

Becoming visible by the late 1960s, a multifaceted women's movement reached its high tide in the 1970s and persisted into the twenty-first century. By that time, despite a powerful countermovement, women had experienced tremendous transformations in their legal status, public opportunities, and personal and sexual

Gay Liberation Front Marches in New York

The Stonewall riots energized a generation of young gay men and lesbians, whose ideas and tactics resembled those of other radical movements of the 1960s. Shortly after Stonewall, the Gay Liberation Front came to life, advertising itself as a "revolutionary group" demanding "complete sexual liberation for all people." Here, in June 1970, members march down Christopher Street, the site of the Stonewall Inn. © Ellen Shumsky/The Image Works.

relationships, while popular expectations about appropriate gender roles had shifted dramatically.

A Multifaceted Movement Emerges

Beginning in the 1940s, large demographic changes laid the preconditions for a resurgence of feminism. As more and more women took jobs, the importance of their paid work to the economy and their families challenged traditional views of women and awakened many women workers, especially labor union women, to the inferior conditions of their employment. The democratization of higher education brought more women to college campuses, where their aspirations exceeded the confines of domesticity and of routine, subordinate jobs.

Policy initiatives in the early 1960s reflected both these larger transformations and the efforts of women's rights activists. In 1961, Assistant Secretary of Labor Esther Peterson persuaded President Kennedy to create the President's Commission on the Status of Women (PCSW). Its 1963 report documented widespread discrimination against women and recommended remedies, although it did not challenge women's domestic roles. One of the commission's concerns was addressed even before its report came out, when Congress passed the Equal Pay Act of 1963, making it illegal to pay women less than men for the same work.

Like other movements, the rise of feminism owed much to the black freedom struggle. Women gained protection from employment discrimination through Title VII of the Civil Rights Act of 1964 and the extension of affirmative action to women by piggybacking onto civil rights measures. They soon grew impatient when the government failed to take these new policies seriously. Determining the need for "an NAACP for women" to put pressure on the government and other institutions, Betty Friedan, civil rights activist Pauli Murray, several union women, and others founded the **National Organization for Women (NOW)** in 1966.

Simultaneously, a more radical feminism grew among mostly white young women active in the black freedom struggle and the New Left. Frustrated when male leaders dismissed and ridiculed their claims of sex discrimination, many women walked out of New Left organizations and created independent women's liberation groups throughout the nation.

Women's liberation began to gain public attention, especially when dozens of women picketed the Miss America beauty pageant in 1968, protesting against being forced "to compete for male approval [and] enslaved by ludicrous 'beauty' standards." Women began to speak publicly about personal experiences that had always been shrouded in secrecy, such as rape and abortion. Throughout the country, women joined consciousness-raising groups, where they discovered that what they had considered "personal" problems reflected an entrenched system of discrimination against and devaluation of women.

Radical feminists, who called their movement "women's liberation," differed from feminists in

Transnational Feminisms

International organizations of women originated in the nineteenth century, but global connections among women increased dramatically in 1945 with the creation of the United Nations, whose charter affirmed "the equal rights of men and women." In 1947, the UN established a Commission on the Status of Women, creating a forum for women from around the globe to meet and be heard; in 1948, it adopted a Universal Declaration of Human Rights, which explicitly condemned sex discrimination. These commitments to justice for women went far beyond any rights guaranteed to women in the United States or most other nations, thereby setting standards and raising expectations.

The UN helped launch a global feminist movement of unparalleled size and diversity when it declared 1975 International Women's Year and sponsored a conference in Mexico City. In addition to official delegates from 125 nations, six thousand women came to Mexico City on their own. The assembly approved the World Plan of Action for Women and prompted the UN to declare 1976 to 1985 the UN Decade for Women.

In response to the call for action in individual countries, the U.S. government funded the National Women's Conference in Houston, Texas, in 1977. More than two thousand state delegates attended, representing a cross section of American womanhood. They adopted the National Plan of Action, not only supporting ratification of the ERA and reproductive freedom but also addressing the needs of specific groups of women, including the elderly, lesbians, racial minorities, women with disabilities, rural women, and homemakers. For the first time, the U.S. women's movement had a comprehensive national agenda setting goals for decades to come.

The three themes of the UN Decade for Women—equality, development, and peace—reflected an effort to address the enormously diverse needs

NOW and other more mainstream groups in several ways. NOW focused on equal treatment for women in the public sphere; women's liberation emphasized ending women's subordination in family and other personal relationships. Groups such as NOW wanted to integrate women into existing institutions; radical groups insisted that women's liberation required a total transformation of economic, political, and social institutions. Differences between these two strands of feminism blurred in the 1970s, as NOW and other mainstream groups embraced many of the issues raised by radicals.

Although NOW elected a black president, Aileen Hernandez, in 1970, the new feminism's leadership and constituency were predominantly white and middle-class. Women of color criticized white feminists for their inadequate attention to the disproportionate poverty experienced by minority women and to the particular forms of oppression women of color experienced when gender combined with race or ethnicity. To black women, who were much more frequently compelled to work in the lowest-paying jobs for their families' survival, employment did not necessarily look like liberation.

In addition to struggling with vast differences among women, feminism also contended with the media's refusal to take women's grievances seriously. For instance, when the House of Representatives passed an equal rights amendment to the U.S. Constitution in 1970, the *New York Times* criticized it in an editorial titled "The Henpecked House." After Gloria Steinem founded *Ms.: The New Magazine for Women* in 1972, feminists had their own mass-circulation periodical controlled by women and featuring articles on a broad range of feminist issues.

Ms. reported on a multifaceted movement that reflected the tremendously diverse experiences, backgrounds, and goals of American women. New women's organizations represented ethnic and racial minorities, labor union women, religious women, welfare mothers, lesbians, and more. Other new groups focused on single issues such as health, education, abortion rights, and violence against women. In addition, U.S. women connected with women abroad, joining a movement that crossed national boundaries. (See "Beyond America's Borders," above.)

Common threads underlay the great diversity of organizations, issues, and activities. Feminism represented the belief that women were barred from, unequally treated in, or poorly served by the entire male-dominated public arena, including politics, medicine, law, education, culture, and religion. Many feminists also sought equality in the private sphere, challenging traditional norms that identified women primarily as wives and mothers or sex objects who accommodated themselves to men's needs and interests.

Feminist Gains Spark a Countermovement

Although more an effect than a cause of women's rising employment, feminism lifted female aspirations and helped lower barriers to occupations of women throughout the world. Feminists from Western nations who focused on equal rights met criticism from women who represented colonized, impoverished third world countries and insisted that "to talk feminism to a woman who has no water, no food, and no home is to talk nonsense." Ever-larger UN-sponsored meetings followed Mexico City—Copenhagen in 1980, Nairobi in 1985, and Beijing in 1995, where twenty thousand women gathered. These global exchanges taught American feminists that to participate in a truly international movement, they would have to revise their Western-centered perspective on women's needs and understand that women's issues must include economic development and anticolonialism.

American feminists also learned that theirs was not always the most advanced nation when it came to women's welfare and status. Employed women in most industrialized countries had access to paid maternity leave and publicly subsidized child care. By 2015, women had headed governments in more than thirty countries, including India, Israel, Britain, and Germany. Many nations, such as Argentina, Egypt, and members of the European Union, had some form of affirmative action to increase the numbers of women in government. And whereas American women held just 20 percent of the seats in Congress, women constituted more than 35 percent of national legislatures in such countries as Sweden, South Africa, Costa Rica, and Belgium.

Despite enormous differences among women around the world, internationally minded feminists continued to seek common ground. As Gertrude Mongella, secretary general of the Beijing conference, insisted in 1995, "A revolution has begun and there is no going back. . . . This revolution is too just, too important, and too long overdue."

Questions for Analysis

Analyze the Evidence: What were the three themes of the UN Decade for Women? How were these three themes related to women's status and well-being?

Recognize Viewpoints: How and why did the agendas of women from richer countries differ from those of women from the developing world?

Consider the Context: What goals did women's movements in the United States and abroad have in common with other protest movements of the 1960s?

monopolized by men. By 2010, women's share of law and medical degrees had shot up from 5 percent and 10 percent, respectively, to around 50 percent, though they earned much less than men in those fields. Women gained political offices very slowly; yet by 2016, they constituted about 20 percent of Congress and nearly 25 percent of all state legislators.

Despite outnumbering men in college enrollments and making some inroads into male-dominated occupations, women still concentrated in low-paying, traditionally female jobs, and an earnings gap between men and women persisted into the twenty-first century. Employed women continued to bear primary responsibility for taking care of their homes and families, thereby working a "double day." Unlike in other advanced countries, women in the United States were not entitled to paid maternity leave, and government provisions for child care lagged far behind.

By the mid-1970s, feminism faced a powerful countermovement, organized around opposition to an Equal Rights Amendment (ERA) to the Constitution that would outlaw differential treatment of men and women under all state and federal laws. After Congress passed the ERA in 1972, Phyllis Schlafly, a conservative activist in the Republican Party, mobilized thousands of antifeminist women who feared that the ERA would devalue what they believed were their God-given roles as wives and mothers. These women, marching on state capitols, persuaded enough male legislators to block ratification so that when the time limit ran out in 1982, only thirty-five states had ratified it, three short of the necessary three-fourths majority (see chapter 30, "Making Historical Arguments," page 882).

Powerful opposition likewise arose to feminists' quest for abortion rights. "Without the full capacity to limit her own reproduction," abortion rights activist Lucinda Cisler insisted, "a woman's other 'freedoms' are tantalizing mockeries that cannot be exercised." In 1973, the Supreme Court ruled in the landmark *Roe v. Wade* decision that the Constitution protects the right to abortion, which states cannot prohibit in the early stages of pregnancy. This decision galvanized many Americans who believed that abortion constituted murder. Like ERA opponents, with whom they often overlapped, right-to-life activists believed that abortion disparaged motherhood and that feminism threatened their traditional roles. Beginning in 1977, abortion foes pressured Congress to restrict the right to abortion by prohibiting coverage under all government-financed health programs, and the Supreme Court allowed states to impose additional obstacles.

Despite resistance, feminists won other lasting gains. Title IX of the Education Amendments Act of 1972 banned sex discrimination in all aspects of education, such as admissions, athletics, and hiring. Congress also outlawed sex discrimination in credit in 1974, opened U.S. military academies to women in 1976, and prohibited discrimination against pregnant workers in 1978. Moreover, the Supreme Court struck down laws

that treated men and women differently in Social Security, welfare and military benefits, and workers' compensation.

At the state and local levels, women saw reforms in areas that radical feminists had first introduced. They won laws forcing police departments and the legal system to treat rape victims more justly and humanely. Activists also pushed domestic violence onto the public agenda, obtaining government financing for shelters for battered women as well as laws ensuring both greater protection for victims of domestic violence and more effective prosecution of abusers.

REVIEW   What were the key goals of feminist reformers, and why did a countermovement arise to resist them?

▶ Liberal Reform in the Nixon Administration

Opposition to civil rights measures, Great Society reforms, and protest groups—along with frustrations over the war in Vietnam (see "A Nation Polarized" in chapter 29)—delivered the White House to Republican Richard M. Nixon in 1968. Nixon attacked the Great Society for "pouring billions of dollars into programs that have failed" and promised to represent the "forgotten Americans, the non-shouters, the non-demonstrators." Yet his administration either promoted or accepted important elements of the liberal reform agenda, including greater federal assistance to the poor, new protections for women and minorities, and environmental reforms.

Extending the Welfare State and Regulating the Economy

A number of factors shaped the liberal policies of the Nixon administration. Democrats continued to control Congress, the Republican Party contained many liberals and moderates, and Nixon saw political advantages in accepting some liberal programs, especially those promoted by grassroots movements that persisted into the 1970s. Serious economic problems also compelled new approaches, and although Nixon's real passion lay in foreign policy, he was eager to establish a domestic legacy.

Under Nixon, government assistance programs such as Social Security, housing, and food stamps grew, and Congress enacted a new billion-dollar program that provided Pell grants for low-income students to attend college. Noting the disparity between what Nixon said and what he did, his speechwriter, the archconservative Pat Buchanan, grumbled, "Vigorously did we inveigh against the Great Society, enthusiastically did we fund it."

Nixon also acted contrary to his antigovernment rhetoric when economic crises and energy shortages induced him to increase the federal government's power in the marketplace. By 1970, both inflation and unemployment had surpassed 6 percent, an unprecedented combination dubbed "stagflation." Domestic troubles were compounded by the decline of American dominance in the international economy. With Japan and Western Europe fully recovered from the devastation of World War II, foreign cars, electronic equipment, and other products now competed favorably with American goods. In 1971, for the first time in decades, the United States imported more than it exported. Because the amount of dollars in foreign hands exceeded U.S. gold reserves, the nation could no longer back up its currency with gold.

In 1971, Nixon abandoned the convertibility of dollars into gold and devalued the dollar to increase exports by making them cheaper. To protect domestic manufacturers, he imposed a 10 percent surcharge on most imports, and he froze wages and prices, thus enabling the government to stimulate the economy without fueling inflation. In the short run, these policies worked, and Nixon was resoundingly reelected in 1972. Yet by 1974, unemployment had crept back up and inflation soared.

Skyrocketing energy prices intensified stagflation. Throughout the post–World War II economic boom, abundant domestic oil deposits and access to cheap Middle Eastern oil had encouraged the building of large cars and skyscrapers with no concern for fuel efficiency. By the 1970s, the United States was consuming one-third of the world's fuel resources.

In the fall of 1973, the United States faced its first energy crisis. Arab nations, furious at the administration's support of Israel during the Yom Kippur War (see "Shoring Up U.S. Interests around the World" in chapter 29), cut off oil shipments to the United States. Long lines formed at gas stations, where prices had nearly doubled, and many homes were cold. In response, Nixon authorized temporary emergency measures allocating petroleum and establishing a national 55-mile-per-hour speed limit to save gasoline. The energy crisis eased, but the nation had yet to come to grips with its seemingly unquenchable demand for fuel and dependence on foreign oil.

Responding to Environmental Concerns

The oil crisis dovetailed with a rising environmental movement, which was pushing the government to conserve energy and protect nature and human beings from the hazards of rapid economic growth. Like the conservation movement born in the Progressive Era (see "Roosevelt and Conservation" in chapter 21), the new environmentalists sought to preserve natural areas for recreational and aesthetic purposes and to conserve natural resources for future use. Especially in the West, the post–World War II explosion of economic and population growth, with the resulting demands for electricity and water, made such efforts seem even more critical. Already in the 1950s, environmental groups mobilized to stop construction of dams that would disrupt national parks and wilderness.

The new environmentalists, however, went beyond conservationism to attack the ravaging effects of industrial and technological advances on human life and health. The polluted air and water and spread of deadly chemicals attending economic growth threatened wildlife, plants, and the ecological balance that sustained human life. Biologist Rachel Carson drew national attention in 1962 with her best seller *Silent Spring*, which described the harmful effects of toxic chemicals such as the pesticide DDT. The Sierra Club and other older conservation organizations expanded their agendas, and a host of new groups arose. Millions of Americans expressed environmental concerns on the first observation of Earth Day in April 1970. The locally organized, grassroots events addressed a host of topics, including oil spills, water pollution, recycling, industrial waste, automobile emissions, and many more.

Responding to these concerns, Nixon built on efforts begun under Johnson. He called "clean air, clean water, open spaces . . . the birthright of every American" and urged Congress to "end the plunder of America's natural heritage." In 1970, he created the **Environmental Protection Agency (EPA)** to enforce environmental laws, conduct research, and reduce human health and environmental risks from pollutants. He also signed the landmark Occupational Safety and Health Act (OSHA), protecting workers against job-related accidents and disease; the Clean Air Act of 1970, restricting factory and automobile emissions of carbon dioxide and other pollutants; and the Endangered Species Act of 1973. Although environmentalists claimed that Nixon failed to do enough, pointing particularly to his veto of the Clean Water Act of 1972, which Congress overrode, his environmental initiatives far surpassed those of previous administrations.

Expanding Social Justice

Nixon's 1968 campaign had appealed to southern Democrats and white workers by exploiting hostility to black protest and new civil rights policies, but his administration had to answer to the courts and to Congress. In 1968, fourteen years after the *Brown* decision, school desegregation had barely touched the South. Like Eisenhower, Nixon was reluctant to use federal power to compel integration, but the Supreme Court overruled the administration's efforts to delay court-ordered desegregation. By 1974, fewer than one

in ten southern black children attended totally segregated schools.

Nixon also began to implement affirmative action among federal contractors and unions, and his administration awarded more government contracts and loans to minority businesses. Congress took the initiative in other areas. In 1970, it extended the Voting Rights Act of 1965, and in 1972 it strengthened the Civil Rights Act of 1964 by enlarging the powers of the Equal Employment Opportunity Commission. In 1971, Congress also responded to the massive youth movement with the Twenty-sixth Amendment to the Constitution, reducing the voting age to eighteen. And in 1973, Nixon signed legislation outlawing discrimination against people with disabilities in all programs receiving federal funds.

VISUAL ACTIVITY

Earth Day 1970

Building on the success of teach-ins about the Vietnam War, Democratic senator Gaylord Nelson of Wisconsin came up with the idea of Earth Day "to shake up the political establishment and force this issue [environmentalism] onto the national agenda." As a result, on April 22, 1970, some twenty million people participated in grassroots demonstrations throughout the country. Above are demonstrators in New York City. Dennis Stock/Magnum Photos.

READING THE IMAGE: What aspects of environmentalism are reflected in the colored faces in the forefront and in the banner behind? Why might young people have been especially drawn to the environmental movement?

CONNECTIONS: What new environmental policies were enacted in the early 1970s?

Several measures of the Nixon administration also specifically attacked sex discrimination, as the president confronted a growing feminist movement that included Republican women. Nixon vetoed a comprehensive child care bill and publicly opposed abortion, but he signed the landmark Title IX, guaranteeing equality in all aspects of education, and allowed his Labor Department to push affirmative action.

President Nixon advocated for Native Americans more than for any other protest group. He told Congress that Indians were "the most deprived and most isolated minority group . . . the heritage of centuries of injustice." While not bowing to radical demands, his administration dealt cautiously with extreme protests such as the occupations of Alcatraz and the Bureau of Indian Affairs. Nixon signed measures recognizing claims of Alaskan and New Mexican Indians, returned tribal status to groups that had undergone termination, and set in motion legislation restoring tribal lands and granting Indians more control over their schools and other service institutions.

REVIEW How did liberal reform fare under President Nixon?

► Conclusion: Achievements and Limitations of Liberalism

Senate majority leader Mike Mansfield was not alone in concluding that Lyndon Johnson "has done more than FDR ever did, or ever thought of doing." Taking up goals of John F. Kennedy's New Frontier, the Great Society expanded the New Deal's focus on economic security, refashioning liberalism to embrace individual rights and to extend material well-being to groups left out of or discriminated against in New Deal programs. Yet opposition to Johnson's leadership grew so strong that by 1968 his liberal vision lay in ruins. "How," he asked, "was it possible that all these people could be so ungrateful to me after I have given them so much?"

Fannie Lou Hamer could have pointed out how slowly the government acted when efforts to win civil rights met with violence. In addition, Hamer's failed attempts to use Johnson's antipoverty programs to help poor blacks in Mississippi reflected, in part, some of the more general shortcomings of the War on Poverty. Hastily planned and inadequately funded, antipoverty programs focused more on remediating individual shortcomings than on structural reforms that would ensure adequately paying jobs for all. Because Johnson launched an all-out war in Vietnam and refused to ask for sacrifices from prosperous Americans, the Great Society never commanded the resources necessary for victory over poverty.

Furthermore, black aspirations exceeded white Americans' commitment to genuine equality. Most whites supported overturning the crude and blatant forms of racism in the South, but when the civil rights movement attacked racial barriers long entrenched throughout the nation and sought equality in fact as well as in law, it faced a powerful backlash. By the end of the 1960s, the revolution in the legal status of African Americans was complete, but the black freedom struggle had lost momentum, and African Americans remained, with Native Americans and Latinos, at the bottom of the economic ladder.

Johnson's critics overlooked the Great Society's more successful and lasting elements. Medicare and Medicaid continue to provide access to health care for the elderly and the poor. Federal aid for education and housing became permanent elements of national policy. Moreover, Richard Nixon's otherwise conservative administration implemented school desegregation in the South and affirmative action, initiated environmental reforms, and secured new rights for Native Americans and women. Women benefited from the decline of discrimination, and significant numbers of African Americans and other minority groups began to enter the middle class.

Yet the perceived shortcomings of government programs contributed to social turmoil and fueled the resurgence of conservative politics. Young radicals launched direct confrontations with the government and universities that, together with racial conflict, escalated into political discord and social disorder. The Vietnam War polarized American society as much as did domestic change; it devoured resources that might have been used for social reform and undermined faith in government.

See the Selected Bibliography for this chapter in the Appendix.

28 Chapter Review

KEY TERMS

Civil Rights Act of 1964 (p. 805)
War on Poverty (p. 806)
Medicare and Medicaid (p. 807)
Voting Rights Act of 1965 (p. 807)
Immigration and Nationality Act of 1965 (p. 807)
Warren Court (p. 808)
black power movement (p. 816)
American Indian Movement (AIM) (p. 817)
Chicano movement (p. 818)
National Organization for Women (NOW) (p. 823)
Roe v. Wade (p. 825)
Environmental Protection Agency (EPA) (p. 827)

REVIEW QUESTIONS

1. How did the Kennedy and Johnson administrations exemplify a liberal vision of the federal government? (pp. 803–810)

2. How and why did the civil rights movement change in the mid-1960s? (pp. 810–817)

3. What other movements emerged in the 1960s, and how were they influenced by the black freedom struggle? (pp. 817–822)

4. What were the key goals of feminist reformers, and why did a countermovement arise to resist them? (pp. 822–826)

5. How did liberal reform fare under President Nixon? (pp. 826–829)

MAKING CONNECTIONS

1. Why were Lyndon Johnson's reforms so much more far-reaching than John F. Kennedy's?

2. What specific gains did the civil rights movement achieve in the 1960s, and how were those gains limited?

3. What characteristics did all reform movements of the 1960s share?

LINKING TO THE PAST

1. How was Lyndon Johnson's approach to poverty different from Franklin Roosevelt's? Which was more successful? (See chapter 24.)

2. What changes that had been taking place in the United States since 1940 laid a foundation for the rise of a feminist movement in the 1960s? (See chapters 25 and 26.)

29 Vietnam and the End of the Cold War Consensus

1961–1975

CAMOUFLAGE HELMET
The antiwar buttons on this military helmet reflect the bitter divisions that the Vietnam War produced in the United States, even among some of the soldiers themselves.
Doug Steley B/Alamy.

LIEUTENANT FREDERICK DOWNS JR. GREW UP ON AN INDIANA farm and enlisted in the army after three years of college. Leaving a ten-month-old daughter behind, he completed officer training and arrived in Vietnam in September 1967. The infantry platoon leader and his men went to Vietnam "cocky and sure of our destiny, gung ho, invincible."

That confidence was tempered by what they found in Vietnam. Unlike most of America's previous wars, there was no fixed battlefront; helicopters ferried fighting units all over South Vietnam, as U.S. and South Vietnamese troops attempted to defeat the South Vietnamese insurgents and their North Vietnamese allies. In a civil war characterized by guerrilla tactics, Downs and his men struggled to distinguish civilians from combatants and destroyed villages just because they might be used by the enemy. He had faith that his country could win the war, but he found the South Vietnamese army to be lazy and ineffective. "Maybe the people in Nam are worth saving, but their army isn't worth shit," he wrote in his memoir. Downs won several medals for bravery, but his one-year stint in Vietnam ended when a land mine blew off his left arm and wedged shrapnel into his legs and back.

Downs served in Vietnam at the height of a U.S. engagement that began with the Cold War commitments made by Presidents Harry S. Truman and Dwight D. Eisenhower. John F. Kennedy wholeheartedly took on those commitments, promising more flexible and vigorous efforts to thwart communism, declaring that the United States would "pay any price, bear any burden, meet any hardship, support any friend, oppose any foe to assure the survival and the success of liberty."

Kennedy sent increasing amounts of American arms and personnel to sustain the South Vietnamese government, and Lyndon B. Johnson dramatically escalated that commitment in 1965, turning a civil war among the Vietnamese into America's war. At peak strength in 1968, 543,000 U.S. military personnel served in Vietnam; all told, some 2.6 million saw duty there. Yet this massive intervention failed to defeat North Vietnam and created intense discord at home, "poisoning the soul of America," in Downs's words. Some Americans supported the government's goal in Vietnam and decried only the failure to pursue it effectively. Others believed that preserving a non-Communist South Vietnam was neither a vital interest of the United States nor within its capacity or moral right to achieve. Back home in college after months of surgery, Downs encountered a man who asked about the hook descending from his sleeve. When he said that he had lost his arm in Vietnam, the man shot back, "Serves you right."

This internal conflict was just one of the war's great costs. Like Downs, more than 150,000 soldiers suffered severe wounds, and more than 58,000 lost their lives. The war derailed domestic reform, depleted the federal budget, disrupted the economy, kindled domestic discord, and led to the violation of protesters' rights, leaving a lasting mark on the nation.

Even while fighting communism in Vietnam and in other third world countries, American leaders moved to ease Cold War tensions. After a tense standoff with the Soviet Union during the Cuban missile crisis, the United States began to cooperate with its Cold War enemy to limit the spread of nuclear weapons. In addition, Richard M. Nixon made a historic visit to China in 1972, abandoning the policy of isolating China and paving the way for normal diplomatic relations by the end of the 1970s.

▶ New Frontiers in Foreign Policy

John F. Kennedy moved quickly to pursue containment more aggressively and with more flexible means. In contrast to the Eisenhower administration's emphasis on nuclear weapons, Kennedy expanded both the nation's nuclear capacity and its ability to fight conventional battles and engage in guerrilla warfare. Kennedy also accelerated the nation's space exploration program and increased engagement with the third world. When the Soviets tried to establish a nuclear outpost in Cuba in 1962, Kennedy took the United States to the brink of war. Less dramatically, Kennedy sent increasing amounts of American arms and personnel to save the South Vietnamese government from Communist insurgents.

Meeting the "Hour of Maximum Danger"

Underlying Kennedy's foreign policy was an assumption that the United States had "gone soft—physically, mentally, spiritually soft," as he put it in 1960. Calling the Eisenhower era "years of drift and impotency," Kennedy warned in his inaugural address that the nation faced a grave peril: "Each day the crises multiply. . . . Each day we draw nearer the hour of maximum danger."

Although the president exaggerated the threat to national security, several developments in 1961 heightened the sense of crisis and provided a rationalization for his military buildup. Shortly before Kennedy's inauguration, Soviet premier Nikita Khrushchev publicly encouraged "wars of national liberation," thereby aligning the Soviet Union with independence movements in the third world that were often anti-Western. His statement reflected in part the Soviet competition with China for the allegiance of emerging nations, but U.S. officials saw it as a threat to the status quo of containment.

Cuba, just ninety miles off the Florida coast, posed the first crisis for Kennedy. The revolution led by Fidel Castro had moved Cuba into the Soviet orbit, and Eisenhower's Central Intelligence Agency (CIA) had planned an invasion of the island by Cuban exiles living in Florida. Kennedy ordered the invasion to proceed even though his military advisers deemed its success uncertain.

In April 1961, about 1,400 anti-Castro exiles trained and armed by the CIA landed at the **Bay of Pigs** on the south shore of Cuba (Map 29.1). Contrary to U.S. expectations, no popular uprising

CHRONOLOGY

1961	• Bay of Pigs invaded. • Berlin Wall erected. • Kennedy increases military aid to South Vietnam. • Peace Corps created.
1962	• Cuban missile crisis occurs.
1963	• President Kennedy assassinated; Lyndon B. Johnson becomes president.
1964	• Gulf of Tonkin Resolution passed.
1965	• Operation Rolling Thunder begins. • First combat troops sent to Vietnam. • U.S. troops invade Dominican Republic.
1967	• Arab-Israeli Six-Day War fought.
1968	• Demonstrations against Vietnam War increase. • Tet Offensive launched. • Johnson decides not to seek second term. • Violence erupts near Democratic convention in Chicago. • Richard M. Nixon elected president.
1969	• American astronauts land on moon.
1970	• Nixon orders invasion of Cambodia. • Students killed at Kent State and Jackson State.
1971	• Portions of *Pentagon Papers* published.
1972	• Nixon becomes first U.S. president to visit China. • Nixon signs arms limitation treaties with Soviets.
1973	• Paris Peace accords end U.S. fighting in Vietnam. • CIA backs military coup in Chile. • Arab oil embargo follows Yom Kippur War.
1975	• North Vietnam takes over South Vietnam, ending the war. • Helsinki accords signed.

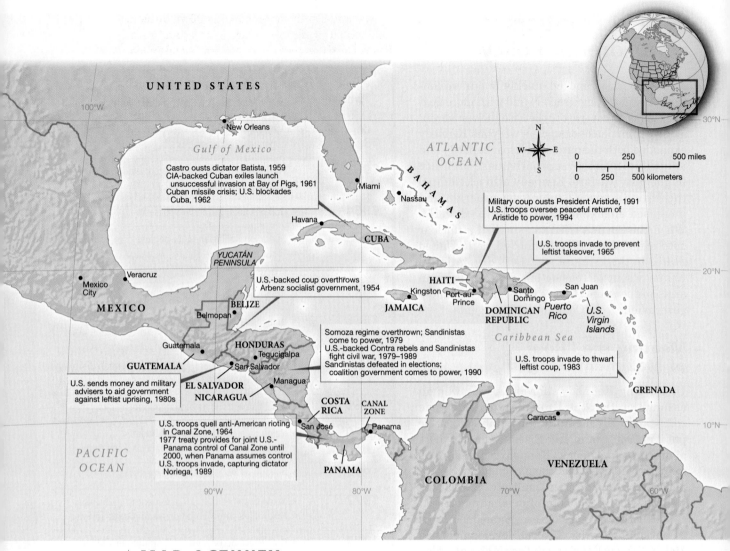

UNITED STATES

100°W

New Orleans

Gulf of Mexico

Castro ousts dictator Batista, 1959
CIA-backed Cuban exiles launch
 unsuccessful invasion at Bay of Pigs, 1961
Cuban missile crisis; U.S. blockades
 Cuba, 1962

Miami

Nassau

Havana

CUBA

Veracruz

Mexico
City

YUCATÁN
PENINSULA

U.S.-backed coup overthrows
Arbenz socialist government, 1954

MEXICO

BELIZE

Belmopan

Guatemala

HONDURAS

Tegucigalpa

GUATEMALA

San Salvador

U.S. sends money and military
advisers to aid government
against leftist uprising, 1980s

EL SALVADOR
NICARAGUA

Managua

Somoza regime overthrown; Sandinistas
 come to power, 1979
U.S.-backed Contra rebels and Sandinistas
 fight civil war, 1979–1989
Sandinistas defeated in elections;
 coalition government comes to power, 1990

U.S. troops quell anti-American rioting
 in Canal Zone, 1964
1977 treaty provides for joint U.S.-
 Panama control of Canal Zone until
 2000, when Panama assumes control
U.S. troops invade, capturing dictator
 Noriega, 1989

San José

COSTA
RICA

CANAL
ZONE

Panama

PANAMA

*PACIFIC
OCEAN*

90°W

80°W

COLOMBIA

ATLANTIC
OCEAN

N
W E
S

B A H A M A S

0   250   500 miles
0   250   500 kilometers

Military coup ousts President Aristide, 1991
U.S. troops oversee peaceful return of
 Aristide to power, 1994

U.S. troops invade to prevent
 leftist takeover, 1965

20°N

HAITI

Kingston

Port-au-
Prince

JAMAICA

Santo
Domingo

San Juan

DOMINICAN
REPUBLIC

Puerto
Rico

U.S.
Virgin
Islands

Caribbean Sea

U.S. troops invade to thwart
 leftist coup, 1983

GRENADA

Caracas

VENEZUELA

10°N

70°W

60°W

30°N

MAP ACTIVITY

Map 29.1   U.S. Involvement in Latin America and the Caribbean, 1954–1994
During the Cold War, the United States frequently intervened in Central American and Caribbean countries
to suppress Communist or leftist movements.

READING THE MAP: How many and which Latin American countries did the United States invade directly?
What was the extent of indirect U.S. involvement in other upheavals in the region?
CONNECTIONS: What role, if any, did geographic proximity play in U.S. policy toward the region? What was
the significance of the Cuban missile crisis for U.S. foreign policy?

materialized to support the anti-Castro brigade.
Kennedy refused to provide direct military support,
and the invaders quickly fell to Castro's forces.
The disaster humiliated Kennedy and the United
States, posing a stark contrast to the president's
inaugural promise of a new, more effective foreign
policy. And it alienated Latin Americans who saw
it as another example of Yankee imperialism.

Days before the Bay of Pigs invasion, the
Soviet Union dealt a psychological blow when a
Soviet astronaut became the first human to orbit

the earth. Kennedy then called for a huge new
commitment to the space program, with the goal
of sending a man to the moon by 1970. Congress
authorized the **Apollo program** and boosted
appropriations for space exploration. John H.
Glenn orbited the earth in 1962, and the United
States beat the Soviets to the moon, landing two
astronauts there in 1969.

Kennedy was determined to show American
toughness to Khrushchev, but when the two met
in June 1961 in Vienna, Austria, Khrushchev took

the offensive. The stunned Kennedy reported privately, "He just beat [the] hell out of me. . . . If he thinks I'm inexperienced and have no guts ... we won't get anywhere with him." Khrushchev demanded an agreement recognizing the existence of two Germanys, and he threatened U.S. occupation rights in and access to West Berlin.

The Soviet premier was concerned about the massive exodus of East Germans into West Berlin, a major embarrassment for the Communists. To stop this flow, in August 1961 East Germany erected a wall between the sectors. With the **Berlin Wall** stemming the tide of escapees and Kennedy declaring West Berlin "the great testing place of Western courage and will," Khrushchev backed off from his threats. A decade later the superpowers recognized East and West Germany as separate nations and guaranteed Western access to West Berlin.

Kennedy used the Berlin crisis to add $3.2 billion to the defense budget. He increased draft calls and mobilized the reserves and National Guard, adding 300,000 troops to the military. This buildup of conventional forces provided for a "flexible response," offering "a wider choice than humiliation or all-out nuclear action," yet Kennedy also more than doubled the nation's nuclear force within three years.

New Approaches to the Third World

Complementing Kennedy's hard-line policy toward the Soviet Union were fresh approaches to the nationalist movements that had multiplied since the end of World War II. In 1960 alone, seventeen African nations gained their independence. Much more than his predecessors, Kennedy publicly supported third world aspirations, believing that the United States could win the hearts and minds of people in developing nations by helping to fulfill hopes for autonomy and material well-being.

Kennedy launched his most popular third world initiative in 1961 with an idea borrowed from Senator Hubert H. Humphrey: the **Peace Corps**. The program recruited young people to work in developing countries, attracting many who had been moved by Kennedy's inaugural address appeal for idealism and sacrifice. One volunteer spoke of having been "born between clean sheets when others were issued into the dust with a birthright of hunger." Peace Corps volunteers worked directly with local people, opening schools, providing basic health care, and assisting with agriculture and small businesses.

By the mid-1970s, more than 60,000 volunteers had served in Latin America, Africa, and Asia. Peace Corps projects were generally welcomed, but they did not address the receiving countries' larger economic and political challenges.

Kennedy also used military means to bring political stability to the third world. He rapidly expanded the elite special forces corps established under Eisenhower to aid groups fighting against Communist-leaning movements. These counterinsurgency forces, including the army's Green Berets and the navy's SEALs, were trained to wage guerrilla warfare and equipped with the

Peace Corps Volunteers Build a School in Gabon
Young Americans who joined the Peace Corps helped increase food production, build public works, and curb diseases in developing countries, but the majority worked on educational projects. In 1964, these volunteers worked side by side with a local resident to build a school in the west-central African nation of Gabon, which had won its independence from France in 1960. James P. Blair/National Geographic/Getty Images.

latest technology. They would get their first test in Vietnam.

The Arms Race and the Nuclear Brink

The final piece of Kennedy's foreign policy was to strengthen American nuclear dominance. He tripled the number of nuclear weapons based in Europe to 7,200 and multiplied fivefold the supply of intercontinental ballistic missiles (ICBMs). Concerned that this buildup would enable the United States to launch a first strike and wipe out Soviet missile sites before they could respond, the Soviet Union stepped up its own ICBM program. Thus began the most intense arms race in history.

The superpowers came perilously close to using their weapons during the **Cuban missile crisis** in 1962. Khrushchev decided to install nuclear missiles in Cuba to protect Castro's regime from further U.S. attempts at invasion and to balance the U.S. missiles aimed at the Soviet Union from Europe. On October 22, after the CIA showed Kennedy aerial photographs of missile launching sites under construction in Cuba, Kennedy announced that the military was on full alert and that the navy would turn back any Soviet vessel suspected of carrying missiles to Cuba. He warned that any attack launched from Cuba would trigger a full nuclear assault against the Soviet Union.

With the superpowers on the brink of nuclear war, both Kennedy and Khrushchev also exercised caution. Kennedy refused advice from the military to bomb the missile sites. On October 24, Russian ships carrying nuclear warheads toward Cuba suddenly turned back. When one ship crossed the blockade line, Kennedy ordered the navy to follow it rather than confront it.

While Americans experienced the Cold War's most dangerous days, Kennedy and Khrushchev negotiated an agreement. The Soviets removed the missiles and pledged not to introduce new offensive weapons into Cuba. The United States promised not to invade the island. Secretly,

Kennedy also agreed to remove U.S. missiles from Turkey. The Cuban crisis contributed to Khrushchev's fall from power two years later, while Kennedy emerged triumphant. The image of an inexperienced president fumbling the Bay of Pigs invasion gave way to that of a strong leader.

Having proved his toughness, Kennedy worked to ease superpower hostilities. In June 1963, Kennedy called for a reexamination of Cold War assumptions, asking Americans "not to see conflict as inevitable." Acknowledging the superpowers' differences, Kennedy stressed what they had in common: "We all breathe the same air. We all cherish our children's future and we are all mortal." In August 1963, the United States, the Soviet Union, and Great Britain signed a limited nuclear test ban treaty, reducing the threat of radioactive fallout and raising hopes for further superpower accord.

A Growing War in Vietnam

In 1963, Kennedy criticized the idea of "a Pax Americana enforced on the world by American weapons of war," but he had already increased the flow of those weapons into South Vietnam. Kennedy's strong anticommunism and attachment to a vigorous foreign policy prepared him to expand the commitment that he had inherited from Eisenhower.

By the time Kennedy took office, more than $1 billion in aid and seven hundred U.S. military advisers had failed to stabilize South Vietnam. Two major obstacles stood in the way. First, the South Vietnamese insurgents— whom Americans derisively called Vietcong—were an indigenous force whose initiative came from within. Because the Saigon government refused to hold elections, the rebels saw no choice but to take up arms. Increasingly, Ho Chi Minh's Communist government in North Vietnam supplied them with weapons and soldiers, aiming eventually to unify all of Vietnam.

Second, the South Vietnamese government refused to satisfy insurgents' demands, but the Army of the Republic of Vietnam (ARVN) could

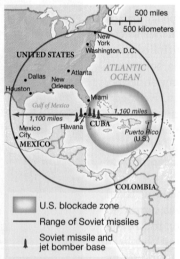

Cuban Missile Crisis, 1962

Cuban Missile Crisis
During the Cuban missile crisis, while many Americans prepared for the worst possible outcome, U.S. Navy pilots dodged antiaircraft fire to conduct low-altitude reconnaissance. This photo, taken on October 23, 1962, shows details of the missile site in Cuba. Bettmann/Corbis.

not defeat them militarily. Ngo Dinh Diem, South Vietnam's premier from 1954 to 1963, chose self-serving military leaders for their personal loyalty rather than for their effectiveness. Many South Vietnamese, the majority of whom were Buddhists, saw the Catholic Diem as a corrupt and brutal tool of the West. In contrast, Ho Chi Minh and his associates consolidated their power through land reform and their anticolonialist credentials on the one hand and imprisonment and mass executions on the other.

Stability and popular support enabled the Hanoi government in the North to wage war in the South. In 1960, it established the National Liberation Front (NLF), composed of South Vietnamese rebels but directed by the northern army. In addition, Hanoi constructed a network of infiltration routes, called the Ho Chi Minh

Trail, in neighboring Laos and Cambodia, through which it sent people and supplies to help liberate the South (Map 29.2). Violence escalated between 1960 and 1963, bringing the Saigon government close to collapse.

In response, Kennedy gradually escalated the U.S. commitment. By spring 1963, military aid had doubled, and 9,000 Americans served in Vietnam as military advisers, occasionally participating in actual combat. The South Vietnamese government promised reform but never made good on its promises.

American officials assumed that technology and sheer power could win in Vietnam. Yet advanced weapons were ill suited to the guerrilla warfare practiced by the enemy, whose surprise attacks were designed to weaken support for the South Vietnamese government. Moreover, U.S. weapons and strategy harmed the very people

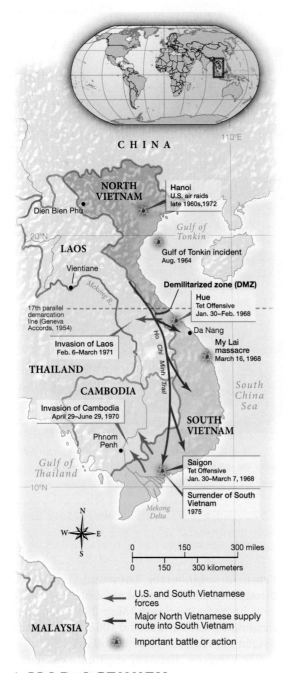

CHINA

NORTH VIETNAM

Dien Bien Phu

Hanoi
U.S. air raids
late 1960s,1972

Gulf of Tonkin

Gulf of Tonkin incident
Aug. 1964

LAOS

Vientiane

Mekong R.

Demilitarized zone (DMZ)

17th parallel demarcation line (Geneva Accords, 1954)

Hue
Tet Offensive
Jan. 30–Feb. 1968

Da Nang

Invasion of Laos
Feb. 6–March 1971

My Lai massacre
March 16, 1968

THAILAND

Ho Chi Minh Trail

CAMBODIA

South China Sea

Invasion of Cambodia
April 29–June 29, 1970

SOUTH VIETNAM

Phnom Penh

Gulf of Thailand

Saigon
Tet Offensive
Jan. 30–March 7, 1968

Surrender of South Vietnam
1975

Mekong Delta

N W E S

0   150   300 miles
0   150   300 kilometers

← U.S. and South Vietnamese forces
← Major North Vietnamese supply route into South Vietnam
✳ Important battle or action

MALAYSIA

MAP ACTIVITY

Map 29.2   The Vietnam War, 1964–1975

The United States sent 2.6 million soldiers to Vietnam and spent more than $150 billion on the longest war in American history, but it was unable to prevent the unification of Vietnam under a Communist government.

READING THE MAP: What accords divided Vietnam into two nations? When were these accords signed, and where was the line of division drawn? Through what countries did the Ho Chi Minh Trail go?

CONNECTIONS: What was the Gulf of Tonkin incident, and how did the United States respond? What was the Tet Offensive, and how did it affect the war?

they were intended to save. Thousands of peasants were uprooted or fell victim to bombs—containing the highly flammable substance napalm—dropped by the South Vietnamese air force to quell the Vietcong. In 1962, U.S. planes began to spray herbicides such as **Agent Orange** to destroy the Vietcong's jungle hideouts and food supply.

With tacit permission from Washington, in November 1963 South Vietnamese military leaders executed a coup against Diem and his brother, who headed the secret police. Kennedy expressed shock at the murders but indicated no change in policy. In a speech to be given on the day he was assassinated, Kennedy referred specifically to Southeast Asia and warned, "We dare not weary of the task." At his death, 16,700 Americans were stationed in Vietnam, and 100 had died there.

REVIEW   Why did Kennedy believe that engagement in Vietnam was crucial to his foreign policy?

► Lyndon Johnson's War against Communism

Lyndon B. Johnson shared the Cold War assumptions underlying Kennedy's foreign policy. Retaining Kennedy's key advisers—Secretary of State Dean Rusk, Secretary of Defense Robert McNamara, and National Security Adviser McGeorge Bundy—Johnson continued the massive buildup of nuclear weapons as well as conventional and counterinsurgency forces. In 1965, he made the fateful decisions to order U.S. troops into combat in Vietnam and to initiate sustained bombing of the North. That same year, Johnson sent U.S. Marines to crush a leftist rebellion in the Dominican Republic.

An All-Out Commitment in Vietnam

The president, who wanted to make his mark on domestic policy, was compelled to deal with the commitments his predecessors had made in Vietnam. Some advisers, politicians, and international leaders questioned the wisdom of greater intervention there, recognizing the situation as a civil war rather than Communist aggression. Most U.S.

Agent Orange
For more than a decade, U.S. planes like these sprayed herbicides in Vietnam, Cambodia, and Laos, destroying 5.5 million acres of forest and farmland to eliminate sources of food and enemy hiding places. The most common chemical used, Agent Orange, contained dioxin, which left land contaminated for decades and ruined the health of civilian Vietnamese and American soldiers.
Dick Swanson/The LIFE Images Collection/Getty Images.

allies did not consider Vietnam crucial to containing communism and were not prepared to share the military burden. Senate majority leader Mike Mansfield wondered, "What national interests in Asia would steel the American people for the massive costs of an ever-deepening involvement?" Disregarding the opportunity for disengagement that these critics saw in 1964, Johnson expressed his own doubt privately: "I don't think it's worth fighting for and I don't think we can get out."

Like Kennedy, Johnson remembered the political blows that Truman had taken when the Communists took over China, and he determined not "to be the president who saw Southeast Asia go the way China did." Like most of his advisers, he saw American credibility as a bulwark against the threat of communism, and he believed that abandoning Vietnam would undermine his ability to achieve his Great Society.

Johnson understood the ineffectiveness of his South Vietnamese allies and agonized over sending young men into combat. Yet he continued to dispatch more military advisers, weapons, and economic aid and, in August 1964, seized an opportunity to increase the pressure on North Vietnam. While spying in the Gulf of Tonkin, off the coast of North Vietnam, two U.S. destroyers reported that North Vietnamese gunboats had fired on them (see Map 29.2). Johnson quickly ordered air strikes on North Vietnamese torpedo bases and oil storage facilities. Concealing the uncertainty about whether the second attack had even occurred, he won

from Congress the **Gulf of Tonkin Resolution**, authorizing him to take "all necessary measures to repel any armed attacks against the forces of the United States and to prevent further aggression."

Soon after winning the election of 1964, Johnson widened the war. He dismissed reservations expressed by prominent Democrats and rejected peace overtures from North Vietnam, which insisted on American withdrawal and a coalition government in South Vietnam as steps toward unification of the country. In February 1965, Johnson authorized Operation Rolling Thunder, a gradually intensified bombing of North Vietnam. Less than a month later, Johnson ordered the first combat troops to South Vietnam, and in July he shifted U.S. troops from defensive to offensive operations, dispatching 50,000 more soldiers (Figure 29.1). Although the administration downplayed the import of these decisions, they marked a critical turning point. Now it was genuinely America's war.

Preventing Another Castro in Latin America

Johnson also faced persistent problems closer to home. Thirteen times during the 1960s, military coups toppled Latin American governments, and local insurgencies grew apace. The administration's response varied from case to case but centered on the determination to prevent any more Castro-type revolutions.

FIGURE 29.1   U.S. Troops in Vietnam, 1962–1972

The steepest increases in the American military presence in Vietnam came with Johnson's escalation of the war in 1965 and 1966. Although Nixon reduced troop levels significantly in 1971 and 1972, the United States continued massive bombing attacks.

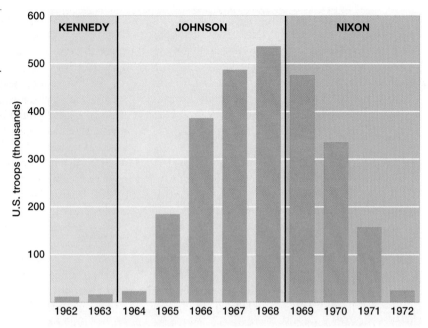

In 1964, riots erupted in the Panama Canal Zone, instigated by Panamanians who viewed the United States as a colonial power because it had held the territory since early in the century (see "The Big Stick" in chapter 21). Johnson sent troops to quell the disturbance, but he also initiated negotiations that eventually returned the canal to Panamanian authority in 2000.

Elsewhere, Johnson's Latin American policy generated new cries of "Yankee imperialism." In 1961, voters in the Dominican Republic ousted a longtime dictator and elected a constitutional government headed by reformist Juan Bosch, who was overthrown by a military coup two years later. In 1965, when Bosch supporters launched an uprising against the military government, Johnson sent more than 20,000 soldiers to suppress what he perceived to be a leftist revolt and to take control of the island.

This first outright show of Yankee force in Latin America in four decades damaged the administration. Although Johnson had justified intervention as necessary to prevent "another

U.S. Troops in the Dominican Republic

These U.S. paratroopers were among the 20,000 troops sent to the Dominican Republic in April and May 1965. The invasion restored peace but kept the popularly elected government of Juan Bosch from regaining office. Dominicans greeted the U.S. troops with anti-American slogans throughout the capital, Santo Domingo. Bosch himself said, "This was a democratic revolution smashed by the leading democracy in the world." Bettmann/Corbis.

Cuba," no Communists were found among the rebels, and U.S. force kept the reform-oriented Boschists from returning to power. Moreover, the president had not consulted the Dominicans or the Organization of American States (OAS), to which the United States had pledged it would respect national sovereignty in Latin America.

The Americanized War

Military success in the Dominican Republic no doubt encouraged the president to press on in Vietnam. From 1965 to early 1968, the U.S. military presence grew to more than 500,000 troops as it escalated attacks on North Vietnam and on its ally, the National Liberation Front, in South Vietnam. To minimize protest at home and avoid provoking Chinese or Soviet involvement, Johnson expanded the war slowly. "I'm going up old Ho Chi Minh's leg an inch at a time," he gloated.

Eventually, U.S. pilots dropped 643,000 tons of bombs on North Vietnam and more than twice that amount in the South, a total surpassing all the explosives the United States dropped in World War II. The North Vietnamese withstood monthly death tolls of more than 2,000 from the bombing. "They turned their hatred into activity," said one North Vietnamese about his comrades, whose ingenuity and sheer effort helped compensate for the destruction of transportation lines, industry sites, and power plants. (See "Making Historical Arguments," page 842.) In South Vietnam, the massive U.S. bombing campaign destroyed villages and fields, alienating the very population that the Americans had come to save and turning the former leading rice producer into a rice importer.

On the ground, General William Westmoreland's strategy of attrition was designed to seek out and kill the Vietcong and North Vietnamese regular army. Because there was no fixed battlefront, helicopters carried troops to conduct offensives all over South Vietnam, and officials calculated progress not in territory seized but in "body counts" and "kill ratios"—the number of enemies killed relative to the cost in American and ARVN lives. "To win a battle, we had to kill them," explained Lieutenant Frederick Downs Jr. "For them to win, all they had to do was survive." After U.S. troops fought and bled to take ground, the enemy would withdraw, only to come back whenever they liked. The Americans "never owned anything except the ground they stood on." And even though U.S.-ARVN forces achieved high kill ratios, North Vietnam sent in or recruited new Communist forces faster than they could be eliminated.

Those Who Served

Teenagers fought the Vietnam War, in contrast to World War II, when the average soldier was twenty-six years old. All the men in Frederick Downs's platoon were between the ages of eighteen and twenty-one, and the average age for all soldiers was nineteen. One eighteen-year-old reflected, "I should have been home

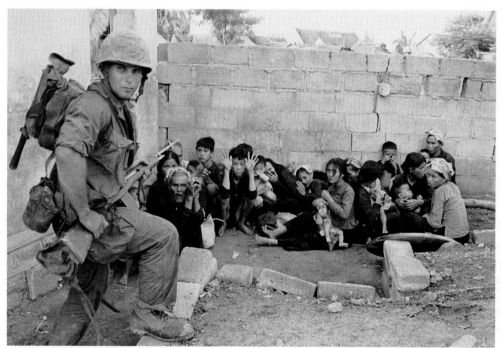

The Toll on Vietnamese Civilians
The guerrilla nature of the Vietnam War made it especially devastating on civilians. Here, in 1965, Vietnamese women try to protect their children while U.S. Marines storm the village of My Son. The soldiers were searching for Vietcong insurgents, who had slipped away before the attack, but were able to get little information from the villagers. Bettmann/Corbis.

Why Couldn't American Bombing Achieve Victory in Vietnam?

"**N**o nation can long survive the free exploitation of air weapons over its homeland," asserted the official U.S. study of strategic bombing during World War II. In the Vietnam War, U.S. planes delivered even more explosives than they had in World War II. Why, then, did strategic bombing not bring victory in Vietnam?

"Our airpower did not fail us; it was the decision makers," asserted Admiral U. S. Grant Sharp, head of the Pacific Command during the Vietnam War. In February 1965, military officials welcomed President Johnson's order to begin bombing North Vietnam to destroy the North's capacity and will to support the Communist insurgents in South Vietnam. But

they chafed at Johnson's strategy of gradual escalation and the restrictions he imposed on Operation Rolling Thunder, the three-and-a-half-year bombing campaign. Military officials believed that the operation should have begun with all-out bombing and continued until the devastation brought North Vietnam to its knees. Instead, they charged, civilian decision makers forced the military to fight with one hand tied behind its back. Their arguments echoed General Douglas MacArthur's criticism of Truman's policy during the Korean War—although these officials did not repeat MacArthur's insubordination (see "From Containment to Rollback to Containment" in chapter 26).

Unlike military officials, who could single-mindedly focus on defeating the enemy, the president had to balance military objectives against political considerations, and he found compelling reasons to limit the use of airpower. Recalling the Korean War, Johnson carefully avoided action that might provoke intervention by the Chinese, who now possessed nuclear weapons. Johnson's strategy also aimed to keep the Soviet Union out of the war, to avoid escalating antiwar sentiment at home, and to minimize international criticism of the United States. Consequently, the president banned strikes on areas that could produce high civilian casualties, and on areas near the Chinese border or airfields and missile sites under construction and likely to contain Chinese or Soviet advisers. Military leaders agreed with Johnson's desire to spare civilian lives, and noncombatant casualties in North Vietnam contrasted sharply with those in World War II. During that war, the Anglo-American bombing of Dresden, Germany, alone killed more than 35,000 civilians, and the firebombing of Japan took 330,000 civilian lives. By comparison, over three and a half years, Operation

getting ready to take a pretty girl to the prom." Until the Twenty-sixth Amendment to the Constitution dropped the voting age from twenty-one to eighteen in 1971, most soldiers could not even vote for the officials who sent them to war. Men of all classes had fought in World War II, but in Vietnam the poor and working class constituted about 80 percent of the troops. More privileged youths avoided the draft with college deferments or family connections to get into the National Guard. Sent from Plainville, Kansas, to Vietnam in 1965, Mike Clodfelter could not recall "a single middle-class son of the town's businessmen, lawyers, doctors, or ranchers from my high school graduating class who experienced the Armageddon of our generation."

More than World War II, Vietnam was a men's war. Because the United States did not undergo full mobilization for Vietnam, officials did not seek women's sacrifices for the war effort. Still, between 7,500 and 11,000 women served in Vietnam, the vast majority of them nurses. Some women were exposed to enemy fire, and eight died. Many more struggled with their helplessness to repair the maimed and dead bodies they attended.

Early in the war, African Americans constituted 31 percent of combat troops, often choosing the military over the meager opportunities in the civilian economy. Special forces ranger Arthur E. Woodley Jr. recalled, "The only way I could possibly make it out of the ghetto was to be the best soldier I possibly could." Death rates

Rolling Thunder killed an estimated 52,000 civilians.

North Vietnam's relatively low level of economic development and its government's ability to mobilize citizens counteracted the military superiority of the United States. Sheer human-power compensated for the demolition of transportation facilities, factories, and electric power plants. When bombs struck a rail line, civilians rushed in with bicycles to unload a train's cargo, carry it beyond the break, and load it onto a second train. Three hundred thousand full-time workers and 200,000 farmers labored to keep the Ho Chi Minh Trail usable in spite of heavy bombing. When bridges were destroyed, the North Vietnamese resorted to ferries and bamboo pontoons and rebuilt bridges slightly underwater to make them harder to detect from the air. They scattered oil storage facilities and production centers throughout the countryside and, when bombs knocked out electric power plants, used portable generators and lit oil lamps and candles in their homes. "The Americans thought that the more bombs they dropped, the quicker we would fall to our knees and surrender. But the bombs heightened

rather than dampened our spirit," remarked one Vietnamese.

North Vietnam's military needs were relatively small, and officials found ample means to meet them. In 1967, North Vietnam had only about 55,000 soldiers in South Vietnam, and because they waged a guerrilla war with only sporadic fighting, the insurgents in the South did not require huge amounts of military supplies. Even after Communist forces in the South increased, the total nonfood needs of these soldiers were estimated at just one-fifth of what a single U.S. division required. What U.S. bombs destroyed, the North Vietnamese replaced with Chinese and Soviet imports. China provided 600,000 tons of rice in 1967 alone, and it supplied small arms and ammunition, vehicles, and other goods throughout the war. Competing with China for influence in North Vietnam and favor in the third world, the Soviets contributed tanks, fighter planes, surface-to-air missiles, and other weapons. In addition, the Soviet-installed modern defense systems made the bombing more difficult and dangerous for the United States, which lost 1,400 planes by 1969.

Short of decimating the civilian population, it is doubtful that

more intense bombing could have completely halted North Vietnamese support for the Vietcong, given the nature of the North Vietnamese economy, the determination and ingenuity of the North Vietnamese people, and the plentiful assistance from China and the Soviet Union. Whether the strategic bombing that worked so well in a world war against major industrial powers could be effective in a third world guerrilla war remained in doubt after the Vietnam War.

Questions for Analysis

Summarize the Argument: What circumstances that prevented U.S. victory in Vietnam does the author attribute to the United States and what factors to North Vietnam?

Analyze the Evidence: What specific conditions in North Vietnam enabled it to withstand heavy bombing and continue to support the insurgency in the South?

Consider the Context: How did other nations influence both the United States' bombing campaign and North Vietnam's response to it?

---

among black soldiers were disproportionately high until 1966, when the military adjusted personnel assignments to achieve a better racial balance.

The young troops faced extremely difficult conditions. Frederick Downs's platoon fought in thick leech-ridden jungles, in rain and oppressive heat, always vulnerable to sniper bullets and land mines. Soldiers in previous wars had served "for the duration," but in Vietnam a soldier served a one-year tour of duty. A commander called it "the worst personnel policy in history," because men had less incentive to fight near the end of their tours, wanting merely to stay alive and whole. American soldiers inflicted great losses on the enemy, yet the war remained a stalemate.

Many Vietnamese saw the South Vietnamese government as a tool of Western imperialism, full of graft and corruption. Moreover, with the difficulty of distinguishing friend from foe, ARVN and American troops killed and wounded thousands of South Vietnamese civilians and destroyed their villages. By 1968, nearly 30 percent of the population had become refugees. According to Downs, "All Vietnamese had a common desire—to see us go home." The failure to stabilize South Vietnam even as the U.S. military presence expanded enormously created grave challenges for the administration at home.

REVIEW Why did massive amounts of airpower and ground troops fail to bring U.S. victory in Vietnam?

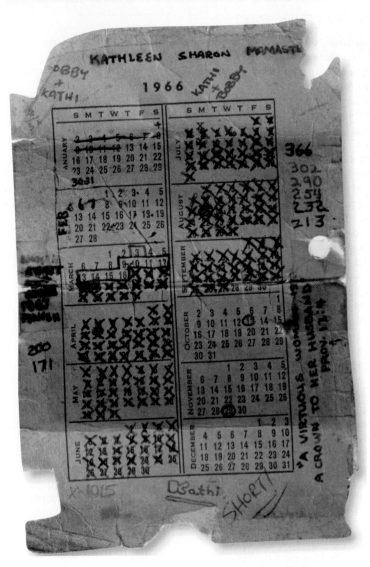

VISUAL ACTIVITY

Counting the Days in Vietnam

Unlike soldiers in previous wars, most soliders in Vietnam served tours of duty lasting just one year. The soldier who carried this calendar expressed a common obsession with time "in country." Soldiers considered themselves "short" when they had fewer than 100 days left. Bobby McMaster was thinking either of his wife or of the woman he would marry when, and if, he returned home. Nathan Benn/Corbis.
READING THE IMAGE: What does the condition of this calendar suggest about how McMaster spent his time in Vietnam? What concerns about the woman he left behind are expressed in the quotation from the Bible?
CONNECTIONS: Besides the length of tours of duty, what other differences existed in the experiences of the soldiers of World War II and those of the Vietnam War?

and criticism into a mass movement against the war. In April 1965, Students for a Democratic Society (SDS) recruited 20,000 people for the first major antiwar protest in Washington, D.C. Thousands of students protested against Reserve Officers Training Corps (ROTC) programs, CIA and defense industry recruiters, and military research projects on their campuses. Environmentalists attacked the use of chemical weapons, such as the deadly Agent Orange.

Antiwar sentiment entered society's mainstream, including, by 1968, the *New York Times,* the *Wall Street Journal, Life* magazine, and popular TV anchorman Walter Cronkite. Clergy, businesspeople, scientists, and physicians formed their own groups to pressure Johnson to stop the bombing and start negotiations. Prominent Democratic senators urged Johnson to substitute negotiation for force.

Opposition to the war took diverse forms, including letter writing, public demonstrations, draft card burnings, and attempts to stop troop trains. Although the peace movement never claimed a majority of the population, it focused media attention on the war and severely limited the administration's options. The twenty-year-old consensus around Cold War foreign policy had shattered.

Many refused to serve. The World Boxing Association stripped Muhammad Ali of his heavyweight title when he refused to "drop bombs and bullets on brown people in Vietnam while so-called negro people in Louisville are treated like dogs." More than 170,000 men gained conscientious objector status and performed nonmilitary duties at home or in Vietnam. About 60,000 fled the country to escape the draft, and more than 200,000 were accused of failing to register or of committing other draft offenses.

► A Nation Polarized

Soon President Johnson was fighting a war on two fronts, as domestic opposition to the war swelled after 1965. In March 1968, torn between his domestic critics and the military's clamor for more troops, Johnson announced a halt to the bombing, a new effort at negotiations, and his decision not to pursue reelection. Throughout 1968, demonstrations, violence, and assassinations convulsed the increasingly polarized nation. Vietnam took center stage in the election, and voters narrowly favored the Republican candidate, former vice president Richard Nixon, who promised to achieve "peace with honor."

The Widening War at Home

Johnson's authorization of Operation Rolling Thunder expanded the previously quiet doubts

VISUAL ACTIVITY

Mothers against the War

Founded in 1961 to work for nuclear disarmament, Women Strike for Peace (WSP) began to protest the Vietnam War in 1963. As "concerned housewives" and mothers, members mobilized around the slogan "Not Our Sons, Not Your Sons, Not Their Sons." In February 1967, more than 2,000 women, some shown here, protested at the Pentagon, banging on doors, which were locked as they approached. Bettmann/Corbis.

READING THE IMAGE: Notice how these women look. Do they appear threatening to you? Why do you think Pentagon officials locked them out? How do their signs draw on their roles as mothers?

CONNECTIONS: How are the antiwar arguments made by WSP similar to and different from those of other opponents of the Vietnam War?

Opponents of the war held diverse views. Those who saw the conflict in moral terms wanted total withdrawal, claiming that their country had no right to interfere in a civil war and stressing the suffering of the Vietnamese people. A larger segment of antiwar sentiment reflected practical considerations—the belief that the war could not be won at a bearable cost. Those activists wanted Johnson to stop bombing North Vietnam and seek negotiations. Working-class people were no more antiwar than other groups, but they recognized the class dimensions of the war and the antiwar movement. A firefighter whose son had died in Vietnam said bitterly, "It's people like us who give up our sons for the country."

The antiwar movement outraged millions of Americans who supported the war. Some members of the generation who had fought against Hitler could not understand younger men's refusal to support their government. They expressed their anger at war protesters with bumper stickers that read "America: Love It or Leave It."

By 1967, the administration realized that "discontent with the war is now wide and deep." President Johnson used various means to silence critics. He equated opposition to the war with communism and assistance to the enemy. His administration deceived the public by making optimistic statements and concealing officials' doubts about the possibility of success. Johnson ordered the CIA to spy on peace advocates, and

1968: A Year of Protest

To many people living through it, 1968 looked like the start of a worldwide political revolution. A surge of protests against the U.S. war in Vietnam and demands for greater democracy and economic justice jumped over borders and challenged authorities in many countries around the world. Although local grievances ignited much of the unrest, a common feature was the central role played by university students. The protests of 1968 unfolded rapidly, giving rise to excitement and apprehension. From February to December, demonstrations erupted in North and South America, Europe, and Asia. Many demonstrators expressed transnational solidarity by carrying the flag of Vietnam's National Liberation Front or placards bearing the image of Ernesto "Che" Guevara, a Latin American radical killed by the Bolivian military in 1967. And yet there was little international coordination of events or any shared plan for remaking the world.

One of the first large-scale protests occurred in February at West Berlin's Free University, where some 10,000 participants from ten countries at the "Vietnam Congress" called for "an international manifestation of solidarity" with the people of Vietnam. Protests continued throughout the spring, prompting the West German government to pass emergency laws to stifle disorder. In February and March, demonstrations flared up in Madrid, Warsaw, Rome, São Paulo, and London, met by police with clubs. Charges of police brutality, disseminated in television and newspaper reports, further fed the cycle of protest.

In April and May, violence erupted in the United States. The assassination of Martin Luther King Jr. on April 4 ignited riots in many U.S. cities. Less than a month later, students at Columbia University in New York City seized buildings and shut down the campus, leading to a bloody showdown between police and protesters.

In May, rebellion paralyzed France. It began with students' complaints about services at a university north of Paris and spread to the Sorbonne in the capital city. Police teargassed a small rally, only to face tens of thousands of students streaming into Paris over the next few days. Violence escalated as protesters barricaded streets. Independent radio stations broadcast live interviews with demonstrators, and soon a million people were in the streets. Workers joined the rebellion, shutting down factories across France. Students proclaimed that "exceptional domestic and international conditions" had brought powerless students and workers together around the world. By late May, France was in deep crisis.

Prague, the capital of Communist Czechoslovakia, also stirred in May. A liberal president, Alexander Dubček, pushed for reforms against heavy-handed Soviet control, giving rise to hopes for greater freedom. Students demonstrated, and thousands signed manifestos. But this "Prague Spring" was cut short in August when Soviet tanks rumbled into the country and Dubček was arrested. Throughout Europe, students marched on Soviet embassies to protest the crackdown. At the same moment in the United States, Chicago police battled young protesters near the Democratic National Convention.

In July, Mexican police attacked marchers carrying posters of Fidel Castro and Che Guevara. When thousands rallied against the violence, police fired into the crowd, killing several students. Violent clashes continued into August and September, as activists protested the Olympic Games, scheduled to open in Mexico City in October. Insisting that the money spent on the Olympics should instead have been used to alleviate the country's widespread poverty, protesters chanted, "We don't want Olympic Games; we want revolution." The upcoming Olympics created pressure for the authorities to clear the city of dissidents. When some 10,000 students assembled for a rally on October 2, jeeps with machine guns arrived. More than 100 protesters were killed, and another several hundred were wounded. The Olympic Games went on as scheduled ten days later.

In the wake of the massacre, protesters staged demonstrations and attacks on Mexican embassies in Latin

without the president's specific authorization, the FBI infiltrated the peace movement, disrupted its work, and spread false information about activists. Even the resort to illegal measures failed to subdue the opposition.

The Tet Offensive and Johnson's Move toward Peace

The year 1968 was marked by violent confrontations around the world. Protests against governments erupted from Mexico City to Paris to Tokyo, usually led by students in collaboration with workers. (See "Beyond America's Borders," page above.) American society became increasingly polarized. The so-called hawks charged that the United States was fighting with one hand tied behind its back and called for intensification of the war. The doves wanted de-escalation or withdrawal. As U.S. troop strength neared half a million and military deaths approached 20,000 by the end of 1967, most

Prague Spring
Czech students march in the capital of Czechoslovakia in support of proposals introduced in the spring of 1968 that would loosen Soviet control of the Communist satellite and promote freedom of speech and economic reform. Their banner reads "Never Again with the Soviet Union," mocking an earlier Czech-Stalinist slogan, "Forever with the Soviet Union." Bettmann/Corbis.

America and Europe. By December, more episodes of violence against protesters occurred in Spain, Pakistan, and Northern Ireland. In the United States, violence diminished generally, but not in urban ghettos.

By year's end, a kind of stunned exhaustion set in. The Soviets had shut down the Prague Spring, the student-led protests in France and Germany had reached a stalemate, and Republican Richard Nixon had won the U.S. presidential election with promises to maintain law and order at home and to end the war in Vietnam. The year of global protest ended with despair and fear on all sides. Student protest did not disappear, but the excitement of worldwide revolutionary solidarity was blunted by the very real threat of fatal consequences faced by protesters.

Questions for Analysis

Analyze the Evidence: What were some of the specific aims of protesters across the world in 1968?

Ask Historical Questions: What did the global protests of 1968 have in common? In what ways were they different?

Consider the Context: What international events prompted many of the protests?

people were torn between weariness with the war and a desire to fulfill the U.S. commitment. As one woman said, "I want to get out but I don't want to give up."

Grave doubts penetrated the administration itself. Secretary of Defense Robert McNamara, a principal architect of U.S. involvement, now believed that the North Vietnamese "won't quit no matter how much bombing we do." He feared for the image of the United States, "the world's greatest superpower, killing or seriously injuring 1,000 noncombatants a week, while trying to pound a tiny, backward nation into submission on an issue whose merits are hotly disputed." McNamara left the administration in early 1968, but he kept his concerns private and did not publicly oppose the war.

A critical turning point came with the **Tet Offensive.** On January 30, 1968, the North Vietnamese and Vietcong launched a campaign of attacks on key cities, every major American base, and the U.S. Embassy in Saigon during

The Battle for Hue
During the Tet Offensive in early 1968, North Vietnamese troops captured the city of Hue, the ancient capital of Vietnam, rich with the country's history and culture. It took nearly a month of brutal house-to-house fighting for U.S. and ARVN troops to retake the city, 80 percent of which had by then been destroyed. Here U.S. Marines are pinned down near the center of Hue. Bettmann/Corbis.

Tet, the Vietnamese New Year holiday. Although the enemy was eventually pushed back and lost ten times as many soldiers as ARVN and U.S. forces, Tet was psychologically devastating to the United States because it exposed the credibility gap between official statements and the war's reality. The attacks created a million more South Vietnamese refugees as well as widespread destruction. Public approval of Johnson's handling of the war dropped to 26 percent.

In the aftermath of Tet, Johnson conferred with advisers in the Defense Department and an unofficial group of foreign policy experts who had been key architects of Cold War policy since the 1940s. Dean Acheson, who had been Truman's secretary of state, summarized their conclusion: "We can no longer do the job we set out to do in the time we have left and we must begin to take steps to disengage."

On March 31, 1968, Johnson announced a sharp reduction in the bombing of North Vietnam and an offer to begin peace talks. He added the stunning declaration that he would not run for reelection. The gradual escalation of the war was over, and military strategy shifted from "Americanization" to "Vietnamization" of the war. But this was not a shift in policy. The goal remained a non-Communist South Vietnam; the United States would simply rely more heavily on the South Vietnamese to achieve it.

Negotiations began in Paris in May 1968. The United States would not agree to recognize the Hanoi government's National Liberation Front, to allow a coalition government in the South, or to withdraw. The North Vietnamese would agree to nothing less. Although the talks continued, so did the fighting.

Meanwhile, violence escalated at home. Protests struck two hundred college campuses in the spring of 1968. In the bloodiest action, students occupied buildings at Columbia University in New York City, condemning the university's war-related research and its treatment of African Americans. (See chapter 28,

Protest in Chicago
The worst violence surrounding the August 1968 Democratic National Convention in Chicago occurred near the Hilton Hotel, where most of the delegates stayed. When some 3,000 protesters marching toward the convention site confronted a line of police, the police attacked not only the demonstrators but also reporters, hotel guests, and bystanders, driving a crowd through a plate-glass hotel window and injuring hundreds. Paul Sequeira/ Getty Images.

"Analyzing Historical Evidence," page 820.) When negotiations failed, university officials called in the city police, who cleared the buildings, injuring scores of demonstrators and arresting hundreds. An ensuing student strike prematurely ended the academic year.

The Tumultuous Election of 1968

Disorder and violence also entered the election process. In June, two months after the murder of Martin Luther King Jr. and the riots that followed, antiwar candidate Senator Robert F. Kennedy, campaigning for the Democratic National Convention, was killed by a Palestinian Arab refugee because of his support for Israel.

In August, protesters battled the police in Chicago, site of the Democratic Party national convention. Several thousand demonstrators came to the city, some to support peace candidate Senator Eugene McCarthy, others to cause disruption. On August 25, when demonstrators jeered at orders to disperse, police attacked them with tear gas and clubs. Street battles continued for three days, culminating in a police riot on the night of August 28. Taunted by the crowd, the police sprayed Mace and clubbed not only those who had come to provoke violence but also reporters, peaceful demonstrators, and convention delegates.

The bloodshed in Chicago had little effect on the convention's outcome. Vice President Hubert H. Humphrey believed that the nation was "throwing lives and money down a corrupt rat hole" in Vietnam, but he kept his views to himself and trounced the remaining antiwar candidate, McCarthy, by nearly three to one for the Democratic nomination.

In contrast to the turmoil in Chicago, the Republican convention met peacefully and nominated former vice president Richard Nixon. In a bid for southern support, Nixon chose Maryland governor Spiro T. Agnew for his running mate. A strong third candidate entered the race when the American Independent Party nominated staunch segregationist George C. Wallace. The former Alabama governor appealed to Americans' dissatisfaction with the reforms and rebellions of the 1960s and their outrage at the assaults on traditional values. Nixon guardedly played on resentments that fueled the Wallace campaign, calling for "law and order" and attacking liberal Supreme Court decisions, busing for school desegregation, and protesters.

The candidates differed little on the central issue of Vietnam. Nixon promised "an honorable end" to the war but did not indicate how to achieve it. Humphrey had reservations about U.S. policy in Vietnam, yet as vice president he was tied to Johnson's policies. Nixon edged out Humphrey by just half a million popular votes but won 301 electoral college votes to Humphrey's 191 and Wallace's 46 (Map 29.3). The Democrats maintained control of Congress.

The 1968 election revealed deep cracks in the coalition that had maintained Democratic dominance in Washington since the 1930s. Johnson's liberal policies on race shattered a century of Democratic Party rule in the South, which delivered all its electoral votes to Wallace and Nixon. Elsewhere, large numbers of

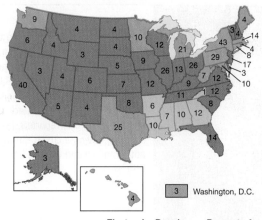

Candidate	Electoral Vote	Popular Vote	Percent of Popular Vote
Richard M. Nixon (Republican)	301	31,770,237	43.4
Hubert H. Humphrey (Democrat)	191	31,270,533	42.7
George C. Wallace (American Independent)	46	9,906,141	13.5

Note: North Carolina split its vote, with one elector voting for Wallace.

Map 29.3
The Election of 1968

blue-collar workers broke their traditional alliance with the Democrats to vote for Wallace or Nixon, as did other groups that associated the Democrats with racial turmoil, poverty programs, changing sexual mores, and failure to turn the tide in Vietnam. Autoworker Dewey Burton voted for Wallace, objecting to paying "high taxes and more for a home so that somebody can [bus] my son 30 miles away to get an inferior education." These resentments would soon be mobilized into a resurging right in American politics (see chapter 30).

> **REVIEW** How did the war in Vietnam polarize the nation?

▶ Nixon, Détente, and the Search for Peace in Vietnam

Richard M. Nixon hoped to make his mark on history by applying his broad understanding of international relations to a changing world. Diverging from Republican orthodoxy, he made dramatic overtures to the Soviet Union and China.

Yet anticommunism remained central to U.S. policy. Nixon backed repressive regimes around the world and aggressively pursued the war in Vietnam, despite mounting opposition. He expanded the conflict into Cambodia and Laos and ferociously bombed North Vietnam. In the end, however, he was forced to settle for peace without victory.

Moving toward Détente with the Soviet Union and China

Nixon perceived that the "rigid and bipolar world of the 1940s and 1950s" was changing, and America's European allies were seeking to ease East-West tensions. Moreover, Nixon and his national security adviser Henry A. Kissinger believed they could exploit the increasing discord between the Soviet Union and China. In addition, these two nations might be used to help the United States extricate itself from Vietnam.

Following two years of secret negotiations, in February 1972 Nixon became the nation's first president to set foot on Chinese soil, an astonishing move by one who had built his career on anticommunism. Although his visit was largely symbolic, cultural and scientific exchanges followed, and American manufacturers began to find markets in China—small steps in the process of globalization that would take giant strides in the 1990s (as discussed in chapter 31). In 1979, the United States and China established formal diplomatic relations.

As Nixon and Kissinger had hoped, the warming of U.S.-Chinese relations furthered their strategy of **détente**, their term for easing conflict with the Soviet Union. Détente did not mean abandoning containment; instead it focused on issues of common concern, such as arms control and trade. Containment now would be achieved not just by military threat but also by ensuring that the Soviets and Chinese had stakes in a stable international order. Nixon's goal was "a stronger, healthy United States, Europe, Soviet Union, China, Japan, each balancing the other."

Arms control, trade, and stability in Europe were three areas where the United States and the Soviet Union had common interests. In May 1972, Nixon visited Moscow, signing agreements on trade and cooperation in science and space. Most significantly, the two superpowers concluded the **Strategic Arms Limitation Treaty (SALT)** in 1972, agreeing to limit antiballistic missiles (ABMs) to two each. Giving up pursuit of a defense against nuclear weapons was a crucial move

Nixon in China
During his surprise visit to China in February 1972, Nixon, alluding to his anti-Communist credentials, remarked to Chinese leader Mao Zedong, "Those on the right can do what those on the left only talk about." Here, Mao, Nixon, and Kissinger meet at Mao's residence in Beijing. In the preceding months, Kissinger had traveled secretly to China to lay the groundwork for the visit. Bettmann/Corbis.

because it denied both nations an ABM defense so secure against a nuclear attack that they would risk a first strike.

Although détente made little progress after 1974, U.S., Canadian, Soviet, and European leaders signed a historic agreement in 1975 in Helsinki, Finland, that formally recognized the post–World War II boundaries in Europe. Conservatives excoriated the **Helsinki accords** because they acknowledged the status quo: Soviet domination over Eastern Europe. Yet the agreement also committed the signing countries to recognize "the universal significance of human rights and fundamental freedoms." Dissidents in the Soviet Union and its Eastern European satellites used this official promise of rights to challenge the Soviet dictatorship and help force its overthrow fifteen years later.

Shoring Up U.S. Interests around the World

Despite the thaw in U.S. relations with the Soviet Union and China, in other parts of the world Nixon and Kissinger continued to view left-wing movements as threats to U.S. interests and actively resisted social revolutions that might lead to communism. For example, the Nixon administration helped overthrow Salvador Allende, a self-proclaimed Marxist who was elected president of Chile in 1970. Since

1964, the CIA and U.S. corporations concerned about nationalization of their Chilean properties had assisted Allende's opponents. After Allende's election, Nixon ordered the CIA director to destabilize Allende's government and the economy, and in 1973 the CIA helped the Chilean military engineer a coup, resulting in Allende's death and a brutal dictatorship under General Augusto Pinochet.

In other parts of the world, too, the Nixon administration backed repressive regimes. In southern Africa, it eased pressures on white minority governments that tyrannized blacks. In the Middle East, the United States sent massive arms shipments to support the shah of Iran's harsh regime because Iran had enormous petroleum reserves and seemed a stable anti-Communist ally.

Like his predecessors, Nixon pursued a delicate balance between defending Israel's security and seeking the goodwill of Arab nations strategically and economically important to the United States. Conflict between Israel and the Arab nations had escalated into the **Six-Day War** in 1967, when Israel attacked Egypt after Egypt had massed troops on the Israeli border and cut off sea passage to Israel's southern port. Although Syria and Jordan joined the war on Egypt's side, Israel won a stunning victory, seizing the Sinai Peninsula and Gaza Strip from Egypt, the Golan Heights from Syria, and the West Bank, where

Chile

GUYANA
SURINAME
FRENCH GUIANA
VENEZUELA
COLOMBIA
ECUADOR
PERU
BRAZIL
BOLIVIA
PACIFIC OCEAN
PARAGUAY
Santiago
URUGUAY
ARGENTINA
CHILE
ATLANTIC OCEAN

0 250 500 mi.
0 500 km.

hundreds of thousands of Palestinians lived, from Jordan.

That decisive victory did not quell Middle Eastern turmoil. In October 1973, on the Jewish holiday Yom Kippur, Egypt and Syria surprised Israel with a full-scale attack. When the Nixon administration sided with Israel, Arab nations retaliated with an oil embargo that created severe shortages in the United States. After Israel repulsed the attack, tensions remained high. The Arab countries refused to recognize Israel's right to exist, Israel began to settle its citizens in the West Bank and other territories it had seized during the Six-Day War, and no solution could be found for the Palestinian refugees who had been displaced by the creation of Israel in 1948. The simmering conflict contributed to anti-American sentiment among Arabs who viewed the United States as Israel's supporter.

Israeli Territorial Gains in the Six-Day War, 1967

Vietnam Becomes Nixon's War

"I'm going to stop that war. Fast," Nixon asserted. He gradually withdrew ground troops, but he was no more willing than his predecessors to be the president who let South Vietnam fall to the Communists. (See "Analyzing Historical Evidence," page 854.) That goal was tied to the larger objective of maintaining American credibility. Regardless of the wisdom of the initial intervention, Kissinger asserted, "the commitment of 500,000 Americans has settled the importance of Vietnam. For what is involved now is confidence in American promises."

From 1969 to 1972, Nixon and Kissinger pursued a three-pronged approach. First, they tried to strengthen the South Vietnamese military and government. ARVN forces grew to more than a million, and the South Vietnamese air force

U.S. Invasion of Cambodia, 1970

became the fourth largest in the world. The United States also promoted land reform, village elections, and the building of schools, hospitals, and transportation facilities.

Second, Nixon gradually reduced the U.S. presence in Vietnam, a move that somewhat disarmed the antiwar movement at home. American forces decreased from 543,000 in 1968 to 140,000 by the end of 1971, although casualties remained high. Third, the United States replaced U.S. forces with intensive bombing. In the spring of 1969, Nixon began a ferocious air war in Cambodia, hiding it from Congress and the public for more than a year. Seeking to knock out North Vietnamese sanctuaries in Cambodia, Americans dropped more than 100,000 tons of bombs but succeeded only in sending the enemy to other hiding places. Echoing Johnson, Kissinger believed that a "fourth-rate power like North Vietnam" had to have a "breaking point," but the massive bombing failed to find it.

To support a new, pro-Western Cambodian government installed through a military coup and "to show the enemy that we were still serious about our commitment in Vietnam," Nixon ordered a joint U.S.-ARVN invasion of Cambodia in April 1970. He accompanied that action with a belligerent speech emphasizing the importance of U.S. credibility: "If when the chips are down, the world's most powerful nation acts like a pitiful helpless giant, the forces of totalitarianism and anarchy will threaten free nations" everywhere.

In response to this escalation of the war, more than 100,000 people protested in Washington, D.C., and students boycotted classes on hundreds of campuses. At a rally on May 4 at Kent State University in Ohio, National Guard troops opened fire, killing four and wounding ten others. "They're starting to treat their

VISUAL ACTIVITY

Pro-War Demonstrators

Supporters as well as opponents of the war in Vietnam took to the streets, as these New Yorkers did in support of the U.S. invasion of Cambodia in May 1970. Construction workers—called "hard hats"—and other union members marched with American flags and posters championing President Nixon's policies and blasting New York mayor John Lindsay for his antiwar position. Paul Fusco/Magnum Photos. READING THE IMAGE: What do the hard hats in the photograph symbolize in terms of identity and politics? CONNECTIONS: How were these union members related to the unraveling of the Democratic Party coalition?

own children like they treat us," commented a black woman in Harlem. In a confrontation at Jackson State College in Mississippi on May 14, police shot into a dormitory, killing two black students.

Congressional reaction to the invasion of Cambodia revealed increasing concern about abuses of presidential power. In the name of national security, presidents since Franklin Roosevelt had conducted foreign policy without the consent or sometimes even the knowledge of Congress—for example, Eisenhower in Iran and Kennedy in Cuba. But in their determination to win the war in Vietnam, Johnson and Nixon had taken extreme measures to deceive the public and silence their critics. The aggression into Cambodia infuriated enough legislators that the Senate voted to terminate the Gulf of Tonkin Resolution and to cut off funds for the Cambodian operation. The House refused to go along, but by the end of June 1970 Nixon had pulled all U.S. troops out of Cambodia.

In 1971, Vietnam veterans became a visible part of the peace movement, the first men in U.S. history to protest a war in which they had fought. They held a public investigation of "war crimes" in Vietnam, rallied in front of the Capitol, and cast away their war medals. In May 1971, veterans numbered among the 40,000 protesters who engaged in civil disobedience in an effort to shut down Washington. Officials made more than 12,000 arrests, which courts later ruled violations of protesters' rights.

After the spring of 1971, there were fewer massive antiwar demonstrations, but opposition to the war continued. Public attention focused on the court-martial of Lieutenant William Calley, which began in November 1970. During the trial, Americans learned that in March 1968 Calley's company had killed every inhabitant of the hamlet of My Lai, even though it had encountered no enemy forces and the four hundred villagers were nearly all old men, women, and children. The military covered up the massacre for more than a year before a journalist exposed it. Eventually, twelve officers and enlisted men were charged with murder or assault, but only Calley was convicted.

Administration policy suffered another blow in June 1971 when the *New York Times* published portions of the **Pentagon Papers**, a secret internal study of the war begun in 1967. Nixon sent government lawyers to court to stop further publication, in part out of fear that other information would be leaked. The Supreme Court, however, ruled that suppression of the publication violated the First Amendment. Subsequent circulation of the *Pentagon Papers*, which revealed pessimism among officials even as they made rosy promises, heightened disillusionment with the war by casting doubts on the government's credibility. More than 60 percent of Americans polled in 1971 considered it a mistake to have sent American troops to Vietnam; 58 percent believed the war to be immoral.

Military morale sank in the last years of the war. Having been exposed to the antiwar

Ending the War in Vietnam

By 1969, a clear majority of Americans wanted their country out of Vietnam. As these documents suggest, disagreement raged over how to get out and what would be the consequences of U.S. withdrawal.

DOCUMENT 1
Richard Nixon Explains His Policy of Vietnamization, November 3, 1969

Elected on the promise of ending the war, Nixon adopted a plan of Vietnamization, strengthening South Vietnam so that it could take over its own defense and U.S. forces could come home. Here Nixon explains why he chose Vietnamization over immediate withdrawal.

But the question facing us today is: Now that we are in the war, what is the best way to end it?

In January I could only conclude that the precipitate withdrawal of American forces from Vietnam would be a disaster not only for South Vietnam but for the United States and for the cause of peace.

For the South Vietnamese, our precipitate withdrawal would inevitably allow the Communists to repeat the massacres which followed their takeover in the North 15 years before. . . .

For the United States, this first defeat in our Nation's history would result in a collapse of confidence in American leadership, not only in Asia but throughout the world. Three American Presidents have recognized the great stakes involved in Vietnam and understood what had to be done. . . .

For the future of peace, precipitate withdrawal would thus be a disaster of immense magnitude.

—A nation cannot remain great if it betrays its allies and lets down its friends.

—Our defeat and humiliation in South Vietnam without question would promote recklessness in the councils of those great powers who have not yet abandoned their goals of world conquest.

—This would spark violence wherever our commitments help maintain the peace in the Middle East, in Berlin, eventually even in the Western Hemisphere. . . .

I pledged in my campaign for the Presidency to end the war in a way that we could win the peace. I have initiated a plan of action which will enable me to keep that pledge.

The more support I can have from the American people, the sooner that pledge can be redeemed; for the more divided we are at home, the less likely the enemy is to negotiate at Paris.

Let us be united for peace. Let us also be united against defeat. Because let us understand: North Vietnam cannot defeat or humiliate the United States. Only Americans can do that.

Source: Excerpt from *Public Papers of the Presidents of the United States: Richard Nixon, 1969* (Washington, D.C.: U.S. Government Printing Office, 1971), 901–9.

DOCUMENT 2
A Vietnam Veteran Urges Congress to End the War, April 22, 1971

John Kerry was a decorated navy lieutenant who served in Vietnam in 1968 and 1969 and later became a U.S. senator and secretary of state. He provided this testimony as a leader of Vietnam Veterans against the War.

movement at home, many soldiers had less faith in the war than their predecessors had had. Racial tensions among the troops mounted, many soldiers sought escape in illegal drugs, and enlisted men committed hundreds of "fraggings," attacks on officers. In a 1971 report, *The Collapse of the Armed Forces*, a retired Marine colonel described the lack of discipline: "Our army that now remains in Vietnam [is] near mutinous."

The Peace Accords

Nixon and Kissinger continued to believe that intensive firepower could bring the North Vietnamese to their knees. In March 1972, responding to a North Vietnamese offensive, the United States resumed sustained bombing of the North, mined Haiphong and other harbors for the first time, and announced a naval blockade. With peace talks stalled, in December

. . . In our opinion, and from our experience, there is nothing in South Vietnam, nothing which could happen that realistically threatens the United States of America. And to attempt to justify the loss of one American life in Vietnam, Cambodia, or Laos by linking such loss to the preservation of freedom . . . is to us the height of criminal hypocrisy, and it is that kind of hypocrisy which we feel has torn this country apart. . . .

We found that not only was it a civil war, an effort by a people who had for years been seeking their liberation from any colonial influence whatsoever, but also we found that the Vietnamese . . . were hard put to take up the fight against the threat we were supposedly saving them from.

We found most people didn't even know the difference between communism and democracy. They only wanted to work in rice paddies without helicopters strafing them and bombs with napalm burning their villages and tearing their country apart. They wanted everything to do with the war, particularly with this foreign presence of the United States of America, to leave them alone in peace, and they practiced the art of survival by siding with whichever military force was present at a particular time, be it Vietcong, North Vietnamese, or American.

We found also that all too often American men were dying in those rice paddies for want of support from their allies. We saw firsthand how money from American taxes was used for a corrupt dictatorial regime. We saw that many people in this country had a one-sided idea of who was kept free by our flag, as blacks provided the highest percentage of casualties. We saw Vietnam ravaged equally by American bombs as well as by search and destroy missions, as well as by Vietcong terrorism, and yet we listened while this country tried to blame all of the havoc on the Vietcong. . . .

We watched the U.S. falsification of body counts, in fact the glorification of body counts. We listened while month after month we were told the back of the enemy was about to break. We fought using weapons against "oriental human beings," with quotation marks around that. We fought using weapons against those people which I do not believe this country would dream of using were we fighting in the European theater. . . .

Now we are told that the men who fought there must watch quietly while American lives are lost so that we can exercise the incredible arrogance of Vietnamizing the Vietnamese. . . .

Each day to facilitate the process by which the United States washes her hands of Vietnam someone has to give up his life so that the United States doesn't have to admit something that the entire world already knows, so that we can't say that we have made a mistake. Someone has to die so that President Nixon won't be, and these are his words, "the first President to lose a war."

We are asking Americans to think about that because how do you ask a man to be the last man to die in Vietnam? How do you ask a man to be the last man to die for a mistake?

Source: Excerpt from *Legislative Proposals Relating to the War in Southeast Asia, Hearings before the U.S. Senate Committee on Foreign Relations*, 92nd Cong. 180–210 (April–May 1971).

Questions for Analysis

Summarize the Argument: Why did President Nixon consider it crucial to remain engaged until South Vietnam's freedom from Communist control was assured? What reasons did Kerry give for placing U.S. withdrawal from Vietnam above all other considerations?

Recognize Viewpoints: Both Nixon and Kerry considered the effects of U.S. actions in Vietnam on particular nations or groups. With which people was each of them most concerned?

Consider the Context: In which ways were Nixon and Kerry both correct about what happened when the United States left Vietnam?

Nixon ordered the most devastating bombing yet. Though costly to both sides, it brought renewed negotiations. On January 27, 1973, representatives of the United States, North Vietnam, South Vietnam, and the Vietcong (now called the Provisional Revolutionary Government) signed a formal peace accord in Paris. The agreement required removal of all U.S. troops and military advisers from South Vietnam but allowed North Vietnamese forces to remain.

Both sides agreed to return prisoners of war. Nixon called the agreement "peace with honor," but in fact it allowed only a face-saving withdrawal. Unlike the ending of World War II, "There's nothing to celebrate," said an American Legion commander.

Fighting resumed immediately among the Vietnamese. Nixon's efforts to support the South Vietnamese government, and indeed his ability to govern at all, were increasingly eroded by

U.S. Involvement in Vietnam

1954	French colonial presence ends with Vietnamese victory at Dien Bien Phu.
	Geneva accords establish temporary division of North and South Vietnam at seventeenth parallel and provide for free elections.
	United States joins with European, East Asian, and other nations to form Southeast Asia Treaty Organization.
	Eisenhower administration begins to send weapons and military advisers to South Vietnam to bolster Diem government.
1961–1963	Under Kennedy administration, military aid to South Vietnam doubles, and number of military advisers reaches 9,000.
1963	Military coup ousts South Vietnamese premier Ngo Dinh Diem.
1964	President Johnson uses Gulf of Tonkin incident to escalate war.
1965	Johnson administration initiates Operation Rolling Thunder, strategic bombing of North Vietnam.
1965–1967	Number of U.S. troops in Vietnam increases, reaching 543,000 in 1968, but U.S. and ARVN forces make only limited progress against the guerrilla forces.
1968	Tet Offensive causes widespread destruction and heavy casualties.
	Johnson announces reduction in bombing of North Vietnam, plans for peace talks, and his decision not to run for reelection.
1969	Nixon administration initiates secret bombing of Cambodia, increases bombing of North Vietnam while reducing U.S. troops in the South, and pursues peace talks.
1970	Nixon orders joint U.S.-ARVN invasion of Cambodia.
1970–1971	U.S. troops in Vietnam decrease from 334,600 to 140,000.
1972	With peace talks stalled in December, Nixon administration orders the war's most devastating bombing of North Vietnam.
1973	On January 27, United States, North Vietnam, and South Vietnam sign formal accord in Paris marking end of U.S. involvement.
1975	North Vietnam launches new offensive in South Vietnam, defeating ARVN. Vietcong troops occupy Saigon, renaming it Ho Chi Minh City.

what came to be known as the Watergate scandal, which forced him to resign in 1974 (as discussed in chapter 30). In 1975, North Vietnam launched a new offensive, seizing Saigon on April 30. The Americans remaining in the U.S. Embassy and their Marine guard hastily evacuated, along with 150,000 of their South Vietnamese allies. Confusion, humiliation, and tragedy marked the rushed departure. The United States lacked sufficient transportation capacity and time to evacuate all those who had supported the South Vietnamese government and were desperate to leave. A U.S. diplomat who escaped Saigon commented, "The rest of our lives we will be haunted by how we betrayed those people." Eventually more than 600,000 Vietnamese fled to the United States, but others lost their lives trying to escape, and many who could not get out suffered from political repression or poverty.

During the four years it took Nixon to end the war, he had expanded the conflict into Cambodia and Laos and launched massive bombing campaigns. Although increasing numbers of legislators criticized the war, Congress never denied the funds to fight it. Only after the peace accords did the legislative branch try to reassert its constitutional authority in the making of war. The War Powers Act of 1973 required the president to secure congressional approval for any substantial, long-term deployment of troops abroad. The new law, however, did little to dispel the distrust of government that resulted from Americans' realization that their leaders had not told the truth about Vietnam.

The war produced widespread criticism of the draft from both the left and right. As the United States withdrew from Vietnam, Nixon and Congress agreed to abandon conscription, which had been part of the Cold War since its beginning. Replacing the principle of obligation with the offer of opportunity, military leaders predicted that an all-volunteer army would make a more disciplined and professional fighting force. At the same time, ending service as a common sacrifice distanced most Americans from the horrors of warfare and from the military, whose ranks would be disproportionately filled by poorer Americans and people of color.

The Legacy of Defeat

Four presidents had declared that the survival of South Vietnam was critical to U.S. containment policy. Yet their predictions that a Communist

VISUAL ACTIVITY

Evacuating South Vietnam

As Communist troops approached Saigon in the spring of 1975, desperate South Vietnamese attempted to flee along with the departing Americans. Here they attempt to scale the wall of the U.S. Embassy to reach evacuation helicopters. Thousands were left behind, while South Vietnamese president Nguyen Van Thieu fled with fifteen tons of baggage on a U.S. plane. AP Images/Neal Ulevich.

READING THE IMAGE: What in the photo suggests the desperation of the South Vietnamese? How might this kind of photo have been viewed in the United States by war supporters and opponents?

CONNECTIONS: What besides the hasty departure from Saigon left a bitter taste in the mouths of Americans about the Vietnam War?

victory in South Vietnam would set the dominoes cascading did not materialize. Although Vietnam, Laos, and Cambodia all fell within the Communist camp in the spring of 1975, the rest of Southeast Asia did not. When China and Vietnam reverted to their historically hostile relationship, the myth of a monolithic Communist power overrunning Asia evaporated.

Antigovernment sentiment was just one of the war's legacies. Vietnam also left bitter divisions among Americans and diverted money from domestic programs. The war created federal budget deficits and triggered inflation that contributed to ongoing economic crises throughout the 1970s (see chapter 30).

The long pursuit of victory in Vietnam complicated the United States' relations with other nations, as even its staunchest ally, Britain, doubted the wisdom of the war. The use of terrifying American power against a small Asian country alienated many in the third world and compromised efforts to win the hearts and minds of people in developing nations.

The cruelest legacy of Vietnam fell on those who had served. "The general public just wanted to ignore us," remembered Frederick Downs, while opponents of the war "wanted to argue with us until we felt guilty about what we had done over there." Many veterans believed in the war's purposes and felt betrayed by the government for not letting them win it. Others blamed the government for sacrificing the nation's youth in an immoral, unnecessary war, expressing their sense of the war's futility by referring to their dead comrades as having been "wasted." Veterans of color had more reason to doubt the nobility of their purpose. A Native American soldier assigned to resettle Vietnamese civilians found it to be "just like when they moved us to the rez [reservation]. We shouldn't have done that."

Because the Vietnam War was a civil war involving guerrilla tactics, combat was especially brutal (Table 29.1). The terrors of conventional

TABLE 29.1	VIETNAM WAR CASUALTIES
United States	
Battle deaths	47,434
Other deaths	10,786
Wounded	153,303
South Vietnam	
Killed in action	110,357
Military wounded	499,026
Civilians killed	415,000
Civilians wounded	913,000
Communist Regulars and Guerrillas	
Killed in action	66,000

Source: U.S. Department of Defense.

warfare were multiplied, and so were the motivations to commit atrocities. The 1968 massacre at My Lai was only the most widely publicized war crime. To demonstrate the immorality of the war, peace advocates stressed the atrocities, contributing to a distorted image of the Vietnam veteran as dehumanized and violent.

Most veterans came home to public neglect. Government benefits were less generous to Vietnam veterans than they had been to those of previous wars. While two-thirds of Vietnam veterans said that they would serve again, and while most veterans readjusted well to civilian life, some suffered long after the war ended. The Veterans Administration estimated that nearly one-sixth of the veterans suffered from post-traumatic stress disorder, experiencing recurring nightmares, feelings of guilt and shame, violence, substance abuse, and suicidal tendencies. Thirty years after performing army intelligence work in Saigon, Doris Allen "still hit the floor sometimes when [she heard] loud bangs." Some who had served in Vietnam began to report birth defects, cancer, severe skin disorders, and other ailments. Veterans claimed a link between those illnesses and Agent Orange, which had exposed many to the deadly poison dioxin in Vietnam. In 1991, Congress began to provide assistance to veterans with diseases linked to the poison.

By then, the climate had changed. The war began to enter the realm of popular culture, with novels, TV shows, and hit movies depicting a broad range of military experience—from soldiers reduced to brutality, to men and women serving with courage and integrity. The incorporation of the Vietnam War into the collective experience was symbolized most dramatically in the Vietnam Veterans Memorial unveiled in Washington, D.C., in November 1982. Designed by Yale architecture student Maya Lin, the black, V-shaped wall inscribed with the names of 58,200 men and women lost in the war became one of the most popular sites in the nation's capital. In an article describing the memorial's dedication, a Vietnam combat veteran spoke to and for his former comrades: "Welcome home. The war is over."

> **REVIEW**   What strategies did Nixon implement to bring American involvement in Vietnam to a close?

► Conclusion: An Unwinnable War

Lieutenant Frederick Downs Jr. fought in America's longest war. The United States spent $111 billion (more than $600 billion in 2014 dollars) and sent 2.6 million men and women to Vietnam. Of those, 58,200 never returned, and 150,000, like Downs, suffered serious injury. The war shattered consensus at home, increased presidential power at the expense of congressional authority and public accountability, weakened the economy, diminished trust in government, and contributed to the downfall of two presidents.

Even as Nixon and Kissinger took steps to ease Cold War tensions with the major Communist powers—the Soviet Union and China—they also acted vigorously throughout the third world to install or prop up anti-Communist governments. They embraced their predecessors' commitment to South Vietnam as a necessary Cold War engagement: To do otherwise would threaten American credibility and make the United States appear weak. Defeat in Vietnam did not make the United States the "pitiful helpless giant" predicted by Nixon, but it did signify a relative decline of U.S. power and the impossibility of containment on a global scale.

One of the constraints on U.S. power was the tenacity of revolutionary movements determined to achieve national independence. Overestimating the effectiveness of American technological superiority, U.S. officials badly underestimated the sacrifices that the enemy was willing to make and failed to realize how easily the United States could be perceived as a colonial intruder. A second constraint on Eisenhower, Kennedy, Johnson, and Nixon was their resolve to avoid a major confrontation with the Soviet Union or China. For Johnson, who conducted the largest escalation of the war, caution was critical so as not to provoke direct intervention by the Communist superpowers. After China exploded its first atomic bomb in 1964, the potential heightened for the Vietnam conflict to escalate into worldwide disaster.

Third, in Vietnam the United States sought to prop up an extremely weak ally engaged in a civil war. The South Vietnamese government failed to win the support of its people, and the intense devastation the war brought to civilians only made things worse. Short of taking over the

South Vietnamese government and military, the United States could do little to strengthen South Vietnam's ability to resist communism.

Finally, domestic opposition to the war, which by 1968 had spread to mainstream America, constrained the options of Johnson and Nixon. As the war dragged on, with increasing American casualties and growing evidence of the damage being inflicted on innocent Vietnamese, more and more civilians wearied of the conflict. Even some who had fought in the war joined the peace movement, sending their military ribbons and bitter letters of protest to the White House. In 1973, Nixon and Kissinger bowed to the resoluteness of the enemy and the limitations of U.S. power. As the war wound down, passions surrounding it contributed to a rising conservative movement that would substantially alter the post–World War II political order.

See the Selected Bibliography for this chapter in the Appendix.

29 Chapter Review

REVIEW QUESTIONS

1. Why did Kennedy believe that engagement in Vietnam was crucial to his foreign policy? (pp. 833–838)

2. Why did massive amounts of airpower and ground troops fail to bring U.S. victory in Vietnam? (pp. 838–843)

3. How did the war in Vietnam polarize the nation? (pp. 844–850)

4. What strategies did Nixon implement to bring American involvement in Vietnam to a close? (pp. 850–858)

MAKING CONNECTIONS

1. How did Cuba figure into President Kennedy's Cold War policies?

2. Explain the Gulf of Tonkin incident and its significance to American foreign policy. How did President Johnson respond to the incident, and why?

3. Discuss the range of American responses to the war in Vietnam. How did they change over time?

LINKING TO THE PAST

1. What commitments were made in the Truman and Eisenhower administrations that resulted in the United States' full-scale involvement in Vietnam? (See chapters 26 and 27.)

2. Compare American public sentiment during World War II to that during the Vietnam War. What policies, events, attitudes, and technological advancements contributed to the differences? (See chapter 25.)

30 America Moves to the Right

1969–1989

CONTENT LEARNING OBJECTIVES

After reading and studying this chapter, you should be able to:

- Explain the emergence of a grassroots conservative movement and how Nixon courted the right. Identify the events that led to Nixon's resignation.

- Describe the "outsider" presidency of Jimmy Carter and explain his approach to energy and environmental regulation, human rights, and the Cold War.

- Explain how Ronald Reagan's presidency represented ascendant conservatism and the factors behind Reagan's broad appeal.

- Explain how minority groups, feminists, gays and lesbians, and lower-income Americans struggled during the 1980s.

- Describe Reagan's foreign policies, including increased militarization and interventions in the Middle East, Latin America, and Asia. Explain what led to a thaw in Soviet-American relations.

MAKING AMERICA "REAGAN COUNTRY"
This delegate badge from the 1980 Republican National Convention displayed key themes of Ronald Reagan's presidency and politics in the 1980s—patriotism and the rugged individualism of the West. Division of Political History, National Museum of American History, Smithsonian Institution.

ONE OF THE "MOST EXCITING DAYS" OF PHYLLIS SCHLAFLY'S life was hearing Republican Barry Goldwater address the Federation of Republican Women in 1963. Schlafly wanted the United States to do more than just contain communism; like Goldwater, she wanted to eliminate that threat entirely. She also wanted to cut back the federal government, especially its role in providing social welfare and enforcing civil rights. Goldwater's loss to Lyndon Johnson in 1964 did not diminish Schlafly's conservative commitment. She added new issues to the conservative agenda, cultivating a grassroots movement that would redefine the Republican Party and American politics well into the twenty-first century.

Phyllis Stewart was born in St. Louis in 1924, attended Catholic schools, and worked her way through Washington University testing ammunition at a World War II defense plant. After earning a master's degree in government from Radcliffe College, she worked at the American Enterprise Institute, where she imbibed the think tank's conservatism. Returning to the Midwest, she married Fred Schlafly, an Alton, Illinois, attorney, and bore six children. "I don't think there's anything as much fun as taking care of a baby," Schlafly claimed.

Yet while insisting that caring for home and family was women's most important career, Schlafly spent much of her time writing or on the road, speaking, leading Republican women's organizations, and testifying before legislative committees. She ran twice for Congress but lost in her heavily Democratic district in Illinois. Her 1964 book, *A Choice Not an Echo*, pushed Barry Goldwater for president and sold more than three million copies. In 1967, she began publishing the *Phyllis Schlafly Report*, a monthly newsletter about current political issues. Throughout the 1950s and 1960s, Schlafly advocated stronger efforts to combat communism, a more powerful military, and limited government action in domestic affairs.

In the 1970s, Schlafly expanded the agenda of conservatism to address new issues such as feminism, abortion, gay rights, busing for racial integration, and religion in the schools. Her ideas resonated with Americans who were fed up with the expansion of government, liberal Supreme Court decisions, protest movements, and the loosening of moral standards that seemed to define the 1960s. Although Richard Nixon did not embrace the entire conservative agenda, he won the presidency in 1968 on a platform that sought to make the Republicans the dominant party by appealing to disaffected blue-collar and southern white Democrats. The Watergate revelations forced Nixon to resign the presidency in 1974, and his Republican successor, Gerald Ford, served only two years; but the political spectrum continued to shift right even when Democrat Jimmy Carter captured the White House in 1976. Carter advanced environmental and energy legislation, but an economy beset by both inflation and unemployment and a crisis in U.S.-Iranian relations burdened his campaign for reelection.

Consequently, Schlafly's call for "a choice not an echo" was realized when Ronald Reagan won the presidency in 1980. Cutting taxes, government regulations, and social programs; expanding the nation's military capacity; and pressuring the Soviet Union and communism in the third world, Reagan addressed the hopes of the traditional right. Like Schlafly, he also championed the concerns of Christian conservatives, opposing abortion and sexual permissiveness and favoring a larger role for religion in public life.

In the face of resistance from feminists, civil rights groups, environmentalists, and others, Reagan failed to enact the entire conservative agenda. Although he enormously increased the national debt, and his aides engaged in illegal activities to thwart communism in Latin America, his popularity boosted the Republican Party. And Reagan's optimism and spirited leadership contributed to a revival in national pride and confidence.

The *Phyllis Schlafly Report*

Phyllis Schlafly began her newsletter in 1967. When Congress passed the ERA in 1972, the *Report* added antifeminism and other concerns of the religious right to its agenda. Schlafly had more than 35,000 newsletter subscribers in the mid-1970s; she also had many adversaries, including feminist leader Betty Friedan, who called her "a traitor to your sex." Courtesy of Phyllis Schlafly.

The Phyllis Schlafly Report

VOL. 5, NO. 10, SECTION 2   Box 618, ALTON, ILLINOIS 62002   MAY, 1972

The Fraud Called The Equal Rights Amendment

If there ever was an example of how a tiny minority can cram its views down the throats of the majority, it is the Equal Rights Amendment, called ERA. A noisy claque of women's lib agitators rammed ERA through Congress, intimidating the men into voting for it so they would not be labeled "anti-woman."

The ERA passed Congress with big majorities on March 22, 1972 and was sent to the states for ratification. When it is ratified by 38 states, it will become the law of the land. Within two hours of Senate passage, Hawaii ratified it. New Hampshire and Nebraska, both anxious to be second, rushed their approval the next day. Then in steady succession came Iowa, Idaho, Delaware, Kansas, Texas, Maryland, Tennessee, Alaska, Rhode Island, and New Jersey. As this goes to press, 13 states have ratified it and others are on the verge of doing so.

Three states have rejected it: Oklahoma, Vermont and Connecticut.

What is ERA? The Amendment reads: "Equality of rights under the law shall not be denied or abridged by the United States or by any state on account of sex."

Does that sound good? Don't kid yourself. This innocuous-sounding amendment will take away far more important rights than it will ever give. This was made abundantly clear by the debate in Congress. Senator Sam Ervin (D., N.C.) called it "the most drastic measure in Senate history." He proved this by putting into the *Congressional Record* an article from the *Yale Law Journal* of April 1971.

The importance of this *Yale Law Journal* article is that both the proponents and the opponents of ERA agree that it is an accurate analysis of the consequences of ERA. Congresswoman Martha Griffiths, a leading proponent of ERA, sent a copy of this article to every member of Congress, stating that "It will help us understand the purposes and effect of the Equal Rights Amendment.... The article tells us how the ERA will work in practice....

the most important of all women's rights.

"In all states husbands are primarily liable for the support of their wives and children.... The child support sections of the criminal nonsupport laws ... could not be sustained where only the male is liable for support." (YLJ, pp. 944-945)

"The Equal Rights Amendment would bar a state from imposing greater liability for support on a husband than on a wife merely because of his sex." (YLJ, p. 945)

"Like the duty of support during marriage and the obligation to pay alimony in the case of separation or divorce, nonsupport would have to be eliminated as a ground for divorce against husbands only...." (YLJ, p. 951)

"The Equal Rights Amendment would not require that alimony be abolished but only that it be available equally to husbands and wives." (YLJ, p. 952)

2. ERA will wipe out the laws which protect only women against sex crimes such as rape.

"Courts faced with criminal laws which do not apply equally to men and women would be likely to invalidate the laws rather than extending or rewriting them to apply to women and men alike." (YLJ, p. 966)

"Seduction laws, statutory rape laws, laws prohibiting obscene language in the presence of women, prostitution and 'manifest danger' laws ... The Equal Rights Amendment would not permit such laws, which base their sex discriminatory classification on social stereotypes." (YLJ, p. 954)

"The statutory rape laws, which punish men for having sexual intercourse with any woman under an age specified by law ... suffer from a defect under the Equal Rights Amendment ....

"To be ... singling out ...

► Nixon, Conservatism, and Constitutional Crisis

Richard Nixon acquiesced in continuing most Great Society programs and even approved path-breaking environmental, minority, and women's rights measures (see "Liberal Reform in the Nixon Administration" in chapter 28), prompting Phyllis Schlafly to call him "too liberal." Yet his public rhetoric and some of his actions signaled the country's rightward move. Whereas John F. Kennedy had summoned Americans to contribute to the common good, Nixon invited Americans to "ask—not just what will government do for me, but what can I do for myself?" invoking individualism and reliance on private enterprise, not on government. These preferences would grow stronger in the nation during the 1970s and beyond, as a new strand of conservatism joined the older movement that focused on anticommunism, a strong national defense, and limited government. New conservatives wanted to restore what they considered traditional moral values.

Just two years after Nixon won reelection by a huge margin, his abuse of power and efforts to cover up crimes committed by subordinates, revealed in the so-called Watergate scandal, forced the first presidential resignation in history. His successor, Gerald Ford, faced the aftermath of Watergate and severe economic problems, which returned the White House to the Democrats in 1976.

Emergence of a Grassroots Movement

Hidden beneath Lyndon B. Johnson's landslide victory over Arizona senator Barry Goldwater in 1964 lay a rising conservative movement. Defining his purpose as "enlarging freedom at home and safeguarding it from the forces of tyranny abroad," Goldwater argued that government intrusions into economic life hindered prosperity, stifled personal responsibility, and interfered with citizens' rights to determine their own values. Conservatives assailed big government in domestic affairs but demanded a strong military to eradicate "Godless communism."

The grassroots movement supporting Goldwater's nomination was especially vigorous in the South and West, and it included middle-class suburban women and men, members of the

CHRONOLOGY

1968	• Richard Nixon elected president.
1969	• Warren E. Burger appointed chief justice of Supreme Court.
1971	• Nixon vetoes child care bill.
1972	• Watergate scandal begins. • Nixon reelected president.
1974	• Nixon resigns; Vice President Gerald Ford becomes president. • Ford pardons Nixon.
1976	• Jimmy Carter elected president.
1977	• United States signs Panama Canal treaty.
1978	• *Regents of the University of California v. Bakke* decided. • Congress deregulates airlines.
1979	• Carter facilitates Camp David accords. • Carter establishes formal diplomatic relations with China. • Soviet Union invades Afghanistan. • Iranian hostage crisis begins. • Moral Majority founded.
1980	• Congress deregulates banking, trucking, and railroad industries. • Congress passes Superfund legislation. • Ronald Reagan elected president.
1981	• AIDS virus discovered. • Economic Recovery Tax Act passes.
1983	• Terrorist bomb kills 241 U.S. Marines in Beirut, Lebanon. • Family Research Council founded.
1984	• Reagan reelected president.
1986	• Iran-Contra scandal uncovered.
1987	• Intermediate-range nuclear forces agreement signed.
1988	• Civil Rights Restoration Act passes.

rabidly anti-Communist John Birch Society, and college students in the new Young Americans for Freedom (YAF). In 1966, California conservatives helped Ronald Reagan defeat the liberal incumbent governor, whom Reagan linked to the Watts riot, student disruptions at California universities, and rising taxes.

A number of Sun Belt characteristics made conservatism strong in places such as Orange County, California; Dallas, Texas; and Scottsdale, Arizona. These predominantly white areas contained relatively homogeneous, skilled, and economically comfortable populations, as well as military bases and defense plants. The West harbored a long-standing tradition of Protestant morality, individualism, and opposition to interference by a remote federal government, although

that tradition was hardly consistent with the Sun Belt's economic dependence on defense spending and on huge federal projects providing water and power for the burgeoning region. The South, which also benefited from military bases and the space program, shared the West's antipathy toward the federal government, but hostility to racial change was much more central to the South's conservatism. After signing the Civil Rights Act of 1964, President Johnson remarked privately, "I think we just delivered the South to the Republican Party."

Grassroots movements proliferated around what conservatives believed marked the "moral decline" of their nation. For example, in 1962 Mel and Norma Gabler got the Texas Board of Education to drop books that they believed undermined "the Christian-Judeo morals, values, and standards as given to us by God through . . . the Bible." Sex education roused the ire of Eleanor Howe in Anaheim, California, who felt that "nothing [in the sex education curriculum] depicted my values." (See "Experiencing the American Promise," page 866.) The U.S. Supreme Court's liberal decisions on school prayer, obscenity, and abortion also galvanized conservatives to restore "traditional values."

In the 1970s, grassroots protests against taxes grew alongside concerns about morality. As Americans struggled with inflation and unemployment, many found themselves paying higher taxes, especially higher property taxes as the value of their homes increased. Some were incensed to see their taxes fund government programs for people they considered undeserving. In 1978, Californians revolted in a popular referendum, slashing property taxes and limiting the state legislature's ability to raise other taxes. What a newspaper called a "primal scream by the People against Big Government" spread to other states.

Law and order was yet another rallying cry of the right, reflecting concerns about rising rates of crime, which were due in part to baby boomers maturing into the age group most prone to crime. Conservatives lumped common crime with civil disobedience and antiwar protest into a cry for law and order, and blamed liberals for Great Society programs that had failed to reduce crime, permissive attitudes toward protesters, and Supreme Court decisions that coddled criminals. A Pennsylvania man called "crime, the streets being unsafe, strikes, the trouble with the colored, all this dope-taking . . . a breakdown of the American way of life."

VISUAL ACTIVITY

The Tax Revolt

Neighbors gather in Los Angeles to rally for Proposition 13, an initiative launched by conservative Howard Jarvis in 1978. Many homeowners rallied to Jarvis's antitax movement because rising land values had increased their property taxes sharply. After Californians passed Proposition 13, some thirty-seven states cut property taxes, and twenty-eight reduced income taxes. The tax issue helped the Republican Party end decades of Democratic dominance. Tony Korody/The LIFE Images Collection/Getty Images.

READING THE IMAGE: Considering the signs, what is the main concern of the people pictured here? What kinds of people are pictured here, and what are their stakes in the property tax issue?

CONNECTIONS: What other issues did Republicans capitalize on in the 1970s and 1980s?

Nixon Courts the Right

Highlighting law and order in his 1968 presidential campaign, Nixon appealed to "forgotten Americans, those who did not indulge in violence, those who did not break the law." He also exploited hostility to black protest and new civil rights policies to woo white southerners and a considerable number of northern voters away from the Democratic Party. As president, he used this "southern strategy" to make further inroads into traditional Democratic strongholds in the 1972 election.

Nixon reluctantly enforced court orders to achieve high degrees of integration in southern schools, but he resisted efforts to deal with segregation outside the South. In northern and western cities, where segregation resulted from discrimination in housing and in the drawing of school district boundaries, half of all African American children attended nearly all-black schools. After courts began to order the transfer of students between schools in white and black neighborhoods to achieve desegregation, busing became a hot-button issue. "We've had all we can take of judicial interference with local schools," Phyllis Schlafly railed in 1972.

Percent of black students statewide attending schools more than 50% white

	60% or more		30–40%
	50–60%		20–30%
	40–50%		20% or less

Integration of Public Schools, 1968

Children had been riding buses to school for decades, but busing for racial integration provoked fury. Violence erupted in Boston in 1974 when a district judge found that school officials had maintained what amounted to a dual system based on race and ordered busing "if necessary to achieve a unitary school system." The whites most affected by busing came from working-class families. Left in cities abandoned by the more affluent, their children often rode buses to predominantly black, overcrowded schools with deficient facilities. Clarence McDonough denounced the liberal officials who bused his "kid half way around Boston so that a bunch of politicians can end up their careers with a clear conscience." African Americans themselves were conflicted about sending their children on long rides to schools where white teachers might not welcome or respect them.

Whites eventually became more accepting of integration, especially after the creation of schools with specialized programs and other new mechanisms for desegregation offered greater choice. Nonetheless, integration propelled white flight to the suburbs. Nixon failed to persuade Congress to end court-ordered busing, but after he had appointed four new justices, the Supreme

School Busing
Controversy over busing as a means of integration erupted in Boston in 1974 after a federal judge ruled that Boston officials had deliberately constructed a segregated school system. Antibusing outrage was especially virulent at historically white South Boston High School, where one black student recalled that "it was like a war zone." Here Tactical Patrol Force officers protect black students at the high school. Jack O'Connell/The *Boston Globe* via Getty Images.

A Mother Campaigns for a Say in Her Children's Education

Although historians usually trace the rise of conservatism through national politics, the most intense political battles of the 1970s and 1980s often raged at the local level. None were more impassioned than those mounted by parents over what their children should be taught in public schools. The introduction of sex education and new textbooks in the Kanawha County, West Virginia, school district in 1969 prompted Alice Moore to challenge instruction she deemed harmful to her children and to organize a parents' movement to gain control over their children's education.

The sprawling school district of Kanawha County encompassed the state capital of Charleston as well as surrounding towns and rural areas containing chemical plants, coal mines, and small hamlets. Alice Moore, a native of Mississippi, and her husband, a fundamentalist minister, lived in a small town on the outskirts of Charleston, where their four children attended local schools. Her disgust with the sex education program prompted her to run for the school board in 1970, and she won a seat as the only woman on a five-person board. Moore failed to terminate the sex education program, which she found a "humanistic, atheistic attack on God," but did manage to dilute the curriculum.

The district's adoption of a new English language arts curriculum in 1974 provoked even greater controversy. The program, similar to those gaining adoption across the country, sought to teach children about the larger world, incorporated writings by African Americans and other minority groups, and encouraged students to think critically and independently.

Objecting to both the philosophy and the content of the new curriculum, Moore began to mobilize opposition, calling on fundamentalist ministers and holding meetings in churches. In June 1974, at a meeting before an impassioned crowd of more than a thousand, she persuaded the school board to eliminate 8 of the curriculum's 325 books but failed to prevent adoption of the curriculum by a vote of three to two. Opponents then redoubled their efforts, echoing concerns that were energizing the Christian Right across the country.

Protesters charged that the new materials in the curriculum constituted an assault on Christianity, authority, patriotism, and the system of free enterprise. One of Moore's allies, a conservative chemical company owner, vilified the curriculum as "liberal, socialist, even communist-inspired." Textbook opponents also challenged the authority of distant "experts" to decide what was best for their children.

Furthermore, Moore and her supporters objected to the curriculum's multicultural materials, designed to illustrate the diversity of American society. They disliked the nonstandard English that appeared in some of the literature, as well as what they considered the "trashy" aspects of urban ghetto life. "Why the hell do we have to indoctrinate our children out here in semi-rural communities with the problems of the inner city?" a protester asked.

The new sexual permissiveness of the 1960s also aroused anti-textbook forces. The sexual realism in some of the materials inflamed fundamentalist protesters, above all because it defied their belief in the system of right and wrong laid out in the Bible, which they interpreted literally. To Moore, morality was not a relative issue: "God's law is absolute."

Such deeply held beliefs inspired opponents to keep their children home when school opened in September, achieving a 20 percent absentee rate. Defying their union leadership, thousands of miners went out on a sympathy strike while protesters set up picket lines and staged demonstrations. Three schools were bombed, district headquarters were dynamited, and guns were fired on both sides. Anti-textbook supporters streamed into Charleston, including representatives from the Heritage Foundation, the John Birch Society, and the Ku Klux Klan. The violence gradually

Court imposed strict limits on the use of that tool to achieve racial balance.

Nixon's judicial appointments also reflected the southern strategy. He criticized the Supreme Court under Chief Justice Earl Warren for being "unprecedentedly politically active . . . using their interpretation of the law to remake American society according to their own social, political, and ideological precepts." When Warren resigned in 1969, Nixon replaced him with Warren E. Burger, a federal appeals court judge who was a strict constructionist, inclined to interpret the Constitution narrowly and to limit government intervention on behalf of individual rights. The Burger Court curbed somewhat the protections of individual rights established

RE-ELECT

ALICE MOORE

FOR

BOARD of EDUCATION

Dear Friends,

The schools belong to the people who pay for them, not Washington Bureaucrats, not School Administrators, not National Education Organizations.

Nationally, education is costing us more than **61 billion dollars** a year, more than is spent on education by all the rest of the world combined. This is a **1000 percent increase** in 20 years while enrollment has barely doubled. Yet, almost **one third** of our high school graduates cannot pass college placement exams and this number increases annually.

Are your children getting the education you want for them? I am convinced most parents expect the schools, for which we pay and for which we provide the children, to:

- Offer the best academic education possible with emphasis on basic skills.

- Respect family privacy and our right as parents to rear our children according to **our own moral, ethical and religious beliefs** without interference.

- Provide a disciplined and morally up-lifting educational climate for the safety and peace of mind for both students and teachers. **Stop coddling the class trouble-makers at the expense of serious minded students.**

- Operate the schools as efficiently as private enterprise.

As a board member, I have tried to represent the public interest, not an Educational Bureaucracy. This is the kind of education I want for my five children. If this is what you want, please give me your vote and contact your friends on my behalf.

Sincerely yours,

(Mrs.) Alice Moore

The **final** board vote is at the May 11 primary. Democrats, Republicans and Independents can vote for me, for this non-partisan position.

Alice Moore Campaigns for the School Board

Alice Moore's 1976 campaign for reelection to the Kanawha County Board of Education emphasized moral issues and attacked government bureaucrats and expenditures. Her first campaign's slogan had been "We need a mother on the board of education." She bore her fifth child while on the board, but one of the policies she championed prohibited pregnant girls from attending high school because she considered them "disruptive." West Virginia State Archives.

retreated from the public schools entirely. By 2013, parents were homeschooling 1.7 million children, and the number of private Christian schools soared, accommodating parents who, in Moore's words, "can't put their children in public schools and allow them to have their beliefs torn away." Those who believed that students should be exposed to a diversity of ideas to form their own beliefs were in the majority, but Christian conservatives such as Moore continued to fight for control over what their children were taught.

Questions for Analysis

Analyze the Evidence: What specific features of the new English language arts curriculum did Alice Moore and her supporters object to?

Recognize Viewpoints: What values of the new conservatives were reflected in the anti-textbook campaign? How might other groups have viewed the debate differently?

Consider the Context: What larger tensions of the 1970s did the textbook fight reflect?

subsided, but protests went on through April 1975.

The school board ended up keeping most of the new curriculum, but parents were allowed to designate those books they did not want their children to read. Many teachers avoided hassles by not using any of the new books. The board also set new guidelines for choosing textbooks, which included banning materials that contained profanity, that

looked favorably on different forms of government, or that "intrude[d] into the privacy of students' homes by asking personal questions about the inner feelings or behavior of themselves or their parents."

Conflicts over public school curricula, involving such topics as evolution, continued to strike communities throughout the nation, although none equaled the war in Kanawha County. Some conservative parents

by its predecessor, but it upheld many of the liberal programs of the 1960s. For example, *Regents of the University of California v. Bakke* (1978) limited the range of affirmative action but allowed universities to attack the results of past discrimination as long as they did not use strict quotas and racial classifications to do so.

Nixon's southern strategy and other repercussions of the civil rights revolution ended the Democratic hold on the "solid South." Beginning in 1964, a number of conservative southern Democrats changed their party affiliation; by 2015, Republicans controlled every southern state legislature, every governorship, and every Senate seat.

In addition to exploiting racial fears, Nixon appealed to anxieties about women's changing roles and new demands. In 1971, he vetoed a bill providing federal funds for day care centers with a message that combined the old and new conservatism. Parents should purchase child care services "in the private, open market," he insisted, not rely on government. He appealed to social conservatives by warning about the measure's "family-weakening implications." In response to the movement to liberalize abortion laws, Nixon sided with "defenders of the right to life of the unborn," anticipating the Republican Party's eventual embrace of the issue.

The Election of 1972

Nixon's ability to attract Democrats and appeal to concerns about Vietnam, race, law and order, and traditional morality heightened his prospects for reelection in 1972. Although the war in Vietnam continued, antiwar protests ebbed with the decrease in American ground forces and casualties. Nixon's economic initiatives had temporarily checked inflation and unemployment (see "Extending the Welfare State and Regulating the Economy" in chapter 28), and his attacks on busing and antiwar protesters had won increasing support from the right.

South Dakota senator George S. McGovern came to the Democratic convention as the clear leader and was easily nominated by the delegates, who included unprecedented numbers of women, minorities, and youth. But McGovern struggled as Republicans portrayed him as a left-wing extremist, while his support for busing, a generous welfare program, and immediate withdrawal from Vietnam alienated some Democrats.

Nixon achieved a landslide victory, winning 60.7 percent of the popular vote and every state except Massachusetts. Although the Democrats held on to Congress, Nixon won majorities among traditional Democrats—southerners, Catholics, urbanites, and blue-collar workers. The president, however, had little time to savor his triumph, as revelations began to emerge about crimes committed to ensure the victory.

Watergate

During the early-morning hours of June 17, 1972, five men working for Nixon's reelection crept into Democratic Party headquarters in the Watergate complex in Washington, D.C. Intending to repair a bugging device installed in an earlier break-in, they were discovered and arrested. Nixon and his aides then tried to cover up the burglars' connection to administration officials, setting in motion the scandal reporters dubbed **Watergate**.

Nixon was not the first president to lie to the public or misuse power. Every president since Franklin D. Roosevelt had enlarged the powers of his office in the name of national security. This expansion of executive powers, often called the "imperial presidency," weakened traditional checks and balances on the executive branch and opened the door to abuses. No president, however, had dared go as far as Nixon, who saw opposition to his policies as a personal attack and was willing to violate the Constitution to stop it.

Upon learning of the Watergate arrests, Nixon plotted to manipulate the Central Intelligence Agency (CIA) and Federal Bureau of Investigation (FBI) to conceal links between the burglars and the White House, while publicly denying any connection. In April 1973, after investigations by a grand jury and the Senate suggested that White House aides had been involved in the

Watergate

In this drawing, famed political cartoonist Herbert Lawrence Block, known as Herblock, cleverly combined two elements of the Watergate scandal that felled Nixon. During the investigation, the president declared, "I am not a crook," and the tapes of conversations in the Oval Office that he was forced to turn over to investigators showed an eighteen-minute gap at a critical moment. © The Herb Block Foundation.

cover-up effort, Nixon accepted official responsibility for Watergate but denied any knowledge of the break-in or cover-up. He also announced the resignations of three White House aides and the attorney general. In May, he authorized the appointment of an independent special prosecutor, Archibald Cox, to conduct an investigation.

Meanwhile, speaking before a Senate investigating committee headed by Democrat Samuel J. Ervin of North Carolina, White House counsel John Dean described projects to harass "enemies" through tax audits and other illegal means and implicated the president in efforts to cover up the Watergate break-in. Another White House aide struck the decisive blow when he disclosed that all conversations in the Oval Office were taped. Both Cox and Ervin immediately asked for the tapes related to Watergate. When Nixon refused, citing executive privilege and separation of powers, they won a unanimous decision from the Supreme Court ordering him to release the recordings.

Additional disclosures exposed Nixon's misuse of federal funds and tax evasion. In August 1973, Vice President Spiro Agnew resigned after an investigation uncovered his acceptance of bribes while governor of Maryland. Nixon's choice of House minority leader Gerald Ford of Michigan to succeed Agnew won widespread approval, but Agnew's resignation further tarnished the administration, and Nixon's popular support plummeted.

In February 1974, the House of Representatives began an impeachment investigation. In April, Nixon began to release edited transcripts of the tapes. The transcripts revealed Nixon's orders to aides in March 1973: "I don't give a shit what happens. I want you all to stonewall it, let them plead the Fifth Amendment, cover up or anything else, if it'll save it—save the plan." House Republican leader Hugh Scott of Pennsylvania called the documents a "deplorable, shabby, disgusting, and immoral performance by all."

In July 1974, the House Judiciary Committee voted to impeach the president on three counts: obstruction of justice, abuse of power, and contempt of Congress. Seven or eight Republicans on the committee sided with the majority, and it seemed certain that the House would follow suit. Georgia state legislator and civil rights activist Julian Bond commented, "The prisons of Georgia are full of people who stole $5 or $10, and this man tried to steal the Constitution."

To avoid impeachment, Nixon announced his resignation to a national television audience on August 8, 1974. Acknowledging some incorrect judgments, he insisted that he had always tried to do what was best for the nation. The next morning, Nixon ended a rambling, emotional farewell to his staff with some advice: "Always give your best, never get discouraged, never get petty; always remember, others may hate you, but those who hate you don't win unless you hate them, and then you destroy yourself." Had he followed his own advice, he might have saved his presidency.

The Ford Presidency and the 1976 Election

Upon taking office, Gerald R. Ford announced, "Our long national nightmare is over." But he shocked many Americans one month later by granting Nixon a pardon "for all offenses against the United States which he . . . has committed or may have committed or taken part in" during his presidency. Prompted by Ford's concern for Nixon's health and by his hope to get the country beyond Watergate, this sweeping pardon saved Nixon from nearly certain indictment and trial, and it provoked a tremendous outcry from Congress and the public. Democrats made impressive gains in the November congressional elections, while Ford's action gave Nixon a new political life. Without having to admit that he had violated the law, Nixon rebuilt his image over the next two decades into that of an elder statesman. Thirty of his associates ultimately pleaded guilty to or were convicted of crimes related to Watergate.

Congress's efforts to guard against the types of abuses revealed in the Watergate investigations had only limited effects. The Federal Election Campaign Act of 1974 established public financing of presidential campaigns and imposed some restrictions on contributions to curtail the selling of political favors. Yet politicians found other ways of raising money—for example, through political action committees (PACs), to which individuals could contribute more than they could to candidates. Moreover, the Supreme Court struck down limitations on campaign spending as violations of freedom of speech. Ever-larger campaign donations flowed to candidates from interest groups, corporations, labor unions, and wealthy individuals.

Congressional investigating committees discovered a host of illegal FBI and CIA activities stretching back to the 1950s, including surveillance of American citizens such as Martin Luther King Jr., harassment of political dissenters, and plots to assassinate Fidel Castro and other foreign leaders. In response to these revelations, President Ford placed new controls on covert operations, and Congress created permanent committees to oversee the intelligence agencies. Yet these measures did little to diminish the public's cynicism about their government or to curtail massive government surveillance of private communications that accompanied terrorist threats to the United States in the twenty-first century.

Disillusionment grew as the Ford administration struggled with serious economic problems: a low growth rate, high unemployment, a foreign trade deficit, and soaring energy prices. Ford carried these burdens into the election campaign of 1976, while contending with a major challenge from the Republican right. Blasting Nixon's and Ford's foreign policy of détente for causing the "loss of U.S. military supremacy," California governor Reagan came close to capturing the nomination.

The Democrats nominated James Earl "Jimmy" Carter Jr., former governor of Georgia. A graduate of the U.S. Naval Academy, Carter spent seven years as a nuclear engineer in the navy before returning to Plains, Georgia, to run the family peanut farming business. Carter stressed his faith as a "born-again Christian" and his distance from the government in Washington. Although he selected liberal senator Walter F. Mondale of Minnesota as his running mate, Carter's nomination nonetheless marked a rightward turn in the party.

Carter had considerable appeal as a candidate who carried his own bags, lived modestly, and taught a Bible class at his Baptist church. He also benefited from Ford's failure to solve the country's economic problems, which helped him win the traditional Democratic coalition of blacks, organized labor, and ethnic groups and even recapture some of the white southerners who had voted for Nixon in 1972. Still, Carter received just 50 percent of the popular vote to Ford's 48 percent, while Democrats retained substantial margins in Congress (Map 30.1).

REVIEW   How did Nixon's policies reflect the increasing influence of conservatives on the Republican Party?

▶ The "Outsider" Presidency of Jimmy Carter

Jimmy Carter promised a government that was "competent" as well as "decent, open, fair, and compassionate." He also warned Americans "that even our great Nation has its recognized limits, and that we can neither answer all questions nor solve all problems." Carter's humility and personal integrity helped revive trust in the presidency, but he faltered in the face of domestic and foreign crises.

Energy shortages and stagflation worsened, exposing Carter's deficiencies in working with Congress and rallying public opinion. He achieved notable advances in environmental and energy policies, and he oversaw foreign policy successes concerning the Panama Canal, China, and the Middle East. Yet near the end of his term, Soviet-American relations deteriorated, new crises emerged in the Middle East, and the economy plummeted.

Retreat from Liberalism

Carter vowed "to help the poor and aged, to improve education, and to provide jobs," but at the same time "not to waste money." When these goals conflicted, budget balancing took priority over reform. Carter's approach pleased Americans unhappy about their tax dollars being used to benefit the disadvantaged while stagflation eroded their own standard of living. But his fiscal stringency frustrated liberal Democrats pushing for

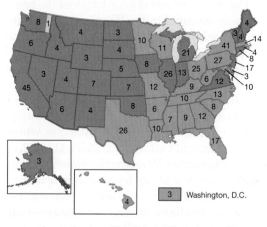

Candidate	Electoral Vote	Popular Vote	Percent of Popular Vote
Jimmy Carter (Democrat)	297	40,830,763	50.1
Gerald R. Ford (Republican)	240	39,147,793	48.0
Ronald Reagan (Independent Republican)	1	n/a	n/a

Map 30.1
The Election of 1976

major welfare reform and a national health insurance program. Carter himself said, "In many cases I feel more at home with the conservative Democratic and Republican members of Congress than I do with the others."

Although Carter did fulfill liberals' desire to make government more inclusive by appointing unprecedented numbers of women and minorities to cabinet, judicial, and diplomatic posts, a number of factors thwarted Carter's policy goals. His outsider status helped him win the election but left him without strong ties to party leaders in Congress. Democrats complained that Carter flooded them with comprehensive proposals without consultation or a strategy to get them enacted. Even if he had possessed Lyndon Johnson's political skills, Carter might not have done much better. The economic problems he inherited—unemployment, inflation, and sluggish economic growth—confounded economic doctrine. Usually, rising prices accompanied a humming economy with a strong demand for labor. Now, however, stagflation burdened the economy with both steep inflation and high unemployment, enlarging the federal budget deficit.

Carter first targeted unemployment, signing bills that pumped $14 billion into the economy through public works and public service jobs programs and cutting taxes by $34 billion. Unemployment receded, but then inflation surged. Working people, wrote one journalist, "winced and ached" as their paychecks bought less and less, "hollowing their hopes and dreams, their plans for a house or their children's college education." To curb inflation, Carter curtailed federal spending, and the Federal Reserve Board tightened the money supply. Not only did these measures fail to halt inflation, which surpassed 13 percent in 1980, but they also contributed to rising unemployment, reversing the gains made in Carter's first two years.

Carter's commitment to restraining the federal budget frustrated Democrats pushing for comprehensive welfare reform, national health insurance, and a substantial jobs program that would make government the employer of last resort. His refusal to propose a comprehensive national health insurance plan, long a key Democratic Party objective, led to a bitter split with Massachusetts senator Ted Kennedy, who fought Carter for the 1980 presidential nomination. Carter's agreement to legislation to ensure solvency in the Social Security system resulted in higher payroll taxes on lower- and middle-income Americans.

Jimmy Carter's Inauguration
At the close of his inauguration in January 1977, Carter was the first president to walk from the Capitol to the White House, to symbolize his connection with ordinary people. As he said subsequently, "Government officials can't be sensitive to your problems if we are living like royalty here." Here he is shown hand in hand with his daughter Amy and wife Rosalynn. Bernard Gotfryd/Getty Images.

By contrast, corporations and wealthy individuals gained from new legislation, such as a sharp cut in the capital gains tax. When the Chrysler Corporation approached bankruptcy, Congress provided $1.5 billion in loan guarantees to bail out the auto giant. Congress also acted on Carter's proposals to deregulate airlines in 1978 and the banking, trucking, and railroad industries in 1980, beginning a policy turn toward implementing conservatives' insistence on a free market and unfettered private enterprise.

Energy and Environmental Reform

Complicating the government's battle with stagflation was the nation's enormous energy

VISUAL ACTIVITY

The Fuel Shortage

This billboard appeared in 1980 while Iran held Americans hostage in Tehran (see page 876). The Iranian revolution brought to power Ayatollah Ruholla Khomeini, pictured on the billboard, and created gasoline shortages and rising gas prices, vexing motorists all over the United States. The ad urges drivers to observe the fuel-saving 55-mile-per-hour speed limit imposed in 1974 during the first oil crisis. Outdoor Advertising Association of America (OAAA) Archives, David M. Rubenstein Rare Book & Manuscript Library, Duke University.

READING THE IMAGE: What assumptions does the billboard make about Americans' reactions to the Iran hostage crisis? What reasons does the ad give for drivers to respect the speed limit? What reasons are not mentioned?

CONNECTIONS: What impact did the hostage and oil crises have on American politics?

consumption and dependence on foreign sources for one-third of its energy demands. Consequently, Carter proposed a comprehensive program to conserve energy, and he elevated its importance by establishing the Department of Energy. Beset with competing demands among energy producers and consumers, Congress picked Carter's program apart. The **National Energy Act of 1978** penalized manufacturers of gas-guzzling automobiles and provided other incentives for conservation and development of alternative fuels, such as wind and solar power, but the act fell far short of a long-term, comprehensive program.

In 1979, a new upheaval in the Middle East, the Iranian revolution, created the most severe energy crisis yet. In midsummer, shortages caused 60 percent of gasoline stations to close down, resulting in long lines and high prices. In response, Congress reduced controls on the oil and gas industry to stimulate American production and imposed a windfall profits tax on producers to redistribute some of the profits they would reap from deregulation.

European nations were no less dependent on foreign oil than the United States, but they more successfully controlled consumption. They levied high taxes on gasoline, encouraging people to use public transportation and manufacturers to produce more energy-efficient cars. In the automobile-dependent United States, however, with inadequate public transit, a sprawling population, and an aversion to taxes, politicians dismissed that approach. By the end of the century, the United States, with 6 percent of the world's population, would consume more than 25 percent of global oil production (Figure 30.1 and Map 30.2).

A vigorous environmental movement opposed nuclear energy as an alternative fuel, warning of radiation leakage, potential accidents, and the hazards of radioactive wastes. In 1976, hundreds of members of the Clamshell Alliance went to jail for attempting to block construction of a nuclear power plant in Seabrook, New Hampshire; other groups sprang up across the country to demand an environment safe from nuclear radiation and waste. The perils of nuclear energy claimed international attention in March 1979, when a meltdown of the reactor core was narrowly averted at the nuclear facility near Harrisburg, Pennsylvania. Popular opposition and the great expense of building nuclear power plants limited development of the industry, which provided 20 percent of the nation's electricity in 2015.

A disaster at Love Canal in Niagara Falls, New York, advanced other environmental goals by underscoring the human costs of unregulated development. Residents suffering high rates of serious illness discovered that their homes sat atop highly toxic waste products from a nearby chemical company. Finally responding to the residents' claims in 1978, the state of New York agreed to help families relocate, and the Carter administration sponsored legislation in 1980 that created the so-called Superfund, $1.6 billion for cleanup of hazardous wastes left by the chemical industry around the country.

Carter also signed bills to improve clean air and water programs; to expand the Arctic National Wildlife Refuge (ANWR) preserve in Alaska; and to control strip mining, which left destructive scars on the land. During the 1979 gasoline crisis, Carter attempted to balance the development of domestic fuel sources with environmental concerns, winning legislation to conserve

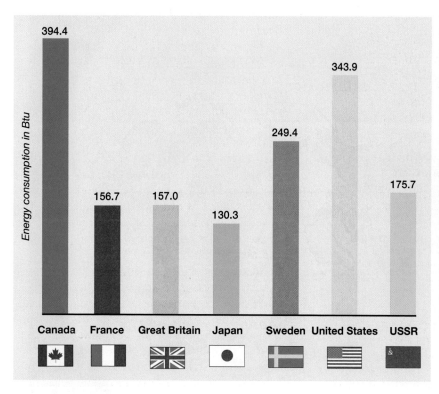

FIGURE 30.1 Global Comparison: Energy Consumption Per Capita, 1980 By 1980, the United States consumed more energy than most other industrialized nations, with a per capita rate of consumption that was more than double that of Britain, France, and Japan and nearly twice as high as that of the Soviet Union. A number of factors influence a nation's energy consumption, including standard of living, climate, size of landmass, population distribution, availability and price of energy, and government policies.

energy and to provide incentives for the development of solar energy and environmentally friendly alternative fuels.

Promoting Human Rights Abroad

"We're ashamed of what our government is as we deal with other nations around the world," Jimmy Carter charged, promising to reverse U.S. support of dictators, secret diplomacy, interference in the internal affairs of other countries, and excessive reliance on military solutions. Human rights formed the cornerstone of his approach. The Carter administration applied economic pressure on governments that denied their citizens basic rights, refusing aid or trading privileges to nations such as Chile and El Salvador, as well as to the white minority governments of Rhodesia and South Africa. Yet in other instances, Carter sacrificed human rights ideals to strategic and security considerations, invoking no sanctions against repressive governments in Iran, South Korea, and the Philippines.

Carter's human rights principles faced another test when a popular movement overthrew an oppressive dictatorship in Nicaragua. U.S. officials were uneasy about the leftist Sandinistas who led the rebellion and had ties to Cuba. Once the Sandinistas assumed power in 1979, however, Carter recognized the new government and sent economic aid, signaling that how a government treated its citizens was as important as how anti-Communist and friendly to American interests it was.

Applying moral principles to relations with Panama, Carter sped up negotiations over control of the Panama Canal, and in 1977 signed a treaty providing for Panama's takeover of the canal in 2000. Supporters viewed the treaty as restitution for the use of U.S. power to gain control of the territory in 1903. Opponents insisted on retaining the vital waterway. "We bought it, we paid for it, it's ours," claimed Ronald Reagan during the presidential primaries of 1976. It took a massive effort by the administration to get Senate ratification of the **Panama Canal treaty**.

Seeking to promote peace in the Middle East, Carter seized on the courage of Egyptian president Anwar Sadat, the first Arab leader to risk his political career by talking directly with Israeli officials. In 1979, Carter invited Sadat and Israeli prime minister Menachem Begin to Camp David, Maryland, where he applied his tenacious diplomacy for thirteen days. These talks led to the **Camp David accords**, whereby Egypt became the first Arab state to recognize Israel, and Israel agreed to gradual withdrawal from the Sinai

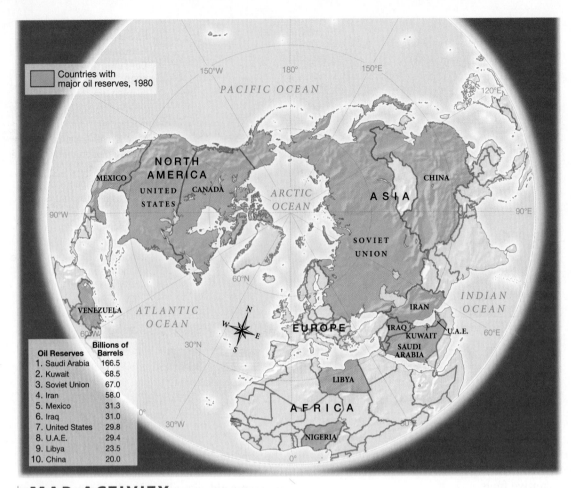

MAP ACTIVITY

Map 30.2   Worldwide Oil Reserves, 1980

Geologists and engineers can estimate the size of "proved oil reserves," quantities recoverable with existing technology and prices. In 1980, worldwide reserves were estimated at 645 billion barrels. Recovery of reserves depends on many factors, including the location of the oil. Large portions of U.S. reserves, for example, lie under the Gulf of Mexico, where it is expensive to drill and where hurricanes can disrupt operations.

READING THE MAP: Where did the United States rank in 1980 in the possession of oil reserves? About what portion of the total oil reserves were located in the Middle East?

CONNECTIONS: When during the 1970s did the United States experience oil shortages? What caused these shortages?

Peninsula, which it had seized in the 1967 Six-Day War (Map 30.3). Although Israel maintained control of other Palestinian land (the West Bank and Gaza) and continued to settle Israelis there, Carter had nurtured the first meaningful steps toward peace in the Middle East (see "Shoring Up U.S. Interests around the World" in chapter 29).

The Cold War Intensifies

Consistent with his human rights approach, Carter preferred to pursue national security through nonmilitary means and initially sought accommodation with the nation's Cold War enemies. Following up on Nixon's initiatives, in 1979 he opened formal diplomatic relations with the People's Republic of China and signed a second strategic arms reduction treaty with Soviet premier Leonid Brezhnev.

Yet that same year, Carter decided to pursue a military buildup when the Soviet Union invaded neighboring Afghanistan, whose recently installed Communist government was threatened by Muslim opposition (see Map 30.3). Carter imposed economic sanctions on the Soviet Union, barred U.S. participation in the 1980 Summer Olympic

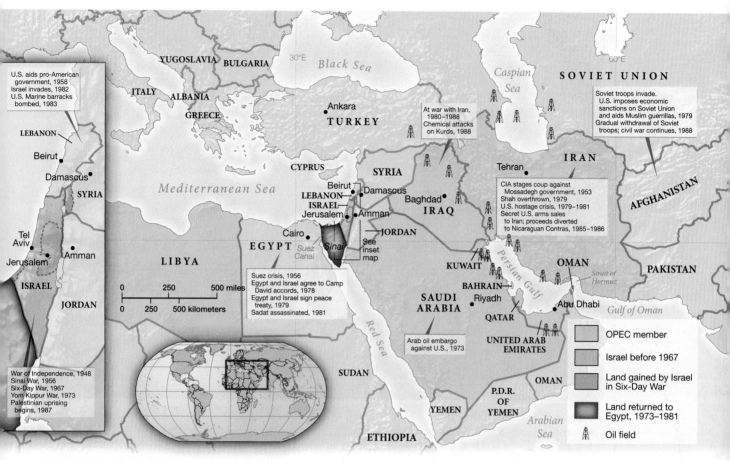

U.S. aids pro-American
government, 1958
Israel invades, 1982
U.S. Marine barracks
bombed, 1983

LEBANON

Beirut

Damascus

SYRIA

Tel
Aviv

Jerusalem   Amman

ISRAEL

JORDAN

War of Independence, 1948
Sinai War, 1956
Six-Day War, 1967
Yom Kippur War, 1973
Palestinian uprising
begins, 1987

YUGOSLAVIA   BULGARIA   30°E   Black Sea   60°E   SOVIET UNION

ITALY   ALBANIA   Soviet troops invade.
                                                                          U.S. imposes economic
GREECE   Ankara   sanctions on Soviet Union
                                 TURKEY   At war with Iran,   and aids Muslim guerrillas, 1979
                                               1980–1988   Gradual withdrawal of Soviet
                                               Chemical attacks   troops; civil war continues, 1988
                                               on Kurds, 1988

CYPRUS   SYRIA   Tehran   IRAN
Mediterranean Sea   AFGHANISTAN
                   Beirut   Damascus   CIA stages coup against
                   LEBANON   Baghdad   Mossadegh government, 1953
                   ISRAEL   IRAQ   Shah overthrown, 1979
                   Jerusalem   Amman   U.S. hostage crisis, 1979–1981
                   Cairo   JORDAN   Secret U.S. arms sales
EGYPT   Suez   to Iran; proceeds diverted
        Canal   Sinai   to Nicaraguan Contras, 1985–1986
LIBYA   See
                        inset   PAKISTAN
                        map   KUWAIT   OMAN   Strait of
0   250   500 miles   Hormuz
                                           BAHRAIN
0   250   500 kilometers   SAUDI   OMAN
                                           ARABIA   Riyadh
Suez crisis, 1956   Abu Dhabi   Gulf of Oman
Egypt and Israel agree to Camp   QATAR
David accords, 1978
Egypt and Israel sign peace   UNITED ARAB   OPEC member
treaty, 1979   EMIRATES
Sadat assassinated, 1981   Israel before 1967
                   Arab oil embargo
                   against U.S., 1973   Land gained by Israel
                                                         in Six-Day War
SUDAN   OMAN
                                                         Land returned to
                                    P.D.R.   Egypt, 1973–1981
                                    OF
                   YEMEN   YEMEN   Arabian   Oil field
ETHIOPIA   Sea

MAP ACTIVITY

Map 30.3 The Middle East, 1948–1989

Determination to preserve access to the rich oil reserves of the Middle East and commitment to the security of Israel were fundamental—and often conflicting—principles of U.S. foreign policy in that region.

READING THE MAP: Where did the United States become involved diplomatically or militarily in the Middle East between 1948 and 1989?

CONNECTIONS: What role did U.S. foreign policy regarding the Middle East and events in Israel play in provoking the 1973 Arab oil embargo against the United States? What precipitated the taking of U.S. hostages in Iran in 1979?

Games in Moscow, and obtained legislation requiring all nineteen-year-old men to register for the draft.

Claiming that Soviet actions jeopardized oil supplies from the Middle East, the president announced the "Carter Doctrine," threatening the use of any means necessary to prevent an outside force from gaining control of the Persian Gulf. His human rights policy fell by the wayside as the United States stepped up aid to the military dictatorship in Afghanistan's neighbor, Pakistan, and the CIA funneled secret aid through Pakistan to the Afghan rebels. Finally, Carter called for hefty increases in defense spending.

Events in Iran also encouraged this hard-line approach. Generous U.S. arms and aid had not

enabled the shah to crush Iranian dissidents who still resented the CIA's role in the overthrow of the Mossadegh government in 1953 (see "Interventions in Latin America and the Middle East" in chapter 27), condemned the shah's brutal attempts to silence opposition, and detested his adoption of Western culture and values. These grievances erupted into a revolution in 1979 that forced out the shah and brought to power Shiite Islamic fundamentalists led by Ayatollah Ruholla Khomeini, whom the shah had exiled in 1964.

Carter's decision to allow the shah into the United States for medical treatment enraged Iranians, who believed that the United States would restore him to power as it had done in

American Hostages in Iran
Less than a month after Iranian militants seized the U.S. Embassy in Tehran and took Americans hostage, the Iranian leader Ayatollah Khomeini ordered the release of thirteen hostages, all women or African Americans, because he believed they were not spies and had already endured "the oppression of American society." Here, in front of propaganda, they are presented to the press shortly before their release. Bettmann/Corbis.

1953. On November 4, 1979, a crowd broke into the U.S. Embassy in Iran's capital, Tehran, and seized sixty-six U.S. diplomats, CIA officers, citizens, and military attachés. Refusing the captors' demands to return the shah to Iran for trial, Carter froze Iranian assets in U.S. banks and placed an embargo on Iranian oil. In April 1980, he sent a small military operation into Iran, but the rescue mission failed.

The disastrous rescue attempt and scenes of blindfolded U.S. citizens paraded before TV cameras fed Americans' feelings of impotence, simmering since the defeat in Vietnam. These frustrations in turn increased support for a more militaristic foreign policy. Opposition to Soviet-American détente, combined with the Soviet invasion of Afghanistan, nullified the thaw in superpower relations that had begun in the 1960s. Iran released a handful of the captives (primarily women and African Americans), but the **Iran hostage crisis** dominated the news during the 1980 presidential campaign and contributed to

Carter's defeat. Iran freed the remaining fifty-

> **REVIEW**   How did Carter implement his commitment to human rights, and why did human rights give way to other priorities?

▶ Ronald Reagan and the Conservative Ascendancy

The election of Ronald Reagan in 1980 marked the most important turning point in politics since Franklin D. Roosevelt's election in 1932. Reagan's victory established conservatism's dominance in the Republican Party, while Democrats searched for votes by moving toward the right. The United

States was not alone in this political shift. Conservatives rose to power in Britain with the election of Prime Minister Margaret Thatcher, and they led governments in Germany, Canada, and Sweden, while social democratic governments elsewhere trimmed their welfare states.

The Reagan administration embraced the values of the New Christian Right, but it left its most important mark on the economy: victory over inflation, deregulation of industry, enormous tax cuts, and a staggering federal budget deficit. Popular culture celebrated financial success, but poverty increased and economic inequality grew. Although the Reagan era did not see a policy revolution comparable to that of the New Deal, it dealt a sharp blow to the liberalism that had informed American politics since the 1930s.

Appealing to the New Right and Beyond

Sixty-nine-year-old Ronald Reagan was the oldest candidate ever nominated for the presidency. Gaining national attention first as a movie actor, he initially shared the politics of his staunchly Democratic father but moved to the right in the 1940s and 1950s and campaigned for Barry Goldwater in 1964.

Reagan's political career took off when he was elected governor of California in 1966. He ran as a conservative, but in office he displayed flexibility, approving a major tax increase, a strong water pollution bill, and a liberal abortion law. Displaying similar agility in the 1980 presidential campaign, he softened earlier attacks on programs such as Social Security and chose the moderate George H. W. Bush as his running mate.

Some Republicans balked at his nomination and the party platform, which reflected the concerns of the party's right wing. For example, after Phyllis Schlafly persuaded the party to reverse its forty-year support for the Equal Rights Amendment, moderate and liberal Republicans protested outside the convention hall. Moderate John B. Anderson, congressman from Illinois, deserted his party to run as an independent.

Reagan's campaign capitalized on the economic recession and the international challenges symbolized by the American hostages in Iran. Repeatedly, Reagan asked voters, "Are you better off now than you were four years ago?" He promised to "take government off the backs of the people" and to restore Americans' morale and other nations' respect. Reagan won the election, and Republicans took control of the Senate for the first time since the 1950s.

While the economy and the Iran hostage crisis sealed Reagan's victory, he also benefited from the burgeoning grassroots conservative movement that had pushed Goldwater's candidacy in 1964. That movement grew with the politicization of religious conservatives, predominantly Protestants who had traditionally refrained from partisan politics and who came to be known as the **New Christian Right**. During the 1970s, evangelical and fundamentalist Christianity claimed thousands of new adherents. Evangelical ministers such as Pat Robertson preached to huge television audiences, attacking feminism, abortion, and homosexuality. They called for the restoration of old-fashioned "family values." A considerable number of Catholics, such as Phyllis Schlafly, shared the fundamentalists' goal of a return to "Christian values."

Conservatives created political organizations such as the Moral Majority, founded by the Reverend Jerry Falwell in 1979, to fight "left-wing, social welfare bills, . . . pornography, homosexuality, [and] the advocacy of immorality in school textbooks." Dr. James Dobson, a psychologist with a popular Christian talk show, founded the Family Research Council in 1983 to lobby Congress for measures to curb abortion, divorce, homosexuality, and single motherhood. The instruments of more traditional conservatives, who stressed limited government at home and militant anticommunism abroad, likewise flourished, while Schlafly's newsletter merged the sentiments of the old and new right.

Reagan spoke for the Christian Right on such issues as abortion and school prayer, but he did not push hard for so-called moral policies. Instead, his major achievements fulfilled goals of the older right—strengthening the nation's anti-Communist posture and reducing taxes and government restraints on free enterprise. "In the present crisis," Reagan declared, "government is not the solution to our problem; government is the problem."

Reagan was extraordinarily popular, appealing even to Americans who opposed his policies but warmed to his optimism, confidence, and easygoing humor. Ignoring the darker moments of the American past, he presented a version of history that Americans could feel good about. Declaring that it was "morning in America," he promised an even more glorious future.

Ronald Reagan Addresses Religious Conservatives
Reagan's victory in 1980 helped to reshape the Republican Party by attracting millions of evangelical Christians. In his 1983 address to the National Association of Evangelicals, Reagan called the Soviet Union an "evil empire" and appealed to religious conservatives with strong words about abortion and prayer in the schools, rejoicing that "America is in the midst of a spiritual awakening and a moral renewal." Ronald Reagan Presidential Library.

Unleashing Free Enterprise

Reagan's first domestic objective was a massive tax cut. To justify tax cuts in the face of a large budget deficit, Reagan relied on a new theory called **supply-side economics**, which held that cutting taxes would actually increase revenue by enabling businesses to expand, encouraging individuals to work harder because they could keep more of their earnings (especially the wealthy, who enjoyed the greatest tax savings), and increase the production of goods and services—the supply—which in turn would boost demand. Reagan promised that the economy would grow so much that the government would recoup the lost taxes, but instead it incurred a galloping deficit.

In the summer of 1981, Congress passed the **Economic Recovery Tax Act**, the largest tax reduction in U.S. history. Rates were cut from 14 percent to 11 percent for the lowest-income individuals and from 70 percent to 50 percent for the wealthiest, who also benefited from reduced levies on corporations, capital gains, gifts, and inheritances. A second measure, the Tax Reform Act of 1986, cut taxes still further. Although the 1986 law narrowed loopholes used primarily by the wealthy, affluent Americans saved far more on their tax bills than did average taxpayers, and the distribution of wealth tipped further in favor of the rich.

Carter had confined deregulation to particular industries, such as air transportation and banking, while increasing health, safety, and environmental regulations. The Reagan administration, by contrast, pursued across-the-board deregulation. It declined to enforce the Sherman Antitrust Act (see "Railroads, Trusts, and the Federal Government" in chapter 18), which limited monopolies, against an unprecedented number of business mergers and takeovers. Reagan also loosened regulations protecting employee health and safety, and he weakened labor unions. When members of the Professional Air Traffic Controllers Organization—one of the few unions to support Reagan in 1980—struck in 1981, the president fired them, destroying the union and intimidating organized labor.

Reagan blamed environmental laws for the nation's sluggish economic growth and targeted them for deregulation. His first secretary of the interior, James Watt, declared, "We will mine more, drill more, cut more timber," and released federal lands to private exploitation. Meanwhile, the head of the Environmental Protection Agency relaxed enforcement of air and water pollution standards. Of environmentalists, Reagan wisecracked, "I don't think they'll be happy until the White House looks like a bird's nest," but their numbers grew in opposition to his policies. Popular support for environmental protection forced several officials to resign and blocked full realization of Reagan's deregulatory goals.

Deregulation of the banking industry, begun under Carter with bipartisan support, created a crisis in the savings and loan (S&L) industry. Some of the newly deregulated S&L institutions extended enormous loans to real estate developers and invested in other high-yield but risky ventures. The lenders reaped lavish profits, and their depositors enjoyed high interest rates, but when real estate values plunged, hundreds of S&Ls went bankrupt, creating the largest financial scandal in U.S. history thus far. The government bailout of the industry in 1989 cost American taxpayers more than $100 billion.

The S&L crisis deepened the federal deficit. Reagan cut funds for food stamps, job training, student aid, and other social welfare programs, and hundreds of thousands of people lost benefits. Yet increases in defense spending far exceeded the budget cuts and, along with the tax cuts, caused the deficit to soar. The nation's debt tripled to $2.3 trillion, consuming one-seventh of all federal expenditures. Despite Reagan's antigovernment rhetoric, the number of federal employees increased from 2.9 million to 3.1 million during his presidency.

It took the severest recession since the 1930s to squeeze inflation out of the U.S. economy. Unemployment approached 11 percent late in 1982, and record numbers of banks and businesses closed. The threat of unemployment further undermined organized labor, forcing unions to make concessions that management insisted were necessary for industry's survival. In 1983, the economy recovered and entered a period of unprecedented growth.

That economic upswing and Reagan's own popularity posed a formidable challenge to the Democrats in the 1984 election. They nominated Carter's vice president, Walter F. Mondale, to head the ticket, but even his precedent-breaking choice of a woman as his running mate—New York representative Geraldine A. Ferraro—did not save the Democrats from a humiliating defeat. Reagan charged his opponents with concentrating on America's failures, while he emphasized success and possibility. Democrats, he claimed,

"see an America where every day is April 15th [the deadline for income tax returns] . . . we see an America where every day is the Fourth of July." Reagan was reelected in a landslide victory, winning 59 percent of the popular vote and every state but Mondale's Minnesota.

Winners and Losers in a Flourishing Economy

After the economy took off in 1983, some Americans won great fortunes. Popular culture celebrated making money and displaying wealth. Books by business wizards topped best seller lists, the press described lavish million-dollar parties, and a new television show, *Lifestyles of the Rich and Famous*, drew large audiences. College students listed making money as their primary ambition.

Many of the newly wealthy got rich from moving assets around rather than from producing goods, making money by manipulating debt and restructuring corporations through mergers and takeovers. Notable exceptions included Steven Jobs, who invented the Apple computer in his garage; Bill Gates, who transformed the software industry; and Liz Claiborne, who created a billion-dollar fashion enterprise. Most financial wizards operated within the law, but greed sometimes led to criminal convictions.

Older industries faced increasing international pressures, as German and Japanese corporations overtook U.S. manufacturing in steel, automobiles, and electronics. International competition forced the collapse of some companies, while others moved factories and jobs abroad to be closer to foreign markets or to benefit from the low wages in countries such as Mexico and Korea. Service industries expanded and created new jobs at home, but at substantially lower wages. The number of full-time workers earning wages below the poverty level ($12,195 for a family of four in 1990) rose from 12 percent to 18 percent of all workers in the 1980s.

The weakening of organized labor combined with the decline in manufacturing to erode the position of blue-collar workers. Chicago steelworker Ike Mazo, who contemplated the $6-an-hour jobs available to him, fumed, "It's an attack on the living standards of workers." Increasingly, a second income was needed to stave off economic decline. By 1990, nearly 60 percent of married women with young children worked outside the home. Yet even with two incomes, families struggled. Speaking of her children, Mazo's wife confessed, "I worry about their future every day. Will we be able to put them through college?" The average $10,000 gap between men's and women's annual earnings made things even harder for the nearly 20 percent of families headed by women.

In keeping with conservative philosophy, Reagan adhered to trickle-down economics, insisting that the benefits of a booming economy would trickle down to everyone. Average personal income did rise during his tenure, but the trend toward greater economic inequality that had begun in the 1970s intensified in the 1980s, encouraged in part by his tax policies. During Reagan's presidency, the percentage of Americans living in poverty increased from 11.7 to 13.5, the highest poverty rate in the industrialized world. Social Security and Medicare helped to stave off destitution among the elderly. Less fortunate were other groups that the economic boom had bypassed: racial minorities, female-headed families, and children. One child in five lived in poverty.

> **REVIEW**   What conservative goals were realized in the Reagan administration?

▶ Continuing Struggles over Rights

The rise of conservatism put liberal social movements on the defensive, as the government abandoned the commitment to equal opportunity undertaken in the 1960s and the president's federal court appointments reflected that shift. Feminists and minority groups fought to keep protections they had recently won, and the newer gay and lesbian rights movement made some gains.

Battles in the Courts and Congress

Ronald Reagan agreed with conservatives that the nation had moved too far in guaranteeing rights to minority groups. Crying "reverse discrimination," conservatives maintained that affirmative action unfairly hurt whites, ignoring statistics showing that minorities and white women still lagged far behind white men in opportunities and income. Black labor leader Cleveland Robinson pointed to the difficulty of achieving equal opportunity in a faltering economy, calling full employment "the basic ingredient of successful affirmative

action." Without it, "you will have both blacks and whites fighting for the same job." Intense mobilization by civil rights groups, educational leaders, labor, and even corporate America prevented the administration from abandoning affirmative action, and the Supreme Court upheld important antidiscrimination policies. Moreover, against Reagan's wishes, Congress extended the Voting Rights Act with veto-proof majorities. The administration did, however, limit civil rights enforcement by appointing conservatives to the Justice Department, the Civil Rights Commission, and other agencies as well as by slashing their budgets.

Congress stepped in to defend antidiscrimination programs after the Justice Department, in the case of *Grove City v. Bell* (1984), persuaded the Supreme Court to severely weaken Title IX of the Education Amendments Act of 1972, a key law promoting equal opportunity in education. In 1988, Congress passed the Civil Rights Restoration Act over Reagan's veto, reversing the administration's victory in *Grove City* and banning government funding of any organization that practiced discrimination on the basis of race, color, national origin, sex, disability, or age.

The *Grove City* decision reflected a rightward movement in the federal judiciary, on which liberals had counted as a powerful ally. With the opportunity to appoint half of the 761 federal court judges and three new Supreme Court justices, President Reagan encouraged the rightward trend by carefully selecting conservative candidates. The full impact of these appointments became clear after Reagan left office, as the Court allowed states to impose restrictions that weakened access to abortion for poor and rural women, reduced protections against employment discrimination, and whittled down legal safeguards against the death penalty.

Feminism on the Defensive

A signal achievement of the New Right was capturing the Republican Party's position on women's rights. For the first time in its history, the party took an explicitly antifeminist tone, opposing both the **Equal Rights Amendment (ERA)** and abortion rights, key goals of women's rights activists. When the time limit for ratification of the ERA ran out in 1982, Phyllis Schlafly and her followers celebrated the defeat of a central feminist objective. (See "Making Historical Arguments," page 882.)

Ratified the ERA

Did not ratify the ERA

Ratified and then voted to rescind ratification

The Fight for the Equal Rights Amendment

Cast on the defensive, feminists focused more on women's economic and family problems, where they found some common ground with the Reagan administration. The Child Support Enforcement Amendments Act helped single and divorced mothers collect court-ordered child support payments from absent fathers. The Retirement Equity Act of 1984 benefited divorced and older women by strengthening their claims to their husbands' pensions and enabling women to qualify more easily for private retirement pensions.

Reagan's advisers had their own concerns about women, specifically about the gender gap in voting—women's tendency to support liberal and Democratic candidates in larger numbers than men did. Reagan appointed three women to cabinet posts and, in 1981, selected the first woman, Sandra Day O'Connor, a moderate conservative, for the Supreme Court, despite the Christian Right's objection to her support of abortion. But these actions accompanied a general decline in the number of women and minorities in high-level government positions. And with higher poverty rates than men, women suffered most from Reagan's cuts in social programs.

Although Supreme Court decisions allowed increasing restrictions on women's ability to obtain abortions, feminists fought successfully to retain the basic principles of *Roe v. Wade*. Moreover, they won a key decision from the Supreme Court ruling that sexual harassment in the workplace constituted sex discrimination. Feminists also made some gains at the state level on such issues as pay equity, rape, and domestic violence.

VISUAL ACTIVITY

The Abortion Debate
After the *Roe v. Wade* decision in 1973, several states enacted restrictions on abortion. In 1989, the Supreme Court upheld a Missouri law prohibiting public employees from performing abortions except to save a woman's life. It also banned abortions in public buildings and required physicians to perform viability tests on the fetus after twenty weeks. Here, activists on both sides rally before the Supreme Court. AP Photo/Ron Edmonds.
READING THE IMAGE: What arguments do the signs of the abortion opponents make?
CONNECTIONS: How did other elements of the feminist agenda fare in the 1980s?

The Gay and Lesbian Rights Movement

In contrast to feminism and other social movements, gay and lesbian rights activism grew during the 1980s, galvanized in part by the

VISUAL ACTIVITY

Gay Rights Parade
Annual gay rights parades in the United States began in June 1970, the first anniversary of Stonewall (see chapter 28). More than 150,000 people marched in this parade in New York City in 1989, including many friends and relatives of homosexuals. Here, E. G. Smith wears the "rainbow" colors of the movement, while his grandmother, Norma Isaacs, demonstrates her support. AP Photo/Sergio Florez.
READING THE IMAGE: Notice the building on the parade route. Why would the organizers have chosen this street? How might bystanders have responded to the presence of Norma Isaacs?
CONNECTIONS: What gains did the gay and lesbian rights movement make during the 1980s?

Why Did the ERA Fail?

The proposed Equal Rights Amendment to the U.S. Constitution guaranteed that "equality of rights under the law shall not be denied or abridged by the United States or by any State on account of sex." Two more short sections gave Congress enforcement powers and provided that the ERA would take effect two years after ratification. By the 1970s, it had become the symbol of the women's movement, and the controversy it sparked revealed profound differences in beliefs and values among Americans.

The National Woman's Party, a militant suffrage organization that had helped win the vote for women in 1920, first proposed an equal rights amendment to the Constitution in 1923. It won little support, however, before the resurgence of feminism in the late 1960s, when the National Organization for Women and other women's groups made the ERA a key objective.

Both houses of Congress passed the ERA in March 1972 by overwhelming margins, 354–23 in the House and 84–8 in the Senate. Within three hours, Hawai'i rushed to become the first state to ratify, and twenty-three states quickly followed. Public opinion heavily favored ratification, peaking at 74 percent in favor in 1974 and never falling below 52 percent, while opposition never topped 31 percent. Yet even after Congress extended the ratification period until 1982,

the ERA fell three short of the three-fourths of the states required by the Constitution (see The Fight for the Equal Rights Amendment spot map on page 880). Why did a measure with so much congressional and popular support fail?

The ERA encountered well-organized and passionate opposition linked to the growing conservative forces in the 1970s. Conservatives' opposition to the ERA reflected in part their distaste for big government, but even more it signaled the Christian Right's determination to preserve traditional gender roles and "family values." What feminists saw as a simple measure to ensure equal rights for all citizens, ERA opponents saw as a threat to women's God-given and natural right to be protected and supported by men. They raised fears by suggesting extravagant ways in which courts might interpret the amendment. Phyllis Schlafly claimed that the ERA would put abortion rights and gay rights into the Constitution, deprive women of alimony and child support, and send them into combat.

Anti-ERA arguments drew on conservative Christian beliefs. Evangelical minister and politician Jerry Falwell declared the ERA "a definite violation of holy Scripture [and its] mandate that 'the husband is the head of the wife.'" Anti-ERA rhetoric also appealed to some women's understanding of their own self-interest. Many ERA opponents

were full-time housewives who had no stake in equal treatment in the marketplace and who feared that the amendment would eliminate the duty of men to support their families.

Schlafly and other conservatives skillfully mobilized women who saw their traditional roles threatened. In October 1972, she established a national movement called STOP (Stop Taking Our Privileges) ERA, whose members deluged legislators with letters and lobbied them personally in state capitols. In Illinois, they gave lawmakers apple pies with notes that read, "My heart and my hand went into this dough / For the sake of the family please vote 'no.'" Opponents also brought baby girls to the legislature wearing signs that pleaded, "Please don't draft me."

ERA opponents had an easier task than supporters because the framers of the Constitution had stacked the odds against revision. All opponents had to do was convince a minority of legislators in a minority of states to preserve the status quo. In addition, unlike their suffragist predecessors, pro-ERA forces had concentrated on winning Congress and were not prepared for the state campaigns.

The very gains that feminists made in the 1960s and 1970s also worked against ratification. Congress had banned sex discrimination in employment, education, and other areas, and the Supreme Court had struck down several discriminatory laws, thus making it harder for ERA advocates to demonstrate the urgency of constitutional revision.

The ERA failed because a handful of men in a handful of state legislatures voted against it. The shift of only a few votes in states such as Illinois and North Carolina would have meant ratification. Schlafly's

discovery in 1981 of a devastating disease, acquired immune deficiency syndrome (AIDS). Because initially the disease disproportionately affected male homosexuals in the United States, activists mobilized to promote public

funding for AIDS education, prevention, and treatment.

The gay and lesbian rights movement encouraged closeted homosexuals to "come out," and their visibility increased awareness,

Feminists did not leave the ERA battle empty-handed, however. Thousands of women were mobilized on both sides of the issue, participating in the public arena for the first time. Fourteen states passed their own equal rights amendments after 1970. And feminists continued to fight legislative and judicial battles for the expansion of women's rights into the twenty-first century.

Questions for Analysis

Summarize the Argument: What different values were expressed by opponents and supporters of the ERA? What did both sides gain from the campaigns?

Analyze the Evidence: What structural features of the U.S. Constitution made ratification difficult for ERA advocates? What other specific obstacles prevented ERA's passage?

Consider the Context: Why were woman suffrage supporters more successful than ERA advocates in gaining a constitutional amendment?

forces played a key role in the defeat because men could vote no and take cover behind the many women who opposed it. And those women proved willing to commit time, energy, and money to block ratification because they were convinced that the ERA threatened their very way of life.

if not always acceptance, of homosexuality among the larger population. Beginning with the election of Elaine Noble to the Massachusetts legislature in 1974, several openly gay politicians won offices ranging from mayor to member of Congress, and the Democrats began to include gay rights in their party platforms. Activists organized gay rights marches throughout the country, turning out half a million people in New York City in 1987.

Protecting Gay and Lesbian Rights

Since the 1970s, the gay and lesbian rights movement has sought measures to protect homosexuals from discrimination. In 1982, Wisconsin became the first state to ban discrimination on the basis of sexual orientation, following several cities that passed gay rights ordinances in the 1970s. By 2015, twenty-two states and the District of Columbia outlawed employment discrimination against gays, and more than 250 cities and counties did so.

DOCUMENT 1
Ordinance of the City of Minneapolis, 1974

In 1974, the city council of Minneapolis amended its civil rights ordinance to include discrimination based on sexual orientation. The law provided a rationale for banning discrimination and covered a broad range of activities.

It is determined that discriminatory practices based on race, color, creed, religion, national origin, sex, or affectional or sexual preference, with respect to employment, labor union membership, housing accommodations, property rights, education, public accommodations, and public services, or any of them, tend to create and intensify conditions of poverty, ill health, unrest, civil disobedience, lawlessness, and vice and adversely affect the public health, safety, order, convenience, and general welfare; such discriminatory practices threaten the rights, privileges, and opportunities of all inhabitants of the city and such rights, privileges, and opportunities are hereby to be declared civil rights.

Source: From *The Rights of Gay People: The Basic ACLU Guide to a Gay Person's Rights*, ed. E. Carrington Boggan et al. (New York: Avon Books, 1975), 251.

DOCUMENT 2
Paul Moore, Letter to the Editor of the *New York Times*, November 23, 1981

Paul Moore, Episcopal bishop of New York, made a religious argument for gay rights.

I quote our diocesan resolution: "Whereas this Convention, without making any judgment on the morality of homosexuality, agrees that homosexuals are entitled to full civil rights. Now therefore be it resolved this Convention supports laws guaranteeing homosexuals all civil rights guaranteed to other citizens." The Bible stands for justice and compassion for all of God's children. To deny civil rights to anyone for something he or she cannot help is against the clear commandment of justice and love, which is the message of the word of God. As a New Yorker I find it incredible that this great city, populated by more gay persons than any other city in the world, still denies them basic human rights. They make an enormous contribution to the commercial, artistic, and religious life of our city.

Source: Paul Moore, reprinted with the permission of The Archives of the Episcopal Church.

DOCUMENT 3
Vatican Congregation for the Doctrine of the Faith, August 6, 1992

The following statement from the Roman Catholic Church reflects the views of many religious groups that deem homosexuality immoral.

"Sexual orientation" does not constitute a quality comparable to race, ethnic background, etc., in respect to nondiscrimination. Unlike these, homosexual orientation is an objective disorder and evokes moral concern.

There are areas in which it is not unjust discrimination to take sexual orientation into account, for example, in the placement of children for adoption or foster care, in employment of teachers or athletic coaches, and in military recruitment.

Source: From Vatican Doctrine of the Faith, *Origins*, August 6, 1992. Copyright © Libreria Editrice Vaticana. Reprinted by permission.

Popular attitudes about homosexuality moved toward greater tolerance but remained complex, leading to uneven changes in policies. (See "Analyzing Historical Evidence," above.) Dozens of cities banned job discrimination against homosexuals, and beginning with Wisconsin in 1982, some states made sexual orientation a protected category under civil rights laws. Local governments and large corporations began to offer health insurance and other benefits to same-sex domestic partners.

Yet a strong countermovement challenged the drive for gay rights. The Christian Right targeted gays and lesbians as symbols of national immorality, and when the AIDS epidemic appeared, some fundamentalists believed that

DOCUMENT 4
Charles Cochrane Jr., Testimony before the House Subcommittee on Employment Opportunities of the Committee on Education and Labor, January 27, 1982

Congress has considered, but never enacted, legislation banning discrimination on the basis of sexual orientation. Charles Cochrane Jr., an army veteran and police sergeant, testified on behalf of such a bill.

I am very proud of being a New York City policeman. And I am equally proud of being gay. I have always been gay.

I have been out of the closet for 4 years. November 6 was my anniversary. It took me 34 years to muster enough courage to declare myself openly.

We gays are loathed by some, pitied by others, and misunderstood by most. We are not cruel, wicked, cursed, sick, or possessed by demons. We are artists, business people, police officers, and clergymen. We are scientists, truck drivers, politicians; we work in every field. We are loving human beings who are in some ways different. . . .

During the early years of my association with the New York City Police Department a great deal of energy did go into guarding and concealing my innermost feelings. I believed that I would be subjected to ridicule and harassment were my colleagues to learn of my sexual orientation. Happily, when I actually began to integrate the various aspects of my total self, those who knew me did not reject me.

Then what need is there for such legislation as H.R. 1454? The crying need of others, still trapped in their closets, who must be protected, who must be reassured that honesty about themselves and their lives will not cost them their homes or their jobs. . . .

The bill before you will not act as a proselytizing agent in matters of sexual orientation or preference. It will not include affirmative action provisions. Passage of this bill will protect the inherent human rights of all people of the United States, while in no way diminishing the rights of those who do not see the need for such legislation.

Source: *Hearing on H.R. 1454 before the U.S. House Subcommittee on Employment Opportunities of the Committee on Education and Labor*, 97th Cong. 54–56 (1982).

DOCUMENT 5
Carl F. Horowitz, "Homosexuality's Legal Revolution," May 1991

Carl Horowitz, a policy analyst at the Heritage Foundation, a conservative think tank, argues against gay rights.

Homosexual activists have all but completed their campaign to persuade the nation's educational establishment that homosexuality is normal "alternative" behavior, and thus any adverse reaction to it is akin to a phobia, such as fear of heights, or an ethnic prejudice, such as anti-Semitism.

The movement now stands on the verge of fully realizing its use of law to . . . intimidate heterosexuals uncomfortable about coming into contact with it. . . . The movement seeks to win sinecures through the state, and over any objections by "homophobic" opposition. With a cloud of a heavy fine or even a jail sentence hanging over a mortgage lender, a rental agent, or a job interviewer who might be discomforted by them, homosexuals under these laws can win employment, credit, housing, and other economic entitlements. Heterosexuals would have no right to discriminate against homosexuals, but apparently, not vice versa. . . .

Heterosexuals and even "closeted" homosexuals will be at a competitive disadvantage for jobs and housing. . . .

The new legalism will increase heterosexual anger—and even violence—toward homosexuals.

Source: Carl F. Horowitz, "Homosexuality's Legal Revolution," *Freeman*, May 1991.

Questions for Analysis

Analyze the Evidence: Which of these documents discusses how heterosexuals would be affected by laws protecting gay and lesbian rights? What effects do they anticipate?

Consider the Context: Based on these documents, how might the civil rights movement have influenced the authors' views on homosexual rights?

Recognize Viewpoints: What underlying assumptions about gay men and lesbians can you find in the arguments for and against laws to protect homosexual rights?

---

it represented "the wrath of God upon homosexuals." Conservatives succeeded in overturning some homosexual rights measures, which already lagged far behind protections for women and minorities. Many states removed anti-sodomy laws from the books, but in 1986 the Supreme Court upheld the constitutionality of such laws. Until the Court reversed that opinion in 2003, more than a dozen states retained statutes that left homosexuals vulnerable to criminal charges for private consensual behavior.

REVIEW   What gains and setbacks did minorities, feminists, and gays and lesbians experience during the Reagan years?

▶ Ronald Reagan Confronts an "Evil Empire"

Reagan accelerated Carter's arms buildup and harshly censured the Soviet Union, calling it "an evil empire." Yet despite the new aggressiveness— or, as some argued, because of it—Reagan presided over the most impressive thaw in superpower conflict since the Cold War had begun. On the periphery of the Cold War, Reagan practiced militant anticommunism, assisting anti-leftist movements in Asia, Africa, and Central America and dispatching troops to the Middle East and the Caribbean.

Militarization and Interventions Abroad

Reagan expanded the military with new bombers and missiles, an enhanced nuclear force in Europe, a larger navy, and a rapid-deployment force. Throughout Reagan's presidency, defense spending averaged $216 billion a year, up from $158 billion in the Carter years and higher even than in the Vietnam era.

Reagan justified the military buildup as a means to negotiate with the Soviets from a position of strength, but he provoked an outburst of pleas to halt the arms race. In 1982, 750,000 people marched in New York City, demanding a freeze on additional nuclear weapons. That same year the National Conference of Catholic Bishops issued a strong call for nuclear disarmament. Hundreds of thousands demonstrated across Europe, stimulated by fears of new U.S. missiles scheduled for deployment there in 1983.

The U.S. military buildup was powerless before the growing threat of terrorism by nonstate organizations seeking to gain political objectives by attacking civilian populations. Terrorism had a long history throughout the world, but in the 1970s and 1980s Americans

Nuclear Freeze Campaign
In the early 1980s, millions of Europeans and Americans worked to end the nuclear arms race. People marched even in the Soviet Union, where they passed the U.S. Embassy to make sure that news of their demonstration could not be censored. Here 750,000 march in New York City in 1982. The movement pushed Reagan and Gorbachev toward the nuclear arms limitation treaty signed in 1987. Lee Frey/Authenticated News/Getty Images.

saw it escalate among groups hostile to Israel and Western policies. In 1972, for example, after the Israeli occupation of the West Bank, Palestinian terrorists murdered eleven Israeli athletes at the Munich Olympics. The terrorist organization Hezbollah, composed of Shiite Muslims and backed by Iran and Syria, arose in Lebanon in 1982 after Israeli forces invaded that country to stop the Palestine Liberation Organization from using sanctuaries in Lebanon to launch attacks on Israel.

Reagan's effort to stabilize Lebanon by sending 2,000 Marines to join an international peacekeeping mission failed. In April 1983, a suicide attack on the U.S. Embassy in Beirut killed 63 people, and in October a Hezbollah fighter drove a bomb-filled truck into a U.S. barracks there, killing 241 Marines. The attack prompted the withdrawal of U.S. troops, signaling that political violence could affect U.S. policy. Lebanon remained in chaos, while incidents of murder, kidnapping, and hijacking by various Middle Eastern extremist groups continued.

Following a Cold War pattern begun under Dwight D. Eisenhower, the Reagan administration sought to contain leftist movements across the globe. In October 1983, 5,000 U.S. troops invaded Grenada, a small Caribbean nation where Marxists had staged a successful coup. In Asia, the United States covertly aided the Afghan rebels' war against Afghanistan's Soviet-backed government. In the African nation of Angola, the United States armed rebel forces against the government supported by the Soviet Union and Cuba. Reagan also sided with the South African government, which was brutally suppressing black protest against apartheid, forcing Congress to override his veto to impose economic sanctions against South Africa.

Administration officials were most fearful of left-wing movements in Central America, which Reagan claimed could "destabilize the entire region from the Panama Canal to Mexico." When a leftist uprising occurred in El Salvador in 1981, the United States sent money and military advisers to prop up the authoritarian government. In neighboring Nicaragua, the administration secretly aided the Contras, an armed coalition seeking to

El Salvador and Nicaragua

unseat the left-wing Sandinistas, who had toppled a long-standing dictatorship.

The Iran-Contra Scandal

Fearing being drawn into another Vietnam, many Americans opposed aligning the United States with reactionary forces not supported by the majority of Nicaraguans. Congress repeatedly instructed the president to stop aiding the Contras, but the administration continued to secretly provide them with weapons and training. It also helped wreck the Nicaraguan economy. With support for his government undermined, Nicaragua's president, Daniel Ortega, agreed to a political settlement, and when he was defeated by a coalition of all the opposition groups, he stepped aside.

Secret aid to the Contras was part of a larger project that came to be known as the **Iran-Contra scandal**. It began in 1985 when officials of the National Security Council and the CIA covertly arranged to sell arms to Iran, then in the midst of an eight-year war with neighboring Iraq, even while the United States openly supplied Iraq with funds and weapons. The purpose was to get Iran to pressure Hezbollah to release American hostages being held in Lebanon. Profits from the arms sales were then channeled through Swiss bank accounts to aid the Nicaraguan Contras. Over the objections of his secretaries of state and defense, Reagan approved the arms sales to Iran, but the three subsequently denied knowing that the proceeds were diverted to the Contras.

When news of the affair surfaced in November 1986, the Reagan administration faced serious charges. The president's aides had defied Congress's express ban on military aid to the Contras. Investigations by an independent prosecutor led to a trial in which seven individuals pleaded guilty or were convicted of lying to Congress and destroying evidence. One felony conviction was later overturned on a technicality, and President George H. W. Bush pardoned the other six officials in December 1992. The independent prosecutor's final report found no evidence that Reagan had broken the law, but it concluded that he had known about the diversion of

...ures the ...oped between ...d Reagan and ...r Mikhail Gorbachev, ...ere at their first meeting ...neva in November 1985. Al- ...ugh the meeting did not produce any key agreements, the two men began to appreciate each other's concerns and to build trust, launching a relationship that would lead to nuclear arms reductions and the end of the Cold War. Ronald Reagan Presidential Library.

funds to the Contras and had "knowingly participated or at least acquiesced" in covering up the scandal.

A Thaw in Soviet-American Relations

A momentous reduction in Cold War tensions soon overshadowed the Iran-Contra scandal. The new Soviet-American accord depended both on Reagan's flexibility and profound desire to end the possibility of nuclear war and on an innovative Soviet head of state who recognized that his country's domestic problems demanded an easing of Cold War antagonism. Mikhail Gorbachev assumed power in 1985 determined to revitalize an economy incapable of satisfying basic consumer needs. Hoping to stimulate production and streamline distribution of consumer goods, Gorbachev lifted some economic regulations and proclaimed a new era of *glasnost* (greater freedom of expression), eventually allowing contested elections and challenges to Communist rule.

Concerns about immense defense budgets moved both Reagan and Gorbachev to the negotiating table. Enormous military expenditures stood between the Soviet premier and his goal of economic revival. With growing popular support for arms reductions, Reagan made disarmament

a major goal in his last years in office and readily responded when Gorbachev took the initiative. A positive personal chemistry developed between them, and the two leaders met four times between 1985 and 1988. Reagan had to fend off criticism from the hard anti-Communist right, but by December 1987 the superpowers had completed an **intermediate-range nuclear forces (INF) agreement**, marking a major turning point in U.S.-Soviet relations. The treaty eliminated all short- and medium-range missiles from Europe and provided for on-site inspection for the first time. This was also the first time that either nation had agreed to eliminate weapons already in place.

In 1988, Gorbachev further reduced tensions by announcing a gradual withdrawal from Afghanistan, which had become the Soviet equivalent of America's Vietnam. In addition, the Soviet Union, the United States, and Cuba agreed on a political settlement of the civil war in Angola. In the Middle East, both superpowers supported a cease-fire and peace talks in the eight-year war between Iran and Iraq. Within three years, the Cold War that had defined the world for nearly half a century would be history.

REVIEW How did anticommunism shape Reagan's foreign policy?

► Conclusion: Reversing the Course of Government

"Ours was the first revolution in the history of mankind that truly reversed the course of government," boasted Ronald Reagan in his farewell address in 1989. The word *revolution* exaggerated the change, but his administration did mark the slowdown or reversal of expanding federal budgets for domestic programs and regulations that had taken off in the 1930s. Although he did not deliver on the social or moral issues dear to the heart of the New Right, Reagan represented the "choice not an echo" that Phyllis Schlafly had called for in 1964, using his skills as "the Great Communicator" to cultivate antigovernment sentiment and undermine the liberal assumptions of the New Deal.

Antigovernment sentiment grew along with the backlash against the reforms and cultural changes of the 1960s and the conduct of the Vietnam War. Watergate and other lawbreaking by Nixon administration officials further disillusioned Americans. Presidents Ford and Carter restored morality to the White House, but neither could solve the gravest economic problems since the Great Depression—slow economic growth, stagflation, and an increasing trade deficit. Even the Democrat Carter gave higher priority to fiscal austerity than to social reform, stressed the limitations of what government could or should do, and began the government's retreat from regulation of key industries.

A new conservative movement helped Reagan win the presidency and flourished during his administration. Reagan's tax cuts, combined with hefty increases in defense spending, created a federal deficit crisis that justified cuts in social welfare spending, made new federal initiatives unthinkable, and burdened the country for years to come. These policies also contributed to a widening income gap between the rich and poor, weighing especially heavily on minorities, female-headed families, and children. Many Americans continued to support specific federal programs—especially those, such as Social Security and Medicare, that reached beyond the poor—but public sentiment about the government in general had taken a U-turn from the Roosevelt era. Instead of seeing the government as a helpful and problem-solving institution, many believed that it was ineffective at solving national problems and often made things worse. As Reagan appointed new justices, the Supreme Court retreated from liberalism, curbing the government's authority to protect individual rights and regulate the economy.

With the economic recovery that set in after 1982 and his optimistic rhetoric, Reagan lifted the confidence of Americans about their nation and its promise—confidence that had eroded with the economic and foreign policy blows of the 1970s. Beginning his presidency with harsh rhetoric against the Soviet Union and a huge military buildup, he left office having helped move the two superpowers to the highest level of cooperation since the Cold War began. Although that accord was not welcomed by strong anti-Communist conservatives like Phyllis Schlafly, it signaled developments that would transform American-Soviet relations—and the world—in the next decade.

See the Selected Bibliography for this chapter in the Appendix.

Chapter Review

~~~ergate (p. 868)
~~ational Energy Act of 1978 (p. 872)
Panama Canal treaty (p. 873)
Camp David accords (p. 873)
Iran hostage crisis (p. 876)
New Christian Right (p. 877)
supply-side economics (p. 878)
Economic Recovery Tax Act (p. 878)
Equal Rights Amendment (ERA) (p. 880)
Iran-Contra scandal (p. 887)
intermediate-range nuclear forces (INF) agreement
(p. 888)

REVIEW QUESTIONS

1. How did Nixon's policies reflect the increasing in-fluence of conservatives on the Republican Party? (pp. 863–870)

2. How did Carter implement his commitment to human rights, and why did human rights give way to other priorities? (pp. 870–876)

3. What conservative goals were realized in the Reagan administration? (pp. 876–880)

4. What gains and setbacks did minorities, feminists, and gays and lesbians experience during the Reagan years? (pp. 880–885)

5. How did anticommunism shape Reagan's foreign policy? (pp. 886–888)

MAKING CONNECTIONS

1. What was Watergate's legacy for American politics in the following decade? In your answer, explain what led to Nixon's resignation.

2. How did the Republican and Democratic parties change in the 1970s and 1980s? Discuss how those changes shaped American politics.

3. How did Americans' memory of the Vietnam War affect foreign policy in the 1970s and 1980s?

4. Why was grassroots conservatism particularly strong in the Sun Belt in the 1970s and 1980s?

LINKING TO THE PAST

1. How were the conservatives of the 1980s similar to and different from the conservatives who opposed the New Deal in the 1930s? (See chapter 24.)

2. Presidents Jimmy Carter and Woodrow Wilson both claimed human rights as a central principle of their foreign policies. Which one was more suc-cessful in advancing human rights? Explain your answer. (See chapter 22.)

31 The Promises and Challenges of Globalization

Since 1989

After reading and studying this chapter, you should be able to:

- Explain the limited domestic initiatives of George H. W. Bush's presidency, and explain U.S. interventions in Central America and the Persian Gulf.

- Explain the Clinton administration's search for a middle ground in domestic policy, and outline the factors that guided the administration's military interventions around the world.

- Describe the debates over globalization and its effects on the United States.

- Explain George W. Bush's key domestic initiatives and his foreign policy of preemption and unilateralism, including the invasion of Iraq in 2003.

- Describe the historic 2008 presidential election and President Obama's response to domestic and foreign challenges.

CONTAINER BOX
Using truck-size boxes to move goods without loading and unloading individual items became the norm by the 1980s. The container box's efficiency stimulated global industrial development and increased Americans' access to cheaper goods. Oleksiy Mark/Shutterstock.

IN HIS MOSCOW HOTEL ROOM IN APRIL 1988, RONALD REAGAN'S national security adviser, Colin L. Powell, contemplated Soviet premier Mikhail Gorbachev's reforms that would dramatically alter the Soviet Union's government and economy. Powell recalled, "I realized that one phase of my life had ended, and another was about to begin. Up until now, as a soldier, my mission had been to confront, contain, and, if necessary, combat communism. Now I had to think about a world without a Cold War."

Colin Powell was born in Harlem in 1937, the son of Jamaican immigrants who worked in a garment factory. At the City College of New York, he joined the army's Reserve Officers Training Corps (ROTC) program and, on graduation in 1958, began a lifelong career in military and public service, rising to the highest rank of four-star general. He stayed in the army because "I loved what I was doing," but he also knew that "for a black, no other avenue in American society offered so much opportunity." Powell's service in Vietnam taught him that "you do not squander courage and lives without clear purpose, without the country's backing, and without full commitment." In his subsequent positions as national security adviser to Ronald Reagan, chairman of the Joint Chiefs of Staff under George H. W. Bush and William Jefferson (Bill) Clinton, and secretary of state under George W. Bush, Powell endeavored to keep his country out of "halfhearted warfare for half-baked reasons that the American people could not understand or support."

Powell's sense that Gorbachev's reforms would transform the Cold War became a reality more quickly than anyone anticipated. Eastern Europe threw off communism in 1989, and the Soviet Union disintegrated in 1991. Throughout the 1990s, as the lone superpower, the United States deployed military and diplomatic power during episodes of instability in Latin America, the Middle East, Eastern Europe, and Asia, almost always in concert with other major nations. In 1991, the United States led a United Nations–authorized force of twenty-eight nations to repel Iraq's invasion of Kuwait.

In the 1990s, Powell remarked that "neither of the two major parties fits me comfortably." Many Americans seemed to agree: From 1988 to 2016, they elected two Republicans—George H. W. Bush and George W. Bush— and two Democrats—Bill Clinton and Barack Obama—as president, and each faced Congresses where the opposing party controlled at least one house. Bipartisan cooperation produced a few initiatives, including disability rights legislation, welfare reform, drug benefits under Medicare, and expanded federal involvement in public education. But the most far-reaching law—expansion and reform of health care—passed without one Republican vote. In the face of congressional stalemate, Obama used executive powers to achieve modest reforms in the areas of immigration, environmental protection, minimum wage, and gay and transgender rights.

All four presidents supported globalization. As capital, products, information, and people crossed national boundaries in greater numbers and at greater speed, a surge of immigration rivaled the stream that had brought Powell's parents to the United States. Powell shared the worldwide shock when in September 2001 terrorist attacks in New York City and Washington, D.C., exposed American vulnerability to horrifying threats. The United States sent soldiers into Afghanistan to overthrow the government that had harbored the attackers. The administration's response to terrorism overwhelmed Secretary of State Powell's commitments to internationalism, multilateralism, and military restraint when, in 2003, George W. Bush began a second war against Iraq. The unpopularity of that war and a severe financial crisis helped the Democrats regain power and elect Barack Obama as the first African American president in 2008. Obama pursued a more multilateral approach and improved the U.S. image abroad. Nonetheless, although the Iraq War ended, the Middle East grew more unstable and terrorism remained a threat around the world.

► Domestic Stalemate and Global Upheaval: The Presidency of George H. W. Bush

Vice President George H. W. Bush announced his bid for the presidency in 1988, declaring, "We don't need radical new directions." As president, Bush proposed few domestic initiatives, but he signed key environmental and disability rights legislation. More dramatic changes swept through the world, shattering the free-world-versus-communism framework of the Cold War years. Most Americans approved of Bush's handling of the disintegration of the Soviet Union and its hold over Eastern Europe and of his response to Iraq's invasion of Kuwait. But voters' concern over a sluggish economy limited him to one term as president.

Gridlock in Government

The son of a wealthy U.S. senator from New England, George Herbert Walker Bush fought in World War II, served in Congress, and headed the Central Intelligence Agency under Richard Nixon. When Ronald Reagan tapped him for second place on the Republican ticket in 1980, Bush tailored his more moderate positions to Reagan's conservative agenda. At the end of Reagan's second term, Republicans rewarded him with the presidential nomination.

In the Democratic primaries in 1988, civil rights leader Reverend Jesse Jackson—whose Rainbow Coalition campaign centered on the needs of minorities, women, the working class, and the poor—won several primaries and seven million votes. But the centrist candidate, Massachusetts governor Michael Dukakis, won the nomination. On election day, Bush won 54 percent of the vote while the Democrats gained seats in Congress.

Promising "a kinder, gentler nation," President Bush was more inclined than Reagan to approve government activity in the private sphere. For example, Bush approved the **Clean Air Act of 1990**, the strongest, most comprehensive environmental law in history. Some forty million Americans benefited when Bush signed another regulatory measure in 1990, the **Americans with Disabilities Act (ADA)**, banning discrimination against people with disabilities and requiring that private businesses and public facilities be accessible to them. As a breeze rippled over the White House lawn

CHRONOLOGY

1988	• George H. W. Bush elected president.
1989	• Communism collapses in Eastern Europe.
1990	• Americans with Disabilities Act passes.
1991	• Persian Gulf War fought.
1992	• William Jefferson "Bill" Clinton elected president.
1993	• Israel and PLO sign peace accords. • North American Free Trade Agreement signed.
1994	• World Trade Organization established.
1995	• Federal building in Oklahoma City bombed.
1996	• Temporary Assistance for Needy Families program established. • President Clinton reelected.
1998–2000	• United States bombs Iraq.
1999	• Senate trial rejects impeachment of Clinton.
2000	• George W. Bush elected president.
2001	• Terrorists attack World Trade Center and Pentagon. • U.S.-led coalition drives Taliban government out of Afghanistan. • USA Patriot Act passes. • Federal taxes cut by $1.35 trillion.
2002	• No Child Left Behind Act passes.
2003	• United States attacks Iraq.
2004	• President Bush reelected.
2005	• Hurricane Katrina devastates Gulf states.
2008	• Financial crisis leads to Great Recession. • Barack Obama elected president.
2009	• American Recovery and Reinvestment Act passes.
2010	• Patient Protection and Affordable Care Act passes. • Wall Street Reform and Consumer Protection Act passes. • United States ends combat operations in Iraq, increases troops in Afghanistan. • *Citizens United v. FEC* guts regulations on campaign financing.
2011	• Osama bin Laden killed. • Arab Spring uprisings begin.
2012	• President Obama reelected.
2015	• U.S. Supreme Court declares that same-sex couples have constitutional right to marriage. • Iran nuclear deal signed. • United States restores diplomatic relations with Cuba.

Suing for Access: Disability and the Courts

When the ADA passed in 1990, Beverly Jones expressed her elation: "For me, the passage of the ADA was like opening a door that had been closed to me for so long." The measure banned discrimination against people with disabilities by private employers, public agencies, and state and local governments. This civil rights act providing equal access and opportunity followed in a long tradition of Americans fighting for their rights, struggling not only to enact laws but also to see them enforced.

Jones, a single mother with two children, joined the ranks of the 2.2 million wheelchair-users after an automobile accident in 1984 left her with paraplegia. Determined not to "allow what I wanted in life to be denied because of . . . physical limitations," she trained as a court reporter and went to work to support her family. But Jones discovered that despite the requirements of the ADA, in Tennessee seven out of ten courthouses were not wheelchair accessible. "I was often forced to ask complete strangers to carry me up the stairs,"

Jones recalled, and she found the experiences "humiliating and frightening."

Jones pleaded in vain with local, state, and federal officials to obtain compliance with the law. "The door that I thought had been opened was still closed and my freedom to live my dream was turning into a nightmare," she said. Finally, in 1998, after having to ask a judge to carry her to a restroom, she decided to appeal to the courts.

Jones filed a lawsuit against the state of Tennessee, joining five other plaintiffs who alleged that the state was in violation of Title II of the ADA, which prohibits governmental entities from denying public services, programs, and activities to individuals with a disability. A co-plaintiff, George Lane, had injured his hip and pelvis in a car accident. Cited for reckless driving, he went to the courthouse in a wheelchair but had to crawl up the stairs. When the court adjourned for lunch, he crawled back down. That afternoon, he refused to crawl upstairs again and was jailed for failing to appear

in court. He never forgot the humiliation of having to drag his body up the thirty tile steps of the Polk County Courthouse. Lane, Jones, and the four other plaintiffs sought legal redress and damages of $250,000 each.

Tennessee immediately countersued, challenging the constitutionality of the ADA's requirement that states make public facilities accessible to people with disabilities and arguing that the Eleventh Amendment to the Constitution granted states sovereign immunity (protection from lawsuits). Carol Westlake, executive director of the Tennessee Disability Coalition, pointed out that Tennessee's claim of states' rights was the same argument used to deny civil rights to African Americans in the 1950s and 1960s. After six years of litigation, the case of *Tennessee v. Lane* reached the Supreme Court in 2004. As the justices heard arguments, activists demonstrated outside the Court, chanting, "Justice for all: we won't crawl."

At stake was not only the right of people with disabilities to sue a state when denied access to public

at the signing ceremony, disability advocate Cynthia Jones said, "It was kind of like a new breath of air was sweeping across America. . . . People knew they had rights. That was wonderful." (See "Experiencing the American Promise," above.)

Yet Bush also needed to satisfy party conservatives to whom he had pledged "Read my lips: No new taxes." Bush vetoed thirty-six bills, including those extending unemployment benefits, raising taxes, and mandating family and medical leave for workers. Press reports increasingly used the words *stalemate* and *divided government*.

Continuing a trend begun during the Reagan years, some states compensated for this paraly-

sis with their own innovations. State legislatures enacted laws to establish parental leave policies, improve food labeling, and protect the environment. Dozens of cities passed ordinances requiring businesses receiving tax abatements or other benefits to pay wages well above the federal minimum. In 1999, California passed a much tougher gun control bill than reformers had been able to get through Congress.

The huge federal budget deficit inherited from Reagan impelled Bush in 1990 to abandon his "no new taxes" pledge, outraging conservatives. The new law modestly raised taxes on high-income Americans and increased levies on gasoline, cigarettes, alcohol, and luxury items,

facilities, but also the right of Congress to make federal laws binding on the states. In May 2004, the Supreme Court ruled in a five-to-four decision that states failing to make their courthouses accessible to people with disabilities could be sued for damages under federal disability law. But it confined its ruling to the specific context presented in the case: access to courts. By the narrowest possible margin, with the crucial fifth vote cast by Justice Sandra Day O'Connor, the Court focused on one narrow application of the ADA and upheld it in the face of Tennessee's claim of constitutional immunity.

Jones recognized that she was part of a larger struggle. "This Supreme Court ruling wasn't about Beverly Jones; it means equal access to the justice system for 54 million Americans with disabilities." While she rejoiced in having "accomplished what we wanted to be achieved," she was also sobered by the narrow grounds on which the Court decided her case. A year after *Tennessee v. Lane*, Jones testified before the Senate Judiciary Committee on the nomination of John Roberts to the position of chief justice of the United States. Pointing to the fragility of her victory, she urged the senators to "pay close attention to whether John Roberts has proven that he would ensure that the rights [that] people with disabilities fought so hard to secure are not stripped away."

Beverly Jones

Beverly Jones is shown here next to one of the courthouse stairways that made her job as a court reporter so difficult. She filed suit under the ADA in 1998, and in 2004, the Supreme Court upheld her right to enforce the protections the ADA granted to people with disabilities. AP Photo/John Russell.

Questions for Analysis

Recognize Viewpoints: On what basis did Tennessee oppose Jones's lawsuit? What argument did the state present, and how did it support that argument?

Ask Historical Questions: In what ways was the struggle for disability rights similar to and different from other minority rights movements? Provide another historical example of how an individual's struggle on her or his own behalf affected a much larger population.

Consider the Context: Why was disability rights legislation one of the few pieces of reform legislation that passed in the 1990s?

---

while leaving intact most of Reagan's massive tax cuts. Neither the new revenues nor controls on spending curbed the deficit, however, which was boosted by rising costs for Social Security, Medicare, Medicaid, and natural disaster relief.

Like Reagan, Bush created a more conservative Supreme Court. His first nominee was a moderate, but in 1991, when the only African American on the Court, Thurgood Marshall, retired, Bush nominated Clarence Thomas, a conservative black appeals court judge who had opposed affirmative action when he headed the Equal Employment Opportunity Commission (EEOC) under Reagan. Charging that Thomas would not protect minority rights, civil rights groups and other liberal organizations fought the nomination. Then Anita Hill, a black law professor and former EEOC employee, accused Thomas of sexual harassment. Thomas angrily denied the charges, and the Senate voted narrowly to confirm him. The hearings angered many women, who noted that only two women sat in the Senate and denounced the male senators for not taking sexual harassment seriously.

The Cold War Ends

While domestic policy remained fairly constant during Bush's presidency, the world experienced enormous changes. In 1989, the progressive forces

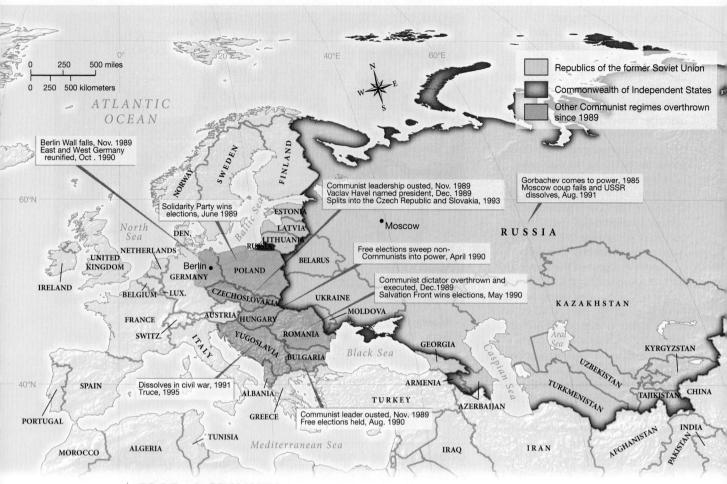

MAP ACTIVITY

Map 31.1   Events in Eastern Europe, 1989–2002

The overthrow of Communist governments throughout Eastern Europe and the splintering of the Soviet Union into more than a dozen separate nations were among the most momentous changes in world history since World War II.

READING THE MAP: Which country was the first to overthrow its Communist government? Which was the last? In which nations did elections usher in a change in government?

CONNECTIONS: What problems did Mikhail Gorbachev try to solve, and how did he try to solve them? What made President Reagan ready to reach an accommodation with Gorbachev? (See "Ronald Reagan Confronts an 'Evil Empire'" in chapter 30.)

that Gorbachev had encouraged in the Communist world (see "A Thaw in Soviet-American Relations" in chapter 30) swept through Eastern Europe, where popular uprisings demanded an end to state repression and inefficient economic bureaucracies. Communist governments toppled like dominoes (Map 31.1), virtually without bloodshed, because Gorbachev refused to prop them up with Soviet armies. East Germany opened its border with West Germany, and in November 1989 ecstatic Germans danced on the Berlin Wall.

Unification of East and West Germany sped to completion in 1990. Soon Poland,

Hungary, and other former iron curtain countries lined up to join the North Atlantic Treaty Organization (NATO), a development that Russia found threatening. Eight former Soviet satellites joined the European Union and the common economic market it had established in 1992. Inspired by the liberation of Eastern Europe, republics within the Soviet Union soon established their own independence. With nothing left to govern, Gorbachev resigned. The Soviet Union had dissolved, and with it the Cold War conflict that had defined U.S. foreign policy for decades.

Fall of the Berlin Wall
After 1961, the Berlin Wall became the prime symbol of the Cold War and the iron grip of communism over Eastern Europe and the Soviet Union. When Communist authorities opened the wall on November 9, 1989, Berliners on both sides rushed to the gate to celebrate. Here thousands gather at the Brandenburg Gate, Berlin's most famous landmark. AP Photo.

Democracy also prevailed in South Africa, which began to dismantle apartheid; this process led in 1994 to the election of the country's first black president, Nelson Mandela. Colin Powell joked that he was "running out of villains. I'm down to Castro and Kim Il-sung," the North Korean dictator who, along with China's leaders, resisted the liberalizing tides sweeping the world. In 1989, Chinese soldiers killed hundreds of pro-democracy demonstrators in Beijing, and the Communist government arrested some ten thousand reformers. North Korea remained a Communist dictatorship, committed to developing nuclear weapons.

"The post–Cold War world is decidedly not post-nuclear," declared one U.S. official. In 1990, the United States and the Soviet Union signed the Strategic Arms Reduction Talks (START) treaty, which cut about 30 percent of each superpower's nuclear arsenal. And in 1996, the United Nations General Assembly overwhelmingly approved a total nuclear test ban treaty. Yet India and Pakistan, hostile neighbors, refused to sign the treaty, and both exploded atomic devices in 1998. Moreover, the Republican-controlled U.S. Senate defeated ratification of the treaty. The potential for rogue nations and terrorist groups to develop nuclear weapons posed an ongoing threat.

Going to War in Central America and the Persian Gulf

Near its borders, the United States continued to exercise its military power. In Central America, U.S. officials had supported Panamanian dictator Manuel Noriega, whom they valued for his anticommunism. But in 1989, after an American grand jury indicted Noriega for drug trafficking and after his troops killed an American Marine, Bush ordered 25,000 military personnel into Panama to capture him. U.S. forces quickly overcame Noriega's troops, sustaining 23 deaths, while hundreds of Panamanians, including many civilians, died. Colin Powell noted that "our euphoria over our victory was not universal." Both the United Nations and the Organization of American States condemned the unilateral action by the United States.

By contrast, Bush's second military engagement rested solidly on international approval. Viewing Iran as America's major enemy in the Middle East, U.S. officials had quietly assisted the Iraqi dictator Saddam Hussein in the Iran-Iraq war, which began in 1980 and ended inconclusively in 1988. Struggling with an enormous war debt, in August 1990 Hussein invaded the small country of Kuwait (Map 31.2), and his

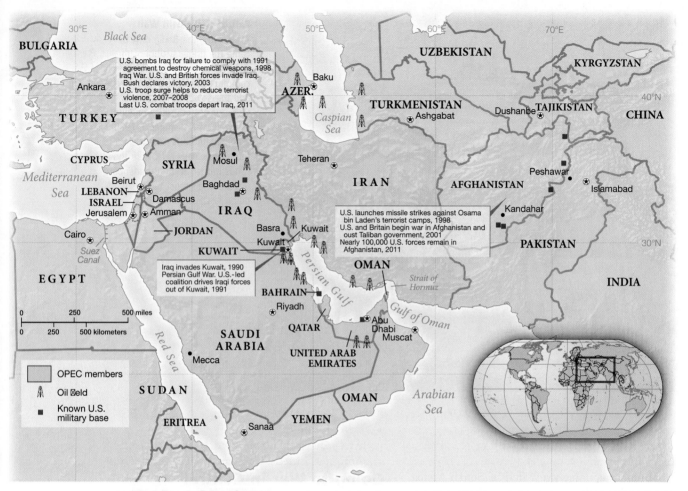

MAP ACTIVITY

Map 31.2   Events in the Middle East, 1989–2011

The Arab League supported the war to liberate Kuwait in 1991, and after September 11, 2001, it also approved of U.S. military operations in Afghanistan. Yet only the countries where the United States had military bases supported the American invasion of Iraq in 2003. Arab hostility toward the United States also reflected the deterioration of Israeli-Palestinian relations after 1999.

READING THE MAP: In what countries are the sources of oil located? In what countries does the United States have military bases?

CONNECTIONS: What conditions prompted the U.S. military interventions in Iraq and Afghanistan in 1991, 2001, and 2003? What were the U.S. goals in each of these interventions? To what extent were those goals realized?

troops soon neared the Saudi Arabian border. Faced with this threat to the world's largest oil reserves, President Bush quickly ordered a massive military mobilization and assembled an international coalition to stand up to Iraq. He invoked principles of national self-determination and international law, but access to Middle Eastern oil was also a key concern.

Reflecting the easing of Cold War tensions, the Soviet Union supported a UN embargo on Iraqi oil and authorization for using force if Iraq

did not withdraw from Kuwait by January 15, 1991. By then, the United States had deployed more than 400,000 soldiers to Saudi Arabia, joined by 265,000 troops from two dozen other nations, including several Arab states. "The community of nations has resolutely gathered to condemn and repel lawless aggression," Bush announced. "With few exceptions, the world now stands as one."

When the UN-imposed deadline for Iraqi withdrawal expired, Bush asked Congress to

The Gulf War
On Thanksgiving 1990, during the buildup to the Gulf War, President George H. W. Bush visited U.S. troops deployed to Saudi Arabia. Here he talks with one of the 33,000 women stationed throughout the area. For the first time, women served in combat support positions, piloting planes and helicopters, directing artillery, and fighting fires. Diana Walker/Time Life Pictures/Getty Images.

approve war. Many legislators favored waiting to see whether the embargo would force Hussein to back down, a position quietly urged within the administration by Colin Powell. Congress debated for three days and then authorized war by a margin of five votes in the Senate and sixty-seven in the House, with most Democrats opposed. On January 17, 1991, U.S. forces led a forty-day bombing campaign against Iraqi military targets, power plants, oil refineries, and transportation networks. Having severely crippled Iraq by air, the coalition then stormed into Kuwait, forcing Iraqi troops to withdraw (see Map 31.2).

"By God, we've kicked the Vietnam syndrome once and for all," President Bush exulted on March 1. Most Americans found no moral ambiguity in the **Persian Gulf War** and took pride in the display of military prowess. The United States stood at the apex of global leadership, steering a coalition in which Arab nations fought beside their former colonial rulers.

Some Americans wondered why Bush ended the war without deposing Hussein. Bush pointed to the limited UN mandate and to Middle Eastern leaders' concerns that invading Iraq would destabilize the region. His secretary of defense, Richard Cheney, doubted that a stable government could be created to replace Hussein and considered the price of a long occupation too high. Instead, administration officials counted on Hussein's pledge not to rearm or develop weapons of mass

destruction, secured by a system of UN inspections, to contain him.

After the war, Israel, which had endured Iraqi missile attacks, was more secure, but the Israeli-Palestinian conflict seethed. Despite military losses, Hussein remained in power and turned his war machine on Iraqi Kurds and Shiite Muslims, whom the United States had encouraged to rebel. Hussein also found ways to conceal arms from UN inspectors before he threw the inspectors out in 1998. Finally, the decision to keep U.S. troops based in Saudi Arabia, the holy land of Islam, fueled the hatred and determination of Muslim extremists like Osama bin Laden.

The 1992 Election

Bush's popularity after the Gulf War caused the most prominent Democrats to opt out of the presidential race of 1992. But that did not deter William Jefferson "Bill" Clinton, who at age forty-five had served as governor of Arkansas for twelve years. Like Carter in 1976, Clinton and his running mate, Tennessee senator Albert Gore Jr., presented themselves as "New Democrats" and sought to rid the party of its liberal image.

Clinton cultivated the "forgotten middle class," who "do the work, pay the taxes, raise the kids, and play by the rules." He promised a tax cut for the middle class, pledged to reinvigorate government and the economy, and vowed "to put an end to welfare as we know it." Bush was vulnerable to an unemployment rate of 7 percent and to a challenge from self-made Texas billionaire H. Ross Perot, whose third-party organization revealed Americans' frustrations with government and the major parties. Clinton won 43 percent of the popular vote, Bush 38 percent, and Perot 19 percent—the strongest third-party finish in eighty years.

> **REVIEW** How did George H. W. Bush respond to threats to U.S. interests as the Cold War came to an end?

▶ The Clinton Administration's Search for the Middle Ground

Bill Clinton's assertion that "the era of big government is over" reflected the Democratic Party's move to the right that had begun with Jimmy Carter, but Clinton did not completely abandon liberal principles. He extended benefits for the working poor; delivered incremental reforms to feminists, environmentalists, and other groups; and spoke out for affirmative action and gay rights. Yet his administration restricted welfare benefits and attended more to the concerns of middle-class Americans than to the needs of the disadvantaged.

Clinton's two-term presidency witnessed the longest economic boom in history and ended with a budget surplus. Although various factors generated the prosperity, many Americans identified Clinton with the buoyant economy, elected him to a second term, and supported him even when his reckless sexual behavior led to impeachment, which crippled his leadership in his last years in office.

Clinton's Reforms

Clinton wanted to restore confidence in government as a force for good while not alienating antigovernment voters. Yet he inherited a huge budget deficit—$4.4 trillion in 1993—that precluded substantial federal initiatives. Moreover, Clinton never won a majority of the popular vote,

and the Republicans controlled Congress after 1994. Throughout his presidency, Clinton was burdened by investigations into past financial activities and private indiscretions.

Despite these obstacles, Clinton achieved a number of reforms. He issued executive orders easing restrictions on abortion and signed several bills that Republicans had previously blocked. In 1993, Congress enacted gun control legislation and the Family and Medical Leave Act, which mandated unpaid leave for childbirth, adoption, and family medical emergencies for workers in larger companies. The Violence against Women Act of 1994 authorized $1.6 billion and new remedies for combating sexual assault and domestic violence. Clinton won stricter air pollution controls and greater protection for national forests and parks. Other liberal measures included a minimum-wage increase and a large expansion of aid for college students. Most significantly, Clinton pushed through a substantial increase in the **Earned Income Tax Credit (EITC)**. Begun in 1975, EITC gave tax breaks to people who worked full-time at meager wages or, if they owed no taxes, a subsidy to lift their family income above the poverty line. By 2003, some fifteen million low-income families were benefiting from the EITC, almost half of them minorities. One expert called it "the largest antipoverty program since the Great Society." The program implicitly recognized the inability of the free market to secure a living wage for all workers.

Shortly before Clinton took office, the economy had begun to rebound. Economic expansion, along with spending cuts, tax increases, and declining unemployment, produced in 1998 the first budget surplus since 1969. Clinton failed, however, in his major domestic initiative to provide universal health insurance and to curb skyrocketing medical costs. Congress enacted important smaller reforms, such as underwriting health care for five million uninsured children, yet forty million Americans remained uninsured.

Pledging to make the face of government "look like America," Clinton built on the gradual progress women and minorities had made since the 1960s. For example, African Americans and women had become mayors in major cities from New York to San Francisco. Virginia had elected the first black governor since Reconstruction, and Florida the first Latino. Clinton's cabinet appointments included six women, three African Americans, two Latinos, and an Asian American. His judicial appointments had a similar cast, and in 1993 he named the second woman to the

Supreme Court, Ruth Bader Ginsburg, whose arguments as an attorney had won key women's rights rulings from that Court.

Accommodating the Right

The 1994 midterm elections swept away the Democratic majorities in Congress and helped push Clinton to the right. Republicans claimed the 1994 election as a mandate for their conservative platform to end "government that is too big, too intrusive, and too easy with the public's money" and for "a Congress that respects the values and shares the faith of the American family."

The most extreme antigovernment sentiment developed far from Washington in the form of grassroots armed militias that celebrated white Christian supremacy and reflected conservatives' hostility to such diverse institutions as taxes and the United Nations. The militia movement grew after passage of new gun control legislation and after government agents stormed the headquarters of an armed religious cult in Waco, Texas, in April 1993, killing more than 80. On the second anniversary of that event, two militia sympathizers bombed a federal building in Oklahoma City, taking 168 lives in the worst terrorist attack in the nation's history up to that point.

Bowing to conservative views on gay and lesbian rights and following the advice of military leaders, Clinton backed away from his promise to lift the ban on gays in the military. Cathleen Glover, an army specialist in Arabic who lost her position along with thousands of other soldiers, lamented, "The army preaches integrity, but asks you to lie to everyone around you." In addition, in 1996, Clinton signed the Defense of Marriage Act (DOMA), prohibiting the federal government from recognizing state-licensed marriages between same-sex couples.

Yet attitudes and practices relating to homosexuality were changing rapidly, and the years following Clinton's presidency would witness a number of significant victories for gay rights. By 2006, a majority of the largest companies provided health benefits to same-sex domestic partners and included sexual orientation in their nondiscrimination policies. A majority of states banned discrimination in public employment, and many of those laws extended to private employment, housing, and education. In 2015, the Supreme Court in *Obergefell v. Hodges* declared by a vote of five to four that same-sex

Domestic Terrorism
The most devastating product of antigovernment extremism was the explosion of the Alfred P. Murrah Federal Building in Oklahoma City in April 1995. The building housed a day care center, and 19 infants and toddlers were among the 168 people killed. The driver of the truck carrying the explosives was executed in 2001, and his co-conspirator was sentenced to life imprisonment without parole. Greg Smith/REA/Redux.

couples had a constitutional right to marry, making gay marriage legal in all fifty states. The gay rights movement continued to fight other forms of discrimination, including job bias, which was still legal in many states, and worked for the rights of transgender people.

In the 1990s, hardening attitudes about poverty were reflected in Clinton's handling of the New Deal program Aid to Families with Dependent Children (AFDC), popularly called welfare. Using the term *welfare queen* to stigmatize AFDC recipients, critics encouraged voters to blame poverty on the poor themselves and on welfare programs that fostered dependency, rather than on external circumstances such as lack of adequate jobs and child care. Many questioned why they should subsidize poor mothers when so many women worked outside the home. Defenders of AFDC doubted that the economy could provide sufficient jobs at decent wages and pointed to the much greater subsidies the government provided to other groups, such as large farmers, corporations, and homeowners. After vetoing two

VISUAL ACTIVITY

The End of Welfare

After signing the bill that sharply curtailed government support for poor mothers and their children, Bill Clinton made it a part of his 1996 campaign for reelection. He highlighted the issue especially when campaigning in more conservative regions, as this photo from a campaign stop in Daytona, Florida, shows. Paul J. Richards/AFP/Getty Images.

READING THE IMAGE: What does the poster behind Clinton say about the importance of welfare as an issue in 1996? What American "values" do you think it refers to?

CONNECTIONS: What other programs that addressed the issue of poverty did Clinton advance?

welfare bills, Clinton signed a less punitive measure as the 1996 election approached. The **Temporary Assistance for Needy Families (TANF) program** replaced AFDC and limited welfare payments to two consecutive years, with a lifetime maximum of five years.

Clinton's signature on the new law denied Republicans a partisan issue in the 1996 presidential campaign. The Republican Party also moved to the center, nominating Kansan Robert Dole, a World War II hero and former Senate majority leader. Clinton won 49 percent of the votes; 41 percent went to Dole and 9 percent to third-party candidate Ross Perot. Voters sent a Republican majority back to Congress.

In 1999, Clinton and Congress further deregulated the financial industry by repealing key aspects of the Glass-Steagall Act, passed during the New Deal to avoid another Great Depression. The Financial Services Modernization Act ended the separation between banking, securities, and insurance services, allowing financial institutions to engage in all three areas, practices that contributed to the severe financial meltdown of 2008.

Impeaching the President

Clinton's magnetism, his ability to capture the middle ground, and the nation's economic resurgence enabled him to survive scandals and impeachment. Early in his presidency, charges related to firings of White House staff, political use of FBI records, and the Clintons' real estate investments in Arkansas led to an official investigation by an independent prosecutor.

In January 1998, the independent prosecutor, Kenneth Starr, began to investigate a charge that Clinton had had sexual relations with a twenty-one-year-old White House intern and then lied about it to a federal grand jury. Starr prepared a case for the House of Representatives, which in December 1998 voted to impeach the president for perjury and obstruction of justice. Clinton became the second president (after Andrew Johnson, in 1868) to be impeached by the House and tried by the Senate.

Most Americans condemned the president's behavior but approved of the job he was doing and opposed his removal from office. One man said, "Let him get a divorce. . . . Don't take him out of office and disrupt the country." Some saw Starr as a fanatic invading individuals' privacy. Those favoring removal insisted that the president must set a high moral standard and that lying to a grand jury, even over a private matter, was a serious offense. The Senate votes fell far short of the two-thirds majority needed for conviction on either count. A majority, including some Republicans, seemed to agree with a Clinton supporter that the president's behavior, though "indefensible, outrageous, unforgivable, shameless," did not warrant his removal from office.

The Booming Economy of the 1990s

Clinton's ability to weather impeachment owed much to the prosperous economy, which in 1991 began a period of tremendous expansion. During the 1990s, the gross domestic product grew by more than one-third, thirteen million new jobs were created, inflation remained in check, unemployment reached 4 percent—its lowest point in twenty-five years—and the stock market soared.

Clinton's policies contributed to the boom. He made deficit reduction a priority, and in exchange the Federal Reserve Board and bond market traders encouraged economic expansion by lowering interest rates. Businesses also prospered because they had lowered their costs through corporate restructuring and employee layoffs. Economic problems in Europe and Asia helped American firms become more competitive in the international market. And the computer revolution and the application of information technology boosted productivity.

People at all income levels benefited from the economic boom, but income inequality, rising

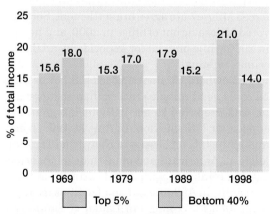

FIGURE 31.1   The Growth of Inequality: Changes in Family Income, 1969–1998
For most of the post–World War II period, income increased for all groups on the economic ladder. But after 1969, the income of the poorest families actually declined, while the income of the richest 20 percent of the population grew substantially. Adapted from the *New York Times*, 1989.

since the 1970s, endured (Figure 31.1). The growing use of computer technology increased demand for highly skilled workers, while the movement of manufacturing jobs abroad diminished opportunities and wages for the less skilled. Moreover, deregulation and the continuing decline of unions hurt lower-skilled workers, tax cuts favored the better-off, and the minimum wage failed to keep up with inflation.

Although more minorities than ever attained middle-class status, people of color overall remained lowest on the economic ladder. For instance, in 1999 the median income for white households surpassed $45,000, but it stood at only $29,423 and $33,676 for African American and Latino households, respectively. In 2000, poverty afflicted more than 20 percent of African Americans and Latinos, in contrast to 7.5 percent of whites.

> **REVIEW**   How did President Clinton seek a middle ground in American politics?

▶ The United States in a Globalizing World

America's economic success in the 1990s was linked to its dominance in a world economy that was undergoing tremendous transformations in a process called globalization—the growing integration and interdependence of national citizens and economies. President Clinton lowered a number of trade barriers, despite heated arguments about whether that was in the country's best interest. Debates likewise arose over the large numbers of immigrants entering the United States.

Clinton agreed with Bush that the United States must retain its supreme position in the world. He used military force in Somalia, the Middle East, and Eastern Europe, and he pushed hard to ease the conflict between Israelis and Palestinians. Clinton also strove to safeguard American interests from terrorist attacks around the world, a challenge in some ways more difficult than combating communism.

Defining America's Place in a New World Order

In 1991, President George H. W. Bush declared a "new world order" emerging from the ashes of the Cold War. As the sole superpower, the United

States was determined to let no nation challenge its military superiority or global leadership: It spent ten times more on defense than its nearest competitor, the United Kingdom (Figure 31.2). Defining principles for the use of that power in a post–Cold War world remained a challenge.

Africa, where civil wars and extreme human suffering rarely evoked a strong U.S. response, was a case in point. In 1992, President Bush had attached U.S. forces to a UN operation in the northern African country of Somalia, where famine and civil war raged. In 1993, President Clinton allowed that humanitarian mission to turn into "nation building"—an effort to establish a stable government—and eighteen U.S. soldiers were killed. The outcry after Americans saw film of a soldier's corpse dragged through the streets suggested that most citizens were unwilling to sacrifice lives when no vital interest was threatened. Indeed, both the United States and the UN stood by in 1994 when more than half a million people were massacred in a brutal civil war in Rwanda.

In Eastern Europe, the collapse of communism ignited a severe crisis when, after the Communists were swept out of power in Yugoslavia in 1989, ruthless leaders exploited ethnic differences to bolster their power. Yugoslavia splintered into separate states and fell into civil war. The Serbian aggression under President Slobodan Milosevic against Bosnian Muslims, which included rape, torture, and mass killings, horrified much of the world, but European and U.S. leaders hesitated to use military force. Finally, in 1995, Clinton ordered U.S. fliers to join NATO forces in intensive bombing of Serbian military con-

Breakup of Yugoslavia

centrations. That effort and successful offensives by the Croatian and Bosnian armies forced Milosevic to the bargaining table, where representatives from Serbia, Croatia, and Bosnia hammered out a peace treaty.

In 1998, new fighting broke out in the southern Serbian province of Kosovo, where ethnic Albanians, who constituted 90 percent of the population, demanded independence. When the Serbian army retaliated, in 1999, NATO launched a U.S.-led bombing attack on Serbian military and government targets that, after three months, forced Milosevic to agree to a settlement. Serbians voted Milosevic out of office in 2000, and he died in 2006 while on trial for genocide by a UN war crimes tribunal.

Elsewhere, Clinton deployed U.S. power when he could send missiles rather than soldiers, and he was prepared to act without international support or UN sanction. In August 1998, bombings at the U.S. embassies in Kenya and Tanzania killed 12 Americans and more than 250 Africans. Clinton retaliated with missile attacks on training camps in Afghanistan and facilities in Sudan controlled by Osama bin Laden, a Saudi-born millionaire who financed Al Qaeda, the Islamic-extremist terrorist network linked to the embassy attacks. Clinton also bombed Iraq in 1993 when a plot to assassinate former president Bush was uncovered, in 1996 after Saddam Hussein attacked the Kurds in northern Iraq, and repeatedly between 1998 and 2000 after Hussein expelled UN weapons inspectors. Whereas Bush had acted in the Gulf War with the support of an international

United States
$478.2 billion

United Kingdom
$48.3 billion

France
$46.2 billion

Japan
$42.1 billion

China
$41.0 billion

Germany
$33.2 billion

Italy
$27.2 billion

Saudi Arabia
$25.2 billion

Russia
$21.0 billion

India
$20.4 billion

FIGURE 31.2 Global Comparison: Countries with the Highest Military Expenditures, 2005
During the Cold War, the military budgets of the United States and the Soviet Union were relatively even. Even before the Iraq War began in 2003, the U.S. military budget constituted 47 percent of total world military expenditures. Massive defense budgets reflected the determination of Democratic and Republican administrations alike to maintain dominance in the world, even while the capacities of traditional enemies shrank.

force that included Arab states, Clinton acted unilaterally and in the face of Arab opposition.

To defuse the Israeli-Palestinian conflict, Clinton applied diplomatic rather than military power. In 1993, Norwegian diplomats had brokered an agreement between Yasir Arafat, head of the Palestine Liberation Organization (PLO), and Yitzhak Rabin, Israeli prime minister, to recognize the existence of each other's states. Israel agreed to withdraw from the Gaza Strip and Jericho, allowing for Palestinian self-government there. In July 1994, Clinton presided over another turning point as Israel and Jordan signed a declaration of peace. Yet difficult issues remained, especially control of Jerusalem and the presence of more than 200,000 Israeli settlers in the West Bank, the land seized by Israel in 1967, where three million Palestinians were determined to establish their own state.

Events in Israel since 1989

First Persian Gulf War, 1991
Israel and PLO sign accords, 1993
Israel and Jordan sign peace treaty, 1994
Progress of Israeli-Palestinian negotiations halts and violence escalates, 2000
Israel withdraws from Gaza, 2005
Israel at war with Hezbollah in Lebanon, 2006
Israel invades Gaza, 2008

Debates over Globalization

Building on efforts by Reagan and Bush, Clinton sought to speed up the growth of a "global marketplace" with new measures to ease restrictions on international commerce. Although the process of globalization was centuries old, new communications technologies such as the Internet and cell phones connected nations, corporations, and individuals at much faster speeds and much lower costs. To advance globalization and the U.S. economy, in 1993 Clinton won congressional approval of the **North American Free Trade Agreement (NAFTA)**, which eliminated all tariffs and trade barriers among the United States, Canada, and Mexico. Fearing loss of jobs and industries to Mexico, a majority of Democrats opposed NAFTA, but Republican support ensured approval. In 1994, the Senate ratified the General Agreement on Tariffs and Trade, establishing the **World Trade Organization (WTO)** to enforce substantial tariff and import quota reductions among some 135 member nations. In 2005, Clinton's successor, George W. Bush, lowered more trade barriers with the Central American–Dominican Republic Free Trade Agreement. The Obama administration negotiated the largest trade pact ever, the Trans-Pacific Partnership, but struggled to obtain Congressional approval.

The free trade issue was intensely contested. Much of corporate America welcomed the elimination of trade barriers and opportunities to lower their taxes. "Ideally, you'd have every plant you own on a barge," remarked Jack Welch, CEO of General Electric. Critics, including many Democrats, linked globalization to the loss of good jobs, the weakening of unions, and the growing gap between rich and poor. (See "Making Historical Arguments," page 908.) Demanding "fair trade" rather than simply free trade, critics wanted treaties to require decent wage and labor standards. Environmentalists wanted countries seeking increased commerce with the United States to reduce pollution and prevent the destruction of endangered species.

Globalization controversies often centered on relationships between the United States, which dominated the world's industrial core, and developing nations on the periphery, whose cheap labor and lax environmental standards attracted investors. United Students against Sweatshops, for example, attacked Nike, which paid Chinese workers $1.50 per hour to produce shoes selling for more than $100 in the United States. Yet leaders of developing nations actively sought foreign investment because wages deemed pitiful by Americans often provided their impoverished people a higher standard of living. At the same time, developing countries often pointed to American hypocrisy in advocating free trade in industry while heavily subsidizing the U.S. agricultural sector. "When countries like America, Britain and France subsidize their farmers," complained a grower in Uganda, "we get hurt."

While globalization's cheerleaders pointed to the cheap consumer goods available to Americans and argued that everyone would benefit in the long run, critics focused on the short-term victims. American businessman George Soros recognized that international trade and investments generated wealth but could not meet other needs, "such as the preservation of peace, alleviation of poverty, protection of the environment, labor conditions, or human rights." According to World Bank president James D. Wolfensohn, "Our challenge is to make globalization an instrument of opportunity and inclusion—not fear."

The Internationalization of the United States

The United States experienced the dynamic forces of globalization in many ways. Already in the 1980s, Japanese, European, and Middle Eastern investors had purchased U.S. stocks and bonds, real estate, and corporations. Local communities welcomed foreign capital, and states competed to recruit foreign automobile plants. By 2002, the paychecks of nearly four million American workers came from foreign-owned companies such as Honda and BMW.

Globalization was also transforming American society, as the United States experienced a tremendous surge of immigration, part of a worldwide movement of some 214 million immigrants in 2010 alone. By 2014, the United States' 42.2 million immigrants constituted 13.2 percent of the population. In contrast to earlier immigrants, who had come largely from Europe, by the 1980s

Luke Sharrett/Bloomberg via Getty Images.

VISUAL ACTIVITY

Migrant Workers

Mexican immigrants constituted more than two-thirds of crop workers in 2015 and a sizable share of tobacco workers. These migrant workers labor in a tobacco curing barn in Finchville, Kentucky, where tobacco hangs from rafters. The labor not only was long and arduous but also exposed workers to nicotine and other poisons that could be absorbed directly through the skin.

READING THE IMAGE: What makes tobacco curing hazardous for these workers? What do their dress and gestures suggest about the nature of their work?

CONNECTIONS: What other kinds of labor did immigrants from Latin America and Asia perform?

the vast majority came from Asia, Latin America, and the Caribbean. Consequently, immigration changed the racial and ethnic composition of the nation. By 2014, 55 million Latinos constituted the largest U.S. minority group, at 17 percent of the population. But since 2010, more immigrants have come from Asia than from Latin America.

The promise of economic opportunity, as always, lured immigrants to America, and the Immigration and Nationality Act of 1965 enabled them to come. The law allowed close relatives of U.S. citizens to enter above the annual ceiling of 270,000 immigrants, thus creating family migration chains. Moreover, during the Cold War, U.S. immigration policy was generous to refugees from communism, welcoming more than 800,000 Cubans and more than 600,000 Vietnamese, Laotians, and Cambodians.

The racial composition of the new immigration heightened the long-standing wariness of native-born Americans toward newcomers. Pressure for more restrictive policies stemmed from beliefs that immigrants took jobs from the native-born, suppressed wages by accepting low pay, strained social services, or eroded the dominant culture and language. Americans expressed particular hostility toward immigrants who were in the country illegally, estimated at 11.3 million in 2014, even though the economy depended on their cheap labor.

The new immigration was making America an international, interracial society. The largest numbers of immigrants flocked to California, New York, Texas, Florida, New Jersey, and Illinois, but new immigrants dispersed throughout the country. Taquerias, sushi bars, and Vietnamese restaurants appeared in southeastern and midwestern towns; cable TV companies added Spanish-language stations; and the international sport of soccer soared in popularity. Mixed marriages displayed the growing fusion of cultures, recognized in 2000 on Census Bureau forms, where Americans could check more than one racial category. Like their predecessors, the majority of post-1965 immigrants were unskilled and poor. They took the lowest-paying jobs, constituting nearly half of all farmworkers and housekeepers. Yet a significant number of immigrants were highly skilled workers, sought after by burgeoning high-tech industries. By 2006, nearly one-third of all software developers were foreign-born, as were 28 percent of all physicians.

REVIEW   What were the costs and benefits to the United States of globalization in the 1990s and early 2000s?

What Happened to American Manufacturing Jobs, and Why Did It Matter?

In 2001, Paul Sufronko, a supervisor at Rocky Shoes and Boots in Nelsonville, Ohio, handed out final paychecks to the company's last sixty-seven employees in the United States, thereby ending a process of outsourcing that had begun in the 1980s. Before his own job ended, Sufronko traveled to Rocky plants in Puerto Rico and the Dominican Republic to train local workers to replace him. Asked about his job loss, the thirty-six-year-old said, "Things just didn't work out." Other Americans did not take the loss of their jobs to foreign workers quite so philosophically. An autoworker in Michigan believed that "corporations are looking for a disposable workforce. . . . No commitment to community; no commitment to country." Sufronko's displacement reflected a pattern across industrial America: In 1960, 96 percent of all shoes bought in the United States were made within the country; by 2000, nearly all came from abroad.

Beginning in the 1970s, the process of de-industrialization affected huge segments of the U.S. economy, including steel, appliances, machine tools, computers, furniture, clothing, and more. From a peak of 19.5 million in 1977, the number of manufacturing jobs fell below 12 million by 2012. The proportion of American workers in manufacturing jobs dropped from one-third in the 1950s to 10 percent by the twenty-first century. Although factory work was often grueling and tedious, blue-collar wages provided a middle-class existence for millions of families. Industrial labor unions had boosted wages, even among those whose workplaces were not organized, and provided other benefits such as health insurance and pensions for their members. As factories closed, union membership plummeted from nearly one in three workers in the 1950s to less than one in ten in 2015. Both the decline of manufacturing and the decline of unions contributed to a widening income gap. Once the industrial heartland of America, the region fringing the Great Lakes and stretching from New York to Illinois soon became known as the Rust Belt.

This dramatic transformation of the American economy was the product of many forces. As nations abroad recovered after World War II, some U.S. manufacturers curtailed production or simply shut down as they lost increasing shares of their markets to foreign products. Japanese and German factories, newly built and equipped after the war, adopted innovative production processes that enabled their steel and automobile

▶ President George W. Bush: Conservatism at Home and Radical Initiatives Abroad

Although losing the popular vote in 2000, George W. Bush made his mark in domestic policy with key legislation to improve public school education, subsidize prescription drugs for elderly citizens, and greatly reduce taxes for the wealthy. The tax cuts, along with spending on new crises, created the largest budget deficit in the nation's history, and a financial crisis near the end of his presidency sent the economy into a recession.

As Islamist terrorism replaced communism as the primary threat to U.S. security, the Bush administration invaded Afghanistan in 2001 and Iraq in 2003. Bush won reelection in 2004, but stability in Iraq and Afghanistan remained elusive, and he confronted serious foreign and domestic crises in his second term. Democrats capitalized on widespread dissatisfaction with his administration to gain control of Congress in 2006 and the White House in 2008.

The Disputed Election of 2000

The oldest son of former president George H. W. Bush, George W. Bush was the governor of Texas when he won the Republican presidential nomination. Inexperienced in national and international affairs, Bush chose for his running mate a seasoned official, Richard B. Cheney, who had served in three previous Republican administrations. Many observers predicted that the thriving

makers to compete with General Motors and U.S. Steel. By 2015, both China and Japan manufactured more cars than the United States, and China produced more than five times as much steel.

While some companies built plants abroad to be close to burgeoning markets there, more often companies decided to move production offshore to take advantage of cheaper labor, a constant goal of managers. Even before factory jobs began to move abroad, the Rust Belt experienced a kind of de-industrialization as companies moved production from cities like Detroit to southern states, where labor unions were weak or nonexistent and where they could pay lower wages. The athletic shoe manufacturer Nike was one of the first to exploit the advantages of production abroad, turning to Japan in the 1960s. When labor costs there began to rise, Nike shifted production to South Korea. When Korean workers demanded better wages and working conditions, it turned to China and other Asian countries. Local contractors in Indonesia paid workers as little as fifteen cents an hour as they produced seventy million pairs of shoes in 1996. Many companies, like Nike, contracted out production to foreign companies

rather than employing foreign workers directly, and as a result the precise number of U.S. jobs lost to foreign workers is difficult to calculate.

Charles Seitz, who lost his job at Eastman Kodak when the company moved some of its operations to China and Mexico, was not entirely wrong when he said, "There's nothing made here [in the United States] anymore." Of course, not all the job losses resulted from outsourcing production. Some corporations chose another way to cut costs: increasing productivity so that they could downsize their workforces. At Kodak, for example, a machine replaced fourteen workers who previously had mixed filmmaking ingredients. The invention of smartphones dealt a further blow to Kodak, and virtually none of the phones that came with built-in cameras were made in the United States. Whether a job was lost to a foreign worker, to automation, or to a work speed-up, millions of workers saw the job security and standard of living that they had been used to for decades slip away.

In 2004, the 150-year-old company Levi Strauss, whose product had become an iconic American garment in the 1960s, shut down its last plants in the United States, contracting out

the manufacture of jeans in fifty other countries from Latin America to Asia. Marivel Gutierez, a side-seam operator in the San Antonio plant, acknowledged that workers in Mexico and elsewhere would benefit, suggesting the globalization of the American dream. "But," she worried, "what happens to our American dream?" Workers like Gutierez stood as reminders that as many reaped the benefits of free enterprise across national borders, globalization left multitudes of victims in its wake.

Questions for Analysis

Summarize the Argument: What are three reasons for the loss of manufacturing jobs in the United States? What were some of the effects of de-industrialization?

Analyze the Evidence: Did the number of manufacturing jobs in the United States fall in actual numbers, in percentage of the workforce, or both?

Consider the Context: The loss of manufacturing jobs in the United States was part of the process of globalization. What benefits did U.S. residents gain from globalization?

economy would benefit the Democratic contender, Vice President Al Gore, and he did surpass Bush by more than half a million votes. But Florida's 25 electoral college votes would decide the presidency. Bush's tiny margin in Florida prompted an automatic recount of the votes, which eventually gave him an edge of 537 votes in that state.

The Democrats asked for hand-counting of Florida ballots in several heavily Democratic counties where machine errors and confusing ballots may have left thousands of Gore votes unrecorded. The Republicans, in turn, went to court to try to stop the hand-counts. The outcome of the 2000 election hung in the balance for weeks as cases went up to the Supreme Court. Finally, the sharply divided justices ruled five to four against allowing the state to conduct further recounts. While critics charged partisanship, noting that the conservative justices had

abandoned their principle of favoring state over federal authority, Gore conceded to Bush. For the first time since 1888, a president who failed to win the popular vote took office (Map 31.3).

The Domestic Policies of a "Compassionate Conservative"

Bush had promised to govern as a "compassionate conservative." Embracing the nation's diversity and following in Clinton's footsteps, he appointed African Americans, Latinos, and Asian Americans to his cabinet. A devout born-again Christian, he immediately established the White House Office of Faith-Based and Community Initiatives, funding religious groups to run programs for prison inmates, the unemployed, and others. Conservatives praised the initiatives, which encouraged private institutions to replace

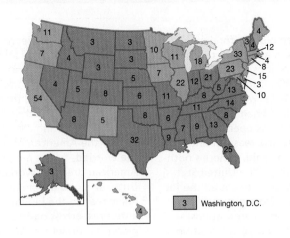

Candidate	Electoral Vote	Popular Vote	Percent of Popular Vote
George W. Bush (Republican)	271	50,456,062	47.8
Al Gore (Democrat)	267	50,996,862	48.4
Ralph Nader (Green Party)	0	2,858,843	2.7
Patrick J. Buchanan (Reform Party)	0	438,760	0.4

3 Washington, D.C.

Map 31.3
The Election of 2000

government as the provider of welfare, but others charged that they violated the constitutional separation of church and state. Federal courts ruled in several dozen cases that faith ministries were using government funds to indoctrinate the people they served. More substantial was Bush's achievement of legislation authorizing a $15 billion anti-AIDS program in Africa that eventually saved millions of lives.

By contrast, Bush's fiscal policies were more compassionate toward the rich. In 2001, he signed a bill reducing taxes over the next ten years by $1.35 trillion. A 2003 tax law slashed another $320 billion. The laws heavily favored the wealthy by reducing income taxes, phasing out estate taxes, and cutting tax rates on capital gains and dividends. They also provided benefits for married couples and families with children and offered tax deductions for college expenses.

The tax cuts helped turn the budget surplus that Bush had inherited into a mushrooming federal deficit—the highest in U.S. history. In 2009, the deficit surpassed $1 trillion as the government struggled to combat a recession. By then, the national debt had risen to $9.6 trillion, making the United States increasingly dependent on China and other foreign investors, who held more than half of the debt.

Bush used executive powers to weaken environmental protection as part of his larger agenda to reduce government regulation, promote

economic growth, and increase energy production. The administration opened millions of wilderness acres to mining, oil, and timber industries and relaxed standards under the Clean Air and Clean Water Acts. To worldwide dismay, the administration withdrew from the Kyoto Protocol, signed in 1997 by 178 nations to reduce greenhouse gas emissions that cause global warming.

Conservatives hailed Bush's two appointments to the Supreme Court. In 2005, John Roberts, who had served in the Reagan and George H. W. Bush administrations, was named chief justice. When the moderate Sandra Day O'Connor resigned, Bush nominated Samuel A. Alito, a staunch conservative who was narrowly confirmed. While the Court upheld the rights of homosexuals and stood up to the administration on the rights of accused terrorists, it also upheld increasing restrictions on abortion and struck down regulations in the areas of voting rights, gun control, sex discrimination in employment, and business practices. Its five-to-four ruling in *Citizens United v. FEC* (2010) gutted regulation of election campaign financing by holding that such spending was a form of speech protected by the First Amendment.

In contrast to the partisan conflict over judicial appointments and tax and environmental policy, Bush won bipartisan support for the **No Child Left Behind Act** of 2002, a substantial expansion of the federal government into public education. Promising to end, in Bush's words, "the story of children being just shuffled through the system," the law set national standards and imposed penalties on failing schools. But the law was never adequately funded; school officials criticized the one-size-fits-all approach and pointed to poverty as a source of student deficiencies, which schools alone could not overcome. In 2015, Congress returned considerable control to the states and local districts.

President Bush's second effort to co-opt Democratic Party issues constituted what he hailed as "the greatest advance in health care coverage for America's seniors" since Medicare began in 1965. In 2003, Bush signed a bill providing prescription drug benefits for the elderly and also expanding the role of private insurers in the Medicare system. Most Democrats opposed the legislation because it subsidized private insurers with federal funds, banned imports of low-priced drugs, and prohibited the government from negotiating with drug companies to reduce prices. The law was a boon to the elderly, but medical costs overall continued to soar, and 40 million Americans remained uninsured.

One domestic undertaking of the Bush administration found little approval anywhere: its response to Hurricane Katrina, which in August

Hurricane Katrina
Residents of the poverty-stricken Lower Ninth Ward of New Orleans pleaded for help in the flooding that followed Hurricane Katrina in August 2005. The boat was useless because it had lost its motor. Some residents waited as long as five days to be rescued. A historian of the disaster wrote, "Americans were not used to seeing their country in ruins, their people in want." AP Photo/David J. Phillip.

2005 devastated the coasts of Alabama, Louisiana, and Mississippi and ultimately took some fifteen hundred lives. The catastrophe that ensued when the levees broke, flooding 80 percent of New Orleans, shook many Americans' deeply rooted assumption that government would protect citizens from natural disasters. New Orleans residents who were too old, too poor, or too sick to evacuate spent days waiting on rooftops for help; wading in filthy, toxic water; and enduring the heat and disorder at the centers where they had been told to go for help. "How can we save the world if we can't save our own people?" wondered one Louisianan. Since so many of Katrina's hardest-hit victims were poor and black, the disaster also highlighted racial injustices and deprivations remaining in American society.

The Globalization of Terrorism

The response to Hurricane Katrina contrasted sharply with the government's decisive reaction to the horror that had unfolded four years earlier on the morning of September 11, 2001. Nineteen terrorists hijacked four planes and flew two of them into the twin towers of New York City's World Trade Center and one into the Pentagon in Washington, D.C.; the fourth crashed in a field in Pennsylvania. The attacks took nearly 2,800 lives, including people from ninety different countries.

The hijackers belonged to Osama bin Laden's Al Qaeda international terrorist network. Organized in Afghanistan then ruled by the radical Muslim Taliban government, the attacks expressed Islamic extremists' rage at the spread of Western culture and values into the Muslim world, as well as their opposition to the 1991 Persian Gulf War against Iraq and the stationing of American troops in Saudi Arabia. Bin Laden sought to rid the Middle East of Western influence and install puritanical Muslim control.

The 9/11 terrorists and others who came after them ranged from poor to well-off; many lived in Middle Eastern homelands governed by undemocratic and corrupt governments, others in Western cities where they felt alienated and despised. All saw the West, especially the United States, as the evil source of their humiliation and the supporter of Israel's oppression of Palestinian Muslims.

In the wake of the September 11 attacks, President Bush sought a global alliance against terrorism and won at least verbal support from most governments. On October 11, with NATO support, the United States and Britain began bombing Afghanistan, and American forces aided the Northern Alliance, the Taliban government's main opposition. By December, the Taliban government was destroyed, but bin Laden eluded capture until U.S. special forces killed him in Pakistan in 2011. Afghans elected a new national government, but the Taliban remained strong in large parts of the country and contributed to ongoing economic instability and insecurity. When the Taliban retook the city of Kunduz in 2015, a U.S. soldier who had fought there wrote, "You wonder what all that effort and sacrifice was for."

After the September 11 attacks, anti-immigrant sentiment revived throughout the United States, and residents appearing to be Middle Eastern or practicing Islam often aroused suspicion. Authorities arrested more than a thousand Arabs and Muslims; a Justice Department study later found that many people with no connection to terrorism spent months in jail, denied their rights. "I think America overreacted . . . by singling out Arab-named men like myself," said Shanaz Mohammed, who was jailed for eight months for an immigration violation.

In October 2001, Congress passed the **USA Patriot Act**, giving the government new powers to monitor suspected terrorists, including the ability to access all Americans' personal information. It soon provoked calls for revision from both conservatives and liberals. Kathleen MacKenzie, a councilwoman in Ann Arbor, Michigan, explained why the council opposed the Patriot Act: "As concerned as we were about national safety, we felt that giving up [rights] was too high a price to pay." A security official countered, "If you don't violate someone's human rights some of the time, you probably aren't doing your job." A decade past 9/11, the government continued to gather personal information on individual citizens, seeming to some to have sacrificed too much liberty for security.

Insisting that presidential powers were virtually limitless in times of national crisis, Bush stretched his authority until he met resistance from the courts and Congress. The United States detained more than 700 prisoners captured in

Afghanistan

Afghanistan and taken to the U.S. military base at Guantánamo, Cuba, where, until the courts acted, they had no rights and were sometimes tortured. Although President Barack Obama promised to close the detention camp, he met resistance from Congress, and more than fifty prisoners remained there in 2016.

The government also sought to protect Americans from future terrorist attacks through the greatest reorganization of the executive branch since 1948. In November 2002, Congress authorized the new Department of Homeland Security, combining 170,000 federal

9/11
The magnitude of the destruction and loss of lives in the 9/11 attacks made Americans feel more vulnerable than they had since the Cold War ended. The attacks also affected people around the world, who streamed to U.S. embassies or expressed their shock and sympathy in other ways. Steve Ludlum/The *New York Times*/Redux.

employees from twenty-two agencies responsible for various aspects of domestic security. Chief among the department's duties were intelligence analysis; immigration and border security; chemical, biological, and nuclear countermeasures; and emergency preparedness and response.

Unilateralism, Preemption, and the Iraq War

The Bush administration sought collective action against the Taliban, but on most international issues it adopted a go-it-alone approach. In addition to withdrawing from the Kyoto Protocol on global warming and violating international rules about the treatment of military prisoners, it withdrew from the UN's International Criminal Court and rejected an agreement to enforce bans on biological weapons that all of America's European allies had signed.

Nowhere was the policy of unilateralism more striking than in a new war against Iraq, a war pushed by Vice President Dick Cheney and Secretary of Defense Donald H. Rumsfeld, but not by Secretary of State Colin Powell. Addressing West Point graduates in June 2002, President Bush proclaimed a new strategy based not on containment but on preemption: "Traditional concepts of deterrence will not work against a terrorist enemy whose avowed tactics are wanton destruction and the targeting of innocents; whose so-called soldiers seek martyrdom in death and whose most potent protection is statelessness." Because even weak countries and small groups could strike devastating blows at the United States, as Al Qaeda had done on 9/11, the nation had to "be ready for preemptive action." The president's claim that the United States had the right to start a war was at odds with international law and with many Americans' understanding of their nation's ideals. It distressed most of America's great-power allies.

Nonetheless, the Bush administration soon applied the doctrine of preemption to Iraq, whose dictator, Saddam Hussein, appeared to be violating UN restrictions on Iraqi development of nuclear, chemical, and biological weapons. In November 2002, the United States obtained a UN Security Council resolution demanding that Iraq disarm or face "serious consequences." When Iraq failed to comply fully with UN inspections, the Bush administration decided on war. Making claims—later proved false—that

Hussein had links to Al Qaeda and held weapons of mass destruction, the president insisted that the threat was immediate and great enough to justify preemptive action. Despite the absence of UN approval and opposition from the Arab world and most major nations—including France, Germany, China, and Russia—the United States and Britain invaded Iraq on March 19, 2003, supported by some thirty nations (see Map 31.2). Coalition forces won an easy victory, and Bush declared the end of the **Iraq War** on May 1. Saddam Hussein was captured in December 2003, tried by an Iraqi court, and executed.

Chaos followed the quick victory. Damage from U.S. bombing and widespread looting resulting from the failure of U.S. troops to secure order and provide basic necessities left Iraqis wondering how much they had gained. "With Saddam there was tyranny, but at least you had a salary to put food on your family's table," said a young father. A Baghdad hospital worker complained, "They can take our oil, but at least they should let us have electricity and water." Five years after the invasion, continuing violence had caused 2 million to flee their country and displaced 1.9 million within Iraq.

The administration had not planned adequately for the occupation and failed to send sufficient troops to Iraq. The 140,000 American forces there came under attack almost daily from remnants of the former Hussein regime, religious extremists, and hundreds of foreign terrorists now entering the chaotic country. Seeking to divide Iraqis and undermine the occupation, terrorists launched assaults that killed tens of thousands of Iraqis. By the end of the Iraq War, nearly 4,500 U.S. soldiers had lost their lives, and many returned home grievously wounded.

The war became an issue in the presidential campaign of 2004. U.S. senator John Kerry, the Democratic nominee, criticized Bush's unilateralist foreign policy and the administration's conduct of the war. A slim majority of voters, however, indicated their belief that Bush would better protect American security than Kerry, giving the president a 286 to 252 victory in the electoral college, 50.7 percent of the popular vote, and Republican majorities in Congress.

In June 2004, the United States transferred sovereignty to a Shiite-dominated Iraqi government, which failed to satisfy Iraq's other major groups—Sunnis and Kurds. Violence escalated against

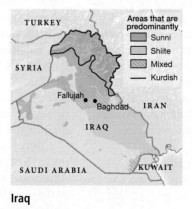

Iraq

government officials, Iraqi civilians, and occupation forces. A nineteen-year-old Iraqi confined to his house by his parents, who feared he could be killed or lured into terrorist activities, said, "If I'm killed, it doesn't even matter because I'm dead right now." By 2006, a majority of Americans believed that the Iraq War was a mistake.

Criticism of the war crossed party lines and included military leaders. Critics acknowledged that the United States had felled a brutal dictator, but coalition forces were not adequately prepared for the turmoil that followed. Nor did they find the weapons of mass destruction or links to Osama bin Laden that administration officials had insisted made the war necessary. Rather, in the chaos induced by the invasion, more than a thousand terrorists entered Iraq— the place, according to one expert, "for fundamentalists to go . . . to stick it to the West."

The war and occupation exacted a steep price in American and Iraqi lives, dollars (more than $750 billion), U.S. relations with other great powers, and the nation's reputation in the world, especially among Arab nations. Revelations of prisoner abuse in the Abu Ghraib prison in Iraq and in the Guantánamo detention camp housing captives from the Afghan war further tarnished the image of the United States, as anti-Americanism rose around the world. The budget deficit swelled, and resources were diverted to Iraq from other national security challenges, including the stabilization of Afghanistan, the elimination of Al Qaeda, and the threats posed by North Korea's and Iran's pursuit of nuclear weapons.

Voters registered their dissatisfaction in 2006, giving Democrats control of Congress for the first time since 1994. A temporary troop surge in Iraq in 2007, along with actions by Iraqi leaders, contributed to a significant reduction in violence, and the administration began planning for the withdrawal of U.S. forces, which was completed at the end of 2011. Peace eluded the Iraqis, however, who continued to live amid sectarian violence. Unrest was exacerbated by the rise of the Islamic State in Iraq and Syria (ISIS), a more brutal and effective offspring of Al Qaeda. By 2016, ISIS controlled key areas of Iraq and Syria and was linked to or inspired terrorist attacks on civilians in Egypt; Turkey; Paris, France; San Bernardino, California; Orlando, Florida; Brussels, Belgium; and elsewhere.

REVIEW What impact did the terrorist attacks on September 11, 2001, have on U.S. foreign and domestic policies?

▶ The Obama Presidency: Reform and Backlash

Bush's successor, Barack Hussein Obama, aimed to turn the page in both domestic and foreign policy. He achieved major health care reform and some antirecession measures, but a determined grassroots movement on the Republican right pushed the party to oppose the president at every turn. In foreign policy, Obama generally sought a less aggressive, more multilateral approach to challenges around the world. His administration reopened diplomatic relations with Cuba in 2015 and negotiated a treaty with five major powers and Iran to keep that nation from developing nuclear weapons. But most of the Middle East remained an unstable and dangerous place, and the United States seemed increasingly vulnerable to terrorist threats.

Governing during Economic Crisis and Political Polarization

Obama won an election that represented momentous changes in American politics. The Republican nominee, Senator John McCain of Arizona, a Vietnam War hero, chose as his running mate Alaska governor Sarah Palin, the first Republican woman vice presidential candidate. In the Democratic Party, for the first time, an African American and a woman were the top two contenders. (See "Analyzing Historical Evidence," page 916.) In a hard-fought primary battle, Obama edged out New York senator and former First Lady Hillary Clinton for the nomination.

Born to a white mother and a Kenyan father and raised in Hawai'i and Indonesia, Obama was the first African American to head the *Harvard Law Review*. He settled in Chicago, taught law, served in the Illinois Senate, and won election to the U.S. Senate in 2004. At the age of forty-seven, he won the Democratic presidential nomination with brilliant grassroots and Internet organizing and by promising a new kind of politics and racial reconciliation. Obama won 53 percent of the popular vote and defeated McCain 365 to 173 in the electoral college, while Democrats increased their majorities in the House and Senate.

Defining "individual responsibility and mutual responsibility" as "the essence of the American promise," Obama hoped to work across party lines to enact reforms in health care, education, the environment, and immigration policy,

Health Care Reform
Repeated breakdowns of the federal government's Web site when it opened for health insurance enrollment in October 2013 added fuel to the critics of the Patient Protection and Affordable Care Act. President Obama chose Faneuil Hall in Boston, where former governor Mitt Romney had signed a similar health reform measure for Massachusetts, to defend the law and promise that the Web site would be fixed. Yoon S. Byun/The *Boston Globe* via Getty Images.

but he confronted a severe economic crisis. A recession had struck in late 2007, fueled by a breakdown in financial institutions that had accumulated trillions of dollars of bad debt, much of it from risky home mortgages. As the recession spread to other parts of the economy and the world, mortgage foreclosures skyrocketed, major companies went bankrupt, and unemployment rose to 9.8 percent in late 2010.

The Great Recession was so severe that Congress passed the Bush administration's $700 billion Troubled Asset Relief Program in 2008 to inject credit into the economy and shore up banks and other businesses. Obama followed with the American Recovery and Reinvestment Act of 2009, $787 billion worth of spending and tax cuts to stimulate the economy and relieve unemployment. He also arranged a federal bailout of General Motors and Chrysler, saving some one million jobs related to the automobile industry. Finally, to address the sources of the financial crisis, Congress expanded governmental regulation with the Wall Street Reform and Consumer Protection Act in 2010. Nonetheless, the recovery was agonizingly slow, and income inequality reached its highest level since the 1920s.

With a Democrat-controlled Congress for only the first two years of his presidency, Obama's domestic achievements fell short of his promises. His judicial appointments increased the number of women on the Supreme Court to three and included the first-ever Latina justice, and he signed legislation that strengthened women's right to equal pay. In addition, Congress ended discrimination against gays in the military and rolled back some of the Bush tax cuts that had disproportionately favored the wealthy.

Obama's paramount achievement was passage of health care reform, putting the United States in step with the other advanced nations that subsidized some kind of health care for all citizens. The **Patient Protection and Affordable Care Act** of 2010 required that nearly everyone carry health insurance, and to that end, it provided subsidies and compelled larger businesses to cover their employees. The law also included protections for health care consumers and contained provisions to limit medical costs. Although liberals failed to get a public option to allow government-managed programs to compete with private insurance plans, the law represented the largest expansion of government since the Great Society. Even though Republicans had previously endorsed key elements of the measure, and it resembled Massachusetts's health care program established under Republican governor Mitt Romney, not a single Republican voted for it. Most Republican governors impeded its implementation in their states.

"Obamacare" (a derisive label later embraced by its supporters), along with the government bailouts of big corporations, helped fuel a grassroots

Caricaturing the Candidates: Clinton and Obama in 2008

In the Democratic presidential primaries of 2008, political cartoonists faced an unfamiliar challenge. As usual, cartoonists had to draw a recognizable image of a subject but exaggerate or enhance it to make it humorous. For the first time in a U.S. presidential primary campaign, a woman and an African American squared off as major rivals, upsetting centuries-old notions of who a president should be. Political cartoonists now faced the challenge of caricaturing a woman and a black man without opening themselves to charges of sexism or racism.

Hillary Clinton had a long history in political cartoons as First Lady and then as senator from New York. A favorite theme of cartoonists who commented on her active involvement in policy during her husband's presidency suggested that she was exerting too much power rather than playing the traditional supporting role of First Lady. During her own campaign in 2008, cartoonists continued to exaggerate her hips, and they took advantage of the lines on the sixty-year-old's face.

Political cartoonists drawing Barack Obama faced the challenge of avoiding obvious racial stereotypes. In contrast to Clinton, long in

"The Clinton Machine" Pat Bagley, The *Salt Lake Tribune*, Cagle Cartoons.

the public eye, Obama was a relative newcomer to the national scene, having spent just two years in the U.S. Senate before announcing his candidacy. Forty-seven years old, with a long, lean face and body and closely clipped hair, he provided fewer opportunities for caricature than did Clinton. Obama had already described himself as "a skinny

kid with big ears and a funny name," and cartoonists pounced on that image.

In the first cartoon, from February 2008, Hillary Clinton is in the driver's seat of "The Clinton Machine," which is about to crush Barack Obama. Note who is providing the power for the steamroller and how his appearance contrasts

movement of mostly white, middle-class, and older voters funded by billionaire conservatives and encouraged by conservative media. These Americans, self-identified as members of the Tea Party movement, raged at what they considered an overreaching government and from the sense that they and their values were being displaced. As one Tea Party supporter put it, "The government is taking over everything—I want my freedom back." Most Tea Party activists defended

Social Security and Medicare as programs they had "earned" but resisted any new federal entitlement programs.

The intensely polarized political environment posed a roadblock to reducing unemployment and thwarted Obama's efforts to reform environmental and immigration policy. Obama carried the burden of a nearly 8 percent unemployment rate into the 2012 election, where he faced Republican Mitt Romney. With the electorate

with that of Obama. Although Obama won two of the four earliest primaries, the cartoonist suggests that Hillary Clinton's campaign was about to clobber Obama. Consider what the cartoon suggests about Bill Clinton's role in his wife's campaign and about Hillary Clinton's ambition.

Political cartoonists sometimes use animal images that have certain associations for their viewers. The second cartoon, showing Hillary Clinton as a wasp who will not let go of Obama, reflects the view of Obama supporters that Clinton should have pulled out of the race earlier. By May 2008, Obama had won the most delegates through state primaries. Yet Clinton hung on, claiming that she had won more of the overall popular vote and that she led Obama in support from the so-called superdelegates, including elected officials and party leaders, whose votes were not tied to primary election results. Even after her concession in early June 2008, some cartoons showed her threatening Obama as he contemplated choosing a running mate. This cartoon here may have tapped into stereotypes of nagging women and into anxieties about an ambitious black man by making him appear weak and deferential.

Although cartoonists tended to portray Clinton and Obama as bitter enemies throughout the primaries, the two politicians began an effective partnership when president-elect

"It's Not My Place" Daryl Cagle, Cagle Cartoons.

Obama selected Clinton for the position of secretary of state in November 2008.

Questions for Analysis

Analyze the Evidence: What is the effect of portraying Obama as oblivious to the Clinton machine's power in the first cartoon and as unable to stand up to Clinton's determination in the second? What stereotypes about women are conveyed in the ways in which Clinton is drawn in each of the cartoons? Would a man have been portrayed as a wasp?

Recognize Viewpoints: What attitude about Bill Clinton's role in his wife's campaign is conveyed in the first cartoon? What message does the second cartoon send about Obama in showing Clinton seeming to overpower him, even though he was ahead of her in the race for the nomination? Do you think that these cartoonists successfully avoided sexist or racist stereotypes?

Consider the Context: In what ways was the election of 2008 groundbreaking?

deeply divided over the role of the federal government, Obama won easily in the electoral college, with 332 votes to Romney's 206, and he captured 51 percent of the popular vote to Romney's 47 percent (Map 31.4). Yet, following the 2014 midterm elections, Republicans took over both houses of Congress.

With Republicans in Congress blocking him at every turn, Obama used his executive authority to raise the minimum wage for federal workers, protect younger undocumented immigrants from deportation, and chip away at some of the racial injustices in the criminal justice system. He stiffened curbs on motor vehicle and power plant emissions, encouraged alternative energy development, and helped make possible a landmark climate change agreement signed in Paris in 2015 by 195 nations, which pledged action to reduce carbon emissions that threatened to devastate the earth.

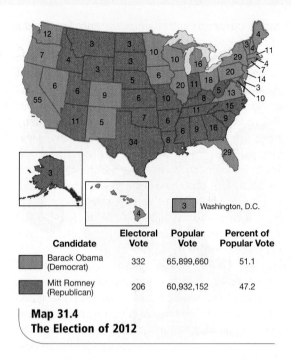

Candidate	Electoral Vote	Popular Vote	Percent of Popular Vote
Barack Obama (Democrat)	332	65,899,660	51.1
Mitt Romney (Republican)	206	60,932,152	47.2

Map 31.4
The Election of 2012

Redefining the War on Terror

Obama criticized much of his predecessor's foreign policy, embodied in Bush's term "global war on terror." Obama believed that that concept exaggerated the threat, rationalized disastrous decisions like the invasion of Iraq, sacrificed American ideals in the pursuit of security, and distracted attention from serious problems at home. In office, however, Obama left some Bush initiatives in place. The Bush administration had ended its use of torture, but Obama failed to convince Congress to close Guantánamo, where sixty prisoners remained, without rights, in 2016. Obama greatly increased the use of unmanned drone strikes in other countries, killing hundreds of people, both terrorists and innocent citizens. Continuing Bush's surveillance programs, the Obama administration secretly collected data about millions of citizens' communications.

Obama followed the Bush administration's plan to withdraw from Iraq, and the last troops departed in 2011, whereupon terrorist violence and sectarian strife grew stronger. He dispatched 50,000 more military personnel to Afghanistan, nearly 10,000 of whom remained there in 2016. In May 2011, U.S. special forces killed Osama bin Laden, who was hiding in Pakistan, weakening but not destroying Al Qaeda and its offshoots.

Obama wanted to regain the trust of Muslim nations, but he sometimes floundered when confronted with difficult decisions about what the United States should do, such as when, in 2011,

popular uprisings, collectively referred to as the "Arab Spring," sought reforms from entrenched dictators in Tunisia, Egypt, Libya, and Syria. Each country had experienced long-standing internal divisions, decades of official corruption, and neglect of its population's basic needs, such as water and food; moreover, terrorists operated in each country, hoping to exploit the situation to install a radical fundamentalist Islamic state. Although some rebellions toppled corrupt dictators, such as Libya's Muammar al-Gaddafi, little progress was made toward stability, constitutional government, equal rights, and economic security. Protests in Syria turned into a civil war that took more than 200,000 lives; sent four million Syrians into exile creating a refugee crisis in Europe; and provided an opening for the spread of the radical Islamist organization ISIS.

The calamity of the Iraq War and the desire to improve the nation's international reputation made Obama wary of intervention. Though reluctant to commit military force beyond air strikes and some special forces on the ground, Obama insisted that the United States must remain engaged in the Middle East. Preferring to attack problems with diplomacy, in 2015 Obama worked with China, Russia, France, the United Kingdom, and Germany to secure a treaty with Iran to keep that nation from developing nuclear weapons. The harsh condemnation of the Iran nuclear deal by most Republicans reflected how much Americans disagreed about where their nation's international interests lay and what the United States could and should do to protect those interests and national security.

REVIEW What obstacles stood in the way of Obama's reform agenda?

▶ Conclusion: Defining the Government's Role at Home and Abroad

More than two hundred years after the birth of the United States, Colin Powell referred to the unfinished nature of the American promise when he declared that the question of America's role in the world "isn't answered yet." In fact, the end of the Cold War, the rise of international terrorism, and the George W. Bush administration's doctrines of preemption and unilateralism sparked new debates over the long-standing question of how the United States should act beyond its borders.

Nor had Americans set to rest questions about the role of government at home. In a population greatly composed of people fleeing oppressive governments, Americans had always debated what responsibilities the government should shoulder and what was best left to private enterprise, families, churches, and other voluntary institutions. Far more than other industrialized democracies, the United States had relied on private rather than public obligation, individual rather than collective solutions. In the twentieth century, Americans had significantly enlarged the federal government's powers and responsibilities, but the years since the 1960s had seen a decline of trust in government's ability to improve people's lives, even as a poverty rate of 20 percent among children continued and a growing gap between rich and poor intensified into the twenty-first century.

The shifting of control of the government back and forth between Republicans and Democrats from 1989 to 2016 revealed a dynamic debate over government's role in domestic affairs. The first Bush administration's civil rights measure for people with disabilities, Clinton's incremental reforms, and Obama's Affordable Care Act built on a deep-rooted tradition that sought to realize the American promise of justice and human well-being. Those who mobilized against the ravages of globalization worked internationally for what populists, progressives, New Deal reformers, and activists of the 1960s had sought for the domestic population: protection of individual rights, curbs on capitalism, assistance for victims of rapid economic change, and fiscal policies that placed greater responsibility on those best able to pay for the collective good. Even the second Bush administration, which sought to limit government's reach, supported the No Child Left Behind Act and the Medicare prescription drug program; it departed from traditional conservative policy in a gigantic program to bail out failing businesses when the Great Recession struck in 2008. The controversy surrounding Obama's efforts to stimulate the economy and reform health care and the financial industry replayed America's long-standing debate about the government's appropriate role.

The United States became more embedded in the global economy as products, information, and people crossed borders with amazing speed and frequency. New waves of immigration altered the face of the American population and the makeup of its culture. Although the end of the Cold War brought about unanticipated cooperation between the United States and its former enemies, globalization also contributed to the threat of deadly terrorism within America's own borders. In response to those dangers, the second Bush administration launched wars in Afghanistan and Iraq. Both Democratic and Republican presidents sought to maintain the preeminence in the world that the United States had held since World War II, but debate continued about how much it could accomplish in other parts of the world and where and how best to use American power.

See the Selected Bibliography for this chapter in the Appendix.

31 Chapter Review

KEY TERMS

Clean Air Act of 1990 (p. 893)
Americans with Disabilities Act (ADA) (p. 893)
Persian Gulf War (p. 899)
Earned Income Tax Credit (EITC) (p. 900)
Temporary Assistance for Needy Families (TANF) program (p. 902)
North American Free Trade Agreement (NAFTA) (p. 905)
World Trade Organization (WTO) (p. 906)
No Child Left Behind Act (p. 910)
USA Patriot Act (p. 912)
Iraq War (p. 913)
Patient Protection and Affordable Care Act (p. 915)

REVIEW QUESTIONS

1. How did George H. W. Bush respond to threats to U.S. interests as the Cold War came to an end? (pp. 893–900)

2. How did President Clinton seek a middle ground in American politics? (pp. 900–903)

3. What were the costs and benefits to the United States of globalization in the 1990s and early 2000s? (pp. 903–907)

4. What impact did the terrorist attacks on September 11, 2001, have on U.S. foreign and domestic policies? (pp. 908–914)

5. What obstacles stood in the way of Obama's reform agenda? (pp. 914–918)

MAKING CONNECTIONS

1. How did the fall of the Soviet Union influence the foreign policy of George H. W. Bush?

2. How did Clinton's policies differ from those of Democrats in the past?

3. Explain what economic globalization is, and describe how it affected the U.S. economy and population in the 1990s.

4. What gave rise to the 9/11 attacks? How did the United States respond?

LINKING TO THE PAST

1. How did George W. Bush's doctrine of preemption differ from the doctrine of containment? (See chapter 26.)

2. What features did immigration after 1980 have in common with immigration between 1880 and 1920? What was different? (See chapter 19.)

Appendix Directory

APPENDIX I. Documents

THE DECLARATION OF INDEPENDENCE

In Congress, July 4, 1776,

THE UNANIMOUS DECLARATION OF THE THIRTEEN UNITED STATES OF AMERICA

When in the course of human events, it becomes necessary for one people to dissolve the political bands which have connected them with another, and to assume, among the powers of the earth, the separate and equal station to which the laws of nature and of nature's God entitle them, a decent respect to the opinions of mankind requires that they should declare the causes which impel them to the separation.

We hold these truths to be self-evident, that all men are created equal; that they are endowed by their Creator with certain unalienable rights; that among these, are life, liberty, and the pursuit of happiness. That, to secure these rights, governments are instituted among men, deriving their just powers from the consent of the governed; that, whenever any form of government becomes destructive of these ends, it is the right of the people to alter or to abolish it, and to institute a new government, laying its foundation on such principles, and organizing its powers in such form, as to them shall seem most likely to effect their safety and happiness. Prudence, indeed, will dictate that governments long established, should not be changed for light and transient causes; and, accordingly, all experience hath shown, that mankind are more disposed to suffer, while evils are sufferable, than to right themselves by abolishing the forms to which they are accustomed. But, when a long train of abuses and usurpations, pursuing invariably the same object, evinces a design to reduce them under absolute despotism, it is their right, it is their duty, to throw off such government and to provide new guards for their future security. Such has been the patient sufferance of these colonies, and such is now the necessity which constrains them to alter their former systems of government. The history of the present King of Great Britain is a history of repeated injuries and usurpations, all having, in direct object, the establishment of an absolute tyranny over these States. To prove this, let facts be submitted to a candid world: He has refused his assent to laws the most wholesome and necessary for the public good.

He has forbidden his governors to pass laws of immediate and pressing importance, unless suspended in their operation till his assent should be obtained; and, when so suspended, he has utterly neglected to attend to them.

He has refused to pass other laws for the accommodation of large districts of people, unless those people would relinquish the right of representation in the legislature; a right inestimable to them, and formidable to tyrants only.

He has called together legislative bodies at places unusual, uncomfortable, and distant from the depository of their public records, for the sole purpose of fatiguing them into compliance with his measures.

He has dissolved representative houses repeatedly for opposing, with manly firmness, his invasions on the rights of the people.

He has refused, for a long time after such dissolutions, to cause others to be elected; whereby the legislative powers, incapable of annihilation, have returned to the people at large for their exercise; the state remaining in the mean-time exposed to all the danger of invasion from without, and convulsions within.

He has endeavored to prevent the population of these States; for that purpose, obstructing the laws for naturalization of foreigners, refusing to pass others to encourage their migration hither, and raising the conditions of new appropriations of lands.

He has obstructed the administration of justice, by refusing his assent to laws for establishing judiciary powers.

He has made judges dependent on his will alone, for the tenure of their offices, and the amount and payment of their salaries.

He has erected a multitude of new offices, and sent hither swarms of officers to harass our people, and eat out their substance.

He has kept among us, in times of peace, standing armies, without the consent of our legislature.

He has affected to render the military independent of, and superior to, the civil power.

He has combined, with others, to subject us to a jurisdiction foreign to our Constitution, and unacknowledged by our laws; giving his assent to their acts of pretended legislation:

For quartering large bodies of armed troops among us:

For protecting them by a mock trial, from punishment, for any murders which they should commit on the inhabitants of these States:

For cutting off our trade with all parts of the world:

For imposing taxes on us without our consent:

For depriving us, in many cases, of the benefit of trial by jury:

For transporting us beyond seas to be tried for pretended offences:

For abolishing the free system of English laws in a neighboring province, establishing therein an arbitrary government, and enlarging its boundaries, so as to render it at once an example and fit instrument for introducing the same absolute rule into these colonies:

For taking away our charters, abolishing our most valuable laws, and altering, fundamentally, the powers of our governments:

For suspending our own legislatures, and declaring themselves invested with power to legislate for us in all cases whatsoever.

He has abdicated government here, by declaring us out of his protection, and waging war against us.

He has plundered our seas, ravaged our coasts, burnt our towns, and destroyed the lives of our people.

He is, at this time, transporting large armies of foreign mercenaries to complete the works of death, desolation, and tyranny, already begun, with circumstances of cruelty and perfidy scarcely paralleled in the most barbarous ages, and totally unworthy the head of a civilized nation.

He has constrained our fellow citizens, taken captive on the high seas, to bear arms against their country, to become the executioners of their friends, and brethren, or to fall themselves by their hands.

He has excited domestic insurrections amongst us, and has endeavored to bring on the inhabitants of our frontiers, the merciless Indian savages, whose known rule of warfare is an undistinguished destruction of all ages, sexes, and conditions.

In every stage of these oppressions, we have petitioned for redress; in the most humble terms; our repeated petitions have been answered only by repeated injury. A prince, whose character is thus marked by every act which may define a tyrant, is unfit to be the ruler of a free people.

Nor have we been wanting in attention to our British brethren. We have warned them, from time to time, of attempts made by their legislature to extend an unwarrantable jurisdiction over us. We have reminded them of the circumstances of our emigration and settlement here. We have appealed to their native justice and magnanimity, and we have conjured them, by the ties of our common kindred, to disavow these usurpations, which would inevitably interrupt our connections and correspondence. They, too, have been deaf to the voice of justice and consanguinity. We must, therefore, acquiesce in the necessity which denounces our separation, and hold them as we hold the rest of mankind, enemies in war, in peace, friends.

We, therefore, the representatives of the United States of America, in general Congress assembled, appealing to the Supreme Judge of the world for the rectitude of our intentions, do, in the name, and by authority of the good people of these colonies, solemnly publish and declare, that these united colonies are, and of right ought to be, free and independent states: that they are absolved from all allegiance to the British Crown, and that all political connection between them and the state of Great Britain is, and ought to be, totally dissolved; and that, as free and independent states, they have full power to levy war, conclude peace, contract alliances, establish commerce, and to do all other acts and things which independent states may of right do. And, for the support of this declaration, with a firm reliance on the protection of Divine Providence, we mutually pledge to each other our lives, our fortunes, and our sacred honor.

The foregoing Declaration was, by order of Congress, engrossed, and signed by the following members:

JOHN HANCOCK

New Hampshire
Josiah Bartlett
William Whipple
Matthew Thornton

Massachusetts Bay
Samuel Adams
John Adams
Robert Treat Paine
Elbridge Gerry

Rhode Island
Stephen Hopkins
William Ellery

Connecticut
Roger Sherman
Samuel Huntington
William Williams
Oliver Wolcott

New York
William Floyd
Phillip Livingston
Francis Lewis
Lewis Morris

New Jersey
Richard Stockton
John Witherspoon
Francis Hopkinson
John Hart
Abraham Clark

Pennsylvania
Robert Morris
Benjamin Rush
Benjamin Franklin
John Morton
George Clymer
James Smith

George Taylor
James Wilson
George Ross

Delaware
Caesar Rodney
George Read
Thomas M'Kean

Maryland
Samuel Chase
William Paca
Thomas Stone
Charles Carroll,
  of Carrollton

North Carolina
William Hooper
Joseph Hewes
John Penn

South Carolina
Edward Rutledge
Thomas Heyward, Jr.
Thomas Lynch, Jr.
Arthur Middleton

Virginia
George Wythe
Richard Henry Lee
Thomas Jefferson
Benjamin Harrison
Thomas Nelson, Jr.
Francis Lightfoot Lee
Carter Braxton

Georgia
Button Gwinnett
Lyman Hall
George Walton

Resolved, That copies of the Declaration be sent to the several assemblies, conventions, and committees, or councils of safety, and to the several commanding officers of the continental troops; that it be proclaimed in each of the United States, at the head of the army.

THE CONSTITUTION OF THE UNITED STATES*

Agreed to by Philadelphia Convention, September 17, 1787. Implemented March 4, 1789.

Preamble

We the people of the United States, in order to form a more perfect union, establish justice, insure domestic tranquility, provide for the common defense, promote the general welfare, and secure the blessings of liberty to ourselves and our posterity, do ordain and establish this Constitution for the United States of America.

Article I

Section 1 All legislative powers herein granted shall be vested in a Congress of the United States, which shall consist of a Senate and a House of Representatives.

Section 2 The House of Representatives shall be composed of members chosen every second year by the people of the several States, and the electors in each State shall have the qualifications requisite for electors of the most numerous branch of the State Legislature.

No person shall be a Representative who shall not have attained to the age of twenty-five years, and been seven years a citizen of the United States, and who shall not, when elected, be an inhabitant of that State in which he shall be chosen.

Representatives and direct taxes shall be apportioned among the several States which may be included within this Union, according to their respective numbers, *which shall be determined by adding to the whole number of free persons, including those bound to service for a term of years and excluding Indians not taxed, three-fifths of all other persons.* The actual enumeration shall be made within three years after the first meeting of the Congress of the United States, and within every subsequent term of ten years, in such manner as they shall by law direct. The number of Representatives shall not exceed one for every thirty thousand, but each State shall have at least one Representative; *and until such enumeration shall be made, the State of New Hampshire shall be entitled to choose three, Massachusetts eight, Rhode Island and Providence Plantations one, Connecticut five, New York six, New Jersey four, Pennsylvania eight, Delaware one, Maryland six, Virginia ten, North Carolina five, South Carolina five, and Georgia three.*

When vacancies happen in the representation from any State, the Executive authority thereof shall issue writs of election to fill such vacancies.

The House of Representatives shall choose their Speaker and other officers; and shall have the sole power of impeachment.

Section 3 The Senate of the United States shall be composed of two Senators from each State, *chosen by the legislature thereof,* for six years; and each Senator shall have one vote.

Immediately after they shall be assembled in consequence of the first election, they shall be divided as equally as may be into three classes. The seats of the Senators of the first class shall be vacated at the expiration of the second year, of the second class at the expiration of the fourth year, and of the third class at the expiration of the sixth year, so that one-third may be chosen every second year; *and if vacancies happen by resignation or otherwise, during the recess of the legislature of any State, the Executive thereof may make temporary appointments until the next meeting of the legislature, which shall then fill such vacancies.*

No person shall be a Senator who shall not have attained to the age of thirty years, and been nine years a citizen of the United States, and who shall not, when elected, be an inhabitant of that State for which he shall be chosen.

The Vice-President of the United States shall be President of the Senate, but shall have no vote, unless they be equally divided.

The Senate shall choose their other officers, and also a President pro tempore, in the absence of the Vice-President, or when he shall exercise the office of President of the United States.

The Senate shall have the sole power to try all impeachments. When sitting for that purpose, they shall be on oath or affirmation. When the President of the United States is tried, the Chief Justice shall preside: and no person shall be convicted without the concurrence of two-thirds of the members present.

Judgment in cases of impeachment shall not extend further than to removal from the office, and disqualification to hold and enjoy any office of honor, trust or profit under the United States: but the party convicted shall nevertheless be liable and subject to indictment, trial, judgment and punishment, according to law.

---

*Passages no longer in effect are in italic type.

Section 4 The times, places and manner of holding elections for Senators and Representatives shall be prescribed in each State by the legislature thereof; but the Congress may at any time by law make or alter such regulations, except as to the places of choosing Senators.

The Congress shall assemble at least once in every year, and such meeting *shall be on the first Monday in December, unless they shall by law appoint a different day.*

Section 5 Each house shall be the judge of the elections, returns and qualifications of its own members, and a majority of each shall constitute a quorum to do business; but a smaller number may adjourn from day to day, and may be authorized to compel the attendance of absent members, in such manner, and under such penalties, as each house may provide.

Each house may determine the rules of its proceedings, punish its members for disorderly behavior, and with the concurrence of two-thirds, expel a member.

Each house shall keep a journal of its proceedings, and from time to time publish the same, excepting such parts as may in their judgment require secrecy; and the yeas and nays of the members of either house on any question shall, at the desire of one-fifth of those present, be entered on the journal.

Neither house, during the session of Congress, shall, without the consent of the other, adjourn for more than three days, nor to any other place than that in which the two houses shall be sitting.

Section 6 The Senators and Representatives shall receive a compensation for their services, to be ascertained by law and paid out of the treasury of the United States. They shall in all cases except treason, felony and breach of the peace, be privileged from arrest during their attendance at the session of their respective houses, and in going to and returning from the same; and for any speech or debate in either house, they shall not be questioned in any other place.

No Senator or Representative shall, during the time for which he was elected, be appointed to any civil office under the authority of the United States, which shall have been created, or the emoluments whereof shall have been increased, during such time; and no person holding any office under the United States shall be a member of either house during his continuance in office.

Section 7 All bills for raising revenue shall originate in the House of Representatives; but the Senate may propose or concur with amendments as on other bills.

Every bill which shall have passed the House of Representatives and the Senate, shall, before it become a law, be presented to the President of the United States; if he approve he shall sign it, but if not he shall return it with objections to that house in which it shall have originated, who shall enter the objections at large on their journal, and proceed to reconsider it. If after such reconsideration two-thirds of that house shall agree to pass the bill, it shall be sent, together with the objections, to the other house, by which it shall likewise be reconsidered, and, if approved by two-thirds of that house, it shall become a law. But in all such cases the votes of both houses shall be determined by yeas and nays, and the names of the persons voting for and against the bill shall be entered on the journal of each house respectively. If any bill shall not be returned by the President within ten days (Sundays excepted) after it shall have been presented to him, the same shall be a law, in like manner as if he had signed it, unless the Congress by their adjournment prevent its return, in which case it shall not be a law.

Every order, resolution, or vote to which the concurrence of the Senate and House of Representatives may be necessary (except on a question of adjournment) shall be presented to the President of the United States; and before the same shall take effect, shall be approved by him, or being disapproved by him, shall be repassed by two-thirds of the Senate and House of Representatives, according to the rules and limitations prescribed in the case of a bill.

Section 8 The Congress shall have power

To lay and collect taxes, duties, imposts, and excises, to pay the debts and provide for the common defense and general welfare of the United States; but all duties, imposts and excises shall be uniform throughout the United States;

To borrow money on the credit of the United States;

To regulate commerce with foreign nations, and among the several States, and with the Indian tribes;

To establish an uniform rule of naturalization, and uniform laws on the subject of bankruptcies throughout the United States;

To coin money, regulate the value thereof, and of foreign coin, and fix the standard of weights and measures;

To provide for the punishment of counterfeiting the securities and current coin of the United States;

To establish post offices and post roads;

To promote the progress of science and useful arts by securing for limited times to authors and inventors the exclusive right to their respective writings and discoveries;

To constitute tribunals inferior to the Supreme Court;

To define and punish piracies and felonies committed on the high seas and offences against the law of nations;

To declare war, grant letters of marque and reprisal, and make rules concerning captures on land and water;

To raise and support armies, but no appropriation of money to that use shall be for a longer term than two years;

To provide and maintain a navy;

To make rules for the government and regulation of the land and naval forces;

To provide for calling forth the militia to execute the laws of the Union, suppress insurrections and repel invasions;

To provide for organizing, arming, and disciplining the militia, and for governing such part of them as may be employed in the service of the United States, reserving to the States respectively the appointment of the officers, and the authority of training the militia according to the discipline prescribed by Congress;

To exercise exclusive legislation in all cases whatsoever, over such district (not exceeding ten miles square) as may, by cession of particular States, and the acceptance of Congress, become the seat of the government of the United States, and to exercise like authority over all places purchased by the consent of the legislature of the State, in which the same shall be, for erection of forts, magazines, arsenals, dock-yards, and other needful buildings;—and

To make all laws which shall be necessary and proper for carrying into execution the foregoing powers, and all other powers vested by this Constitution in the government of the United States, or in any department or officer thereof.

Section 9 *The migration or importation of such persons as any of the States now existing shall think proper to admit shall not be prohibited by the Congress prior to the year one thousand eight hundred and eight; but a tax or duty may be imposed on such importation, not exceeding ten dollars for each person.*

The privilege of the writ of habeas corpus shall not be suspended, unless when in cases of rebellion or invasion the public safety may require it.

No bill of attainder or ex post facto law shall be passed.

No capitation, or other direct, tax shall be laid, unless in proportion to the census or enumeration herein before directed to be taken.

No tax or duty shall be laid on articles exported from any State.

No preference shall be given by any regulation of commerce or revenue to the ports of one State over those of another; nor shall vessels bound to, or from, one State be obliged to enter, clear, or pay duties in another.

No money shall be drawn from the treasury, but in consequence of appropriations made by law; and a regular statement and account of the receipts and expenditures of all public money shall be published from time to time.

No title of nobility shall be granted by the United States: and no person holding any office of profit or trust under them, shall, without the consent of the Congress, accept of any present, emolument, office, or title, of any kind whatever, from any king, prince, or foreign state.

Section 10 No State shall enter into any treaty, alliance, or confederation; grant letters of marque and reprisal;

coin money; emit bills of credit; make anything but gold and silver coin a tender in payment of debts; pass any bill of attainder, ex post facto law, or law impairing the obligation of contracts, or grant any title of nobility.

No State shall, without the consent of Congress, lay any imposts or duties on imports or exports, except what may be absolutely necessary for executing its inspection laws: and the net produce of all duties and imposts, laid by any State on imports or exports, shall be for the use of the treasury of the United States; and all such laws shall be subject to the revision and control of the Congress.

No State shall, without the consent of Congress, lay any duty of tonnage, keep troops, or ships of war in time of peace, enter into any agreement or compact with another State, or with a foreign power, or engage in war, unless actually invaded, or in such imminent danger as will not admit of delay.

Article II

Section 1 The executive power shall be vested in a President of the United States of America. He shall hold his office during the term of four years, and, together with the Vice-President, chosen for the same term, be elected as follows:

Each State shall appoint, in such manner as the legislature thereof may direct, a number of electors, equal to the whole number of Senators and Representatives to which the State may be entitled in the Congress; but no Senator or Representative, or person holding an office of trust or profit under the United States, shall be appointed an elector.

The electors shall meet in their respective States, and vote by ballot for two persons, of whom one at least shall not be an inhabitant of the same State with themselves. And they shall make a list of all the persons voted for, and of the number of votes for each; which list they shall sign and certify, and transmit sealed to the seat of government of the United States, directed to the President of the Senate. The President of the Senate shall, in the presence of the Senate and House of Representatives, open all the certificates, and the votes shall then be counted. The person having the greatest number of votes shall be the President, if such number be a majority of the whole number of electors appointed; and if there be more than one who have such majority, and have an equal number of votes, then the House of Representatives shall immediately choose by ballot one of them for President; and if no person have a majority, then from the five highest on the list said house shall in like manner choose the President. But in choosing the President the votes shall be taken by States, the representation from each State having one vote; a quorum for this purpose shall consist of a member or members from two-thirds of the States, and a majority of all the States shall be necessary to a choice. In every case, after the choice of the President, the person having the greatest number of votes of the electors shall be the Vice-President. But if there should remain two or more who have equal votes, the Senate shall choose from them by ballot the Vice-President.

The Congress may determine the time of choosing the electors, and the day on which they shall give their votes; which day shall be the same throughout the United States.

No person except a natural-born citizen, *or a citizen of the United States at the time of the adoption of this Constitution*, shall be eligible to the office of President; neither shall any person be eligible to that office who shall not have attained to the age of thirty-five years, and been fourteen years a resident within the United States.

In cases of the removal of the President from office or of his death, resignation, or inability to discharge the powers and duties of the said office, the same shall devolve on the Vice-President, and the Congress may by law provide for the case of removal, death, resignation, or inability, both of the President and Vice-President, declaring what officer shall then act as President, and such officer shall act accordingly, until the disability be removed, or a President shall be elected.

The President shall, at stated times, receive for his services a compensation, which shall neither be increased nor diminished during the period for which he shall have been elected, and he shall not receive within that period any other emolument from the United States, or any of them.

Before he enter on the execution of his office, he shall take the following oath or affirmation:—"I do solemnly swear (or affirm) that I will faithfully execute the office of the President of the United States, and will to the best of my ability preserve, protect and defend the Constitution of the United States."

Section 2 The President shall be commander in chief of the army and navy of the United States, and of the militia of the several States, when called into the actual service of the United States; he may require the opinion, in writing, of the principal officer in each of the executive departments, upon any subject relating to the duties of their respective offices, and he shall have power to grant reprieves and pardons for offences against the United States, except in cases of impeachment.

He shall have power, by and with the advice and consent of the Senate, to make treaties, provided two-thirds of the Senators present concur; and he shall nominate, and by and with the advice and consent of the Senate, shall appoint ambassadors, other public ministers and consuls, judges of the Supreme Court, and all other officers of the United States, whose appointments are not herein otherwise provided for, and which shall be established by law: but Congress may by law vest the appointment of such inferior officers, as they think proper, in the President alone, in the courts of law, or in the heads of departments.

The President shall have power to fill up all vacancies that may happen during the recess of the Senate, by granting commissions which shall expire at the end of their next session.

Section 3 He shall from time to time give to the Congress information of the state of the Union, and recommend to their consideration such measures as he shall judge necessary and expedient; he may, on extraordinary occasions, convene both houses, or either of them, and in case of disagreement between them, with respect to the time of adjournment, he may adjourn them to such time as he shall think proper; he shall receive ambassadors and other public ministers; he shall take care that the laws be faithfully executed, and shall commission all the officers of the United States.

Section 4 The President, Vice-President and all civil officers of the United States shall be removed from office on impeachment for, and on conviction of, treason, bribery, or other high crimes and misdemeanors.

Article III

Section 1 The judicial power of the United States shall be vested in one Supreme Court, and in such inferior courts as the Congress may from time to time ordain and establish. The judges, both of the Supreme and inferior courts, shall hold their offices during good behavior, and shall, at stated times, receive for their services a compensation which shall not be diminished during their continuance in office.

Section 2 The judicial power shall extend to all cases, in law and equity, arising under this Constitution, the laws of the United States, and treaties made, or which shall be made, under their authority;—to all cases affecting ambassadors, other public ministers and consuls;—to all cases of admiralty and maritime jurisdiction;—to controversies to which the United States shall be a party;—to controversies between two or more States;—*between a State and citizens of another State*;—between citizens of different States;— between citizens of the same State claiming lands under grants of different States, and between a State, or the citizens thereof, and foreign states, citizens or subjects.

In all cases affecting ambassadors, other public ministers and consuls, and those in which a State shall be party, the Supreme Court shall have original jurisdiction. In all the other cases before mentioned, the Supreme Court shall have appellate jurisdiction, both as to law and fact, with such exceptions, and under such regulations, as the Congress shall make.

The trial of all crimes, except in cases of impeachment, shall be by jury; and such trial shall be held in the State where said crimes shall have been committed; but when not committed within any State, the trial shall be at such place or places as the Congress may by Law have directed.

Section 3 Treason against the United States shall consist only in levying war against them, or in adhering to their enemies, giving them aid and comfort. No person shall be convicted of treason unless on the testimony of two witnesses to the same overt act, or on confession in open court.

The Congress shall have power to declare the punishment of treason, but no attainder of treason shall work corruption of blood, or forfeiture except during the life of the person attainted.

Article IV

Section 1 Full faith and credit shall be given in each State to the public acts, records, and judicial proceedings of every other State. And the Congress may by general laws prescribe the manner in which such acts, records, and proceedings shall be proved, and the effect thereof.

Section 2 The citizens of each State shall be entitled to all privileges and immunities of citizens in the several States.

A person charged in any State with treason, felony, or other crime, who shall flee from justice, and be found in another State, shall on demand of the executive authority of the State from which he fled, be delivered up, to be removed to the State having jurisdiction of the crime.

No Person held to service or labor in one State, under the laws thereof, escaping into another, shall, in consequence of any law or regulation therein, be discharged from such service or labor, but shall be delivered up on claim of the party to whom such service or labor may be due.

Section 3 New States may be admitted by the Congress into this Union; but no new State shall be formed or erected within the jurisdiction of any other State; nor any State be formed by the junction of two or more States, or parts of States, without the consent of the legislatures of the States concerned as well as of the Congress.

The Congress shall have power to dispose of and make all needful rules and regulations respecting the territory or other property belonging to the United States; and nothing in this Constitution shall be so construed as to prejudice any claims of the United States, or of any particular State.

Section 4 The United States shall guarantee to every State in this Union a republican form of government, and shall protect each of them against invasion; and on application of the legislature, or of the executive (when the legislature cannot be convened), against domestic violence.

Article V

The Congress, whenever two-thirds of both houses shall deem it necessary, shall propose amendments to this Constitution, or, on the application of the legislatures of two-thirds of the several States, shall call a convention for proposing amendments, which, in either case, shall be valid to all intents and purposes, as part of this Constitution, when ratified by the legislatures of three-fourths of the several States, or by conventions in three-fourths thereof, as the one or the other mode of ratification may be proposed by the Congress; provided *that no amendments which may be made prior to the year one thousand eight hundred and eight shall in any manner affect the first and fourth clauses in the ninth section of the first article*; and that no State, without its consent, shall be deprived of its equal suffrage in the Senate.

Article VI

All debts contracted and engagements entered into, before the adoption of this Constitution, shall be as valid against the United States under this Constitution, as under the Confederation.

This Constitution, and the laws of the United States which shall be made in pursuance thereof; and all treaties made, or which shall be made, under the authority of the United States, shall be the supreme law of the land; and the judges in every State shall be bound thereby, anything in the Constitution or laws of any State to the contrary notwithstanding.

The Senators and Representatives before mentioned, and the members of the several State legislatures, and all executive and judicial officers, both of the United States and of the several States, shall be bound by oath or affirmation to support this Constitution; but no religious test shall ever be required as a qualification to any office or public trust under the United States.

Article VII

The ratification of the conventions of nine States shall be sufficient for the establishment of this Constitution between the States so ratifying the same.

Done in convention by the unanimous consent of the States present, the seventeenth day of September in the year of our Lord one thousand seven hundred and eighty-seven and of the Independence of the United States of America the twelfth. In witness whereof we have hereunto subscribed our names.

GEORGE WASHINGTON
PRESIDENT AND DEPUTY FROM VIRGINIA

New Hampshire
John Langdon
Nicholas Gilman

Massachusetts
Nathaniel Gorham
Rufus King

Connecticut
William Samuel
 Johnson
Roger Sherman

New York
Alexander Hamilton

New Jersey
William Livingston
David Brearley
William Paterson
Jonathan Dayton

Pennsylvania
Benjamin Franklin
Thomas Mifflin
Robert Morris
George Clymer
Thomas FitzSimons
Jared Ingersoll
James Wilson
Gouverneur Morris

Delaware
George Read
Gunning Bedford, Jr.
John Dickinson
Richard Bassett
Jacob Broom

Maryland
James McHenry
Daniel of St. Thomas
 Jenifer
Daniel Carroll

Virginia
John Blair
James Madison, Jr.

North Carolina
William Blount
Richard Dobbs Spaight
Hugh Williamson

South Carolina
John Rutledge
Charles Cotesworth
 Pinckney
Charles Pinckney
Pierce Butler

Georgia
William Few
Abraham Baldwin

AMENDMENTS TO THE CONSTITUTION WITH ANNOTATIONS (including the six unratified amendments)

▶ *IN THEIR EFFORT TO GAIN Antifederalists' support for the Constitution, Federalists frequently pointed to the inclusion of Article 5, which provides an orderly method of amending the Constitution. In contrast, the Articles of Confederation, which were universally recognized as seriously flawed, offered no means of amendment. For their part, Antifederalists argued that the amendment process was so "intricate" that one might as easily roll "sixes an hundred times in succession" as change the Constitution.*

The system for amendment laid out in the Constitution requires that two-thirds of both houses of Congress agree to a proposed amendment, which must then be ratified by three-quarters of the legislatures of the states. Alternatively, an amendment may be proposed by a convention called by the legislatures of two-thirds of the states. Since 1789, members of Congress have proposed thousands of amendments. Besides the seventeen amendments added since 1789, only the six "unratified" ones included here were approved by two-thirds of both houses and sent to the states for ratification.

Among the many amendments that never made it out of Congress have been proposals to declare dueling, divorce, and interracial marriage unconstitutional as well as proposals to establish a national university, to acknowledge the sovereignty of Jesus Christ, and to prohibit any person from possessing wealth in excess of $10 million.*

Among the issues facing Americans today that might lead to constitutional amendment are efforts to balance the federal budget, to limit the number of terms elected officials may serve, to limit access to or prohibit abortion, to establish English as the official language of the United States, and to prohibit flag burning. None of these proposed amendments has yet garnered enough support in Congress to be sent to the states for ratification.

Although the first ten amendments to the Constitution are commonly known as the Bill of Rights, only Amendments 1–8 actually provide guarantees of individual rights. Amendments 9 and 10 deal with the structure of power within the constitutional system. The Bill of Rights was promised to appease Antifederalists who refused to ratify the Constitution without guarantees of individual liberties and limitations to federal power. After studying more than two hundred amendments recommended by the ratifying conventions of the states, Federalist James Madison presented a list of seventeen to Congress, which used Madison's list as the foundation for the twelve amendments that were sent

---

*Richard B. Bernstein, *Amending America* (New York: Times Books, 1993), 177–81.

to the states for ratification. Ten of the twelve were adopted in 1791. The first on the list of twelve, known as the Reapportionment Amendment, was never adopted (see page A-12). The second proposed amendment was adopted in 1992 as Amendment 27 (see page A-22).

Amendment I

Congress shall make no law respecting an establishment of religion, or prohibiting the free exercise thereof; or abridging the freedom of speech, or of the press; or the right of the people peaceably to assemble, and to petition the government for a redress of grievances.

◆ ◆ ◆

▶ *The First Amendment is a potent symbol for many Americans. Most are well aware of their rights to free speech, freedom of the press, and freedom of religion and their rights to assemble and to petition, even if they cannot cite the exact words of this amendment.*

The First Amendment guarantee of freedom of religion has two clauses: the "free exercise clause," which allows individuals to practice or not practice any religion, and the "establishment clause," which prevents the federal government from discriminating against or favoring any particular religion. This clause was designed to create what Thomas Jefferson referred to as "a wall of separation between church and state." In the 1960s, the Supreme Court ruled that the First Amendment prohibits prayer (see Engel v. Vitale, online) and Bible reading in public schools.

Although the rights to free speech and freedom of the press are established in the First Amendment, it was not until the twentieth century that the Supreme Court began to explore the full meaning of these guarantees. In 1919, the Court ruled in Schenck v. United States (online) that the government could suppress free expression only where it could cite a "clear and present danger." In a decision that continues to raise controversies, the Court ruled in 1990, in Texas v. Johnson, that flag burning is a form of symbolic speech protected by the First Amendment.

Amendment II

A well-regulated militia being necessary to the security of a free State, the right of the people to keep and bear arms shall not be infringed.

◆ ◆ ◆

▶ *Fear of a standing army under the control of a hostile government made the Second Amendment an important part of the Bill of Rights. Advocates of gun ownership claim that the amendment prevents the government from regulating firearms. Proponents of gun control argue that the amendment is designed only to protect the right of the states to maintain militia units.*

In 1939, the Supreme Court ruled in United States v. Miller that the Second Amendment did not protect the right of an individual to own a sawed-off shotgun, which it argued was not ordinary militia equipment. Since then, the Supreme Court has refused to hear Second Amendment cases, while lower courts have upheld firearms regulations. Several justices currently on the bench seem to favor a narrow interpretation of the Second Amendment, which would allow gun control legislation. The controversy over the impact of the Second Amendment on gun owners and gun control legislation will certainly continue.

Amendment III

No soldier shall, in time of peace, be quartered in any house without the consent of the owner, nor in time of war, but in a manner to be prescribed by law.

◆ ◆ ◆

▶ *The Third Amendment was extremely important to the framers of the Constitution, but today it is nearly forgotten. American colonists were especially outraged that they were forced to quarter British troops in the years before and during the American Revolution. The philosophy of the Third Amendment has been viewed by some justices and scholars as the foundation of the modern constitutional right to privacy. One example of this can be found in Justice William O. Douglas's opinion in Griswold v. Connecticut (online).*

Amendment IV

The right of the people to be secure in their persons, houses, papers, and effects, against unreasonable searches and seizures, shall not be violated, and no warrants shall issue but upon probable cause, supported by oath or affirmation, and particularly describing the place to be searched, and the persons or things to be seized.

◆ ◆ ◆

▶ *In the years before the Revolution, the houses, barns, stores, and warehouses of American colonists were ransacked by British authorities under "writs of assistance," or general warrants. The British, thus empowered, searched for seditious material or smuggled goods that could then be used as evidence against colonists who were charged with a crime only after the items were found. The first part of the Fourth Amendment protects citizens from "unreasonable" searches and seizures.*

The Supreme Court has interpreted this protection as well as the words search and seizure in different ways at different times. At one time, the Court did not recognize electronic eavesdropping as a form of search and seizure, though it does today. At times, an "unreasonable" search has been almost any search carried out without a warrant, but in the two decades before 1969, the Court sometimes sanctioned warrantless searches that it considered reasonable based on "the total atmosphere of the case."

The second part of the Fourth Amendment defines the procedure for issuing a search warrant and states the requirement of "probable cause," which is generally viewed as evidence indicating that a suspect has committed an offense.

The Fourth Amendment has been controversial because the Court has sometimes excluded evidence that has been seized in violation of constitutional standards. The justification is that excluding such evidence deters violations of the amendment, but doing so may allow a guilty person to escape punishment.

Amendment V

No person shall be held to answer for a capital, or otherwise infamous crime, unless on a presentment or indictment of a grand jury, except in cases arising in the land or naval forces, or in the militia, when in actual service in time of war or public danger; nor shall any person be subject for the same offence to be twice put in jeopardy of life or limb; nor shall be compelled in any criminal case to be a witness against himself, nor be deprived of life, liberty, or property, without due process of law; nor shall private property be taken for public use without just compensation.

◆ ◆ ◆

► *The Fifth Amendment protects people against government authority in the prosecution of criminal offenses. It prohibits the state, first, from charging a person with a serious crime without a grand jury hearing to decide whether there is sufficient evidence to support the charge and, second, from charging a person with the same crime twice. The best-known aspect of the Fifth Amendment is that it prevents a person from being "compelled . . . to be a witness against himself." The last clause, the "takings clause," limits the power of the government to seize property.*

Although invoking the Fifth Amendment is popularly viewed as a confession of guilt, a person may be innocent yet still fear prosecution. For example, during the Red-baiting era of the late 1940s and 1950s, many people who had participated in legal activities that were associated with the Communist Party claimed the Fifth Amendment privilege rather than testify before the House Un-American Activities Committee because the mood of the times cast those activities in a negative light. Since "taking the Fifth" was viewed as an admission of guilt, those people often lost their jobs or became unemployable. (See chapter 26.) Nonetheless, the right to protect oneself against self-incrimination plays an important role in guarding against the collective power of the state.

Amendment VI

In all criminal prosecutions, the accused shall enjoy the right to a speedy and public trial, by an impartial jury of the State and district wherein the crime shall have been committed, which district shall have been previously ascertained by law, and to be informed of the nature and cause of the accusation; to be confronted with the witnesses against him; to have compulsory process for obtaining witnesses in his favor, and to have the assistance of counsel for his defence.

◆ ◆ ◆

► *The original Constitution put few limits on the government's power to investigate, prosecute, and punish crime. This process was of great concern to the early Americans, however, and of the twenty-eight rights specified in the first eight amendments, fifteen have to do with it. Seven rights are specified in the Sixth Amendment. These include the right to a speedy trial, a public trial, a jury trial, a notice of accusation, confrontation by opposing witnesses, testimony by favorable witnesses, and the assistance of counsel.*

Although this amendment originally guaranteed these rights only in cases involving the federal government, the adoption of the Fourteenth Amendment began a process of applying the protections of the Bill of Rights to the states through court cases such as Gideon v. Wainwright *(online).*

Amendment VII

In suits at common law, where the value in controversy shall exceed twenty dollars, the right of trial by jury shall be preserved, and no fact tried by a jury shall be otherwise reexamined in any court of the United States, than according to the rules of the common law.

◆ ◆ ◆

► *This amendment guarantees people the same right to a trial by jury as was guaranteed by English common law in 1791. Under common law, in civil trials (those involving money damages) the role of the judge was to settle questions of law and that of the jury was to settle questions of fact. The amendment does not specify the size of the jury or its role in a trial, however. The Supreme Court has generally held that those issues be determined by English common law of 1791, which stated that a jury consists of twelve people, that a trial must be conducted before a judge who instructs the jury on the law and advises it on facts, and that a verdict must be unanimous.*

Amendment VIII

Excessive bail shall not be required, nor excessive fines imposed, nor cruel and unusual punishments inflicted.

♦ ♦ ♦

▶ *The language used to guarantee the three rights in this amendment was inspired by the English Bill of Rights of 1689. The Supreme Court has not had a lot to say about "excessive fines." In recent years it has agreed that, despite the provision against "excessive bail," persons who are believed to be dangerous to others can be held without bail even before they have been convicted.*

Although opponents of the death penalty have not succeeded in using the Eighth Amendment to achieve the end of capital punishment, the clause regarding "cruel and unusual punishments" has been used to prohibit capital punishment in certain cases (see Furman v. Georgia, online) and to require improved conditions in prisons.

Amendment IX

The enumeration in the Constitution, of certain rights, shall not be construed to deny or disparage others retained by the people.

♦ ♦ ♦

▶ *Some Federalists feared that inclusion of the Bill of Rights in the Constitution would allow later generations of interpreters to claim that the people had surrendered any rights not specifically enumerated there. To guard against this, Madison added language that became the Ninth Amendment. Interest in this heretofore largely ignored amendment revived in 1965 when it was used in a concurring opinion in Griswold v. Connecticut (online). While Justice William O. Douglas called on the Third Amendment to support the right to privacy in deciding that case, Justice Arthur Goldberg, in the concurring opinion, argued that the right to privacy regarding contraception was an unenumerated right that was protected by the Ninth Amendment.*

In 1980, the Court ruled that the right of the press to attend a public trial was protected by the Ninth Amendment. While some scholars argue that modern judges cannot identify the unenumerated rights that the framers were trying to protect, others argue that the Ninth Amendment should be read as providing a constitutional "presumption of liberty" that allows people to act in any way that does not violate the rights of others.

Amendment X

The powers not delegated to the United States by the Constitution, nor prohibited by it to the States, are reserved to the States respectively, or to the people.

♦ ♦ ♦

▶ *The Antifederalists were especially eager to see a "reserved powers clause" explicitly guaranteeing the states control over their internal affairs. Not surprisingly, the Tenth Amendment has been a frequent battleground in the struggle over states' rights and federal supremacy. Prior to the Civil War, the Democratic Republican Party and Jacksonian Democrats invoked the Tenth Amendment to prohibit the federal government from making decisions about whether people in individual states could own slaves. The Tenth Amendment was virtually suspended during Reconstruction following the Civil War. In 1883, however, the Supreme Court declared the Civil Rights Act of 1875 unconstitutional on the grounds that it violated the Tenth Amendment. Business interests also called on the amendment to block efforts at federal regulation.*

The Court was inconsistent over the next several decades as it attempted to resolve the tension between the restrictions of the Tenth Amendment and the powers the Constitution granted to Congress to regulate interstate commerce and levy taxes. The Court upheld the Pure Food and Drug Act (1906), the Meat Inspection Acts (1906 and 1907), and the White Slave Traffic Act (1910), all of which affected the states, but struck down an act prohibiting interstate shipment of goods produced through child labor. Between 1934 and 1935, a number of New Deal programs created by Franklin D. Roosevelt were declared unconstitutional on the grounds that they violated the Tenth Amendment. (See chapter 24.) As Roosevelt appointees changed the composition of the Court, the Tenth Amendment was declared to have no substantive meaning. Generally, the amendment is held to protect the rights of states to regulate internal matters such as local government, education, commerce, labor, and business, as well as matters involving families such as marriage, divorce, and inheritance within the state.

Unratified Amendment
Reapportionment Amendment (proposed by Congress September 25, 1789, along with the Bill of Rights)

After the first enumeration required by the first article of the Constitution, there shall be one Representative for every thirty thousand, until the number shall amount to one hundred, after which the proportion shall be so regulated by Congress, that there shall be not less than one hundred Representatives, nor less than one Representative for every forty thousand persons, until the number of Representatives shall amount to two hundred; after which the proportion shall be so regulated by Congress, that there shall not be less than two hundred Representatives, nor more than one Representative for every fifty thousand persons.

♦ ♦ ♦

▶ *If the Reapportionment Amendment had passed and remained in effect, the House of Representatives today would have more than 5,000 members rather than 435.*

Amendment XI

[Adopted 1798]

The judicial power of the United States shall not be construed to extend to any suit in law or equity, commenced or prosecuted against one of the United States by citizens of another State, or by citizens or subjects of any foreign state.

◆ ◆ ◆

▶ *In 1793, the Supreme Court ruled in favor of Alexander Chisholm, executor of the estate of a deceased South Carolina merchant. Chisholm was suing the state of Georgia because the merchant had never been paid for provisions he had supplied during the Revolution. Many regarded this Court decision as an error that violated the intent of the Constitution.*

Antifederalists had long feared a federal court system with the power to overrule a state court.

When the Constitution was being drafted, Federalists had assured worried Antifederalists that section 2 of Article 3, which allows federal courts to hear cases "between a State and citizens of another State," did not mean that the federal courts were authorized to hear suits against a state by citizens of another state or a foreign country. Antifederalists and many other Americans feared a powerful federal court system because they worried that it would become like the British courts of this period, which were accountable only to the monarch. Furthermore, Chisholm v. Georgia prompted a series of suits against state governments by creditors and suppliers who had made loans during the war.

In addition, state legislators and Congress feared that the shaky economies of the new states, as well as the country as a whole, would be destroyed, especially if loyalists who had fled to other countries sought reimbursement for land and property that had been seized. The day after the Supreme Court announced its decision, a resolution proposing the Eleventh Amendment, which overturned the decision in Chisholm v. Georgia, was introduced in the U.S. Senate.

Amendment XII

[Adopted 1804]

The electors shall meet in their respective States, and vote by ballot for President and Vice-President, one of whom, at least, shall not be an inhabitant of the same State with themselves; they shall name in their ballots the person voted for as President, and in distinct ballots the person voted for as Vice-President, and they shall make distinct lists of all persons voted for as President, and of all persons voted for as Vice-President, and of the number of votes for each, which lists they shall sign and certify, and transmit sealed to the seat of government of the United States, directed to the President of the Senate;—the President of the Senate shall, in the presence of the Senate and House of Representatives, open all the certificates and the votes shall then be counted;—the person having the greatest number of votes for President shall be the President, if such number be a majority of the whole number of electors appointed; and if no person have such majority, then from the persons having the highest numbers not exceeding three on the list of those voted for as President, the House of Representatives shall choose immediately, by ballot, the President. But in choosing the President, the votes shall be taken by States, the representation from each State having one vote; a quorum for this purpose shall consist of a member or members from two-thirds of the States, and a majority of all the States shall be necessary to a choice. And if the House of Representatives shall not choose a President whenever the right of choice shall devolve upon them, before the fourth day of March next following, then the Vice-President shall act as President, as in the case of the death or other constitutional disability of the President.

The person having the greatest number of votes as Vice-President shall be the Vice-President, if such number be a majority of the whole number of electors appointed; and if no person have a majority, then from the two highest numbers on the list the Senate shall choose the Vice-President; a quorum for the purpose shall consist of two-thirds of the whole number of Senators, and a majority of the whole number shall be necessary to a choice. But no person constitutionally ineligible to the office of President shall be eligible to that of Vice-President of the United States.

◆ ◆ ◆

▶ *The framers of the Constitution disliked political parties and assumed that none would ever form. Under the original system, electors chosen by the states would each vote for two candidates. The candidate who won the most votes would become president, while the person who won the second-highest number of votes would become vice president. Rivalries between Federalists and Antifederalists led to the formation of political parties, however, even before George Washington had left office. Though Washington was elected unanimously in 1789 and 1792, the elections of 1796 and 1800 were procedural disasters because of party maneuvering (see chapters 9 and 10). In 1796, Federalist John Adams was chosen as president, and his great rival, the Antifederalist Thomas Jefferson (whose party was called the Republican Party), became his vice president. In 1800, all the electors cast their two votes as one of two party blocs. Jefferson and his fellow Republican nominee, Aaron Burr, were tied with 73 votes each. The contest went to the House of Representatives, which finally elected Jefferson after 36 ballots. The Twelfth Amendment prevents these problems by requiring electors to vote separately for the president and vice president.*

Unratified Amendment
Titles of Nobility Amendment (proposed by Congress May 1, 1810)

If any citizen of the United States shall accept, claim, receive or retain any title of nobility or honor or shall, without the consent of Congress, accept and retain any present, pension, office or emolument of any kind whatever, from any emperor, king, prince or foreign power, such person shall cease to be a citizen of the United States, and shall be incapable of holding any office of trust or profit under them or either of them.

♦ ♦ ♦

► *This amendment would have extended Article 1, section 9, clause 8 of the Constitution, which prevents the awarding of titles by the United States and the acceptance of such awards from foreign powers without congressional consent. Historians speculate that general nervousness about the power of the emperor Napoleon, who was at that time extending France's empire throughout Europe, may have prompted the proposal. Though it fell one vote short of ratification, Congress and the American people thought the proposal had been ratified, and it was included in many nineteenth-century editions of the Constitution.*

The Civil War and Reconstruction Amendments (Thirteenth, Fourteenth, and Fifteenth Amendments)

► *In the four months between the election of Abraham Lincoln and his inauguration, more than 200 proposed constitutional amendments were presented to Congress as part of a desperate attempt to hold the rapidly dissolving Union together. Most of these were efforts to appease the southern states by protecting the right to own slaves or by disfranchising African Americans through constitutional amendment. None were able to win the votes required from Congress to send them to the states. The relatively innocuous Corwin Amendment seemed to be the only hope for preserving the Union by amending the Constitution.*

    The northern victors in the Civil War tried to restructure the Constitution just as the war had restructured the nation. Yet they were often divided in their goals. Some wanted to end slavery; others hoped for social and economic equality regardless of race; others hoped that extending the power of the ballot box to former slaves would help create a new political order. The debates over the Thirteenth, Fourteenth, and Fifteenth Amendments were bitter. Few of those who fought for these changes were satisfied with the amendments themselves; fewer still were satisfied with their interpretation. Although the

amendments put an end to the legal status of slavery, it took nearly a hundred years after the amendments' passage before most of the descendants of former slaves could begin to experience the economic, social, and political equality the amendments had been intended to provide.

Unratified Amendment
Corwin Amendment (proposed by Congress March 2, 1861)

No amendment shall be made to the Constitution which will authorize or give to Congress the power to abolish or interfere, within any State, with the domestic institutions thereof, including that of persons held to labor or service by the laws of said State.

♦ ♦ ♦

► *Following the election of Abraham Lincoln, Congress scrambled to try to prevent the secession of the slaveholding states. House member Thomas Corwin of Ohio proposed the "unamendable" amendment in the hope that by protecting slavery where it existed, Congress would keep the southern states in the Union. Lincoln indicated his support for the proposed amendment in his first inaugural address. Only Ohio and Maryland ratified the Corwin Amendment before it was forgotten.*

Amendment XIII
[Adopted 1865]

Section 1 Neither slavery nor involuntary servitude, except as a punishment for crime whereof the party shall have been duly convicted, shall exist within the United States, or any place subject to their jurisdiction.

Section 2 Congress shall have power to enforce this article by appropriate legislation.

♦ ♦ ♦

► *Although President Lincoln had abolished slavery in the Confederacy with the Emancipation Proclamation of 1863, abolitionists wanted to rid the entire country of slavery. The Thirteenth Amendment did this in a clear and straightforward manner. In February 1865, when the proposal was approved by the House, the gallery of the House was newly opened to black Americans who had a chance at last to see their government at work. Passage of the proposal was greeted by wild cheers from the gallery as well as tears on the House floor, where congressional representatives openly embraced one another.*

    The problem of ratification remained, however. The Union position was that the Confederate states were part of the country of thirty-six states. Therefore, twenty-seven states were needed to ratify the amendment. When Kentucky and Delaware rejected it, backers realized that without approval from at least four former Confederate states, the amendment would fail. Lincoln's successor, President Andrew Johnson, made ratification of the

Thirteenth Amendment a condition for southern states to rejoin the Union. Under those terms, all the former Confederate states except Mississippi accepted the Thirteenth Amendment, and by the end of 1865 the amendment had become part of the Constitution and slavery had been prohibited in the United States.

Amendment XIV
[Adopted 1868]

Section 1 All persons born or naturalized in the United States, and subject to the jurisdiction thereof, are citizens of the United States and of the State wherein they reside. No State shall make or enforce any law which shall abridge the privileges or immunities of citizens of the United States; nor shall any State deprive any person of life, liberty, or property, without due process of law; nor deny to any person within its jurisdiction the equal protection of the laws.

Section 2 Representatives shall be appointed among the several States according to their respective numbers, counting the whole number of persons in each State, excluding Indians not taxed. But when the right to vote at any election for the choice of Electors for President and Vice-President of the United States, Representatives in Congress, the executive and judicial officers of a State, or the members of the legislature thereof, is denied to any of the male inhabitants of such State, being twenty-one years of age and citizens of the United States, or in any way abridged, except for participation in rebellion, or other crime, the basis of representation therein shall be reduced in the proportion which the number of such male citizens shall bear to the whole number of male citizens twenty-one years of age in such State.

Section 3 No person shall be a Senator or Representative in Congress, or Elector of President and Vice-President, or hold any office, civil or military, under the United States, or under any State, who, having previously taken an oath, as a member of Congress, or as an officer of the United States, or as a member of any State legislature, or as an executive or judicial officer of any State, to support the Constitution of the United States, shall have engaged in insurrection or rebellion against the same, or given aid or comfort to the enemies thereof. Congress may, by a vote of two-thirds of each house, remove such disability.

Section 4 The validity of the public debt of the United States, authorized by law, including debts incurred for payment of pensions and bounties for services in suppressing insurrection or rebellion, shall not be questioned. But neither the United States nor any State shall assume or pay any debt or obligation incurred in aid of insurrection or rebellion against the United States, or any claim for the loss or emancipation of any slave; but all such debts, obligations, and claims shall be held illegal and void.

Section 5 The Congress shall have power to enforce, by appropriate legislation, the provisions of this article.

◆ ◆ ◆

▶ *Without Lincoln's leadership in the reconstruction of the nation following the Civil War, it soon became clear that the Thirteenth Amendment needed additional constitutional support. Less than a year after Lincoln's assassination, Andrew Johnson was ready to bring the former Confederate states back into the Union with few changes in their governments or politics. Anxious Republicans drafted the Fourteenth Amendment to prevent that from happening. The most important provisions of this complex amendment made all native-born or naturalized persons American citizens and prohibited states from abridging the "privileges or immunities" of citizens; depriving them of "life, liberty, or property, without due process of law"; and denying them "equal protection of the laws." In essence, it made all ex-slaves citizens and protected the rights of all citizens against violation by their own state governments.*

As occurred in the case of the Thirteenth Amendment, former Confederate states were forced to ratify the amendment as a condition of representation in the House and the Senate. The intentions of the Fourteenth Amendment, and how those intentions should be enforced, have been the most debated point of constitutional history. The terms due process *and* equal protection *have been especially troublesome. Was the amendment designed to outlaw racial segregation? Or was the goal simply to prevent the leaders of the rebellious South from gaining political power?*

The framers of the Fourteenth Amendment hoped Article 2 would produce black voters who would increase the power of the Republican Party. The federal government, however, never used its power to punish states for denying blacks their right to vote. Although the Fourteenth Amendment had an immediate impact in giving black Americans citizenship, it did nothing to protect blacks from the vengeance of whites once Reconstruction ended. In the late nineteenth and early twentieth centuries, section 1 of the Fourteenth Amendment was often used to protect business interests and strike down laws protecting workers on the grounds that the rights of "persons," that is, corporations, were protected by "due process." More recently, the Fourteenth Amendment has been used to justify school desegregation and affirmative action programs, as well as to dismantle such programs.

Amendment XV
[Adopted 1870]

Section 1 The right of citizens of the United States to vote shall not be denied or abridged by the United States or by any State on account of race, color, or previous condition of servitude.

Section 2 The Congress shall have power to enforce this article by appropriate legislation.

◆ ◆ ◆

▶ *The Fifteenth Amendment was the last major piece of Reconstruction legislation. While earlier Reconstruction acts had already required black suffrage in the South, the Fifteenth Amendment extended black voting rights to the entire nation. Some Republicans felt morally obligated to do away with the double standard between North and South since many northern states had stubbornly refused to enfranchise blacks. Others believed that the freedman's ballot required the extra protection of a constitutional amendment to shield it from white counterattack. But partisan advantage also played an important role in the amendment's passage, since Republicans hoped that by giving the ballot to northern blacks, they could lessen their political vulnerability.*

Many women's rights advocates had fought for the amendment. They had felt betrayed by the inclusion of the word "male" in section 2 of the Fourteenth Amendment and were further angered when the proposed Fifteenth Amendment failed to prohibit denial of the right to vote on the grounds of sex as well as "race, color, or previous condition of servitude." In this amendment, for the first time, the federal government claimed the power to regulate the franchise, or vote. It was also the first time the Constitution placed limits on the power of the states to regulate access to the franchise. Although ratified in 1870, the amendment was not enforced until the twentieth century.

The Progressive Amendments (Sixteenth–Nineteenth Amendments)

▶ *No amendments were added to the Constitution between the Civil War and the Progressive Era. America was changing, however, in fundamental ways. The rapid industrialization of the United States after the Civil War led to many social and economic problems. Hundreds of amendments were proposed, but none received enough support in Congress to be sent to the states. Some scholars believe that regional differences and rivalries were so strong during this period that it was almost impossible to gain a consensus on a constitutional amendment. During the Progressive Era, however, the Constitution was amended four times in seven years.*

Amendment XVI
[Adopted 1913]

The Congress shall have power to lay and collect taxes on incomes, from whatever source derived, without apportionment among the several States, and without regard to any census or enumeration.

◆ ◆ ◆

▶ *Until passage of the Sixteenth Amendment, most of the money used to run the federal government came from customs duties and taxes on specific items, such as liquor. During the Civil War, the federal government taxed incomes as an emergency measure. Pressure to enact an income tax came from those who were concerned about the growing gap between rich and poor in the United States. The Populist Party began campaigning for a graduated income tax in 1892, and support continued to grow. By 1909, thirty-three proposed income tax amendments had been presented in Congress, but lobbying by corporate and other special interests had defeated them all. In June 1909, the growing pressure for an income tax, which had been endorsed by Presidents Roosevelt and Taft, finally pushed an amendment through the Senate. The required thirty-six states had ratified the amendment by February 1913.*

Amendment XVII
[Adopted 1913]

Section 1 The Senate of the United States shall be composed of two Senators from each State, elected by the people thereof, for six years; and each Senator shall have one vote. The electors in each State shall have the qualifications requisite for electors of [voters for] the most numerous branch of the State legislatures.

Section 2 When vacancies happen in the representation of any State in the Senate, the executive authority of such State shall issue writs of election to fill such vacancies: Provided, that the Legislature of any State may empower the executive thereof to make temporary appointments until the people fill the vacancies by election as the Legislature may direct.

Section 3 This amendment shall not be so construed as to affect the election or term of any Senator chosen before it becomes valid as part of the Constitution.

◆ ◆ ◆

▶ *The framers of the Constitution saw the members of the House as the representatives of the people and the members of the Senate as the representatives of the states. Originally senators were to be chosen by the state legislators. According to reform advocates, however, the growth of private industry and transportation conglomerates during the Gilded Age had created a network of corruption in which wealth and power were exchanged for influence and votes in the Senate. Senator Nelson Aldrich, who represented Rhode Island in the late nineteenth and early twentieth centuries, for example, was known as "the senator from Standard Oil" because of his open support of special business interests.*

Efforts to amend the Constitution to allow direct election of senators had begun in 1826, but since any proposal had to be approved by the Senate, reform seemed impossible. Progressives tried to gain influence in the Senate by instituting party caucuses and primary elections, which gave citizens the chance to express their choice of a senator who could then be officially elected by the state legislature. By 1910, fourteen of the country's thirty senators received popular votes through a state primary before the state legislature made its selection. Despairing of getting a proposal through the Senate, supporters of a direct election amendment had begun in 1893 to seek a convention of representatives from two-thirds of the states to propose an amendment that could then be ratified. By 1905, thirty-one of forty-five states had endorsed such an amendment. Finally, in 1911, despite extraordinary opposition, a proposed amendment passed the Senate; by 1913, it had been ratified.

Amendment XVIII
[Adopted 1919; repealed 1933 by Amendment XXI]

Section 1 After one year from the ratification of this article the manufacture, sale, or transportation of intoxicating liquors within, the importation thereof into, or the exportation thereof from the United States and all territory subject to the jurisdiction thereof, for beverage purposes, is hereby prohibited.

Section 2 The Congress and the several States shall have concurrent power to enforce this article by appropriate legislation.

Section 3 This article shall be inoperative unless it shall have been ratified as an amendment to the Constitution by the legislatures of the several States, as provided by the Constitution, within seven years from the date of the submission thereof to the States by the Congress.

◆ ◆ ◆

▶ *The Prohibition Party, formed in 1869, began calling for a constitutional amendment to outlaw alcoholic beverages in 1872. A prohibition amendment was first proposed in the Senate in 1876 and was revived eighteen times before 1913. Between 1913 and 1919, another thirty-nine attempts were made to prohibit liquor in the United States through a constitutional amendment. Prohibition became a key element of the progressive agenda as reformers linked alcohol and drunkenness to numerous*

social problems, including the corruption of immigrant voters. While opponents of such an amendment argued that it was undemocratic, supporters claimed that their efforts had widespread public support. The admission of twelve "dry" western states to the Union in the early twentieth century and the spirit of sacrifice during World War I laid the groundwork for passage and ratification of the Eighteenth Amendment in 1919. Opponents added a time limit to the amendment in the hope that they could thus block ratification, but this effort failed. (See also Amendment XXI.)

Amendment XIX
[Adopted 1920]

Section 1 The right of citizens of the United States to vote shall not be denied or abridged by the United States or by any State on account of sex.

Section 2 Congress shall have the power to enforce this article by appropriate legislation.

◆ ◆ ◆

▶ *Advocates of women's rights tried and failed to link woman suffrage to the Fourteenth and Fifteenth Amendments. Nonetheless, the effort for woman suffrage continued. Between 1878 and 1912, at least one and sometimes as many as four proposed amendments were introduced in Congress each year to grant women the right to vote. While over time women won very limited voting rights in some states, at both the state and federal levels opposition to an amendment for woman suffrage remained very strong. President Woodrow Wilson and other officials felt that the federal government should not interfere with the power of the states in this matter. Others worried that granting suffrage to women would encourage ethnic minorities to exercise their own right to vote. And many were concerned that giving women the vote would result in their abandoning traditional gender roles. In 1919, following a protracted and often bitter campaign of protest in which women went on hunger strikes and chained themselves to fences, an amendment was introduced with the backing of President Wilson. It narrowly passed the Senate (after efforts to limit the suffrage to white women failed) and was adopted in 1920 after Tennessee became the thirty-sixth state to ratify it.*

Unratified Amendment
Child Labor Amendment (proposed by Congress June 2, 1924)

Section 1 The Congress shall have power to limit, regulate, and prohibit the labor of persons under eighteen years of age.

Section 2 The power of the several States is unimpaired by this article except that the operation of State laws shall be suspended to the extent necessary to give effect to legislation enacted by Congress.

♦ ♦ ♦

▶ *Throughout the late nineteenth and early twentieth centuries, alarm over the condition of child workers grew. Opponents of child labor argued that children worked in dangerous and unhealthy conditions, that they took jobs from adult workers, that they depressed wages in certain industries, and that states that allowed child labor had an economic advantage over those that did not. Defenders of child labor claimed that children provided needed income in many families, that working at a young age developed character, and that the effort to prohibit the practice constituted an invasion of family privacy.*

In 1916, Congress passed a law that made it illegal to sell goods made by children through interstate commerce. The Supreme Court, however, ruled that the law violated the limits on the power of Congress to regulate interstate commerce. Congress then tried to penalize industries that used child labor by taxing such goods. This measure was also thrown out by the Court. In response, reformers set out to amend the Constitution. The proposed amendment was ratified by twenty-eight states, but by 1925, thirteen states had rejected it. Passage of the Fair Labor Standards Act in 1938, which was upheld by the Supreme Court in 1941, made the amendment irrelevant.

Amendment XX
[Adopted 1933]

Section 1 The terms of the President and Vice-President shall end at noon on the 20th day of January, and the terms of Senators and Representatives at noon on the 3rd day of January, of the years in which such terms would have ended if this article had not been ratified; and the terms of their successors shall then begin.

Section 2 The Congress shall assemble at least once in every year, and such meeting shall begin at noon on the 3rd day of January, unless they shall by law appoint a different day.

Section 3 If, at the time fixed for the beginning of the term of the President, the President-elect shall have died, the Vice-President-elect shall become President. If a President shall not have been chosen before the time fixed for the beginning of his term, or if the President-elect shall have failed to qualify, then the Vice-President-elect shall act as President until a President shall have qualified; and the Congress may by law provide for the case wherein neither a President-elect nor a Vice-President-elect shall have qualified, declaring who shall then act as President, or the manner in which one who is to act shall be selected, and such person shall act accordingly until a President or Vice-President shall have qualified.

Section 4 The Congress may by law provide for the case of the death of any of the persons from whom the House of Representatives may choose a President whenever the right of choice shall have devolved upon them, and for the case of the death of any of the persons from whom the Senate may choose a Vice-President whenever the right of choice shall have devolved upon them.

Section 5 Sections 1 and 2 shall take effect on the 15th day of October following the ratification of this article.

Section 6 This article shall be inoperative unless it shall have been ratified as an amendment to the Constitution by the Legislatures of three-fourths of the several States within seven years from the date of its submission.

♦ ♦ ♦

▶ *Until 1933, presidents took office on March 4. Since elections are held in early November and electoral votes are counted in mid-December, this meant that more than three months passed between the time a new president was elected and when he took office. Moving the inauguration to January shortened the transition period and allowed Congress to begin its term closer to the time of the president's inauguration. Although this seems like a minor change, an amendment was required because the Constitution specifies terms of office. This amendment also deals with questions of succession in the event that a president- or vice president-elect dies before assuming office. Section 3 also clarifies a method for resolving a deadlock in the electoral college.*

Amendment XXI
[Adopted 1933]

Section 1 The eighteenth article of amendment to the Constitution of the United States is hereby repealed.

Section 2 The transportation or importation into any State, Territory, or Possession of the United States for delivery or use therein of intoxicating liquors, in violation of the laws thereof, is hereby prohibited.

Section 3 This article shall be inoperative unless it shall have been ratified as an amendment to the Constitution by conventions in the several States, as provided in the Constitution, within seven years from the date of the submission thereof to the States by the Congress.

♦ ♦ ♦

▶ *Widespread violation of the Volstead Act, the law enacted to enforce prohibition, made the United*

States a nation of lawbreakers. Prohibition caused more problems than it solved by encouraging crime, bribery, and corruption. Further, a coalition of liquor and beer manufacturers, personal liberty advocates, and constitutional scholars joined forces to challenge the amendment. By 1929, thirty proposed repeal amendments had been introduced in Congress, and the Democratic Party made repeal part of its platform in the 1932 presidential campaign. The Twenty-first Amendment was proposed in February 1933 and ratified less than a year later. The failure of the effort to enforce prohibition through a constitutional amendment has often been cited by opponents to subsequent efforts to shape public virtue and private morality.

Amendment XXII
[Adopted 1951]

Section 1 No person shall be elected to the office of the President more than twice, and no person who has held the office of President, or acted as President, for more than two years of a term to which some other person was elected President shall be elected to the office of President more than once. But this article shall not apply to any person holding the office of President when this Article was proposed by the Congress, and shall not prevent any person who may be holding the office of President, or acting as President, during the term within which this Article becomes operative from holding the office of President or acting as President during the remainder of such term.

Section 2 This article shall be inoperative unless it shall have been ratified as an amendment to the Constitution by the legislatures of three-fourths of the several States within seven years from the date of its submission to the States by the Congress.

◆ ◆ ◆

▶ *George Washington's refusal to seek a third term of office set a precedent that stood until 1912, when former president Theodore Roosevelt sought, without success, another term as an independent candidate. Democrat Franklin Roosevelt was the only president to seek and win a fourth term, though he did so amid great controversy. Roosevelt died in April 1945, a few months after the beginning of his fourth term. In 1946, Republicans won control of the House and the Senate, and early in 1947 a proposal for an amendment to limit future presidents to two four-year terms was offered to the states for ratification. Democratic critics of the Twenty-second Amendment charged that it was a partisan posthumous jab at Roosevelt.*

Since the Twenty-second Amendment was adopted, however, the only presidents who might have been able to seek a third term, had it not existed, were Republicans Dwight Eisenhower, Ronald Reagan, and George W. Bush, and

Democrat Bill Clinton. Since 1826, Congress has entertained 160 proposed amendments to limit the president to one six-year term. Such amendments have been backed by fifteen presidents, including Gerald Ford and Jimmy Carter.

Amendment XXIII
[Adopted 1961]

Section 1 The District constituting the seat of Government of the United States shall appoint in such manner as the Congress may direct: A number of electors of President and Vice-President equal to the whole number of Senators and Representatives in Congress to which the District would be entitled if it were a State, but in no event more than the least populous State; they shall be in addition to those appointed by the States, but they shall be considered for the purposes of the election of President and Vice-President, to be electors appointed by a State; and they shall meet in the District and perform such duties as provided by the twelfth article of amendment.

Section 2 The Congress shall have the power to enforce this article by appropriate legislation.

◆ ◆ ◆

▶ *When Washington, D.C., was established as a federal district, no one expected that a significant number of people would make it their permanent and primary residence. A proposal to allow citizens of the district to vote in presidential elections was approved by Congress in June 1960 and was ratified on March 29, 1961.*

Amendment XXIV
[Adopted 1964]

Section 1 The right of citizens of the United States to vote in any primary or other election for President or Vice-President, for electors for President or Vice-President, or for Senator or Representative in Congress, shall not be denied or abridged by the United States or any State by reason of failure to pay any poll tax or other tax.

Section 2 The Congress shall have the power to enforce this article by appropriate legislation.

◆ ◆ ◆

▶ *In the colonial and Revolutionary eras, financial independence was seen as necessary to political independence, and the poll tax was used as a requirement for voting. By the twentieth century, however, the poll tax was used mostly to bar poor people, especially southern blacks, from voting. While conservatives complained that the amendment interfered with states' rights, liberals thought that the amendment did not go far enough because it barred the poll tax only in national elections and not in state or local elections. The amendment was ratified in 1964, however, and two years later, the Supreme Court ruled that poll taxes in state and local elections also violated the equal protection clause of the Fourteenth Amendment.*

Amendment XXV

[Adopted 1967]

Section 1 In case of the removal of the President from office or of his death or resignation, the Vice-President shall become President.

Section 2 Whenever there is a vacancy in the office of the Vice-President, the President shall nominate a Vice-President who shall take office upon confirmation by a majority vote of both Houses of Congress.

Section 3 Whenever the President transmits to the President pro tempore of the Senate and the Speaker of the House of Representatives his written declaration that he is unable to discharge the powers and duties of his office, and until he transmits to them a written declaration to the contrary, such powers and duties shall be discharged by the Vice-President as Acting President.

Section 4 Whenever the Vice-President and a majority of either the principal officers of the executive departments or of such other body as Congress may by law provide, transmit to the President pro tempore of the Senate and the Speaker of the House of Representatives their written declaration that the President is unable to discharge the powers and duties of his office, the Vice-President shall immediately assume the powers and duties of the office as Acting President.

Thereafter, when the President transmits to the President pro tempore of the Senate and the Speaker of the House of Representatives his written declaration that no inability exists, he shall resume the powers and duties of his office unless the Vice-President and a majority of either the principal officers of the executive department[s] or of such other body as Congress may by law provide, transmit within four days to the President pro tempore of the Senate and the Speaker of the House of Representatives their written declaration that the President is unable to discharge the powers and duties of his office. Thereupon Congress shall decide the issue, assembling within forty-eight hours for that purpose if not in session. If the Congress, within twenty-one days after receipt of the latter written declaration, or, if Congress is not in session, within twenty-one days after Congress is required to assemble, determines by two-thirds vote of both Houses that the President is unable to discharge the powers and duties of his office, the Vice-President shall continue to discharge the same as Acting President; otherwise, the President shall resume the powers and duties of his office.

♦ ♦ ♦

► *The framers of the Constitution established the office of vice president because someone was needed to preside over the Senate. The first president to die in office was William Henry Harrison, in 1841. Vice President John Tyler had himself sworn in as president, setting a precedent that was followed when seven later presidents died in office. The assassination of President James A. Garfield in 1881 posed a new problem, however. After he was shot, the president was incapacitated for two months before he died; he was unable to lead the country, while his vice president, Chester A. Arthur, was unable to assume leadership. Efforts to resolve questions of succession in the event of a presidential disability thus began with the death of Garfield.*

In 1963, the assassination of President John F. Kennedy galvanized Congress to action. Vice President Lyndon Johnson was a chain-smoker with a history of heart trouble. According to the 1947 Presidential Succession Act, the two men who stood in line to succeed him were the seventy-two-year-old Speaker of the House and the eighty-six-year-old president of the Senate. There were serious concerns that any of these men might become incapacitated while serving as chief executive. The first time the Twenty-fifth Amendment was used, however, was not in the case of presidential death or illness, but during the Watergate crisis. When Vice President Spiro T. Agnew was forced to resign following allegations of bribery and tax violations, President Richard M. Nixon appointed House Minority Leader Gerald R. Ford vice president. Ford became president following Nixon's resignation eight months later and named Nelson A. Rockefeller as his vice president. Thus, for more than two years, the two highest offices in the country were held by people who had not been elected to them.

Amendment XXVI

[Adopted 1971]

Section 1 The right of citizens of the United States, who are eighteen years of age or older, to vote shall not be denied or abridged by the United States or by any State on account of age.

Section 2 The Congress shall have power to enforce this article by appropriate legislation.

♦ ♦ ♦

► *Efforts to lower the voting age from twenty-one to eighteen began during World War II. Recognizing that those who were old enough to fight a war should have some say in the government policies that involved them in the war, Presidents Eisenhower, Johnson, and Nixon endorsed* the idea. In 1970, the combined pressure of the antiwar movement and the demographic pressure of the baby boom generation led to a Voting Rights Act lowering the voting age in federal, state, and local elections.

In Oregon v. Mitchell (1970), the state of Oregon challenged the right of Congress to determine the age at which people could vote in state or local elections. The Supreme Court agreed with Oregon. Since the Voting Rights Act was ruled unconstitutional, the Constitution had to be amended to allow passage of a law that would lower the voting age. The amendment was ratified in a little more than three months, making it the most rapidly ratified amendment in U.S. history.

Unratified Amendment

Equal Rights Amendment (proposed by Congress March 22, 1972; seven-year deadline for ratification extended to June 30, 1982)

Section 1 Equality of rights under the law shall not be denied or abridged by the United States or by any State on account of sex.

Section 2 The Congress shall have the power to enforce, by appropriate legislation, the provisions of this article.

Section 3 This amendment shall take effect two years after the date of ratification.

◆ ◆ ◆

▶ In 1923, soon after women had won the right to vote, Alice Paul, a leading activist in the woman suffrage movement, proposed an amendment requiring equal treatment of men and women. Opponents of the proposal argued that such an amendment would invalidate laws that protected women and would make women subject to the military draft. After the 1964 Civil Rights Act was adopted, protective workplace legislation was removed anyway.

The renewal of the women's movement, as a byproduct of the civil rights and antiwar movements, led to a revival of the Equal Rights Amendment (ERA) in Congress. Disagreements over language held up congressional passage of the proposed amendment, but on March 22, 1972, the Senate approved the ERA by a vote of 84 to 8, and it was sent to the states. Six states ratified the amendment within two days, and by the middle of 1973 the amendment seemed well on its way to adoption, with thirty of the needed thirty-eight states having ratified it. In the mid-1970s, however, a powerful "Stop ERA" campaign developed. The campaign portrayed the ERA as a threat to "family values" and traditional relationships between men

and women. Although thirty-five states ultimately ratified the ERA, five of those state legislatures voted to rescind ratification, and the amendment was never adopted.

Unratified Amendment

D.C. Statehood Amendment (proposed by Congress August 22, 1978)

Section 1 For purposes of representation in the Congress, election of the President and Vice-President, and article V of this Constitution, the District constituting the seat of government of the United States shall be treated as though it were a State.

Section 2 The exercise of the rights and powers conferred under this article shall be by the people of the District constituting the seat of government, and as shall be provided by Congress.

Section 3 The twenty-third article of amendment to the Constitution of the United States is hereby repealed.

Section 4 This article shall be inoperative, unless it shall have been ratified as an amendment to the Constitution by the legislatures of three-fourths of the several states within seven years from the date of its submission.

◆ ◆ ◆

▶ The 1961 ratification of the Twenty-third Amendment, giving residents of the District of Columbia the right to vote for a president and vice president, inspired an effort to give residents of the district full voting rights. In 1966, President Lyndon Johnson appointed a mayor and city council; in 1971, D.C. residents were allowed to name a nonvoting delegate to the House; and in 1981, residents were allowed to elect the mayor and city council. Congress retained the right to overrule laws that might affect commuters, the height of federal buildings, and selection of judges and prosecutors. The district's nonvoting delegate to Congress, Walter Fauntroy, lobbied fiercely for a congressional amendment granting statehood to the district. In 1978, a proposed amendment was approved and sent to the states. A number of states quickly ratified the amendment, but, like the ERA, the D.C. Statehood Amendment ran into trouble.

Opponents argued that section 2 created a separate category of "nominal" statehood. They argued that the federal district should be eliminated and that the territory should be reabsorbed into the state of Maryland. Although these theoretical arguments were strong, some scholars believe that racist attitudes toward the predominantly black population of the city were also a factor leading to the defeat of the amendment.

Amendment XXVII

[Adopted 1992]

No law, varying the compensation for the services of the Senators and Representatives, shall take effect, until an election of Representatives shall have intervened.

♦ ♦ ♦

▶ *While the Twenty-sixth Amendment was the most rapidly ratified amendment in U.S. history, the Twenty-seventh Amendment had the longest journey to ratification. First proposed by James Madison in 1789 as part of the package that included the Bill of Rights, this amendment had been ratified by only six states by 1791. In 1873, however, it was ratified by Ohio to protest a massive retroactive salary increase by the federal government. Unlike later proposed amendments, this one came with no time limit on ratification.*

In the early 1980s, Gregory D. Watson, a University of Texas economics major, discovered the "lost" amendment and began a single-handed campaign to get state legislators to introduce it for ratification. In 1983, it was accepted by Maine. In 1984, it passed the Colorado legislature. Ratifications trickled in slowly until May 1992, when Michigan and New Jersey became the thirty-eighth and thirty-ninth states, respectively, to ratify. This amendment prevents members of Congress from raising their own salaries without giving voters a chance to vote them out of office before they can benefit from the raises.

APPENDIX II. Government and Demographics

PRESIDENTIAL ELECTIONS

Year	Candidates	Parties	Popular Vote	Percentage of Popular Vote	Electoral Vote	Percentage of Voter Participation
1789	**GEORGE WASHINGTON (Va.)***				69	
	John Adams				34	
	Others				35	
1792	**GEORGE WASHINGTON (Va.)**				132	
	John Adams				77	
	George Clinton				50	
	Others				5	
1796	**JOHN ADAMS (Mass.)**	Federalist			71	
	Thomas Jefferson	Democratic-Republican			68	
	Thomas Pinckney	Federalist			59	
	Aaron Burr	Dem.-Rep.			30	
	Others				48	
1800	**THOMAS JEFFERSON (Va.)**	Dem.-Rep.			73	
	Aaron Burr	Dem.-Rep.			73	
	John Adams	Federalist			65	
	C. C. Pinckney	Federalist			64	
	John Jay	Federalist			1	
1804	**THOMAS JEFFERSON (Va.)**	Dem.-Rep.			162	
	C. C. Pinckney	Federalist			14	
1808	**JAMES MADISON (Va.)**	Dem.-Rep.			122	
	C. C. Pinckney	Federalist			47	
	George Clinton	Dem.-Rep.			6	
1812	**JAMES MADISON (Va.)**	Dem.-Rep.			128	
	DeWitt Clinton	Federalist			89	
1816	**JAMES MONROE (Va.)**	Dem.-Rep.			183	
	Rufus King	Federalist			34	
1820	**JAMES MONROE (Va.)**	Dem.-Rep.			231	
	John Quincy Adams	Dem.-Rep.			1	
1824	**JOHN Q. ADAMS (Mass.)**	Dem.-Rep.	108,740	30.5	84	26.9
	Andrew Jackson	Dem.-Rep.	153,544	43.1	99	
	William H. Crawford	Dem.-Rep.	46,618	13.1	41	
	Henry Clay	Dem.-Rep.	47,136	13.2	37	
1828	**ANDREW JACKSON (Tenn.)**	Democratic	647,286	56.0	178	57.6
	John Quincy Adams	National Republican	508,064	44.0	83	
1832	**ANDREW JACKSON (Tenn.)**	Democratic	687,502	55.0	219	55.4
	Henry Clay	National Republican	530,189	42.4	49	
	John Floyd	Independent			11	
	William Wirt	Anti-Mason	33,108	2.6	7	

*State of residence when elected president.

Year	Candidates	Parties	Popular Vote	Percentage of Popular Vote	Electoral Vote	Percentage of Voter Participation
1836	**MARTIN VAN BUREN (N.Y.)**	Democratic	765,483	50.9	170	57.8
	W. H. Harrison	Whig			73	
	Hugh L. White	Whig	739,795	49.1	26	
	Daniel Webster	Whig			14	
	W. P. Mangum	Independent			11	
1840	**WILLIAM H. HARRISON (Ohio)**	Whig	1,274,624	53.1	234	78.0
	Martin Van Buren	Democratic	1,127,781	46.9	60	
	J. G. Birney	Liberty	7,069		—	
1844	**JAMES K. POLK (Tenn.)**	Democratic	1,338,464	49.6	170	78.9
	Henry Clay	Whig	1,300,097	48.1	105	
	J. G. Birney	Liberty	62,300	2.3	—	
1848	**ZACHARY TAYLOR (La.)**	Whig	1,360,099	47.4	163	72.7
	Lewis Cass	Democratic	1,220,544	42.5	127	
	Martin Van Buren	Free-Soil	291,263	10.1	—	
1852	**FRANKLIN PIERCE (N.H.)**	Democratic	1,601,274	50.9	254	69.6
	Winfield Scott	Whig	1,386,580	44.1	42	
	John P. Hale	Free-Soil	155,825	5.0	5	
1856	**JAMES BUCHANAN (Pa.)**	Democratic	1,836,169	45.3	174	78.9
	John C. Frémont	Republican	1,341,264	33.1	114	
	Millard Fillmore	American	874,534	21.6	8	
1860	**ABRAHAM LINCOLN (Ill.)**	Republican	1,866,452	39.9	180	81.2
	Stephen A. Douglas	Democratic	1,375,157	29.4	12	
	John C. Breckinridge	Democratic	847,953	18.1	72	
	John Bell	Union	590,631	12.6	39	
1864	**ABRAHAM LINCOLN (Ill.)**	Republican	2,213,665	55.1	212	73.8
	George B. McClellan	Democratic	1,805,237	44.9	21	
1868	**ULYSSES S. GRANT (Ill.)**	Republican	3,012,833	52.7	214	78.1
	Horatio Seymour	Democratic	2,703,249	47.3	80	
1872	**ULYSSES S. GRANT (Ill.)**	Republican	3,597,132	55.6	286	71.3
	Horace Greeley	Democratic; Liberal Republican	2,834,125	43.9	66	
1876	**RUTHERFORD B. HAYES (Ohio)**	Republican	4,036,298	47.9	185	81.8
	Samuel J. Tilden	Democratic	4,288,590	51.0	184	
1880	**JAMES A. GARFIELD (Ohio)**	Republican	4,454,416	48.5	214	79.4
	Winfield S. Hancock	Democratic	4,444,952	48.1	155	
1884	**GROVER CLEVELAND (N.Y.)**	Democratic	4,874,986	48.5	219	77.5
	James G. Blaine	Republican	4,851,981	48.3	182	
1888	**BENJAMIN HARRISON (Ind.)**	Republican	5,439,853	47.9	233	79.3
	Grover Cleveland	Democratic	5,540,309	48.6	168	
1892	**GROVER CLEVELAND (N.Y.)**	Democratic	5,555,426	46.1	277	74.7
	Benjamin Harrison	Republican	5,182,690	43.0	145	
	James B. Weaver	People's	1,029,846	8.5	22	
1896	**WILLIAM McKINLEY (Ohio)**	Republican	7,104,779	51.1	271	79.3
	William J. Bryan	Democratic-People's	6,502,925	47.7	176	
1900	**WILLIAM McKINLEY (Ohio)**	Republican	7,207,923	51.7	292	73.2
	William J. Bryan	Dem.-Populist	6,358,133	45.5	155	
1904	**THEODORE ROOSEVELT (N.Y.)**	Republican	7,623,486	57.9	336	65.2
	Alton B. Parker	Democratic	5,077,911	37.6	140	
	Eugene V. Debs	Socialist	402,283	3.0	—	
1908	**WILLIAM H. TAFT (Ohio)**	Republican	7,678,908	51.6	321	65.4
	William J. Bryan	Democratic	6,409,104	43.1	162	
	Eugene V. Debs	Socialist	420,793	2.8	—	

Year	Candidates	Parties	Popular Vote	Percentage of Popular Vote	Electoral Vote	Percentage of Voter Participation
1912	WOODROW WILSON (N.J.)	Democratic	6,293,454	41.9	435	58.8
	Theodore Roosevelt	Progressive	4,119,538	27.4	88	
	William H. Taft	Republican	3,484,980	23.2	8	
	Eugene V. Debs	Socialist	900,672	6.1	—	
1916	WOODROW WILSON (N.J.)	Democratic	9,129,606	49.4	277	61.6
	Charles E. Hughes	Republican	8,538,221	46.2	254	
	A. L. Benson	Socialist	585,113	3.2	—	
1920	WARREN G. HARDING (Ohio)	Republican	16,143,407	60.5	404	49.2
	James M. Cox	Democratic	9,130,328	34.2	127	
	Eugene V. Debs	Socialist	919,799	3.4	—	
1924	CALVIN COOLIDGE (Mass.)	Republican	15,725,016	54.0	382	48.9
	John W. Davis	Democratic	8,386,503	28.8	136	
	Robert M. La Follette	Progressive	4,822,856	16.6	13	
1928	HERBERT HOOVER (Calif.)	Republican	21,391,381	57.4	444	56.9
	Alfred E. Smith	Democratic	15,016,443	40.3	87	
	Norman Thomas	Socialist	881,951	2.3	—	
1932	FRANKLIN D. ROOSEVELT (N.Y.)	Democratic	22,821,857	57.4	472	56.9
	Herbert Hoover	Republican	15,761,841	39.7	59	
	Norman Thomas	Socialist	881,951	2.2	—	
	William Z. Foster	Communist	102,991	0.3	—	
1936	FRANKLIN D. ROOSEVELT (N.Y.)	Democratic	27,751,597	60.8	523	61.0
	Alfred M. Landon	Republican	16,679,583	36.5	8	
	William Lemke	Union	882,479	1.9	—	
1940	FRANKLIN D. ROOSEVELT (N.Y.)	Democratic	27,244,160	54.8	449	62.5
	Wendell Willkie	Republican	22,305,198	44.8	82	
1944	FRANKLIN D. ROOSEVELT (N.Y.)	Democratic	25,602,504	53.5	432	55.9
	Thomas E. Dewey	Republican	22,006,285	46.0	99	
1948	HARRY S. TRUMAN (Mo.)	Democratic	24,105,695	49.5	303	53.0
	Thomas E. Dewey	Republican	21,969,170	45.1	189	
	J. Strom Thurmond	States'-Rights Democratic	1,169,021	2.4	39	
	Henry A. Wallace	Progressive	1,156,103	2.4	—	
1952	DWIGHT D. EISENHOWER (N.Y.)	Republican	33,936,252	55.1	442	63.3
	Adlai Stevenson	Democratic	27,314,992	44.4	89	
1956	DWIGHT D. EISENHOWER (N.Y.)	Republican	35,575,420	57.6	457	60.6
	Adlai Stevenson	Democratic	26,033,066	42.1	73	
	Other	—	—		1	
1960	JOHN F. KENNEDY (Mass.)	Democratic	34,227,096	49.9	303	62.8
	Richard M. Nixon	Republican	34,108,546	49.6	219	
	Other	—	—		15	
1964	LYNDON B. JOHNSON (Texas)	Democratic	43,126,506	61.1	486	61.7
	Barry M. Goldwater	Republican	27,176,799	38.5	52	
1968	RICHARD M. NIXON (N.Y.)	Republican	31,770,237	43.4	301	60.9
	Hubert H. Humphrey	Democratic	31,270,533	42.7	191	
	George Wallace	American Indep.	9,906,141	13.5	46	
1972	RICHARD M. NIXON (N.Y.)	Republican	47,169,911	60.7	520	55.2
	George S. McGovern	Democratic	29,170,383	37.5	17	
	Other	—	—		1	
1976	JIMMY CARTER (Ga.)	Democratic	40,830,763	50.1	297	53.5
	Gerald R. Ford	Republican	39,147,793	48.0	240	
	Other	—	1,575,459	2.1	—	
1980	RONALD REAGAN (Calif.)	Republican	43,901,812	51.0	489	54.0
	Jimmy Carter	Democratic	35,483,820	41.0	49	
	John B. Anderson	Independent	5,719,722	7.0	—	
	Ed Clark	Libertarian	921,188	1.1	—	

Year	Candidates	Parties	Popular Vote	Percentage of Popular Vote	Electoral Vote	Percentage of Voter Participation
1984	**RONALD REAGAN (Calif.)**	Republican	54,455,075	59.0	525	53.1
	Walter Mondale	Democratic	37,577,185	41.0	13	
1988	**GEORGE H. W. BUSH (Texas)**	Republican	47,946,422	54.0	426	50.2
	Michael S. Dukakis	Democratic	41,016,429	46.0	112	
1992	**WILLIAM J. CLINTON (Ark.)**	Democratic	44,908,254	43.0	370	55.9
	George H. W. Bush	Republican	39,102,282	38.0	168	
	H. Ross Perot	Independent	19,721,433	19.0	—	
1996	**WILLIAM J. CLINTON (Ark.)**	Democratic	47,401,185	49.2	379	49.0
	Robert Dole	Republican	39,197,469	40.7	159	
	H. Ross Perot	Independent	8,085,294	8.4	—	
2000	**GEORGE W. BUSH (Texas)**	Republican	50,456,062	47.8	271	51.2
	Al Gore	Democratic	50,996,862	48.4	267	
	Ralph Nader	Green Party	2,858,843	2.7	—	
	Patrick J. Buchanan	Reform Party	438,760	0.4	—	
2004	**GEORGE W. BUSH (Texas)**	Republican	61,872,711	50.7	286	60.3
	John F. Kerry	Democratic	58,894,584	48.3	252	
	Other	—	1,582,185	1.3	—	
2008	**BARACK OBAMA (Ill.)**	Democratic	69,456,897	52.9	365	56.8
	John McCain	Republican	59,934,314	45.7	173	
2012	**BARACK OBAMA (Ill.)**	Democratic	65,899,660	51.1	332	57.5
	Willard Mitt Romney	Republican	60,932,152	47.2	206	
2016*	**DONALD J. TRUMP (N.Y.)**	Republican	59,704,886	47.5	279	56.5
	Hillary Clinton	Democratic	59,938,290	47.7	228	
	Gary Johnson	Libertarian	4,072,835	3.3	—	
	Jill Stein	Green Party	1,218,065	1.0	—	

*As of 11/10/16

SUPREME COURT JUSTICES

Name	Service	Appointed by	Name	Service	Appointed by
John Jay*	1789–1795	Washington	**Roger B. Taney**	1836–1864	Jackson
James Wilson	1789–1798	Washington	Philip P. Barbour	1836–1841	Jackson
John Blair	1789–1796	Washington	John Catron	1837–1865	Van Buren
John Rutledge	1790–1791	Washington	John McKinley	1837–1852	Van Buren
William Cushing	1790–1810	Washington	Peter V. Daniel	1841–1860	Van Buren
James Iredell	1790–1799	Washington	Samuel Nelson	1845–1872	Tyler
Thomas Johnson	1791–1793	Washington	Levi Woodbury	1845–1851	Polk
William Paterson	1793–1806	Washington	Robert C. Grier	1846–1870	Polk
John Rutledge†	1795	Washington	Benjamin R. Curtis	1851–1857	Fillmore
Samuel Chase	1796–1811	Washington	John A. Campbell	1853–1861	Pierce
Oliver Ellsworth	1796–1799	Washington	Nathan Clifford	1858–1881	Buchanan
Bushrod Washington	1798–1829	J. Adams	Noah H. Swayne	1862–1881	Lincoln
Alfred Moore	1799–1804	J. Adams	Samuel F. Miller	1862–1890	Lincoln
John Marshall	1801–1835	J. Adams	David Davis	1862–1877	Lincoln
William Johnson	1804–1834	Jefferson	Stephen J. Field	1863–1897	Lincoln
Henry B. Livingston	1806–1823	Jefferson	**Salmon P. Chase**	1864–1873	Lincoln
Thomas Todd	1807–1826	Jefferson	William Strong	1870–1880	Grant
Gabriel Duval	1811–1836	Madison	Joseph P. Bradley	1870–1892	Grant
Joseph Story	1811–1845	Madison	Ward Hunt	1873–1882	Grant
Smith Thompson	1823–1843	Monroe	**Morrison R. Waite**	1874–1888	Grant
Robert Trimble	1826–1828	J. Q. Adams	John M. Harlan	1877–1911	Hayes
John McLean	1829–1861	Jackson	William B. Woods	1880–1887	Hayes
Henry Baldwin	1830–1844	Jackson	Stanley Matthews	1881–1889	Garfield
James M. Wayne	1835–1867	Jackson	Horace Gray	1882–1902	Arthur

*Chief Justices appear in bold type.
†Acting Chief Justice; Senate refused to confirm appointment.

Name	Service	Appointed by	Name	Service	Appointed by
Samuel Blatchford	1882–1893	Arthur	**Harlan F. Stone**	1941–1946	F. Roosevelt
Lucius Q. C. Lamar	1888–1893	Cleveland	James F. Byrnes	1941–1942	F. Roosevelt
Melville W. Fuller	1888–1910	Cleveland	Robert H. Jackson	1941–1954	F. Roosevelt
David J. Brewer	1889–1910	B. Harrison	Wiley B. Rutledge	1943–1949	F. Roosevelt
Henry B. Brown	1890–1906	B. Harrison	Harold H. Burton	1945–1958	Truman
George Shiras	1892–1903	B. Harrison	**Frederick M. Vinson**	1946–1953	Truman
Howell E. Jackson	1893–1895	B. Harrison	Tom C. Clark	1949–1967	Truman
Edward D. White	1894–1910	Cleveland	Sherman Minton	1949–1956	Truman
Rufus W. Peckham	1896–1909	Cleveland	**Earl Warren**	1953–1969	Eisenhower
Joseph McKenna	1898–1925	McKinley	John Marshall Harlan	1955–1971	Eisenhower
Oliver W. Holmes	1902–1932	T. Roosevelt	William J. Brennan Jr.	1956–1990	Eisenhower
William R. Day	1903–1922	T. Roosevelt	Charles E. Whittaker	1957–1962	Eisenhower
William H. Moody	1906–1910	T. Roosevelt	Potter Stewart	1958–1981	Eisenhower
Horace H. Lurton	1910–1914	Taft	Byron R. White	1962–1993	Kennedy
Charles E. Hughes	1910–1916	Taft	Arthur J. Goldberg	1962–1965	Kennedy
Willis Van Devanter	1910–1937	Taft	Abe Fortas	1965–1969	L. Johnson
Edward D. White	1910–1921	Taft	Thurgood Marshall	1967–1991	L. Johnson
Joseph R. Lamar	1911–1916	Taft	**Warren E. Burger**	1969–1986	Nixon
Mahlon Pitney	1912–1922	Taft	Harry A. Blackmun	1970–1994	Nixon
James C. McReynolds	1914–1941	Wilson	Lewis F. Powell Jr.	1972–1988	Nixon
Louis D. Brandeis	1916–1939	Wilson	William H. Rehnquist	1972–1986	Nixon
John H. Clarke	1916–1922	Wilson	John Paul Stevens	1975–	Ford
William H. Taft	1921–1930	Harding	Sandra Day O'Connor	1981–2006	Reagan
George Sutherland	1922–1938	Harding	**William H. Rehnquist**	1986–2005	Reagan
Pierce Butler	1923–1939	Harding	Antonin Scalia	1986–2016	Reagan
Edward T. Sanford	1923–1930	Harding	Anthony M. Kennedy	1988–	Reagan
Harlan F. Stone	1925–1941	Coolidge	David H. Souter	1990–2009	G. H. W. Bush
Charles E. Hughes	1930–1941	Hoover	Clarence Thomas	1991–	G. H. W. Bush
Owen J. Roberts	1930–1945	Hoover	Ruth Bader Ginsburg	1993–	Clinton
Benjamin N. Cardozo	1932–1938	Hoover	Stephen Breyer	1994–	Clinton
Hugo L. Black	1937–1971	F. Roosevelt	**John G. Roberts Jr.**	2005–	G. W. Bush
Stanley F. Reed	1938–1957	F. Roosevelt	Samuel Anthony Alito Jr.	2006–	G. W. Bush
Felix Frankfurter	1939–1962	F. Roosevelt			
William O. Douglas	1939–1975	F. Roosevelt	Sonia Sotomayor	2009–	Obama
Frank Murphy	1940–1949	F. Roosevelt	Elena Kagan	2010–	Obama

ADMISSION OF STATES TO THE UNION

State	Date of Admission	State	Date of Admission
Delaware	December 7, 1787	Florida	March 3, 1845
Pennsylvania	December 12, 1787	Texas	December 29, 1845
New Jersey	December 18, 1787	Iowa	December 28, 1846
Georgia	January 2, 1788	Wisconsin	May 29, 1848
Connecticut	January 9, 1788	California	September 9, 1850
Massachusetts	February 6, 1788	Minnesota	May 11, 1858
Maryland	April 28, 1788	Oregon	February 14, 1859
South Carolina	May 23, 1788	Kansas	January 29, 1861
New Hampshire	June 21, 1788	West Virginia	June 19, 1863
Virginia	June 25, 1788	Nevada	October 31, 1864
New York	July 26, 1788	Nebraska	March 1, 1867
North Carolina	November 21, 1789	Colorado	August 1, 1876
Rhode Island	May 29, 1790	North Dakota	November 2, 1889
Vermont	March 4, 1791	South Dakota	November 2, 1889
Kentucky	June 1, 1792	Montana	November 8, 1889
Tennessee	June 1, 1796	Washington	November 11, 1889
Ohio	March 1, 1803	Idaho	July 3, 1890
Louisiana	April 30, 1812	Wyoming	July 10, 1890
Indiana	December 11, 1816	Utah	January 4, 1896
Mississippi	December 10, 1817	Oklahoma	November 16, 1907
Illinois	December 3, 1818	New Mexico	January 6, 1912
Alabama	December 14, 1819	Arizona	February 14, 1912
Maine	March 15, 1820	Alaska	January 3, 1959
Missouri	August 10, 1821	Hawai'i	August 21, 1959
Arkansas	June 15, 1836		
Michigan	January 16, 1837		

Population

FROM AN ESTIMATED 4,600 white inhabitants in 1630, the country's population grew to a total of more than 308 million in 2010. It is important to note that the U.S. census, first conducted in 1790 and the source of these figures, counted blacks, both free and slave, but did not include American Indians until 1860. The years 1790 to 1900 saw the most rapid population growth, with an average increase of 25 to 35 percent per decade. In addition to "natural" growth—birthrate exceeding death rate—immigration was also a factor in that rise, especially between 1840 and 1860, 1880 and 1890, and 1900 and 1910. The twentieth century witnessed slower growth, partly a result of 1920s immigration restrictions and a decline in the birthrate, especially during the depression era and the 1960s and 1970s. The U.S. population is expected to pass 340 million by the year 2020.

POPULATION GROWTH, 1630–2010

Year	Population	Percent Increase	Year	Population	Percent Increase
1630	4,600	—	1830	12,866,020	33.5
1640	26,600	473.3	1840	17,069,453	32.7
1650	50,400	89.1	1850	23,191,876	35.9
1660	75,100	49.0	1860	31,443,321	35.6
1670	111,900	49.1	1870	39,818,449	26.6
1680	151,500	35.4	1880	50,155,783	26.0
1690	210,400	38.9	1890	62,947,714	25.5
1700	250,900	19.3	1900	75,994,575	20.7
1710	331,700	32.2	1910	91,972,266	21.0
1720	466,200	40.5	1920	105,710,620	14.9
1730	629,400	35.0	1930	122,775,046	16.1
1740	905,600	43.9	1940	131,669,275	7.2
1750	1,170,800	30.0	1950	150,697,361	14.5
1760	1,593,600	36.1	1960	179,323,175	19.0
1770	2,148,100	34.8	1970	203,302,031	13.4
1780	2,780,400	29.4	1980	226,542,199	11.4
1790	3,929,214	41.3	1990	248,718,302	9.8
1800	5,308,483	35.1	2000	281,422,509	13.1
1810	7,239,881	36.4	2010	308,745,538	9.7
1820	9,638,453	33.1			

Sources: *Historical Statistics of the U.S.* (1960); *Historical Statistics of the U.S., Colonial Times to 1970* (1975); *Statistical Abstract of the U.S., 1996* (1996); *Statistical Abstract of the U.S., 2003* (2003); and United States Census (2010).

Major Trends in Immigration

THE QUANTITY AND CHARACTER OF IMMIGRATION to the United States has varied greatly over time. During the first major influx, between 1840 and 1860, newcomers hailed primarily from northern and western Europe. From 1880 to 1915, when rates soared even more dramatically, the profile changed, with 80 percent of the "new immigration" coming from central, eastern, and southern Europe. Following World War I, strict quotas reduced the flow considerably. Note also the significant falloff during the years of the Great Depression and World War II. The sources of immigration during the last half century have changed significantly, with the majority of people coming from Latin America, the Caribbean, and Asia. The latest surge during the 1980s and 1990s brought more immigrants to the United States than in any decade except 1901–1910.

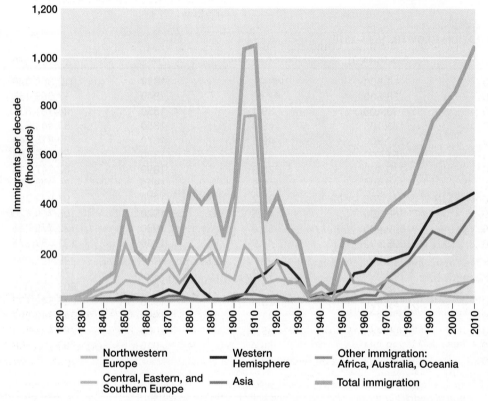

Sources: Data from *Historical Statistics of the U.S., Colonial Times to 1970* (1975); *Statistical Abstract of the U.S., 1999* (1999); and *Statistical Abstract of the U.S., 2011* (2011).

Selected Bibliography

Chapter 1

GENERAL WORKS

Robson Bonnichsen and Karen L. Turnmire, *Ice Age Peoples of North America* (1999).

Karen Olsen Bruhns and Karen R. Stothert, *Women in Ancient America* (1999).

Thomas D. Dillehay, *The Settlement of the Americas: A New Prehistory* (2000).

Brian Fagan, *Ancient North America* (2005).

Tim Flannery, *The Eternal Frontier: An Ecological History of North America and Its Peoples* (2001).

J. C. H. King, *First People, First Contacts: Native Peoples of North America* (1999).

Charles C. Mann, *1491: New Revelations of the Americas before Columbus* (2006).

Francis McManamon et al., eds., *Archaeology in America* (2008).

Steven Mithen, *After the Ice: A Global Human History, 20,000–5000 BC* (2003).

Daniel K. Richter, *Before the Revolution: America's Ancient Pasts* (2011).

Christina Snyder, *Slavery in Indian Country: The Changing Face of Captivity in Early America* (2010).

Nicholas Wade, *Before the Dawn: Recovering the Lost History of Our Ancestors* (2006).

NATIVE AMERICAN CULTURES IN TERRITORY OF PRESENT-DAY UNITED STATES

Kenneth M. Ames and Herbert D. G. Maschner, *Peoples of the Northwest Coast: Their Archaeology and Prehistory* (1999).

Sally A. Kitt Chappell, *Cahokia: Mirror of the Cosmos* (2002).

Linda S. Cordell, *Archaeology of the Southwest* (2009).

Richard J. Dent Jr., *Chesapeake Prehistory: Old Traditions, New Directions* (1995).

E. James Dixon, *Bones, Boats, and Bison: Archeology and the First Colonization of Western North America* (1999).

Thomas E. Emerson et al., eds., *Late Woodland Societies: Tradition and Transformation across the Midcontinent* (2008).

Kendrick Frazier, *People of Chaco: A Canyon and Its Cultures* (1999).

George C. Frison, *Prehistoric Hunters of the High Plains* (2nd ed., 1991).

Sarah A. Kerr, *Beyond Chaco: Great Kiva Communities on the Mogollon Rim Frontier* (2001).

Steven A. LeBlanc, *Prehistoric Warfare in the American Southwest* (1999).

Stephen H. Lekson, *The Chaco Meridian: Centers of Political Power in the Ancient Southwest* (1999).

Jerald T. Milanich, *Archaeology of Precolumbian Florida* (1994).

Timothy R. Pauketat, *Cahokia: Ancient America's Greatest City on the Mississippi* (2009).

Jefferson Reid and Stephanie Whittlesley, *The Archaeology of Ancient Arizona* (1997).

Karl H. Schlesier, *Plains Indians, A.D. 500–1500: The Archaeological Past of Historic Groups* (1994).

Lynne Sebastian, *The Chaco Anasazi: Sociopolitical Evolution in the Prehistoric Southwest* (1992).

Lynda Shaffer, *Native Americans before 1492: The Moundbuilding Centers of the Eastern Woodlands* (1992).

Marvin T. Smith, *Coosa: The Rise and Fall of a Southeastern Mississippian Chiefdom* (2000).

Biloine Whiting Young and Melvin L. Fowler, *Cahokia: The Great Native American Metropolis* (1999).

THE MEXICA

David Carrasco, *City of Sacrifice: The Aztec Empire and the Role of Violence in Civilization* (1999).

Michael D. Coe and Rex Koontz, *Mexico: From the Olmecs to the Aztecs* (6th ed., 2013).

Susan Toby Evans, *Ancient Mexico and Central America: Archaeology and Culture History* (2008).

Eduardo Matos Moctezuma and Felipe Solis Olguin, *Aztecs* (2002).

Chapter 2

GENERAL WORKS

J. H. Elliott, *Empires of the Atlantic World: Britain and Spain in America, 1491–1830* (2006).

Mark G. Hanna, *Pirate Nests and the Rise of the British Empire, 1570–1740* (2015).

John L. Kessell, *Spain in the Southwest: A Narrative History of Colonial New Mexico, Arizona, Texas, and California* (2002).

Diarmaid MacCulloch, *Christianity: The First Three Thousand Years* (2009).

David Parrott, *The Business of War: Military Enterprise and Military Revolution in Early Modern Europe* (2013).

William D. Phillips and Carla Rahn Phillips, *The Worlds of Christopher Columbus* (1992).

Daniel K. Richter, *Before the Revolution: America's Ancient Pasts* (2011).

John K. Thornton, *A Cultural History of the Atlantic World, 1250–1820* (2012).

David J. Weber, *The Spanish Frontier in North America* (2009).

EXPLORERS AND EMPIRES

Roger Crowley, *Conquerors: How Portugal Forged the First Global Empire* (2015).

James Horn, *A Kingdom Strange: The Brief and Tragic History of the Lost Colony of Roanoke* (2010).

Henry Arthur Francis Kamen, *Empire: How Spain Became a World Power, 1492–1763* (2004).

Karen Ordahl Kupperman, *Roanoke: The Abandoned Colony* (2nd ed., 2007).

Francesc Relaño, *The Shaping of Africa: Cosmographic Discourse and Cartographic Science in Late Medieval and Early Modern Europe* (2002).

A. J. R. Russell-Wood, *The Portuguese Empire, 1415–1808: A World on the Move* (1998).

Hugh Thomas, *Rivers of Gold: The Rise of the Spanish Empire from Columbus to Magellan* (2004).

EUROPEANS ENCOUNTER THE NEW WORLD

Ricardo Alegria and Jose Arrom, *Taino: Pre-Columbian Art and Culture from the Caribbean* (1998).

Rebecca Catz, *Christopher Columbus and the Portuguese, 1476–1498* (1993).

Noble David Cook, *Born to Die: Disease and New World Conquest, 1492–1650* (1998).

Charles C. Mann, *1493: Uncovering the New World Columbus Created* (2012).

Michael Leroy Oberg, *The Head in Edward Nugent's Hand: Roanoke's Forgotten Indians* (2008).

Anthony Pagden, *Lords of All the World: Ideologies of Empire in Spain, Britain, and France, 1500–1800* (1995).

Irving Rouse, *The Tainos: Rise and Decline of the People Who Greeted Columbus* (1992).

CONQUEST AND NEW SPAIN

Herman L. Bennett, *Colonial Blackness: A History of Afro-Mexico* (2010).

Louise M. Burkhart, *The Slippery Earth: Nahua-Christian Moral Dialogue in Sixteenth-Century Mexico* (1989).

David Ewing Duncan, *Hernando de Soto: A Savage Quest in the Americas* (1995).

Richard Flint and Shirley Cushing Flint, *The Coronado Expedition* (2003).

Serge Gruzinski, *The Conquest of Mexico: The Incorporation of Indian Societies into the Western World, Sixteenth–Eighteenth Centuries* (1993).

Ramón A. Gutiérrez, *When Jesus Came, the Corn Mothers Went Away: Marriage, Sexuality, and Power in New Mexico, 1500–1846* (1991).

Robert H. Jackson, *Race, Caste, and Status: Indians in Colonial Spanish America* (1999).

John L. Kessell, *Pueblos, Spaniards, and the Kingdom of New Mexico* (2010).

Andrew L. Knaut, *The Pueblo Revolt of 1680: Conquest and Resistance in Seventeenth-Century New Mexico* (1995).

Miguel León-Portilla, *Bernardino de Sahagún: First Anthropologist* (2002).

Jerald T. Milanich, *Laboring in the Fields of the Lord: Spanish Missions and Southwestern Indians* (1999).

Matthew Restall, *Seven Myths of the Spanish Conquest* (2004).

Matthew Restall and Kris Lane, *Latin America in Colonial Times* (2011).

Stuart B. Schwartz, *All Can Be Saved: Religious Tolerance and Salvation in the Iberian Atlantic World* (2009).

Hugh Thomas, *World without End: Spain, Philip II, and the First Global Empire* (2015).

Charles A. Truxillo, *By the Sword and the Cross: The Historical Evolution of the Catholic World Monarchy in Spain and the New World, 1492–1825* (2001).

Stephanie Gail Wood, *Transcending Conquest: Nahua Views of Spanish Colonial Mexico* (2003).

Chapter 3

CHESAPEAKE SOCIETY

Bernard Bailyn, *The Barbarous Years: The Peopling of British North America: The Conflict of Civilizations, 1600–1675* (2012).

Kathleen Brown, *Good Wives, Nasty Wenches, and Anxious Patriarchs: Gender, Race, and Power in Colonial Virginia* (1996).

Alison Games, *The Web of Empire: English Cosmopolitans in the Age of Expansion, 1560–1660* (2009).

April Hatfield, *Atlantic Virginia: Intercolonial Relations in the Seventeenth Century* (2003).

James Horn, *A Land as God Made It: Jamestown and the Birth of America* (2006).

Karen Ordahl Kupperman, *The Jamestown Project* (2010).

Peter C. Mancall, *The Atlantic World and Virginia, 1550–1624* (2007).

Debra Meyers, *Common Whores, Vertuous Women, and Loveing Wives: Free Will Christian Women in Colonial Maryland* (2003).

Marcy Norton, *Sacred Gifts, Profane Pleasures: A History of Tobacco and Chocolate in the Atlantic World* (2010).

Geoffrey Parker, *Global Crisis: War, Climate Change and Catastrophe in the Seventeenth Century* (2013).

Steve Sarson, *British America, 1500–1800: Creating Colonies, Imagining an Empire* (2005).

Terry L. Snyder, *Brabbling Women: Disorderly Speech and the Law in Early Virginia* (2003).

Christopher L. Tomlins, *Freedom Bound: Law, Labor, and Civic Identity in Colonizing English America, 1580–1865* (2010).

Lorena S. Walsh, *Motives of Honor, Pleasure, and Profit: Plantation Management in the Colonial Chesapeake, 1607–1763* (2010).

INDIANS

Alan Gallay, *The Indian Slave Trade: The Rise of the English Empire in the American South, 1670–1717* (2002).

Joseph M. Hall Jr., *Zamuno's Gifts: Indian European Exchange in the Colonial Southeast* (2012).

Karen Ordahl Kupperman, *Indians and English: Facing Off in Early America* (2000).

Andrew Lipman, *The Saltwater Frontier: Indians and the Contest for the American Coast* (2015).

Helen C. Rountree, *Pocahontas, Powhatan, Opechancanough: Three Indian Lives Changed by Jamestown* (2005).

Christina Snyder, *Slavery in Indian Country: The Changing Face of Captivity in Early America* (2010).

Jayme A. Sokolow, *The Great Encounter: Native Peoples and European Settlers in the Americas, 1492–1800* (2003).

Margaret Holmes Williamson, *Powhatan Lords of Life and Death: Command and Consent in Seventeenth-Century Virginia* (2003).

SLAVERY AND INDENTURED SERVITUDE

Susan Dwyer Amussen, *Caribbean Exchanges: Slavery and the Transformation of English Society, 1640–1700* (2007).

James F. Brooks, *Captives and Cousins: Slavery, Kinship, and Community in the Southwest Borderlands* (2002).

Tim Hashaw, *The Birth of Black America: The First African Americans and the Pursuit of Freedom at Jamestown* (2007).

Linda M. Heywood and John K. Thornton, *Central Africans, Atlantic Creoles, and the Foundation of the Americas* (2007).

Russell R. Menard, *Migrants, Servants, and Slaves: Unfree Labor in Colonial British America* (2001).

Jerald T. Milanich, *Laboring in the Fields of the Lord: Spanish Missions and Southeastern Indians* (1999).

Edmund S. Morgan, *American Slavery, American Freedom: The Ordeal of Colonial Virginia* (1975).

Jennifer L. Morgan, *Laboring Women: Reproduction and Gender in New World Slavery* (2004).

Simon P. Newman, *A New World of Labor: The Development of Plantation Slavery in the British Atlantic* (2013).

John Ruston Pagan, *Anne Orthwood's Bastard: Sex and Law in Early Virginia* (2003).

Andrés Reséndez, *The Other Slavery: The Uncovered Story of Indian Enslavement in America* (2016).

CAROLINA SOCIETY AND THE WEST INDIES

Cara Anzilotti, *In the Affairs of the World: Women, Patriarchy, and Power in Colonial South Carolina* (2002).

S. Max Edelson, *Plantation Enterprise in Colonial South Carolina* (2006).

Kirsten Fischer, *Suspect Relations: Sex, Race, and Resistance in Colonial North Carolina* (2002).

Michael Jarvis, *In the Eye of All Trade: Bermuda, Bermudians, and the Maritime Atlantic World, 1680–1783* (2010).

Russell K. Menard, *Sweet Negotiations: Sugar, Slavery, and Plantation Agriculture in Early Barbados* (2006).

Matthew Mulcahy, *Hubs of Empire: The Southeastern Low Country and British Caribbean* (2014).

Chapter 4

GENERAL WORKS

Virginia DeJohn Anderson, *Creatures of Empire: How Domestic Animals Transformed Early America* (2004).

Bernard Bailyn, *The Barbarous Years: The Peopling of British North America: The Conflict of Civilizations, 1600–1675* (2012).

Colin G. Calloway, *New Worlds for All: Indians, Europeans, and the Remaking of Early America* (1998).

Eric Jay Dolin, *Fur, Fortune, and Empire: The Epic History of the Fur Trade in America* (2010).

David D. Hall, *Worlds of Wonder, Days of Judgment: Popular Religious Belief in Early New England* (1989).

Peter Moogk, *La Nouvelle France: The Making of French Canada—A Cultural History* (2000).

Christopher L. Pastore, *Between Land and Sea: The Atlantic Coast and the Transformation of New England* (2014).

Carla Gardina Pestana, *The English Atlantic in the Age of Revolution, 1640–1661* (2004).

James Pritchard, *In Search of Empire: The French in the Americas, 1670–1730* (2007).

Anya Zilberstein, *A Temperate Empire: Making Climate Change in Early America* (2016).

NATIVE AMERICANS

Russell Bourne, *Gods of War, Gods of Peace: How the Meeting of Native and Colonial Religions Shaped Early America* (2002).

Roger M. Carpenter, *The Renewed, the Destroyed, and the Remade: The Three Thought Worlds of the Huron and the Iroquois, 1609–1675* (2004).

Jill Lepore, *The Name of War: King Philip's War and the Origins of American Identity* (1998).

Daniel R. Mandell, *King Philip's War: Colonial Expansion, Native Resistance, and the End of Indian Sovereignty* (2010).

Michael McDonnell, *Masters of Empire: Great Lakes Indians and the Making of America* (2015).

Donna Merwick, *The Shame and the Sorrow: Dutch-Amerindian Encounters in New Netherland* (2006).

Michael Leroy Oberg, *Dominion and Civility: English Imperialism and Native America, 1585–1685* (1999).

Ann Marie Plane, *Colonial Intimacies: Indian Marriages in Early New England* (2000).

NEW ENGLAND

Louise A. Breen, *Transgressing the Bounds: Subversive Enterprises among the Puritan Elite in Massachusetts, 1630–1692* (2001).

Nick Bunker, *Making Haste from Babylon: The Mayflower Pilgrims and Their World* (2010).

James F. Cooper Jr., *Tenacious of Their Liberties: The Congregationalists in Colonial Massachusetts* (1999).

Cornelia Hughes Dayton, *Women before the Bar: Gender, Law, and Society in Connecticut, 1639–1789* (1995).

Lisa M. Gordis, *Opening Scriptures: Bible Reading and Interpretive Authority in Puritan New England* (2003).

Katherine Grandjean, *American Passage: The Communications Frontier in Early New England* (2015).

David D. Hall, *A Reforming People: Transformation of Public Life in New England* (2013).

Jane Kamensky, *Governing the Tongue: The Politics of Speech in Early New England* (1997).

Eve LaPlante, *American Jezebel: The Uncommon Life of Anne Hutchinson, the Woman Who Defied the Puritans* (2005).

Mary Beth Norton, *In the Devil's Snare: The Salem Witchcraft Crisis of 1692* (2002).

Mark A. Peterson, *The Price of Redemption: The Spiritual Economy of Puritan New England* (1998).

Nathaniel Philbrick, *Mayflower: A Story of Courage, Community, and War* (2006).

Wendy Warren, *New England Bound: Slavery and Colonization in Early America* (2016).

Michael P. Winship, *Making Heretics: Militant Protestantism and Free Grace in Massachusetts, 1636–1641* (2002).

MIDDLE COLONIES

Evan Haefeli, *New Netherland and the Dutch Origins of American Religious Liberty* (2012).

Ned C. Landsman, *Crossroads of Empire: The Middle Colonies in British North America* (2010).

Peter C. Mancall, *Fatal Journey: The Final Expedition of Henry Hudson* (2009).

Cathy Matson, *Merchants and Empire: Trading in Colonial New York* (1998).

David E. Narrett, *Inheritance and Family Life in Colonial New York City* (1992).

Russell Shorto, *The Island at the Center of the World: The Epic Story of Dutch Manhattan and the Forgotten Colony That Shaped America* (2004).

Allen Tully, *Forming American Politics: Ideals, Interests, and Institutions in Colonial New York and Pennsylvania* (1994).

Chapter 5

GENERAL WORKS

Jennifer L. Anderson, *Mahogany: The Costs of Luxury in Early America* (2012).

Ira Berlin, *Generations of Captivity: A History of African-American Slaves* (2003).

Stephen R. Berry, *Path in the Mighty Waters: Shipboard Life and Atlantic Crossings to the New World* (2015).

Holly Brewer, *By Birth or Consent: Children, Law, and the Anglo-American Revolution in Authority* (2005).

Eric Jay Dolin, *Fur, Fortune, and Empire: The Epic History of the Fur Trade in America* (2010).

Robert S. DuPlessis, *The Material Atlantic: Clothing, Commerce, and Colonization in the Atlantic World, 1650–1800* (2016).

Kathleen DuVal, *The Native Ground: Indians and Colonists in the Heart of the Continent* (2006).

Adrian Finucane, *The Temptations of Trade: Britain, Spain, and the Struggle for Empire* (2016).

Patrick Griffin, *The People with No Name: Ireland's Ulster Scots, America's Scots Irish, and the Creation of a British Atlantic World, 1689–1764* (2001).

David Hancock, *Oceans of Wine: Madeira and the Emergence of American Trade and Taste* (2009).

Brendan McConville, *The King's Three Faces: The Rise and Fall of Royal America, 1688–1776* (2007).

Anthony Pagden, *The Enlightenment and Why It Still Matters* (2013).

Peter Silver, *Our Savage Neighbors: How Indian War Transformed Early America* (2008).

Christina Snyder, *Slavery in Indian Country: The Changing Face of Captivity in Early America* (2012).

Michael Witgen, *An Infinity of Nations: How the Native New World Shaped Early North America* (2013).

NEW ENGLAND

Richard Aquila, *The Iroquois Restoration: Iroquois Diplomacy on the Colonial Frontier, 1701–1754* (1997).

Elaine Forman Crane, *Ebb Tide in New England: Women, Seaports, and Social Change, 1630–1800* (1998).

Phyllis Whitman Hunter, *Purchasing Identity in the Atlantic World: Massachusetts Merchants, 1670–1780* (2001).

George M. Marsden, *Jonathan Edwards: A Life* (2003).

Lisa Norling, *Captain Ahab Had a Wife: New England Women and the Whale Fishery, 1720–1870* (2000).

Daniel Vickers, *Young Men and the Sea: Yankee Seafarers in the Age of Sail* (2005).

MIDDLE COLONIES

Katherine Carté Engel, *Religion and Profit: Moravians in Early America* (2009).

Leslie M. Harris, *In the Shadow of Slavery: African Americans in New York City, 1626–1863* (2003).

Eric Hinderaker, *Elusive Empires: Constructing Colonialism in the Ohio Valley, 1673–1800* (1997).

Jill Lepore, *New York Burning: Liberty, Slavery, and Conspiracy in Eighteenth-Century Manhattan* (2005).

James H. Merrell, *Into the American Woods: Negotiators on the Pennsylvania Frontier* (1999).

Jane T. Merritt, *At the Crossroads: Indians and Empires on a Mid-Atlantic Frontier, 1700–1763* (2003).

Donna Merwick, *The Shame and the Sorrow: Dutch-Amerindian Encounters in New Netherland* (2006).

Simon P. Newman, *Embodied History: The Lives of the Poor in Early Philadelphia* (2003).

David Waldstreicher, *Runaway America: Benjamin Franklin, Slavery, and the American Revolution* (2004).

SOUTHERN COLONIES

Vincent Carretta, *Equiano the African: Biography of a Self-Made Man* (2005).

Steven W. Hackel, *Children of Coyote, Missionaries of Saint Francis: Indian-Spanish Relations in Colonial California, 1769–1850* (2005).

Robert H. Jackson, *Missions and the Frontiers of Spanish America* (2005).

Catherine Kerrison, *Claiming the Pen: Women and Intellectual Life in the Early American South* (2006).

Philip D. Morgan, *Slave Counterpoint: Black Culture in the Eighteenth-Century Chesapeake and Low Country* (1998).

Gregory E. O'Malley, *Final Passages: The Intercolonial Slave Trade of British America, 1619–1807* (2014).

Brett Rushforth, *Bonds of Alliance: Indigenous and Atlantic Slaveries in New France* (2012).

Jon F. Sensbach, *Rebecca's Revival: Creating Black Christianity in the Atlantic World* (2005).

Randy J. Sparks, *The Two Princes of Calabar: An Eighteenth-Century Atlantic Odyssey* (2004).

———*Africans in the Old South: Mapping Exceptional Lives across the Atlantic World* (2016).

David J. Weber, *Bárbaros: Spaniards and Their Savages in the Age of Enlightenment* (2005).

Bradford J. Wood, *This Remote Part of the World: Regional Formation in Lower Cape Fear, North Carolina, 1725–1775* (2004).

Chapter 6

GENERAL WORKS

Edward Countryman, *The American Revolution* (2003).

Merrill Jensen, *The Founding of a Nation: A History of the American Revolution, 1763–1776* (2004).

Robert Middlekauff, *The Glorious Cause: The American Revolution, 1763–1789* (2005).

Gordon Wood, *The Radicalism of the American Revolution* (1993).

Alfred F. Young, *Liberty Tree: Ordinary People and the American Revolution* (2006).

NATIVE AMERICANS AND THE SEVEN YEARS' WAR

Fred Anderson, *Crucible of War: The Seven Years' War and the Fate of Empire in British North America, 1754–1766* (2001).

Colin G. Calloway, *The Scratch of a Pen: 1763 and the Transformation of America* (2007).

Gregory Evans Dowd, *War under Heaven: Pontiac, the Indian Nations, and the British Empire* (2004).

Eric Hinderaker, *The Two Hendricks: Unraveling a Mohawk Mystery* (2010).

James H. Merrell, *Into the American Woods: Negotiators on the Pennsylvania Frontier* (2000).

Timothy J. Shannon, *Indians and Colonists at the Crossroads of Empire: The Albany Congress of 1754* (2002).

Peter Silver, *Our Savage Neighbors: How Indian War Transformed Early America* (2009).

Richard White, *The Middle Ground: Indians, Empires, and Republics in the Great Lakes Region, 1650–1815* (1991).

THE REVOLUTIONARY CRISIS OF THE 1760S AND 1770S

Richard Archer, *As If an Enemy's Country: The British Occupation of Boston and the Origins of Revolution* (2010).

Bernard Bailyn, *The Ordeal of Thomas Hutchinson* (1976).

Carol Berkin, *Revolutionary Mothers: Women in the Struggle for America's Independence* (2006).

T. H. Breen, *American Insurgents, American Patriots: The Revolution of the People* (2010).

Benjamin L. Carp, *Defiance of the Patriots: The Boston Tea Party and the Making of America* (2010).

John E. Ferling, *The First of Men: A Life of George Washington* (1988).

David Hackett Fischer, *Paul Revere's Ride* (1995).

Robert A. Gross, *The Minutemen and Their World* (2001).

Joan Gundersen, *To Be Useful to the World: Women in Revolutionary America, 1740–1790* (1996).

Woody Holton, *Forced Founders: Indians, Debtors, Slaves, and the Making of the American Revolution in Virginia* (1999).

Pauline Maier, *From Resistance to Revolution: Colonial Radicals and the Development of American Opposition to Britain, 1765–1776* (1992).

Gary B. Nash, *The Unknown American Revolution: The Unruly Birth of Democracy and the Struggle to Create America* (2006).

Mary Beth Norton, *Liberty's Daughters: The Revolutionary Experience of American Women, 1750–1800* (1996).

Andrew Jackson O'Shaughnessy, *The Men Who Lost America: British Leadership, the American Revolution, and the Fate of the Empire* (2013).

Ray Raphael, *The First American Revolution: Before Lexington and Concord* (2002).

Alfred F. Young, *The Shoemaker and the Tea Party: Memory and the American Revolution* (2000).

SLAVERY

Ira Berlin, *Many Thousands Gone: The First Two Centuries of Slavery in North America* (2000).

Douglas R. Egerton, *Death or Liberty: African Americans and Revolutionary America* (2009).

Sylvia Frey, *Water from the Rock: Black Resistance in a Revolutionary Age* (1991).

Philip Morgan, *Slave Counterpoint* (1998).

Chapter 7

GENERAL WORKS

Carol Berkin, *Revolutionary Mothers: Women in the Struggle for America's Independence* (2005).

Edward Countryman, *The American Revolution* (1985).

John E. Ferling, *Almost a Miracle: The American Victory in the War of Independence* (2009).

Gary B. Nash, *The Unknown American Revolution: The Unruly Birth of Democracy and the Struggle to Create America* (2005).

Jack Rakove, *Revolutionaries: A New History of the Invention of America* (2010).

Ray Raphael, *A People's History of the American Revolution: How Common People Shaped the Fight for Independence* (2001).

Charles Royster, *A Revolutionary People at War: The Continental Army and American Character, 1775–1783* (1996).

William B. Warner, *Protocols of Liberty: Communication Innovation and the American Revolution* (2013).

Gordon S. Wood, *The Radicalism of the American Revolution* (1992).

Alfred F. Young, Gary B. Nash, and Ray Raphael, *Revolutionary Founders: Rebels, Radicals, and Reformers in the Making of the Nation* (2011).

THE WARTIME CONFEDERATION AND ITS LEADERS

Ron Chernow, *Washington: A Life* (2010).

Joseph J. Ellis, *His Excellency: George Washington* (2004).

John E. Ferling, *Setting the World Ablaze: Washington, Adams, Jefferson, and the American Revolution* (2000).

Eric Foner, *Tom Paine and Revolutionary America* (2004).

Edith Gelles, *Portia: The World of Abigail Adams* (1992).

Woody Holton, *Abigail Adams* (2010).

Pauline Maier, *American Scripture: Making the Declaration of Independence* (1997).

Jackson Turner Main, *The Sovereign States, 1775–1783* (1973).

Jack N. Rakove, *The Beginnings of National Politics: An Interpretive History of the Continental Congress* (1979).

Sheila L. Skemp, *The Making of a Patriot: Benjamin Franklin at the Cockpit* (2012).

CAMPAIGNS, BATTLES, AND SOLDIERS

Wayne K. Bodle, *The Valley Forge Winter: Civilians and Soldiers in War* (2004).

W. Jeffrey Bolster, *Black Jacks: African American Seamen in the Age of Sail* (1998).

Edwin G. Burrows, *The Prisoners of New York* (2008).

Colin G. Calloway, *The American Revolution in Indian Country: Crisis and Diversity in Native American Communities* (1995).

E. Wayne Carp, *To Starve the Army at Pleasure: Continental Army Administration and American Political Culture, 1775–1783* (1984).

Elizabeth A. Fenn, *Pox Americana: The Great Smallpox Epidemic of 1775–1782* (2002).

David Hackett Fischer, *Washington's Crossing* (2004).

Joseph R. Fischer, *A Well-Executed Failure: The Sullivan Campaign against the Iroquois, July–September 1779* (1997).

Sylvia Frey, *The British Soldier in America: A Social History of Military Life in the Revolutionary Period* (1965).

Robert Gross, *The Minutemen and Their World* (2001).

Myra Jasanoff, *Liberty's Exiles: American Loyalists in the Revolutionary World* (2012).

Sidney Kaplan and Emma Nogrady Kaplan, *The Black Presence in the Era of the American Revolution* (1989).

Richard M. Ketchum, *Saratoga: Turning Point of America's Revolutionary War* (1997).

David G. Martin, *The Philadelphia Campaign: June 1777–1778* (2003).

James Kirby Martin, *Benedict Arnold, Revolutionary Hero: An American Warrior Reconsidered* (1997).

Holly A. Mayer, *Belonging to the Army: Camp Followers and Community during the American Revolution* (1996).

David McCullough, *1776* (2005).

Alfred F. Young, *Masquerade: The Life and Times of Deborah Sampson, Continental Soldier* (2004).

Chapter 8
GENERAL WORKS

Lance Banning, *The Sacred Fire of Liberty: James Madison and the Founding of the Federal Republic* (1995).

Gary B. Nash, *The Unknown American Revolution: The Unruly Birth of Democracy and the Struggle to Create America* (2006).

Peter S. Onuf and Cathy D. Matson, *A Union of Interests: Political and Economic Thought in Revolutionary America* (1990).

Jack Rakove, *Revolutionaries: A New History of the Invention of America* (2010).

Robert E. Shalhope, *The Roots of Democracy: American Thought and Culture, 1760–1800* (2004).

Alan Taylor, *The Divided Ground: Indians, Settlers, and the Northern Borderland of the American Revolution* (2006).

Gordon Wood, *The Creation of the American Republic, 1776–1787* (1969).

Alfred F. Young, ed., *Beyond the American Revolution: Explorations in the History of American Radicalism* (1993).

THE CONFEDERATION GOVERNMENT AND THE STATES

Paul Finkelman, *Slavery and the Founders: Race and Liberty in the Age of Jefferson* (2014).

Daniel M. Friedenberg, *Life, Liberty, and the Pursuit of Land: The Plunder of Early America* (1992).

Marc W. Kruman, *Between Authority and Liberty: State Constitution Making in Revolutionary America* (1997).

Peter S. Onuf, *Statehood and Union: A History of the Northwest Ordinance* (1987).

Charles Rappleye, *Robert Morris, Financier of the American Revolution* (2010).

Jack N. Rakove, *The Beginnings of National Politics: An Interpretive History of the Continental Congress* (1979).

CITIZENSHIP

Ira Berlin, *Many Thousands Gone: The First Two Centuries of Slavery in North America* (1998).

Linda K. Kerber, *Women of the Republic: Intellect and Ideology in Revolutionary America* (1980).

Joanne Pope Melish, *Disowning Slavery: Gradual Emancipation and "Race" in New England, 1780–1860* (1998).

Gary B. Nash and Jean R. Sonderlund, *Freedom by Degrees: Emancipation in Pennsylvania and Its Aftermath* (1991).

Leonard L. Richards, *Shays's Rebellion: The American Revolution's Final Battle* (2002).

Marylynn Salmon, *Women and the Law of Property in Early America* (1986).

Rosemarie Zagarri, *A Woman's Dilemma: Mercy Otis Warren and the American Revolution* (1995).

THE CONSTITUTION AND RATIFICATION

John K. Alexander, *The Selling of the Constitutional Convention: A History of News Coverage* (1990).

Richard Beeman, *Plain, Honest Men: The Making of the American Constitution* (2010).

Carol Berkin, *A Brilliant Solution: Inventing the American Constitution* (2003).

Richard Brookhiser, *Gentleman Revolutionary: Gouverneur Morris, the Rake Who Wrote the Constitution* (2003).

Saul Cornell, *The Other Founders: Anti-Federalism and the Dissenting Tradition in America, 1788–1828* (1999).

Michael Allen Gillespie and Michael Lienesch, eds., *Ratifying the Constitution* (1989).

Woody Holton, *Unruly Americans and the Origins of the Constitution* (2007).

John P. Kaminski and Richard Leffler, *Federalists and Antifederalists: The Debate over the Constitution* (1998).

Leonard W. Levy, *The Establishment Clause: Religion and the First Amendment* (1994).

Pauline Maier, *Ratification: The People Debate the Constitution, 1787–1788* (2011).

Jackson Turner Main, *The Antifederalists: Critics of the Constitution, 1781–1788* (2006).

William Lee Miller, *The First Liberty: Religion and the American Republic* (1986).

Richard B. Morris, *Witnesses at the Creation: Hamilton, Madison, Jay, and the Constitution* (1985).

Jack N. Rakove, *Original Meanings: Politics and Ideas in the Making of the Constitution* (1996).

Chapter 9

POLITICS

Bernard Bailyn, *To Begin the World Anew: The Genius and Ambiguities of the American Founders* (2003).

Ron Chernow, *Alexander Hamilton* (2004).

——*Washington: A Life* (2010).

Jerry A. Clouse, *The Whiskey Rebellion: Southwestern Pennsylvania's Frontier People Test the American Constitution* (1995).

Stanley Elkins and Eric McKitrick, *The Age of Federalism: The Early American Republic, 1788–1800* (1993).

Joseph J. Ellis, *Founding Brothers: The Revolutionary Generation* (2000).

——*American Creation: Triumphs and Tragedies in the Founding of the Republic* (2008).

Todd Estes, *The Jay Treaty Debate, Public Opinion, and the Evolution of Early American Political Culture* (2006).

John E. Ferling, *Adams vs. Jefferson: The Tumultuous Election of 1800* (2005).

——*The Ascent of George Washington: The Hidden Political Genius of an American Icon* (2010).

David P. Geggus, ed., *The Impact of the Haitian Revolution in the Atlantic World* (2002).

David Patrick Geggus and Norman Fiering, eds., *The World of the Haitian Revolution* (2008).

Peter P. Hill, *French Perceptions of the Early American Republic, 1783–1793* (1988).

Ralph Ketcham, *Presidents above Party: The First American Presidency, 1789–1829* (1984).

David McCullough, *John Adams* (2001).

Jeffrey L. Pasley, *The Tyranny of Printers: Newspaper Politics in the Early American Republic* (2001).

Thomas P. Slaughter, *The Whiskey Rebellion: Frontier Epilogue to the American Revolution* (1986).

Larry E. Tise, *The American Counterrevolution: A Retreat from Liberty, 1783–1800* (1999).

Richard J. Twomey, *Jacobins and Jeffersonians: Anglo-American Radicalism in the United States, 1790–1820* (1989).

SOCIETY AND CULTURE

Susan Branson, *These Fiery Frenchified Dames: Women and Political Culture in Early National Philadelphia* (2001).

Richard D. Brown, *Knowledge Is Power: The Diffusion of Information in Early America, 1700–1865* (1989).

Nancy Cott, *The Bonds of Womanhood: Women's Sphere in New England, 1780–1835* (1997).

Joanne B. Freeman, *Affairs of Honor: National Politics in the New Republic* (2001).

Richard R. John, *Spreading the News: The American Postal System from Franklin to Morse* (1996).

Linda Kerber, *Women of the Republic: Intellect and Ideology in Revolutionary America* (1997).

Clare A. Lyons, *Sex among the Rabble: An Intimate History of Gender and Power in the Age of Revolution, Philadelphia, 1730–1830* (2006).

Bruce H. Mann, *Republic of Debtors: Bankruptcy in the Age of American Independence* (2002).

Simon P. Newman, *Parades and the Politics of the Street: Festive Culture in the Early American Republic* (2000).

Sheila L. Skemp, *Judith Sargent Murray: A Brief Biography with Documents* (1998).

David Waldstreicher, *In the Midst of Perpetual Fetes: The Making of American Nationalism, 1776–1820* (1997).

Rosemarie Zagarri, *Revolutionary Backlash: Women and Politics in the Early American Republic* (2007).

INDIANS AND THE FRONTIER

Andrew R. L. Cayton, *Frontier Republic: Ideology and Politics in the Ohio Country, 1780–1825* (1989).

Gregory E. Dowd, *A Spirited Resistance: The North American Indian Struggle for Unity, 1745–1815* (1992).

R. Douglas Hurt, *The Ohio Frontier: Crucible of the Old Northwest, 1720–1830* (1998).

Claudio Saunt, *A New Order of Things: Property, Power, and the Transformation of the Creek Indians, 1733–1816* (1999).

Chapter 10

POLITICS

Andrew Burstein and Nancy Isenberg, *Madison and Jefferson* (2010).

Saul Cornell, *The Other Founders: Anti-Federalism and the Dissenting Tradition in America, 1788–1828* (1999).

Joseph J. Ellis, *American Sphinx: The Character of Thomas Jefferson* (1997).

Joanne B. Freeman, *Affairs of Honor: National Politics in the New Republic* (2001).

Nancy Isenberg, *Fallen Founder: The Life of Aaron Burr* (2008).

Peter J. Kastor, *The Nation's Crucible: The Louisiana Purchase and the Creation of America* (2004).

Alexander Keyssar, *The Right to Vote: The Contested History of Democracy in the United States* (2000).

Edward J. Larson, *A Magnificent Catastrophe: The Tumultuous Election of 1800, America's First Presidential Campaign* (2007).

Jeffrey L. Pasley, Andrew W. Robertson, and David Waldstreicher, *Beyond the Founders: New Approaches to the Political History of the Early American Republic* (2003).

Sean Wilentz, *The Rise of American Democracy: Jefferson to Lincoln* (2005).

Richard Zacks, *The Pirate Coast: Thomas Jefferson, the First Marines, and the Secret Mission of 1805* (2006).

INDIANS, THE WAR OF 1812, AND THE WEST

Stephen E. Ambrose, *Undaunted Courage: Meriwether Lewis, Thomas Jefferson, and the Opening of the American West* (1996).

Carl Benn, *The Iroquois in the War of 1812* (1998).

James F. Brooks, *Captives and Cousins: Slavery, Kinship, and Community in the Southwest Borderlands* (2002).

Kathleen DuVal, *The Native Ground: Indians and Colonists in the Heart of the Continent* (2007).

Albert Furtwangler, *Acts of Discovery: Visions of America in the Lewis and Clark Journals* (1993).

Pekka Hämäläinen, *The Comanche Empire* (2008).

John Sugden, *Tecumseh: A Life* (1997).

Alan Taylor, *The Civil War of 1812: American Citizens, British Subjects, Irish Rebels, and Indian Allies* (2010).

———*The Internal Enemy: Slavery and War in Virginia, 1772–1832* (2013).

Richard White, *The Middle Ground: Indians, Empires, and Republics in the Great Lakes Region, 1650–1815* (1991).

SLAVERY

Douglas Egerton, *Gabriel's Rebellion* (1993).

Annette Gordon-Reed, *The Hemingses of Monticello: An American Family* (2009).

James Oliver Horton and Lois E. Horton, *In Hope of Liberty: Culture, Community, and Protest among Northern Free Blacks, 1700–1860* (1997).

Gary B. Nash, *Forging Freedom: The Formation of Philadelphia's Black Community, 1720–1840* (1988).

Shane White, *Somewhat More Independent: The End of Slavery in New York City, 1710–1810* (1991).

WOMEN, MARRIAGE, AND RELIGION

Catherine Allgor, *Parlor Politics: In Which the Ladies of Washington Help Build a City and a Government* (2000).

Norma Basch, *In the Eyes of the Law: Women, Marriage, and Property in Nineteenth-Century New York* (1982).

———*Framing American Divorce: From the Revolutionary Generation to the Victorians* (1999).

Catherine A. Brekus, *Strangers and Pilgrims: Female Preaching in America, 1740–1845* (1998).

Nancy Cott, *Public Vows: A History of Marriage and the Nation* (2001).

Susan Juster, *Disorderly Women: Sexual Politics and Evangelicalism in Revolutionary New England* (1994).

Mary Kelley, *Learning to Stand and Speak: Women, Education, and Public Life in America's Republic* (2006).

Susan E. Klepp, *Revolutionary Conceptions: Women, Fertility, and Family Limitation in America, 1760–1820* (2009).

Mary Beth Sievens, *Stray Wives: Marital Conflict in Early National New England* (2005).

Chapter 11

THE MARKET REVOLUTION

Edward J. Balleisen, *Navigating Failure: Bankruptcy and Commercial Society in Antebellum America* (2001).

Mary H. Blewett, *Men, Women, and Work: Class, Gender, and Protest in the New England Shoe Industry, 1780–1910* (1988).

Jeanne Boydston, *Home and Work: Housework, Wages, and the Ideology of Labor in the Early Republic* (1990).

Thomas Dublin, *Transforming Women's Work: New England Lives in the Industrial Revolution* (1994).

John Lauritz Larson, *The Market Revolution in America: Liberty, Ambition, and the Eclipse of the Common Good* (2009).

Stephen Mihm, *A Nation of Counterfeiters: Capitalists, Con Men, and the Making of the United States* (2009).

Seth Rockman, *Scraping By: Wage Labor, Slavery, and Survival in Early Baltimore* (2008).

Charles G. Sellers, *The Market Revolution: Jacksonian America, 1815–1846* (1991).

Carol Sheriff, *The Artificial River: The Erie Canal and the Paradox of Progress, 1817–1862* (1996).

POLITICS

Andrew Burstein, *The Passions of Andrew Jackson* (2003).

John Ehle, *Trail of Tears: The Rise and Fall of the Cherokee Nation* (1997).

Daniel Walker Howe, *What Hath God Wrought: The Transformation of America, 1815–1845* (2009).

Jon Meacham, *American Lion: Andrew Jackson in the White House* (2009).

Sean Michael O'Brien, *In Bitterness and in Tears: Andrew Jackson's Destruction of the Creeks and Seminoles* (2003).

Theda Perdue, *Cherokee Women: Gender and Culture Change, 1700–1835* (1998).

Merrill D. Peterson, *The Great Triumvirate: Webster, Clay, and Calhoun* (1987).

Sean Wilentz, *The Rise of American Democracy, Jefferson to Lincoln* (2005).

CULTURE, RELIGION, AND REFORM

Patricia Cline Cohen, Timothy J. Gilfoyle, and Helen Lefkowitz Horowitz, *The Flash Press: Sporting Male Weeklies in 1840s New York (2008)*.

Bruce Dorsey, *Reforming Men and Women: Gender in the Antebellum City* (2002).

Lori D. Ginzberg, *Women and the Work of Benevolence: Morality, Politics, and Class in the Nineteenth-Century United States* (1990).

Nathan O. Hatch, *The Democratization of American Christianity* (1991).

Julie Roy Jeffrey, *The Great Silent Army of Abolitionism: Ordinary Women in the Antislavery Movement* (1998).

Richard R. John, *Spreading the News: The American Postal System from Franklin to Morse* (1995).

Catherine E. Kelly, *In the New England Fashion: Reshaping Women's Lives in the Nineteenth Century* (1999).

Bruce Laurie, *Beyond Garrison: Antislavery and Social Reform* (2005).

Gerda Lerner, *The Grimké Sisters from South Carolina: Pioneers for Women's Rights and Abolition* (2009).

Richard S. Newman, *The Transformation of American Abolitionism: Fighting Slavery in the Early Republic* (2002).

Mark Perry, *Lift Up Thy Voice: The Grimké Family's Journey from Slaveholders to Civil Rights Leaders* (2002).

Alisse Portnoy, *Their Right to Speak: Women's Activism in the Indian and Slave Debates* (2005).

Patrick Rael, *Black Identity and Black Protest in the Antebellum North* (2002).

Stacey M. Robertson, *Hearts Beating for Liberty: Women Abolitionists in the Old Northwest* (2010).

Scott A. Sandage, *Born Losers: A History of Failure in America* (2005).

Kathryn Kish Sklar and James Brewer Stewart, *Women's Rights and Transatlantic Slavery in the Era of Emancipation* (2007).

Richard B. Stott, *Jolly Fellows: Male Milieus in Nineteenth-Century America* (2009).

Daniel S. Wright, *"The First of Causes to Our Sex": The Female Moral Reform Movement in the Antebellum Northeast, 1834–1848* (2006).

Ronald J. Zboray and Mary Saracino Zboray, *Literary Dollars and Social Sense: A People's History of the Mass Market Book* (2005).

Chapter 12

THE ECONOMY AND FREE LABOR

Jeanne Boydston, *Home and Work: Housework, Wages, and the Ideology of Labor in the Early Republic* (1990).

J. Matthew Gallman, *Receiving Erin's Children: Philadelphia, Liverpool, and the Irish Famine Migration, 1854–1855* (2000).

Jonathan A. Glickstein, *Concepts of Free Labor in the Antebellum United States* (1991).

Donald R. Hoke, *Ingenious Yankees: The Rise of the American System of Manufactures in the Private Sector* (1990).

Jonathan Hughes and Louis P. Cain, *American Economic History* (2011).

Robert A. Margo, *Wages and Labor Markets in the United States, 1820–1860* (2000).

David R. Meyer, *The Roots of American Industrialization* (2003).

Scott A. Sandage, *Born Losers: A History of Failure in America* (2005).

Manisha Sinha, *The Slave's Cause: A History of Abolition* (2016).

Kenneth J. Winkle, *The Young Eagle: The Rise of Abraham Lincoln* (2001).

WESTWARD EXPANSION AND THE MEXICAN-AMERICAN WAR

Gary Anderson, *The Conquest of Texas: Ethnic Cleansing in the Promised Land, 1820–1875* (2005).

Juliana Barr, *Peace Came in the Form of a Woman: Indians and Spaniards in the Texas Borderlands* (2007).

Peter J. Blodgett, *Land of Golden Dreams: California in the Gold Rush Decade, 1848–1858* (1999).

H. W. Brand, *Lone Star Nation* (2004).

Richard L. Bushman, *Joseph Smith: Rough Stone Rolling* (2005).

David C. Clary, *Eagles and Empire: The United States, Mexico, and the Struggle for a Continent* (2009).

Christopher Corbett, *The Poker Bride: The First Chinese in the Wild West* (2009).

David Dary, *The Oregon Trail: An American Saga* (2004).

Brian DeLay, *War of a Thousand Deserts: Indian Raids and the U.S.-Mexican War* (2008).

Jared Farmer, *On Zion's Mount: Mormons, Indians, and the American Landscape* (2008).

Paul W. Foos, *A Short, Offhand, Killing Affair: Soldiers and Social Conflict during the Mexican-American War* (2002).

Sarah Barringer Gordon, *The Mormon Question: Polygamy and Constitutional Conflict in Nineteenth-Century America* (2002).

Amy S. Greenberg, *Manifest Manhood and the Antebellum American Empire* (2005).

———*A Wicked War: Polk, Clay, Lincoln and the 1846 U.S. Invasion of Mexico* (2013).

Timothy J. Henderson, *A Glorious Defeat: Mexico and Its War with the United States* (2007).

Albert Hurtado, *John Sutter: A Life on the North American Frontier* (2006).

Benjamin Heber Johnson, *Revolution in Texas: How a Forgotten Rebellion and Its Bloody Suppression Turned Mexicans into Americans* (2003).

Susan Lee Johnson, *Roaring Camp: The Social World of the California Gold Rush* (2000).

Kent G. Lightfoot, *Indians, Missionaries, and Merchants: The Legacy of Colonial Encounters on the California Frontier* (2005).

Robert W. Merry, *A Country of Vast Designs: James K. Polk, the Mexican War, and the Conquest of the American Continent* (2009).

Gregory H. Nobles, *American Frontiers: Cultural Encounters and Continental Conquest* (1997).

Andres Resendez, *Changing National Identities at the Frontier: Texas and New Mexico, 1800–1850* (2005).

Malcolm Rohrbough, *Days of Gold: The California Gold Rush and the American Nation* (1997).

James A. Sandos, *Converting California: Indians and Franciscans in the Missions* (2004).

Virginia Scharff and Carolyn Brucken, *Home Lands: How Women Made the West* (2010).

Joel H. Sibley, *Storm over Texas: The Annexation Controversy and the Road to Civil War* (2005).

Stacey L. Smith, *Freedom's Frontier: California and the Struggle over Unfree Labor, Emancipation, and Reconstruction* (2013).

Michael L. Tate, *Indians and Emigrants: Encounters on the Overland Trail* (2006).

John G. Turner, *Brigham Young: Pioneer Prophet* (2012).

Richard White, *"It's Your Misfortune and None of My Own": A New History of the American West* (1993).

Richard Bruce Winders, *Mr. Polk's Army: The American Military Experience in the Mexican War* (1997).

Steven E. Woodworth, *Manifest Destinies: America's Westward Expansion and the Road to Civil War* (2010).

ANTEBELLUM CULTURE AND REFORM

Bruce Dorsey, *Reforming Men and Women: Gender in the Antebellum City* (2002).

Lori D. Ginzberg, *Elizabeth Cady Stanton: An American Life* (2009).

Bruce Laurie, *Beyond Garrison: Antislavery and Social Reform* (2005).

Sally McMillen, *Seneca Falls and the Origins of the Women's Rights Movement* (2008).

Patrick Rael, *Black Identity and Black Protest in the Antebellum North* (2002).

Susan M. Ryan, *The Grammar of Good Intentions: Race and the Antebellum Culture of Benevolence* (2003).

Beth A. Salerno, *Sister Societies: Women's Antislavery Organizations in Antebellum America* (2005).

Susan Zaeske, *Signatures of Citizenship: Petitioning, Antislavery, and Women's Political Identity* (2003).

Chapter 13

SLAVEHOLDERS AND THE ECONOMY

Edward E. Baptist, *Creating an Old South: Middle Florida's Plantation Frontier before the Civil War* (2002).

Sven Beckert, *Empire of Cotton: A Global History* (2014).

David L. Carlton and Peter A. Coclanis, *The South, the Nation, and the World: Perspectives on Southern Economic Development* (2003).

Steven Deyle, *Carry Me Back: The Domestic Slave Trade in American Life* (2005).

Richard Follett, *The Sugar Masters: Planters and Slaves in Louisiana's Cane World, 1820–1860* (2005).

Walter Johnson, *River of Dark Dreams: Slavery and Empire in the Cotton South* (2013).

Aaron W. Marrs, *Railroads in the Old South: Pursuing Progress in a Slave Society* (2009).

Jonathan Martin, *Divided Mastery: Slave Hiring in the American South* (2004).

James David Miller, *South by Southwest: Planter Emigration and Identity in the Slave South* (2002).

Gavin Wright, *Slavery and American Economic Development* (2006).

SLAVES, SLAVERY, AND RACE RELATIONS

David F. Allmendinger Jr., *Nat Turner and the Rising in Southhampton County* (2014).

Ira Berlin, *Generations of Captivity: A History of African-American Slaves* (2003).

Thomas C. Buchanan, *Black Life on the Mississippi: Slaves, Free Blacks, and the Western Steamboat World* (2004).

Diane Mutti Burke, *On Slavery's Border: Missouri's Small-Slaveholding Households, 1815–1865* (2011).

Stephanie M. H. Camp, *Closer to Freedom: Enslaved Women and Everyday Resistance in the Plantation South* (2004).

Erskine Clarke, *Dwelling Place: A Plantation Epic* (2005).

Sharla Fett, *Working Cures: Healing, Health, and Power on Southern Slave Plantations* (2002).

Sylvia R. Frey and Betty Wood, *Come Shouting to Zion: African American Protestantism in the American South and British Caribbean to 1830* (1998).

Eugene D. Genovese, *Roll, Jordan, Roll: The World the Slave Made* (1974).

Kenneth S. Greenberg, ed., *Nat Turner: A Slave Rebellion in History and Memory* (2003).

Gwendolyn Midlo Hall, *Slavery and African Ethnicities in the Americas: Restoring the Links* (2005).

Anthony E. Kaye, *Joining Places: Slave Neighborhoods in the Old South* (2007).

Tiya Miles, *Ties that Bind: The Story of an Afro-Cherokee Family in Slavery and Freedom* (2005).

Sydney Nathans, *To Free a Family: The Journey of Mary Walker* (2012).

Dylan C. Penningroth, *The Claims of Kinfolk: African American Property and Community in the Nineteenth-Century South* (2003).

Larry Eugene Rivers, *Rebels and Runaways: Slave Resistance in Nineteenth-Century Florida* (2012).

Brenda E. Stevenson, *Life in Black and White: Family and Community in the Slave South* (1996).

Leonard Todd, *Carolina Clay: The Life and Legend of the Slave Potter Dave* (2008).

SOCIETY AND CULTURE

Ira Berlin, *Slaves without Masters: The Free Negro in the Antebellum South* (1974).

Charles C. Bolton and Scott P. Culclasure, eds., *The Confessions of Edward Isham: A Poor White Life of the Old South* (1998).

Christine Jacobson Carter, *Southern Single Blessedness: Unmarried Women in the Urban South, 1800–1865* (2006).

Laura F. Edwards, *The People and Their Peace: Legal Culture and the Transformation of Inequality in the Post-Revolutionary South* (2009).

Craig T. Friend and Lorri Glover, eds., *Southern Manhood: Perspectives on Masculinity in the Old South* (2004).

Steven Hahn, *The Roots of Southern Populism: Yeoman Farmers and the Transformation of the Georgia Upcountry, 1850–1890* (1983).

Christine Leigh Heyrman, *Southern Cross: The Beginnings of the Bible Belt* (1997).

Charles F. Irons, *The Origins of Proslavery Christianity: White and Black Evangelicals in Colonial and Antebellum Virginia* (2008).

Anya Jabour, *Scarlett's Sisters: Young Women in the Old South* (2007).

Michael P. Johnson and James L. Roark, *Black Masters: A Free Family of Color in the Old South* (1984).

Stephanie McCurry, *Masters of Small Worlds: Yeoman Households, Gender Relations, and the Political Culture of the Antebellum South* (1995).

Glenn McNair, *Criminal Injustice: Slaves and Free Blacks in Georgia's Criminal Justice System* (2009).

Seth Rockman, *Scraping By: Wage Labor, Slavery, and Survival in Early Baltimore* (2009).

Adam Rothman, *Slave Country: American Expansion and the Deep South* (2005).

Joshua D. Rothman, *Notorious in the Neighborhood: Sex and Families across the Color Line in Virginia, 1787–1861* (2002).

Loren Schweninger, *Families in Crisis in the Old South: Divorce, Slavery, and the Law* (2012).

Jonathan Daniel Wells, *Origins of the Southern Middle Class, 1800–1861* (2004).

Julie Winch, *Between Slavery and Freedom: Free People of Color in America from Settlement to the Civil War* (2014).

Eva Sheppard Wolf, *Almost Free: A Story about Family and Race in Antebellum Virginia* (2012).

Bertram Wyatt-Brown, *Southern Honor: Ethics and Behavior in the Old South* (1982).

Jeffrey Robert Young, *Domesticating Slavery: The Master Class in Georgia and South Carolina, 1670–1837* (1999).

POLITICS AND POLITICAL CULTURE

Anthony Gene Carey, *Parties, Slavery, and the Union in Antebellum Georgia* (1997).

William J. Cooper Jr., *Liberty and Slavery: Southern Politics to 1860* (1983).

Lacy K. Ford Jr., *Deliver Us from Evil: The Slavery Question in the Old South* (2009).

Michael Perman, *Pursuit of Unity: A Political History of the American South* (2009).

Elizabeth R. Varon, *We Mean to Be Counted: White Women and Politics in Antebellum Virginia* (1998).

Peter Wallenstein, *From Slave South to New South: Public Policy in Nineteenth-Century Georgia* (1987).

Chapter 14

GENERAL WORKS

Don E. Fehrenbacher, *The Slaveholding Republic: An Account of the United States Government's Relations to Slavery* (2001).

Michael Holt, *Fate of Their Country: Politicians, Slavery Extension, and the Coming of the Civil War* (2004).

Bruce C. Levine, *Half Slave and Half Free: The Roots of the Civil War* (1992).

James M. McPherson, *Ordeal by Fire: The Civil War and Reconstruction* (1982).

David M. Potter, *The Impending Crisis: America Before the Civil War, 1848–1861* (2011).

Mark E. Neely, *Boundaries of American Political Culture in the Civil War Era* (2005).

Eric H. Walther, *The Shattering of the Union: America in the 1850s* (2004).

Sean Wilentz, *The Rise of American Democracy: Jefferson to Lincoln* (2005).

NORTHERN SECTIONALISM

Tom Chaffin, *Pathfinder: John Charles Frémont and the Course of American Empire* (2002).

Rodney O. Davis and Douglas L. Wilson, eds., *The Lincoln-Douglas Debates* (2008).

Eric Foner, *Free Labor, Free Soil, Free Men: The Ideology of the Republican Party before the Civil War* (1970).

———*Gateway to Freedom: The Hidden History of the Underground Railroad* (2015).

William E. Gienapp, *The Origins of the Republican Party, 1852–1856* (1987).

R. Blakeslee Gilpin, *John Brown Still Lives! America's Long Reckoning with Violence, Equality, and Change* (2011).

Susan-Mary Grant, *North over South: Northern Nationalism and American Identity in the Antebellum Era* (2000).

David Grimsted, *American Mobbing, 1828–1865: Toward Civil War* (1998).

Joan D. Hedrick, *Harriet Beecher Stowe: A Life* (1994).

Pamela Herr, *Jessie Benton Frémont: A Biography* (1987).

Nancy Isenberg, *Sex and Citizenship in Antebellum America* (1998).

David S. Reynolds, *John Brown, Abolitionist: The Man Who Killed Slavery, Sparked the Civil War, and Seeded Civil Rights* (2005).

Leonard L. Richards, *The California Gold Rush and the Coming of the Civil War* (2007).

Brian Schoen, *The Fragile Fabric of Union: Cotton, Federal Politics, and the Global Origins of the Civil War* (2009).

James Brewer Stewart, *Wendell Phillips, Liberty's Hero* (1986).

Wendy Hamand Venet, *Neither Ballots nor Bullets: Women Abolitionists and the Civil War* (1991).

Douglas L. Wilson, *Honor's Voice: The Transformation of Abraham Lincoln* (1998).

Kenneth J. Winkle, *The Young Eagle: The Rise of Abraham Lincoln* (2001).

SOUTHERN SECTIONALISM

Robert E. Bonner, *Mastering America: Southern Slaveholders and the Crisis of American Nationhood* (2009).

William J. Cooper Jr., *The South and the Politics of Slavery, 1828–1856* (1978).

John Patrick Daly, *When Slavery Was Called Freedom: Evangelicalism, Proslavery, and the Causes of the Civil War* (2002).

Lacy K. Ford Jr., *Origins of Southern Radicalism: The South Carolina Upcountry, 1800–1860* (1988).

William W. Freehling, *The Road to Disunion*, 2 vols. (1990-2007).

Matthew Pratt Guterl, *American Mediterranean: Southern Slaveholders in the Age of Emancipation* (2008).

David S. Heidler and Jeanne T. Heidler, *Henry Clay: The Essential American* (2010).

William A. Link, *Roots of Secession: Slavery and Politics in Antebellum Virginia* (2002).

Robert E. May, *Manifest Destiny's Underworld: Filibustering in Antebellum America* (2002).

Christopher J. Olsen, *Political Culture and Secession in Mississippi: Masculinity, Honor, and the Antiparty Tradition, 1830–1860* (2002).

Edward Rugemer, *The Problem of Emancipation: The Caribbean Roots of the American Civil War* (2008).

Manisha Sinha, *The Counterrevolution of Slavery: Politics and Ideology in Antebellum South Carolina* (2000).

Mitchell Snay, *Gospel of Disunion: Religion and Separatism in the Antebellum South* (1993).

SECESSION

Shearer Davis Bowman, *At the Precipice: Americans North and South during the Secession Crisis* (2010).

Daniel Crofts, *Reluctant Confederates: Upper South Unionists in the Secession Crisis* (1989).

Charles B. Dew, *Apostles of Disunion: Southern Secession Commissioners and the Causes of the Civil War* (2001).

Michael P. Johnson, *Toward a Patriarchal Republic: The Secession of Georgia* (1977).

Russell McClintock, *Lincoln and the Decision for War: The Northern Response to Secession* (2008).

David M. Potter, *Lincoln and His Party in the Secession Crisis* (1942).

Lorman A. Ratner and Dwight L. Teeter Jr., *Fanatics and Fire-Eaters: Newspapers and the Coming of the Civil War* (2003).

Chapter 15

GENERAL WORKS

Orville Vernon Burton, *The Age of Lincoln* (2007).

Allen C. Guelzo, *A New History of the Civil War and Reconstruction* (2012).

James M. McPherson, *The Battle Cry of Freedom: The Civil War Era* (1988).

Scott Nelson and Carol Sheriff, *A People at War: Civilians and Soldiers in America's Civil War* (2007).

Adam I. P. Smith, *The American Civil War* (2007).

MILITARY HISTORY

Michael J. Bennett, *Union Jacks: Yankee Sailors in the Civil War* (2004).

Mark Grimsley, *The Hard Hand of War: Union Military Policy toward Southern Civilians, 1861–1865* (1995).

Joseph T. Glatthaar, *General Lee's Army: From Victory to Collapse* (2008).

Chandra Manning, *What This Cruel War Was Over: Soldiers, Slavery, and the Civil War* (2007).

James M. McPherson, *Tried by War: Abraham Lincoln as Commander in Chief* (2008).

Mark E. Neely Jr., *The Civil War and the Limits of Destruction* (2007).

Christopher Phillips, *The Civil War in the Border South* (2013).

Brooks D. Simpson, *Ulysses S. Grant: Triumph over Adversity, 1822–1865* (2000).

Donald Stoker, *The Grand Design: Strategy and the U.S. Civil War* (2010).

Daniel E. Sutherland, *A Savage Conflict: The Decisive Role of Guerrillas in the American Civil War* (2009).

William G. Thomas, *The Iron Way: Railroads, the Civil War, and the Making of Modern America* (2011).

Joan Waugh, *U. S. Grant: American Hero, American Myth* (2009).

Russell F. Weigley, *A Great Civil War: A Military and Political History, 1861–1865* (2000).

John Fabian Witt, *Lincoln's Code: The Laws of War* (2012).

THE NORTH AND SOUTH AT WAR

Stephen V. Ash, *When the Yankees Came: Conflict and Chaos in the Occupied South, 1861–1865* (1995).

Iver Bernstein, *The New York City Draft Riots: Their Significance for American Society and Politics in the Age of the Civil War* (1990).

William A. Blair, *Virginia's Private War: Feeding Body and Soul in the Confederacy, 1861–1865* (1998).

——*With Malice Toward Some: Treason and Loyalty in the Civil War Era* (2014).

Victoria E. Bynum, *The Long Shadow of the Civil War: Southern Dissent and Its Legacies* (2010).

William J. Cooper, *Jefferson Davis, American* (2000).

Alice Fahs, *The Imagined Civil War: Popular Literature of the North and South, 1861–1865* (2001).

Drew Gilpin Faust, *This Republic of Suffering: Death and the American Civil War* (2008).

William W. Freehling, *The South vs. the South: How Anti-Confederate Southerners Shaped the Course of the Civil War* (2001).

Gary W. Gallagher, *The Confederate War* (1997).

Judith Ann Giesberg, *Civil War Sisterhood: The U.S. Sanitary Commission and Women's Politics in Transition* (2000).

William C. Harris, *Lincoln and the Border States: Preserving the Union* (2012).

Libra R. Hilde, *Worth a Dozen Men: Women and Nursing in the Civil War South* (2012).

Jacqueline Jones, *Saving Savannah: The City and the Civil War* (2008).

Bruce Levine, *The Fall of the House of Dixie: The Civil War and the Social Revolution that Transformed the South* (2013).

Stephanie McCurry, *Confederate Reckoning: Power and Politics in the Civil War* (2010).

Mark E. Neely Jr., *The Fate of Liberty: Abraham Lincoln and Civil Liberties* (1991).

Megan Kate Nelson, *Ruin Nation: Destruction and the American Civil War* (2012).

Mark A. Noll, *The Civil War as a Theological Crisis* (2006).

George C. Rable, *God's Almost Chosen People: A Religious History of the American Civil War* (2010).

Heather Cox Richardson, *The Greatest Nation of the Earth: Republican Economic Policies during the Civil War* (1997).

James L. Roark, *Masters without Slaves: Southern Planters in the Civil War and Reconstruction* (1977).

Anne Sarah Rubin, *A Shattered Nation: The Rise and Fall of the Confederacy, 1861–1868* (2005).

Mark S. Schantz, *Awaiting the Heavenly Country: The Civil War and America's Culture of Death* (2008).

Nina Silber, *Daughters of the Union: Northern Women Fight the Civil War* (2006).

Walter Stahr, *Seward: Lincoln's Indispensable Man* (2012).

Yael A. Sternhell, *Routes of War: The World of Movement in the Confederate South* (2012).

Margaret M. Storey, *Loyalty and Loss: Alabama's Unionists in the Civil War and Reconstruction* (2004).

Harry S. Stout, *Upon the Altar of the Nation: A Moral History of the American Civil War* (2006).

Amy Murrell Taylor, *The Divided Family in Civil War America* (2005).

Jennifer L. Weber, *Copperheads: The Rise and Fall of Lincoln's Opponents in the North* (2008).

THE STRUGGLE FOR FREEDOM

Ira Berlin et al., eds., *Freedom: A Documentary History of Emancipation, 1861–1867,* 5 vols. (1982–2008).

Eric Foner, *The Fiery Trial: Abraham Lincoln and American Slavery* (2010).

Joseph T. Glatthaar, *Forged in Battle: The Civil War Alliance of Black Soldiers and White Officers* (1990).

William B. Gould IV, ed., *Diary of a Contraband: The Civil War Passage of a Black Sailor* (2002).

Allen C. Guelzo, *Lincoln's Emancipation Proclamation: The End of Slavery in America* (2004).

Steven Hahn, *The Political Worlds of Slavery and Freedom* (2009).

Bruce Levine, *Confederate Emancipation: Southern Plans to Free and Arm Slaves during the Civil War* (2006).

William S. McFeely, *Frederick Douglass* (1991).

James Oakes, *The Radical and the Republican: Frederick Douglass, Abraham Lincoln, and the Triumph of Antislavery Politics* (2007).

David Williams, *I Freed Myself: African American Self-Emancipation in the Civil War* (2014).

Chapter 16

GENERAL WORKS

Thomas J. Brown, ed., *Reconstructions: New Perspectives on the Postbellum United States* (2006).

Laura F. Edwards, *A Legal History of the Civil War and Reconstruction: A Nation of Rights* (2015).

Michael W. Fitzgerald, *Splendid Failure: Postwar Reconstruction in the American South* (2007).

Eric Foner, *Reconstruction: America's Unfinished Revolution* (1988).

James M. McPherson, *Ordeal by Fire: The Civil War and Reconstruction* (3rd ed., 2000).

Mark Wahlgren Summers, *The Ordeal of Reunion: A New History of Reconstruction* (2014).

THE MEANING OF FREEDOM

Ira Berlin et al., eds., *Freedom: A Documentary History of Emancipation, 1861–1867*, 5 vols. (1982–2008).

Ronald E. Butchart, *Schooling the Freed People: Teaching, Learning, and the Struggle for Black Freedom, 1861–1876* (2010).

Jim Downs, *Sick for Freedom: African-American Illness and Suffering during the Civil War and Reconstruction* (2012).

John Hope Franklin and Loren Schweninger, *In Search of the Promised Land: A Slave Family in the Old South* (2006).

Thavolia Glymph, *Out of the House of Bondage: The Transformation of the Plantation Household* (2008).

Steven Hahn, *A Nation under Our Feet: Black Political Struggles in the Rural South, from Slavery to the Great Migration* (2003).

Leon F. Litwack, *Been in the Storm So Long: The Aftermath of Slavery* (1979).

Susan Eva O'Donovan, *Becoming Free in the Cotton South* (2007).

Joshua Paddison, *American Heathens: Religion, Race, and Reconstruction in California* (2012).

Howard N. Rabinowitz, *Race Relations in the Urban South, 1865–1890* (1978).

Roger L. Ransom and Richard Sutch, *One Kind of Freedom: The Economic Consequences of Emancipation* (1977).

Leslie Schwalm, *A Hard Fight for We: Women's Transition from Slavery to Freedom in South Carolina* (1997).

Loren Schweninger, *James T. Rapier and Reconstruction* (1978).

Rebecca J. Scott, *Degrees of Freedom: Louisiana and Cuba after Slavery* (2005).

Clarence E. Walker, *A Rock in a Weary Land: The African Methodist Episcopal Church during the Civil War and Reconstruction* (1982).

THE POLITICS OF RECONSTRUCTION

Stephen V. Ash, *A Massacre in Memphis: The Race Riot that Shook the Nation* (2013).

Richard F. Bensel, *Yankee Leviathan: The Origins of Central State Authority in America, 1859–1877* (1990).

Philip Dray, *Capitol Men: The Epic Story of Reconstruction Through the Lives of the First Black Congressmen* (2008).

Ellen Carol DuBois, *Feminism and Suffrage: The Emergence of an Independent Women's Movement in America, 1848–1869* (1978).

Laura Edwards, *Gendered Strife and Confusion: The Political Culture of Reconstruction* (1997).

Martha Hodes, *Mourning Lincoln* (2015).

James K. Hogue, *Uncivil War: Five New Orleans Street Battles and the Rise and Fall of Radical Reconstruction* (2006).

Richard L. Hume and Jerry B. Gough, *Blacks, Carpetbaggers, and Scalawags: The Constitutional Conventions of Radical Reconstruction* (2008).

Heather Cox Richardson, *The Death of Reconstruction: Race, Labor, and Politics in the Post–Civil War North, 1865–1901* (2001).

Leslie A. Schwalm, *Emancipation's Diaspora: Race and Reconstruction in the Upper Midwest* (2009).

Brooks D. Simpson, *The Reconstruction Presidents* (1998).

Mark Wahlgren Summers, *A Dangerous Stir: Fear, Paranoia, and the Making of Reconstruction* (2009).

Michael Vorenberg, *Final Freedom: The Civil War, the Abolition of Slavery, and the Thirteenth Amendment* (2001).

C. Vann Woodward, *Reunion and Reaction: The Compromise of 1877 and the End of Reconstruction* (1951).

THE STRUGGLE IN THE SOUTH

James Alex Baggett, *The Scalawags: Southern Dissenters in the Civil War and Reconstruction* (2003).

Nancy D. Bercaw, *Gendered Freedoms: Race, Rights, and the Politics of Household in the Delta, 1861–1875* (2003).

Stephen Budiansky, *The Bloody Shirt: Terror After the Civil War* (2008).

Jane Turner Censer, *The Reconstruction of White Southern Womanhood, 1865–1895* (2003).

Paul A. Cimbala, *Under the Guardianship of the Nation: The Freedmen's Bureau and the Reconstruction of Georgia, 1865–1870* (1997).

Jane E. Dailey, *Before Jim Crow: The Politics of Race in Post-emancipation Virginia* (2000).

Carole Faulkner, *Women's Radical Reconstruction: The Freedmen's Aid Movement* (2004).

Sarah E. Gardner, *Blood and Irony: Southern White Women's Narratives of the Civil War, 1861–1937* (2004).

Moon-Ho Jung, *Coolies and Cane: Race, Labor, and Sugar in the Age of Emancipation* (2006).

Stephen Kantrowitz, *Ben Tillman and the Reconstruction of White Supremacy* (2000).

Charles Lane, *The Day Freedom Died: The Colfax Massacre, the Supreme Court, and the Betrayal of Reconstruction* (2008).

Amy Feely Morsman, *The Big House After Slavery: Virginian Plantation Families and Their Postbellum Domestic Experiences* (2010).

George C. Rable, *But There Was No Peace: The Role of Violence in the Politics of Reconstruction* (1984).

James L. Roark, *Masters without Slaves: Southern Planters in the Civil War and Reconstruction* (1977).

Hannah Rosen, *Terror in the Heart of Freedom: Citizenship, Sexual Violence, and the Meaning of Race in the Postemancipation South* (2009).

Hyman Rubin III, *South Carolina Scalawags* (2006).

Christopher M. Span, *From Cotton Field to Schoolhouse: African American Education in Mississippi, 1862–1875* (2009).

Peter Wallenstein, *From Slave South to New South: Public Policy in Nineteenth-Century Georgia* (1987).

Chapter 17

GENERAL

Najia Aarin-Heriot, *Chinese Immigrants, African Americans, and Racial Anxiety in the United States, 1848–1882* (2003).

Robert V. Hine and John Mack Faragher, *The American West: A New Interpretive History* (2000).

Patricia Nelson Limerick, *Something in the Soil: Legacies and Reckonings in the New West* (2000).

Valerie Matsumoto and Blake Allmendinger, eds., *Over the Edge: Remapping the American West* (1999).

Louis S. Warren, *Buffalo Bill's America: William Cody and the Wild West Show* (2005).

Richard White, *"It's Your Misfortune and None of My Own": A New History of the American West* (1991).

———*Railroaded: The Transcontinentals and the Making of Modern America* (2011).

David M. Wrobel, *Promised Lands: Promotion, Memory, and the Creation of the American West* (2002).

INDIANS

David Wallace Adams, *Education for Extinction: American Indians and the Boarding School Experience, 1875–1928* (1995).

Gary Clayton Anderson, *The Conquest of Texas: Ethnic Cleansing in the Promised Land, 1820–1875* (2005).

Stuart Banner, *How the Indians Lost Their Land: Law and Power on the Frontier* (2005).

Ned Blackhawk, *Violence over the Land: Indian Empires in the Early American West* (2006).

Colin Calloway, *First Peoples: A Documentary Survey of American Indian History* (3rd ed., 2008).

Jerome A. Greene, *American Carnage: Wounded Knee, 1890* (2014).

James O. Gump, *The Dust Rose like Smoke: The Subjugation of the Zulu and the Sioux* (1994).

Pekka Hämäläinen, *The Comanche Empire* (2008).

Andrew C. Isenberg, *The Destruction of the Bison: An Environmental History, 1730–1920* (2000).

Ari Kelman, *A Misplaced Massacre: Struggling over the Memory of Sand Creek* (2013).

Edward Lazarus, *Black Hills, White Justice: The Sioux Nation versus the United States, 1775 to the Present* (1991).

Jeffrey Ostler, *The Plains Sioux and U.S. Colonialism from Lewis and Clark to Wounded Knee* (2004).

Nathaniel Philbrick, *The Last Stand: Custer, Sitting Bull, and the Battle of the Little Bighorn* (2010).

Francis Paul Prucha, *The Great Father: The United States Government and the American Indian* (1986).

Charles M. Robinson III, *A Good Year to Die: The Story of the Great Sioux War* (1995).

Alan Trachtenberg, *Shades of Hiawatha: Staging Indians, Making Americans, 1880–1930* (2004).

MINING, RANCHING, AND FARMING

Suchen Chan, *This Bittersweet Soil: The Chinese in American Agriculture, 1860–1919* (1986).

Suchen Chan, Douglas Henry Daniels, Mario T. Garcia, and Terry P. Wilson, *Peoples of Color in the American West* (1994).

Roger Daniels, *Asian American: Chinese and Japanese in the United States since 1850* (1997).

Deborah Fitzgerald, *Every Farm a Factory: The Industrial Ideal in American Agriculture* (2003).

Manuel G. Gonzales, *Mexicanos: A History of Mexicans in the United States* (1999).

J. S. Holliday, *Rush for Riches: Gold Fever and the Making of California* (1999).

David Igler, *Industrial Cowboys: Miller & Lux and the Transformation of the Far West, 1850–1920* (2001).

Andrew C. Isenberg, *Mining California: An Ecological History* (2005).

Ronald M. James, *The Roar and the Silence: The History of Virginia City and the Comstock Lode* (1998).

William Loren Katz, *Black West: A Documentary and Pictorial History of the African American Role in the Westward Expansion of the United States* (2005).

Karen R. Merrill, *Public Lands and Political Meaning: Ranchers, the Government, and the Property between Them* (2002).

Rodman Wilson Paul, *Mining Frontiers of the Far West, 1848–1880* (rev. ed., 2001).

William G. Robbins, *Colony and Empire: The Capitalist Transformation of the American West* (1994).

Steven Stoll, *Larding the Lean Earth: Soil and Society in Nineteenth-Century America* (2002).

Chapter 18

GENERAL WORKS

Charles W. Calhoun, ed., *The Gilded Age: Essays on the Origins of Modern America* (1996).

Sean Dennis Cashman, *America in the Gilded Age: From the Death of Lincoln to the Rise of Theodore Roosevelt* (1993).

Rebecca Edwards, *New Spirits: Americans in the Gilded Age, 1865–1905* (2006).

Jackson Lears, *Rebirth of a Nation: The Making of Modern America, 1877–1920* (2009).

Richard White, *Railroaded: The Transcontinentals and the Making of Modern America* (2011).

BUSINESS

Kathleen Brady, *Ida Tarbell: Portrait of a Muckraker* (1984).

Edward Chancellor, *Devil Take the Hindmost: A History of Financial Speculation* (1999).

Ron Chernow, *Titan: The Life of John D. Rockefeller, Sr.* (1998).

Steve Fraser, *Every Man a Speculator: A Cultural History of Wall Street in America* (2005).

Ernest Freeberg, *The Age of Edison: Electric Light and the Invention of Modern America* (2013).

Morton J. Horowitz, *The Transformation of American Law, 1870–1960* (1992).

Christopher F. Jones, *Router of Power: Energy and Modern America* (2014).

Walter Licht, *Industrializing America* (1995).

Carol Marvin, *When Technologies Were New* (1988).

David Nasaw, *Andrew Carnegie* (2006).

T. J. Stiles, *The First Tycoon: The Epic Life of Cornelius Vanderbilt* (2009).

Jean Strouse, *Morgan: American Financier* (1999).

Viviana A. Zelizer, *The Social Meaning of Money* (1994).

POLITICS

Paula Baker, *The Moral Framework of Public Life* (1991).

Richard F. Bensel, *The Political Economy of American Industrialization, 1877–1900* (2000).

Ruth Bordin, *Women and Temperance: The Quest for Power and Liberty, 1873–1900* (1990).

Alyn Brodsky, *Grover Cleveland: A Study in Character* (2000).

Robert W. Cherny, *American Politics in the Gilded Age, 1868–1900* (1997).

Jane Dailey, Glenda Elizabeth Gilmore, and Bryant Simon, eds., *Jumpin' Jim Crow: Southern Politics from the Civil War to Civil Rights* (2000).

Rebecca Edwards, *Angels in the Machinery: Gender in American Party Politics from the Civil War to the Progressive Era* (1997).

Dana Frank, *Buy American: The Untold Story of Economic Nationalism* (1999).

Paula Giddings, *Ida, a Sword among Lions: Ida B. Wells and the Campaign against Lynching* (2008).

Steven Hahn, *A Nation under Our Feet: Black Political Struggles in the Rural South from Slavery to the Great Migration* (2003).

Darlene Clark Hine and Kathleen Thompson, *A Shining Thread of Hope: The History of Black Women in America* (1998).

Ari Hoogenboom, *Rutherford B. Hayes: Warrior and President* (1995).

H. Paul Jeffers, *An Honest President: The Life and Presidencies of Grover Cleveland* (2000).

Ross Evans Paulson, *Liberty, Equality, and Justice: Civil Rights, Women's Rights, and the Regulation of Business, 1865–1932* (1997).

Dorothy Salem, *To Better Our World: Black Women in Organized Reform, 1890–1920* (1990).

Ian Tyrell, *Woman's World, Woman's Empire: The Woman's Christian Temperance Union in International Perspective, 1880–1930* (1991).

LeeAnn Whites, *Gender Matters: Civil War, Reconstruction, and the Making of the New South* (2005).

CULTURE

Ellen Gruber Garvey, *The Adman in the Parlor: Magazines and the Gendering of Consumer Culture, 1880s to 1910s* (1996).

Judy Arlene Hilkey, *Character Is Capital: Success Manuals and Manhood in Gilded Age America* (1997).

Jane H. Hunter, *How Young Ladies Became Girls: The Victorian Origins of American Girlhood* (2002).

Paulette D. Kilmer, *The Fear of Sinking: The American Success Formula in the Gilded Age* (1996).

Alan Trachtenberg, *The Incorporation of America: Culture and Society in the Gilded Age* (anniversary edition, 2009).

Chapter 19

IMMIGRATION

John Bodnar, *The Transplanted: A History of Immigration in Urban America* (1985).

Vincent J. Cannato, *American Passage: The History of Ellis Island* (2010).

Roger Daniels, *Guarding the Golden Door: American Immigration Policy and Immigrants since 1882* (2004).

Allan Dawley, *Struggles for Justice: Social Responsibility and the Liberal State* (1991).

Martha Gardner, *The Qualities of a Citizen: Women, Immigration, and Citizenship, 1870–1965* (2005).

Dirk Hoerder, *Cultures in Contact: World Migrations in the Second Millennium* (2002).

Matthew Frye Jacobson, *Whiteness of a Different Color: European Immigrants and the Alchemy of Race* (1998).

David M. Reimers, *Unwelcome Strangers* (1998).

David R. Roediger, *Working toward Whiteness: How America's Immigrants Became White* (2005).

Ronald Takaki, *Strangers from a Different Shore: A History of Asian Americans* (1998).

WORKERS AND UNIONS

Susan Porter Benson, *Counter Cultures: Saleswomen, Managers, and Customers in American Department Stores, 1890–1940* (1986).

Ileen A. DeVault, *United Apart: Gender and the Rise of Craft Unionism* (2004).

Hasia Diner, *Lower East Side Memories: A Jewish Place in America* (2000).

Leon Fink, *Workingman's Democracy: The Knights of Labor and American Politics* (1983).

Robert J. Gordon, *The Rise and Fall of American Growth: The U.S. Standard of Living Since the Civil War* (2016).

James Green, *Death in the Haymarket: A Story of Chicago, the First Labor Movement, and the Bombing That Divided Gilded Age America* (2006).

Hamilton Hold, ed., *The Life Stories of Undistinguished Americans as Told by Themselves* (2000).

Jacqueline Jones, *American Work: Four Centuries of Black and White Labor* (1998).

Jackson Lears, *Rebirth of a Nation: The Making of Modern America, 1877–1920* (2009).

Susan Levine, *Labor's True Women: Carpet Weavers, Industrialization, and Labor Reform in the Gilded Age* (1984).

David Montgomery, *The Fall of the House of Labor: The Workplace, the State, and American Labor Activism, 1865–1925* (1987).

Roy Rosenzweig, *Eight Hours for What We Will: Workers and Leisure in an Industrial City, 1870–1920* (1983).

Timothy Spears, *Chicago Dreaming: Midwesterners and the City, 1871–1919* (2005).

Carole Srole, *Transcribing Class and Gender: Masculinity and Femininity in Nineteenth-Century Courts and Offices* (2009).

Sharon Hartman Strom, *Beyond the Typewriter: Gender, Class, and the Origins of Modern American Office Work, 1900–1930* (1992).

Robert E. Weir, *Knights Unhorsed: Internal Conflict in a Gilded Age Social Movement* (2000).

THE CITY AND ITS AMUSEMENTS

LeRoy Ashby, *With Amusement for All: A History of American Popular Culture since 1830* (2006).

Sven Beckert, *The Monied Metropolis: New York City and the Consolidation of the American Bourgeoisie, 1850–1896* (2001).

Gary S. Cross and John K. Walton, *The Playful Crowd: Pleasure Places in the Twentieth Century* (2005).

Sarah Deutsch, *Women and the City: Gender, Space, and Power in Boston, 1870–1940* (2000).

Nan Enstad, *Ladies of Labor, Girls of Adventure: Working Women, Popular Culture, and Labor Politics at the Turn of the Twentieth Century* (1999).

Margaret Garb, *City of American Dreams: A History of Home Ownership and Housing Reform in Chicago, 1871–1919* (2005).

Richard Haw, *The Brooklyn Bridge: A Cultural History* (2005).

Elizabeth Hawes, *New York, New York: How the Apartment House Transformed Life in the City, 1869–1930* (1993).

Kathy Peiss, *Cheap Amusements: Working Women and Leisure in Turn-of-the-Century New York* (1986).

Roy Rosenzweig and Elizabeth Blackmar, *The Park and the People: A History of Central Park* (1992).

Witold Rybczynski, *A Clearing in the Distance: Frederick Law Olmsted and America in the Nineteenth Century* (1999).

Jules Tygiel, *Past Time: Baseball as History* (2000).

Chapter 20

THE FARMERS' ALLIANCE, THE LABOR WARS, AND WOMEN'S ACTIVISM

Peter H. Argersinger, *The Limits of Agrarian Radicalism: Western Populism and American Politics* (1995).

Jean H. Baker, *Sisters: The Lives of America's Suffragists* (2005).

Donna A. Barnes, *The Louisiana Populist Movement, 1881–1900* (2011).

Ruth Bordin, *Frances Willard: A Biography* (1986).

Alan Dawley, *Struggles for Justice: Social Responsibility and the Liberal State* (1991).

Ellen Carol DuBois, *Woman Suffrage and Women's Rights* (1998).

Gerald H. Gaither, *Blacks and the Populist Movement* (2013).

Michael Lewis Goldberg, *An Army of Women: Gender and Politics in Gilded Age Kansas* (1997).

Steven Hahn, *A Nation under Our Feet: Black Political Struggles in the Rural South from Slavery to the Great Migration* (2003).

Elizabeth Jameson, *All That Glitters: Class, Conflict, and Community in Cripple Creek* (1998).

Michael Kazin, *The Populist Persuasion: An American History* (rev. ed., 1998).

Paul Krause, *The Battle for Homestead, 1880–1892* (1992).

Connie L. Lester, *Up From the Mudsills of Hell: The Farmers' Alliance, Populism, and Progressive Agriculture in Tennessee, 1870–1915* (2006).

Theodore R. Mitchell, *Political Education in the Southern Farmers' Alliance, 1887–1900* (1987).

David Nasaw, *Andrew Carnegie* (2006).

Nick Salvatore, *Eugene V. Debs: Citizen and Socialist* (1982).

DEPRESSION AND THE ELECTION OF 1896

Louis L. Gould, *The Presidency of Willliam McKinley* (1981).

Stephen Kantrowitz, *Ben Tillman and the Reconstruction of White Supremacy* (2000).

Michael Kazin, *A Godly Hero: The Life of William Jennings Bryan* (2006).

Kenneth L. Kusmer, *Down and Out, on the Road: The Homeless in American History* (2002).

Gretchen Ritter, *Goldbugs and Greenbacks: The Antimonopoly Tradition in the Politics of Finance in America* (1997).

Carol A. Schwantes, *Coxey's Army: An American Odyssey* (1985).

Douglas Steeples and David O. Whitten, *Democracy in Desperation: The Depression of 1892* (1998).

U.S. FOREIGN POLICY AND THE SPANISH-AMERICAN WAR

Fred Anderson and Andrew Cayton, *The Domination of War: Empire and Liberty in North America, 1500–2000* (2005).

Edward P. Crapol, *James G. Blaine: Architect of Empire* (1999).

Kristin Hoganson, *Fighting for American Manhood: How Gender Politics Provoked the Spanish-American and Philippine-American Wars* (1998).

Matthew Frye Jacobson, *Barbarian Virtues: The United States Encounters Foreign Peoples at Home and Abroad, 1876–1917* (2000).

Gregg Jones, *Honor in the Dust: Theodore Roosevelt, War in the Philippines, and the Rise and Fall of America's Imperial Dream* (2013).

Amy Kaplan, *The Anarchy of Empire in the Making of U.S. Culture* (2002).

Stephen Kinzer, *Overthrow: America's Century of Regime Change from Hawaii to Iraq* (2006).

Walter LaFeber, *The Cambridge History of American Foreign Relations*, vol. 2, *The American Search for Opportunity, 1865–1913* (1993).

Brian Linn, *The Philippine War, 1899–1902* (2000).

Paul T. McCartney, *Power and Progress: American National Identity, the War of 1898, and the Rise of American Imperialism* (2006).

Ivan Musicant, *Empire by Default: The Spanish-American War and the Dawn of the American Century* (1998).

Thomas J. Osborne, *Annexation Hawaii* (1998).

Louis A. Perez Jr., *The War of 1898: The United States and Cuba in History and Historiography* (1998).

Diana Preston, *Besieged in Peking: The Story of the 1900 Boxer Uprising* (1999).

Lars Shoultz, *Beneath the United States* (1998).

David J. Silbey, *A War of Frontier and Empire: The Philippine-American War, 1899–1902* (2008).

Margaret Strobel, *Gender, Sex, and Empire* (1993).

Evan Thomas, *The War Lovers: Roosevelt, Lodge, Hearst, and the Rush to Empire, 1898* (2010).

David Traxel, *1898: The Birth of the American Century* (1999).

Walter Zimmerman, *First Great Triumph: How Five Americans Made Their Country a World Power* (2002).

Chapter 21

GENERAL

Geoffrey Cowan, *Let the People Rule: Theodore Roosevelt and the Birth of the Presidential Primary* (2016).

Maureen A. Flanagan, *America Reformed: Progressives and Progressivisms, 1890s–1920s* (2007).

Jackson Lears, *Rebirth of a Nation: The Making of Modern America, 1877–1920* (2009).

Michael McGerr, *A Fierce Discontent: The Rise and Fall of the Progressive Movement in America* (2005).

Eric Ruchway, *Blessed among Nations: How the World Made America* (2006).

Michael Wolraich, *Unreasonable Men: Theodore Roosevelt and the Republican Rebels Who Created Progressive Politics* (2014).

GRASSROOTS PROGRESSIVISM

Victoria Bissell Brown, *The Education of Jane Addams* (2004).

Robert Kanigel, *The One Best Way: Frederick Winslow Taylor* (1997).

Louise W. Knight, *Citizen: Jane Addams and the Struggle for Democracy* (2005).

———*Jane Addams: Spirit in Action* (2010).

Seth Koven and Sonya Michel, eds., *Mothers of a New World: Maternalist Politics and the Origins of the Welfare State* (1993).

Robyn Muncy, *Creating a Female Dominion in American Reform* (1991).

Kathryn Kish Sklar, *Florence Kelley and the Nation's Work: The Rise of Women's Political Culture, 1830–1900* (1995).

Landon R. Y. Storre, *Civilizing Capitalism: The National Consumers' League, Women's Activism, and Labor Standards in the New Deal Era* (2000).

Nancy C. Unger, *Fighting Bob La Follette: The Righteous Reformer* (2000).

David Von Drehle, *Triangle: The Fire That Changed America* (2003).

PROGRESSIVE POLITICS AND DIPLOMACY

Douglas Brinkley, *The Wilderness Warrior: Theodore Roosevelt and the Crusade for America* (2009).

John Milton Cooper, *Woodrow Wilson: A Biography* (2009).

Alan Dawley, *Changing the World: American Progressives in War and Revolution* (2003).

Doris Kearns Goodwin, *The Bully Pulpit: Theodore Roosevelt, William Howard Taft, and the Golden Age of Journalism* (2013).

Lewis L. Gould, *Four Hats in the Ring: The 1912 Election and the Birth of Modern American Politics* (2008).

———*William Howard Taft: Presidency* (2009).

Kristin Hoganson, *Consumers' Imperium: The Global Production of American Domesticity, 1865–1920* (2007).

Matthew Frye Jacobson, *Barbarian Virtues: The United States Encounters Foreign Peoples at Home and Abroad, 1876–1917* (2000).

Robert Johnston, *The Radical Middle Class: Populist Democracy and the Question of Capitalism in Progressive Era Portland, Oregon* (2003).

Walter LaFeber, *The Cambridge History of American Foreign Relations*, vol. 2, *The American Search for Opportunity, 1865–1913* (1993).

Kevin Matson, *Creating a Democratic Public: The Struggle for Urban Participatory Democracy during the Progressive Era* (1998).

Robert W. Righter, *The Battle over Hetch Hetchy: America's Most Controversial Dam and the Birth of Modern Environmentalism* (2005).

Daniel T. Rodgers, *Atlantic Crossings: Social Politics in a Progressive Age* (1998).

RADICALS, RACE RELATIONS, AND WOMAN SUFFRAGE

Mary Jo Buhle, *Women and American Socialism, 1870–1920* (1981).

Ellen Chesler, *Woman of Valor: Margaret Sanger and the Birth Control Movement in America* (1993).

Melvyn Dubofsky, *"Big Bill" Haywood* (1987).

Gary Gerstle, *American Crucible: Race and Nation in the Twentieth Century* (2002).

Glenda Elizabeth Gilmore, *Gender and Jim Crow: Women and the Politics of White Supremacy in North Carolina, 1896–1920* (1996).

David Fort Godshalk, *Veiled Visions: The 1906 Atlanta Race Riot and the Reshaping of American Race Relations* (2005).

Evelyn Higginbotham, *Righteous Discontent: The Women's Movement in the Black Baptist Church, 1880–1920* (1993).

David Levering Lewis, *W. E. B. Du Bois: Biography of a Race, 1868–1919* (1993).

Rebecca J. Mead, *How the Vote Was Won: Woman Suffrage in the Western United States, 1868–1914* (2004).

Nick Salvatore, *Eugene V. Debs: Citizen and Socialist* (1982).

Chapter 22

GENERAL WORKS

John Milton Cooper, *Woodrow Wilson: A Biography* (2009).

Thomas Fleming, *The Illusion of Victory: America in World War I* (2003).

Robert H. Zieger, *America's Great War: World War I and the American Experience* (2000).

"OVER THERE"

Gerald Astor, *The Right to Fight: A History of African Americans in the Military* (1998).

Peter Boyle, *American-Soviet Relations: From the Russian Revolution to the Fall of Communism* (1993).

Edward M. Coffman, *The War to End All Wars: The American Military Experience in World War I* (1968).

Byron Farwell, *Over There: The United States in the Great War, 1917–1918* (1999).

Lloyd C. Gardner, *Safe for Democracy: The Anglo-American Response to Revolution, 1913–1923* (1987).

Judith S. Graham, ed., *"Out Here at the Front": The World War I Letters of Nora Saltonstall* (2004).

Jennifer D. Keene, *Doughboys, the Great War, and the Remaking of America* (2001).

Thomas Knock, *To End All Wars: Woodrow Wilson and the Quest for a New World Order* (1992).

Edward G. Lengel, *To Conquer Hell: The Meuse-Argonne, 1918* (2008).

Margaret Olwen Macmillan, *Paris 1919: Six Months That Changed the World* (2002).

Gary Mead, *The Doughboys: America and the First World War* (2000).

Emily S. Rosenberg, *Financial Missionaries to the World: The Politics and Culture of Dollar Diplomacy, 1890–1930* (1999).

Gene Smith, *Until the Last Trumpet Sounds: The Life of General of the Armies John J. Pershing* (1998).

David L. Snead, ed., *An American Soldier in World War I: George Browne* (2006).

David F. Trask, *The AEF and Coalition Warmaking, 1917–1918* (1993).

Susan Zeiger, *In Uncle Sam's Service: Women with the AEF, 1917–1919* (1999).

THE HOME FRONT

Jean Baker, *Sisters: The Lives of America's Suffragists* (2005).

Nancy Cott, *The Grounding of American Feminism* (1987).

Leslie Midkiff DeBauche, *Reel Patriotism: The Movies and World War I* (1997).

Marc A. Eisner, *From Warfare State to Welfare State: World War I, Compensatory State Building, and the Limits of the Modern Order* (2000).

Ernest Freeberg, *Democracy's Prisoner: Eugene V. Debs, the Great War, and the Right to Dissent* (2008).

Elizabeth Frost and Kathryn Cullen-DuPont, eds., *Women's Suffrage in America: An Eyewitness History* (1992).

Maurine Weiner Greenwald, *Women, War, and Work: The Impact of World War I on Women Workers in the United States* (1980).

James N. Gregory, *Southern Diaspora: How the Great Migrations of Black and White Southerners Transformed America* (2005).

James R. Grossman, *Land of Hope: Chicago, Black Southerners, and the Great Migration* (1989).

David Kennedy, *Over Here: The First World War and American Society* (1980).

David Levering Lewis, *W. E. B. Du Bois: Biography of a Race, 1868–1919* (1993).

Robert K. Murray, *Red Scare: A Study in National Hysteria, 1919–1920* (1955).

Tammy M. Proctor, *Civilians in a World at War, 1914–1918* (2010).

George J. Sanchez, *Becoming Mexican American: Ethnicity, Culture, and Identity in Chicano Los Angeles, 1900–1945* (1993).

William H. Thomas Jr., *Unsafe for Democracy: World War I and the U.S. Justice Department's Covert Campaign to Suppress Dissent* (2008).

Joe William Trotter Jr., ed., *The Great Migration in Historical Perspective* (1991).

Chapter 23

GENERAL WORKS

David M. Kennedy, *Freedom from Fear: The American People in Depression and War, 1929–1945* (1999).

William E. Leuchtenburg, *The Perils of Prosperity, 1914–1932* (1958).

Michael Parrish, *Anxious Decades: America in Prosperity and Depression, 1920–1941* (1992).

POLITICS AND ECONOMY

Kristi Anderson, *After Suffrage: Women in Partisan and Electoral Politics before the New Deal* (1996).

Douglas Brinkley, *Wheels for the World: Henry Ford, His Company, and a Century of Progress, 1903–2003* (2003).

Kendrick A. Clements, *Hoover, Conservation, and Consumerism: Engineering the Good Life* (2000).

Warren I. Cohen, *Empire without Tears: America's Foreign Relations, 1921–1933* (1987).

Steve Fraser, *Every Man a Speculator: A History of Wall Street* (2005).

Colin Gordon, *New Deals: Business, Labor, and Politics in America, 1920–1935* (1994).

David Greenberg, *Calvin Coolidge* (2006).

Owen Gutfreund, *Twentieth-Century Sprawl: Highways and the Reshaping of the American Landscape* (2004).

Jill Jonnes, *Empires of Light: Edison, Tesla, and Westinghouse, and the Race to Electrify the World* (2003).

William E. Leuchtenburg, *Herbert Hoover: Thirty-First President, 1929–1933* (2009).

Martha L. Olney, *Buy Now, Pay Later: Advertising, Credit, and Consumer Durables in the 1920s* (1991).

Lorrai Schuyler, *Weight of Their Votes: Southern Women and Political Leverage in the 1920s* (2006).

Steven Watts, *People's Tycoon: Henry Ford and the American Century* (2005).

SOCIETY AND CULTURE

Douglas Carl Abrams, *Selling the Old-Time Religion: American Fundamentalists and Mass Culture, 1920–1940* (2001).

Francisco E. Balderrama and Raymond Rodriguez, *Decade of Betrayal: Mexican Repatriation in the 1930s* (1995).

Kevin Boyle, *Arc of Justice: A Saga of Race, Civil Rights, and Murder in the Jazz Age* (2004).

Steven Conn, *Americans Against the City: Anti-urbanism in the Twentieth Century* (2014).

Liz Conor, *Spectacular Modern Woman: Feminine Visibility in the 1920s* (2004).

Ruth Schwartz Cowan, *More Work for Mother: The Ironies of Household Technology from the Open Hearth to the Microwave* (1983).

Roger Daniels, *Guarding the Golden Door: American Immigration Policy and Immigrants since 1882* (2004).

Paula S. Fass, *The Damned and the Beautiful: American Youth in the 1920s* (1977).

David J. Goldberg, *Discontented America: The United States in the 1920s* (1999).

David M. Kennedy, *Birth Control in America: The Career of Margaret Sanger* (1970).

David E. Kyvig, *Daily Life in the United States, 1920–1940* (2002).

Edward J. Larson, *Summer of the Gods: The Scopes Trial and America's Continuing Debate over Science and Religion* (1997).

David Levering Lewis, *W. E. B. Du Bois: The Fight for Equality and the American Century, 1919–1963* (2000).

Nancy MacLean, *Behind the Mask of Chivalry: The Making of the Second Ku Klux Klan* (1994).

David E. Nye, *Electrifying America: Social Meanings of a New Technology, 1880–1940* (1990).

Daniel Okrent, *Last Call: The Rise and Fall of Prohibition* (2010).

Thomas R. Pegram, *One Hundred Percent American: The Rebirth and Decline of the Ku Klux Klan* (2011).

David M. Reimers, *Unwelcome Strangers: American Identity and the Turn against Immigration* (1998).

Susan Smulyan, *Selling Radio: The Commercialization of American Broadcasting, 1920–1934* (1994).

Judith Stein, *The World of Marcus Garvey* (1986).

Andrew Wiese, *Places of Their Own: African American Suburbanization in the Twentieth Century* (2004).

Chapter 24

GENERAL WORKS

Gary Dean Best, *The Retreat from Liberalism: Collectivists versus Progressives in the New Deal Years* (2002).

Douglas Brinkley, *Rightful Heritage: Franklin D. Roosevelt and the Land of America* (2016).

William H. Chafe, ed., *The Achievement of American Liberalism: The New Deal and Its Legacies* (2003).

Morris Dickstein, *Dancing in the Dark: A Cultural History of the Great Depression* (2010).

Ronald Edsforth, *The New Deal: America's Response to the Great Depression* (2000).

Alonzo Hamby, *Man of Destiny: FDR and the Making of the American Century* (2015).

Ira Katznelson, *Fear Itself: The New Deal and the Origins of Our Time* (2013).

David M. Kennedy, *Freedom from Fear: The American People in Depression and War, 1929–1945* (1999).

Alan Lawson, *A Commonwealth of Hope: The New Deal Response to Crisis* (2006).

William Edward Leuchtenburg, *Franklin D. Roosevelt and the New Deal, 1932–1940* (2009).

Amity Shlaes, *The Forgotten Man: A New History of the Great Depression* (2008).

NEW DEAL POLITICS

Roger Biles, *The South and the New Deal* (2006).

Jefferson Cowie, *The Great Exception: The New Deal and the Limits of American Politics* (2016).

Kirstin Downey, *The Woman behind the New Deal: The Life and Legacy of Frances Perkins* (2010).

Alonzo L. Hamby, *For the Survival of Democracy: Franklin Roosevelt and the World Crisis of the 1930s* (2004).

Joseph E. Lowndes, *From the New Deal to the New Right: Race and the Southern Origins of Modern Conservatism* (2009).

Marian C. McKenna, *Franklin Roosevelt and the Great Constitutional War: The Court-Packing Crisis of 1937* (2002).

Kim Phillips-Fein, *Invisible Hands: The Businessmen's Crusade against the New Deal* (2010).

Theodore Rosenof, *Economics in the Long Run: New Deal Theorists and Their Legacies, 1933–1993* (1997).

Robert Shogan, *Backlash: The Killing of the New Deal* (2006).

Mary Triece, *On the Picket Line: Strategies of Working-Class Women during the Depression* (2007).

Clyde P. Weed, *The Nemesis of Reform: The Republican Party during the New Deal* (1994).

NEW DEAL POLICIES

Lizbeth Cohen, *Making a New Deal: Industrial Workers in Chicago, 1919–1939* (1990).

Kathleen G. Donohue, *Freedom from Want: American Liberalism and the Idea of the Consumer* (2004).

Timothy Eagan, *The Worst Hard Time: The Untold Story of Those Who Survived the Great American Dust Bowl* (2006).

Jan Goggans, *California on the Breadlines: Dorothea Lange, Paul Taylor, and the Making of a New Deal Narrative* (2010).

Linda Gordon, *Dorothea Lange: A Life beyond Limits* (2009).

Michael R. Grey, *New Deal Medicine: The Rural Health Programs of the Farm Security Administration* (1999).

Janet Irons, *Testing the New Deal: The General Textile Strike of 1934 in the American South* (2000).

Jennifer Klein, *For All These Rights: Business, Labor, and the Shaping of America's Public-Private Welfare State* (2003).

Lawrence Levine et al., *The Fireside Conversations: America Responds to FDR during the Great Depression* (2010).

Neil M. Maher, *Nature's New Deal: The Civilian Conservation Corps and the Roots of the American Environmental Movement* (2009).

Julie Novkov, *Constituting Workers, Protecting Women: Gender, Law, and Labor in the Progressive Era and New Deal Years* (2001).

Sarah Phillips, *This Land, This Nation: Conservation, Rural America, and the New Deal* (2007).

Patrick D. Reagan, *Designing a New America: The Origins of New Deal Planning, 1890–1936* (1999).

John A. Salmond, *The General Textile Strike of 1934: From Maine to Alabama* (2002).

Jason Scott Smith, *Building New Deal Liberalism: The Political Economy of Public Works, 1933–1956* (2005).

Landon R. Y. Stors, *Civilizing Capitalism: The National Consumers' League, Women's Activism, and Labor Standards in the New Deal Era* (2000).

David A. Taylor, *Soul of a People: The WPA Writers' Project Uncovers Depression America* (2010).

Chapter 25

GENERAL WORKS

Max Arthur, ed., *Forgotten Voices of the Second World War: A New History of World War Two in the Words of the Men and Women Who Were There* (2004).

Anthony Beevor, *The Second World War* (2013).

Richard Evans, *The Third Reich at War* (2010).

Thomas Fleming, *The New Dealers' War: Franklin D. Roosevelt and the War within World War II* (2001).

Peter Fritzsche, *Life and Death in the Third Reich* (2009).

Max Hastings, *Inferno: The World at War, 1939–1945* (2011).

David M. Kennedy, *Freedom from Fear: The American People in Depression and War, 1929–1945* (1999).

Ian Kershaw, *To Hell and Back: Europe 1914–1949* (2015).

Mark Mazower, *Hitler's Empire: How the Nazis Ruled Europe* (2008).

Andrew Roberts, *The Storm of War: A New History of the Second World War* (2011).

Paul W. Tibbets Jr., *The Tibbets Story* (1978).

John Toland, *The Rising Sun: The Decline and Fall of the Japanese Empire, 1936–1945* (2001).

Adam Tooze, *The Wages of Destruction: The Making and Breaking of the Nazi Economy* (2006).

FOREIGN POLICY

Tokomo Akami, *Internationalizing the Pacific: The U.S., Japan, and the Institute of Pacific Relations in War and Peace, 1919–1945* (2002).

Elizabeth Borgwardt, *A New Deal for the World: America's Vision for Human Rights* (2005).

Tsuyoshi Hasegawa, *Racing the Enemy: Stalin, Truman, and the Surrender of Japan* (2005).

Adam Hochschild, *Spain in Our Hearts: Americans in the Spanish Civil War, 1936–1939* (2016).

J. Robert Moskin, *Mr. Truman's War: The Final Victories of World War II and the Birth of the Postwar World* (2002).

David Reynolds, *From Munich to Pearl Harbor: Roosevelt's America and the Origins of the Second World War* (2001).

Gaddis Smith, *American Diplomacy during the Second World War, 1941–1945* (1985).

MOBILIZATION AND THE HOME FRONT

Gerald Astor, *The Right to Fight: A History of African Americans in the Military* (1998).

Jeffrey F. Burton et al., *Confinement and Ethnicity: An Overview of World War II Japanese American Relocation Sites* (2002).

Stephanie A. Carpenter, *On the Farm Front: The Women's Land Army in World War II* (2003).

Susan Hartmann, *The Home Front and Beyond: American Women in the 1940s* (1982).

Arthur Herman, *Freedom's Forge: How American Business Produced Victory in World War II* (2012).

John W. Jeffries, *Wartime America: The World War II Home Front* (1996).

Christopher Moore, *Fighting for America: Black Soldiers—The Unsung Heroes of World War II* (2005).

Wendy Ng, *Japanese American Internment during World War II* (2002).

James T. Sparrow, *Warfare State: World War II Americans and the Age of Big Government* (2013).

MILITARY EVENTS

Rick Atkinson, *The Guns at Last Light: The War in Western Europe, 1944–1945* (2013).

Antony Beevor, *D-Day: The Battle for Normandy* (2009).

———*Ardennes 1944: The Battle of the Bulge* (2015).

Jonathan Dimbleby, *The Battle of the Atlantic: How the Allies Won the War* (2016).

John Dower, *War without Mercy: Race and Power in the Pacific War* (1986).

Max Hastings, *Overlord: D-Day and the Battle for Normandy* (2006).

———*The Secret War: Spies, Ciphers, and Guerrillas, 1939–1945* (2016).

Peter Novick, *The Holocaust in American Life* (1999).

Richard Overy, *Why the Allies Won* (1996).

———*The Bombing War: Europe, 1939–1945* (2013).

Mary Louise Roberts, *What Soldiers Do: Sex and the American GI in World War II France* (2013).

Peter Schrijvers, *The GI War against Japan: American Soldiers in Asia and the Pacific during World War II* (2002).

Thomas W. Zeiler, *Unconditional Defeat: Japan, America, and the End of World War II* (2004).

Chapter 26

GENERAL WORKS

Rodolfo Acuña, *Occupied America: A History of Chicanos* (5th ed., 2004).

Carol Anderson, *Eyes off the Prize: The United Nations and the African American Struggle for Human Rights, 1944–1955* (2003).

Margot Canaday, *The Straight State: Sexuality and Citizenship in Twentieth-Century America* (2009).

Peter L. Hahn, *Caught in the Middle East: U.S. Policy toward the Arab-Israeli Conflict, 1945–1961* (2004).

Alonzo L. Hamby, *Man of the People: A Life of Harry S. Truman* (1995).

Ira Katznelson, *When Affirmative Action Was White: An Untold History of Racial Inequality in Twentieth-Century America* (2005).

James T. Patterson, *Grand Expectations: The United States, 1945–1974* (1996).

Brenda Gayle Plummer, *Rising Wind: Black Americans and U.S. Foreign Affairs, 1935–1960* (1996).

Julian E. Zelizer, *Arsenal of Democracy: The Politics of National Security—from World War II to the War on Terrorism* (2010).

DOMESTIC POLITICS AND POLICIES

Glenn C. Altschuler and Stuart M. Blumin, *The GI Bill: A New Deal for Veterans* (2009).

Jonathan Bell, *The Liberal State on Trial: The Cold War and American Politics in the Truman Years* (2004).

Kevin Boyle, *The UAW and the Heyday of American Liberalism, 1945–1968* (1995).

Mark Brilliant, *The Color of America Has Changed: How Racial Diversity Shaped Civil Rights Reform in California, 1941–1978* (2010).

Andrew E. Busch, *Truman's Triumph: The 1948 Election and the Making of Postwar America* (2012).

Griffin Fariello, *Red Scare: Memories of the American Inquisition* (1995).

Kari Frederickson, *The Dixiecrat Revolt and the End of the Solid South, 1932–1968* (2001).

Michael D. Gambone, *The Greatest Generation Comes Home: The Veteran in American Society* (2005).

Ignacio M. García, *Hector P. García: In Relentless Pursuit of Justice* (2002).

Meg Jacobs, *Pocketbook Politics: Economic Citizenship in Twentieth-Century America* (2004).

David K. Johnson, *The Lavender Scare: The Cold War Persecution of Gays and Lesbians in the Federal Government* (2004).

Suzanne Mettler, *Soldiers to Citizens: The G.I. Bill and the Making of the Greatest Generation* (2005).

Henry A. J. Ramos, *The American GI Forum: In Pursuit of the Dream, 1948–1983* (1998).

Ellen W. Schrecker, *Many Are the Crimes: McCarthyism in America* (1998).

Ingrid Winther Scobie, *Center Stage: Helen Gahagan Douglas: A Life* (1992).

Robert Shogan, *Harry Truman and the Struggle for Racial Justice* (2013).

Philippa Strum, *Mendez v. Westminster: School Desegregation and Mexican-American Rights* (2010).

THE COLD WAR

Greg Behrman, *The Most Noble Adventure: The Marshall Plan and the Time When America Helped Save Europe* (2007).

Robert L. Beisner, *Dean Acheson: A Life in the Cold War* (2006).

Iris Chang, *Thread of the Silkworm* (1996).

Campbell Craig and Fredric Logevall, *America's Cold War: The Politics of Insecurity* (2009).

Robert Dallek, *The Lost Peace: Leadership in a Time of Horror and Hope, 1945–1953* (2010).

Carolyn Eisenberg, *Drawing the Line: The American Decision to Divide Germany, 1944–1949* (1996).

John L. Gaddis, *The Cold War: A New History* (2005).

Michael D. Gordin, *Red Cloud at Dawn: Truman, Stalin, and the End of the Atomic Monopoly.* (2010).

Daniel F. Harrington, *Berlin on the Brink: The Blockade, the Airlift, and the Early Cold War* (2012).

Lawrence S. Kaplan, *1948: The Birth of the Transatlantic Alliance* (2007).

Melvyn Leffler, *For the Soul of Mankind: The United States, the Soviet Union, and the Cold War* (2007).

Richard Rhodes, *Dark Sun: The Making of the Hydrogen Bomb* (1995).

Katherine A. S. Sibley, *Red Spies in America: Stolen Secrets and the Dawn of the Cold War* (2004).

Odd Arne Westad, *The Global Cold War* (2005).

ASIA AND THE KOREAN WAR

Gordon H. Chang, *Friends and Enemies: The United States, China, and the Soviet Union, 1948–1972* (1990).

Bruce Cumings, *The Korean War* (2010).

Chae-Jin Lee, *A Troubled Peace: U.S. Policy and the Two Koreas* (2006).

Allen R. Millett, *The War for Korea, 1945–1950: A House Burning* (2005).

——*The War for Korea, 1950–1951: They Came from the North* (2010).

Michael Schaller, *Altered States: The United States and Japan since the Occupation* (1997).

Stanley Weintraub, *MacArthur's War: Korea and the Undoing of an American Hero* (2000).

Chapter 27

EISENHOWER'S ADMINISTRATION

Jeff Broadwater, *Eisenhower and the Anti-Communist Crusade* (2010).

Dino A. Brugioni, *Eyes in the Sky: Eisenhower, the CIA, and Cold War Aerial Espionage* (2010).

Steven Z. Freiberger, *Dawn over Suez: The Rise of American Power in the Middle East, 1953–1957* (1992).

David Halberstam, *The Fifties* (1993).

Stephen Kinzer, *All the Shah's Men: An American Coup and the Roots of Middle East Terror* (2003).

William M. McClenaham Jr. and William H. Becker, *Eisenhower and the Cold War Economy* (2011).

Yanek Mieczkowski, *Eisenhower's Sputnik Moment: The Race for Space and World Prestige* (2013).

David A. Nichols, *Eisenhower 1956: The President's Year of Crisis—Suez and the Brink of War* (2011).

Jean Edward Smith, *Eisenhower: In War and Peace* (2012).

Kathryn C. Statler and Andrew L. Johns, eds., *The Eisenhower Administration, the Third World, and the Globalization of the Cold War* (2006).

Philip Taubman, *Secret Empire: Eisenhower, the CIA, and the Hidden Story of America's Space Espionage* (2003).

Salim Yaqub, *Containing Arab Nationalism: The Eisenhower Doctrine and the Middle East* (2004).

ECONOMIC AND SOCIAL DEVELOPMENTS

Lizabeth Cohen, *A Consumers' Republic: The Politics of Mass Consumption in Postwar America* (2003).

Gail Cooper, *Air-Conditioning America: Engineers and the Controlled Environment, 1900–1960* (1998).

Carlos Eire, *Waiting for Snow in Havana: Confessions of a Cuban Boy* (2004).

Kenneth T. Jackson, *Crabgrass Frontier: The Suburbanization of the United States* (1985).

Michael Johns, *Moment of Grace: The American City in the 1950s* (2002).

Fred Kaplan, *1959: The Year Everything Changed* (2009).

Jennifer Klein, *For All These Rights: Business, Labor, and the Shaping of America's Public-Private Welfare State* (2003).

Tom Lewis, *Divided Highways: Building the Interstate Highways, Transforming American Life* (1999).

David Oshinsky, *Polio: An American Story* (2005).

Adam Rome, *The Bulldozer in the Countryside: Suburban Sprawl and the Rise of American Environmentalism* (2001).

Bruce J. Schulman, *From Cotton Belt to Sunbelt: Federal Policy, Economic Development, and the Transformation of the South, 1938–1980* (1994).

GENDER, THE FAMILY, AND CULTURE

Glenn C. Altschuler, *All Shook Up: How Rock 'n' Roll Changed America* (2004).

Erik Barnouw, *Tube of Plenty: The Evolution of American Television* (rev. ed., 1990).

Stephanie Coontz, *The Way We Never Were: American Families and the Nostalgia Trip* (1992).

Robert Ellwood, *The Fifties Spiritual Marketplace: American Religion in a Decade of Conflict* (1997).

Elizabeth Fraterrigo, *Playboy and the Making of the Good Life in Modern America* (Oxford, 2009).

James Gilbert, *Men in the Middle: Searching for Masculinity in the 1950s* (2005).

James Howard Jones, *Alfred C. Kinsey: A Public/Private Life* (1998).

Elaine Tyler May, *Homeward Bound: American Families in the Cold War Era* (1988).

Anna McCarthy, *The Citizen Machine: Governing by Television in 1950s America* (2010).

Joanne Meyerowitz, ed., *Not June Cleaver: Women and Gender in Postwar America, 1945–1960* (1994).

Lynn Spigel, *Make Room for TV: Television and the Family Ideal in Postwar America* (1992).

Steven Watson, *The Birth of the Beat Generation: Visionaries, Rebels, and Hipsters, 1944–1960* (1995).

MINORITIES AND CIVIL RIGHTS

Melba Patillo Beals, *Warriors Don't Cry: A Searing Memoir of the Battle to Integrate Little Rock's Central High* (1994).

Taylor Branch, *Parting the Waters: America in the King Years, 1954–1963* (1988).

Mary L. Dudziak, *Cold War Civil Rights: Race and the Image of American Democracy* (2000).

David J. Garrow, ed., *The Montgomery Boycott and the Women Who Started It: The Memoir of Jo Ann Gibson Robinson* (1987).

Michael J. Klarman, *From Jim Crow to Civil Rights: The Supreme Court and the Struggle for Racial Equality* (2004).

Richard Kluger, *Simple Justice: The History of Brown v. Board of Education and Black America's Struggle for Racial Equality* (rev. ed., 2004).

David A. Nichols, *A Matter of Justice: Eisenhower and the Beginning of the Civil Rights Revolution* (2007).

James T. Patterson, *Brown v. Board of Education: A Civil Rights Milestone and Its Troubled Legacy* (2001).

Barbara Ransby, *Ella Baker and the Black Freedom Movement* (2003).

Thomas J. Sugrue, *Sweet Land of Liberty: The Forgotten Struggle for Civil Rights in the North* (2008).

Patricia Sullivan, *Lift Every Voice: The NAACP and the Making of the Civil Rights Movement* (2009).

Roberta Ulrich, *American Indian Nations from Termination to Restoration, 1953–2006* (2010).

Juan Williams, *Thurgood Marshall: American Revolutionary* (1998).

Chapter 28

THE BLACK FREEDOM STRUGGLE

Raymond Arsenault, *Freedom Riders: 1961 and the Struggle for Racial Justice* (2006).

Ari Berman, *Give Us the Ballot: The Modern Struggle for Voting Rights in America* (2015).

Martha Biondi, *To Stand and Fight: The Struggle for Civil Rights in Postwar New York City* (2003).

Joshua Bloom and Waldo E. Martin Jr., *Black Against Empire: The History and Politics of the Black Panther Party* (2013).

Taylor Branch, *America in the King Years*, 3 vols. (1988, 1998, 2006).

John D'Emilio, *Lost Prophet: the Life and Times of Bayard Rustin* (2003).

Wesley C. Hogan, *Many Minds, One Heart: SNCC's Dream for a New America* (2009).

William P. Jones, *The March on Washington: Jobs, Freedom, and the Forgotten History of Civil Rights* (2013).

Peniel E. Joseph, *Dark Days, Bright Nights: From Black Power to Barack Obama* (2010).

Chana Kai Lee, *For Freedom's Sake: The Life of Fannie Lou Hamer* (1999).

Manning Marable, *Malcolm X: A Life of Reinvention* (2011).

Gary May, *Bending toward Justice: The Voting Rights Act and the Transformation of American Democracy* (2013).

Charles Payne, *I've Got the Light of Freedom: The Organizing Tradition and the Mississippi Freedom Struggle* (1995).

Barbara Ransby, *Ella Baker and the Black Freedom Movement: A Radical Democratic Vision* (2003).

Timothy Tyson, *Radio Free Dixie: Robert F. Williams and the Roots of Black Power* (1999).

Bruce Watson, *Freedom Summer: The Savage Season That Made Mississippi Burn and Made America a Democracy* (2010).

POLITICS, POLICIES, AND COURT DECISIONS

David C. Carter, *The Music Has Gone Out of the Movement: Civil Rights and the Johnson Administration, 1965–1968* (2009).

Robert Dallek, *An Unfinished Life: John F. Kennedy, 1917–1963* (2003).

Maurice Isserman and Michael Kazin, *America Divided: The Civil War of the 1960s* (2000).

Michael B. Katz, *The Undeserving Poor: From the War on Poverty to the War on Welfare* (1989).

Nancy MacLean, *Freedom Is Not Enough: The Opening of the American Workplace* (2006).

Gerald Posner, *Case Closed: Lee Harvey Oswald and the Assassination of JFK* (1993).

Lucas A. Powe Jr., *The Warren Court and American Politics* (2000).

John D. Skrentny, *The Minority Rights Revolution* (2002).

Melvin Small, *The Presidency of Richard Nixon* (2003).

Irwin Unger, *The Best of Intentions: The Triumph and Failure of the Great Society* (1996).

Randall B. Woods, *LBJ: Architect of American Ambition* (2006).

PROTEST MOVEMENTS

Terry H. Anderson, *The Movement and the Sixties* (1995).

David Barber, *A Hard Rain Fell: SDS and Why It Failed* (2010).

Stefan M. Bradley, *Harlem vs. Columbia University: Black Student Power in the Late 1960s* (2009).

Daniel M. Cobb, *Native Activism in Cold War America: The Struggle for Sovereignty* (2008).

John D'Emilio, William B. Turner, and Urvashi Vaid, *Creating Change: Sexuality, Public Policy, and Civil Rights* (2000).

Lillian Faderman, *The Gay Revolution: The Story of the Struggle* (2015).

Matt Garcia, *From the Jaws of Victory: The Triumph and Tragedy of Cesar Chavez and the Farm Worker Movement* (2012).

Troy R. Johnson, *The American Indian Occupation of Alcatraz Island: Red Power and Self-Determination* (2008).

Ian F. Haney López, *Racism on Trial: The Chicano Fight for Justice* (2003).

Daryl J. Maeda, *Chains of Babylon: The Rise of Asian America* (2009).

Malcolm McLaughlin, *The Long, Hot Summer of 1967: Urban Rebellion in America* (2014).

Adam Rome, *The Genius of Earth Day: How a 1970 Teach-in Unexpectedly Made the First Green Generation* (2013).

F. Arturo Rosales, *Chicano! The History of the Mexican American Civil Rights Movement* (1997).

Bradley G. Shreve, *Red Power Rising: The National Indian Youth Council and the Origins of Native Activism* (2011).

Chapter 29

FOREIGN POLICY UNDER KENNEDY, JOHNSON, AND NIXON

Beth Bailey, *America's Army: Making the All-Volunteer Force* (2009).

Warren Bass, *Support Any Friend: Kennedy's Middle East and the Making of the U.S.-Israel Alliance* (2003).

H. W. Brands, *The Wages of Globalism: Lyndon Johnson and the Limits of American Power* (1995).

Robert Dallek, *Nixon and Kissinger: Partners in Power* (2007).

Michael Dobbs, *One Minute to Midnight: Kennedy, Khrushchev, and Castro on the Brink of Nuclear War* (2008).

Michael Grow, *U.S. Presidents and Latin American Interventions: Pursuing Regime Change in the Cold War* (2008).

Elizabeth Cobbs Hoffman, *All You Need Is Love: The Peace Corps and the Spirit of the 1960s* (1998).

Howard Jones, *The Bay of Pigs* (2008).

Frederick Kempe, *Berlin 1961: Kennedy, Khrushchev, and the Most Dangerous Place on Earth* (2011).

Margaret Macmillan, *Nixon and Mao: The Week That Changed the World* (2007).

Walter A. McDougall, *The Heavens and the Earth: A Political History of the Space Age* (1985).

Keith L. Nelson, *The Making of Détente: Soviet-American Relations in the Shadow of Vietnam* (1995).

Robert B. Rakove, *Kennedy, Johnson, and the Nonaligned World* (2013).

Thomas Alan Schwartz, *Lyndon Johnson and Europe: In the Shadow of Vietnam* (2003).

Jeremi Suri, *Power and Protest: Global Revolution and the Rise of Détente* (2003).

THE WAR IN VIETNAM

Mark Philip Bradley, *Vietnam at War* (2009).

Arnold R. Isaacs, *Vietnam Shadows: The War, Its Ghosts, and Its Legacy* (1997).

David Kaiser, *American Tragedy: Kennedy, Johnson, and the Origins of the Vietnam War* (2000).

Jeffrey P. Kimball, *Nixon's Vietnam War* (1998).

A. J. Langguth, *Our Vietnam / Nuoc Viet Ta: A History of the War, 1954–1975* (2000).

Mark Atwood Lawrence, *The Vietnam War: A Concise International History* (2008).

Fredrik Logevall, *Choosing War: The Lost Chance for Peace and the Escalation of the War in Vietnam* (1999); *Embers of War: The Fall of an Empire and the Making of America's Vietnam* (2013).

Daniel S. Lucks, *Selma to Saigon: The Civil Rights Movement and the Vietnam War* (2014).

David Maraniss, *They Marched into Sunlight: War, Peace, Vietnam, and America, October 1967* (2004).

James Willbanks, *The Tet Offensive: A Concise History* (2008).

THOSE WHO SERVED

Christian G. Appy, *Working-Class War: American Combat Soldiers in Vietnam* (1993).

Philip Caputo, *A Rumor of War* (1977).

David Donovan, *Once a Warrior King: Memories of an Officer in Vietnam* (1985).

Frederick Downs, *The Killing Zone: My Life in the Vietnam War* (1978); *Aftermath: A Soldier's Return from Vietnam* (1984); *No Longer Enemies, Not Yet Friends: An American Soldier Returns to Vietnam* (1991).

Harry Maurer, *Strange Ground: Americans in Vietnam, 1945–1975, an Oral History* (1998).

Tim O'Brien, *If I Die in a Combat Zone, Box Me Up and Ship Me Home* (1992).

Al Santoli, *Everything We Had: An Oral History of the Vietnam War* (1981).

William J. Shkurti, *Soldiering On in a Dying War: The True Story of the Firebase Pace Incidents and the Vietnam Drawdown* (2011).

Kara Dixon Vuic, *Officer, Nurse, Woman: The Army Nurse Corps in the Vietnam War* (2010).

James E. Westheider, *Fighting on Two Fronts: African Americans and the Vietnam War* (1997).

POLITICS AND THE ANTIWAR MOVEMENT

Dan T. Carter, *The Politics of Race: George Wallace, the Origins of the New Conservatism, and the Transformation of American Politics* (1995).

Michael S. Foley, *Confronting the War Machine: Draft Resistance during the Vietnam War* (2007).

Adam Garfinkle, *Telltale Hearts: The Origins and Impact of the Vietnam Anti-War Movement* (1997).

Lewis L. Gould, *1968: The Election That Changed America* (rev. ed., 2010).

Simon Hall, *Rethinking the American Anti-War Movement* (2011).

Andrew E. Hunt, *The Turning: A History of Vietnam Veterans against the War* (1999).

Rhodri Jeffreys-Jones, *Peace Now! American Society and the Ending of the Vietnam War* (1999).

Martin Klimke, *The Other Alliance: Student Protest in West Germany and the United States in the Global Sixties* (2009).

Lorena Orpesa, *Raza Sí!, Guerra No!: Chicano Protest and Patriotism During the Viet Nam War Era* (2005).

David Rudenstine, *The Day the Presses Stopped: A History of the Pentagon Papers Case* (1996).

Sandra Scanlon, *The Pro-War Movement: Domestic Support for the Vietnam War and the Making of Modern American Conservatism* (2013).

Amy Swerdlow, *Women Strike for Peace: Traditional Motherhood and Radical Politics in the 1960s* (1993).

Chapter 30

GENERAL WORKS

Edward D. Berkowitz, *Something Happened: A Political and Cultural Overview of the Seventies* (2006).

Thomas Borstelman, *The 1970s: A New Global History from Civil Rights to Economic Inequality* (2011).

Laura Kalman, *Right Star Rising: A New Politics, 1974–1980* (2010).

Burton I. Kaufman and Scott Kaufman, *The Presidency of James Earl Carter, Jr.* (2006).

Robert Mason, *Richard Nixon and the Quest for a New Majority* (2004).

Keith W. Olson, *Watergate: The Presidential Scandal That Shook America* (2003).

James T. Patterson, *Restless Giant: The United States from Watergate to* Bush v. Gore (2005).

Doug Rossinow, *The Reagan Era: A History of the 1980s* (2015).

Gil Troy, *Morning in America: How Ronald Reagan Invented the 1980s* (2005).

Sean Wilentz, *The Age of Reagan: A History, 1974–2008* (2008).

FOREIGN POLICY

David Crist, *The Twilight War: The Secret History of America's Thirty-Year Conflict with Iran* (2012).

Marc Ensalaco, *Middle Eastern Terrorism: From Black September to September 11* (2008).

David Farber, *Taken Hostage: The Iran Hostage Crisis and America's First Encounter with Radical Islam* (2004).

Scott Kaufman, *Plans Unraveled: The Foreign Policy of the Carter Administration* (2008).

William M. LeoGrande, *Our Own Backyard: The United States in Central America, 1977–1992* (1998).

Douglas Little, *American Orientalism: The United States and the Middle East since 1945* (2002).

James Mann, *The Rebellion of Ronald Reagan: A History of the End of the Cold War* (2009).

THE ECONOMY, ENERGY, AND THE ENVIRONMENT

W. Carl Biven, *Jimmy Carter's Economy: Policy in an Age of Limits* (2003).

Elizabeth D. Blum, *Love Canal Revisited: Race, Class, and Gender in Environmental Activism* (2008).

Phillip J. Cooper, *The War against Regulation: From Jimmy Carter to George W. Bush* (2009).

Jefferson Cowie, *Stayin' Alive: The 1970s and the Last Days of the Working Class* (2010).

Samuel P. Hays, *A History of Environmental Politics since 1945* (2000).

Meg Jacobs, *Panic at the Pump: The Energy Crisis and the Transformation of American Politics in the 1970s* (2016).

John W. Sloan, *The Reagan Effect: Economics and Presidential Leadership* (1999).

Judith Stein, *Pivotal Decade: How the United States Traded Factories for Finance in the Seventies* (2010).

SOCIAL MOVEMENTS AND CONTESTS OVER RIGHTS

Terry H. Anderson, *The Pursuit of Fairness: A History of Affirmative Action* (2004).

John A. Andrew, *The Other Side of the Sixties: Young Americans for Freedom and the Rise of Conservative Politics* (1997).

Donald T. Critchlow, *Phyllis Schlafly and Grassroots Conservatism: A Woman's Crusade* (2005).

J. Brooks Flippen, *Jimmy Carter, the Politics of Family, and the Rise of the Religious Right* (2011).

Linda Hirshman, *Victory: The Triumphant Gay Revolution—How a Despised Minority Pushed Back, Beat Death, Found Love, and Changed America for Everyone* (2012).

J. Anthony Lukas, *Common Ground: A Turbulent Decade in the Lives of Three American Families* (1986).

Bradford Martin, *The Other Eighties: A Secret History of America in the Age of Reagan* (2011).

Carol Mason, *Reading Appalachia from Left to Right: Conservatives and the 1974 Kanawha County Textbook Controversy* (2009).

Donald G. Mathews and Jane Sherron De Hart, *Sex, Gender, and the Politics of the ERA* (1990).

Lisa McGirr, *Suburban Warriors: The Origins of the New American Right* (2001).

Kim Phillips-Fein, *Invisible Hands: The Making of the Conservative Movement from the New Deal to Reagan* (2009).

Robert O. Self, *All in the Family: The Realignment of American Democracy since the 1960s* (2012).

James F. Simon, *The Center Holds: The Power Struggle inside the Rehnquist Court* (1995).

Daniel K. Williams, *God's Own Party: The Making of the Christian Right* (2010).

Chapter 31

DOMESTIC POLITICS, POLICIES, AND ECONOMIC CHANGE

Jonathan Alter, *The Center Holds: Obama and His Enemies* (2013).

Alan S. Blinder, *After the Music Stopped: The Financial Crisis, the Response, and the Work Ahead* (2013).

Douglas Brinkley, *The Great Deluge: Hurricane Katrina, New Orleans, and the Mississippi Gulf Coast* (2006).

Alfred D. Chandler Jr., *Inventing the Electronic Century: The Epic Story of the Consumer Electronics and Computer Science Industries* (2001).

John F. Harris, *The Survivor: Bill Clinton in the White House* (2005).

John Meacham, *Destiny and Power: The American Odyssey of George Herbert Walker Bush* (2015).

Bruce D. Meyer and Douglas Holtz-Eakin, *Making Work Pay: The Earned Income Tax Credit and Its Impact on America's Families* (2002).

Jack N. Rakove, ed., *The Unfinished Election of 2000* (2001).

Richard K. Scotch, *From Good Will to Civil Rights: Transforming Federal Disability Policy* (rev. ed., 2001).

David K. Shipler, *The Working Poor: Invisible in America* (2004).

Theda Skocpol and Vanessa Williamson, *The Tea Party and the Remaking of Republican Conservatism* (2012).

Jean Edward Smith, *Bush* (2016).

Paul Starr, *Remedy and Reaction: The Peculiar American Struggle over Health Care Reform* (2011).

Joseph E. Stiglitz, *The Price of Inequality* (2012).

GLOBALIZATION AND IMMIGRATION

Frank D. Bean and Gillian Stevens, *America's Newcomers and the Dynamics of Diversity* (2003).

Jeremy Brecher, Tim Costello, and Brendan Smith, *Globalization from Below* (2000).

Otis L. Graham, *Unguarded Gates: A History of America's Immigration Crisis* (2004).

John R. MacArthur, *The Selling of "Free Trade": NAFTA, Washington, and the Subversion of American Democracy* (2000).

David M. Reimers, *Other Immigrants: The Global Origins of the American People* (2005).

Joseph E. Stiglitz, *Globalization and Its Discontents* (2002).

FOREIGN POLICY AFTER THE COLD WAR

Andrew J. Bacevich, *American Empire: The Realities and Consequences of U.S. Diplomacy* (2002).

Ivo H. Daalder and James M. Lindsay, *America Unbound: The Bush Revolution in Foreign Policy* (2003).

Karen DeYoung, *Soldier: The Life of Colin Powell* (2006).

David Halberstam, *War in a Time of Peace: Bush, Clinton, and the Generals* (2001).

James Mann, *Rise of the Vulcans: The History of Bush's War Cabinet* (2004).

Christopher Maynard, *Out of the Shadow: George H. W. Bush and the End of the Cold War* (2008).

Richard Sale, *Clinton's Secret Wars: The Evolution of a Commander in Chief* (2009).

TERRORISM AND THE AFGHAN AND IRAQ WARS

Beth Bailey and Richard H. Immerman, *Understanding the U.S. Wars in Iraq and Afghanistan* (2015).

Peter L. Bergen, *The Longest War: The Enduring Conflict Between America and Al Qaeda* (2011).

Peter Hahn, *Missions Accomplished?: The United States and Iraq Since World War I* (2011).

Seth G. Jones, *In the Graveyard of Empires: America's War in Afghanistan* (2009).

Daniel Levitas, *The Terrorist Next Door: The Militia Movement and the Radical Right* (2002).

Jane Mayer, *The Dark Side: The Inside Story of How the War on Terror Turned into a War on American Ideals* (2008).

National Commission on Terrorist Attacks, *The 9/11 Commission Report: Final Report of the National Commission on Terrorist Attacks upon the United States* (2004).

George Packer, *The Assassins' Gate: America in Iraq* (2005).

Anthony Shadid, *Night Draws Near: Iraq's People in the Shadow of America's War* (2005).

Scott Shane, *Objective Troy: A Terrorist, a President, and the Rise of the Drone* (2015).

Joby Warrick, *Black Flags: The Rise of Isis* (2015).

Lawrence Wright, *The Terror Years: From Al-Qaeda to the Islamic State* (2016).

Glossary

Acoma pueblo revolt Revolt against the Spaniards by Indians living at the Acoma pueblo in 1599. Juan de Oñate violently suppressed the uprising, but the Indians revolted again later that year, after which many Spanish settlers returned to Mexico.

Agent Orange Herbicide used extensively during the Vietnam War to destroy the Vietcong's jungle hideouts and food supply. Its use was later linked to a wide range of illnesses that veterans and the Vietnamese suffered after the war, including birth defects, cancer, and skin disorders.

Agricultural Adjustment Act (AAA) New Deal legislation passed in May 1933 aimed at cutting agricultural production and raising crop prices and, consequently, farmers' income. Through the "domestic allotment plan," the AAA paid farmers to not grow crops.

Algonquian Indians People who inhabited the coastal plain of present-day Virginia, near the Chesapeake Bay, when English colonists first settled the region.

Alien and Sedition Acts 1798 laws passed to suppress political dissent. The Sedition Act criminalized conspiracy and criticism of government leaders. The two Alien Acts extended the waiting period for citizenship and empowered the president to deport or imprison without trial any foreigner deemed a danger.

American Colonization Society An organization dedicated to sending freed slaves and other black Americans to Liberia in West Africa. Although some African Americans cooperated with the movement, others campaigned against segregation and discrimination.

American Expeditionary Force (AEF) American armed forces under the command of General John Pershing who fought under a separate American command in Europe during World War I. They helped defeat Germany when they entered the conflict in full force in 1918.

American Federation of Labor (AFL) Organization created by Samuel Gompers in 1886 that coordinated the activities of craft unions throughout the United States. The AFL worked to achieve immediate benefits for skilled workers. Its narrow goals for unionism became popular after the Haymarket bombing.

American Indian Movement (AIM) Organization established in 1968 to address the problems Indians faced in American cities, including poverty and police harassment. AIM organized Indians to end relocation and termination policies and to win greater control over their cultures and communities.

American system The practice of manufacturing and then assembling interchangeable parts. A system that spread quickly across American industries, the use of standardized parts allowed American manufacturers to employ cheap, unskilled workers.

American Temperance Society Organization founded in 1826 by Lyman Beecher that linked drinking with poverty, idleness, ill-health, and violence. Temperance lecturers traveled the country gaining converts to the cause. The temperance movement had considerable success, contributing to a sharp drop in American alcohol consumption.

Americans with Disabilities Act (ADA) Legislation signed by President George W. Bush in 1990 that banned discrimination against the disabled. The law also required handicapped accessibility in public facilities and private businesses.

Antifederalists Opponents of ratification of the Constitution. Antifederalists feared that a powerful and distant central government would be out of touch with the needs of citizens. They also complained that the Constitution failed to guarantee individual liberties in a bill of rights.

antinomians Individuals who believed that Christians could be saved by faith alone and did not need to act in accordance with God's law as set forth in the Bible. Puritan leaders considered this belief to be a heresy.

Apollo program Project initiated by John F. Kennedy in 1961 to surpass the Soviet Union in space exploration and send a man to the moon.

appeasement British strategy aimed at avoiding a war with Germany in the late 1930s by not objecting to Hitler's policy of territorial expansion.

Archaic Indians Hunting and gathering peoples who descended from Paleo-Indians and dominated the Americas from 10,000 BP to between 4000 and 3000 BP, approximately.

Articles of Confederation The written document defining the structure of the government from 1781 to 1788 under which the union was a confederation of equal states, with no executive and limited powers, existing mainly to foster a common defense.

baby boom The surge in the American birthrate between 1945 and 1965, which peaked in 1957 with 4.3 million births. The baby boom both reflected and promoted Americans' postwar prosperity.

Bacon's Rebellion An unsuccessful rebellion against the colonial government in 1676, led by frontier settler Nathaniel Bacon, that arose when increased violence between Indians and colonists pushing westward was met with government refusal to protect settlers or allow them to settle Indian lands.

Barbados Colonized in the 1630s, this island in the English West Indies became an enormous sugar producer and a source of wealth for England. The island's African slaves quickly became a majority of the island's population despite the deadliness of their work.

battle of Antietam Battle fought in Maryland on September 17, 1862, between the Union forces of George McClellan and Confederate troops of Robert E. Lee. The battle, a Union victory that left 6,000 dead and 17,000 wounded, was the bloodiest day of the war.

battle of Bull Run (Manassas) First major battle of the Civil War, fought at a railroad junction in northern Virginia on July 21, 1861. The Union suffered a sobering defeat, while the Confederates felt affirmed in their superiority and the inevitability of Confederate nationhood.

battle of Bunker Hill Second battle of the Revolutionary War, on June 16, 1775, involving a massive British attack on New England militia units on a hill facing Boston. The militiamen finally yielded the hill, but not before inflicting heavy casualties on the British.

battle of Gettysburg Battle fought at Gettysburg, Pennsylvania (July 1–3, 1863), between Union forces under General Meade and Confederate forces under General Lee. The Union emerged victorious, and Lee lost more than one-third of his men. Together with Vicksburg, Gettysburg marked a major turning point in the Civil War.

Battle of the Little Big Horn 1876 battle begun when American cavalry under George Armstrong Custer attacked an encampment of Indians who refused to remove to a reservation. Indian warriors led by Crazy Horse and Sitting Bull annihilated the American soldiers, but their victory was short-lived.

battle of Long Island First major engagement of the new Continental army, defending against 45,000 British troops newly arrived on western Long Island (today Brooklyn). The Continentals retreated, with high casualties and many taken prisoner.

Battle of Midway June 3–6, 1942, naval battle in the Central Pacific in which American forces surprised and defeated the Japanese who had been massing an invasion force aimed at Midway Island. The battle put the Japanese at a disadvantage for the rest of the war.

battle of New Orleans The final battle in the War of 1812, fought and won by General Andrew Jackson and his militiamen against the much larger British army in New Orleans. The celebrated battle made no difference since the peace had already been negotiated.

battle of Oriskany A punishing defeat for Americans in a ravine named Oriskany near Fort Stanwix in New York in August 1777. German American militiamen aided by allied Oneida warriors were ambushed by Mohawk and Seneca Indians, and 400 on the revolutionary side were killed.

battle of Saratoga A multistage battle in New York ending with the decisive defeat and surrender of British general John Burgoyne on October 17, 1777. France was convinced by this victory to throw its official support to the American side in the war.

battle of Shiloh Battle at Shiloh Church, Tennessee, on April 6–7, 1862, between Albert Sidney Johnston's Confederate forces and Ulysses S. Grant's Union army. The Union army ultimately prevailed, though at great cost to both sides. Shiloh ruined the Confederacy's bid to control the war in the West.

battle of Tippecanoe An attack on Shawnee Indians at Prophetstown on the Tippecanoe River in 1811 by American forces headed by William Henry Harrison, Indiana's territorial governor. The Prophet Tenskwatawa fled with his followers. Tecumseh, his brother, deepened his resolve to make war on the United States.

battle of Yorktown October 1781 battle that sealed American victory in the Revolutionary War. American troops and a French fleet trapped the British army under the command of General Charles Cornwallis at Yorktown, Virginia.

Bay of Pigs Failed U.S.-sponsored invasion of Cuba by anti-Castro forces in 1961 who planned to overthrow Fidel Castro's government. The disaster humiliated Kennedy and the United States. It alienated Latin Americans who saw the invasion as another example of Yankee imperialism.

Beringia The land bridge between Siberia and Alaska that was exposed by the Wisconsin glaciation, allowing people to migrate into the Western Hemisphere.

Berlin Wall Structure erected by East Germany in 1961 to stop the massive exodus of East Germans into West Berlin, which was an embarrassment to the Communists.

Bill of Rights The first ten amendments to the Constitution, officially ratified by 1791. The First through Eighth Amendments dealt with individual liberties, and the Ninth and Tenth concerned the boundary between federal and state authority.

birth control movement Movement launched in 1915 by Margaret Sanger in New York's Lower East Side. Birth control advocates hoped contraception would alter social and political power relationships by reducing the numbers of the working class to induce higher wages and by limiting the supply of soldiers to end wars.

black codes Laws passed by state governments in the South in 1865 and 1866 that sought to keep ex-slaves subordinate to whites. At the core of the black codes lay the desire to force freedmen back to the plantations.

Black Death A disease that in the mid-fourteenth century killed about a third of the European population and left a legacy of increased food and resources for the survivors as well as a sense of a world in precarious balance.

Black Hills Mountains in western South Dakota and northeast Wyoming that are sacred to the Lakota Sioux. In the 1868 Treaty of Fort Laramie, the United States guaranteed Indians control of the Black Hills, but it broke its promise after gold was discovered there in 1874.

black power movement Movement of the 1960s and 1970s that emphasized black racial pride and autonomy. Black power advocates encouraged African Americans to assert community control, and some within the movement also rejected the ethos of nonviolence.

"Bleeding Kansas" Term for the bloody struggle between proslavery and antislavery factions in Kansas following its organization in the fall of 1854. Corrupt election tactics led to a proslavery victory, but free-soil Kansans established a rival territorial government, and violence quickly ensued.

Bolshevik Russian revolutionary. Bolsheviks forced Czar Nicholas II to abdicate and seized power in Russia in 1917. In a separate peace with Germany, the Bolshevik government withdrew Russia from World War I.

Bonus Marchers World War I veterans who marched on Washington, D.C., in 1932 to lobby for immediate payment of the pension ("bonus") promised them in 1924. President Herbert Hoover believed the bonuses would bankrupt the government and sent the U.S. Army to evict the veterans from the city.

bossism Pattern of urban political organization that arose in the late nineteenth century in which an often corrupt "boss" maintains an inordinate level of power through command of a political machine that distributes services to its constituents.

Boston Massacre March 1770 incident in Boston in which British soldiers fired on an American crowd, killing five. The Boston Massacre became a rallying point for colonists who increasingly saw the British government as tyrannical and illegitimate.

Boxer uprising Uprising in China led by the Boxers, an antiforeign society, in which 30,000 Chinese converts and 250 foreign Christians were killed. An international force rescued foreigners in Beijing, and European powers imposed the humiliating Boxer Protocol on China in 1901.

Brown v. Board of Education 1954 Supreme Court ruling that overturned the "separate but equal" precedent established in *Plessy v. Ferguson* in 1896. The Court declared that separate educational facilities were inherently unequal and thus violated the Fourteenth Amendment.

burial mounds Earthen mounds constructed by ancient American peoples, especially throughout the gigantic drainage of the Ohio and Mississippi rivers, after about 2500 BP and often used to bury important leaders and to enact major ceremonies.

Cahokia The largest ceremonial site in ancient North America, located on the eastern bank of the Mississippi River across from present-day St. Louis, where thousands of inhabitants built hundreds of earthen mounds between about AD 700 and AD 1400.

California gold rush Mining rush initiated by James Marshall's discovery of gold in the foothills of the Sierra Nevada in 1848. The hope of striking it rich drew over 250,000 aspiring miners to California between 1849 and 1852 and accelerated the push for statehood.

Calvinism Christian doctrine of Swiss Protestant theologian John Calvin. Its chief tenet was predestination, the idea that God had determined which human souls would receive eternal salvation. Despite this, Calvinism promoted strict discipline in daily and religious life.

Camp David accords Agreements between Egypt and Israel reached at the 1979 talks hosted by President Carter at Camp David. In the accords, Egypt became the first Arab state to recognize Israel, and Israel agreed to gradual withdrawal from the Sinai Peninsula.

Carlisle Indian School Institution established in Pennsylvania in 1879 to educate and assimilate American Indians. It pioneered the "outing system," in which Indian students were sent to live with white families in order to accelerate acculturation.

carpetbaggers Southerners' pejorative term for northern migrants who sought opportunity in the South after the Civil War. Northern migrants formed an important part of the southern Republican Party.

Central Intelligence Agency (CIA) Agency created by the National Security Act of 1947 to expand the government's espionage capacities and ability to thwart communism through covert activities, including propaganda, sabotage, economic warfare, and support for anti-Communist forces around the world.

Chicano movement Mobilization of Mexican Americans in the 1960s and 1970s to fight for civil rights, economic justice, and political power and to combat police brutality. Most notably, the movement worked to improve the lives of migrant farmworkers and to end discrimination in employment and education.

chiefdom Hierarchical social organization headed by a chief. Archaeologists posit that the Woodland cultures were organized into chiefdoms because the construction of their characteristic burial mounds likely required one person having command over the labor of others.

Chinese Exclusion Act 1882 law that effectively barred Chinese immigration and set a precedent for further immigration restrictions. The Chinese population in America dropped sharply as a result of the passage of the act, which was fueled by racial and cultural animosities.

chivalry The South's romantic ideal of male-female relationships. Chivalry's underlying assumptions about the weakness of white women and the protective authority of men resembled the paternalistic defense of slavery.

Civil Rights Act of 1866 Legislation passed by Congress in 1866 that nullified the black codes and affirmed that black Americans should have equal benefit of the law. This expansion of black rights and federal authority drew a veto from President Andrew Johnson, which Congress later overrode.

Civil Rights Act of 1964 Law that responded to demands of the civil rights movement by making discrimination in employment, education, and public accommodations illegal. It was the strongest such measure since Reconstruction and included a ban on sex discrimination in employment.

Civilian Conservation Corps (CCC) Federal relief program established in March 1933 that provided assistance in the form of jobs to millions of unemployed young men and a handful of women. CCC workers worked on conservation projects throughout the nation.

civil service reform Effort in the 1880s to end the spoils system and reduce government corruption. The Pendleton Civil Service Act of 1883 created the Civil Service Commission to award government jobs under a merit system that required examinations for office and made it impossible to remove jobholders for political reasons.

Clean Air Act of 1990 Environmental legislation signed by President George H. W. Bush. The legislation was the strongest and most comprehensive environmental law in the nation's history.

Clovis point Distinctively shaped spearhead used by Paleo-Indians and named for the place in New Mexico where it was first excavated.

Coercive (Intolerable) Acts Four British acts of 1774 meant to punish Massachusetts for the destruction of three shiploads of tea. Known in America as the Intolerable Acts, they led to open rebellion in the northern colonies.

Cold War Term given to the tense and hostile relationship between the United States and the Soviet Union from 1947 to 1989. The term *cold* was apt because the hostility stopped short of direct armed conflict.

Columbian exchange The transatlantic exchange of goods, people, and ideas that began when Columbus arrived in the Caribbean, ending the age-old separation of the hemispheres.

Comanchería Indian empire based on trade in horses, hides, guns, and captives that stretched from the Canadian plains to Mexico in the eighteenth century. By 1865, fewer than five thousand Comanches lived in the empire, which ranged from west Texas north to Oklahoma.

Committee for Industrial Organization (CIO) Coalition (later called the Congress of Industrial Organizations) of mostly unskilled workers formed in 1935 that mobilized massive union organizing drives in major industries. By 1941, through the CIO-affiliated United Auto Workers, organizers had overcome violent resistance to unionize the entire automobile industry.

committees of correspondence A communications network established among towns in Massachusetts and also among colonial capital towns in 1772–1773 to provide for rapid dissemination of news about important political developments. These committees politicized ordinary townspeople, sparking a revolutionary language of rights and duties.

Common Sense Pamphlet written by Thomas Paine in 1776 that laid out the case for independence. In it, Paine rejected monarchy, advocating its replacement with republican government based on the consent of the people. The pamphlet influenced public opinion throughout the colonies.

Compromise of 1850 Laws passed in 1850 meant to resolve the dispute over the spread of slavery in the territories. Key elements included the admission of California as a free state and the Fugitive Slave Act. The Compromise soon unraveled.

Compromise of 1877 Informal agreement in which Democrats agreed not to block Hayes's inauguration and to deal fairly with freedmen, and Hayes vowed not to use the army to uphold the remaining Republican regimes in the South and to provide the South with substantial federal subsidies for railroads. The Compromise brought the Reconstruction era to an end.

Comstock Lode Silver ore deposit discovered in 1859 in Nevada. Discovery of the Comstock Lode touched off a mining rush that brought a diverse population into the region and led to the establishment of a number of boomtowns, including Virginia City, Nevada.

Confederate States of America Government formed by Lower South states on February 7, 1861, following their secession from the Union. Secessionists argued that the election of a Republican to the presidency imperiled slavery and the South no longer had political protection within the Union.

conquistadors Term, literally meaning "conquerors," that refers to the Spanish explorers and soldiers who conquered lands in the New World.

containment The post–World War II foreign policy strategy that committed the United States to resisting the influence and expansion of the Soviet Union and communism. The strategy of containment shaped American foreign policy throughout the Cold War.

Continental army The army created in June 1775 by the Second Continental Congress to oppose the British. Virginian George Washington, commander in chief, had the task of turning local militias and untrained volunteers into a disciplined army.

contraband of war General Benjamin F. Butler's term for runaway slaves, who were considered confiscated property of war, not fugitives, and put to work in the Union army. This policy proved to be a step on the road to emancipation.

cotton kingdom Term for the South that reflected the dominance of cotton in the southern economy. Cotton was particularly important in the tier of states from South Carolina west to Texas. Cotton cultivation was the key factor in the growth of slavery.

court-packing plan Law proposed by Franklin Roosevelt to add one new Supreme Court justice for each existing judge who was over the age of seventy. Roosevelt wanted to pack the Court with up to six New Dealers who could protect New Deal legislation, but the Senate defeated the bill in 1937.

Coxey's army Unemployed men who marched to Washington, D.C., in 1894 to urge Congress to enact a public works program to end unemployment. Jacob S. Coxey of Ohio led the most publicized contingent. The movement failed to force federal relief legislation.

Creek War Part of the War of 1812 involving the Creek nation in Mississippi Territory and Tennessee militiamen. General Andrew Jackson's forces gained victory at the Battle of Horseshoe Bend in 1814, forcing the Creeks to sign away much of their land.

creoles Children born to Spanish parents in the New World who, with the *peninsulares*, made up the tiny portion of the population at the top of the colonial social hierarchy.

Cripple Creek miners' strike of 1894 Strike led by the Western Federation of Miners in response to an attempt to lengthen their workday to ten hours. With the support of local businessmen and the Populist governor of Colorado, the miners successfully maintained an eight-hour day.

Cuban missile crisis 1962 nuclear standoff between the Soviet Union and the United States when the Soviets attempted to deploy nuclear missiles in Cuba. In a negotiated settlement, the Soviet Union agreed to remove its missiles from Cuba, and the United States agreed to remove its missiles from Turkey.

Cuban revolution Uprising led by Fidel Castro that drove out U.S.-supported dictator Fulgencio Batista and eventually allied Cuba with the Soviet Union.

cult of domesticity Nineteenth-century belief that women's place was in the home, where they should create havens for their families. This sentimentalized ideal led to an increase in the hiring of domestic servants and freed white middle-class women to spend time in pursuits outside the home.

Dawes Allotment Act 1887 law that divided up reservations and allotted parcels of land to individual Indians as private property. In the end, the American government sold almost two-thirds of "surplus" Indian land to white settlers. The Dawes Act dealt a crippling blow to traditional tribal culture.

D Day June 6, 1944, the date of the Allied invasion of northern France. D Day was the largest amphibious assault in world history. The invasion opened a second front against the Germans and moved the Allies closer to victory in Europe.

Declaration of Independence A document containing philosophical principles and a list of grievances that declared separation from Britain. Adopted by the Second Continental Congress on July 4, 1776, it ended a period of intense debate with moderates still hoping to reconcile with Britain.

Declaratory Act 1766 law issued by Parliament to assert Parliament's unassailable right to legislate for its British colonies "in all cases whatsoever," putting Americans on notice that the simultaneous repeal of the Stamp Act changed nothing in the imperial powers of Britain.

Democrats Political party that evolved out of the Democratic Republicans after 1834. Strongest in the South and West, the Democrats embraced Andrew Jackson's vision of limited government, expanded political participation for white men, and the promotion of an ethic of individualism.

détente Term given to the easing of conflict between the United States and the Soviet Union during the Nixon administration by focusing on issues of common concern, such as arms control and trade.

domino theory Theory of containment articulated by President Eisenhower in the context of Vietnam. He warned that the fall of a non-Communist government to communism would trigger the spread of communism to neighboring countries.

Double V campaign World War II campaign in America to attack racism at home and abroad. The campaign pushed the federal government to require defense contractors to integrate their workforces. In response, Franklin Roosevelt authorized a committee to investigate and prevent racial discrimination in employment.

***Dred Scott* decision** 1857 Supreme Court decision that ruled the Missouri Compromise unconstitutional. The Court ruled against slave Dred Scott, who claimed travels with his master into free states made him and his family free. The decision also denied the federal government the right to exclude slavery in the territories and declared that African Americans were not citizens.

Earned Income Tax Credit (EITC) Federal antipoverty program initiated in 1975 that assisted the working poor by giving tax breaks to low-income, full-time workers or a subsidy to those who owed no taxes. President Clinton pushed through a significant increase in the program in 1993.

Economic Recovery Tax Act Legislation passed by Congress in 1981 that authorized the largest reduction in taxes in the nation's history. The tax cuts benefited affluent Americans disproportionately and widened the distribution of American wealth in favor of the rich.

Eighteenth Amendment (prohibition) Amendment banning the manufacture, transportation, and sale of alcohol. Congress passed the amendment in December 1917, and it was ratified in January 1920. World War I provided a huge boost to the crusade to ban alcohol.

Eisenhower Doctrine President Eisenhower's 1957 declaration that the United States would actively combat communism in the Middle East. Following this doctrine, Congress approved the policy, and Eisenhower sent aid to Jordan in 1957 and troops to Lebanon in 1958.

Ellis Island Immigration facility opened in 1892 in New York harbor that processed new immigrants coming into New York City. In the late nineteenth century, some 75 percent of European immigrants to America came through New York.

Emancipation Proclamation President Lincoln's proclamation issued on January 1, 1863, declaring all slaves in Confederate-controlled territory free. The proclamation made the Civil War a war for abolition, though its limitations—exemptions for loyal border states and Union-occupied areas of the Confederacy—made some ridicule the act.

Embargo Act of 1807 Act of Congress that prohibited U.S. ships from traveling to foreign ports and effectively banned overseas trade in an attempt to deter Britain from halting U.S. ships at sea. The embargo caused grave hardships for Americans engaged in overseas commerce.

encomienda A system for governing used during the Reconquest and in New Spain. It allowed the Spanish *encomendero*, or "owner" of a town, to collect tribute from the town in return for providing law and order and encouraging "his" Indians to convert to Christianity.

English Reformation Reform effort initiated by King Henry VIII that included banning the Catholic Church and declaring the English monarch head of the new Church of England but little change in doctrine. Henry's primary concern was consolidating his political power.

Enlightenment An eighteenth-century philosophical movement that emphasized the use of reason to reevaluate previously accepted doctrines and traditions. Enlightenment ideas encouraged examination of the world and independence of mind.

Environmental Protection Agency (EPA) Federal agency created by President Nixon in 1970 to enforce environmental laws, conduct environmental research, and reduce human health and environmental risks from pollutants.

Equal Rights Amendment (ERA) Constitutional amendment passed by Congress in 1972 requiring equal treatment of men and women under federal and state law. Facing fierce opposition from the New Right and the Republican Party, the ERA was defeated as time ran out for state ratification in 1982.

Erie Canal Canal finished in 1825, covering 350 miles between Albany and Buffalo and linking the port of New York City with the entire Great Lakes region. The canal turned New York City into the country's premier commercial city.

family economy Economic contributions of multiple members of a household that were necessary to the survival of the family. From the late nineteenth century into the twentieth, many working-class families depended on the wages of all family members, regardless of sex or age.

Farmers' Alliance Movement to form local organizations to advance farmers' collective interests that gained wide popularity in the 1880s. Over time, farmers' groups consolidated into the Northwestern Farmers' Alliance and the Southern Farmers' Alliance. In 1892, the Farmers' Alliance gave birth to the People's Party.

Federal Deposit Insurance Corporation (FDIC) Regulatory body established by the Glass-Steagall Banking Act that guaranteed the federal government would reimburse bank depositors if their banks failed. This key feature of the New Deal restored depositors' confidence in the banking system during the Great Depression.

Federalists One of the two dominant political groups that emerged in the 1790s. Federalist leaders supported Britain in foreign policy and commercial interests at home. Prominent Federalists included George Washington, Alexander Hamilton, and John Adams.

feme covert Legal doctrine grounded in British common law that held that a wife's civic life was subsumed by her husband's. Married women lacked independence to own property, make contracts, or keep wages earned. The doctrine shaped women's status in the early Republic.

Fifteenth Amendment Constitutional amendment passed in February 1869 prohibiting states from depriving any citizen of the right to vote because of "race, color, or previous condition of servitude." It extended black suffrage nationwide. Woman suffrage advocates were disappointed the amendment failed to extend voting rights to women.

finance capitalism Investment sponsored by banks and bankers that typified the American business scene at the end of the nineteenth century. After the panic of 1893, bankers stepped in and reorganized major industries to stabilize them, leaving power concentrated in the hands of a few influential capitalists.

fireside chats Series of informal radio addresses Franklin Roosevelt made to the nation in which he explained New Deal initiatives. The chats helped bolster Roosevelt's popularity and secured popular support for his reforms.

First Continental Congress September 1774 gathering of colonial delegates in Philadelphia to discuss the crisis precipitated by the Coercive Acts. The congress produced a declaration of rights and an agreement to impose a limited boycott of trade with Britain.

first transcontinental railroad Railroad completed in 1869 that was the first to span the North American continent. Built in large part by Chinese laborers, this railroad and others opened access to new areas, which fueled land speculation and actively recruited settlers.

Five-Power Naval Treaty of 1922 Treaty that committed Britain, France, Japan, Italy, and the United States to a proportional reduction of naval forces, producing the world's greatest success in disarmament up to that time. Republicans orchestrated its development at the 1921 Washington Disarmament Conference.

Fort Sumter Union fort on an island at the entrance to Charleston harbor in South Carolina. After Confederate leaders learned President Lincoln intended to resupply Fort Sumter, Confederate forces attacked the fort on April 12, 1861, thus marking the start of the Civil War.

Fourteen Points Woodrow Wilson's plan, proposed in 1918, to create a new democratic world order with lasting peace. Wilson's plan affirmed basic liberal ideals, supported the right to self-determination, and called for the creation of a League of Nations. Wilson compromised on his plan at the 1919 Paris peace conference, and the U.S. Senate refused to ratify the resulting treaty.

Fourteenth Amendment Constitutional amendment passed in 1866 that made all native-born or naturalized persons U.S. citizens and prohibited states from abridging the rights of national citizens. The amendment hoped to guarantee equality before the law for black citizens.

free black An African American who was not enslaved. Southern whites worried about the increasing numbers of free blacks. In the 1820s and 1830s, state legislatures stemmed the growth of the free black population and shrank the liberty of free blacks.

free labor Term referring to work conducted free from constraint and according to the laborer's own inclinations and will. The ideal of free labor lay at the heart of the North's argument that slavery should not be extended into the western territories.

free silver Term used in the late nineteenth century by those who advocated minting silver dollars in addition to supporting the gold standard and the paper currency backed by gold. Western silver barons and poor farmers from the West and South hoped this would result in inflation, effectively providing them with debt relief.

Freedmen's Bureau Government organization created in March 1865 to distribute food and clothing to destitute Southerners and to ease the transition of slaves to free persons. Early efforts by the Freedmen's Bureau to distribute land to the newly freed blacks were later overturned by President Andrew Johnson.

Fugitive Slave Act A law included in the Compromise of 1850 to help attract southern support for the legislative package. Its strict provisions for capturing runaway slaves provoked outrage in the North and intensified antislavery sentiment in the region.

Ghost Dance Religion founded in 1889 by Paiute shaman Wovoka that combined elements of Christianity and traditional Indian religion and served as a nonviolent form of resistance for Indians in the late nineteenth century. The Ghost Dance frightened whites and was violently suppressed.

GI Bill of Rights Legislation passed in 1944 authorizing the government to provide World War II veterans with funds for education, housing, and health care, as well as loans to start businesses and buy homes.

Gilded Age A period of enormous economic growth and ostentatious displays of wealth during the last quarter of the nineteenth century. Industrialization dramatically changed U.S. society and created a newly dominant group of rich entrepreneurs and an impoverished working class.

global migration Movement of populations across large distances such as oceans and continents. In the late nineteenth century, large-scale immigration from southern and eastern Europe into the United States contributed to the growth of cities and changes in American demographics.

good neighbor policy Foreign policy announced by Franklin Roosevelt in 1933 that promised the United States would not interfere in the internal or external affairs of another country, thereby ending U.S. military interventions in Latin America.

gospel of wealth The idea that the financially successful should use their wisdom, experience, and wealth as stewards for the poor. Andrew Carnegie promoted this view in an 1889 essay in which he maintained that the wealthy should serve as stewards of society as a whole.

gradual emancipation A law passed in five northern states that balanced civil rights against property rights by providing a multistage process for freeing slaves, distinguishing persons already alive from those not yet born and providing benchmark dates when freedom would arrive for each group.

Great Awakening Wave of revivals that began in Massachusetts and spread through the colonies in the 1730s and 1740s. The movement emphasized vital religious faith and personal choice. It was characterized by large, open-air meetings at which emotional sermons were given by itinerant preachers.

Great Railroad Strike A violent multicity strike that began in 1877 with West Virginia railroad brakemen who protested against sharp wage reductions and quickly spread to include roughly 600,000 workers. President Rutherford B. Hayes used federal troops to break the strike. Following the strike's failure, union membership surged.

Gulf of Tonkin Resolution Resolution passed by Congress in 1964 in the wake of a naval confrontation in the Gulf of Tonkin. It gave the president virtually unlimited authority in conducting the Vietnam War. The Senate terminated the resolution following outrage over the U.S. invasion of Cambodia in 1970.

Haitian Revolution The 1791–1804 conflict involving diverse Haitian participants and armies from three European countries. At its end, Haiti became a free, independent, black-run country. The Haitian Revolution fueled fears of slave insurrections in the United States.

Halfway Covenant A Puritan compromise established in Massachusetts in 1662 that allowed the unconverted children of visible saints to become "halfway" members of the church and baptize their own children even though they were not full members of the church themselves.

Hartford Convention A secret meeting of New England Federalist politicians held in late 1814 to discuss constitutional changes to reduce the South's political power and thus help block policies that injured northern commercial interests.

Haymarket bombing May 4, 1886, conflict in which both workers and policemen were killed or wounded during a labor demonstration in Chicago. The violence began when someone threw a bomb into the ranks of police at the gathering. The incident created a backlash against labor activism.

headright Fifty acres of free land granted by the Virginia Company to planters for each indentured servant they purchased.

Helsinki accords 1975 agreement signed by U.S., Canadian, Soviet, and European leaders, recognizing the post–World War II borders in Europe and pledging the signatories to respect human rights and fundamental freedoms.

Hernandez v. Texas 1954 Supreme Court decision that found that the systematic exclusion of Mexican Americans from juries violated the constitutional guarantee of equal protection.

Holocaust German effort during World War II to murder Europe's Jews, along with other groups the Nazis deemed "undesirable." Despite reports of the ongoing genocide, the Allies did almost nothing to interfere. In all, some 11 million people were killed in the Holocaust, most of them Jews.

Homestead Act of 1862 Act that promised 160 acres in the trans-Mississippi West free to any citizen or prospective citizen who settled on the land for five years. The act spurred American settlement of the West. Altogether, nearly one-tenth of the United States was granted to settlers.

Homestead lockout 1892 lockout of workers at the Homestead, Pennsylvania, steel mill after Andrew Carnegie refused to renew the union contract and workers prepared to strike. Union supporters attacked the Pinkerton National Detective Agency guards hired to protect the mill, but the National Guard soon broke the strike.

House of Burgesses Organ of government in colonial Virginia made up of an assembly of representatives elected by the colony's male inhabitants. It was established by the Virginia Company and continued by the crown after Virginia was made a royal colony.

House Un-American Activities Committee (HUAC) Congressional committee especially prominent during the early years of the Cold War that investigated

Americans who might be disloyal to the government or might have associated with Communists or other radicals. It was one of the key institutions that promoted the second Red scare.

Housing Act of 1949 Law authorizing the construction of 810,000 units of government housing. This landmark effort marked the first significant commitment of the federal government to meet the housing needs of the poor.

hunter-gatherer A way of life that involved hunting game and gathering food from naturally occurring sources, as opposed to engaging in agriculture and animal husbandry. Archaic Indians and their descendants survived in North America for centuries as hunter-gatherers.

Immigration and Nationality Act of 1965 Legislation passed during Lyndon Johnson's administration abolishing discriminatory immigration quotas based on national origins. Although it did limit the number of immigrants, including those from Latin America for the first time, it facilitated a surge in immigration later in the century.

impressment A British naval practice of seizing sailors on American ships under the claim they were deserters from the British navy. Some 2,500 British and American men were taken by force into service, a grievance that helped propel the United States to declare war on Britain in 1812.

Incan empire A region under the control of the Incas and their emperor, Atahualpa, that stretched along the western coast of South America and contained more than nine million people and a wealth in gold and silver.

indentured servants Poor immigrants who signed contracts known as indentures, in which they committed to four to seven years of labor in North America in exchange for transportation from England, as well as food and shelter after they arrived in the colony.

Indian Removal Act of 1830 Act that directed the mandatory relocation of eastern tribes to territory west of the Mississippi. Jackson insisted his goal was to save the Indians. Indians resisted the controversial act, but in the end most were forced to comply.

Industrial Workers of the World (IWW) Umbrella union and radical political group founded in 1905 that was dedicated to organizing unskilled workers to oppose capitalism. Members, nicknamed the Wobblies, advocated direct action by workers, including sabotage and general strikes, in hopes of triggering a widespread workers' uprising.

intermediate-range nuclear forces (INF) agreement Nuclear disarmament agreement reached between the United States and the Soviet Union in 1987, signifying a major thaw in the Cold War. The treaty eliminated all short- and medium-range missiles from Europe and provided for on-site inspection for the first time.

internment camps Makeshift prison camps, to which Americans of Japanese descent were sent as a result of Roosevelt's Executive Order 9066, issued in February 1942. In 1944, the Supreme Court upheld this blatant violation of constitutional rights as a "military necessity."

Interstate Commerce Commission (ICC) Federal regulatory agency designed to oversee the railroad industry. Congress created it through the 1887 Interstate Commerce Act after the Supreme Court decision in *Wabash v. Illinois* (1886) effectively denied states the right to regulate railroads. The ICC proved weak and did not immediately pose a threat to the industry.

Interstate Highway and Defense System Act of 1956 Law authorizing the construction of a national highway system. Promoted as essential to national defense and an impetus to economic growth, the national highway system accelerated the movement of people and goods and changed the nature of American communities.

Iran-Contra scandal Reagan administration scandal that involved the sale of arms to Iran in exchange for Iran's help securing the release of hostages held in Lebanon and the redirection of the sale's proceeds to finance the Nicaraguan Contras who wanted to unseat an elected government.

Iran hostage crisis Crisis that began in 1979 after the deposed shah of Iran was allowed into the United States following the Iranian revolution. Iranians broke into the U.S. Embassy in Tehran and took sixty-six Americans hostage, imprisoning most of them for more than a year.

Iraq War War launched by the United States, Britain, and several smaller countries in March 2003 against the government of Iraqi dictator Saddam Hussein. It was based on claims (subsequently refuted) that Hussein's government had links to Al Qaeda, harbored terrorists, and possessed weapons of mass destruction.

iron curtain Metaphor coined by Winston Churchill in 1946 to demark the line dividing Soviet-controlled countries in Eastern Europe from democratic nations in Western Europe following World War II.

Jamestown The first permanent English settlement in North America, established in 1607 by colonists sponsored by the Virginia Company.

Jay Treaty 1795 treaty between the United States and Britain, negotiated by John Jay. It secured limited trading rights in the West Indies but failed to ensure timely removal of British forces from western forts and reimbursement for slaves removed by the British after the Revolution.

Jim Crow System of racial segregation in the South lasting from after the Civil War into the twentieth century. Jim Crow laws segregated African Americans in public facilities such as trains and streetcars, curtailed their voting rights, and denied them other basic civil rights.

Johnson-Reed Act 1924 law that severely restricted immigration to the United States to no more than 161,000 a year with quotas for each European nation. The racist restrictions were designed to staunch the flow of immigrants from southern and eastern Europe and Asia.

Kansas-Nebraska Act 1854 law that divided Indian Territory into Kansas and Nebraska, repealed the Missouri Compromise, and left the new territories to decide the issue of slavery on the basis of popular sovereignty. The law led to bloody fighting in Kansas.

King Cotton diplomacy Confederate diplomatic strategy built on the hope that European nations starving for cotton would break the Union blockade and recognize the Confederacy. This strategy failed as Europeans held stores of surplus cotton and developed new sources outside the South.

King Philip's War War begun by Metacomet (King Philip), in which the Wampanoag Indians attacked colonial settlements in western Massachusetts in 1675. Colonists responded by attacking the Wampanoag and other tribes they believed conspired with them. The colonists prevailed in the brutal war.

Knights of Labor The first mass organization of America's working class. Founded in 1869, the Knights of Labor attempted to bridge the boundaries of ethnicity, gender, ideology, race, and occupation to build a "universal brotherhood" of all workers.

Korean War Conflict between North Korean forces supported by China and the Soviet Union and South Korean and U.S.-led United Nations forces over control of South Korea. Lasting from 1950 to 1953, the war represented the first time that the United States went to war to implement containment.

Ku Klux Klan Secret society that first thwarted black freedom after the Civil War as a paramilitary organization supporting Democrats. It was reborn in 1915 to fight against perceived threats posed by blacks, immigrants, radicals, feminists, Catholics, and Jews. The new Klan spread well beyond the South in the 1920s.

Ladies Association A women's organization in Philadelphia that collected substantial money donations in 1780 to reward Continental soldiers for their service. A woman leader authored a declaration, "The Sentiments of an American Woman," to justify women's unexpected entry into political life.

League of Nations International organization proposed in Woodrow Wilson's Fourteen Points that was designed to secure political independence and territorial integrity for all states and thus ensure enduring peace. The U.S. Senate refused to ratify the Treaty of Versailles, and the United States never became a member.

Lend-Lease Act Legislation in 1941 that enabled Britain to obtain arms from the United States without cash but with the promise to reimburse the United States when the war ended. The act reflected Roosevelt's desire to assist the British in any way possible, short of war.

Lewis and Clark expedition 1804–1806 expedition led by Meriwether Lewis and William Clark that explored the trans-Mississippi West for the U.S. government. The expedition's mission was scientific, political, and geographic.

Lincoln-Douglas debates Series of debates on the issue of slavery and freedom between Democrat Stephen Douglas and Republican Abraham Lincoln, held as part of the 1858 Illinois senatorial race. Douglas won the election, but the debates helped catapult Lincoln to national attention.

Lone Star Republic Independent republic, also known as the Republic of Texas, that was established by a rebellion of Texans against Mexican rule. The victory at San Jacinto in April 1836 helped ensure the region's independence and recognition by the United States.

Louisiana Purchase 1803 purchase of French territory west of the Mississippi River that stretched from the Gulf of Mexico to Canada. The Louisiana Purchase nearly doubled the size of the United States and opened the way for future American expansion west.

Lowell mills Water-powered textile mills constructed along the Merrimack River in Lowell, Massachusetts, that pioneered the extensive use of female laborers. By 1836, the eight mills there employed more than five thousand young women, living in boardinghouses under close supervision.

loyalists Colonists who remained loyal to Britain during the Revolutionary War, probably numbering around one-fifth of the population in 1776. Colonists remained loyal to Britain for many reasons, and loyalists could be found in every region of the country.

Lusitania British passenger liner torpedoed by a German U-boat on May 7, 1915. The attack killed 1,198 passengers, including 128 Americans. The incident challenged American neutrality during World War I and moved the United States on a path toward entering the war.

Manhattan Project Top-secret project authorized by Franklin Roosevelt in 1942 to develop an atomic bomb ahead of the Germans. The thousands of Americans who worked on the project at Los Alamos,

New Mexico, succeeded in producing a successful atomic bomb by July 1945.

manifest destiny Term coined in 1845 by journalist John L. O'Sullivan to justify American expansion. O'Sullivan claimed that it was the nation's "manifest destiny" to transport its values and civilization westward. Manifest destiny framed the American conquest of the West as part of a divine plan.

Marbury v. Madison 1803 Supreme Court case that established the concept of judicial review in finding that parts of the Judiciary Act of 1789 were in conflict with the Constitution. The Supreme Court assumed legal authority to overrule acts of other branches of the government.

Marshall Plan Aid program begun in 1948 to help European economies recover from World War II. Between 1948 and 1953, the United States provided $13 billion to seventeen Western European nations in a project that helped its own economy as well.

Mason-Dixon line A surveyor's mark that had established the boundary between Maryland and Pennsylvania in colonial times. By the 1830s, the boundary divided the free North and the slave South.

mechanical reapers Tools usually powered by horses or oxen that enabled farmers to harvest twelve acres of wheat a day, compared to the two or three acres a day possible with manual harvesting methods.

Medicare and Medicaid Social programs enacted as part of Lyndon Johnson's Great Society. Medicare provided the elderly with universal compulsory medical insurance financed primarily through Social Security taxes. Medicaid authorized federal grants to supplement state-paid medical care for poor people of all ages.

Mexica An empire that stretched from coast to coast across central Mexico and encompassed as many as six million people. Their culture was characterized by steep hierarchy and devotion to the war god Huitzilopochtli.

Middle Passage The crossing of the Atlantic by slave ships traveling from West Africa to the Americas. Slaves were crowded together in extremely unhealthful circumstances, and mortality rates were high.

military-industrial complex A term President Eisenhower used to refer to the military establishment and defense contractors who, he warned, exercised undue influence in city, state, and federal government.

Military Reconstruction Act Congressional act of March 1867 that initiated military rule of the South. Congressional reconstruction divided the ten unreconstructed Confederate states into five military districts, each under the direction of a Union general. It also established the procedure by which unreconstructed states could reenter the Union.

miscegenation Interracial sex. Proslavery spokesmen played on the fears of whites when they suggested that giving blacks equal rights would lead to miscegenation. In reality, slavery led to considerable sexual abuse of black women by their white masters.

Missouri Compromise 1820 congressional compromise engineered by Henry Clay that paired Missouri's entrance into the Union as a slave state with Maine's as a free state. The compromise also established Missouri's southern border as the permanent line dividing slave from free states.

Monroe Doctrine President James Monroe's 1823 declaration that the Western Hemisphere was closed to further colonization or interference by European powers. In exchange, Monroe pledged that the United States would not become involved in European struggles. The United States strengthened the doctrine during the late nineteenth century.

Montgomery bus boycott Yearlong boycott of Montgomery's segregated bus system in 1955–1956 by the city's African American population. The boycott brought Martin Luther King Jr. to national prominence and ended in victory when the Supreme Court declared segregated transportation unconstitutional.

Mormons Members of the Church of Jesus Christ of Latter-Day Saints founded by Joseph Smith in 1830. Most Americans deemed the Mormons heretics. After Smith's death at the hands of an angry mob in 1844, Brigham Young moved the people to what is now Utah in 1846.

muckraking Early-twentieth-century style of journalism that exposed the corruption of big business and government. Theodore Roosevelt coined the term after a character in *Pilgrim's Progress* who was too busy raking muck to notice higher things.

mutually assured destruction (MAD) Term for the standoff between the United States and Soviet Union based on the assumption that a nuclear first strike by either nation would result in massive retaliation and mutual destruction for each. Despite this, both countries pursued an ever-escalating arms race.

National American Woman Suffrage Association (NAWSA) Organization formed in 1890 that united the National Woman Suffrage Association and the American Woman Suffrage Association. The NAWSA pursued state-level campaigns to gain the vote for women. With successes in Idaho, Colorado, and Utah, woman suffrage had become more accepted by the 1890s.

National Energy Act of 1978 Legislation that penalized manufacturers of gas-guzzling automobiles and provided additional incentives for energy conservation and development of alternative fuels, such as wind and solar power. The act fell short of the long-term, comprehensive program that President Carter advocated.

National Organization for Women (NOW) Women's civil rights organization formed in 1966. Initially, NOW focused on eliminating gender discrimination in public institutions and the workplace, but by the 1970s it also embraced many of the issues raised by more radical feminists.

National Recovery Administration (NRA) Federal agency established in June 1933 to promote industrial recovery. It encouraged industrialists to voluntarily adopt codes that defined fair working conditions, set prices, and minimized competition. In practice, large corporations developed codes that served primarily their own interests rather than those of workers or the economy.

natural increase Growth of population through reproduction, as opposed to immigration. In the eighteenth century, natural increase accounted for about three-fourths of the American colonies' population growth.

Navigation Acts English laws passed in the 1650s and 1660s requiring that English colonial goods be shipped through English ports on English ships in order to benefit English merchants, shippers, and seamen.

neutrality acts Legislation passed in 1935 and 1937 that sought to avoid entanglement in foreign wars while protecting trade. It prohibited selling arms to nations at war and required nations to pay cash for nonmilitary goods and to transport them in their own ships.

New Christian Right Politically active religious conservatives who became particularly vocal in the 1980s. The New Right religious conservatives criticized feminism, opposed abortion and homosexuality, and promoted a larger role for religion in public life, "family values," and military preparedness.

New Deal coalition Political coalition that supported Franklin D. Roosevelt's New Deal and the Democratic Party, including farmers, factory workers, immigrants, city folk, women, African Americans, and progressive intellectuals. The coalition dominated American politics during and long after Roosevelt's presidency.

"The New Freedom" Woodrow Wilson's 1912 campaign slogan, which reflected his belief in limited government and states' rights. Wilson promised to use antitrust legislation to eliminate big corporations and to improve opportunities for small businesses and farmers.

New Jersey Plan Alternative plan for the structure of the national government drafted by delegates from small states, retaining the confederation's single-house congress with one vote per state. It shared with the Virginia Plan enhanced congressional powers, including the right to tax, regulate trade, and use force to stop popular uprisings.

"The New Nationalism" Theodore Roosevelt's 1912 campaign slogan, which reflected his commitment to federal planning and regulation. Roosevelt wanted to use the federal government to act as a "steward of the people" to regulate giant corporations.

New Negro Term referring to African Americans who challenged American racial hierarchy through the arts. The New Negro emerged in New York City in the 1920s in what became known as the Harlem Renaissance, which produced dazzling literary, musical, and artistic talent.

new Negroes Term given to newly arrived African slaves in the colonies. Planters usually maintained only a small number of recent arrivals among their slaves at any given time in order to accelerate their acculturation to their new circumstances.

New Netherland Dutch colony on Manhattan Island. New Amsterdam was its capital and headquarters.

New Spain Land in the New World held by the Spanish crown. Spain pioneered techniques of using New World colonies to strengthen the kingdom in Europe and would become a model for other European nations.

new woman Alternative image of womanhood that came into the American mainstream in the 1920s. The mass media frequently portrayed young, college-educated women who drank, smoked, and wore skimpy dresses. New women also challenged American convictions about separate spheres for women and men and the sexual double standard.

New York City draft riots Four days of rioting in New York City in July 1863 triggered by efforts to enforce the military draft. Democratic Irish workingmen, suffering economic hardship, infuriated by the draft, and opposed to emancipation, killed at least 105 people, most of them black.

New York Female Moral Reform Society An organization of religious women inspired by the Second Great Awakening to eradicate sexual sin and male licentiousness. Formed in 1833, it spread to hundreds of auxiliaries and worked to curb male licentiousness, prostitution, and seduction.

Newburgh Conspiracy A bogus threatened coup staged by Continental army officers and leaders in the congress in 1782–1783, who hoped that a forceful demand for military back pay and pensions would create pressure for stronger taxation powers. General Washington defused the threat.

Nineteenth Amendment (woman suffrage) Amendment granting women the vote. Congress passed the amendment in 1919, and it was ratified in August 1920. Like proponents of prohibition, the advocates of woman suffrage triumphed by linking their cause to the war.

No Child Left Behind Act 2002 legislation championed by President George W. Bush that expanded the role of the federal government in public education. The law required every school to meet annual testing standards, penalized failing schools, and allowed parents to transfer their children out of such schools.

North American Free Trade Agreement (NAFTA) 1993 treaty that eliminated all tariffs and trade barriers among the United States, Canada, and Mexico. NAFTA was supported by President Clinton, a minority of Democrats, and a majority of Republicans.

North Atlantic Treaty Organization (NATO) Military alliance formed in 1949 among the United States, Canada, and Western European nations to counter any possible Soviet threat. It represented an unprecedented commitment by the United States to go to war if any of its allies were attacked.

Northwest Ordinance Land act of 1787 that established a three-stage process by which settled territories would become states. It also banned slavery in the Northwest Territory. The ordinance guaranteed that western lands with white population would not become colonial dependencies.

NSC 68 Top-secret government report of April 1950 warning that national survival required a massive military buildup. The Korean War brought nearly all of the expansion called for in the report, and by 1952 defense spending claimed nearly 70 percent of the federal budget.

nullification Theory asserting that states could nullify acts of Congress that exceeded congressional powers. South Carolina advanced the theory of nullification in 1828 in response to an unfavorable federal tariff. A show of force by Andrew Jackson, combined with tariff revisions, ended the crisis.

Oneida community Utopian community organized by John Humphrey Noyes in New York in 1848. Noyes's opposition to private property led him to denounce marriage as the root of the problem. The community embraced sexual and economic communalism, to the dismay of its mainstream neighbors.

Open Door policy Policy successfully insisted upon by Secretary of State John Hay in 1899–1900 recommending that the major powers of the United States, Britain, Japan, Germany, France, and Russia all have access to trade with China and that Chinese sovereignty be maintained.

Oregon Trail Route from Independence, Missouri, to Oregon traveled by American settlers starting in the late 1830s. Disease and accidents caused many more deaths along the trail than did Indian attacks, which migrants feared.

Paleo-Indians Archaeologists' term for the first migrants into North America and their descendants who spread across the Americas between 15,000 BP and 13,500 BP, approximately.

Panama Canal treaty 1977 agreement that returned control of the Panama Canal from the United States to Panama in 2000. To pass the treaty, President Carter overcame stiff opposition in the Senate from conservatives who regarded control of the canal as vital to America's interests.

panic of 1837 First major economic crisis of the United States that led to several years of hard times from 1837 to 1841. Sudden bankruptcies, contraction of credit, and runs on banks worked hardships nationwide. Causes were multiple and global and not well understood.

partible inheritance System of inheritance in which land was divided equally among sons. By the eighteenth century, this practice in Massachusetts had subdivided plots of land into units too small for subsistence, forcing children to move away to find sufficient farmland.

paternalism The theory of slavery that emphasized reciprocal duties and obligations between masters and their slaves, with slaves providing labor and obedience and masters providing basic care and direction. Whites employed the concept of paternalism to deny that the slave system was brutal and exploitative.

Patient Protection and Affordable Care Act Sweeping 2010 health care reform bill that established nearly universal health insurance by providing subsidies and compelling larger businesses to offer coverage to employees. Championed by President Obama, it also imposed new regulations on insurance companies and contained provisions to limit health care costs.

Peace Corps Program launched by President Kennedy in 1961 through which young American volunteers helped with education, health, and other projects in developing countries around the world. More than 60,000 volunteers had served by the mid-1970s.

Pennsylvania Dutch Name given by other colonists to German immigrants to the middle colonies; an English corruption of the German term *Deutsch*. Germans were the largest contingent of migrants from continental Europe to the middle colonies in the eighteenth century.

Pentagon Papers Secret government documents published in 1971 containing an internal study of the Vietnam War. The documents further disillusioned the public by revealing that officials harbored pessimism about the war even as they made rosy public pronouncements about its progress.

People's Party (Populist Party) Political party formed in 1892 by the Farmers' Alliance to advance the goals of the Populist movement. Populists sought economic democracy, promoting land, electoral, banking, and monetary reform. Republican victory in the presidential election of 1896 effectively destroyed the People's Party.

Persian Gulf War 1991 war between Iraq and a U.S.-led international coalition. The war was sparked by the 1990 Iraqi invasion of Kuwait. A forty-day bombing campaign against Iraq followed by coalition troops storming into Kuwait brought a quick coalition victory.

plantation Large farm worked by twenty or more slaves. Although small farms were more numerous, plantations produced more than 75 percent of the South's export crops.

plantation belt Flatlands that spread from South Carolina to east Texas and were dominated by large plantations.

planter A substantial landowner who tilled his estate with twenty or more slaves. Planters dominated the social and political world of the South. Their values and ideology influenced the values of all southern whites.

Plessy v. Ferguson 1896 Supreme Court ruling that upheld the legality of racial segregation. According to the ruling, blacks could be segregated in separate schools, restrooms, and other facilities as long as the facilities were "equal" to those provided for whites.

Pontiac's Rebellion A coordinated uprising of Native American tribes in 1763 in the Northwest (Great Lakes region) after the end of the Seven Years' War. The rebellion heightened Britain's determination to create a boundary between Americans and Indians, embodied in the Proclamation of 1763.

popular sovereignty The idea that government is subject to the will of the people. Applied to the territories, popular sovereignty meant that the residents of a territory should determine, through their legislature, whether to allow slavery.

predestination Doctrine stating that God determined whether individuals were destined for salvation or damnation before their birth. According to the doctrine, nothing an individual did during his or her lifetime could affect that person's fate.

presidios Spanish forts built to block Russian advance into California.

progressivism A reform movement that often advocated government activism to mitigate the problems created by urban industrialism. Progressivism reached its peak in 1912 with the creation of the Progressive Party. The term *progressivism* has come to mean any general effort advocating for social welfare programs.

prohibition The ban on the manufacture and sale of alcohol that went into effect in January 1920 with the Eighteenth Amendment. Prohibition proved almost impossible to enforce. By the end of the 1920s, most Americans wished it to end, and it was finally repealed in 1933.

Protestant Reformation The reform movement that began in 1517 with Martin Luther's critiques of the Roman Catholic Church, which precipitated an enduring schism that divided Protestants from Catholics.

Pueblo Bonito The largest residential and ceremonial site, containing more than 600 rooms and thirty-five kivas, in the major Anasazi cultural center of Chaco Canyon in present-day New Mexico.

Pueblo Revolt An effective revolt of Pueblo Indians in New Mexico, under the leadership of Popé, against the Spaniards in 1680. Particularly targeting symbols of Christianity, they succeeded in killing two-thirds of Spanish missionaries and driving the Spaniards out of New Mexico.

pueblos Multiunit dwellings, storage spaces, and ceremonial centers—often termed *kivas*—built by ancient Americans in the Southwest for centuries around AD 1000.

Pullman boycott Nationwide railroad workers' boycott of trains carrying Pullman cars in 1894 after Pullman workers, suffering radically reduced wages, joined the American Railway Union (ARU) and union leaders were fired in response. The boycott ended after the U.S. Army fired on strikers and ARU leader Eugene Debs was jailed.

Puritan Revolution English civil war that arose out of disputes between King Charles I and Parliament, which was dominated by Puritans. The conflict began in 1642 and ended with the execution of Charles I in 1649, resulting in Puritan rule in England until 1660.

Puritans Dissenters from the Church of England who wanted a genuine Reformation rather than the partial Reformation sought by Henry VIII. The Puritans' religious principles emphasized the importance of an individual's relationship with God developed through Bible study, prayer, and introspection.

Quakers Epithet for members of the Society of Friends. Their belief that God spoke directly to each individual through an "inner light" and that neither ministers nor the Bible was essential to discovering God's Word put them in conflict with orthodox Puritans.

Reconquest The centuries-long drive to expel Muslims from the Iberian Peninsula undertaken by the Christian kingdoms of Spain and Portugal. The military victories of the Reconquest helped the Portuguese gain greater access to sea routes.

Reconstruction Finance Corporation (RFC) Federal agency established by Herbert Hoover in 1932 to help American industry by lending government funds to endangered banks and corporations, which Hoover hoped would benefit people at the bottom through trickle-down economics. In practice, this provided little help to the poor.

Red scare The widespread fear of internal subversion and Communist revolution that swept the United States in 1919 and resulted in suppression of dissent. Labor unrest, postwar recession, the difficult peacetime readjustment, and the Soviet establishment of the Comintern all contributed to the scare.

Redeemers Name taken by southern Democrats who harnessed white rage in order to overthrow Republican rule and black political power and thus, they believed, save southern civilization.

redemptioners A variant of indentured servants. In this system, a captain agreed to provide passage to Philadelphia, where redemptioners would obtain money to pay for their transportation, usually by selling themselves as servants.

reform Darwinism Sociological theory developed in the 1880s that argued humans could speed up evolution by altering their environment. A challenge to the laissez-faire approach of social Darwinism, reform Darwinism insisted the liberal state should play an active role in solving social problems.

Report on Manufactures A proposal by Treasury Secretary Alexander Hamilton in 1791 calling for the federal government to encourage domestic manufacturers with subsidies while imposing tariffs on foreign imports. Congress initially rejected the measure.

Report on Public Credit Hamilton's January 1790 report recommending that the national debt be funded—but not repaid immediately—at full value. Hamilton's goal was to make the new country creditworthy, not debt-free. Critics of his plan complained that it would benefit speculators.

republicanism A social philosophy that embraced representative institutions (as opposed to monarchy), a citizenry attuned to civic values above private interests, and a virtuous community in which individuals work to promote the public good.

Republican Party Antislavery party formed in 1854 following passage of the Kansas-Nebraska Act. The Republicans attempted to unite all those who opposed the extension of slavery into any territory of the United States.

Republicans One of the two dominant political groups that emerged in the 1790s. Republicans supported the revolutionaries in France and worried about monarchical Federalists at home. Prominent Republicans included Thomas Jefferson and James Madison.

reservations Land assigned by the federal government to American Indians beginning in the 1860s in an attempt to reduce tensions between Indians and western settlers. On reservations, Indians subsisted on meager government rations and faced a life of poverty and starvation.

rock and roll A music genre created from country music and black rhythm and blues that emerged in the 1950s and captivated American youth.

Roe v. Wade 1973 Supreme Court ruling that the Constitution protects the right to abortion, which states cannot prohibit in the early stages of pregnancy. The decision galvanized social conservatives and made abortion a controversial policy issue for decades to come.

Roosevelt Corollary Theodore Roosevelt's 1904 follow-up to the Monroe Doctrine in which he declared the United States had the right to intervene in Latin America to stop "brutal wrongdoing" and protect American interests. The corollary warned European powers to keep out of the Western Hemisphere.

royal colony A colony ruled by a king or queen and governed by officials appointed to serve the monarchy and represent its interests.

scalawag A derogatory term that Southerners applied to southern white Republicans, who were seen as traitors to the South. Most were yeoman farmers.

Schenck v. United States 1919 Supreme Court decision that established a "clear and present danger" test for restricting free speech. The Court upheld the conviction of socialist Charles Schenck for urging resistance to the draft during wartime.

Scopes trial 1925 trial of John Scopes, a biology teacher in Dayton, Tennessee, for violating his state's ban on teaching evolution. The trial created a nationwide media frenzy and came to be seen as a showdown between urban and rural values.

Scots-Irish Protestant immigrants from northern Ireland, Scotland, and northern England. Deteriorating economic conditions in their European homelands contributed to increasing migration to the colonies in the eighteenth century.

Scottsboro Boys Nine African American youths who were arrested for the alleged rape of two white women in Scottsboro, Alabama, in 1931. After an all-white jury sentenced the young men to death, the Communist Party took action that saved them from the electric chair.

second Bank of the United States National bank with multiple branches chartered in 1816 for twenty years. Intended to help regulate the economy, the bank became a major issue in Andrew Jackson's reelection campaign in 1832, framed in political rhetoric about aristocracy versus democracy.

Second Continental Congress Legislative body that governed the United States from May 1775 through the war's duration. It established an army, created its own money, and declared independence once all hope for a peaceful reconciliation with Britain was gone.

Second Great Awakening Unprecedented religious revival in the 1820s and 1830s that promised access to salvation. The Second Great Awakening proved to be a major impetus for reform movements of the era, inspiring efforts to combat drinking, sexual sin, and slavery.

Selective Service Act Law enacted in 1940 requiring all men who would be eligible for a military draft to register in preparation for the possibility of a future conflict. The act also prohibited discrimination based on "race or color."

Seneca Falls Declaration of Sentiments Declaration issued in 1848 at the first national woman's rights convention in the United States, which was held in Seneca Falls, New York. The document adopted the style of the Declaration of Independence and demanded equal rights for women, including the franchise.

Separatists People who sought withdrawal from the Church of England. The Pilgrims were Separatists.

settlement houses Settlements established in poor neighborhoods beginning in the 1880s. Reformers like Jane Addams and Lillian Wald believed that only by living among the poor could they help bridge the growing class divide. College-educated women formed the backbone of the settlement house movement.

Seven Years' War War (1754–1763) between Britain and France that ended with British domination of North America; known in America as the French and Indian War. Its high expense laid the foundation for conflict that would lead to the American Revolution.

sharecropping Labor system that emerged in the South during Reconstruction. Under this system, planters divided their plantations into small farms that freedmen rented, paying with a share of each year's crop. Sharecropping gave blacks some freedom, but they remained dependent on white landlords and country merchants.

Shays's Rebellion Uprising (1786–1787) led by farmers centered in western Massachusetts. Dissidents protested taxation policies of the eastern elites who controlled the state's government. Shays's Rebellion caused leaders throughout the country to worry about the confederation's ability to handle civil disorder.

Sherman Antitrust Act 1890 act that outlawed pools and trusts, ruling that businesses could no longer enter into agreements to restrict competition. Government inaction, combined with the Supreme Court's narrow reading of the act in the *United States v. E. C. Knight Company* decision, undermined the law's effectiveness.

Sherman's March to the Sea Military campaign from September through December 1864 in which Union forces under General Sherman marched from Atlanta, Georgia, to the coast at Savannah. Carving a path of destruction as it progressed, Sherman's army aimed at destroying white Southerners' will to continue the war.

siege of Vicksburg Six-week siege by General Grant intended to starve out Vicksburg. On July 4, 1863, the 30,000 Confederate troops holding the city surrendered. The victory gave the Union control of the Mississippi River and, together with Gettysburg, marked a major turning point of the war.

Six-Day War 1967 conflict between Israel and the Arab nations of Egypt, Syria, and Jordan. Israel attacked Egypt after Egypt had massed troops on its border and cut off the sea passage to Israel's southern port. Israel won a stunning victory, seizing territory that amounted to twice its original size.

slave codes Laws enacted in southern states in the 1820s and 1830s that required the total submission of slaves. Attacks by antislavery activists and by slaves convinced southern legislators that they had to do everything in their power to strengthen the institution of slavery.

slavery Coerced labor. African slavery became the most important form of coerced labor in the New World in the seventeenth century.

social Darwinism A social theory popularized in the late nineteenth century by Herbert Spencer and William Graham Sumner. Proponents believed only relentless competition could produce social progress and wealth was a sign of "fitness" and poverty a sign of "unfitness" for survival.

social gospel A vision of Christianity that saw its mission as not simply to reform individuals but to reform society. Emerging in the early twentieth century, it offered a powerful corrective to social Darwinism and the gospel of wealth, which fostered the belief that riches signaled divine favor.

Social Security A New Deal program created in August 1935 that was designed to provide a modest income for elderly people. The act also created unemployment insurance with modest benefits. Social Security provoked sharp opposition from conservatives and the wealthy.

Socialist Party Political party formed in 1900 that advocated cooperation over competition and promoted the breakdown of capitalism. Its members, who were largely middle-class and native-born, saw both the Republican and the Democratic parties as hopelessly beholden to capitalism.

Spanish-American War 1898 war between Spain and the United States that began as an effort to free Cuba from Spain's colonial rule. This popular war left the United States an imperial power in control of Cuba and colonies in Puerto Rico, Guam, and the Philippines.

spoils system System in which politicians doled out government positions to their loyal supporters. This patronage system led to widespread corruption during the Gilded Age.

Stamp Act 1765 British law imposing a tax on all paper used for official documents, for the purpose of raising revenue. Widespread resistance to the Stamp Act led to its repeal in 1766.

Stono Rebellion Slave uprising in Stono, South Carolina, in 1739 in which a group of slaves armed themselves, plundered six plantations, and killed more than twenty whites. Whites quickly suppressed the rebellion.

Strategic Arms Limitation Treaty (SALT) A 1972 agreement between the United States and the Soviet Union, limiting antiballistic missiles (ABMs) to two each. The treaty prevented either nation from building an ABM system defense so secure against a nuclear attack that it would risk a first strike.

Strategic Defense Initiative (SDI) Project launched by President Reagan to deploy lasers in space that would prevent enemy missiles from reaching their targets. Critics protested that it violated the 1972 Antiballistic Missile Treaty. The project cost billions of dollars without producing a working system.

Sugar (Revenue) Act 1764 British law that decreased the duty on French molasses, making it more attractive for shippers to obey the law, and at the same time raised penalties for smuggling. The Sugar Act regulated trade but was also intended to raise revenue.

Sun Belt Name applied to the West, Southwest, and parts of the South, which grew rapidly after World War II as a center of defense industries and non-unionized labor.

supply-side economics Economic theory that justified the Reagan administration's large tax cuts on the grounds that they would encourage investment and production (supply) and stimulate consumption (demand) because individuals could keep more of their earnings. Reagan's supply-side economics created a massive federal budget deficit.

sweatshop A small room used for clothing piecework beginning in the late nineteenth century. As mechanization transformed the garment industry with the introduction of foot-pedaled sewing machines and mechanical cloth-cutting knives, independent tailors were replaced with sweatshop workers hired by contractors to sew pieces into clothing.

Taft-Hartley Act Law passed by the Republican-controlled Congress in 1947 that amended the Wagner Act and placed restrictions on organized labor that made it more difficult for unions to organize workers.

Tainos The Indians who inhabited San Salvador and many Caribbean islands and who were the first people Columbus encountered after making landfall in the New World.

task system A system of labor in which a slave was assigned a daily task to complete and allowed to do as he wished upon its completion. This system offered more freedom than the carefully supervised gang-labor system.

Tea Act of 1773 British act that lowered the existing tax on tea to entice boycotting Americans to buy it. Resistance to the Tea Act led to the passage of the Coercive Acts and imposition of military rule in Massachusetts.

Teapot Dome Nickname for scandal in which Interior Secretary Albert Fall accepted $400,000 in bribes for leasing oil reserves on public land in Teapot Dome, Wyoming. It was part of a larger pattern of corruption that marred Warren G. Harding's presidency.

Temporary Assistance for Needy Families (TANF) program Program established by the Personal Responsibility and Work Opportunity Reconciliation Act of 1996. Replacing Aid to Families with Dependent Children, TANF provided grants to the states to assist the poor and limited welfare payments to two consecutive years, with a lifetime maximum of five years.

Tet Offensive Major campaign of attacks launched throughout South Vietnam in early 1968 by the North Vietnamese and Vietcong. A major turning point in the war, it exposed the credibility gap between official statements and the war's reality, and it shook Americans' confidence in the government.

three-fifths clause Clause in the Constitution that stipulated that all free persons plus "three-fifths of all other Persons" would constitute the numerical base for apportioning both representation and taxation. The clause tacitly acknowledged the existence of slavery in the United States.

Townshend duties British law that established new duties on tea, glass, lead, paper, and painters' colors imported into the colonies. The Townshend duties led to boycotts and heightened tensions between Britain and the American colonies.

Trail of Tears Forced westward journey of Cherokees from their lands in Georgia to present-day Oklahoma in 1838. Despite favorable legal action, the Cherokees endured a grueling 1,200-mile march overseen by federal troops. Nearly a quarter of the Cherokees died en route.

Treaty of Fort Stanwix 1784 treaty with the Iroquois Confederacy that established the primacy of the American confederation (and not states) to negotiate with Indians and resulted in large land cessions in the Ohio Country (northwestern Pennsylvania and eastern Ohio). Tribes not present at Fort Stanwix disavowed the treaty.

Treaty of Greenville 1795 treaty between the United States and various Indian tribes in Ohio. The United States gave the tribes treaty goods valued at $25,000. In exchange, the Indians ceded most of Ohio to the Americans. The treaty brought only temporary peace to the region.

Treaty of Guadalupe Hidalgo February 1848 treaty that ended the Mexican-American War. Mexico gave up all claims to Texas north of the Rio Grande and ceded New Mexico and California to the United States. The United States agreed to pay Mexico $15 million and to assume American claims against Mexico.

Treaty (Peace) of Paris, 1783 September 3, 1783, treaty that ended the Revolutionary War. The treaty acknowledged America's independence, set its boundaries, and promised the quick withdrawal of British troops from American soil. It failed to recognize Indians as players in the conflict.

Treaty of Tordesillas The treaty negotiated in 1494 to delineate land claims in the New World. The treaty drew an imaginary line west of the Canary Islands; land discovered west of the line belonged to Spain, and land to the east belonged to Portugal.

tribute The goods the Mexica collected from conquered peoples, from basic food products to candidates for human sacrifice. Tribute engendered resentment among the Mexica's subjects, creating a vulnerability the Spaniards would later exploit.

Triple Alliance Early-twentieth-century alliance between Germany, Austria-Hungary, and Italy, formed as part of a complex network of military and diplomatic agreements intended to prevent war in Europe by balancing power. In actuality, such alliances made large-scale conflict more likely.

Triple Entente Early-twentieth-century alliance between Great Britain, France, and Russia, which was formed as part of a complex network of military and diplomatic agreements intended to prevent war in Europe by balancing power. In actuality, such alliances made large-scale conflict more likely.

Truman Doctrine President Harry S. Truman's commitment to "support free peoples who are resisting attempted subjugation by armed minorities or by outside pressures." First applied to Greece and Turkey in 1947, it became the justification for U.S. intervention into many countries during the Cold War.

trust A system in which corporations give shares of their stock to trustees who hold the stocks "in trust" for their stockholders, thereby coordinating the industry to ensure profits to the participating corporations and curb competition.

"typewriters" Women who were hired by businesses in the decades after the Civil War to keep records and conduct correspondence, often using equipment such as typewriters. Secretarial work constituted one of the very few areas where middle-class women could use their literacy for wages.

Uncle Tom's Cabin Enormously popular antislavery novel written by Harriet Beecher Stowe and published in 1852. It helped to solidify northern sentiment against slavery and to confirm white Southerners' sense that no sympathy remained for them in the free states.

underconsumption New Dealers' belief that the root cause of the country's economic paralysis was that factories and farms produced more than they could sell, causing factories to lay off workers and farmers to lose money. The only way to increase consumption, they believed, was to provide jobs that put wages in consumers' pockets.

underground railroad Network consisting mainly of black homes, black churches, and black neighborhoods that helped slaves escape to the North by supplying shelter, food, and general assistance.

Union blockade The United States' use of its navy to patrol the southern coastline to restrict Confederate access to supplies. Over time, the blockade became increasingly effective and succeeded in depriving the Confederacy of vital supplies.

United States Constitution The document written in 1787 and subsequently ratified by the original thirteen states that laid out the governing structure of the United States in separate legislative, executive, and judicial branches.

upcountry The hills and mountains of the South whose higher elevation, colder climate, rugged terrain, and poor transportation made the region less hospitable than the flatlands to slavery and large plantations.

USA Patriot Act 2001 law that gave the government new powers to monitor suspected terrorists and their associates, including the ability to access personal information. Critics charged that it represented an unwarranted abridgment of civil rights.

Versailles treaty Treaty signed on June 28, 1919, that ended World War I. The agreement redrew the map of the world and assigned Germany sole responsibility for the war, saddling it with a debt of $33 billion in war damages. Many Germans felt betrayed by the treaty.

Virginia and Kentucky Resolutions Condemning the Alien and Sedition Acts, the 1798 resolutions submitted to the federal government by the Virginia and Kentucky state legislatures. The resolutions tested the idea that state legislatures could judge the constitutionality of federal laws and nullify them.

Virginia Company A joint-stock company organized by London investors in 1606 that received a land grant from King James I in order to establish English colonies in North America. Investors hoped to enrich themselves and strengthen England economically and politically.

Virginia Plan Plan drafted by James Madison, presented at the opening of the Philadelphia constitutional convention. Designed as a powerful three-branch government, with representation in both houses of the congress to be tied to population, this plan eclipsed the voice of small states in national government.

virtual representation The theory that all British subjects were represented in Parliament, whether they had elected representatives in that body or not. American colonists rejected the theory of virtual representation, arguing that only direct representatives had the right to tax the colonists.

visible saints Puritans who had passed the tests of conversion and church membership and were therefore thought to be among God's elect.

Voting Rights Act of 1965 Law passed during Lyndon Johnson's administration that empowered the federal government to intervene to ensure minorities access to the voting booth. As a result of the act, black voting and officeholding in the South shot up, initiating a major transformation in southern politics.

Wagner Act 1935 law that guaranteed industrial workers the right to organize into unions; also known as the National Labor Relations Act. Following passage of the act, union membership skyrocketed to 30 percent of the workforce, the highest in American history.

War Hawks Young men newly elected to the Congress of 1811 who were eager for war against Britain in order to end impressments, fight Indians, and expand into neighboring British territory. Leaders included Henry Clay of Kentucky and John C. Calhoun of South Carolina.

War on Poverty President Lyndon Johnson's efforts, organized through the Office of Economic Opportunity, to ameliorate poverty primarily through education and training as well as by including the poor in decision making.

Warren Court The Supreme Court under Chief Justice Earl Warren (1953–1969), which expanded the Constitution's promise of equality and civil rights. It issued landmark decisions in the areas of civil rights, criminal rights, reproductive freedom, and separation of church and state.

Watergate Term referring to the 1972 break-in at Democratic Party headquarters in the Watergate complex in Washington, D.C., by men working for President Nixon's reelection, along with Nixon's efforts to cover it up. The Watergate scandal led to President Nixon's resignation.

welfare capitalism Industrial programs for workers that became popular in the 1920s. Some businesses improved safety and sanitation inside factories. They also instituted paid vacations and pension plans. This encouraged loyalty to companies rather than to independent labor unions.

Whigs Political party that evolved out of the National Republicans after 1834. With a northeastern power base, the Whigs supported federal action to promote commercial development and generally looked favorably on the reform movements associated with the Second Great Awakening.

Whiskey Rebellion July 1794 uprising by farmers in western Pennsylvania in response to enforcement of an unpopular excise tax on whiskey. The federal government responded with a military presence that caused dissidents to disperse before blood was shed.

Wilmot Proviso Proposal put forward by Representative David Wilmot of Pennsylvania in August 1846 to ban slavery in territory acquired from the Mexican-American War. The proviso enjoyed widespread support in the North, but Southerners saw it as an attack on their interests.

Woman's Christian Temperance Union (WCTU) All-women organization founded in 1874 to advocate total abstinence from alcohol. The WCTU provided important political training for women, which many used in the suffrage movement.

Works Progress Administration (WPA) Federal New Deal program established in 1935 that provided government-funded public works jobs to millions of unemployed Americans during the Great Depression, in areas ranging from construction to the arts.

World Trade Organization (WTO) International economic body established in 1994 through the General Agreement on Tariffs and Trade to enforce substantial tariff and import quota reductions. Many corporations welcomed these trade barrier reductions, but critics linked them to job loss and the weakening of unions.

World's Columbian Exposition World's fair held in Chicago in 1893 that attracted millions of visitors. The elaborately designed pavilions of the "White City" included exhibits of technological innovation and of cultural exoticism. They embodied an urban ideal that contrasted with the realities of Chicago life.

Wounded Knee 1890 massacre of Sioux Indians by American cavalry at Wounded Knee Creek, South Dakota. Sent to suppress the Ghost Dance, the soldiers opened fire on the Sioux as they attempted to surrender. More than two hundred Sioux men, women, and children were killed.

XYZ affair 1797 incident in which American negotiators in France were rebuffed for refusing to pay a substantial bribe. The incident led the United

States into an undeclared war with France, known as the Quasi-War, which intensified antagonism between Federalists and Republicans.

yellow journalism Term first given to sensationalistic newspaper reporting and cartoon images rendered in yellow. A circulation war between two New York City papers provoked the tactics of yellow journalism that fueled popular support for the Spanish-American War in 1898.

yeomen Farmers who owned and worked on their own small plots of land. Yeomen living within the plantation belt were more dependent on planters than were yeomen in the upcountry, where small farmers dominated.

Index

ATLAS OF THE TERRITORIAL GROWTH OF THE UNITED STATES

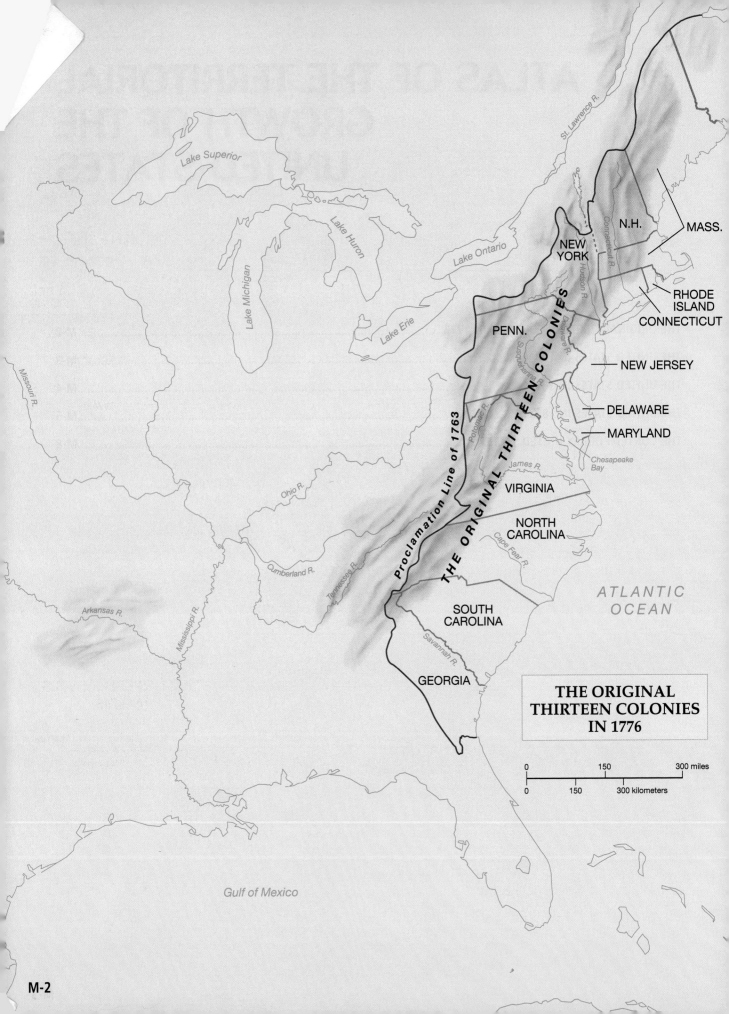

THE ORIGINAL
THIRTEEN COLONIES
IN 1776

0   150   300 miles

0   150   300 kilometers

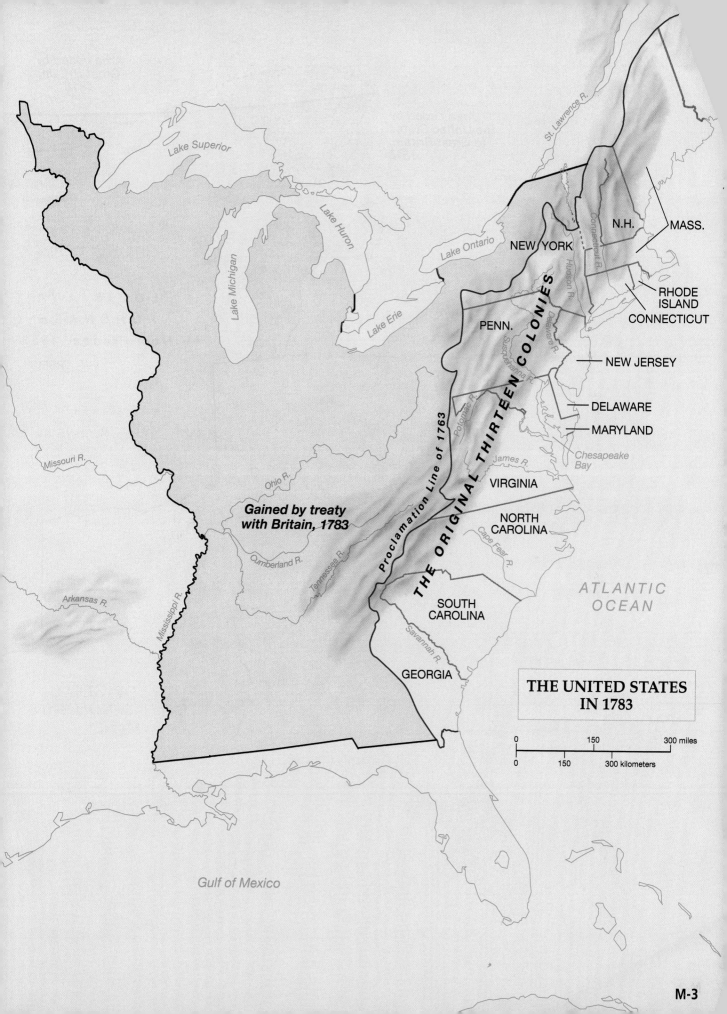

Lake Superior

Lake Michigan

Lake Huron

Lake Erie

Lake Ontario

St. Lawrence R.

N.H.

MASS.

NEW YORK

Connecticut R.

Hudson R.

RHODE ISLAND

CONNECTICUT

PENN.

Susquehanna R.

Delaware R.

NEW JERSEY

DELAWARE

MARYLAND

Potomac R.

Chesapeake Bay

Proclamation Line of 1763

THE ORIGINAL THIRTEEN COLONIES

James R.

VIRGINIA

Missouri R.

Gained by treaty with Britain, 1783

Ohio R.

NORTH CAROLINA

Cape Fear R.

ATLANTIC OCEAN

Cumberland R.

Tennessee R.

Arkansas R.

SOUTH CAROLINA

Mississippi R.

Savannah R.

GEORGIA

THE UNITED STATES IN 1783

0   150   300 miles

0   150   300 kilometers

Gulf of Mexico

M-3

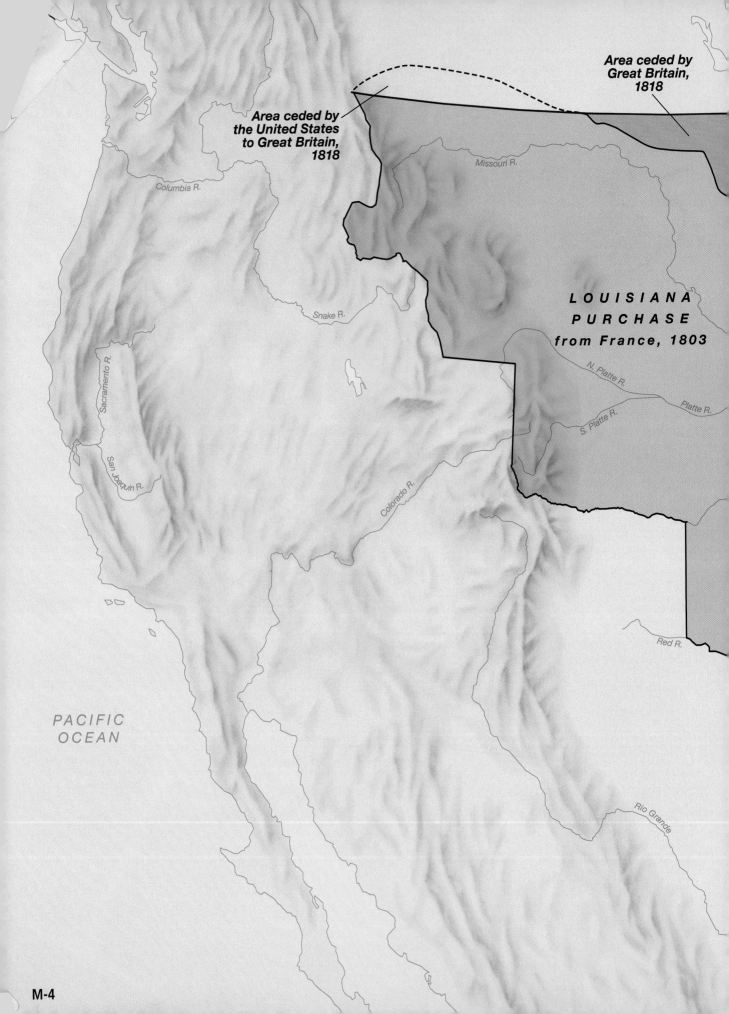

Area ceded by
Great Britain,
1818

Area ceded by
the United States
to Great Britain,
1818

Missouri R.

Columbia R.

LOUISIANA
PURCHASE
from France, 1803

Snake R.

N. Platte R.

Platte R.

S. Platte R.

Sacramento R.

San Joaquin R.

Colorado R.

Red R.

PACIFIC
OCEAN

Rio Grande

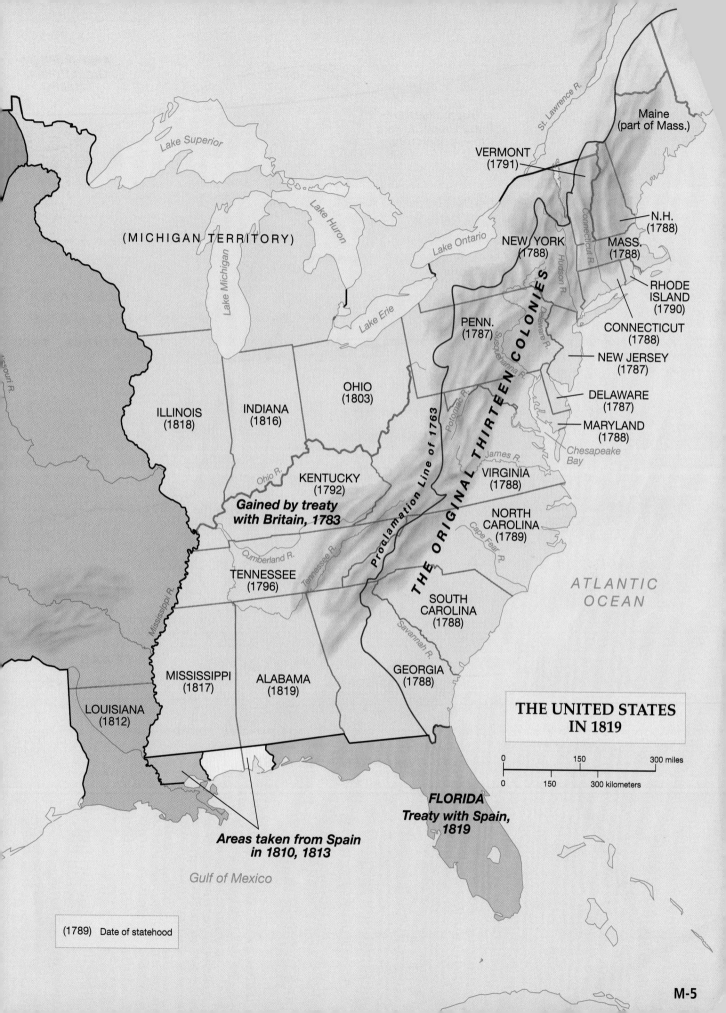

Lake Superior

Lake Huron

St. Lawrence R.

Maine
(part of Mass.)

(MICHIGAN TERRITORY)

Lake Michigan

VERMONT
(1791)

Lake Ontario

Lake Erie

NEW YORK
(1788)

Hudson R.

Connecticut R.

N.H.
(1788)

MASS.
(1788)

RHODE
ISLAND
(1790)

CONNECTICUT
(1788)

PENN.
(1787)

Delaware R.

Susquehanna R.

NEW JERSEY
(1787)

DELAWARE
(1787)

OHIO
(1803)

INDIANA
(1816)

ILLINOIS
(1818)

Ohio R.

KENTUCKY
(1792)

*Gained by treaty
with Britain, 1783*

Proclamation Line of 1763

Potomac R.

MARYLAND
(1788)

Chesapeake
Bay

James R.

VIRGINIA
(1788)

THE ORIGINAL THIRTEEN COLONIES

NORTH
CAROLINA
(1789)

Cape Fear R.

ATLANTIC
OCEAN

Missouri R.

Mississippi R.

Cumberland R.

TENNESSEE
(1796)

Tennessee R.

SOUTH
CAROLINA
(1788)

Savannah R.

MISSISSIPPI
(1817)

ALABAMA
(1819)

GEORGIA
(1788)

LOUISIANA
(1812)

*Areas taken from Spain
in 1810, 1813*

*FLORIDA
Treaty with Spain,
1819*

**THE UNITED STATES
IN 1819**

0   150   300 miles

0   150   300 kilometers

Gulf of Mexico

(1789)   Date of statehood

M-5

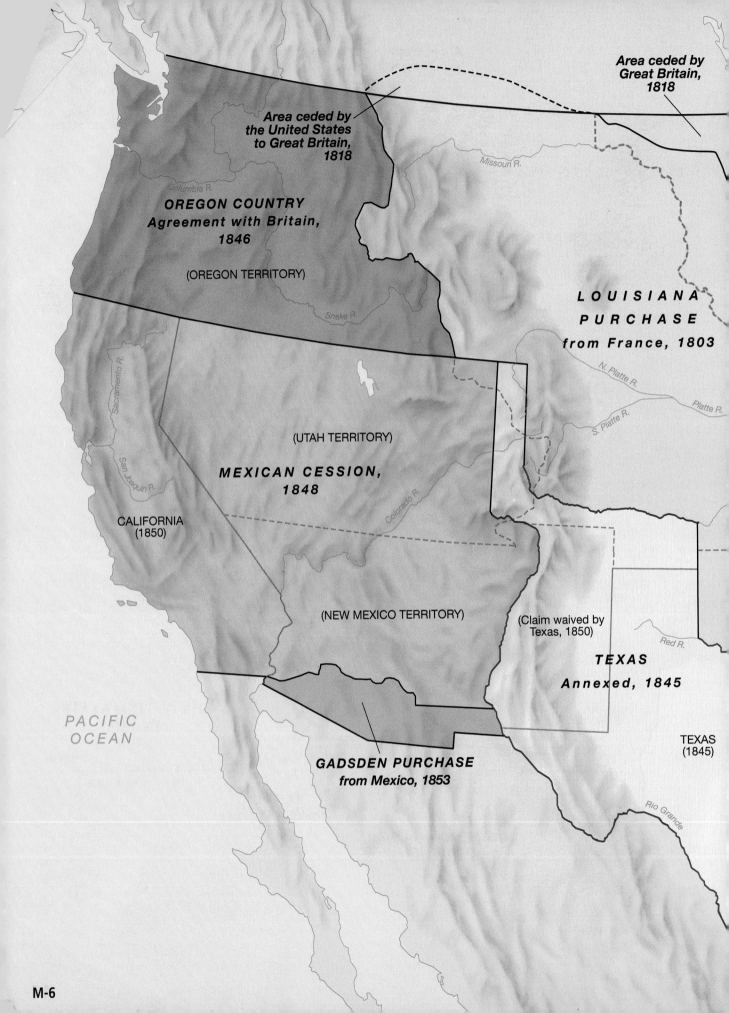

Area ceded by
Great Britain,
1818

Area ceded by
the United States
to Great Britain,
1818

Columbia R.

OREGON COUNTRY
Agreement with Britain,
1846

(OREGON TERRITORY)

Snake R.

Missouri R.

LOUISIANA
PURCHASE
from France, 1803

N. Platte R.

S. Platte R.

Platte R.

Sacramento R.

(UTAH TERRITORY)

MEXICAN CESSION,
1848

San Joaquin R.

Colorado R.

CALIFORNIA
(1850)

(NEW MEXICO TERRITORY)

(Claim waived by
Texas, 1850)

Red R.

TEXAS
Annexed, 1845

TEXAS
(1845)

PACIFIC
OCEAN

GADSDEN PURCHASE
from Mexico, 1853

Rio Grande

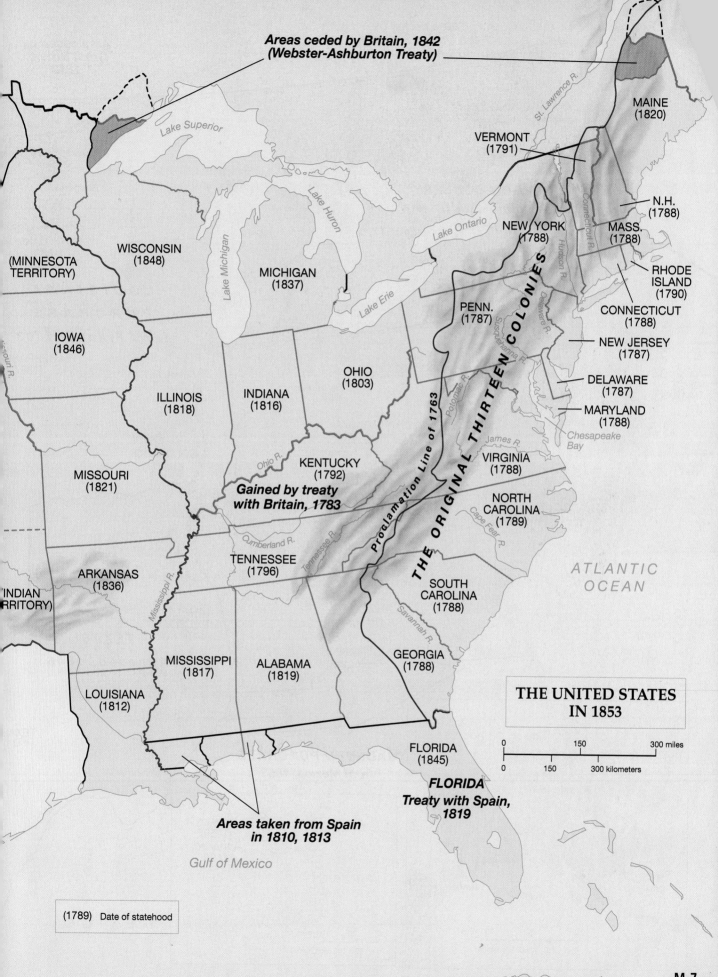

Areas ceded by Britain, 1842
(Webster-Ashburton Treaty)

Lake Superior

St. Lawrence R.

MAINE
(1820)

VERMONT
(1791)

Lake Huron

Connecticut R.

N.H.
(1788)

Lake Ontario

NEW YORK
(1788)

MASS.
(1788)

Lake Michigan

Lake Erie

RHODE
ISLAND
(1790)

Hudson R.

CONNECTICUT
(1788)

(MINNESOTA
TERRITORY)

WISCONSIN
(1848)

MICHIGAN
(1837)

PENN.
(1787)

Delaware R.

NEW JERSEY
(1787)

IOWA
(1846)

OHIO
(1803)

Susquehanna R.

DELAWARE
(1787)

ILLINOIS
(1818)

INDIANA
(1816)

Potomac R.

MARYLAND
(1788)

Missouri R.

MELILLA

*Chesapeake
Bay*

Ohio R.

KENTUCKY
(1792)

James R.

VIRGINIA
(1788)

MISSOURI
(1821)

Gained by treaty
with Britain, 1783

Proclamation Line of 1763

THE ORIGINAL THIRTEEN COLONIES

NORTH
CAROLINA
(1789)

Cumberland R.

Cape Fear R.

Tennessee R.

TENNESSEE
(1796)

ATLANTIC
OCEAN

ARKANSAS
(1836)

Mississippi R.

SOUTH
CAROLINA
(1788)

INDIAN
TERRITORY)

Savannah R.

MISSISSIPPI
(1817)

ALABAMA
(1819)

GEORGIA
(1788)

LOUISIANA
(1812)

THE UNITED STATES
IN 1853

FLORIDA
(1845)

0	150	300 miles
0	150	300 kilometers

FLORIDA
Treaty with Spain,
1819

Areas taken from Spain
in 1810, 1813

Gulf of Mexico

(1789)   Date of statehood

M-7

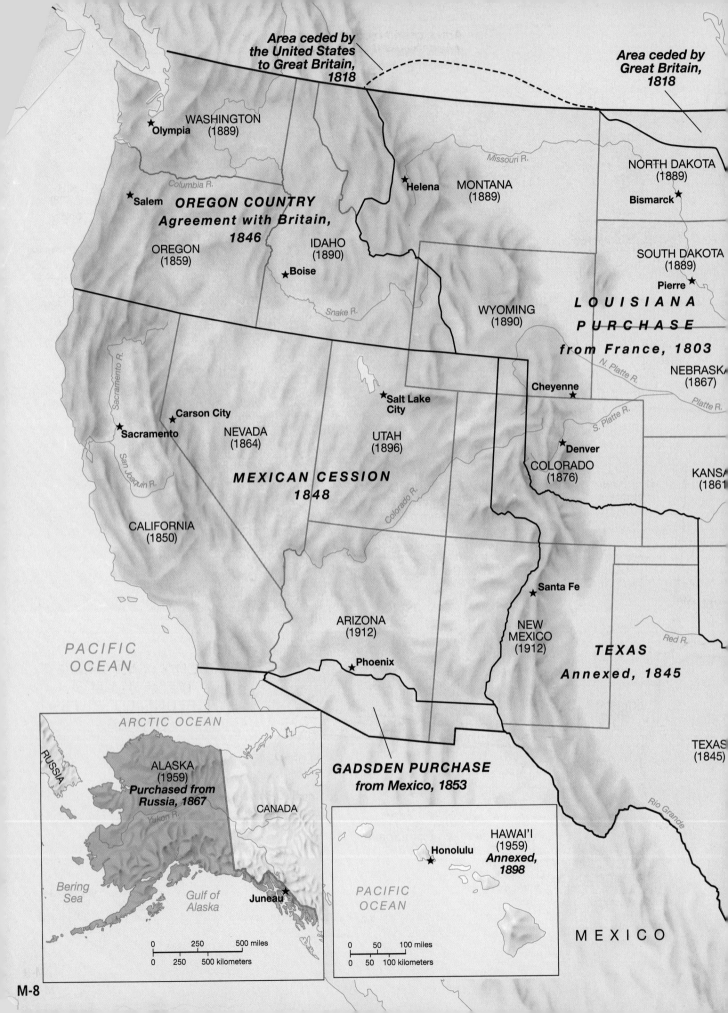

Area ceded by
the United States
to Great Britain,
1818

Area ceded by
Great Britain,
1818

WASHINGTON
(1889)
★ Olympia

Missouri R.

NORTH DAKOTA
(1889)
Bismarck ★

Helena ★ MONTANA
(1889)

★ Salem
Columbia R.
OREGON COUNTRY
**Agreement with Britain,
1846**

OREGON
(1859)

IDAHO
(1890)
★ Boise

SOUTH DAKOTA
(1889)

Pierre ★

Snake R.

WYOMING
(1890)

**L O U I S I A N A
P U R C H A S E**
from France, 1803

N. Platte R.

NEBRASKA
(1867)
Platte R.

Sacramento R.

★ Carson City

★ Sacramento

NEVADA
(1864)

San Joaquin R.

★ Salt Lake
City

Cheyenne
★

S. Platte R.

UTAH
(1896)

Denver
★
COLORADO
(1876)

KANSAS
(1861)

Colorado R.

**MEXICAN CESSION
1848**

CALIFORNIA
(1850)

**PACIFIC
OCEAN**

ARIZONA
(1912)

★ Phoenix

★ Santa Fe

NEW
MEXICO
(1912)

TEXAS
Annexed, 1845

Red R.

TEXAS
(1845)

GADSDEN PURCHASE
from Mexico, 1853

Rio Grande

ARCTIC OCEAN

RUSSIA

ALASKA
(1959)
**Purchased from
Russia, 1867**

CANADA

Yukon R.

*Bering
Sea*

*Gulf of
Alaska*

Juneau ★

HAWAI'I
(1959)
*Annexed,
1898*

★ Honolulu

*PACIFIC
OCEAN*

M E X I C O

| 0 | 250 | 500 miles |
| 0 | 250 | 500 kilometers |

| 0 | 50 | 100 miles |
| 0 | 50 | 100 kilometers |

M-8

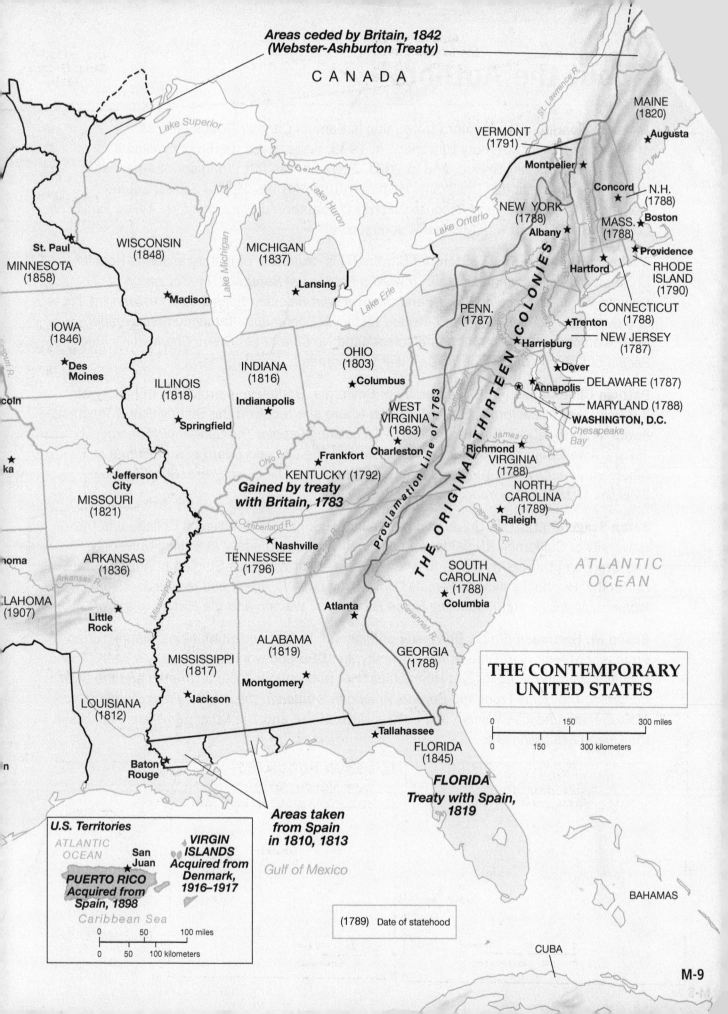

Areas ceded by Britain, 1842
(Webster-Ashburton Treaty)

CANADA

Lake Superior

Lake Huron

Lake Ontario

Lake Michigan

Lake Erie

St. Lawrence R.

VERMONT
(1791)

MAINE
(1820)
★ Augusta

Montpelier ★

Concord ★   N.H.
            (1788)

NEW YORK
(1788)

Albany ★

MASS. ★ Boston
(1788)

★ Providence

Hartford ★

RHODE
ISLAND
(1790)

WISCONSIN
(1848)

MICHIGAN
(1837)

★ St. Paul

MINNESOTA
(1858)

★ Madison

Lansing ★

PENN.
(1787)

CONNECTICUT
(1788)

★ Trenton

NEW JERSEY
(1787)

IOWA
(1846)

★ Des
Moines

ILLINOIS
(1818)

INDIANA
(1816)

OHIO
(1803)

★ Columbus

Harrisburg ★

★ Dover

DELAWARE (1787)

Annapolis ★

★ Indianapolis

Springfield ★

★ Frankfort

KENTUCKY (1792)

WEST
VIRGINIA
(1863)

Charleston ★

⊗ WASHINGTON, D.C.

MARYLAND (1788)

*Chesapeake
Bay*

Ohio R.

Richmond ★

VIRGINIA
(1788)

THE ORIGINAL THIRTEEN COLONIES

Proclamation Line of 1763

Gained by treaty
with Britain, 1783

MISSOURI
(1821)

★ Jefferson
City

ka ★

Missouri R.

Cumberland R.

Nashville ★

TENNESSEE
(1796)

NORTH
CAROLINA
(1789)

★ Raleigh

Cape Fear R.

ATLANTIC
OCEAN

ARKANSAS
(1836)

oma

LAHOMA
(1907)

★ Little
Rock

Arkansas R.

Mississippi R.

Atlanta ★

SOUTH
CAROLINA
(1788)

★ Columbia

Savannah R.

ALABAMA
(1819)

MISSISSIPPI
(1817)

★ Jackson

Montgomery ★

GEORGIA
(1788)

LOUISIANA
(1812)

Baton
Rouge ★

★ Tallahassee

FLORIDA
(1845)

FLORIDA
Treaty with Spain,
1819

Areas taken
from Spain
in 1810, 1813

Gulf of Mexico

BAHAMAS

CUBA

THE CONTEMPORARY UNITED STATES

| 0 | 150 | 300 miles |
| 0 | 150 | 300 kilometers |

(1789) Date of statehood

U.S. Territories

*ATLANTIC
OCEAN*

San
Juan ★

VIRGIN
ISLANDS
Acquired from
Denmark,
1916–1917

PUERTO RICO
Acquired from
Spain, 1898

Caribbean Sea

| 0 | 50 | 100 miles |
| 0 | 50 | 100 kilometers |

About the Authors

James L. Roark (Ph.D., Stanford University) is Samuel Candler Dobbs Professor of American History at Emory University. In 1993, he received the Emory Williams Distinguished Teaching Award, and in 2001–2002 he was Pitt Professor of American Institutions at Cambridge University. He has written *Masters without Slaves: Southern Planters in the Civil War and Reconstruction* and coauthored *Black Masters: A Free Family of Color in the Old South* with Michael P. Johnson.

Michael P. Johnson (Ph.D., Stanford University) is professor of history at Johns Hopkins University. His publications include *Toward a Patriarchal Republic: The Secession of Georgia*; *Abraham Lincoln, Slavery, and the Civil War: Selected Speeches and Writings*; and *Reading the American Past: Selected Historical Documents*, the documents reader for *The American Promise*. He has also coedited *No Chariot Let Down: Charleston's Free People of Color on the Eve of the Civil War* with James L. Roark.

Patricia Cline Cohen (Ph.D., University of California, Berkeley) is professor of history at the University of California, Santa Barbara, where she received the Distinguished Teaching Award in 2005–2006. She has written *A Calculating People: The Spread of Numeracy in Early America* and *The Murder of Helen Jewett: The Life and Death of a Prostitute in Nineteenth-Century New York*, and she has coauthored *The Flash Press: Sporting Male Weeklies in 1840s New York*.

Sarah Stage (Ph.D., Yale University) has taught U.S. history at Williams College and the University of California, Riverside, and she was visiting professor at Beijing University and Szechuan University. Currently she is professor of Women's Studies at Arizona State University. Her books include *Female Complaints: Lydia Pinkham and the Business of Women's Medicine* and *Rethinking Home Economics: Women and the History of a Profession*.

Susan M. Hartmann (Ph.D., University of Missouri) is Arts and Humanities Distinguished Professor of History at Ohio State University. In 1995 she won the university's Exemplary Faculty Award in the College of Humanities. Her publications include *Truman and the 80th Congress*; *The Home Front and Beyond: American Women in the 1940s*; *From Margin to Mainstream: American Women and Politics since 1960*; and *The Other Feminists: Activists in the Liberal Establishment*.